H

NORTHERN CALIFORNIA

HEATHER C. LISTON & ELIZABETH LINHART MONEY

NORTHERN CALIFORNIA

© AVALON TRAVEL

Contents

Discover
Northern California

If you can't decide between the beach or the mountains, city nightlife or quaint historic towns, wining and dining or roughing it, then Northern California is your ultimate destination—rich in history, dense in urban culture, awash in vineyards, and all in some of the most scenic landscapes in the world. Yosemite National Park, Lake Tahoe, Big Sur, and San Francisco are among the top 10 of most travelers' bucket lists. But beyond these headlining pleasures are lesser-known discoveries: towering coast redwoods, historic ghost towns, a smoldering volcano, pounding surf, and Gold Rush-era mines.

Culturally, San Francisco is the beating heart of Northern California. Fine art, radical ideas, and world-class cuisine mix easily in this cosmopolitan city that loves its politics as much as its nightlife. In Wine Country, culture meets nature where locals enjoy life one sip at a time. Sacramento, the sometimes cantankerous capital, is surrounded by the historic Gold Country, dotted with mines and preserved 19th-century towns that reveal the state's early days—and the events that shaped it into the dynamic place it is now.

Natural wonders and wide-open spaces draw visitors and locals to climb Yosemite's granite peaks, hike among redwoods in Sequoia and Kings Canyon, surf the beaches of Santa Cruz, scale the spines of Shasta, Lassen, and Whitney, ski the slopes of Tahoe, and dip their toes into the sea in Big Sur.

Whether you're a visitor discovering its wonders for the first time or a seasoned native looking to explore its hidden treasures, enchanting Northern California awaits.

Planning Your Trip

▶ WHERE TO GO

San Francisco

The politics, the culture, the food—these are what make San Francisco world-famous. Dine on cutting-edge cuisine at high-end restaurants and off-beat food-trucks, tour classical and avant-garde museums, bike through Golden Gate Park and explore its hidden treasures, and stroll along Fisherman's Wharf where barking sea-lions and loud street performers compete for attention.

San Francisco Bay Area

Surrounding San Francisco is a region as diverse as the city itself. To the north, Marin offers wilderness seekers a quick reprieve from the city, while ethnic diversity and intellectual curiosity give the East Bay a hip urban edge. On the southern Peninsula, beaches and farmland are within quick driving distance of the entrepreneurial culture of Silicon Valley and San Jose.

Wine Country

Northern California's Wine Country is famous for a reason. This is the place to pamper yourself with excellent wines, fantastic food, and luxurious spas. Napa offers all of the above in spades, while Sonoma is the place to catch a bit of history and to enjoy a mellower atmosphere. The Russian River adds redwoods and a bit of river rafting to the mix.

North Coast

For deserted beaches, towering redwoods, and scenic coastal towns, cruise north along The Redwood Coast. Explore Russian history at Fort Ross on the grassy bluffs of the Sonoma Coast, be romanced by Mendocino's small-town charm and nearby wineries, and take a detour east to Clear Lake, where fishing, boating, and other recreational opportunities await on California's largest freshwater lake.

Shasta and Lassen

At the southern end of the volcanic Cascade Range are geologic wonders alongside plentiful outdoor recreation. Rent a houseboat on

IF YOU HAVE...

Humboldt Redwoods State Park

- **A WEEKEND:** Visit San Francisco.
- **FIVE DAYS:** Add the Wine Country or visit Monterey and Big Sur.
- **ONE WEEK:** Add Yosemite and Tahoe.
- **TWO WEEKS:** Add the North Coast as well as Sacramento and the Gold Country.

Shasta Lake or spend a few days climbing or skiing dramatic Mount Shasta. You can traverse nearby lava tunnels or travel south to hike through boiling mud pots and fumaroles at Lassen Volcanic National Park.

Lake Tahoe

Bright blue skies, granite mountaintops, and evergreen forests surround jewel-like Lake Tahoe. Glossy hotels and casinos line the South Shore, while the low-key North and West Shores beckon with quiet beaches and miles of hiking, biking, and ski trails. The Truckee-Donner area adds a bit of Old West flavor to the outdoor scene, while the Nevada Shore specializes in uninhibited good times.

Sacramento and Gold Country

The political beating heart of California is the Gold Rush–era town of Sacramento. History abounds here as well as on the winding scenic highways that crisscross Northern Gold Country. Tour abandoned mines, raft some high-octane white water, go wine-tasting in the Shenandoah Valley, or explore the caves, caverns, and big trees of Southern Gold Country.

Yosemite and the Eastern Sierra

The work of Ansel Adams and John Muir has made Yosemite a worldwide icon. Thousands crowd into Yosemite Valley to view the much-photographed Half Dome, Bridalveil

Fisherman's Wharf in San Francisco

Mist Trail in Yosemite

Santa Cruz Beach Boardwalk

Falls, and El Capitan. On the eastern side of the Sierras, Mono Lake and Mammoth Lakes provide more scenic wilderness to explore.

Sequoia and Kings Canyon

Aside from the dramatic rugged terrain, the real draws to this central Sierra region are the giant sequoias in the General Grant Grove and the General Sherman Tree. Visit the Giant Forest Museum, take an invigorating hike up to Moro Rock, and duck into glittering Crystal Cave, which is as beautiful as its name suggests.

Central Coast

Some of the most beautiful and most adventurous coastline in the world is along Highway 1—the Pacific Coast Highway. Go surfing and wine-tasting in Santa Cruz. Witness gray whales and sea lions off the rugged Monterey Bay, and then explore their environment at the Monterey Bay Aquarium. Camp and hike the unspoiled wilderness of Big Sur, and then tour grandiose Hearst Castle in San Simeon.

▶ WHEN TO GO

Northern California's best feature is its all-season appeal. Yosemite's waterfalls are at their peak in spring, when the crowds are fewer. This is also a great time to visit Big Sur—lodging rates drop, as do the number of visitors, while blooming wildflowers make for colorful road trips.

"The coldest winter I ever spent was a summer in San Francisco," a quote falsely attributed to Mark Twain, still holds true as the wind and fog that blows through the city June–August surprises unsuspecting visitors. Regardless, summer remains Northern California's travel season; expect crowds at popular attractions, wineries, national parks, and campgrounds.

wine country in autumn

Yosemite Valley

Fall is a wonderful time to visit as the summer crowds have left but winter rain and snow have not yet closed Yosemite, Shasta, or Tahoe. September in particular is San Francisco's "summer," with warm sunny days and little summer fog.

In winter, Tahoe draws crowds for skiing and snowboarding. Unfortunately, it also draws heavy traffic along I-80, which can close due to snow and related accidents. Yosemite's roads likewise close in winter, including Highway 120 and the Tioga Pass, which links the Eastern Sierra to the west entrance of the park. Heavy rains can also flood Wine Country roads, leaving travelers stranded (although there are worse places to be stuck).

▶ BEFORE YOU GO

The most central place to fly into is San Francisco International Airport (SFO), but you can avoid some of the hassle of this large facility by flying into smaller airports in Oakland, San Jose, or even Sacramento.

Unless your trip is focused on San Francisco, plan to rent a car to explore the rest of the region. Winter drivers should carry tire chains for unexpected snows in the high Sierras.

Book hotels early and buy tickets for big-name attractions in advance, especially in summer. If you plan to visit any big-name restaurants, make those reservations early as well. Lodging and campground reservations are particularly essential in Yosemite and Big Sur.

Summer fog is likely along the coast and is pretty much guaranteed in San Francisco, making the air damp and chilly. Bring layered clothing, especially a wind-resistant coat and a warm sweater, as well as sunscreen.

Visiting the United States from abroad, you'll need your passport and possibly a visa.

Explore Northern California

▶ BEST DAY TRIPS

Many of California's most famous destinations are within a short drive of San Francisco. Less than two hours away, Wine Country is one of the best day trips out of San Francisco. You can indulge and pamper yourself all day and still have time to fall asleep in the city that night. Though doable in a day, Big Sur and Yosemite are better suited to an overnight stay or a weekend getaway.

San Francisco

Three days are perfect for a whirlwind romance with the city of San Francisco.

DAY 1

Start your day with breakfast at the Ferry Building. Grab a latté at Blue Bottle Coffee or graze from one of the many on-site vendors before taking a stroll along Fisherman's Wharf. Near Pier 39, buy ferry tickets to Alcatraz to tour the former island prison. Back at the foot of Beach and Hyde Streets, board the Powell-Hyde cable car and hop off for some window shopping at Union Square.

In the afternoon, head to the Sunset District to explore verdant Golden Gate Park. The fabulous de Young museum is directly across from the California Academy of Sciences. Art lovers and science geeks can part ways here or squeeze in a trip to enjoy both! Near Golden Gate Park, visit the Haight, the hippie enclave made famous in the 1960s. Enjoy the finely crafted cocktails and nibbles at Alembic or head back downtown to splurge on dinner at Farallon. End the day with martinis at the swank Top of the Mark.

Tartine Bakery

Lombard Street

Muir Woods National Monument

DAY 2

North Beach is home to Mama's on Washington Square, whose specialty "m'omelettes" have made this joint a local favorite for decades. After brunch, stop in at City Lights, the legendary Beat Generation bookstore, then enjoy an old-school cappuccino at Caffé Trieste. Work off that omelette with a climb to the top of Coit Tower to catch a great view of the city skyline—look west to find crooked Lombard Street.

Spend the afternoon in the hip Mission district. Order an authentic Mission burrito at Papalote Mexican Grill or sweets from Tartine Bakery. History buffs should visit 18th-century Mission Dolores. End your stay in the Mission with thin-crust pizzas and classic cocktails at Beretta.

DAY 3

Get an early start for breakfast at popular Dottie's True Blue Café. Afterwards, head to the Palace of Fine Arts for one of the city's top photo-ops. Spend a few hours discovering the world of science at the Exploratorium or, if the weather cooperates, explore The Presidio and take a hike along Crissy Field. Stop for coffee and a snack at Warming Hut Bookstore & Café, then it's off to the ultimate San Francisco photo-op, the Golden Gate Bridge.

MARIN DAY TRIP

Extend the love affair with a side trip to wander the redwoods in Marin. Muir Woods National Monument comprises acres of staggeringly beautiful redwood forest nestled in Marin just north of San Francisco. The Muir Woods Visitors Center is a great place to begin your exploration. Hike the Main Trail, a paved boardwalk through the beautiful redwoods; pick up a self-guided trail leaflet at the visitors center and follow the interpretive numbers along the way to learn about the flora and fauna of this unique ecosystem.

Sonoma County

After your hike, fill up on a hearty lunch of British comfort food at The Pelican Inn. Dark wood and a long trestle table give a proper Old English feel to the dimly lit dining room. It's just a short walk from the restaurant to lovely Muir Beach, perfect for wildlife-watching and beachcombing. End the day with oysters and drinks at the Farley Bar at Cavallo Point Lodge. Snag a blanket and a seat on the porch to watch the fog roll in over the Golden Gate Bridge.

Wine Country

The Napa Valley is less than 100 miles north of San Francisco, making it an ever-popular day-trip destination. If you plan to tour Wine Country, choose one region to explore. Napa and Sonoma are closest to San Francisco, about one hour's drive. Traffic on the winding two-lane roads in these regions can easily become clogged with wine-tasting day-trippers, especially on weekends. To avoid the crowds, try to get an early start or visit on a weekday. Note that most wineries close by 4 p.m., and some are open only by appointment.

ONE DAY IN NAPA
50 Miles, 1-1.5 Hours from San Francisco

In downtown Napa, get your bearings at the Napa General Store and sample some Napa vintages. Have lunch or just pick up some picnic supplies at Oxbow Public Market before hopping back on Highway 29. Drive north to Rutherford and enjoy a tasting at Grgich Hills, which offers a relaxed Napa experience. Continue north on Highway 29 to St. Helena and the palatial estate of Beringer Vineyards. Many of Beringer's wines are only available here.

After a full day of wine-tasting, give your taste buds a rest with dinner at the Culinary Institute of America, where the country's top chefs are trained. The Greystone Restaurant is where that food is served; you can even watch as it's prepared in the open kitchen. From St. Helena, the drive back to San Francisco will take 1.5–2 hours.

Overnight: Spend the night at the aptly named Zinfandel Inn before spending a second day exploring Sonoma.

ONE DAY IN SONOMA
40-50 Miles, 1-1.5 Hours from San Francisco
From Napa, Highway 121 winds west through the Carneros wine region. Stop off for a bit of bubbly at gorgeous Domaine Carneros, where the views and gardens are almost as impressive as the sparkling wines. From Highway 121, Highway 12 twists north into Sonoma. Stretch your legs in Sonoma Plaza and explore the charming downtown area. Stop in at the Sonoma Mission for a bit of history, then grab a lunch at the girl and the fig, housed in the historic Sonoma Hotel.

After lunch it may be time for a massage at the Garden Spa at MacArthur Place, or try some Sonoma vintages at the Charles Creek Vineyard tasting room right on the square. For more wine-tasting, take Highway 12 north to quaint Glen Ellen and stop in at the Valley of the Moon Winery, where the landmark winery will enchant with its stone buildings and unusual sangiovese rosé.

If you have time for one more winery, be sure to visit Muscardini and Ty Caton, whose joint tasting room in Kenwood pours undoubtedly the best and most affordable vintages in the valley. From here, it is only 11 miles to downtown Santa Rosa, where you can catch U.S. 101 south to San Francisco, 52 miles and a little over an hour away. You may decide to grab a bite before you head back; if so, the quirky and excellent Dóce Lunas is the best bet in town.

Overnight: Spend the night at the Gaige House in Glen Ellen, or the Sonoma Hotel on the plaza in Sonoma.

Monterey and Big Sur
1-2 DAYS IN MONTEREY BAY
112 Miles, 2 Hours from San Francisco
Attractions in Santa Cruz and Monterey, plus the charm of Carmel, can easily fill your itinerary. From San Francisco, take U.S. 101

Big Sur coastline

Big Sur, where spirit meets nature

south to Highway 17 through the redwoods to the laid-back town of Santa Cruz. Ride the rides on the Santa Cruz Beach Boardwalk and dig your toes in the sand on the beach. Once you've got your fill of sun, continue an hour south to Monterey and the Monterey Bay Aquarium. Dine at Montrio, or splurge at Casanova in quaint Carmel.

Overnight: The delightful Cypress Inn in Carmel provides a quick launch to the coastal wonders of Big Sur the next day.

1-2 DAYS IN BIG SUR
140 Miles, 3 Hours from San Francisco
Big Sur captures the best qualities of the Northern California coast: windswept beaches and pounding surf, verdant state parks with majestic redwoods, and the literary solitude of the Beats. Although possible to do as a day trip, two days will allow you to better enjoy the splendor of this region.

Part of Big Sur's appeal is the drive along Highway 1, the Pacific Coast Highway, lined with historic bridges, pastures of grazing sheep, and breathtaking cliffs. The Bixby Bridge marks the official entrance to Big Sur. Stop at Pfeiffer Big Sur State Park to hike through the redwoods to Pfeiffer Falls, or walk the short trail to McWay Falls farther south in Julia Pfeiffer Burns State Park. Thumb through the books at Henry Miller Memorial Library, drink in the sunset at Nepenthe, and don't miss breakfast at Deetjens.

Overnight: Deetjen's has rustic accommodations in a historic setting, or pitch a tent at Pfeiffer Big Sur State Park. Make reservations in advance for both on summer weekends.

RETURN OPTION VIA HIGHWAY 1
70 Miles, 1.5 Hours from
Pescadero to San Francisco
Add some variety to your return route by following coastal Highway 1 north of Santa Cruz. Turn east in Pescadero onto Pescadero Creek Road and follow it to the town's sole stop sign. Enjoy lunch at Duarte's or pick up a loaf of delicious artichoke garlic bread at Arcangeli's Bakery to take home. Continue

east on Pescadero Creek Road until it meets Highway 84 in La Honda. Follow gorgeous Highway 84 east as it twists and turns through coastal redwoods, eventually coming to a crossroads in Woodside. Stop at Alice's Restaurant for biker-themed burgers and a beer, then roll north along Skyline Boulevard (Hwy. 35) through more scenic redwoods and past numerous county parks before returning to the urban landscape of I-280 north to San Francisco.

Yosemite and Tahoe

From San Francisco, it's just a four-hour drive to either Lake Tahoe or Yosemite National Park; from Sacramento, it's even closer. Combine a trip to both in summer by crossing through Yosemite via the Tioga Pass Road (Hwy. 120). On the eastern side of the Sierra, scenic U.S. 395 leads north almost to the Nevada border, and road-trippers can take forested Highway 89 west to its junction with U.S. 50 to continue to South Lake Tahoe.

ONE DAY IN YOSEMITE
200 Miles, 4 Hours

From the north, Yosemite National Park is most easily accessed from Highway 120 through the Big Oak Flat entrance; in winter, use Highway 140 through the main Arch Rock entrance.

In Yosemite Valley, hop on board the Valley Shuttle for a scenic car-free exploration of the Valley's sights, especially Bridalveil Falls, El Capitan, and Half Dome. The best way to experience Yosemite's beauty is on one of its many trails; enjoy a leisurely stroll around Mirror Lake, scale a waterfall on the Mist Trail, or test your powers of endurance on the way to Upper Yosemite Falls. Afterward, reward your efforts with a pit stop at the Ahwahnee bar to soak in the valley views.

Overnight: It takes advance planning to score a campground reservation in Yosemite Valley, especially in summer. Try your luck with one of the first-come, first-served campgrounds such as Tamarack Flat or Tuolumne Meadows (summer only)—but be sure to get there before noon.

Yosemite Valley

TWO DAYS IN YOSEMITE

Highway 120 becomes Tioga Road as it continues east through Yosemite's high country. This seasonal road is only open late spring–late fall; plan your trip in the shoulder seasons (spring and fall) to avoid the crowds. Along the way, gape at jaw-dropping vistas from Olmstead Point, gaze at crystal-clear alpine lakes and grassy Tuolumne Meadows, and explore some of Yosemite's rugged high-elevation backcountry on hikes to Cathedral Lakes. Tioga Road peaks at Tioga Pass as it leaves the park, descending to the arid desert along U.S. 395. Here, abandoned ghost towns like Bodie State Historic Park and saline Mono Lake characterize the drier eastern Sierras.

ONE DAY IN TAHOE
190 Miles, 3.5-4 Hours from
San Francisco or Yosemite Valley

U.S. 50 enters the Tahoe region on the popular South Shore of Lake Tahoe. Stop in at one of the casinos across the Nevada state line, or take in the lay of the land on the Heavenly gondola. Highway 89 heads west to glittering Emerald Bay, where you can hike the Rubicon Trail to Vikingsholm Castle. Continue north on Highway 89 to reach the North and West Shores, which hold Tahoe's legendary appeal. The lively center of Tahoe City has plenty of restaurants, hotels, and campgrounds to keep you close to the lake for the night.

BEST OF NORTHERN CALIFORNIA

- **Best Attraction for Kids of All Ages:** Monterey Bay Aquarium (p. 722)
- **Best Bubbly:** Domain Chandon (p. 211)
- **Best Escape:** Alcatraz (p. 37)
- **Best Ghost Town:** Bodie State Historic Park (p. 640)
- **Best Place to Bring a Flashlight:** Crystal Cave (p. 679)
- **Best Place to Bring a Lunch:** Donner Memorial State Park (p. 473)
- **Best Place to Contemplate the Past:** Columbia State Historic Park (p. 569)
- **Best Place to Develop House Envy:** Hearst Castle (p. 782)
- **Best Place to Get Lost:** Winchester Mystery House (p. 189)
- **Best Place to Hug a Tree:** Redwood State and National Parks (p. 352)
- **Best Waterfall:** Bridalveil Fall (p. 586)
- **Bluest Lake:** Lake Tahoe (p. 429)
- **Most Devilish:** Devils Postpile National Monument (p. 646)
- **Most Heavenly:** Angel Island State Park (p. 123)
- **Most Iconic Landmark:** Golden Gate Bridge (p. 45)
- **Most Volcanic:** Lassen Peak (p. 393)

Monterey Bay Aquarium

Volcanic rock hangs from a Mono Lake signpost.

Overnight: Spend the night at the Pepper Tree Inn in Tahoe City, or camp at General Creek Campground in Sugar Pine Point State Park (reservations recommended in summer).

TWO DAYS IN TAHOE

In the morning, take Highway 89 east to Truckee. Along the way you'll pass Squaw Valley, which may merit a detour through The Village at Squaw Valley. While in Truckee, enjoy the Old West vibe and stop for lunch at the Bar of America, a Truckee institution since 1974. On your way home, stop by Donner Memorial State Park. While the park history tells a grim tale, the hiking trails around the lake are quite beautiful. After your last taste of the Sierras, it is 184 miles back to San Francisco (3.5 hours) or 100 miles to Sacramento (2 hours).

TAHOE IN WINTER

Nothing says winter like sliding down the slopes at Tahoe. Numerous ski resorts line the lake and mountains. Heavenly rules the roost on the South Shore, while Squaw Valley draws boarders and skiers on the North and West Shores. Cross-country skiers should head to Royal Gorge in the Truckee-Donner area.

Highway 89 and U.S. 50 are the main arteries to the Tahoe area, and they can become congested and blocked by snow into spring. Bring tire chains and plenty of patience—in inclement weather, it can take up to eight hours to drive here from San Francisco.

▶ BEST ROAD TRIPS

The classic tour of Northern California is behind the wheel. Don't miss a chance to drive up the Pacific Coast Highway, with its quaint towns, giant redwoods, and untamed beaches. Cruising down Highway 49 in the Gold Country is another favorite, where mining towns, some seemingly preserved in amber, detail California's boom-time beginnings. But less-visited destinations like Mount Lassen and Mount Shasta, with their glaciers, steaming fumaroles, and

the Mendocino Coast

beautiful desolation, celebrate the state's wild side. To add to the experience, a multitude of scenic two-lane highways makes driving from one destination to the next a treat in and of itself.

North Coast
HIGHWAY 1 NORTH TO
U.S. 101 IN CRESCENT CITY
400 Miles, 9 Hours

Crashing surf, towering redwoods, and rocky beaches typify the rugged Northern California coast. Highway 1 and U.S. 101 twist apart and converge again for almost 400 miles from San Francisco to Crescent City, culminating in one of the state's best and most scenic road trips.

From San Francisco, travel north over the Golden Gate Bridge to the Bay Area's playground, Marin County. Following Highway 1, stop for a short hike amid coastal redwoods at Muir Woods National Monument before continuing north past Stinson Beach to Point Reyes National Seashore, where a wealth of hiking and biking opportunities await. Slurp oysters at Hog Island Oyster Co. or stock up on gourmet cheese at Cowgirl Creamery for

a picnic later. Just an hour north lies Bodega Bay, where Alfred Hitchcock's *The Birds* was filmed. January–May you may even spot whales off the coast.

Guerneville makes a fun detour inland from Highway 1. Spend the night at Creekside Inn and Lodge and dip your toes—or a canoe—in the Russian River. Back on Highway 1, stop for a dose of history at Fort Ross State Historic Park, a reconstructed Russian fort. As Highway 1 winds north, the artsy enclave of Mendocino beckons. Wander through the Mendocino Coast Botanical Gardens and consider spending the night at one of the many quaint B&Bs.

Highway 1 rejoins U.S. 101 in Leggett and enters the famed Redwood Coast. From Humboldt Redwoods State Park near Garberville to Del Norte Coast Redwoods south of Crescent City, this 150-mile stretch is rich with hiking and camping opportunities. Cruise the Avenue of the Giants and pitch a tent in Humboldt Redwoods State Park or snag a campsite at Prairie Creek Redwoods. Del Norte Coast Redwoods State Park is the last of the redwoods before Crescent City.

Shasta Dam

Shasta and Lassen

These northern peaks and parklands are some of the state's most spectacular and least visited. Mount Shasta is a paradise for outdoor enthusiasts year-round. You can hike or climb to the summit in the summer and ski down its slopes in winter. Shasta Lake, by contrast, is best in summer, when boating, fishing, and waterskiing can fully be enjoyed. Because of its high elevation and rocky terrain, Mount Lassen's roads are closed late fall–spring, making it a mid-late–summer destination.

Most services are found in Redding and Red Bluff, which are also the best access points from I-5. Each destination can be a road trip in itself, but you can also make a loop via Highway 89. It is a thrilling way to see both peaks and to make the most of a trek this far north.

SACRAMENTO TO MOUNT SHASTA
220 Miles, 3.5-4 Hours

From Sacramento, it takes about 2.5 hours driving north on I-5 to get to the small city of Redding, the gateway for both Shasta Lake and Mount Shasta. From Redding, continue north on I-5 for just eight miles until you come to Shasta Lake. Turn west on Highway 151 to explore looming Shasta Dam. After marveling at its size, head over to the other side of I-5 to experience another kind of wonder, this one made by the hand of nature, and tour the Lake Shasta Caverns.

Next, take advantage of what Shasta Lake does best: watery summertime fun. Head over to the Bridge Bay Resort where you can rent all you need to go boating, waterskiing, or fishing out on the lake's many fingers and inlets; you can even book a room for the night. Or make the most of you time on the lake by renting a houseboat or camping at the Hirz Mountain Lookout Tower, with views of both Mount Shasta and Mount Lassen.

From Shasta Lake, head north on I-5 for 40 miles to Castle Crags State Park, where you can trying your hand at rock climbing and scale granite faces, domes, and spires. Or you can hike the Crags Trail to Castle Dome, a 5.5-mile round-trip with spectacular views.

Next stop is Mount Shasta, only 15 miles up I-5, where more climbing and hiking opportunities await. The Gray Butte Trail is a moderate 3.4-mile hike to this small peak, but if the big peak is too irresistible, you can opt for a multiday trek summiting Mount Shasta. Winter offers equally fun outdoor adventures, when you can spend all day skiing and snowboarding at Mount Shasta Ski Park.

After a full day on the hiking, climbing, or skiing trails, snag a campsite at Lake Siskiyou Camp & Resort or opt for a greater indulgence and reward at the Shasta MountInn Retreat & Spa.

MOUNT SHASTA TO LASSEN
100 Miles, 2 Hours
Once you have had your fill of Mount Shasta, head east on Highway 89. The scenic two-lane road winds through mountainous terrain and across wild rivers. One of the best sights along the way is McArthur-Burney Falls, claimed to be the most beautiful waterfall in California. This can either be a quick stop, as the falls are near the parking lot, or you can take the time to do a short hike nearby.

You'll enter Lassen Volcanic National Park shortly after leaving McArthur-Burney Falls. Because you are entering from the north, you can make a quick stop at the Loomis Museum before pressing south to Lassen Peak; the beauty and the views on the trail make the effort worthwhile. Nearby is another treat—Bumpass Hell—where you can hike surrounded by smoking fumaroles and boiling mud pots.

Camp at either Manzanita Lake or Summit Lake Campground. From the park, it is less than 200 miles (3–3.5 hours) back to Sacramento.

Gold Country
SACRAMENTO TO NORTHERN AND SOUTHERN GOLD COUNTRY
180 Miles, 4-4.5 Hours
A tour through Gold Country is a road trip rich in history, beautiful scenery, outdoor adventure, and even wine-tasting. Highway 49 runs for 127 miles through the heart of Gold Country from Nevada City to Jamestown. Sacramento is near the northern Gold

Mount Shasta

BEST OUTDOOR ADVENTURES

Half Dome, Yosemite

Northern California is rich with opportunities for getting outdoors. From surfing the Pacific coast to climbing the tallest mountain, you can do it all. Choose your own adventure to begin.

- **Backpacking:** Lost Coast (p. 336), Pacific Crest Trail (p. 398), Yosemite (p. 592)

- **Bicycling:** Point Reyes National Seashore (p. 139)

- **Camping:** Yosemite's Tuolumne Meadows (p. 614), Humboldt Redwoods State Park (p. 340)

- **Canoeing:** The Russian River (p. 265)

- **Caving:** Mercer Caverns (p. 564), Crystal Cave (p. 679)

- **Fishing:** Lake Berryessa (p. 220), Clear Lake (p. 327), Mendocino Coast (p. 307)

- **Hiking:** Yosemite Valley (p. 587), Sequoia National Park (p. 680), Big Sur (p. 772)

- **Horseback riding:** Mount Shasta (p. 413), Yosemite Valley Stables (p. 593), Grant Grove Stables (p. 669)

- **Mountain climbing:** Mount Shasta (p. 410), Mount Whitney (p. 675)

- **Rock climbing:** El Capitan (p. 593), Half Dome (p. 591), and Sentinel Dome (p. 602) in Yosemite.

- **Skiing:** Tahoe's North Shore (p. 463), Badger Pass in Yosemite (p. 600)

- **Snowboarding:** Mount Shasta (p. 412), Tahoe (p. 463)

- **Surfing:** Santa Cruz (p. 706)

- **Swimming:** Eel River (p. 340), Lake Tahoe (p. 492), Yuba River (p. 531)

- **Tidepooling:** Fitzgerald Marine Reserve (p. 165)

- **Whale-watching:** Bodega Bay (p. 282)

- **White-water rafting:** South Fork American River (p. 543)

Country and is a great place to start a historic tour. You can easily extend this trip to Yosemite via Highway 120 (2 hours), or continue east on U.S. 50 in Placerville to reach Lake Tahoe in a mere 1.5 hours.

In Sacramento, start your day early with a tour of the Capitol Building and see where all the big decisions are made. Walk over to Old Sacramento, where you'll find the Gold Rush–era part of this town lovingly preserved. To really drink in the atmosphere, step into Fat City Bar and Café to enjoy comfort food served in a 19th-century dining room.

Take I-80 east for 32 miles until you reach Auburn in Northern Gold Country, then detour north on Highway 49 for 23 miles to Grass Valley. Stop at the Empire Mine State Historic Park and get a feel for the toil, hardship, dreams, and occasional wild luck that shaped the Gold Country. Charming Grass Valley offers food and shopping, or go straight to Nevada City, only three miles away, and spend the afternoon strolling its narrow streets. The Outside Inn offers unique guest rooms that border the creek.

historic Nevada City

Head back south on Highway 49 for one hour to reach Placerville. Take a thrilling white-water rafting trip on the American River near Coloma, or tour Marshall Gold Discovery State Historic Park, the site where James Marshall discovered gold in 1848. Next, hit the wineries and orchards around Apple Hill and taste the Gold Country's best vintages. Consider staying nearby at the Historic Cary House Hotel. If you plan to stick by the river, the American River Resort has campsites as well as cabins.

It is 60 winding miles from Placerville down Highway 49 to Angels Camp, the heart of Southern Gold Country. Visit the Angels Camp Museum and Carriage House, which beautifully showcases 30 carriages and wagons from the Gold Rush era. Grab a bite at the Sidewinder Café, then venture east for eight miles on Highway 4 to Murphys and descend 162 feet below the ground into Mercer Caverns.

Head down to Columbia, where most of downtown is part of the Columbia State Historic Park. Stroll the preserved streets of this Gold Rush boomtown to get a feel for what life was like when the mines operated. Stick around for dinner at the Columbia City Hotel Restaurant, where fine dining meets Old West elegance.

Accommodations await a short jog west on Highway 108 in Jamestown, where the National Hotel has been in operation since 1859. In the morning, stop by the Mother Lode Coffee Shop for a hearty breakfast before returning to Sacramento (2 hours, 114 miles).

SAN FRANCISCO

When engineers laid out the streets of San Francisco, they modeled the city after America's board-flat urban centers. They may as well have tried to fit a siren into a schoolgirl's uniform. The regular grid pattern found on maps leaves visitors unprepared for the precipitous inclines and stunning water views in this town built on 43 hills.

Geographically and culturally, San Francisco is anything but flat, and what level ground exists might at any moment give way. While earthquakes remake the land, social upheavals play a similar role in reminding that the only constant here is change. In the 1950s, the Beats challenged postwar conformity and left a legacy of incantatory poems and independent bookstores. The late 1960s saw a years-long Summer of Love, which shifted consciousness as surely as quakes shift tectonic plates. Gay and lesbian liberation movements sprung forth in the 1970s, as did a renewed push for women's rights. Since then, a vibrant culture of technological innovation has taken root and continues to rapidly evolve as groundbreaking companies and tech visionaries choose to make the City their home.

Although San Francisco is one of the most visited cities in the United States, it often seems like a provincial village, or a series of villages that share a downtown and a roster of world-class icons. Drive over the Golden Gate or the Bay Bridge as the fog is lifting and your heart will catch at the ever-changing beauty of the scene. Stand at the base of the Transamerica

© DOMINI DRAGOONE

SAN FRANCISCO

HIGHLIGHTS

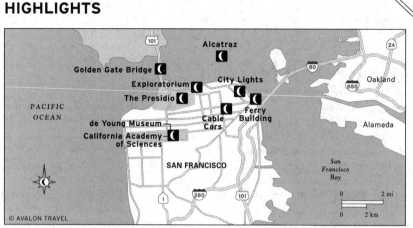

LOOK FOR ☾ TO FIND RECOMMENDED SIGHTS, ACTIVITIES, DINING, AND LODGING.

☾ **Cable Cars:** Nothing is more iconic than climbing San Francisco's steep hills on an historic cable car (page 30).

☾ **Ferry Building:** The 1898 Ferry Building has been renovated and reimagined as the foodie mecca of San Francisco. The Tuesday and Saturday farmers market is not to be missed (page 33).

☾ **Alcatraz:** Spend the day in prison...at the historically famous former maximum security penitentiary in the middle of the Bay. Audio tours bring to life the cells that Al Capone, George "Machine Gun" Kelly, and Robert "Birdman of Alcatraz" Stroud called home (page 37).

☾ **Exploratorium:** Kids and adults alike love to explore San Francisco's innovative and interactive science museum. The exhibits are meant to be touched, heard, and felt (page 43).

☾ **The Presidio:** The original 1776 El Presidio de San Francisco is now a dormant military installation and national park. Tour the historic buildings that formerly housed a military hospital, barracks, and fort—all amid a peaceful and verdant setting (page 43).

☾ **Golden Gate Bridge:** Nothing beats the view from one of the most famous and fascinating bridges in the country. Pick a fogless day for a stroll or bike ride across the span (page 45).

☾ **de Young Museum:** The revamped de Young has become the showpiece of Golden Gate Park. A mixed collection of media and regions is highlighted by the 360-degree view from the museum's tower (page 50).

☾ **California Academy of Sciences:** With a four-story rainforest, a state-of-the-art planetarium, and an underwater aquarium home to 38,000 animals, the Academy of Sciences is a thrill for visitors of all ages (page 51).

☾ **City Lights:** The Beat generation lives on at this landmark bookstore, widely considered the best in the City (page 70).

PHOTO COURTESY OF PRAYITNO

the cable car turnaround at Market and Powell Streets

Pyramid, hang off the side of a cable car, or just walk through the neighborhoods that make the city more than the sum of its parts. Despite the hills, San Francisco is a city that cries out to be explored on foot.

PLANNING YOUR TIME

Try to spend at least one weekend in San Francisco, and focus your time downtown. Union Square makes a great home base, thanks to its plethora of hotels, shops, and easy access to public transportation, but it can be fairly dead at night. Spend your time grazing the sumptuous offerings at the Ferry Building, then hop a crowded cable car to Fisherman's Wharf to catch the ferry to Alcatraz. At night, relax at one of San Francisco's many well-regarded restaurants. With a full week, you can explore Golden Gate Park's excellent museums—the de Young and the California Academy of Sciences. You can easily spend another full day exploring The Presidio, visiting the nearby Exploratorium, and taking a scenic, foggy stroll across the Golden Gate Bridge.

San Francisco's weather tends toward blanket fog and chilly windy days with bright spots of sun the exception. Come prepared with a warm coat and a sweater and leave the shorts at home.

Sights

UNION SQUARE AND NOB HILL

Wealth and style mark these areas near the center of San Francisco. Known for their lavish shopping areas, cable cars, and mansions, Union Square and Nob Hill draw both local and visiting crowds all year long. Sadly, the stunning 19th-century mansions built by the robber barons on Nob Hill are almost all gone—shaken then burned in the 1906 earthquake and fire. But the area still exudes a certain elegance; restaurants are particularly good on Nob Hill.

If you shop in only one part of San Francisco,

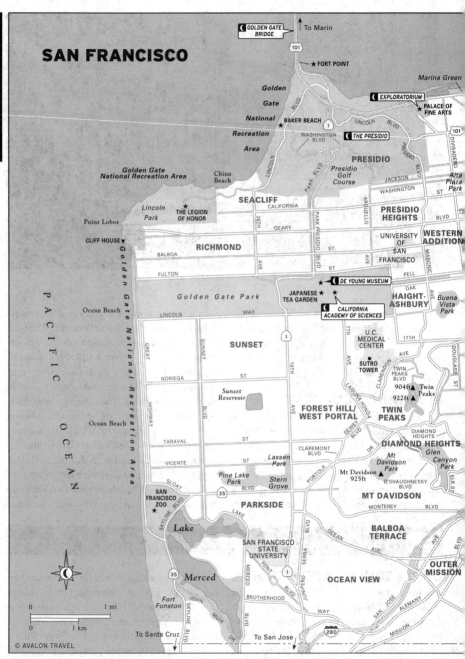

SAN FRANCISCO

GOLDEN GATE BRIDGE
To Marin
101
★ FORT POINT
Marina Green
Golden
Gate
EXPLORATORIUM
PALACE OF FINE ARTS
National
BAKER BEACH ★
LINCOLN BLVD
101
Recreation
1
WASHINGTON BLVD
THE PRESIDIO
DIVISADERO
Area
PRESIDIO
Golden Gate National Recreation Area
China Beach
Presidio Golf Course
JACKSON
Alta Plaza Park
WASHINGTON ST
SEACLIFF
CALIFORNIA
PRESIDIO HEIGHTS
BLVD
Lincoln Park
THE LEGION OF HONOR ★
Point Lobos
26TH
GEARY
Park Presidio Blvd
UNIVERSITY OF SAN FRANCISCO
WESTERN ADDITION
MASONIC
CLIFF HOUSE ▼
BALBOA
RICHMOND
AVE
ST
FELL
FULTON
OAK
DE YOUNG MUSEUM
Ocean Beach
Golden Gate Park
JAPANESE TEA GARDEN ★ ★
HAIGHT-ASHBURY
Buena Vista Park
CALIFORNIA ACADEMY OF SCIENCES
LINCOLN
WAY
PACIFIC
GREAT
SUNSET
7TH
U.C. MEDICAL CENTER
17TH
DOUGLASS
OCEAN
SUNSET
ST
19TH
AVE
SUTRO TOWER ■
TWIN PEAKS BLVD
904ft ▲ Twin Peaks
NORIEGA
ST
LAGUNA HONDA
922ft ▲
Sunset Reservoir
HIGHWAY
FOREST HILL/ WEST PORTAL
TWIN PEAKS
OCEAN
Ocean Beach
BLVD
DIAMOND HEIGHTS
TARAVAL
ST
CLAREMONT BLVD
DEWEY
DIAMOND HEIGHTS
Glen Canyon Park
Lassen Park
Mt Davidson Park
VICENTE
ST
PORTOLA
ELK ST
Pine Lake Park
Stern Grove
Mt Davidson ▲ 925ft
O'SHAUGHNESSY BLVD
SAN FRANCISCO ZOO ★
35
SLOAT
BLVD
LAKE
MT DAVIDSON
SKYLINE BLVD
PARKSIDE
MONTEREY
BLVD
Lake
BALBOA TERRACE
SAN FRANCISCO STATE UNIVERSITY
SERRA
MERCED
OCEAN
AVE
BLVD
35
Merced
FONT
JUNIPERO
1
OUTER MISSION
OCEAN VIEW
Fort Funston
JOHN MUIR
BROTHERHOOD
WAY
SAN JOSE
ALEMANY
0   1 mi
0   1 km
SKYLINE BLVD
DR
280
MISSION
To Santa Cruz
To San Jose

© AVALON TRAVEL

SAN FRANCISCO

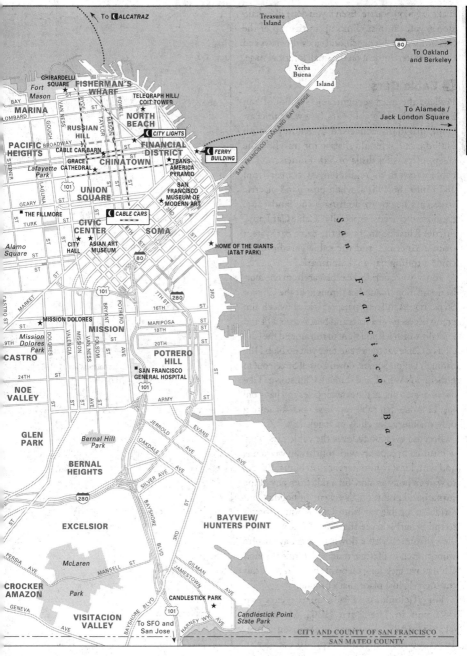

To **ALCATRAZ**

Treasure Island

Yerba Buena Island

To Oakland and Berkeley

To Alameda / Jack London Square

GHIRARDELLI SQUARE
Fort Mason
FISHERMAN'S WHARF

TELEGRAPH HILL/ COIT TOWER

MARINA

NORTH BEACH

RUSSIAN HILL

CITY LIGHTS

CABLE CAR BARN

PACIFIC HEIGHTS

GRACE CATHEDRAL

CHINATOWN

FINANCIAL DISTRICT

FERRY BUILDING

TRANS AMERICA PYRAMID

Lafayette Park

UNION SQUARE

SAN FRANCISCO MUSEUM OF MODERN ART

THE FILLMORE

CABLE CARS

CIVIC CENTER

SOMA

Alamo Square

CITY HALL

ASIAN ART MUSEUM

HOME OF THE GIANTS (AT&T PARK)

San Francisco Bay

MISSION DOLORES

MISSION

Mission Dolores Park

CASTRO

POTRERO HILL

SAN FRANCISCO GENERAL HOSPITAL

NOE VALLEY

GLEN PARK

Bernal Hill Park

BERNAL HEIGHTS

EXCELSIOR

BAYVIEW/ HUNTERS POINT

McLaren Park

CROCKER AMAZON

CANDLESTICK PARK

Candlestick Point State Park

VISITACION VALLEY

To SFO and San Jose

SAN FRANCISCO

make it Union Square. Even if you don't like chain stores, you can just climb up to the top of the Square itself, grab a bench, and enjoy the views and the live entertainment on the small informal stage.

◖ Cable Cars

Perhaps the most recognizable symbol of San Francisco is the cable cars (www.sfcablecar.com), originally conceived by Andrew Smith Hallidie as a safer alternative for traveling the steep, often slick hills of San Francisco. The cable cars ran as regular mass transit from 1873 into the 1940s, when buses and electric streetcars began to dominate the landscape. Dedicated citizens, especially "Cable Car Lady" Friedel Klussmann, saved the cable car system from extinction, and the cable cars have become a rolling national landmark.

Today, you can ride the cable cars from one tourist destination to another throughout the City for $6 per ride. A full day "passport" ticket (which also grants access to streetcars and buses) costs $14 and is totally worth it if you want to run around the City all day. Cable car routes can take you up Nob Hill, through Union Square, down Powell Street, out to Fisherman's Wharf, and through Chinatown. Take a seat, or grab one of the exterior poles and hang on! Just be aware that cable cars have open-air seating only, making a ride chilly on foggy days.

Because everybody loves the cable cars, they get stuffed to capacity with tourists on weekends and with local commuters at rush hours. Expect to wait an hour or more for a ride from any of the turnaround points on a weekend or holiday. But a ride on a cable car from Union Square down to the Wharf is more than worth the wait. The views from the hills down to the Bay inspire wonder even in lifetime residents. A ride through Chinatown feels long on bustle but in fact reveals the lifestyle in a place that's unique.

For aficionados, a ride on the cars can take you to **The Barn** (1201 Mason St., 415/474-1887, www.cablecarmuseum.org, 10 A.M.–6 P.M. daily Apr.–Sept., 10 A.M.–5 P.M.

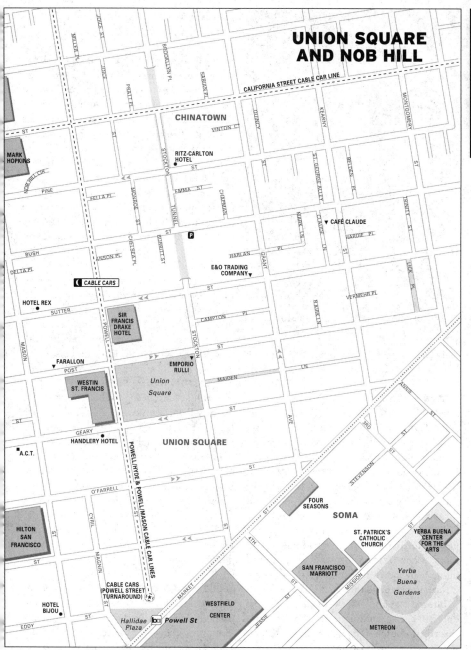

UNION SQUARE AND NOB HILL

CALIFORNIA STREET CABLE CAR LINE

MILLER PL
JOICE ST
BROOKLYN PL
PRATT PL
SABIAN PL

MONTGOMERY

CHINATOWN

VINTON CT
QUINCY
KEARNY
ST

MARK HOPKINS

NOB HILL CIR
PINE
FELLA PL
EMMA ST
CHAPMAN
ST
ST. GEORGE ALLEY
BELDEN
ST
TRINITY
ST

RITZ-CARLTON HOTEL
STOCKTON
MONROE
TUNNEL
CHELSEA PL

P

MARK LN
CLAUDE LN
▼ CAFÉ CLAUDE
HARDIE PL

BUSH
ANSON PL
BURRITT ST
HARLAN
GRANT
PL
CLAUDE LN
ST
LICK PL

DELTA PL

☾ CABLE CARS

E&O TRADING COMPANY ▼

ST

VERMEHR PL

H KREBS PL

HOTEL REX ●
SUTTER

SIR FRANCIS DRAKE HOTEL

CAMPTON PL

ST

POWELL

MASON
▼ FARALLON
POST
EMPORIO RULLI
STOCKTON
ST
MAIDEN
LN

WESTIN ST. FRANCIS

Union Square

AVE

ST

ANNIE

■ A.C.T.
GEARY ●
HANDLERY HOTEL

UNION SQUARE

ST

STEVENSON
3RD
ST

O'FARRELL
CYRIL

FOUR SEASONS

SOMA

YERBA BUENA CENTER FOR THE ARTS

HILTON SAN FRANCISCO
MAGNIN
ST

POWELL/HYDE & POWELL/MASON CABLE CAR LINES

4TH

ST. PATRICK'S CATHOLIC CHURCH

SAN FRANCISCO MARRIOTT

MISSION

Yerba Buena Gardens

HOTEL BIJOU ●
CABLE CARS (POWELL STREET TURNAROUND) ★
MARKET
Hallidae Plaza 🚇 *Powell St*
WESTFIELD CENTER
JESSIE
ST

METREON

EDDY

© AARON KOHR /123RF.COM

SAN FRANCISCO

Grace Cathedral is one of the largest Episcopal cathedrals in the United States.

daily Oct.–Mar., free), a museum depicting the life and times of the San Francisco cable cars.

Grace Cathedral

A local icon, Grace Cathedral (1100 California St., 415/749-6300, www.gracecathedral.org, 7 A.M.–6 P.M. Mon.–Sat., 8 A.M.–6 P.M. Sun.) is many things to many people. The French Gothic–style edifice, completed in 1964, attracts architecture and beaux arts lovers by the thousands with its facade, stained glass, and furnishings. The labyrinths—replicas of the Chartres Cathedral labyrinth in France—appeal to meditative walkers seeking spiritual solace. Concerts featuring world music, sacred music, and modern classical ensembles draw audiences from around the Bay and farther afield.

But most of all, Grace Cathedral opens its doors to the community as a vibrant, active Episcopal church. The doctrine of exploration and tolerance matches well with the San Francisco community, of which the church remains an important part.

FINANCIAL DISTRICT AND SOMA

The skyscrapers of the Financial District create most of the San Francisco skyline, which extends out to the waterfront, locally called the Embarcadero. It's here that the major players of the San Francisco business world make and spend their money. The Stock Exchange sits in the middle of the action, making San Francisco not just rich but important on the international financial scene. But even businesspeople have to eat, and they certainly like to drink, so the Financial District offers a wealth of restaurants and bars. Hotels tend toward expensive tall towers, and the shopping here caters to folks with plenty of green.

SoMa (local shorthand for the South of Market area) was once a run-down postindustrial mess that rented warehouses to artists. Urban renewal and the ballpark have turned it into *the* neighborhood of the 21st century, complete with upscale restaurants and chichi wine bars.

Transamerica Pyramid

The single most recognizable landmark on the San Francisco skyline, the Transamerica Pyramid (600 Montgomery St.) was originally designed to look a little like a tree and to be taller and prouder than the nearby Bank of America building. Designed by William Pereira, the pyramid has four distinctive wings, plus the 212-foot aluminum-plated spire, which is lit up for major holidays. Visitors can no longer ride up to the 27th-floor observation deck (a post-9/11 precaution), but a "virtual observation deck" can be viewed via cameras in the lobby.

Wells Fargo Bank History Museum

One of a number of Wells Fargo museums in California and the West, the Wells Fargo Bank History Museum (420 Montgomery St., 415/396-2619, www.wellsfargohistory.com, 9 A.M.–5 P.M.

Mon.–Fri., free) in San Francisco boasts the distinction of sitting on the site of the original Wells Fargo office, opened in 1852. Here you'll see an 1860s Concord stagecoach, gold dust and ore from the Gold Rush era, and an exhibit called "Wells Fargo CSI Officers in Pursuit." Enjoy the history of the stagecoach line that became one of the country's most powerful banks.

Ferry Building

In 1898, the City of San Francisco created a wonderful new Ferry Building to facilitate commuting from the East Bay. But the rise of the automobile after World War II rendered the gorgeous construction obsolete, and its aesthetic ornamentation was covered over and filled in. But then the roads jammed up and ferry service began again, and the 1989 earthquake led to the removal of the Embarcadero Eyesore (an elevated freeway). Restored to glory in the 1990s, the San Francisco Ferry Building

San Francisco's Ferry Building provides upscale food and drink as well as ferry services.

(1 Ferry Bldg., 415/983-8030, www.ferrybuildingmarketplace.com, 10 A.M.–6 P.M. Mon.–Fri., 9 A.M.–6 P.M. Sat., 11 A.M.–5 P.M. Sun., check with businesses for individual hours) stands at the end of the Financial District at the edge of the water. You can get a brief lesson in the history of the edifice just inside the main lobby, where photos and interpretive plaques describe the life of the Ferry Building.

Inside the handsome structure, it's all about the food. The famous **Farmers Market** (415/291-3276, www.ferrybuildingmarketplace.com/farmers_market.php, 10 A.M.–2 P.M. Tues. and Thurs., 8 A.M.–2 P.M. Sat.) draws crowds. Accompanying the fresh produce, the permanent shops provide top-tier artisanal food and drink, from wine to cheese to high-end kitchenware. Local favorites Cowgirl Creamery and Acme Bread Company maintain storefronts here. For immediate gratification, a few incongruous quick-and-easy restaurants offer reasonable eats.

Perhaps surprisingly, out on the water side of the Ferry Building, you can actually catch a ferry. Boats come in from Larkspur, Sausalito, Tiburon, Vallejo, and Alameda each day. Check with the Blue and Gold Fleet (www.blueandgoldfleet.com), Golden Gate Ferry (www.goldengateferry.org), and Bay Link Ferries (www.baylinkferry.com) for information about service, times, and fares.

AT&T Park

The name changes every few years, but the place remains the same. AT&T Park (24 Willie Mays Plaza, 415/972-1800, http://sanfrancisco.giants.mlb.com/sf/ballpark) is home to the San Francisco Giants, endless special events, several great restaurants, and arguably California's best garlic fries. From the ballpark, you can look right out onto the Bay. During baseball games, a motley collection of boats float beside the stadium, hoping that an out-of-the-park fly ball will come sailing their way.

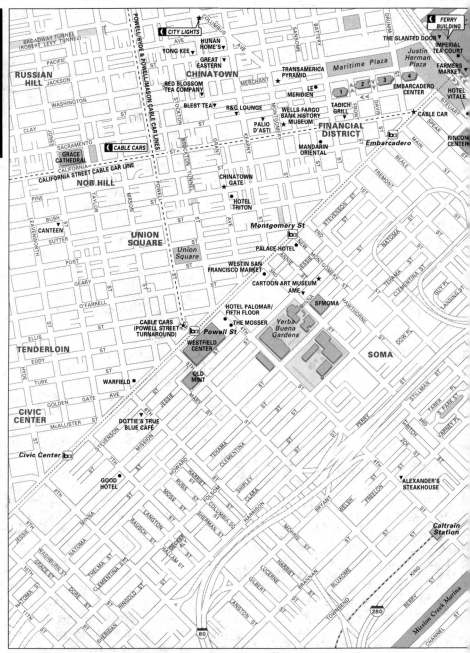

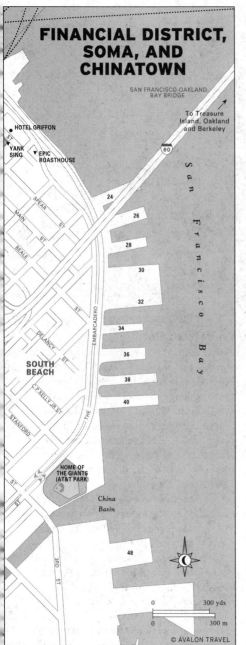

FINANCIAL DISTRICT, SOMA, AND CHINATOWN

SAN FRANCISCO-OAKLAND BAY BRIDGE

To Treasure Island, Oakland and Berkeley

HOTEL GRIFFON

YANK SING

EPIC ROASTHOUSE

80

San Francisco Bay

SPEAR ST

MAIN ST

BEALE ST

EMBARCADERO

DELANCY ST

SOUTH BEACH

C.P. KELLY JR ST

STANFORD

THE EMBARCADERO

HOME OF THE GIANTS (AT&T PARK)

China Basin

3RD ST

24
26
28
30
32
34
36
38
40
48

0   300 yds
0   300 m

© AVALON TRAVEL

Cartoon Art Museum

The Cartoon Art Museum (655 Mission St., 415/227-8666, http://cartoonart.org, 11 A.M.–5 P.M. Tues.–Sun., adults $7, seniors and students $5, children $3) offers a fun and funny outing for the whole family. The 20-year-old museum displays both permanent and traveling exhibits of original cartoon art, including international newspaper cartoons, high-quality comics, and Pixar Studios' big-screen animated wonders. Even young children are captivated by the beauty and creativity found here.

San Francisco Museum of Modern Art

SFMOMA (151 3rd St., 415/357-4000, www.sfmoma.org, 10 A.M.–5:45 P.M. Fri.–Tues., 10 A.M.–8:45 P.M. Thurs., opens at 11 A.M. in winter, adults $18, seniors $13, students $11, children under 12 free), as it's fondly called, is a local favorite. Even if modern art isn't your favorite, MOMA has a wonderful array of pieces to suit every taste. Amazing permanent collections include works by Ansel Adams, Henri Matisse, and Shiro Kuramata. Enjoy the paintings and sculptures in the fine arts collections, the wonderful photography, the funky modern furniture, and some truly bizarre installation art. SFMOMA brings in a number of special exhibitions each year, featuring the works of the hottest current artists and retrospectives of post-1900 legendary figures.

CHINATOWN

The massive Chinese migration to California began almost as soon as the news of easy gold in the mountain streams made it to East Asia. And despite rampant prejudice and increasingly desperate attempts on the part of "good" Americans to rid their pristine country of these immigrants, the Chinese not only stayed but persevered and eventually prospered. Many never made it to the gold fields, preferring instead to remain in bustling San Francisco to

bustling Chinatown

open shops and begin the business of commerce in their new home. They were basically segregated to a small area beneath Nob Hill, where they created a motley collection of wooden shacks that served as homes, restaurants, shops, and more. This neighborhood quickly became known as Chinatown. Along with much of San Francisco, the neighborhood was destroyed in the 1906 earthquake and fire. Despite xenophobic attempts to relocate Chinatown as far away from downtown San Francisco as possible, the Chinese prevailed and the neighborhood was rebuilt where it originally stood.

Today, visitors see the post-1906 visitor-friendly Chinatown that was built after the quake. Beautiful Asian architecture mixes with more mundane blocky city buildings to create a unique skyscape. Small alleyways wend between the broad touristy avenues, creating an atmosphere that speaks of the secrecy and closed culture of the Chinese in San Francisco.

Chinatown Gate

Visible from the streets leading into Union Square, the Chinatown Gate (Grant Ave. and Bush St.) perches at the southern "entrance" to the famous Chinatown neighborhood. The gate, built in 1970, is a relatively recent addition to this history-filled neighborhood. The design features Chinese dragons, pagodas, and other charming details. The inscription reads "All under heaven is for the good of the people," a quote from Dr. Sun Yat-sen. Its gaudy colorful splendor draws droves of visitors with cameras each day; on weekends it can be tough to find a quick moment to get your own picture taken at the gate.

Chinatown truly is a sight in and of itself. Visitors stroll the streets, exploring the tiny alleys and peeking into the temples, admiring the wonderful Asian architecture on occasionally unlikely buildings. Among the best known of these is the **Bank of America Building** (701 Grant Ave.)—an impressive edifice with a

Chinese tiled roof and 60 dragon medallions decorating the facade. The **East West Bank** (743 Washington St.) is even more traditional in its look. The small, beautiful building that acted as the Chinatown Telephone Exchange was constructed in this ultra-Chinese style just after 1906, when the Great Earthquake demolished the original structure. The Bank of Canton purchased the derelict building in 1960 and rehabilitated it; like many banks, it has changed hands since then. The **Sing Chong Building** (601 Grant Ave. at California St.) was another 1906 quick-rebuild, the reconstruction beginning shortly after the ground stopped shuddering and the smoke cleared.

NORTH BEACH AND FISHERMAN'S WHARF

"The Rock"

© BTMEDIA/123RF.COM

The Fisherman's Wharf and North Beach areas are an odd amalgam of old-school residential neighborhood and total tourist mecca. North Beach has long served as the Italian district of San Francisco, reflected in the restaurants in the area. Fisherman's Wharf was the spot where 19th-century Italians came to work; they were a big part of the fishing fleet that provided San Francisco with its legendary supply of fresh seafood.

Today, Fisherman's Wharf is *the* spot where visitors to San Francisco come to visit and snap photos. If you're not into crowds, avoid the area in the summer. For visitors who can hack a ton of other people, some of the best views of the air show during Fleet Week and the fireworks on the Fourth of July can be found down on the Wharf.

◖ Alcatraz

Going to Alcatraz (www.nps.gov/alcatraz), one of the most famous landmarks in the City, feels a bit like going to purgatory; this military fortress turned maximum-security prison, nicknamed "The Rock," has little warmth or welcome on its craggy forbidding shores. The fortress became a prison in the 19th century while it still

belonged to the military, which used it to house Civil War prisoners. The isolation of the island in the Bay, the frigid waters, and the nasty currents surrounding Alcatraz made it a perfect spot to keep prisoners contained with little hope of escape and near-certain death if the attempt was ever made. In 1934, after the military closed down their prison and handed the island over to the Department of Justice, construction began to turn Alcatraz into a new style of prison ready to house a new style of prisoner: Depression-era gangsters. A few of the honored guests of this maximum-security penitentiary were Al Capone, George "Machine Gun" Kelly, and Robert Stroud, "the Birdman of Alcatraz." The prison closed in 1963, and in 1964 and 1969 occupations were staged by Indians of All Tribes, an exercise that eventually led to the privilege of self-determination for North America's original inhabitants.

Today, Alcatraz acts primarily as an attraction for visitors to San Francisco. **Alcatraz Cruises** (Pier 33, 415/981-7625, www.alcatrazcruises.com, 9:10 A.M.–3:55 P.M., 6:15 and 6:45 P.M. daily, adults $28–35, children $17–21)

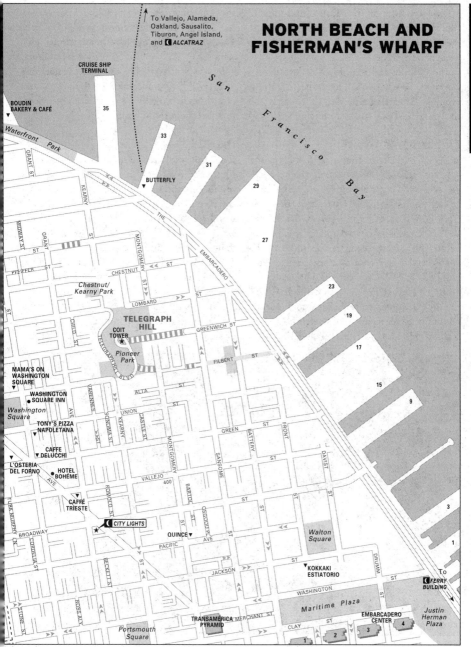

To Vallejo, Alameda, Oakland, Sausalito, Tiburon, Angel Island, and **(** ALCATRAZ

NORTH BEACH AND FISHERMAN'S WHARF

San Francisco Bay

CRUISE SHIP TERMINAL

BOUDIN BAKERY & CAFÉ ▼

Waterfront Park

35

33

31

29

27

BUTTERFLY ▼

THE EMBARCADERO

GRANT ST

MIDWAY ST

KEARNY ST

GRANT ST

ST

MONTGOMERY ST

PFEIFFER ST

CHESTNUT ST

Chestnut / Kearny Park

LOMBARD ST

CHILD ST

23

19

17

15

9

TELEGRAPH HILL

COIT TOWER ★

TELEGRAPH HILL BLVD

Pioneer Park

GREENWICH ST

FILBERT ST

MAMA'S ON WASHINGTON SQUARE ▼

WASHINGTON SQUARE INN ●

Washington Square

VARENNES ST

ALTA ST

UNION ST

ST

KEARNY ST

CASTLE ST

MONTGOMERY ST

SANSOME ST

BATTERY ST

FRONT ST

DAVIST ST

TONY'S PIZZA NAPOLETANA ●

SONOMA ST

GREEN ST

CAFFE DELUCCHI ▼

L'OSTERIA DEL FORNO ▼

HOTEL BOHÉME ●

AVE

VALLEJO 400 ST

BAETTO ST

ST

ST

3

CAFFÉ TRIESTE ▼

ROMOLO ST

OSGOOD PL

ST

(CITY LIGHTS ★

QUINCE ▼

AVE

PACIFIC ST

Walton Square

1

TURK MURPHY LN

BROADWAY

CORDELIA ST

BECKETT ST

JACKSON ST

DRUMM ST

KOKKAKI ESTIATORIO ▼

WASHINGTON ST

To **(** FERRY BUILDING

STONE ST

ROSSI ALY

Maritime Plaza

EMBARCADERO CENTER

Justin Herman Plaza

4

TRANSAMÉRICA PYRAMID

MERCHANT ST

CLAY ST

ST

1

2

3

Portsmouth Square

offers ferry rides out to Alcatraz and tours of the island and the prison. Tours depart from Pier 33. It's a good idea to buy tickets at least a week in advance, especially if you'll be in town in the summer and want to visit Alcatraz on a weekend. Tours often sell out, especially in the evening. Be careful after dark; the prison and the island are both said to be haunted!

Fisherman's Wharf

Welcome to the tourist mecca of San Francisco! Just don't go looking for an actual wharf or single pier when you come to visit Fisherman's Wharf. In fact, the Fisherman's Wharf area (Beach St. from Powell St. to Van Ness Ave., backs onto Bay St., www.fishermanswharf.org), reachable by Muni F line, sprawls along the waterfront and inland several blocks, creating a large tourist neighborhood. The Wharf, as it's called by locals, who avoid the area at all costs, features all crowds, all the time. Be prepared to push through a sea of humanity to see sights, buy souvenirs, and eat seafood. Fisherman's Wharf includes many of

the sights that people come to San Francisco to see: Pier 39, Ghirardelli Square, and, of course, **The Wax Museum of Fisherman's Wharf** (145 Jefferson St., 800/439-4305, www.waxmuseum. com, 10 A.M.–9 P.M. daily, adults $16, seniors and ages 12–17 $12, under age 12 $8), the presence of which tells most serious travelers all they need to know about the Wharf.

Pier 39

One of the most-visited spots in San Francisco, Pier 39 (www.pier39.com) hosts a wealth of restaurants and shops. If you've come down to the pier to see the sealife, start with the unusual **Aquarium of the Bay** (415/623-5300, www.aquariumofthebay.com, 9 A.M.–8 P.M. daily summer, call for off-season hours, adults $18, seniors and children $10). This 300-foot clear-walled tunnel lets visitors see thousands of species native to the San Francisco Bay, including sharks, rays, and plenty of fish. For a special treat, take the Behind the Scenes Tour or sign up for a Sleeps with the Sharks family

the sea lions at Pier 39

sleepover. Farther down the pier, get personal (but not *too* close) to the local colony of **sea lions**. These big, loud mammals tend to congregate at K-Dock in the West Marina. The best time to see the sea lions is winter, when the population grows into the hundreds. To learn more about the sea lions, head for the interpretive center on Level 2 of the **Marine Mammal Center** (415/289-7325, www.marinemammal-center.org, 10 A.M.–5 P.M. daily, free).

A perennial family favorite, the **San Francisco Carousel** ($3 per ride) is painted with beautiful scenes of San Francisco. Riders on the moving horses, carriages, and seats can look at the paintings or out onto the pier. Kids also love the daily shows by local street performers. Depending on when you're on the pier, you might see jugglers, magicians, or stand-up comedians on the **Alpine Spring Water Center Stage** (show times vary, free).

San Francisco Maritime National Historical Park

San Francisco Maritime National Historical Park comprises several waterfront offerings. The **visitors center** (499 Jefferson St., 415/447-5000, 9:30 A.M.–5 P.M. daily) presents some of the long and amazing maritime history of San Francisco, but the real fun comes from climbing aboard the historic ships at permanent dock across the street at the **Hyde Street Pier**. The shiniest jewel of the collection is the 1886 square-rigged *Balclutha,* a three-masted schooner that recalls times gone by. There are also several steamboats, including the workhorse ferry *Eureka* and a cool old steam paddle-wheel tugboat called the *Eppleton Hall.* Be careful if you're tall—as with most ships, these all have very short doorways and sometimes low ceilings.

The **Aquatic Bathhouse Building** (900 Beach St., 415/561-7100, www.nps.gov/safr, 10 A.M.–4 P.M. daily, adults $5, children free), built in 1939, houses the Maritime Museum with small exhibits and WPA murals.

Ghirardelli Square

Jammed in with Fisherman's Wharf and Pier 39, Ghirardelli Square (900 North Point St., www.ghirardellisq.com), pronounced "GEAR-ah-DEL-ee," reinvented itself as an upscale shopping, dining, and living area. Its namesake, the famous **Ghirardelli Chocolate Factory** (900 North Point St., 415/775-5500, www.ghirardelli.com, 9 A.M.–11 P.M. Sun.–Thurs., 9 A.M.–midnight Fri.–Sat.) sits at the corner of the square. Here you can browse the rambling shop and pick up truffles, wafers, candies, and sauces for all your friends back home. Finally, get in line at the ice cream counter to order a hot-fudge sundae. These don't travel well, so you'll have to enjoy it here. Once you've finished gorging on chocolate, you can wander out into the square to enjoy more shopping (there's even a cupcake shop if your teeth haven't dissolved yet) and the sight of an unbelievably swank condo complex overlooking the Bay.

Lombard Street

You've no doubt seen it in movies, on TV, and on postcards: Lombard Street, otherwise known as "the crookedest street in the world." The truth is, Lombard Street is a major artery running through San Francisco. So why bother braving the bumper-to-bumper cars navigating its zigzag turns? For one, you can't beat the view from the top. With its 27 percent grade, Lombard Street offers unobstructed vistas of San Francisco Bay, Alcatraz Island, Fisherman's Wharf, Coit Tower, and the City.

The section that visitors flock to spans only one block, from Hyde Street at the top to Leavenworth Street at the bottom. Lombard was originally created to keep people from rolling uncontrolled down the treacherously steep grade. Brave pedestrians can walk up and down the sides of the brick-paved street, enjoying the hydrangeas and Victorian mansions that line the roadway. For convenience during the peak summer months, take a cable car directly to the top of Lombard Street and walk down the noncurvy stairs on either side.

Coit Tower

It's big, it's phallic, and it may or may not have been designed to look like a fire-hose nozzle or a power station. But since 1933, Coit Tower (1 Telegraph Hill Blvd., 415/362-0808, http://sfrecpark.org, 10 A.M.–5:30 P.M. daily in summer, adults $7, ages 12–17 $5, under age 12 $2, call for tour times) has beautified the City just as benefactor Lillie Hitchcock Coit intended when she willed San Francisco one-third of her monumental estate. Inside, murals depicting city life and works of the 1930s cover the walls. From the top of the tower on a clear day, you can see the whole of the City and the Bay. Part of what makes Coit Tower special is the walks up to it. Rather than contributing to the acute congestion in the area, consider taking public transit to the area and walking up the Filbert Steps to the tower. It's steep, but there's no other way to see the lovely little cottages and gardens that mark the path up from the streets to the top of Telegraph Hill.

MARINA AND PACIFIC HEIGHTS

The Marina and Pacific Heights shelter some of the amazing amount of money that flows in the City by the Bay. The Marina is one of the San Francisco neighborhoods constructed on landfill (sand dredged up from the bottom of the ocean and piled in what was once a marsh). It was badly damaged in the 1989 Loma Prieta earthquake, but you won't see any of that damage today. Instead, you'll find a wealthy neighborhood, a couple of yacht harbors, and lots of good museums, dining, and shopping.

Palace of Fine Arts

The Palace of Fine Arts (3301 Lyon St., 415/567-6642) was originally meant to be nothing but a temporary structure—part of the Panama Pacific Exposition in 1915. But the lovely building won the hearts of San Franciscans, and a fund was started to preserve the Palace beyond the Exposition. Through the first half of the 20th century, efforts could not keep it from crumbling, but in the 1960s and 1970s, serious rebuilding work took place, and

The Palace of Fine Arts was originally intended to be a temporary structure.

today the Palace of Fine Arts stands proud and strong and beautiful. It houses the **Palace of Fine Arts Theater** (www.palaceoffinearts. org), which hosts events nearly every day, from beauty pageants to conferences on the future of artificial intelligence. Until Spring 2013, it also housed the Exploratorium.

☾ Exploratorium

Kids around the Bay Area have loved the Exploratorium (3601 Lyon St., 415/561-0360, www.exploratorium.edu, 10 A.M.–5 P.M. Tues.–Sun., also some Mon. holidays, adults $25, youth $19) for decades. This innovative museum makes science the most fun thing ever for kids of all ages; adults are welcome to join in on the interactive exhibits too. You can learn about everything from frogs to the physics of baseball, sound, and seismology. The Exploratorium seeks to be true to its name and encourage exploration into all aspects of science. For an utterly unusual experience, pay an extra $5 and walk bravely (and blindly) into the Tactile Dome, a lightless space where you can "see" your way only by reaching out and touching the environment around you.

In Spring 2013, the Exploratorium will move to new digs at Piers 15 and 17, between the Ferry Building and Fisherman's Wharf. Check the website for details.

Fort Mason

Once the Port of Embarkation from which the United States waged World War II in the Pacific, Fort Mason Center (Buchanan St. and Marina Blvd., 415/345-7500, www.fort-mason.org, 9 A.M.–8 P.M. daily, parking up to $10) now acts as home to numerous non-profit, multicultural, and artistic organizations. Where soldiers and guns departed to fight the Japanese, visitors now find dance performances, independent theatrical productions, art galleries, and the annual **San Francisco Blues Festival** (www.sfblues.com). At any time

of year, a number of great shows go on in the renovated historic white and red buildings of the complex; check the online calendar to see what's coming up during your visit.

Other fun features include installations of the **Outdoor Exploratorium** (www.exploratorium.edu/outdoor, dawn–dusk daily). Ranging all over Fort Mason, the Exploratorium exhibits appeal to all five senses (yes, even taste) and teach visitors about the world around them—right there around them, in fact. You'll taste salt in local water supplies, hear a foghorn, and see what causes the parking lot to crack and sink. It's free, and it's fascinating—download a map from the website, or grab a guide from installation 5, Portable Observatories.

☾ The Presidio

It seems strange to think of progressive, peace-loving San Francisco as a town with tremendous military history, yet the City's warlike past is nowhere more evident than at The Presidio (Bldg. 105, Montgomery St. and Lincoln Blvd., 415/561-4323, www.nps.gov/prsf, visitors center 10 A.M.–4 P.M. Thurs.–Sun., free). This sweeping stretch of land running along the San Francisco Headlands down to the Golden Gate has been a military installation since 1776, when the Spanish created their El Presidio del San Francisco fort on the site. In 1846 the United States army took over the site (peacefully), and in 1848 the American Presidio military installation formally opened. It was finally abandoned by the military and became a national park in 1994. The Presidio had a role in every Pacific-related war from the Civil War through Desert Storm.

To orient yourself among the more than 800 buildings that make up the Presidio, start at the visitors center or the **Warming Hut Bookstore & Café** (983 Marine Dr., 415/561-3040, 9 A.M.–5 P.M. daily). As you explore the huge park, you can visit the pioneering aviation area **Crissy Field,** Civil War–era fortifications

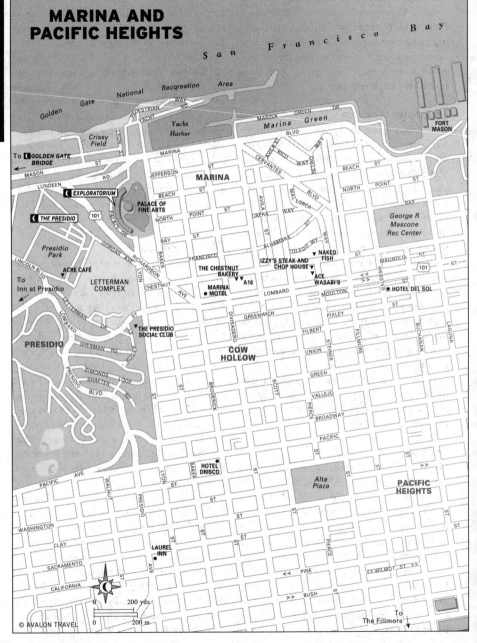

MARINA AND PACIFIC HEIGHTS

San Francisco Bay

National Recreation Area

Golden Gate

Crissy Field

Yacht Harbor

Marina Green

MARINA BLVD

FORT MASON

To GOLDEN GATE BRIDGE

EXPLORATORIUM

THE PRESIDIO

PALACE OF FINE ARTS

Presidio Park

ACRE CAFÉ

To Inn at Presidio

LETTERMAN COMPLEX

George R Moscone Rec Center

HOTEL DEL SOL

MARINA

NAKED FISH

THE CHESTNUT BAKERY

IZZY'S STEAK AND CHOP HOUSE

ACE WASABI'S

A16

MARINA MOTEL

PRESIDIO

THE PRESIDIO SOCIAL CLUB

COW HOLLOW

HOTEL DRISCO

Alta Plaza

PACIFIC HEIGHTS

LAUREL INN

To The Fillmore

0   200 yds
0   200 m

© AVALON TRAVEL

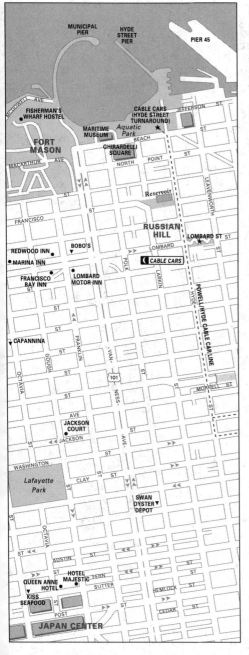

at **Fort Point,** and the **Letterman Digital Arts Center** (Chestnut St. and Lyon St., www.lucas-film.com), built on the site of the Letterman Army Hospital, which served as a top-notch care facility for returning wounded soldiers over more than a century's worth of wars.

◖ Golden Gate Bridge

People come from the world over to see and walk the Golden Gate Bridge (U.S. 101/Hwy. 1 at Lincoln Blvd., 415/923-2000, http://goldengatebridge.org, cars $6, pedestrians free). A marvel of human engineering constructed in 1936 and 1937, the suspension bridge spans the narrow "gate" from which the Pacific Ocean enters the San Francisco Bay. On a clear day, pedestrians can see the whole Bay from the east sidewalk, then turn around to see the Pacific Ocean spreading out on the other. Or take in the stunning bridge view from the Marin Headlands barracks, looking down from the northwest and in toward the City skyline.

The bridge itself is not golden, but a rich orange color called "international orange" that shines like gold when the sun sets behind it on a clear evening. But newcomers to the City beware—not all days and precious few evenings at the bridge are clear. One of the most beautiful sights in San Francisco is the fog blowing in over the Golden Gate late in the afternoon. Unfortunately, once the fog stops blowing and settles in, the bridge is cold, damp, and viewless, so plan to come early in the morning, or pick spring or autumn for your best chance of a clear sight of this most famous and beautiful of artificial structures.

CIVIC CENTER AND HAYES VALLEY

Some of the most interesting neighborhoods in the City cluster toward its center. The Civic Center functions as the heart of San Francisco; the beautiful building actually houses the mayor's office and much of San Francisco's government.

CIVIC CENTER, HAYES VALLEY, MISSION, AND CASTRO

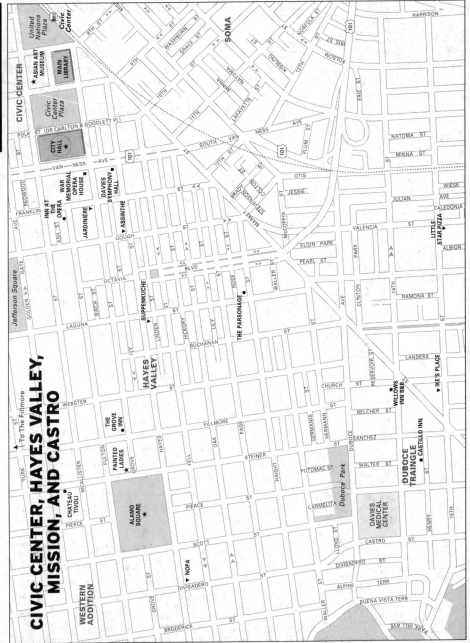

United Nations Plaza
Civic Center
CIVIC CENTER
ASIAN ART MUSEUM
MAIN LIBRARY
Civic Center Plaza
POLK ST
DR CARLTON B GOODLETT PL
CITY HALL
VAN NESS AVE
INN AT THE OPERA
WAR MEMORIAL OPERA HOUSE
DAVIES SYMPHONY HALL
ASH ST
REDWOOD ST
FRANKLIN AVE
JARDINIÈRE
ABSINTHE
GOUGH ST
Jefferson Square
GOLDEN GATE AVE
OCTAVIA
LAGUNA
BIRCH ST
SUPPENKUCHE
LINDEN ST
HICKORY
LILY
IVY
BUCHANAN
ROSE ST
THE PARSONAGE
HAYES VALLEY
WEBSTER
THE GROVE INN
FILLMORE
PAGE
PAINTED LADIES
HAYES
GROVE
OAK
FELL
STEINER
HAIGHT
POTOMAC ST
CHATEAU TIVOLI
FULTON
McALLISTER
TURK ST
To The Fillmore
WESTERN ADDITION
ALAMO SQUARE
PIERCE
SCOTT
NOPA
DIVISADERO
GROVE ST
BRODERICK ST
WALLER ST
PARK HILL AVE
BUENA VISTA TERR
ALPINE TERR
CARMELITA
Duboce Park
GERMANIA
HERMANN
SANCHEZ
DUBOCE
WALTER ST
BELCHER ST
CHURCH ST
RESERVOIR ST
WILLOWS INN B&B
IKE'S PLACE
LANDERS
DUBOCE TRIANGLE
CASTILLO INN
DAVIES MEDICAL CENTER
CASTRO ST
DIVISADERO ST
LLOYD ST
HENRY ST
15TH
SOMA
8TH ST
9TH ST
10TH
11TH
12TH ST
WASHBURN ST
GRACE ST
NATOMA
MINNA
LAFAYETTE
SOUTH VAN NESS AVE
OTIS
COLTON
STEVENSON AVE
BRADY
JESSIE
MARKET
McCOPPIN
ELGIN PARK
PEARL ST
VALENCIA
PARK AVE
WALLER ST
CLINTON
14TH
RAMONA ST
ALBION
LITTLE STAR PIZZA
CALEDONIA
WIESE
JULIAN AVE
MINNA ST
NATOMA ST
HARRISON
NORFOLK ST
SIRIS ST
FOLSOM
ERIE ST
KISSLING
PLUM ST

TREAT AVE

AVE

LUCKY ST

FOLSOM ST

SHOTWELL ST

SOUTH VAN NESS AVE

MISSION

CYPRESS ST

LA TAQUERIA

CAPP ST

24th St

LILAC

16th St

MISSION ST

OSAGE ALY

HOFF ST

SAN CARLOS ST

BARTLETT

ORANGE ALY

CLARION ALY

SYCAMORE ST

LEXINGTON

PAPALOTE MEXICAN GRILL

BAR TARTINE

POPLAR ST

VALENCIA

JOSE AVE

25TH

ALBION ST

LAPIDGE ST

RANGE

DEARBORN

LINDA

ST

GUERRERO

TARTINE BAKERY

OAKWOOD

AMES ST

FAIR OAKS ST

BI-RITE CREAMERY AND BAKESHOP

DELORINA

CUMBERLAND

QUANE ST

DOLORES

MERSEY ST

CHATTANOOGA ST

MISSION DOLORES

Dolores Park

CHULA LN

17TH

CHURCH

NELLIE ST

IKE'S PLACE

DORLAND ST

LIBERTY

VICKSBURG ST

SANCHEZ

NOE VALLEY

DINOSAURS

16TH

PROSPER ST

18TH

HANCOCK

19TH

CUMBERLAND

21ST

ELIZABETH

JERSEY

POND

NOE

FRANCES

HARTFORD ST

CASTRO

HILL

22ND

ALVARADO

LA MEDITERRANEE

INN ON CASTRO

MARKET

CASTRO

ANCHOR OYSTER BAR

COLLINGWOOD

20TH

BEAVER

FLINT ST

STATES ST

DIAMOND ST

EUREKA ST

23RD

24TH

300 yds

300 m

RANDALL MUSEUM

MUSEUM WAY

DOUGLASS

21ST

© AVALON TRAVEL

Visitors who last visited San Francisco a decade or more ago will notice that the Civic Center has been cleaned up quite a lot in the last few years. It's now safe to walk here—at least in the daytime.

As the Civic Center melts toward Hayes Valley, the high culture of San Francisco appears. Near the border you'll find Davies Symphony Hall, home of the world-famous San Francisco Symphony, and the War Memorial Opera House. And serving these, you'll find fabulous Hayes Valley hotels and restaurants.

City Hall

Look at San Francisco's City Hall (1 Dr. Carlton B. Goodlett Place, 415/554-6079, www.sfgov. org, 8 A.M.–8 P.M. Mon.–Fri., free) and you'll think you've somehow been transported to Europe. The stately building with the gilded dome is the pride of the City and houses much of its government. Enjoy walking through the parklike square in front of City Hall (though this area can get a bit sketchy after dark). The inside has been extensively renovated after being damaged in the Loma Prieta earthquake in 1989. You'll find a combination of historical grandeur and modern accessibility and convenience as you tour the Arthur Brown Jr.–designed edifice.

Asian Art Museum

Across from City Hall is the Asian Art Museum (200 Larkin St., 415/581-3500, www.asianart. org, 10 A.M.–5 P.M. Tues.–Fri., adults $12, seniors $8, ages 13–17 $7, under age 13 free). Yup, that's it right there with the enormous Ionic columns and Eurocentric facade. But inside you'll have an amazing metaphorical window into the Asian cultures that have shaped and defined San Francisco and the Bay Area. The second and third floors of this intense museum are packed with great art from all across Asia, including a Chinese gilded Buddha dating from A.D. 338. Sit down on a padded bench to admire paintings, sculpture, lacquered jade, textiles, jewels, and every type of art object

© DOMINI DRAGOONE

San Francisco's City Hall

imaginable. The breadth and diversity of Asian culture may stagger you; the museum's displays come from Japan and Vietnam, Buddhist Tibet, and ancient China. Special exhibitions cost extra—check the website to see what will be displayed on the ground floor galleries when you're in town. Even if you've been to the museum in the past, come back for a browse. The curators regularly rotate items from the permanent collection, so you'll probably encounter new beauty every time you visit.

Alamo Square

Possibly the most photographed neighborhood in San Francisco, Alamo Square (Hayes St. and Steiner St.) is home to the "painted ladies" on "postcard row." This is a row of stately Victorian mansions, all painted brilliant colors and immaculately maintained, that appear in many images of the City. Stroll in Alamo Square's green park and enjoy the serenity of this charming residential neighborhood.

MISSION AND CASTRO

Perhaps the most famous, or infamous, neighborhoods in the City are the Mission district and the Castro district. The Castro is the heart of gay San Francisco, complete with naughty shops, leather bars, and all sorts of, uh...adult festivals. It has become pretty touristy, but you can still find the occasional jewel here. Just don't expect the Halloween party you've heard about—the City has cracked down, and Halloween has become sedate in this party-happy neighborhood.

With its mix of Latino immigrants, working artists, and urban professionals, the Mission is a neighborhood bursting at the seams with idiosyncratic energy. Changing from block to block, the zone manages to be blue-collar, edgy, and gentrified all at once. The heart of the neighborhood is still very much Latin American, with delicious burritos and *pupusas* around every corner. It's a haven for international restaurants and real bargains in thrift shops, along with the hippest clubs in the City.

the "painted ladies" of Alamo Square

Mission Dolores

Mission Dolores

Mission Dolores (3321 16th St., 415/621-8203, www.missiondolores.org, 9 A.M.–4:30 P.M. daily May–Oct., 9 A.M.–4 P.M. daily Nov.–Apr., donation adults $5, children $3), formally named Mission San Francisco de Asís, was founded in 1776. Today, the Mission is the oldest intact building in the City, survivor of the 1906 earthquake and fire, the 1989 Loma Prieta quake, and more than 200 years of use. You can attend Roman Catholic services here each Sunday, or you can visit the Old Mission Museum and the Basilica, which house artifacts from the Native Americans and Spanish of the 18th century. The beauty and grandeur of the Mission recall the heyday of the Spanish empire in California, so important to the history of the state as it is today.

GOLDEN GATE PARK AND THE HAIGHT

Perhaps the most spectacular sight in Golden Gate Park is, well, Golden Gate Park (main entrance at Stanyan St. at Fell St., McLaren Lodge Visitors Center at John F. Kennedy Dr., 415/831-2700, www.golden-gate-park.com). Acres of land include forest, desert, formal gardens, museums, and buffalo pasture. Enjoy a free concert in the summer or a walk under the trademark fog in the winter.

Haight-Ashbury

The neighborhood surrounding the intersection of Haight and Ashbury Streets (known locally as "the Haight") is best known for the wave of countercultural energy that broke out in the 1960s. The area initially was a magnet for drifters, dropouts, and visionaries who preached and practiced a heady blend of peace, love, and psychedelic drugs.

The door to the promised new consciousness never swung fully open, and then it swung shut with a resounding bang. Today, thousands of visitors stand at the iconic intersection, and what they see is Ben & Jerry's. The district is still home to plenty of independent businesses, including vintage stores, lots of places to get pierced and tattooed, and, of course, head shops. Plenty of chain stores are interspersed with the indies, reminding visitors that the power of capitalism can intrude anywhere—even in a countercultural center.

A prettier aspect of local gentrification appears in the form of restored Victorian houses in the Haight. You can actually stay in a bright, funky Red Victorian, or check out the private homes on Page Street and throughout the neighborhood. To learn more about the history of the Haight and to walk past the famed homes of the Grateful Dead and Jefferson Airplane, take the **Flower Power Walking Tour** (intersection of Stanyan St. and Waller Sts., 415/863-1621, www.hippygourmet.com, 9:30 A.M. Tues. and Sat., 11 A.M. Fri., $20).

◖ de Young Museum

Haven't been to the City in a while? Take

some time out to visit the completely rebuilt de Young Museum (50 Hagiwara Tea Garden Dr., 415/750-3600, http://deyoung.famsf.org, 9:30 A.M.–5:15 P.M. Tues.–Thurs. and Sat.–Sun., 9:30 A.M.–8:45 P.M. Fri., adults $10, seniors $7, children $6) in Golden Gate Park. Everything from the striking exterior to the art collections and exhibitions and the 360-degree panoramic view of San Francisco from the top of the tower has been renewed, replaced, or newly recreated. The reason for the recent renewal was the 1989 earthquake, which damaged the original de Young beyond simple repair. The renovation took more than 10 years, and the results are a smashing success. For a special treat, brave the lines and grab a meal at the museum's café.

The collections at the de Young include works in various media: painting, sculpture, textiles, ceramics, and more modern graphic designs and "contemporary crafts." Some collections focus on artists from the United States, while many others contain art from around the world. The exhibitions that come through the de Young range from the William Morris art nouveau from Britain to the exquisite Jean-Paul Gautier collection.

◖ California Academy of Sciences

A triumph of the sustainable scientific principles it exhibits, the California Academy of Sciences (55 Music Concourse Dr., 415/379-8000, www.calacademy.org, 9:30 A.M.–5 P.M. Mon.–Sat., 11 A.M.–5 P.M. Sun., adults $30, children 4–11 $20, students and seniors $25) drips with ecological perfection. From its grass-covered roof to its underground aquarium, visitors can explore every part of the universe. Wander through a steamy endangered rainforest contained inside a giant glass bubble, or travel through an all-digital outer space in the high-tech planetarium. More studious nature lovers can spend days examining every inch of the Natural History Museum, including favorite exhibits like the 87-foot-long blue whale skeleton, from the older incarnation of the Academy of Science. Though it might look and sound like an adult destination, in fact the new Academy of Sciences takes pains to make itself kid-friendly, with interactive exhibits, thousands of live animals, and endless opportunities for learning. How could kids not love a museum where the guards by the elevators have butterfly nets to catch the occasional "exhibit" that's trying to escape?

Japanese Tea Garden

The Japanese Tea Garden (7 Hagiwara Tea Garden Dr., 415/752-4227, http://japanese-teagardensf.com, 9 A.M.–6 P.M. daily Mar.–Oct., 9 A.M.–4:45 P.M. daily Nov.–Feb., adults $7, seniors $5, children $2) is a haven of peace and tranquility that's a local favorite within the park. The planting and design of the garden began in 1894 for the California Exposition.

a large bronze Buddha in the Japanese Tea Garden

© RAFAEL RAMIREZ LEE/123RF.COM

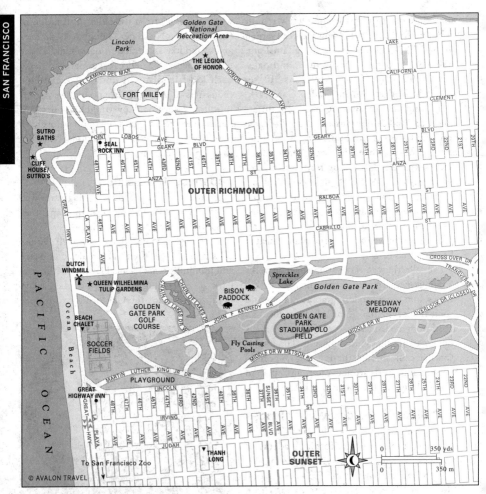

© AVALON TRAVEL

Today the flourishing garden displays a wealth of beautiful flora, including stunning examples of rare Chinese and Japanese plants, some quite old. As you stroll along the paths, you'll come upon sculptures, bridges, ponds, and even traditional *tsukubai* (a tea ceremony sink). You can visit the tea house, the brilliant pagoda and temple, and the gift shop as well.

San Francisco Botanical Gardens

Take a bucolic walk in the middle of Golden Gate Park by visiting the San Francisco Botanical Gardens (1199 9th Ave. at Lincoln Way, 415/661-1316, www.sfbotanicalgarden.org, 9 A.M.–6 P.M. daily Mar.–Sept., 10 A.M.–5 P.M. daily Oct.–early Mar., adults $7, students and seniors $5, ages 5–11 $2, families $15, under age 5 and city residents with ID free). The 55-acre gardens play home to more than 8,000 species of plants from around the world, including a California Natives garden and a shady redwood forest. Fountains, ponds,

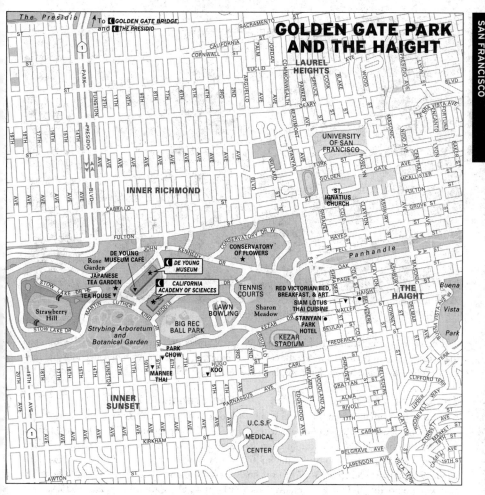

GOLDEN GATE PARK AND THE HAIGHT

meadows, and lawns are interwoven with the flowers and trees to create a peaceful, serene setting in the middle of the crowded city. The Botanical Gardens are a great place to kick back with a book and a snack; the plants will keep you in quiet company as you rev up to tackle another round of touring.

Conservatory of Flowers

Lying at the northeastern entrance to Golden Gate Park, the Conservatory of Flowers (100 John F. Kennedy Dr., 415/831-2090, www. conservatoryofflowers.org, 10 A.M.–4:30 P.M. Tues.–Sun., adults $7, students and seniors $5, ages 5–11 $2) blooms year-round. The exotic flowers grow in several "galleries" within the enormous glassy white Victorian-style greenhouse. Rare, slightly scary orchids twine around rainforest trees, eight-foot lily pads float serenely on still waters, and cheerful seasonal flowers spill out of containers in the potted plant gallery.

© SABRINA YOUNG

the lush interior of the Conservatory of Flowers

If you're traveling with small kids, be aware that strollers are not permitted inside the conservatory; wheelchairs and power chairs are allowed.

The Legion of Honor

A beautiful museum in a town filled with beauty, The Legion of Honor (100 34th Ave. at Clement St., 415/750-3600, http://legionofhonor.famsf. org, 9:30 A.M.–5:15 P.M. Tues.–Sun., adults $10, seniors $7, students and ages 13–17 $6) sits on its lonely promontory in Lincoln Park, overlooking the Golden Gate. A gift to the City from philanthropist Alma Spreckels in 1924, this French beaux arts–style building was built to honor the memory of California soldiers who died in World War I. From its beginning, the Legion of Honor was a museum dedicated to bringing European art to the population of San Francisco. Today, visitors can view gorgeous collections of European paintings, sculpture, and decorative arts, ancient artifacts from around the Mediterranean, thousands of paper drawings by great artists, and much more. Special exhibitions come from the Legion's own collections and museums of the world.

San Francisco Zoo

Lions and tigers and bears...and lemurs and meerkats and penguins, oh, my! Located farther out in the Sunset "avenues," the San Francisco Zoo (Sloat Blvd. at 47th Ave., 415/753-7080, www.sfzoo.org, 10 A.M.–5 P.M. daily summer, 10 A.M.–4 P.M. daily winter, adults $15, seniors $12, ages 4–14 $9) has them all and more, making it a favorite excursion for locals and visitors all year long. Over the last several years the zoo has undergone a transformation, becoming an example of naturalized habitats and conservatory zoo practices. Today, animal lovers can enjoy the native plants and funny faces in the lemur habitat, the families of meerkats, and the bird sanctuary. Families come to check out the wealth of interactive children's exhibits as well as the various exotic animals.

Entertainment and Events

NIGHTLIFE
Bars
UNION SQUARE AND NOB HILL

These ritzy neighborhoods are better known for their shopping than their nightlife, but a few bars hang in there, plying weary shoppers with good drinks. Most tend toward the upscale. Some inhabit the upper floors of the major hotels, like the **Tonga Room and Hurricane Bar** (950 Mason St., 415/772-5278, www.tongaroom.com, 5–11:30 P.M. Wed.–Thurs. and Sun., 5 P.M.–12:30 A.M. Fri.–Sat.), where an over-the-top tiki theme adds a whimsical touch to the stately Fairmont Hotel on Nob Hill. Enjoy the tropical atmosphere with a fruity rum drink topped with a classic paper umbrella.

Just outside the Union Square area in the sketchy Tenderloin neighborhood, brave souls can find a gem. **Cafe Royale** (800 Post St., 415/441-4099, www.caferoyale-sf.com, 3 P.M.–2 A.M. daily) isn't a typical watering hole by any city's standards, but its intense focus on art fits perfectly with the endlessly eclectic ethos of San Francisco. Local artists exhibit their work in Café Royale on a monthly basis, and plenty of live performers grace the space. Live music tends toward the folksy and indie unplugged. In among the artwork, some liquor lurks—think trendy sake and *soju* cocktails, good glasses of wine, and imported beers. The menu includes French sandwiches, gourmet salads, and small plates.

Part live-music venue, part elegant bar, **Top of the Mark** (Mark Hopkins, 1 Nob Hill, 415/616-6940, www.intercontinentalmark-hopkins.com, 2:30–11:30 P.M. Mon.–Thurs., 2:30 P.M.–12:30 A.M. Fri.–Sat., 5–11:30 P.M. Sun.) has something for every discerning taste in nighttime entertainment. Since World War II, the views and drinks in this wonderful lounge at the top of the InterContinental Mark Hopkins Hotel have drawn visitors from around the world. The lounge doubles as a restaurant that serves breakfast and lunch, but the best time for cocktails is, of course, at night. That's when live bands play almost every night of the week. The dress code is business casual or better and is enforced, so leave the jeans in your room. Have a top-shelf martini, and let your toes tap along.

The cocktail craze is alive and well at the **Rickhouse** (246 Kearny St., 415/398-2827, www.rickhousesf.com, 5 P.M.–2 A.M. Mon. and Sat., 3 P.M.–2 A.M. Tues.–Fri.). Voted one of the best bars in the world by *Food & Wine* magazine in 2010, Rickhouse excels in the creative and classic cocktail. Grab a seat upstairs or down, and sample a Rye Maple Fizz or go in on a massive rum punch, served in a hollow clam shell. Just get here before the after-work crowd, or you may not get in at all.

FINANCIAL DISTRICT AND SOMA

All those high-powered business suit–clad executive types working in the Financial District need places to drink too. One of these is the **Royal Exchange** (301 Sacramento St., 415/956-1710, http://royalexchange.com, 11 A.M.–11 P.M. Mon.–Fri.). This classic pub-style bar has a green-painted exterior, big windows overlooking the street, and a long, narrow barroom. The Royal Exchange serves a full lunch and dinner menu, a small wine list, and a full complement of top-shelf spirits. But most of all, the Exchange serves beer. With 73 taps pouring out 32 different types of beer, the hardest problem will be choosing one. This businesspeople's watering hole is open to the public only on weekdays; on weekends they host private parties.

The Cosmopolitan (121 Spear St., Suite B8, 415/543-4001, http://cosmopolitansf. com, 3:30 P.M.–midnight Mon.–Tues., 11:30 A.M.–2 A.M. Wed.–Fri., 5:30 P.M.–2 A.M. Sat.) offers the best of both worlds: a bar and piano lounge serving top-shelf liquors and reasonably priced well drinks, and a large dining room serving an ever-changing menu of California cuisine. You're more than welcome to enjoy drinks only at the bar, or make a reservation for a complete upscale dinner in the restaurant. If you're lucky, you might even get some live entertainment from a local musician plying the lounge piano.

In urban-renewed SoMa (meaning South of Market), upscale wine bars have become an evening institution. Among the trendiest you'll find is **District** (216 Townsend St., 415/896-2120, http://districtsf.com, 4 P.M.–2 A.M. Mon.–Fri., 5 P.M.–2 A.M. Sat.). A perfect example of its kind, District features bare brick walls, simple wooden furniture, and a big U-shaped bar at the center of the room with wine glasses hanging above it. While you can get a cocktail or even a beer here, the point of coming to District is to sip the finest wines from California, Europe, and beyond.

The **House of Shields** (39 New Montgomery St., 415/284-9958, www.thehouseofshields.com, 2 P.M.–2 A.M. Mon.–Fri., 3 P.M.–2 A.M. Sat.–Sun.) has been in the City since 1908. The original incarnation was an illegal speakeasy during the prohibition era (it even has an under-street tunnel to the neighboring Sheraton Hotel). After an extensive remodeling in 2010 by celebrity chef Dennis Leary, the House of Shields has reopened serving upscale cocktails (with upscale prices) in the gorgeous interior. Expect a huge crowd during happy hour, which thins out after about 8 P.M. or so.

Secret passwords, a hidden library, and an art deco vibe make **Bourbon and Branch** (505 Jones St., 415/346-1735, www.bourbonandbranch.com, 6 P.M.–2 A.M. Mon.–Sat., reservations suggested) a must for lovers of the brown stuff. Tucked behind a nameless brown door, this resurrected 1920s-era speakeasy evokes its prohibition-era past with passwords and secret passages. A business-class elite sips rare bourbon and scotch in secluded booths while those without reservations step into the hidden library.

CHINATOWN

Nightlife in Chinatown runs to dark, quiet dive bars filled with locals. Perhaps the perfect Chinatown dive, **Li Po Lounge** (916 Grant Ave., 415/982-0072, 2 P.M.–2 A.M. daily, cash only) has an appropriately dark and slightly spooky atmosphere that recalls the opium dens of another century. Cheap drinks and Chinese dice games attract locals, and it's definitely helpful to speak Cantonese. But even an English-speaking out-of-town visitor can get a good cheap (and strong!) mai tai or beer. The hanging lantern and Buddha statue behind the bar complete the picture. Another great local hangout worth checking out is the **Buddha Cocktail Lounge** (901 Grant Ave., 415/362-1792, 1 P.M.–2 A.M. daily, cash only).

NORTH BEACH AND FISHERMAN'S WHARF

For a good time down on the Wharf, you can choose from a number of popular bars. **Rosewood** (732 Broadway, 415/951-4886, 5 P.M.–2 A.M. Mon.–Sat.) glows with its namesake wood paneling and soft lighting. Join the young, hip, urban crowd and sip a specialty cocktail, or quaff a draft beer inside the bar or out on the bamboo-strewn patio. A popular hangout, Rosewood can get crowded (and service can get spotty) on weekends.

One of the oldest and most celebrated bars in the City, **Tosca** (242 Columbus Ave., 415/986-9651, http://toscacafesf.com, 5 P.M.–2 A.M. Tues.–Sun.) loves its unpretentious yet glam 1940s style. Hunter S. Thompson once tended bar here when the owner was out at the dentist. The jukebox plays grand opera to the patrons clustered in the big red booths. Locals love the lack of trendiness, the classic cocktails, and the occasional star sightings.

Almost across the street from Tosca is **Vesuvio** (255 Columbus Ave., 415/362-3370, www.vesuvio.com, 6 A.M.–2 A.M. daily). Jack Kerouac loved Vesuvio, which is why it's probably North Beach's most famous saloon. This cozy bi-level hideout is an easy place to spend the afternoon with a pint of Anchor Steam.

Dress up a little for a night out at **15 Romolo** (15 Romolo Place, 415/398-1359, www.15romolo.com, 5 P.M.–2 A.M. daily). You'll have to hike up the steep little alley (Fresno St. crosses Romolo Place, which can be a little hard to find) to this hotel bar, but once you're here you'll love the fab cosmos, edgy jukebox music, and often mellow crowd. The bar is smallish and can get crowded on the weekend, so come on a weeknight if you prefer a quiet drink. 15 Romolo also serves brunch (11:30 A.M.–3:30 P.M. Sat.–Sun.).

MARINA AND PACIFIC HEIGHTS

Marina and Pacific Heights denizens enjoy a good glass of vino, and the wine bars in the area cater to local tastes. The **Bacchus** (1954 Hyde St., 415/928-2633, www.bacchussf.com, 5:30 P.M.–midnight daily) is a tiny local watering hole that offers an array of wines, sake cocktails, and even delivered-to-your-table sushi from nearby Sushi Groove. DJs sometimes spin on Thursday and Friday nights.

Another favorite bar is the **City Tavern** (3200 Fillmore St., 415/567-0918, www. citytavernsf.com, 3 P.M.–2 A.M. Mon.–Fri., 11 A.M.–2 A.M. Sat.–Sun.). Here you'll get a mix of sports, drinks, and good company. Good solid American food comes at reasonable prices, while weekend brunch features an array of tasty classics as well as some health-conscious fare. The full bar pours an array of beers, wines, liquors, and cocktails.

All that's really left of the original Matrix is the ground you stand on, but the **MatrixFillmore** (3138 Fillmore St., 415/563-4180, www.matrixfillmore.com, 8 P.M.–2 A.M. daily) does claim huge mid-20th-century musical fame. The Matrix, then a live music venue,

was opened by Marty Balin so that his freshly named band, Jefferson Airplane, would have a place to play. Subsequent acts included the Grateful Dead, Janis Joplin, and the Doors. Today, the MatrixFillmore's Lincoln-log fireplace and top-shelf cocktails appeal to the quiet drinking crowd on weeknights and the bridge-and-tunnel singles scene on the weekend. DJs spin techno most nights, though you can catch an occasional live act here too. There's valet parking at the Balboa Cafe down the street.

CIVIC CENTER AND HAYES VALLEY

Hayes Valley bleeds into Lower Haight (Haight St. between Divisadero St. and Octavia Blvd.) and supplies most of the neighborhood bars. For proof that the independent spirit of the Haight lives on in spite of encroaching commercialism, stop in and have a drink at the **Toronado** (547 Haight St., 415/863-2276, www.toronado.com, 11:30 A.M.–2 A.M. daily). This dimly lit haven maintains one of the finest beer selections in the nation, with a changing roster of several dozen microbrews on tap, including many hard-to-find Belgian ales.

The bar scene heads upscale with the **Pause Wine Bar** (1666 Market St., 415/437-1770, www.pausesf.com, 4:30 P.M.–midnight Tues.–Sat.), in the former site of Cav. The focus is on the food as much as the wine—the small plates menu is pleasantly diverse, and the bar closes at midnight, encouraging an earlier night for a slightly older crowd.

Longtime classic bar Jade has given way to the hipster-tiki-cocktail stylings of **Smuggler's Cove** (650 Gough St., 415/869-1900, http://smugglerscovesf.com, 5 P.M.–2 A.M. daily). Yes, it's all about the rum.

If what you really want is a dive bar, **Place Pigalle** (520 Hayes St., 415/552-2671, http://placepigallesf.com, 2 P.M.–2 A.M. Wed.–Sun., 5 P.M.–2 A.M. Mon.–Tues.) is the place for you. This hidden gem in Hayes Valley offers beer and wine only, a pool table, lots of sofas for lounging, and an uncrowded, genuinely laid-back vibe even on weekends.

MISSION AND CASTRO

These neighborhoods seem to hold a whole city's worth of bars. The Mission, despite a recent upswing in its economy, still has plenty of no-frills bars, many with a Latino theme. And, of course, men seeking men flock to the Castro's endless array of gay bars. For lesbians, the Mission might be a better bet.

Dalva (3121 16th St., 415/252-7740, 4 P.M.–2 A.M. daily) is a small but sophisticated oasis in an ocean of overcrowded Mission hipster hangouts. You'll find dramatic high ceilings, modern paintings, and a jukebox stuffed with indie rock and electronica. Way back in the depths of the club, the Hideaway bar serves up a delectable array of cocktails poured by a rotating staff of local celebrity mixologists.

Excellent draft beers, tasty barbecue plates, and a motorcycle-inclined crowd give **Zeitgeist** (199 Valencia St., 415/255-7505, http://zeitgeistsf.com, 9 A.M.–2 A.M. daily) a punk-rock edge. This Mission favorite endears itself to all

sorts, thanks to its spacious outdoor beer garden and Friday barbecues.

The cocktails at **Beretta** (1199 Valencia St., 415/695-1199, www.berettasf.com, 5:30 P.M.–1 A.M. Mon.–Fri., 11 A.M.–1 A.M. Sat.–Sun.) consistently win raves from locals and visitors alike. Order a Rattlesnake—and a pizza to suck up the venom of that bite.

You'll have no trouble finding a gay bar in the Castro. One of the best is called simply **Q Bar** (456 Castro St., 415/864-2877, www.qbarsf.com, 4 P.M.–2 A.M. Mon.–Fri., 2 P.M.–2 A.M. Sat.–Sun.). Just look for the red neon "Bar" sign set in steel out front. Inside, expect to find the fabulous red decor known as "retro-glam," delicious top-shelf cocktails, and thrumming beats spun by popular DJs almost every night of the week. Unlike many Castro establishments, the Bar caters to pretty much everybody: gay men, gay women, and gay-friendly straight folks.

GOLDEN GATE PARK AND THE HAIGHT

Haight Street crowds head out in droves to the **Alembic** (1725 Haight St., 415/666-0822,

Zeitgeist, a Mission favorite

www.alembicbar.com, noon–2 A.M. daily) for artisanal cocktails laced with American spirits. On par with the whiskey and bourbon menu is the cuisine: Wash down beef-tongue sliders with a Sazerac.

Club Deluxe (1511 Haight St., 415/552-6949, www.sfclubdeluxe.com, 4 P.M.–2 A.M. Tues.–Sun.) is the perfect place to discover your inner Sinatra. Pull up a stool at this dark retro-style bar and order something classic while listening to live jazz or watching burlesque. A pizza menu gives patrons something to buffer those strong drinks.

The **Beach Chalet Brewery** (1000 Great Hwy., 415/386-8439, www.beachchalet.com, 9 A.M.–11 P.M. Mon.–Thurs., 9 A.M.–midnight Fri., 8 A.M.–midnight Sat., 8 A.M.–11 P.M. Sun.) is an attractive brewpub and restaurant directly across the street from Ocean Beach. Sip a pale ale while watching the sunset, and check out the historic murals downstairs.

Clubs

Some folks are surprised at the smallish list of San Francisco clubs. The truth is, San Francisco just isn't a see-and-be-seen, hip-new-club-every-week kind of town. In the City, you'll find gay clubs, vintage dance clubs, Goth clubs, and the occasional underground rave mixed in with the more standard dance floor and DJ fare.

If you're up for a full night of club-hopping and don't want to deal with transit headaches, several bus services can ferry your party from club to club. Many of these offer VIP entrance to clubs and will stop wherever you want to go. **Think Escape** (800/823-7249, www.thinkescape.com, from $30 pp) has buses and limos with drivers and guides to get you to the hottest spots with ease.

UNION SQUARE AND NOB HILL

Defying San Francisco expectation, **Ruby Skye** (420 Mason St., 415/693-0777, www.rubyskye.com, 9 P.M.–2 A.M. Thurs.–Sat., cover $15–20,

dress code enforced) books top DJs and occasional live acts into a big, crowded dance club. The building, built in 1890, was originally the Stage Door Theatre, but it has been redone to create dance floors, bars, DJ booths, and VIP spaces. Crowds can get big on the weekend, and the patrons tend to be young and pretty and looking for action. The sound system rocks, so conversation isn't happening, and the drinks tend toward overpriced vodka and Red Bull.

For a chic New York–style club experience, check out **Vessel** (85 Campton Place, 415/433-8585, www.vesselsf.com, 10 P.M.–2 A.M. Wed.–Thurs. and Sat., 9:30 P.M.–2 A.M. Fri., cover $10–30). With old-school bottle service at some tables, Vessel caters to an upscale crowd that likes postmodern decor, top-shelf liquors, and a bit of dancing to round out the evening. Dress up if you plan to get in.

Down the brightly lit staircase in the aptly named **The Cellar** (685 Sutter St., 415/441-5678, http://cellarsf.com, 5 P.M.–2 A.M. Mon.–Fri., 10 P.M.–2 A.M. Sat.–Sun., cover from $25), you'll find a combo bar and club. Two dance floors share the space with pool tables favored by the after-work happy hour crowd (beer is $2 during happy hour, 5–9 P.M. Mon.–Fri.). With regular theme nights, this red-and-blue plush velvet club often attracts a slightly older crowd. An online guest list, reserved tables, and bottle and cocktail service are available through the website. The Cellar is a favorite with many local urbanites.

Harry Denton's Starlight Room (450 Powell St., 21st Fl., 415/395-8595, www.harrydenton.com, 6 P.M.–2 A.M. Tues.–Sat., cover up to $20) brings the flamboyant side of San Francisco downtown. Enjoy a cocktail in the early evening or a nightcap and a bite of dessert after the theater in this truly old-school nightclub. Dress in your best to match the glitzy red-and-gold decor and mirrors. Whoop it up at Sunday's a Drag shows (noon and 2:30 P.M. Sun.). Reservations are recommended.

FINANCIAL DISTRICT AND SOMA

111 Minna Street Gallery (111 Minna St., 415/974-1719, www.111minnagallery.com, noon–11 P.M. Wed., noon–2 A.M. Thurs.–Fri., 5 P.M.–2 A.M. Sat., cover $5) really is an art gallery, but it's also one of the hottest dance clubs in SoMa. Art lovers who come to 111 Minna to enjoy the changing exhibitions of new art in peace and quiet do so during the day. After 5 P.M. the gallery transforms into a nightclub, opening the full bar and bringing in DJs who spin late into the weekend nights. Guests must be 21 and older due to the liquor license and because they often showcase explicit artworks.

It's dark, it's dank, and it's very, very Goth. The **Cat Club** (1190 Folsom St., 415/703-8964, www.sfcatclub.com, 9 P.M.–3 A.M. Tues.–Sun., cover $6–10) gets pretty energetic on '80s dance nights, but it's still a great place to go after you've donned your best down-rent black attire and painted your face deathly pale, especially on Goth-industrial-electronica nights.

You'll find a friendly crowd, decent bartenders, strong drinks, and easy access to smoking areas. Each of the two rooms has its own DJ, which somehow works perfectly even though they're only a wall apart from each other. Check the website to find the right party night for you, and expect the crowd to heat up after 11 P.M.

Looking for *the* DJs and dance parties? You'll find them at the **DNA Lounge** (375 11th St., 415/626-1409, www.dnalounge.com, 9 P.M.–3:30 A.M. Sun.–Thurs., 9 P.M.–5 A.M. Fri.–Sat., cover varies). With Bootie twice a month, '80s parties, and live music, the DNA Lounge has been one of the City's perpetual hot night spots for decades. It's also one of the few clubs that's open after hours.

NORTH BEACH AND FISHERMAN'S WHARF

The North Beach neighborhood has long been San Francisco's best-known red-light district. To this day, Broadway Avenue is lined with the neon signs of strip clubs and adult stores, all

© DOMINI DRAGOONE

the Cat Club

promising grown-up good times. Do be aware that cover charges at most of the strip clubs tend to be on the high side, and lone women should approach this area with extreme caution after dark.

If you're just looking for a good time at a dance club, check out the **Bamboo Hut** (479 Broadway, 415/989-8555, www.maximumproductions.com, 8 P.M.–2 A.M. Mon., 5 P.M.–2 A.M. Wed.–Fri., 7 P.M.–2 A.M. Sat.). It's part tacky tiki bar, part impromptu dance club, and has a cheerful vibe and friendly scene that can be hard to come by in this part of town. You'll see the tiki god, the bamboo decor, and the fun umbrella-clad fruity rum drinks. The house specialty is the Flaming Volcano Bowl—yes, it's really on fire, and it's probably a good idea to share one with a friend—or three

MARINA AND PACIFIC HEIGHTS
The **Hi-Fi Lounge** (2125 Lombard St., 415/345-8663, www.maximumproductions.com, 8 P.M.–2 A.M. Wed.–Sat.) personifies the fun that can be had in smaller San Francisco venues. This one-floor wonder with a tiny dance floor gets incredibly crowded. Yet even the locals have a good time when they come out to the Hi-Fi. The decor is funky and fun, and the patrons are young and affluent. Most visitors find the staff friendly and the bartenders attentive. It being the Marina, come early to get decent parking and to avoid the cover charge. On Thursday and Friday, early birds get $1 draft beer.

CIVIC CENTER AND HAYES VALLEY
Not your slick, shiny nightclub, the **Rickshaw Stop** (155 Fell St., 415/861-2011, www.rickshawstop.com, cover $5–18) in the Hayes Valley neighborhood welcomes one and all with a cavernous lower bar, stage area, and dance floor, and a quirky balcony area complete with comfy old sofas. Up-and-coming live acts play here, DJs spin, and special events

and parties add to the action almost every week. Have a drink, enjoy the music, and get comfortable!

The most famous gentlemen's club in the City is **Mitchell Brothers O'Farrell Theatre** (895 O'Farrell St., 415/776-6686, www.ofarrell.com, 12:30 P.M.–1:30 A.M. Mon.–Thurs., 12:30 P.M.–2:30 A.M. Fri.–Sat., 5:30 P.M.–midnight Sun., cover $20 before 7 P.M., $40 after 9 P.M.). The O'Farrell started out as an adult movie house in 1969, featuring its own productions on the silver screen. Live shows began in 1976, though films still run in the CineStage room. Today, patrons can choose between five different show rooms, plus VIP booths. Unlike many City strip clubs, Mitchell Brothers offers full nudity and features live shows. Many of the performers and dancers are major adult film stars who perform limited engagements at the O'Farrell. The catch? No liquor.

MISSION AND CASTRO
The Mission and the Castro are popular clubbing districts in San Francisco, and as the urban renewal continues, SoMa is making its own play to create a hot nightlife rep. Naturally the biggest concentration of gay clubs is in the Castro.

Fans of the hipster lounge scene flock to the **Fluid Ultra Lounge** (662 Mission St., 415/385-2547, www.fluidsf.com, 9 P.M.–2 A.M. Thurs.–Sat., cover varies). The second you walk in, you'll probably feel you're not chic enough for this David Oldroyd–designed postmodern wonderland. Gleaming metal meets fascinating floral-esque accessories in a series of rooms that boast really uncomfortable white chairs. If you're not up for lots of young and ultra-cool clubsters, you may find the decor to be the best part of Fluid. You can definitely dance on an interestingly lit floor, though it can be tough to pry a drink out of the bartenders at times. Come early or get your name on the guest list (you can sign up online) to avoid the hefty cover charge.

GOLDEN GATE PARK AND THE HAIGHT

In the infamous Haight, the club scene is actually an eclectic mix of everything from trendy to retro. **Milk** (1840 Haight St., 415/387-6455, www.milksf.com, 9 P.M.–2 A.M. Mon.–Sat., 3 P.M.–close Sun., cover up to $5) counts itself among the trendy. It's tiny, and it's often empty on weekdays and packed solid on weekends. The music ranges from reggae to hip-hop to '80s, depending on the night and the DJ. Milk attracts more locals than out-of-towners, but if that's what you're looking for in your visit to the City, a night of Milk might be just what the doctor ordered.

Gay and Lesbian

San Francisco's gay nightlife has earned a worldwide rep for both the quantity and quality of options. In fact, the gay club scene totally outdoes the straight club scene for frolicsome fabulous fun. While the City's queer nightlife caters more to gay men than to lesbians, there's plenty of space available for partiers of all persuasions. For a more comprehensive list of San Francisco's queer bars and clubs, visit www.sf-gaybarlist.com.

Looking for a stylin' gay bar turned club, Castro style? Head for **Badlands** (4121 18th St., 415/626-9320, www.sfbadlands.com, 2 P.M.–2 A.M. daily). This Castro icon was once an old-school bar with pool tables on the floor and license plates on the walls. Now you'll find an always-crowded dance floor, au courant peppy pop music, ever-changing video screens, and plenty of gay men out for a good time. Any number of local straight women count themselves among the regulars at this friendly establishment, which attracts a youngish but mixed-age crowd. Do be aware that Badlands gets incredibly crowded, complete with a hot and packed dance floor, especially on weekend nights. There's a coat check on the bottom level.

The **Lexington Club** (3464 19th St., 415/863-2052, www.lexingtonclub.com, 5 P.M.–2 A.M. Mon.–Thurs., 3 P.M.–2 A.M. Fri.–Sun.) calls itself "your friendly neighborhood dyke bar." In truth, the Lex offers a neighborhood dive environment and cheap

© DOMINI DRAGOONE

the Lexington Club

drinks—think $1 margaritas on Friday nights and Pabst on Mondays. Friendly? Depends on how dyke you are—tats, piercings, short hair, and tank tops make for a better Lex experience.

Unlike some of the harder-core Castro gay clubs, **Truck** (1900 Folsom St., 415/252-0306, www.trucksf.com, 4 P.M.–2 A.M. Mon.–Fri., 2 P.M.–2 A.M. Sat.–Sun.) offers a friendly neighborhood vibe. Truck lures in patrons with cheap drinks, friendly bartenders, and theme nights every week. Food is served 4–9 P.M. weekdays and 2–9 P.M. weekends, when the bar tends to be quieter. Oh, and yes, that's a shower. Stop by late on Friday night for the Truck Wash to see it in action.

The Lookout (3600 16th St., 415/431-0306, www.lookoutsf.com, 3:30 P.M.–2 A.M. Mon.–Fri., 12:30 P.M.–2 A.M. Sat.–Sun., cover $2–5) gets its name and much of its rep from its balcony overlooking the iconic Castro neighborhood. Get up there for some primo people watching as you sip your industrial-strength alcoholic concoctions and nibble on surprisingly edible bar snacks and pizza. Do be aware that the Lookout hosts quite a few "events" that come complete with a cover charge.

Yes, there's a Western-themed gay bar in San Francisco. **Cinch** (1723 Polk St., 415/776-4162, until 2 A.M. daily) has a laid-back (no pun intended), friendly, male-oriented vibe that's all but lost in the once gay, now gentrified Polk Street hood. Expect fewer females and strong drinks to go with the unpretentious decor and atmosphere.

For after-hours dancing on weekends, many SF clubsters end up in SoMa at **The EndUp** (401 6th St., 415/646-0999, www.theendup.com, 10 P.M.–4 A.M. Thurs., 11 P.M.–9 A.M. Fri., 10 P.M.–4 A.M. Sat.).

Live Music
ROCK AND POP
Opened in the late 1960s, **The Fillmore** (1805 Geary Blvd., 415/346-6000, www.thefillmore.com) ignited the careers of legendary bands such as Santana and the Grateful Dead. This popular venue now hosts everything from concerts to theme parties.

Started by rock veteran Boz Scaggs in 1988, **Slim's** (333 11th St., 415/255-0333, www.slims-sf.com, $15–60) showcases everything from the Subhumans to Billy Bob Thornton. Dinner tickets are the only way to score an actual seat.

The **Warfield** (982 Market St., 415/345-0900, http://thewarfieldtheatre.com) is one of the older rock venues in the City. It started out as a vaudeville palace in the early 1900s, booking major jazz acts as well as variety shows. The Warfield's configuration is that of a traditional theater, with a raised stage, an open orchestra section below it, and two balconies rising up and facing the stage. There's limited table seating on the lowest level (mostly by reservation), reserved seats in the balconies, and open standing in the orchestra below the stage. The Warfield books all sorts of acts, from Bill Maher to alternative rock; the likes of Evanescence, Lyle Lovett, and Death Cab for Cutie have played here.

Given the dense crowd of tourists in the Fisherman's Wharf area, it's no surprise that a few bars and clubs offer live music to entertain the masses and keep them buying drinks late into the evening. Despite its locale, **Bimbo's 365 Club** (1025 Columbus Ave., 415/474-0365, www.bimbos365club.com) retains its reputation as a favorite venue for locals. Bimbo's was opened in 1931 by an Italian immigrant looking to create a fun and fabulous club to help San Francisco residents take their minds off the gloom of the Depression. The club moved to the Columbus Avenue location in 1951 and became a favorite of San Francisco legend Herb Caen as well as many other local socialites. Today, major accessible acts such as Chris Isaak and the Brian Setzer Orchestra play Bimbo's. The club itself, with its shabby chic interior and atmosphere, remains a beloved elder statesman with a heavy local following.

Mezzanine (444 Jessie St., 415/625-8880, www.mezzaninesf.com) brings top acts to San Francisco. This vast club inside a renovated warehouse showcases a veritable who's who of DJs and live acts, from Public Enemy to the Chemical Brothers. Art parties, fashion shows, and film installations round out the monthly calendar.

BLUES AND JAZZ

The neighborhood surrounding Union Square is one of the most fertile areas in San Francisco for live music. Whether you're into blues, rock, or even country, you'll find a spot to have a drink and listen to some wonderful live tunes.

Biscuits and Blues (401 Mason St., 415/292-2583, www.biscuitsandblues.com, 6 P.M.–2 A.M. daily) is a local musicians' favorite. Just around the corner from the big live drama theaters, this house dedicates itself to jazz and blues. Headliners have included Joe Louis Walker, Jimmy Thackery, and Jim Kimo. One of the best things about this club is that you can, in fact, get biscuits as well as blues. Dinner is served nightly and features a surprisingly varied and upscale menu combining California cuisine with the mystical flavors of New Orleans. Yum!

At the **Boom Boom Room** (1601 Fillmore St., 415/673-8000, www.boomboomblues.com, 4 P.M.–2 A.M. Tues.–Sat., 2 P.M.–1 A.M. Sun.), you'll find the latest in a legacy of live blues, boogie, groove, soul, and funk music.

In the same neighborhood is **Yoshi's** (1330 Fillmore St., 415/655-5600, www.yoshis.com). Both a restaurant and live music venue, Yoshi's attracts some big names—Natalie Cole, Hiroshima, and the Bad Plus—as well as Fillmore locals for drinks and sushi in the stunning lounge.

Comedy

San Francisco's oldest comedy club, the **Punch Line** (444 Battery St., 415/397-7573, www.punchlinecomedyclub.com, shows 8 P.M. and 10 P.M. Tues.–Sun., cover varies) is an elegant and intimate venue that earned its top-notch reputation with stellar headliners such as Robin Williams, Ellen DeGeneres, and Dave Chappelle. An on-site bar keeps the audience primed.

Cobb's Comedy Club (915 Columbus Ave., 415/928-4320, www.cobbscomedy.com, shows 8 P.M. and 10:15 P.M. Thurs.–Sun., cover varies, 2-drink minimum) has played host to star comedians such as Jerry Seinfeld, Sarah Silverman, and Margaret Cho since 1982. The 425-seat venue offers a full dinner menu and a bar to slake your thirst. Be sure to check your show's start time—some comics don't follow the usual Cobb's schedule.

THE ARTS
Theater

For a great way to grab last-minute theater tickets, walk right up to the **Union Square TIX** booth (Union Square, 415/430-1140, www.tixbayarea.com, 10 A.M.–6 P.M. daily). TIX sells same-day, half-price, no-refund tickets to all kinds of shows across the City. If you've got your heart set on a specific musical or play in a big theater, get to the booth early in the day and steel yourself for possible disappointment—especially on weekends, when many top-shelf shows sell out. TIX also sells half-price tickets to same-day shows online—check the website at 11 A.M. daily for up-to-date deals.

If you really, really need to see a major musical while you're in San Francisco, check out **SHN** (www.shnsf.com). SHN operates the Orpheum, the Curran, and the Golden Gate Theater—the three venues where big Broadway productions land when they come to town.

UNION SQUARE AND NOB HILL

Just up from Union Square, on Geary Street, the traditional San Francisco theater district continues to entertain crowds almost every day of the week. The old Geary Theater is now the permanent home of **A.C.T.** (415 Geary St., 415/749-2228, www.act-sf.org, shows Tues.–Sun.,

$22–82). A.C.T. puts on a season filled with big-name, big-budget productions. Each season sees an array of high-production-value musicals such as *Urinetown,* American classics by the likes of Sam Shepard and Somerset Maugham, and intriguing new works; you might even get to see a world premiere. Don't expect to find street parking on Geary. Discount parking is available with a ticket stub from A.C.T. at the Mason-O'Farrell garage around the corner. Tickets can be reasonably priced, especially on weeknights, but do be aware that the second balcony seats are truly high altitude—expect to look nearly straight down to the stage, and take care if you're prone to vertigo.

The **Curran Theater** (445 Geary St., 888/746-1799, www.curran-theater.com, $105–250), next door to A.C.T., has a state-of-the-art stage for classic, high-budget musicals. Audiences have watched *Les Misérables, Phantom of the Opera,* and *High School Musical* from the plush red velvet seats. Expect to pay a premium for tickets to these musicals, which can sometimes run at the Curran for months or even years. Check the schedule for current shows, and leave children under age five at home—they won't be permitted in the Curran.

FINANCIAL DISTRICT AND SOMA

Focusing on short works by new writers, **Three Wise Monkeys** (415/776-7427, http://bayone-acts.org, $19–25) productions usually run at the Boxcar Theater (505 Natoma St.). Each year Three Wise Monkeys hosts the Bay One Acts (BOAs) as well as the Short Leaps Festival, where all plays read last 10 minutes or less.

NORTH BEACH AND FISHERMAN'S WHARF

There's one live show that's always different, yet it's been running continuously for three and a half decades. This musical revue is crazy, wacky, and offbeat, and it pretty much defines live theater in San Francisco. It's **Beach Blanket Babylon** (678 Green St., 415/421-4222, www.beachblanketbabylon.com, shows Wed.–Sun.,

$25–100). Even if you saw Beach Blanket Babylon 10 years ago, you should come to see it again; because it mocks current pop culture, the show evolves almost continuously to take advantage of tabloid treasures. While minors are welcome at the Sunday matinees, evening shows can get pretty racy, and liquor is involved, so these are restricted to attendees 21 and over.

The hats. Oh, the hats. You'll never forget the hats.

MARINA AND PACIFIC HEIGHTS

Beyond the bright lights of Geary and Market Streets lie any number of tiny up-and-coming (or down-and-going, depending) theaters, many of which produce new plays by local playwrights. One of the best known of the "small" theaters, the **Magic Theatre** (Fort Mason Center, Bldg. D, 415/441-8822, http://magictheatre.org, $30–60) produced Sam Shepard's new works back before he was anyone special. They're still committed to new works, so when you go to a show at the Magic you're taking a chance or having an adventure, depending on how you look at it.

At the **Palace of Fine Arts Theatre** (3301 Lyon St., 415/567-6642, www.palaceoffinearts. org, cover varies) you'll find accessible avant-garde performing arts pieces, live music performance, dance recitals, and the occasional children's musical recital or black-and-white film.

CIVIC CENTER AND HAYES VALLEY

Down on Market Street, the **Orpheum Theater** (1192 Market St., 888/746-1799, www.shnsf. com, $50–200) runs touring productions of popular Broadway musicals. At the **EXIT Theatre** (156 Eddy St., 415/673-3847, www. theexit.org), down in the Tenderloin, you'll see plenty of unusual experimental plays, many by local playwrights. The EXIT also participates in the annual San Francisco Fringe Festival (www.sffringe.org).

MISSION AND CASTRO

Take care getting to **Theatre Rhinoceros** (1360 Mission St., Suite 200, 800/838-3006, www.therhino.org, $15–35), as it's in a less-than-ritzy part of town. But it's worth it: The Rhino puts on a wonderfully entertaining set of gay and lesbian plays and has branched out to explore the whole spectrum of human sexuality, especially as it's expressed in anything-goes (even conservative Republicans!) San Francisco.

Classical Music and Opera

Right around the Civic Center, music takes a turn for the upscale. This is the neighborhood where the ultrarich and not-so-rich classics lovers come to enjoy a night out. Acoustically renovated in 1992, **Davies Symphony Hall** (201 Van Ness Ave., 415/864-6000, www.sfsymphony. org) is home to Michael Tilson Thomas's world-renowned San Francisco Symphony. Loyal patrons flock to performances that range from the classic to the avant-garde. Whether you love Mozart or Mahler, or you want to hear classic rock blended with major symphony orchestra, the San Francisco Symphony does it.

The **War Memorial Opera House** (301 Van Ness Ave., 415/621-6600, www.sfwmpac.org, performances Tues.–Sun.), a beaux arts–style building designed by Coit Tower and City Hall architect Arthur Brown Jr., houses the **San Francisco Opera** (415/864-3330, http://sfopera.com) and **San Francisco Ballet** (415/865-2000, www.sfballet.org). Tours are available (415/552-8338, 10 A.M.–2 P.M. Mon., $5–7).

Cinema

A grand movie palace from the 1920s, the **Castro Theatre** (429 Castro St., 415/621-6120, www.castrotheatre.com, $8.50–11) has enchanted San Francisco audiences for almost a century. The Castro Theater hosts everything from revival double features (from black-and-white through 1980s classics) to musical movie sing-alongs, live shows, and even the

War Memorial Opera House

occasional book signing. Naturally, the Castro also screens current releases and documentaries about queer life in San Francisco and beyond. Check the calendar online to figure out what's going to be playing when you're in town before buying tickets. Then plan your Muni route to the theater, which doesn't have a dedicated parking lot. Once inside, be sure to admire the lavish interior decor.

Expect an upscale moviegoing experience at the **Sundance Kabuki Theater** (1881 Post St., www.sundancecinemas.com/kabuki.html, $9–13). The "amenity fee" pays for reserved seating, film shorts rather than commercials, and bits of bamboo decor. The Kabuki has eight screens, all of which show mostly big blockbuster Hollywood films, plus a smattering of independents and the occasional filmed opera performance. The Over 21 shows, in the two theaters connected to the full bars, encompass the most compelling reason to see a typical first-run movie for several dollars extra.

Shopping

UNION SQUARE AND NOB HILL

For the biggest variety of chain and department stores, plus a few select designer boutiques, locals and visitors alike flock to Union Square (bounded by Geary St., Stockton St., Post St., and Powell St.). The shopping area includes more than just the square proper: More designer and brand-name stores cluster for several blocks in all directions.

Department Stores

Several big high-end department stores call Union Square home. **Macy's** (170 O'Farrell St., 415/397-3333, www.macys.com, 10 A.M.–9 P.M. Mon.–Fri., 9 A.M.–10 P.M. Sat., 11 A.M.–8 P.M. Sun.) has two immense locations, one for women's clothing and another for the men's store and housewares. **Neiman Marcus** (150 Stockton St., 415/362-3900, www.neimanmarcus.com, 10 A.M.–7 P.M. Mon.–Wed. and Fri.–Sat., 10 A.M.–8 P.M. Thurs., noon–6 P.M. Sun.) is a favorite among high-budget shoppers, while **Saks Fifth Avenue** (384 Post St., 415/986-4758, www.saksfifthavenue.com, 10 A.M.–7 P.M. Mon.–Wed., 10 A.M.–8 P.M. Thurs.–Sat., noon–7 P.M. Sun.) adds a touch of New York style to funky-but-wealthy San Francisco.

Clothing and Shoes

Levi's (300 Post St., 415/501-0100, www.levi.com, 10 A.M.–9 P.M. Mon.–Sat., 11 A.M.–8 P.M. Sun.) may be a household name, but this three-floor fashion emporium offers incredible customization services while featuring new music and emerging art. Guys should head to the outpost of **Ben Sherman** (55 Stockton St., 415/593-0671, www.bensherman.com, 10 A.M.–8 P.M. Mon.–Sat., 11 A.M.–7 P.M. Sun.) for stylish threads from the British-based outfitter that has been dressing cool mods for almost five decades.

A gem of a boutique is the original shop of the San Francisco designer **Margaret O'Leary** (1 Claude Lane, 415/391-1010, www.margaretoleary.com, 10 A.M.–5 P.M. Tues.–Sat.), who launched a knitwear-inspired line in her name. Women's fine sweaters—from sleeveless to cardigans—and chic fabric designs are featured in the cozy, European-inspired space.

An elegant space on boutiquey Maiden Lane houses **Wolford** (115 Maiden Lane, 415/391-6727, www.wolford.com, 10 A.M.–6 P.M. Mon.–Sat.), the top name in hosiery. Stockings laced with elegant seams and zigzag patterns usually run $65, but sales can offer bargain prices. Upscale and inventive lingerie at **Agent**

© DOMINI DRAGOONE

Macy's in Union Square

Provocateur (54 Geary St., 415/421-0229, www.agentprovocateur.com, 11 A.M.–7 P.M. Mon.–Sat., noon–5 P.M. Sun.) promises a most unique and memorable souvenir to go with those Wolford stockings.

Fluevogers unite! There's an outpost of the popular **John Fluevog Shoes** (253 Grant Ave., 415/296-7900, www.fluevog.com, 10 A.M.–6 P.M. Mon.–Thurs., 10 A.M.–7 P.M. Fri.–Sat., noon–6 P.M. Sun.) here. The Canadian designer's artistic creations have appeared on the pages of *Vogue* and on the feet of notable celebrities like Scarlett Johansson and the White Stripes.

Gift and Home
Britex Fabrics (146 Geary St., 415/392-2910, www.britexfabrics.com, 10 A.M.–6 P.M. Mon.–Sat.) draws fashion designers, quilters, DIYers, and costume geeks from all over the Bay Area to its legendary monument to fabric. If you're into any sort of textile crafting, a visit to Britex has the qualities of a religious experience. All four

floors are crammed floor-to-ceiling with bolts of fabric, swaths of lace, and rolls of ribbon. From $1-per-yard grosgrain ribbons to $95-per-yard French silk jacquard and $125-per-yard Italian wool coating, Britex has it all.

Health and Beauty
One of the most rarified salons in Union Square is the **Elizabeth Arden Red Door** (126 Post St., Suite 4, 415/989-4888, 9 A.M.–7 P.M. Mon.–Wed. and Sat., 9 A.M.–8 P.M. Thurs.–Fri., 10 A.M.–6 P.M. Sun.). You'll definitely need an appointment to get a trim or a color touch-up here.

FINANCIAL DISTRICT AND SOMA
Is there any place in San Francisco where you *can't* shop? Even the Financial District has plenty of retail opportunities. Antiques, art, and design lovers come down to **Jackson Square** (Jackson St. and Montgomery St.) for the plethora of high-end shops and galleries. Don't expect to find much in the way of cheap

tchotchkes—the objets d'art and interior accessories find places in the exquisite homes of the wealthy buyers who can afford such luxuries. But as always, it's free to look, to imagine, and to dream. **Kathleen Taylor—The Lotus Collection** (445 Jackson St., 415/398-8115, www.ktaylorlotus.com, 10 A.M.–5 P.M. Mon.–Fri., by appointment Sat.) specializes in antique textiles from around the world. Whether you fancy a medieval tapestry for your wall or an ancient Asian table runner, this is the place to find it.

The **Montgomery Gallery** (406 Jackson St., 415/788-8300, www.montgomerygallery.com, 10 A.M.–5:30 P.M. Tues.–Fri., 11 A.M.–5 P.M. Sat.) seems like a museum, displaying works of the old masters as well as the top tier of more modern artists.

For tea, visit the **Imperial Tea Court** (1 Ferry Bldg. Plaza, Suite 27, 415/544-9830, www.imperialtea.com, 10 A.M.–6 P.M. Mon.–Fri., 9 A.M.–6:30 P.M. Sat., 10:30 A.M.–6 P.M.) at the Ferry Building. This intensely Chinese tea shop sells black teas in bulk, beautiful Asian tea ware, and, of course, serves hot tea at its six Chinese rosewood tables. If you want to get into the tea experience, consider signing up for a class with owner Ray Fong, who is a published author and tea consultant. You'll learn about the traditions of tea from plant to cup, including the Chinese ceremonial modes of serving.

CHINATOWN

Chinatown is one of the most popular shopping districts in San Francisco. Shopping in Chinatown isn't about seeking out a specific store; instead, it's an experience of strolling from shop to endless shop. It can take hours just to get a few blocks up Grant Street, and a thorough perusal of all the side streets might take days. Narrow, cluttered T-shirt and tchotchke shops stand between jewelry stores offering genuine gems and antiques shops crammed with treasures. Clothing boutiques run to slippery silks, while home-decor stores offer table

linens made out of real linen as well as statuary, art, tea sets—everything a dedicated shopper could dream of and more.

If you've only got a short time to shop, the epic **Chinatown Bazaar** (667 Grant Ave., 415/391-6369, 10 A.M.–9:30 P.M. daily) has pretty much everything you can imagine coming from Chinatown and a lot of things beyond imagination. They've got some of the best prices in the district for pottery items, Chinese and Buddhist-inspired statuary, chopsticks, tea sets, and much more. Prices for small, pretty items run $2–10.

Fine jewelry stores abound in Chinatown—you'll have no trouble finding a strand of matching pearls if that's to your taste. **Royal Fine Jewelry** (730 Grant Ave., 415/397-8868, 11 A.M.–6:30 P.M. daily) has a particularly fine selection of semiprecious and precious jewelry, some of it fairly unusual in style.

Gourmet Goodies

For a sense (and a scent) of the more local side of Chinatown, head off the main drag to Stockton Street and seek out the local food markets. Or visit the **Red Blossom Tea Company** (831 Grant Ave., 415/395-0868, www.redblossomtea.com, 10 A.M.–6:30 P.M. Mon.–Sat., 10 A.M.–6 P.M. Sun., $10–20). You'll find top-quality teas of every type you can think of and probably some you've never heard of. Red Blossom has been in business for more than 25 years importing the best teas available from all over Asia. For the tea adventurous, the blossoming teas, specific varieties of oolong, and *pu-erh* teas make great souvenirs to bring home and share with friends. And if you fall in love, never fear; Red Blossom takes advantage of Bay Area technology to offer all their loose teas on the Internet.

The **Golden Gate Fortune Cookie Company** (56 Ross Alley, 415/781-3956, 9 A.M.–midnight daily) makes a great stop, especially if you've brought the kids along. Heck, even if you're alone, the delicious aromas wafting from the building as you pass the alley on Jackson Street may draw you inside. Expect to have a tray of sample cookies pressed on you as soon as you enter. Inside the factory, you'll see the cookies being folded into their traditional shapes by workers, but the best part is checking out all the different types of fortune cookies. Yes, there are lots of kinds you'll never see on the tablecloth at a restaurant: chocolate and strawberry flavors, funky shapes, various sizes, and don't forget the cookies with the X-rated fortunes, perfect to bring home and share with friends. Bags of cookies cost only $3–4, making them attractive souvenirs to pick up—although with their lovely scent, they might not make it all the way home.

NORTH BEACH AND FISHERMAN'S WHARF

The best thing about the souvenir stores in Fisherman's Wharf is that they know what tourists to San Francisco really *need*: sweatshirts, hats, gloves, and fuzzy socks. For last-minute warm clothes on foggy days, just take a walk from the cable car turnaround down Hyde Street to Jefferson Street and then over to Mason Street. For souvenirs, try **Pier 39**. Funky boutiques crowd both sides and both stories of the buildings that line the pier.

The North Beach district is filled with fun, beauty, and great Italian restaurants and cafés. The Italian district also boasts some of the hippest shops in the City, so it's a great place for shoppers who eschew chains to seek out thrift shops and funky independents.

◖ City Lights

One of the most famous independent bookshops in a city famous for its literary bent is City Lights (261 Columbus Ave., 415/362-8193, www.citylights.com, 10 A.M.–midnight daily). It opened in 1953 as an all-paperback bookstore with a decidedly Beat aesthetic, focused on selling modern literary fiction and progressive political tomes. As the Beats flocked to San Francisco and to City Lights, the shop put on another hat—that of publisher. Allen Ginsberg's *Howl* was published by the erstwhile independent, which never looked back. Today, they're still selling and publishing the best of cutting-edge fiction and nonfiction. The store is still in its original location on the point of Columbus Avenue, though it's expanded somewhat since the '50s. Expect to find your favorite genre paperbacks along with the latest intriguing new works. The nonfiction selections can really make you take a step back and think about your world in a new way, which is just what the founders of City Lights wanted.

Clothing

For hip dressers who prefer classic style to the latest stuff fresh out of the sweatshops, **Old Vogue** (1412 Grant Ave., 415/392-1522, 11 A.M.–6 P.M. Mon.–Tues. and Thurs., 11 A.M.–8 P.M. Wed., 11 A.M.–10 P.M. Fri.–Sat., noon–6 P.M. Sun.) is the perfect North Beach destination. Stop in at the funky little storefront and plan to spend a little while browsing through the racks of vintage apparel: one floor dedicated to comfy old jeans and pants, the other to coats, blouses, dresses, and accessories. Old Vogue can provide you with just the perfect hat to top off your favorite clubbing outfit.

Eye-catching **Alla Prima** (1420 Grant Ave., 415/397-4077, www.allaprimalingerie.com, 11 A.M.–7 P.M. Tues.–Sat., 12:30–5 P.M. Sun.) sells nothing but lingerie from the likes of Cosabella, La Perla, and Dolce & Gabbana. Pieces range from delicate and frilly to sturdy and functional. Hayes Valley boasts a second location (539 Hayes St., 415/864-8180, 11 A.M.–7 P.M. Mon.–Sat., noon–5 P.M. Sun.).

Music

For the ultimate hip North Beach shopping

trip, stop in at **101 Music** (1414 Grant Ave., 415/382-6369, 10 A.M.–8 P.M. Tues.–Sat., noon–8 P.M. Sun.). This independent shop is short on copies of the latest pop CDs and long on vintage vinyl and secondhand instruments and musical equipment. Expect to see turntables, keyboards, and all sorts of fun arcane stuff as soon as you walk in the door. The vinyl collection hides downstairs. The organization of the records and CDs could be better, but isn't browsing for treasure in the bins part of the fun at such a shop? Customer service, much of it provided by the owner, keeps locals coming back.

MARINA AND PACIFIC HEIGHTS

Pacific Heights and its neighbor Presidio Heights, two quiet residential areas, are connected by Sacramento Street, home to interior design and clothing boutiques that display high-end wares that appeal to the well-heeled residents of this area. With 12 blocks' worth of shops, galleries, salons, and eateries, the main trouble folks have is getting through all of it in one shopping session.

Clothing

If you prefer fashions from earlier decades, browse through **GoodByes Consignment Shop** (3483 Sacramento St., 415/674-0151, www. goodbyessf.com, 10 A.M.–6 P.M. Mon.–Wed. and Fri.–Sat., 10 A.M.–8 P.M. Thurs., 11 A.M.–5 P.M. Sun.). GoodByes also has a men's store (3464 Sacramento St.) just across the street.

Rabat (2080 Chestnut St., 415/929-8868, http://rabatshoes.com, 10:30 A.M.–6:30 P.M. Mon.–Fri., 10:30 A.M.–6 P.M. Sat., 11 A.M.– 5:30 P.M. Sun.) is awash in stylish, colorful shoes for men and women, artfully displayed in a mininalist setting.

Yoga purists swear by the comfortable and reliable clothing at **Lululemon Athletica** (1981 Union St., 415/776-5858, 10 A.M.–8 P.M. Mon.–Sat., 10 A.M.–7 P.M. Sun.). From yoga

pants to in-store classes, men and women alike come here to sweat it out in style.

Gift and Home

It takes a ritzy San Francisco neighborhood to support a six-days-a-week orchid store. **Beautiful Orchids** (3319 Sacramento St., 415/567-2443, www.beautifulorchids.com, 10 A.M.–6 P.M. daily) specializes in rarified live orchid plants. Every color of the rainbow, amazing shapes, and waterfall figures spill from elegant planters. Expect to pay a premium for these rare hand-tended flowers, and to spend even more to ship them home. You can also find elegant home accessories here, most picked to complement the orchids rather than the other way around.

CIVIC CENTER AND HAYES VALLEY

In the Hayes Valley neighborhood adjacent to the Civic Center, shopping goes uptown, but the unique scent of counterculture creativity somehow makes it in. This is a fun neighborhood to get your stroll on, checking out the art galleries and peeking into the boutiques for clothing and upscale housewares, and then stopping at one of the lovely cafés for a restorative bite to eat.

Clothing and Shoes

Ver Unica (437B Hayes St. and 526 Hayes St., 415/431-0688, www.verunicasf.com, 11 A.M.–7 P.M. Mon.–Sat., noon–6 P.M. Sun.) is a vintage boutique that attracts locals and celebrities with high-quality men's and women's clothing and accessories dating from the 1920s to the 1980s, along with a small selection of new apparel by up-and-coming designers.

The corset takes center stage at unique **Dark Garden** (321 Linden St., 415/431-7684, www. darkgarden.net, open daily, call for hours). Custom fitting and design doesn't come cheap, but you'll get quality. An assortment of lingerie is also sold here.

Paolo Iantorno's boutique **Paolo Shoes** (524 Hayes St., 415/552-4580, http://paoloshoes. com, 11 A.M.–7 P.M. Mon.–Sat., 11 A.M.–6 P.M. Sun.) showcases his collection of handcrafted shoes, for which all leather and textiles are conscientiously selected and then inspected to ensure top quality.

On the same street is **Bulo** (418 Hayes St., 415/255-4939, http://buloshoes.com). Italian for hip, fresh, and attractive, Bulo caters to the fashion- and quality-conscious foot fetishist.

Gourmet Goodies

Those with a sweet tooth flock to **Miette** (449 Octavia St., 415/626-6221, www.miette.com, noon–7 P.M. Sun.–Fri., 11 A.M.–7 P.M. Sat.), a cheery European-inspired candy shop, sister store to the Ferry Plaza bakery (415/837-0300). From double-salted licorice to handmade English toffee, the quality confections include imports from England, Italy, and France.

Nosa Ria (500 Laguna St., 415/529-1506, www.nosaria.com, 11 A.M.–7 P.M. Tues.-Sat., 11 A.M.–5 P.M. Sun.) sells "quintessential Spanish foods"—from cured meats and an assortment of cheeses to sweets and specialty oils. A trip here might be the closest thing to visiting Spain.

MISSION AND CASTRO

In the 21st century, the closest you can come to the old-school Haight Street shopping experience is in the Mission. The big shopping street with the coolest selections is definitely Valencia Street, which has all the best thrift shops and funky stuff.

On Castro Street, shopping is sexy. Whether you want toys or leather, fetish or lace, or just a pair of fabulous spike-heeled boots, you can find it in one of the racy shops found in the City's notoriously "everything goes" district.

Books

There's a **Books Inc.** (2275 Market St.,

415/864-6777, www.booksinc.net, 10 A.M.–10 P.M. daily) in the Castro. This small independent Bay Area bookseller's chain hosts numerous author events and stocks plenty of local authors. You can also find your favorite paperbacks. At this location, the managers stock lots of great gay fiction and nonfiction, in keeping with the neighborhood. You're welcome to stay as long as you like, browsing through the books.

Clothing and Shoes

A local favorite vintage and secondhand clothing store in the Mission is **Schauplatz** (791 Valencia St., 415/864-5665, 1–7 P.M. Wed.–Mon.). It might be a bit more expensive than your average Goodwill, but you'll be wowed by the fabulous and unusual apparel. Surf the racks for everything from 1940s dresses to vintage sunglasses.

At quirky designer boutique **Dema** (1038 Valencia St., 415/206-0500, www.godemago. com), you'll find a range of cotton goodies that include Velvet, Blended, and Orla Kiely as well as fine cashmere blends and silk dresses.

Sunhee Moon (3167 16th St., 415/355-1800, www.sunheemoon.com, noon–7 P.M. Mon.–Fri., noon–6 P.M. Sat.–Sun.) showcases San Francisco designer Sunhee's own line of classic separates with a twist, which fit petite gals perfectly. Her boutique also carries jewelry, bags, sunglasses, and other accessories from local designers.

Therapy (545 Valencia St., 415/865-0981, www.shopattherapy.com, 11:30 A.M.–9:30 P.M. Mon.–Thurs., 10:30 A.M.–11 P.M. Fr.–Sat., 10:30 A.M.–9:30 P.M. Sun.) surpasses the nearby competition with its well-priced mix of clothing, accessories, and goofy gifts.

Need shoes? One of the few honest-to-goodness local family-owned shoe stores, **De La Sole** (549 Castro St., 415/255-3140, www. delasole.com, 11 A.M.–7 P.M. Sun.–Thurs., 11 A.M.–8 P.M. Fri.–Sat.) in the Castro proffers

© DOMINI DRAGOONE

Schauplatz

both men's and women's foot fashions. The shoes shine with the latest fashions, from sneakers to formals. Even the shop's interior carries on the theme of fun, fashionable modernity, making visitors feel hip just by walking in the door.

Gift and Home

Five and Diamond (510 Valencia St., 415/255-9747, www.fiveanddiamond.com, noon–8 P.M. Mon.–Thurs., 11 A.M.–9 P.M. Fri.–Sat., 11 A.M.–7 P.M. Sun.) can bring you every aspect of the stereotypical San Francisco experience all in one storefront. Inside this unique space, you'll find off-the-wall art, unusual clothing, and downright scary jewelry. Those who make an appointment in advance can also get a tattoo here, or purchase some keen body jewelry. A trip inside Five and Diamond can be an exciting adventure for the bold, but might be a bit much for the faint of heart. Decide for yourself whether you dare to take the plunge.

Author Dave Eggers's tongue-in-cheek storefront at **826 Valencia** (826 Valencia St., 415/642-5905, www.826valencia.org/store, noon–6 P.M. daily) doubles as a pirate supply shop and youth literacy center. While you'll find plenty of pirate booty, you'll also find a good stock of literary magazines and books. Almost next door, **Paxton Gate** (824 Valencia St., 415/824-1872, www.paxtongate.com, 11 A.M.–7 P.M. daily) takes the typical gift shop to a new level with taxidermy. This quirky spot is surprisingly cheery, with garden supplies, books, and candles filling the cases in addition to the fossilized creatures.

Cliff's Variety (479 Castro St., 415/431-5365, www.cliffsvariety.com, 8:30 A.M.–8 P.M. Mon.–Fri., 9:30 A.M.–8 P.M. Sat., 11 A.M.–6 P.M. Sun.) is no ordinary hardware store, though it does carry jigsaws and wrenches. Check out its delightful array of bric-a-brac, including toys, wigs, and lava lamps.

Good Vibrations (899 Mission St.,

© DOMINI DRAGOONE

Good Vibrations

800/289-8423, www.goodvibrations.com, 10 A.M.–9 P.M. Sun.–Thurs., 10 A.M.–11 P.M. Fri.–Sat.) is a woman-owned, woman-operated, woman-centric sex shop. The well-lit house of sex succeeded in creating a sex-positive cultural center in the Mission, then expanded to two more stores in San Francisco (603 Valencia St. and 1620 Polk St.) and one in Berkeley. In addition to selling every kind of sex toy you can imagine, and probably a bunch you'd never even fantasized about, Good Vibration hosts classes and seminars aimed at improving the human sexual experience. And GV prides itself on its sex-positive, female-friendly, hand-picked collection of adult videos.

GOLDEN GATE PARK AND THE HAIGHT

The Haight-Ashbury shopping district isn't what it used to be, but if you're willing to poke around a bit, you can still find a few bargains in the remaining thrift shops. One relic of the 1960s counterculture still thrives on the Haight: head shops. However, all pipes, water pipes, and other paraphernalia are strictly for use in smoking legal tobacco, you understand.

Books and Music

Music has always been a part of the Haight. To this day you'll find homeless folks pounding out rhythms on *doumbeks* and congas on the sidewalks. Located in an old bowling alley, **Amoeba** (1855 Haight St., 415/831-1200, www.amoeba.com, 10:30 A.M.–10 P.M. Mon.–Sat., 11 A.M.–9 P.M. Sun.) is a larger-than-life record store that promotes every type of music imaginable. Amoeba's staff, many of whom are musicians themselves, are among the most knowledgeable in the business.

The award-winning **Booksmith** (1644 Haight St., 800/493-7323, www.booksmith.com, 10 A.M.–10 P.M. Mon.–Sat., 10 A.M.–8 P.M. Sun.) boasts a helpful and informed staff, a fabulous magazine collection, and Northern

California's preeminent calendar of readings by internationally renowned authors.

Technically in the Richmond neighborhood, **Green Apple Books & Music** (506 Clement St., 415/387-2272, www.greenapplebooks.com, 10 A.M.–10:30 P.M. Sun.–Thurs., 10 A.M.–11:30 P.M. Fri.–Sat.) is worth the trek. Locals head to this fog belt location to get their fill of thousands of titles that include staff picks, new releases, and used nonfiction. Friendly sales staff are on hand to assist with navigating the myriad stacks.

Clothing

Join the countless bargain shoppers who prowl the racks for fabulous forgotten garments, but don't expect to pay $0.25 for that great 1930s bias-cut dress or $0.50 for a cast-off Dior blouse; the merchants in the Haight are experienced used clothiers who know what the good stuff is worth. The same is true at the **Buffalo Exchange** (1555 Haight St., 415/431-7733, www.buffaloexchange.com, 11 A.M.–8 P.M.

daily), another Haight institution filled with a mix of new and used überhip clothes.

Originally a vaudeville theater, the capacious **Wasteland** (1660 Haight St., 415/863-3150, www.shopwasteland.com, 11 A.M.–8 P.M. Mon.–Sat., noon–7 P.M. Sun.) has a traffic-stopping art nouveau facade, a distinctive assortment of vintage hippie and rock-star threads, and a glamour-punk staff.

For more upscale (and unworn) threads, head to **Ambiance** (1458 Haight St., 415/552-5095, www.ambiancesf.com, 10 A.M.–7 P.M. Mon.–Sat., 11 A.M.–7 P.M. Sun.). The two-level store is packed with everything from evening dresses to jeans—and tons of customers.

From the grungy, make for the glam at **Piedmont Boutique** (1452 Haight St., 415/864-8075, www.piedmontsf.com, 11 A.M.–7 P.M. daily). The narrow store is a riot of color, filled with feather boas, sequined shorts, fantastic wigs—and those who wear them. This is where San Francisco's drag queens shop. (Tip: Avoid the crowds during Halloween.)

Sports and Recreation

PARKS

The largest park in San Francisco is **Golden Gate Park** (main entrance at Stanyan St. and Fell St., McLaren Lodge Visitors Center at John F. Kennedy Dr., 415/831-2700, www.golden-gate-park.com). In addition to popular sights like the Academy of Sciences, the de Young, and the Japanese Tea Garden, Golden Gate Park is San Francisco's unofficial playground. There are three botanical gardens, a children's playground (Martin Luther King Jr. Dr. and Bowling Green Dr.), tennis courts, and a golf course. Stow Lake offers paddleboats for rent (415/752-0347, 10 A.M.–4 P.M. daily, $13–17 per hour), and the park even has its own bison paddock (off John F. Kennedy Dr.). Weekends, find the park filled with locals roller-skating,

biking, hiking, and even Lindy Hopping. Note that the main entrance at John F. Kennedy Drive off Fell Street is closed to motorists every Sunday for pedestrian-friendly fun.

Crissy Field (1199 E. Beach, Presidio, 415/561-7690, www.crissyfield.org, 9 A.M.–5 P.M. daily), in the Golden Gate National Recreation Area, is a park with a mission. In partnership with the National Park Service, ecology programs are the centerpiece. Check the website for a list of classes, seminars, and fun hands-on activities for all ages. Many of these include walks out into the marsh beyond the center and the landscape of the Presidio and beyond.

Expect to see lots of locals when you visit **Mission Dolores Park** (Dolores St. and

18th St., 415/554-9529, http://sfrecpark.org/MissionDoloresPark.aspx), usually called Dolores Park and a favorite of Mission district denizens. Bring a beach blanket to sprawl on the lawn, enjoy the views, and do some serious people watching; wear walking shoes and stroll on the paved pedestrian paths; or take your racket and balls and grab a game of tennis up at one of the six courts. On weekends, music festivals and cultural events often spring up at Dolores Park.

Many people who like to hike prefer it with some semblance of solitude. That can be tough to come by in the ever-crowded Golden Gate Park and Presidio. **McLaren Park** (Mansell St. between Excelsior District and Visitacion Valley, 415/239-7735, www.jennalex.com/projects/fomp/homepage) is something of a hidden gem in the busy City—a crowd-free park with miles of hiking trails, dozens of picnic tables, athletic fields, an indoor pool, and even a nine-hole golf course. You can enjoy a set of tennis, swim some laps, or play a quick round. But most of all, you can walk. Seven miles of trails are asphalt paved, and plenty of undeveloped

trails wend off into the brush and trees all around. If you've got the stamina, you can circle the whole park by following its trails. Feel free to bring your canine companion with you to this dog-friendly park. On the other hand, take care walking here if you're a woman alone; McLaren Park is generally quite safe in the daylight hours, but at night it becomes much less safe, so plan to finish up your hiking, picnicking, and playing by sunset.

BEACHES

San Francisco boasts of being a city that has everything, and it certainly comes close. This massive urban wonderland even claims several genuine sand beaches within its city limits. No doubt the biggest and most famous of these is **Ocean Beach** (Great Hwy., parking at Sloat Blvd., Golden Gate Park, and the Cliff House, www.parksconservancy.org/visit/parksites/ocean-beach.html). This five-mile stretch of sand forms the breakwater for the Pacific Ocean along the whole west side of the City. Because it's so large you're likely to find a spot to sit down and maybe even a parking place

© KATHRYN OSGOOD

Baker Beach

along the beach, except perhaps on that rarest of occasions in San Francisco: a sunny, warm day. Don't go out for an ocean swim at Ocean Beach: Extremely dangerous rip currents kill at least one person every year.

The beach at **Aquatic Park** (Beach St. and Hyde St., www.nps.gov/safr) sits right in the middle the Fisherman's Wharf tourist area. This makes Aquatic Park incredibly convenient for visitors who want to grab a picnic on the Wharf to enjoy down on the beach. The coolest part of Aquatic Park is its history rather than its current presence. It was built in the late 1930s as a bathhouse catering to wealthy San Franciscans, and today, one of the main attractions of Aquatic Park remains swimming: Triathletes and hard-core swimmers brave the frigid waters to swim for miles in the protected cove. More sedate visitors can find a seat and enjoy a cup of coffee, a newspaper, and some people watching.

Baker Beach (Golden Gate Point and the Presidio, www.parksconservancy.org/visit/park-sites/baker-beach.html) is best known for its scenery, and that doesn't just mean the lovely views of the Golden Gate Bridge. Baker is San Francisco's own clothing-optional (that is, nude) beach. But don't worry, plenty of the denizens of Baker Beach wear clothes while flying kites, playing volleyball and Frisbee, and even just strolling on the beach. Baker Beach was the original home of the Burning Man festival before it moved out to the Black Rock Desert of Nevada. Because Baker is much smaller than Ocean Beach, it gets crowded in the summer. Whether you choose to sunbathe nude or not, don't try to swim here. The currents get seriously strong and dangerous because it is so close to the Golden Gate.

BIKING

In other places, bicycling is a sport or a mode of transportation. In San Francisco, bicycling is a religion. As a newcomer to biking in the City, it may be wise to start off gently, perhaps with a guided tour that avoids areas with dangerous traffic. The fabulously named **Blazing Saddles** (2715 Hyde St., 415/202-8888, www.blazingsaddles.com) rents bikes and offers guided bicycling tours all over the Bay Area. If you prefer the safety of a group, take the guided tour (10 A.M. daily, 3 hours, reservations required) through San Francisco and across the Golden Gate Bridge into Marin County. With five Blazing Saddles locations, most in the Fisherman's Wharf area, it's easy to find yourself a cruiser and head out for a spin.

If you're not a serious cyclist, or you're a serious cyclist who's new to the City, take the easy and flat nine-mile ride across the **Golden Gate Bridge** and back. This is a great way to see the Bridge and the Bay for the first time, and it takes only an hour or two to complete. Another option is to ride across the bridge and into the town of Sausalito (8 miles) or Tiburon (16 miles), enjoy an afternoon and dinner, and then ride the ferry back into the City (bikes are allowed on board).

If you've got a bit more time and leg strength, consider a scenic ride on the paved paths of **Golden Gate Park** (main entrance at Stanyan St. and Fell St., McLaren Lodge Visitors Center at John F. Kennedy Dr., 415/831-2700, www.golden-gate-park.com) and **The Presidio** (Montgomery St. and Lincoln Blvd., 415/561-4323, www.nps.gov/prsf). A bike makes a perfect mode of transportation to explore the various museums and attractions of these two large parks, and you can spend all day and never have to worry about finding parking.

Looking for some great urban mountain biking? Miles of unpaved roads and trails inside the city limits provide technically challenging rides for adventurous cyclists willing to take a risk or two. Check out the website for **San Francisco Mountain Biking** (www.sfmtb.com) for information about trails, roads, routes, and regulations.

GOLF

A number of golf courses hide in the parks of San Francisco. The premier golf course in the City, the **Presidio Golf Course** (Arguello St., 50 yards from Arguello Gate, 415/561-4653, www.presidiogolf.com) was once reserved for the exclusive use of military officers, government officials, and visiting dignitaries. Since 1995 the 18-hole, par-72 course, driving range, practice putting greens, and clubhouse have been available to the public. Reserve your tee time by phone or online. Lessons are available, offered by the Arnold Palmer Golf Academy (the Arnold Palmer Management Company operates the course).

Lincoln Park Golf Course (34th Ave. and Clement St., 415/221-9911) is an 80-year-old public 18-hole, par-68 course in the Outer Richmond district. It hosts the annual San Francisco City Golf Championships. For tee times at any municipal course, call 415/750-4653.

HIKING

Yes, you can go for a hike inside the city of San Francisco. Most of the parks in the City offer hiking trails to suit various tastes and ability levels. The City also boasts some longer and more interesting trails that present serious hikers with a real challenge.

For an easy nature walk in the Presidio, try the easy **Lobos Creek Trail** (Lincoln St. at Bowley St., www.bahiker.com, dawn–dusk daily). Less than a mile long, this flat boardwalk trail is wheelchair-accessible and shows off the beginning successes of the ecological restoration of the Presidio. You'll get to see restored sand dunes and native vegetation, which has attracted butterflies and other insects, in turn bringing birds to the trail area. Another easy Presidio hike goes way back into the region's history. The one-mile (one-way) **Lover's Lane** (Funston Ave. and Presidio Blvd., www.nps.gov/prsf/planyourvisit/lovers-lane.htm) once served soldiers stationed at

the Presidio who beat down the path into the City proper to visit their sweethearts. Today, you'll have a peaceful tree-shaded walk on a flat semipaved path that passes the former homes of the soldiers, crosses El Polin Creek, and ends at the Presidio Gate.

Want to hike the whole **Bay Area Ridge Trail** (415/561-2595, www.ridgetrail.org)? Prepare to get serious—the whole trail runs more than 325 miles and grows longer annually. It crosses the city of San Francisco from south to north. The easy Presidio section (Arguello Blvd. and Jackson St.) runs 2.7 miles from the Arguello Gate to the foot of the Golden Gate Bridge. If you've been trudging the sidewalks and climbing the hills of the difficult seven-mile section from Stern Grove (Wawona St. and 21st Ave.) to the Presidio's Arguello Gate, you'll be happy to find the gently sloping dirt footpaths through unpopulated forests and meadows of the Presidio. Round out the City section of the trail with the moderate 3.2-mile (one-way) section from Fort Funston (hang glider viewing deck off Fort Funston Rd.) to Stern Grove. If the weather is right, you can watch the hang gliders fly at the fort before pointing your boots north to hike the paved trails through protected glens and residential neighborhoods that most visitors to San Francisco never see.

The **Land's End Trail** (Merrie Way, 415/561-4323, www.parksconservancy.org) winds, drops, and rises from the ruins of the Sutro Baths, past the Legion of Honor, and on out to the rugged cliffs and beaches where the North American continent ends. At low tide, you can stand out in the wind and see the leftover bits of three ships that all wrecked on the rocks of Point Lobos. Smaller side trails lead down to little beaches, and the views of the Golden Gate are the stuff of legend. The **El Camino Del Mar** trail intersects Land's End, creating a mostly paved loop for enthusiastic hikers who want to take on a three-plus-mile trek that hits most of the major landmarks of Land's End. The views from this trail are some of the best in the city.

It isn't surprising that Golden Gate Park is riddled with paved pedestrian paths. The **Golden Gate Park and Ocean Beach Hike** (trailhead at Fell St. and Baker St., www.traillink.com) trail runs from the Golden Gate Park Panhandle all the way to the ocean, then down Ocean Beach to the San Francisco Zoo. You'll pass close by the Conservatory of Flowers, the de Young Museum, Stow Lake, Bercut Equitation Field, and several children's play areas.

Probably the closest thing to a true serene backwoods hike in San Francisco can be found at the easy 0.5-mile trail at **Mount Davidson** (Dalewood St., West Portal, 6 A.M.–10 P.M. daily, www.bahiker.com). Park in the adjacent West Portal residential area and wander through the gate and into the woods. Take the main fire road straight up the gentle slope to the top of the mountain, then find the smaller track off to the left that leads to the famous "cross at the top of the mountain." To extend your stay in this pleasant place, either walk down the other side of the mountain or head back to find the smaller branch trails that lead off into the trees.

The difficult 10.5-mile **California Coastal Trail** (Golden Gate National Recreation Area, www.californiacoastaltrail.info) runs through the city of San Francisco on its way down the state. Originating beneath the Golden Gate Bridge, the trail meanders all the way down the west side of the City. It passes by many major monuments and parks, so you can take a break from hiking to visit Fort Point, the Palace of the Legion of Honor, and the site of the Sutro Baths. You'll get to walk along the famous beaches of San Francisco as well, from Baker Beach to China Beach and on down to Ocean Beach, which account for five miles of the Coastal Trail. You can keep on walking all the way down to Fort Funston; the San Francisco portion of the trail terminates at Philip Burton Memorial State Beach. You can enter the trail from just about anywhere and exit where it feels convenient. Get a current trail map to be aware of any partial trail closures.

KAYAKING

For the adventurous, kayaking on San Francisco Bay is a great way to experience the famous waterway on a personal level. **City Kayak** (415/357-1010, www.citykayak.com) has locations at South Beach Harbor (Pier 40, Embarcadero and Townsend St., 10 A.M.–7 P.M. daily), with rental equipment available, and at Fisherman's Wharf (Pier 39, Slip A21). Beginners can take guided paddles along the shoreline, getting a new view of familiar sights. More advanced kayakers can take trips out to the Golden Gate and around Alcatraz Island.

WHALE WATCHING

With day-trip access to the marine sanctuary off the Farallon Islands, whale watching is a year-round activity in San Francisco. **San Francisco Whale Tours** (Pier 39, Dock B, 800/979-3370, www.sanfranciscowhaletours.com, tours daily, $60–89, advance purchase required) offers six-hour trips out to the Farallons almost every Saturday and Sunday, with almost-guaranteed whale sightings on each trip. Shorter whale-watching trips along the coastline run on weekdays, and 90-minute quickie trips out to see slightly smaller local wildlife, including elephant seals and sea lions, also go out daily. Children ages 3–15 are welcome on boat tours (for reduced rates), and kids often love the chance to spot whales, sea lions, and pelicans. Children under age three are not permitted for safety reasons.

SPECTATOR SPORTS

Lovers of the big leagues will find fun in San Francisco and around the Bay Area. The City is home to the National Football League's **San Francisco 49ers** (www.49ers.com). The 49ers play at **Candlestick Park** (490 Jamestown Ave., tickets 415/656-4900, parking 415/656-4949, parking $30), far from the center of the City on Candlestick Point. This doesn't seem to matter to "the Faithful," the loyal fans who've seen the team through their dismal beginnings, rejoiced in their domination of the NFL through the 1980s and 1990s, and continued to cheer as the team "rebuilds" (that is, loses a lot) in the 21st century. Check the website for current single-ticket prices. And be sure to bring a coat to the games—the fog rolls in off the Bay and makes the park chilly and windy. (Note that as of press time, the team is planning to move to a new—and hotly debated—stadium in Santa Clara.)

Major League Baseball's **San Francisco Giants** (http://sanfrancisco.giants.mlb.com) play out the long summer baseball season at **AT&T Park** (24 Willie Mays Plaza, 3rd St. and King St., 415/972-2000). Come out to enjoy the game, the food, and the views at San Francisco's still shiny and new ballpark. Giants games take place on weekdays and weekends, both day and night. It's not hard to snag last-minute tickets to a regular season game.

Accommodations

San Francisco has plenty of accommodations to suit every taste and most budgets. The most expensive places tend to be in Union Square, SoMa, and the Financial District. Cheaper digs can be had in the neighborhoods surrounding Fisherman's Wharf. You'll find the most character in the smaller boutique hotels, but plenty of big chain hotels have at least one location in town if you prefer a known quantity. In fact, a number of chain motels have moved into historic San Francisco buildings, creating a more unusual experience than you might expect from the likes of a Days Inn.

Free parking with a hotel room is rare in the City, existing mostly in motor lodges and chain motels down by the wharf. Overnight garage parking downtown can be excruciatingly expensive. Check with your hotel to see if they have a "parking package" that includes this expense (and possibly offers valet service as well). If you don't plan to leave the City on your trip, consider saving a bundle by skipping the rental car altogether and using public transit. On the other hand, to explore outside the City limits, a car is a necessity.

UNION SQUARE AND NOB HILL

In and around Union Square and Nob Hill, you'll find approximately a zillion hotels. As a rule, those closest to the top of the Hill or to Union Square proper are the most expensive. For a 1–2-block walk, you get more personality and genuine San Francisco experience for less money and less prestige. There are few inexpensive options in these areas; hostels appear in the direction of the Tenderloin, where safety becomes an issue after dark.

Under $150

While the best bargains aren't in these neighborhoods, you can still find one or two budget-conscious lodgings in the Union Square and Nob Hill area. Just off Union Square, the **Handlery Hotel** (351 Geary St., 800/995-4874, www.handlery.com, $135–330) offers a wide variety of guest rooms for all different price ranges. Value rooms in the historical section of the hotel tend to be small and the appointments a bit sterile, but the amenities are as good as those in the newer, pricier Club section of the complex. For a serious splurge, rent the Rooftop Garden Suite, complete with an outdoor patio overlooking the City. A heated outdoor pool is available to all, and the Daily Grill restaurant serves up large portions of standard California cuisine all day long.

The **Hotel Bijou** (111 Mason St.,

800/771-1022, www.hotelbijou.com, $116–200) might be the most fun of the inexpensive lot. Whimsical decor mimics an old-fashioned movie theater, and in fact a tiny "movie house" downstairs runs double features, free to guests, every night—with only movies shot in San Francisco. The guest rooms are small, clean, and nicely appointed.

$150-250

C Hotel Rex (562 Sutter St., 800/433-4434, www.jdvhotels.com/rex, $190–430) has a classic feel, evoking a hotel in San Francisco early in the 1900s. Guest rooms are comfortable and spacious, decorated with the work of local artists and artisans. The dimly lit lobby bar is famous in the City for its literary bent—you may find yourself embroiled in a fascinating conversation as you enjoy your evening glass of wine. Amenities include a small elevator (not all boutique hotels in SF have them), access to a nearby gym, and valet parking packages for an additional fee. The attached Café Andrée serves dinner each night; ask at the desk about reservations.

The **C Hotel Monaco** (501 Geary St., 415/292-0100, www.monaco-sf.com, $179–300) shows the vibrant side of San Francisco. Big guest rooms are whimsically decorated with bright colors, while baths are luxurious and feature cushy animal-print bathrobes. Friendly service comes from purple-velour-coated staff, who know the hotel and the City and will cheerfully tell you all about both. Chair massage complements the free wine and cheese in the large open guest lounge. Be sure to check out the Grand Café and the dining room as well. Because the Hotel Monaco is located a couple of blocks from Union Square, you get more, and more fun, for your money.

Only half a block down from the square, the **Sir Francis Drake** (450 Powell St., 800/795-7129, www.sirfrancisdrake.com, $220–360) has its own history beginning in the late 1920s. Here at the Drake you'll find a bit less opulence in the lobby, compared to the St. Francis, and a bit more in the guest rooms. The Beefeater doorman (almost always available for a photo), the unique door overhang, and the red-and-gold interior all add to the character of this favorite.

Over $250

A San Francisco legend, the **Clift** (495 Geary St., 415/775-4700, www.clifthotel.com, $315–500) has a lobby worth walking into, whether you're a guest of the hotel or not. The high-ceilinged, gray industrial space is entirely devoted to modern art. Yes, you really are supposed to sit on the antler sofa and the metal chairs, though most folks avoid the seriously oversize vintage seat. By contrast, the big Philippe Starck–designed guest rooms are almost Spartan in their simplicity, with colors meant to mimic the City skyline. Stop in for a drink at the Redwood Room, done in brown leather and popular with a younger crowd. For dinner, a branch of Jeffrey Chodorow's Asia de Cuba restaurant is located inside the hotel. The Clift is perfectly located for theatergoers, and the Square is an easy walk away.

The opulence of the lobby at the **Westin St. Francis** (335 Powell St., 415/397-7000, www.westinstfrancis.com, $295–370) matches its elegant address. With more than a century of history as San Francisco's great gathering spot, the St. Francis still garners great prestige. Guest rooms are attractive but small. The cost of a stay pays mainly for the decadent fixtures of the common areas, the four eateries (including Michael Mina, the executive chef's signature restaurant), the state-of-the-art gym, top-quality meeting and banquet spaces, and the address on Union Square.

Certain names just mean luxury in the hotel world. The **Fairmont San Francisco** (950 Mason St., 415/772-5000, www.fairmont.com, $270–420) is among the best of these. With a rich history, above-and-beyond service, and spectacular views, the Fairmont makes any stay in the City memorable. Check online for

SAN FRANCISCO

COURTESY OF PRAYITNO

the Westin St. Francis

package specials or to book a tee time or spa treatment, and note that some of the guest rooms in this rarified hostelry actually allow smoking.

Another Nob Hill contender with a top name, the **Ritz-Carlton** (600 Stockton St., 415/296-7465, www.ritzcarlton.com, $430–560) provides patrons with ultimate pampering. From the high-thread-count sheets to the five-star dining room and the full-service spa, guests at the Ritz all but drown in sumptuous amenities. Even the "standard" guest rooms are exceptional, but if you've got the bread, spring for the Club Floors, where they'll give you an iPod, a personal concierge, and possibly the kitchen sink if you ask for it.

FINANCIAL DISTRICT AND SOMA

Top business execs make it their, well...business to stay near the towering offices of the Financial District, down by the water on the Embarcadero, or in SoMa. Thus, most of the lodgings in these areas cater to the expense-account set. The big-name chain hotels run expensive; book one if you're traveling on an unlimited company credit card. Otherwise, look for smaller boutique and indie accommodations that won't tear your wallet to bits or laugh at your checking account.

Under $150

No, really, there's a place to stay in SoMa that's cheap, fastidious, and safe. It's the surprisingly eponymous **Good Hotel** (112 7th St., 800/444-5819, www.thegoodhotel.com, $139–159). The guest rooms here are small and are starting to turn shabby around the edges of the eyeball-searing modern decor, but they've got scrupulously clean private baths, and it's hard to beat the location at the corner of 7th and Mission Streets, an easy walk to the Civic Center or the Asian Art Museum, places to enjoy good cheap food, and quick access to BART. Just don't wander up one block to 6th Street, because the "safe" thing comes to an abrupt halt between the two numbered streets. If you're slightly suicidal, you can borrow one of the cruiser bikes in the lobby from the friendly desk staff. The Good Hotel is noisy at night, but if you're going to stay at a major intersection in a major city, you have to expect some traffic noise.

Should you find the need for a full-service professional recording studio in your hotel, head straight for **The Mosser** (54 4th St., 800/227-3804, www.themosser.com, $79–189, parking $35). The Mosser's inexpensive guest rooms have European-style shared baths in the hallway and spare Asian-inspired interior decor. Pricier options include bigger guest rooms with private baths; on the other hand, solo travelers can trim their costs by getting a teensy room with a single twin bed. With a rep for cleanliness and pleasant amenities, including morning coffee and comfy bathrobes, this hotel fulfills its goal—to provide visitors to the City with cheap crash space in a great location convenient to sights, shops, and public transportation.

$150-250

An unlikely hotel in the middle of the stuffy suit-clad Financial District, the █**Hotel Triton** (342 Grant Ave., 800/800-1299, www.hotel-triton.com, $160–300) welcomes guests with whimsical decor and an ecological theme. Jerry Garcia and Carlos Santana both decorated guest rooms here, and the environmentally friendly practices developed at the Triton are being adopted by sister hotels all over the world. You'll find the guest rooms tiny but comfortable and well stocked with ecofriendly amenities and bath products. The flat-panel TVs offer a 24-hour yoga channel, and complimentary yoga props can be delivered to your room on request. For the most eco-zany experience at the Triton, book a Celebrity Eco-Suite. Or if you're traveling alone, consider reserving a Zen Den—specially designed for solo travelers and offering the finest Buddhist-inspired amenities.

And don't forget to adopt a rubber ducky for the duration of your stay!

For something posh but not overwhelmingly huge, check out **Hotel Griffon** (155 Steuart St., 800/321-2201, www.hotelgriffon.com, $245–350). A boutique business hotel with a prime vacation locale, the Griffon offers business and leisure packages to suit any traveler's needs. They're a bit pricier, but the best guest rooms overlook the Bay, with views of the Bay Bridge and Treasure Island.

Over $250

Le Méridien San Francisco (333 Battery St., 415/296-2900, $300–570) stands tall in the Embarcadero Center, convenient to shopping, dining, and the streetcar and cable car lines to all the favorite downtown destinations. This expensive luxury hotel pampers guests with Frette sheets, plush robes, marble baths, and stellar views. Expect nightly turndown service, free newspapers, and 24-hour room service.

It may be part of a chain, but at the **Westin San Francisco Market** (50 3rd St., 415/974-6400, www.westinsf.com, $260–670) you'll find plenty of San Francisco charm at your doorstep. Guests stay in pleasant rooms with pretty cityscapes at this large hotel (formerly known as the Argent). Amenities mimic the more expensive SoMa hotels, and seasonal special rates dip down into the genuinely affordable. The attached restaurant, Ducca, serves three meals daily, and the lounge is open until midnight for nightcaps.

Hotel Vitale (8 Mission St., 888/890-8688, www.hotelvitale.com, $300–520) professes to restore guests' vitality with its lovely guest rooms and exclusive spa, complete with rooftop hot soaking tubs and a yoga studio. Many of the good-size guest rooms also have private deep soaking tubs. If you happen to reside in the greater Bay Area, check out the deeply discounted "Sunday Locals Only" package.

The only problem with staying at the

◖ **Mandarin Oriental San Francisco** (222 Sansome St., 415/276-9888, www.mandarinoriental.com, $520–860) is that you may never leave your room. Redefining decadence, the Mandarin Oriental includes raised beds in all rooms so guests can enjoy the panoramic city and bay views while snuggling under the covers. In the swank corner guest rooms and suites, raised bathtubs let bathers enjoy stunning sights (such as the Transamerica Pyramid, Alcatraz, and the Golden Gate Bridge) from the warmth of the bubbly water. All guest rooms boast top amenities and Asian-inspired decor, and families are welcome. You can find the best room rates on the hotel's website (the prices will make a budget-minded traveler's eyes bleed) along with various stay-and-play packages with an emphasis on golf and spa treatments.

For a unique San Francisco hotel experience, book a room at the famous **Hotel Palomar** (12 4th St., 866/373-4941, www.hotelpalomar-sf.com, $250–575). You'll find every amenity imaginable, from extra-long beds for taller guests to in-room spa services and temporary pet goldfish. The overall decorative motif evokes M. C. Escher, and whimsical colorful touches accent each room. Be sure to make reservations for dinner at the award-winning Fifth Floor restaurant during your stay. Check the website for special deals, some quite reasonably priced, that focus on shopping and spa-style relaxation. You can even book a spa package with your dog!

The **Palace Hotel** (2 New Montgomery St., 415/512-1111, www.sfpalace.com, $260–600) enjoys its reputation as the grande dame of all San Francisco hotels. The original Palace was the dream of William Ralston, who bankrupted himself creating the immense hotel. The rich history of the Palace began when its doors opened in 1875. It was gutted by fires following the 1906 earthquake, rebuilt and reopened in 1909, and refurbished for the new millennium during 1989–1991. In 1919, President Woodrow Wilson negotiated the terms of the Treaty of Versailles over lunch at the Garden Court. Today, guests take pleasure in beautiful bedrooms, exercise and relax in the full-service spa and fitness center, and dine in the Palace's three restaurants. If you're staying at the Palace, having a meal in the exquisite Garden Court dining room is a must, although you may forget to eat as you gaze upward at the stained-glass domed ceiling.

NORTH BEACH AND FISHERMAN'S WHARF

Perhaps it's odd, but the tourist mecca of San Francisco is not a district of a zillion hotels. Most of the major hostelries sit down nearer to Union Square. But you can stay near the Wharf or in North Beach if you choose; you'll find plenty of chain motels here, plus a few select boutique hotels in all price ranges.

Under $150

The **San Remo Hotel** (2237 Mason St., 800/352-7366, www.sanremohotel.com, $70–100) is one of the best bargains in the City. The blocky old yellow building has been around since just after the 1906 earthquake, offering inexpensive guest rooms to budget-minded travelers. One of the reasons for the rock-bottom pricing is the baths—you don't get your own. Four shared baths with shower facilities located in the hallways are available to guests day and night. The guest rooms boast the simplest of furnishings and decorations as well as clean white-painted walls and ceilings. Some rooms have their own sinks, all have either double beds or two twin beds, and none have telephones or TVs—so this might not be the best choice of lodgings for large media-addicted families. Couples on a romantic vacation can rent the Penthouse, a lovely room for two with lots of windows and a rooftop terrace boasting views of North Beach and the Bay.

$150-250

Hotel Bohème (444 Columbus Ave.,

415/433-9111, www.hotelboheme.com, $175–195) offers comfort, history, and culture at a pleasantly low price for San Francisco. The Bohème's long history has included a recent renovation to create an intriguing, comfortable lodging. Guest rooms are small but comfortable, Wi-Fi is free, and the spirit of the 1950s bohemian Beats lives on. The warmly colored and gently lit guest rooms are particularly welcoming to solo travelers and couples, with their retro brass beds covered by postmodern geometric spreads. All guest rooms have private baths, and the double-queen rooms can sleep up to four people for an additional charge.

The **Washington Square Inn** (1660 Stockton St., 800/388-0220, www.wsisf.com, $195–350) doesn't look like a typical California B&B. With its city-practical architecture and canopy out on the sidewalk, it's more a small, elegant hotel. The inn offers 16 guest rooms with queen or king beds, private baths, elegant appointments, and fine linens. Some guest rooms have spa bathtubs, and others have views of Coit Tower and Grace Cathedral. Only the larger guest rooms and junior suites are spacious; the standard guest rooms are "cozy" in the European urban style. A few of the amenities include a generous continental breakfast brought to your room daily, afternoon tea, a flat-screen TV in every guest room, and free Wi-Fi. To stay at the Washington Square Inn is to get a true sense of the beauty and style of San Francisco.

It may be part of a chain, but the **Hyatt at Fisherman's Wharf** (555 North Point St., 415/563-1234, www.fishermanswharf.hyatt.com, $210–390) still merits a visit. The brick facade, unusual for San Francisco, hides an ultramodern lobby and matching guest rooms. Although not too big, guest rooms are elegantly appointed with lots of decadent white linens. Many packages aim at both business travelers and visiting families. Perhaps the best of these is the Summer Parking Package, which includes overnight valet parking in the room rate.

Another great upscale hotel in the heart of San Francisco's visitors' district is the **Best Western Tuscan Inn** (425 North Point St., 800/648-4626, www.tuscaninn.com, $200–290). This

the Hyatt at Fisherman's Wharf

luxurious Italian-inspired hotel offers great amenities and prime access to Fisherman's Wharf, Pier 39, Alcatraz, and all the local shopping and dining. The attractive and very modern exterior gives way to earth tones and country-style charm in the common areas. The guest rooms boast bright colors and up-to-date furnishings—much fancier than you might be accustomed to from a Best Western. All guest rooms have private baths. They've also got Internet access, cable TV, and limo service to the Financial District three times daily. Check online for discount rates if you're coming during the middle of the week or booking more than two weeks in advance.

Over $250

For an ultra-luxurious stay in the City, save up for a room at **The Argonaut** (495 Jefferson St., 800/790-1415, www.argonauthotel.com, $250–350). With stunning Bay views from its prime Fisherman's Wharf location, in-room spa services, and a yoga channel, The Argonaut is all San Francisco, all the time. Bold patterns in blues, golds, and black and white dominate guest-room decor. Guest rooms range from cozy standards up to posh suites with separate bedrooms and whirlpool tubs. The hotel is located steps from the Maritime Museum and Ghirardelli Square.

MARINA AND PACIFIC HEIGHTS

These areas are close enough to Fisherman's Wharf to walk there for dinner, and the lodgings are far more affordable than downtown digs.

Under $100

For an unexpected, bucolic park hostel within walking and biking distance of frenetic downtown San Francisco, stop for a night at the **Fisherman's Wharf Hostel** (Fort Mason Bldg. 240, 415/771-7277, www.sfhostels.com/fishermans-wharf, dorm $26–30, private room $75–125). The hostel sits on Golden Gate National Recreation Area land, pleasantly far from the problems that plague other SF hostels. The best amenities (aside from the free linens, breakfast, and no curfews or chores) are the views of the Bay and Alcatraz, and the sweeping lawns and mature trees all around the hostel.

Few frills clutter the clean, comfortable guest rooms at the **Redwood Inn** (1530 Lombard St., 800/221-6621, www.sfredwoodinn.com, $80–110), but if you need a reasonably priced motel room in ever-expensive San Francisco, this is a great place to grab one. From the location on Lombard Street, you can get to points of interest throughout the City.

Another one of the many motels lining Lombard Street is the **Lombard Motor Inn** (1475 Lombard St., 415/441-6000, www.lombardmotorinn.com, $90–150). It's got the standard-issue amenities: reasonably sizable guest rooms, dark 1990s-era motel colors, free parking, and location, location, location. Of course, the location means there's plenty of nighttime noise pouring in through the windows, especially on weekends.

The **Marina Inn** (3110 Octavia St., 800/274-1420, www.marinainn.com, $80–130), built in 1924, exudes old-fashioned San Francisco charm but boasts pleasant modern amenities. This small family-friendly hotel offers continental breakfast, concierge services, and free Wi-Fi. The Inn is within walking distance of major City attractions, including Fisherman's Wharf, Ghirardelli Square, and the cable cars. And if you're feeling a bit scruffy and want to freshen up before your big night on the town, visit the Inn's attached barbershop or salon.

The **Francisco Bay Inn** (1501 Lombard St., 800/410-7007, www.franciscobayinn.com, $80–125) offers good motel lodgings at reasonable-for-San Francisco rates. The stellar location provides easy access to the Golden Gate Bridge, famously crooked Lombard Street, and Fisherman's Wharf. Best of all, the Francisco Bay offers free parking—a City rarity worth upward of $50 per day.

$100-150

The stately **Queen Anne Hotel** (1590 Sutter St., 800/227-3970, www.queenanne.com, $130–230) brings the elegance of downtown San Francisco out to Pacific Heights. Sumptuous fabrics and rich colors in the guest rooms and common areas add to the feeling of decadence and luxury in this boutique hotel. Small, moderate guest rooms offer attractive accommodations on a budget, while superior rooms and suites are more upscale. Continental breakfast is included, as are a number of high-end services such as courtesy car service and afternoon tea and sherry.

The exterior and interior amenities of the **Hotel Majestic** (1500 Sutter St., 415/441-1100, www.thehotelmajestic.org, $120–140) evoke the grandeur of early-20th-century San Francisco. The Edwardian-style 1902 building boasts antique furnishings and decorative items from England and France. Cozy guest rooms, junior suites, and one-bedroom suites are available. If you're in the City on business or just want to go shopping, take advantage of free car service to Union Square and the Financial District on weekday mornings. The Cafe Majestic serves breakfast and dinner, with a focus on local, healthful ingredients.

$150-200

The guest rooms at the 【**Marina Motel** (2576 Lombard St., 800/346-6118, www.marinamotel.com, $150–200) may be small, but the place is big on charm and character. This friendly little motel, decorated in French-country style, welcomes smokers, families with kids, and dogs. Just ask for the room type that best suits your needs when you make your reservations. Guest rooms are pleasantly priced for budget travelers, and several vacation packages offer deep discounts on tours, spa treatments, and outdoor adventures.

Pack the car and bring the kids to the **Hotel del Sol** (3100 Webster St., 877/433-5765, www.thehoteldelsol.com, $150–180). This unique hotel-motel embraces its origins as a 1950s motor lodge, with the guest rooms decorated in bright, bold colors with whimsical accents, a heated courtyard pool, and the ever-popular free parking. Family suites and larger guest rooms have kitchenettes. The Marina locale offers trendy cafés, restaurants, bars, and shopping within walking distance as well as access to major attractions.

The **Inn at Presidio** ($195–350) opened in 2011 inside historic Pershing Hall right in the center of The Presidio. Built in 1903, the large brick builiding was formerly home to single military officers. Today, singles and couples alike can book one of the classic rooms or suites, whose subtle contemporary furnishings complement the framed photos and other Presidio memorabilia sprinkled throughout. On-site amenities include a breakfast buffet, wine and cheese reception, free Wi-Fi, a covered front porch with rocking chairs overlooking the Main Post, and an outdoor deck with fire pit. There is a $6 fee for self-parking, or take advantage of the PresidoGo shuttle into downtown.

Over $200

A small, cute inn only a short walk from the Presidio, the **Laurel Inn** (444 Presidio Ave., 800/552-8735, www.jdvhotels.com/laurel_inn, $215–250) provides the perfect place for people with pets or for travelers who want to stay a bit longer in the City. Many of the guest rooms have kitchenettes, and all are comfortable and modern. The G Bar lounge next door offers a nice place to stop and have a cocktail, and the exclusive boutiques of Pacific Heights beckon visitors looking for a way to part with their cash.

Another Pacific Heights jewel, the **Jackson Court** (2198 Jackson St., 415/929-7670, www.jacksoncourt.com, $210) presents a lovely brick facade in the exclusive neighborhood. The 10-room inn offers comfortable, uniquely decorated queen rooms and a luscious continental breakfast each morning.

Tucked in with the money-laden mansions of Pacific Heights, **Hotel Drisco** (2901 Pacific Ave., 800/634-7277, www.jdvhotels.com/drisco, $300–475) offers elegance to discerning visitors. Away from the frenzied pace and noise of downtown, at the Drisco you get quiet, comfy guest rooms with overstuffed furniture, breakfast with a latte, and a glass of wine in the evening. Economy rooms have detached baths, and lavish suites have stellar views.

CIVIC CENTER AND HAYES VALLEY

You'll find a few reasonably priced accommodations and classic inns in the Civic Center and Hayes Valley areas.

$100-150

The Grove Inn (890 Grove St., 800/829-0780, www.grovinn.com, $138) offers simple, quiet guest rooms with double-paned windows, fluffy feather beds, TVs, and phones. A continental breakfast is served every morning. You can walk from the Inn to "postcard row" (ask the innkeepers for directions), take a longer stroll down to the Civic Center, or take public transit or a cab to any of the City's attractions.

Take a step back into an older San Francisco at the **Chateau Tivoli** (1057 Steiner St., 800/228-1647, www.chateautivoli.com, $114–340). The over-the-top colorful exterior matches perfectly with the American Renaissance interior decor. Each unique guest room and suite showcases an exquisite style evocative of the Victorian era. Most guest rooms have private baths, although the two least expensive share a bath. With a reasonable price tag even for the most opulent suites, this B&B is perfect for families (though there are no TVs in any room) and for longer stays. Try to get a room for a weekend so you can partake of the gourmet champagne brunch.

$150-250

Located in Hayes Valley a few blocks from the Opera House, the **Inn at the Opera** (333 Fulton St., 888/298-7198, www.shellhospitality.com/, $205) promises to have guests ready for a swanky night of San Francisco culture. In fact, overnight shoeshine and clothes-pressing services count among the inn's many amenities. French interior styling in the guest rooms and suites once impressed visiting opera stars and now welcomes guests from all over the world.

It might seem strange to stay at an inn called **The Parsonage** (198 Haight St., 415/863-3699, www.theparsonage.com, from $210). But this classy Victorian bed-and-breakfast exemplifies the bygone elegance of the City in one of its most colorful neighborhoods. Guest rooms are decorated with antiques, and baths has stunning marble showers. Enjoy pampering, multicourse breakfasts, and brandy and chocolates when you come "home" each night.

MISSION AND CASTRO

Accommodations in these neighborhoods are few and tend to run toward modest B&Bs.

Under $100

For a sweet, affordable little Castro inn experience, try the **Castillo Inn** (48 Henry St., 800/865-5112, $95). With only four guest rooms and shared baths, you'll imagine you've found a family pension in Tuscany transported to San Francisco. In the midst of the Castro, you've got all sorts of queer-life entertainment options only a short stroll way.

$100-150

For a romantic visit to the Castro with your partner, stay at the **Willows Inn Bed & Breakfast** (710 14th St., 800/431-0277, www.willowssf.com, $114–220). The Willows has European-style shared baths and comfortable guest rooms with private sinks and bent willow furnishings, and serves a yummy continental breakfast each morning. Catering to the queer community, the innkeepers at the Willows can help you with nightclubs, restaurants, and festivals in the City and locally in the Castro. One of the best amenities is the friendship and camaraderie you'll find with the other guests and staff at this great Edwardian B&B.

At the **Inn on Castro** (321 Castro St., 415/861-0321, www.innoncastro.com, $145–230), you've got all kinds of choices. You can pick an economy room with a shared bath, a posh private suite, or a self-service apartment. Once ensconced, you can chill out on the cute patio, or go out into the Castro to take in the legendary entertainment and nightlife. The self-catering apartments can sleep up to four and have fully furnished and appointed kitchens and dining rooms. Amenities include LCD TVs with cable, DVD players, and colorful modern art.

GOLDEN GATE PARK AND THE HAIGHT

Accommodations around Golden Gate Park are surprisingly reasonable. Leaning toward Victorian and Edwardian inns, most lodgings are in the middle price range for well above average guest rooms and services. However, getting downtown from the quiet residential spots can be a trek; ask at your inn about car services, cabs, and the nearest bus lines.

Out on the ocean side of the park, motor inns of varying quality cluster on the Great Highway. They've got the advantages of more space, low rates, and free parking, but they range from drab all the way down to seedy; choose carefully.

$100-150

The Summer of Love seems endless to guests at the **Red Victorian Bed, Breakfast, and Art** (1665 Haight St., 415/864-1978, www.redvic. com, $114–220). The Red Vic serves up peace, love, and literature along with breakfast, while community and color (but absolutely no TVs) decorate the guest rooms. Part of the economy of this B&B includes shared, named baths for

some guest rooms, although many guest rooms have their own private baths. Enjoy the intellectual, peaceful conversations over breakfast, browse the Peace Arts Gift Shop, and if you can, get in a chat with owner Sami Sunchild.

To say the **Seal Rock Inn** (545 Point Lobos Ave., 888/732-5762, www.sealrockinn.com, $130–200) is near Golden Gate Park pushes even the fluid San Francisco neighborhood boundaries a bit. In fact, this pretty place perches near the tip of land's end, only a short walk from the Pacific Ocean. All guest rooms at the Seal Rock Inn have ocean views, private baths, free parking, free Wi-Fi, and recent remodels that create a pleasantly modern ambiance. With longer stays in mind, the Seal Rock offers rooms with kitchenettes (two-day minimum stay to use the kitchen part of the room; weird but true). You can call and ask for a fireplace room that faces the Seal Rocks, so you can stay warm and toasty while training your binoculars on a popular mating spot for local sea lions. The restaurant downstairs serves breakfast and lunch; on Sunday you'll be competing with brunch-loving locals for a table.

$150-250

The **Stanyan Park Hotel** (750 Stanyan St., 415/751-1000, www.stanyanpark.com, $175–230) graces the Upper Haight area across the street from Golden Gate Park. This renovated 1904–1905 building, listed on the National Register of Historic Places, shows off its Victorian heritage both inside and out. Guest rooms can be small but are elegantly decorated, and a number of multiple-room suites are available. For a special treat, ask for a room overlooking the park.

Way over on the other side of the park, the **Great Highway Inn** (1234 Great Hwy., 800/624-6644, www.greathwy.com, $150–200) sits across the street from Ocean Beach. Actually an old motor-lodge style motel, the Inn has big clean guest rooms, decent beds,

SAN FRANCISCO

road noise, some language problems with the desk when checking in, and a short walk out to the Pacific Ocean. Guest rooms have standard-issue floral bedspreads, industrial-strength carpets, and private baths. A better option for travelers with cars, the Great Highway Inn has free parking in an adjacent lot. An on-site coffee shop offers decent food but weird hours. The motel offers discounted rates to families visiting patients at the nearby UCSF Medical Center.

SAN FRANCISCO AIRPORT

San Francisco Airport (SFO) is actually 13 miles south of San Francisco, situated on the peninsula. If you're hunting for an urban chic boutique hotel or a funky and unique hostel, the airport is *not* the place to motel-shop. SFO's hotel row, however, has many mid-priced chain motels.

Don't expect ritzy accommodations at the **Ritz Inn** (151 El Camino Real, San Bruno, 800/799-7489, www.ritzinnsfo.com, $58–70). At this cheap plain Jane you'll get a bed with an uncomfortable mattress and a loud floral spread, a bathroom, a microwave, a fridge, and a TV. Many other businesses along the El Camino are other airport motels.

The **Villa Montes Hotel** (620 El Camino Real, San Bruno, 650/745-0111, www.ascend-collection.com, $143–170) offers mid-tier accommodations and amenities on a fairly nice block. Both the exterior and the interior are attractive and modern, complete with slightly wacky lobby decor and an indoor hot tub. Guest rooms have one or two beds, complete with bright white duvets and pillow-top mattresses. Focusing on business travelers, the motel has free in-room Wi-Fi, multiline phones with voice mail, and copy and fax machines for guest use.

Millwood Inn & Suites (1375 El Camino Real, Millbrae, 800/516-6738, www.mill-woodinn.com, $125–150) offers contemporary decor and big guest rooms designed for the comfort of both business and vacation travelers. Amenities include free Wi-Fi and satellite TV with an attached DVD player. Gorge on a bigger-than-average free buffet breakfast in the morning. Perhaps best of all, the Millwood Inn offers a complementary airport shuttle—not all airport motels near SFO do.

A generous step up both in price and luxury is the **Bay Landing Hotel** (1550 Bayshore Hwy., Burlingame, 650/259-9000, www.bay-landinghotel.com, $165–185). Updated guest rooms include pretty posted headboards, granite sinks in the baths, tub-shower combos, in-room safes, and free Wi-Fi. Free continental breakfast is served in the lobby, which has a lending library for guests.

Food

One of the main reasons people come to San Francisco from near and far is to eat. Some of the greatest culinary innovation in the world comes out of the kitchens in the City. The only real problem is how to choose which restaurant to eat dinner at tonight.

UNION SQUARE AND NOB HILL
Bakeries and Cafés

With a monopoly on the coffee available in the middle of Union Square, business is brisk at **Emporio Rulli** (333 Post St., 415/433-1122, www.rulli.com, 7 A.M.–7 P.M. daily, $10–20). This local chain offers frothy coffee, pastries, and upscale sandwiches, plus wine and beer. Expect everything to be overpriced at Rulli. In the summer, sitting at the outdoor tables feels comfortable. In the winter, it's less pleasant, but it's fun to watch the skaters wobble around the tiny outdoor ice rink in the square.

Asian

It seemed unlikely that anything worthy could possibly replace Trader Vic's, but **Le Colonial** (20 Cosmo Pl., 415/931-3600, www.lecolonialsf.com, 5:30–10 P.M. Sun.–Wed., 5:30–11 P.M. Thurs.–Sat., $25–40) does it. This Vietnamese-fusion hot spot takes pride in its tiki lounge, which features live music acts and house DJs six nights a week. Cocktails are big and tropical, and they pay proper homage to the building's illustrious former occupant. But don't skip the food; the lush French-Vietnamese fare comes family-style and blends flavors in a way that seems just perfect for San Francisco.

You'll find all of Southeast Asia in the food at **E&O Trading Company** (314 Sutter St., 415/693-0303, www.eosanfrancisco.com, 11:30 A.M.–10 P.M. Mon.–Wed., 11:30 A.M.–11 P.M. Thurs.–Sat., 5–10 P.M. Sun., $12–26). This fusion grill serves up small plates like Indonesian corn fritters, mixed in with larger grilled dishes such as black pepper shaking beef. Enjoy the wine list, full bar, and French colonial decor. Reservations are recommended.

California

Make reservations in advance if you want to dine at San Francisco legend **Farallon** (450 Post St., Suite 4, 415/956-6969, www.farallonrestaurant.com, 5:30–9:30 P.M. Mon.–Thurs., 5:30–11 P.M. Fri.–Sat., 5–10 P.M. Sun., $30–55). Dark, cave-like rooms are decorated in an under-the-sea theme—complete with the unique Jellyfish Bar. The cuisine, on the other hand, is out of this world. Chef Mark Franz has made Farallon a 10-year fad that just keeps gaining ground. The major culinary theme, seafood, dominates the pricey-but-worth-it menu. Desserts by award-winning pastry chef Emily Luchetti round out what many consider to be the perfect California meal.

Another local mainstay of San Francisco haute cuisine is Wolfgang Puck's **Postrio** (545 Post St., 415/776-7825, www.postrio.com,

6:30 A.M.–10:30 P.M. daily, $30–40). Here you'll find everything from Puck's famed pizzas to the best of rarified local sustainable fare. The restaurant has three levels, all of which see their share of celebrities. Not surprisingly, reservations are strongly recommended if you want to dine chez Puck.

French

The famed **Fleur de Lys** (777 Sutter St., 415/673-7779, www.hubertkeller.com, 6–9:30 P.M. Tues.–Thurs., 5:30–10 P.M. Fri.–Sat., prix fixe $72–95, reservations strongly recommended) is one of the longest-running and finest dining establishments in San Francisco, and chef Hubert Keller (Keller may be *the* best name in Bay Area dining ever) continues to create delectable and inventive dishes. The dining room is magnificent, with its elaborate tented ceiling, lushly upholstered chairs, and perfect glass accent pieces. But the reason people flock to Fleur de Lys is, and has always been, the food. The absolutely cream-of-the-crop menu isn't really à la carte—instead, you're encouraged to peruse the items and create your own three-, four-, or five-course feast. Vegetarians aren't left out, since Keller creates vegetable-only (and fish-only) dishes with the same love he dedicates to his meats. You'll probably want wine with your meal, which means it's going to cost a bundle. But it's worth the money to splurge at this world-famous spot.

Tucked away in a tiny alley that looks like it might have been transported from Saint-Michel in Paris, **C Café Claude** (7 Claude Ln., 415/392-3505, www.cafeclaude.com, 11:30 A.M.–10:30 P.M. Mon.–Sat., 5:30–10:30 P.M. Sun., $18–28) serves classic brasserie cuisine to French expatriates and Americans alike. Much French is spoken here, but the simple food tastes fantastic in any language. Café Claude is open for lunch through dinner, serving an attractive post-lunch menu for weary shoppers looking for sustenance at 3 or 4 P.M.

Indian

On the more affordable end of the Indian food spectrum you'll find **Chutney** (511 Jones St., 415/931-5541, www.chutneysf.com, noon–midnight daily, $3–10). With a menu emphasizing curries and masalas—some vegetarian and some meat-laden—Chutney offers a good quick bite, especially late at night.

FINANCIAL DISTRICT AND SOMA

Bakeries and Cafés

One of the Ferry Building mainstays, the **Acme Bread Company** (1 Ferry Plaza, Suite 15, 415/288-2978, 6:20 A.M.–7:30 P.M. Mon.–Fri., 8 A.M.–7 P.M. Sat.–Sun.) remains true to its name. You can buy bread here, but not sandwiches, croissants, or froufrou pastries. All the bread that Acme sells is made with fresh organic ingredients in traditional style; the baguettes are traditionally French, so they start to go stale after only 4–6 hours. Eat fast!

For a quick bite, stop in at **The Grove Café** (690 Mission St., 415/957-0558, 7 A.M.–11 P.M. Mon.–Fri., 8 A.M.–11 P.M. Sat.–Sun.), in Yerba Buena. This local chain offers fresh soups, salads, and sandwiches as well as coffee and Wi-Fi in an airy and relaxed setting.

Blue Bottle Café (66 Mint St., 415/495-3394, www.bluebottlecoffee.net, 7 A.M.–7 P.M. Mon.–Fri., 8 A.M.–6 P.M. Sat., 8 A.M.–4 P.M. Sun., $5–10), a popular local chain with multiple locations around the city, takes its equipment very seriously. Whether you care about the big copper thing that made your mocha or not, you can get a good cup of joe and a small if somewhat pretentious meal at the Mint Plaza. Other locations include the Ferry Building (1 Ferry Bldg., Suite 7) and the SFMOMA (151 3rd St., 5th Fl.).

American

Looking for a good old-fashioned American breakfast? Walk on down to **Dottie's True Blue Café** (28 6th St., 415/885-2767, http://dotties.

biz, 7:30 A.M.–3 P.M. Mon.–Wed. and Thurs.–Fri., 7:30 A.M.–4 P.M., $6–12). The menu is simple: classic egg dishes, light fruit plates, and an honest-to-goodness blue-plate special for breakfast as well as salads, burgers, and sandwiches for lunch. The service is friendly, and the portions are huge. So what's the catch? Everyone in San Francisco knows that there's a great breakfast to be had at Dottie's. Expect lines up to an hour long for a table at this locals' mecca, especially at breakfast on weekend mornings.

Asian

It may not be in Chinatown, but the dim sum at **Yank Sing** (101 Spear St., 415/957-9300, www.yanksing.com, 11 A.M.–3 P.M. Mon.–Fri., 10 A.M.–4 P.M. Sat.–Sun., $39) is second to none. The family owns and operates both this restaurant and its sister location (49 Stevenson St., 415/541-4949), and now the third generation is training to take over. In addition to the traditional steamed pork buns, shrimp dumplings, egg custard tarts, and such, the "Creative Collection" offers unique bites you won't find elsewhere in the city. Note that it's open for lunch only.

California

From an impossibly small kitchen, chef Dennis Leary turns out some of the biggest flavors in town at **Canteen** (817 Sutter St., 415/928-8870, www.sfcanteen.com, 6 P.M. and 8 P.M. Tues., 6 P.M., 7:30 P.M., and 9:15 P.M. Wed.–Sat., $20–27). Sidle up to the lime-green counter or squeeze into one of the tiny booths to enjoy his eclectic menu—from black cod with couscous to velvety vanilla soufflé. Reserve early: Seats are in short supply.

French

There's no question that **Fifth Floor** (12 4th St., 415/348-1555, www.fifthfloorrestaurant.com, 5:30–10 P.M. Tues.–Sat., $30–40) is one of the top French restaurants in San Francisco. Which is saying something. The restaurant sits on the fifth floor of the Hotel Palomar and has both a casual café and a full-scale formal dining room to serve as many diners as possible. The cuisine exemplifies the best of southern France—the chef specializes in Gascon food and loves to create dishes that show off his early life and training. An ultra-expensive dinner at Fifth Floor is the perfect excuse to dress to the nines. Don't worry, the dining room decor can take it.

For the lower end of the French cuisine spectrum, check out **Crepes A Go-Go** (350 11th St., 415/503-1294, 11 A.M.–10 P.M. daily, $3.50–6) in SoMa. Believe it or not, the tiny but clean premises, lone guy working the crepes, and late-night hours (call to check what the *real* closing hours are) are all quite reminiscent of Paris. Crepes A Go-Go can make you some quick and hearty nighttime sustenance or perhaps a fruity dessert. The house special is the turkey, egg, and cheese—a great way to fuel a full night of drinking and clubbing.

Italian

Palio d'Asti (640 Sacramento St., 415/395-9800, www.paliodasti.com, 11:30 A.M.–2:30 P.M. and 5:30–9 P.M. Mon.–Fri., 5:30–9 P.M. Sat., $15–33) is one of the City's elder statesmen. The restaurant has been around since just after the 1906 earthquake, and the decor in the dining areas recreates another bygone era in the old country. Try either lunch or dinner, and enjoy the classic Italian menu, which includes wood-fired handmade pizzas as well as homemade pastas and classic Italian entrées. If you're in the City in the fall, be sure to stop in and sample the luscious, expensive, and exceedingly rare Piedmont white truffles.

Japanese

In these neighborhoods you'll find plenty of sushi restaurants to choose from, from the most ultracasual walk-up lunch places to the fanciest fusion joints. **Ame** (St. Regis Hotel, 689 Mission St., 415/284-4040, www.

amerestaurant.com, 6–9:30 P.M. Mon.–Thurs., 5:30–10 P.M. Fri.–Sat., 5:30–9:30 P.M. Sun., $35–40) is one of the latter. Appropriately situated in stylish SoMa, this upscale eatery serves a California-Japanese fusion style of seafood. Raw fish fanciers can start with the offerings from the sashimi bar, while folks who prefer their food cooked will find a wealth of options in the appetizers and main courses. The blocky, attractively colored dining room has a modern flair that's in keeping with the up-to-date cuisine coming out of the kitchen. You can either start out or round off your meal with a cocktail from the shiny black bar.

Forget your notions of the plain Jane sushi bar; **Ozumo** (161 Steuart St., 415/882-1333, www.ozumo.com, 11:30 A.M.–2 P.M. Mon.–Wed., 11:30 A.M.–2 P.M. and 5:30–10:30 P.M. Thurs., 11:30 A.M.–2 P.M. and 5:30–11 P.M. Fri., 5:30–11 P.M. Sat., 5:30–10:30 P.M. Sun., $28–46) takes Japanese cuisine upscale, San Francisco style. Order some classic *nigiri,* a small-plate *izakaya* pub dish, or a big chunk of meat off the traditional *robata* grill. The high-quality sake lines the shelves above the bar and along the walls. For nonimbibers, choose from a selection of premium teas. If you're a night owl, enjoy a late dinner on weekends and drinks in the lounge nightly.

Seafood

One of the very first restaurants established in San Francisco during the Gold Rush in 1849, the ◖ **Tadich Grill** (240 California St., 415/391-1849, www.tadichgrill.com, 11 A.M.–9:30 P.M. Mon.–Fri., 11:30 A.M.–9:30 P.M. Sat., $20–40) still serves fresh-caught fish and classic miner fare. The menu combines perfectly sautéed sand dabs, octopus salad, and corned beef hash. Mix that with the business lunch crowd in suits, out-of-towners, and original dark wooden booths from the 1850s and you've got a fabulous San Francisco stew of a restaurant. Speaking of stew, the Tadich cioppino enjoys worldwide fame—and deserves it, even in a city that prides itself on the quality of its seafood concoctions.

Steak

Alexander's Steakhouse (448 Brannan St., 415/495-1111, www.alexanderssteakhouse.com, 5:30–10 P.M. Mon.–Sat., 5:30–9 P.M. Sun., $35–200) describes itself as "where East meets beef." It's true—the presentation at Alexander's looks like something you'd see on *Iron Chef,* and the prices of the *wagyu* beef look like the monthly payment on a small Japanese car. This white-tablecloth steak house that's managed to succeed even in beef-loving SoMa is the very antithesis of a bargain, but the food, including the steaks, is more imaginative than most, and the elegant dining experience will make you feel special as your wallet quietly bleeds out. Console yourself with a cone of cotton candy after dessert—the delicate spun sugar will help make you feel like a kid who blew his allowance at a carnival.

How could you not love a steak house with a name like **Epic Roasthouse** (369 Embarcadero, 415/369-9955, www.epicroasthouse.com, 5:30–9:30 P.M. Mon.–Tues., 11:30 A.M.–2:30 P.M. and 5:30–9:30 P.M. Wed.–Thurs., 11:30 A.M.–2:30 P.M. and 5:30–10 P.M. Fri., 11 A.M.–3 P.M. and 5:30–10 P.M. Sat., 11 A.M.–3 P.M. and 5:30–9:30 P.M. Sun.,, $20–50)? Come for the wood-fired grass-fed beef; stay for the prime views over San Francisco Bay. The Epic Roasthouse sits almost underneath the Bay Bridge, where the lights sparkle and flash over the deep black water at night. On weekends, the steak house offers the hipster City crowd what it wants—an innovative prix fixe brunch menu complete with hair-of-the-dog cocktails. Epic!

Vietnamese

Probably the single most famous Asian restaurant in a city filled with eateries of all types is **The Slanted Door** (1 Ferry Plaza, Suite 3, 415/861-8032, http://slanteddoor.com, 11 A.M.–2:30 P.M. and 5:30–10 P.M. Mon.–Sat., 11:30 A.M.–3 P.M. and 5:30–10 P.M. Sun., $20–30). If all you know of Vietnamese cuisine is rubbery summer rolls and tripe-and-tendon *pho,* you are in for some seriously tasty reeducation. Owner Charles Phan, along with more than 20 family members and the rest of his staff, pride themselves on welcoming service and top-quality food. Organic local ingredients get used in both traditional and innovative Vietnamese cuisine, creating a unique dining experience. Even experienced foodies remark that they've never had green papaya salad, glass noodles, or shaking beef like this before. The light afternoon tea menu (2:30–4:30 P.M. daily) can be the perfect pick-me-up for weary travelers who need some sustenance to get them through the long afternoon until dinner, and Vietnamese coffee is the ultimate Southeast Asian caffeine experience.

Farmers Markets

While farmers markets litter the landscape in just about every California town, the **Ferry Plaza Farmers Market** (1 Ferry Plaza, 415/291-3276, www.ferrybuildingmarketplace.com, 10 A.M.–2 P.M. Tues. and Thurs., 8 A.M.–2 P.M. Sat.) is special. At the granddaddy of Bay Area farmers markets, you'll find a wonderful array of produce, cooked foods, and even locally raised meats and locally caught seafood. Expect to see the freshest fruits and veggies from local growers, grass-fed beef from Marin County, and seasonal seafood pulled from the Pacific beyond the Golden Gate. Granted, you'll pay for the privilege of purchasing from this market—if you're seeking bargain produce, you'll be better served at one of the weekly suburban farmers markets. Even locals flock downtown to the Ferry Building on Saturday mornings, especially in the summer when the variety of California's agricultural bounty becomes staggering.

CHINATOWN
Chinese Banquets

The "banquet" style of Chinese restaurant may be a bit more familiar to American travelers. Banquet restaurants offer tasty meat, seafood, and veggie dishes along with rice, soups, and appetizers, all served family-style. Tables are often round, with a lazy Susan in the middle to facilitate the passing of communal serving bowls around the table. In the City, most banquet Chinese restaurants have at least a few dishes that will feel familiar to the American palate, and menus often have English translations.

The **R&G Lounge** (631 Kearny St., 415/982-7877, www.rnglounge.com, 11:30 A.M.–9:30 P.M. daily, $12–40, reservations suggested) takes traditional Chinese American cuisine to the next level. The menu is divided by colors that represent the five elements, according to Chinese tradition and folklore. In addition to old favorites like moo shu pork, chow mein, and lemon chicken, you'll find spicy Szechuan and Mongolian dishes and an array of house specialties. Salt-and-pepper Dungeness crab, served whole on a plate, is the R&G signature dish, though many of the other seafood dishes are just as special. Expect your seafood to be fresh since it comes right out of the tank in the dining room. California-cuisine mores have made their way into the R&G Lounge in the form of some innovative dishes and haute cuisine presentations. This is a great place to enjoy Chinatown cuisine in an American-friendly setting.

Another great banquet house is the **Hunan Home's Restaurant** (622 Jackson St., 415/982-2844, http://hunanhome.ypguides.net, 11:30 A.M.–9:30 P.M. Sun.–Thurs., 11:30 A.M.–10 P.M. Fri.–Sat., $10–15). It is a bit more on the casual side, and it even has another location in suburban Los Altos. You'll find classic items on the menu such as broccoli beef and kung pao chicken, but do take care if something you plan to order has a "spicy" notation next to it.

At Hunan Home's, and in fact at most Bay Area Chinese restaurants, they mean *really* spicy.

Dim Sum

The Chinese culinary tradition of dim sum is literally translated as "touch the heart," meaning "order to your heart's content" in Cantonese. In practical terms, it's a light meal—lunch or afternoon tea—composed of small bites of a wide range of dishes. Americans tend to eat dim sum at lunchtime, though it can just as easily be dinner or even Sunday brunch. In a proper dim sum restaurant, you do not order anything or see a menu. Instead, you sip your oolong and sit back as servers push loaded steam trays out of the kitchen one after the other. Servers and trays make their way around the tables; you pick out what you'd like to try as it passes, and enough of that dish for everyone at your table is placed before you.

One of the many great dim sum places in Chinatown is the **Great Eastern** (649 Jackson St., 415/986-2500, 10 A.M.–midnight daily, $15–25). It's not a standard dim sum place; instead of the steam carts, you'll get a menu and a list. You must write down everything you want on your list and hand it to your waiter, and your choices will be brought out to you, so family style is undoubtedly the way to go here. Reservations are strongly recommended for diners who don't want to wait 30–60 minutes or more for a table. This restaurant jams up fast, right from the moment it opens, especially on weekends. The good news is that most of the folks crowding into Great Eastern are locals. You know what that means.

Another well-known dim sum spot, **Yong Kee** (732 Jackson St., 415/986-3759, www.yongkeecompany.com, 7 A.M.–6 P.M. Tues.–Sun., $10, cash only), offers a completely different dim sum experience. This Cantonese-only hole-in-the-wall caters primarily to locals, but if you've ever had dim sum or even just Chinese steamed buns before, you'll want to try them here. They're famous for their enormous fresh-made chicken buns *(gai bow)*, which is what the Chinese women lined up at the take-out counter have come for. You can also get a great pork bun, and the rest of the dim sum nibbles are tasty too. Reservations are not taken, but they aren't necessary. Do be aware that Yong Kee isn't a good beginner's dim sum place unless you've got a Cantonese-speaking friend to guide you. But if you're already a fan of the cuisine, you'll love Yong Kee even if you can't understand the menu or the staff.

Tea Shops

While black tea, often oolong, is the staple in California Chinese restaurants, you'll find an astonishing variety of teas if you step into one of Chinatown's small tea shops. You can enjoy a hot cup of tea or buy some loose tea to take home with you. Most tea shops also sell lovely imported teapots and other implements for proper tea-making.

One option is **Blest Tea** (752 Grant Ave., 415/951-8516, http://blesttea.com, tasting $3), which boasts of the healthful qualities of their many varieties of tea. You're welcome to taste what's available for a nominal fee to be sure you're purchasing something you'll really enjoy. If you're lucky enough to visit when the owner is minding the store, ask her lots of questions—she'll tell you everything you ever needed to know about tea.

NORTH BEACH AND FISHERMAN'S WHARF
Bakeries and Cafés

Serving some of the most famous sourdough in the City, the **Boudin Bakery & Café** (Pier 39, Space 5-Q, 415/421-0185, www.boudinbakery. com, 8 A.M.–8 P.M. Sun.–Thurs., 8 A.M.–9 P.M. Fri.–Sat., $6–8) is a Pier 39 institution. Grab a loaf of bread to take with you, or order in one of the Boudin classics. Nothing draws tourists like the fragrant clam chowder in a bread bowl, but if you prefer, you can try another soup, a

Boudin Bakery & Café

COURTESY OF PRAYITNO

signature sandwich, or even a fresh salad. For a more upscale dining experience with the same great breads, try **Bistro Boudin** (160 Jefferson St., 415/351-5561, 11:30 A.M.–9:30 P.M. Sun.–Thurs., 11:30 A.M.–10 P.M. Fri.–Sat., $18–30).

Widely recognized as the first espresso coffeehouse on the West Coast, family-owned **Caffé Trieste** (601 Vallejo St., 415/392-6739, www.caffetrieste.com, 6:30 A.M.–10 P.M. Sun.–Thurs., 6:30 A.M.–11 P.M. Fri.–Sat., cash only) first opened its doors in 1956. Sip a cappuccino, munch on Italian pastries, and enjoy Saturday afternoon concerts by the Giotta family at this treasured North Beach institution.

American

Smack-dab in the middle of North Beach, **Mama's on Washington Square** (1701 Stockton St., 415/362-6421, www.mamas-sf.com, 8 A.M.–3 P.M. Tues.–Sun., $8–10) is the perfect place to fuel up on gourmet omelets, freshly baked breads—including a delectable cinnamon brioche—and daily specials like crab Benedict before a day of sightseeing. Arrive early, or be prepared to wait...and wait.

California

San Francisco culinary celebrity Gary Danko has a number of restaurants around town, but perhaps the finest is the one that bears his name. **Gary Danko** (800 North Point St., 415/749-2060, www.garydanko.com, 5:30–10 P.M. daily, prix fixe $69–102) offers the best of Danko's California cuisine, from the signature horseradish-crusted salmon medallions to the array of delectable fowl dishes. The herbs and veggies come from Danko's own farm in Napa. Make reservations in advance to get a table, and consider dressing up a little for your sojourn in the elegant white-tablecloth dining room.

A local favorite, especially for weekend brunch, **Butterfly** (Pier 33, 415/864-8999, www.butterflysf.com, 11:30 A.M.–10 P.M. Tues.–Fri., 11 A.M.–10 P.M. Sat., 11 A.M.–3 P.M. Sun.,

$19–40) attracts a young, hip crowd with its ultramodern decor and cocktails for both lunch and dinner. You can sit at a window table enjoying the Asian-inspired California cuisine and watching the city-size cruise ships dock next door. The brunch menu offers fun breakfast-type dishes. Butterfly can draw a crowd, so make reservations to get a seat at your favorite time.

European

With a culinary style perhaps best described as European fusion, **Luella** (1896 Hyde St., 415/674-4343, www.luellasf.com, 5:30–10 P.M. Mon.–Sat., 5–9 P.M. Sun., $13–28) brings the flavors of Italy, France, and Spain to the City. The tasty original dishes, most with a distinctive splash of California style that complements the European roots, are best enjoyed with a glass of wine from the extensive wine bar. If you're out late or on the run, dinner is served at the wine bar, and a bar menu offers tasty treats after the dining room closes.

French

The **Hyde Street Bistro** (1521 Hyde St., 415/292-4415, www.hydestreetbistrosf.com, 5:30–10 P.M. Sun.–Thurs., 5:30–10:30 P.M. Fri.–Sat., $27) definitely belongs in San Francisco, what with the cable car clanging by outside the front door and the fog blowing past overhead. But in romance and cuisine, it's all Parisian splendor. A prix fixe menu offers economy, while the à la carte menu provides a variety of traditional French bistro fare, including snails, foie gras, and coq au vin. This is a perfect place to bring a date for romantic night out, or to celebrate an anniversary.

Greek

In the Greek fishing village of Kokkari, wild game and seafood hold a special place in the local mythology. At **Kokkari Estiatorio** (200 Jackson St., 415/981-0983, www.kokkari.com, 11:30 A.M.–2:30 P.M. and 5:30–10 P.M.

Mon.–Thurs., 11:30 A.M.–2:30 P.M. and 5:30–11 P.M. Fri., 5–11 P.M. Sat., 5–10 P.M. Sun., $22–42), patrons enjoy Mediterranean delicacies made with fresh California ingredients amid rustic elegance, feasting on such classic dishes as zucchini cakes and grilled lamb chops.

Italian

North Beach is San Francisco's own version of Little Italy. Poke around and find one of the local favorite mom-and-pop pizza joints, or try a bigger, more upscale Italian eatery.

At busy **Caffe Delucchi** (500 Columbus Ave., 415/393-4515, www.caffedelucchi.com, 10 A.M.–10 P.M. Mon.–Fri., 8 A.M.–11 P.M. Sat.–Sun., $12–24), down-home Italian cooking meets fresh San Francisco produce to create affordable, excellent cuisine. You can get hand-tossed pizzas, salads, and entrées for lunch and dinner, plus tasty traditional American breakfast fare with an Italian twist on the weekends. Drinks run to *soju* cocktails and artisanal Italian and California wines.

Trattoria Contadina (1800 Mason St., 415/982-5728, www.trattoriacontadina.com, 5:30–9:30 P.M. Sun.–Thurs., 5:30–10:30 P.M. Fri.–Sat., $17–27) presents mouthwatering Italian fare in a fun, eclectic dining room. Dozens of framed photos line the walls, and fresh ingredients stock the kitchen in this San Francisco take on the classic Italian trattoria. Kids are welcome, and vegetarians will find good meatless choices on the menu.

A teensy neighborhood place, **L'Osteria del Forno** (519 Columbus Ave., 415/982-1124, www.losteriadelforno.com, 11:30 A.M.–10 P.M. Sun.–Mon. and Wed.–Thurs., 11:30 A.M.–10:30 P.M. Fri.–Sat., $10–18) serves up a small menu to match its small dining room and small tables and small (but full) bar. The delectable northern Italian–style pizzas and pastas paired with artisanal cocktails go a long way toward warming up frozen fog-drenched visitors from the Wharf and the beach. Locals love L'Osteria,

which means it's next to impossible to get a table at lunchtime or dinnertime, and doubly impossible on weekends. Your best bet is to drop by during the off-hours—L'Osteria stays open all afternoon and makes a perfect haven for travelers who find themselves in need of a very late lunch.

Want a genuine world-champion pizza while you're in town? Nine-time World Pizza Champion Tony Gemignani can hook you up. **Tony's Pizza Napoletana** (1570 Stockton St., 415/835-9888, www.tonyspizzanapoletana.com, noon–11 P.M. Wed.–Sun., $15–30) has four different pizza ovens that cook eight distinct styles of pizza. You can get a classic American pie loaded with pepperoni, a California-style pie with lamb and eucalyptus (if you really must), or a Sicilian pizza smothered in meat and garlic. The chef's special Neapolitan-style pizza margherita is a simple-sounding pizza made of perfection. The wood-fired atmosphere of this temple to the pie includes marble-topped tables, dark woods, and white linen napkins stuck into old tomato cans. The long full bar dominates the front dining room—grab a fancy bottle of wine or a cocktail to go with that champion pizza.

For fine Italian-influenced cuisine, make a reservation at **Quince** (470 Pacific Ave., 415/775-8500, www.quincerestaurant.com, 5:30–10 P.M. Mon.–Sat., $25–95). Chef-owner Michael Tusk blends culinary aesthetics to create his own unique style of cuisine. It's best to arrive at Quince hungry; the menu is divided into four different courses, or you can try the chef's tasting menu ($125). Once you've had a look at the dishes, made with the finest local and sustainable ingredients, you'll want to try at least one from every course.

Japanese

Even in a town with hundreds of sushi bars, **Sushi Groove** (1916 Hyde St., 415/440-1905, www.sushigroove.com, 5:30–10 P.M.

Sun.–Tues., 5:30–10:30 P.M. Fri.–Sat., $15–23) stands out. With an immense sushi bar, friendly chefs, and innovative sushi that blends traditional Japanese fish with unusual California touches, the Groove finds favorites with locals and visitors alike. For a treat, order one of the chef's choice specials.

Seafood

It's tough to walk down the streets of the Wharf without tripping over at least three big shiny seafood restaurants. You can pick just about any of the big ones and come up with a decent (if touristy) meal. A good way to choose is to stroll past the front doors and take a look at the menus.

It has the look of a big tourist trap, but at **McCormick and Kuleto's** (900 North Point St., 415/929-1730, www.mccormickandschmicks.com, 11:30 A.M.–10 P.M. Sun.–Thurs., 11:30 A.M.–11 P.M. Fri.–Sat., $20–35), the chefs know how to cook seafood to satisfy even the pickiest foodie. In the grand dining room, with slightly scary light fixtures and stellar views out to the Bay, you'll find an array of fresh fish and a list of innovative preparations.

Steak

A New York stage actress wanted a classic steak house in San Francisco, and so **Harris'** (2100 Van Ness Ave., 415/673-1888, www.harris-restaurant.com, 5:30 P.M.–close Mon.–Fri., 5 P.M.–close Sat.–Sun., $43–54) came to be. The fare runs to traditional steaks and prime rib as well as a bit of upscale, with a Kobe rib eye and surf-and-turf featuring a whole Maine lobster. Music lovers can catch live jazz in the lounge most evenings.

MARINA AND PACIFIC HEIGHTS
Bakeries and Cafés

Just looking for a quick snack to tide you over? Drop in at **The Chestnut Bakery** (2359 Chestnut St., 415/567-6777, www.chestnutbakery.com, 7 A.M.–noon Mon., 7 A.M.–6 P.M.

Tues.–Sat., 8 A.M.–5 P.M. Sun.). Only a block and a half from Lombard Street, this small family-owned storefront is a perfect spot for weary travelers to take the weight off their feet and enjoy a cookie, pastry, or one of the bakery's famous cupcakes. If you come in the morning, you'll find scones, croissants, and other favorite breakfast pastries. Be aware that this is a favorite local spot, which means that some items sell out each day.

Visitors to the Presidio can enjoy a quick bite or a leisurely lunch at the **Acre Café** (1013 Torney Ave., 415/561-2273, 7:30 A.M.–3 P.M. Mon.–Fri., $10). This simple café serves up fresh food for almost (but not quite) reasonable prices. Open for both breakfast and lunch, it's also a good spot to grab a cup of coffee to enjoy with a morning walk along the paths of the Presidio. Just keep in mind that this is a walk-up style café, so don't expect much by way of customer service.

California

Tucked away in a quiet corner of The Presidio, **The Presidio Social Club** (563 Ruger St., 415/885-1888, http://presidiosocialclub.com, 11:30 A.M.–10 P.M. Mon.–Fri., 10 A.M.–10 P.M. Sat., 10 A.M.–9 P.M. Sun., $20–25) serves locally sourced cuisine in an historic military barrack. The open space manages to feels intimate, with period details such as helicopter fans, stainless steel medicine cabinets behind the lengthy marble cocktail bar, and large picture windows overlooking the park. Menu favorites include steak and seafood, a creamy macaroni and cheese dish, and even a Sunday pig roast (3–5 P.M., $20). The inventive cocktail menu is a highlight.

Italian

The name **A 16** (2355 Chestnut St., 415/771-2216, www.a16sf.com, 5:30–10 P.M. Mon.–Tues., 11:30 A.M.–2:30 P.M. and 5:30–10 P.M. Wed.–Thurs., 11:30 A.M.–2:30 P.M. and 5:30–11 P.M. Fri., 5–11 P.M. Sat., 5–10 P.M. Sun.,

$13–30) refers to the major road cutting through the Campania region of southern Italy. At A 16 in San Francisco, you'll find fabulous southern Italian food. Handmade artisanal pizzas, pastas, and entrées tempt the palate with a wealth of hearty flavors. Pasta dishes come in two sizes—a great thing for those with smaller appetites. A wonderful wine list complements the food.

For a southern Italian meal with a soft touch, **Capannina** (1809 Union St., 415/409-8001, www.capanninasf.com, 5–10 P.M. Mon.–Thurs., 5–10:30 P.M. Fri.–Sun., $17–30) is the place. Soft green walls with marble and glass accents provide a sense of peace. The menu features classic Italian with an emphasis on the fruits of the sea. Many of the ingredients are imported directly from Italy, enhancing the authenticity of each dish.

Japanese

For a super-hip San Francisco sushi experience, strut on down to **Ace Wasabi's** (3339 Steiner St., 415/567-4903, http://acewasabisf.com, 5:30–10:30 P.M. Mon.–Thurs., 5:30–11 P.M. Fri.–Sat., 5–10 P.M. Sun., $6–13 per item). Advertising "rock 'n' roll sushi" and created with the atmosphere of an *izakaya* (a Japanese bar and grill), Ace Wasabi's appeals to a young, fun crowd. Be aware that the party can get loud on weekends.

On the other hand, the ◖**Naked Fish** (2084 Chestnut St., 415/771-1168, www.nakedfishsf.com, 5:30–10 P.M. Mon.–Thurs., 5:30–11 P.M. Fri.–Sat., 5:30–9:30 P.M. Sun., $5–12 per item) proffers an upscale Japanese dining experience. In a fine dining room, taste the sushi, *robata* grill skewers, Hawaiian-style tapas, and spicy appetizers. Don't skip the sake—Naked Fish has a stellar menu of premium brands, including unfiltered and high-quality bottles rarely found outside of Japan. Consider bringing a date for dinner to start an elegant night on the town.

If you're in Pacific Heights, give **Kiss**

Seafood (1700 Laguna St., 415/474-2866, 5:30–9:30 P.M. Tues.–Sat., $30–60) a try. This tiny restaurant (12 seats in total) boasts some of the freshest fish in town—no mean feat in San Francisco. The lone chef prepares all the fish himself, possibly due to the tiny size of the place. Obviously, reservations are a good idea. When it comes to the menu, anything seafood is recommended, but if you're up for sashimi, you'll be in raw-fish heaven. Round off your meal with a glass of chilled premium sake.

Seafood

Located in the somewhat grimy Polk Gulch area, tiny **Swan Oyster Depot** (1517 Polk St., 415/673-1101, 8 A.M.–5:30 P.M. daily, $10–20, cash only) packs in the lunchtime crowd with the freshest oysters, crab, and lobster you can eat.

Steak

The Marina is a great place to find a big thick steak. One famed San Francisco steak house, **Bobo's** (1450 Lombard St., 415/441-8880, www.boboquivaris.com, 5–10 P.M. daily, $30–50) prides itself on its dry-aged beef and fresh seafood. In season, enjoy whole Dungeness crab. But most of all, enjoy "The Steak," thickly cut and simply prepared to enhance the flavor of the beef.

Another great house of beef is **Izzy's Steak and Chop House** (3345 Steiner St., 415/563-0487, www.izzyssteaks.com, 5–10 P.M. Sun.–Thurs., 5:30–10:30 P.M. Fri.–Sat., $20–32). Here you'll find an array of tasty steak preparations, seafood, and selected nonsteak entrées. Be sure to save room for one of Izzy's classic desserts.

CIVIC CENTER AND HAYES VALLEY
California

Housed in a former bank, **Nopa** (500 Divisadero St., 415/864-8643, http://nopasf.com, 6 P.M.–1 A.M. daily, $18–25) brings together the neighborhood that the restaurant is named after with a whimsical mural by a local artist, a communal table, and a crowd as diverse as the surrounding area. A creative and inexpensive menu offers soul-satisfying dishes—and keeps tables full into the wee hours. The cocktails are legendary. On weekends Nopa also serves brunch (11 A.M.–2:30 P.M. Sat.–Sun.).

French

◖ Jardinière (300 Grove St., 415/861-5555, www.jardiniere.com, 5–10:30 P.M. daily, $20–40) was the first restaurant opened by local celebrity chef Traci Des Jardins. The bar and dining room blend into one another and feature stunning art deco decor. The ever-changing menu is a masterpiece of French California cuisine, and Des Jardins has long supported the sustainable restaurant movement. Eating at Jardinière is not only a treat for the senses, it is a way to support the best of trends in San Francisco restaurants. Make reservations if you're trying to catch dinner before a show.

Absinthe (398 Hayes St., 415/551-1590, www.absinthe.com, 11:30 A.M.–midnight Tues.–Fri., 11 A.M.–midnight Sat., 11 A.M.–10 P.M. Sun., $23–35) takes its name from the notorious "green fairy" drink made of liquor and wormwood. Absinthe indeed does serve absinthe—including locally made St. George Spirits Absinthe Verte. It also serves upscale French bistro fare, including what may be the best french fries in the City. The French theme carries on into the decor as well—expect the look of a Parisian brasserie or perhaps a café in Nice, with retro-modern furniture and classic prints on the walls. The bar is open until 2 A.M., so if you want drinks or dessert after a show at the Opera or Davies Hall, just walk around the corner.

German

Suppenküche (525 Laguna St., 415/252-9289, www.suppenkuche.com, 5–10 P.M. Mon.–Sat., 10 A.M.–2:30 P.M. and 5–10 P.M. Sun., $15–20) brings a taste of Bavaria to the Bay Area. The beer list is a great place to start, since you can enjoy a wealth of classic German brews on tap and in bottles, plus a few Belgians thrown in for variety. For dinner, expect German classics with a focus on Bavarian cuisine. Spaetzle, pork, sausage—you name it, they've got it, and it will harden your arteries right up. Suppenküche also has a Biergarten (424 Octavia St., http://biergartensf.com, 3–9 P.M. Wed.–Sun.) two blocks away.

MISSION AND CASTRO
Bakeries and Cafés

Need to grab a quick sandwich before heading off on another San Francisco adventure? Get it at **Ike's Place** (3489 16th St., 415/553-6888, http://ilikeikesplace.com, 10 A.M.–7 P.M. Mon.–Sat., $10). An independent deli, Ike's serves big hearty homemade sandwiches that will fuel up even the most energetic travelers. Ike's is the perfect place to buy your daily take-out lunch.

Locals love the artful pastries and fresh breads at **◖ Tartine Bakery** (600 Guerrero St., 415/487-2600, www.tartinebakery. com, 8 A.M.–7 P.M. Mon., 7:30 A.M.–7 P.M. Tues.–Wed., 7:30 A.M.–8 P.M. Thurs.–Fri., 8 A.M.–8 P.M. Sat., 9 A.M.–8 P.M. Sun., $4–13). Tartine's bakers use organic flour, sea salt, and locally sourced produce and cheeses to craft their culinary creations, and the French-Italian-Californian fusion pastries and paninis have brought this bakery its word-of-mouth success. With hours that extend into early evening, Tartine makes an attractive alternative for a light dinner or fixings for an evening picnic.

Speaking of dinner, sister property **Bar Tartine** (561 Valencia St., 6–10 P.M. Tues.–Thurs., 6–11 P.M. Fri., 10:30 A.M.–2:30 P.M. and 6–11 P.M. Sat., 10:30 A.M.–2:30 P.M. and 6–10 P.M. Sun., $10–25) serves gourmet dinners and weekend brunches.

Satisfy your sweet tooth at **Bi-Rite Creamery & Bakeshop** (3692 18th St., 415/626-5600,

© CHAD ROBERTSON/COURTESY TARTINE BAKERY AND POSTCARDPR

the mushroom tart at Tartine Bakery

11 A.M.–10 P.M. Sun.–Thurs., 11 A.M.–11 P.M. Fri.–Sat.). The ice cream is made by hand with organic milk, cream, and eggs; inventive flavors include maple walnut, salted caramel, and white chocolate raspberry swirl. Pick up a scoop to enjoy at nearby Mission Dolores Park.

California
Range (842 Valencia St., 415/282-8283, 6 P.M.–close Mon.–Thurs., 5:30 P.M.–close Fri.–Sun., $20–26) may have lost its Michelin Guide star in 2011, but it's no less popular. Consistently rated one of the top Bay Area restaurants, Range serves up expertly crafted California cuisine such as coffee-rubbed pork shoulder and halibut cheeks à la nage. An inventive cocktail list doesn't hurt either.

French
Frances (3870 17th St., 415/621-3870, 5–10 P.M. Sun.–Thurs., 5–10:30 P.M. Fri.–Sat., $26–28) has been winning rave reviews ever since it opened its doors. The California-inspired French cuisine is locavore-friendly, with an emphasis on sustainable ingredients and local farms. The short-but-sweet menu changes daily and includes such temptations as caramelized Atlantic scallops and bacon beignets. Reservations are strongly advised, especially since Frances received its Michelin Guide star.

Italian
Sometimes even the most dedicated culinary explorer needs a break from the endless fancy food of San Francisco. When the time is right for a plain ol' pizza, head for **Little Star Pizza** (400 Valencia St., 415/551-7827, www.little-starpizza.com, noon–10 P.M. Mon.–Thurs. and Sun., noon–11 P.M. Fri.–Sat., $10–15). A jewel of the Mission district, this pizzeria specializes in Chicago-style deep-dish pies, but also serves thin-crust pizzas for devotees of the New York style. Once you've found the all-black building

and taken a seat inside the casual eatery, grab a beer or a cocktail from the bar if you have to wait for a table. Pick one of Little Star's specialty pizzas, or create your own variation from the toppings they offer. Can't get enough of Little Star? They've got a second location (846 Divisadero St., 415/441-1118).

Delfina (3621 18th St., 415/552-4055, www.delfinasf.com, 5:30–10 P.M. Mon.–Thurs., 5:30–11 P.M. Fri.–Sat., 5–10 P.M. Sun., $18–26) gives Italian cuisine a hearty California twist. From the antipasti to the entrées, the dishes speak of local farms and ranches, fresh seasonal produce, and the best Italian American taste that money can buy. With both a charming, warm indoor dining room and an outdoor garden patio, there's plenty of seating at this lovely restaurant.

Mediterranean

La Méditerranée (288 Noe St., 415/431-7210, www.lamednoe.com, 11 A.M.–10 P.M. Sun.–Thurs., 11 A.M.–11 P.M. Fri.–Sat., $9–14) serves delicious Greek and Middle Eastern dishes at reasonable prices. You can get kebabs or baba ghanoush, tabbouleh and baklava, vegetarian dishes, and meatballs. Locals love La Méditerranée for the quality of the food, the quantity provided, and the flexible hours. In warm weather, ask to be seated outside.

Mexican

Much of the rich heritage of the Mission district is Hispanic, thus leading to the Mission being *the* place to find a good taco or burrito. **Farolito Taqueria** (2950 24th St., 415/641-0758, www.elfarolitoinc.com, 10 A.M.–12:45 A.M. Sun.–Thurs., 10 A.M.–2:45 A.M. Fri.–Sat., $10) has found favor with the ultra-picky locals who have dozens of taqueria options within a few blocks. It seems that every regular has a different favorite—the burritos, the enchiladas, the quesadillas. Whatever your pleasure, you'll find a tasty version of it at Farolito. A totally

casual spot, you order at the counter and sit at picnic-style tables to chow down on the properly greasy Mexican fare. (Don't confuse this Farolito with the taqueria by the same name on Mission Street.)

La Taqueria (2889 Mission St., 415/285-7117, 11 A.M.–9 P.M. Mon.–Sat., 11 A.M.–8 P.M. Sun., $5–10) is a local Mission favorite for burritos.

For a famous iteration of the classic Mission district burrito joint, join the crowd at **Papalote Mexican Grill** (3409 24th St., 415/970-8815, www.papalote-sf.com, 11 A.M.–10 P.M. Mon.–Sat., 11 A.M.–9 P.M. Sun., $5–12). Build your own plate of tacos or a burrito from a list of classic and specialty ingredients—carne asada, *chile verde,* grilled vegetables, and tofu—whatever makes you happy. What will make you even happier is the price: It's possible to get a filling meal for less than $10.

Seafood

For great seafood in a lower-key atmosphere, locals eschew the tourist traps on the Wharf and head for the **Anchor Oyster Bar** (579 Castro St., 415/431-3990, www.anchoroysterbar.com, 11:30 A.M.–10 P.M. Mon.–Fri., noon–10 P.M. Sat., 4–9:30 P.M. Sun., $15–30) in the Castro. The raw bar features different varieties of oysters, but not so many as to be overwhelming or pretentious. The dining room serves seafood, including local favorite Dungeness crab. Service is friendly, as befits a neighborhood spot, and it sees fewer large crowds. This doesn't diminish its quality, and it makes for a great spot to get a delicious meal before heading out to the local clubs for a late night out.

Vietnamese

Even casual international food aficionados find that the *banh mi* (Vietnamese sandwiches on French-style baguette bread) at **Dinosaurs** (2275 Market St., 415/503-1421, 10 A.M.–10 P.M. daily, $5) makes the grade. Dinosaurs makes good sandwiches, it makes them fast, and it sells them cheap. Diners love the barbecued pork, but the vegan crispy tofu gets mixed reviews. Dinosaurs is a great idea if you don't need a huge meal but want a taste of something you might not be able to get elsewhere.

GOLDEN GATE PARK AND THE HAIGHT
Bakeries and Cafés

The Sunset lends itself to a proliferation of cafés. Among the best of these is the **de Young Museum Café** (50 Hagiwara Tea Garden Dr., 415/750-2613, http://deyoung.famsf.org, 9:30 A.M.–4 P.M. Tues.–Sun., 9:30 A.M.–8 P.M. Fri., $10–20). Situated inside the museum on the ground floor, with a generous dining room plus outdoor terrace seating, the Café was created with the same care that went into the de Young's galleries. From the day it opened, the focus has been on local sustainable food that's often organic but always affordable. Service is cafeteria-style, but the salads and sandwiches are made fresh daily on the premises. Just be sure to get lunch early, or pick an off-hour to eat; the lines at lunchtime can extend for miles.

One of the prettiest spots in Golden Gate Park is the Japanese Tea Garden. Within the garden is the famous **Tea House** (7 Hagiwara Tea Garden Dr., 415/752-1171, http://japaneseteagardensf.com, 9 A.M.–6 P.M. daily Mar.–Oct., 9 A.M.–4:45 P.M. daily Nov.–Feb., $10–20), where you can purchase a cup of hot tea and a light Japanese meal within the beautiful and inspiring garden.

American

Adjacent to Golden Gate Park, **Park Chow** (1240 9th Ave., 415/665-9912, 8 A.M.–10 P.M. Sun.-Thurs., 8 A.M.–11 P.M. Fri.–Sat., $10–15) does a brisk business with locals and visitors alike. The cozy interior complements the organic yet comfort food menu featuring everything from wood-fired pizzas to steak frites. Opt for the rooftop garden on the rare sunny day.

California

One of the most famous restaurant locations on the San Francisco coast is the Cliff House. The high-end eatery inhabiting the famed facade is **Sutro's** (1090 Point Lobos

the Tea House in Golden Gate Park's Japanese Tea Garden

DELECTABLE DUNGENESS

COURTESY OF PRAYITNO

You can find traditional whole cracked Dungeness at Fisherman's Wharf.

Dungeness crabs enjoy celebrity status in San Francisco. Although the crabs are named for a place on the Washington coast, the Dungeness came to fame in San Francisco, where Italian immigrant fishers caught crabs in and around the Bay, cooked them up in steaming cauldrons, and sold the meat in paper cones as "crab cocktail." These entrepreneurs also sold whole cooked crabs to families, who took them home and held crab feeds for their families. Although Dungeness crabs no longer live in San Francisco Bay, the fishery as a whole is remarkably well managed. The famously strict **Monterey Bay Seafood Watch** program (www.montereybay-aquarium.org/cr/SeafoodWatch) rates Northern California-caught Dungeness crab as a "Best Choice."

Dungeness season usually runs November–June, but the freshest crabs are caught and cooked from the start of the season (usually the second Tuesday of Nov.) through New Year's. You can still buy Dungeness crab cocktails and whole-cooked crabs from crab shacks along Fisherman's Wharf. Famed Italian seafood restaurant **Alioto's** (8 Fisherman's Wharf, 415/673-0183, www.aliotos.com, 11 A.M.-11 P.M. daily, $17-48) serves whole cracked Dungeness in the traditional style. They've also got crab soups, salads, sandwiches, and stews. Dungeness has a firm white flesh with a delicate, sweet flavor; it tastes lovely dipped in a little drawn butter, but it also has enough oomph to stand up in complex and spicy Asian preparations. In Chinatown, **R&G Lounge** (631 Kearny St., 415/982-7877, http://rnglounge.com, 11:30 A.M.-9:30 P.M. daily, $12-40, reservations suggested) offers deep-fried and salt-and-pepper crabs. In the Outer Sunset, **Thanh Long** (4101 Judah St., 415/665-1146, www.anfamily.com, 4:30-9:30 P.M. Sun.-Thurs., 4:30-10:30 P.M. Fri.-Sat., $20-30) is famous for its roast crab soaked in garlic and butter.

Ave., 415/386-3330, www.cliffhouse.com, 11:30 A.M.–3:30 P.M. and 5–9:30 P.M. Mon.–Sat., 11 A.M.–3:30 P.M. and 5–9:30 P.M. Sun., $18–36). The appetizers and entrées are mainly seafood in somewhat snooty preparations. Although the cuisine is expensive and fancy, in all honesty it's not the best in the City. What *is* amazing are the views from the floor-to-ceiling windows out over the vast expanse of the Pacific Ocean. These views make Sutro's a perfect spot to enjoy a romantic dinner while watching the sun set over the sea.

The Cliff House also houses the more casual **Bistro** (9 A.M.–3:30 P.M. and 4:15–9:30 P.M. Mon.–Sat., 8:30 A.M.–3:30 P.M. and 4:15–9:30 P.M. Sun., $15–30).

Japanese

Sushi restaurants are immensely popular in these residential neighborhoods. **Koo** (408 Irving St., 415/731-7077, www.sushikoo.com, 5:30–10 P.M. Tues.–Thurs., 5:30–10:30 P.M. Fri.–Sat., 5–9:30 P.M. Sun., $30–50) is a favorite in the Sunset. While sushi purists are happy with the selection of *nigiri* and sashimi, lovers of fusion and experimentation will enjoy the small plates and unusual rolls created to delight diners. Complementing the Japanese cuisine is a small but scrumptious list of premium sakes. Only the cheap stuff is served hot, as high-quality sake is always chilled.

Thai

Dining in the Haight? If the touristy cafés don't appeal to you, check out the flavorful dishes at **Siam Lotus Thai Cuisine** (1705 Haight St., 415/933-8031, www.siamlotussf.com, noon–9 P.M. Sun.–Mon. and Wed.–Thurs., noon–9:30 P.M. Fri.–Sat., $7–13). You'll find a rainbow of curries, pad Thai, and all sorts of Thai meat, poultry, and vegetarian dishes. Look to the lunch specials for bargains, and to the Thai iced tea for a lunchtime pick-me-up.

Behind its typical storefront exterior, **Marnee Thai** (1243 9th Ave., 415/731-9999, www.marneethaisf.com, 11:30 A.M.–10 P.M. daily, $10–20) cooks up some of the best Thai food in San Francisco, with a location convenient to Golden Gate Park. The corn-cake appetizer is a must.

Vietnamese

Thanh Long (4101 Judah St., 415/665-1146, www.anfamily.com, 4:30–9:30 P.M. Sun.–Thurs., 4:30–10:30 P.M. Fri.–Sat., $20–30) was the first family-owned Vietnamese restaurant in San Francisco. Since the early 1970s, Thanh Long has been serving one of the best preparations of local Dungeness crab in the City—roasted crab with garlic noodles. This isn't a $5 *pho* joint—expect white tablecloths and higher prices at this stately small restaurant in the outer Sunset neighborhood.

Information and Services

INFORMATION
Visitor Information

The main San Francisco **Visitor Information Center** (900 Market St., 415/391-2000, www.sanfranciscotravel.com, 9 A.M.–5 P.M. Mon.–Fri., 9 A.M.–3 P.M. Sat.–Sun. May–Oct., 9 A.M.–5 P.M. Mon.–Fri., 9 A.M.–3 P.M. Sat. Nov.–Apr.) can help you even before you arrive. See the website for information about attractions and hotels, and to order a visitors' kit. Once you're in town, you can get a San Francisco book at the Market Street location as well as the usual brochures and a few useful coupons.

If English is not your first language, you'll find materials at the Visitor Information Center in 12 different languages along with multilingual staff.

Media and Communications

The major daily newspaper in San Francisco is the *San Francisco Chronicle* (www.sfgate. com). With an appropriately liberal slant on the national political news, a free website, and separate food and wine sections, it's the right paper for its city.

San Francisco also has about a zillion alternative papers, free at newsstands all over town. The *San Francisco Bay Guardian* (www.sfbg. com) and the *SF Weekly* (www.sfweekly.com) are the best-known and most reputable of these. The alternative rags often have the best up-to-date entertainment information available, so if you're looking for nighttime fun, be sure to pick one up while you're out and about.

SERVICES
Banks and Post Offices

Every major national bank and many regional and international banks have branches in San Francisco. ATMs abound, especially in well-traveled areas like Fisherman's Wharf and Union Square. Ask at your hotel or restaurant for the location of the nearest branch or ATM.

Post offices and mailing centers are common in San Francisco. The **Civic Center Post Office** (1390 Market St., 415/931-1053, 9 A.M.–5:30 P.M. Mon.–Fri.) offers passort services in addition to postage and shippin. If you've been shopping for things that don't easily fit into the overhead bin, hit the well-placed post office branch in the basement of Macy's (170 O'Farrell St., 415/552-2330, 10 A.M.–5:30 P.M. Mon.–Sat., 11 A.M.–5 P.M. Sun.). Yes, you read that right—it's open on Sunday.

Luggage and Laundry

If your hotel doesn't have valet service, you can take your dirty linen down to a coin laundry. The most entertaining laundry in the City is **BrainWash Café and Laundromat** (1122 Folsom St., 415/255-4866, www.brainwash. com, 7 A.M.–10 P.M. Mon.–Thurs., 7 A.M.–11 P.M. Fri.–Sat., 8 A.M.–10 P.M. Sun.). Enjoy a BrainWash salad or a Burger of Doom with a cold beer and kick back to the sounds of live bands and open mike (7–8 P.M. most nights).

Store your bags through the **Airport Travel Agency** (650/877-0422, 7 A.M.–11 P.M. daily, no reservations necessary) on the Departures-Ticketing Level of the International Terminal at the San Francisco Airport, near Gates G91–G102. Fees vary by the size of the object stored, from $3 for a purse to $6–10 for a suitcase, up to $15 for surfboards or bicycles. All rates are for 24 hours' storage. If traveling by bus, rent a locker at the **Greyhound** bus terminal (200 Folsom St., 415/495-1569, www. greyhound.com, 5:30 A.M.–midnight daily).

Medical Services

The **San Francisco Police Department** (766 Vallejo St., 415/315-2400, www.sf-police.org) is headquartered in Chinatown, on Vallejo Street between Powell and Stockton Streets.

San Francisco boasts a large number of full-service hospitals. The **UCSF Medical Center at Mount Zion** (1600 Divisadero St., 415/567-6600, www.ucsfhealth.org) is renowned for its research and advances in cancer treatments and other important medical breakthroughs. The main hospital is at the corner of Divisadero and Geary Streets. Right downtown, **St. Francis Memorial Hospital** (900 Hyde St., 415/353-6000, www.saintfrancismemorial.org), at the corner of Hyde and Bush Streets, has an emergency department.

Getting There and Around

GETTING THERE
Air

San Francisco International Airport (SFO, 800/435-9736, www.flysfo.com) isn't within the City of San Francisco; it is actually about 13 miles south in the town of Millbrae, right on the Bay. You can easily get a taxi ($35) or other ground transportation into the heart of the City from the airport. Both Caltrain and BART are accessible from SFO, and some San Francisco hotels offer complimentary shuttles from the airport as well. You can also rent a car here.

As one of the 30 busiest airports in the world, SFO has long check-in and security lines much of the time and dreadful overcrowding on major travel holidays. On an average day, plan to arrive at the airport about two hours before your domestic flight, three hours before an international flight.

Train and Bus

Amtrak does not run directly into San Francisco. You can ride into San Jose, Oakland, or Emeryville stations, then take a connecting bus into San Francisco.

Greyhound (200 Folsom St., 415/495-1569, www.greyhound.com, 5:30 A.M.–1 A.M. daily) offers bus service to San Francisco from all over the country.

GETTING AROUND
Car

The **Bay Bridge** (toll $6) links I-80 to San Francisco from the east, and the **Golden Gate Bridge** (toll $7) connects Highway 1 from the north. From the south, U.S. 101 and I-280 snake up the peninsula and into the City. Be sure to get a detailed map and good directions to drive into San Francisco—the freeway interchanges, especially surrounding the east side of the Bay Bridge, can be confusing, and the traffic

congestion is legendary. For traffic updates and route planning, visit **511.org** (www.511.org).

A car of your own is not necessarily beneficial in San Francisco. The hills are daunting, traffic is excruciating, and parking prices are absurd. If you plan to spend all of your time in the City, consider dispensing with a car and using cabs and public transit options. Rent a car when you're ready to leave San Francisco, or turn your rental in early if the City is your last stop.

If you absolutely must have your car with you, try to get a room at a hotel with a parking lot and either free parking or a parking package for the length of your stay.

CAR RENTAL

All the major car rental agencies have a presence at the San Francisco Airport (SFO, 800/435-9736, www.flysfo.com). In addition, most reputable hotels can offer or recommend a car rental. Rates tend to run $90–160 per day and $250–550 per week (including taxes and fees), with discounts for weekly and longer rentals. If you're flying into Mineta San José Airport (SJC, www.flysanjose.com) or Oakland Airport (OAK, www.flyoakland.com), the cost can drop to $110–250 per week for budget agencies. Premium agencies like Hertz and Avis are much pricier—you'll pay $375–650 for the same car. Off-site locations may offer cheaper rates, in the range of about $375 per week.

PARKING

To call parking in San Francisco a nightmare is to insult nightmares. Every available scrap of land that can be built on has been built on, with little left over to create parking for the zillions of cars that pass through on a daily basis. Parking a car in San Francisco can easily cost $50 per day or more. Most downtown and

modern bus and vintage streetcar on Market Street

Union Square hotels do not include free parking with your room. Expect to pay $35–45 per night for parking, which may not include in-and-out privileges.

Street parking spots are as rare as unicorns and often require permits (which visitors cannot obtain). Lots and garages fill up quickly, especially during special events. You're more likely to find parking included at the motels along the edge of the city—Fisherman's Wharf, the Marina, the Richmond, and the Sunset district have the most motor inns with parking included.

Muni

Local opinion about the Muni (www.sfmta.com, adults $2, $0.75 youths and seniors) light rail system isn't printable in guidebooks. The truth is, Muni can get you where you want to go in San Francisco as long as time isn't a concern. A variety of lines snake through the City—those that go down to Fisherman's Wharf use vintage streetcars to heighten the

fun for visitors. See the website for a route map, ticket information, and (ha-ha) schedules.

To buy tickets, use one of the vending machines placed near some stops. Muni ticket machines are also outside the Caltrain station. See the website for more information about purchasing tickets.

Muni also runs the bus lines, which require the same fares; they can be slightly more reliable than the trains and go all over the City.

BART

Bay Area Rapid Transit, or BART (www.bart.gov, $3–10 one-way), is the Bay Area's late-coming answer to major metropolitan underground railways like Chicago's L trains and New York's subway system. Sadly, there's only one arterial line through the City. However, service directly from San Francisco Airport into the City runs daily, as does service to Oakland Airport, the cities of Oakland and Berkeley, plus many other East Bay destinations. BART connects to the

Caltrain system and San Francisco Airport in Millbrae. See the website for route maps, schedules (BART usually runs on time), and fare information.

To buy tickets, use the vending machines found in every BART station. If you plan to ride more than once, you can "add money" to a single ticket, and then keep that ticket and reuse it for each ride.

Caltrain

This traditional commuter rail line runs along the peninsula into Silicon Valley, from San Francisco to San Jose, with limited continuing service to Gilroy. Caltrain (www.caltrain.com, $2.75–13 one-way) Baby Bullet trains can get you from San Jose to San Francisco in under an hour during commuting hours. Extra trains are often added for San Francisco Giants, San Francisco 49ers, and San Jose Sharks games.

You must purchase a ticket in advance at the vending machines found in all stations, or get your 10-ride card stamped before you board a train. The main Caltrain station in San Francisco is at the corner of 4th and King Streets, within walking distance of AT&T Park and Moscone Center.

Taxi

You'll find plenty of taxis scooting around all the major tourist areas of the City. Feel free to wave one down or ask your hotel to call you a cab. If you need to call a cab yourself, try **City Wide Dispatch** (415/920-0700).

SAN FRANCISCO BAY AREA

San Francisco may steal the spotlight, but the rest of the Bay Area is home to nearly seven million people and is just as dynamic as the city it surrounds. It is home to captains of industry, towering redwoods, prestigious universities and their earnest and cantankerous college towns, ethnically diverse cities, and old Portuguese fishing and dairy communities. You can find some of the best minds, most spectacular scenery, and tastiest food found anywhere. And much of it lies outside the seven-by-seven mile perimeter of San Francisco.

Thanks to the foresight of previous generations much of the coast and ridgelines in the Bay Area have been preserved as open space. In the North Bay and the Peninsula south of the city, you can hike to quiet beaches, stroll among ancient stands of redwoods, and enjoy the fruits of generations-old family farms that still operate on some of the most beautiful (and expensive) land in the world.

Across the Bay, the cities of Berkeley and Oakland rival San Francisco in cultural diversity, radical thinking, and cutting-edge gastronomy. Historically centered around the university and the war effort of the 1940s, the East Bay has grown to become as cosmopolitan as it gets.

From the Campanile at the University of California, Berkeley, you can see the Hoover Tower at Stanford University, Cal's bitter rival. While undergraduates at Berkeley may protest everything from nuclear power to tuition hikes,

SAN FRANCISCO BAY AREA

HIGHLIGHTS

◖ Angel Island State Park: A visit to the largest island of the bay packs a lot into a short amount of time. Catch a bit of history, natural wonder, and unparalleled views when you make the trek to this rarely visited treasure (page 123).

◖ Muir Woods National Monument: Stand among trees nearly 1,000 years old and 200 feet tall in one of the nation's earliest national monuments (page 126).

◖ Mount Tamalpais State Park: The Bay Area's backyard is awash in hiking and biking trails, stellar views, and redwood groves—all topped by Mt. Tam's 2,571-foot peak (page 129).

◖ Point Reyes National Seashore: Home to tule elk, desolate beaches, dairy and oyster farms, one of the oldest West Coast lighthouses, and scores of remote wilderness trails, Point Reyes is one of the most diverse parks in the Bay Area (page 134).

◖ Oakland Museum: Taking a multidisciplinary approach to tell California's story, the East Bay's latest cultural institution offers a fascinating take on the state. You'll see contemporary art, skeletons of long-extinct local fauna, and ephemera from California's early days (page 156).

◖ USS *Hornet*: For a taste of the military history that helped build the Bay Area, visit this retired aircraft carrier docked in Alameda, now also famous for its ghosts and swing-dancing parties (page 157).

◖ San Gregorio General Store: Drinks, books, live music, and every type of houseware under the sun fill this local institution, frequented by cowboys, environmentalists, and farmers (page 176).

◖ Año Nuevo State Reserve: Watch giant elephant seals, sea otters, endangered red-legged frogs, or any number of marine birds at this reserve's 4,000 acres (page 176).

◖ Filoli: This Gregorian-style mansion is now

a museum, home to 16 acres of stunning gardens (page 180).

◖ Winchester Mystery House: It may be a bit touristy, but the weirdness and creepiness of this sprawling manic mansion are no gimmick. Built by the widow to the Winchester rifle fortune, it is a testament to the dark side of the Wild West (page 189).

© AVALON TRAVEL

LOOK FOR ◖ TO FIND RECOMMENDED SIGHTS, ACTIVITIES, DINING, AND LODGING.

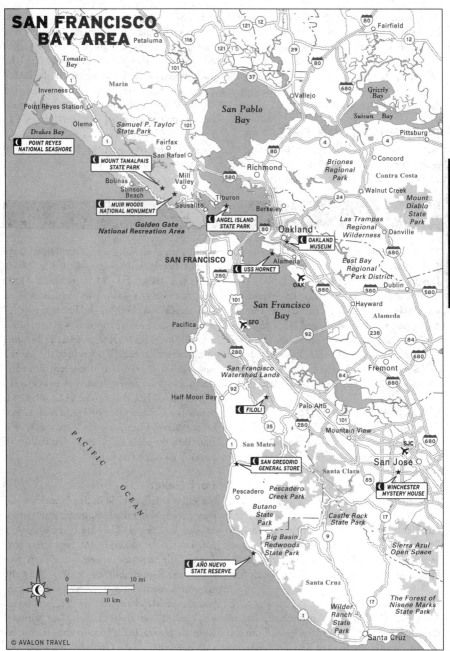

SAN FRANCISCO BAY AREA

Petaluma

Tomales Bay

Inverness

Marin

Point Reyes Station

Olema

Samuel P. Taylor State Park

Drakes Bay

POINT REYES NATIONAL SEASHORE

Fairfax

San Rafael

MOUNT TAMALPAIS STATE PARK

Bolinas

Mill Valley

Stinson Beach

MUIR WOODS NATIONAL MONUMENT

Sausalito

Tiburon

Berkeley

Golden Gate National Recreation Area

ANGEL ISLAND STATE PARK

SAN FRANCISCO

USS HORNET

Alameda

OAK

OAKLAND MUSEUM

Pacifica

San Francisco Bay

SFO

Half Moon Bay

San Francisco Watershed Lands

FILOLI

Palo Alto

San Mateo

Mountain View

SAN GREGORIO GENERAL STORE

Santa Clara

SJC

San Jose

Pescadero

Pescadero Creek Park

WINCHESTER MYSTERY HOUSE

Butane State Park

Castle Rock State Park

Sierra Azul Open Space

Big Basin Redwoods State Park

AÑO NUEVO STATE RESERVE

Santa Cruz

Wilder Ranch State Park

The Forest of Nisene Marks State Park

Santa Cruz

PACIFIC OCEAN

San Pablo Bay

Vallejo

Fairfield

Grizzly Bay

Suisun Bay

Pittsburg

Briones Regional Park

Concord

Contra Costa

Richmond

Walnut Creek

Mount Diablo State Park

Las Trampas Regional Wilderness

Danville

Oakland

East Bay Regional Park District

Dublin

Hayward

Alameda

Fremont

0   10 mi
0   10 km

© AVALON TRAVEL

students at Stanford are busy trying to become the next Mark Zuckerberg. Planted firmly at the epicenter of the "new economy," Stanford and its home, Palo Alto, are saturated in the entrepreneurial ethos, while Silicon Valley's work horse, San Jose, is home to some of the biggest names in the tech world.

PLANNING YOUR TIME

You can cross the Golden Gate Bridge and explore Marin County on a day trip, but you may spend more time in the car than strolling its beaches or forests. To better enjoy the parks and hiking trails, plan an overnight stay. The East Bay is fairly spread out and is often clogged by commuter traffic in the afternoon. Oakland and Berkeley offer easier access via the BART commuter rail system, and have concentrated sights in their downtown areas. On the peninsula, Palo Alto is an easy drive from San Francisco. If all you have is an afternoon, take scenic Highway 1 past the beaches only 30 minutes from the city.

North Bay

Marin County, in the North Bay, is the Bay Area's backyard. Beginning with the Marin Headlands at the terminus of the Golden Gate Bridge, there is a nearly unbroken expanse of wildlands from San Francisco Bay to Tomales Bay. Here you'll find rugged cliffs plunging into the Pacific, towering redwoods, the area's tallest mountain, and verdant pastures home to the Bay Area's celebrated grass-fed beef and award-wining cheese–producing dairy cows.

MARIN HEADLANDS

The Marin Headlands lie north of San Francisco at the north end of the Golden Gate Bridge. The land here encompasses a wide swath of virgin wilderness, former military structures, and a historic lighthouse.

Once over the bridge, the Alexander Avenue exit offers two options for exploring the Headlands: follow Alexander Avenue to Fort Baker and the Bay Area Discovery Museum, or turn left onto Bunker Road for the Marin Headlands Visitors Center and Nike Missile Site.

Vista Point

Aptly named Vista Point, at the north end of the Golden Gate Bridge, offers views from the Marin Headlands toward San Francisco. If you dream of walking across the **Golden Gate Bridge** (gates daily 5 A.M.–6:30 P.M. Nov.–mid-Mar., daily 5 A.M.–9 P.M. mid-Mar.–Oct.), be sure to bring a warm coat as the wind and fog can really whip through. The bridge is 1.7 miles long, so a round-trip walk will turn into a 3.4-mile hike. Bikes are allowed daily 24 hours on the west side. Bicycle riders may also use the east side but must be careful to watch for pedestrians. Dogs are never allowed on either side.

To reach Vista Point, take U.S. 101 north across the Golden Gate Bridge. The first exit on the Marin County side is Vista Point; turn right into the parking lot. Note that this small parking lot often fills early.

Fort Baker

Standing at Crissy Field in San Francisco, you may wonder about those charming white buildings across the Bay. They are Fort Baker (435 Murray Circle, 415/331-1540, www.nps.gov/goga, daily sunrise–sunset), a 335-acre former Army Post established in 1905. With the transfer of many of the Bay Area's military outposts to parkland and civilian use, Fort Baker was handed over to the Golden Gate National Recreation Area and is open to visitors. The location, just east of the Golden Gate Bridge but

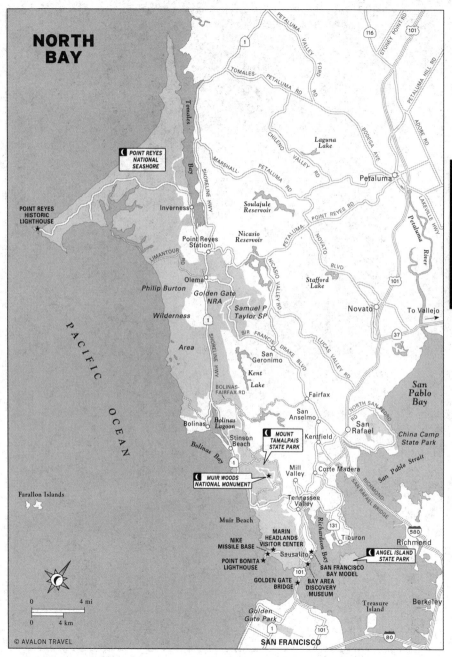

NORTH BAY

POINT REYES NATIONAL SEASHORE

POINT REYES HISTORIC LIGHTHOUSE

Tomales Bay

SHORELINE HWY

MARSHALL

Inverness

Point Reyes Station

LIMANTOUR RD

Olema

Philip Burton

Golden Gate NRA

Wilderness

Samuel P Taylor SP

Area

SHORELINE HWY

SIR FRANCIS DRAKE BLVD

San Geronimo

Kent Lake

BOLINAS-FAIRFAX RD

Bolinas

Bolinas Lagoon

Stinson Beach

MOUNT TAMALPAIS STATE PARK

MUIR WOODS NATIONAL MONUMENT

Bolinas Bay

P A C I F I C   O C E A N

Farallon Islands

Muir Beach

NIKE MISSILE BASE

POINT BONITA LIGHTHOUSE

MARIN HEADLANDS VISITOR CENTER

Sausalito

SAN FRANCISCO BAY MODEL

GOLDEN GATE BRIDGE

BAY AREA DISCOVERY MUSEUM

Golden Gate Park

SAN FRANCISCO

PETALUMA VALLEY FORD RD

TOMALES-PETALUMA RD

STONEY POINT RD

PETALUMA HILL RD

CHILENO VALLEY RD

Laguna Lake

RODEGA AVE

ADOBE RD

Petaluma

PETALUMA RD

Soulajule Reservoir

POINT REYES RD

LAKEVILLE HWY

Petaluma River

Nicasio Reservoir

NICASIO VALLEY RD

PETALUMA

NOVATO

Stafford Lake

BLVD

Novato

To Vallejo

LUCAS VALLEY RD

Fairfax

NORTH SAN PEDRO RD

San Anselmo

San Rafael

Kentfield

San Pablo Bay

China Camp State Park

San Pablo Strait

Mill Valley

Corte Madera

RICHMOND-SAN RAFAEL BRIDGE

Tennessee Valley

Richardson Bay

Tiburon

Richmond

ANGEL ISLAND STATE PARK

Berkeley

Treasure Island

0   4 mi

0   4 km

© AVALON TRAVEL

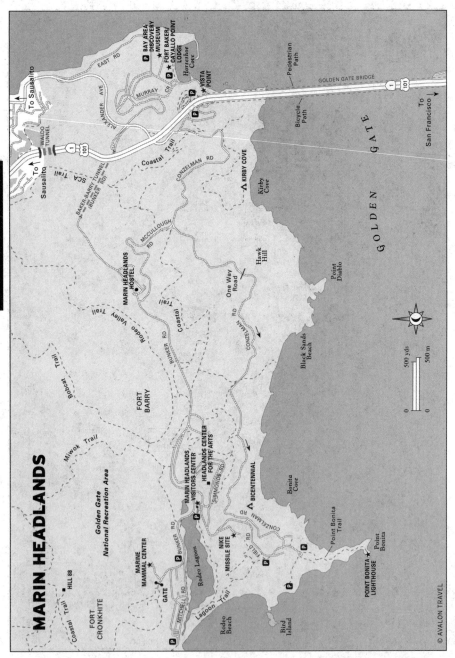

MARIN HEADLANDS

FORT CRONKHITE

HILL 88

Golden Gate
National Recreation Area

FORT BARRY

Coastal Trail

Miwok Trail

Bobcat Trail

Rodeo Valley Trail

Coastal Trail

BUNKER RD

MARIN HEADLANDS HOSTEL

MCCULLOUGH RD

One Way Road

CONZELMAN RD

CONZELMAN RD

Hawk Hill

Point Diablo

Black Sands Beach

KIRBY COVE

Kirby Cove

Coastal Trail

SCA Trail

BAKER-BARRY TUNNEL
BUNKER RD

WALDO TUNNEL

To Sausalito

To Sausalito

101

101

EAST RD

ALEXANDER AVE

MURRAY CR

BAY AREA DISCOVERY MUSEUM

FORT BAKER/CAVALLO POINT LODGE

Horseshoe Cove

VISTA POINT

GOLDEN GATE BRIDGE

Pedestrian Path

Bicycle Path

101

To San Francisco

GOLDEN GATE

500 yds

500 m

0

0

MARINE MAMMAL CENTER

MARIN HEADLANDS VISITORS CENTER

HEADLANDS CENTER FOR THE ARTS

SIMMONDE RD

BICENTENNIAL

Bonita Cove

Point Bonita Trail

CONZELMAN RD

FIELD RD

NIKE MISSILE SITE

GATE

BUNKER RD

MITCHELL RD

Rodeo Lagoon

Lagoon Trail

Rodeo Beach

Bird Island

Point Bonita

POINT BONITA LIGHTHOUSE

© AVALON TRAVEL

© MATT TILGHMAN/123RF.COM

SAN FRANCISCO BAY AREA

Rodeo Beach in the Marin Headlands

secluded in a shallow valley, makes it a great destination to enjoy city views and a wind-free beach. The fort is the best example of military architecture from the Endicott Period. It includes many elegant homes with large sweeping porches centered around the oval parade grounds. As with many of the "posts to parks" in the Golden Gate National Recreation Area system, Fort Baker houses a hotel, Cavallo Point Lodge, and a nonprofit called the Institute at the Golden Gate. The Bay Area Discovery Museum is also nearby, along with the tiny Presidio Yacht Club, where all are welcome for a quick drink by the water. But the real attractions are views from or below the bluffs, the sheltered and unpopulated beach, and the graceful architecture.

Bay Area Discovery Museum

The Bay Area Discovery Museum (557 McReynolds Rd., Sausalito, 415/339-3900, www.baykidsmuseum.org, 9 A.M.–4 P.M. Tues.–Fri., 10 A.M.–5 P.M. Sat.–Sun., $11) offers kids of all ages a chance to explore the world they live in. The focus is definitely on the younger set; most of the permanent exhibits are geared toward small children, with lots of interactive components and places to play. Kids can check out easy-to-understand displays that describe the natural world, plus lots of Bay Area–specific exhibits. The Discovery Museum also boasts a theater and a café.

Marin Headlands Visitors Center

A great place to start your exploration of the Marin Headlands is at the visitors center (Field Rd. and Bunker Rd., 415/331-1540, www.nps.gov/goga, daily 9:30 A.M.–4:30 P.M.), located in the old chapel at Fort Barry. The park rangers can give you the current lowdown on the best trails, beaches, and campgrounds in the Headlands.

Point Bonita Lighthouse

The Point Bonita Lighthouse (415/331-1540,

Point Bonita Lighthouse

www.nps.gov/goga, Sat.–Mon. 12:30–3:30 P.M.) has been protecting the Headlands for over 150 years. It remains an active light station to this day. You need some dedication to visit Point Bonita, since it's only open a few days each week and there's no direct access by car. A 0.5-mile trail with steep sections leads from the trailhead on Field Road. Along the way, you'll pass through a hand-cut tunnel chiseled from the hard rock by the original builders of the lighthouse, then over the bridge that leads to the building. Point Bonita was the third lighthouse built on the West Coast and is now the last staffed lighthouse in California. Today, the squat hexagonal building shelters automatic lights, horns, and signals. For a special treat, call the Marin Headlands Visitors Center to book a spot on a romantic 1.5-hour full-moon tour.

Marine Mammal Center

Inspired by the ocean's beauty and want to learn more about the animals that live in it? Visit the Marine Mammal Center (2000 Bunker Rd., 415/289-7325, www.marinemammalcenter.org, daily 10 A.M.–5 P.M., free) at Fort Cronkhite in the Marin Headlands. The center is a hospital for sick and injured seals and sea lions. Visitors are free to wander around and look at the educational displays to learn more about what the center does, but the one-hour docent-led tours (Fri.–Mon., adults $7, seniors and ages 5–17 $5, under age 5 free) explain the program in greater depth. Visitors will also get an education on the impact of human activity on marine mammals, and maybe a chance for close encounters with some of the center's patients.

Nike Missile Site

Military history buffs jump at the chance to tour a restored Cold War–era Nike missile base, known in military speak as SF-88. The Nike Missile Site (Field Rd. past the Headlands Visitors Center, 415/331-1453, www.nps.gov/goga, Wed.–Fri. 12:30–3:30 P.M. and 1st Sat. each month) is the only such restored Nike base in the United States. Volunteers continue the restoration and lead tours every 30 minutes at the base, which is overseen by the Golden Gate National Recreation Area. On the tour, you'll get to see the fueling area, the testing and assembly building, and even take a ride on the missile elevator down into the pits that once stored missiles built to defend the United States from the Soviet Union. Because restoration work continues endlessly, the tour changes as new areas become available to visitors.

Hiking

Folks come from all over the world to hike the trails that thread through the Marin Headlands. The landscape is some of the most beautiful in the state, with unparalleled views of the Golden Gate Bridge and the Pacific Ocean.

From the Marin Headlands Visitors Center parking lot (Field Rd. and Bunker Rd.), the **Lagoon Trail** (1.75 miles, easy) encircles Rodeo Lagoon and gives bird-watchers an eagle's-eye view of the egrets, pelicans, and other seabirds that call the lagoon home. The trailhead is near the restrooms.

An easy spot to get to, **Rodeo Beach** draws many visitors on summer weekends—do not expect solitude on the beach or the trails, or even in the water. Locals come out to surf when the break is going, while beachcombers watch from the shore. Note that the wind can really howl out here. The Lagoon Trail accesses the beach, but there is also a fairly large parking lot on Bunker Road that is much closer.

At Rodeo Beach is a trailhead for the **Coastal Trail.** To explore some of the battery ruins that pockmark these hills, follow the Coastal Trail (1.5 miles, easy) north to its intersection with Old Bunker Road Trail and return to Bunker Road near the Marine Mammal Center. Or extend this hike by continuing 2.3 miles up the Coastal Trail to the summit of **Hill 88** and stellar views. You can loop this trail by linking it with Wolf Ridge Trail to Miwok Trail for a moderate 5.5-mile round-trip hike.

To reach the trailheads and parking lots, follow Bunker Road west to either Rodeo Beach or the Marin Headlands Visitors Center and their adjoining parking lots.

Biking

If you prefer two wheels to two feet, you'll find the road and trail biking in the Marin Headlands both plentiful and spectacular. From the Tennessee Valley Trailhead, there are many multiuse trails designated for bikers as well as hikers. The **Valley Trail** (4 miles round-trip) takes you down the Tennessee Valley and all the way out to Tennessee Beach. A longer ride runs up the **Miwok Trail** (2 miles) northward. Turn southwest onto the **Coyote Ridge Trail** (0.9 mile), then catch the **Coastal Fire Road** (2 miles) the rest of the way west to Muir Beach. Another fun ride leads from just off U.S. 101 at the Rodeo Avenue exit. Park your car on the side of Rodeo Avenue, then bike down the

short **Rodeo Avenue Trail,** which ends in a T intersection after 0.7 mile at **Alta Trail.** Take a left, and access to **Bobcat Trail** is a few yards away. Continue on Bobcat Trail for 2.5 miles straight through the Headlands to the **Miwok Trail** for just 0.5 mile, and you'll find yourself out at Rodeo Beach.

Need to rent a bicycle for your travels? In San Francisco, **Bike and Roll** (899 Columbus Ave., 415/229-2000, www.bikeandroll.com/sanfrancisco, daily 8 A.M.–5 P.M.) offers off-road biking tours of the Marin Headlands, plus bicycle rentals that let you go wherever the spirit moves you.

Accommodations

Lodging options are fairly limited in the Marin Headlands. Many luxury-minded travelers choose to stay in Tiburon or Sausalito, while budget-motel seekers head for San Rafael.

Travelers who want budget accommodations indoors often choose the **Marin Headlands Hostel** (Bldg. 941, Fort Barry, 415/331-2777, www.norcalhostels.org/marin, dorm $25, private room $80). You'll find full kitchen facilities, Internet access, laundry rooms, and a rec room—all the amenities you'd expect from a high-end U.S. hotel. Surprisingly cozy and romantic, the hostel is sheltered in the turn-of-the-20th-century buildings of Fort Barry, creating a unique atmosphere. And, of course, with the Headlands right outside your door and 24-hour access for registered guests, there is no lack of activities or exploration opportunities.

To stay in a national park with the luxury of a well-appointed hotel and spa, book a room at the ◖ **Cavallo Point Lodge** (601 Murray Circle, Fort Baker, Sausalito, 415/339-4700, www.cavallopoint.com, $500), a luxury hotel at Fort Baker. Stay in the beautiful historic homes that feature elegant early-20th-century woodwork, box-beam ceilings, and wraparound porches. Inside are 21st-century amenities such as lush carpets, plush beds dressed in organic linens, flat-screen TVs, wireless Internet, gas fireplaces, and bathtubs so deep you can get lost. For those interested in more modern furnishings, Cavallo Lodge also has accommodations in the two-story green buildings. You'll find floor-to-ceiling windows to take advantage of the spectacular views, radiant floor heating, and private porches. The lodge also boasts environmental credentials, as is fitting in a national park, and dog-friendly accommodations. The excellent Murray Circle Restaurant and Farley Bar are on-site, and the spa offers treatments such as massages, wraps, and facials in addition to a tea bar.

Camping

Camping here requires some planning; lots of other people have the same idea. Be forewarned about pitching a tent, as Marin can be foggy, cold, and windy at any time of year, even July–August. Bring your warm camping gear if you plan to seek out one of the precious few campsites.

The most popular campground is **Kirby Cove** (877/444-6777, www.recreation.gov, reservations required, $25). Secluded and shaded campsites provide a beautiful respite complete with bay views and a private beach. Make reservations well in advance for summer weekends, since this popular campground fills up fast.

The **Bicentennial Campground** (Battery Wallace parking lot, 415/331-1540, free) boasts a whopping three campsites easily accessible from the parking lot. Each site can accommodate a maximum of two people, and there's no water available or fires allowed on-site. A nearby picnic area has barbecue grills that campers can use to cook.

Food

End a day of historic hiking with oysters and drinks at the ◖ **Farley Bar** at Cavallo Point Lodge (601 Murray Circle, Fort Baker, Sausalito, 415/339-4750, www.cavallopoint. com, 11 A.M.–11 P.M. Sun.–Thurs., 11 A.M.–midnight Fri.–Sat., $20). Snag a blanket and a

seat on the porch to watch the fog roll in over the Golden Gate Bridge. With only 12 drinks on the menu (all $12), the bar boasts one of the most classic and contemporary cocktail menus around. If you find you are not ready to leave after the sun goes down, mosey on inside, where lush leather chairs and sofas are arranged to maximize privacy and where a server is sure to hand you a bar menu.

Also on-site is the equally excellent **Murray Circle Restaurant** (Cavallo Point Lodge, 601 Murray Circle, Fort Baker, Sausalito, 415/339-4750, www.cavallopoint.com, 7–11 A.M., 11:30 A.M.–2 P.M., and 5:30–10 P.M. Mon.–Thurs., 7–11 A.M., 11:30 A.M.–2 P.M., and 5:30–11 P.M. Fri., 7–11 A.M., 11:30 A.M.–2:30 P.M., and 5:30–11 P.M. Sat., 7–11 A.M., 11:30 A.M.–2:30 P.M., and 5:30–10 P.M. Sun., $14–30). The long slender dining room is draped in muted greens and golds, creating an effect that perfectly matches the simple elegant style of the historic building. The menu is based on the best Marin produce, seafood, meat, and dairy. Simple dishes are executed with French technique. You'll find plenty of oyster options, but you'll also find smoked pork shank paired with California-grown black rice and red snapper with artichokes.

Information and Services

Aside from the visitors centers and museums, there isn't much in the way of services in the Headlands. Likewise, cell phone reception can be spotty. For a post office, hospital, or bank, you'll have to go to Sausalito or across the bridge to San Francisco.

Getting There and Around

Fort Baker and the Marin Headlands are located just north of the Golden Gate Bridge on Highway 1 and U.S. 101. To get to the Headlands from San Francisco, take the Alexander Avenue exit, the second exit after you cross the bridge. From the north, Alexander

© LEAADA/123RF.COM

a tugboat in the quaint town of Sausalito

Avenue is the last Sausalito exit. If the visitors center is the first stop on your agenda, turn left onto Bunker Road and go through the one-way tunnel. If you want to hit Fort Barry and the Bonita Lighthouse first, follow Alexander Avenue right and travel under the highway to Conzelman Road, which leads up the hill along the edge of the Headlands. Keep in mind that many of the roads are very narrow and become one-way in places.

Traffic in this area, particularly in the Headlands, can be heavy on beautiful weekend days, so try and plan to get here early and spend the time that other people are stuck in theirs cars exploring the area on foot. Another option is to take **Muni** bus route 76 (415/701-2311, www.sfmta.com, 10 A.M.–7 P.M. Sun., $2 one-way). Making stops throughout downtown San Francisco and the north end of the city, this Sunday-only Muni line crosses the Golden Gate and ventures as far as Rodeo Cove in the Headlands. It makes frequent trips, and you can even load bikes on the front.

SAUSALITO

The affluent town of Sausalito wraps around the north end of San Francisco Bay. The main drag runs along the shore, and the concrete boardwalk is perfect for strolling and biking. A former industrial fishing town, Sausalito still has a few old cannery buildings and plenty of docks, most now lined with pleasure boats.

San Francisco Bay Model

One of the odder attractions you'll find in the North Bay is the San Francisco Bay Model (2100 Bridgeway, 415/332-3871, www.spn. usace.army.mil/bmvc, call or check website for hours). It is a scale model of the way the Bay works, complete with currents and tides. Scientists and engineering types love to see how the waters of the Bay move and work.

Accommodations

The Gables Inn (62 Princess St., 415/289-1100, www.gablesinnsausalito.com, $225) opened in

1869 and is the oldest B&B in the area. Each of the nine guest rooms is appointed in tasteful earth tones, with white linens and several baths. Although this inn honors its long history, it has also kept up with the times, adding cable TV and Internet access. Genial innkeepers serve a buffet breakfast, available for a few hours each morning, and host a wine and cheese soiree each evening.

With a checkered history dating back to 1915, the **Hotel Sausalito** (16 El Portal, 888/442-0700, www.hotelsausalito.com, $165–210) was a speakeasy, a bordello, and a home for the writers and artists of the Beat generation. Today, this tiny boutique hotel, with its yellow walls and locally built furnishings, evokes the Mediterranean coast. Sink into your cozy room after a day spent walking or biking along the water and a scrumptious dinner out.

The **Casa Madrona Hotel and Spa** (801 Bridgeway, 800/288-0502, www.casamadrona.com, $270–390) is a sprawling collection of structures housing contemporary luxury hotel rooms and suites that satisfy even the pickiest celebrity guest. Poggio, the on-site restaurant, serves award-winning Italian food, and the full-service spa pampers guests with a full menu of body and salon treatments. If you're treating yourself to a room at Casa Madrona, be sure to ask for one with a view overlooking the Bay or the harbor.

For a taste of the life of the richest residents of the area, stay at Sausalito's **Inn Above Tide** (30 El Portal, 800/893-8433, www.innabovetide.com, $350). Billed as the only hotel in the Bay Area that's actually on the Bay, the inn sits over the edge of the water looking out at the San Francisco skyline. Most guest rooms have private decks that allow guests to take advantage of the sublime views (well, except when it's foggy). Inside the guest rooms, the appointments look like something you'd find in an upscale home rather than a hotel. Guests love the rooms with oversized bathtubs set by windows to take advantage of the Bay views. From the hotel, you can walk downtown to enjoy the shops, spas, and restaurants of Sausalito.

Food

If you're jonesing for some Chinese food, go to **Tommy's Wok Chinese Cuisine** (3001 Bridgeway, 415/332-5818, http://tommyswok.com, 11:30 A.M.–3 P.M. and 4–9 P.M. Mon.-Thurs., 11:30 A.M.–3 P.M. and 4–9:30 P.M. Fri.-Sat., 4–9 P.M. Sun., $10–20). Unlike a typical Chinese restaurant, Tommy's is into the swing of California cuisine fashions. This includes organic free-range chicken, organic tofu, and a heavy emphasis on fresh vegetables—even in the meat dishes. Don't expect to find too many of your sweet syrupy favorites; instead, take a chance on some tasty broccoli or asparagus.

It's hard to get away from the sea when you're visiting Sausalito. **Fish** (350 Harbor Dr., 415/331-3474, www.331fish.com, daily 11:30 A.M.–4:30 P.M. and 5:30–8:30 P.M., $10–25) can hook you up with some of the best sustainable seafood in the North Bay. No farmed salmon, overfished swordfish, or other more-harm-than-good seafood makes its way into the kitchen. Fresh wild fish prepared perfectly using a California-style mix of international cooking techniques results in amazing dishes you can't find anywhere else, even in the Bay Area.

Information and Services

To get started, make a stop at the **Sausalito Visitors Center** (780 Bridgeway, 415/332-0505, www.sausalito.org, Tues.–Sun. 11:30 A.M.–4 P.M.). Also known as the Ice House, this tiny building, used to store ice in the days before refrigeration technology, has loads of Sausalito materials to browse and purchase. The helpful staff has free maps and tips and sells books, cards, and souvenirs.

In the downtown area are a few cafés with Internet access, and to get cash, there is a **Bank of America** (750 Bridgway). Sausalito also has a **post office** (150 Harbor Dr.). For a newspaper even more local than the *San Francisco Chronicle,* pick up a copy of the *Marin Independent Journal* (www.marinij.com).

Getting There and Around

Sausalito is just over the Golden Gate Bridge from San Francisco and is easily accessible by bicycle on side roads or by car on U.S. 101. Once in town, navigating by car can be a challenge, as the narrow oceanfront main road gets very crowded on weekends. If you can, park and walk around town, both for your own comfort and to do your part to minimize traffic congestion. Street parking is mostly metered.

If you have the time, a great way to get to Sausalito from San Francisco is by ferry. Two companies make the trip daily, which takes roughly an hour or less. The scenery is beautiful, and it is a great chance to get out on the Bay a lot more cheaply than a bay tour. The **Blue and Gold Fleet** (415/705-8200, http://blueandgoldfleet.com, 11:20 A.M.–8:20 P.M. Mon.–Fri., 9:45 A.M.–6 P.M. Sat.–Sun., adults $10.50, children and seniors $6.25, under age 5 free) makes the trip from Pier 41. Largely serving commuters, the **Golden Gate Ferry** (415/455-2000, http://goldengate.org, 7:40 A.M.–7:20 P.M. Mon.–Fri., 10:40 A.M.–6:50 P.M. Sat.–Sun., adults $9.25, children and seniors $4.50, under age 5 free) leaves from the Ferry Building, closer to downtown San Francisco. The trip across of the Bay is cheaper and a bit faster.

TIBURON

Once a simple fishing town, Tiburon now has some of the most expensive waterfront real estate in the world. The small downtown area that backs onto the marina is popular with the young and affluent crowd as well as longtime yacht owners. Aside from the views, one of the greatest draws to Tiburon is its proximity to Angel Island, the largest in the Bay and one of the most unique state parks around.

◖ Angel Island State Park

Angel Island (415/435-1915, www.parks.ca.gov, daily 8 A.M.–sunset, rates vary by ferry company) has a long history, beginning with

Angel Island State Park

regular visits (though no permanent settlements) by the Coastal Miwok people. During the Civil War the U.S. Army created a fort on the island in anticipation of Confederate attacks from the Pacific. The attacks never came, but the Army maintained a base here. Today, many of the 19th-century military buildings remain and can be seen on the tram tour (1 hour, $10–15), on foot, or on a docent-led Segway or Digger electric scooter tour (both 2 hours, $68 pp). Later, the Army built a Nike missile base on the island to protect strategically important San Francisco from possible Soviet attacks. The missile base is not open to the public, but it can be seen from roads and trails.

Angel Island's history also has a shameful side—it served as an immigration station for inbound ships and a concentration camp for the flood of Chinese attempting to escape turmoil in their homeland. While Europeans were waved through with little more than a head-lice check, the Chinese were herded into barracks while government officials scrutinized their papers. After months and sometimes years of waiting, many were shipped back to China. Today, poetry lines the walls of the barracks, expressing the despair of the immigrants who had hoped for a better life and found little more than prison. Docent-led tours show this poetry and the buildings of the camps.

Angel Island is a major destination for both casual and serious hikers. Trails of varying difficulty crisscross the island, creating fun for hikers and bikers alike. Adventurous trekkers can scale Mount Livermore via either the **North Ridge Trail** or the **Sunset Trail.** Each runs about 4.5 miles round-trip for a moderate, reasonably steep hike. Stop at the top for a rest and some gorgeous Bay views. For the best experience, make a loop, taking one trail up the mountain and the other back down. If you're up for a long paved-road hike, take the **Perimeter Road** (5 miles, moderate) all the way around the island.

While there is no store on the island for supplies, the **Cove Café** (415/435-3392, www.angelisland.com, 11 A.M.–3 P.M. Mon.–Fri., 11 A.M.–4 P.M. Sat.–Sun. Mar.–Oct., $10) serves hot sandwiches, wraps, salads, and even a gourmet cheese platter from Cowgirl Creamery. Craving oysters and a beer? Stroll next door to the **Cove Cantina Oyster Bar** (11 A.M.–5:30 P.M. Fri.–Sun. Memorial Day–Oct.).

CAMPING

Camping is available at nine primitive campsites (800/444-7275 or www.reserveamerica.com, $30) that fill up quickly; successful campers reserve their campsites six months in advance. The campsites themselves are characterized as "environmental sites"; each is equipped with food lockers (a must), surprisingly nice outhouses, running water, and a barbecue. You must bring your own charcoal, as wood fires are strictly prohibited. Three of the sites, the **Ridge Sites**, sit on the southwest side of the island, known to be fairly windy. The other six sites, the **East Bay** and **Sunrise Sites**, face the East Bay. Wherever you end up, plan on walking up to 2.5 miles from the ferry to your campsite. Despite the dramatic urban views, camping here is a little like backpacking.

GETTING THERE

Angel Island State Park is located in the middle of San Francisco Bay. To get here, you must either boat in or take one of the ferries that serve the island. The harbor at Tiburon is the easiest place to access Angel Island. The private **Angel Island–Tiburon Ferry** (21 Main St., Tiburon, 415/435-2131, www.angelislandferry.com, adults $13.50, ages 6–12 $11.50, ages 3–5 $3.50, bicycles $1) can get you out to the island in about 10 minutes and runs several times a day. You can also take the **Blue and Gold Fleet** (415/703-8200, www.blueandgoldfleet.com, $8.50 one-way) to Angel Island if you are departing from either Oakland-Alameda

(2990 Main St., Alameda, summer–fall only) or San Francisco (Pier 41). Be aware however, that scheduling the ferry can be a little tight. Blue and Gold leave once in the morning (10 A.M. Mon.–Fri., 9:40 A.M. Sat.–Sun.) from San Francisco, and the last ferry back departs at 2:25 P.M. Monday–Friday and 4:10 P.M. Saturday–Sunday. While the ferry out of Tiburon has more sailings during the day, they last ferry is still early (daily 3–5 P.M.), with very few sailings on weekdays during the winter.

Ferries have plenty of room for you to bring your own bicycle, or you can rent one (Sat.–Sun. Mar.–Nov., daily Apr.–Oct., $12.50 per hour, $40 per day) at the main visitors area near the ferry dock. Rentals must always be returned at 4 P.M. Grab a map from the gift shop. Not all trails are open to bikes, but those that are include the easy five-mile paved Perimeter Road around the island, perfect for newcomers.

Accommodations

The lovely **Waters Edge Hotel** (25 Main St., 415/789-5999, www.marinhotels.com, $199–279) is a boutique lodging that lives up to its name, backing onto the marina and docks. You can stumble right out of your guest room onto the dock and over to the Angel Island ferry. Inside, you'll love the feather beds, cushy robes, and breakfast delivered to your guest room each morning.

Also wonderfully close to the water and attractions of downtown Tiburon, the **Lodge at Tiburon** (1651 Tiburon Blvd., 415/435-3133, www.thelodgeattiburon.com, $229–289) offers the comforts and conveniences of a larger hotel while providing the personal attention and atmosphere of a boutique inn. All the guest rooms are soothing and pretty, but for a special treat, book a Spa Room with a huge raised whirlpool tub set in an alcove overlooking the water. Have dinner or a drink at the attached Tiburon Grill in the evening, or take a walk downtown to look at the shops.

Food

There are many visitor-friendly restaurants in downtown Tiburon. For a surprisingly good Italian meal, head for **Servino** (9 Main St., 415/435-2676, www.bestservino.com, lunch 11:30 A.M.–3 P.M. Mon.–Fri., brunch 11:30 A.M.–4 P.M. Sat.–Sun., dinner 5–10 P.M. Sun.–Thurs., 5–11 P.M. Fri.–Sat., $13–25) on the waterfront. A huge outdoor patio offers diners stunning views of the Bay, Angel Island, and the San Francisco cityscape. Service is as warm and friendly as the classic Italian cuisine. A full bar caters to locals and visitors alike. The menu runs to hearty, somewhat Americanized Italian dishes. You can eat yourself senseless by trying all the courses, or choose just an entrée to keep the meal a bit lighter. The full bar makes a great place to sit should you need to wait for a table, and Servino's hosts live music on Thursday–Friday nights.

A Tiburon mainstay is **Sam's Anchor Café** (27 Main St., 415/435-4527, www.samscafe.com, 11 A.M.–9:30 P.M. Mon.–Fri., 9:30 A.M.–9:30 P.M. Sat.–Sun., $14–28). Sitting on the water with a large glassed-in deck, Sam's specializes in seafood, liberally poured glasses of wine, and lounging in the sun on beautiful weekend afternoons. You'll find many locals and visitors catching some rays over oysters on the half shell, fish-and-chips, or a burger. At night, the fare becomes a bit fancier, moving indoors with white tablecloths and low lighting. You'll find more elegantly plated dishes, but seafood still reigns, as the does the good-time vibe.

Information and Services

To get maps and recommendations, the **Tiburon Chamber of Commerce** (96 Main St., 415/435-5633, 9 A.M.–4 P.M. Mon.–Fri.) is a small office, but the staff will be able to answer any questions you may have. The town of Tiburon is small, so don't expect a whole lot in the way of services. There is a **Bank of America** (1601 Tiburon Blvd.), a **Wells Fargo Bank** (1550 Tiburon Blvd.), and a **post office** (6 Beach Rd.).

Getting There and Around

Tiburon is located on a peninsula about eight

miles north of the Golden Gate Bridge. From San Francisco, take U.S. 101 north to the Tiburon Boulevard exit. Stay to the right and follow the road along the water for nearly six miles until you reach the small downtown area.

Like Sausalito, Tiburon is very walkable and is a great destination via ferry from San Francisco. The **Blue and Gold Fleet** (415/705-8200, http://blueandgoldfleet.com) runs daily trips (30 minutes, 10:10 A.M.–8 P.M. Mon.–Fri., 9:45 A.M.–6:30 P.M. Sat.–Sun., adults $10.50, children and seniors $6.25, under age 5 free) to Tiburon from San Francisco's Pier 41.

TENNESSEE VALLEY

After U.S. 101 enters Marin County, the Stinson Beach/Mill Valley exit leads through barely noticed and unincorporated Tamalpais Valley. One of the most popular—and crowded, especially on summer weekends—places to start hiking is the **Tennessee Valley Trailhead** (end of Tennessee Valley Rd.), which has portable toilets but no water. A wealth of trails spring from this trailhead. A quick hike from the trailhead can take you out to the **Haypress Campground** (about 1.5 miles, moderate), which has picnic tables and pretty views. For a nice long hike, take the **Old Springs Trail** (1.3 miles) down to the **Miwok Trail.** Turn right and after 0.3 mile and take another right at **Wolf Ridge Trail** (0.7 mile) to the **Coastal Trail.** Taking a right, you'll intersect the **Tennessee Valley Trail** after 1.3 miles, which, taking another right toward the east, takes you back to the trailhead (1.4 miles).

A nice 2.5-mile hike from the Tennessee Valley Trailhead leads to **Hawk Campground** (415/331-1540, free) with three primitive sites. Your reward for the work of packing in all your gear and water is a near-solitary camping experience that lets you kick back and get to know the wilderness surrounding you. Amenities include chemical toilets but no water, and fires are not allowed.

To reach the Tennessee Valley Trailhead, take the Stinson Beach/Highway 1 exit off U.S. 101 and drive 0.6 mile, passing under the freeway and continuing straight. Turn left on Tennessee Valley Road and continue two miles to the trailhead.

Immediately after passing under U.S. 101, you may notice the **Buckeye Roadhouse** (15 Shoreline Hwy., Mill Valley, 415/331-2600, www.buckeyeroadhouse.com, 11:30 A.M.–10:30 P.M. Mon.–Sat., 10:30 A.M.–10 P.M. Sun., $24) hidden off to the left. Dating from 1937, this classic building is the local go-to for steaks, barbecue, and classic cocktails, and you'll find it filled every weekend. Valet parking is offered at the entrance, or park for free in the lot to the left (but you'll have to walk across the busy freeway entrance).

◖ MUIR WOODS NATIONAL MONUMENT

Established in 1908 and named for naturalist and author John Muir, Muir Woods National Monument (Panoramic Hwy., off Hwy. 1, 415/388-2596, www.nps.gov/muwo, daily 8 A.M.–sunset, adults $7, under age 15 free) comprises acres of staggeringly beautiful redwood forest nestled in Marin County. More than six miles of trails wind through the redwoods and accompanying Mount Tamalpais area, crossing verdant creeks and the lush forest. These are some of the most stunning—and accessible—redwoods in the Bay Area.

If you're new to Muir Woods, the visitors center is a great place to begin your exploration. The **Muir Woods Visitors Center** (1 Muir Woods Rd., daily 9 A.M.–5:30 P.M., closing hours vary) abuts the main parking area and marks the entrance to Muir Woods. In addition to maps, information, and advice about hiking, you'll also find a few amenities. Inside the park, slightly past the visitors center, is the **Muir Woods Trading Company Gift Shop and Cafe** (415/388-7059, www.

© KATHRYN OSGOOD

Muir Woods National Monument

muirwoodstradingcompany.com, daily 9 A.M.–5:30 P.M., closing hours vary) where you can purchase souvenirs and sustenance made from high-quality local ingredients.

Hiking

Muir Woods boasts many lovely trails that crisscross the gorgeous redwood forest. First-time visitors should follow the wheelchair- and stroller-accessible **Main Trail Loop** (1 mile, easy). Leading from the visitors center on an easy and flat walk through the beautiful redwoods, this trail has an interpretive brochure (pick one up at the visitors center) with numbers along the trail that describe the flora and fauna. Hikers can continue the loop on the **Hillside Trail** for an elevated view of the valley.

One of the first side trails off the Main Trail, the **Ocean View Trail** (3.4 miles, moderate) soon appears to the left. Some advice: Either bring water, or pick up a bottle at the Visitors Center before starting up the trail. The trail climbs through the redwoods for 1.5 miles until its junction with **Lost Trail**. Turn right on Lost Trail and follow it downhill for 0.7 mile to **Fern Creek Trail.** Bear left onto the Fern Creek trail for a lush and verdant return to the Main Trail. Along the way you'll see the much-lauded Kent Tree, a 250-foot-tall Douglas fir.

Alternatively, you can continue on the Main Trail to where Fern Creek Trail starts and hike in the opposite direction to the junction with **Alice Eastwood Camp,** after a brief westward jog on Lost Trail. There you can get a drink of water, use the restrooms, and even have a picnic in this developed area. Follow the **Camp Eastwood Trail** back to the starting point.

It's easier to avoid the crowds by following the Main Trail to its terminus with the **Bootjack Trail** (6.4 miles, moderate). The Bootjack Trail climbs uphill for 1.3 miles before its junction with the **TCC Trail.** Bear left for the TCC Trail and meander through the quiet Douglas firs. At 1.4 miles, the trail meets up with the **Stapleveldt Trail;** turn left again to follow this trail for 0.5 mile to **Ben Johnson Trail,** which continues downhill for one more mile to meet up with the Main Trail.

You may notice signs in this area for the **Dipsea Trail,** an out-and-back hike to Stinson Beach. This is a strenuous, unshaded 7.1-mile hike, and the only way back is the way you came—but uphill.

Getting There

Muir Woods is accessed via the long and winding Muir Woods Road. From U.S. 101, take the Stinson Beach/Highway 1 exit. On Highway 1, also named the Shoreline Highway, follow the road under the freeway and proceed until the road splits in a T-junction at the light. Turn left, continuing on Shoreline Highway for 2.5 miles. At the intersection with Panoramic Highway, make a sharp right turn and continue climbing uphill. At the junction of Panoramic Highway and Muir Woods Road, turn left and follow the road 1.5 twisty miles down to the Muir Woods parking lots on the right.

If you're visiting on a holiday or a summer weekend, get to the Muir Woods parking areas early—they fill fast, and afternoon hopefuls often cannot find a spot. Lighted signs on U.S. 101 will alert you to parking conditions at the main parking lot. To avoid the traffic hassle, there is a **Muir Woods Shuttle** (415/455-2000, http://goldengatetransit.org/services/muirwoods.php, Sat.–Sun. summer, $3 pp round-trip) that leaves from various points in southern Marin County, including the Sausalito ferry terminal.

MUIR BEACH

Few coves on the California coast can boast as much beauty as Muir Beach (just south of the town of Muir Beach, www.nps.gov/goga, daily sunrise–sunset). From the overlook above Highway 1 to the edge of the ocean beyond the dunes, Muir Beach is a haven for both wildlife and beachcombers. In the wintertime, beachgoers bundle up against the chill and walk the sands of the cove or along the many trails that lead from the beach. If you're lucky, you might find a Monterey pine tree filled with sleepy monarch butterflies, here to overwinter before making their long migration back north in the spring. Springtime brings rare rays of sunshine to Muir Cove, and as the air grows (a little bit) warmer in summer, the north end of the cove attracts another breed of beach life: nudists. If the clothing-optional California lifestyle makes you uncomfortable, stick to the south side, the brackish Redwood Creek lagoon, and the windswept picnic grounds.

Muir Beach is directly off Highway 1. The most direct route is to take U.S. 101 to the Stinson Beach/Highway 1 exit and follow Highway 1 (also called Shoreline Highway) for 6.5 miles to Pacific Way (look for the Pelican Inn). Turn left onto Pacific Way and continue straight to the Muir Beach parking lot. If arriving from Muir Woods, simply continue following Muir Woods Road down to the junction with Highway 1 and turn left onto Pacific Way.

Accommodations and Food

One fine Marin lodging is **The Pelican Inn** (10 Pacific Way, Muir Beach, 415/383-6000, www.pelicaninn.com, $235). Inside the Tudor structure, the guest room decor continues the historic ambiance, with big-beam construction, canopy beds, and historic portrait prints. The seven mostly small guest rooms each come with private baths and full English-style breakfast, but no TVs or phones. The Pelican Inn is a perfect spot to unplug, disconnect, and truly get away from it all.

In addition to quaint bedchambers, you can also get hearty food at The Pelican Inn (lunch daily 11:30 A.M.–3 P.M., dinner daily 5:30–9 P.M., $15–30). Dark wood and a long trestle table give the proper old English feeling to the dimly lit dining room. The cuisine brings home the flavors of old England, with dishes like beef Wellington, shepherd's pie, and fish-and-chips. Breakfast is served only to overnight guests, but lunch and dinner are available to nonguests. True fans of the British Isles will round off the meal with a pint of Guinness.

◖ MOUNT TAMALPAIS STATE PARK

To see the whole Bay Area in a single day, go to Mount Tamalpais State Park (801 Panoramic Hwy., Mill Valley, 415/388-2070, www.parks. ca.gov, daily 7 A.M.–sunset, day-use parking $8). Known as Mount Tam, this park boasts stellar views of the San Francisco Bay Area—from Mount St. Helena in Napa down to San Francisco and across to the East Bay. The Pacific Ocean peeks from around the corner of the western peninsula, and on a clear day you can just make out the foothills of the Sierra Nevada mountains to the east. This park is the Bay Area's backyard, with hiking, biking, and camping opportunities widely appreciated for both their beauty and easy access. Ample parking, interpretive walks, and friendly park rangers make a visit to Mount Tam a hit even for less outdoorsy travelers.

In addition to recreation, Mount Tam also provides the perfect setting for the arts. The **Mountain Theater** (E. Ridgecrest Blvd. at Pan Toll Rd.), also known as the Cushing Memorial Amphitheater, built in the 1930s, still hosts plays at its outdoor stone seating. Performances and dates vary; contact the Mountain Play Association (415/383-1100, www.mountainplay.org, May–June, $30–47) for information and tickets. Plan to arrive early, as both parking and seating fill completely well before the show starts. The Mountain Theater also serves as the meeting place for the **Mount Tam Astronomy Program** (415/289-6636, www. mttam.net). Held every Saturday from April to October near the new and first quarter moon, the group hosts a talk by an astronomer that lasts about 45 minutes, after which is a tour of the night sky and star viewing through telescopes. Bring flashlights.

The **East Peak Visitors Center** (11 A.M.–4 P.M. Sat.–Sun.) is located at the top of Mount Tam, with a small museum and gift shop as well as a picnic area with tables and restrooms, and even a small refreshment stand. The on-site staff can assist with hiking tips or guided walks. The **Pantoll Ranger Station** (Panoramic Hwy. at Pantoll Rd., 415/388-2070, 9 A.M.–5 P.M. Fri.–Mon.), which anchors the western and larger edge of the park, provides hikers with maps and camping information.

Enjoy the views without setting out on the trail at the **Bootjack Picnic Area** (Panoramic Hwy.), which has tables, grills, water, and restrooms. The small parking lot northeast of the Pantoll Ranger Station fills quickly and early in the day.

Hiking

Up on Mount Tam, you can try anything from a leisurely 30-minute interpretive stroll up to a strenuous hike up and down one of the many deep ravines. Mount Tam's hiking areas are divided into three major sections: the East Peak, the Pantoll area, and the Rock Springs area. Each of these regions offers a number of beautiful trails, so you'll want to grab a map from the visitors center or online to get a sense of the mountain and its hikes. For additional hikes, visit the Mount Tamalpais Interpretive Association website (www.mttam.net).

EAST PEAK

The charming, interpretive **Verna Dunshee Trail** (0.75 mile, easy) offers a short, mostly flat walk along a wheelchair-accessible trail. The views are fabulous, and you can get a leaflet at the visitors center that describes many of the things you'll see along the trail. Turn this into a loop hike by continuing on Verna Dunshee counterclockwise; once back at the visitors center, make the climb up to **Gardner Lookout** for stellar views from the top of Mount Tam's East Peak (2,571 feet).

PANTOLL

The Pantoll Ranger Station is ground zero for some of the best and most challenging hikes in the park. The **Old Mine Trail** (across Panormaic Hwy.) leads up to Mountain Theater via the Easy Grade Trail (2 miles, easy–moderate). Eager hikers can continue on the **Rock Springs Trail** to West Point Inn and back via **Old Stage Road** for a more challenging 4.7 miles.

The **Steep Ravine Trail** (3.8 miles, moderate) descends through lush Webb Creek and gorgeous redwoods to meet with the Dipsea Trail. To return to the Pantoll parking area, turn left onto Dipsea Trail and climb the demanding steps back to the **Coastal Fire Road.** Turn left again, then right on the Old Mine Trail for an exhilarating 3.8-mile hike.

The **Dipsea Trail** loop (7.3 miles round-trip, strenuous) is part of the famous Dipsea Race Course (second Sun. in June), a 7.4-mile course renowned for both its beauty and its challenging stairs. The trailhead that begins in Muir Woods, near the parking lot, leads through Mount Tam all the way to Stinson Beach. Hikers can pick up the Dipsea on the Old Mine Trail or at its intersection with the Steep Ravine Trail in Mount Tam, but a common loop is to take the **Matt Davis Trail** (across Panoramic Hwy. from the Pantoll parking area) west all the way to Stinson Beach and then return via the Dipsea Trail to Steep Ravine Trail. This is a long, challenging hike, especially on the way back, so bring water and endurance.

ROCK SPRINGS

Rock Springs is conveniently located near the Mountain Theater, and a variety of trails lead off from this historic venue. Cross Ridgecrest Boulevard and take the **Mountain Theater Fire**

trail marker on the strenuous Dipsea Trail

© MARK RASMUSSEN/123RF.COM

The summit of Mount Tamalpais offers stunning views of San Francisco Bay.

Trail to Mountain Theater. Along the top row of the stone seats, admire the vistas while looking for **Rock Springs Trail** (it's a bit hidden). Once you find it, follow Rock Springs Trail all the way to historic West Point Inn. The views here are stunning, and you'll see numerous cyclists flying downhill on Old Stage Road below. Cross this road to pick up Nora Trail, following it until it intersects with **Matt Davis Trail.** Turn right to reach the Bootjack day-use area. Follow the **Bootjack Trail** right (north) to return to the Mountain Theater for a 4.6-mile loop.

Here's your chance to see waterfalls via the lovely **Cataract Trail** (3 miles, easy–moderate). From the trailhead, follow Cataract Trail for a short bit before heading right on **Bernstein Trail.** Shortly, turn left onto **Simmons Trail** and continue to Barth's Retreat, site of a former camp that is now a small picnic area with restrooms. Turn left on **Mickey O'Brien Trail** (a map can be helpful here), returning to an intersection with the Cataract Trail. It's worth the

short excursion to follow Cataract Trail to the right through the Laurel Dell picnic area and up to Cataract Falls. Enjoy a picnic at Laurel Dell before returning to Cataract Trail to follow it down to the Rock Springs trailhead.

Biking

To bike up to the peak of Mount Tam is a mark of local cyclists' strength and endurance. Rather than driving up to the East Peak or the Mountain Home Inn, sturdy cyclists pedal up the paved road to the East Peak. It's a long hard ride, but for an experienced cyclist the challenge and the views make it more than worthwhile. Just take care, since this road is open to cars, many of which may not realize that bikers frequent the area.

A hard but satisfying trip up the mountain begins at the Lagunitas Trailhead in Ross (15.8 miles, strenuous). From here you take the **Eldridge Grade Fire Road** all the way to East Peak. The scenery is as beautiful as the ride is challenging and technical. To make the trip into a loop, turn onto paved **Ridgecrest Boulevard** for a little over four miles. On the right is the **Rock Springs Lagunitas Fire Road.** Take it all the way back to the trailhead. To reach the peak when you are already up on the mountain, consider parking at the Pantoll Ranger Station and taking **Old Stage Grade** north to either Middle Peak or East Peak (6 miles, moderate). You can make the ride into a longer loop by jumping on **Eldridge Grade** at East Peak, taking it to **Wheeler Trail,** where you will have to walk your bike a short distance and then turn right on **E-Koo Fire Road.** After a couple of miles it will intersect with **Old Railroad Grade** (stay right), which will then meet **Old Stage Grade.** Turn left and head down to the trailhead.

Accommodations

It is quite likely that the **West Point Inn** (1000 Panoramic Hwy., Mill Valley, 415/388-9955, www.westpointinn.com, $35–50, Tues.–Sat.) has changed very little since it was built in 1904. The only change is perhaps that guests would take the old train to its doorstep, while today they must hike two miles on a dirt road. The inn has no electricity; instead, it is lit by gaslights and warmed by fires in the large fireplaces in the downstairs lounge and parlor, where guests are encouraged to read, play games, and enjoy each other's company. There are seven guest rooms upstairs and five rustic cabins nearby. All guests must bring their own linens, flashlights, and food, which can be prepared in the communal kitchen. One Sunday a month during the summer, the inn hosts a pancake breakfast (9 A.M.–1 P.M., adults $10, children $5) that draws local hikers. The wait can be long, but it is a lot of fun.

Also with terrific views, albeit far less rustic, is **Mountain Home Inn** (810 Panoramic Hwy., 415/381-9000, www.mtnhomeinn. com, $195–345), also built during the heyday of the railroad. You don't have to hike in, however; in fact, the innkeepers would prefer that you relax as much as possible. With 10 guest rooms, many with jetted tubs, wood-burning fireplaces, and private decks, it would be hard to exert yourself. If you do feel like leaving your private hideaway, you can opt for a massage, slip downstairs for a complimentary breakfast, or dine on a three-course prix fixe dinner ($38) in the cozy and warmly lit dining room.

Camping

With spectacular views of the Pacific Ocean it's no wonder that the rustic accommodations at ◖ **Steep Ravine** (800/444-7275, www.reserveamerica.com, cabins $100, campsites $25) stay fully booked. On the steep ravine (the name is no exaggeration) there are six primitive campsites and nine cabins. The cabins are considered rustic but each comes equipped with a small wood stove, a table, a sleeping platform, and a grill; the campsites are also spare but each has a table, a fire pit, and a food locker. Restrooms and drinking water are nearby. To book either a cabin or a campsite you need to be on the phone at 8 A.M. six months before the date you intend to go. The word is out.

If Steep Ravine is full or you want to camp within hiking distance of the top of the mountain, the **Pantoll Campground** (1393 Panoramic Hwy., 415/388-2070, http://mttam.net/activities/camping.html, $25) has 16 sites with drinking water, firewood, and restrooms. Camping here operates on a first-come, first-served basis, paid for at the ranger station, so get here early. The sites are pleasantly removed from the parking lot, which means that once you have gone to the trouble of hauling in all your gear, you will enjoy the quiet of car-free camping.

Food

Is a gourmet meal at the end of a long hike your idea of the perfect end to the perfect day? Luckily, the **Mountain Home Inn**

(810 Panoramic Hwy., 415/381-9000, www.
mtnhomeinn.com, lunch 11:30 A.M.–3 P.M.
Wed.–Mon. Apr.–Nov. and 11:30 A.M.–3 P.M.
Wed.–Sun. Nov.–Apr., dinner daily 5:30–
8:30 P.M., prix fixe dinner $38) opens its
kitchen to the public. Enjoy a three-course prix
fixe dinner of French-California cuisine overlooking the surrounding mountains and mist-
filled valleys. Or, if you are spending the day
in the Mount Tam area and don't want to pack
a lunch, the Mountain Home Inn also offers
grilled sandwiches and fresh salads. The Wine
Bar (3:30–8 P.M. Wed.–Sun.) is open between
meals. You can nibble on lighter fare such as a
local cheese plate, ceviche, or paella while sipping fantastic local wine on the expansive deck.

Information and Services
For more information, contact the volunteer-run
Mount Tamalpais Interpretive Association
(415/258-2410, www.mttam.net). Because the
ongoing California state budget crisis has left
the Mount Tam's visitors center and ranger station with limited hours, you may be visiting
when both are closed, but the state park did
manage to set up free Wi-Fi; if you arrive at the
park and need information, you can access the
Web just 150–200 feet from the ranger station.

Getting There and Around
Panoramic Highway is a long and winding two-
lane road across the Mount Tamalpais area and
extending all the way to Stinson Beach. Once
upon a time, well-heeled visitors could take a
scenic train ride up to and across Mount Tam.
Today, you'll probably want to drive up to one
of the parking lots, from which you can explore
the trails. Take Highway 1 to the Stinson Beach
exit, then follow the fairly good signs up the
mountain. Turn right at Panoramic Highway
at the top of the hill. Follow the road for five
winding miles until you reach the Pantoll
Ranger Station. To get to the East Peak Visitors
Center, take a right on Pantoll Road, and

another right on East Ridgecrest Boulevard.
To access the park from Stinson Beach, take a
right on Panorama Highway at the T intersection with Highway 1 just south of town.

Bus access to the park is available via route
61 of the **West Marin Stagecoach** (415/226-
0855, www.marintransit.org, daily, $2), provid-
ing public transit from Stinson Beach or Mill
Valley to Mount Tam, dropping and picking
visitors up at the Pantoll Ranger Station.

STINSON BEACH
The primary attraction at Stinson Beach is
the tiny town's namesake: a broad 3.5-mile-
long sandy stretch of coastline that's unusually (for Northern California) congenial to
visitors. Although it's as plagued by fog as anywhere else in the Bay Area, on rare clear days
Stinson Beach is the favorite destination for San
Franciscans seeking some surf and sunshine.

To get out on the water, swing by **Stinson
Beach Surf and Kayak** (3605 Hwy. 1, 415/868-
2739, www.stinsonbeachsurfandkayak.com,
10 A.M.–6 P.M. Sat.–Sun., $20–40 per day).
The owner, Bill, will set you up with a surfboard, kayak, boogie board, or stand-up paddle
boat. Wetsuits, which you will certainly need,
are available. He also offers surf lessons and is
happy to give pointers to novices out on the
lagoon about the general etiquette of paddling
around wildlife. While he keeps regular store
hours on weekends and on holiday Mondays,
during the week the shop is "on call." This may
mean a bit of planning on your part if you are
in Stinson Beach during the week; you can call
or page him (415/257-1831) and he'll be happy
to help you out.

Accommodations
Given its status as a beach resort town, you will
find a few inns and motels to stay the night.
The **Sandpiper Inn** (1 Marine Way, 415/868-
1632, www.sandpiperstinsonbeach.com, $120–
170) has six guest rooms and four cabins, and

you can choose between motel-style accommodations with comfortable queen beds, private baths, and gas fireplaces or the four individual redwood cabins, which offer additional privacy, bed space for families, and full kitchens.

Another nice spot is the **Stinson Beach Motel** (3416 Shoreline Hwy. 1, 415/868-1712, www.stinsonbeachmotel.com, $150). It features eight vintage-y beach bungalow-style guest rooms that sleep 2–4 guests each. Some guest rooms have substantial kitchenettes; all have private baths, garden views, TVs, and blue decor. The motel is a great spot to bring the family for a beach vacation.

Food

A few small restaurants dot the town of Stinson Beach, most of which serve seafood. Among the best is the **Sand Dollar Restaurant** (3458 Hwy. 1, 415/868-0434, www.stinsonbeachrestaurant.com, daily lunch and dinner, $10–25). This so-called fish joint actually serves more land-based dishes than seafood, but perhaps the fact that the dining room is constructed out of three old barges makes up the difference. In addition to lunch and dinner, the Sand Dollar serves a popular Sunday brunch.

Getting There

Stinson Beach is an unbelievably beautiful place to get to. First, take the Stinson Beach exit off U.S. 101. Follow the Shoreline Highway (Hwy. 1) as it snakes up the hill past the turnoffs for Tennessee Valley, Muir Woods, and Mount Tamalpais State Park. The road will pass through Green Gulch, where produce is grown for the legendary Greens Restaurant in San Francisco; Muir Beach; and eventually along cliffs high above the Pacific. After about five miles, the highway descends into Stinson Beach. Most of the town is strung along the highway, and signs make it easy to navigate to the beach.

So what's the catch with this idyllic recreation spot? As with so many other places in and near large metropolitan areas in California, it's the traffic. You'll quickly experience this problem if you try to drive into Stinson Beach on a sunny weekend day in summer. With only one lane in each direction and a couple of intersections with stop signs, traffic backups that stretch for miles are all too common. Your best bet is to drive in on a weekday or in the evening when everyone else is leaving the beach.

Fortunately, an alternative to driving is **West Marin Stagecoach** (415/226-0855, www.marintransit.org, daily, $2) route 61, a daily bus that runs from Mill Valley into Stinson Beach.

POINT REYES NATIONAL SEASHORE

A haven for wilderness buffs, the Point Reyes area boasts acres of unspoiled forest and beach country. Expect cool weather even in the summer, but enjoy the lustrous green foliage and spectacular scenery that result. Point Reyes National Seashore (1 Bear Valley Rd., 415/464-5100, www.nps.gov/pore, daily dawn–midnight) stretches for miles between Tomales Bay and the Pacific, north from Stinson Beach to the tip of the land at the end of the bay. Dedicated hikers can trek from the bay to the ocean, or from the beach to land's end. The protected lands shelter a range of wildlife. In the marshes and lagoons, a wide variety of birds—including three different species of pelicans—make their nests. The pine forests shade shy deer and larger elk. There are also a number of ranches, dairy farms, and even an oyster farm that still operate inside the park. Grandfathered in at the time the park was created, these sustainable, generations-old family farms give added character and historical depth to Point Reyes.

The Point Reyes area includes the tiny towns of Olema, Point Reyes Station, and Inverness.

Visitors Centers

The **Bear Valley Visitors Center** (1 Bear Valley Rd., 415/464-5100, 9 A.M.–5 P.M.

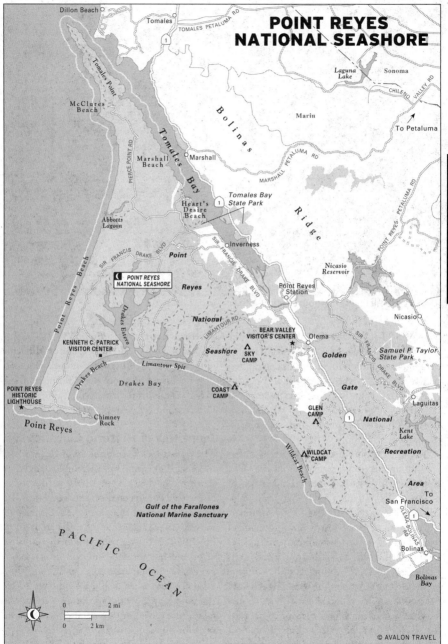

POINT REYES NATIONAL SEASHORE

Dillon Beach
Tomales
TOMALES PETALUMA RD
1
Laguna Lake
Sonoma
CHILENO VALLEY RD
Tomales Point
Bolinas
Marin
To Petaluma
McClures Beach
Marshall Beach
MARSHALL PETALUMA RD
Tomales Bay
PIERCE POINT RD
Marshall
Ridge
POINT REYES PETALUMA RD
Heart's Desire Beach
Tomales Bay State Park
Abbotts Lagoon
SIR FRANCIS DRAKE BLVD
Inverness
SIR FRANCIS DRAKE BLVD
Point
Nicasio Reservoir
Point Reyes Station
POINT REYES NATIONAL SEASHORE
Reyes
Nicasio
Point Reyes Beach
KENNETH C. PATRICK VISITOR CENTER
National
LIMANTOUR RD
BEAR VALLEY VISITOR'S CENTER
Olema
SIR FRANCIS DRAKE BLVD
Samuel P. Taylor State Park
Drakes Estero
Seashore
SKY CAMP
Golden
Drakes Beach
Limantour Spit
COAST CAMP
Gate
Laguitas
POINT REYES HISTORIC LIGHTHOUSE
Drakes Bay
1
National
Point Reyes
Chimney Rock
GLEN CAMP
Kent Lake
Recreation
WILDCAT CAMP
Wildcat Beach
Area
To San Francisco
OLEMA BOLINAS RD
1
Gulf of the Farallones National Marine Sanctuary
Bolinas
PACIFIC OCEAN
Bolinas Bay
0   2 mi
0   2 km

© AVALON TRAVEL

Point Reyes Historic Lighthouse

© HARRIS SHIFFMAN/123RF.COM

Mon.–Fri., 8 a.m.–5 p.m. Sat.–Sun.) acts as the central visitors center for Point Reyes National Seashore. In addition to maps, fliers, and interpretive exhibits, you can watch a short video introducing the Point Reyes region. You can also talk to the park rangers, either to ask advice or to obtain beach fire permits and backcountry camping permits.

Two other visitors centers are located at different spots in the vast acreage of Point Reyes. The **Ken Patrick Visitors Center** (Drakes Beach, 415/669-1250, 10 a.m.–5 p.m. Sat.–Sun. fall–spring, usually daily 10 a.m.–5 p.m. summer) sits right on the beach in a building made of weathered redwood. Its small museum focuses on the maritime history of the region, and it acts as the host area for the annual Sand Sculpture event held on the beach. The **Drake Beach Café** (415/669-1297, www.drakescafe.com, hours vary) serves delicious food with an appropriate focus on the local, organic, and sustainable.

Finally, the **Historic Lighthouse and**

Visitors Center (415/669-1534, 10 a.m.–4:30 p.m. Thurs.–Mon.) is the most difficult of the three to access. You must walk about 0.5 mile up a steep hill from the parking lot to get to this visitors center. You'll find the lighthouse right at your feet once you arrive.

Point Reyes Historic Lighthouse

The jagged rocky shores of Point Reyes make for great sightseeing but incredibly dangerous maritime navigation. In 1870 the first lighthouse was constructed on the headlands. Its first-order Fresnel lens threw light far enough for ships to see and avoid the treacherous granite cliffs. Yet the danger remained, and soon after, a lifesaving station was constructed alongside the light station. It wasn't until the 20th century, when a ship-to-shore radio station and newer lifesaving station were put in place, that the Point Reyes shore truly became safer for ships.

The Historic Lighthouse (415/669-1534,

www.nps.gov/pore, 10 A.M.–4:30 P.M. Thurs.–Mon., light room 2:30–4 P.M. Thurs.–Mon.) still stands today on a point past the visitors center, accessed by descending a sometimes treacherous, cold, and windblown flight of 300 stairs, which often closes to visitors during bad weather for safety reasons. Still, it's worth a visit; the Fresnel lens and original machinery all remain in place, and the adjacent equipment building contains foghorns, air compressors, and other safety implements from decades gone by. Check the website for information about twice-monthly special events when the light is switched on.

Tomales Bay State Park

At the northeast edge of the Point Reyes Peninsula, Tomales Bay State Park (1208 Pierce Point Rd., 415/669-1140, www.park.ca.gov, daily 8 A.M.–sunset, $8) is shrouded in pine forests and is home to four lovely beaches. Protected from the wind and waves by the Inverness Ridge to the west, the beaches are calm, gently slopping, and partially secluded, which is unusual on the peninsula. They are the perfect place to read and sunbathe while the kids splash around in the gently lapping surf. There are also places to picnic or hike, if you are eager to hit the woods. An easy one-mile trail leads to the **Jepson Memorial Grove**, home to the last virgin groves of Bishop pine trees in California. Access is via the Jepson Trail, which leads to **Heart's Desire Beach**, perhaps the most popular beach in the park. All the beaches require a walk from the parking lots, but the walks are through meadows and forest, and the beach is a great reward.

Hiking

One of the main reasons people make the trip out to Point Reyes is to explore its beautiful scenery up close. Hikers fan out on the trails winding through the national seashore and surrounding state parks. To list all the hikes in Point Reyes would require a book in itself. For just a taste of what the area has to offer, start at the Bear Valley Visitors Center; this is the trailhead for several simple hikes, and the visitors center can provide maps and trail information. From the visitors center, hiking is accessed along four main roads (south to north): Olema–Bolinas Road, Limantour Road, Sir Francis Drake Boulevard, and Pierce Point Road.

OLEMA-BOLINAS ROAD

At the very south end of Point Reyes, Olema–Bolinas Road leads to the Palomarin Trailhead. Located at the end of Mesa Road, the trailhead provides access to the **Coastal Trail** (8 miles, moderate), which offers opportunities for both day hiking and overnight backpacking to **Wildcat Camp** (12.4 miles, permit required). Day hikers in good physical condition can follow the trail out past Bass Lake, Pelican Lake, and Crystal Lake (note that the trail to Alamere Falls remains closed). To reach the trailhead, take Olema–Bolinas Road west to Mesa Road and the Palomarin Trailhead.

BEAR VALLEY VISITORS CENTER

From the visitors center, the **Bear Valley Trail** runs south all the way to the ocean and the dramatic perch of **Arch Rock** (8.2 miles, moderate). For a shorter hike, follow Bear Valley Trail to **Divide Meadow** (3.2 miles, moderate) and then return to the visitors center.

Bear Valley Trail also provides access to **Mount Wittenberg** (5 miles, strenuous), although there is an easier trailhead off Limantour Road. This is the highest point in the park (1,407 feet), and you'll feel it on the climb up. From Bear Valley Trail, turn right at the intersection with Mount Wittenberg Trail and follow it to the top. Hikers can return via either the **Meadow Trail** (turn left on Sky Trail, then left again on Meadow Trail) or take **Z Ranch Trail** (left) to return via **Horse Trail**.

LIMANTOUR ROAD

Limantour Road is north of the Bear Valley Visitors Center; take Bear Valley Road north

Search for seals on the Chimney Rock Trail.

and turn west on Limantour Road. One of the first trailheads along this road is for the **Sky Trail** (4.3 miles, moderate). The Sky Trail provides easier access to Mount Wittenberg with the bonus of passing by Sky Camp, one of the area's most popular hike-in campgrounds.

Limantour Road eventually passes Point Reyes Hostel, where you'll find the Laguna Trailhead for the **Coast-Laguna Loop** (5 miles, moderate). Follow Laguna Trail down to Drakes Bay, where it hugs the shoreline until reaching Coast Camp, another backpacking campsite. From Coast Camp, take **Fire Lane Trail** north to **Laguna Trail** and return to the trailhead. Almost across Limantour Road from the hostel, **Muddy Hollow Trail** (4 miles) is an easy hike to Limantour Beach.

Birders will want to make a beeline for the **Limantour Spit Trail** (2 miles, easy). From the parking lot at Limantour Beach, it's a quick short hike to the beach; look for a spur trail headed west.

SIR FRANCIS DRAKE BOULEVARD

The Estero Trailhead is located off Sir France Drake Boulevard, shortly after the junction with Pierce Point Road. **Estero Trail** offers several options for hikers. For a short two-mile hike, follow the trail to Home Bay and turn around there. You can extend the hike to **Sunset Beach** (7.8 miles round-trip, moderate) which overlooks Drakes Estero; or continue farther to **Drakes Head** (9.4 miles round-trip), via Estero Trail and **Drakes Head Trail,** with views overlooking Estero de Limantour and Drakes Bay.

Sir Francis Drake Boulevard continues rolling through pastures south and west until it ends at the Point Reyes Lighthouse. From the parking area on Chimney Rock Road, just south of the Point Reyes Lighthouse, follow the **Chimney Rock Trail** (1.6 miles, easy) through grassy cliffs to a wooden bench at the tip of the peninsula. The views of the Pacific and the Point Reyes coast are stunning even though the wind tends to whip mercilessly here. Return the way you came, but take the short spur trail left to the headlands overlook, where you may see and hear seals on the beach far below.

PIERCE POINT ROAD

Pierce Point Road extends to the northern end of the park where windswept sandy beaches, lagoons, and tule elk await. To reach Pierce Point Road from the Bear Valley Visitors Center, take Sir Francis Drake Boulevard north past Inverness until it intersects with Pierce Point Road. Turn right on Pierce Point Road and continue to the trailhead for **Abbots Lagoon** (2 miles round-trip), an easy hike that will be a hit with bird lovers. Pierce Point Road continues north to another hiking option at **Kehoe Beach** (1 mile, easy), where a gravel trail descends to the beach. (Note that this is the only trail in Point Reyes where leashed dogs are permitted.)

Pierce Point Road runs almost to the tip of Tomales Point. From the trailhead at Pierce Point Ranch, there are two hiking options.

For a short and easy hike to the beach, follow **McClures Beach Trail** (1 mile, easy) to explore tide pools bordered by granite cliffs. A bit longer, **Tomales Point Trail** is a wide smooth path through the middle of the Tule Elk Reserve to a viewpoint at Bird Rock. From Bird Rock, the "trail" to Tomales Point (9.5 miles round-trip, moderate) becomes trickier and less defined, but it is worth it for the views north to Bodega Bay.

Biking

Cyclists, sometimes in big packs, ply the area's many small roads. For a stout mountain-bike ride, take the **Bolinas Ridge Trail** (11 miles one-way, moderate), open to both bikers and hikers and offering stunning views down toward the Olema Valley. You'll find access to the trail off Sir Francis Drake Boulevard, east of Olema on the south side of the road. Bolinas–Fairfax Road, which intersects Highway 1 at the tip of Bolinas Lagoon, provides access from the south. An easier trail, more suitable for families, runs west down to **Marshall Beach** on Tomales Bay. To get to the trailhead, take Pierce Point Road to the unpaved L Ranch Road.

For road biking, most paved roads in Point Reyes are open to both bicycles and cars. Ask at one of the local bike shops for information about this year's hot biking spots and any trail closures.

You can find bike rentals in the heart of Point Reyes Station at **Point Reyes Outdoors** (11401 Hwy. 1, Point Reyes Station, 415/663-8192, www.pointreyesoutdoors.com, 9 A.M.–6 P.M. Mon.–Fri., 9 A.M.–5 P.M. Sat.–Sun., half day $35, full day $42). The small shop only offers mountain bikes, but they also rent child trailers and car racks if you don't want to start cycling right in the town. In addition to rentals, the staff will also point you to the best roads and trails for your skill level and mood.

Kayaking

The calm water of Tomales Bay practically calls out to be explored by kayak. **Blue Waters** (60 4th St., Suite C, Point Reyes Station, 415/669-2600, www.bwkayak.com, $25–45 per hour) offers both kayak tours and rentals with two launch sites, one in Inverness and one in Marshall, on the east side of the bay. In addition to paddles around the bay, tours include exploring Drake's Estero in Point Reyes, and some tours incorporate hikes into the afternoon. If you want to go it alone, Blue Waters rents one-, two-, and three-person kayaks, and rates include all the gear you need plus a paddle lesson to make sure everyone is safe on the water.

Sea Trek (415/488-1000, www.seatrek.com, $20–35 per hour, tours $80) also offers tours of Tomales Bay and Drakes Estero. You can opt for a day out in the sunshine, the full moon paddle tour, or the Saturday night tour, where the stars shine unhindered by city lights as you cruise along the bay. Tours last 3–4 hours and often include a meal at a local eatery. While Sea Trek is based in Sausalito, all tours meet at the launch location.

In addition to renting out bikes, **Point Reyes Outdoors** (415/663-8192, www.pointreyesoutdoors.com) also provides the widest variety of kayak tours ($75–110) in the area. You can choose a day out in the wetlands of the southern part of the bay, where excellent birding awaits; a night paddling in water with bioluminescent creatures along Point Reyes Seashore; or a tour around Hog Island among the harbor seals and shorebirds. Tours generally last 3–6 hours and include a picnic of gourmet goodies from local businesses.

Horseback Riding

To tour the area on horseback, **Five Brook Ranch** (8001 Hwy. 1, 415/663-1570, www.fivebrooks.com, daily 9 A.M.–5 P.M., $30–40 per hour) can get you saddled up to ride through Point Reyes's forests and grasslands, up ridges and down to beaches on tours that last 1–6 hours. The most popular tour is up to an ospreys' nest along Inverness Ridge, then dropping down for a peaceful amble along Olema Creek. If you're up for an all-day adventure, opt for the Wildcat Beach Ride, which includes a picnic at the remote white-sand beach.

Accommodations

OLEMA

The **Point Reyes Seashore Lodge** (10021 Hwy. 1, 415/663-9000, www.pointreyesseashorelodge. com, $135–225) offers both budget and luxury lodging in its 23 guest rooms. Attractive floral patterns mix with clean white walls and attractive wooden accents. All guest rooms have private baths, some with whirlpool tubs, and a couple of suites with special amenities are located away from the main lodge for extra privacy. Outside, guests can enjoy the attractive gardens with winding brick pathways that roll out to Olema Creek. The Farm House Restaurant, Bar, and Deli adjoin the hotel, providing plenty of food and drink options for the tiny town of Olema.

For something a little quieter, the **Olema Druid's Hall** (9870 Shoreline Hwy./Hwy. 1, 415/663-8727, www.olemadruids.com, $185–385) has only three guest rooms and one cottage. Housed in the 1885 meeting hall of the Druids Association, the inn has a distinct architectural charm, and the surrounding gardens are sculpted with lush flower beds, stands of mature cypresses and pines, and green lawns. Despite the area's reputation for cool nights, you will keep warm with the inn's radiant floor heating while wrapped in the 300-thread-count sheets. Each of the guest rooms is decorated in a style that melds with the Victorian building but is modern enough for any discerning traveler. You can also expect to find a wood-burning fireplace, wireless Internet access, and a minibar. All guests can enjoy a complimentary continental breakfast comprised of local ingredients.

POINT REYES STATION

In Point Reyes Station, you can find a guest room and tasty board for a reasonable price at **One Mesa Bed & Breakfast** (1 Mesa Rd., 415/663-8866, www.onemesa.com, $147–189). All three guest rooms have private baths, down comforters, and feather beds, along with included all-day and all-night coffee service. Each guest room is decorated in a different style—most have fireplaces, some have soaking tubs, and all have TVs and VCRs. Guests can make use of the inn's hot tub and enjoy a self-service breakfast on weekdays and a basket of goodies delivered to your door on weekends.

In the heart of Point Reyes Station is the **Point Reyes Station Inn** (11591 Hwy. 1, 415/663-9372, www.pointreyesstationinn. com, $125–225). The five-room inn is light and airy with turn-of-the-20th-century charm. The guest rooms are decorated in heavy antique furnishings that are lightened by the vaulted ceilings, large windows, and glass doors leading to private porches. All but one have fireplaces and private en suite baths. There is a communal hot tub in the garden, and the continental breakfast features eggs from the inn's own chickens.

Lingonberry Farm B&B (12430 Hwy. 1, 415/663-1826, www.lingonberryfarm.com, $145–165) is outfitted in bright, simple Swedish style. Each of the guest rooms is distinctively decorated in blues, yellows, and crisp whites with trim farm-style furniture and minimalist artwork. All have private baths. Downstairs in the sunny dining area, guests are treated to a Swedish-style continental breakfast during the week and a full hot breakfast on weekends.

The reason to choose the far less quaint **Point Reyes Hostel** (1390 Limantour Spit Rd., 415/663-8811, www.norcalhostels.org/reyes, $24–120) is for what's next door: Located just off Limantour Road a few miles from the beach, the hostel is steps from fantastic hiking and lush natural scenery. Like most hostels, the accommodations are spare but comfortable. You can pick the überaffordable dorm rooms ($24) or opt for a private room ($82–120). The hostel has a communal kitchen and three lounge areas, furnished in furniture funky enough to fit in any college-age group house, and there is a place to lock up bicycles.

INVERNESS

Perhaps the most famous lodging around is ◖ **Manka's Inverness Lodge** (30 Callendar Way, 415/669-1034, www.mankas.com, $215–615). Partially burned down in 2006, the lodge has been rebuilt in the woodsy charm that has made it a favorite of Bay Area weekenders. But Manka's is not so much a lodge as a compound dressed in an oddly ethereal combination of hunting lodge and arts and crafts styles. Stay in the lodge, where four upstairs guest rooms are decked out with deep reading chairs, plush beds with tree-limb posts, and antique fixtures. Four similar guest rooms are in the Annex. Two cabins are nearby, and two others are perched on the Inverness Ridge to make the most of the views. All feature large sitting rooms complete with stone fireplaces. Some have private hot tubs or luxurious outdoor showers. Most have private decks overlooking the tree-covered hills. Two more modern lodgings can be found a few miles from the main compound hanging over the edge of Tomales Bay. The Boat House is akin to a small lushly appointed loft with two baths and multiple sleeping spaces. The smaller Boatman's Quarters has equally lovely views of the bay, a private deck, and a fireplace. As you would expect in such a carefully crafted lodge, there is an equally celebrated dining room that features a prix fixe multicourse dinner ($58).

Located in the center of the village of Inverness, **Ten Inverness Way** (10 Inverness Way, 415/669-1648, www.teninvernessway.com, $145–170) shares Manka's love of the Craftsman style but with considerably less ambition. The lodge itself is a 1904 craftsman building, and each of the five guest rooms is dressed in antiques and colorful quilts that border on country kitsch. Part of the true charm of the place is the way the building's coved ceilings, cute multipaned windows, and built-in benches add to the feeling of coziness. In each guest room, you'll also find a queen feather bed and a private bath. In the morning, enjoy coffee, a newspaper, and a full breakfast; evenings see complimentary wine and refreshments with the other guests.

Motel Inverness (12718 Sir Francis Drake Blvd., 415/236-1967, www.motelinverness.com, $99–190) sits handsomely on the bay. Constructed of natural wood with lovely and fanciful flourishes, Motel Inverness is more like a classic lodge than a typical motel. There are guest rooms or more spacious suites available with full kitchens, and all are decorated in light colors with striped bedspreads and minimal fuss. The parking lot abuts the entrance to each room, but the rooms open onto the breathtaking serenity of wetlands bordering the bay. Inside the main lodge is a grand lounge, where you can play pool on the antique pool table, read in front of the great stone fireplace, or relax with a glass of wine on the expansive deck.

Camping

While you would expect the Point Reyes area to abound in camping opportunities, finding a place to pitch a tent is a tall order. The only camping nearby is in the Point Reyes National Seashore (www.nps.gov/pore, 415/663-8054, reservations www.recreation.gov, $20), and all are hike-in sites that require reservations months in advance. All campsites have a pit toilet, a water faucet, a picnic table, a charcoal grill, and a food locker.

Sky Camp is the closest to the Bear Valley Visitors Center and is accessed via a trail on Limantour Road. The hike is a moderate 1.4 miles uphill, and the campground includes 11 individual sites and one group site. From its location, you'll get great views of the Pacific Ocean and Drake's Bay, provided it's not foggy.

Near the end of Limantour Road before the beach is the trailhead for the aptly named **Coast**

Camp. While not directly on the beach, the campground is in a quiet valley of coastal scrub and willow trees. There are 12 individual camp-sites and 2 group sites. There are two routes to get here: one that is 1.8 miles uphill along the Laguna and Firelane Trails, and the longer 2.7-mile Coast Trail route, which is flat and considerably easier for carrying camping gear.

The other coastal campground is **Wildcat Camp.** It has five individual sites and three group sites. Like Coast Camp, it is set away from the beach on an open bluff-top meadow. From Bear Valley it is a 5.5-mile hike or an easier but longer 6.7-mile stroll on the Coast Trail.

The most secluded campground is **Glen Camp.** Hidden deep within a valley and protected from ocean winds, the campground is a healthy 4.6 miles from the Bear Valley Trailhead. There are only five individual sites and no group sites, keeping this a quiet getaway.

Food
OLEMA
Attached to the Point Reyes Seashore Lodge, the **Farm House Restaurant and Bar** (10021 Hwy. 1, 415/663-1264, www.pointreyesseashore.com, 11:30 A.M.–9 P.M. Mon.–Thurs., 11:30 A.M.–10 P.M. Fri.–Sun., $12–29) is the oldest operating business in Olema. In the elegant bright dining room you can enjoy a pleasant range of fresh California cuisine. There is a heavy emphasis on seafood, as you would expect with so many great oyster farms and fishing waters nearby. There are a number of pasta dishes as well as meat-heavy plates such as pork chops, steaks, and roast chicken. You can also get a burger or other classic hot sandwiches if you are looking for a lighter and cheaper meal. There is also a bar menu that features specialty cocktails, locally brewed beer, and oysters prepared half a dozen different ways.

POINT REYES STATION
If you're seeking a rarified organic California meal, you are in the right town. The star of the Point Reyes Station restaurant scene is the ◖ **Station House Café** (11180 Hwy. 1, 415/663-1515, www.stationhousecafe.com, 8 A.M.–9 P.M. Thurs.–Tues., $12–21), which is both casual and upscale. Since 1974, long before "organic" and "local" were foodie credos, the Station House Café has been dedicated to serving food with ingredients that reflect the agrarian culture of the area. The restaurant still has to the same mission, and the food culture around Point Reyes has gotten even better, making the very reasonably priced California cuisine top-notch. More comfort food than haute cuisine, you'll find lots of familiar dishes and fantastic takes on old classics. Hint: The oyster stew is not to be missed. The dining room is open and unpretentious with large multipaned windows letting in tons of light. On the left side of the restaurant is a full bar, where bartenders deftly mix cocktails and pours beer and glasses of wine. There is also an outside patio dripping with wisteria.

Osterina Stellina (11285 Hwy. 1, 415/663-9988, http://osteriastellina.com, lunch 11:30 A.M.–2:30 P.M., dinner 5–9 P.M. Fri.–Wed., $15–44) has brought white-tablecloth dining to Point Reyes Station. The Italian eatery has plenty of local items on the menu prepared in a rustic yet elegant Mediterranean fashion. There are thin-crust pizzas, robust pastas with seafood and organic vegetables, and hearty main dishes of osso buco and saffron-buttered halibut. Lunch is a bit more scaled down, but not by much. The wine list is a nice blend of Italian and California wines. Nearly all are available by the glass, but for a price.

Right off Highway 1 along Tomales Bay is the unassuming **Point Reyes Vineyard** (12700 Hwy. 1, 415/663-1011, www.ptreyesvineyard-inn.com, noon–5 P.M. Sat.–Sun. mid-Nov.–May, noon–5 P.M. Fri.–Mon. June–mid-Nov., and by appointment). This small winery pours some surprisingly tasty vintages. Staff can tell you about the wines as well as direct you to their favorite local restaurants and recreation spots.

If you need a *real* drink (and a bit of local color), slip through the swinging doors of the **Old Western Saloon** (11201 Hwy. 1, 415/663-1661, daily 10 A.M.–2 A.M.). At this crusty old West Marin haunt you'll see ranchers yukking it up with park rangers, young and old, longtime natives, and recent transplants. It's the place where everyone goes, despite its divey appearance.

Traveling out of Point Reyes Station north along the bay, a stop at **Nick's Cove** (23240 Hwy. 1, 415/663-1033, www.nickscove.com, 11 A.M.–9 P.M. Mon.–Fri., 10 A.M.–9 P.M. Sat.–Sun. $14–29) may be in order. Overlooking the bay in an expansive weathered redwood building, Nick's Cove has recently been revamped. Its combination of charm, relaxed atmosphere, and good-quality classic American food with a slightly modern twist has made this a popular stop for folks passing though the area. The menu is well designed to accommodate all types of diners, from those who want a light nibble with their Bloody Mary to those eager for a high-end meal. Out back is a long deck and a boathouse, perfect to explore with the little ones.

There is no better place to stock a picnic basket than the **Bovine Bakery** (11315 Hwy. 1, 415/663-9420, 6:30 A.M.–5 P.M. Mon.–Fri., 7 A.M.–5 P.M. Sat.–Sun.), where you can pick up a cup of coffee, loaves of bread, and cookies.

Around the corner is **Cowgirl Creamery** (80 4th St., 415/663-9335, www.cowgirlcreamery. com, 10 A.M.–6 P.M. Wed.–Sun.), which produces the best cheese in the Bay Area. All of their cheese is made on-site in the French brie style. Tours of the facility are available Friday mornings by appointment only. At the retail shop inside, you can pick up a stinky but oh-so-good round of Red Hawk, the milder Mount Tam and Pierce Point, or the subtle and seasonal St. Pat's. The store also sells other gourmet treats, from jams to crackers and even pasta and some sandwiches.

The **Tomales Bay Oyster Co.** (15479 Hwy. 1, 415/663-1242, http://tomalesbayoysters.com, 9 A.M.–5 P.M. Mon.–Fri., 8 A.M.–5 P.M. Sat.–Sun.) is a low-key affair where you can buy a wide selection of oysters, clams, and mussels in an open air market a feet from the bay from where they are harvested. The smaller oysters tend to be sweeter, but the bigger, meatier ones better lend themselves to barbecuing. And if that is what you have in mind, you're in luck: Tomales Bay Oyster Company is set up with grills and picnic tables ready to host your oyster party. You can bring in whatever other food and drink you see fit, and an afternoon spent here is always a good time.

Dining around the Bay Area, you may have seen **Hog Island** (20215 Hwy. 1, 415/663-9218, www.hogislandoysters.com, daily 9 A.M.–5 P.M.) oysters appear on many upscale menus. They are the big boys in the oyster world around here and also have an open-air stand where you can buy and barbecue oysters. While they have excellent oysters, Hog Island gets insanely busy on weekends as many Bay Area folks come to get their raw-oyster fix. Parking can be tricky, and unless you get here really early, you'll have to wait to get a grill and picnic table.

INVERNESS

Vladimir's Czechoslovakian Restaurant (12785 Sir Francis Drake Blvd., 415/669-1021, noon A.M.–9 P.M. Tues.–Sun., prix fixe $27, cash only) is a favorite of both locals and visitors. Enter the cool old dining room, complete with stuffed deer heads on the walls, and take a seat. The late Vladimir, who owned the restaurant, could be rude one minute and the next hand you the best pint of beer you ever had. After his death, the restaurant went to his daughter, and the rest of his family still works here, so the atmosphere is the same. The mugs of beer are generous, and the kitchen produces a prix fixe meal of serious Czech food: borscht, rabbit, duck, and all manner of things that might seem heavy or strange to the American palate—but they're delicious. And for those not quite ready to brave Eastern European cuisine, the bar menu offers Americanized concessions such as burgers and quesadillas. Vladimir's is very serious about its no-children policy, which makes it a perfect retreat for romantic couples.

A great convenient coffee stop is the **Busy Bee Bakery** (12301 Sir Francis Drake Blvd., 415/663-9496, 7:30 A.M.–4 P.M. Mon. and Thurs.–Fri., 8 A.M.–5 P.M. Sat.–Sun.). This owner-run shop offers good espresso drinks, delectable home-made (in the back of the shop) pastries, and some lovely photo prints done by the owner.

Priscilla's (12781 Sir Francis Drake Blvd., 415/669-1244, 11 A.M.–8 P.M. Wed.–Mon., $9–16) doses out mainstream fare for very reasonable prices. The charming board-and-bat building also houses a gift store and the post office. The restaurant has an outdoor deck covered just enough to keep you from getting burned while enjoying a sunny afternoon. Both beer and wine are available, and the menu includes salads, hot sandwiches, and a couple of seafood specialties.

If you want some of the region's famed oysters, take a beautiful drive out to **Drakes Bay Oyster Co.** (17171 Sir Francis Drake Blvd., 415/669-1149, www.drakesbayoyster.com, daily 8:30 A.M.–4:30 P.M.), located in Point Reyes National Seashore. One of the agrarian businesses grandfathered into the park, the location of the farm, at the edge of Drake's Estero, is stunning and well worth the drive, and so are the oysters. They may be muddier than their Tomales Bay counterparts, but many argue that they are superior in flavor. This is a small-scale family operation with a few grills and picnic benches. The friendly staff will set you up with enough ice to ensure a spoil-free trip home.

Information and Services

The Point Reyes area tends toward the remote and charmingly rural—there's not much out in the wilderness here. You can get gas only in Point Reyes Station. There are full-service grocery stores in Point Reyes Station (Palace Market) and in Inverness (the aptly named Inverness store). For any other shopping needs, the biggest nearby towns are Novato and Petaluma. The tiny **West Marin Chamber of Commerce** (Point Reyes Station, 415/663-9232, www.pointreyes.org, 11 A.M.–4 P.M. Fri.–Sun.) can provide information on the region.

Cell phones do not work in most parts of Point Reyes National Seashore and the adjoining parklands. Check with your inn or hotel for information about Internet access. There is a **post office** (11260 Hwy. 1, 415/663-1305) in the town of Point Reyes Station, and the closest hospital is **Novato Community Hospital** (180 Rowland Way, Novato, 415/209-1300, www.novatocommunity.sutterhealth.org).

Getting There and Around

Point Reyes is only about an hour north of San Francisco by car, but getting here can be quite a drive for newcomers. From the Golden Gate Bridge, take U.S. 101 north to just south of San Rafael. Take the Sir Francis Drake Boulevard exit toward San Anselmo. Follow Sir Francis Drake Boulevard west for 20 miles to the small town of Olema and Highway 1. At the intersection with Highway 1, turn right (north) to Point Reyes Station and the Bear Valley Visitors Center.

A slower but more scenic route follows Highway 1 into Point Reyes National Seashore and provides access to the trails near Bolinas in the southern portion of the park. From the Golden Gate Bridge, take U.S. 101 north to the Mill Valley/Stinson Beach exit. Follow the road under the freeway, and when the road splits at the stoplight, turn left onto Shoreline Highway (Hwy. 1). Follow Shoreline Highway, and do not turn right onto Panoramic Highway, for almost 30 miles through Stinson Beach and past Bolinas Lagoon to the coast. From the lagoon, it's 11 miles north to Point Reyes Station. Expect twists, turns, and general slow going as you approach Point Reyes.

East Bay

The East Bay is unique not only because of its ethnic and economic diversity but for the way its divergent groups come together, making it feel like a true melting pot. In addition to the world-class University of California, Berkeley, the Oakland Museum of California gives the museums across the Bay a run for their money. Big music names are drawn to Berkeley's Greek Theater and Oakland's recently reopened Fox Theatre, and nearly every old neighborhood has a classic movie house showing art-house and foreign flicks, an erudite independent bookstore, and multiple cafés where you can hear patrons arguing over ideas big and small.

BERKELEY

There's no place quite like Berkeley. While the Haight in San Francisco nurtured the creative side of the 1960s flower children, Berkeley brought out their fire. The town has long been known for its radical, liberal, progressive activism. The youthful urban culture tends to revolve around the University of California, Berkeley. Yet well-heeled foodies also flock to town to sample some of the finest cuisine in Northern California.

University of California, Berkeley

Berkeley is a college town, and fittingly the University of California, Berkeley (www.berkeley.edu) offers the most interesting places to go and things to see. If your visit to the area includes your teenagers, think about taking a free guided campus tour (510/642-5215, www.berkeley.edu, 10 A.M. Mon.–Sat., 1 P.M. Sun., by reservation only) to acquaint them with the university and all it has to offer. To get a great view of the campus from above, take an elevator ride up the **Campanile** (10 A.M.–3:45 P.M. Mon.–Fri., 10 A.M.–4:45 P.M. Sat., 10 A.M.–1:30 P.M. and 3–5 P.M. Sun., adults $2, seniors

and ages 4–17 $1, under age 4 free), formally called Sather Tower. If you prefer, you can wander around campus on your own, discovering the halls where students live and learn; the newly renovated stadium, which is listed in the National Register of Historic Places; and architectural details such as Sather Gate and South Hall, built in 1873. Or stop in at the **Lawrence Hall of Science** (1 Centennial Dr., 510/642-5132, www.lawrencehallofscience.org, daily 10 A.M.–5 P.M., adults $12, seniors and students $9, ages 3–6 $60, under age 3 free) for a look at the latest exhibits and interactive displays.

Also on campus is the **University of California Botanical Garden** (end of Centennial Dr., 510/643-2755, http://botanicalgarden.berkeley.edu, adults $10, seniors $8, ages 13–17 $5, ages 5–12 $2, free under age 5, daily 9 A.M.–5 P.M.), an immense space with an astounding array of wild plants from around the world. Botany buffs love to spend hours in this place, studying and examining plants outdoors, in the greenhouses, and in the arid house (a habitat for plants requiring extremely hot and dry conditions). Others just come to amble through the peaceful plantings and perhaps stop to sniff a flower or two. You can see over 1,000 different kinds of sunflowers, nearly 2,500 types of cacti, thousands of native California plants, and hundreds of rare and endangered plants collected from around the world.

Entertainment and Events

There's a reasonable variety of evening entertainment to be had in Berkeley. The major regional theater is the **Berkeley Repertory Theatre** (2025 Addison St., 510/647-2949, www.berkeleyrep.org, Tues.–Sun., $27–69). Appropriate to its hometown, the Berkeley Rep puts on several unusual shows, from world premieres of edgy new works to totally different

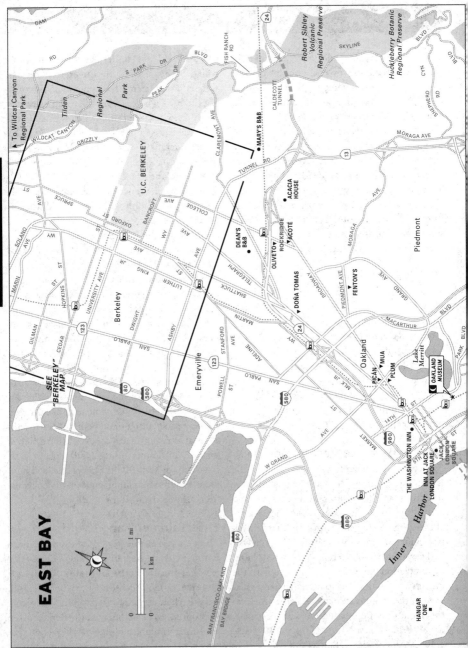

EAST BAY

To Wildcat Canyon Regional Park

SEE "BERKELEY" MAP

1 mi

1 km

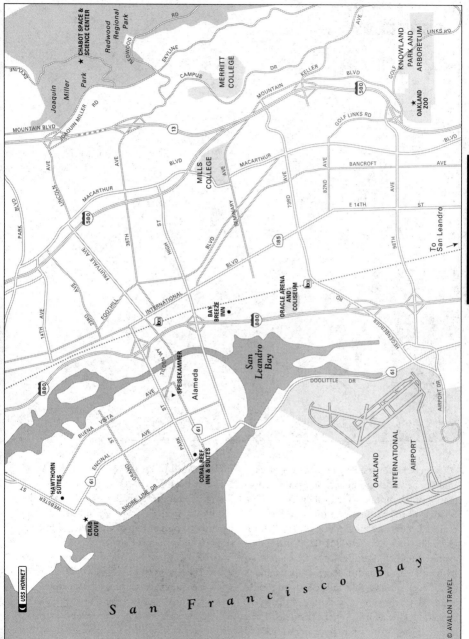

© AVALON TRAVEL

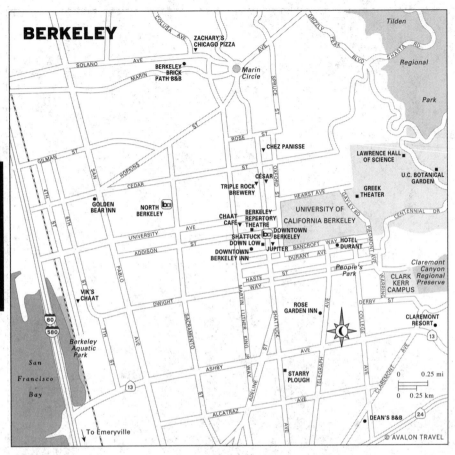

© AVALON TRAVEL

takes on old favorites. Recent offerings have included a new adaptation of *Figaro* and a performance of the hit one-woman show *No Child*.

Some of the best entertainment in Berkeley is at its live music venues. The **Starry Plough** (3101 Shattuck Ave., 510/841-0282, www.starryploughpub.com, daily 4 P.M.–2 A.M.) is an Irish pub with a smallish stage setup. Fabulous Celtic rock groups, folk musicians, and indie bands play here almost every day of the week. Despite lacking a formal dance floor, dedicated fans find ways to create an impromptu space to move to their favorite bands. Every Wednesday

night instead of music you'll find the famed Berkeley Poetry Slam—there's nothing like it. Hungry music and spoken-word fans can order a full meal from the kitchen, while the thirsty can quaff a pint or two of Guinness while they sit back and watch the stage.

In Berkeley, the big-name acts come to the **Greek Theater** (2001 Gayley Rd., 800/745-3000, www.apeconcerts.com). This outdoor amphitheater, constructed in the classic Greek style, sits on the UC Berkeley campus. Expect to see top-tier performers playing the Greek, including artists such as Paul Simon, Primus, and Spearhead.

© ELIZABETH LINHART MONEY

Sather Gate at UC Berkeley

For a slightly less formal outing, Berkeley has any number of bars and clubs that offer DJs, dancing, or just a quiet drink. **The Shattuck Down Low Lounge** (2284 Shattuck Ave., 510/455-4735, www.shattuckdownlow.com, daily 9 P.M.–2 A.M.) is a big dance club that often has live musical acts to get the audience up and moving. The bar serves up cocktails, wine, and beer, and there's plenty of room to sit when you're tired and have a drink or two.

At **Jupiter** (2181 Shattuck Ave., 510/843-8277, www.jupiterbeer.com, 11:30 A.M.–1 A.M. Mon.–Thurs., 11:30 A.M.–1:30 A.M. Fri., noon–1:30 A.M. Sat., noon–midnight Sun.), your evening out can include excellent wood-fired pizzas and a wide selection of locally brewed beer. This bistro and nightspot features an outdoor beer garden where jazz ensembles play or cool DJs spin the night away.

Shopping

Berkeley's citizens grow fierce at the very thought of big chain stores invading their precious downtown area. A few have succeeded, but you'll still find a variety of funky independent shops on **Telegraph Avenue** (between the UC campus and Parker Ave.). One of the best bookstores in the area is **Shakespeare & Co.** (2499 Telegraph Ave., 510/841-8916, http://shakespeareandcobooks.tumblr.com, 10 A.M.–8 P.M. Mon.–Thurs., 10 A.M.–9 P.M. Fri.–Sat., 11 A.M.–8 P.M. Sun.). This new-and-used store definitely has an old-school vibe, complete with the dust and the semi-organized shelves and the musty smell. True bibliophiles can spend hours browsing for treasures.

Moe's Books (2476 Telegraph Ave., 510/849-2087, http://moesbooks.com, daily 10 A.M.–10 P.M.) is another Berkeley institution. Also a new-and-used bookstore, Moe's has a newer vibe, including a online retail presence, with lots of hip up-to-date titles. Moe's also attracts literary talent to read and give talks for its regular active reading series. If you drop in on a

© ELIZABETH JANG

The Gardener features beautifully crafted home and garden treasures.

random Thursday you may get to see Jonathan Lethem, Dave Eggers, or Lawrence Ferlinghetti.

A shopping experience in Berkeley just wouldn't be complete without a quick browse inside a head shop. At **Hi Times** (2374 Telegraph Ave., 510/486-0988, 11 A.M.–8 P.M. Mon.–Sat., 11 A.M.–7 P.M. Sun.), employees tend to be friendly and attentive, so feel free to ask for whatever you need. **Annapurna** (2416 Telegraph Ave., 510/841-6187, 10 A.M.–9 P.M. Sun.–Thurs., 10 A.M.–10 P.M. Fri.–Sat.) is the oldest head shop in Berkeley, offering an array of different items including adult toys, posters, T-shirts, vaporizers, and grinders.

Clothing stores run to funky foreign stuff, like the apparel sold in **Kathmandu Imports** (2515 Telegraph Ave., 510/665-8970, 11 A.M.–6 P.M. Mon.–Sat., noon–6:30 P.M. Sun.), which specializes in Tibetan arts and crafts. Secondhand stores such as **Mars Mercantile** (2398 Telegraph Ave., 510/843-6711, daily 11 A.M.–7 P.M.) are another option.

While it bills itself as a vintage store, the selection actually feels more like a downscale thrift shop. The provocative window displays lure shoppers inside, where a few solid basic items can be had for reasonable prices.

In true Berkeley fashion, the best Berkeley shopping mall is the revitalized **4th Street** between Delaware Street and University Avenue. Here in this once-shady part of town, scores of stores have set up shop and have created a slightly upscale shopping district. You won't find much in the way of large national chains (except for Anthropologie and Crate and Barrel), but there are also smaller retailers like Sur La Table and Papyrus. **The Gardener** (1836 4th St., 510/548-4545, www.thegardener.com, 10 A.M.–6 P.M. Mon.–Sat., 11 A.M.–6 P.M. Sun.) stocks inspired treasures for your home and garden, including beautifully crafted gardening tools, salad bowls made from unique and reclaimed wood, luscious soaps, and sweet knickknacks to beautify your home. For a bit of whimsy, step into **Castle in the Air** (1805 4th St., 510/204-9801, www.castleintheair. biz, 10 A.M.–6 P.M. Mon.–Sat., 11 A.M.–6 P.M. Sun.) for specialty pens, stationery, and notebooks as well as quirky gifts, cards, and art books. **Books Inc.** (1760 4th St., 510/525-7777, 9:30 A.M.–7 P.M. Sun.–Thurs., 9:30 A.M.–8 P.M. Fri.–Sat.) is the local independent bookstore, with special events and readings many nights.

Sports and Recreation
TILDEN REGIONAL PARK
Tilden Regional Park (Grizzly Peak Blvd., 888/327-2757, www.ebparks.org, daily 5 A.M.–10 P.M.) covers the ridge directly above Berkeley. Within its more than 2,000 acres, the park has a celebrated botanical garden, the swimmable Lake Anza and its sandy beaches, an antique carousel, and miniature steam trains, perfect to thrill the little ones. But aside from the attractions, Tilden also offers scores

of hiking and mountain biking trails that, except for the breathtaking views of the Bay Area, almost convince you that you are in absolute wilderness. And while this isn't really wilderness, taking a trail map is advisable, as multiple trails crisscross one another, allowing for more adventure but also potential confusion.

For a simple stroll, consider taking the **Jewel Lake Nature Trail** (1 mile, easy). Located in the Nature Area of the park, generally a quiet area where no dogs are allowed, you'll need to park at the trailhead at the intersection of Central Park Drive and Canon Drive, near the Little Farm and Environmental Education Center. From the parking lot, the trail heads north along Wildcat Creek and out to Jewel Lake. You won't gain much elevation, and although there are exposed patches, the trail is mostly lush and leafy, surrounded by bay laurels, blackberries, and buckeye trees.

For a more rigorous climb, the **Wildcat Peak**

© ELIZABETH LINHART MONEY

Miniature steam trains are one of the treasures found in Tilden Regional Park.

SAN FRANCISCO BAY AREA

Loop (3.5 miles, moderate) leaves from the same trailhead behind the Environmental Education Center. Take **Laurel Canyon Trail** through eucalypti and California bay laurels up through the canyon, which is a gentle grade most of the way. The trail then turns left toward the Rotary Peace Grove and on to Wildcat Peak (1,211 feet). From the stony vista, you'll be able to see the Golden Gate Bridge, San Pablo Bay, and Mount Diablo, depending on which direction you're facing. To get back down the mountain, take **Wildcat Peak Trail** for about one mile. You'll hit **Jewel Lake Nature Trail.** Turn left, and it will take you back to the trailhead.

If you want to spend some time on the **Bay Area Ridge Trail** (3.5 miles, moderate), a pleasant loop starts at the Quarry Trailhead off Wildcat Canyon Road. Take **Wildcat Canyon Trail** to **Seaview Trail** and turn right. After some time, the trail changes names to **East Bay Skyline National Trail** and **Bay Area Ridge Trail.** At **Big Springs Trail,** take a right back down the mountain. You'll come to a parking lot, but the trail continues on the other side. After nearly one mile, take a left on **Quarry Trail;** it will take you back to the parking lot.

Tilden offers a great many roads and trails for cyclists. The paved roads snaking through the park (Wildcat Canyon Rd., Grizzly Peak Blvd., and South Park Dr.) twist and turn while gaining and losing enough elevation to keep any cyclist busy. As for mountain biking, many of the big trails are shared with hikers. The Bay Area Ridge, Meadows Canyon, and Big Springs Trails are some of the most popular.

WILDCAT CANYON REGIONAL PARK
North of Tilden, the equally large Wildcat Canyon Regional Park (5755 Mcbryde Ave., Richmond, 510/544-3092, www.ebparks.org, daily sunrise–sunset) is filled with wide fire roads, all of which are open to cyclists. **Nimitz Way** is a paved trail along the ridgeline that is popular with cyclists young and old. **Harvey**

Canyon Trail is a single-track trail also open to cyclists that descends from Nimitz Way down to Wildcat Creek. The only significant restriction for cyclists is that access via the south end of the park is only through the Tilden Nature Area, which allows limited bicycle access. The only route from the south starts at the Little Farm and Environmental Education Center. Bicycles are only permitted on Loop Road, which at Jewel Lake connects with Wildcat Creek Trail.

Wildcat Canyon has fewer trails than Tilden, but it is quieter, and the trails traverse a more challenging topography and allow for longer treks. A healthy loop (7 miles, moderate–strenuous) that allows you to see most of the park and some ridge-top views begins at the Alvarado Trailhead at the north end of the park. Start by taking **Wildcat Creek Trail** to **Harvey Canyon Trail,** which ascends sharply to the ridge. At the top you'll come to the paved **Nimitz Way.** After nearly one mile, continue straight (Nimitz Way veers slightly right) on **San Pablo Ridge Trail** until **Belgium Trail,** and turn left. This trail leads back down to the trailhead.

Accommodations
UNDER $100
Offering great value for surprisingly low rates, the **Golden Bear Inn** (1620 San Pablo Ave., 510/525-6770, www.goldenbearinn.com, $90) has myriad small unique touches that make it special among budget motels. A family-friendly place, parents can rent an inexpensive guest room with two twin beds in a separate bedroom, providing privacy and relaxation for everyone. There is even a cottage available ($150) that has two bedrooms, a living room, and a full kitchen for those looking for a longer stay. Cute guest rooms are nicely decorated and have TVs and wireless Internet access. Restaurants and attractions cluster comfortably nearby.

$100-150
The **Downtown Berkeley Inn** (2001 Bancroft Way, 510/843-4043, www.

downtownberkeleyinn.com, $110) brings the inn concept into the city. The location, exterior, and guest room design all mimic the urban style that defines downtown Berkeley. Guest rooms boast top amenities, such as high-end beds and 42-inch plasma TVs. If you're out till the wee hours, pull the blackout drapes and sleep in.

$150-250

Mary's Bed and Breakfast (47 Alvarado Rd., 510/848-1431, weekend 2-day minimum, $150) feels a bit like a tropical resort with its rattan furnishing and light, airy decor. Mary's offers three guest rooms with a deluxe continental breakfast each morning in the dining room. An apartment is also available by the week or the month. In the Claremont district of south Berkeley, Mary's is within walking distance to the Claremont Hotel's spa and restaurant as well as the neighborhood's posh restaurants and shops.

The **Rose Garden Inn** (2740 Telegraph Ave., 510/549-2145, www.rosegardeninn.com, Sat. 2-night minimum, $155–210) is a large rambling structure with 40 guest rooms and gorgeous rose bushes (don't worry—the bushes are not inside the guest rooms). If you come in the spring, take the time to stroll in the lush gardens and smell the pungent jasmine. Guest rooms are decorated in floral themes, many with light wood, white wicker, and other cute garden cottage–style touches. All guest rooms have private baths and TVs, and a hearty buffet breakfast is included.

Book a room at the **Berkeley Brick Path Bed & Breakfast** (1805 Marin Ave., 510/524-4277, www.thebrickpath.com, $170–215). The garden is the pride of this inn, and you can stroll down the namesake brick path among the lush greenery and gorgeous flowers, take a seat out on the patio to enjoy your breakfast, or sip an afternoon glass of wine in the gazebo. Each of the three guest rooms has a unique style: one with a brick fireplace, one with a huge whirlpool tub, and the East-West cottage with a full kitchen and private entrance.

The **Hotel Durant** (2600 Durant St., 510/845-8981, www.hoteldurant.com, $220) has it all: location, location, views, and location. If you can, get a guest room on the upper floors to take in a view of Oakland, San Francisco, or the Bay. From the lobby, you can walk to the university, Telegraph Avenue, and the Elmwood shopping district.

Since 1915, the **Claremont Resort and Spa** (41 Tunnel Rd., 510/843-3000, www.claremontresort.com, $180–280) has catered to rich and famous East Bay visitors. No two of the 279 elegantly furnished guest rooms look quite the same, so you'll have a unique experience even in this large resort hotel. The guest rooms may be plush, but the real focus at the Claremont is fitness and pampering. A full-fledged health club, complete with yoga, Pilates, and spinning classes, takes up part of the huge complex. And the full-service spa, which offers all the current popular body treatments plus aesthetic services, finds favor with visitors and locals alike.

Food
CASUAL DINING

A downscale ethnic enclave that is well worth a visit is the **Chaat Café** (1902 University Ave., 510/845-1431, www.chaatcafes.com, 11:30 A.M.9 P.M. Sun.–Thurs., 11:30 A.M.–9:30 P.M. Fri.–Sat., $10) offers spicy Indian cuisine for the right price. This local Bay Area chain serves *chaat* (small plates and appetizers), of course, and you can also get a meaty curry, a tandoori dish, stuffed naan, and more. Although you'll find a few vegetarian specialties on the menu, this particular Indian place sticks more to the meat-eating tradition.

For Indian food with plenty of veggie options, **Viks Chaat** (2390 4th St., 510/644-4432, www.vikschaatcorner.com, 11 A.M.–6 P.M. Mon.–Thurs., 11 A.M.–8 P.M. Fri.–Sat., $12) has been a Berkeley mainstay for nearly 20 years. You'll find plenty of authentic

Indian street food, including *dosas,* flat *papdis* topped with potatoes and chutney, and puffed puri filled with mint water, garbanzo beans, and tamarind.

Thin-crust wood-fired pizzas are all the rage among Bay Area foodies, but a trip to the north end of Berkeley to savor **Zachary's Chicago Pizza** (1853 Solano Ave., 510/525-5950, www. zacharys.com, 11 A.M.–9:30 P.M. Sun.–Thurs., 11 A.M.–10:30 P.M. Fri.–Sat., $20) is well worth the effort. Their deep-dish cornmeal crust pies come with the standard Italian toppings (pepperoni, sausage, green peppers, mushrooms), or you can opt for the more inventive offerings such as barbecue chicken and Mexican chorizo. But don't worry, all pizzas come slathered in tomato sauce to complete the authentic Chicago style. You can even get a thin-crust pizza, if that is what truly calls to you. Be aware that this small old-school pizzeria fills up quickly, especially on weekend nights. Luckily, if there is a long wait, you can put in your order when you put in your name. Your pizza might make it to your table as you finally sit down to eat.

To get a flavor of the Berkeley college and family scenes, grab a table at north Berkeley's **Triple Rock Brewery** (1920 Shattuck Ave., 510/843-2739, http://triple-rock.com, 11:30 A.M.–1 A.M. Mon.–Wed., 11:30 A.M.–2 A.M. Thurs.–Sat., 11:30 A.M.–midnight Sun., $9). Like all good Northern California brewpubs, you can pick from an ever-evolving menu of beer that includes seasonal specialties and favorites ranging from the light Pinnacle Pale Ale to the heavy Stonehenge Stout. And like all great brewpubs in the region, the food is not only exceptional, it is also made from local and organic ingredients. You'll find juicy free-range burgers, a great reuben sandwich featuring beer-braised corned beef, and a variety of hand-cut fries. The interior has the charm of a seasoned pub with a well-worn wood bar, low lighting, large windows, and a rooftop beer garden.

FINE DINING

The very best fine-dining venue, and Alice Waters's baby, is ◖ **Chez Panisse** (1517 Shattuck Ave., restaurant 510/548-5525, café 510/548-5049, www.chezpanisse.com, restaurant prix fixe $55–85, café $19–25). If you plan to dine in the restaurant at Chez Panisse, you need to make your reservations early and possibly plan your entire trip to Berkeley around the date on which you get a table. You can make a dinner reservation up to one month in advance. And no, we're not exaggerating. You should try to get a reservation at French Laundry if you think this is ridiculous. The desk takes phone calls 9 A.M.–9:30 P.M. Monday–Saturday and a $25 deposit is required. You'll get the chance to enjoy some of the best cuisine that's ever graced a plate in Berkeley or anywhere else. Waters and her successors create French-California dishes at the cutting edge of current trends—Waters doesn't follow trends, she sets them.

Upstairs, the café offers food that's a bit more casual but just as good as the rarified dining room downstairs. It's much easier to get a reservation in the bustling, energetic café than the restaurant, and the casual atmosphere is less intimidating for diners who are new to all this California haute cuisine excess.

Also in north Berkeley, **César** (1515 Shattuck Ave., 510/883-0222, http://cesarberkeley.com, daily noon–midnight, $30) is a refreshingly modern tapas bar started by three Chez Panisse alumni. As tapas implies, the menu is geared toward small-plate Spanish cuisine, but many of the dishes, such as lamb chops with lentils and steak with caramelized red onions, plus all the *bocadillos* (fresh Spanish-style sandwiches), could stand in for a modest entrée. The bright indoor-outdoor space also lends itself to enjoying one of the many Spanish and California wines or classic and inventive collection of cocktails.

Information and Services

Newcomers to Berkeley can start at the

© NORA JANG

the leafy entrance to Chez Panisse

Visitors Information Center (2030 Addison St., 510/549-7040, http://visitberkeley.com, 9 A.M.–5 P.M. Mon.–Fri.). You can read about the goings on in Berkeley in the *Daily Californian* and the fledgling *Berkeley Times,* published once a week. For live entertainment listings and reviews, check out the free *East Bay Express,* also published once a week.

As a major metropolitan area, you'll find most services you need in Berkeley. ATMs for major banks appear on Shattuck and Telegraph Avenues, and near all the major heavily trafficked areas. Just be wary using ATMs, especially after dark. There are two convenient **post offices** (1521 Shattuck Ave.; 2515 Durant Ave.).

For medical assistance, the **Alta Bates Summit Medical Center** (2450 Ashby Ave., 510/204-4444, www.altabatessummit.org) has a 24-hour emergency room.

Getting There and Around

Berkeley is north of Oakland and Alameda along the east side of the San Francisco Bay. If you're driving into Berkeley, take the Bay Bridge from San Francisco, then turn north onto I-580/I-80. Major roads in town include San Pablo, Ashby, Shattuck, Telegraph, and University Avenues. Be warned that parking in Berkeley can be a bona fide nightmare. If you're visiting for the day or for an evening show, consider taking the BART train to avoid the parking hassle.

BART (www.bart.gov, $1.75–5 one-way) is a major form of transit in and around the Bay Area. The Downtown Berkeley station is located underneath Shattuck Avenue in the heart of Berkeley. Other stations in the city include North Berkeley, Ashby, and Rockridge.

The closest airport is **Oakland International Airport** (OAK, 1 Airport Dr., Oakland, 510/563-3300, www.flyoakland.com). From the Oakland airport, you can rent a car, catch a cab, or take the AirBART shuttle from the terminals to the BART Colesium/Airport station. If you fly into San Francisco, you can take BART from the airport across the Bay to Berkeley.

OAKLAND AND ALAMEDA

The view across the Bay from San Francisco includes both Oakland and Alameda. Oakland is the biggest city in the East Bay, and although its reputation hasn't always been perfect (and travelers should probably stay in the popular visitor areas), today a great deal of downtown urban renewal has made it a visitor-friendly place with plenty of attractions, accommodations, and good food.

Long ago, Alameda grew up around its naval base, providing a residential community for sailors, their families, and support businesses. The base closed in the 1990s, but the quiet, pleasant community remains.

◖ Oakland Museum

The Oakland Museum of California (1000 Oak St., Oakland, 510/318-8400, www.museumca. org, 11 A.M.–5 P.M. Wed.–Sun., adults $12, students and seniors $9, children $6, parking $1 per hour) has undergone a renovation that has launched it into the stratosphere of must-see museums. Its uniquely multidisciplinary approach tells California's story through art, history, and science. Within its modernist concrete walls you'll be able to see Thiebaud's and Diebenkorn's take on the urban California landscape, a rare and authentic Ohlone basket, home furnishings from elite homes of California's early days, and a casting of a once-endemic mastodon. The museum also hosts special theme-based exhibits that compliment its three-pronged approach. You may stumble into one celebrating the social consciousness of street art, a video installation exploring life as a black man in the United States, or retrospectives of the comic-book artist Daniel Clowes or the jewelry maker Margaret de Patta. While it

OAKLAND MUSEUM OF CALIFORNIA, 2012

Oakland Museum

may seem that anything goes at the Oakland Museum, the one caveat is that it must somehow reflect the character of California. Like all good museums, this one has a café, the Blue Oak, which serves wine, espresso, and a selection of salads and sandwiches.

Chabot Space and Science Center

One of the most spectacular sights in the East Bay, Chabot Space and Science Center (10000 Skyline Blvd., Oakland, 510/336-7300, www.chabotspace.org, 10 A.M.–5 P.M. Tues.–Thurs., 10 A.M.–10 P.M. Fri.–Sat., 10 A.M.–5 P.M. Sun. summer, 10 A.M.–5 P.M. Wed.–Thurs., 10 A.M.–10 P.M. Fri.–Sat., 10 A.M.–5 P.M. Sun. fall–spring, adults $16, students and seniors $13, youths $12) makes science and space super cool. Up in the Oakland Hills, the Chabot complex includes observatories, a planetarium, a museum, and the Megadome theater, all open to the public (most Bay Area observatory telescopes are private). Unlike the other science museums in the area, which focus mainly on life on earth, Chabot focuses on the life *of* earth and the rest of the universe. You and your family can create your own solar system in an interactive exhibit, ride a space shuttle in the Megadome, and check out Saturn's rings through the telescopes. If your visit runs long, grab a bite to eat and a cup of coffee at the on-site Celestial Café.

Oakland Zoo

For a day with creatures of the land, go to the Oakland Zoo (9777 Golf Links Rd., Oakland, 510/632-9525, www.oaklandzoo.org, daily 10 A.M.–4 P.M., adults $13.75, youths and seniors $9.75, under age 2 free), where you'll discover an astounding 660 different types of amphibians, mammals, reptiles, and birds living in humane and well-maintained enclosures around the lush and beautiful grounds. There are children's rides, including a carousel, a roller coaster, and a train to keep the excitement high.

If you prefer sealife, head for the **Crab Cove Visitors Center** (1252 McKay Ave., Alameda, 510/544-3178, www.ebparks.org, 10 A.M.–4 P.M. Wed.–Sun., parking $5) in Alameda. Find out what the Bay looks like from the fish's perspective, say hello to the world under the sea, or take a peek at the exhibit on local Alameda history.

◖ USS *Hornet*

Military historians, ghost hunters, and swing dancers meet aboard the USS *Hornet* museum (Ferry Point, Alameda, 510/521-8448, www.uss-hornet.org, daily 10 A.M.–4 P.M., adults $15, students, seniors, and military $12, children $5, under age 4 free) moored at the former naval base in Alameda. Small by comparison to modern aircraft carriers, the *Hornet* doesn't seem so small when you stand on the hangar deck staring at the half dozen planes and helicopters on display. Several open decks reveal what cramped steel-clad life was like aboard the Constitution-class carriers. Bring a map; it's easy to get lost in the mazelike lower decks. Claustrophobic visitors can spend their time up on the flight deck or touring the island, imagining what it must have been like to experience the stress and action of one plane launching from the carrier every 45 seconds all day long.

The *Hornet* is reputed to be one of the most haunted structures in the Bay Area, with the ghosts of sailors who lost their lives on duty floating through their favorite spots aboard ship. Most ghost activity seems to occur at night, and overnight visits and flashlight tours are available (check the website for dates and times). Finally, the *Hornet* acts as a local dance hall and event center for Alameda, hosting swing dance soirees and holiday parties on a regular basis.

Entertainment and Events

Ballroom dancers from all around the Bay Area gather in Oakland on a regular basis to attend the famous **Ye Gaskell Occasional Dance**

© ELIZABETH LINHART MONEY

the USS *Hornet* docked in Alameda

Society ball (1547 Lakeside Dr., Oakland, www.gaskellball.com, check website for schedule, $20). This fabulous fancy-dress event encourages everybody to wear their finest (from any era from 1800 through today, but Victorian is encouraged) to create a picture of beauty swirling around the dance floor. You don't need to be an accomplished dancer to enjoy Gaskell's: Dance classes are offered during the afternoon before the ball, and a quick brushup takes place before the official opening dance—always a Viennese waltz.

If you prefer a more modern beat to dance to, you can find some good live music and dancing in Oakland. Perhaps the best-known venue is **Yoshi's** (510 Embarcadero W., Oakland, 510/238-9200, www.yoshis.com, 5:30–9 P.M. Mon.–Thurs., 5:30–10 P.M. Fri.–Sat., 5–9 P.M. Sun., shows daily 8 P.M. and 10 P.M.). With a sushi restaurant in one room and the legendary jazz club next door, it's possible to enjoy the sushi without attending the concert, or

vice versa. If you're a dinner patron, it's a very good idea to make reservations for the show and claim a seat before you sit down for your meal. Performers at Yoshi's have included Otis Taylor and Kurt Elling.

The renovated **Fox Theater** (1807 Telegraph Ave., 510/302-2250, www.thefoxoakland. com) attracts big names to this city landmark. Originally opened in 1928 and closed for nearly 40 years, it was designed in the Moorish style in favor during the decade of the flapper. The theater is now in league with some of the more venerated venues across the Bay like the Filmore, Warfield, and Great American Music Hall. Recent acts in this relatively intimate venue have included Tenacious D, Death Cab for Cutie, and Rufus Wainwright. It also has a bar and café where you can get champagne to go with your fish tacos.

Luka's Taproom & Lounge (2221 Broadway, Oakland, 510/451-4677, www.lukasoakland. com, 11:30 A.M.–midnight Mon.–Wed.,

11:30 A.M.–2 A.M. Thurs.–Fri., 5:30 P.M.–2 A.M. Sat., 11 A.M.–midnight Sun.) is a restaurant during the day and early evening, then becomes a lounge and dance club with a full bar after the sun sets. With a separate room for DJs and dancing, another space that serves as a full-on pool room with a 45-playing jukebox, and the Taproom with its brasserie-style food and 16 beers on tap, almost everyone can find something to enjoy at Luka's.

A bit more high-minded is the art house and lounge **Era Art Bar** (19 Grand Ave., Oakland, 510/832-4400, www.oaklandera.com, 4:30 P.M.–1:30 A.M. Tues.–Fri., 9 P.M.–1:30 A.M. Sat., cover charge Mon.–Fri. $5, Sat.–Sun. $10). With a big emphasis on style, Era Art Bar is carefully crafted with modern and antique furnishings, blown-glass chandeliers, and rotating art shows. Its cocktails follow the modern fashion of unique spirits combined with fresh ingredients. The evenings are usually booked with DJs, live music, and unusual acts.

If you just want a beer, head downtown to **The Trappist** (460 8th St., Oakland, 510/238-8900, www.thetrappist.com, noon–midnight Sun.–Thurs., noon–1 A.M. Fri.–Sat.). There are no fancy cocktails, just excellent Belgian brews along with loads of local microbrews and fantastic gastropub fare. The Trappist also hosts events, but they tend to be geared toward all things beer.

Out in Alameda, you'll find some nightlife at the **Lost Weekend Lounge** (2320 Santa Clara Ave., Alameda, 510/523-4700, 9 A.M.–2 A.M. Mon.–Fri., 5:30 P.M.–2 A.M. Sat., 11 A.M.–midnight Sun.). This beloved dive bar has everything a local haunt should have: cheap, heavily poured drinks, occasional live music, a smoking patio, and a juke box. Nearby, **Lucky 13** (1301 Park St., 510/523-2118, www.lucky13alameda.com, daily 11:30 A.M.–2 A.M.) has a decidedly more hipster vibe. There are plenty of great beers on tap and plenty of upper-crust spirits. The red-lit interior gives an "insiders club" feel, while a beer garden, awesome juke box, and black-and-white photo booth also add to the fun.

To get to the source of it all, visit **Hangar One Vodka** (2601 Monarch St., Alameda Point, Alameda, 510/769-1601, www.hangarone.com, noon–7 P.M. Wed.–Sat., noon–5 P.M. Sun.) tasting room. Look out over the view of San Francisco Bay as you sip the vodkas named for the building in which they are created; they'll surprise you with their elegance and variety.

Shopping

Jack London Square (www.jacklondonsquare.com), down on Oakland's surprisingly pretty waterfront, is a bustling crowd of visitors and locals who've come to eat, catch a movie, and shop. The absolute best time to shop is during the weekly farmers market (9 A.M.–2 P.M. Sun.). In addition to picking up great local food, including bread, pastries, fruits, and vegetables, you can enjoy cooking demonstrations, live music, and free yoga on the green.

For more local specialized shops with a neighborhood feel, head to **Rockridge** (College Ave. between Alcatraz Ave. and 51st St., Oakland). Foodies will want to explore epicurean **Rockridge Market Hall** (5655 College Ave., 510/250-6000, http://rockridgemarkethall.com, 9 A.M.–8 P.M. Mon.–Fri., 9 A.M.–7 P.M. Sat., 10 A.M.–6 P.M. Sun.), where multiple gourmet shops share one roof. Inside the brick building, you'll find a coffee roaster, a bakery, a fresh pasta shop, a fish market, a butcher, wine, and flowers. Every store is known for its adherence to the "eat local" ethos and for its quality. Nearby, bookworms can get their fix at well-regarded and independent **Diesel Bookstore** (5433 College Ave., 510/653-9965, www.dieselbookstore.com, 10 A.M.–9 P.M. Mon.–Thurs., 10 A.M.–10 P.M. Fri.–Sat., 10 A.M.–6 P.M. Sun.). And if you're looking for some quirky gifts to take home or a little something to add to your home, **Rockridge Home** (5418 College Ave., 510/420-1928, www.rockridgehome.com, daily 11 A.M.–8 P.M.) has something for everyone. You can find colorful paper lanterns, a French press coffeemaker, and deluxe skin treatments to turn you bathroom into a mini spa. The Rockridge area boasts a number of fantastic places to eat, but if you need a quick stop to refuel, **Bittersweet** (5427 College Ave., Oakland, 510/654-7159, http://bittersweetcafe.com, 8 A.M.–7 P.M. Mon.–Wed., 8 A.M.–9 P.M. Thurs.–Fri., 9 A.M.–9 P.M. Sat., 9 A.M.–7 P.M. Sun.) sells cups of rich and velvety hot chocolate.

The **Piedmont Avenue District** is an old Oakland neighborhood with a historic movie theater and mom-and-pop stores. **Phillipa Roberts Jewelry** (4176 Piedmont Ave., 510/655-0656, www.philipparoberts. com, 10 A.M.–6 P.M. Mon.–Sat.) is a charming jewelry and gift store owned and operated by a local jewelry maker. While she stocks an eclectic assortment of housewares and gifts, her handmade jewelry, made largely from silver and semiprecious stones in simple elegant designs,

are the real treat. If you are into fiber arts, **Piedmont Yarn and Apparel** (4171 Piedmont Ave., 510/595-9595, www.piedmontyarn.com, 11 A.M.–7 P.M. Mon.–Sat., 11 A.M.–5 P.M. Sun.) is your place. With a wide variety of yarn, including its own hand-dyed line, along with classes and workshops, this is a great DIY find. **Spectator Books** (4163 Piedmont Ave., 510/653-7300, www.spectatorbooks.com, 11 A.M.–8 P.M. Sun.–Thurs., 11 A.M.–9 P.M. Fri., 11 A.M.–10 P.M. Sat.) specializes in new, used, and rare books. The multiple rooms, stacked high with disheveled books, are a bibliophile's delight.

Sports and Recreation

The jewel of Oakland is **Lake Merritt** (650 Bellevue Ave., 510/238-7275). Here you can take a walk around the lake, play a few holes of golf, rent a kayak for a peaceful paddle, or even get in a set of tennis. For families, **Children's**

Take a stroll around Lake Merritt.

Fairyland (699 Bellevue Ave., 510/452-2259, www.fairyland.org, 10 A.M.–4 P.M. Mon.–Fri., 10 A.M.–5 P.M. Sat.–Sun. summer, 10 A.M.–4 P.M. Wed.–Sun. spring–fall, 10 A.M.–4 P.M. Fri.–Sun. winter, $8) provides hours of entertainment and diversion on 10 acres at the edge of the lake.

If you're eager to get out on the water, the **Lake Merritt Boating Center** (568 Bellevue Ave., 510/238-2196, http://www2.oakland-net.com, daily 10:30 A.M.–5 P.M., spring–fall, 10:30 A.M.–4 P.M. Sat.–Sun. winter, $12–24 per hour, cash only) has everything from canoes to catamarans, kayaks, and sailboats. On the lake at Lakeside Park off Grand Avenue, it is run by the city, so the prices are fair; the only hitch is that it is cash only. You can also hit the water of the Oakland Estuary off Jack London Square at **California Canoe and Kayak** (CCK, 409 Water St., 510/893-7833, www.calkayak.com, daily 10 A.M.–6 P.M.). CCK carries not only kayaks and equipment but also a wide selection of outdoor fashions.

If you'd rather watch than play, Oakland is home to several professional sports teams of varying reputations and records. The best consistent players are the Major League Baseball **Oakland A's** (510/638-4900, http://oakland.athletics.mlb.com). Part of the American League, the A's have seen their ups and downs, but they almost always put on a good show for their fans. The most notorious team in pro football, the **Oakland Raiders** (800/724-3377, www.raiders.com) calls the East Bay home again after a stint in Los Angeles. If you get tickets to a game, be aware that the home side of the stadium can get rowdy and rough.

All three teams play at the **Oracle Arena and Coliseum** (7000 Coliseum Way, Oakland, 510/569-2121, www.coliseum.com), a complex with both a covered basketball arena and an open-air stadium that hosts both the A's and the Raiders. Though the vast majority of event and game-goers are perfectly safe, the Coliseum isn't in the best neighborhood, so pay attention as you walk out to your car.

Accommodations
OAKLAND
In Oakland, try the **Bay Breeze Inn** (4919 Coliseum Way, Oakland, 510/536-5972, www.baybreezeinnoakland.com, $95–150). With all the amenities of a higher-priced chain motel, the Bay Breeze offers both comfort and convenience. Located just down the street from the Oakland Coliseum and only a few miles from Oakland Airport, this is the perfect place to stay if you're into football, baseball, basketball, live concerts, or just need to be near the airport. Do be aware that the Coliseum area can be sketchy after dark, so take care if you're walking alone.

Located in the thick of the Jack London Square District, the **Inn at Jack London Square** (233 Broadway, Oakland, 510/452-4565, www.innatthesquare.com, $129–159) offers comfortable digs for reasonable rates. In addition to its clean and modestly stylish decor, the hotel has the standard amenities of complimentary Wi-Fi, local shuttle service, and room service. There is also an exercise room and an outdoor pool perfect for relaxing during Oakland's hot summer days. Best of all, the hotel is within easy walking distance of many of the popular eateries, entertainment venues, and other attractions around Oakland's recently revitalized waterfront.

At the **Acacia House** (6276 Acacia Ave., Oakland, 510/610-2928, www.acaciahousebb.com, 2-night minimum, $125–225), you'll find a lovely three-room suite with soaring windows overlooking the Oakland Hills, native trees, and the upscale Rockridge neighborhood. A stay at the Acacia House feels more like visiting a friend's home than checking into an anonymous motel. Walk to the Rockridge BART station to explore the area, or sit in the garden, sipping a drink from the wet bar and relaxing. Book early during high season.

The Washington Inn (495 10th St., Oakland, 510/452-1776, www.thewashingtoninn.com, $79–124) brings a hint of European elegance to Oakland. Guest rooms are done in clean lines, simple furnishings, and bright white linens with touches of brilliant color. This inn prides itself on pampering its guests, so be sure to take advantage of the extras. And make a dinner reservation at TWIST, the hotel's wonderful white-tablecloth California-Italian restaurant. The inn's location in the heart of downtown makes it perfect for business and pleasure travelers alike.

An unique lodging, **Dean's Bed & Breakfast** (480 Pedestrian Way, Oakland, 510/652-5024, $140) is in the heart of charming Rockridge. It is actually a cottage stocked with fresh food and coffee, making each guest's stay completely private. You'll enjoy the heated pool and Japanese garden in summertime as well as the sights and attractions of Oakland and nearby Berkeley.

ALAMEDA

If you prefer to stay in Alameda, the **Hawthorn Suites** (1628 Webster St., Alameda, 510/522-1000, www.oaklandhs.com, $150) has all the appointments and amenities of a good motel along with big, extra-nicely decorated guest rooms. Sure, it's a chain, but it's one of the nicer ones and conveniently located in downtown Alameda, only a short drive from the USS *Hornet* museum.

Stay right on the water at the **Coral Reef Inn & Suites** (400 Park St., Alameda, 800/533-2330, www.coralreefinn.com, $95–115). This down-to-earth motel has large guest rooms with kitchenettes and small dining tables—perfect for a longer stay in the area.

Food
OAKLAND

The **Home of Chicken and Waffles** (444 Embarcadero W., Oakland, 510/836-4446, http://homeofchickenandwaffles.com, 10 A.M.–midnight Mon.–Thurs., 8 A.M.–4 A.M. Fri.–Sat., 9 A.M.–midnight Sun., $7–14) serves up good ol' Southern comfort food late into the night. Specialties of the house include the gooey mac and cheese, true Southern sides (lots of grits), and, of course, chicken and waffles—served together, if you please. Note that after 11:30 P.M. you must prepay for your meal.

At **Phnom Penh House** (251 8th Ave., Oakland, 510/893-3825, 11 A.M.–9:15 P.M. Mon.–Thurs., 11 A.M.–9:45 P.M. Fri.–Sat., $7–14) you can give Cambodian food a whirl in the heart of Oakland's Chinatown. Dishes are similar to Thai cooking with some different spice combinations. At Phnom Penh, the fish, soup, and green papaya salad all draw rave reviews from frequent diners. The curries are worth trying as well.

At the foot of the Oakland Hills, the Piedmont district's main draw is the delightfully retro **Fenton's Creamery** (4226 Piedmont Ave., 510/658-7000, www.fentonscreamery.com, 11 A.M.–11 P.M. Sun.–Thurs., 9 A.M.–midnight Fri.–Sat., $10) which has been serving scoops since 1894. There are scores of flavors, including Swiss milk chocolate, run raisin, black walnut, and pomegranate, sold by the scoop, in classic waffle cones, or made up into a sinful sundae. But you can also opt for a burger, grilled ham and cheese, or a Cobb salad. Fenton's also serves breakfast throughout the day.

Doña Tomas (5004 Telegraph Ave., Oakland, 510/450-0522, www.donatomas.com, 5:30–9:30 P.M. Tues.–Thurs., 5:30–10 P.M. Fri., 9:30 A.M.–2:30 P.M. and 5:30–10 P.M. Sat., 9:30 A.M.–2:30 P.M. Sun., $20), in the Temescal neighborhood, retains a loyal following, and for good reason. The food is authentic, fresh, based on local handmade ingredients, and very affordable. The bar is stocked with a great selection of wine and tequilas, indicating general good taste, while the interior is bright and filled with Mexican textiles and heavy Mission-style tables and chairs. There can be a wait, particularly at dinner, but it is worth it.

Mua (2442A Webster Ave., Oakland,

510/238-1100, http://muaoakland.com, 11:30 A.M.–midnight Mon.–Thurs., 11:30 A.M.–2 A.M. Fri., 4:30 P.M.–2 A.M. Sat., 4:30 P.M.–midnight Sun., $10–30) is closer to downtown and serves smart California fare and hip cocktails to the young urban set. Its interior is modern and industrial, and it is one of the few places in the Bay Area that serves food late into the evening. While you'll find fresh offerings such as lamb cheeks and ahi sashimi, the burger is one of the best things on the menu.

Practically around the corner, **Picán** (2295 Broadway, Oakland, 510/834-1000, www.picanrestaurant.com, 11:30 A.M.–2 P.M. and 5–9:30 P.M. Mon.–Thurs., 11:30 A.M.–2 P.M. and 5–11 P.M. Fri., 5–11 P.M. Sat., 10:30 A.M.–3 P.M. and 4:30–9 P.M. Sun., $13–35) also serves food late, but here the emphasis is on Southern cooking with a fresh California twist. Most plates are filled with Southern staples such as grits, sorghum, and catfish. The interior is a bit old-school, with high-back cane chairs, cream-colored walls, traditional woodwork, and a gleaming chrome kitchen. You may feel like you've stepped into an old Savannah eatery.

Also in this uptown area is **C Plum** (2214 Broadway, Oakland, 510/444-1586, www.plumoakland.com, 5–10 P.M. Sun.–Thurs., 5–11 P.M. Fri.–Sat., $10–22), the most recent creation by celebrated chef and restaurateur Daniel Patterson. In his first East Bay foray, Patterson focuses solely on bar food, but this is not a typical nachos-and-Buffalo-wings joint. Instead, the menu is limited but highly crafted. Fried duck egg is richly plated with duck confit, there is lamb mole with spaetzle, polenta accented with candied garlic, and for dessert, choose between white-chocolate parfait or brown-butter brioche. The elevation of bartenders to "mixologists" in recent years has led to an astounding revolution in cocktails, but here it is taken a step further: Plum even hand-cuts its own ice cubes to impart the perfect temperature for its elixirs. Plum's smart food and cocktails are equally matched by its interior. Spare, like the menu, the bar takes center stage, elevated by high ceilings and walls papered in lacquered pages of poetry.

At the nearby **Lake Chalet Seafood Bar and Grill** (1520 Lakeside Dr., 510/208-5253, www.thelakechalet.com, 11 A.M.–10 P.M. Mon.–Thurs., 11 A.M.–11 P.M. Fri., 10 A.M.–11 P.M. Sat., 10 A.M.–10 P.M. Sun., $16–28), the biggest draw is the location. Sitting directly on Lake Merritt in a historic building, the Lake Chalet has the atmosphere of an early-20th-century private club. The dining room, with dark wood, white walls, and a marble-topped bar with gleaming chrome fixtures, looks out over the lake and its elegant "necklace of lights." The food is standard country club fare with an emphasis on seafood, and the drinks (lots of beer, wine, and cocktail selections) are enough to keep you put, either in the dining room or on the spacious back deck overlooking the lake and downtown.

Near Jack London Square, **Chop Bar** (247 4th St., 510/834-2467, www.oaklandchopbar.com, 7 A.M.–10 P.M. Mon.–Thurs., 7 A.M.–11 P.M. Fri., 9 A.M.–11 P.M. Sat., 9 A.M.–10 P.M. Sun., $12–23) serves breakfast, lunch, and dinner in a cozy, warmly lit space accented in recycled wood and old brass instruments. The food is simple but excellent with an emphasis on artisanal ingredients. The bar has local beer and wines on tap, which is a way to get quality and affordable wines by the glass. Whether you decide to go for a plate of charcuterie with a glass of wine late in the afternoon, or for a sumptuous dinner of oxtail *poutine* or pan-seared trout, Chop Bar won't disappoint.

Commitment to sustainable food is nothing new in Bay Area restaurants, but few are as dedicated to the mission as **Oliveto** (5655 College Ave., 510/547-5356, www.oliveto.com, restaurant 11:30 A.M.–2 P.M. and 5:30–9 P.M. Mon.–Thurs., 11:30 A.M.–2 P.M. and 5:30–9:30 P.M.

Fri., 5:30–10 P.M. Sat., 5–9 P.M. Sun., $16–32; café 7 A.M.–9 P.M. Mon.–Thurs., 7 A.M.–10 P.M. Fri., 8 A.M.–10 P.M. Sat., 8 A.M.–9 P.M. Sun., $5–16). Chefs cook "snout to tail" and enlist local farmers to grow heritage corn and wheat for their polenta, pasta, and pizza. The menu is both inventive and traditional, where pan-roasted duck breast is served with a kumquat *sugo* and tortellini is accented by red-lupine honey. For those seeking a more casual experience, the downstairs café serves simpler fare such as pizza, polenta, roast chicken, soups, and salads. Every dish, upstairs and down, is executed with the same skill that has earned this eatery the reputation as one of the country's top Italian restaurants.

Also in Rockridge is **À Côté** (5478 College Ave., 510/655-6469, www.acoterestaurant.com, 5:30–10 P.M. Sun.–Tues., 5:30–11 P.M. Wed.–Thurs., 5:30–midnight Fri.–Sat., $25), which serves small-plate French, Basque, and Italian Mediterranean food. The quality and the price range imply that this is a fine-dining sort of a place, but the communal tables, outdoor patio, and general relaxed atmosphere demonstrate that this is a place where everyone can be comfortable. There are an astounding 40 wines offered by the glass, perfect to pair with each little dish, including mussels in Pernod and Basque pork ribs. Of course, no meal here would be complete without an order of the *pommes frites*, a proud specialty.

ALAMEDA

If you're out on the island of Alameda and you're looking for a tasty meal, consider sampling the German food at **Speisekammer** (2424 Lincoln Ave., Alameda, 510/522-1300, www.speisekammer.com, noon–9 P.M. Tues.–Sun., $17). This Old World eatery specializes in sausages, marinated meat, red cabbage, and sauerkraut—and, of course, beer. Check the website for information about the beer-drinking contests. Just to make your dining experience that much more fun, Speisekammer hosts live entertainment Thursday–Saturday night—mostly jazz combos, but you might find a country band or even a showcase of local musicians to enjoy with your wiener schnitzel.

Information and Services

Start at the **Oakland Convention and Visitors Bureau** (463 11th St., Oakland, 510/839-9000, www.oaklandcvb.com, 9 A.M.–5 P.M. Mon.–Fri.) to get good advice, maps, restaurant recommendations, and traffic tips. You'll find plenty of banks and ATMs scattered around Oakland; it's a good idea to stick to the ATMs in well-lit visited areas rather than picking a random spot along the freeway at night. The same goes for gas stations and minimarts. Oakland boasts many **post offices,** including one downtown at 1301 Clay Street. Internet access should be easy in a city filled with Starbucks outlets and wired hotels.

For medical attention, head out to **Alameda Hospital** (2070 Clinton Ave., Alameda, 510/522-3700, www.alamedahospital.org), which has a 24-hour emergency room. In Oakland, **Alta Bates** (350 Hawthorne Ave., 510/655-4000, www.altabatessummit.org) has a summit campus that also has a 24-hour emergency room.

Getting There and Around

Oakland is across the Bay from San Francisco and slightly south of Berkeley. Alameda is actually *in* San Francisco Bay—by car the island is accessed from downtown Oakland via the Webster Street Tube. Oakland is accessed by car from San Francisco via I-80 over the Bay Bridge (westbound toll $5). From I-80, I-580 borders Oakland to the north, while I-880 parallels I-80 downtown with access to Alameda. Try to avoid driving I-80, I-880, or I-580 during the commuting hours (8–10 A.M. and 4–7 P.M.). To reach Alameda, take I-880 south to the Broadway/Alameda exit. Turn right onto 5th Street and follow it to the Broadway intersection. Veer left to enter the Webster Street Tube. Webster Street will take you to the heart of the island.

The **Oakland International Airport** (OAK, 1 Airport Dr., Oakland, 510/563-3300, www.flyoakland.com) sees less traffic than San Francisco's airport and has shorter security lines and fewer delays. Major airlines include Alaska, Delta, JetBlue, Southwest, and Spirit.

Bay Area Rapid Transit or **BART** (www.bart.gov) is a good means of public transportation for visitors to Oakland, Berkeley, and San Francisco. The 12th Street/Oakland City Center station is convenient to downtown Oakland, but there are also trains out to 19th Street, Lake Merritt, and the Oakland Airport (via AirBART shuttle bus, $3). BART fares (most East Bay destinations $1.75–5 one-way) are based on distance, and ticket machines that accept cash and debit or credit cards are in every station. Alameda is not served by BART.

Bus service in Oakland and Alameda is run by **AC Transit** (510/891-4706, www.actransit.org, adults $2.10, children and seniors $0.85). Transbay routes connect the East Bay and San Francisco (adults $4.20, children and seniors $2.10).

The Peninsula

The San Francisco peninsula encompasses the coastal area from Pacifica down to Año Nuevo State Reserve and inland to Palo Alto. Many Bay Area locals escape to the coast for weekend vacations, enjoying the small-town atmosphere in Half Moon Bay and Pescadero along with the unspoiled beauty of the dozens of miles of undeveloped coastline. Peak seasons for major attractions include October's pumpkin season and winter, when elephant seals return to Año Nuevo.

The San Andreas Fault splits the coastal and inland peninsula, with dramatic views and curves from aptly named Skyline Boulevard (Hwy. 35). Nestled amid redwoods, quaint and beautiful Woodside sits midway between the coast and inland peninsula, while nearby Palo Alto provides eastern access via U.S. 101.

MOSS BEACH

Midway down the coast between San Francisco and Half Moon Bay on Highway 1, Moss Beach is one of several residential towns that line the coast south of the imposing Devil's Slide. There is little here besides stunning scenery, a few small businesses, and the Fitzgerald Marine Reserve. North of Moss Beach is the lovely Montara, while south is the Half Moon Bay Airport, El Granada, Princeton, and then Half Moon Bay.

Fitzgerald Marine Reserve

For tide-pooling on the coast, the Fitzgerald Marine Reserve (200 Nevada Ave., Moss Beach, 650/728-3584, www.co.sanmateo.ca.us, daily sunrise–sunset) is the place to go. The 32-acre reserve extends from the Montara Lighthouse south to Pillar Point and is considered one of the most diverse intertidal zones in the Bay Area. On its rocky reefs, you can hunt for sea anemones, starfish, eels, and crabs—there's even a small species of red octopus. The reserve is also home to egrets, herons, an endangered species of butterfly, and a slew of sea lions and harbor seals that enjoy sunning themselves on the beach's outer rocks. Rangers are available to answer any questions and, if need be, to remind you of the strict tide pool etiquette. This includes an unyielding no-dog policy, staying 300 feet from marine mammals, and not removing any plants, animals, shells or even rocks from the reserve. Persistent ocean spray and blankets of seaweed can keep the reefs slick, so wear shoes with good traction. For the best viewing, come at low tide (tide logs are available at most local bookstores, but for a quick reference, check out www.protides.com) and on weekdays, as this is a popular

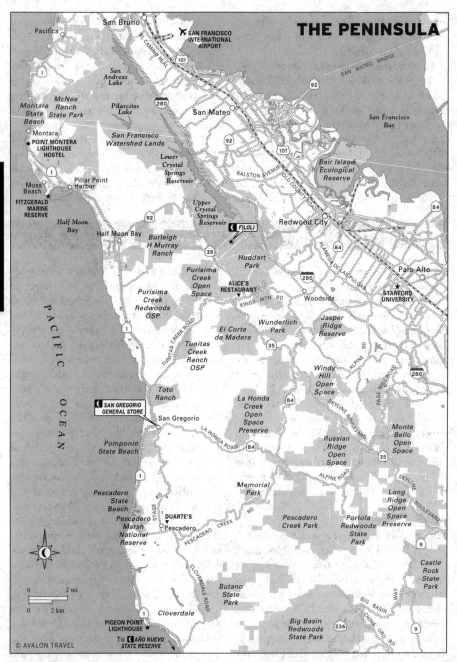

THE PENINSULA

SAN FRANCISCO BAY AREA

© ELIZABETH LINHART MONEY

a cypress-lined trail through the Fitzgerald Marine Reserve

destination for families. For a more leisurely and drier experience, numerous trails crisscross the windswept bluffs and through sheltering groves of cypress and eucalyptus trees.

Montara State Beach

Just north of Moss Beach and the Marine Reserve is Montara State Beach (2nd St. and Hwy. 1, Montara, www.parks.ca.gov, 650/726-8819, daily 8 A.M.–sunset), one of the most beautiful beaches in this area. It is as popular with tide-poolers, surfers, and anglers as it is with picnickers and beachcombers. It is also dog-friendly, which is a big plus as many state beaches have restrictions on canines in the interest of preserving the endangered snowy plover. Thankfully, the beach also remains relatively uncrowded compared to many of the other beaches to the south; it has a tendency to get windy, and there is limited parking.

McNee Ranch State Park

For those who want sweeping views of the coast as well as a heart-pounding hike, McNee Ranch (Hwy. 1, across from Montara State Beach, 650/726-8819, www.parks.ca.gov, daily 8 A.M.–sunset) fits the bill. The big hike is eight miles up Montara Mountain, through dry California chaparral along a series of fire roads. The peak itself is 1,900 feet high (the parking lot is at 100 feet), and it is an arduous but worthwhile climb to the top. Although the trail is unmarked, there are maps at the information board just past the parking lot. Still, it's easy to wing it—just follow the roads uphill. From the top, you can see all the way across the Golden Gate and south past Half Moon Bay. Unfortunately, there is no loop trail, so you must return down the mountain. But with the crisscrossing trails, you won't have to come back the same way. Parking is in a small and poorly marked dirt lot directly across Highway 1 from Montara Beach. An easier option is to park at the beach (free) and walk across the road to the trailhead. McNee Ranch is also a popular mountain biking area, and dogs are welcome on leash.

Accommodations

For an indulgent hideaway, make a reservation at the **Seal Cove Inn** (221 Cypress Ave., Moss Beach, 800/995-9987, www.sealcoveinn.com, $235–350). Tucked away in the cypress and pine forest of Moss Beach, this highly regarded 10-room B&B bills itself a "European Sanctuary." Outside, the gabled roof, climbing ivy, and expansive gardens let guests know they have entered the inn's rarified world, as do the interior's warm colors, creamy soft linens, private decks and fireplaces, pre-breakfast coffee and newspaper room service, and complimentary wine stocked in the mini fridge.

In the neighboring community of Montara, the **Goose and Turrets** (835 George St., Montara, 650/728-5451, http://goose.montara.com, $160–210) is a local getaway favorite. A rambling old building houses the inn; inside, decor runs to the eclectic. The Clipper Room is perfect for aviation buffs, and guests who like their space will love the sweeping expanse of hardwood floor in the Hummingbird Room. The food and accommodations involve ecologically friendly choices, and the owners are active in local park and community environmental organizations.

The **Point Montara Lighthouse Hostel** (16th St. and Hwy. 1, Montara, 650/728-7177, www.norcalhostels.org, dorm $25–27, private room $73, nonmembers add $3 per night) offers even better views at a fraction of the price, albeit with a bit less luxury. You can stay in the shared dorm rooms, each with 3–6 beds and either coed or gender-specific. You can also spring for a private room. Either way, you can enjoy use of the shared kitchen, common areas with wood-burning fireplaces, the eclectic garden perched on the cliff, and the private cove beach. Other amenities include Wi-Fi, laundry facilities, an espresso bar, and complimentary linens.

Food

As many people come to the **Moss Beach** **Distillery** (140 Beach Way, Moss Beach, 650/728-5595, www.mossbeachdistillery.com, noon–8:30 P.M. Mon.–Thurs., noon–9 P.M. Fri.–Sat., 11 A.M.–8:30 P.M. Sun., $15–38) for the ghost stories as for the hearty food and terrific ocean views. The Distillery operated as a speakeasy during Prohibition, with the basement rooms in the cliff-side building storing cases of illegal alcohol. The restaurant offers something of a cross between traditional American food and California cuisine. Portions tend to be large, and service is friendly if occasionally slow during peak times. Folks who want to soak up the old-school speakeasy atmosphere like to sit in the bar, while visitors who want to stare out over the ocean prefer the terrace, where, thankfully, plenty of blankets are on hand to ward off the Pacific chill as the sun goes down.

Looking to pack a picnic lunch before you head out to the Fitzgerald Marine Reserve or Montara State Beach? Swing by **Gherkin's Sandwich Shop** (171 7th St., Montara, 650/728-2211, daily 7 A.M.–7 P.M., $10) for everything you can imagine between two slices of bread. You'll find oddities like breakfast frittata sandwiches and the Ooey Gooey, with peanut butter, Nutella, and marshmallows. For the less adventurous, there are also classics like BLTs, burgers, and pastrami and swiss cheese. You can also order a variety of sides that include garlic fries and macaroni salad, but beware: The sandwiches are huge and can easily be split between two people or saved for a later snack.

You might decide to stumble into **La Costanera** (8150 Cabrillo Hwy., Montara, 650/728-1600, www.lacostanerarestaurant.com, 5–10:30 P.M. Tues.–Sun., $25) because of the location. But this place, poised above Montara Beach, is about more than just the view. Skillfully designed with grand sloping picture windows and sunken dining rooms, La Costanera is a sophisticated Peruvian restaurant and the only eatery on this part of the coast to earn a Michelin star two years in a row. There

THE BLUE LADY

With all its history, it's easy to get lost in the ghost stories that haunt San Francisco. Yet two of the most famous Bay Area hauntings aren't anywhere close to Chinatown or Nob Hill. Instead, strange stories and creepy occurrences perch nearer to the perilous cliffs of the Pacific Coast and lurk in the Santa Cruz Mountain forests.

Just north of Half Moon Bay, the **Moss Beach Distillery** (140 Beach Way, Moss Beach, 650/728-5595, www.mossbeachdistillery.com) has been featured on *Unsolved Mysteries* and *Ghost Hunters* and written up in countless publications not for its food but for its famous ghost: the Blue Lady. Rumor has it that a beautiful young woman walked the cliffs of Moss Beach from her home to a coast-side speakeasy then known as Frank's Place, now Moss Beach Distillery, to meet her lover, a handsome piano player who worked in the bar. The Blue Lady, whose name has never been discovered, perished one night on the cliffs under suspicious circumstances. Some say that her lover had left her, and she threw herself onto the rocks out of grief; others claim that her seafaring husband came home, discovered his wife's infidelity, and shoved her off. However it happened, in the middle of the 20th century, odd things started occurring at the distillery. A storage room with only one door and a barred-over window became stuck from the inside. Eventually, several men bashed it open, only to discover that several heavy cases of spirits had been shoved up against the door to keep it closed. But by whom? No one was in the room, and no one could have gotten out. Many years and a major reconstruction later (the building sits on a slowly eroding cliff that will eventually fall into the ocean), an accountant was working late one night in the restaurant's offices. She was startled to hear her printer turn itself on...startled because she was in another office using a different computer and was alone in the building. On examination, the printer yielded a single piece of paper with a tiny heart printed on it. The accountant believes this means the ghost likes her.

Today, the distillery is a favorite with ghost-hunting groups, who often come to spend the night in an old building that gets decidedly creepy after the lights go out. Restaurant patrons rarely have ghostly experiences, unless you count those created by the owner for the entertainment of his customers.

are a variety of ceviches to choose from as well as slow-cooked pork shoulder and lobster, all accented in Peruvian sauces and spices. If you only want a quick bite while soaking in the sunset, the bar menu offers hearty plates that could serve as a light dinner.

Getting There and Around

Moss Beach is 23 miles directly south of San Francisco on Highway 1 (Cabrillo Hwy.). From San Francisco, the easiest and most direct—not to mention scenic—route is to follow Highway 1 south all the way to Moss Beach. Alternatively, if you are coming from I-280 on the peninsula, take Highway 92 west to Half Moon Bay and Highway 1. From Half Moon Bay, Moss Beach is only seven miles north on Highway 1.

HALF MOON BAY

To this day, the coastal city of Half Moon Bay retains its character as an "ag" (agricultural) town. The locals all know each other, even though the majority of residents commute "over the hill" to more lucrative peninsula and Silicon Valley jobs. For those who farm the area, strawberries, artichokes, and Brussels sprouts are the biggest crops, along with flowers, pumpkins, and Christmas trees, making the coast the place to come for holiday festivities. Half Moon Bay enjoys a beautiful natural setting and earns significant income from tourism, especially during the world-famous Pumpkin Festival each October.

Four miles north are Pillar Point Harbor and the neighboring town of

© ELIZABETH LINHART MONEY

The Moss Beach Distillery is known more for its location than its food.

Princeton-by-the-Sea, the other work-horse on the coast. Here, anglers haul in crab, salmon, and herring, and local businesses cater to their needs. This is the place to rent kayaks, go on a chartered fishing trip, and buy fresh fish, sometimes straight off the boat (especially during crab season).

Beaches

The beaches of Half Moon Bay draw visitors from over the hill and farther afield all year long. As with most of the North Pacific region, summer can be a chilly foggy time on the beaches. For the best beach weather, plan your Half Moon Bay trip for September–October. **Half Moon Bay State Beach** (www.parks. ca.gov, parking $10 per day) actually encompasses three discrete beaches stretching four miles down the coast, each with its own access point and parking lot. **Francis Beach** (95 Kelly Ave.) has the most developed amenities, including a good-size campground with grassy

areas to pitch tents and enjoy picnics, a visitors center, and indoor hot showers. **Venice Beach** (Venice Blvd., off Hwy. 1) offers outdoor showers and flush toilets. **Dunes Beach** (Young Ave., off Hwy. 1) is the southernmost major beach in the chain and the least developed.

Perhaps the most famous beach in the area is one that has no name. At the end of West Point Avenue in Princeton is the Pillar Point Marsh and a long stretch of beach the wraps around the edge of the point. This beach is the launch pad for surfers paddling out to tackle the infamous **Mavericks Break** (Pillar Point Marsh parking lot, past Pillar Point Harbor). Formed by unique underwater topography, the giant waves are the site of the legendary **Mavericks Surf Contest** (http://maverickssurf.com). The competition is always held in winter, when the swells reach their peak, and left until the last minute to ensure that they are the biggest of the year. When perfect conditions present themselves, the best surfers in the world are given 48

SAN FRANCISCO BAY AREA

© JAY GRAHAM/VISITHALFMOONBAY.ORG

Pillar Point Harbor, near Half Moon Bay

hours' notice to make it to Mavericks to compete. Unfortunately, you can't see the breaks all that well from the beach, but there are dirt trails that crisscross the point, where breathtaking views can be had. Just walk up West Point Avenue past the yellow gate and catch any number of dirt trails heading west toward the bluffs. But for those eyeing the big waves, beware: Mavericks is not a beginner's break, especially in winter, and the giant breakers can be deadly. If you aren't positive you're up to the challenge, don't paddle out.

Entertainment and Events

Locals may complain that there is not a lot going on in Half Moon Bay, but the city boasts one of the best jazz venues and two of the biggest annual events in the Bay Area. Since it opened in 1964, the **Bach Dancing and Dynamite Society** (311 Mirada Rd., Half Moon Bay, 650/726-2020, www.bachddsoc. org) has been a hangout for bohemians and

jazz aficionados, hosting the biggest names in jazz—Bill Evans, Dizzy Gillespie, Etta James, and Duke Ellington. Not only is the music fantastic, but the venue, the Douglas Beach House, can't be beat.

In contrast to the Bach's cool vibe, the **Pacific Coast Dream Machines** (Half Moon Bay Airport, 9850 Hwy. 1, www.miramarevents.com) is all muscle and revving engines. This two-day event includes a demolition derby, a flying motorcycle, World War II–era fighter planes, ultra-lightweight and antique biplanes, and automobiles from peddle cars to homemade kit cars. The event generally takes place on the last weekend in April, so plan accordingly; whether or not you plan to attend, the traffic congestion is equally legendary.

The biggest annual event in this small agricultural town is the **Half Moon Bay Art & Pumpkin Festival** (www.miramarevents.com). Every October, nearly 250,000 people trek to Half Moon Bay to pay homage to the big orange squash. The festival includes live music, food, artists' booths, contests, activities for kids, an adults lounge area, and a parade. Perhaps the best-publicized event is the pumpkin weigh-off, which takes place before the festivities begin. Farmers bring their tremendous squash in on flatbed trucks from all over the country to determine which is the biggest of all. The winner gets paid per pound, a significant prize when the biggest pumpkins weigh over 1,000 pounds.

Shopping

Strolling Main Street is another reason folks come to Half Moon Bay. A holdover from the town's agricultural roots is **Half Moon Bay Feed and Fuel** (331 Main St., 650/726-4814, http://halfmoonbay-feedandfuel.com, 8:30 A.M.–6 P.M. Mon.–Fri., 9 A.M.–5 P.M. Sat., 10 A.M.–4 P.M. Sun.). Even if you don't need a new saddle or a bale of hay, stopping by the Feed and Fuel is a fun little detour. There are often baby chicks and bunnies as well as quirky gift items that any Western fanatic or wannabe cowboy would love.

Just on the next block, you can step into a whole other world in **Abode** (417 Main St., 650/726-6060, http://abodehalfmoonbay.com, 10 A.M.–5 P.M. Sun.–Thurs., 10 A.M.–6 P.M. Fri.–Sat.). Carefully crafted, Abode almost feels like a treatise on home decorating in which the goal is fluidity of between the outside and the inside spaces. There are no bright plastic or enamel wares here, but instead furniture and home accents are all in an earthy palette and are largely made from glass, wood, and other natural materials and designed artistic quality, craftsmanship, and utility.

Another Half Moon Bay treasure is **Toque Blanche** (604 Main St., 650/726-2898, www.mytoque.com, 10 A.M.–6 P.M. Mon.–Sat., 10 A.M.–5 P.M. Sun.), perhaps the best kitchen store in the Bay Area. They have everything from coffeemakers to panini presses, cookie cutters to knives, dinner plates to linens. Some of the bonuses include free cooking demos, super soft French dishtowels, a wall full of different types of salt, and La Chamba Cookware, extremely versatile and attractive Colombian cooking pottery.

To see what Half Moon Bay does best, drop by the **Coastside Farmer's Market** (Shoreline Station, Hwy. 1 and Kelly Ave., www.coastsidefarmersmarket.org, 9 A.M.–1 P.M. Sat. May–Dec.). There is plenty of local meat, bread, produce, pottery, art, and even wool skeins, spun and dyed by hand. Local bands are always at the market, and there is plenty of street food. The **Half Moon Bay Flower Market** (650/712-9439, www.explorer1.com, 10 A.M.–4 P.M. third Sat. of the month) is even more of an institution, where local flower growers show off a multitude of blooms and houseplants that range from the domestic to the exotic.

Sports and Recreation

There are plenty of great trails around Half Moon Bay. A local favorite is **Purisima Creek Redwoods** (4.4 miles up Higgins Canyon Rd., 650/619-1200, www.openspace.org). There are a multitude of trails in this 3,000-acre preserve, and many ascend to Skyline Boulevard for an elevation gain of 1,700 feet. You can take a leisurely stroll through the redwoods, complete with dripping ferns, flowering dogwood and wood sorrel, along **Purisima Creek Trail** (3.9 miles, easy–strenuous), until it turns steep and eventually takes you to its literally breathtaking Skyline terminus. If you don't want to crest the ridge of the Santa Cruz Mountains, you can opt for Harkins Ridge Trail (6 miles, moderate), which rises out of the canyon shortly past the trailhead. You'll hike through redwoods, then oaks and chaparral, and back again into firs, pines, and redwoods as you gain 800 feet in elevation over 2.5 miles. To make a loop, cut down Craig Britton Trail, which meets Purisima Creek Trail. To feel like you've conquered a mountain, make the climb to

© JAY GRAHAM/VISITHALFMOONBAY.ORG

SAN FRANCISCO BAY AREA

biking around Half Moon Bay

2,102-foot **Bald Knob** (9.6 miles, strenuous). From Purisima Creek Trail, take Borden Hatch Mill Trail to Bald Knob Trail, where you will find a flat clearing among the dry madrones, live oaks, and chaparral. You will be rewarded with terrific coastal views.

Fortunately for mountain bikers, nearly all the trails in the preserve are open to cyclists. As you can imagine, the trails are steep and knotted with rocks and trees roots, which makes for an exhausting, exhilarating, or terrifying ride, depending on your experience and attitude.

The most popular trail in Half Moon Bay is the **Coastside Trail** (www.parks.ca.gov). Extending five miles from Miramar Beach to Poplar Beach, this flat paved trail follows the coast and is filled with joggers, dog walkers, and bikes. There are a multitude of beach-access points along the way, and if you want to go downtown, jump off at Kelly Avenue and take it across Highway 1 to the heart of Half Moon Bay. Beyond the Poplar Beach parking lot, the trail crosses a wooden bridge and turns into a dirt trail. This area is known as the **Wavecrest Open Space** and goes all the way down to the Ritz Carlton. It is much less traveled than the paved Coastside Trail and is a great place to spot herons, egrets, and gray whales off the coast during their spring migration. Parking is plentiful at Poplar Beach ($2 per hour), at the end of Poplar Street on the south end of town.

For a sedate ocean adventure, take a winter whale-watching cruise or a shallow-water rockfish fishing trip on board the *Queen of Hearts* (Pillar Point Harbor, 510/581-2628, www.fishingboat.com, reservations strongly recommended, adults $69, children $60). Whale-watching trips (Jan.–Apr.) cost a bit less than fishing trips on the *Queen of Hearts*. Deep-sea fishing for albacore and salmon (if the season isn't canceled) makes for a more energetic day out on the Pacific, although motion-sickness medication is often recommended.

Bait and Switch Sportfishing (Pillar Point

Harbor, 650/726-7133, www.huckfinnsportfishing.com, tackle $5–14, 1-day license $12) offers eight boats for a wide variety of whale-watching and deep-sea fishing trips, and even trips to watch the Mavericks Surf Contest; call for rates.

One of the coolest ways to see the coast is from the deck of a sea kayak. Many kayak tours with the **Half Moon Bay Kayaking Company** (2 Johnson Pier, 650/773-6101, www.hmb-kayak.com) require no previous kayaking experience. For an easy first paddle, try the Pillar Point tour, the full-moon tour, or the sunset paddle. If you're looking for a wilder ride, sign up for a kayak surfing class—you'll learn how to catch waves safely in specially designed kayaks. The company also offers beginner through advanced classes in closed-deck kayaks.

Sea Horse and Friendly Acres Ranches (1828 Hwy. 1, 650/726-9903, www.seahorseranch.com, daily from 8 A.M., $55 per hour) offers one-hour, 90-minute, and two-hour guided tours that take you along the cliffs and down onto the sands at Half Moon Bay's state beaches. Children over the age of five are welcome, as are riders of all ability levels. The horses here are sedate rental nags who know the routes in their sleep, allowing riders to sit back and enjoy the stunning views and the company of fellow riders.

Accommodations

Half Moon Bay offers several lovely bed-and-breakfasts and one luxury resort hotel. The **Ritz-Carlton Half Moon Bay** (1 Miramontes Point Rd., 650/712-7000, www.ritzcarlton.com, $500) looms large over the Pacific and resembles a medieval castle. Inside, guests enjoy the finest of modern amenities. The Ritz-Carlton has a top-tier restaurant (Navio), a world-class day spa, and posh guest rooms that really are worth the rates. If you can, get a guest room facing the ocean. While you're here, enjoy free access to the spa's bathing rooms, an outdoor hot tub overlooking the ocean, tennis courts, and the basketball court. Golf at the Ritz is second to none in the Bay Area.

For a more personal lodging experience, try the ❰ **Old Thyme Inn** (779 Main St., 650/726-1616, www.oldthymeinn.com, $195–375), located right downtown next door to the Cetrella Bistro. Each uniquely decorated guest room has its own garden theme and luxurious amenities. Downstairs, guests can enjoy the common sitting rooms and the gorgeous garden. Each morning the owners serve up a sumptuous breakfast using fresh ingredients.

Somewhere between the Ritz and the Old Thyme Inn is the **Cypress Inn** (407 Miranda Rd., 650/726-6002, www.cypressinn.com, $209–409). Built out of weathered redwood, the inn is a neat compound where most of the guest rooms come with fireplaces, private decks, jetted tubs, and fridges. Adding to the luxury are a full-service breakfast and a cocktail hour offered in the Main House. The inn is an easy bike ride to downtown Half Moon Bay, a pleasant stroll to many beaches, and the modest yet lovely mix of galleries, restaurants, and cafés in the Miramar area.

Food

The quality of food in Half Moon Bay is superb. Open since 1987, ❰ **Pasta Moon** (315 Main St., 650/726-5125, www.pastamoon.com, 11:30 A.M.–2 P.M. and 5:30–9 P.M. Mon.–Thurs., 11:30 A.M.–2 P.M. and 5:30–9:30 P.M. Fri., noon–3 P.M. and 5:30–9:30 P.M. Sat., noon–3 P.M. and 5:30–9 P.M. Sun., $14–34) is the godmother of fine dining. While managing to be both casual and upscale at once, Pasta Moon serves updated Italian cuisine with an emphasis on fresh, light dishes. Their wood-fired pizzas are particularly good and affordable, as are any of the pasta dishes, made with house-made noodles. The rustic dining room, with a view of the woods and the creek, completes the experience, while the bar and new lounge, humming with live jazz, offers a more casual and urbane evening out.

Cetrella (845 Main St., 650/726-4090, www.ce-trella.com, 5:30–9:30 P.M. Tues.–Thurs. and Sun., 5:30–10 P.M. Fri.–Sat., $22–40) also bills itself as a Mediterranean bistro. In truth, the menu includes a range of Mediterranean-themed California cuisine, and the big-beam construction looks like something out of the redwood forests up north. The chef uses local, often organic ingredients to create stunning fare that varies by season. Look for Dungeness crab in winter and artichokes in the spring.

For seafood, come to **Sam's Chowder House** (4210 N. Cabrillo Hwy., Pillar Point Harbor, 650/712-0371, www.samschowderhouse.com, 11:30 A.M.–9 P.M. Mon.–Thurs., 11:30 A.M.–9:30 P.M. Fri.–Sat., 11 A.M.–9 P.M. Sun., $12–35). Owner Paul Shenkman, a veteran restaurateur once associated with Pasta Moon and Cetrella, is a New Jersey native who takes seafood very seriously. The perpetually full parking lot out front points to Shenkman's golden touch. Inside, Sam's offers everything from a stiff drink at the bar to light appetizers and champagne on the deck, steaming plates of whole lobster, seafood paella, and seared tuna served in the ample yet cozy dining room. Sam's is also known for its kid-friendly vibe and its $1 oyster nights that are not to be missed.

When all you need is a quick bite or a casual lunch, the **Moonside Bakery & Cafe** (604 Main St., 650/726-9070, www.moonsidebakery.com, daily 7 A.M.–5 P.M.) can fix you up. Stop in the morning for breakfast pastries and espresso. In the afternoon and evening, expect sandwiches and hand-fired pizzas.

Information and Services

Visit the **Half Moon Bay Chamber of Commerce** (235 Main St., 650/726-8389, www.halfmoonbaychamber.org, 9 A.M.–5 P.M. Mon.–Fri., 10 A.M.–3 P.M. Sat.–Sun.), in the red house just after you turn on Main Street from Highway 92. The chamber also doubles as a visitors center where you can find maps, brochures, and a schedule of events.

Two local publications are the *Half Moon Bay Review* (www.hmbreview.com) and *CoastViews Magazine* (www.coastviewsmag.com). The *Review,* published weekly, provides the best information about live local entertainment. The free *CoastViews* comes out monthly and is available around this region.

The **post office** (500 Stone Pine Rd.) is off Main Street before the bridge heading south. Cell phones work fine in the town of Half Moon Bay, but coverage can be spotty up in the hills above town and out on the undeveloped coastline and beaches along Highway 1.

There is a 24-hour emergency room at the **Seton Coastside Hospital** (600 Marine Blvd., Moss Beach, 650/563-7100, www.setoncoastside.org). For less serious health services, the **Coastside Clinic** (Shoreline Station, Suite 100A, 225 S. Hwy. 1, Half Moon Bay, 650/573-3941, www.sanmateomedicalcenter.org) is located just north of the intersection of Kelly Avenue and Highway 1.

Getting There and Around

Half Moon Bay is on Highway 1 about 45 minutes south of San Francisco. From San Francisco, take I-280 south to Highway 92 west to Half Moon Bay and Highway 1. You can also take the scenic route by following Highway 1 directly south from San Francisco all the way to Half Moon Bay.

Parking in downtown Half Moon Bay is usually a fairly easy proposition—except, of course, if you're in town for the Pumpkin Festival, when parking is a nightmare of epic proportions. Your best bet is to stay in town with your car safely stowed in a hotel parking lot before the festival.

PESCADERO

Pescadero is a tiny dot on the coastline, south of Half Moon Bay and well north of Santa Cruz, with one main street, one side street, and several smallish farms. Despite its tiny size, many

Bay Area denizens visit Pescadero for the twisty roads that challenge motorcyclists and bicyclists, fresh produce, and, of course, the legendary Duarte's Tavern.

Pescadero State Beach

Pescadero State Beach (Hwy. 1, north of Pescadero Rd., 650/879-2170, www.parks.ca.gov, daily 8 A.M.–sunset) is the closest beach to the town of Pescadero. It's a great spot to walk in the sand and stare out at the Pacific, but near-constant winds make it less than ideal for picnics or sunbathing. It does have some facilities, including public restrooms.

Bird lovers flock to **Pescadero Marsh Natural Preserve** (Hwy. 1, www.smcnha.org), located on Highway 1 right across the highway from Pescadero State Beach. This protected wetland, part of Pescadero State Beach, is home to a variety of avian species, including blue herons, great and snowy egrets, and northern harriers. For the best birding, visit the marsh early in the morning or in late fall or early spring, when migration is in full swing.

San Gregorio State Beach

North of Pescadero, at the intersection of Highway 84 and Highway 1, San Gregorio State Beach (650/879-2170, www.parks.ca.gov, daily 8 A.M.–sunset, $10 per car) stretches farther than it seems. Once you're walking toward the ocean, the small-seeming cove stretches out beyond the cliffs that bound it to create a long stretch of beach perfect for contemplative strolling. San Gregorio is a local favorite in the summer, despite the regular appearance of thick, chilly fog over the sand. Brave beachgoers can even swim and bodysurf here, although you'll quickly get cold if you do so without a wetsuit. Picnic tables and restrooms cluster near the parking lot, although picnicking can be hampered by the wind.

◖ San Gregorio General Store

San Gregorio is a tiny picturesque town of rolling rangeland, neat patches of colorful crops, and century-old homes, including a one-room schoolhouse and an old brothel. Its beating heart is the San Gregorio General Store (Hwy. 84 and Stage Rd., 650/726-0565, www.sangregoriostore.com, 10:30 A.M.–6 P.M. Mon.–Thurs., 10:30 A.M.–7 P.M. Fri., 10 A.M.–7 P.M. Sat., 10 A.M.–6 P.M. Sun.). Open since 1889, the San Gregorio General Store has an eclectic book section and a variety of cast-iron cookery, oil lamps, and raccoon traps. In the back of the store are coolers stocked with juice, soda, bottled water, and deli sandwiches made in the back kitchen. The real centerpiece is the bar, serving beer, wine, and a large selection of spirits to ranchers and farmers out for a coffee break in the mornings and locals just getting off work. On the weekends the store is packed by mostly out-of-towners, and the live music keeps things moving. The deep picture windows out front make it a comfy place to watch the afternoon pass by with a cold beer. The San Gregorio General Store lives up to its name: You can even buy stamps or mail a letter at the full-service post office next door.

Pigeon Point Lighthouse

South of Pescadero is Pigeon Point Lighthouse (210 Pigeon Point Rd., at Hwy. 1, 650/879-2120, www.parks.ca.gov, daily 8 A.M.–sunset). First lit in 1872, Pigeon Point is one of the most photographed lighthouses in the United States. Sadly, visitors find the lighthouse itself in a state of disrepair, and recent earthquakes have made climbing to the top unsafe. Yet the monument stands, its hostel still shelters travelers, and visitors still marvel at the incomparable views from the point. Winter guests can look for migrating whales from the rocks beyond the tower.

◖ Año Nuevo State Reserve

Año Nuevo State Reserve (Hwy. 1, south of Pescadero, 650/879-2025, reservations 800/444-4445, www.parks.ca.gov, daily

© SABRINA YOUNG

an elephant seal at Año Nuevo State Reserve

8 A.M.–sunset, $10 per car) is world-famous as the winter home and breeding ground of the once-endangered elephant seals. The reserve also has extensive dunes and marshland. The beaches and wilderness are open year-round. The elephant seals start showing up in late November and stay to breed, birth pups, and loll on the beach until early March. Visitors are not allowed down to the elephant seal habitats on their own and must sign up for a guided walking tour. Once you see two giant males crashing into one another in a fight for dominance, you won't want to get too close. Book your tour at least a day or two in advance since the seals are popular with both locals and travelers.

Accommodations

Pescadero has a small but surprisingly good array of lodging options. If budget is a factor, try the **Pigeon Point Hostel** (210 Pigeon Point Rd., at Hwy. 1, 650/879-0633, http://norcal-hostels.org/pigeon, dorm $25–27, private room $73). This Hostelling International hostel has simple but comfortable accommodations, both private and dorm-style. Amenities include three kitchens, free Wi-Fi, and beach access. But the best amenity of all is the cliff-top hot tub, which makes this hostel more than special.

At **Costanoa Lodge and Campground** (2001 Rossi Rd., at Hwy. 1, 650/879-1100, www.costanoa.com, campsite $55, rooms $120–380), pitch a tent in the campground or rent a whirlpool suite in the lodge. Other lodging options include log-style cabins with shared baths, small tent cabins with shared baths, and private guest rooms. Costanoa's many nature programs seek to educate visitors about the ecology of the San Mateo coast and the preservation efforts underway. A small general store offers s'mores fixings and souvenirs, while "Comfort Stations" provide outdoor fireplaces, private indoor-outdoor showers, baths with heated floors, and saunas that are open daily 24 hours to all guests.

For a little more luxury, the **Pescadero**

Creek Inn Bed & Breakfast (393 Stage Rd., 888/307-1898, www.pescaderocreekinn.com, $190–225) is conveniently located in downtown Pescadero, an easy walk from Duarte's, the grocery stores, the local cemetery, and the creek. While the house isn't completely soundproof, the guest rooms have high ceilings and are prettily appointed. The owners serve up a delectable breakfast each morning, plus wine and cheese in the afternoon.

If you want something unique, Pescadero has lodgings available year-round. The **Pescadero Creekside Barn** (248 Stage Rd., 650/879-0868, www.pescaderolodging.com, call for rates) is nestled in the loft of an old barn downtown. This studio apartment–style space sleeps two and has a TV with a DVD player, a kitchen, and a claw-foot tub. The seclusion and charm make the space perfect for a romantic getaway or a solitary weekend retreat.

Camping

Most of the camping in Pescadero is inland, deep in the redwoods. **Butano State Park** (1500 Cloverdale Rd., Pescadero, 650/879-2040, www.parks.ca.gov, Apr.–Nov., $35) offers 21 drive-in and 18 walk-in campsites. While there are no showers, there are clean restrooms, fire pits, and drinking water. Perhaps the best amenity is the proximity to fantastic hiking in the park. There are quiet strolls through the canopy of redwoods or more athletic treks up dusty ridgelines. The most scenic is the **Butano Fire Road** that summits at an abandoned airstrip.

Farther inland, past the tiny town of Loma Mar, is **Memorial Park** (9500 Pescadero Creek Rd., 650/879-0238, www.co.sanmateo.ca.us, year-round, $37) with 158 campsites open. Each site, which accommodates as many as eight people, has a fire pit, picnic tables, and a metal locker to store food and sundries. There is also drinking water, baths with coin-operated showers, and a general store within the park that sells firewood in addition to hot dog buns, ice cream, and soap. While there are fewer hiking trails than at Butano, Memorial boasts an amphitheater and swimming holes in Pescadero Creek.

Food

◖**Duarte's Tavern** (202 Stage Rd., Pescadero, 650/879-0464, www.duartestavern.com, daily 7 A.M.–9 P.M., $13–25) has been honored by the James Beard Foundation as "An American Classic," and once you walk through the doors you'll see why. The rambling building features sloping floors and age-darkened wooden walls. The food is good, the service friendly, and the coffee plentiful. And while almost everybody in the Bay Area comes to Duarte's eventually for a bowl of artichoke soup or a slice of olallieberry pie, it is really the atmosphere that is the biggest draw. Here, locals of all stripes—farmers, farmhands, ranchers, and park rangers—sit shoulder to shoulder with travelers from "over the hill" sharing conversation and a bite to eat, particularly in the dimly lit bar. The greatest assets are the outdated jukebox and excellent Bloody Marys, garnished with a pickled green bean.

If Duarte's is too crowded, venture cross the street to the **Pescadero Country Store** (251 Stage Rd., 650/879-0410, daily 8 A.M.–6 P.M., $12). This converted grocery store has a pizza counter serving wood-fired pies, a full-service deli, a beer and wine bar uniquely decorated in a deep blue nautical theme, and a small grocery store. While Duarte's is still the local hangout, many opt to come here for an occasional reprieve.

If you're heading to Pescadero from Half Moon Bay, stop at **Bob's Vegetable Stand** (Hwy. 1, 5 miles south of Half Moon Bay, 650/712-7740) which has a selection of local produce rivaling any grocery store. Once in Pescadero, **Harley Farms** (205 North St., 650/879-0480, www.harleyfarms.com, call for tour information) boasts of being the last working dairy on the San Mateo coast. Its goat cheese is locally famous and is sold in its farm

© SABRINA YOUNG

SAN FRANCISCO BAY AREA

Duarte's has been in business since 1894.

store as well as at high-end grocery stores in the Bay Area. During your stop, you can even assist in the cheese-making process, taking a tour that teaches you how to milk a goat and then create fresh artisanal cheese.

Farther up Pescadero Road at **Phipp's Country Store and Farm** (2700 Pescadero Rd., 650/879-1032, www.phippscountry.com), you can pick your own warm-from-the-sun strawberries and olallieberries (spring–summer only). Phipp's also has a quaint country store where they sell homemade jams, jellies, herbal vinegars, and a whole host of heritage beans, grown and dried on the farm.

To round out your picnic, drop by **Arcangeli Grocery** (287 Stage Rd., 650/879-0147, www. normsmarket.com) across the street from Duarte's. All the breads are homemade and delicious, and the pastries—especially the raspberry twists—are great.

Getting There and Around

Pescadero is 17 miles south of Half Moon Bay.

At Pescadero State Beach, Highway 1 intersects Pescadero Road. Turn east on Pescadero Road and drive two miles to the stop sign (the only one in town). Turn left onto Stage Road to find the main drag. Parking is free and generally easy to find on Stage Road or in the Duarte's parking lot. On weekends, you might need to park down the road a ways and walk a block or two.

WOODSIDE

If the Bay Area had a landed gentry, they would reside in Woodside. Here among the bucolic grasslands and oak groves are well-heeled equestrian estates. While this has been a moneyed area since its inception as a private club retreat at the turn of the 20th century, Woodside really boomed with the recently minted dot-com millionaires of the 1990s. Huge mansions replaced the relatively more modest abodes, many of which can be seen through low fences in Woodside proper. The serene scenery, good food, and hiking and cycling options are the real draw.

◖ Filoli

Built in 1917, Filoli (86 Cañada Rd., Woodside, 650/364-8300, www.filoli.org, 10 A.M.–3:30 P.M. Tues.–Sat., 11 A.M.–3:30 P.M. Sun., $15) was the country manor of William Bowers Bour II, one of San Francisco's richest people at the time. It is now owned by the National Trust for Historic Preservation and can be toured. The house itself was designed by Willis Polk in the Gregorian style and is now a museum of 17th- and 18th-century antiques. Many of the rooms reflect the truly rarefied world of the very wealthy, especially the Ballroom, a 70- by 32-foot space decorated in murals and gold leaf.

The gardens are what Filoli is best known for. Of its nearly 700 acres, 16 acres are carefully cultivated plots that form an outdoor museum of sorts that celebrates American horticultural style and botanical diversity. There are the manicured West Terraces, dripping in wisteria and shaped by sharply cut lawns and pruned trees and shrubs that would serve perfectly as a set for *Upstairs Downstairs*. Botanists and epicureans will marvel at the Gentleman's Orchard, which boasts the largest collection of heirloom fruit in North America. The grounds also host an olive orchard, a bonsai collection, a camellia and citrus collection, and a native plant garden designed and built in 2005. For the price of admission, you can wander the grounds on your own, or join a docent-led tour. Some tours offer a leisurely and informative stroll around the house and the gardens, while others take guests on robust orchard and nature hikes, many of which reach deep into Filoli's wilder corners.

Sports and Recreation

The official sport of Woodside is road cycling. There are no easy roads to bike in Woodside proper, except maybe Mountain Home and Whiskey Hill Roads, but both have appreciable hills. True biking enthusiasts instead opt for the most perilous roads to peddle: Old La Honda, Alpine, King's Mountain, and Bear Gulch Roads are all narrow, curvy, and sharply ascend through oaks and redwoods up to Highway 35. Many riders then come back down Highway 84, where they can cruise at the speed of traffic; it's a heart-stopping sight, so drivers beware.

Crystal Springs Trail (17.6 miles, easy), on the other hand, is the perfect fit for novice cyclists and those looking for a mellow afternoon bike ride. The trail starts in Woodside and follows Cañada Road past Filoli and the Pulgas Water Temple to the Crystal Springs Reservoir, where it skirts its eastern edge. While the trail, which is paved and neatly divided into two lanes, does not circumvent the reservoir, you can continue on to San Andreas Lake and ride alongside it to the lake's terminus in San Bruno. There are some gaps in the trail, meaning you have to jump onto Cañada Road or Skyline Boulevard, but thankfully both have wide bike lanes. Despite these inconveniences, the trail is a largely flat ride through stunning scenery and is often far from any roads, providing peaceful seclusion.

There are a number of open-space preserves in the Woodside area, but the most accessible, user-friendly, and diverse is **Huddart Park** (1100 Kings Mountain Rd., Woodside, 650/851-1210, www.co.sanmateo.ca.us). Crystal Springs Trail (9 miles, strenuous) starts at the eastern end of the park and zigzags its way west. To reach Skyline Boulevard, you can turn on either Richards Road or Summit Springs Trails. The latter is longer, but it joins **Purisima Creek Trail** to descend down the western side of the mountains. Despite the 1,200-foot elevation gain, Crystal Springs Trail is wide, evenly graded, and a pleasant but invigorating hike. You certainly don't have to go all the way to Skyline Boulevard. For a shorter loop (4.5 miles, moderate), turn onto Dean Trail after 2.5 miles. The trail drops across McGarvey Gulch and hugs King's Mountain

Road, but the heavily wooded trail is lovely despite the traffic noise. If you want to further shorten your trip, Archery Fire Road is a cutoff for the longer Dean Trail. For those who simply want a taste of the outdoors, Huddart Park's 900 acres have a number of picnic areas, including covered spots, as well as a playground, group campsites, an archery range, and Chickadee Nature Trail (0.5 mile, easy), which crisscrosses a seasonal gorge.

Food

Alice's Restaurant (Hwy. 84 and Hwy. 35, 650/851-0303, www.alicesrestaurant.com, 8:30 A.M.–9 P.M. Mon.–Fri., 8 A.M.–9 P.M. Sat.–Sun., $10) has more than a whiff of counterculture to it. Located on Skyline Boulevard in the redwoods that were once home to Ken Kesey and the Merry Pranksters, it is still a hangout for bikers and locals. The menu features eggs served 10 different ways, 20 different burgers, garlic fries, quesadillas, prime-rib sandwiches, and a whole slew of beers on tap. The portions are big, and the outside deck is a favorite Bay Area spot on sunny weekend afternoons.

Opened in 1954, **The Village Pub** (2967 Woodside Rd., 650/851-9888, http://thevillage-pub.net, 11:30 A.M.–2:30 P.M. and 5–10 P.M. Mon.–Fri., 5–10 P.M. Sat., 10 A.M.–2 P.M. and 5–10 P.M. Sun., $35) is a longtime institution reinvented as a Michelin-starred restaurant where dinner for two can easily cost $200. The country-estate elegance is articulated with box-beam ceilings, red velvet chairs, and clean white walls accented by dark wood trim. The cuisine is based on the restaurant's partnership with a local farm and is executed in the French and Mediterranean styles that have come to characterize high-end California cooking; you'll find lots of charcuterie, cornichons, and cassoulets. In addition to dinner and lunch, there is a pub menu (11:30 A.M.–10 P.M. Mon.–Fri.).

© SABRINA YOUNG

Alice's Restaurant is a popular stop for hikers, bikers, and cyclists.

The **Woodside Bakery and Café** (3052 Woodside Rd., 650/851-7247, http://woodside-bakery.com, daily 6 A.M.–9 P.M., $15–30) still holds on to its earthy roots. For breakfast, order eggs, home fries, and waffles; for lunch, opt for a salad, a grilled sandwich, or wood-fired pizza. Dinner has carpaccio, rack of lamb, and scampi risotto on the menu. You'll also have your pick of pies, pastries, muffins, cakes, cupcakes, and, of course, plenty of coffee options to wash it down. All the choices are well executed, but the casual atmosphere makes for an incongruous dining experience.

Robert's Market (3015 Woodside Rd., 650/851-1511, www.robertsmarket.com, daily 6:30 A.M.–8 P.M.), across the street from the Woodside Bakery, has one of the best delis around with traditional sandwich fixings along with specials of the house. The French ham and brie and the avocado BLT are particularly tasty. You can also pick up a variety of premade pasta salads, antipasti salads, and grilled or marinated vegetables as sides, along with chips, soft drinks, and sweets.

Getting There and Around

Woodside is along Highway 84 between Highway 35 (Skyline Blvd.) and I-280. From San Francisco, take I-280 for 30 miles south to Highway 84 (Woodside Rd.) west. From the coast, take Highway 1 south to San Gregorio, about 14 miles south of Half Moon Bay. Turn onto Highway 84 east and follow it all the way to Woodside.

PALO ALTO

Palo Alto owes much of its prosperity and character to neighboring Stanford University, which was founded by Leland and Jane Stanford in memory of their deceased son. In the 1990s Palo Alto went through a not entirely welcome transformation when it became a center for venture capitalists funding the emerging dot-com start-up companies.

Stanford University

Stanford University (end of University Ave., Stanford, 650/723-2560, www.stanford.edu) is one of the top universities in the world, and fewer than 10 percent of the high school students who apply each year are accepted. The **visitors center** (295 Galvez St., www.stanford.edu, 8:30 A.M.–5 P.M. Mon.–Fri., 10 A.M.–5 P.M. Sat.–Sun.) is in a handsome one-story brick building; inside, well-trained staff can help you with campus maps and tours. Definitely download or procure a map of campus before getting started on your explorations, as Stanford is infamously hard for newcomers to navigate.

For a taste of the beauty that surrounds the students on a daily basis, begin your tour with **The Quad** (Oval at Palm Dr.) and **Memorial Church.** Located at the center of campus, these architectural gems are still in active use. Classes are held in the quad every day, and services take place in the church each Sunday. Almost

© ELIZABETH LINHART MONEY

Stanford's Hoover Tower

next door to the Quad is **Hoover Tower** (daily 10 A.M.–4 P.M.), the tall tower that's visible from up to 30 miles away. For great views of the Bay Area, head up to its observation platform.

On the other side of the Quad, just past the Oval, is the **Cantor Arts Center** (Lomita Dr. and Museum Way, 650/723-4177, www.museum.stanford.edu, 11 A.M.–5 P.M. Wed.–Sun., 11 A.M.–8 P.M. Thurs.). This free art museum features both permanent collections of classic paintings and sculpture donated by the Cantors and other philanthropists, along with traveling exhibitions. One of the center's highlights is the **Rodin Sculpture Garden,** pieces cast in France from Rodin's originals that include *The Burghers of Calais* and *The Gates of Hell.* The most famous member of this collection, *The Thinker,* can be found in the Susan and John Diekman Gallery inside the museum.

Farther toward the edges of campus lurk two more treasures. **The Dish** (http://dish.stanford.edu) is a radio telescope that perches high on the Stanford hills, visible from Palm Drive and many other spots on the peninsula. Along Junipero Serra Boulevard and Campus Drive East, several trails run up the hillside to the Dish. Once up the hill, you can hike back down—the observatory and radio telescope are not open to visitors. Built by the Stanford Research Institute in 1966 to study earth's atmosphere and later used to communicate with spacecraft and satellites, the Dish rarely sees any action these days. But hiking the Dish along the many pedestrian trails is a time-honored Stanford tradition.

The second monument to science stretches for a full mile across Stanford land into the hills. The **Stanford Linear Accelerator Center** (SLAC, 2575 Sand Hill Rd., Menlo Park, www.slac.stanford.edu) is one of only a few research facilities of its kind in the world. Here atoms are launched at one end of the building and reach high speeds before smashing into a barrier at the other end. Stanford researchers study the smashed pieces, increasing knowledge about the subatomic world. The work at SLAC is serious, and so is visiting. Unscheduled guests are promptly turned away at the gate. The only way to enter the facility is by registering with a pre-scheduled tour (4 times per month, maximum 25 people). To book a spot on a tour, check online on the third Friday the month before 9 A.M. At that time, the next month's tour schedule will be posted, and you can register for a spot.

Entertainment and Events

Palo Alto enjoys a vibrant entertainment scene. **Stanford Lively Arts** (650/725-2787, http://livelyarts.stanford.edu, prices and locations vary) puts on an array of concerts and live staged entertainment each season. Expect to see several jazz ensembles each year, some world music, a world premiere or two, and perhaps an unusual dance piece.

In town, the small **Dragon Theatre** (535 Alma St., 650/493-2006, www.dragonproductions.net) puts on both well-known plays and premieres by local playwrights. Recent offerings have included *Rough Crossing* by Tom Stoppard and *The Underpants* by Steve Martin. The acting pool is deep, since nearby Foothill College has an award-winning theater conservatory program that turns out excellent actors, directors, and stagehands.

Many students and longtime residents of Palo Alto enjoy seeing classic black-and-white movies back up on the big screen where they belong. Old-school movie house **The Stanford Theatre** (221 University Ave., 650/324-3700, www.stanfordtheatre.org) has plush red velvet seats, beautifully painted walls and ceiling, and a year-round schedule of fabulous old films. The Stanford Theatre often hosts festivals to highlight a specific star or genre.

Shopping

Once populated by bookstores and boutiques, **University Avenue** is now dominated

SAN FRANCISCO BAY AREA

by restaurants of all stripes. The side streets off University Avenue hide some of the most unique stores, like **Five Ten Gifts** (510 Waverly St., 650/322-4510, www.fivetengifts.com, 11 A.M.–5 P.M. Tues.–Fri., noon–5 P.M. Sat.). Among its overstocked shelves, you'll find six-foot-long watches, brightly hand-painted teacups, an assortment of gag gifts, and paper lanterns. Equally unique but with a fine-art twist is **De Novo Fine Contemporary Jewelry** (250 University Ave., 650/327-1256, www.de-novo.com, 10 A.M.–6 P.M. Mon.–Sat.). Two doors down from University Avenue on Ramona Street, this jewelry store eschews flashy baubles in favor of handcrafted jewelry made by artisans from around the world. Nearby is one of the best art-supply stores—**University Arts** (267 Hamilton St., 650/328-5000, www.university-art.com, 9:30 A.M.–5:30 P.M. Mon.–Wed. and Fri.–Sat., 9:30 A.M.–7 P.M. Thurs., noon–4 P.M. Sun.). Even out-of-town artists make it a point to check out the vast shelves filled with the finest brushes, colors, and raw materials.

The serious shopping happens at the open-air **Stanford Shopping Center** (Sand Hill Rd. and El Camino Real, www.stanfordshop.com, 10 A.M.–9 P.M. Mon.–Fri., 10 A.M.–7 P.M. Sat., 11 A.M.–6 P.M. Sun.), with upscale boutiques and top-tier department stores befitting the affluence of the area. Big stores include Bloomingdale's, Nordstrom, Macy's, and Neiman Marcus.

Sports and Recreation

Stanford University (www.stanford.edu) enjoys a reputation for athletics almost as great as its rep for academics. The women's basketball program is legendary, as is the men's baseball team. The golf team boasts Tiger Woods as an alumnus, and more than a few Olympians have swum in the pools and run on the tracks.

After a long day of exploring the Stanford campus, a dip in hot tub followed by a luxurious spa treatment makes the perfect end to the day. **Watercourse Way** (165 Channing Ave., 650/462-2000, www.watercourseway.com, 8 A.M.–11:30 P.M. Sun.–Thurs., 8 A.M.–12:30 A.M. Fri.–Sat., $18–28) enjoys the title of the Silicon Valley's premier day spa. It stands out for its amazing tiled tub rooms, range of treatments, and array of top-tier products. Each rentable hot-tub room boasts unique and serene decor. The spa treatments are relatively reasonably priced, and the pampering is second to none.

Accommodations

Lodgings near Palo Alto on the cheap can be found in the serene farm setting of **Hidden Villa Hostel** (26870 Moody Rd., Lost Altos Hills, 650/949-8648, www.hiddenvilla.org, Sept.–May, $27–60). A sustainably constructed hostel building and a private cabin that's perfect for families and romantic honeymooners, the Hidden Villa Hostel also has access to beautiful wilderness hiking trails, the surrounding organic farm, and the small wealthy town of Los Altos Hills. Hidden Villa is the oldest operating youth hostel in the United States, and it's incredibly popular. The newer buildings are more unique and attractive than those of most hostels, and were created to showcase features such as the radiant floor heating and bale wall construction. Reservations are required on weekends and a good idea even on weekdays.

Down on El Camino Real, **Dinah's Garden Hotel** (4261 El Camino Real, 800/227-8220, www.dinahshotel.com, $199–250) doesn't quite feel like a chain despite its location and basic shape. The cute koi ponds and gardens mix with the bright floral interior decor to create a tropical paradise theme. The basic guest rooms are the size and shape of a motel, but the high-priced suites are something to behold. Attached to the hotel are both a casual poolside grill and an upscale restaurant, a branch of the legendary Trader Vic's.

The **Creekside Inn** (3400 El Camino Real, 650/493-2411, www.creekside-inn.com,

$100–160) provides garden accommodations set back a bit from the noisy road. The guest rooms are a bit more upscale than many motels in the same price range, with stylish fabrics and up-to-date amenities. This larger boutique hotel has more than 100 guest rooms, an outdoor heated pool, and an exercise room. All guest rooms have free Wi-Fi, fully stocked private baths, refrigerators, coffeemakers, in-room safes, and comfy bathrobes. You can get a package deal that includes breakfast with your room.

Much closer to the Stanford campus, the **Stanford Terrace Inn** (531 Stanford Ave., 650/857-0333, www.stanfordterraceinn.com, $200–250) provides appropriate luxury to visiting parents. The Terrace has eco-conscious guest rooms with all hypoallergenic and sustainable furnishings, linens, and toiletries, plus filtered water and air. All guest rooms, even the standard ones, are huge and come with attractive furnishings and luxury amenities. The lovely indoor-outdoor restaurant is popular with the locals on holiday weekends.

Food

A historic favorite often associated with Stanford, **Sundance the Steakhouse** (1921 El Camino Real, 650/321-6798, http://sundancethesteakhouse.com, 11:30 A.M.–2 P.M. and 5–10 P.M. Tues.–Sat., 5–9 P.M. Sun.–Mon., $19–39) reeks of old boys' club. The dimly lit interior features dark wood, dark booths, black-and-white prints, and antique sporting equipment. The food tends toward steaks; order a big cut of beef complete with traditional sides, or opt for the more interesting California-style seafood preparation. The salads and starters are tempting, but save room for dessert.

The **Rose and Crown** (457 Emerson Ave., 650/327-7673, www.roseandcrownpa.com, 11:30 A.M.–2 P.M. and 6–9 P.M. Mon.–Fri., 11:30 A.M.–9 P.M. Sat.–Sun., $8–10) is a pub in every sense of the word, with a serious selection of beer and a menu of British food. The Rose and Crown is cozy, dark, and cluttered, perfect to wile away an afternoon over a pitcher of beer or catch a soccer game with some noisy fans.

Palo Alto is home to a venerable seafood institution: **Scott's Seafood Grill & Bar** (Town and Country Village, Suite 1, 855 El Camino Real, 650/323-1555, www.scottsseafoodpa.com, 11 A.M.–9 P.M. Mon.–Tues., 11 A.M.–9:30 P.M. Wed.–Fri., 9 A.M.–9:30 P.M. Sat., 9 A.M.–9 P.M. Sun., $20–36). This elegant white-tablecloth restaurant has a large window-lined dining room and a bar on the other side. At breakfast and lunch, Scott's caters to the business set—many power lunches take place here over salmon and sole. The seafood at Scott's runs to a good variety of fish done up in fine preparations, often with exotic sauces. The wine list is worth perusing, with fine California vintages and European wines.

The kitschy decor at the **Palo Alto Creamery** (566 Emerson St., 650/323-3131, www.paloaltocreamery.com, 7 A.M.–10 P.M. Mon.–Wed., 7 A.M.–11 P.M. Thurs., 7 A.M.–midnight Fri., 8 A.M.–midnight Sat., 8 A.M.–10 P.M. Sun., $7–13) makes diners feel they're in a genuine 1950s soda shop. Red vinyl, shiny chrome, a black-and-white checked floor, a long counter, and funky booths help complete the picture. The food runs to burgers, sandwiches, and American classic entrées, but what you really come for is the house-made ice cream. Be aware that the Creamery gets crowded, especially on weekends. Locals know it's open pretty late and often fill the place to the brim for an after-show meal.

Information and Services

The **Palo Alto Visitors Center** (400 Mitchell Lane, 650/324-3121, www.destinationpaloalto.com, 9 A.M.–5 P.M. Mon.–Sat.) is conveniently located, complete with ample parking. Inside, you'll find plenty of helpful tips on local sights, restaurants, and events. Also grab a couple of maps, specifically of Stanford University.

For a taste of local entertainment listings, check out the *Daily Post* or the *Palo Alto Weekly* (published Fri.), the older of the two and known for producing more in-depth features.

The nearest 24-hour emergency room is **Stanford University Hospital** (300 Pasteur Dr., 650/723-5111, http://stanfordhospital.org). For nonlife-threatening emergencies visit the **Palo Alto Medical Foundation Urgent Care Center** (795 El Camino Real, 650/321-4121, www.pamf.org, daily 7 A.M.–9 P.M.).

Getting There and Around

Palo Alto is easily accessed via U.S. 101 and I-280 and is equidistant between **Mineta San Jose International Airport** (SJC, 1667–2077 Airport Blvd., 408/501-0979, www.sjc.org) and **San Francisco International Airport** (SFO, 800/435-9736, www.flysfo.com). **Caltrain** (800/660-4287, www.caltrain.com, $3–13) can get you here as well; the commuter rail line runs from Gilroy to San Francisco with a hub in San Jose. That same hub has access to **VTA Light Rail** (408/321-2300, www.vta.org, $2–4), serving San Jose up to Mountain View.

San Jose

Sprawled across the south end of Silicon Valley, San Jose proudly claims the title of biggest city in the Bay Area. It is the beating heart of the valley's high-tech industry and is home to eBay, Cisco, Adobe, IBM, and many others. Long considered a cultural wasteland, in the last decade San Jose has worked to change its image, supporting local art and attracting high-end restaurants. If you want to get a sense of how Silicon Valley residents really live, spend a few days in San Jose.

SIGHTS
San Jose Museum of Art

The highly regarded San Jose Museum of Art (110 S. Market St., 408/271-6840, www.sjmusart.org, 11 A.M.–5 P.M. Tues.–Sun., adults $8, students and seniors $5, under age 6 free) is right downtown. Housed in a historic sandstone building that was added on to in 1991, the beautiful light-filled museum features modern and contemporary art. Its permanent collection focuses largely on West Coast artists, but major retrospectives of works by the likes of Andy Warhol, Robert Mapplethorpe, and Alexander Calder come through often, giving the museum a broader scope. As a

bonus, the Museum Store offers perhaps the best gift shopping in downtown San Jose. Likewise, the café, with both an indoor lounge and outside sidewalk tables, is a great place to grab a quick bite.

the historic San Jose Museum of Art

© CSP/123RF.COM

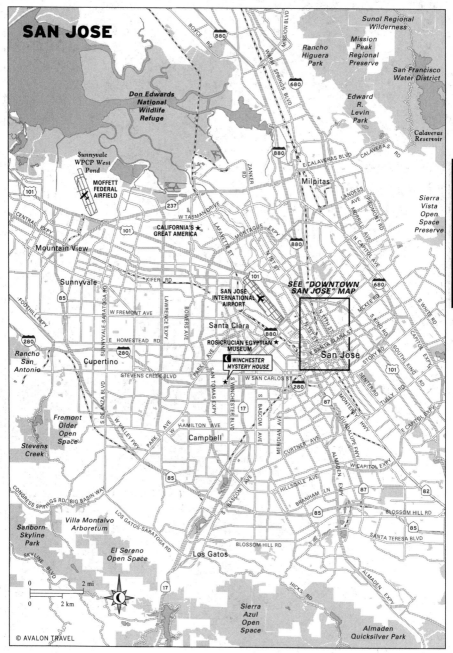

SAN JOSE

Sunol Regional Wilderness

Mission Peak Regional Preserve

San Francisco Water District

Rancho Higuera Park

Don Edwards National Wildlife Refuge

Edward R. Levin Park

Calaveras Reservoir

Sunnyvale WPCP West Pond

MOFFETT FEDERAL AIRFIELD

Milpitas

Sierra Vista Open Space Preserve

Mountain View

CALIFORNIA'S GREAT AMERICA ★

Sunnyvale

SAN JOSE INTERNATIONAL AIRPORT

SEE "DOWNTOWN SAN JOSE" MAP

Santa Clara

ROSICRUCIAN EGYPTIAN MUSEUM ★

San Jose

Rancho San Antonio

Cupertino

WINCHESTER MYSTERY HOUSE ★

STEVENS CREEK BLVD

Fremont Older Open Space

Stevens Creek

Campbell

Sanborn-Skyline Park

Villa Montalvo Arboretum

BLOSSOM HILL RD

El Sereno Open Space

Los Gatos

BLOSSOM HILL RD

SANTA TERESA BLVD

0   2 mi

0   2 km

Sierra Azul Open Space

Almaden Quicksilver Park

© AVALON TRAVEL

SAN FRANCISCO BAY AREA

SAN FRANCISCO BAY AREA

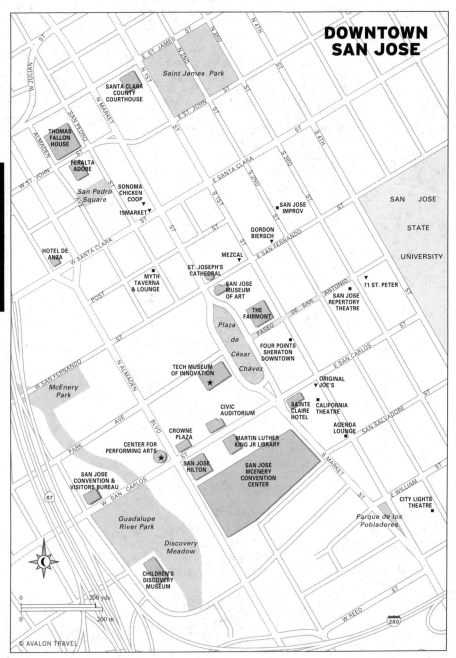

DOWNTOWN
SAN JOSE

Saint James Park

SANTA CLARA
COUNTY
COURTHOUSE

THOMAS
FALLON
HOUSE

PERALTA
ADOBE

San Pedro
Square

SONOMA
CHICKEN
COOP

19MARKET

HOTEL DE
ANZA

SAN JOSE
IMPROV

GORDON
BIERSCH

MEZCAL

MYTH
TAVERNA
& LOUNGE

ST. JOSEPH'S
CATHEDRAL

SAN JOSE
MUSEUM
OF ART

THE
FAIRMONT

Plaza
de
César
Chávez

SAN JOSE   STATE   UNIVERSITY

71 ST. PETER

SAN JOSE
REPERTORY
THEATRE

FOUR POINTS
SHERATON
DOWNTOWN

TECH MUSEUM
OF INNOVATION

McEnery
Park

CIVIC
AUDITORIUM

ORIGINAL
JOE'S

SAINTE
CLAIRE
HOTEL

CALIFORNIA
THEATRE

AGENDA
LOUNGE

CROWNE
PLAZA

CENTER FOR
PERFORMING ARTS

SAN JOSE
HILTON

MARTIN LUTHER
KING JR LIBRARY

SAN JOSE
MCENERY
CONVENTION
CENTER

SAN JOSE
CONVENTION &
VISITORS BUREAU

CITY LIGHTS
THEATRE

Guadalupe
River Park

Parque de los
Pobladores

Discovery
Meadow

CHILDREN'S
DISCOVERY
MUSEUM

0   200 yds
0   200 m

© AVALON TRAVEL

Tech Museum of Innovation

The Tech Museum of Innovation (201 S. Market St., 408/294-8324, www.thetech.org, daily 10 A.M.–5 P.M., adults $12, children $9) brings technology of all kinds to kids, families, and science lovers. The interactive displays at the Tech invite touching, letting children explore, and learn about medical technology, computers, biology, chemistry, physics, and more using all their senses. Traveling exhibits also make the rounds here and help to flesh out the Tech's somewhat aging displays. Recently, these have included *Islamic Science Rediscovered* and the (to some) stomach-churning but eye-opening (no pun intended) *Body Worlds Vital*. The IMAX theater (additional $4) shows films dedicated to science, learning, technology, and adventure.

Rosicrucian Egyptian Museum

Perhaps San Jose's most unusual attraction is the imposing Rosicrucian Egyptian Museum

the Rosicrucian Egyptian Museum

(1660 Park Ave., 408/947-3635, www.egyptianmuseum.org, 9 A.M.–5 P.M. Wed.–Fri., 10 A.M.–6 P.M. Sat.–Sun., adults $9, students and seniors $7, children $5). The museum was opened by the Rosicrucian Order in 1928 and has a wonderful collection of ancient Egyptian artifacts, including several mummies—partly unwrapped, a rarity today. Local children and adults love the Rosicrucian's jewels, tomb artifacts, tools, and textiles. The complex also boasts a planetarium, but at the time of writing it is temporarily closed; call for current information on shows and showtimes.

◖ Winchester Mystery House

For good old-fashioned haunted fun, stop in at the Winchester Mystery House (525 S. Winchester Blvd., 408/247-2101, www.winchestermysteryhouse.com, daily 9 A.M.–5 P.M., adults $27, children $20). A San Jose attraction that predates the rise of Silicon Valley, the huge bizarre mansion was built by famous eccentric Sarah Winchester. Kids love the doors that open onto brick walls, stairwells that go nowhere, and oddly shaped rooms, while adults enjoy the story of Sarah and the antiques displayed in many of the rooms. Sarah married into the gun-making Winchester family and became disturbed later in life by the destruction and death wrought by her husband's products. She designed the house to both facilitate communication with the spirits of the dead and to confound them and keep herself safe. Whether or not ghosts still haunt the mansion is a matter of debate and of faith—visit and make up your own mind. Admission to the grounds is free, but to get a peek inside the house, you must be on one of the many tours ($27–35). For an extra-spooky experience, take a Friday the 13th or Halloween flashlight tour (book early, as these tours fill up fast).

Winchester Mystery House

DOOR TO NOWHERE

ENTERTAINMENT AND EVENTS

Cultural travelers can get seats to **Ballet San Jose** (408/288-2800, www.balletsanj.org, $30–85) at the Center for the Performing Arts (255 Almaden Blvd.) or to **Opera San Jose** (408/437-4450, www.operasj.org, $51–101) at the California Theatre (345 S. First St.).

Live theater options also abound in downtown San Jose. The big pro company is the **San Jose Repertory Theatre** (101 Paseo de San Antonio, 408/367-7255, www.sjrep.com, $30–74), locally known as the Rep. The theater space has been rebuilt and the company made over in an attempt to lure a younger audience with edgy new works. This has only been partly successful—the audience still leans toward their canes, and shows sometimes get so close to the edge that they fall off into the abyss of bad theater. Still, it can be fun to see the action in the gorgeous newer space. On the other hand, **City Lights Theatre** (529 S. 2nd St., 408/295-4200, www.cltc.org, $15–40), just down the block from the Rep, has a

tiny black box–style theater and little money to spend on fancy lobby light fixtures. But the shows, mostly featuring up-and-coming local performers, never fail to entertain. Their take on everything from *Lysistrata* to *The Waiting Room* is fresh and original, providing a perfect local theater experience with a definite Silicon Valley flavor.

The clubs in San Jose certainly are suburban, but the lack of self-conscious hipness can make a night out at **Agenda Lounge** (399 S. 1st St., 408/287-3991, www.agendalounge.com, 5:30 P.M.–2 A.M. Wed.–Sat., 9 P.M.–2 A.M. Sun.) or **Myth Taverna and Lounge** (152 Post St., 408/286-7678, www.mythsj.com) more relaxed than a trek up to San Francisco.

Live comedy is another popular Silicon Valley option. The **San Jose Improv** (62 S. 2nd St., 408/280-7475, www.improv.com), located in the historic San Jose Theatre, often hosts major-league headliners like Margaret Cho and Kevin Nealon while also granting stage time to local talent in showcases and contests.

SHOPPING

A variety of big shopping malls and an endless series of mini malls fan out over San Jose's miles of terrain. The top place to shop is **Santana Row** (Stevens Creek Blvd. and Winchester Blvd., www.santanarow.com). This upscale outdoor center dazzles the eye with its array of chic chain and one-off boutiques, shops, and restaurants. Shops include Sur La Table, Anthropologie, Brooks Brothers, and many more.

SPORTS AND RECREATION

For a straight-up thrill ride–heavy amusement park, go to **California's Great America** (4701 Great America Pkwy., Santa Clara, 408/988-1776, www.cagreatamerica.com, 10 A.M.–8 P.M. Sun.–Fri., 10 A.M.–10 P.M. Sat. June–Aug., adults $46–56, children $36, parking $12). With roller coasters from classic to legs-dangling, a vertical drop, water rides, a full-fledged water park, a slime-filled kid's zone, and much more, Great America makes for an energetic, often hot, all-day romp. To cool down, head to **Raging Waters** (2333 S. White Rd., 408/238-9900, www.rwsplash.com, daily 10:30 A.M.–6 P.M. June–Aug., adults $30, children $22). This sprawling water park features up-to-date slides and rides, plus plenty of serene pools for relaxing on a hot and sunny San Jose summer day. For both parks, be sure to check out the website before you visit: Not only do hours vary, but significant deals on ticket prices can be had if purchased online.

San Jose may be mocked by its cousins in San Francisco and the East Bay, but there are some great and different professional sports worth seeing. The big dog in the area is the **San Jose Sharks** (http://sharks.nhl.com) National Hockey League team. They haven't won a Stanley Cup yet, but everyone gets into the games at the downtown HP Pavilion (525 W. Santa Clara St.), making San Jose one of the loudest and liveliest places to watch a game in the league.

ACCOMMODATIONS

The **Arena Hotel** (817 The Alameda, 408/294-6500, www.pacifichotels.com, $100–150) is conveniently near HP Pavilion, making it perfect for hockey fans and concertgoers. It's more motel than hotel, since guest rooms tend toward the small and the decor toward chain-motel floral ticky-tacky. You do get the standard TV, mini fridge, coffeemaker, and a surprise whirlpool tub.

The Hotel Montgomery was promoted as San Jose's first luxury hotel when it opened in 1911. Now rechristened as the **Four Points Sheraton Downtown San Jose** (211 S. 1st St., 408/282-8800, www.fourpoints.com, $100–140), it still prides itself on its old-school elegance and hospitality. Guest rooms echo the elegance and add a touch of comfort, with Egyptian cotton linens and cushy comforters on the beds. Local original art and a standard-issue red leather chair round out the room decor. Posh amenities include an on-site gym, restaurant and bar, room service, and Wi-Fi in the public areas of the hotel.

The **Sainte Claire Hotel** (302 S. Market St., 408/295-2000, www.thesainteclaire.com, $155) offers big city–style accommodations. Standard guest rooms are small but attractive, with carved wooden furniture and rich linens and draperies. The suites are more luxurious. Amenities include a flat-screen TV with a DVD player, a CD and MP3 player, free Wi-Fi, plush robes, and turndown service.

For a taste of true Silicon Valley luxury, stay at **The Fairmont San Jose** (170 S. Market St., 408/998-1900, www.fairmont.com, $150–180). With a day spa and limousine service, it's no surprise that the 731 guest rooms at the Fairmont are something special. Even the standard guest rooms have plenty of space, elegant fabrics and appointments, and a marble-clad private bath with a separate shower and bathtub. Of the Fairmont's two towers, the South Tower has the more luxurious guest rooms.

© ELIZABETH LINHART MONEY

the Sainte Claire Hotel

Consumer culture takes a turn for the absurd at the **Hotel Valencia Santana Row** (355 Santana Row, 408/551-0010, www.hotelvalencia-santanarow.com, $225). This top-tier hotel is right in the middle of the prestigious shopping mall incongruously named for a local musical legend. Ultramodern elegance and convenience includes everything from Internet-enabled phones on the desks to fuzzy black throw blankets on the beds. The lavish baths with upscale toiletries help to make the hotel experience pleasing to all the senses.

FOOD

A remarkable array of restaurants tempt visitors and locals alike in San Jose. The only problem is that many are not open for lunch on the weekend, as downtown San Jose largely caters to the business crowd. Still, places like **71 Saint Peter** (71 N. San Pedro St., 408/971-8523, www.71saintpeter.com, 11:30 A.M.–2 P.M. and 5–9 P.M. Mon.–Fri., 5–9 P.M. Sat., $15–28)

are worth holding out for dinner. Billed as a Mediterranean grill, the cuisine takes inspiration from Europe and blends it with the flavors and fresh ingredients of California. While the à la carte menus are fine, the real treat in this charming indoor-outdoor dining room is the seasonal tasting menu. Featuring the best available produce of the current season, this four-course dinner is not only delicious, it's a bargain.

For folks who want tasty food without the white tablecloths, the **Sonoma Chicken Coop** (31 N. Market St., 408/287-4098, www.sonomachickencoop.com, 11 A.M.–9 P.M. Sun.–Thurs., 11 A.M.–10 P.M. Fri.–Sat., $7–12) offers a fun alternative to upscale California cuisine. At the Coop, you walk up to the counter to order, then find your own table either inside the always-packed dining room or out on the back terrace. Your order number is called, and you must grab your own tray of food. Choose from roast chicken (of course), fondue appetizers, duck, homemade pizzas, and other items, which you can pair with tasty side dishes. Plenty of interesting salads make a somewhat lighter meal.

Open seven days a week, **Gordon Biersch** (33 E. San Fernando St., 408/294-6785, www.gordonbiersch.com, 11:30 A.M.–11 P.M. Sun.–Wed., 11:30 A.M.–midnight Thurs., 11:30 A.M.–1 A.M. Fri.–Sat., $12–28) is always busy, and the food and beer are tasty. Try the blackened ahi tacos or the Cajun pasta, but don't miss out on one of the handcrafted German-style beers brewed on-site. It has a lively happy hour, particularly if a local sports team is playing on the large overhead TVs in the bar.

Just a few doors down, **Mezcal** (25 W. San Fernando St., 408/283-9595, http://mezcal-restaurantsj.com, 11:30 A.M.–9 P.M. Mon., 11:30 A.M.–10 P.M. Tues.–Thurs., 11:30 A.M.–11:30 P.M. Fri., 4–11:30 P.M. Sat., 4–9 P.M. Sun., $10–19) offers something a bit spicier. Specializing in food from the Oaxaca region of Mexico, the menu is full of moles, pork cracklings, and fresh fish, fruit, and vegetables. Handmade corn tortillas accompany many menu items. One of Mezcal's standout dishes and a local favorite is the *chapulines* appetizer (sautéed grasshoppers). High ceilings, exposed brick and beams, smart lighting, and trim tables and chairs give Mezcal a dynamic, urban touch.

Further upscale and up Market Street, **19Market** (19 N. Market St., 408/280-6111, www.19market.com, 11:30 A.M.–3 P.M. and 5–10 P.M. Mon.–Thurs., 11:30 A.M.–3 P.M. and 5 P.M.–midnight Fri., 5 P.M.–midnight Sat., 5–10 P.M. Sun., $18) serves traditional Vietnamese food with a high polish. The high-end interior features white tablecloths and a bar noteworthy for its inventive cocktails. Happily, the food—such as duck spring rolls and tamarind prawns—matches this sophistication.

A good reason to venture up to Japantown is **Gombei** (193 E. Jackson St., 408/279-4311, http://gombei.com, 11:30 A.M.–2:30 P.M. and 5–9:30 P.M. Mon.–Sat., $9) for traditional Japanese food at good prices. The menu is as minimal as the decor, with simple headers such as *udon,* tofu, and curry rice.

At **Original Joe's** (301 S. 1st St., 408/292-7030, www.originaljoes.com, daily 11 A.M.–1 A.M., $27), little has changed—from the decor to the food—in the 56 years since it opened. Veal parmigiana and pot roast share the menu with calf's liver served four different ways. There is a variety of pasta and steaks as well as the mid-century bar, The Hideout.

INFORMATION AND SERVICES

Before you come to San Jose, visit www.sanjose.org to get all the information you need about the Silicon Valley region and its attractions. Once in town, you can stop in at the **San Jose Convention and Visitors Bureau** (408 Almaden Blvd., 408/295-9600) for maps, brochures, guidebooks, and local advice.

San Jose has its own major daily newspaper that competes for business with its more famous northern neighbor. The *San Jose Mercury News* (www.mercurynews.com) covers national news and wire service stories along with plenty of local events and happenings. The entertainment section can provide some local events info. But when it comes to nightlife, most locals pick up a copy of *San Jose Metro* (www.metroactive.com), a free rag that proclaims itself the hippest of the Silicon Valley entertainment publications.

San Jose has plenty of **post offices,** including downtown at 200 South 3rd Street.

Here in the heart of Silicon Valley, it's tough to find a patch of air that doesn't have some Wi-Fi flowing through it. Expect to pay for Internet access at Starbucks and some of the luxury hotels. If that's not to your taste, warchalking is practically an art form here (but you didn't hear that from us).

For medical attention, **Good Samaritan Hospital** (2425 Samaritan Dr., 408/559-2011, www.goodsamsj.org) has 24-hour emergency services.

GETTING THERE AND AROUND

Travelers heading straight for Silicon Valley should skip San Francisco International Airport and fly into **Mineta San Jose International Airport** (SJC, 1667–2077 Airport Blvd., 408/501-0979, www.sjc.org) if at all possible. This suburban commercial airport has shorter lines, less parking and traffic congestion, and is convenient to downtown San Jose.

Amtrak (800/872-7245, www.amtrak.com) trains come into San Jose, and you can catch either the once-daily Seattle–Los Angeles *Coast Starlight* or the commuter *Capitol Corridor* to Sacramento at the **San Jose-Diridon Station** (65 Cahill St.). See the Amtrak website for information about scheduling and fares.

San Jose–Diridon station is also a hub for **Caltrain** (800/660-4287, www.caltrain.com, $3–13), a commuter train that runs from Gilroy to San Francisco. If you'd like to spend a day or even two in San Francisco but base yourself in Silicon Valley, taking Caltrain is an excellent way to go.

At Diridon station you can even catch the **VTA Light Rail** (408/321-2300, www.vta.org, $2–4), a streetcar network that serves San Jose and some of Silicon Valley as far north as Mountain View.

The VTA also operates Silicon Valley **buses** (408/321-2300, www.vta.org, $2–4), which can get you almost anywhere you need to go if you're patient enough.

As with most of the Bay Area, it's best to avoid San Jose's freeways 7–9:30 A.M. and 4–7:30 P.M. Monday–Friday. Arterial U.S. 101 is a dank, dirty stretch of road that's convenient to much of the peninsula. I-280 is much prettier and less convenient, but definitely the easiest, but not the shortest, driving route north to San Francisco. Highway 17 is the fast, treacherous route over the hills from the coast and Santa Cruz; it turns into I-880 in the middle of San Jose and runs past the end of the Bay and then north along the east side of the water all the way to Oakland. Highway 87, sometimes called the Guadalupe Parkway, can provide

Caltrain is a great way to travel to and from San Jose.

convenient access to downtown San Jose and the airport.

Parking in San Jose isn't anywhere near as bad as in San Francisco, but you should still be prepared to pay a premium for event parking and enclosed lots at the fancier hotels.

LOS GATOS

Charming Los Gatos is 10 miles west of San Jose along Highway 17 at the gateway to the Santa Cruz Mountains. Quaint shops and a stellar restaurant make it worth the trek.

Los Gatos boasts a picturesque downtown filled with restaurants, cafés, boutiques, and blue-blood retail chains. The best shopping can be found on University and Santa Cruz Avenues as well as on Main Street, where toy stores, cooking stores, and funky mom-and-pop shops line the sidewalks. **The French Cellar** (32 E. Main St., 408/354-0993, www.thefrenchcellar.com, 11 A.M.–6 P.M. Tues.–Sat., 11 A.M.–4 P.M. Sun.) sells all things French in a cluttered, homey storefront. You can find a wide selection of Native American art and jewelry at the **Indian Store** (68 W. Main St., 408/354-9988, www.theindianstore.com, 10 A.M.–6 P.M. Mon.–Sat., 11 A.M.–5 P.M. Sun.). A real Los Gatos one-of-a-kind is **Gina's Shop** (25 W. Main St., 408/354-3189, call for hours), with African ceremonial masks, woven baskets from Indonesia, and a whole shelf devoted to Mexican Day of the Dead figurines.

The most venerated restaurant in the South Bay is **⬛ Manresa** (320 Village Lane, 408/354-4330, www.manresarestaurant.com, 5:30–9 P.M. Wed.–Sun.). Chef and proprietor David Kinch has earned Manresa two Michelin stars for five consecutive years for his haute cuisine entirely derived from the California coast. The menu features such delicate oddities as *panna cotta* topped with abalone "petals," a "winter tidal pool" of shellfish, fois gras, and seaweed, or duck roasted in hay. Diners can choose from the four-course prix fixe menu ($125) or the "seasonal and spontaneous" tasting menu ($175). Surprisingly, Manresa accepts walk-ins, but if you're looking for a special Saturday-night affair, don't wait until the last minute; these coveted spots can be fully booked a month in advance.

For an entirely different dining experience, the **Los Gatos Coffee Roasting Company** (101 W. Main St., 408/354-3263, www.lgcrc.com, 6 A.M.–6 P.M. Mon.–Sat., 6:30 A.M.–6 P.M. Sun., $10) offers freshly roasted coffee, espresso drinks, crepes, paninis, and pastries to a devoted following. Always crowded with locals, this is a great place to cool your heels after a day shopping and walking around town.

WINE COUNTRY

Entering California's Wine Country is an unmistakable experience. From the crest of the last hill, sunlight paints golden streaks on endless rows of grapevines that stretch in every direction for as far as the eye can see. Trellises run along both sides of every road, tempting visitors to question the unpicked weeds beneath the vines, the rose bushes capping each row, and the strange motionless fans standing guard high above. A heady aroma of earth and grapes permeates the area. Welcome to the Napa and Sonoma Valleys.

The area's beautiful grapevines are renowned worldwide for producing top-quality vintages and economical varietal table wines. But foodies also know the area as a center for stellar cuisine. Yountville, a tiny upscale town in the middle of Napa Valley, is the favorite haven of celebrity chef Thomas Keller. The food served at his French Laundry restaurant is legendary, as are the prices. Keller's influence helped to usher in a culinary renaissance, and today the lush flavors of local sustainable produce are available throughout the region.

Sonoma Valley has long played second fiddle to Napa in terms of viticultural prestige, but the wines coming out of the area are second to none. The Russian River Valley wineries are often friendlier and less crowded than their Napa counterparts, while the wineries in the southern Carneros region are few and far between. Each offers visitors a more personal experience than Napa and the chance to

HIGHLIGHTS

LOOK FOR **(** TO FIND RECOMMENDED SIGHTS, ACTIVITIES, DINING, AND LODGING.

(**Domaine Chandon:** This Yountville winery offers a gorgeous setting in which to sample its premier California champagne. Their tour is one of the best in Napa (page 211).

(**Grgich Hills:** Home of the California chardonnay that won the Paris Wine Tasting of 1976, Grgich Hills uses a biodynamic farming process to produce exquisite wines (page 219).

(**Mumm:** This sophisticated yet down-to-earth winery excels in friendly service, sparkling wines, and generous pours (page 219).

(**Culinary Institute of America:** The ancient gray stonework and quietly forested surroundings belie the culinary activity inside. Stop by for cooking classes and demonstrations, to peruse the museum, or to indulge in a meal at the exemplary restaurant (page 225).

(**Mission San Francisco Solano de Sonoma:** The final Spanish mission built in California is the centerpiece of Sonoma State Historic Park (page 240).

(**Kendall-Jackson Wine Center:** Kendall-Jackson's food-and-wine pairing tasting option is the best example of this Wine Country trend: excellent small bites paired with a daily selection of wines, served in a elegant tasting room (page 253).

(**The Russian River:** Rafting, canoeing, and kayaking make this area as much a destination for outdoors enthusiasts as for wine fans (page 265).

(**A. Rafanelli:** The best Sonoma reds are produced at this unpretentious appointment-only winery. Be sure to pick up one of their stunning cabs (page 269).

sample unique and amazing varietals. Sonoma County's craggy coastline and natural beauty provide great recreation opportunities for visitors more fond of the outdoors than the grapes.

PLANNING YOUR TIME

Napa and Sonoma form the beating heart of California's great Wine Country. Many visitors plan a weekend in Napa, with weekend trips back to explore Sonoma and the Russian River. If you come during the summer or fall, you'll find a crush in almost every tasting room in the valley;

even the smaller boutique labels do big business during the six-month high season (May–Oct.).

Be aware that Highway 29, which runs through the heart of Napa Valley, gets jammed up around St. Helena and can be very slow on weekends. U.S. 101 slows through Santa Rosa during the weekday rush-hour commutes and late in the day on sunny summer weekend afternoons. If you're not up for driving, downtown tasting rooms in the cities of Napa, Sonoma, and Santa Rosa are good alternatives to the slow trek up and down the wine roads.

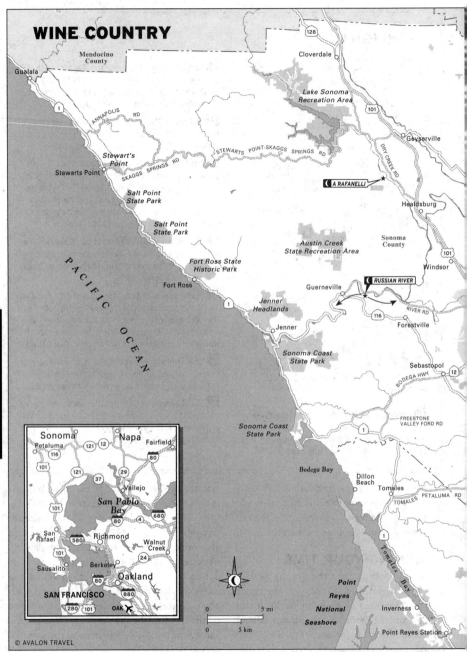

WINE COUNTRY

Mendocino County

Gualala

128

Cloverdale

Lake Sonoma Recreation Area

101

Geyserville

ANNAPOLIS RD

STEWARTS POINT-SKAGGS SPRINGS RD

DRY CREEK RD

Stewart's Point

Stewarts Point

SKAGGS SPRINGS RD

A RAFANELLI

Healdsburg

Salt Point State Park

Salt Point State Park

Austin Creek State Recreation Area

Sonoma County

101

Windsor

Fort Ross State Historic Park

Fort Ross

1

RUSSIAN RIVER

Guerneville

116

RIVER RD

Forestville

P A C I F I C   O C E A N

Jenner Headlands

Jenner

Sebastopol

12

Sonoma Coast State Park

BODEGA HWY

FREESTONE VALLEY FORD RD

Sonoma Coast State Park

1

Bodega Bay

Dillon Beach

Tomales

PETALUMA RD

TOMALES

Point Reyes National Seashore

Inverness

Point Reyes Station

Tomales Bay

Inset map:

Sonoma

Petaluma

121

12

Napa

Fairfield

116

80

101

121

29

37

Vallejo

San Pablo Bay

680

4

San Rafael

580

Richmond

Walnut Creek

101

24

Sausalito

Berkeley

80

SAN FRANCISCO

Oakland

880

280

101

OAK

0   5 mi

0   5 km

© AVALON TRAVEL

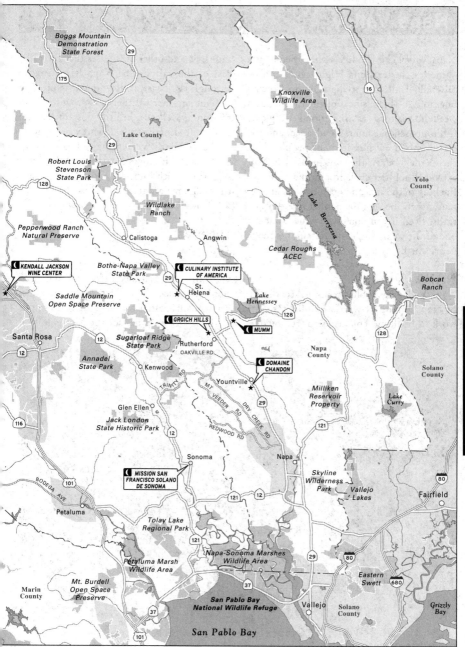

Boggs Mountain
Demonstration
State Forest

29

175

Knoxville
Wildlife Area

16

29

Lake County

Yolo
County

Robert Louis
Stevenson
State Park

Lake
Berryessa

128

Wildlake
Ranch

Pepperwood Ranch
Natural Preserve

Cedar Roughs
ACEC

Bobcat
Ranch

Calistoga

Angwin

KENDALL JACKSON
WINE CENTER

Bothe-Napa Valley
State Park

CULINARY INSTITUTE
OF AMERICA

29

St.
Helena

Lake
Hennessey

Saddle Mountain
Open Space Preserve

128

GRGICH HILLS

MUMM

Santa Rosa

12

Sugarloaf Ridge
State Park

Rutherford

OAKVILLE RD.

Napa
County

128

12

Annadel
State Park

Kenwood

DOMAINE
CHANDON

Solano
County

Lake
Curry

TRINITY RD.

Yountville

MT. VEEDER RD.

DRY CREEK RD.

116

Glen Ellen

Jack London
State Historic Park

12

REDWOOD RD.

29

Milliken
Reservoir
Property

121

Sonoma

MISSION SAN
FRANCISCO SOLANO
DE SONOMA

Napa

Skyline
Wilderness
Park

Vallejo
Lakes

Fairfield

80

BODEGA AVE.

101

121

12

Petaluma

Tolay Lake
Regional Park

121

Napa-Sonoma Marshes
Wildlife Area

29

80

Eastern
Swett

680

Marin
County

Mt. Burdell
Open Space
Preserve

Petaluma Marsh
Wildlife Area

37

San Pablo Bay
National Wildlife Refuge

Vallejo

Solano
County

Grizzly
Bay

101

37

San Pablo Bay

Napa Valley

Napa Valley can feel like a wine theme park. Wineries cluster along Highway 29 and the Silverado Trail, each trying to outdo its neighbors to win the business of the thousands of weekend visitors. Tasting rooms are plentiful, tours sell out hours in advance, and special events draw hundreds of people. Then there's the food: As the wine industry in Napa exploded, top-tier chefs rose to the challenge, flocking to the area and opening amazing restaurants in the tiny towns that line the wine trails. Even if you don't love wine, a meal at one of the many high-end restaurants makes Napa worth a visit.

NAPA

Napa Valley has a blue-collar heart, the city of Napa, many of whose 80,000 residents work in banking, construction, the medical industry, and other businesses that serve the rest of the valley. The Napa River snakes through the heart of downtown, tempering the hot summer weather and providing recreation as well as a healthy dose of natural beauty. It also gives the downtown a historic feel, particularly with its many 19th-century buildings. The town boasts sparkling new structures with high-end clothiers and cutting-edge restaurants as well as the Oxbow Market—a one-of-a-kind culinary treat.

Wineries
TRINITAS
Situated in a cool cave beneath a hilltop vineyard, the Trinitas Tasting Room (875 Bordeaux Way, 707/251-3012, www.trinitas-cellars.com, daily 11 A.M.–7 P.M.) functions as the resort wine bar for the Meritage Inn.

springtime in Napa

© ELIZABETH LINHART MONEY

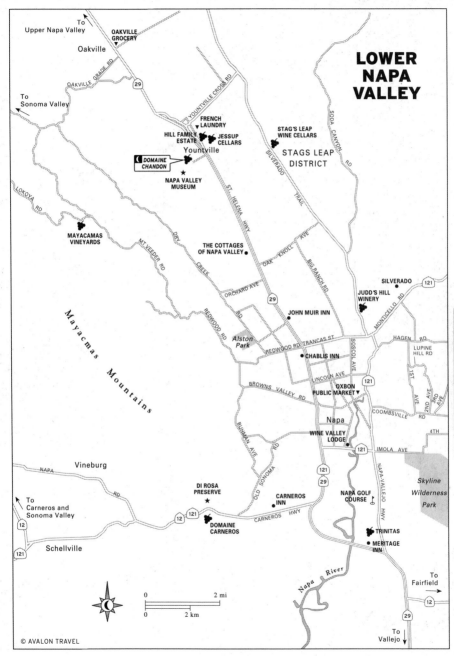

LOWER NAPA VALLEY

To Upper Napa Valley

Oakville

OAKVILLE GROCERY

OAKVILLE GRADE RD

To Sonoma Valley

YOUNTVILLE CROSS RD

FRENCH LAUNDRY

HILL FAMILY ESTATE
JESSUP CELLARS

Yountville

DOMAINE CHANDON

NAPA VALLEY MUSEUM

STAG'S LEAP WINE CELLARS

STAGS LEAP DISTRICT

SODA CANYON RD

SILVERADO TRAIL

LOKOYA RD

MAYACAMAS VINEYARDS

MT VEEDER RD

DRY CREEK RD

ST HELENA HWY

THE COTTAGES OF NAPA VALLEY

OAK KNOLL AVE

BIG RANCH RD

SILVERADO

JUDD'S HILL WINERY

121

MONTICELLO RD

ORCHARD AVE

REDWOOD RD

29

JOHN MUIR INN

HAGEN RD

LUPINE HILL RD

1ST AVE

2ND AVE

3RD AVE

M a y a c m a s   M o u n t a i n s

Alston Park

REDWOOD RD

TRANCAS ST

CHABLIS INN

LINCOLN AVE

SOSCOL AVE

121

BROWNS VALLEY RD

OXBON PUBLIC MARKET

COOMBSVILLE RD

Napa

WINE VALLEY LODGE

4TH

121

IMOLA AVE

BURMAN AVE

OLD SONOMA RD

Skyline Wilderness Park

To Carneros and Sonoma Valley

Vineburg

NAPA RD

DI ROSA PRESERVE

CARNEROS INN

121

29

NAPA GOLF COURSE

NAPA-VALLEJO HWY

12

121

DOMAINE CARNEROS

CARNEROS HWY

TRINITAS

MERITAGE INN

121

Schellville

0   2 mi
0   2 km

Napa River

To Fairfield

12

To Vallejo

29

© AVALON TRAVEL

WINE COUNTRY

WINE COUNTRY

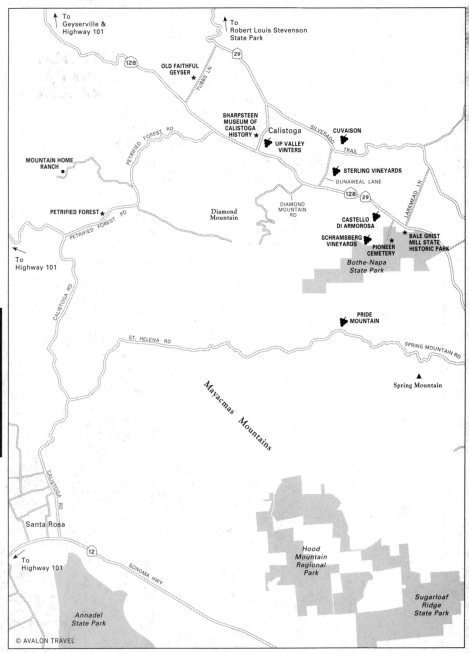

To
Geyserville &
Highway 101

To
Robert Louis Stevenson
State Park

128

29

OLD FAITHFUL
GEYSER

TUBBS LN

SHARPSTEEN
MUSEUM OF
CALISTOGA
HISTORY   Calistoga

CUVAISON

SILVERADO

UP VALLEY
VINTERS

PETRIFIED FOREST RD

MOUNTAIN HOME
RANCH

STERLING VINEYARDS

TRAIL

DUNAWEAL LANE

PETRIFIED FOREST

PETRIFIED FOREST RD

Diamond
Mountain

DIAMOND
MOUNTAIN
RD

128   29

LARKMEAD LN

CASTELLO
DI ARMOROSA

BALE GRIST
MILL STATE
HISTORIC PARK

To
Highway 101

SCHRAMSBERG
VINEYARDS

PIONEER
CEMETERY

Bothe-Napa
State Park

CALISTOGA RD

PRIDE
MOUNTAIN

ST. HELENA RD

SPRING MOUNTAIN RD

Mayacmas Mountains

Spring Mountain

CALISTOGA RD

Santa Rosa

12

To
Highway 101

SONOMA HWY

Hood
Mountain
Regional
Park

Sugarloaf
Ridge
State
Park

Annadel
State Park

© AVALON TRAVEL

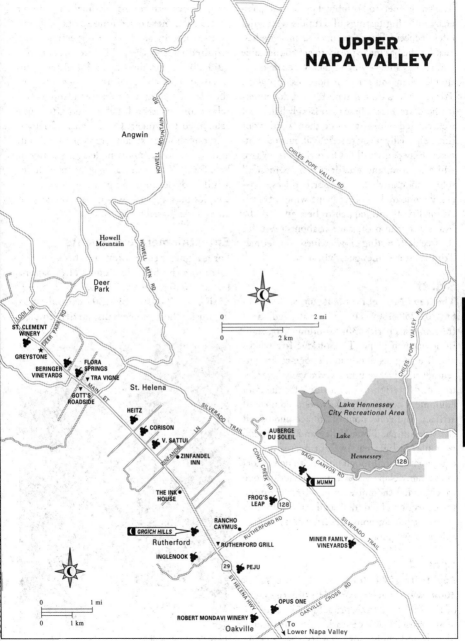

UPPER NAPA VALLEY

Angwin

CHILES POPE VALLEY RD

HOWELL MOUNTAIN RD

Howell
Mountain

HOWELL MTN RD

Deer
Park

LODI LN

DEER PARK RD

ST. CLEMENT
WINERY

GREYSTONE

FLORA
SPRINGS

BERINGER
VINEYARDS

TRA VIGNE

MAIN ST

GOTT'S
ROADSIDE

St. Helena

HEITZ

SILVERADO TRAIL

CHILES POPE VALLEY RD

0   2 mi

0   2 km

CORISON

V. SATTUI

ZINFANDEL LN

ZINFANDEL
INN

THE INK
HOUSE

CONN CREEK RD

AUBERGE
DU SOLEIL

Lake Hennessey
City Recreational Area

Lake

Hennessey

128

SAGE CANYON RD

MUMM

FROG'S
LEAP   128

RANCHO
CAYMUS

RUTHERFORD RD

SILVERADO TRAIL

GRGICH HILLS

Rutherford

RUTHERFORD GRILL

MINER FAMILY
VINEYARDS

INGLENOOK

29   PEJU

ST HELENA HWY

OAKVILLE CROSS RD

OPUS ONE

ROBERT MONDAVI WINERY

Oakville

To
Lower Napa Valley

0   1 mi

0   1 km

The bar is open to both hotel guests and pass-ersby, offering tastings of Trinitas wines and bites of cheese, fruit, and tiny gourmet goodies. Seats at the bar make it easy to get comfortable and stay awhile—which quickly becomes desirable when you get your nose inside a glass. Trinitas wines do not tend toward downmarket hotel freebies. These surprisingly balanced, well-crafted wines are more than worth your time, especially if you're serious about your vintages. Expect a small list featuring one or two whites, a rosé, and one or two red wines, all sold at shockingly low per-bottle prices, especially compared to other Napa wines of similar quality. If you happen to be a guest at the inn, wander into the cave at about 5 P.M. for the free daily tasting of two wines—sometimes Trinitas, sometimes guest vintners.

Sights

The **Napa Firefighters Museum** (1201 Main St., 707/259-0609, 11 A.M.–4 P.M. Wed.–Sat., free) makes a perfect 30–60-minute stop right in downtown Napa. The antique fire trucks and fire engines dominate the one-room museum, staffed by volunteers who truly love history and firefighting. But don't let the cool equipment completely overwhelm you; small artifacts and collections of vintage photos tell the story of the Napa Valley and the crucial part played by area firefighting teams and equipment. Flip through poster-size news shots of the many Napa Valley floods, including one that flooded the museum building; examine the collection of old tools; and ask the docents about the incongruous collection of insurance-company plaques.

Spas

Spa Terra (875 Bordeaux Way, 707/251-3000, www.spaterra.com, $130) is the jewel of the Meritage Inn's property. The interior of an artificial cave beneath a vineyard seems like an odd choice for a luxury spa, but the gorgeous cavern rooms will make a believer of even the most discerning spa-goer. Begin your pampering with a warm greeting and a required tour of the public areas from your guide. Be sure to show up at least 30 minutes in advance of an appointment—you'll have the run of a tiled hot tub, steam room, and relaxation space both before and after your scheduled treatment. Grab a glass of lemon water, a cool moist cloth for your forehead, and warm out (it's not the least bit chilly in Spa Terra). The menu of treatments includes a full-body scrub using grape-seed extracts, couples massages in two-person rooms, and an espresso-based facial.

Entertainment and Events

For a night of entertainment, check out the lineup at the historic **Napa Valley Opera House** (1030 Main St., 707/226-7372, http://nvoh.org, $7–40). This 130-year-old Napa institution hosts comedians, jazz ensembles,

Historic Napa Mill

© ELIZABETH LINHART MONEY

musical acts, theater performances, and even old-movie nights; you can count on something going on nearly every night of the week. Countless cultural icons, from Jack London to Steve Martin, have walked the stage over its long history, but the building itself is also a treat. With antique tile floors, curving banisters, classical flourishes, a café, and two lounges, the 500-seat venue feels intimate for a romantic or elegant evening out. Pricing and showtimes vary; visit the website for more information.

Shopping

Downtown Napa strives to be a shopping destination, yet despite some redevelopment efforts, it's still not quite there. The north end of Main Street has some flashy buildings with equally flashy clothiers, but the place to go is the **Historic Napa Mill** (Main St., www.historicnapamill.com), one block down. Formerly the Hatt Warehouse, the mill has since been converted into a lovely shopping and dining center, decorated with rustic touches—weathered redwood, an abundance of trailing vines, and blooming planter boxes and hanging baskets. The historic Napa River Inn is located here, as is the **Vintage Sweet Shoppe** (530 Main St., 707/224-2986, http://vintagesweetshoppe.com, 10 a.m.–6 p.m. Sun.–Wed., 8 a.m.–10 p.m. Thurs.–Sat.), which specializes in chocolate but has enough treats to make anyone's teeth ache. In the same complex, the **Napa General Store** (540 Main St., 707/259-0762, www.napageneralstore.com, daily 8 a.m.–5 p.m.) next door offers a bite to eat, a glass of wine, wine-related knickknacks, and other gifts. The store also sells local artwork, including leather crafts and fiber art, all of which has an arty ecological bent.

With so much natural beauty in the Napa Valley, is it any wonder that there are so many artists living here? The **Napa Valley Art Association** (1307 1st St., 707/254-2085,

WINE COUNTRY

© ELIZABETH LINHART MONEY

Whole Spice Company at the Oxbow Public Market

www.nvart.org/gallery.html, 10 A.M.–6 P.M. Sun.–Thurs., 10 A.M.–9 P.M. Fri.–Sat.) showcases some of the best. The gallery presents pen-and-ink drawings, watercolors, photography, glass jewelry, fiber art, and oil paintings. While there are plenty of lush portraits of vineyards, you'll also find some unusual subjects— jellyfish, abstract aerial photographs, or watery self-portraits. The association plans events that often pair wine tasting with art shows; check the website before visiting.

Across the River from downtown Napa, the **Oxbow Public Market** (610–644 1st St., 707/226-6529, www.oxbowpublicmarket. com, daily 9 A.M.–7 P.M.) is a well-used piece of real estate. Located next to the now-defunct COPIA museum, the Oxbow Public Market has once again breathed life into this "across the tracks" section of Napa. The market is a food lover's delight. Grab a cup of **Ritual Coffee** and browse through the epicurean wares; pick through beautiful cooking- and kitchen-related antiques at the **Heritage Culinary Artifacts;** or get lost in the myriad spices and seasonings at the **Whole Spice Company.** There is also a chocolatier, an olive-oil company, and the venerable **Wine Merchant,** where you can pick up some vino, cheese, and other treats for the road.

Sports and Recreation

Once you're on the trails of **Skyline Wilderness Park** (2201 Imola Ave., 707/252-0481, www.skylinepark.org, daily 8 A.M.–7 P.M.), you may forget you're even in the Wine Country. Up at this park, no vineyards encroach on the natural chaparral landscape of Napa's high country. This park includes the Martha Walker Garden—a botanical garden planted with California and Napa native plants in honor of a legendary figure in the local horticultural community. The rest of this 850-acre park is given over to multiple community uses. You'll find campgrounds, hiking trails, horse and bicycle paths, a disc golf course, halls suitable for events, and more. Be aware that it gets hot here in the summertime, and not all the campgrounds and trails offer adequate shade to cool off. Even so, the natural beauty of this protected wilderness makes Skyline Park a favorite with both locals and travelers.

Since you're in a land of entertainment options, it seems only natural to enjoy a round of golf during your Wine Country vacation. At the par-72 **Napa Golf Course** (2295 Streblow Dr., 707/255-4333, www.playnapa.com, $29–39), golfers of all levels—even beginners—can enjoy a full 18 holes. More experienced players will enjoy (or curse) the plethora of water features and full-size trees on this course, known locally as a bargain.

Napa River Adventures (Oxbow Public Market, 610 1st St., Suite 4, 707/259-1833, www.naparyiveradventures.com/river-cruise, adults $50, children $25) offers 2.5-hour tours of the Napa River, through wetlands and alongside the historic downtown. Float along the river in a lovely small covered motor launch in cushy seats, enjoying the view out the massive wraparound windows. The trip takes you right into the heart of downtown Napa and back to the dock.

A unique experience is rising in the morning sun over the valley in a brightly colored hot-air balloon. **Balloons Above the Valley** (3425 Solano Ave., 800/464-6824, www. balloonrides.com, $220) offers the full experience—lodging packages that include transportation to the launch site and a champagne brunch after you touch down. You'll float serenely over the vineyards of Napa Valley on your trip before a gentle descent at a predetermined spot. Be sure to make reservations in advance as trips can fill up quickly, especially during high season (May–Oct.). You must be an early riser too, since most balloon trips depart shortly after dawn.

Accommodations

$100-150

While it may not be the most exciting lodging in Napa, the **John Muir Inn** (1998 Trower Ave., 888/522-8999, www.johnmuirnapa.com, $100–150) is certainly one of the most affordable. Standard amenities include complimentary Wi-Fi, and an outdoor pool sweetens the deal. Pricier guest rooms might boast a fridge, a wet bar, and a kitchenette. A DVD rental library gives exhausted wine-tasting travelers an excuse to stay in for the night.

$150-250

At the **Chablis Inn** (3360 Solano Ave., 800/443-3490, www.chablisinn.com, $150), the guest rooms include all the usual amenities: a wet bar with a mini fridge, an in-room coffeemaker, a TV with cable, and more. Guest rooms are simply decorated, but the beds are comfortable, the carpets are dark (making it safe to drink just a little bit of red wine in your room), and the address is central to both the attractions of downtown Napa and the famous Highway 29 wine road. Dogs are welcome.

The pretty, unassuming **Wine Valley Lodge** (200 S. Coombs St., 707/224-7911, www.winevalleylodge.com, $170) welcomes guests with its redbrick and adobe-tile exterior. Inside, guests enjoy serene guest rooms with unobtrusive art, pale yellow walls, and soothing pastel comforters. Guest rooms are a nice size, and you can choose a king bed, two doubles, or a suite, depending on your needs. The Wine Valley Lodge also boasts a significant past: In the late 1950s and early 1960s, several movies were filmed in Napa, and various A-list stars, including Rock Hudson, Jean Simmons, and even Elvis stayed at the lodge during filming.

For a different style of historic lodging experience, stay at the **Napa Inn** (1137 Warren St., 800/435-1144, www.napainn.com, $250), which comprises two Victorian houses, both painted blue, in historic downtown Napa. You can walk from either to downtown shops and restaurants, and the Wine Train depot is a very short drive. As bed-and-breakfasts go, the Napa Inn is a big one, with more than 10 guest rooms and suites. If you plan to travel with your pet, talk to the inn well in advance to get one of the two pet-friendly guest rooms. Elegant fabrics and lush modern textures moderate the floral and carved-wood decor of the Victorian era. The nicest guest rooms have corner whirlpool tubs and king beds. Breakfast at the Napa Inn is an event, with multiple courses served by candlelight.

For another charming and conveniently located option, consider the **Arbor Guest House** (1436 G St., 707/252-8144, www.arborguesthouse.com, $175–300). The prim white exterior betrays little of the inn's lush Victorian decor. Rich fabric drapes the windows and beds, and polished antiques grace even the smallest corner, while soft lighting and flower-filled vases lend warm touches. There are only five guest rooms, each distinctively decorated; two offer gas fireplaces and two-person jetted tubs for a romantic stay. Guests are invited to a complimentary hot breakfast in the morning and wine and appetizers in the evening.

OVER $250

The ◖ **Napa River Inn** (500 Main St., 877/251-8500, www.napariverinn.com, $250–350) has one of the best locations in Napa—right inside the Historic Napa Mill. You can practically fall out of your guest room and hit the General Store, restaurant, several galleries, the candy store, and at least one other restaurant on the way down. Located steps from the center of Napa's bustling downtown, your guest room might even afford you a view of the Napa River. The interior of this luxury hotel is crammed with high-end antiques and reproductions. Best of all, you can choose from three styles of room decor: Historic Victorian rooms feature canopy beds, floral prints, cushy chairs, and slipper tubs; the nautical rooms, many of

WINE COUNTRY

which face the river, resemble the inside of a yacht, with wood paneling, porthole-style mirrors, and rope-style accents; and the Wine Country rooms echo the natural wealth of the Napa Valley with floral linens, marble baths, and oak moldings.

The king of Napa lodging is the **Silverado** (1600 Atlas Peak Rd., 707/257-0200, www.silveradoresort.com, $275). You'll find the finest in modern amenities and decorations in your suite (all guest rooms at the Silverado are full suites with kitchens and dining rooms), including high-thread-count linens, complimentary Wi-Fi, and a private patio or deck overlooking the grounds. Pale colors with eye-popping jewel-toned accents speak of the best current designers. Outside your guest room, there's so much to do at the Silverado that you'll find it hard to pry yourself away from the grounds to go wine tasting. Choose from the immense spa with full fitness and salon services, two 18-hole golf courses, two restaurants, 17 tennis courts, 10 pools, and—believe it or not—more.

The **Carneros Inn** (4048 Sonoma Hwy., 707/299-4900, www.thecarnerosinn.com, $450–720) is an expansive and expensive cottage resort. The immense property, which backs onto real countryside, has three restaurants, a spa, two pools, a fitness center, and even a small market. On arrival, follow the signs to the registration area and then just keep driving—the lobby is at the very top of the resort's hill. Your persistence is rewarded with a charming greeting complete with drinks. The unprepossessing (from the outside) cottages spread out in small clusters for acres, each group surrounding its own garden paths and water features. Inside, the cozy (yes, that does mean "smallish") cottages sparkle with white linens, tile floors, and windows overlooking sizeable private backyards with decks and comfy chaises. But it's the baths that bring Carneros Inn clients back again and again.

The **Meritage Inn** (875 Bordeaux Way, 707/251-1900, www.themeritageresort.com, $200–575) is beside the small Napa Valley airport, convenient to businesspeople and travelers who want easy access to both the Napa Valley and Sonoma-Carneros wine regions. This big motel got a Wine Country makeover—now the grounds, common spaces, and guest rooms have the deep harvest colors and country-elegant style of Tuscany. The lush garden pool is the literal centerpiece of the property, which also includes a wine-tasting room, a fabulous spa, and a refreshingly down-to-earth restaurant. The basic shape of the guest rooms remains true to the Meritage's motel roots, but the Tuscan-style decor and trimmings make a play for elegance, with comfortable beds, deep soaking tubs in the baths, and posh amenities. Expect a fridge stocked with free water and sodas, a coffeemaker, and a complimentary bottle of wine.

Food

The FARM (4048 Sonoma Hwy., 707/299-4880, www.thecarnerosinn.com, daily 4–10 P.M., $35) at the Carneros Inn serves up the expected upscale California cuisine, complete with a chef's tasting menu and big white service plates topped with tiny artistic piles of food. The food may be a touch pretentious, but it's cooked perfectly, and the chef has put some imagination into his dishes that really works well. Expect unusual but deftly created flavor combinations, smaller portions appropriate to the number of courses you'll get, and just a touch of molecular gastronomy thrown in for color and interest. The dining room feels more comfortable than many of its ilk, with cushy banquettes and padded chairs. Do dress up a little—the FARM has a distinctly upscale vibe. If you want to soak in the atmosphere with a more casual experience, ask about the bar menu.

For classic breakfast dishes and almost down-to-earth salad and sandwich fare, the **Boon Fly Café** (4048 Sonoma Hwy., 707/299-4870, www.thecarnerosinn.com, daily 7 A.M.–9 P.M., $25–40) offers an upscale California diner experience at the Carneros Inn. If you're staying at the inn, skip the mediocre service of the café itself and order the Boon Fly menu via room service—the prices are the same in-cottage as in the diner. Eggs are cooked competently, salads are enormous, and the carefully designed down-home dining room is cute. Sadly, the Boon Fly does not serve breakfast all day—be sure to arrive and order before 11 A.M. if you're dying for an omelet.

The restaurant at the Meritage Inn, **Siena** (875 Bordeaux Way, 707/251-1950, www.themeritageresort.com, 6:30 A.M.–3 P.M. Mon.–Fri., 6:30 A.M.–3 P.M. and 5–10 P.M. Sat., 5–10 P.M. Sun., brunch 6:30–10:30 A.M. Sun., $25), doesn't serve typical Wine Country cuisine. The food is mostly Italian, much of it hot, hearty, and welcome after a long day of wine tasting. Choose from fresh salads, pasta dishes, and big entrées, though if you've been in Napa for a while, you may not be able to resist a macaroni-and-cheese appetizer or a cheeseburger; both of these comforting dishes stand out for their simplicity and their quality. Desserts also tend toward the dense and filling—consider sharing one among your tablemates. The upholstered booths and dim lighting make a romantic dining experience possible, but the vibe in the dining room manages to stay low-key enough to make jeans-clad diners comfortable.

When Napa locals need a diner-style breakfast or lunch, they head to the **Butter Cream Bakery & Diner** (2297 Jefferson St., 707/255-6700, www.buttercreambakery.com, diner daily 5:30 A.M.–3 P.M., bakery 5:30 A.M.–6:30 P.M. Mon.–Sat., 5:30 A.M.–4:30 P.M. Sun., $10–15). It's not in the ritzy part of downtown, but the brilliant pink- and white-striped building is hard to miss. On the diner side, breakfast is served all day; choose between a small table in the fluorescent-lit linoleum dining room or a stool at the old-school counter. Service is indifferent, but you'll get decently cooked eggs, tasty sandwiches, reasonable portions, and best

of all, reasonable prices. Over on the bakery side, mouthwatering turnovers, danishes, and fruit rings make it easy to get a good breakfast on the go. Dessert pastries, cookies, and cakes tempt even dieters.

Sake in Wine Country? Not a bad idea, particularly if it's paired with dinner at **Morimoto's** (610 Main St., Napa, 707/252-1600, www.morimotonapa.com, 11:30 A.M.–2:30 P.M. and 5–10 P.M. Sun.–Thurs., 11:30 A.M.–2:30 P.M. and 5–11 P.M. Fri.–Sat., $25–40). Celebrity chef Masaharu Morimoto, who has appeared on the *Iron Chef* TV show, recently relocated to Napa to open this esoteric and sleek Japanese eatery. The elegant interior features steel highlighted by bright yellow accents. The food includes traditional Japanese dishes, all with a unique and modern twist—*gyoza* with bacon cream and duck confit–fried rice are just some of the menu items. There are also a handful of non sequiturs like steak, lobster, and roasted fingerling potatoes. For a full idea of the chef's culinary vision, order the tasting menu ($120).

For simple Italian fare, go to **Azzurro** (1260 Main St., 707/255-5552, www.azzurropizzeria.com, 11:30 A.M.–9:30 P.M. Mon.–Wed., 11:30 A.M.–10 P.M. Thurs.–Sat., 11:30 A.M.–9:30 P.M. Sun., $15). Veterans of Tra Vigne in St. Helena, Michael and Christina Gyetvan opened Azzurro with the intention of bringing their style of Italian food to downtown Napa. A favorite with locals, this trattoria offers wood-fired pizzas in addition to hearty pasta dishes and big rustic salads. The warm and modern interior welcomes diners with wood and stone tables and an open kitchen. Wines by the glass are affordable.

For a bit of this and a bit of that, venture across the Napa River to the █ **Oxbow Public Market** (610–644 1st St., 707/226-6529, www.oxbowpublicmarket.com, daily 9 A.M.–7 P.M.). Inside this large open space you can snack on oysters at the **Hog Island Oyster Company**, lunch on tacos from **Pica Pica Maize Kitchen**, or blow your diet at **Kara's Cupcakes.**

Hamburgers are just out the side door at **Gott's Roadside,** and around the corner you can find some of the best charcuterie around in delectable take-out sandwiches at the **Fatted Calf** or pizza by the slice at **The Model Bakery.** The bacon *levain,* made with hunks of bacon and bacon fat from next door, is irresistible.

Perhaps the most acclaimed of these options is the **Kitchen Door** (707/226-6529, www.kitchendoornapa.com, 11 A.M.–9 P.M. Mon.–Fri., 9 A.M.–9 P.M. Sat.–Sun., $10–20). Unlike the market's loud and congested interior, the Kitchen Door has an air of calm. The white-tile wood oven, open seating, and large picture windows draw light in for an illuminating meal. Comfort food comes in all stripes, including some Armenian dishes, rice and noodle bowls, roast chickens, burgers, and sundaes.

Information and Services

The **Napa Valley Destination Council** (600 Main St., 707/251-5895, Napa, www.napavalley.org/nvcvb.html, daily 9 A.M.–5 P.M.), in the middle of downtown Napa, has complimentary maps, guidebooks, and wine tasting passes. Chat with a friendly local who can direct you to the favorite wineries and restaurants.

For current events, *Wine Country This Week* (www.winecountrythisweek.com) has the best up-to-date information. You can find local news in the daily *Napa Valley Register* (www.napanews.com). Napa has a **post office** (1351 2nd St., 707/255-0621). For medical treatment (including alcohol poisoning), the **Queen of the Valley** (1000 Trancas St., 707/252-4411, www.thequeen.org) has both a 24-hour emergency room and trauma center and a by-appointment urgent-care clinic.

Getting There and Around

Napa, in all its bucolic beauty, does not have infrastructure designed for the number of visitors it receives. This is part of its charm—unless you spend your visit sitting in bumper-to-bumper traffic. The best way to experience the valley is to avoid the ever-popular autumn crush and summer weekend afternoons. November and early spring are beautiful seasons to see the valley. But if a summer Saturday spent wine tasting is impossible to resist, hit the wineries early and stay off the roads from mid-afternoon to early evening. With great restaurants and seductive spas everywhere, you'll easily be able to pass the extra time.

BY CAR

Considering the number of people that go to Napa, it is not all that easy to get to. Most of the highways in this region are two lanes and frequently go by colloquial names. They are also susceptible to gridlocked traffic thanks to the numerous wine-lovers and the occasional race at nearby Infineon Raceway.

Highway 29 is the central conduit that runs north into the valley from the city of Napa. It is also known as the Napa–Vallejo Highway between the two cities, and as the St. Helena Highway from Napa to Calistoga, where it becomes Foothill Boulevard. To reach Highway 29 from San Francisco, take U.S. 101 north across the Golden Gate Bridge to Novato. In Novato, take the exit for Highway 37 east to Napa. Highway 37 skirts the tip of the San Pablo Bay and runs all the way to Vallejo. From Vallejo, take Highway 29 (Sonoma Blvd.) north for seven miles until you reach downtown Napa. Highway 29 will take you as far north as Calistoga.

Highway 37 in Vallejo is especially easy if you're coming from the East Bay, Lake Tahoe, and Sacramento. Highway 37 intersects I-80 at the north end of Vallejo at the exit for Six Flags Discovery Kingdom.

Highway 128 connects the north end of Napa Valley near Rutherford with U.S. 101 in Geyserville. From Geyserville, you can follow this beautiful two-lane road south to Calistoga, where it joins Highway 29.

Coming from **Highway 121** in Sonoma, **Highway 12** east leads directly to Napa. Highway 121 then picks up again at West Imola Avenue and leads east to the **Silverado Trail,** an alternate route north–south in the Napa Valley.

BY BUS
To avoid the potential headache of driving in Napa, take the **VINE** bus (800/696-6443, http://nctpa.net, adults $1.50–5.50, children $1–2.50), which provides public transportation around Napa Valley, including Napa, Yountville, Oakville, Rutherford, St. Helena, and Calistoga. If you don't want to drive at all, jump aboard the commuter VINE 29 Express, which runs all day Monday–Friday. The Express travels from the El Cerrito BART station in the East Bay and from the Vallejo Ferry Terminal into Napa Valley. Fares are cash-only and require exact change.

NAPA VALLEY WINE TRAIN
If trying to decide which wineries to visit, which restaurants are worth a stop, and how best to avoid weekend traffic sounds exhausting, consider taking the Napa Valley Wine Train (1275 McKinstry St., Napa, 800/427-4124, www.winetrain.com, $54–189). The Wine Train offers a relaxing sightseeing experience aboard vintage train cars, where you can sit back and enjoy the food, wine, and views. The train runs from Napa to St. Helena and back, a 36-mile three-hour round-trip tour. The least expensive option includes only wine. More amenities at higher prices include a gourmet three-course lunch or dinner, with the option of taking a winery tour along the way. Each package includes seating in a different historic railcar—you might lunch in the 1917 Pullman Car, or take an evening tour of Grgich Hills aboard the 1952 Vista Dome Car. Advance reservations are strongly suggested.

YOUNTVILLE
Named for George Calvert Yount, who planted the first vineyard in Napa Valley, Yountville is the quintessential wine-loving town. There are not even 3,000 residents, but the town has earned widespread fame for its epicurean spirit. you'll find a number of prestigious wineries and champagneries, but it is really restaurateur Thomas Keller who put this postage stamp–size town on the map. First came the French Laundry, then Bouchon and the Bouchon Bakery, and eventually Ad Hoc. But it's not just a Keller company town; other notable eateries have opened up and keep pace with the big boy. Still, with so many fantastic dining options, you might wish there was more to do in Yountville to extend your stay in order to accommodate as many meals out as possible.

Wineries
◖ DOMAINE CHANDON
One of the premier champagneries in Napa Valley, Domaine Chandon (1 California Dr., 707/944-2280, www.chandon.com, daily 10 A.M.–5 P.M., $12–32) offers one of the best tours in Napa—it's a perfect introduction to the process of wine- and champagne-making. Walk out into the vineyards to look at the grapes, head down to the tank- and barrel-filled cellars to learn about the champagne-making process, then proceed into the aging rooms to see the racked bottles, tilted and dusty, aging to the point of drinkability. Finally, you'll adjourn to the tasting room to sample the bubbly concoctions. Chandon also makes still wines, which you can also taste. Reservations are required for tours, and booking in advance is a good idea.

Domaine Chandon also boasts lovely gardens, a stream, and an immense estate. Visitors can walk the open paths among the vineyards, enjoy the delights of the tasting room ($18–25), and make a reservation for dinner at Étoile, the on-site California-French restaurant.

HILL FAMILY ESTATE
Right on Washington Street in downtown Yountville, the Hill Family Estate (6512

WINE COUNTRY

Washington St., 707/944-9580, www.hillfamilyestate.com, daily 10 A.M.–6 P.M., $10) tasting room and antiques shop offers an elegant tasting and shopping experience. The most affordable item in the room is the tasting glass; you can get two free tastes if you first stop by the Yountville Visitors Center on the next block, or you can just purchase your tastes for $5 each. Roam among the pricey French antiques as you sip, or stand at the bar to enjoy the company of the Hill family and a small selection of light, balanced red and white wines. The cabernet sauvignons are not made in the typical heavy-handed Napa style, so even tasters with delicate palates will find them drinkable. Ask about the Double Barrel Cab, which is sold in a box that the younger sons of the winery family have blasted with buckshot with their grandfather's double-barrel shotgun.

JESSUP CELLARS
Located in downtown Yountville, the tiny tasting room at Jessup Cellars (6740 Washington St., 707/944-8523, www.jessupcellars.com, daily 10 A.M.–6 P.M.) offers tastes of incredible boutique red wines that you'll have a hard time finding anyplace else. There are no tours here, no picnic grounds or fancy gardens, but you'll find lush, rich zinfandels and deep, smoky cabernets that are more than worth the sometimes-steep price tag. The tasting room boasts a cute little bar, a few shelves with items for purchase, and staff that love their jobs. If you chat them up, you may find yourself tasting rare Jessup vintages that are not on the usual list.

ROBERT SINSKEY VINEYARDS
Robert Sinskey Vineyards (6320 Silverado Tr., 707/944-9090, www.robertsinskey.com, daily 10 A.M.–4:30 P.M., $25–75) is getting into the foodie act that's sweeping Wine Country, offering a menu of small bites alongside their list of current wines. The appointment-only tastings include a tour of the cave and cellar, and

discussions about the art of wine-making make the extra effort worthwhile. With or without the food, the red wines themselves are worth dropping in at this attractive stone-and-wood edifice.

Sights
The small **Napa Valley Museum** (55 Presidents Circle, 707/944-0500, www.napavalleymuseum.org, 10 A.M.–4 P.M. Tues.–Sun., $5) is tucked behind Domaine Chandon on the other side of Highway 29 in Yountville. Here you'll find perhaps the most complete description of the wine-making process available in Wine Country. The main feature of the downstairs gallery is a big high-tech multimedia display that categorizes each step and month in the life of a wine (and the winemaker). If you're interested in learning the details of the grape, plan on spending at least 30 minutes reading the left-hand wall. Next, you can test what you've learned with a variety of interactive quizzes on wine-making. Finally, you can examine information about how different types of wine taste and how to appreciate and drink them. A tiny exhibit tells the history of Napa Valley, from the earliest pioneers through the current wine boom. The upstairs gallery provides space for rotating exhibitions; you're likely to find the work of local artists or art depicting food and wine.

Spas
An easy walk from anywhere in downtown Yountville, the newly reimagined **Spa Villagio** (6481 Washington St., 800/351-1133, daily 7:30 A.M.–9 P.M.) has a beautiful space in which to pamper its patrons. You don't need to be a guest at the Villagio Inn to book a treatment at the spa, although you may want to try one of the five Spa Suites—private spaces where singles, couples, and friends can relax before, during, and after their treatments. Be sure to show up an hour early for your massage, facial, or treatment package—at the price you're paying for treatments, you'll want to take advantage

of the saunas and hot tubs, relaxation rooms, and the other chichi amenities. The spa recommends making reservations for your treatment at least three weeks in advance, especially during the summer–fall high season.

Entertainment and Events

More than 50 years ago, the **Lincoln Theater** (100 California Dr., 707/944-1300, www.lincolntheatre.org, $10–125) ran its first show at the Veterans Home in Yountville. Today, a packed year-round season brings top-end live entertainment of all kinds to the Wine Country. You can see touring Broadway shows, locally produced plays, stand-up comedy, dance productions, music nights, and more. Many of the productions at the Lincoln welcome family audiences. Although this large theater seats hundreds, purchase tickets in advance if you can—especially for one-night-only special performances or if you'll be in the area for only one weekend. The theater recommends arriving 30 minutes ahead of showtime to ensure that you've got time to park your car, walk from the parking lot, and find your seat before the curtain goes up.

Shopping

Step inside **Masonrie Napa Valley** (6711 Washington St., 707/944-0889, tasting $20–40), an honestly unique art gallery and tasting room inhabiting the old stone building that was the Burgundy House. Taste rare Napa vintages while sitting at an antique wooden table topped with a chunk of mammoth bone or browse ultramodern leather and metal furniture paired with objets d'art, including an inlaid human skull. An ever-rotating collection of modern and antique decorative art has a distinctly industrial and almost macabre feel that you won't find anywhere else in the Napa Valley. You'll also get the chance to taste local wines made by Napa vintners who don't have their own tasting rooms. Tastings aren't cheap, but you can get a 2-for-1 ticket from the Yountville Chamber of Commerce (6484 Washington St., 707/944-0904), and you'll have the undivided attention of your pourer, who will seat you in a small gallery and discuss the wines with you as you sip. Tasting selections are forever changing, so frequent visitors to the region can keep coming back to try something new.

Sports and Recreation

Biking is a popular way to see the vineyards, forests, and wineries of Napa. You can get away from the highways and the endless traffic of the wine roads on two wheels. If you don't know the area, the best way to bike it is to take a tour. **Napa Valley Bike Tours** (6795 Washington St., 707/944-2953, www.napavalleybiketours.com, $139) offers standard and custom tours all over the area, from central Napa to Calistoga. You'll get a brand-name bike, a map, a helmet, and an orientation before beginning your trek. Then you'll be off on your chosen tour: a pedal through the vineyards, a half-day or full-day tour that includes both wine tasting and meals, or a multiplesport "adventure package" that includes kayaking, or a balloon ride.

Accommodations

If you've come to Napa Valley to dine at the French Laundry or immerse yourself in the food scene, you'll want to stay in Yountville if you can. Several inns are within stumbling distance of the French Laundry, which is convenient for gourmands who want to experience a range of wines with the meal.

$100-150

A French-style inn, the **Maison Fleurie** (6529 Yount St., 800/788-0369, www.foursisters.com, $150) offers the best of small-inn style for a more reasonable nightly rate. It is in a perfect location for walking to Bouchon, the Bouchon Bakery, and the many other amazing

WINE COUNTRY

restaurants, boutiques, and tasting rooms in town. The 13 guest rooms in this "house of flowers" have an attractive but not overwhelming floral decorative theme. The more economical rooms, described as "cozy," are small but attractive. If you've got the budget to splurge, opt for a room in the Bakery Building, where you'll get a fireplace, a jetted spa tub, and a king bed. All guests can enjoy a full breakfast each morning as well as an afternoon wine reception, fresh cookies, and complimentary access to the inn's bicycles.

$150-250

For a motel with a historic twist, book a room at the **Napa Valley Railway Inn** (6503 Washington St., 707/944-2000, www.napavalleyrailwayinn.com, $125–260). The nine guest rooms are converted 100-year-old train cars tightly packed together, making a unique type of hotel. The rooms themselves are funky and narrow but carefully decorated in classic style with rich bedspreads. Some of the perks include the Coffee Caboose, where you can start your day with pastries and coffee, access to the nearby Yountville Fitness Center to burn off any unwanted calories, and a "Napa Valley Travel Packet" ($20), which includes tasting vouchers, maps, bottled water, and Advil.

The **Bordeaux House** (6600 Washington St., 707/944-2855, www.bordeauxhouse.com, $150–250) has it all: a beautiful brick facade, lovely French country interiors, and a location literally three doors down from the French Laundry. The amenities in each individually decorated room will make you feel as though you're staying in a quaint country inn in the south of France. During your stay, take a stroll through the inn's gardens, enjoy a splash in the outdoor spa, and partake of the better-than-continental breakfast in the common area each morning. Perhaps best of all, the location on Washington Street makes a walk from the inn through the best of downtown Yountville an easy prospect.

OVER $250

Located next to Bouchon Bakery, wake up to mouthwatering smells at the cozy five room **Petit Logis Inn** (6527 Yount St., 877/944-2332, www.petitlogis.com, $135–295). Each room has a fireplace, a jetted tub, and a fridge and is decorated in warm creamy colors with an occasional wall mural. Low-key and unpretentious, the inn is best described as "the place to come to pretend you live in Yountville." Unlike many other inns, breakfast is not included but can be arranged for an additional charge at a nearby restaurant.

The **Napa Valley Lodge** (2230 Madison St., 888/944-3545, www.napavalleylodge.com, $335), a stunning Mediterranean-style hotel with stucco walls and red tile roofs, loves the sunshine and warmth of the Napa Valley summer. Guests are steeped in the luxury that the Wine Country in general, and Yountville in particular, is known for. Book a spa treatment either in your guest room or out beside the heated pool. Start each day with the complimentary champagne buffet breakfast, or order from the California cuisine room-service menu. Finish each night in the luxury of your guest room—including the Parkside Terrace rooms, with king beds topped with European-style duvets; the Vineyard Courtyard Terrace rooms, with their own patios and sweeping views of the surrounding vineyards; and the luxurious King Suite, with a fireplace, two-person soaking tub, and the ubiquitous valley vineyard views.

At **The Cottages of Napa Valley** (1012 Darms Lane, 2 miles south of Yountville, 707/252-7810, www.napacottages.com, $450), you'll pay a princely sum to gain a home away from home in the heart of Wine Country. Each cottage has its own king bed, private garden, outdoor fireplace, and kitchenette. Every morning the quiet staff drops off a basket of fresh pastries from Bouchon Bakery and a pot of great coffee for breakfast to greet you whenever you feel like waking up. Simple yet luxurious country-cottage furnishings feel welcoming and homey, and the staff can help you plan and execute the ultimate Wine Country vacation.

If you're splurging on a no-expenses-spared trip to Napa Valley, enjoy the location and luxury of the **Vintage Inn** (6541 Washington St., 707/944-1112, www.vintageinn.com, $330–650). Guest rooms in the elegant hexagonal buildings feature the softest sheets ever, L'Occitane toiletries in a big beautiful bath with plenty of storage for longer stays, and a prettily hidden TV and fridge. The French country–meets–Wine Country decor extends to a private patio or deck overlooking the lush gardens. Once you make your way off the property (it's easy to get lost in the landscaping and identical structures of this big resort space), you're at the center of the main drag in Yountville. Walk to wine-tasting rooms, galleries, and of course, the legendary restaurants. But before making reservations for lunch someplace pricey, take a look at the fabulous food offerings at the Vintage Inn. The dining room serves what might be the best complimentary

hotel buffet breakfast in California, with buttery French pastries, fresh fruit, and made-to-order omelets. Then, at 3 P.M., the staff sets out a free full-fledged afternoon tea, complete with finger sandwiches, homemade scones, and organic teas—plus wine, of course. As a sister property of the nearby Villagio, Vintage Inn guests get use of the Villagio's fitness center, tennis courts, and spa.

Food

The tiny town of Yountville boasts perhaps the biggest reputation for culinary excellence in California—a big deal when you consider the offerings of San Francisco and Los Angeles. The reason for this reputation starts and ends with restaurateur Thomas Keller's indisputably amazing **◖ French Laundry** (6640 Washington St., 707/944-2380, www.frenchlaundry.com, dinner daily 5:30–9 P.M., lunch 11 A.M.–1 P.M. Fri.–Sun., by reservation only, $240). Once you've obtained that all-important reservation, the fun begins. From the moment you walk in the door of the rambling

The French Laundry grows most of its own produce right across the street.

© ELIZABETH LINHART MONEY

RESERVATIONS FOR FRENCH LAUNDRY

Most people familiar with the world of high-end food know that the best restaurant in California, and possibly in the United States, is the **French Laundry**. Thomas Keller's culinary haven in tiny Yountville was the only restaurant in the greater Bay Area to earn the coveted three-star Michelin Guide rating in 2007. The restaurant is in a charming vintage house, and the kitchen garden is right across the street, where you can walk among the rows of vegetables and herbs. It may sound like a foodie paradise, but there's just one problem: getting a table.

The difficulty in getting reservations to the French Laundry is almost as legendary as the French Laundry itself. Rather than expecting to dine at the French Laundry during a planned trip to the Wine Country, savvy travelers expect to plan their whole trip around whatever French Laundry reservation they manage to get.

The bare facts: The French Laundry takes reservations *precisely* two months in advance by phone, online, and via local concierges. Reservations are accepted for parties of two, four, or six only. Diners can choose between lunch and dinner seatings that offer the same menu. It's easier to get a table for lunch than for dinner; both take 2.5-4 hours. Budget $500 pp for your meal if you plan to drink wine, and $300-350 if you don't.

The French Laundry starts taking **phone reservations** at 9 A.M. daily. Between 8:30 and 8:45 A.M., program their number on your speed-dial and begin calling; continue calling until you get an answer. If you get a continuous busy signal past 11 A.M., you'll probably need to try again the next day, and maybe the day after that.

Making **reservations online** works much the same way as on the phone, only it's harder. Each day the French Laundry offers only one table, for lunch, online. Visit OpenTable (www.opentable.com) at about 8:30 A.M. and start trying to snag that table. If you're still trying at 9:30 A.M., it's probably already gone.

Hands-down the low-stress way to get a coveted French Laundry table is to hire a concierge to do it for you. The French Laundry lets concierges walk downtown to the restaurant each day to put in bookings for their clients. Call or email a concierge and expect to pay a nominal fee ($20-30), but if you can afford to dine at the French Laundry, that's pocket change. Give your new best friend a range of dates and times that will suit you, and he or she will do their best to accommodate your request. Do not expect to get your first choice of times; flexible diners will find themselves with a remarkably trouble-free reservation experience.

So, is it really worth all this rigmarole just to get into one restaurant, then pay a sizeable amount of money for a single meal? Yes. With the gracious welcome at the door, stunning service throughout, the meal, and the food that can be found nowhere else, dining at the French Laundry is worth both the hassle and the price tag.

Victorian, you're treated like royalty. You'll be led to your seat in one of the small dining rooms by one of the many immaculate black-and-white-clad staff. Even if you're new to this level of dining—and most people are—you'll be made to feel more than welcome. The menu, which changes often, offers two main selections: the regular nine-course tasting menu and the vegetarian nine-course tasting menu. You'll have a few either-or choices as you run down each list—usually you'll see two options for the fish course and two options for the entrée. The waitstaff can help you identify anything you don't recognize or if you're having trouble making a decision. The sommelier is at your beck and call to assist with a wine list that weighs several pounds.

Then the meal begins. From the start, waiters and footmen ply you with extras—an *amuse-bouche* here, an extra middle course there—and if you mention that someone else has something on their plate that you'd like to try, it appears in front of you as if by magic. Finally, the desserts come, and come, and come. After the fourth separate dessert course, you may want to ask for a white flag to signal your surrender. All together, a meal at the French Laundry can run up to 13 courses and take four hours to eat. Afterward, you might not eat normally for a couple of days, and you'll have spent a good deal of money on a single meal, but it will seem worth it.

Departing from Yountville's ever-present Wine Country cuisine formula, **Bistro Jeanty** (6510 Washington St., 707/944-0103, www. bistrojeanty.com, daily 11:30 A.M.–10:30 P.M., $26) gets lots of recommendations from locals. Certainly the interior works on the theory of whimsy rather than prestige, with a life-size toy man "riding" a bicycle down the middle of the front dining room. Parisian posters on the walls evoke just the atmosphere the proprietors are aiming for—an authentic French bistro. Jeanty's heart is the menu, a single page devoted to the classics of Parisian bistro cuisine. Tomato bisque served with a puff pastry shell, traditional salads, cassoulet, coq au vin, and even a *croque monsieur* are all crafted with obvious joy. Local Yountville residents can lovingly describe their own favorite dishes. Service is friendly, and you'll see a few locals hanging out at the bar, watching the TV tuned to a sports channel—something of a non sequitur. Jeanty has two dining rooms, making walk-in dining easy on off-season weeknights, but definitely make a dinner reservation if you're in town on the weekend or in high season (May–Oct.).

Étoile (1 California Dr., 888/242-6366, www.chandon.com, 11:30 A.M.–2:30 P.M. and 6–9 P.M. Thurs.–Mon., $35) is another high-end restaurant in Yountville, set inside the tasting facility at the prestigious Domaine Chandon champagnery. Lovely white tablecloths sparkle in the sunlight and overlook Chandon's lush green gardens. The menu at Étoile is inventive even for Napa, and each dish is prepared to utter perfection. Order the chef's tasting menu (4 courses, $90) and add wine pairings (an additional $65) to sample Chandon's wine list.

If you can't access the French Laundry, try Thomas Keller's other Yountville option, **Bouchon** (6534 Washington St., 707/944-8037, www.bouchonbistro.com, 11:30 A.M.–midnight Mon.–Fri., 11 A.M.–midnight Sat.–Sun., $34). Reservations are still strongly recommended, but you should be able to get one just a week in advance. Bouchon's atmosphere and food scream Parisian bistro. Order traditional favorites such as the *croque monsieur* or steak frites, or opt for a California-influenced specialty salad or entrée made with local sustainable ingredients.

If you're just looking for a breakfast pastry or a sandwich, walk from Bouchon next door to the **Bouchon Bakery** (6528 Washington St., 707/944-2253, www.bouchonbakery. com, daily 7 A.M.–7 P.M.). This ultra-high-end bakery supplies both Bouchon and the French Laundry with pastries and breads and operates a retail storefront. Locals and visitors flock to the bakery at breakfast and lunchtime, so expect a line.

Situated in the V Market Place (formerly Vintage 1870), **Bottega** (6525 Washington St., Suite A9, 707/945-1050, www.bottega-napavalley.com, 5–9:30 P.M. Mon., 11:30 A.M.–2:30 P.M. and 5–9:30 P.M. Tues.–Thurs., 11:30 A.M.–2:30 P.M. and 5–10 P.M. Fri.–Sat., 11:30 A.M.–2:30 P.M. and 5–9:30 P.M. Sun., $15–30) is the return to the kitchen for celebrity chef Michael Chiarello. The former host of *Easy Entertaining* on the Food Network has come back to Napa Valley with his flair for Italian cuisine. The exposed brick and bare ceiling beams of the dining room pair nicely with such classic dishes as *tagliarini* with veal and porcini *sugo,* duck served with pickled pomegranates, and braised short ribs with spaetzle. The prices, particularly the wine list, are fairly reasonable for the area. While the menu changes with the seasons, try to finish your meal with the ricotta *zeppole*—Italian doughnuts fried to order and topped with praline cream.

Information and Services

Right in the thick of the epicurean madness, the **Yountville Chamber of Commerce** (6484 Washington St., 707/944-0904, http://yountville.com, daily 10 A.M.–5 P.M.) also doubles as a visitors center. There are maps available along with always helpful tips, but swing by to purchase the two-for-one tasting ($5) at Hill Family Estate just down the street. There is also a **post office** (6514 Washington St.).

Getting There and Around

BY CAR

Yountville is on Highway 29, just nine miles north of Napa. Downtown Yountville is on the east side of Highway 29, and Washington Street is the main drag, connecting with Highway 29 at the south and north ends of town; to reach the heart of Yountville, exit on California Drive in the south and Madison Street in the north. The Yountville Cross Road will take you from the north end of town to the Silverado Trail.

BY BUS AND TROLLEY

To reach Yountville by bus, jump aboard the **VINE** (800/696-6443, http://nctpa.net, adults $1.50–5.50, children $1–2.50), a commuter bus service that runs from the East Bay north through Calistoga.

Around town, consider taking the **Yountville Trolley** (707/944-1234, http://nctpa.net, 10 A.M.–2 P.M. and 4–7 P.M. Wed.–Fri., 10 A.M.–7 P.M. Sat.–Sun., free). The trolley runs on a fixed track from Yountville Park along Washington Street to California Drive, conveniently near Domaine Chandon. It may also be a convenient way to get back to your hotel after imbibing too much.

RUTHERFORD AND OAKVILLE

Driving along on Highway 29, you might not even notice the tiny hamlets of Oakville and Rutherford. Neither town has much in the way of a commercial or residential district, and both have tiny populations. Oakville earned a spot on the map in 1903 when the U.S. Department of Agriculture planted an experimental vineyard. Since then, it has garnered distinction as a unique American Viticultural Area (AVA) known for its Bordeaux-style varietals. Oakville is also home to the outstanding Oakville Grocery, opened in 1881.

Rutherford was named for the 1,000 acres given to Thomas Rutherford by his father-in-law, George Yount. The area now has the distinction of growing some of the best cabernet grapes around. Yountville is also home to Grgich Hills, whose chardonnay crashed the Paris Wine Tasting of 1976. Like Oakville, Rutherford is also its own designated AVA.

Wineries

FROG'S LEAP

With so much outrageous winery architecture in the valley, Frog's Leap Winery (8815 Conn Creek Rd., Rutherford, 800/959-4704, www.frogsleap.com, daily 10 A.M.–4 P.M., tasting $20) is an understated breath of fresh air. Its historic red barn and modest home and vineyard sit among gardens and vines. This big producer is just west of the Silverado Trail in the flats of Napa Valley; it has been a producer since 1981 and a leader in organic wine production and environmental stewardship. Tasting here is relaxing; sample a flight of four wines on the wraparound porch or inside the vineyard house, accompanied by cheese, crackers, and jam. The highly recommended tour ($20) also provides a tasting of four wines, and each tasting is enjoyed somewhere different along the tour—the garden, the red barn, or in the vineyard, for example. Tours are by appointment only and last about one hour.

MINER FAMILY VINEYARDS

The estate tasting room at Miner Family Vineyards (7850 Silverado Trail, Oakville, 800/366-9463, www.minerwines.com, daily

11 A.M.–5 P.M., tasting $25) provides Silverado Trail travelers with a typical taste of the Napa Valley. You'll need to climb a flight of stairs or take the elevator up to the oddly small tasting room that still manages to display an array of upscale souvenirs for sale. The winery mostly makes standard Napa Valley varietal wines such as chardonnay and cabernet sauvignon, with a viognier and a sangiovese thrown in. Most of the wines aren't bad, but they aren't remarkable either—certainly not as remarkable as the prices might indicate. If you've never tasted California wines before, Miner Family might make for a good baseline. If you're an experienced oenophile, you can give this one a pass.

OPUS ONE

Yup, that huge thing on the rise that looks like a missile silo really is a winery. Opus One (7900 Hwy. 29, Oakville, 800/292-6787, www.opusonewinery.com, daily 10 A.M.–4 P.M., reservations required) boasts a reputation as one of the most prestigious, and definitely one of the most expensive, vintners in Napa. The echoing halls inside the facility add to the grandeur of the place, as does the price of a tasting, $35 for a three-ounce pour of a single wine. You're unlikely to find a bottle of Opus One for under $250. If you don't mind the price tag or just can't get enough of the Opus One experience, tours ($50–70) of the estate are also available, and like the tastings, are by appointment only.

◖ GRGICH HILLS

The tasting room at Grgich Hills Winery (1829 St. Helena Hwy., Rutherford, 800/532-3057, www.grgich.com, daily 9:30 A.M.–4:30 P.M., $15) isn't housed in the most elaborate building. The gardens aren't showy, and the working vineyards run right up to the back of the winemaking facility. Active aging barrels crowd the main building and narrow the path to the tasting room's restrooms. If you're looking for a showy Napa Valley experience, this might not be the best place for you. What you will find at Grgich are some of the best wines in the valley, an entirely biodynamic wine-making operation, and the rich history of fine wine from California taking its rightful place alongside or even ahead of the great French vintages. Mike Grgich took his California chardonnay to the Paris Wine Tasting of 1976 and entered it in the white burgundy blind-tasting competition. It won, and French winemakers were incensed; they demanded that the contest be held again, and Grgich's chardonnay won again. That same year, Robert Mondavi's cabernet sauvignon also took top honors in its category at the same contest. The quality of California wines could no longer be ignored, even by the most xenophobic of French wine connoisseurs.

Today, you'll learn about this history when visiting Grgich Hills. You'll also see plenty of information about biodynamic farming, a process that takes organic practices to the next level using all-natural processes and including phenomenon such as the phases of the moon in the growing and harvesting cycles of the vineyards. All Grgich wines are biodynamically grown and made. The best wine might be the descendants of Mike's legendary chardonnay—arguably the best chardonnay made in Napa or anywhere else. But don't ignore the reds; Grgich offers some lovely zinfandels and cabernets. And the Violetta, a dessert wine named for Mike's daughter, is a special treat that's only made in years when the grape conditions are perfect. None of the Grgich wines are cheap, and there's a fee for tasting, but it's more than worth it when you sip these rare exquisite vintages.

◖ MUMM

You may have already tasted the sparkling wines produced by Mumm (8445 Silverado Trail, Rutherford, 800/686-6272, http://mummnapa.com, daily 10 A.M.–4:45 P.M., tasting $7–25). Even for genuine wine aficionados, it's worth spending an hour or two at Mumm Napa, a friendly and surprisingly down-to-earth winery among the often pretentious estates on the Silverado Trail. First, get on the list and take the free tour (10 A.M.) of the sample vineyard and the working production facility, and learn from the knowledgeable and articulate tour guides, who will describe the process of making sparkling wine in detailed comprehensible English. All tours wind up in a special treat of a place—the only gallery showing original Ansel Adams prints outside Yosemite Valley. Even if you skip the tour, you can hang out in the gallery as long as you like. Perhaps best of all, after finishing the tour, you'll get a tag that gives you 15 percent off all bottle purchases in the winery.

Tastings happen at tables, with menus and service in restaurant fashion. The prices may look very Napa Valley, but you'll get more wine and service for your money at Mumm. Each pour is three ounces of wine—some of it high-end—and you get three pours per tasting. Good news for designated drivers: Nonalcoholic gourmet grape sodas or bottled water are complementary as a thank-you for keeping the Silverado Trail safe. If you've brought your dog, you can bring him into the tasting room too; dogs get water, gourmet doggie bones, and plenty of petting from the tasting-room staff.

PEJU

Peju (8466 St. Helena Hwy., Rutherford, 800/446-7358, www.peju.com, daily 10 A.M.–6 P.M., $15) embodies the ultimate success of the Napa Valley—a 30-year-old family winery that has, through hard work, created great wines that have garnered the attention of international magazines and judging bodies. Today, visitors to Peju see gorgeous sycamore trees, hand-pruned by Tony Peju, running up the drive; a fabulous garden tended by Herta Peju; and solar panels on the roof of the elegant winery building. Inside you'll get tastes

of an array of aromatic and award-winning red wines—from the lighter Bordeaux-varietal cabernet franc to the many vintages of classic California cabernet sauvignon. A few whites and perhaps a rosé or a port round out Peju's list.

INGLENOOK

Wine lovers come to enjoy the grand tasting room and museum at Inglenook (1991 St. Helena Hwy., Rutherford, 800/782-4266, www.inglenook.com, daily 10 A.M.–5 P.M., reservations required, tasting $50), formerly Rubicon and Niebaum-Coppola. Reservations are required for tastings in the large elegant tasting room, where you'll find a generous bar area with plenty of staff to help you navigate the wine list. The winemakers take their job seriously, and the results can be spectacular. This estate winery also houses the small Centennial Museum, showcasing old Inglenook wines, zoetropes, and magic lanterns.

RUTHERFORD HILL

If you're planning in advance to visit Rutherford Hill (200 Rutherford Hill Rd., Rutherford, 707/963-1871, www.rutherfordhill.com, daily 10 A.M.–5 P.M., $15–30), book a spot on the winery-and-cave tour. The winery is pretty standard for a Napa facility, but the caves impress even experienced wine lovers. Dug back into the hillside, Rutherford's caves provide a natural temperature-controlled space in which to age their array of wines, mostly hearty reds. (If you're looking for a place to hold a special dinner or midsize event, Rutherford rents out space in the caves.) Contrary to the myth perpetuated by the movie *Sideways,* Rutherford produces a fine merlot as well as rich cabernet sauvignons and other tasty varietals.

Sports and Recreation

For a lake vacation adjacent to Wine Country, drive a few miles out to **Lake Berryessa** (Berryessa–Knoxville Rd., east of Rutherford).

On this largish lake you can ride powerboats, personal watercraft, kayaks, and canoes, and fish—or just sunbathe on the shore and splash around in the shallows with the family. If you've got your own boat, launch it at one of the marinas or the **Capell Cove Boat Ramp** (Knoxville Rd.), or rent one from one of the lakeside resorts. The **Markley Cove Resort** (7521 Hwy. 128, Napa, 707/966-4204, www. lakeberryessaboats.com) offers all kinds of boats, including patio cruisers, high-end ski-tow boats, personal watercraft, and kayaks. Make reservations well in advance to get the boat you want. You can also rent water skis, wakeboards, and ski tubes.

Lake Berryessa also boasts some of the best fishing in California. You can fish for cold- and warm-water fish, including bass, rainbow trout, and kokanee salmon. Rent a boat from one of the resorts, launch your own, or enjoy some relaxed fishing from the shore. The resorts sell California fishing licenses and bait and can advise you about the season's hottest fishing holes.

Accommodations

Courtyards dripping in wisteria, earth-tone stucco, tiled roofs, and rustic stonework draw guests back in time to **Rancho Caymus** (1140 Rutherford Rd., Rutherford, 800/845-1777, www.ranchocaymus.com, $180–389) and Napa Valley's Spanish past. Each of the 26 suites is named for early Napa adventurers, and many include a separate sitting area, wood-burning fireplaces, Spanish tiled baths, a refrigerator, and a private outdoor area. While the decor many be a bit outdated, you can't beat the price in this central part of Napa.

Perched above the valley and located off the Silverado Trail, **Auberge du Soleil** (180 Rutherford Hill Rd., St. Helena, 707/963-1211, www.aubergedusoleil.com, $700) is the ultimate in Wine Country luxury. Even the most ardent oenophile will be hard-pressed to leave the lush sun-drenched grounds. And why would you leave? The compound features multiple high-end wine-tasting and dining options in addition to a pool, a fitness room, a store, and well-kept gardens accented by modern art. The guest rooms are appointed with Italian sheets, private patios, fireplaces, and TVs in both the living room and the bath. The smallest guest room is 500 square feet, suites can top 1,400 square feet, and the Private Maison is 1,800 square feet. Auberge du Soleil is definitely the place to stay if you have the cash to focus on the inn's amenities and less interest in exploring the area.

Food

The historic **Auberge du Soleil** (180 Rutherford Hill Rd., St. Helena, 800/348-5406, www.aubergedusoleil.com, daily 7–11 A.M., 11:30 A.M.–2:30 P.M., and 5:30–9:30 P.M., tasting menu $150) has an inn where you can stay the night, but some visitors come just for the food—the charming Mediterranean-style dining room has drawn visitors from all over the world for decades. Sunny yellow tablecloths, a central fireplace, exposed wooden beams, and wall-to-wall picture windows welcome diners. Executive Chef Robert Curry, a legend of the Napa Valley culinary scene, uses the finest local ingredients to create his own take on Mediterranean and California cuisine. Choose one item from each course list on the short but exquisite tasting menu to create a four-course dinner. If you ask, you can also dine à la carte from any of the courses. After all that rich food and fine wine, you might find yourself at the inn's desk, begging to be allowed to stay the night within staggering distance of the restaurant. If you're not ready to commit to such an indulgent meal, consider visiting the adjacent **Bistro & Bar** (daily 11 A.M.–11 P.M., $20). Choose from braised short ribs, a charcuterie plate, or a light salad to accompany the wide and rotating selection of wines. You can still soak in

WINE COUNTRY

the luxurious atmosphere—the wraparound deck, the open fireplace—without quite as big a pinch on your wallet.

A long-standing Wine Country favorite is the **Rutherford Grill** (1180 Rutherford Rd., Rutherford, 707/963-1792, www.hillstone. com, 11:30 A.M.–9:30 P.M. Sun.–Thurs., 11:30 A.M.–10:30 P.M. Fri.–Sat., $10–30), which is more casual than many of its Napa Valley peers. Some of the best seats in the house cluster outside the dining room on the wide deck; sheltered by a collection of umbrellas, guests enjoy the pretty gardens with their classic grill fare—cheeseburgers, salads with grilled items, bangers and mash, and a whole array of grilled meats—as well as an extensive and impressive wine list. Perhaps the best part: You can escape from the Rutherford Grill for well under $100 pp.

For a picnic lunch or just a few munchies for the road, stop by the **Oakville Grocery** (7856 St. Helena Hwy., Oakville, 707/944-8802, www. oakvillegrocery.com, 7 A.M.–5 P.M. Mon.–Thurs., 7 A.M.–6 P.M. Fri.–Sat., 8 A.M.–5 P.M. Sun., $10). A long-standing Napa Valley institution, the Oakville Grocery has a reputation for stocking only the best food, wine, cheese, and other goodies along Highway 29. Browse the tightly packed shelves or order a hot lunch at the center counter; they have everything from crab cakes to chimichangas and boxed lunches. To find the building from the northbound highway, look for the large Coca-Cola sign painted on the south side of the building.

Getting There and Around

Oakville is four miles north of Yountville on Highway 29; Rutherford is another two miles north. Both can be easy to miss because of their loose organization and rural character. The Silverado Trail runs parallel to Highway 29 along this stretch. To reach it from Oakville, take Oakville Road east; in Rutherford, take Rutherford Road (Hwy. 128) east.

ST. HELENA

There are few Northern California towns as picturesque and well-groomed as St. Helena. Bolstered by the lucrative wine industry, St. Helena has the glossy sheen of a reinvented old California farm town. It is filled with fine eateries and quaint expensive shops housed in historic buildings and surrounded block upon block by well-maintained craftsman homes. The Napa campus of the Culinary Institute of America is a major employer in the area, as is the St. Helena Hospital. Highway 29 runs north–south through the center of town, which can give you a quick peek at the sights, but it's not so nice when sitting in traffic on a sunny weekend.

Wineries
BERINGER VINEYARDS

You may recognize the Beringer name, as this winery sells large quantities of wine across the country. The palatial stone estate buildings of Beringer Vineyards (2000 Main St., 707/967-4412, www.beringer.com, daily 10 A.M.–5 P.M.,

downtown St. Helena

© ELIZABETH LINHART MONEY

KNOW YOUR GRAPES

© THOMAS BARRAT/123RF.COM

Follow the sign to the pinot noir grapes.

Chardonnay: Most of the white wine made and sold in California is chardonnay. The grapes grow best in a slightly cooler climate, such as the vineyards closer to the coast. Most California chardonnays taste smooth and buttery and a bit like fruit, and they often take on the oak flavor of the barrels they sit in. Chardonnay doesn't keep (age), so most chards are sold the year after they're bottled and consumed within a few months of purchase.

Sauvignon blanc: This pale-green grape is used to make both sauvignon blanc and fumé blanc wines. Sauvignon blanc grapes grow well in Napa, Sonoma, and other warm-hot parts of the state. The difference between a sauvignon blanc and a fumé blanc is in the wine-making

more than in the grapes. Fumé blanc wines tend to have a strong odor and the taste of grapefruit; they pair well with fish dishes and spicy Asian cuisine. The California sauvignon blanc wine goes well with salads, fish, vegetarian cuisine, and even spicy international dishes.

Pinot noir: Pinot noir grapes do best in a cool coastal climate with limited exposure to high heat. The Anderson Valley and the Monterey coastal growing regions tend to specialize in pinot noir, although many Napa and Sonoma wineries buy grapes from the coast to make their own versions. California vintners make up single-varietal pinot noir wines that taste of cherries, strawberries, and smoke.

Zinfandel: These grapes grow best when tortured by their climate; a few grow near Napa, but most come from the Gold Country and the inland Central Coast. A true zinfandel is a hearty deep-red wine, and boasts the flavors and smells of blackberry jam and the dusky hues of venous blood. Zinfandel often tastes wonderful on its own, but it's also good with beef, buffalo, and even venison.

Cabernet sauvignon: Cabernet sauvignon, a grape from the Bordeaux region of France, creates a deep, dark, strong red wine. The grapes that get intense summer heat make the best wine, which makes them a perfect fit for the scorching Napa Valley. In California, especially in Napa, winemakers use cabernet sauvignon on its own to brew some of the most intense single-grape wines in the world. A good dry cab might taste of leather, tobacco, and bing cherries. Cabs age well, often hitting their peak of flavor and smoothness more than a decade after bottling.

$20–30) belie the reasonably priced Beringer vintages available in supermarkets. Inside, you'll find an array of wines for tasting, many of which are not readily available outside the tasting room. Outdoors, you can stroll in the beautiful estate gardens that stretch for acres on prime land next to Highway 29. Tours take

you into the wine-making facilities and show off the highlights of the vast estate.

CORISON

A rarity among Napa Valley's large-scale producers, Corison (987 St. Helena Hwy., 707/963-0826, www.corison.com, daily 10 A.M.–5 P.M., tasting $20) is the genuine article—a tiny single-proprietor winery producing great wines in small quantities. Technically, Corison takes tasters by appointment only, but in truth they've never turned away a drop-in during regular business hours. After turning onto a short gravel driveway, you pass a vintage home to reach the small barn that serves as a tasting room. Open the huge white door (it's easier than it looks) and enter the tasting-, barrel-, and stock room. A tiny bar next to the entrance offers tastings from the 3,000 cases the winery produces each year. Expect the attentive staff to talk in loving and knowledgeable terms about the delicious wines they're pouring. Corison's flagship cabernet sauvignon tastes of luscious fruit and perfect balance. The other wines are not distributed—you must buy them here, join the wine club, or long for them from afar.

FLORA SPRINGS

This winery straddles the line between boutiques and big-deal Napa players. You'll find Flora Springs (677 S. St. Helena Hwy., 707/967-8032, www.florasprings.com, daily 10:30 A.M.–5 P.M., $20–55) on a few menus in upscale restaurants and here in the open, airy tasting room that sweeps in a half circle around the bar, with plenty of windows letting in the Napa sunlight. You'll taste a variety of reds and whites, but the cabernet sauvignons are the Flora Springs standouts.

HEITZ

One of the oldest wineries in the valley, Heitz (436 St. Helena Hwy., 707/963-3542, www.heitzcellar.com, daily 11 A.M.–4:30 P.M., free) brings sincere elegance to the glitz and glamour of Napa. The high-ceilinged tasting room is dominated by a stone fireplace with comfy chairs. A low bar off to the right sets the stage for an array of Napa Valley cabernet sauvignons. To the happy surprise of many, Heitz's cabernets are well balanced and easy to drink,

and though costly, they approach affordable by Napa standards. Most of the grapes used for these wines grow right in the Napa Valley. If you're lucky enough to visit Heitz in February, you can taste the current release of the Martha's Vineyard Cabernet—a vintage grown in the first wine-designated vineyard (the first vineyard to grow grapes for wine rather than eating) in the valley.

PRIDE MOUNTAIN VINEYARDS

Take advantage of some of Wine Country's scenic drives with a visit to Pride Mountain Vineyards (4026 Spring Mountain Rd., 707/963-4949, www.pridewines.com, daily 10 A.M.–3:45 P.M., reservations required, tour and tasting $15, tasting only $10–20), located at the top of a scenic winding road six miles from the turnoff on Highway 29. In addition to the wine, the views are the reward for the effort. Wine tasting is by appointment only, so once you arrive you'll have the pourer's full attention. It's worth it to take the tour, as you'll see the vineyard and the caves and will be able to taste the wine straight out of the barrel. It's a great education in how wine matures with age.

ST. CLEMENT VINEYARDS

St. Clement (2867 Hwy. 29, 866/877-5939, www.stclement.com, daily 10 A.M.–5 P.M., tasting $10–30) is all about the cabs: While they produce one chardonnay for good measure, the rest of St. Clement's wine menu features 11 different vintages of cabernet sauvignon. This translates into a good fun instruction to the variety and qualities of the grape. But this is not the only reason to visit; St. Clement's elegant two-story Victorian farmhouse perched on a hill above Highway 29 and is beautifully surrounded by sloping vineyards. The grounds are lush with English gardens and heavy-limbed oaks; in front, tables dot the split-level decks, affording both privacy and a splendid place for a picnic. The winery's deep-blue interior features more modern touches such as the unique art deco chandeliers. The juxtaposition is unexpected, but it works.

V. SATTUI

A boutique winery that doesn't distribute to retailers, V. Sattui (1111 White Lane, 707/963-7774, www.vsattui.com, daily 9 A.M.–6 P.M., $10–15) won the Best Winery award at the California State Fair in 2006, 2007, and 2012—a mighty feat in a state filled with excellent vintners. V. Sattui produces a wide selection of varietals—everything from light-bodied whites to full-flavored cabernet sauvignons. The dessert madeira is particularly fine—if it's not on the tasting menu, ask your pourer at the bar if they've got a bottle open, and you might just get lucky.

The big tasting room on Highway 29 boasts three spacious bar areas, endless stacks and cases of wine out and ready for purchase, a separate register, and a full deli. The gardens surrounding the facility include a number of picnic tables, and Sattui is a popular lunchtime stop for all-day tasters. But beware: All the recent good press makes even the big Sattui tasting room fill up on weekends in high season (May–Oct.).

Sights

Up under the cool shade trees of the Napa hills, the gristmill at **Bale Grist Mill State Historic Park** (3369 N St./Hwy. 29, 3 miles north of St. Helena, 707/942-4575, www.parks.ca.gov, grounds daily, buildings 10 A.M.–5 P.M. Sat.–Sun.) is quiet: The huge water wheel no longer turns, and the vast network of elevated and ground-level wooden pipes and ducts have dried out. Today, visitors can take a pleasant nature walk from the parking lot down to the site of Dr. Edward Bale's old wheel and its associated mill structures. On weekends, take a tour inside the flour mill with a docent who will tell the story of the gristmill and show off the facility that the good doctor built using local stone,

redwood, and fir. Once you've soaked in the local history and perhaps enjoyed a picnic at one of the scattered tables, take a hike farther out into the woods along several shady trails.

For a literary detour, the **Robert Louis Stevenson Museum** (1490 Library Lane, St, Helena, 707/963-3757, www.silveradomuseum. org, noon–4 P.M. Tues.–Sat., free) is a rich collection of all things related to the celebrated 19th-century author. The museum boasts 9,000 items and is a draw for Stevenson scholars. In addition to original manuscripts, letters, and early and rare editions of his books, visitors will be pleased to see the elegantly carved wooden desk on which Stevenson wrote *Treasure Island* as well as his wedding ring and the lead toy soldiers he played with as a boy. The museum is managed as a wing of the St. Helena Library, which also has an impressive collection of 19th-century art adorning the walls.

◖ CULINARY INSTITUTE OF AMERICA

The premier institute for training professional chefs in the United States has only three campuses: one in upstate New York, one in Texas, and this one, the Culinary Institute of America at Greystone (2555 Main St., 707/967-1010, www. ciachef.edu, 11:30 A.M.–9 P.M. Sun.–Thurs., 11:30 A.M.–10 P.M. Fri.–Sat.), with a restaurant, a café, a gourmet shop, one-day cooking classes and demos, a food-history museum, and a stunning set of campus buildings nestled in the forests and vineyards near the town of St. Helena on Highway 29. If Napa is the perfect place to introduce newcomers to the world of high-end food and wine, Greystone takes it to the intermediate and advanced levels. Most people love the De Baun Café and the Spice Islands Marketplace and want to make a reservation to dine in the *Wine Spectator* Greystone Restaurant. Serious foodies or cork dorks should consider signing up in advance to attend a cooking demo or even a seminar at this haven for haute cuisine. Be sure to take a few minutes to wander the charming grounds and marvel at the imposing structures of the campus—made from, of course, gray stonework.

Shopping

As you may be able to tell from the traffic in town, downtown St. Helena is hopping. Quaint and historic storefronts line Highway 29, housing galleries, clothiers, jewelers, kitchen stores, and, of course, wine shops, many of which offer wine tasting. If you are looking to give your palate a rest from the onslaught of wine, two stores in particular are eager to remind you that grapes are not the only crop that grow well here. Over the years, olive trees have begun spreading across the landscape, which makes perfect sense—Napa Valley has an ideal Mediterranean climate for these trees. The resulting olive oil offers one more thing to taste.

The **St. Helena Olive Oil Company** (1351 Main St., 800/939-9880, www.sholiveoil.com, daily 10:30 A.M.–5 P.M.) gives you the opportunity to parse out notes of grass, citrus, or pepper in the region's oils. The historic building was once the Bank of Italy and has been redone in perfect Wine Country fashion; an exposed stone wall and the old bank's interior details have been infused with a rustic Mediterranean touch. The selection of at least a dozen different house-made olive oils is terrific, as are the local vinegars and the array of delicious bath and body products. Tasting is encouraged, and it's likely you'll walk away with something.

Out of downtown St. Helena's hubbub, the **Napa Valley Olive Oil Manufacturing Co.** (835 Charter Oak Ave., 707/963-4173, daily 9 A.M.–5:30 P.M.) is one of those amazing off-the-beaten-path treasures that travelers feel lucky to find. The tiny, funky old storefront is two blocks off Highway 29 and features a motley collection of plastic-covered picnic tables out front and a faded hand-lettered sign on the door. Inside, take care not to trip over the uneven floor in the cramped, meandering rooms of the shop. Those in the know dart in, grab plainly labeled

quart jugs of olive oil, and pay cash for what's obviously a year's supply of the good stuff. You can't taste the oils and vinegars; you'll just have to go on faith that this Italian-owned and operated shop sells the best. The tiny store also has fabulous cheeses and fresh-baked breads, making it a great stop for would-be picnickers who don't mind the less-than-elegant surroundings. Napa Valley Olive Oil Manufacturing Co. has its own bottling facilities, just as the St. Helena Olive Oil Company does—although here the "facility" consists of the cashier in the back room with a funnel.

Accommodations

The charming small village of St. Helena is right on Highway 29, and its stop signs and traffic signals are often the cause of the endless weekend Wine Country traffic jams. But if you're staying here, you can avoid the worst of the traffic and enjoy the wooded central Napa Valley area.

For the best rates in St. Helena, the **El Bonita Motel** (195 Main St./Hwy. 29, 800/541-3284, www.elbonita.com, $80–300) can't be beat. It is within walking distance of the historic downtown and has a 1950s motel charm. The low-slung 42-room hotel wraps about a patio shaded by oak trees, bordered by a clipped lawn, and filled with tables, chairs, and umbrellas. In the center is a pool, a hot tub, and a sauna, which all guest are encouraged to enjoy. The rooms may not match the indulgence of other Napa inns, but they are clean, comfortable, and pet-friendly, with refrigerators and microwave ovens; some even boast kitchenettes.

At the **Zinfandel Inn** (800 Zinfandel Lane, 707/963-3512, www.zinfandelinn.com, $175), you'll find yourself in a 1980s reproduction of a Shakespearean castle. Lavish stonework adorns the outside of this unique structure. Inside, you'll stay in one of three exquisitely decorated suite-like guest rooms. Each guest room boasts a unique design, complete with antique bedsteads and dressers, feather beds, fireplaces, and tiled whirlpool tubs. All guests enjoy a full breakfast every morning of their stay, plus the rich amenities suited to a Wine Country inn.

A less imposing structure, **The Ink House** (1575 St. Helena Hwy., at Whitehall Lane, 707/963-3890, www.inkhouse.com, $200) prides itself on its more casual elegance. A pretty yellow facade looks almost like a wedding cake. Inside, the breakfast room is on the ground floor, all the guest rooms are on the 2nd floor, and the small 3rd-floor solarium is open as a parlor to guests. There are many amenities to enjoy at the Ink House, including a full gourmet breakfast, an afternoon wine social, complimentary nightcaps, and loaner bicycles. The lounge areas include a pool table and a dartboard; outside, a croquet course and a horseshoe pit afford some gentle recreation. Guest rooms are individually decorated, and each has a view of the surrounding forest and vineyards. Furnishings tend toward American and European antiques, and all the beds are queens.

Food

A highlight of the St. Helena dining scene is the *Wine Spectator* **Greystone Restaurant** (2555 Main St., 707/967-1010, http://ciachef.edu, 11:30 A.M.–9 P.M. Sun.–Thurs., 11:30 A.M.–10 P.M. Fri.–Sat., $21–34), better known to its friends as "the restaurant at the CIA," where the world's top aspiring chefs practice their craft. It's easier to get a reservation here than at Thomas Keller's hallowed French Laundry and Bouchon; with several big dining rooms, the CIA can seat large numbers. If you get the right table, you can watch your food being prepared in the open kitchen. The ever-changing menu highlights the best of each season, and the wine list features the best of Napa Valley's vintages; the student chefs plan menus with an eye to wine pairings.

The imposing stone building draped in ivy and surrounded by grapevines is home to **Tra Vigne** (1050 Charter Oak Ave., 707/963-4444, www.travignerestaurant.com,

Culinary Institute of America

11:30 A.M.–9 P.M. Mon.–Sat., 11 A.M.–9 P.M. Sun., $18–30). When it opened, Tra Vigne helped bring a modern California culinary sensibility to Napa Valley. Today, it has been overshadowed by the profusion of high-end eateries and celebrity chefs, but its reputation for excellent Italian food is still intact. The warm dining room features white tablecloths, cream walls, plush leather booths, and wooden chairs. The food is equally comfortable, with crisply executed thin-crust pizzas, wood oven–roasted meats, and silky pasta dishes. The extensive wine list includes a number of Italian grappas.

Craving pizza or a low-key meal? **Pizzeria Tra Vigne** (1016 Main St., 707/967-9999, www.travignerestaurant.com, 11:30 A.M.–9 P.M. Sun.–Thurs., 11:30 A.M.–9:30 P.M. Fri.–Sat., $9–18), next door to Tra Vigne, is considerably more relaxed than its renowned sibling. Inside are long tables opposite the open kitchen, where a huge wood-fired oven sits center stage. The famous thin-crust Italian pizzas lure locals many weekend nights; you can also enjoy hearty plates of pasta or heavy Italian salads. Wash it all down with a pitcher of any number of beers on tap. There are also a number of beers by the bottle in addition to a healthy selection of wine. If you're traveling with kids, Pizzeria Tra Vigne is a great place to stop and relax over a meal. There is even a pool table.

Until recently, **Gott's Roadside** (933 Main St., 707/963-3486, http://gotts.com, 10:30 A.M.–10 P.M. daily summer, 10:30 A.M.–9 P.M. daily winter, $10) was known as Taylor's Refresher, which explains the wooden sign on Highway 29. This classic roadside diner has been around since 1949, but the food has been updated with a modern local-organic sensibility; the burgers, fries, and milk shakes are made with quality ingredients. The Gott brothers, who took over the business in 1999, have added more California-eclectic comfort food like fish tacos, smoked chicken po'boys, and Chinese chicken salad. They have also earned three James Beard awards for bringing fast food up to the quality of well-respected sit-down restaurants.

Information and Services

Pick up maps, information, and discounted wine-tasting vouchers at the **St. Helena Welcome Center** (657 Main St., 707/963-4456, www.sthelena.com, 9 A.M.–5 P.M. Mon.–Fri., 10 A.M.–5 P.M. Sat.–Sun.). Thankfully, there is parking in back; turn on Vidovich Lane just north of the visitors center.

For health concerns, the **St. Helena Hospital** (10 Woodland Rd., 707/963-6425, http://sthelenanowaiter.org) has a 24-hour emergency room for quick and reliable service. St. Helena also has a **post office** (1461 Main St., between Pine St. and Adams St.).

Getting There and Around

St. Helena is on Highway 29 in the middle of Napa Valley, eight miles south of Calistoga. To reach the Silverado Trail from St. Helena, take Zinfandel Lane or Pope Street east.

To avoid the constant headache of parking and driving around town, consider hopping aboard **The VINE St. Helena Shuttle** (707/963-3007, http://nctpa.net, 7:45 A.M.–5 P.M. Mon.–Fri., $0.50–1). Unfortunately, the shuttle doesn't run on weekends when traffic congestion is heaviest.

CALISTOGA

Despite their proximity, Calistoga and St. Helena couldn't be more different. While St. Helena leans toward the boutique side of the wine scene and often feels permanently congested, Calistoga has a more laid-back, almost mountain-town crunchiness to it. Located far from the city of Napa, it is one of the most economically diverse towns in the valley, which is reflected in its restaurants, businesses, and hotels. You can browse books, grab great barbecue, or sit at a sidewalk café to enjoy a cheap beer and even forget you are in Wine Country.

It is also the land of great and affordable spas, where soaking is treated more as therapy than beauty treatment.

Wineries

CASTELLO DI AMOROSA

When you first spy the ramshackle house and its sweetly tended garden near the entrance to Castello di Amorosa (4045 Hwy. 29, 707/967-6272, www.castellodiamorosa. com, daily 9:30 A.M.–6 P.M. Mar.–Oct., daily 9:30 A.M.–5 P.M. Nov.–Feb., adults $18–28, children $8), you might imagine you are stopping in at one of those delightfully rustic north-valley wineries. You couldn't be more wrong. After passing through the gates and ascending a steep hill lined in vineyards and Italian cypress trees, you'll reach the castle at the top. The steep prices for tasting include access to the main floors of the castle; tours, in addition to barrel-tasting, take visitors to the armory and torture chamber. Who knew these were necessities in Wine Country? In terms of wine, Castello di Amorosa produces a number of varietals, such as pinot grigio and muscat, that are overshadowed by their environs. Children are permitted on the tour, however, indicating that the owners are eager to draw in more than just wine lovers. And certainly your kids will oblige, particularly if you give them a sword and call them Lancelot.

CUVAISON

This small winery harks back to the Napa of decades past. The intimate tasting room at Cuvaison (4550 Silverado Trail N., 707/942-6268, www.cuvaison.com, 11 A.M.–4 P.M. Sun.–Thurs., 10 A.M.–5 P.M. Fri.–Sat., $15–20) doesn't hold busloads of visitors, and the bar might show a few scars, but the tasting room staff know quite a bit about the wine they're pouring, and they want to tell you all about it. This isn't a place for esoteric wine tasting; you quickly get the feeling that everyone, regardless of their background, is on the same ground and here to have a good time. The quaint building sits on the slope of the mountains bordering Napa Valley and shelters several friendly cats. A picnic area invites a longer stop to enjoy the vineyard views with your lunch and a nice bottle of Cuvaison chardonnay, or just to relax and sip one of their light tasty reds.

SCHRAMSBERG VINEYARDS

At the other end of the Calistoga winery spectrum is Schramsberg Vineyards (1400 Schramsberg Rd., 707/942-4558, www.schramsberg.com, tours and tasting 10 A.M.–2:30 P.M., reservations required, $45), founded in 1862 and considered to be one of the best producers of sparkling wine in California. Tastings include four wines, a tour of the 120-year old caves, and an education in the art of making sparkling wines in the Champagne style. Schramsberg can be visited by appointment only and does not allow pets or children, no matter how small or quiet.

STERLING VINEYARDS

Sterling Vineyards (1111 Dunaweal Lane, 800/726-6136, www.sterlingvineyards.com, 10:30 A.M.–4:30 P.M. Mon.–Fri., 10 A.M.–5 P.M. Sat.–Sun., $25–40) is more appealing for folks who are touring Wine Country for the first time than for serious wine aficionados. The jewel of the new "Disneyland with wine" culture of Napa, Sterling features a gondola ride and an obligatory tasting tour through the estate rather than a traditional tasting room experience. It's expensive, and the lines can be long on weekends in high season (May–Oct.).

To be fair, once you've stood in line and bought your tickets, the gondola ride up the mountain to the estate shows off Napa Valley at its best. Take advantage of the time to admire the stellar views of forested hills and endless vineyards. Once up at the estate, you'll be guided around by signs to each tasting venue.

WINE COUNTRY

tasting at Up Valley Vintners

Frankly, the wine isn't worth the effort or the high per-bottle price tag, but the estate has some charm, and the views from the deck match those from the gondola.

UP VALLEY VINTNERS

For every winery with a tasting room and tours, there are several smaller boutique vineyards whose wines can only be found and tasted in select restaurants—until now. Up Valley Vintners (1371 Lincoln Ave., 707/942-1004, www.upvalleyvintners.com, daily noon–5 P.M.) is a co-op of sorts where smaller winemakers can sell their wine and offer tastings directly to the public. The long and narrow shop features a dark wood bar that extends one-third of the way down. Here you will find locals and travelers happily sitting on bar stools, chatting with the pourer. Past the bar is a retail section where each winery has a profile and plenty of bottles for sale. There is a comfortable lounge area inside and a patio with a table and chairs

outside. While all the wines featured come from veteran winemakers of the Calistoga AVA, a real standout is the Dyer cabernet blend. Made from grapes grown on a 2.2-acre vineyard on Diamond Mountain, the blends have a Bordeaux quality and a reputation for excellence, and they are difficult to come by.

Sights
OLD FAITHFUL GEYSER

No, that's not a typo, and you haven't accidentally driven east to Yellowstone. The Napa Valley has its own Old Faithful Geyser (1299 Tubbs Lane, 707/942-6463, www.oldfaithfulgeyser.com, daily 9 A.M.–6 P.M. summer, daily 9 A.M.–5 P.M. winter, adults $10, seniors $7, ages 6–12 $3, under age 6 free). Unlike its more famous counterpart, this geothermal geyser is artificial. In the 19th and early 20th centuries, more than 100 wells were drilled into the geothermal springs of the Calistoga area, and many of these created geysers. Old Faithful is one of the few that wasn't eventually capped off, and it's the only one that erupts with clockwork regularity. When you visit the geyser, expect no more than a 40-minute wait to see it erupt 60 feet or higher into the air. A grassy area surrounds the geyser, with benches and chairs scattered around to allow visitors an easy wait for the show. A bamboo garden surrounds the grassy spot (bamboo is one of the few plants that can tolerate the hot mineral water of this area). Also at Old Faithful you'll find an incongruous but cute petting zoo that houses several fainting goats, plus a few sheep and llamas. A coin-operated feeder lets visitors feed and pet the animals—perfect for children who may grow tired of waiting for the geyser to erupt. Note that the water in the pool from which the geyser erupts as well as the geyser itself are very hot. It's not safe to wade in the water or to stand too close when the geyser goes off. Keep an eye on small children.

© ELIZABETH LINHART MONEY

Petrified Forest

PETRIFIED FOREST

The petrified trees of the Petrified Forest (4100 Petrified Forest Rd., 707/942-6667, www. petrifiedforest.org, daily 9 A.M.–7 P.M. summer, daily 9 A.M.–6 P.M. spring and fall, daily 9 A.M.–5 P.M. winter, adults $6, seniors and students $5, children $3) no longer stand—technically this is an archaeological dig that uncovered a forest that existed more than three million years ago. A volcano that no longer exists erupted, blowing over the trees and covering them with ash. During hundreds of thousands of years, the minerals in the ash traded places with the contents of the cells that made up the wood of the trees, petrifying them; now these long-dead trees are made of stone. When you visit the forest, you'll see plenty of upright living trees. Follow your trail map along a 0.5-mile loop to visit the various excavated petrified trees and chunks of trees. You can touch some of the chunks of petrified wood, but most of the large stone trees are protected by fences to preserve their pristine state. You'll get to see one rare petrified pine tree and a number of petrified coast redwoods, almost all of which have been given names. A fun note: All the trees fell in the same direction and still face that way, showing the direction the blast came from when the volcano erupted. Inside the visitors center and gift shop, you'll find lots of rocks and minerals, books on geology, and a few rare shards of the petrified trees from this forest.

SHARPSTEEN MUSEUM OF CALISTOGA HISTORY

The Sharpsteen Museum of Calistoga History (1311 Washington St., 707/942-5911, www. sharpsteen-museum.org, daily 11 A.M.–4 P.M., $3 donation) takes its name from its founder, Ben Sharpsteen, an Academy Award–winning animator for Disney who had a passion for dioramas. It was through his desire and funding that the immense, exquisitely detailed dioramas depicting the 1860s Calistoga hot springs resort and life in 19th-century Calistoga were built. The other major player in the museum, Sam Brannan, was the first pioneer in Calistoga to build a hot-springs resort using the geothermal springs in the area. At the museum, you'll learn of Brannan's success and subsequent ruin in the resort business as well as his unsuccessful attempt to convert the Napa Valley to Mormonism. Other museum exhibits highlight daily life in 19th-century Napa, complete with artifacts and a nod to the Wappo people, the Native American first residents of this area.

PIONEER CEMETERY

If you're looking for your Napa ancestors or just enjoy prowling through historic graveyards, stop at the Napa Valley Pioneer Cemetery (Bothe–Napa Valley State Park, 3801 St. Helena Hwy. N., www.parks.ca.gov, $8), where you'll find the graves of many of Napa's earliest nonnative settlers and some of the more prominent early pioneer families. The cemetery seems to undergo regular maintenance, since paths between plots are kept clear and walkable. But many of the graves are overgrown with vines—some even have full-size oak trees growing through them. The whole area is covered by a dense canopy of forest foliage, making it a pleasantly cool place to visit on hot summer days. You can explore up the hillside, where the paths get more overgrown and some of the tombstones are old wooden planks, their lettering worn away. If you're interested in genealogy, start at the front entrance of the cemetery, where a map and an alphabetical survey of the cemetery are posted. One warning about visiting this cemetery: No, not ghosts, but a lack of parking. There's enough room at the front for one small car; otherwise, you have to park elsewhere and walk carefully along and across Highway 29 to the gate.

Spas

For an old-school Calistoga spa experience, head down the main drag to **Dr. Wilkinson's Hot Springs Resort** (1507 Lincoln Ave., 707/942-4102, www.drwilkinson.com, daily 8:30 A.M.–5:30 P.M., $69–167). Tucked into a charmingly run-down 1950s motel building, this spa was opened by "Doc" Wilkinson in 1952. Doc's proprietary blend of Calistoga mineral water and volcanic ash, Canadian peat, and lavender is still the gold standard for the Calistoga mud bath today. "The Works" includes the mud bath, complete with a soothing mud mask for your face, a mineral bath, and a finishing blanket wrap. And, of course, you can also get or add a facial and a massage to your treatment. The men's and women's spa areas are separate. If you're a guest of the hotel, be sure to take a swim or a soak in one of the three mineral-water pools: There are two outdoor pools and one huge spa inside.

At the **Calistoga Hot Springs Spa** (1006

There are plenty of spas in Calistoga.

Washington St., 707/942-6269, www.calistogaspa.com, 8:30 A.M.–4:30 P.M. Tues.–Thurs., 8:30 A.M.–9 P.M. Fri.–Mon.), indulge in a mud bath, a mineral bath, or other typical spa treatments. Also available to the public and guaranteed with a spa reservation is access to Calistoga Hot Springs's four outdoor mineral pools. The lap pool is the coolest at 80°F and is set up for serious swimmers. The 90°F wading pool with fountains offers fun and health benefits for the whole family. Another large soaking pool is set to 100°F and meant primarily for adults. Finally, the enormous octagonal 104°F jetted spa is under a gazebo—the perfect location to relax and enjoy the serenity of spa country.

Two other lovely Calistoga spas, both of which offer full mud and mineral baths as well as spa services, are **Golden Haven** (1713 Lake St., 707/942-8000, www.goldenhaven. com, daily 8 A.M.–11 P.M.) and **Indian Springs** (1712 Lincoln Ave., 707/942-4913, www.indianspringscalistoga.com, daily 9 A.M.–8 P.M.). The **Lincoln Avenue Spa** (1339 Lincoln Ave., 707/942-2950, www.lincolnavenuespa.com, 10 A.M.–6 P.M. Sun.–Thurs., 10 A.M.–7 P.M. Fri.–Sat.) does not have mud bath facilities but offers a wider array of spa and esthetic treatments.

Entertainment and Events

The **Napa County Fair** (1435 North Oak St., 707/942-5111, www.napacountyfair.org, adults $10, ages 7–12 $5, under age 7 free) is held every July 4th weekend at the Napa County Fairgrounds and is open to all. The annual fair features live music, a parade, carnival rides for the kids, and plenty of food and wine for everyone.

Sports and Recreation

Not every bit of open space in the Napa Valley is dedicated to grapes. There are several great state parks where you can indulge in the beauty of the valley and not just what it produces. **Bothe-Napa State Park** (3801 St. Helena Hwy., 707/942-4575, www.parks.ca.gov, daily 8 A.M.–sunset) is south of Calistoga on the west side of Highway 29. The park's 2,000-foot elevation provides fantastic views of the valley below and the craggy Mayacamas Mountains beyond, and the nearly 2,000 acres include oak woodlands, coastal redwoods, and occasional open grassland. There are a number of great hikes in the park. **Coyote Peak Trail** climbs to 1,170 feet and forms a 6.5-mile loop with **Upper Ritchey Canyon Trail,** providing great views and a backcountry feel.

Robert Louis Stevenson State Park (Hwy. 29, north of Calistoga, 707/942-4575, www. parks.ca.gov, daily sunrise–sunset) is named for the author who spent his honeymoon in a tiny cabin here. The park offers fewer amenities than nearby Bothe–Napa State Park, but it does have a trail to the top of Mount St. Helena. The 11.2-mile round-trip hike is strenuous, especially when the trail rises above the lush canopy of bay, Douglas fir, and madrone trees to exposed chaparral. All that huffing and puffing is rewarded at the 4,300-foot summit, where great views of the valley unfold. If it's a clear day, you may even see the San Francisco skyline or Mount Shasta, 192 miles north. The park also has picnic tables for those simply looking for a lovely outdoor place to lunch.

As elsewhere in the valley, biking in Calistoga is a fun and scenic alternative to sitting in congested traffic; it's a great way to get around any time of year. **Calistoga Bikeshop** (1318 Lincoln Ave., 707/942-9687, http://calistogabikeshop.com, $15–95 per day) offers guided tours, self-guided tours, and bike rentals. With cruisers and touring bikes, mountain and road bikes, tandems and trailers, and even electric bikes, this bike shop has everything you need to suit your travel plans. Ask at the shop for directions, maps, and suggestions—from a couple of hours in the vineyards to the most challenging mountain-bike tracks in the area.

Feel like a few rounds of golf? The **Mount St. Helena Golf Course** (2025 Grant St.,

707/942-9966, www.napacountyfairgrounds. com, daily 7 A.M.–sunset, $12–26) is a charming and inexpensive par-34 nine-hole course; it's the perfect spot for younger or less experienced golfers. The course is flat and straight, with easier lines than many other courses. On the other hand, all those trees along the fairways and the small greens make it interesting for intermediate players.

If you care to take in Calistoga's dramatic scenery from the air, **Calistoga Balloons** (888/995-7700, www.calistogaballoons.com) is the only company offering regular flights in the north end of Napa Valley. In addition to the vineyards, wineries, spas, and the charming town of Calistoga, you'll also see Mount St. Helena and the lush forested hills surrounding this lovely area.

Accommodations

A plethora of places to stay cluster at the north end of Napa Valley, where you'll find most of the hotel-and-spa combos plus plenty of mineral-water pools and hot tubs for your pleasure. Calistoga also has some of the best lodging rates around.

UNDER $100

The **Calistoga Inn** (1250 Lincoln Ave., 707/942-4101, www.calistogainn.com, $80–120) has been in continuous operation since 1882, giving guests an old-school hotel experience complete with shared baths and showers, but with sinks in each guest room. The inn provides some of the best bargain accommodations in Napa Valley. Each of the 18 guest rooms is a small cozy haven with a queen bed, simple but charming furnishings, and a view of the town. Amenities include a continental breakfast each morning and an English pub downstairs that serves lunch and dinner. Be sure to make reservations in advance—at these rates, rooms go quickly, especially in summer and fall. Be aware that the pub downstairs has live music four nights a week, so the party can get loud on weekends.

Mountain Home Ranch (3400 Mountain Home Ranch Rd., 707/942-6616, www.mountainhomeranch.com, $70–145) almost feels like summer camp. Set deep in the thickly forested mountains above Calistoga, it has an unpolished charm difficult to find elsewhere. Guests can choose a guest room with a full bath, a rustic cabin, or a cottage with a full bath, a fireplace, and a kitchen. There are two pools, a lake, volleyball and tennis courts, table-tennis tables, a basketball hoop, and a number of hiking trails on the property. There is also a menagerie of barnyard animals to keep any animal-loving kid happy. The main house serves a dinner of eggplant parmesan (adults $22, children $16), a lunch of grilled sandwiches (adults $17, children $12), and a complimentary breakfast of eggs, waffles, and fresh fruit. Needless to say, staying here is a relaxed, funky, and old-fashioned type of family vacation.

$100-150

With these bargain rates, don't expect modern luxury at the **Golden Haven Hot Springs** (1713 Lake St., 707/942-8000, www.goldenhaven. com, $115–149). Still, the rooms are spacious and clean, and all come with complimentary use of the hotel's sundeck, hot tubs, and a swimming pool fed by Calistoga hot springs water. Golden Haven also has mud baths, massage services, facials, and body wraps for very reasonable prices. Keep your eyes peeled for specials featured on its website.

$150-250

Dr. Wilkinson's Hot Springs Resort (1507 Lincoln Ave., 707/942-4102, www.drwilkinson.com, $149–300) is an affordable, unpretentious place to stay. There are multiple lodgings to choose from at the funky 1950s-era resort. Motel rooms are decorated in brown, orange, and beige; bungalows include kitchens; and guest rooms in the restored Victorian do not lack for ruffles and floral patterns. In addition to plush bathrobes, all guest rooms have coffee-makers, cable TV, and hypoallergenic bedding. Guests are welcome to use the pools and patio area. Dr. Wilkinson's even has bathing suits on loan if you forgot yours.

Equally old-school are the **Hideaway Cottages** (1412 Fair Way, 707/942-4108, www.hideawaycottages.com, $164–305), a collection of 1940s-era bungalows primly decorated in cream with the occasional plaid bedspread. The cottages retain their original details, such as scalloped-edged kitchen cupboards, tile countertops, and charming built-in glass cabinets. Many of the cottages include sitting rooms, full kitchens, and outdoor seating; all are painted crisp white with country-blue trim. The cottages face communal leafy grounds where lawns offer plenty of spots to lounge around the pool and hot tub. In the interest of quiet, no pets or children under age 18 are allowed.

If you're looking for a more traditional bed-and-breakfast experience, you can't miss **The Pink Mansion** (1415 Foothill Blvd., 800/238-7465, www.pinkmansion.com, $225–345), literally: The 1875 mansion is painted unmistakably bright pink from stem to stern, making it a local landmark. Each lush guest room features a unique theme suitable to romance and wine. The more economical guest rooms have queen beds and pretty antique furnishings; the larger suites are spacious enough to dwarf their king beds, and you'll also find fireplaces, whirlpool tubs, and top-tier amenities. You can enjoy the heated indoor pool and spa, a full breakfast each morning, and use of the various TVs and DVD players, plus a movie library, secreted around the house.

The **Roman Spa Hot Springs Resort** (1300 Washington St., 707/942-4441, www.romanspahotsprings.com, $150–310) in the heart of downtown Calistoga has it all: three mineral-water pools, each set at a different temperature (no children under age 4 are allowed in any pool, and the 105°F spa is adults-only),

plus saunas to inspire guests to relax and refresh themselves with daily soaks and swims. Guest rooms run the gamut from inexpensive motel-style rooms with floral comforters, whirlpool rooms that include a private two-person mineral bath, to kitchen suites (pots, pans, and dishes provided) that beckon families or groups who plan to stay awhile. The Roman Spa connects to the Calistoga Oasis, which offers an array of spa treatments, including the famous mud baths.

OVER $250

Mount View Hotel and Spa (1457 Lincoln Ave., 800/816-6877, www.mountviewhotel.com, $279) is perfectly located on Calistoga's main drag. Guest rooms, suites, and cottages are decorated with tasteful 19th-century antiques and soothing colors inspired by the vines and vintages of the local area. Guest rooms have either two twins, a queen, or a king bed, all feather beds with down comforters. An on-site spa offers facials, body wraps, steam showers, and scrubs. Enjoy the outdoor pool at your leisure.

Food

Small, homey Calistoga offers a pleasing combination of high-end California cuisine and simple delicious fare. If you need a break from rich, expensive food, a great place to stop for a meal is at the corner of Lincoln Street and Highway 29. **◖ Buster's Barbecue and Bakery** (1207 Foothill Blvd., 707/942-5605, http://busters-southernbbq.com, $10) brings unpretentious barbecue to Wine Country. You may find lines of mostly locals looking for a good, quick meal at this walk-up eatery at both lunch and dinner. The simple fare includes huge hot dogs, homemade barbecued tri-tip sandwiches, barbecue pork, and chicken. You'll also have your pick of traditional sides (baked beans, slaw, potato salad, corn bread) and Southern-style baked goods. The sweet-potato pie is a reputable local favorite.

Pacifico Mexican Restaurant (1237

Lincoln Ave., 707/942-4400, 11 A.M.–9 P.M. Mon.–Thurs., 11 A.M.–10 P.M. Fri., 10 A.M.–10 P.M. Sat., 10 A.M.–9 P.M. Sun., $15) serves great south-of-the-border fare in a relaxed easy-going atmosphere. The restaurant feels cool, dark, and cavernous; be sure to order a margarita at the full bar. Or, if the weather is nice, take advantage of the outdoor seating along Cedar Street. Staff are very friendly and attentive, and the fajitas are especially good, as is the chile relleno.

Brannan's Grill (1374 Lincoln Ave., 707/942-2233, www.brannanscalistoga.com, 11:30 A.M.–9:30 P.M. Sun.–Thurs., 11:30 A.M.–10:30 P.M. Sat.–Sun., $20–35) is the only restaurant in Calistoga with a polished Wine Country vibe. The dining room, decorated in rich browns and whites, complements the warm wood bar and seating area. Large picture windows open onto the street when weather permits, adding to the restaurant's indoor-outdoor feel. The classic California cuisine is seasonal and sourced from local producers, with an emphasis on high-end fare. Start with a selection of Hog Island Oysters before moving on to a salads or entrées, or take it easy with a burger and a side of mac and cheese ($15). Desserts are particularly good, especially the crème brûlée.

Information and Services

For discounted wine-tasting vouchers, maps, or tips on the best mud bath, swing by the **Calistoga Visitors Center** (1133 Washington St., 707/942-6333, www.calistogavisitors.org, 9 A.M.–5 P.M. daily), located in the heart of downtown Calistoga. You can even grab the *Weekly Calistogan* for a dose of local news and events.

The **post office** (1013 Washington St.) is located one block south of Lincoln Street. A block away, the **Vermeil House Clinic** (913 Washington St., 707/942-6233, 9 A.M.–5 P.M. Mon.–Fri.) is affiliated with the St. Helena Hospital and treats nonemergency health concerns.

Getting There and Around

Calistoga is eight miles north of St. Helena on Highway 29. In Calistoga, Highway 29 turns east, becoming Lincoln Avenue. To reach the northern end of the Silverado Trail, follow Lincoln Avenue east through town and turn right to intersect it.

Highway 128 also runs through Calistoga, connecting to U.S. 101 north near Healdsburg. To reach Calistoga from U.S. 101 in Santa Rosa, take the exit for Highway 12 east. Turn left on Farmers Lane, and then turn right on Sonoma Highway (Highway 12). Continue driving east on Highway 12 for 2.4 miles to Calistoga Road. Turn left on Calistoga Road and drive 7.1 miles. Calistoga Road intersects Porter Creek Road, becoming Petrified Forest Road for 4.4 miles. Petrified Forest Road intersects with Foothill Boulevard (Hwy. 128) in Calistoga. Turn right and follow Highway 128 south for one mile to Lincoln Avenue, Calistoga's main drag.

Sonoma Valley

The Sonoma and Carneros wine regions are in the southeast part of Sonoma Valley. The scenery features oak forests and vineyard-covered open spaces. The terminus of El Camino Real is in the small city of Sonoma, which includes the famed Sonoma Mission Inn, historical sights, and a charming town square with plenty of shopping and great places to grab a bite. Wineries cluster in this region, though not as many as in the Russian River Valley; the tasting rooms still have plenty of traffic, but the crowds can be less vicious than in the ultra-popular Napa and Dry Creek Valleys.

SONOMA AND CARNEROS
Sonoma Wineries
CHARLES CREEK VINEYARD
Conveniently located on the square in downtown Sonoma, the tasting room at Charles Creek Vineyard (483 1st St. W., Sonoma, 707/935-3848, www.charlescreek.com, daily 11 A.M.–6 P.M.) beckons visitors with a giant cork cow standing proudly in the middle of the floor. This only-in-Wine-Country objet d'art was won at a charity auction and now entices people to wander into the tasting room to take a closer look. Once inside, it's worth your time to taste the wines. This smaller-production winemaker purchases grapes from Napa and Sonoma to create boutique chardonnays, merlots, and cabernet sauvignons. The winemaker takes care to produce vintages that are easy to drink, especially with food.

RAVENSWOOD WINERY
Ravenswood Winery (18701 Gehricke Rd., Sonoma, 888/669-4679, www.ravenswood-wine.com, daily 10 A.M.–4:30 P.M., $10–15) prides itself on making "no wimpy wines." Although the company is now owned by a large conglomerate, Ravenswood wines are still overseen by the original winemaker, Joel Peterson, who began making California zinfandel in 1976. To this day, zinfandel remains the signature varietal under the Ravenswood label. Many of the prized zins come from individual vineyards in Sonoma County, while others are blends of grapes purchased from growers throughout California. When you come to taste, you won't find a stereotypical winery. Unlike many in Napa and Sonoma, Ravenswood sponsors a race car, hosts a bevy of summer barbecues (yep, you can drink zin with ribs), and strives to make tasters of all types feel at home in the winery. Tours and barrel tastings teach newcomers the process of wine-making, while "blend your own" seminars beckon to serious wine connoisseurs. Perhaps best of all, Ravenswood wines are easy on the pocketbook, ranging $13–50 per bottle.

Carneros Wineries
The Carneros region might be described as the "lost" area of Wine Country. Although the wines are spectacular, the wineries are a bit more spread out than in the Napa and Russian River Valleys, and fewer visitors cram into tasting rooms every weekend. Some prestigious California names make their homes here, and some small boutique vintners quietly produce amazing varietals you won't find outside their tasting rooms. If you come to Carneros on a weekday, you might be the only person in some of the tasting rooms, able to chat in depth with the staff about each wine you taste.

DOMAINE CARNEROS
The Sonoma-Carneros region has perfect conditions for champagne-style grapes, and so the glorious Domaine Carneros (1240 Duhig Rd., Napa, 800/716-2788, www.domaine.com, daily 10 A.M.–5:45 P.M., $16–30) makes its

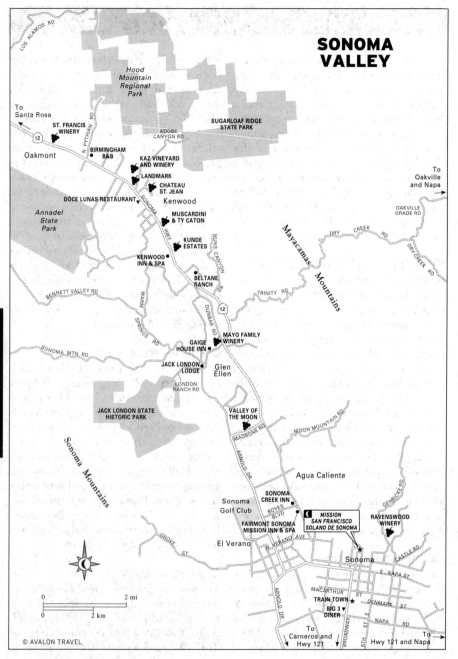

SONOMA VALLEY

To Santa Rosa

ST. FRANCIS WINERY

Oakmont

BIRMINGHAM B&B

KAZ VINEYARD AND WINERY

LANDMARK

CHATEAU ST. JEAN

DÓCE LUNAS RESTAURANT

Kenwood

MUSCARDINI & TY CATON

KUNDE ESTATES

KENWOOD INN & SPA

BELTANE RANCH

Annadel State Park

Hood Mountain Regional Park

SUGARLOAF RIDGE STATE PARK

To Oakville and Napa

OAKVILLE GRADE RD

Mayacamas Mountains

MAYO FAMILY WINERY

GAIGE HOUSE INN

JACK LONDON LODGE

Glen Ellen

JACK LONDON STATE HISTORIC PARK

VALLEY OF THE MOON

Sonoma Mountains

Agua Caliente

MOON MOUNTAIN RD

SONOMA CREEK INN

Sonoma Golf Club

FAIRMONT SONOMA MISSION INN & SPA

MISSION SAN FRANCISCO SOLANO DE SONOMA

RAVENSWOOD WINERY

El Verano

Sonoma

TRAIN TOWN

BIG 3 DINER

To Carneros and Hwy 121

To Hwy 121 and Napa

0   2 mi

0   2 km

© AVALON TRAVEL

estate home here. Visitors rarely fail to be impressed by the grand estate structure, styled in both its architecture and garden setting like the great châteaux of France. Even more impressive are the finely crafted sparkling wines (for legal reasons Domaine Carneros prefers not to use the term *champagne*) and a few still pinot noirs the winery creates using grapes from the Carneros region. The Art of Sparkling Wine Tour ($25) is an excellent opportunity to sample the best wines, tour the grounds, and see how bubbly is made. Domaine Carneros also offers a seated tasting, adding to the overall atmosphere of sophistication and indulgence. If you want to nibble on something while sipping, select from a cheese or charcuterie plate or a selection of caviar and smoked salmon.

GLORIA FERRER

For a taste of some of the upscale sparkling wines Sonoma can produce, take a long drive through immense estate vineyards to the tasting room at Gloria Ferrer (23555 Hwy. 121/ Arnold Dr., Sonoma, 707/996-7256, www. gloriaferrer.com, daily 10 A.M.–5 P.M., $2–10). Ferrer also adheres to the popular format for sparkling wineries—there's no traditional tasting. Instead, visitors order one or more full flutes of sparkling wine, then take a seat at an available table either inside the tasting room or out on the patio overlooking the Sonoma Valley. This style of tasting isn't cheap, but the wines here make the cost worth it for any serious sparkling-wine lover. Just be sure that someone is designated as driver—Ferrer doesn't pour stingy flutes.

SCHUG CARNEROS ESTATE

You might recognize the labels at the Schug Carneros Estate (602 Bonneau Rd., Sonoma, 800/966-9365, www.schugwinery.com, daily 10 A.M.–5 P.M., $5–10). One of the Carneros

© KERI HANSON/SONOMA COUNTY TOURISM BOARD

Gloria Ferrer

region's elders, Walter Schug has made wine that has set the tone for California vintages for many years. The estate itself is worth a visit; the Tudor-esque barn sits in the middle of barns and fields of brilliant-yellow flowering mustard on the valley floor with views of the surrounding mountains all around. Schug's hallmarks are chardonnays and pinot noirs, grapes that grow well in this cooler region, so be sure to try the latest releases of both.

Sights

C MISSION SAN FRANCISCO SOLANO DE SONOMA

Mission San Francisco Solano de Sonoma (114 E. Spain St., Sonoma, 707/938-9560, www.parks.ca.gov, 10 A.M.–5 P.M. Tues.–Sun.), also called simply the Sonoma Mission, is the northernmost of the chain of Spanish missions in California. It is at the corner of the historic plaza in downtown Sonoma—a low,

surprisingly unpretentious block of buildings without much in the way of decoration or crowds. The last mission established, in 1823, and one of the first restored as a historic landmark, in 1926, the Sonoma Mission isn't the prettiest or most elaborate of the 21 missions. But visitors can see museum-style exhibits depicting the life of the later missionaries and Native Americans who lived here, and a unique series of watercolor paintings depicting all of the California missions. Outdoors, guests can rest on benches by the fountain, observe a moment of silence at the Native American mortuary monument, or check out the cactus "wall" that has been growing on the property since the mission era.

It's a little-known fact that California's state flag—the Bear Flag depicting a now-extinct California grizzly bear—first came to be in the tiny rural mission town of Sonoma. To commemorate that historic beginning, the **Bear**

© ELIZABETH LINHART MONEY

Mission San Francisco Solano de Sonoma

WINE COUNTRY

Flag Monument (Sonoma Plaza, E. Spain St. and 1st St. E.) was erected. Visit the monument as you stroll the plaza or explore the various sites of the Sonoma State Historic Park.

CORNERSTONE GARDENS

For a break from all the history of Sonoma's main attractions, take a walk in the modern gardens of Cornerstone Place (23570 Hwy. 121, Sonoma, 707/933-3010, www.cornerstonegardens.com, daily 10 A.M.–5 P.M.). This unique installation combines an art gallery with the work of the foremost landscape and garden designers in the world. Stroll these unusual gardens, which range from traditional plantings to postmodern multimedia installations, and then finish up your excursion with a crawl through the boutiques, upscale food shops, and wine bars that have recently sprung up around the gardens. Daily wine tastings and various snacks and non-alcoholic drinks provide welcome refreshment, especially on hot Sonoma summer afternoons.

DEPOT PARK MUSEUM

If you haven't had enough of history in Sonoma, make a stop by the Depot Park Museum (270 1st St. W., Sonoma, 707/938-1762, www.vom.com/depot, Wed.–Sun. 1–4:30 P.M., free) right down the street from the plaza and around the corner from the mission. The museum hosts a small set of exhibits inside a reproduction of the historic Northwestern Pacific Railroad depot, hence the name. Inside are reconstructions of the active depot in the Rand Room, a showcase of the Bear Flag Rebellion, and the life of the indigenous Miwok people.

TRAIN TOWN

Got a train enthusiast in the family? Take them to Sonoma's own Train Town (20264 Broadway/Hwy. 12, Sonoma, www.traintown.com, daily 10 A.M.–5 P.M. June–Sept., 10 A.M.–5 P.M. Fri.–Sun. Sept.–May, $5.25). Ride the 15-inch scale railroad that winds through the park's 10 cool forested acres, take a spin on the roller coaster or the Ferris wheel, or climb the clock tower for a magnificent view of the park and beyond.

DI ROSA PRESERVE

At the unique di Rosa Preserve (5200 Sonoma Hwy., 707/226-5991, www.dirosapreserve.org, 10 A.M.–4 P.M. Wed.–Sat., $5–15), you'll see the cutting edge of modern California art. With 217 acres, Di Rosa has ample room for three galleries, an outdoor sculpture meadow, and a lake. Take in the festival of color and creativity in the galleries and sculpture garden, or wander the undeveloped portion of the preserve to soak in the colors and shapes of nature.

Spas

The most famous spa in the area is the **Willow Stream Spa** (100 Boyes Blvd., Sonoma, 707/938-9000, www.fairmont.com/sonoma, daily 7:30 A.M.–8 P.M., $89–200). A natural mineral hot spring beneath the Sonoma Mission Inn provides warm water for the indoor and outdoor pools and whirlpools that create the center of the spa's signature Bathing Ritual. Whether you choose a relaxing massage or a challenging yoga class, be sure to arrive at least an hour early to allow time for each step of the ritual, which will relax and focus you for your next treatment or activity. The spa offers an almost bewildering variety of massages, scrubs, wraps, facials, and even more rarified treatments designed to pamper even the most discerning spa-goer. The facilities are surrounded by the inn and a gourmet restaurant, both of which draw visitors from around the world.

At the **Garden Spa at MacArthur Place** (29 E. MacArthur St., Sonoma, 707/933-3193, www.macarthurplace.com/spa.php, 9 A.M.–7 P.M. Mon.–Sat., 9 A.M.–6 P.M. Sun., $118–345), you won't just take in the serene beauty of the inn's lush garden; you will be healed, rejuvenated, and beautified. All of the spa's signature treatments are made from the flowers, herbs, and fruit found in the garden, distilled into such luscious effusions as pomegranate body polish, golden passion-flower body wrap, peppermint foot soak, and the red-wine grape-seed bath. The spa also offers a mud-bath soak, a number of different massages, and facial and waxing treatments. Book treatments at least two weeks in advance as space in this fragrant spa fills up fast.

If you're just looking for a lift for your face, visit **The Pampered Pout** (678 Broadway, Sonoma, 707/938-9396, www.thepampered-pout.com, by appointment Tues.–Fri., $80–120). Choose from among a dozen different 30–90-minute facials to beautify your skin. Esthetician and owner Bridgene Raftery can provide treatments that include a classic European pampering facial, a series of micro-dermabrasion treatments, and makeup lessons for teens. Specialty facials for teens and men along with eyebrow design round out a complete menu of face-perfect services.

Entertainment and Events

For a fun evening of drinking and live entertainment, head to **Murphy's Irish Pub** (464 1st St. E., Sonoma, 707/935-0660, www.sonoma-pub.com, 11 A.M.–11 P.M. Fri.–Sat., 11 A.M.–10 P.M. Sun.–Mon.) on Sonoma Plaza. Grab an imported Irish pint or a glass of local wine, some barbecued oysters or down-home pub fare, and enjoy an evening of live music, literary entertainment, or perhaps a lively trivia game. Unlike many pubs and wine bars in Wine Country, Murphy's welcomes kids in its dining room, so feel free to bring the whole family for a meal and a good time.

Vineyards and olive groves have been associated for thousands of years. Celebrating the symbiosis of these two historic crops is the **Sonoma Valley Olive Festival** (www.sonoma-valley.com/olivefestival, Dec.–Feb.). Sonoma

hosts a variety of annual events that highlight the growth, curing, pressing, and many uses of the noble olive. Check the online calendar for a list of olive-curing classes, olive-themed wine-maker's dinners, and other celebrations. The "hot" olive weekend each year is the festival finale on President's Day weekend (the weekend before the 3rd Monday in Feb.). Expect to make your lodging reservations early and buy tickets to your favorite events in advance—this popular event is rife with classes, dinners, parties, and crowds.

Shopping

There's no more pleasant place to stroll, window shop, or browse for an extravagant trinket than in Sonoma. Around its leafy square are famous structures and state parks, little cafés and eateries, and yes, shops. Lots and lots of shops. Many are on the four main streets bordering the square, but most you will have to hunt for in the nooks and crannies inside the remodeled historic buildings and tiny retail alleyways on each block.

Despite the name, **Large Leather** (481 1st St. W., Sonoma, 707/938-1042, www.large-leather.biz, daily 10 A.M.–6 P.M.) is a pint-size store filled with purses, backpacks, belts, wallets, and bracelets. Anything you can think of that is or can be made out of leather can be found here. All items are handcrafted and designed by the owners, Paul Terwilliger and Jessica Zoutendijk.

A different kind of cooking store, **Bram** (493 1st St. W., 707/935-3717, www.bram-cookware.com, 10 A.M.–6 P.M. Thurs.–Mon., 10 A.M.–5 P.M. Tues.) is devoted entirely to clay-pot cooking. Dark shelves are stocked with a beautiful selection of deep skillets, stew pots, rondeaux, open casseroles, tagines, rectangular bakers, brams, and roasters. Shoppers will be astounded by the range and diversity of the clay pots available. If you are at a loss how to use such a beautiful pot, stacks of cookbooks

utilitarian art in Sonoma Plaza

fill the other side of the shop. The extremely knowledgeable staff are eager to share their experiences and preferences.

For handcrafted artistry with a bit more polish, stroll down to **Sonoma Silver Company** (491 1st St. W., Sonoma, 707/933-0999, www.sonomasilver.com, daily 11 A.M.–6 P.M.), a slender shop awash in silver rings, pendants, bracelets, and earrings. Multiple local jewelers sell and showcase their work here, but many of the shiny trinkets are made in-house by the company's resident jeweler of 20 years.

You can see other local artwork at the **Fairmont Gallery** (447 1st St. W., Sonoma, 707/996-2667, www.fairmontgallery.com, noon–5 P.M. Thurs.–Sun.). Mostly concentrating in oil paintings and other classic brush-on-canvas fine art, the intimate space, set up in an old A-frame house, is a pleasant reprieve from other bustling shops.

Around the corner from the square is **PK Sonoma** (120 W. Napa St., Sonoma, 707/935-6767, www.pksonoma.com, 10 A.M.–6 P.M. daily), where you can buy a spa treatment to take home with you. PK Sonoma's skincare products—including Eye and Lip Silk, made with rose and German chamomile, and Goat's Milk Soap—are made in small batches from locally sourced herbs (lavender is a popular ingredient), giving the store a pleasant farm-to-bath feel. There are even herbal shampoos for your pet.

Sports and Recreation

Not every inch of ground in Sonoma County grows grapes or houses inns and restaurants. One huge plot of invaluable dirt has long been given over to the **Infineon Raceway** (29355 Arnold Dr., Sonoma, 800/870-7223, www.infineonraceway.com), known locally as Sears Point. This massive motor-sports complex hosts almost every sort of vehicular race possible, with several NASCAR events each year, various American Motorcyclist Association motorcycle races, an Indy car race, and, of course, an National Hot Rod Association drag race. Infineon sees more action than many of the country's most popular racetracks, with events scheduled 340 days per year, although many of these are local track days and small-time club races. Ticket prices vary widely, so check the website for the cost of events.

The turnoff to Infineon Raceway is near the intersection of Highways 37 and 121, and wretched traffic jams, truly more stop than go, can last for hours as people exit the racetrack into the unsignaled intersection. Check the race schedule online to avoid this area for at least four hours after the scheduled or estimated end of a big race.

If you happen to be staying at the Sonoma Mission Inn, you can access the **Sonoma Golf Club** (17700 Arnold Dr., Sonoma, 707/939-4100, www.sonomagolfclub.com) for a quieter sporting afternoon. This private par-72 18-hole course offers tee times only to guests of Sonoma Mission Inn or its spa. On the other hand, the public **Los Arroyos Golf Club** (5000 Stage Gulch Rd., Sonoma, 707/938-8835, call for rates) is open to all comers. The par-29 nine-hole course is great for newer players.

There are several fabulous hikes in Sonoma County. One of the best is the easy two-mile **Overlook Trail.** You can reach the trailhead from the center of downtown Sonoma; follow 1st Street West to the Veterans Hall and Cemetery, then look for signs describing the trail route. As you walk along this gentle path, you'll have fabulous views of Sonoma plus the chance to encounter locals out on their favorite jogging route. In wet weather, be sure to wear sturdy hiking boots for navigating the clay mud.

Accommodations

For a charming guest room at reasonable rates within the Sonoma town limits, stay at **Sonoma Creek Inn** (239 Boyes Blvd., 888/712-1289, www.sonomacreekinn.com, $145–199). The whimsical, colorful decor and unique art pieces brighten each guest room and each guest's stay. Amenities include cable TV, free wireless Internet access, a fridge, and private garden patios. Located a few minutes from downtown Sonoma and convenient to the Carneros wineries, the inn is perfect for travelers who want to spend on wine and dining rather than a motel room.

Right on Sonoma Plaza in the heart of Sonoma, **Les Petites Maisons** (1190 E. Napa St., 800/291-8962, www.lespetitesmaisons. com, $230) offers four cute cottages for a homey stay in the Wine Country. Each cottage has its own style, but all have warm colors and comfy furniture to evoke the relaxation needed for a perfect vacation. All the cottages have fully equipped kitchens or kitchenettes that allow you to cook your own fresh food after a visit to the fabulous Sonoma farmers markets. You can eat at the girl and the fig or one of the other wonderful restaurants on the plaza.

In 1850 one of the first Spanish settlers in the Sonoma area built a home for his family on the town square, and for most of the last century, the **Swiss Hotel** (18 W. Spain St., 707/938-2884, www.swisshotelsonoma.com, $110–240) in the structure has offered beds and meals to travelers. With a renovation in the 1990s the guest rooms have plenty of modern amenities, while the exterior and the public spaces retain the historic feel of the original adobe building. You'll find your guest room light, bright, and airy, with fresh paint and pretty floral comforters. Downstairs, enjoy a meal at the restaurant or have a drink at the historic bar. Step outside to take a walk around the historic plaza.

For the price and the character, the **Sonoma Hotel** (110 W. Spain St., Sonoma, 800/468-6016, www.sonomahotel.com, $110–198) can't be beat. Built in 1880, the hotel is one of Sonoma's landmark buildings. The interior is decorated in the fashion of the era, with high wood wainscoting, cream-colored walls, polished antiques, and elegant light fixtures. The guest rooms, all with private baths (a rarity in historical digs), are similarly outfitted in trim Victorian fixtures, and many have slopped ceilings, creating a cozy intimate atmosphere.

Not nearly as historic but conveniently located just a few blocks from the square is **El Pueblo Inn** (896 W. Napa St., 707/996-3651, www.elpuebloinn.com, $179–244). In true Spanish style, all guest rooms face a lush central courtyard with a pool and a hot tub. Some of the guest rooms boast walls of adobe bricks or lounge areas with fireplaces, but many are standard hotel accommodations—clean and modestly decorated. For the price and location, not to mention views of the garden, it's a good deal. The inn also offers a fitness room, complimentary breakfast, and an in-room safe. Another standout is the down comforters.

Neither historic nor centrally located, the **Fairmont Sonoma Mission Inn & Spa** (100 Boyes Blvd., 707/938-9000, www.fairmont. com/sonoma, $300–400) has another appeal: luxury. Of course, there is the spa, an 18-hole golf course, and the Michelin-starred restaurant, but the guest rooms themselves are enough. Your guest room is the kind of place you'll want to return to after a long day sipping wine or soaking in a mud bath, decorated in smooth Provençal yellows with the occasional brown or red thrown in and featuring four-poster beds with deep mattresses covered in down comforters. Some guest rooms have fireplaces, while others feature marble bathtubs; many overlook gardens. If you can tear yourself away, you may be able to enjoy the other amenities of the hotel or Sonoma.

Food

A favorite with the local-sustainable-organic food crowd, **◖the girl and the fig** (110 W. Spain St., Sonoma, 707/938-3634, www.thegirlandthefig. com, 11:30 A.M.–11 P.M. Fri.–Sat., 11:30 A.M.–10 P.M. Sun.–Mon., $20) is right on Sonoma Plaza. The menu changes often to take advantage of the best local seasonal ingredients; for a special treat, order one of the amazing cheese plates or the three-course Bistro Plat du Jour ($34). If you love the sauces and jams, look for the girl and the fig products on-site and at wineries and high-end food shops throughout Wine Country.

Another California cuisine hot spot with a beautiful outdoor patio and a seasonal local-focused menu is the **Harvest Moon Café** (487 1st St. W., Sonoma, 707/933-8160, www. harvestmoonsonoma.com, 5:30–9 P.M. Mon. and Wed.–Thurs., 5:30–9:30 P.M. Fri.–Sat., 10 A.M.–2 P.M. and 5:30–9 P.M. Sun., $17–25). The menu of this charmingly casual restaurant changes daily to take advantage of the best ingredients available.

It's rare when locals and travelers agree on the best restaurant in any given town. The fact that it's a traditional Portuguese eatery in a sea of California cuisine makes it all the more special. **◖LaSalette** (452 1st St. E., Sonoma, 707/938-1927, www.lasalette-restaurant.com, 11:30 A.M.–2:30 P.M. and 5–9 P.M. Mon.–Thurs., 11:30 A.M.–9 P.M. Sat.–Sun., $17–24) has a simple charming atmosphere with a wood-fired oven facing a curving bar that serves drinks and friendly chatter to regulars, along with a full dinner menu. A large outdoor patio is the most popular seating area in summer, although the meandering tile-floored dining room offers plenty of appeal plus a bonus view of the open kitchen. The undisputed star of LaSalette is the food. The unswervingly Portuguese menu features fresh fish and hearty meat dishes plus some good meatless options. Simple yet delectable preparations let the flavors of the principal ingredients shine through. Just ask if you want to make a substitution or leave something out—they're happy to accommodate special requests.

Need a hearty breakfast or down-home lunch before you get going on a full day of wine tasting? Stop in at the **Big 3 Diner** (18140

WINE COUNTRY

Hwy. 12, Sonoma, 707/939-2410, www.fairmont.com/sonoma, daily 7 A.M.–9 P.M., $8–20). The restaurant is part of the Fairmont Sonoma Mission Inn property, which explains both the high prices and the upscale cuisine. But it's good stuff—the kitchen uses high-quality, often organic and local ingredients to create its fancy benedicts and sandwiches. Even locals approve, coming in to be greeted by name by the friendly and efficient staff. If you're staying at the Sonoma Mission Inn, order room service from Big 3 or walk over to the large dining room, outfitted with wooden chairs and tables and a pleasant casual atmosphere.

If you just need a cup of coffee and maybe a quick pastry, stop in at the **Barking Dog Coffee Roasters** (201 W. Napa St., Sonoma, 707/996-7446, www.barkingdogcoffee.com, 6 A.M.–7 P.M. Mon.–Fri., 7 A.M.–7 P.M. Sat.–Sun.). Barking Dog is where locals go to get their morning mochas. Sip a latte or indulge in a scoop of Caffe Classico gelato or a smoothie, take a seat on a comfy old couch, and maybe even enjoy some live music.

For travelers preparing most of their own meals, or if you're looking for gluten-free grains to take home, the **Fruit Basket** (24101 Arnold Dr., Sonoma, 707/938-4332, daily 7 A.M.–7:15 P.M.) open-air market has a great selection. This isn't a local farm stand—much of the produce is emphatically not local, especially in the winter. But the array of dried beans and grains would put a San Francisco health-food store to shame, making it easy for people with celiac disease and those with food allergies to find great make-it-yourself food options. Despite its suggestive name, the Fruit Basket actually serves as a fully stocked market, selling imported Italian and Mexican foods, dairy products, somewhat superfluous wines, and, of course, fresh fruits and vegetables. The only staple they don't stock is fresh meat. Prices are reasonable, and the market is easy to see and access at the south end of the Sonoma-Carneros wine region.

Information and Services

Before you begin your Sonoma and Carneros wine-tasting adventure, stop in at the **Sonoma Valley Visitors Center** (453 1st St. E., Sonoma, 866/996-1090, www.sonomavalley.com, 9 A.M.–5 P.M. Mon.–Sat., 10 A.M.–5 P.M. Sun.). Ask the volunteers for advice on which wineries to visit, and be sure to pick up some complimentary tasting passes. One of the local papers in the Sonoma Valley is the *Sonoma Index-Tribune* (www.sonomanews.com). Turn to the Do and Shop sections for visitor information.

For medical attention in Sonoma, head for the **Sonoma Valley Hospital** (347 Andrieux St., Sonoma, 707/935-5000, www.svh.com), which has a full-service emergency room.

Getting There and Around

The town of Sonoma is over the mountains west of the Napa Valley. The main route through the valley is Highway 12, also called the Sonoma Highway. To reach Sonoma from Napa, drive south on Highway 29 and turn west onto Highway 12/121. Turn north on Highway 12 to reach downtown Sonoma.

From the Bay Area, take U.S. 101 north to Highway 37 east. Highway 37 branches sharply north to become Highway 121, then Highway 116 as it winds into the city of Sonoma. Driving south on U.S. 101, you can turn onto Highway 12 south in Santa Rosa and take a scenic journey down into the Sonoma-Carneros wine region.

Parking in downtown Sonoma is easy in the off-season and tougher in the high season (May–Oct.). Expect to hunt for a spot during local events and be prepared to walk several blocks. Most wineries provide ample free parking on their grounds.

For your public transit needs, use the buses run by **Sonoma County Transit** (SCT, 707/576-7433, www.sctransit.com, $1.25–3.45). Several routes serve the Sonoma Valley daily. You can use SCT to get from Sonoma Valley to Santa Rosa, Guerneville, and other parts of the Russian River Valley as well.

It's fitting that in Wine Country, a place at the cutting edge of sustainable agriculture in a state known for its eco-mindedness, you can take a vineyard tour on a Segway. **Sonoma Segway** (524 Broadway, Sonoma, 707/938-2080, www.sonomasegway.com, tour $99–129, rental $40 per hour) offers a 3.5-hour tour that includes a visit to a local winery, a stop at a local food-based business, and a full visit to historic Sonoma. The tour starts with a lesson on the Segway, and when you finish you'll get a complimentary bottle of wine if you're of age. If you'd prefer to explore the Sonoma streets and paths on your own, rent a Segway—from two hours and up.

GLEN ELLEN

North of the town of Sonoma, the valley becomes more and more rural. The next hamlet on Highway 12 is Glen Ellen (population 784), surrounded by a couple of regional parks and Jack London State Historic Park, named for one of the town's famous residents (the other big name is Hunter S. Thompson). Downtown Glen Ellen has not caught the Wine County bug of boutique shops, Michelin-starred restaurants, and over-the-top spas; instead, it still feels like a rural farm town with a few historic structures thrown in for character.

Wineries

MAYO FAMILY WINERY

The Mayo Family Winery (13101 Arnold Dr., at Hwy. 12, 707/938-9401, www.mayofamilywinery.com, daily 10:30 A.M.–6:30 P.M.) breaks from the chardonnay-cab-merlot juggernaut of Sonoma and produces an array of interesting Italian-style varietals. Here you might taste smoky rich carignan or barbera, enjoy a fruity white viognier, or savor the chianti-based sangiovese. Mayo Family boasts a big presence in the region, with an on-site tasting room, a small downtown-Sonoma storefront tasting room (1395 Broadway, Sonoma, 4–6 P.M. Tues.–Wed., 11 A.M.–6 P.M. Thurs.–Mon.),

and up north in Kenwood the prized reserve tasting room (9200 Sonoma Hwy., Kenwood, 10:30 A.M.–6:30 P.M. Thurs.–Mon., reservations recommended, fee). At the reserve tasting room, your experience includes seven pours of Mayo's best wines, each paired with a small bite of gourmet California cuisine created by chefs on-site. Bon appétit!

VALLEY OF THE MOON

At Valley of the Moon (777 Madrone Rd., 707/939-4510, www.valleyofthemoonwinery.com, daily 10 A.M.–4:30 P.M., $5–10), 150 years of history mixes with the highest wine-making technology California has to offer. Since the Civil War era, this Sonoma institution has passed through many hands and produced hundreds of wines. The circa-1860s stone buildings house late-model stainless-steel fermentation tanks as well as classic oak barrels. In the tasting room is a small list of boutique wines, from an unusual sangiovese rosé to a classic California cabernet. Valley of the Moon takes pride in its awards, and you'll find that almost every wine you taste has its own list of medals. Check the website for a list of upcoming wine events that show off this great Sonoma landmark at its best.

Jack London State Historic Park

Literary travelers come to Sonoma not just for the fine food and abundant wine but for the chance to visit Jack London State Historic Park (2400 London Ranch Rd., 707/938-5216, www.parks.ca.gov, 10 A.M.–5 P.M. Fri.–Mon., $8). Famed author Jack London did in fact live and write in rural Sonoma County at the beginning of the 20th century. Docents offer tours of the park, which include talks on London's life and history. Explore the surviving buildings on London's prized Beauty Ranch or hike up Sonoma Mountain and check out the artificial lake and bathhouse. The pretty stone House of Happy Walls, a creation of London's

WINE COUNTRY

© SABRINA YOUNG

Author Jack London lived in Glen Ellen from 1905 until his death in 1916.

wife, houses a small museum (10 A.M.–4 P.M. Sat.–Sun.). There's no camping at Jack London State Historic Park, but you can bring a picnic to enjoy on the attractive grounds.

With its vineyards, open spaces, and state parks, the Sonoma Valley begs to be explored on horseback in homage to its pioneering history. The **Triple Creek Horse Outfit** (707/887-8700, www.triplecreekhorseoutfit.com, $60–100) offers guided rides at Jack London State Historic Park that last from one hour up to half a day, taking you beyond what you can see from the windows of your car. A ride through the park takes you through the writer's life in Sonoma County and the literary history of the region. To turn it into an epicurean outing, take the popular Picnic Lunch Tour or the Mountain-top Tasting and Ride combo that features a visit to Kunde Winery.

Accommodations

With its wraparound porches and lush gardens, the **Beltane Ranch** (11775 Hwy. 12, 707/996-6501, www.beltaneranch.com, $150–240) looks like it belongs near Savannah, Georgia, rather than Sonoma. But this Valley of the Moon charmer sits in the middle of Wine Country, with five guest rooms and a detached cottage. After a good night's sleep in the pristine country-style guest rooms, guests enjoy a sumptuous breakfast in the dining room or on the porch overlooking the gardens and vineyards beyond.

For a bit of Asian-infused relaxation, stay at one of the best-reviewed inns in Wine Country: the ◧ **Gaige House Inn** (13540 Arnold Dr., 800/935-0237, www.gaige.com, $330), which offers comfort and luxury built into the design of the guest rooms and common spaces. Special attention is paid to every detail, and each of the 23 guest rooms and suites resemble a spread in an interior-design magazine; suites have baths the size of bedrooms and their own tiny garden spaces. Be aware that breakfast and spa treatments cost extra.

WINE COUNTRY

Attached to the redbrick Jack London Saloon and Wolf House Restaurant, the **Jack London Lodge** (13740 Arnold Dr., 707/938-8510, www.jacklondonlodge.com, $95–185) anchors this part of downtown Glen Ellen. The 22-room lodge is modern, with a broad patio, a kidney-shaped pool, and groomed lawns. The inn's interior offers a more Victorian feel with dark wood furniture, rich floral linens, and low lighting, but the history of the building shines through. Vines draping the balcony are a nice touch, as is the hot tub and the creek running through the back of the property.

Food

At the **Glen Ellen Inn Restaurant** (13670 Arnold Dr., 707/996-6409, www.glenelleninn.com, 11:30 A.M.–9 P.M. Thurs.–Tues., 5–9 P.M. Wed., $12–20), French bistro cuisine meets California gastropub. You'll find this self-described oyster grill and martini bar's dining room inside a cute low building. In addition to the seafood-heavy gourmet menu, the Glen Ellen Inn boasts a full bar and a wine list worthy of its location.

the fig café (13690 Arnold Dr., 707/938-2130, www.thegirlandthefig.com, daily 5:30 P.M.–close, brunch 10 A.M.–3 P.M. Sat.–Sun., $13–20) serves the same excellent food as its namesake restaurant in Sonoma but slightly scaled down. The menu leans toward comfort food, with grilled sandwiches, thin-crust pizzas, and a laid-back wine bar. The warm interior and weekend brunch makes it a sure bet.

Information and Services

The small town of Glen Ellen does not have a visitors center, so stock up on maps and tips before you leave Sonoma; the **Sonoma Valley Visitors Center** (453 1st St. E., Sonoma, 866/996-1090, www.sonomavalley.com, 9 A.M.–5 P.M. Mon.–Sat., 10 A.M.–5 P.M. Sun.) has information for Glen Ellen. Some of the local inns and hotels can also provide some information.

Likewise, don't expect to find much in the way of wireless Internet access or reliable cell-phone reception. If you need to communicate the old-fashioned way, there is a **post office** (13720 Arnold Dr.) next to Jack London Lodge.

Getting There and Around

Glen Ellen is located just off Highway 12, seven miles north of Sonoma. Arnold Drive is the main street through town, and it runs all the way south to Sonoma. To reach Glen Ellen from Santa Rosa, take Highway 12 east through Kenwood for 15.7 miles.

It is also possible to jump over to Glen Ellen from Highway 29 in Oakville. In Oakville, turn west onto Oakville Grade. After 3.2 miles, Oakville Grade becomes Dry Creek Road; the name changes again to Trinity Road in 2.8 miles. Keep to the right on Trinity Road, and in three miles you'll reach Sonoma Highway (Hwy. 12), where you turn left toward Glen Ellen.

KENWOOD

Like Glen Ellen, Kenwood is a small town, but unlike Glen Ellen it has a bit more of the Wine Country polish. The wineries can be a little more expensive, and Kenwood is also home to one of the most luxurious inns and spas in the valley. There are plenty of hiking opportunities, as Kenwood is near Sugarloaf Ridge State Park, with 25 miles of trails to engage hikers of any fitness level.

Wineries

CHATEAU ST. JEAN

True to its name, Chateau St. Jean (8555 Hwy. 12, 707/833-4134, www.chateaustjean.com, daily 10 A.M.–5 P.M., tasting $15–25) is built in the style of a miniature French château, with flat graveled walks in straight lines through formally styled gardens. Stroll under the arbors to reach both tasting rooms—the regular one (on the right) and the one for reserve wines (on the left). In the regular, cheaper tasting room you'll find the story of the first winemaker to come to Sonoma along with a selection of traditional California wines—chardonnay, cabernet, pinot noir, and the like. Although Chateau St. Jean wines are sold in stores and at restaurants, the single-vineyard varietals that tasters enjoy at the estate can't be purchased anywhere but here. Visitors can tour the winery's grounds but not the winery production facilities.

KAZ VINEYARD AND WINERY

At the other end of the spectrum from the big businesses of Wine Country that produce many thousands of barrels, there's Kaz (233 Adobe Canyon Rd., 877/833-2536, www.kazwinery.com, by appointment Tues.–Thurs., 11 A.M.–5 P.M. Fri.–Mon.), a tiny winery that is a goofy family affair in its vineyards, winery, and tasting room. You'll find a broad array of small-production wines—sometimes only one barrel of a particular wine gets made. Reds are the Kaz specialty, including a number of blends and unusual varietals you won't see at other Sonoma wineries, including mourvèdre, grenache, and a barbera-tannat blend. Kaz also makes several unique ports—even whites and rosés. Inside the simple brown barn that has been made over into a tasting room, you'll get 6–9 tastes ($5), and if you're lucky, Kaz himself will be pouring and commenting on his wines.

KUNDE ESTATES

One of the large wineries on Sonoma's major tasting road, Kunde Estates (9825 Hwy. 12, 707/833-5501, www.kunde.com, call for reservations, tour and tasting $30–40) has a typically enormous and elegant tasting room, hilly estate vineyards, and tasty but not spectacular wines. What Kunde offers that others don't is a sense of humor and fun—and a tasting room 1,400 feet above the valley floor. Be sure to watch for Blossom, the gaily painted fiberglass cow that the staff moves to different places around the property. But don't climb or

sit on her; she has been broken several times by careless visitors. Tours (read: hikes) are led up the mountain, through the caves, and around vineyards, which use for sustainable practices. Tours require a reservation and do not come cheap. Still, once you reach the tasting bar, you'll get not only a few sips of Kunde's wines but a few stories from the often entertaining characters working the tasting room.

LANDMARK

It seems appropriate that Landmark (101 Adobe Canyon Rd., 707/833-0053, www.landmarkwine.com, daily 10 A.M.–4:30 P.M.) provides wine to the entire country. Owned and operated by the descendents of manufacturer John Deere, Landmark seeks to continue the agricultural traditions of the United States while producing top 21st-century wines. In the tasting room, you'll find premium chardonnays and pinot noirs—wines that grow best in the cooler Sonoma region. Outside the tasting room, you can walk in some of the most spectacular gardens in a region noted for its landscaping. If you're visiting in the summer, take a horse-drawn wagon ride through the vineyards. Or bring a picnic and enjoy a game of bocce ball, a popular local pastime, on the grassy court surrounded by flowers and fountains and grapes. You can also arrange in advance to stay in either the guest suite or the cottage on the estate grounds.

MUSCARDINI AND TY CATON

These two tiny wineries maintain a tasting room in a stylish strip mall in the village of Kenwood. As you drive down the highway it's easy to miss the tiny bar, which would be a pity for any true oenophile. The Muscardini and Ty Caton tasting room (8910 Hwy. 12, 707/938-3224, www.tycaton.com, www.muscardinicellars.com, daily 11 A.M.–6 P.M.) pours some of the best wines in Sonoma County. Ty Caton's $17-per-bottle Pizza Wine puts $50 cabernets from the bigger estates to shame. And their big syrahs, perfect pinots, and astonishing cabernets are also remarkable. Be aware that if you seem interested in the wines you're sipping, the tasting room staff will not only give you a long story about each vintage they pour, they'll start opening and pouring everything they've got in the shop. If you're visiting on an off-season weekday, you may find yourself alone in the shop, discussing the wine regions of California and various varietals for more than an hour. Even in high season (May–Oct.) this small tasting room preserves the kind of wine-tasting experience that wine lovers have been coming to Sonoma for decades to enjoy.

ST. FRANCIS WINERY

It is believed that the Franciscan order of Roman Catholic monks brought wine production to California. In their honor, the St. Francis Winery (100 Pythian Rd., at Hwy. 12, 888/675-9463, www.stfranciswine.com, daily 10 A.M.–5 P.M., $10) sells thick rich wines that appeal to lovers of reds. The estate is built in the light adobe with red roofs style of the California missions, complete with a square bell tower. Inside, visitors drink classic Sonoma chardonnays and an array of yummy reds that show off the lush flavors of Sonoma grapes in both single varietals and blends. For an additional $15, order a plate of charcuterie to accompany your Franciscan wine. If you are eyeing the winery for lunch, call and make a reservation for a full wine-and-food pairing ($38).

Sports and Recreation

Mossy waterfalls, hillside grasslands bordered by oaks, exposed rock outcroppings, and even Sonoma Creek's headwaters can be found at **Sugarloaf Ridge State Park** (2605 Adobe Canyon Rd., 707/833-5712, www.parks.ca.gov, daily sunrise–sunset), just outside Kenwood. Despite its beauty, Sugarloaf is rarely visited, so if you're seeking solitude in nature, this may be your place. There are plenty of trails

to suit your mood and hiking ability; meander down **Creekside Nature Trail** (1 mile, easy) or take **Canyon Trail** (1.6 miles, easy) to the waterfall, which descends 25 feet through mossy boulders beneath a canopy of redwoods. More athletic hikers can take **Vista Trail Loop** (4.1 miles, moderate–difficult) to the Indian Rock outcropping, which has a lovely view of the canyon below. To hike this trail, take Stern Trail to Bald Mountain Trail and turn right. Eventually, take another right on Vista Trail and cross the mountain, taking another right on Grey Pine Trail. Turn right again on Meadow Trail to return to the parking lot.

The crown jewel of the park, however, is Bald Mountain. Although only 2,729 feet high, the mountain sports views of nearly all of Wine Country as well as the Golden Gate and Sierra Nevada on clear days. The hike to the summit is not that challenging: **Bald Mountain Loop** (6.6 miles, moderate–difficult) begins at Stern Trail, and eventually you take a right turn onto Bald Mountain Trail and follow it to the top. To descend, turn right on Grey Pine Trail, and then make another right onto Meadow Trail.

While the lower part of the park has a lush, heavy canopy, the upper trails are quite exposed and can get hot in the summer and early fall. Be sure to bring sunscreen, a hat, plenty of water, and a map, as the trails can be somewhat confusing.

Accommodations

For a fabulous wine-and-spa retreat away from anything resembling a city, stay at the **Kenwood Inn & Spa** (10400 Hwy. 12, 707/833-1293, www.kenwoodinn.com, no children under 18, no pets, $250–400). This Tuscan-style villa has 29 plush guest rooms, a world-renowned spa, and a rustic-elegant Italian restaurant on-site. The only problem is that you may have trouble prying yourself away long enough to go wine tasting. Expect to pay premium room rates during the summer–fall high season.

If an extravagant inn and spa is not

WINE COUNTRY

within your budget, consider staying at the **Birmingham Bed and Breakfast** (8790 Hwy. 12, 800/819-1388, www.birminghambb.com, $175–205). Built in 1915 and now a National Historic Landmark, this five-room bed-and-breakfast exudes plenty of charm. Each guest room is warm, light, and filled with plenty of antiques, including many craftsman touches. Guests enjoy a two-course hot breakfast served on china and crystal and a complimentary gift card for free wine tastings at 30 wineries in the Sonoma Valley.

Though children are not permitted in the main house, the Monroe Cottage, attached to the old water tower, has a full kitchen and living room and accommodates children ages 6–12. Pets are also welcome in the Monroe Cottage for an additional $10 per night.

Food
Despite its Hispanic name, the cuisine at **Dóce Lunas** (8910 Sonoma Hwy., 707/833-4000, www.docelunasrestaurant.com, 11:30 A.M.–2:30 P.M. and 5–8:30 P.M. Wed.–Sat., 10 A.M.–2:30 P.M. and 5–8:30 P.M. Sun., $17–20) is all over the map. Menu items like short ribs, *kalua* pork, and schnitzel are served with a typical Wine Country flair that includes specialty salts, truffle oil, and a carefully selected wine list. Complete your meal with sticky toffee pudding for dessert, and then wander upstairs to ramble through the Dóce Lunas antiques store, which sells country-style kitsch and collectibles.

Information and Services
Kenwood has few services for visitors, but many of the hotels and wineries can direct you to the best places to see. The *Kenwood Press* (www.kenwoodpress.com), where you can find out about local events and get a taste of the town, is published twice a month. Cell-phone reception is better here than in Glen Ellen, but don't count on finding reliable wireless Internet access.

Getting There and Around
Kenwood is located 11 miles east of downtown Santa Rosa on Highway 12, and four miles north of Glen Ellen. To reach Kenwood from U.S. 101 in Santa Rosa, take the exit for Highway 12 east.

Russian River Valley

The Russian River Valley may be the prettiest part of Wine Country. The Russian River runs through it, providing ample water for forests and meadows as well as wide calm spots with sandy banks. Rafting, canoeing, and kayaking opportunities abound on the zippier stretches of the river. If you are visiting for the vino, the area called the Russian River Valley actually encompasses several prestigious American Viticultural Areas, including Dry Creek, Alexander Valley, and, of course, Russian River. Wineries are clustered along three main roads: the Gravenstein Highway (Hwy. 116), River Road, and U.S. 101.

A little to the west of the area's concentrated wine region, you'll reach the river in Guerneville, a noted gay and lesbian resort destination. Even if you're straight (but not narrow), you'll love the kitschy downtown, clothing-optional resorts, and general sense of friendliness and fun that permeates the area.

SANTA ROSA
Santa Rosa is the biggest city in Wine Country and the largest in the North Bay. As such, it is more preoccupied with big-city issues than with wine tasting. This is a mixed-income area where many people work in building trades and other blue-collar professions. It is also ethnically diverse, with a large Latino population

as well as strong Southeast Asian communities. Developed at the turn of the 20th century, the older neighborhoods are filled with charming Craftsman-style bungalows. Downtown boasts some historic buildings, but many did not survive the big earthquakes of 1906 and 1969. Santa Rosa's large size means that there are plenty of things to do with the kids, such as the Charles Shultz and Pacific Air Museums.

Wineries
BATTAGLINI ESTATE WINERY

Many large Russian River wineries make wine out of every varietal under the hot Sonoma sun, but Battaglini Estate Winery (2948 Piner Rd., 707/578-4091, www.battagliniwines.com, daily 10 A.M.–5 P.M., $10) has chosen instead to specialize. Inside the cute wood-paneled tasting room with its homey cluttered bar, you'll find only zinfandels, chardonnays, and petit sirahs. The expression of each of these grapes approaches perfection. You'll also see a few unusual manifestations, such as a late-harvest dessert chardonnay. For the most fun possible during the crowded harvest season in the fall,

join Battaglini for a "stomp" event, during which you'll literally take off your shoes and start stomping in a bucket of grapes.

HANNA

The first thing you'll notice when you drive up to Hanna (5353 Occidental Rd., 707/575-3371, www.hannawinery.com, daily 10 A.M.–4 P.M., $10–20) is the stunning view down the hillside into Alexander Valley. The tasting room is surrounded by vineyards climbing the hills and flowing down to the bottom of the valley. The tasting room has plenty of windows and a broad wraparound porch to help you take in the vistas. But don't neglect the wines: Hanna offers a large list, along with a reserve tasting of the finest vintages. In addition to the inevitable cabernet sauvignons and chardonnays, you might find some unusual varieties, such as malbec—ask nicely and you might even sneak a taste.

◖ KENDALL-JACKSON WINE CENTER
Kendall-Jackson Wine Center (5007 Fulton Rd., Fulton, 707/571-7500, www.kj.com, daily

WINE COUNTRY

© SONOMA COUNTY TOURISM BOARD

Kendall-Jackson Wine Center

WINE COUNTRY

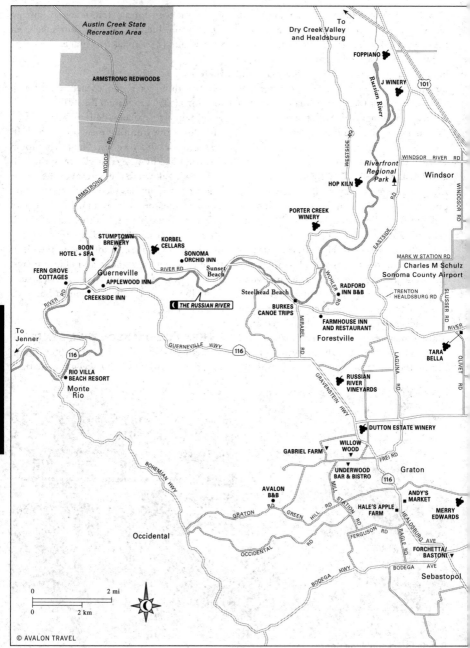

Austin Creek State
Recreation Area

ARMSTRONG REDWOODS

To
Dry Creek Valley
and Healdsburg

FOPPIANO

J WINERY

101

Russian River

Riverfront
Regional
Park

Windsor

WINDSOR RIVER RD

WESTSIDE RD

HOP KILN

PORTER CREEK
WINERY

MARK W STATION RD

Charles M Schulz
Sonoma County Airport

STUMPTOWN
BREWERY

KORBEL
CELLARS

SONOMA
ORCHID INN

BOON
HOTEL + SPA

FERN GROVE
COTTAGES

Guerneville

RIVER RD

APPLEWOOD INN

CREEKSIDE INN

RIVER RD

Sunset
Beach

Steelhead Beach

THE RUSSIAN RIVER

BURKES CANOE TRIPS

WOHLER RD

RADFORD
INN B&B

TRENTON
HEALDSBURG RD

SUSSER RD

FARMHOUSE INN
AND RESTAURANT

Forestville

MIRABEL RD

LAGUNA RD

OLIVET RD

RUSSIAN
RIVER
VINEYARDS

TARA
BELLA

RIVER RD

To
Jenner

116

RIO VILLA
BEACH RESORT

Monte
Rio

GUERNEVILLE HWY

116

GRAVENSTEIN HWY

DUTTON ESTATE WINERY

BOHEMIAN HWY

GABRIEL FARM

WILLOW
WOOD

FREI RD

Graton

UNDERWOOD
BAR & BISTRO

116

AVALON
B&B

GRATON RD

GREEN HILL RD

STATION RD

HALE'S APPLE
FARM

ANDY'S
MARKET

MERRY
EDWARDS

HEALDSBURG AVE

Occidental

OCCIDENTAL RD

FERGUSON RD

BAGLE RD

FORCHETTA/
BASTONI

BODEGA AVE

BODEGA HWY

Sebastopol

0   2 mi

0   2 km

© AVALON TRAVEL

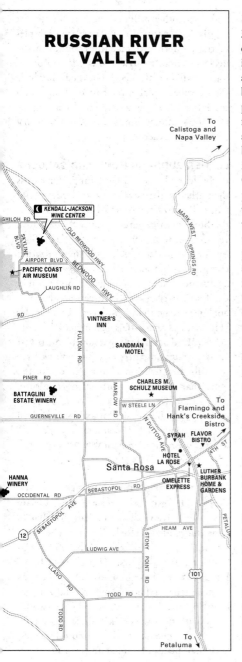

RUSSIAN RIVER VALLEY

To Calistoga and Napa Valley

KENDALL-JACKSON WINE CENTER

SHILOH RD

SKYLINE BLVD

OLD REDWOOD HWY

AIRPORT BLVD

PACIFIC COAST AIR MUSEUM

LAUGHLIN RD

REDWOOD HWY

MARK WEST SPRINGS RD

RD

VINTNER'S INN

FULTON RD

SANDMAN MOTEL

PINER RD

BATTAGLINI ESTATE WINERY

MARLOW RD

CHARLES M. SCHULZ MUSEUM

GUERNEVILLE RD

W STEELE LN

To Flamingo and Hank's Creekside Bistro

DUTTON AVE

SYRAH

FLAVOR BISTRO

4TH ST

HOTEL LA ROSE

Santa Rosa

HANNA WINERY

OCCIDENTAL RD

SEBASTOPOL RD

OMELETTE EXPRESS

LUTHER BURBANK HOME & GARDENS

SEBASTOPOL AVE

HEAM AVE

PETALUMA

12

LUDWIG AVE

STONY POINT RD

101

LLANO RD

TODD RD

TODD RD

To Petaluma

---

10 A.M.–5 P.M., tours daily 11 A.M., 1 P.M., and 3 P.M., tasting $5–15) surprises even serious oenophiles with the quiet elegance of its tasting room and the extensive sustainable gardens and demonstration vineyards surrounding the buildings. Inside, choose between moderately priced regular wine tasting and the $30 pp food-and-wine pairing (order at the tasting bar, and then wait to be seated at one of the small bistro tables nearby). KJ's food-and-wine pairing might be the best example of this new Wine Country tasting trend. A staff of full-time chefs prepares a fresh selection of small bites that pair with the day's selection of reserve and estate wines. The wines are delicate and tasty, but it's the food that stands out—brought out hot and perfect by one of the chefs, who will tell you about the preparation of each luscious mouthful; expect one or two goodies that aren't on the menu. Locals sometimes stop by the high-ceilinged tasting room and make a lunch out of the food-and-wine pairing. Just be aware that in high season (May–Oct.) you might need to make a reservation in advance—KJ doesn't have too many tables. Take a tour of the gardens in spring and summer, and try a taste of fresh wine grapes during the fall harvest season.

TARA BELLA WINERY

You have to call ahead to arrange a private appointment if you want to visit the tiny exclusive Tara Bella Winery (3701 Viking Rd., 707/544-9049, www.tarabellawinery.com). Tara Bella represents the ultimate in intimate family-owned wineries; the husband-and-wife team, Tara and Rich, tend their own vineyard, press their own grapes by hand, and make their own wine. From their eight-acre Russian River vineyard, they create just one cabernet sauvignon each year. Each November they release a new vintage—most of which is snapped up by their wine club, although you can purchase a bottle if you taste at the winery. A visit to Tara Bella is a visit to the roots of California

WINE COUNTRY

wine—family-owned and handcrafted, with a flavor all its own.

Sights

CHARLES M. SCHULZ MUSEUM

Schulz drew the world-famous *Peanuts* comic strip for almost 50 years, and from 1958 until his death in 2000 he lived in Sonoma County. In honor of Schulz and the *Peanuts* gang, the Charles M. Schulz Museum (2301 Hardies Lane, 707/579-4452, www.schulzmuseum.org, 11 A.M.–5 P.M. Mon. and Wed.–Fri., 10 A.M.–5 P.M. Sat.–Sun., adults $10, seniors and ages 4–18 $5, under age 4 free) opened in 2002. Inside the 27,000-square-foot building, which somehow manages to look like it comes from a four-inch comic strip, you'll find an incredible wealth of multimedia art, original drawings, and changing exhibitions based on the works of Schulz. Plenty of permanent collections provide stability and a base for the museum's theme. The museum owns most of the original *Peanuts* strips, a large collection of Schulz's personal possessions, and an astonishing array of tribute artwork from other comic-strip artists and urban installation designers the world over. Outside the building, the grounds include attractive gardens, the Snoopy Labyrinth, and even the infamous Kite-eating Tree.

PACIFIC COAST AIR MUSEUM

Even if you're not an aviation buff, the Pacific Coast Air Museum (2230 Becker Blvd., 707/575-7900, www.pacificcoastairmuseum.org, 10 A.M.–4 P.M. Tues., Thurs., and Sat.–Sun., adults $9, ages 6–17 $5, under age 5 free) is worth a visit. Learn about the history of aviation in the United States through interpretive and photographic exhibits. Spend some time studying the cutaways and bits and pieces to enhance your understanding of the mechanics of powered flight. And finally, fantasize about flying the fine examples of F-series fighters and many other military and civilian aircraft on display. Many of the planes are examples of the modern war machines found on the decks of aircraft carriers today. If you prefer to see civilian craft, check out the funky little Pitts aerobatic plane, the sort of thing you'll see doing impossible-looking tricks during the museum's annual **Wings over Wine Country** air show, held each August.

LUTHER BURBANK HOME AND GARDENS

If you love plants and gardening, don't miss the Luther Burbank Home and Gardens (204 Santa Rosa Ave., 707/524-5445, www.lutherburbank.org, gardens daily 8 A.M.–dusk year-round, tours 10 A.M.–4 P.M. Tues.–Sun. Apr.–Oct., gardens free). Using hybridization techniques, Luther Burbank personally created some of the most popular plants grown in California gardens and landscapes today. You don't have to go to his gardens to see examples of his famous Shasta daisy, an incredibly hardy pure-white daisy hybrid that now blankets vast areas throughout the state. But you will see them in the Luther Burbank gardens in the more than one acre's worth of horticulture, which includes medicinal herbs and showy roses. Check the website for a list of what's in bloom during your visit, as something is sure to be showing its finest flowers every month of the year.

Entertainment and Events

One way to taste wines from a wider variety of vineyards is to stop in at a wine bar. **Willi's Wine Bar** (4404 Old Redwood Hwy., 707/526-3096, www.williswinebar.net, 11:30 A.M.–9:30 P.M. Tues.–Thurs., 11:30 A.M.–10 P.M. Fri.–Sat., 5–9:30 P.M. Sun.–Mon.) offers flights of small pours and bottles of high-end vintages from Sonoma, Napa, and the rest of the world. To go with their wines, this upscale establishment offers cheese plates, charcuterie plates, and small plates of haute cuisine. Your server should be able to advise you on which plates pair best with which wines.

Want to find a bar that doesn't pander to the ubiquitous wine trade? Check out the **Russian River Brewing Company** (725 4th St., 707/545-2337, www.russianriverbrewing.com, 11 A.M.–midnight Sun.–Thurs., 11 A.M.–1 A.M. Fri.–Sat.), which both brews and serves lots of beer. And what goes better with beer than pizza? The food menu leans heavily on pizza and calzones to satisfy folks who build up their appetites trying the various strong local brews. The brewpub also acts as a venue for local and regional blues, funk, and jazz bands: Saturday, Sunday, and Wednesday nights feature live music.

The **Lounge at the Flamingo** (2777 4th St., 707/545-8530, www.flamingoresort.com) draws a significant crowd even on weekday evenings. This retro-style nightspot does have a good-size dance floor bathed in fuchsia light, plenty of seating, and an endless stream of live bands and nighttime fun that appeals to locals and visitors alike. Expect an older, but not senior, crowd for live jazz, oldies cover bands, and weekly West Coast swing classes. The atmosphere exudes geniality, bar food is served all day, and the evening crowd isn't afraid to get out on the floor and dance. All in all it's a fun scene.

Outside the local bar and club circuit, big-time live-music venues are few and far between in the Russian River region, but the **Wells Fargo Center for the Arts** (50 Mark West Springs Rd., 707/546-3600, http://wellsfargo-centerarts.org, ticket prices vary) is a full-size theater that hosts any number of national acts on tour each year, plus the occasional play or headlining comic. Recent acts have included Melissa Etheridge and the Beach Boys.

One of the biggest annual events in this agricultural region is the **Sonoma County Fair** (Sonoma County Fairgrounds, 1350 Bennett Valley Rd., 707/545-4200, www.

sonomacountyfair.com), held during two weeks at the end of July. Even the biggest Sonoma wineries prize the awards they win at their local county fair, and you'll see fair ribbons displayed proudly in many Russian River tasting rooms. If you're lucky enough to be able to attend, you'll find far more than just wine—live entertainment, family shows, and an amazing array of contests and exhibitions featuring the work of folks from all over the Sonoma region. Live horse racing and an adjacent golf course round out the many attractions.

The **Harvest Fair** (1350 Bennett Valley Rd., www.sonomacountyfair.com, Oct.), also held on the Sonoma County Fairgrounds, focuses almost exclusively on competition among wineries and farmers in Sonoma County. Growers and vintners bring their finest produce.

Sports and Recreation

Just as in Napa, one of the popular ways to get a great view of the Russian River Valley is from the basket of a hot-air balloon. Granted, you and your hangover must fall out of bed before dawn for this particular treat—so you might want to make this a first-day adventure before you start wine tasting. **Wine Country Balloons** (meeting site Kal's Kaffe Mocha, 397 Aviation Blvd., 707/538-7359, www.balloontours.com, daily, adults $225, children $195) can get you up in the air to start the day high above Wine Country. This big company maintains a whole fleet of balloons that can carry 2–16 passengers. Expect the total time to be 3–4 hours, with 1–1.5 hours in the air.

For a bit of open space during your visit, **Spring Lake** (393 Violetti Dr., 707/539-8092, www.sonoma-county.org, parking $7 June–Aug., $6 Sept.–May) has a little something for everyone. Picnic tables and hiking and paved cycling trails skirt this 72-acre lake. Anglers out to stalk the wily largemouth bass can launch electric-motor boats (but not gas-powered boats) into the water, while lifeguards watch over a cordoned swimming lagoon that's perfect for kids. A nearby concession stand rents paddleboats and canoe-like craft during summer, and the Environmental Discovery Center boasts interactive displays eager to teach kids and adults alike about the lake's ecosystem and environmental stewardship in general.

Between Santa Rosa and Kenwood, check out the **Bennett Valley Golf Course** (3330 Yulupa Ave., 707/528-3673, www.srcity.org/golf, $16–37). This par-72 medium-length 18-hole course provides challenging play for beginners and intermediates and some fun for advanced golfers too. Practically next door are two 18-hole courses at the **Oakmont Golf Club** (7025 Oakmont Dr., 707/539-0415, www.oakmontgc.com, $19–68). The Oakmont East course offers executive-length par-63 play—perfect for a shorter or slightly easier game. Oakmont West is a little bigger and more challenging, at regulation length and par 72.

Accommodations

In the city of Santa Rosa, you'll find all the familiar chain motels. You'll also see a few charming inns and upper-tier hotels that show off the unique aspects of the city that serves as the transition from the Bay Area to true Northern California.

The **Sandman Motel** (3421 Cleveland Ave., 707/544-8570, www.sandmansantarosa.com, $90–110) offers clean, comfortable motel rooms for reasonable prices. The guest rooms are decorated in standard motel style, with dark carpets and floral bedspreads. Amenities include a big heated swimming pool, outdoor whirlpool tub that is heated year-round, coffee and continental breakfast in the lobby each morning, and in-room fridges and satellite TV. The Sandman is a great place to bring the family.

At the corner of Historic Railroad Square, **Hotel la Rose** (308 Wilson St., 800/527-6738, www.hotellarose.com, $130–170) exemplifies the luxury-hotel concept as it has evolved over

the last century. The stone-clad main building rises high over Railroad Square, with more guest rooms available in the more modern carriage house just across the street. Because Hotel la Rose has only 47 guest rooms, you'll see an attention to detail and a level of service that's missing in the larger motels and hotels in the area. The carriage house offers modern decor and amenities, and each large room and suite feels light and bright. In the main building you'll find an older style of elegance, with antique furniture and floral wallpaper appealing to guests who want a taste of what the hotel might have been like back in 1907. A quick trip downstairs takes you to Hotel la Rose's restaurant, the **Iron Stone** (daily 7 A.M.–10:30 P.M.).

At the north end of Santa Rosa, convenient to the major Russian River wine roads, you can stay at the lovely upscale **Vintners Inn** (4350 Barnes Rd., 800/421-2584, http://vintnersinn.com, $300). The low, attractive red-tile-roof buildings of the inn and the fabulous John Ash & Co. restaurant are adjacent to a large stretch of vineyard. Every guest room has a king bed, fluffy down bedding, and a patio or balcony overlooking a cute garden-like courtyard. Many guest rooms boast fireplaces and spa tubs, and all feature luxurious appointments. Your stay includes a full breakfast each morning, plus access to the inn's outdoor whirlpool tub and the common den, which has a fireplace. The only downside to the Vintners Inn is its regrettable proximity to a local power station; just try to look in the other direction when admiring the view.

Don't worry—the guest room interiors at the kitschy **Flamingo** (2777 4th St., 707/545-8530, www.flamingoresort.com, $150) are decorated in soothing modern style without a hint of virulent pink. The heavy-duty 1950s styling is only at the front of the property inside the lobby and lounge and, of course, on the giant rotating neon sign with the flamingo perched on top. Guest rooms are in spokes surrounding a central garden and immense swimming pool. Each sizeable motel-style guest room has comfortable beds, a clean bath, and nearby parking. The Flamingo is a great place to bring the kids during the hot Sonoma summer—they'll love the pool, while grownups will love the easy access to the Russian River wine roads.

Food

◖ **John Ash & Co.** (4350 Barnes Rd., 707/527-7687, www.vintnersinn.com, 5–9 P.M. Sun.–Tues., 11:30 A.M.–2:30 P.M. and 5–9 P.M. Wed.–Thurs., 11:30 A.M.–2:30 P.M. and 5–9:30 P.M. Fri., 5–9:30 P.M. Sat., $33) stands out as one of the best high-end California cuisine restaurants in the Russian River region. The large elegant dining room, done up in Mediterranean style, is part of the Vintners Inn, and the only unappetizing thing about it is its location across the street from a power plant. The food runs to pure California cuisine with lots of local and sustainable produce prepared to show off the natural flavors. The menu is fairly short, making it easy to choose from each of the three courses that often highlight seafood, beef, lamb, and seasonal specialties. And, of course, the wine list at John Ash & Co. is something special, with some amazing local vintages that are tough to find anywhere outside the Russian River Valley.

Need something a bit more casual? Get in line for breakfast, brunch, or lunch at the ◖ **Omelette Express** (112 4th St., 707/525-1690, www.omelette.com, 6:30 A.M.–3 P.M. Mon.–Fri., 7 A.M.–4 P.M. Sat.–Sun.). Owned by local character Don Taylor, who might even be acting as host at the front door on the weekend, this spot is definitely favored by locals. Don calls many of his customers by their first names, but he also welcomes newcomers with enthusiasm. The very casual dining rooms are decorated with the front ends of classic cars, and the menu—no surprise—involves lots of omelets. Portions are huge and come with a side of toast made with homemade bread, so consider splitting one with a friend.

Syrah (205 5th St., 707/568-4002, www.syrahbistro.com, daily 5 P.M.–close, $20–45) is in central Santa Rosa, making it easy to experience high-end Wine Country cuisine in a nice downtown locale. The chef-owner often works the exposed grill area to one side of the small dining room, putting a perfect char on the meat to be served in the imaginative entrées on the tasting menus and the à la carte list. But it's the appetizers, salads, and sides that really make Syrah's offerings great. Salads are fresh and imaginative, and entrée plates include side dishes that both balance and enhance the main meats. The pastry chef does a fantastic job on the final course, creating a selection of classic chocolate and local seasonal desserts. The California-centric wine list evolves constantly—expect a different array of vintages each time you return.

Also downtown is **Flavor Bistro** (96 Old Courthouse Square, 707/573-9600, http://flavorbistro.com, 11 A.M.–10 P.M. Mon.–Thurs., 11 A.M.–11 P.M. Fri., 8 A.M.–11 P.M. Sat., 8 A.M.–10 P.M. Sun., $15–22). Serving an eclectic mix of California comfort food made from organic and locally sourced ingredients, Flavor is all over the map in terms of cuisine but right on the mark for price. The mellow atmosphere makes it an easy place to take kids, particularly if you are hankering for a spruced-up steak and the little ones just want a burger and fries. Thursday nights offer wine pairing with a four-course meal ($25), while weekends include a full breakfast complete with french toast and eggs wrapped in puff pastry. Sidewalk seating is available for those hot Santa Rosa afternoons.

Information and Services

The serious local daily newspaper is the **Santa Rosa Press Democrat** (www.pressdemocrat.com). Check the Living and Entertainment sections for visitor information. You can also

WINE COUNTRY

check out the many Wine Country guides that proliferate in the tasting rooms, motels, and inns of the region.

As a major city, Santa Rosa has plenty of medical services available. If you need help, try **Santa Rosa Memorial Hospital** (1165 Montgomery Ave., 707/546-3210, www.stjosephhealth.org), which has an emergency room.

Getting There and Around

Santa Rosa is 50 miles north of San Francisco on U.S. 101. Be aware that traffic on this major corridor can get congested, particularly during the morning commute and 3–7 P.M. Monday–Friday. It also slows on sunny summer afternoons when people go to cool themselves along the Russian River. Fortunately, the side roads that lead to various tasting rooms and recreation spots are seldom crowded.

From U.S. 101, take exit 489 toward downtown Santa Rosa to reach the historic district; downtown is east of the freeway. Wineries are on the west side of town and can be accessed by taking Highway 12 west as well as the U.S. 101 exits for River Road and Guerneville.

Golden Gate Transit (415/455-2000, http://goldengatetransit.org, $10.25) runs buses between San Francisco and Santa Rosa on routes 70, 71, 72, and 80. These routes are geared toward commuters who work in San Francisco, so the southbound buses run in the morning and those going north run in the afternoon.

SEBASTOPOL

Low-key and a bit alternative, Sebastopol is undoubtedly the artistic heart of Sonoma County. The relatively modest digs, low cost of living, liberal politics, natural beauty, and small-town vibe have attracted artists that include heavyweights like Tom Waits and Jerry Garcia as well as independent painters, sculptors, and ceramists. Downtown Sebastopol contains a number of shops where local artists sell their works, along with bookstores, record stores,

and the odd place selling tie-dyed T-shirts. The surrounding farmland was once devoted to orchards, particularly apples, but that has changed over the years; now grapes dominate the Gravensteins. Still, the few remaining orchards give fragrance and beauty to the already scenic country roads, especially during the spring bloom.

Wineries
DUTTON ESTATE

A small winery along the comparatively undiscovered Gravenstein Highway, Dutton Estate (8757 Green Valley Rd., 707/829-9463, www.duttonestate.com, daily 10 A.M.–5 P.M., tasting $10) is in the middle of its own vineyards (don't pick the grapes). Tasters enjoy plenty of personal attention from pourers, along with a small list of white and rosé wines, moving into the red pinots and syrahs that do so well in this area. Dutton's syrahs stand out among the offerings, which can include a few extra pours for those who seem genuinely interested in the wines.

MERRY EDWARDS

Merry Edwards was the first woman to earn a degree in enology (wine-making) from the prestigious University of California, Davis, program in 1993. After working as a winemaker for numerous Sonoma vintners and developing her own pinot noir grape clone with the help of the facilities and staff at Davis, Merry finally opened her own winery. The Merry Edwards Winery (2959 Gravenstein Hwy., 707/823-7466, www.merryedwards.com, daily 9:30 A.M.–4:30 P.M., free) offers tastings in its two glass-walled tasting rooms. Anxious to avoid the overcrowded Napa tasting model, each member of Merry Edwards's tasting staff works with only one party of tasters at a time. You'll be led to a table with comfortable chairs already set with four glasses ready for four different pinot noirs. There are four samples of the same varietal plus a bonus sauvignon blanc served at the end of the tasting. It's easy to spend an hour at Merry Edwards, soaking up the luxury of a completely different tasting experience. Perhaps most amazingly of all, tasting at Merry Edwards is free.

Accommodations

In Sebastopol, the best place to stay is the expensive but lovely **Avalon Bed and Breakfast** (11910 Graton Rd., 707/824-0880, www.avalonluxuryinn.com, $239–329). With only three guest rooms, it offers the ultimate in private and romantic accommodations. All guest rooms have king beds, hot tubs or access to the garden hot tub, fireplaces, air-conditioning, and many luxurious amenities. Because Avalon was purpose-built as a bed-and-breakfast, each guest room is actually a suite with plenty of space to spread out and enjoy a longer stay. At breakfast time, you'll be served an organic feast, with produce purchased from a local community-shared agriculture group and loving attention to the details of preparation.

Food

A great break from the endless fancy food is to find a nice ethnic restaurant. In Sebastopol, one of the best is the **Himalayan Tandoori and Curry House** (969 Gravenstein Hwy. S., 707/824-1800, 11 A.M.–2 P.M. and 5–9 P.M. Mon.–Sat., 5–9 P.M. Sun., $16), which serves up Indian food in the Himalayan style. You'll find vegetable curries and meat tandoori here, both properly spicy, as well as fresh naan, spicy rice pudding, and all sorts of treats. You'll even get a break from the endless river of wine, since there's plenty of beer on the drinks menu.

Walking into downtown's **◖ Forchetta/ Bastoni** (6948 Sebastopol Ave., 707/829-9500, http://forchettabastoni.com, $12–30) presents a difficult decision. On one side is Southeast Asian street food (*bánh mi* sandwiches, noodle bowls, and curry plates). On the other side is rustic Italian fare in the form of wood-fired pizzas, pastas, and salads, all with the usual California cuisine twist. The twin restaurants are both

WINE COUNTRY

© ELIZABETH JANG

the Italian side of Forchetta/Bastoni, with its warm, rustic ambiance

smartly decorated. The Asian side, Bastoni (11:30 A.M.–9 P.M. Sun.–Thurs., 11:30 A.M.–10 P.M. Fri.–Sat.) features skinny communal tables, colorfully worn stools, and cans of chopsticks. Over on the Italian side, Forchetta (5–9 P.M. Thurs.–Mon., 11:30 A.M.–2 P.M. Sun.), the decor is a bit more urbane with warm wood walls, exposed vents, and simple but artsy glass chandeliers. A full bar takes up most of Bastoni and is filled by happy locals grabbing a quick bite, a drink, or chatting. If you are torn between the two, Bastoni is frequently less busy, but both sides often have space at the chef's counters that face the open kitchens.

The **Underwood Bar and Bistro** (9113 Graton Rd., Graton, 707/823-7023, www. underwoodgraton.com, 11:30 A.M.–10 P.M. Tues.–Sat., 5–10 P.M. Sun., $20) serves the upscale cuisine in the tiny town of Graton. Plush red velvet and dark wood tables grace the Underwood's dining room, which is recommended by many locals as the best spot in this wine region to sit down to a serious dinner. With a heavy seafood focus, including raw oysters on the half shell, and top-quality meats and produce, Underwood does in fact exemplify Wine Country cuisine. The so-called tapas are actually small plates and appetizers, meant to be shared around the table, but you can share the larger salads and entrées just as easily. The wine list leans heavily toward small local vintners; ask your server to recommend some of the best local wines with dinner. One especially spiffy thing about Underwood: The bar stays open late (10–11 P.M.) on Friday–Saturday nights, serving a pared-down but still satisfying late-night menu.

Calling the **Willow Wood** (9020 Graton Rd., Graton, 707/823-0233, www.willow-woodgraton.com, 8 A.M.–9 P.M. Mon.–Sat., 9 A.M.–3 P.M. Sun., $10–25) a deli is somewhat misleading. Sure, they've got a counter, a take-out business, and well-trodden old wooden floors. But really, Willow Wood is an upscale California-Italian restaurant for lunch, featuring souped-up versions of traditional deli sandwiches accompanied by pasta and pickled veggies. Diners sit on wooden benches to enjoy the large meals, which can also include giant salads and tureens of fresh soup. You can get a beer or a glass of Sonoma wine with your meal, or use the sugar found in the silver alien pod on your table to sweeten the locally beloved hot teas. If you're having trouble making a choice, the open-faced hot sandwich with egg salad and pesto is a favorite.

Information and Services

For maps of the area, souvenirs, newspapers, and wine-tasting coupons, swing by the **Sebastopol Chamber of Commerce Visitors Center** (265 S. Main St., 707/823-3032, www. sebastopol.org, 9 A.M.–5 P.M. Mon.–Fri.). Although it's closed on weekends, they do have a 24-hour information kiosk outside.

Published in Sebastopol, the **Sonoma West Times and News** covers local happenings and upcoming events; it comes out every Thursday. On the same block as the visitors center but on the opposite side of the street is the **post office** (290 Main St.).

Getting There and Around

Sebastopol is west of Santa Rosa, accessed by Highways 116 and 12. The heart of downtown Sebastopol is at the intersection of Sebastopol Avenue (Hwy. 12) and Main Street (Hwy. 116). Note that Sebastopol Avenue becomes the Bodega Highway once it hits downtown Sebastopol and extends all the way to, you guessed it, Bodega Bay.

To reach Sebastopol from U.S. 101, take either the exit for Highway 12 west in Santa Rosa or the exit for Highway 116 west at Cotati, eight miles south of Santa Rosa. Highway 116 is the most direct route to continue to the Russian River from Sebastopol.

GUERNEVILLE AND VICINITY

There are a few wineries in the Guerneville area, but most people come here to float, canoe, or kayak the gorgeous Russian River that winds from Healdsburg all the way through Monte Rio to the Pacific Ocean at Jenner. In addition to its busy summertime tourist trade, Guerneville is also a very popular gay and lesbian resort area. The rainbow flag flies proudly here, and the friendly community welcomes all.

Wineries
FOPPIANO

One of the oldest wineries in the Russian River Valley, Foppiano (12707 Old Redwood Hwy., 707/433-7272, www.foppiano.com, daily 11 A.M.–5 P.M., $5) dates from 1896. Today, Foppiano is still making a small list of premium red wines. Their signature wine is a legendary petit sirah, unusual for the area. They've also got a great sangiovese, a zin, a cab, and a merlot under the Foppiano label. A second label, Riverside, encompasses a few tasty but exceedingly inexpensive varietals that let drinkers on a budget enjoy Foppiano wines. Inside the farmhouse-style tasting room, enjoy sips of the various vintages, but also be sure to ask for Susan's recipes; the hospitality director and fourth-generation member of the Foppiano family creates and adapts dishes to match the family wines.

HOP KILN

Bringing truth in advertising to Sonoma, Hop Kiln (6050 Westside Rd., 707/433-6491, www.hopkilnwinery.com, daily 10 A.M.–5 P.M.) winery is housed in an old hop kiln. Earlier in its history, the Russian River Valley grew more beer-making ingredients than grapes, and this distinctively shaped hop kiln dried the valley's crop each year. Today, you'll find a gift shop inside the main kiln along with an extensive wine tasting bar that includes typical Wine Country varietals. Hop Kiln also produces unique wines, such as their malbec, grenache, and award-winning pinot noir.

J WINERY

Unlike many wineries that cling to Old World traditions, J Winery (11447 Old Redwood Hwy., 707/431-3646, www.jwine.com, 11 A.M.–5 P.M. Thurs.–Tues., $20–65) loves the cutting edge of the California wine scene. J specializes in California-style sparkling wines. The tasting room is a triumph of modern design, and the tasting experience gives visitors a sample of the best that Wine Country has to offer. Make a reservation at the Bubble Lounge, where, instead of the standard tasting bar and pouring staff, there are tables and waitstaff. Instead of the standard one-ounce pours, you'll enjoy wines specially paired with small bites of high-end California cuisine prepared in J's kitchens by their own team of gourmet chefs. You'll get the chance to taste the sparkly vintages as they are meant to be enjoyed—with an array of often spicy foods.

KORBEL CELLARS

Champagne grapes like cooler climates, so it makes sense that Korbel Cellars (13250 River Rd., Guerneville, 707/824-7000, www.korbel.com, daily 10 A.M.–4:30 P.M., four tastes free), the leading producer of California champagne-style sparkling wines, maintains a winery and tasting room on the Sonoma coast. The large, lush estate welcomes visitors with elaborate landscaping and attractive buildings, including a small area serving as a visitors center. Tours of the estate are offered several times daily for a fee. Inside the tasting room, visitors get to sample far more than the ubiquitous Korbel Brut that appears each New Year's. Korbel makes and sells a wide variety of high-end California champagnes, plus a few boutique still wines and a line of brandies. You can't taste the brandy (that involves a different and harder-to-obtain liquor license), but you can purchase it from the winery store. The facility also has a full-service gourmet deli and picnic grounds for tasters who want to stop for lunch.

PORTER CREEK WINERY

Serious cork dorks recommend the tiny tasting room at Porter Creek Winery (8735 Westside

WINE COUNTRY

© ELIZABETH LINHART MONEY

Korbel Cellars

Rd., 707/433-6321, www.portercreekvineyards.com, daily 10:30 A.M.–4:30 P.M., free), which casual tasters might otherwise miss at a bend on a winding road. Turn onto the dirt driveway, pass the farm-style house (actually the owner's family home), and park in front of a small converted shed—the tasting room. This is old-school Sonoma wine tasting. Porter Creek has been making its precious few cases of rich red wine each year for the last 30 years or so. You can occasionally find it at local restaurants, but if you like what you taste, buy it here at the winery. Porter Creek's wines are almost all reds, made from grapes grown organically within sight of the tasting room. You might even see the owner-winemaker walking through his vineyards with his family on a sunny afternoon in the off-season.

RUSSIAN RIVER VINEYARDS

Ironically, Russian River Vineyards (5700 Gravenstein Hwy., Forestville, 707/887-3344, www.russianrivervineyards.com, daily 11:30 A.M.–4:30 P.M., free) really isn't on the Russian River; it is in the coastal hills of nearby Forestville that nurture the Sonoma Coast American Viticultural Area vineyards and wineries. The property doesn't look like a typical high-end winery—the aging wooden buildings seem almost to be falling apart. (Don't worry, the tasting room has recently been shored up.) Sadly, the funky old Victorian house behind the tasting room isn't open for tours—it's part of the private production facility.

The friendly staff help create a classy small-winery tasting experience. Russian River Vineyard's small list of only red wines reflects the locale—tasters enjoy full-bodied, fruity pinot noirs and interesting varietals from the southern reaches of Europe. The charbono tastes especially good. For lunch, ask for a table in one of the two small dining rooms, divided by the brushed-metal tasting bar. Brunch or light afternoon fare is available every day, as

© SABRINA YOUNG

The Russian River is perfect for canoeing, kayaking, and swimming.

is dinner, which includes a three-course prix fixe option.

◖ The Russian River

Guerneville and its surrounding forest are the center for fun on the river. In summer the water is usually warm and dotted with folks swimming, canoeing, or simply floating tubes serenely downriver amid forested riverbanks and under blue skies. **Burke's Canoe Trips** (8600 River Rd., Forestville, 707/887-1222, www. burkescanoetrips.com, Memorial Day–mid-Oct., $60) rents canoes and kayaks on the Russian River. The put-in is at Burke's beach in Forestville; paddlers then canoe downriver 10 miles to Guerneville, where a courtesy shuttle picks them up. Burkes also offers overnight campsites for tents, trailers, and RVs.

On the north bank, **Johnsons Beach & Resort** (16241 1st St., 707/869-2022, www. johnsonsbeach.com, daily 10 A.M.–6 P.M. May–Oct.) rents canoes, kayaks, pedal boats, and inner tubes for floating the river. There is a safe kid-friendly section of the riverbank that is roped off for small children; parents and beachcombers can rent beach chairs and umbrellas for use on the small beach. The boathouse sells beer and snacks.

Fly fishers can cast their lines nearby off **Wohler Bridge** (9765 Wohler Rd., Forestville) and **Steelhead Beach** (9000 River Rd., Forestville).

Armstrong Redwoods

Armstrong Redwoods (17000 Armstrong Woods Rd., Guerneville, 707/869-2015, www.parks.ca.gov, daily 8 A.M.–sunset, $8 per vehicle), is an easy five-minute drive from Guerneville on one mostly straight road. This little redwoods park often gets overlooked, which makes it a bit less crowded than some of the most popular North Coast and Sierra redwood forests. But you can still take a fabulous hike—either a short stroll in the shade of the trees or a multiple-day backcountry adventure. The easiest walk ever to a big tree is the 0.1-mile stagger from the visitors center to the tallest tree in the park, named the **Parson Jones Tree**. If you saunter another 0.5 mile, you'll reach the **Colonel Armstrong Tree**, which grows next to the Armstrong Pack Station—your first stop if you're doing heavy-duty hiking. From the Pack Station, another 0.25 mile of moderate hiking leads to the Icicle Tree.

Right next to Armstrong is the **Austin Creek State Recreation Area** (17000 Armstrong Woods Rd., Guerneville, 707/869-2015, www.parks.ca.gov, daily 8 A.M.–sunset, $8 per vehicle). It's rough going on 2.5 miles of steep, narrow, treacherous dirt road to get to the main entrance and parking area; no vehicles over 20 feet long and no trailers of any kind are permitted. But once you're in, some great—and very difficult—hiking awaits you. The eponymous Austin Creek Trail (4.7 miles one-way) leads down from the hot meadows into the cool forest fed by Austin Creek. To avoid monotony on this challenging route, create a loop by taking the turn onto Gilliam Creek Trail (4 miles one-way). This way you get to see another of the park's cute little creeks as you walk back to the starting point.

Entertainment and Events

Guerneville wouldn't be a proper gay resort town without at least a couple of good gay bars that create proper nightlife for visitors and locals alike. The most visible and funky-looking of these is the **Rainbow Cattle Company** (16220 Main St., Guerneville, 707/869-0206, www.queersteer.com, daily 6 A.M.–2 A.M.). Mixing the vibes of a down-home country saloon with a happening San Francisco nightspot, the Rainbow has cold drinks and hot men with equal abandon. Think cocktails in Mason jars, wood paneling, and leather nights. This is just the kind of queer bar where you can bring your

mom or your straight-but-not-narrow friends, and they'll have just as much fun as you will.

It may not look like much from the road, but the **Stumptown Brewery** (15045 River Rd., 707/869-0705, www.stumptown.com, 11 A.M.–midnight Sun.–Thurs., 11 A.M.–2 A.M. Fri.–Sat.) is *the* place to hang out on the river. Inside this atypical dive bar is a pool table, Naugahyde barstools, and a worn wooden bar crowded with locals. Out back are the second bar and an outdoor deck with scattered tables overlooking the river. The brewery only makes a few of the beers sold on tap, but they are all great and perfect to enjoy by the pitcher. If you are feeling a little woozy from the beer and sunshine, Stumptown also serves a menu of burgers and grilled sandwiches; the food is a perfect excuse to stay put.

If you in the area in mid-August, you may be able to get tickets for the brewery's annual **Russian River Beer Revival and BBQ Cook Off** (www.stumptown.com/revival, Sat. mid-Aug.). The event takes place along the river on a grassy field below the restaurant and noon–6 P.M. Saturday. Enjoy live music, beer tastings from 30 different breweries, and lots and lots of barbecue. Tickets generally go on sale in June and sell out quickly.

Held at Johnson's Beach in Guerneville, the **Russian River Jazz and Blues Festival** (www.omegaevents.com, 707/869-1595, $50–60 each day, Sept.) is a two-day affair with jazz one day and blues the next. The main stage has some pretty big acts, including Buddy Guy, Al Green, and Taj Mahal, but there is plenty of music to groove to throughout the festival grounds. In addition to live acts, food vendors showcase regional fare, local artists hawk their wares, and tents serve glass after glass of wine while sunburned devotees splash around in the river. Much more than just a music festival, this event is the last big bash of the summer season; it takes place at the end of September, just before the weather reliably turns cold. If you plan to stay both days, consider camping here. **Johnson's**

Beach (707/869-2011) has designated campsites available on a first-come, first-served basis.

Accommodations

Because it's the major resort town for lovers of Russian River recreation, you'll find a few dozen bed-and-breakfasts and cabin resorts in town. Many of these spots are gay-friendly, some with clothing-optional hot tubs.

The **Creekside Inn & Lodge** (16180 Neeley Rd., 800/776-6586, www.creeksideinn.com, $175) is right along the Russian River outside of downtown Guerneville. Cabins and cottages at the lodge run short on upscale amenities but long on woodsy kitsch. Every cabin, even the studios, has a full kitchen with a fridge, plenty of space, a comfortable bath, and some of the best complimentary coffee you'll ever get in a hotel room. Choose from economical studios, multiple-bedroom family units, and brand-new eco-cabins that were designed and constructed to have minimal impact on the delicate local environment. The property is large and has a swimming pool for summertime refreshment, but it does not have good river frontage for swimmers. The owners, who know and love their area, will provide good suggestions for local beaches. They'll also make appointments for wine tasting at their favorite private local wineries.

The ◖ **Sonoma Orchid Inn** (12850 River Rd., Guerneville, 888/877-4466, www.sonomaorchidinn.com, pets welcome, $149–245) experience is made by its amazing owners. They've created beautiful guest rooms with elegant linens and furniture, plus just enough tchotchkes to keep things interesting. The best (and spendiest) rooms have satellite TV with DVRs as well as DVD players and VCRs, along with microwaves and small fridges. On the economy end of the spectrum, the guest rooms are tiny but cute, with private baths and pretty decorations. Best of all, the owners of the Orchid will offer to help you with absolutely

anything you need. They not only recommend restaurants and spas, they'll make reservations for you. They've got knowledge about the local wineries, hikes, river spots, and just about everything else in the region. The Orchid makes a perfect inn for visitors who've never been to the area—they're dog friendly, clothing mandatory, and welcoming to travelers of all stripes.

The **Farmhouse Inn & Spa** (7871 River Rd., Forestville, 707/887-3300, www.farmhouseinn.com, $400) is along River Road in the middle of prime wine-tasting country. The yellow-painted farmhouse is the inn's restaurant and contains the two most luxurious guest rooms; most of the guest accommodations march up the gently sloped hillside in the form of a row of cottages. The cute little cabins have upscale decor, warm fireplaces, private baths, and precious little space. The pool area and restaurant aren't big either but make up what they lack in size with charm and an adorable outdoor fireplace area. A gourmet breakfast is available, but reservations are necessary.

Riverfront balconies, a private beach, and beautifully landscaped grounds combine to make **Rio Villa Beach Resort** (20292 Hwy. 116, Monte Rio, 877/746-8455, www.riovilla.com, $119–179) an ideal Russian River getaway. With only 11 guest rooms—including some with kitchens—you're guaranteed both privacy with your companion and intimacy with the resort guests as well as the warm owners. A generous continental breakfast is available in the morning, and the Russian River is mere steps away.

On the road to Armstrong Redwoods, **boon hotel + spa** (14711 Armstrong Woods Rd., Guerneville, 707/869-2721, www.boonhotels.com, $165–260) is the antithesis of Guerneville's woodsy funkiness. In almost a rebuff to its environs, boon hotel + spa is minimal in the extreme, with white walls devoid of artwork, square armless couches, and beds vast enough to get lost in the fair-trade organic cotton sheets. The slate,

© SABRINA YOUNG

Rio Villa offers accommodations on the Russian River.

chrome, and white palette is offset by bright slashes of red and orange. Many of the 14 guest rooms have freestanding cast-iron fireplaces, private patios, and fridges. True to its name, there is a pool and hot tub (both saltwater, for a little twist) and plenty of facial and massage options to work out the kinks. In the morning, wake up to a pressed pot of locally roasted coffee; in the evening, chill out with a cocktail by the pool.

Raford Inn Bed and Breakfast Inn (10630 Wohler Rd., Healdsburg, 800/887-9503, www.rafordinn.com, $165–260) offers Healdsburg-level luxury at slightly less stratospheric prices than its nearby competitors. Each of the six guest rooms has a queen bed, air-conditioning, a CD player, and a private bath. Some have fireplaces, oversize showers, and other luxury amenities. All guest rooms have been decorated in attractive minimalist Victorian style that feels historic but doesn't overwhelm the modern guest. Every morning, the Raford serves up a hearty country breakfast—the perfect start to a day of wine tasting.

Food

River Inn Grill (16141 Main St., Guerneville, 707/869-0481, daily 8 A.M.–2 P.M., $10) is the first eatery you'll see when entering downtown Guerneville. In operation since 1946, this classic diner is the place for breakfast in Guerneville—the heavenly biscuits and gravy is a favorite.

A focal point of downtown Guerneville, **Main Street Station** (16280 Main St., 707/869-0501, www.mainststation.com, noon–9:30 P.M. Mon.–Thurs., noon–10:30 P.M. Fri.–Sun. May–Oct., noon–8 P.M. Mon.–Thurs., noon–9 P.M. Fri.–Sun. Nov.–Apr., $16) offers a big menu filled with homey, casual grub. The mainstay is handmade pizza; you can grab a quick slice for lunch, or bring friends and order a whole pie for dinner. In the evenings, locals and visitors come down to munch sandwiches and pizza, drink beer, and listen to live entertainment on the small stage.

Pat's Restaurant (16236 Main St., 707/869-9905, www.pats-restaurant.com, daily 6 A.M.–3 P.M., $10) is the kind of diner that travelers hope to find. It's homey, casual, and a place locals come to sit at the counter and have breakfast all day long. It sure doesn't look like much from the outside—a small storefront in the middle of downtown Guerneville—but when you peer in the plate-glass windows you'll notice quite a number of diners inside. Classic diner food (eggs, sandwiches, and burgers) is served fresh—the eggs are done perfectly, the hash browns are homemade, and the kitchen actually runs out of favorites like sausage gravy because it's made from scratch daily.

Light, airy, and open, tiny 🄲 **boon eat + drink** (16248 Main St., Guerneville, 707/869-0780, www.eatatboon.com, $20) lures diners to line up on the sidewalk in anticipation of local, organic, and sustainable cuisine served with simple elegance. Lunch usually consists of a simple menu of paninis, small plates, and the grass-fed Boon burger ($11). For dinner, hearty main courses combine lamb shank with mint pesto or a flatiron steak with truffle fries. You really can't go wrong here—unless you can't get in.

Information and Services

Off the beaten wine path is the **Russian River Chamber of Commerce and Visitors Center** (16209 1st St., Guerneville, 707/869-9000, http://russianriver.com, daily 10 A.M.–5 P.M.) in downtown Guerneville. Here you'll find local staff who can give you serious local recommendations not only for wineries but for river recreation, restaurants, and other less-traveled local attractions.

Getting There and Around

Guerneville is on Highway 116, alternately named River Road. In downtown Guerneville, Highway 116 is briefly called Main Street. The most direct access is via U.S. 101 north of Santa Rosa; take the River Road/Guerneville exit and follow River Road west for 15 miles to downtown Guerneville.

Alternately, a more scenic and often less crowded route is to take U.S. 101 to Highway 116 near Cotati, south of Santa Rosa. Named the Gravenstein Highway for its route through the apple orchards of Sebastopol, Highway 116 winds about 22 twisty miles through Sebastopol, Graton, and Forestville to emerge onto River Road in Guerneville.

Sonoma County Transit (http://sctransit.com) runs a Russian River Express bus, route 20, from downtown Santa Rosa to Guerneville ($2.90).

HEALDSBURG AND VICINITY

Healdsburg, a small city of 11,000 that is so charming it's easy to forget that people live and work here. The plaza anchors downtown and the wide and slow Russian River, creating the town's natural southern border. Boutiques, chic restaurants, and galleries dot the town, and fresh paint brightens the historic storefronts and planters filled lush with flowers and trailing vines. Healdsburg is also the nexus of three American Viticulture Areas (AVAs): the Russian River AVA, best known for producing pinot noir and chardonnay; Dry Creek AVA, famous for its zinfandel and sauvignon blanc; and the Alexander Valley AVA, which produces predominantly cabernet sauvignon and merlot.

Wineries
🄲 A. RAFANELLI

Tasting at A. Rafanelli (4685 W. Dry Creek Rd., 707/433-1385, www.arafanelliwinery.com, daily 10 A.M.–4 P.M., by appointment only) feels just about as different from the standard big-business high-end wineries of Wine Country as possible. You can't just walk in, as tastings are by appointment only; there's no marble-covered bar, no chic tasting room. Instead,

WINE COUNTRY

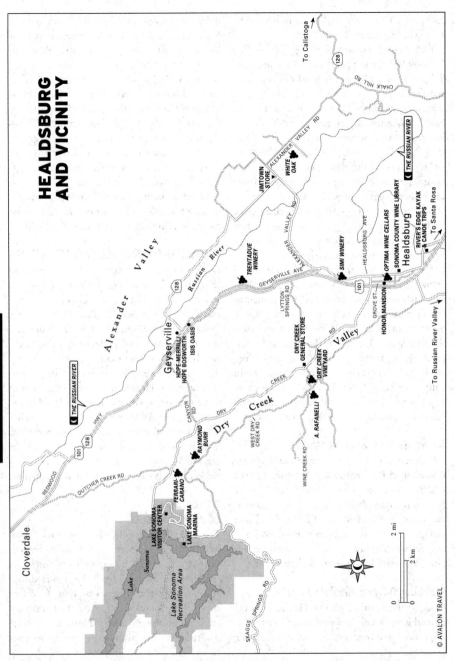

HEALDSBURG AND VICINITY

To Calistoga

128

CHALK HILL RD

ALEXANDER VALLEY RD

THE RUSSIAN RIVER

Alexander Valley

Russian River

JIMTOWN STORE

WHITE OAK

To Santa Rosa

ALEXANDER VALLEY RD

SIMI WINERY

HEALDSBURG AVE

OPTIMA WINE CELLARS

SONOMA COUNTY WINE LIBRARY

Healdsburg

RIVER'S EDGE KAYAK & CANOE TRIPS

TRENTADUE WINERY

GEYSERVILLE AVE

128

Geyserville

HOPE-MERRILL
HOPE BOSWORTH
ISIS OASIS

LYTTON SPRINGS RD

101

GROVE ST

HONOR MANSION

To Russian River Valley

THE RUSSIAN RIVER

DRY CREEK GENERAL STORE

DRY CREEK VINEYARD

RD

Valley

DRY CREEK

REDWOOD HWY

101 128

CANYON RD

DRY CREEK

Dry Creek Valley

WEST DRY CREEK RD

A. RAFANELLI

RAYMOND BURR

WINE CREEK RD

DUTCHER CREEK RD

FERRARI-CARANO

Cloverdale

LAKE SONOMA VISITOR CENTER

LAKE SONOMA MARINA

Lake Sonoma

Lake Sonoma Recreation Area

SKAGGS SPRINGS RD

2 mi

2 km

0

0

© AVALON TRAVEL

you walk into the barrel room of the working winery and stand on the concrete floor in the oak- and grape-scented air. The owner-winemaker will hand out glasses to your group, and you'll begin to taste some of the best red wines produced anywhere in Sonoma County. In a region where the phrase "cab is king" comes up at almost every winery, Rafanelli's cabernet sauvignons are still special. If you can't taste at Rafanelli, look for their zins and cabs at local Sonoma restaurants, to whom they sell the bulk of their wholesale wines.

ARMIDA

Come to the Armida (2201 Westside Rd., 707/433-2222, www.armida.com, daily 11 A.M.–5 P.M.) tasting room for the gorgeous scenery and the funky facilities, but stay for the wonderful wines. The driveway meanders up a Russian River hillside to a cluster of geodesic domes set among lovely and sustainable landscaping. Bring a picnic to enjoy on the big deck overlooking the duck pond and the valley beyond. Before you start eating, wander into the tasting room to check out some of the truly tasty Russian River red wines. You'll have your choice of smoky syrahs and jammy zinfandels. The flagship wine, Poizin, is well represented in the wines and logo-wear in the small gift shop that shares space with the tasting bar. Armida sells Poizin in a coffin-shaped box—ask nicely and they might open a bottle for you to taste (and even if they don't, it's still worth buying).

DRY CREEK VINEYARD

It seems odd that a winery named Dry Creek should have sailboats on all its labels, but that's the signature icon on each bottle produced by Dry Creek Vineyard (3770 Lambert Bridge Rd., 800/864-9463, www.drycreekvineyard. com, daily 10:30 A.M.–4:30 P.M., $5–15). This midsize winery focuses much effort within its own AVA (Dry Creek, of course), producing many single-vineyard wines from grapes grown

within a few miles of the estate. Other wines include grapes from the Russian River Valley AVA. Dry Creek prides itself on both its classic California varietals such as chardonnay, cabernet, and merlot, and on occasionally hopping out of that box and producing something unusual, like a musqué, a chenin blanc, or a Sauternes-style dessert wine. Try as many as you can when you enter the ivy-covered tasting room, styled after a French château.

FERRARI-CARANO

One of the best large wineries in Dry Creek Valley, Ferrari-Carano (8761 Dry Creek Rd., 707/433-6700, www.ferrari-carano.com, daily 10 A.M.–5 P.M., $5–15) provides great standard and reserve wines in an upscale tasting room and winery facility. Upstairs you'll get to taste from Ferrari-Carano's extensive menu of large-production, moderately priced whites and reds. Downstairs, enjoy the elegant lounge area, which includes comfortable seating and a video describing the Ferrari-Carano winemaking process, from grape to glass. Look down into one of the major barrel storage areas, where Ferrari-Carano's wines age right before your eyes. And finally, open the glass doors and enter the reserve tasting room, where for an additional fee you can taste the best of Ferrari-Carano's vintages—smaller runs that are mostly bold assertive reds.

OPTIMA WINE CELLARS

Mike Duffy started making homemade wine with his dad when he was a kid. He got his degree in enology (wine-making) from the prestigious University of California, Davis, program, and it was only a matter of time before he opened his own winery. Today, Optima Wine Cellars (498 Moore Lane, 707/431-8222, www. optimawinery.com, by appointment) makes a small list of premium wines from single AVAs within the Russian River Valley wine area. These include cabernet sauvignon, zinfandel, and chardonnay. Optima also produces a luscious zinfandel port—perfect for dessert or at the end of a long day of wine tasting.

RAYMOND BURR

As well as portraying detective Perry Mason on the famous 1960s TV series, Raymond Burr had a second life as a wine connoisseur and orchid lover. Along with his partner, Robert Benevides, he combined these loves to create the Raymond Burr Vineyards (8339 West Dry Creek Rd., 888/900-0024, www.raymondburrvineyards.com, daily 11 A.M.–5 P.M.). Drive up a bumpy driveway past the greenhouse to reach the parking lot. Wine seekers enter the tiny (by Wine Country standards) tasting room to sip a few of the Burr label vintages. Frankly, most of the wines are tasty but not amazing compared to some other Sonoma products, but the staff and the winery's cats are fun and friendly, the views from the tasting room porch out over the valley are stunning, and the tiny bar and small-town experience are reminiscent of an earlier time in the Wine Country.

Flower lovers must come on specific days or make an appointment in advance to tour of the greenhouses. Burr and Benevides bred more than 1,000 new orchid varieties, and you can see many of them here on the estate.

WHITE OAK

At White Oak (7505 Hwy. 128, 707/433-8429, www.whiteoakwinery.com, daily 10 A.M.–5 P.M., $5), you'll find a wonderful combination of whimsy and wine. This Spanish mission–inspired winery complex is surrounded by green gardens dotted with fun sculptures. Beyond the gardens, estate vineyards grow grapes for Old Vine zinfandel and other fine wines. Go inside to taste some of the wines—the tasting list is small but prestigious. While white-wine drinkers enjoy the sauvignon blanc and chardonnay, big reds are the specialty of the house. Cabernet sauvignon

and zinfandel lovers flock to White Oak for the fabulous regular releases and occasional special library selections. Tours at White Oak provide a look at wine tasting, describing and illustrating the various components that make up a wine's fragrance.

Sights

If you're a serious student of wine, don't miss out on the **Sonoma County Wine Library** (Healdsburg Regional Library, 139 Piper St., 707/433-3772, www.sonomalibrary.org/wine, 10 A.M.–6 P.M. Tues. and Thurs.–Fri., 10 A.M.–8 P.M. Wed., 10 A.M.–4 P.M. Sat.). This public library extension contains a collection of over 5,000 books on wine and subscriptions to more than 80 wine periodicals, along with photos, prints, wine labels, and an online resource for wine lovers (http://winefiles.org). Among the 1,000 or so rare wine books, you'll find treatises on the history, business, and art of wine from as far back as 1512. The library is a perfect place for wine drinkers who want to take their habit or hobby to the next level.

Yes, you really can visit a museum dedicated exclusively to the display and description of hand fans. The tiny **Hand Fan Museum of Healdsburg** (Healdsburg Hotel, 219 Healdsburg Ave., 707/431-2500, www.handfanmuseum.com, 11 A.M.–4 P.M. Wed.–Sun.) seeks to tell the cultural histories of Europe, America, and Asia through the creation, decoration, and use of fans. It doesn't take long to view and enjoy both the permanent collection and seasonal exhibits at this fun little museum. You might be surprised to discover the level of artistry put into some of the fans here, be they paper or lace, antique or modern. You'll learn a little bit about how fans were and are used in various societies: The 17th–19th-century courting practices and sexual invitations in some European countries included intricate movements of a woman's fan, directed at the man of the hour.

Entertainment and Events

For casual-wine bar atmosphere, drop in to **The Wine Shop** (331 Healdsburg Ave., 707/433-0433, 10 A.M.–6 P.M. Mon.–Sat., noon–6 P.M. Sun.). The **Raven Players** (115 North St., 707/433-6335, www.ravenplayers.org, adults $15–26) ply their art in the boutique town of Healdsburg. This ambitious company stages five plays per year—primarily award-winning and established works; recent offerings have included Arthur Miller's *After the Fall* and Christopher Durang's *Beyond Therapy*. For the last show each season, the Ravens produce a big dramatic musical; recent productions have included *Evita* and *Gypsy*.

Sports and Recreation

Newcomers to bicycle touring in the area can choose among several reputable touring companies that will get them on two wheels and pointed in the right direction. **Wine Country Bikes** (61 Front St., 866/922-4537, www.winecountrybikes.com, $139 pp) is on the square in downtown Healdsburg. Its Classic Wine Tour starts at 10 A.M. and runs until 3:30 P.M. During your leisurely pedal through the Dry Creek region, you'll stop and taste wine, take walks in vineyards, and learn more about the history of wine in this small, proud AVA. A gourmet picnic lunch is included with the tour. For independent souls who prefer to carve their own routes, Wine Country Bikes also rents road bikes, tandem bikes, and hybrids ($35–125 per day) that you can also take on moderately difficult park trails where biking is permitted.

To become part of the larger bicycling culture in the area, consider participating in the annual **Harvest Century Bicycle Tour** (Healdsburg Chamber of Commerce, 707/433-6935, www.healdsburg.com, July, $75). This event requires some degree of physical fitness, as riders register to ride 23, 37, or 60 miles. The roads are of moderate difficulty, however; while you'll find some inclines, experienced cyclists won't be so tortured as to preclude enjoying the rest of the day with great food, wine, and the companionship of plenty of like-minded souls.

Healdsburg also provides access to water sports on the Russian River. **Russian River Adventures** (20 Healdsburg Ave., 707/433-5599, www.rradventures.info, adults $50, children $25) offers guided paddles down a secluded section of the river in stable, sturdy inflatable canoes. Dogs, children, and even infants are welcome. The trip usually lasts 4–5 hours, with little white water and lots of serene shaded pools.

Accommodations

Travelers planning to stay a night in Healdsburg will find that none of the boutique inns and hotels in town come cheap. If you take a room at the **Honor Mansion** (891 Grove St., 707/433-4277, www.honormansion.com, $300–7,000), you'll probably feel that you are getting your money's worth. Each of the 13 guest rooms and suites has been furnished and decorated with exquisite attention to even the smallest details. All guest rooms have private baths stocked with high-end toiletries, TVs, CD players, bathrobes, phones, air-conditioning, turn-down service, and more. Naturally, all guest rooms come with a full gourmet breakfast each morning. The Honor Mansion also has a lap pool, a tennis court, a croquet lawn, a boccie pit, and outdoor professional massage service.

On the central town plaza, the **Hotel Healdsburg** (25 Matheson St., 800/889-7188, www.hotelhealdsburg.com, $300–460) is a local icon. The 55-room boutique hotel offers the most upscale amenities, including Frette towels and linens, TVs with DVD players, soaking tubs and walk-in showers, and beautiful decor. Guest rooms have shining wooden floors and furniture, Tibetan throw rugs, and spotless white down comforters. All

WINE COUNTRY

guest rooms include free Wi-Fi and a gourmet breakfast, among other amenities, and guests can enjoy the outdoor pool, fitness center, and full-service day spa.

Food

In a sea of self-conscious chichi restaurants, the **Healdsburg Charcuterie** (335 Healdsburg Ave., 707/431-7213, http://charcuteriehealdsburg.com, 11:30 A.M.–3 P.M. and 5–9 P.M. Mon.–Thurs., 11:30 A.M.–3 P.M. and 5:30–9:30 P.M. Fri., noon–3:30 P.M. and 5:30–9:30 P.M. Sat., noon–3:30 P.M. and 5–9 P.M. Sun., $20) makes diners feel at home. With a cute but not annoying pig theme, local art on the walls, and a softly romantic atmosphere, the Charcuterie makes a great option for a romantic but not overwhelming dinner out. The house-cured pork tenderloin sandwich is the house specialty, but vegetarians certainly can find a tasty and well-prepared meal as well. The Charcuterie pours some lovely local vintages and offers wine flights.

The most famous restaurant in Healdsburg is probably **Dry Creek Kitchen** (317 Healdsburg Ave., 707/431-0330, www.charliepalmer.com, 5:30–9:30 P.M. Mon.–Thurs., noon–2:30 P.M. and 5:30–10 P.M. Fri.–Sat., noon–2:30 P.M. and 5:30–9:30 P.M. Sun., $33), a chic Charlie Palmer dining room that takes the concept of California cuisine to the next level. Expect to see foam, froth, jus, and coulis splattered across the menu, which can range from upscale but recognizable to totally bizarre. Dry Creek Kitchen serves brunch and lunch on the weekend, offering its own unique take on eggs benedict, sliders, and other standards. This is a great place to check out some Dry Creek AVA vintages.

For an upscale eco-friendly California restaurant without the green propaganda, head to fabulous ◖**Zin** (344 Center St., 707/473-0946, www.zinrestaurant.com, 11:30 A.M.–2 P.M. and 5:30–9 P.M. Mon.–Thurs., 11:30 A.M.–2 P.M. and 5:30–9:30 P.M. Fri., 5:30–9:30 P.M. Sat.,

5:30–9 P.M. Sun., $25), just off the square in downtown Healdsburg. The cavernous dining room takes advantage of its existing antique features for decor, the tables are made with recycled and repurposed materials, and the art on the walls comes from local artists and is for sale. But the real reason to eat lunch or dinner at Zin is undoubtedly the food. The chef creates a menu that fuses upscale Wine Country with Mexican and Southern cuisines, giving Zin a unique twist that sets it apart from a plethora of other upscale restaurants in the region. Most return diners recommend starting with the Mexican beer-battered green beans—fabulous french fries with a guilt-reducing green-vegetable interior. If you've overdosed on haute cuisine, check out the Blue Plate specials for dinner, offering something down-home at a reasonable price each night—think spaghetti with meatballs or chicken and dumplings. For dessert, the homemade jelly doughnuts bring home the best of Wine Country: The chef makes his own jelly from local zinfandel grapes each fall, and the doughnuts ooze with deliciousness you won't find anyplace else.

For an independent cup of coffee in Healdsburg, head across the town square to **Flying Goat Coffee** (324 Center St., 707/433-9081, www.flyinggoatcoffee.com, daily 7 A.M.–7 P.M.). This attractive West Coast coffeehouse serves above-average lattes, defaults to "no whip" on the mochas, and doesn't make them too sweet either. The relaxed feel and pleasant seating area make it easy to stop and stay awhile.

Oakville Grocery (124 Matheson St., 707/433-3200, www.oakvillegrocery.com, daily 8 A.M.–6 P.M.), like its cousin in the Napa Valley, sells high-end groceries and local gourmet products to well-heeled customers. It's a great place to pick up gifts for friends back home—they carry fine expensive local olive oils, vinegars, soaps, and bath products. You can also get the goods for a proper picnic, with a great selection of cheeses, fresh local breads, an upscale deli counter, a somewhat redundant wine selection, and a few fine nonalcoholic beverages.

A funkier alternative to the Oakville Grocery is the **Jimtown Store** (6706 Hwy. 128, 707/433-1212, www.jimtown.com, 7:30 A.M.–4 P.M. Mon.–Thurs., 7:30 A.M.–5 P.M. Fri.–Sun. May–Dec., 7:30 A.M.–3 P.M. Mon. and Thurs., 7:30 A.M.–5 P.M. Fri.–Sun. Jan.–Apr., $12), six miles out of town on a dusty country road. When owners Carrie Brown and her husband, the late John Werner, decided to leave New York City, they landed at this general store, in operation since 1895. The couple brought their gourmet sensibilities and turned the store into a quirky combination of old-fashioned American country store with house-made gourmet jams, jellies, and condiments; penny toys; housewares; and, best of all, hot lunches. The chalkboard menu presents a tasty assortment of smoked-brisket sandwiches, chili, buttermilk coleslaw, and chorizo and provolone grilled-cheese sandwiches. The benches and picnic tables outside are a great place to unwrap your sandwich, or you pick up one of their prepared box lunches to go.

Information and Services

Befitting such a desirable destination, the **Healdsburg Chamber of Commerce and Visitors Bureau** (217 Healdsburg Ave., 707/433-6935, www.healdsburg.com, 9 A.M.–5 P.M. Mon.–Fri., 9 A.M.–3 P.M. Sat., 10 A.M.–2 P.M. Sun.) is centrally located just off U.S. 101, just as you come into town on Healdsburg Avenue. The friendly staff are happy to load you up with maps, brochures, and helpful tips.

For a bit of local flavor, the *Healdsburg Tribune* is published every Thursday. If you need to mail a letter, the folks at the **post office** (160 Foss Creek Circle) will be happy to oblige. And for health issues, the **Healdsburg District Hospital** (1375 University Ave., 707/431-6300) has a 24-hour emergency room.

While cell-phone reception is reliable in town, don't expect it to be on Healdsburg's back roads. But unlike the rest of the Russian River Valley region, getting online in Healdsburg is fairly easy. Most hotels and cafés offer access for free or at a price, and the plaza has free Wi-Fi service set up by the city so you can open your laptop and start surfing in the sunshine.

Getting There and Around

Healdsburg is an easy destination, as it is 14 miles north of Santa Rosa on U.S. 101. To reach downtown Healdsburg from U.S. 101, take exit 503, for Central Healdsburg. Healdsburg can also be accessed from Calistoga: Drive north of Calistoga on Highway 128 for 17.4 miles, and at Jimtown, Highway 128 intersects Alexander Valley Road. Continue straight on Alexander Valley Road as Highway 128 turns right, heading north to Geyserville. In 3.3 miles, turn left onto Healdsburg Avenue, which runs to downtown Healdsburg.

GEYSERVILLE

At the tip of Wine Country, Geyserville is also at the edge of California's great northern redwood forest and has a small mountain-town feel. Fewer than 900 people call Geyserville home, and despite its name, which inspires images of healing waters, you won't find any big spas or rejuvenating fountains—at least not anymore. The town got its name for the Geysers, a series of hot springs and fumaroles (vents in the earth's crust) deep in the Mayacamas Mountains east of town. It became a tourist attraction at the turn of the 20th century, and Geyserville sprang up as a result. Now the Geysers is a complex of geothermal power plants, the largest in the world, but Geyserville retains its Old West charm. The downtown is tiny, with a few shops and restaurants and a number of historic buildings. In many ways, Geyserville feels like a snapshot of an earlier time.

WINE COUNTRY

Wineries

TRENTADUE

As you walk up to the magnificent Italianate tasting room at Trentadue (19170 Geyserville Ave., 707/433-3104, www.trentadue.com, daily 10 A.M.–5 P.M., $5), the first thing you'll notice is the gardens sweeping out toward the vineyards. Many of Trentadue's vintages are made from estate-grown grapes, and the gorgeous grounds surrounding the winery are used for weddings and events almost every weekend. Inside the high narrow tasting room, you'll find European-style decor, the usual gifts (including bottled water and nonalcoholic drinks), and a tasting bar that is sometimes too small for the crowd. The winery offers a wide variety of still wines and a couple of sparkling varieties, but the stars of the show are unquestionably the ports; Trentadue makes an array of different styles and flavors of the famed fortified dessert wines.

Sports and Recreation

At the north end of the valley, **Lake Sonoma** (3333 Skaggs Springs Rd., 707/431-5433, www.parks.sonoma.net) sprawls in a series of skinny fingers and is used for both recreation and more practical purposes. A public boat launch (707/433-2200) at Warm Springs Bridge lets you launch your own ski or fishing boat for a $3 fee. A marina (Stewarts Point Rd., www.lakesonoma.com, 707/433-2200) offers boat and slip rentals for guests who don't have their own. Bass anglers gather at the Warm Springs Creek and Dry Creek fingers of the lake, where trees shade the water and create a hospitable home for bass, perch, catfish, and sunfish.

Accommodations

In tiny Geyserville, the bed-and-breakfasts to visit are the ◖ **Hope-Merrill and Hope-Bosworth Houses** (21238 and 21253 Geyserville Ave., 800/825-4233, www.

beautiful Lake Sonoma

© ROY LUCK/FLICKR

hope-inns.com, $149–289). This Victorian charmer, which comprises two historic houses across the street from one another, harks back to classic bed-and-breakfasts on the East Coast. The owners come from the East, and they've brought their traditions and aesthetics with them to the Alexander Valley. If loud floral wallpaper covering every surface of your guest room causes nightmares and hallucinations, this might not be the inn for you, but true aficionados of the Victorian style will love the flowers, lace, frills, and gewgaws. Amenities include a pool and two hot tubs, plenty of common space in both houses, Friday-evening wine tastings out in the yard, and an enormous multicourse homemade breakfast each morning. At breakfast, the owners preside over the tables, offering touring advice to guests. Each guest room has its own private bath—most in the same room, and one or two just across the hall from your room. The most comfortable guest

rooms with the best mattresses tend to be the spendier rooms—if you're in a less expensive room, you may find yourself with less than plush pillows. But overall, the Hope Houses make for a great base from which to explore the Alexander, Dry Creek, and Russian River Valley wineries.

For a completely different, although equally Californian, experience, visit the **Isis Oasis** (20889 Geyserville Ave., 707/857-4747, www. isisoasis.org, $100–150). This retreat center and hostel is dedicated to the Egyptian goddess Isis; the grounds are littered with statues, bright Egyptian art, and paintings, and the interior is filled with funky furniture. There is a pool and hot tub, and errant peacocks patrol the lawns dotted with lounge chairs and picnic tables. Guest rooms are decorated in a homespun Egyptian earth goddess style. In the lodge there are 12 guest rooms with communal baths. For more privacy, opt for the retreat

WINE COUNTRY

Isis Oasis

house, which has two private guest rooms, each with their own bath. The owner lives on-site in an old farmhouse where she raises exotic cats and officiates goddess-related ceremonies. You won't find anything like Isis Oasis anywhere in Wine Country.

Food

There aren't that many places to eat in Geyserville, but that is no indication of the quality you'll find. Until recently, **Catelli's** (21047 Geyserville Ave., 707/857-3471, www.mycatellis.com, 11:30 A.M.–8 P.M. Tues.–Thurs., 11:30 A.M.–9 P.M. Fri., noon–9 P.M. Sat., noon–8 P.M. Sun., $15–32) was originally known as Taverna Santa. It has since been reclaimed by the next generation of Catelli's and rechristened under their name. It also happens that one of the Catellis is a celebrity chef who has appeared on TV's *Iron Chef* and *Oprah*. Steering the restaurant back to her family's roots but with an added dedication to healthy local food, Domenica Catelli and her brother Nick have created an earthy high-quality Italian eatery. Homey sides like fries get a touch of truffle oil, and meatball sliders are made with local organic beef. There are plenty of pasta dishes, and entrées are geared toward sophisticated comfort food.

Just a few doors down is another great Italian joint, **Diavola Restaurant** (21021 Geyserville Ave., 707/814-0111, www.diavolapizzeria.com, daily 11:30 A.M.–9 P.M., $14–25). Decorated in wood and chrome and centered around a wood-burning oven, this small restaurant is all about pizzas and its house-made *salumis* and sausages. The chef's true passion is the art of butchering and curing meat, learned during his seven-year apprenticeship in Italy. So in addition to pasta and meat dishes like lamb chops, you'll find traditional dishes accented with crispy pork belly or pork cheek and thin-crust pizzas topped with various sausages. Diavola has a well-stocked deli case if you are eager to take some cured meats home with you.

Information and Services

For information on where to go and what to do in Geyserville, stop at the visitors center in Healdsburg before trekking north. The small **Geyserville Chamber of Commerce** (707/857-3745, www.geyservillecc.com) does not have an active visitors center. Still, you can call or check out the website for more information. Cell phone reception and Internet access are not the best here, but there is a **post office** (116 School House Lane) off Geyserville Avenue in the center of town.

Getting There and Around

Geyserville is located eight miles north of Healdsburg at the junction of U.S. 101 and Highway 128. It is also 25 miles north of Calistoga via Highway 128.

NORTH COAST

The rugged North Coast of California is a spectacular place. Its wild beauty is in many places unspoiled and almost desolate. This is not the California coast of surfer movies, though hardy souls do ride the chilly Pacific waves as far north as Crescent City. The cliffs are forbidding, the beaches are rocky and windswept, and the surf thunders in with formidable authority.

From Bodega Bay, Highway 1 twists and turns north along hairpin curves that will take your breath away. The Sonoma and Mendocino coasts offer lovely beaches and forests, top-notch cuisine, and a friendly, uncrowded wine region. Along the way, tiny coastal towns—Jenner, Gualala, Mendocino, Fort Bragg—dot the hills and valleys, beckoning travelers with bed-and-breakfasts, organic farms, and relaxing respites from the road. Inland, Mendocino's hidden wine region offers the rural and relaxed pace missing from that other famous wine district. Anderson Valley and Hopland can quench your thirst, while nearby Clear Lake—California's largest natural freshwater lake—provides more than 100 miles of sunny shoreline to cool off. Where Highway 1 merges with U.S. 101 is the famous Lost Coast, accessed only via steep narrow roads and on foot along the scenic California Coastal Trail that runs 64 miles over mountains and across beaches.

For most travelers, the North Coast means redwood country, and U.S. 101 marks the gateway to those redwoods. South of the

© HEATHER C. LISTON

HIGHLIGHTS

◖ Whale-Watching: Bodega Bay offers the perfect coastal setting for spying Pacific gray whales during their migration to Alaska (page 282).

◖ Fort Ross State Historic Park: For a taste of historic California, explore this fortified outpost that served as a waypoint for 19th-century traders (page 287).

◖ Mendocino Coast Botanical Gardens: Stretching out to the sea, 47 acres of botanical gardens offer a vast variety of flowers and plants and the butterflies who love them (page 298).

◖ Clear Lake: The largest freshwater lake in the state is a gorgeous playground for boaters, anglers, hikers, and beachgoers (page 323).

◖ Avenue of the Giants: This aptly named scenic drive parallels U.S. 101 for 31 miles through Humboldt Redwoods State Park and the last remaining stands of virgin redwoods (page 339).

◖ Blue Ox Historic Park: The rambling buildings of this working lumber mill and historic park are filled with 19th-century tools used to customize historic homes. A school offers opportunities to learn about the lives and work of these craftspeople and even work a piece of your own (page 343).

◖ Redwood National and State Parks: Northern California's legendary redwoods stretch along the coast from Garberville to Crescent City, offering unlimited photo ops of redwood giants (page 352).

LOOK FOR ◖ TO FIND RECOMMENDED SIGHTS, ACTIVITIES, DINING, AND LODGING.

NORTH COAST

attractive little college town of Eureka, the famously immense coastal sequoias loom along the highway. A plethora of state and national parks lure travelers with numerous hiking trails, forested campgrounds, kitschy redwood tourist traps, and some of the tallest and oldest trees on the continent. Pitch a tent in Humboldt Redwoods State Park, cruise the Avenue of the Giants, and gaze in ancient wonder at the primordial Founders Grove. Crescent City marks the northern terminus of the North Coast, a coastal seaside town known for fishing, seafood, and for surviving a tsunami.

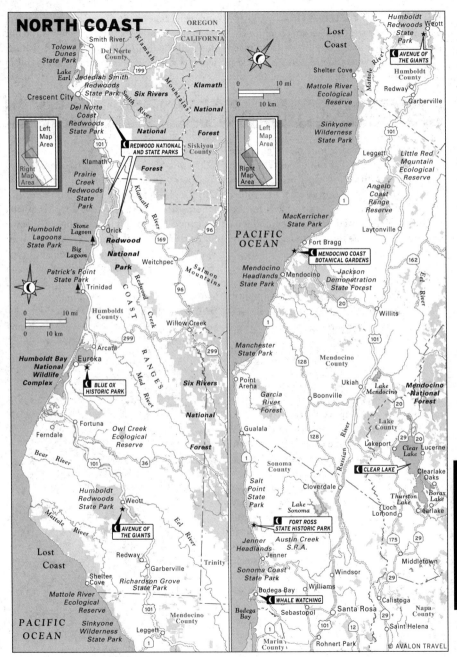

NORTH COAST

OREGON
CALIFORNIA

Lost Coast

Humboldt Redwoods State Park Weott

AVENUE OF THE GIANTS

Smith River

Tolowa Dunes State Park

Del Norte County

Klamath River

Klamath Mountains

Klamath National

Humboldt County

Shelter Cove

Mattole River Ecological Reserve

Mattole River

Redway

Garberville

Lake Earl

Jedediah Smith Redwoods State Park

Six Rivers

Redwood

Sinkyone Wilderness State Park

Crescent City

Del Norte Coast Redwoods State Park

National Forest

Siskiyou County

Leggett

Little Red Mountain Ecological Reserve

REDWOOD NATIONAL AND STATE PARKS

Angelo Coast Range Reserve

Klamath

Prairie Creek Redwoods State Park

Klamath River

MacKerricher State Park

Laytonville

Ed River

PACIFIC OCEAN

Fort Bragg

MENDOCINO COAST BOTANICAL GARDENS

Humboldt Lagoons State Park

Stone Lagoon

Orick

Redwood National Park

Big Lagoon

Patrick's Point State Park

Trinidad

Weitchpec

Salmon Mountains

Mendocino Headlands State Park

Mendocino

Jackson Demonstration State Forest

Willits

Redwood Creek

Willow Creek

Humboldt County

Arcata

Eureka

BLUE OX HISTORIC PARK

Fortuna

Ferndale

Bear River

Mad River

Six Rivers

National Forest

Manchester State Park

Mendocino County

Point Arena

Garcia River Forest

Ukiah

Boonville

Lake Mendocino

Mendocino National Forest

Lake County

Lakeport

Clear Lake

Lucerne

CLEAR LAKE

Clearlake Oaks

Owl Creek Ecological Reserve

Gualala

Sonoma County

Thurston Lake

Borax Lake

Clearlake

Humboldt Redwoods State Park

Weott

AVENUE OF THE GIANTS

Salt Point State Park

Lake Sonoma

Cloverdale

Loch Lomond

Redway

Garberville

Mattole River

Ed River

Trinity

FORT ROSS STATE HISTORIC PARK

Middletown

Lost Coast

Jenner Headlands

Austin Creek S.R.A.

Jenner

Windsor

Shelter Cove

Richardson Grove State Park

Sonoma Coast State Park

Williams

Calistoga

Napa County

Mattole River Ecological Reserve

Bodega Bay

WHALE WATCHING

Santa Rosa

PACIFIC OCEAN

Sinkyone Wilderness State Park

Leggett

Mendocino County

Bodega Bay

Sebastopol

Saint Helena

Marin County

Rohnert Park

© AVALON TRAVEL

Lost Coast

Klamath Mountains

Del Norte County

PACIFIC OCEAN

Left Map Area

Right Map Area

Left Map Area

Right Map Area

COAST RANGES

Humboldt Bay National Wildlife Complex

PLANNING YOUR TIME

The outdoors is the primary attraction in this region. Driving is the way to get from place to place, unless you're a hard-core backpacker. Make time to explore the redwoods in the parks and spend time on the rugged beaches (in warm waterproof clothes) as well. Hiking is the one don't-miss activity. Close seconds are fishing, whale-watching, and watching the fog roll in as you sit in a cozy café.

Sonoma Coast

One good way to begin your meander up the coast is to take U.S. 101 out of San Francisco as far as Petaluma, and then head west toward Highway 1, on this stretch also called the Shoreline Highway. As you travel toward the coast, you'll leave urban areas behind for a while, but you'll pass through some of the most pleasant villages in California.

BODEGA BAY

Bodega Bay is popular for its coastal views, whale watching, and seafood—but it's most famous as the filming locale of Alfred Hitchcock's *The Birds*.

◖ Whale-Watching

The best sight you could hope to see is a close-up view of Pacific gray whales migrating home to Alaska with their newborn calves. The whales head past January–May on their way from their summer home off Mexico. If you're lucky, you can see them from the shore. **Bodega Head,** a promontory just north of the bay, is a place to get close to the migration route. To get to this prime spot, travel north on Highway 1 about one mile past the visitors center and turn left onto Eastshore Road; make a right at the stop sign, and then drive three more miles to the parking lot. On weekends, volunteers from **Stewards of the Coast and Redwoods** (707/869-9177, ext. 1., www.stewardsofthe-coastandredwoods.org) are available to answer questions. Contact them for organized whale-watching tours or to learn more about their various educational programs.

Doran Regional Park

When you arrive in Bodega Bay, you'll see a sign pointing left for Doran Regional Park (201 Doran Beach Rd., 707/875-3540, www.sonoma-county.org, day use $6 per vehicle, camping $26–32). It is less than one mile down the road and worth the trip. You can even swim at Doran Beach; although it's cold, it's protected from the open ocean waves, so it's much safer than most of the beaches along the coast.

Sonoma Coast State Park

Seventeen miles of coast are within Sonoma Coast State Park (707/875-3483, www.parks.

Spot whales off Bodega Bay.

© HEATHER C. LISTON

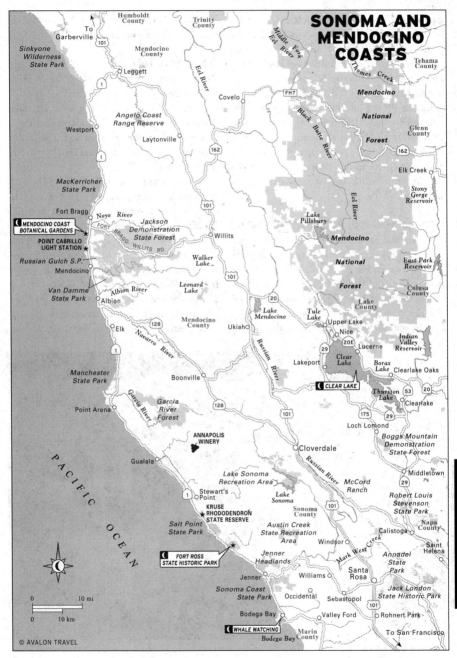

SONOMA AND MENDOCINO COASTS

Humboldt County

To Garberville

Sinkyone Wilderness State Park

Trinity County

Mendocino County

Leggett

Middle Fork Eel River

Thomes Creek

Tehama County

Mendocino

Covelo

FH7

National

Eel River

Angelo Coast Range Reserve

Westport

Laytonville

162

Black Butte River

Forest

Glenn County

162

Elk Creek

MacKerricher State Park

Fort Bragg

Noyo River

Jackson Demonstration State Forest

Willits

Eel River

Lake Pillsbury

Stony Gorge Reservoir

🌙 MENDOCINO COAST BOTANICAL GARDENS

POINT CABRILLO LIGHT STATION ★

Russian Gulch S.P.

Mendocino

FORT BRAGG WILLITS RD

Mendocino

National

East Park Reservoir

Van Damme State Park

Albion River

Albion

Leonard Lake

Walker Lake

101

Forest

Colusa County

Elk

128

Navarro River

Mendocino County

Ukiah

20

Lake Mendocino

Tule Lake

Russian River

Upper Lake

Nice

Lake County

20E

Lucerne

Lakeport

Clear Lake

29

Indian Valley Reservoir

Manchester State Park

Boonville

🌙 CLEAR LAKE

Borax Lake

Clearlake Oaks

Thurston Lake

53

20

Point Arena

Garcia River

Garcia River Forest

128

101

175

Clearlake

Loch Lomond

29

ANNAPOLIS WINERY

Cloverdale

Boggs Mountain Demonstration State Forest

PACIFIC OCEAN

Gualala

Lake Sonoma Recreation Area

Russian River

McCord Ranch

Middletown

29

Stewart's Point

KRUSE RHODODENDRON STATE RESERVE ★

Lake Sonoma

Sonoma County

101

Robert Louis Stevenson State Park

Napa County

Calistoga

Salt Point State Park

Austin Creek State Recreation Area

Windsor

Annadel State Park

Saint Helena

🌙 FORT ROSS STATE HISTORIC PARK ★

Jenner Headlands

Williams

Mark West Creek

Santa Rosa

Jack London State Historic Park

Jenner

Sonoma Coast State Park

Occidental

Sebastopol

101

Bodega Bay

Valley Ford

Rohnert Park

🌙 WHALE WATCHING

Bodega Bay

Marin County

To San Francisco

0   10 mi

0   10 km

© AVALON TRAVEL

NORTH COAST

ca.gov, day use $8 per vehicle). The park's boundaries extend from Bodega Head at the south up to the Vista Trailhead, four miles north of Jenner. As you drive up Highway 1, you'll see signs for various beaches. Although they're lovely places to walk, fish, and maybe sunbathe on the odd hot day, it is not advisable to swim here. If you go down to the water, bring your binoculars and your camera. The cliffs, crags, inlets, whitecaps, mini islands, and rock outcroppings are fascinating in any weather, and their looks change with the shifting tides and fog.

Bodega Seafood, Art, & Wine Festival

This annual festival (707/824-8717, www. winecountryfestivals.com, $12–15) takes place the last weekend in August, combining all the best elements of the Bodega lifestyle with includes live music in addition to tastings, special dinners, and much more. The proceeds help benefit two worthy organizations: the Bodega

Volunteer Fire Department and Stewards of the Coast and Redwoods.

Accommodations

Bodega Bay Lodge (103 Hwy. 1, 707/875-4212 or 888/875-3525, www.bodegabaylodge. com, $215–450) is one of the more luxurious places to stay in the area. It is a large resort with long rows of semidetached cabins. The facility also has a spa, a pool, a fitness center, two fine restaurants, and a library.

Sonoma Coast State Park (707/875-3483, www.parks.ca.gov, day use $8 per vehicle) encompasses several campgrounds along its 17-mile expanse. Some of these have been casualties (let's hope temporarily) of the ongoing state budget crisis, but as of this writing, you can still get a lovely, sandy spot in the trees in **Bodega Dunes Campground** (2585 Hwy. 1, $35), complete with hot showers and flush toilets. To get up-to-date information on closings or reopenings related to Sonoma Coast State

© HEATHER C. LISTON

Bodega Bay Lodge

Park, call the district office (707/865-2391), or stop in at the **Salmon Creek Ranger Station** a little farther north.

Food

《 Gourmet au Bay (913 Hwy. 1, 707/875-9875, www.gourmetaubay.com, 11 A.M.–7 P.M. Sun.–Thurs., 11 A.M.–8 P.M. Fri.–Sat.) is a shop and tasting bar in the coastal town of Bodega Bay. The good news is that you get to taste wines from a variety of different vintners—some are major players in the Napa wine scene, and some are from wineries so small they don't have tasting rooms of their own. You might even get to taste the odd French or Australian wine when you "wine surf," tasting three wines poured and laid out on a miniature surfboard for you to carry out to the deck to admire the view. Inside, you can sip as you peruse the gift shop, which includes some local artisanal foods plus plenty of handmade ceramics and pottery and an array of toys for wine lovers.

Bodega Bay Lodge's **Duck Club Restaurant** (103 Hwy. 1, 707/875-3525, www.bodegabay-lodge.com, breakfast daily 7:30–11 A.M., dinner daily 6–9 P.M., $18–36) offers a warm and elegant dining experience featuring hearty American entrées like steak, chicken, and halibut with seasonal vegetables. There's a fireside lounge overlooking the bay, and even some outdoor seating for warmer days.

One of the best restaurants in the area is **Terrapin Creek** (1580 Eastshore Dr., 707/875-2700, www.terrapincreekcafe.com, 4:30–9 P.M. Thurs.–Sun., $22–29), where they make creative use of the abundance of fresh seafood available.

Information and Services

The **Sonoma Coast Visitors Center** (850 Hwy. 1, 9 A.M.–5 P.M. Mon.–Sat., 10 A.M.–5 P.M. Sun.) in Bodega Bay may look small, but it's chock-full of exactly what you came for: maps, brochures, lists, suggestions, trail guides, events schedules, and even live advice from a local expert.

Getting There and Around

Bodega Bay is located on Highway 1 north of Point Reyes National Seashore and west of Petaluma. It's a beautiful drive north, hugging the coast, but the cliffs and the road's twists and turns mean taking it slow. A faster way to get here is to take U.S. 101 to Petaluma, take the exit for East Washington Street, and follow Bodega Avenue to Valley Ford Road, cutting across to the coast. You'll hit Bodega Bay just about two miles after you pass through Valley Ford. The latter route takes about 1.5 hours, since some of the route is slow and winding.

VALLEY FORD

This is one of those places where the word *town* feels like an overstatement. Valley Ford may be, as one local says, "just a little dairy community," but it has some fairly sophisticated food. In 2010 the **Sonoma Coast Fish Bank** (14435 Hwy. 1, 707/876-3474, www.sonomacoastfishbank.com, daily 11:30 A.M.–6 P.M.) opened its doors in the historic Dairyman's Bank building, built in 1893. It sells fresh sustainable fish and seafood; when possible, offerings are labeled with the name of the fishing vessel, the method of catch, and the area in which it was caught. The Fish Bank also sells local cheeses, charcuterie, and produce and provides picnic tables outside.

Under the same ownership is the **Valley Ford Hotel** (14415 Hwy. 1, 707/876-1983, www.vfordhotel.com, $115) and **Rocker Oysterfeller's Kitchen + Saloon** (14415 Hwy. 1, 707/876-1983, www.rockeroysterfellers.com, 4:30–8:30 P.M. Mon.–Fri., 11:30 A.M.–8:30 P.M. Sat., 10 A.M.–2 P.M. Sun., $14–26). The six guest rooms in the historic 1864 Valley Ford Hotel building include old-fashioned touches like handmade soap. In the restaurant, the creative menu brings a New Orleans flavor to locally raised and harvested Sonoma County bounty.

The **Valley Ford Market** (14400 Hwy. 1, Valley Ford, 707/876-3245, daily 7:30 A.M.–8 P.M.) is a classic old grocery store

Sonoma Coast Fish Bank in Valley Ford

© HEATHER C. LISTON

carrying pies, cakes, homemade beef jerky (ask for a free sample), seeds, ice, lottery tickets, books, and greeting cards. The butcher case carries Petaluma's original Bateman meats, and organic Coast Roast Coffee is available ground or as beans. This place is always crowded with local ranchers, who trust it to have pretty much everything they need.

JENNER

Jenner is on Highway 1 at the Russian River. It's a beautiful spot for a quiet honeymoon or a paddle in a kayak. **Goat Rock State Park** (Goat Rock Rd., 707/875-3483, www.parks.ca.gov, day use $8) is at the mouth of the Russian River. A colony of Harbor Seals breed and frolic here, and you may also see gray whales, sea otters, elephant seals, and a variety of sealife. Pets are not allowed, and swimming is prohibited.

Accommodations and Food

Both the food and the views are memorable at ◖ **River's End** (11048 Hwy. 1, 707/865-2484, www.ilovesunsets.com, noon–3:30 P.M. and 5–8:30 P.M. Sun.–Mon. and Thurs. winter, noon–3:30 P.M. and 5–8:30 P.M. Sun.–Thurs., noon–3:30 P.M. and 5–9 P.M. Fri.–Sat. summer, $25–45). The restaurant is perched above the spot where the Russian River flows into the Pacific, and it's a beautiful sight to behold over, say, oysters or filet mignon. Prices are high, but if you get a window table at sunset, you may forget to think about it.

The **Jenner Inn Café & Wine Bar** (10400 Hwy. 1, 707/865-2377, www.jennerinn.com, 5:30–9:30 P.M. Fri.–Sat., 10 A.M.–8 P.M. Sun., $14–28) serves local and sustainable food in a lovely dining room with coastal views.

The **Jenner Inn and Cottages** (10400 Hwy. 1, 707/865-2377 or 800/732-2377, www.jennerinn.com, $118–348) has a variety of quiet, beautifully furnished guest rooms mere steps from the river. Some guest rooms have hot tubs and private decks, and breakfast is included.

© HEATHER C. LISTON

patio at the Jenner Inn Café & Wine Bar

A few miles north of Jenner proper is the large and luxurious **Timber Cove Inn** (21780 N. Hwy. 1, 707/847-3231 or 800/987-8319, www.timbercoveinn.com, $199–320), with a capacious bar and lounge, an oceanfront patio, guest rooms with spa tubs and fireplaces, and hiking trails nearby.

Information and Services

The small but friendly **Jenner Visitors Center** (10439 Hwy. 1, 707/865-9757, www.steward-softhecoastandredwoods.org, 11 A.M.–3 P.M. Sat.–Sun.) is located across the street from the Jenner Inn. The visitors center is staffed by volunteers, so hours can be unpredictable; call ahead to confirm.

Getting There and Around

Jenner is located on Highway 1, right along the ocean. There is no public transportation to get here, but it is a pretty drive from just about anywhere. The fastest route from San Francisco (about 1.75 hours) is to drive up U.S. 101, make a left onto Washington Street in Petaluma, and continue north on Highway 1.

NORTH OF JENNER

As you hug the shore north of Jenner, you'll soon pass through Fort Ross State Historic Park, Salt Point State Park, and Kruse Rhododendron State Reserve.

〔 Fort Ross State Historic Park

There is no historic early American figure named Ross who settled here; believe it or not, "Ross" is short for "Russian," and this park commemorates the history of Russian settlement on the North Coast. A quick rundown of the story: In the 19th century Russians came to the wilds of Alaska and worked with native Alaskans to develop a robust fur trade, killing seals, otters, sea lions, and land mammals for their pelts. The enterprise required sea travel as the hunters chased the animals

NORTH COAST

© MICHAEL VOROBIEV/123RF.COM

Fort Ross State Historic Park

NORTH COAST

as far as California. Eventually, a group of fur hunters and traders came ashore on what is now the Sonoma coast and developed a fortified outpost that became known as Fort Ross (19005 Hwy. 1, Jenner, 707/847-3286, www.parks.ca.gov, Sat.–Sun. and holidays, parking $8). The area gradually became not only a thriving Russian American settlement but also a center for agriculture and shipbuilding and the site of California's first windmills. Learn more at the park's large visitors center, which provides a continuous film and a roomful of exhibits.

You can also walk into the reconstructed fort buildings and see how the settlers lived. (U.S. 101 was originally built through the middle of the fort area, but it was moved to make way for the historic park.) The only original building still standing is the captain's quarters—a large, luxurious house for that time and place. The other buildings, including the large bunkhouse, the chapel, and the two cannon-filled blockhouses, were rebuilt using much of the original

lumber used by the Russians. Be aware that a serious visit to the whole fort and the beach beyond is a level but long walk; wear comfortable shoes and consider bringing a bottle of water.

Salt Point State Park

Stretching for miles along the Sonoma coastline, Salt Point State Park (25050 Hwy. 1, Jenner, 707/847-3221, www.parks.ca.gov, visitors center 10 A.M.–3 P.M. Sat.–Sun., day use $8) provides easy access from U.S. 101 to more than a dozen sandy state beaches. You don't have to visit the visitors center to enjoy this park and its many beaches—just follow the signs along the highway to the turnoffs and parking lots. If you're looking to scuba dive or free dive, head for **Gerstle Cove,** accessible from the visitors center just south of Salt Point proper. The cove was designated one of California's first underwater parks, and divers who can deal with the chilly water have a wonderful time exploring the diverse undersea wildlife.

Kruse Rhododendron State Reserve

For a genteel experience, head east off Highway 1 to the Kruse Rhododendron State Reserve (707/847-3221, www.parks.ca.gov), where you can meander along the China Gulf Trail in the spring, admiring the profusion of pink rhododendron flowers blooming beneath the second-growth redwood forest. If you prefer a picnic, you'll find tables at many of the beaches—just be aware that the North Coast can be quite windy in the summer.

Stewart's Point

Stewart's Point is home to a post office, a small store, and a restaurant—and that's it. **Stewart's Point Store** (32000 S. Hwy. 1, 707/785-2406, www.stewartspoint.net, daily 6 A.M.–8 P.M., hours vary by season) sells groceries, wine, collectible dishes, hand-knitted hats, and Hostess Zingers. They've also got a deli and a bakery on-site. Upstairs, locally grown dinners are served in a historic dancehall (6:15 P.M. Fri.–Sat., $10–32).

Annapolis Winery

Annapolis Winery (26055 Soda Springs Rd., Annapolis, 707/886-5460, www.annapoliswinery.com, daily noon–5 P.M., tasting free) is a

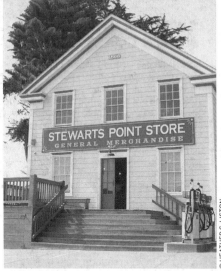

Stewart's Point Store

© HEATHER C. LISTON

small family-owned winery seven miles east of Sea Ranch. You'll find a pleasant coastal climate and a small list of classic California wines. You can usually taste pinot, cabernet, zinfandel, and port, depending on what they've made this year and what's in stock when you arrive.

Mendocino Coast

The Mendocino coast is a popular retreat for those who've been introduced to its specific charms. On weekends, Bay Area residents flock north to their favorite hideaways to enjoy windswept beaches, secret coves, and luscious cuisine. This area is ideal for deep-sea anglers, wine aficionados, and fans of luxury spas. Art is especially prominent in the culture; from the 1960s onward, aspiring artists have found supportive communities, sales opportunities, and homes in Mendocino County, and a number of small galleries display local artworks.

Be aware that the most popular inns fill up fast many weekends year-round. Fall–winter can be high season, with the Crab Festival, the Mushroom Festival, and the various harvest and after-harvest wine celebrations. If you want to stay someplace specific on the Mendocino coast, book your room at least a month in advance for weekday stays and six months or more in advance for major festival weekends.

GUALALA

With a population of 585, Gualala ("wa-LA-la") feels like a metropolis along the Highway 1 corridor in this region. While it's not the most

NORTH COAST

SWEATPANTS, PARKAS, AND NORTH COAST BEACHES

The Hollywood view of California beaches is all about long stretches of sugary-white sand drenched in warm sunshine, populated by beautiful blonds in teeny bikinis and studly surfers riding the photogenic waves. Nothing could be farther from the reality of the Northern California coast. Make no mistake—you'll find gorgeous beaches, but it's a different kind of beauty. Craggy cliffs tower over narrow rocky sand spits teeming with tide pools and backing into ever-changing sea caves. Wide swaths of beach are covered with driftwood, semiprecious minerals, polished sea glass, and ancient fossils. Nonetheless, hardy beachgoers bring their folding chairs, umbrellas, coolers, wetsuits, and surfboards to these beaches to enjoy a day on the sand and surf. Here are some tips to help you prepare for your North Coast beach trip:

· **Dress in layers:** North Coast beach temperatures can hover in the 50s even in the middle of summer. Wear a sweatshirt and warm pants over shorts and a T-shirt, and wear all that over your swimsuit.

· **Prepare for dampness:** Fog and drizzle are ubiquitous on the coast, even when it's sunny and hot only a few miles inland. Bring a wool or fleece cap in addition to your optimistic sunhat. And toss a warm synthetic jacket in your pack (not a down jacket, as down doesn't keep you warm when it's wet).

· **Bring appropriate footwear:** Most North Coast beaches are not barefoot-friendly. Exploration of rocky beaches and tide pools demands either specialized water shoes or good broken-in hiking boots. Jellyfish sometimes wash ashore on California's northern beaches, making bare feet or even beach sandals a painful proposition. And on beaches where fires are allowed, some people just cover over an abandoned fire with a little sand, which could give a hot foot to the next beachcomber to walk by. Even if you choose to go barefoot on the sand, carry a pair of closed-toed shoes with you, just in case the going gets tough farther down the beach.

· **The water is cold:** Going swimming or surfing? Wear a wetsuit and flippers if you don't want to experience hypothermia and possibly even the hospitality of the a Coast Guard rescue team.

· **Learn about fire restrictions:** Fires are illegal on many California beaches. Check restrictions for the beach you are visiting before lighting a driftwood bonfire to keep warm.

· **Wear sunscreen:** Even if a layer of fog covers the sun, you are still at risk of sunburn; locals call it a "cloud tan."

· **Prepare your kids:** Bring plenty of beach toys and talk up tide pool walks, but don't promise the little ones a swim in the ocean. The reality is that it may be too cold, too rough, or otherwise unsafe to swim.

---

charming coastal town, it does have some of the services other places may lack.

Since 1961, the **Art in the Redwoods Festival** (46501 Gualala Rd., 707/884-1138, www.gualalaarts.org, adults $6, under age 18 free) and its parent organization, Gualala Arts, have been going strong. This major event takes place over the course of a long weekend in mid-August and is run by the same people who bring you the Whale and Jazz Festival in April. Now featuring gallery exhibitions, special dinners, a champagne preview, bell ringers, a quilt raffle, and awards for the artists, this is a great reason to get the whole family to Sonoma for some renewal and inspiration.

Sports and Recreation

Two nearby parks provide good camping options. One is **Gualala River Redwood Park** (46001 Gualala Rd., 707/884-3533, www.gualalapark.com, May–Oct., day use $5 pp, camping $38–45 for 2 people); the other is

Gualala Point Regional Park (46001 Gualala Rd., 707/785-2377 or 707/884-3533, www.sonoma-county.org, day use $6 per vehicle, camping $28–32), one mile south of the town of Gualala, technically in Sonoma County. Both places offer redwoods, the ocean, and the river.

Accommodations and Food

For the budget-conscious, a good option is **The Surf Motel** (39170 Hwy. 1, 707/884-3571 or 888/451-7873, www.surfinngualala.com, $99–209). Only a few of the more expensive guest rooms have ocean views, but a full hot breakfast and wireless Internet access are included for all guests.

The **Breakers Inn** (39300 Hwy. 1, 707/884-3200, www.breakersinn.com, $175–225) resembles a series of large seaside cottages, each with flower boxes in the windows and a private deck overlooking the ocean.

The **Whale Watch Inn** (35100 Hwy. 1, 800/942-5342, www.whalewatchinn.com, $190–280) specializes in romance. Each of its 18 individually decorated, luxuriously appointed guest rooms has an ocean view, and most have whirlpool tubs.

If you're hungry when you hit town, try **Bones Roadhouse** (39080 Hwy. 1, 707/884-1188, www.bonesroadhouse.com, daily 7:30 A.M.–10 P.M., $15–25) for barbecue and pulled pork in giant portions, served in a casual atmosphere with ocean views. For a more upscale experience, the **Top o' the Cliff** (39140 S. Hwy. 1, 707/884-1539, noon–4 P.M. and 5:30–8 P.M. Thurs.–Sun., $8–23) has views as well as good food.

Getting There and Around

Gualala is located 115 miles north of San Francisco on Highway 1, and 60 miles south of Fort Bragg. The **Mendocino Transit Authority** (707/462-1422 or 800/696-4682, www.4mta.org) has a bus line that connects Gualala to Fort Bragg.

POINT ARENA
Point Arena Lighthouse

Although its magnificent Fresnel lens no longer turns through the night, the Point Arena Lighthouse (45500 Lighthouse Rd., 707/882-2777 or 877/725-4448, www.pointarenalighthouse.com, daily 10 A.M.–4:30 P.M. summer, daily 10 A.M.–3:30 P.M. winter, adults $13.50, children $1) remains a Coast Guard light and fog station. But what makes this beacon special is its history. When the 1906 earthquake hit San Francisco, it jolted the land all the way up the coast, severely damaging the Point Arena Lighthouse. When the structure was rebuilt two years later, engineers devised the aboveground foundation that gives the lighthouse both its distinctive shape and additional structural stability.

Visitors can enjoy the Lighthouse's extensive interpretive museum, which is housed in the fog station beyond the gift shop. Docent-led tours up to the top of the lighthouse are well worth the trip, both for the views of the lighthouse from the top and for the fascinating story of its destruction and rebirth through the 1906 earthquake as told by the knowledgeable staff. Tour groups also have the opportunity to climb right up to the Fresnel lens, taking a rare close look at an astonishing invention that reflected pre-electric light far enough out to sea to protect passing ships.

Arena Theater

If you prefer your entertainment on a screen but still like a little atmosphere, take in a show at the Arena Theater (210 Main St., 707/882-3456, www.arenatheater.org). This onetime vaudeville theater was also a movie palace of the old school when it opened in 1928. In the 1990s, the old theater got a restorative facelift that returned it to its art deco glory. Today, you can see all kinds of films at the Arena, from recent box office toppers to new documentaries and unusual independent films. If a film

© HEATHER C. LISTON

Point Arena Lighthouse

isn't playing, you might find a live musical or theatrical show.

Entertainment and Events

The annual **Whale and Jazz Festival** (707/884-1138, www.gualalaarts.org/whale-jazz) takes place all around Mendocino Country in April each year. Some of the nation's finest jazz performers play in a variety of venues, while the whales put on their own show out in the Pacific. Point Arena Lighthouse offers whale-watching from the shore each day, and the wineries and restaurants of the region provide refreshment and relaxation every evening of the festival weekend.

Accommodations

The attractively plainspoken **Coast Guard House** (695 Arena Cove, 707/882-2442 or 800/524-9320, www.coastguardhouse.com, $165–265) has quite a history. It was originally built in 1901 as housing for the U.S.

Life-Saving Service, which later became part of the Coast Guard. After it was decommissioned in 1957, it spent some time as a hippie commune and then as the base for Columbia University's underwater seismic research center. Now it's an appealing bed-and-breakfast, with four guest rooms in the main building and two cottages. Some guest rooms have ocean views. Check online for last-minute specials—you may get a deal if they're not booked up.

The **Lighthouse Pointe Resort** (22900 S. Hwy. 1, 707/882-2440 or 800/357-6467, www.vacapedia.com, $150) comprises mostly timeshares, but you can sometimes rent a little cabin here, even at the last minute, that sleeps up to four people and includes a kitchen, living room, and bedroom. No pets are allowed, and there's no smoking, but there is a swimming pool and playground, plus easy access to the beach.

Food

Arena Market & Café (185 Main St.,

© HEATHER C. LISTON

cottages at the Lighthouse Pointe Resort

707/882-3663, www.arenaorganics.org, 7:30 A.M.–7 P.M. Mon.–Sat., 8:30 A.M.–6 P.M. Sun.) is a co-op committed to a philosophy of local, sustainable, and organic food, and they do their best to compensate farmers fairly and keep money in the community. This is a medium-size grocery store, so you can stock up on staples or sit at one of the tables in the front of the store and enjoy a bowl of homemade soup.

The **Uneda Eat Café** (206 Main St., 707/882-3800, www.pangaeacatering.com, 5–9 P.M. Wed.–Fri., $8–20) preserves the sign of the former owner, who was an Italian butcher: The storefront still says "Uneda Meat Market." Now a dine-in, take-out, and catering operation run by Jill and Rob Hunter, who previously owned the popular Pangaea Restaurant, the menu is decidedly locavore.

Blue on the outside, pink on the inside, **Franny's Cup and Saucer** (213 Main St., 707/882-2500, www.frannyscupandsaucer. com, 8 A.M.–4 P.M. Wed.–Sat.) is whimsical and welcoming. The owners, Franny and her mother, Barbara, do all their own baking and they even make truffle and other candies from scratch. It's takeout only, so stop in and pick up a picnic before you go to the lighthouse or one of the parks.

Slightly north of town is **Rollerville Café** (22900 S. Hwy. 1, 707/882-2077, www.roller-villecafe.com, 8 A.M.–2 P.M. Sun.–Thurs., 8 A.M.–7:30 P.M. Fri.–Sat., lunch $8–10, dinner $19–28). Dinner may seem a little pricey, but lunch is available all day; breakfast is 8–11 A.M. This is a small homey place catering to guests at the adjacent timeshare resort as well as locals and travelers.

Information and Services

The **Coast Community Library** (225 Main St., 707/882-3114, www.coastcommunitylibrary. org, hours vary Mon.–Thurs. and Sat.) is a real hub of activity thanks to its central location, the impressive 1928 Point Arena Mercantile Company building, and its free Internet access.

NORTH COAST

Getting There and Around

Point Arena is located 10 miles north of Gualala on Highway 1, and about 120 miles north of San Francisco. The **Mendocino Transit Authority** (800/696-4682, www.4mta.org) runs the route 75 bus to connect Point Arena south to Gualala and north to Fort Bragg. The bus usually runs once a day, although schedules are subject to change; contact the transit authority for details.

ELK

The town of Elk used to be called Greenwood, after the family of Caleb Greenwood, who settled here in about 1850. Details of the story vary, but it is widely believed that Caleb was part of a mission to rescue survivors of the Donner Party after their rough winter near Truckee.

Greenwood State Beach

Greenwood State Beach (Hwy. 1, 707/937-5804, www.parks.ca.gov, visitors center 11 A.M.–1 P.M. Sat.–Sun. Memorial Day–Labor Day) is an intriguing place to visit. From the mid-19th century until the 1920s, this stretch of shore was a stop for large ships carrying timber to points of sale in San Francisco and sometimes even China. The visitors center displays photographs and exhibits about Elk's past in the lumber business. It also casts light on the Native American heritage of the area and the natural resources that are still abundant.

A short hike demonstrates what makes this area so special. From the parking lot, follow the trail down toward the ocean. You'll soon come to a fork; to the right is a picnic area. Follow the left fork to another picnic site and then, soon afterward, the beach. Turn left and walk about 0.25 mile to reach Greenwood Creek. Shortly past it is a cliff, at which point you have to turn around and walk back up the hill. Even in the short amount of time it takes to do this walk,

NORTH COAST

© HEATHER C. LISTON

Greenwood State Beach

you'll experience lush woods, sandy cliffs, and dramatic ocean overlooks. In winter, the walk can be dark and blustery and even more intriguing, although it's a pleasure in any season.

Greenwood State Beach is alongside the town of Elk, 10–15 miles north of Point Arena and about 17 miles south of Mendocino.

Accommodations and Food

The **❰ Elk Cove Inn** (6300 S. Hwy. 1, 800/275-2967, www.elkcoveinn.com, $155–305) is the perfect spot for a secluded getaway. Choose antique-furnished guest rooms in the historic main building or plush spa cabins overlooking the lawn. Best of all, the tiny restaurant serves an innovative dinner menu and a sumptuous breakfast. To work off all that rich cuisine, take a hike down to Elk Cove, the secluded beach beside the inn.

Elk is also home to the luxurious **Griffin House Inn** (5910 S. Hwy. 1, 707/877-3422, www.griffinn.com, $138–325). There are no TVs or phones in these lovely cottages with oceanfront decks. A full breakfast is delivered to your guest room, but there's also a lively dining room. **Bridget Dolan's Pub** (5910 S. Hwy. 1, 707/877-1820, www.griffinn.com/dolans.htm, 4:30–9 P.M. Thurs.–Tues., $12–20) is a warm, neighborly place to get a good meal at a reasonable price.

For basic American food, **Queenie's Roadhouse Café** (6061 Hwy. 1, 8 A.M.–3 P.M. Thurs.–Sun.) is the place to go. The food is hot, the atmosphere is friendly, and the location is perfect—in the center of town and across the street from the ocean.

Not only is the **Beacon Light by the Sea** (7401 S. Hwy. 1, south of Elk, 707/877-3311, 5–11 P.M. Fri.–Sat.) the best bar in the area, its colorful owner, R. D. Beacon, claims it's the only place you can get hard liquor for 14 miles in any direction. Beacon, who was born in Elk, has run the Beacon Light since 1971. With 54 different brands of vodka, 20 whiskeys, and 15

tequilas on offer, there's something for every sort of drinker. On a clear day, the views stretch all the way to the Point Arena Lighthouse.

Getting There and Around

Elk is on Highway 1 just south of the junction with Highway 128, about 23 miles south of Fort Bragg. The nearest airport is the **Charles M. Schultz-Sonoma County Airport** (STS, 2290 Airport Blvd., Santa Rosa, 707/565-7243, www.sonomacountyairport.org) in Santa Rosa. From Santa Rosa, the two-hour drive to Elk is along U.S. 101 north for 27 miles to Highway 128 north before reaching Highway 1 in another 56 miles.

ALBION AND LITTLE RIVER

Tiny Albion is along Highway 1 almost 30 miles north of Point Arena and about eight miles south of Mendocino. Little River is about five miles farther north, also on Highway 1. There is a **post office** (7748 Hwy. 1, Albion, 707/937-5547, www.usps.com, 8:15 A.M.–1 P.M. and 2–4:30 P.M. Mon.–Fri.), a state park, and several plush places to stay.

Van Damme State Park

At Van Damme State Park (Hwy. 1, 3 miles south of Mendocino, 707/937-5804, www.parks.ca.gov, free), take a walk to the park's centerpiece, the **Pygmy Forest,** on the wheelchair-accessible loop trail (0.25 mile, easy). Here you'll see a true biological rarity: mature yet tiny cypress and pine trees perpetually stunted by a combination of always-wet ground and poor soil-nutrient conditions. You can get to the Pygmy Forest from the **Fern Canyon Trail** (6 miles one-way, difficult), or drive Airport Road to the trail parking lot (opposite the county airport) directly to the loop.

Kayak Mendocino (707/937-0700, www.kayakmendocino.com, board surfing $30 per hour) launches four Sea Cave Nature Tours (9 A.M., 11:30 A.M., 2 P.M., and sunset daily, $50 pp) from Van Damme State Park. No previous experience is necessary, as the expert guides provide all the equipment you need and teach you how to paddle your way through the sea caves and around the harbor seals.

Accommodations and Food

◖**Ledford House Restaurant** (3000 N. Hwy. 1, Albion, 707/937-0282, www.ledfordhouse. com, 5 P.M.–close Wed.–Sun., $19–30) is beautiful even from a distance; you'll see it on the hill as you drive up Highway 1. With excellent food and nightly jazz performances, it's one of the truly "special occasion" choices in the area. The **Albion River Inn** (Hwy. 1, 6 miles south of Mendocino, 707/937-1919 or 800/479-7944, www.albionriverinn.com, $195–325) is a gorgeous and serene setting for an away-from-it-all vacation. A full breakfast is included in the room rates, but pets and smoking are not allowed, and there are no TVs.

The **Little River Inn** (7901 N. Hwy. 1, Little River, 707/937-5942 or 888/466-5683, www.littleriverinn.com, $130–375) appeals to coastal vacationers who like a little luxury. It has a nine-hole golf course and two lighted tennis courts, and all its recreation areas overlook the Pacific, which crashes on the shore just across the highway from the inn. The sprawling white Victorian house and barns hide the sprawl of the grounds, which also has a great restaurant and a charming sea-themed bar. Relax even more at the in-house Third Court Salon and Day Spa.

The **Auberge Mendocino** (8200 N. Hwy. 1, Little River, 888/493-4142, www.aubergecottages.com, $299–499) is an elegant Victorian with a sweeping common area and four generous guest rooms. The lovely room appointments mix antiques and modern items, and the beds are supremely comfortable. Be prepared for a huge breakfast in the morning, and try to snag a slice of the owner's pear bread. A pretty garden leads out to a path that in turn picks up a trail out to the ocean.

One of the more luxurious B&Bs around is the **Glendeven Inn** (8205 N. Hwy. 1, 707/937-0083 or 800/822-4536, www.glendeven. com, $148–315), situated in a historic farmhouse with ocean views. The hosts will help you settle in with a complimentary wine and hors d'oeuvres hour in the late afternoon, and they wake you in the morning with a three-course made-to-order breakfast, delivered to your guest room exactly when you want it. If you like the food (you will), consider joining them on-site for a five-course "farm-to-table" dinner (6 P.M. Sat.–Mon., by reservation only, dinner $65, with wine $90).

Stevenswood Spa Resort (8211 N. Hwy. 1, Little River, 800/421-2810, www.stevenswood. com, $299–499) is a modern facility with contemporary decor. A fine on-site restaurant, **The Restaurant at Stevenswood** (8200 N. Hwy. 1, Little River, 707/937-2810, www.stevenswood. com, 6 P.M.–close Thurs.–Tues., $22–28) and a day spa help you feel relaxed and pampered, as does Van Damme State Park, which surrounds the resort on three sides. Be sure to book one of the outdoor in-ground hot tubs at the spa for a relaxing evening.

Camping is available in **Van Damme State Park** (Hwy. 1, 3 miles south of Mendocino, 800/444-7275, www.parks.ca.gov, $35); reservations are strongly encouraged.

MENDOCINO

The charming town of Mendocino is a favorite for romantic weekend getaways, quaint bed-and-breakfasts, art colonies, and local sustainable dining along the coast.

Mendocino Art Center

The town of Mendocino has long been an inspiration and a gathering place for artists of many varieties, and the Mendocino Art

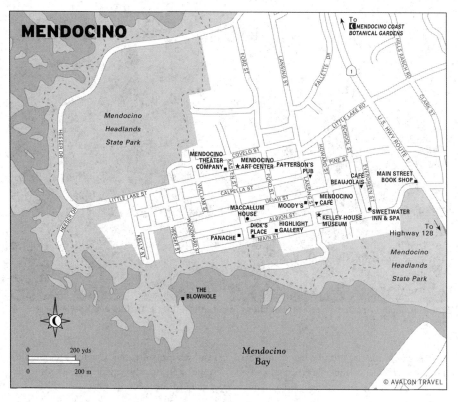

Center (45200 Little Lake St., 707/937-5818 or 800/653-3328, www.mendocinoartcenter. org, daily 10 A.M.–5 P.M., donation) is the main institution that gives these diverse artists a community, provides them with opportunities for teaching and learning, and displays the work of contemporary artists for the benefit of both the artists and the general public. Since 1959 the center has offered artist workshops and retreats. Today it has a flourishing schedule of events and classes, five galleries, and a sculpture garden. You can even drop in and make some art of your own. Supervised "open studios" in ceramics, jewelry making, watercolor, sculpture, and drawing take place throughout the year (call for specific schedules, $5–15 per session).

Kelley House Museum

The mission of the lovely, stately Kelley House Museum (45007 Albion St., 707/937-5791, www.kelleyhousemuseum.org, 11 A.M.–3 P.M. Thurs.–Tues. summer, 11 A.M.–3 P.M. Fri.–Mon. Oct.–May, free, tours 11 A.M. Sat., $10) is to preserve the history of Mendocino for future generations. The new addition to the historic house is home to the village archives, which include thousands of photos. In the museum, antique furniture and fixtures grace the rooms. A collection of Victorian clothing, photos, and documents illuminate the story of historic Mendocino, and knowledgeable docents are available to offer more information. Ask about the town's water-rights issues for a great lesson

The Mendocino Art Center offers workshops in ceramics, fiber arts, fine art, jewelry, and sculpture.

COURTESY OF MENDOCINO ART CENTER

in the untold history of the Mendocino coast. For a special treat, come on a weekend and ask about a tour of the nearby Presbyterian Church.

◖ Mendocino Coast Botanical Gardens

Mendocino Coast Botanical Gardens (18220 N. Hwy. 1, Fort Bragg, 707/964-4352, www. gardenbythesea.org, 9 A.M.–5 P.M. daily Mar.– Oct., 9 A.M.–4 P.M. daily Nov.–Feb., adults $14, seniors $10, ages 6–17 $5) is a vast expanse of land with an astonishing variety of vegetation. Stretching 47 acres down to the sea, these gardens offer miles of walking through careful plantings and wild landscapes. The garden map is also a seasonal guide, useful for those who aren't sure whether it's rhododendron season or whether the dahlia garden might be in bloom. Butterflies flutter and bees buzz, and good labels teach novice botany enthusiasts the names of the plants they see. Children can pick up

their own brochure, the "Quail Trail: A Child's Guide", and enjoy an exploratory adventure designed just for them.

Point Cabrillo Light Station

Whether you're into scenery or history, nautical or otherwise, you won't want to miss a visit to the Point Cabrillo Light Station Historic Park (12301 N. Hwy. 1, 707/937-6122, www.point-cabrillo.org, daily 10 A.M.–4 P.M., $5), north of Mendocino and south of Caspar and Fort Bragg. This beautiful lighthouse has been functioning for more than 100 years since it was built, in part to facilitate the movement of lumber and other supplies south to San Francisco to help rebuild the city after the massive 1906 earthquake. The light station was absorbed into the California State Park system in 2002, and in 2009 became a victim of state budget cuts and saw its services curtailed. The site is currently being managed by a volunteer organization, the

Point Cabrillo Lightkeepers Association. You can take a tour of the famous Fresnel lens, learn about the infamous *Frolic* shipwreck of 1850, and explore the tide-pool aquarium.

Entertainment and Events

For a place to hunker down over a pint in Mendocino, saunter over to **Patterson's Pub** (10485 Lansing St., 707/937-4782, www.pattersonspub.com, bar daily 10 A.M.–midnight, restaurant daily 11 A.M.–11 P.M.). This traditional Irish-style pub is in the former rectory of a 19th-century Catholic church. It nods to the 21st century with six plasma TVs that screen current games. You can order a pleasantly simple and filling meal at the tables or at the bar, and you'll find a dozen beers on tap, a full-fledged wine list, and hard liquor imported from around the world.

So where do the locals go for a drink in heavily visited Mendocino? That would be **Dick's Place** (45080 Main St., 707/937-6010, daily until 2 A.M.), sometimes called Richard's by the Sea. The crowd is a little younger than at Patterson's, and they're always having a good time. Dick's is easy to find, next to the hotel with the only neon sign on Main Street, in the shape of a martini glass.

For live music on the Mendocino coast, the center of nightlife is the **Caspar Inn** (14957 Caspar Rd., Caspar, 707/964-5565, www.casparinn.com, 5 P.M.–2 A.M. Tues.–Sat., 6 P.M.–1 A.M. Sun., cover under $15). The Caspar offers a full bar and a good restaurant menu ($15–22, cash only) in addition to its lineup of bands and other special events, including the "Pool Challenge," open-mike night, and "micro-midget wrestling." The town of Caspar is on the coast, about five miles north of Mendocino and seven miles south of Fort Bragg.

The **Mendocino Theater Company** (45200 Little Lake St., 707/937-4477, www.mendocinotheatre.org, shows 8 P.M. Thurs.–Sat., 2 P.M. Sun., $10–25) offers a genuine small community-theater experience. All plays are staged in the 81-seat Helen Schoeni Theater for an intimate night of live drama or comedy. The small, old weathered building exudes just the right kind of charm to draw in lovers of quirky community theater. But this little theater company has big goals, and it tends to take on thought-provoking work by contemporary playwrights.

For two weekends every March, the Point Cabrillo Light Station is host to the annual **Whale Festival** (707/937-6123, www.pointcabrillo.org, $5), a chance to get expert guidance as you scan the sea for migrating gray whales headed north for the summer.

Art is a big deal in Mendocino. Accordingly, the area hosts a number of art events each year. **Art in the Gardens** (18220 N. Hwy. 1, Fort Bragg, www.gardenbythesea.com, $20 at the door, $15 in advance) takes place each August at the Mendocino Coast Botanical Gardens, for which it is an annual fund-raiser. The gardens are decked out with the finest local artwork, food, and wine, and there is music to entertain the crowds who come to eat, drink, view, and purchase art.

In July, musicians of all types descend on the temporarily warmish coast for the **Mendocino Music Festival** (707/937-2044, www.mendocinomusic.com, each concert $10–49). For two weeks, live performances are held at venues around the area. There's always chamber music, orchestral concerts, opera, jazz, and bluegrass, and there's usually world music, blues, singer-songwriters, and dance performances. A centerpiece of the festival is the famed big-band concert. In addition to 13 evenings of music, there are three series of daytime concerts: piano, jazz, and village chamber concerts. No series passes are available; all events require separate tickets.

If restaurants are the heart of the Mendocino food scene, festivals are its soul. **Taste of Mendocino** (707/961-3460, www.mendocino.com) comprises several subfestivals. **Mendocino Crab & Wine Days** takes place in January and offers a burst of crab-related events (prices vary). In November, the focus is on the wild mushroom season, and you can come to the **Wine & Mushroom Festival** for classes, tastings, and tours (prices vary) to learn to cook or just to eat. Check the website for this year's plethora of other special events.

Shopping

On the coast, the best place to browse is **Mendocino Village.** Not only are the galleries and boutiques welcoming and fun, the whole downtown area is beautiful. It seems that every shop in the Main Street area has its own garden, and each fills with a riotous cascade of flowers in the summer. Even if you hate to shop, make the trip down to the village just to literally smell the roses.

Nothing makes a weekend getaway more enjoyable than a delicious book. Pick one up at the **Main Street Book Shop** (990 Main St., 707/937-1537, 10:30 A.M.–5 P.M. Mon.–Sat., 11 A.M.–4 P.M. Sun.). Next door to the funky Sweetwater, this used bookshop harks back to Mendocino's days as an art colony. The books are only vaguely organized into sections, but the cluttered tables and overstuffed shelves offer a welcome sense of abundance.

Panache (45120 Main St., 707/937-0947, www.thepanachegallery.com, daily 10 A.M.–5 P.M.) displays and sells beautiful works of art in all sorts of media. You'll find paintings, jewelry, sculpture, and art glass. Much of the artistic focus is reminiscent of the sea crashing just outside the large multiple-room gallery. The wooden furniture and boxes are a special treat: handmade treasures using rare woods are combined and then sanded and polished to silk-smooth finishes.

If you love fine woodworking and handcrafted furniture, you will not want to miss the **Highlight Gallery** (45052 Main St., 707/937-3132, www.thehighlightgallery.com, daily 10 A.M.–5 P.M.). Although the gallery has branched out in recent years to feature glasswork, ceramics, painting, and sculpture, its roots are in woodwork, which it maintains as a focus.

Sports and Recreation

Some of the most popular hiking trails in coastal Mendocino wind through **Russian Gulch State Park** (Hwy. 1, 2 miles north of Mendocino, 707/937-5804, www.parks.ca.gov, $8). Russian Gulch has its own **Fern Canyon Trail** (3 miles round-trip), winding into the second-growth redwood forest filled with lush green ferns. At the four-way junction, turn left to hike another 0.75 mile to the ever-popular waterfall. Be aware that you're likely to be part of a crowd visiting the falls on summer weekends. To the right at the four-way junction you can take a three-mile loop for total hike to six miles that leads to the top of the attractive little waterfall. If you prefer the shore to the forest, hike west rather than east to take in the lovely wild headlands and see blowholes, grasses, and even trawlers out seeking the day's catch.

Kayak and canoe trips are a popular summer activity on the Mendo coast. To explore the relatively sedate waters of the Big River estuary, consider renting an outrigger or even a sailing canoe from **Catch a Canoe & Bicycles Too** (Hwy. 1 and Comptche Ukiah Rd., 707/937-0273, www.catchacanoe.com, daily 9 A.M.–5 P.M., boat and bike rentals adults $28 pp for 1–3 hours, ages 6–17 $14 pp, guided tours June–Sept. $55–75 pp) at the Stanford Inn. For an adventurous day on the ocean, consider taking a sea-cave tour by kayak.

A good spot for abalone is **The Blowhole** (end of Main St.), a favorite summer lounging spot for locals. In the water, you'll find abalone and their empty shells, colorful tiny nudibranchs, and occasionally, overly friendly seals. The kelp beds just off the shore attract divers who don't fear cold water and want to check out the complex ecosystem. Check with the state Department of Fish and Game (888/773-8450, www.dfg.ca.gov) for the rules about taking abalone, which is strictly regulated; most species are endangered and can't be harvested. Game wardens can explain the abalone season opening and closing dates, catch limits, licensing information, and the best spots to dive each year.

Of all the reasons people choose to vacation on the Mendocino coast, the main one seems to be plain old relaxation. The perfect way to do so is to seek out one of the many nearby spas. The **Sweetwater** day spa (44840 Main St., 800/300-4140, www.sweetwaterspa.com, 1–9 P.M. Mon.–Fri., noon–9 P.M. Sat.–Sun.) rents indoor hot tubs by the hour and offers a range of massage services ($90–140) at reasonable rates. The rustic buildings and garden setting complete the experience. Appointments are required for massage and private tubs, but walk-ins are welcome to use the communal tub and sauna.

For a massage in the comfort of your own accommodations, make an appointment for a foot rub, herbal facial, full-body massage, or acupuncture with **The Body Works** (707/758-3252, www.massagetime.biz, $125 per hour).

Accommodations

The warm and welcoming **Blackberry Inn** (44951 Larkin Rd., 800/950-7806, www.blackberryinn.biz, $125–275) is in the hills, slightly out of the center of Mendocino. You may be a little confused when you first pull in, since it looks as though you're in a town—a perfectly stylized one from the Old West but without the shooting and the bank robberies. Each of the 17 guest rooms has a different storefront outside, including the bank, the saloon, the barber shop, the land-grant office. Each is charmingly decorated and beautifully maintained with plush, comfortable bedding cozied up with colonial-style quilts, along with the modern convenience of microwaves, fridges, sunken bathtubs, and free wireless Internet. The manager-hosts are the nicest you'll find anywhere, and they deliver freshly baked goods, fruit, and coffee to your guest room in the morning. Four guest rooms are pet-friendly, and the Storybook Cottage ($275) can accommodate the whole family—or a substantial part of a wedding party.

Sweetwater Inn and Spa (44840 Main St., 800/300-4140, www.sweetwaterspa.com, $125–295) harks back to the days when Mendocino was a colony of starving artists rather than a weekend retreat for city dwellers. A redwood water tower was converted into a guest room, joined by a motley connection of detached cottages that guarantee guests great privacy. Every guest room and cottage has its own style—you'll find a spiral staircase in the water tower, a two-person tub set in a windowed alcove in the Zen Room, and fireplaces in many of the cottages. The eclectic decor makes each room different, and many return guests request their favorite guest room again. Thick gardens surround the building complex, and a path leads back to the Garden Spa. The location, just past downtown on Main Street, is perfect for dining, shopping, and art walks.

If you've got the resources, the place to stay is **MacCallum House** (45020 Albion St., 707/936-0289 or 800/609-0492, www.maccallumhouse.com, $149–400), the king of luxury on the Mendo coast. The facility includes several properties in addition to the main 1882 inn building in Mendocino Village, and you can choose from private cottages with hot tubs, suites with jetted tubs, and regular guest rooms with opulent antique appointments. The woodwork gleams, and the service pleases. Note that a two-night minimum is required on weekends, and a three-night minimum goes into effect for most holidays. Room rates include a cooked-to-order breakfast, a $14-per-room credit toward dinner, and passes to the Redwood Health Club.

The **Stanford Inn** (44850 Comptche Ukiah Rd., 0.5 mile east of Hwy. 1, 707/937-5615 or 800/331-8884, www.stanfordinn.com, $211–555) is one of the largest accommodations in the Mendocino area. This resort hotel sits up

NORTH COAST

COURTESY OF PRAYITNO

LODGING

MacCallum House

and away from the beaches in a redwood forest. Gardens surround the resort (there's a nursery on the property), perfect for an after-dinner stroll. The location is convenient to hiking and only a short drive down to Mendocino Village and the coast. Guest rooms have beautiful honey wood-paneled walls, pretty furniture, and puffy down comforters for the feel of an upscale forest lodge in both the basic Big River Rooms and the many configurations of suites. If you're traveling with a group, consider one of the elegant two-bedroom suites, but be aware that "executive suite" means a junior suite. All guest rooms include breakfast at Ravens, a wood-burning fireplace, a TV with a DVD player, a stereo, free use of mountain bikes, and Internet access. The place also prides itself on its exceptional cell phone service and its commitment to green practices.

If you like your vacation to come with a perfect vantage point for watching the sunset over the Pacific, consider the **Sea Rock Bed & Breakfast Inn** (11101 Lansing St., 707/937-0926 or 800/906-0926, www.searock. com, $179–385). This little village of cottages, junior suites, and suites sleep 2–4 people each. After you check in, you can sit outside on the Adirondack chairs to watch the lights change, or you can take the bottle of Husch Vineyard wine from your guest room, stroll across the street, and take it all in from the viewing platform right above the beach. The inn's breakfast room, where hot quiche and fresh fruit, included in the room rates, is served every morning, is also perfectly situated for optimal ocean views. The Sea Rock has been around in its current incarnation for about 20 years, but the site has a long history—it was a brewery before Prohibition.

To stay somewhere really unusual in the kind of home-away-from-home that you might really want to write home about, reserve the **Point Cabrillo Head Lightkeeper's House** (Hwy. 1 between Mendocino and Fort Bragg, 707/937-5033, www.mendocinovacations.com, 2-night minimum, $833–1,030 for 2 nights). This

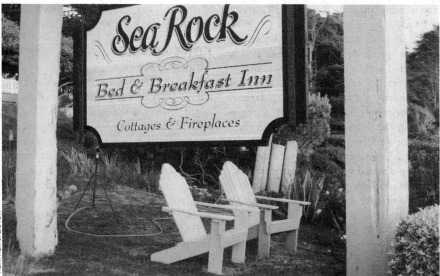

Sea Rock Bed & Breakfast Inn in Mendocino Village

1909 house is located atop a cliff beside the Pacific, so you can watch for whales, dolphins, and seabirds without leaving the porch. The beautifully restored house sleeps eight people in four bedrooms, and it has 4.5 baths and a very modern kitchen, so you and your family or friends can enjoy the vacation of a lifetime. If you want to accommodate a larger group for a family reunion or a wedding party, you can also rent two of the cottages nearby.

Food

One of the most appealing and dependable places to get a good meal any day of the week is the **Mendocino Café** (10451 Lansing St., 707/937-6141, www.mendocinocafe.com, lunch daily 11 A.M.–4 P.M., dinner daily from 5 P.M., $14–32). The café has good simple well-prepared food, a small kids menu, a wine list, and a beer list. Enjoy a Thai burrito, a fresh salmon fillet, or a steak in the warm well-lit dining room. Or sit outside: The café is in the gardens of Mendocino Village, and thanks to

a heated patio, you can enjoy outdoor dining any time of day.

Café Beaujolais (961 Ukiah St., 707/937-5614, www.cafebeaujolais.com, lunch 11:30 A.M.–2:30 P.M. Wed.–Sun., dinner daily from 5:30 P.M., $24–42) is a standout French-California restaurant in an area dense with great upscale cuisine. This charming out-of-the-way spot is a few blocks from the center of Mendocino Village in an older creeper-covered home. Despite the white tablecloths and fancy crystal, the atmosphere is casual at lunchtime and gets only slightly more formal at dinner. The giant salads and delectable entrées are made with organic produce, humanely raised meats, and locally caught seafood. Beware: The portions can be enormous, but you can get them half-size just by asking. Reservations are available on the website.

Vegetarians and carnivores alike rave about **Ravens Restaurant** (Stanford Inn, 44850 Comptche Ukiah Rd., 0.5 mile east of Hwy. 1, 707/937-5615 or 800/331-8884, www.

NORTH COAST

ravensrestaurant.com, 8 A.M.–10:30 A.M. and 5:30 P.M.–close Mon.–Sat., 8 A.M.–noon and 5:30 P.M.–close Sun., $18–23). Inside the lodge, which is surrounded by lush organic gardens, you'll find a big open dining room. Many of the vegetarian and vegan dishes served use produce from the inn's own organic farm. At breakfast, enjoy delectable vegetarian (or vegan, with tofu) scrambles, omelets, and florentines, complete with homemade breads and English muffins. At dinner, try one of the unusual salads or a seasonal vegetarian entrée. Even the wine list reflects organic, biodynamic, and sustainable-practice wineries.

Information and Services
Mendocino Village has a **post office** (10500 Ford St., 707/937-5282, www.usps.com, 7:30 A.M.–4:30 P.M. Mon.–Fri.). **Moody's Internet Café, Art Gallery, and Coffee Bar** (10450 Lansing St., 707/937-4843, www.moodyscoffeebar.com, daily 6 A.M.–8 P.M.) charges $2 per day for wireless Internet access if you bring your own laptop, and an hourly rate to use its computers.

Getting There and Around
It's simplest to navigate to and within Mendocino with your own vehicle. From U.S. 101 near Cloverdale, take Highway 128 northwest for 60 miles. Highway 128 becomes Highway 1 on the coast; Mendocino is another 10 miles north. A slower, more scenic alternative is to take Highway 1; from San Francisco to Mendocino via Highway 1 takes at least 4.5 hours. Mendocino has a fairly compact downtown area, Mendocino Village, with a concentration of restaurants, shops, and inns just a few blocks from the beach.

The **Mendocino Transit Authority** (800/696-4682, www.4mta.org) operates a dozen bus routes that connect Mendocino and Fort Bragg with larger cities like Santa Rosa and Ukiah, where you can make connections to Amtrak, Greyhound, and airports for access to farther-away points.

FORT BRAGG
Skunk Train
One of the famed attractions in Mendocino County is the California Western Railroad, popularly called the Skunk Train (depot at end of Laurel St., 866/457-5865, www.skunktrain.com, daily 8 A.M.–8 P.M.), perfect for rail buffs and traveling families. The restored steam locomotives pull trains from the coast at Fort Bragg 40 miles through the redwood forest to the town of Willits and back. The adventure lets passengers see the true majesty of the redwoods while giving a hint about life in Northern California before the era of highways. The gaily painted trains appeal to children, and the historic aspects and scenery call to adults. You can board in either Fort Bragg or Willits, making a round-trip to return to your lodgings for the night. Fares vary, but a round-trip without a special meal or other event is usually about adults $49, under age 13 $24.

MacKerricher State Park
Three miles north of Fort Bragg, MacKerricher State Park (Hwy. 1, 707/964-9112, district office 707/937-5804, visitors center 707/964-8898, www.parks.ca.gov, daily 9 A.M.–3 P.M., day use free) offers the small duck-filled Cleone Lake, six miles of sandy ocean beaches, four miles of cliffs and crags, and camping (reservations 800/444-7275, www.reserveamerica.com, $35). The main attraction for some is a gigantic, almost complete skeleton of a whale near the park entrance. Because there's no day use fee, you can stop in to see the whale even if you don't have time to hang out at the park. If you're lucky, you can also spot live whales and harbor seals frolicking in the ocean. The coast can be rough here, so don't swim or even wade unless it's what the locals call a "flat day"—no big waves and undertow. If the kids want to

© HEATHER C. LISTON

MacKerricher State Park

play in the water, take them to **Pudding Creek Beach** in the park, about 2.5 miles south of the campground, where they can play in the relatively sheltered area under the trestle bridge.

Triangle Tattoo Museum

This is not your grandmother's art museum, so enter at your own risk. For more than 20 years, the Triangle Tattoo Museum (356B N. Main St., 707/964-8814, www.triangletattoo. com, daily noon–6 P.M., free) has displayed the implements of tattooing and photos of their results. To enter, walk up a flight of narrow stairs and stare at the walls, which are completely covered with photos of tattoos. All forms of the art are represented, from those done by indigenous people to those done at carnivals and in prisons. In glass cases upstairs are all types of tattooing devices, some antique. More photos grace the walls of the warren of small rooms in a never-ending collage. The street-side rooms house a working tattoo parlor, and you can find intrepid artists and their canvases working late into the evening.

Glass Beach

The most famous beach in the Mendo area, Glass Beach (Elm St. and Glass Beach Dr.) is not a miracle of nature. The unpleasant origin of this fascinating beach strewn with sea glass was the Fort Bragg city dump. As the ocean rose over the landfill, the heavy glass that had been dumped there stayed put. Years of pounding surf polished and smoothed the broken edges, and now the surf returns our human refuse to the shore.

Beachcombers used to collect the smooth coated shards of glass, found in hues of green, blue, brown, and clear; now that the beach is under the management of MacKerricher State Park, and it's against the rules remove the glass, but it's still quite a sight. The trail down to Glass Beach is short but steep and treacherous; don't wear sandals—good walking or hiking shoes and attention to safety are a must.

Lost Coast Culture Machine

Devotees of contemporary art will want to make a pilgrimage to the Lost Coast Culture

NORTH COAST

Machine (190 E. Elm St., 707/961-1600, www.lostcoastculturemachine.org, 11 A.M.–6 P.M. Wed.–Sun., donation). Calling itself an "artist-run culture space, papermaking facility, and shop," the exhibitions, presentations, demonstrations, and events here vary widely. There's always something interesting going on, and visitors are welcome to drop in.

Pacific Star Winery

The only winery on the Mendocino coast, Pacific Star Winery (33000 N. Hwy. 1, 707/964-1155, www.pacificstarwinery.com, daily 11 A.M.–5 P.M., tasting free) makes the most of its location. Barrels of wine are left out in the salt air to age, incorporating a hint of the Pacific into each vintage. Friendly tasting-room staffers will tell you how much they like their bosses, the winemaker, and which of the winery cats most likes to be picked up. Wines are tasty and reasonably priced, and you can bring your own picnic to enjoy on the nearby bluff, which overlooks the ocean.

Entertainment and Events

The **North Coast Brewing Company** (455 N. Main St., 707/964-3400, www.northcoastbrewing.com) opened in 1988, aiming at the then-nascent artisanal beer market. As of this writing, they were in the process of renovating, and the brewery was not open for tours. Check before you go; they expect to reopen at an undetermined date. You can see the magic that produces Red Seal Ale, Old Rasputin Russian Imperial Stout, Scrimshaw Pilsner, and the recently resurrected Acme beer, first introduced in the 1860s. Meanwhile, you can enjoy North Coast's wares at the brewery's **Taproom & Grill** (444 N. Main St., 707/964-3400, www.northcoastbrewing.com, 11:30 A.M.–9:30 P.M. Mon.–Fri., 11:30 A.M.–10 P.M. Fri.–Sat., 11:30 A.M.–5 P.M. Sun., $17–30) across the street.

The **Gloriana Opera Company** (210 N. Corry St., 707/964-7469, www.gloriana.org) focuses more on musicals than true operas, but their shows still delight young and old theatergoers alike. Gloriana seeks to bring music and theater to young people, so they produce major musicals that appeal to kids, such as *The Aristocats* and *Charlotte's Web*. On the other hand, *Into the Woods* and the *Rock 'N Roll Revue* appeal mostly to people past their second decade. Local performers star in the two major shows and numerous one-off performances that Gloriana puts on each year.

Shopping

If you really enjoyed Glass Beach, you may want to stop in at the **Sea Glass Gallery & Museum** (17801 N. Hwy. 1, 707/962-0590, www.glassbeachjewelry.com, daily 9 A.M.–5 P.M.), 1.1 miles south of Fort Bragg. You can see a wide array of found treasures from over the years, hear stories from Captain Cass, a retired sailor and expert glass scavenger, and also buy sea glass set in pendants and rings.

Vintage clothing enthusiasts will love **If the Shoe Fits** (337 N. Franklin St., 707/964-2580, 10 A.M.–5:30 P.M. Mon.–Sat. summer, 10 A.M.–5 P.M. Mon.–Sat. winter). Its eclectic collection of used clothing and accessories for men and women usually includes interesting pieces, well preserved and in good condition.

The place to go on the North Coast to feed your vacation reading habit is—where else—**The Bookstore** (206 E. Redwood Ave., 707/964-6559, 10:15 A.M.–5 P.M. Mon.–Sat., noon–3 P.M. Sun.), a small shop with a well-curated selection of new and used books likely to please discriminating readers.

Sports and Recreation

The Mendocino coast is an ideal location to watch whales dance, or try to land the big one (salmon, halibut, rock cod, or tuna). During Dungeness crab season, you can even go out on a crab boat, learn to set pots, and catch your own delectable delicacy.

Many charters leave out of Noyo Harbor in Fort Bragg. The *Trek II* (Noyo Harbor, 707/964-4550, www.anchorcharterboats. com, daily 7 A.M.–8 P.M.) offers five-hour fishing trips ($60–90) and two-hour whale-watching jaunts (Dec.–May, $35). They'll take you rockfishing in summer, crabbing in winter, and chasing after salmon and tuna in season.

The **Noyo Fishing Center** (32440 N. Harbor Dr., Noyo Harbor, 707/964-3000, www.fortbraggfishing.com, half-day fishing trip $75, 2-hour whale-watching excursion $35) will take you out on its boat, the *Profish'nt,* where you can watch a demonstration of crab fishing or look for whales in the winter from the comfort of the heated cabin. They'll help you fish for cod and various deep-sea dwellers in season (May 15–Aug. 15). The crew can even clean and vacuum-pack your catch on the dock before you leave.

The hike to take in MacKerricher State Park (Hwy. 1, 707/964-9112, www.parks.ca.gov, visitors center daily 9 A.M.–3 P.M., day use free), three miles north of Fort Bragg, is the **Ten Mile Beach Trail** (14 miles round-trip, moderate), starting at the Beachcomber Motel at the north end of Fort Bragg and running seven miles up to the Ten Mile River. Most of this path is fairly level and paved. It's an easy walk you can take at your own pace and turn around whenever you want. Street bikes and inline skates are also allowed on this trail.

What better way to enjoy the rugged cliffs, windy beaches, and quiet forests of the coast than on the back of a horse? **Ricochet Ridge Ranch** (24201 N. U.S. 101, 707/964-7669, www.horse-vacation.com) has 10-mile beach trail rides ($45) departing four times a day, morning and afternoon. They also offer longer beach and trail rides, sunset beach rides, and full-fledged riding vacations by reservation (private guided rides $80–295).

Mountain bikers will want to time a visit here to coincide with the annual **Mendocino Coast**

Fat Tire Festival (www.mendocinocoastfattire-festival.com) in early October. It begins with a "poker ride"; you pedal through MacKerricher State Park collecting cards as you go and then speed back to Town Hall to see who has the winning hand. The next day is the Jughandle Juggernaut, a 10- or 20-mile race that is part of the Caspar Cup Series. And finally, on Sunday, there's a half- or full-century ride.

The **Bamboo Garden Spa** (303 N. Main St., Suite C, 707/962-9396, www.bamboogardenspa.com, 11 A.M.–6:30 P.M. Sun.–Tues., 10 A.M.–8 P.M. Wed.–Sat.) pampers its guests with a wide array of massage, skin, and beauty treatments. Get a 50-minute massage ($85), or try the Balinese Soul Soother ($85), the Vanilla Bean Sugar Scrub ($100), or Bonsai Bliss (1 person $145, 2 people $280).

Accommodations

Stringent zoning laws about development and expansion of businesses in the coastal zone are the main reason you're not likely to find a lot of lodging bargains here; only a few chain hotels have managed to build in Fort Bragg.

One budget option is the **Surf Motel** (1220 S. Main St., 707/964-5361 or 800/339-5361, www.surfmotelfb.com, $59–275). There's no pool, but the hotel pleases a variety of vacationers by providing a bike-washing station, a fish-cleaning station, an outdoor shower for divers, a garden to stroll through, and an area set aside for horseshoes and barbecues. Your spacious modern guest room comes with breakfast, free wireless access, a microwave, a fridge, and a blow-dryer. If you rent one of the two apartments, you get a whole kitchen and room for four people.

The **Beachcomber Motel** (1111 N. Main St., 707/964-2402, www.thebeachcombermotel. com, $109–259) is clean and decent, offering many rooms with ocean views; pets are allowed. Amenities are minimal but acceptable, similar to a low-end chain motel. Expect shampoo and

© HEATHER C. LISTON

the pleasant garden at the Surf Motel in Fort Bragg

soap in your tiny bath, but little else. Guest rooms are big enough to satisfy, although some visitors find them a bit dark and sparsely furnished. Thin walls and shared patios make noise a problem, and the location at the north end of town makes it a little inconvenient if your goal is to be near downtown Fort Bragg. What really makes the Beachcomber worthwhile, besides its lower-than-B&B prices, is that it's right on the beach, so ground-floor guests can walk straight out the back door, across the pedestrian and bike path, and onto the sand.

◖**Weller House** (524 Stewart St., 707/964-4415, www.wellerhouse.com, $160–210) is a picture-perfect B&B with elegantly restored Victorian-style guest rooms, ocean views, and sumptuous home cooking. There are even a few gloriously secluded guest rooms for rent up in the old water tower, which is the high point in the whole city of Fort Bragg. If you can't finish writing your novel here, you're just not trying. But that's not all: The owner, Vivien LaMothe,

is also a tango dancer, and the third floor of the main building—a gorgeous 1886 mansion listed on the National Register of Historic Places—is, believe it or not, a ballroom. The virgin redwood floor, the outstanding acoustics, and the spacious porch where dancers can step out for a breath of air make it a marvelous place for a *milonga*. Weller House is one block west of Main Street, in view of the Skunk Train depot, and an easy walk to good restaurants and shopping.

The stately **Grey Whale Inn** (615 N. Main St., 800/382-7244, www.greywhaleinn.com, $150–195) was once a community hospital. The blocky craftsman-style building was erected by the Union Lumber Company in 1915. Today, 13 spacious, simply appointed guest rooms welcome travelers. Whether you get a view of the water or a more pedestrian city view, you'll have a lovely, individually decorated guest room with a private bath and queen or king bed, perhaps covered by an old-fashioned quilt. The inn prides itself on simplicity and friendliness, and its perfect

Weller House in Fort Bragg

location in downtown Fort Bragg makes visitors feel at home walking to dinner or the beach.

Camping

There's appealing camping on the coast at **Van Damme State Park** (Hwy. 1, 707/937-5804, www.parks.ca.gov, reservations 800/444-7275, www.reserveamerica.com, $35), three miles south of Mendocino. The campground offers picnic tables, fire rings, and food lockers, as well as restrooms and hot showers. The park's 1,831 acres includes beachfront property as well as forest, so there's lots of natural beauty to enjoy.

MacKerricher State Park (Hwy. 1, 707/964-9112, www.parks.ca.gov, reservations 800/444-7275, www.reserveamerica.com, $35), three miles north of Fort Bragg, is also a fine place to spend a night or two as you explore the area. Reservations are recommended April 1–October 15, and they're site-specific. In the winter season, camping is available on a first-come, first-served basis. The park has 107 sites suitable for tents and RVs up to 35 feet in its wooded and pleasant West Pinewood Campground; there are also a group campground and walkin hike-and-bike sites. Restrooms with flush toilets as well as hot showers are provided, and each campsite has a fire ring, a picnic table, and a food storage locker.

Food

It used to be that you had to go to the village of Mendocino for a meal, but lately Fort Bragg has developed a more-than-respectable culinary scene of its own. Many excellent restaurants are available within a few blocks of the town center and beach.

The exquisitely hip **⊏ Mendo Bistro** (301 N. Main St., 707/964-4974, www.mendobistro.com, daily 5–9 P.M., $15–28) has everything you want in a restaurant: The food is fresh, original, and delicious, from homemade pasta to right-out-of-the-ocean catches of the day to creative medleys like barbecued lamb

NORTH COAST

shoulder with cornmeal-fried tomatoes. Guest creativity is encouraged by Zagat-rated chef Nicholas Petti, who owns this place and runs it with his wife, Jaimi Parsons. Pick a meat (or tofu or portobello) from the Choice Menu, decide how you want it prepared, and then choose a sauce; they'll do it your way. And even if you usually don't, save room for dessert, which includes homemade mini doughnuts with dipping sauces, a fried banana split, and the light and lovely gelato sampler. The high-ceilinged, many-windowed mezzanine of the historic Company Store building in the center of Fort Bragg is the perfect place for this reasonably priced, family-friendly, great-night-out local institution. The service is outstanding, the atmosphere is airy and happily not loud, and even the butter is delicious. Sometimes a place just works.

With the small fishing and crabbing fleet of Fort Bragg's Noyo Harbor, it's natural that lots of seafood restaurants are clustered nearby. For the most authentic, freshest, and simplest fish preparations, head down to the harbor to any one of the several casual restaurants and fish markets. This harbor deals in salmon, mussels, and Dungeness crab in season. One of the better restaurants, surprisingly enough, is the shabby-looking **Carine's Fish Grotto** (32430 N. Harbor Dr., 707/964-2429, daily 11:30 A.M.–9 P.M. Memorial Day–Labor Day, 11:30 A.M.–9 P.M. Thurs.–Sun. Labor Day–Memorial Day, $8–32); try the clam chowder. Another option is **Sharon's by the Sea** (32096 N. Harbor Dr., 707/962-0680, www.sharons-bythesea.com, daily 11:30 A.M.–3 P.M. and 5 P.M.–close, $16–26), which combines expensive prices, good service, and fabulous views.

Small and unassuming, but well worth a visit, **Nit's Café** (322 Main St., 707/964-7187, 5:30–9 P.M. Wed.–Sun., $14–26, cash only) specializes in Thai and Asian fusion. Noted for its beautiful presentations of both classic and creative dishes, Nit's gets rave reviews from nearly everyone who tries it.

For Japanese food that equals anything you'll find in the Bay Area, see **Taka's Grill** (250A N. Main St., 707/964-5204, daily 4:30–9 P.M., $12–20). They make use of very fresh seafood like *uni* (sea urchin) direct from nearby waters and fashion it expertly into sushi and other delectable dishes.

The **Taproom & Grill** (444 N. Main St., 707/964-3400, www.northcoastbrewing.com, 11:30 A.M.–9:30 P.M. Mon.–Thurs., 11:30 A.M.–10 P.M. Fri.–Sat., 11:30 A.M.–5 P.M. Sun., $17–30) serves seafood, steak, and local microbrews on tap, right across the street from its parent, the North Coast Brewing Company.

Perched improbably beside the entrance of MacKerricher State Park, **Purple Rose Mexican Restaurant** (24300 N. Hwy. 1, 707/964-6507, 5–9 P.M. Tues.–Sat., $10–30) is reputed to have the best margaritas in Mendocino County. While some people find the food only average, it's said that if you just have a margarita or two beforehand, you won't care too much about the cuisine.

Despite the often drizzly overcast weather, Mendocino coast residents and visitors crave ice cream in the summer just like anyone else. **Cowlick's Ice Cream** (250 N. Main St., 707/962-9271, www.cowlicksicecream.com, daily 11 A.M.–9 P.M.) serves delectable handmade ice cream in a variety of flavors. Yes, they really do serve mushroom ice cream during the famous fall Mendo mushroom season. You can get the perennial favorite flavors such as vanilla, chocolate, coffee, and strawberry. If you're lucky, you might also find your favorite seasonal flavor (banana daiquiri, cinnamon, green tea) when you visit. If you're not in downtown Fort Bragg, you can also find this local family-owned chain at the Mendocino Botanical Gardens (18220 N. Hwy. 1), at **Frankie's Ice Cream Parlor** (44951 Ukiah St., Mendocino, 707/937-2436, www.frankiesmendocino.com, daily 11 A.M.–9 P.M.) in Mendocino Village, on the Skunk Train, and at **J. D. Redhouse**

Egghead's, home of the "flying monkey potatoes"

stay as long as you like in the large atrium area they share with several other businesses, which has free Internet access, plenty of electrical outlets, and elbow room. Oh, and the fresh-baked cookies taste as good as they smell.

Egghead's (362 N. Main St., 707/964-5005, www.eggheadsrestaurant.com, daily 7 A.M.–2 P.M., $7.50–20) has been serving an enormous menu of breakfast, lunch, and brunch items to satisfy diners for more than 30 years. The menu includes every imaginable omelet combination, cinnamon raisin toast, burritos, reuben sandwiches, and "flying-monkey potatoes," derived from the *Wizard of Oz* theme that runs through the place.

The most popular burger in town is at **Jenny's Giant Burger** (940 N. Main St., 707/964-2235, daily 10:30 A.M.–9 P.M., $5–7). This little place has a 1950s hamburger-stand feel, but there's nothing stale about it. The food is good, simple, and cheap. Jenny's devoted followers tend to fill the place, but there are a few outdoor tables, and you can always get your treats to go if it's too crowded.

Information and Services

The **Mendocino Coast Chamber of Commerce and Visitors Center** (217 S. Main St., 707/961-6302, www.mendocinocoast.com, 9 A.M.–5 P.M. Mon.–Fri., 10 A.M.–5 P.M. Sat.–Sun.) has unusually attentive and well-trained staff in addition to all the maps, brochures, and ideas you could possibly want. This operation also serves as the Mendocino coast film office, which strongly encourages filmmaking in the area. Come in and get the inside story on where to see some of the famous filming locations.

Of all the towns on the Mendocino coast, Fort Bragg has the most urban atmosphere, complete with supermarkets, big-box stores, and a **post office** (203 N. Franklin St., 707/964-2302, www.usps.com, 8:30 A.M.–5 P.M. Mon.–Fri.).

The **Mendocino Coast District Hospital** (700

(212 S. Main St., Willits, 707/459-1214, daily 10 A.M.–6 P.M.).

If it's coffee and pastry you want as opposed to temporary office space, the **Headlands Coffeehouse** (120 E. Laurel St., 707/964-1987, www.headlandscoffeehouse.com, 7 A.M.–10 P.M. Mon.–Sat., 7 A.M.–7 P.M. Sun.) is unquestionably the place to go. The big windows give it a sunny cheerful atmosphere, the blueberry danishes, from the nearby Mendo Bakery, may be the biggest and best you'll ever have, and the place even smells delicious. There's live music in the evenings and free Internet access.

If what you're really looking for is a place to spread out and work while having coffee and snacks as a bonus, head to the **Mendocino Cookie Company/Zappa's Coffee** (301 N. Main St., 707/964-0282, www.menodcino-cookies.com, daily 7 A.M.–7 P.M.). For a minimal fee they'll let you rent one of their computers, or

River Dr. at Cypress St., 707/961-4652, www.mcdh. org) has the nearest full-service emergency room.

Getting There and Around

Fort Bragg is located on Highway 1, and driving here from San Francisco or Sacramento takes about four hours, from Ukiah 1.5 hours. There is no "fast" way to reach Fort Bragg. The road from any direction is narrow and full of curves, at least for an hour or two, so be prepared to make the scenic journey part of the fun. From Willits, take Highway 20 (Fort Bragg–Willits Rd.) west for 30 miles. If ever a road could be described as sun-dappled, this is one. The sun pops in and out among the redwood forest and makes you want to use all the pullouts to take photos. Keep in mind that there is no cell-phone service along this road, so it is not a good place to run out of gas. Allow plenty of time—it takes longer than you'd expect to travel these 30 miles.

As one of the largest towns in the region, Fort Bragg has access to more public transportation. The most enjoyable way to get here is to take the **Skunk Train** (866/457-5865, www. skunktrain.com) from Willits. The **Mendocino Transit Authority** (707/462-1422 or 800/696-4682, www.mta4.org) has a number of bus lines that pass through Fort Bragg, and it also offers Dial-a-Ride Curb-to-Curb Service (707/964-1800). The most common way to get to and around Fort Bragg, however, is by car.

Westport

The next town north along Highway 1 is Westport, 16 miles north of Fort Bragg, with its own patch of ocean, a few essential services, and one gem. The motto at the ◖ **Westport Hotel** (3892 Hwy. 1, Westport, 707/964-3688 or 877/964-3688, www.westporthotel.us, $140–195) is, "At last, you've found nowhere." The Westport Hotel is marvelous and private,

Westport Hotel

© HEATHER C. LISTON

perfect for a honeymoon spent in luxury and comfort. Each of the six guest rooms has one bed and a bath with fixtures that blend perfectly into the historic 1890 house. Some guest rooms have small private balconies overlooking the waves, and all guests have access to the redwood sauna. Fresh scones, fruit, and coffee are delivered to your room in the morning, and a full hot breakfast is served in the dining room.

Inside the Westport Hotel is the **Old Abalone Pub** (dinner 5–9 P.M. Thurs.–Sat., afternoon tea 3–5 P.M. Sat., brunch 10 A.M.–2 P.M. Sun., dinner $10–25). Thanks to a large mirror over the bar, everyone in the dining room gets an ocean view—even those seated with their backs to the sea.

Camping is available two miles north of Westport at **Westport-Union Landing State Beach** (Hwy. 1, 707/937-5804, www.parks.ca.gov, $25), with 86 first-come, first-served sites. There are no showers or other amenities, just the cliffs, the waves, the sunsets, and the views.

Mendocino Wine Country

Mendocino's interior valley might not be quite as glamorous as the coast, but it is home to history, art, and liquor. The Anderson Valley is the apex of Mendocino's wine region, although the tiny town of Hopland also has its share of tasting rooms. Ukiah, the county seat, is home to a number of microbreweries and a thriving agricultural industry. Up in determinedly funky Willits, a late-1960s art vibe thrives in the 21st century.

Unlike the chilly windy coast, the interior valleys of Mendocino get hot in the summer. Bring shorts, a swimsuit, and an air-conditioned car if you plan to visit June–September.

ANDERSON VALLEY

The Anderson Valley wine trail, also known as Highway 128, begins in Boonville and continues northwest toward the coast, with most of the wineries clustered between Boonville and Navarro.

Wineries

A big name in the Anderson Valley, **Scharffenberger Cellars** (8501 Hwy. 128, Philo, 707/895-2957, www.scharffenbergercellars.com, daily 11 A.M.–5 P.M., tasting $3) makes wine in Mendocino. The tasting room is elegant and unusually child-friendly.

A broad-ranging winery with a large estate vineyard and event center, **Navarro Vineyards** (5601 Hwy. 128, Philo, 707/895-3686 or 800/537-9463, www.navarrowine.com, daily 9 A.M.–6 P.M., tasting free) offers a range of tasty wines as well as some interesting specialty products such as verjuice.

In a valley full of great wineries, **Roederer Estate** (4501 Hwy. 128, 707/895-2288, www.roedererestate.com, daily 11 A.M.–5 P.M., tasting $6) sparkles. The California sparkling wines it creates are some of the best you'll taste. The large tasting room features a bar with sweeping views of the estate vineyards and huge cases filled with Roederer's well-deserved awards. Pourers are knowledgeable, and you'll get to taste from magnum bottles—a rarity at any winery. Be sure to ask for a taste of Roederer's rarely seen still wines; you might find something wonderful.

Small boutique wineries are clustered in the Anderson Valley, an area less crowded than Napa or Sonoma. Any of these are worth a visit to seek out gem wines that aren't available in shops. **Esterlina** (1200 Holmes Ranch Rd., Philo, 707/895-2920, www.esterlinavineyards.com, tasting by appointment only, reserve tasting $15 pp, waived with purchase) offers the best view in the valley—come around sunset if you can. Beyond the spectacular vineyard vistas, Esterlina provides tastes of a selection

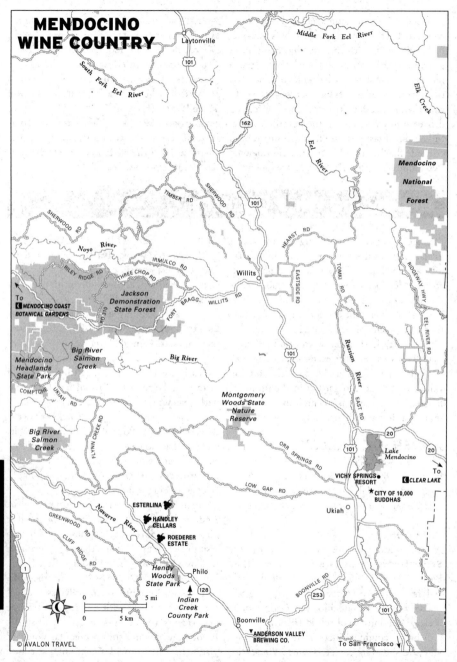

MENDOCINO WINE COUNTRY

Laytonville

Middle Fork Eel River

101

Elk Creek

162

South Fork Eel River

Eel River

Mendocino National Forest

TIMBER RD

SHERWOOD RD

101

HEARST RD

SHERWOOD RD

Noyo River

IRMULCO RD

RILEY RIDGE RD

THREE CHOP RD

RIDGEWAY HWY

EEL RIVER RD

RD 310

Willits

EASTSIDE RD

Jackson Demonstration State Forest

TOMKI RD

To MENDOCINO COAST BOTANICAL GARDENS

FORT BRAGG. WILLITS RD

Big River Salmon Creek

Big River

Russian River

EAST RD

Mendocino Headlands State Park

Montgomery Woods State Nature Reserve

COMPTCHE UKIAH RD

20

Lake Mendocino

20

Big River Salmon Creek

FLYNN CREEK RD

ORR SPRINGS RD

101

VICHY SPRINGS RESORT

To CLEAR LAKE

LOW GAP RD

CITY OF 10,000 BUDDHAS

Navarro River

GREENWOOD RD

ESTERLINA

Ukiah

HANDLEY CELLARS

ROEDERER ESTATE

CLIFF RIDGE RD

1

Hendy Woods State Park

Philo

128

Indian Creek County Park

BOONVILLE RD

253

0   5 mi

0   5 km

Boonville

101

ANDERSON VALLEY BREWING CO.

To San Francisco

© AVALON TRAVEL

BOONTLING: THE NORTH COAST DIALECT

Take oddly broken English, throw in some old Scottish and Irish, add a pinch of Spanish and a dash of Pomo, then season with real names and allusions to taste. Speak among friends and family in an isolated community for a dozen years or more. The result: Boontling.

Boontling is an unusual and almost dead language developed by the denizens of the then-remote town of Boonville in the Anderson Valley late in the 19th century. The beginnings of Boontling are obscured by time, since all the originators of the language are "piked for dusties"—that is, in the cemetery. And many Boonters—speakers of Boontling—are intensely protective of the local lingo. But in the 1960s,

Professor Charles C. Adams of California State University, Chico, came to town to study the language. He gradually gained the trust of the locals and was able to write a doctoral thesis eventually published as a book, *Boontling: An American Lingo*, which documents the history of the language and also supplies a dictionary for the more than 1,000 Boontling terms.

So if you find yourself sitting around over a "horn of zeese" (the Boontling term for a cup of coffee) and hear older folks speaking a language like none you've ever heard, you might just be listening to a rare and endangered conversation in Boontling.

of sparkling and still wines that make it well worth the trip to the top of its hill.

Handley Cellars (3151 Hwy. 128, Philo, 707/895-3876 or 800/733-3151, www.handleycellars.com, daily 10 A.M.–6 P.M. May–Oct., daily 10 A.M.–5 P.M. Nov.–Apr.) offers a complimentary tasting of handcrafted wines you probably won't see in grocery stores. The intriguing Handley tasting room features folk art from around the world for sale. Books on wine are sold too, especially those that focus on women making and drinking wine.

For visitors who prefer a cold beer to a glass of wine, **Anderson Valley Brewing Company** (17700 Hwy. 253, Boonville, 707/895-2337 or 800/207-2337, www.avbc.com, 11 A.M.–6 P.M. Sat.–Thurs., 11 A.M.–7 P.M. Fri. fall–spring, longer hours summer) serves up an array of microbrews that changes each year and each season. The warehouse-size beer hall has a bar, a number of tables, and a good-size gift shop. A beer garden out back is comfortable in spring and fall, and the disc golf course is popular with travelers and locals alike.

Sports and Recreation

The best hiking and biking trails in the area are in and around the Anderson Valley, where evergreen forests shade hikers from the worst of the summer heat. At **Hendy Redwoods State Park** (Philo–Greenwood Rd., 0.5 mile south of Hwy. 128, 707/895-3141 in summer, Mendocino district office 707/937-5804, www.parks.ca.gov, $8), you can hike to two old-growth redwood groves. For an easy, shaded walk, visit the **Big Hendy** grove and enjoy its self-guided nature trail, wheelchair accessible and perfect for a sedate forest walk. Another good short hike with just a little slope is the moderate **Hermit's Hut Trail**—yes, Hendy used to have its very own hermit. No one resides in the tree-stump hut anymore, although it remains a curiosity for hikers. Fit hikers who want a longer trek can weave around the whole park; **Big Hendy Loop** connects to the Fire Road, which connects to the Hermit's Hut Trail, which intersects the Azalea Loop and runs down to the **Little Hendy Loop** for a complete survey of the park's best regions.

Accommodations

Lodging options in and around the Anderson Valley vary widely. In the valley proper you're

NORTH COAST

likely to find funky hotels and cabins and for-est-shaded campgrounds. Ukiah specializes in generic national chain motels from the modest to the mid-tier, while Willits tends to have more old-school independent hotels and motels.

The **Anderson Valley Inn** (8480 Hwy. 128, Philo, 707/895-3325, www.avinn.com, $85–180), between Boonville and Philo, makes the perfect spot from which to divide your time between the Anderson Valley and the Mendocino coast. Eight small guest rooms are done up in bright colors, homey bedspreads, and attractive appointments in this small multiple-building inn. The two two-bedroom suites have full kitchens and are perfect for travelers looking to stay in the area a bit longer. The friendly owners welcome children and dogs in the suites—both must be attended at all times—and can be very helpful with hints about how best to explore the region. This inn often fills quickly on summer weekends, as it's one of the best-value accommodations in the region. There's a two-night minimum on weekends April–November.

In the middle of Boonville, the quaint **Boonville Hotel** (14050 Hwy. 128, 707/895-2210, www.boonvillehotel.com, $125–370) has a rough weathered exterior that contrasts interestingly with the 12 updated contemporary guest rooms, each of which is bright and airy with earth-tone furniture and an attractive collection of mismatched decorations. If you're traveling with children or pets, request one of the guest rooms set up to accommodate them. Downstairs, you'll find comfortable spacious common areas and a huge garden suitable for strolling. Amenities include a bookshop and a gift shop, a good-size bar, and a dining room. For a relaxing treat, book one of the guest rooms with a balcony, which comes with a hammock set up and ready for napping.

Camping

Stylish lodgings aren't common in the Anderson Valley, but you can still find a pleasant place to stay near the wineries. For wine and nature lovers on a budget, the campgrounds at **Indian Creek County Park** (Hwy. 128 at mile marker 23.48, 1 mile east of Philo, 707/463-4291, www.co.mendocino.ca.us, $20) and **Hendy Woods State Park** (Philo–Greenwood Rd., 0.5 mile south of Hwy. 128, 8 miles northwest of Boonville, 707/895-3141, www.parks.ca.gov, $35) provide woodsy, shady campsites.

Food

A picnic makes a perfect lunch in the Anderson Valley, and farmers markets and farm stands can supply fresh local ingredients. The **Boonville farmers market** (14050 Hwy. 128, Boonville, www.mcfarm.org, 9:30 A.M.–noon Sat.) draws a crowd, so be prepared to hunt for parking. For fresh fruit and vegetables every day, try **Gowan's Oak Tree Farm Stand** (6600 Hwy. 128, 2.5 miles north of Philo, 707/895-3353, daily 8 A.M.–7 P.M.). The stand belongs to the local Gowan's Oak Tree Farm and sells only in-season local produce and homemade products made with the same fruits and veggies.

For an elegant full-service dining experience, enjoy **Table 128** (14050 Hwy. 128, Boonville, 707/895-2210, www.boonvillehotel.com, by reservation only Thurs.–Mon. Apr.–Nov., Fri.–Sun. Dec.–Mar., $40–50), the restaurant at the Boonville Hotel. Table 128 is family-style and the menu is prix fixe. The food is so fresh and seasonal that the chef won't commit to a menu more than a week in advance, but you can sign up on the website to receive regular menus by email. Reservations are required and must be secured with a credit card for parties of five or more.

Getting There and Around

You can see pretty much all of Anderson Valley from the "wine road" (Hwy. 128). You can get to Highway 128 from U.S. 101 either directly out of Hopland or from Ukiah on Highway 253. From Hopland, take Mountain House Road west for nine miles. Turn right onto Highway 128 and continue north for about 20 miles.

From Ukiah, take U.S. 101 south for three miles. Merge onto Highway 253 and head west for about 17 miles. When you reach Highway 128, turn right. The center of Boonville is less than one mile away.

Many of the major wine-country touring outfits that operate from San Francisco and the Napa Valley also offer trips in the Anderson Valley. **Mendo Wine Tours** (707/937-6700 or 888/805-8687, www.mendowinetours.com, group tours $175 pp, private limo tour $550 for 2 people) is a regional specialist that offers a Lincoln Town Car for small groups and an SUV limo for groups of up to 10.

HOPLAND

Hopland is inland on U.S. 101 about 15 miles south of Ukiah and 28 miles east of the Anderson Valley via Highway 253. Highway 175 leads east to Clear Lake, under 20 miles away.

Solar Living Center

The Solar Living Center (13771 S. U.S. 101, 707/472-2450, http://solarliving.org) is a "12-acre sustainable living demonstration site," showing, among other things, what life might be like without petroleum. The center has exhibits on permaculture, an organic garden, and a demonstration of solar-powered water systems. The **Real Goods** store (707/472-2403) on-site is also a draw for visitors, and the completely recycled restrooms are worth a look even if you don't need one. If your vehicle happens to run on biodiesel, you can fill your tank here.

For more than 15 years, the Solar Living Center has taken a weekend in August to put on "the greenest show on earth," **MoonDance Eco-Fest** (www.solarliving.org). The hundreds of displays, demonstrations, and workshops go far beyond solar power to teach and exemplify the ever-expanding world of permaculture and renewable energy. Keynote speakers each year include top names from the world of ecological activism and science. But it's not all serious

business at Eco-Fest; musicians perform on the main stage, and the Saturday Night Moondance features entertainment and DJs for eco-lovers who want to dance deep into the night.

Wineries

To get to the best wineries in Hopland, you don't even need to leave U.S. 101. The highway runs through the center of town, and almost all the tasting rooms are located along it. For those who love wine but not crowds, the tiny wineries and tasting rooms in Hopland are the perfect place to relax, enjoy sipping each vintage, and really chat with the pourer, who just might be the winemaker and owner. **Graziano** (13251 S. U.S. 101, 707/744-8466, www.grazianofamilyofwines.com, daily 10 A.M.–5 P.M.), for example, provides a great small-winery experience.

McDowell Valley Vineyards (13380 S. U.S. 101, 707/744-8911, www.mcdowellsyrah.com, 11 A.M.–5 P.M. Mon.–Fri., tasting free) inhabits a weathered old general store complete with a central counter that's now the wine bar. Check out the cool kitchen kitsch as you enjoy your tasting.

The star of this mini region is **Brutocao Cellars** (13500 S. U.S. 101, 707/744-1664 or 800/433-3689, www.brutocaocellars.com, daily 10 A.M.–5 P.M., tasting free), whose vineyards crowd the land surrounding the town. It took over the old high school to create its tasting room and restaurant complex. The wide stone-tiled tasting room houses exceptional wines poured by knowledgeable staff. A sizeable gift shop offers gourmet goodies under the Brutocao label. And if you can't get enough of Brutocao, there is another tasting room in the Anderson Valley (7000 Hwy. 128, Philo, 707/895-2152, www.brutocaocellars.com, daily 10 A.M.–5 P.M., tasting free).

Heading north out of town, the highway passes through acres of vineyards spreading out toward the forest in all directions. Many of these grapes belong to **Jeriko** (12141 Hewlett and Sturtevant Rd., 707/744-1140, www.

© HEATHER C. LISTON

the Sun House at the Grace Hudson Museum

jeriko.us, daily 10 A.M.–5 P.M. Apr.–Oct., daily 11 A.M.–4 P.M. Nov.–Mar., tour and tasting $10, with lunch $30). Visitors drive between the chardonnay and the cabernet to get to the immense Napa-style tasting room. A glass wall exposes the barrel room with aging wines stacked high, tempting tasters to learn their secrets.

Food
With the closing of the Hopland Inn, Hopland lost some of its best dining and one of its only places to stay. A casual place that most people enjoy is the **Bluebird Café & Catering Company** (13340 S. U.S. 101, 707/744-1633, 7 A.M.–2 P.M. Mon.–Thurs., 7 A.M.–7 P.M. Fri.–Sun., $17–20). Your best bet for a good night's sleep is to stay in Ukiah or Lakeport.

UKIAH
City of 10,000 Buddhas
There's plenty to interest the spiritually curious at the **Sagely City of 10,000 Buddhas** (4951 Bodhi Way, 707/462-0939, www.cttbusa.org). This active Buddhist college and monastery asks that guests wear modest clothing (avoid short shorts and short skirts, bare chests, and skimpy tank tops) and keep their voices down out of respect for the nuns and monks who make their lives here. The showpiece is the temple, which really does contain 10,000 golden Buddha statues. An extensive gift- and bookshop provides slightly silly souvenirs as well as serious scholarly texts on Buddhism. For a treat, stop in for lunch at the **Jyun Kang Vegetarian Restaurant** (707/468-7966, 11:30 A.M.–3 P.M. Wed.–Mon., $7), open to the public on the grounds most afternoons.

Grace Hudson Museum and Sun House
One of the few truly cultural offerings in Ukiah is the Grace Hudson Museum (431 S. Main St., 707/467-2836, www.gracehudsonmuseum.org, 10 A.M.–4:30 P.M. Wed.–Sat., noon–4:30 P.M.

Sun., adults $4, seniors and students $3, family $10). This small set of galleries focuses on the life and work of the artist Grace Hudson and her husband, Dr. John Hudson. The life's work of this couple included the study of the Pomo people and other Native American groups. The museum's permanent collection includes many of Grace's paintings, a number of Pomo baskets, and the works of dozens of other California artists. The 1911 craftsman-style Sun House, adjacent to the main museum building, was the Hudsons' home, and docent-guided tours are available.

Entertainment and Events

Ukiah Brewing Company (102 S. State St., 707/468-5898, www.ukiahbrewingco.com, kitchen 11 A.M.–9 P.M. Sun.–Thurs., 11 A.M.–9:30 P.M. Fri.–Sat., bar 11 A.M.–11 P.M. Mon.–Thurs., 11 A.M.–1 A.M. Fri.–Sun., $8–11) offers good beer and good entertainment several nights each week. Settle in with a pilsner or amber ale and enjoy the live music and other weekend-evening entertainment. You might even get a chance to strut yourself at an open-mike night.

Sports and Recreation

Lake Mendocino (www.lakemendocino.com) is an artificial lake along the Russian River that is held in place by Coyote Dam. It's just off U.S. 101 north of Ukiah, allowing residents and visitors the chance to powerboat, water-ski, canoe, kayak, and fish. Shockingly uncrowded even on the hottest summer afternoons, this is a great spot to cool off. You can even find a few beaches and lawns on which to spread out a blanket and lie down, and shaded picnic tables where you can enjoy lunch. You can access the lake from Lake Mendocino Drive, Calpella Drive, and a few other local roads off U.S. 101. Five marinas catering to boaters and two boat ramps are along the shores of the lake. A number of campgrounds also circle the lake—some are boat-in only.

A great place to take a nice cool and shady hike is **Montgomery Woods State Nature Reserve** (Orr Springs Rd., 707/937-5804, www.parks.ca.gov, free), 13 miles west of Ukiah. This remote redwoods park is less crowded than its more accessible and more popular brethren. The quintessential hike at Montgomery runs along **Montgomery Creek** (3 miles, moderate), where you get a chance to see something special and unusual—both the coastal and giant-sequoia species of redwood tree growing in the same park. Montgomery's location and climate make it hospitable to both types, which usually grow hundreds of miles apart.

There is a tranquil and serene (most of the time) historic spa at the edge of Ukiah. Since its establishment in 1854, **Vichy Springs** (2605 Vichy Springs Rd., 707/462-9515, www.vichysprings.com, accommodations $195–390, treatments $105–150 per hour, baths $50 per day) has been patronized by Mark Twain, Jack London, Ulysses S. Grant, Teddy Roosevelt, and California governor Jerry Brown. The hot springs, mineral-heavy and naturally carbonated, closely resemble the world-famous waters of their namesake at Vichy in France. Services include the baths, a hot pool, and an Olympic-size swimming pool as well as a day spa.

In downtown Ukiah, **Tranquility Day Spa** (203 S. State St., 707/463-2189, http://tranquilitydayspaukiah.com) caters to the hippie side of this culturally mixed town. Swirling curtains and sandalwood incense pervade the big warehouse space. Tranquility has both salon and spa services for one-stop shopping for a mud mask, a hot-stone massage, a haircut, a Brazilian wax, a reflexology treatment, and even a "Tango Paraffin Bodyfango," with specific services for men, women, and teens.

Accommodations

There are plenty of lodgings in Ukiah, although they tend to be mostly standard chain motels. Out by the airport, the **Fairfield Inn** (1140

© HEATHER C. LISTON

Schat's Bakery Café

Airport Park Blvd., 707/463-3600, www.mar-riott.com, $115–165) is a good choice. With an elegant lobby, an indoor pool and spa, a small exercise room, and a generous complimentary continental breakfast, it has what you need to be comfortable. Next door, the **Hampton Inn** (1160 Airport Park Blvd., 707/462-6555, www.hamptoninn.com, $129–149) offers attractive guest rooms, an outdoor pool and spa, high-speed Internet access, and a buffet breakfast.

If you're coming to town for a peaceful retreat, the best choice may be **Vichy Springs Resort** (2605 Vichy Springs Rd., 707/462-9515, www.vichysprings.com, $195–390). The guest rooms, in a genteel and rustic old inn and nearby cottages, are small but comfortable, with private baths, warm bedspreads, and cool breezes, and many have views of the mountains or creek. Use of all the pools and hiking trails on the 700-acre grounds along with Internet access and a buffet breakfast are included in the rates.

Food

A local favorite, the **Maple Restaurant** (295 S. State St., 707/462-5221, 7 A.M.–2 P.M. Mon.–Sat., 7 A.M.–1:30 P.M. Sun., $10) serves excellent and inexpensive breakfasts and lunches. Excellent service complements good uncomplicated American-style food. Shockingly good coffee is a final charming touch to this lovely find.

For a cool relaxing breather on a hot Ukiah day, stop in at one of the three locations of **Schat's Bakery Café** (113 W. Perkins St., 707/462-1670; 1255A Airport Park Blvd., 707/468-5850; 1000 Hensley Creek Rd., 707/468-3145, www.schat's.com, 5 A.M.–5 P.M. Mon.–Fri., 5 A.M.–6 P.M. Sat., $5–12). They'll make you a quick filling sandwich on fresh-baked bread, and you can hang out as long as you want in the large airy dining rooms.

Ellie's Mutt Hut & Vegetarian Café (732 S. State St., 707/468-5376, 6:30 A.M.–8 P.M. Mon.–Sat., $8–15) has great vegetarian entrées and an impressive hot dog list. It's one of the best places in California for a mixed group of conscientious vegans and couldn't-care-less carnivores to have a good time together; Ellie's is one of the things that make Ukiah Ukiah. The atmosphere is hamburger-stand casual, and the food is mostly healthy.

Of the dining options in Ukiah, one of the very best is **Patrona** (130 W. Standley St., 707/462-9181, www.patronarestaurant.com, 11 A.M.–9:30 P.M. Tues.–Fri., 10:30 A.M.–9:30 P.M. Sat., $13–29), where especially innovative California cuisine is served in a bistro-casual atmosphere by attentive servers. Portions are a good size but not enormous, and the kitchen's attention to detail is impressive. The wine list features all sorts of Mendocino County vintages, plus a good range of European wines. Most wines are available by the bottle only, but the servers will gladly cork an unfinished bottle so you can take it home to enjoy later.

Information and Services

If you need assistance with local lodging,

NORTH COAST

dining, or wine tasting, try the visitors center at the **Ukiah Valley Conference Center** (200 S. School St., 707/467-5766, 9 A.M.–5 P.M. Mon.–Fri.). Since Ukiah is the county seat, you can find information here about both the city of Ukiah and the Mendocino County.

For local flavor, pick up a copy of the local daily *Ukiah Daily Journal* (www.ukiahdaily-journal.com, Tues.–Sun., daily $0.50, Sun. $1), with the best in up-to-date entertainment and events during your visit.

Ukiah has branches of many major banks. You can also find a **post office** (224 N. Oak St., 707/462-8814, www.usps.com, 8:30 A.M.–5 P.M. Mon.–Fri.). Internet access is available, often for a fee, at many of the chain motels and, of course, at the various Starbucks and other cafés. The **Ukiah Valley Medical Center** (275 Hospital Dr., 707/462-3111, www.uvmc.org) has a 24-hour emergency room as part of its full-service facility.

Getting There and Around

Ukiah is about 110 miles north of San Francisco (2 hours), a straight shot on U.S. 101. It's also about 60 miles north of Santa Rosa (1 hour) on U.S. 101.

The **Mendocino Transit Authority** (800/696-4682, www.4mta.org) runs bus service throughout the county, with Ukiah as the hub; you can catch buses here and in Mendocino and Fort Bragg. Private pilots can land at **Ukiah Municipal Airport** (UKI, 1411 S. State St., www.cityofukiah.com).

NORTH OF UKIAH
Willits

Seabiscuit enthusiasts might remember that the world-famous racehorse lived out his final years a few miles south of Willits at **Ridgewood Ranch** (16200 N. U.S. 101, 707/459-5992, www.seabiscuitheritage.org). Seabiscuit came here in 1939 to recover from his injuries and

© HEATHER C. LISTON

NORTH COAST

The town of Willits prides itself on being the "Gateway to the Redwoods."

stayed until his death in 1947. You can take a walking tour (9:30 A.M.–noon 1st and 3rd Sat. May–Oct., adults $20, under age 11 free) to see Seabiscuit's stud barn, learn about the history of his career and his jockey, Red Pollard, and even meet some of the horse's descendants, who still live here.

The **Mendocino County Museum** (400 E. Commercial St., 707/459-2736, www.co.mendocino.ca.us/museum, 10 A.M.–4:30 P.M. Wed.–Sun., adults $4, ages 6–18 $1) has intriguing permanent exhibits on local history. Highlights include a psychedelic van to celebrate Willits's hippie past, a showcase of the town's railroad heritage, information on the 1850 shipwreck of the *Frolic,* and a complete re-creation of the 1950s Willits Creamery soda fountain, complete with period advertisements and waitress uniforms.

The **Book Juggler** (182 S. Main St., 707/459-4075, www.thebookjuggler.com, 10 A.M.–7 P.M. Mon.–Thurs., 10 A.M.–8 P.M. Fri., 10 A.M.–6 P.M. Sat.) carries both new and used books.

There's no question where the coolest coffee bar in Willits is: **Mendonesia** (3 S. Main St., 707/459-1001, 11 A.M.–7 P.M. Mon.–Thurs., 11 A.M.–11 P.M. Fri.–Sat., noon–6 P.M. Sun.). In addition to the usual coffee, scones, and sandwiches, there's a baby grand piano, an upright bass, and a drum kit. It's always open-mike night at Mendonesia, run by the bass player Tom Girdauskas.

The fine-dining niche in Willits is filled by the small and sweet **Purple Thistle** (50 S. Main St., 707/459-4750, 5–9 P.M. Wed.–Thurs. and Sun., 5–9:30 P.M. Fri.–Sat., $14–23). Centrally located with good food and unusually good service, this place also has a pleasant back patio for outdoor dining.

Burrito Exquisito (42 S. Main St., 707/459-5421, 11 A.M.–9 P.M. daily, $6–10) serves fast, inexpensive, and very good food. This is a small place, with just one table and a few stools at the counter, so takeout is sometimes the best option.

© HEATHER C. LISTON

Burrito Exquisito

Willits has a modern big-box retail area at its south end, where you can find one or two ATMs. You can also find a **post office** (315 S. Main St., 707/459-5255, www.usps.com, 8:30 A.M.–5 P.M. Mon.–Fri.).

Willits is on U.S. 101, about midway between Ukiah to the south and Laytonville to the north. Driving from San Francisco takes 2.5–3 hours, depending on traffic. To get here from Fort Bragg, take Highway 20 (Fort Bragg–Willits Rd.) for about 30 miles of twists and turns through redwood forests. Several **Mendocino Transit Authority** (707/462-1422 or 800/696-4682, www.mta4.org) bus lines provide service to Willits.

Laytonville

Laytonville is about 23 miles north of Willits on U.S. 101 and has a few more services than points north. If you're heading up into the trees, this is a good place to stop and gas up. The town has several gas stations and banks, mostly right along the highway. For a burger and a break, you could do worse than **Wheels Café and Pub** (44930 U.S. 101, 707/984-8811, daily 7 A.M.–11 P.M., $8–18, cash only). There is a **post office** (50 Ramsey Rd., 707/984-6722, www.usps.com, 8:30 A.M.–5 P.M. Mon.–Fri.) and **Geigers Long Valley Market and Ace Hardware Store** (44951 U.S. 101, 707/984-6911, 7 A.M.–9 P.M. Mon.–Sat., 8 A.M.–8 P.M. Sun.) has some necessities.

Clear Lake

Clear Lake, in the heart of Lake County, is California's largest natural freshwater lake, with more than 100 miles of shoreline and an average summer temperature of 76°F, making it a delight for swimmers, boaters, and water-skiers. It's also heavily stocked with largemouth bass, among other fish, leading ESPN to name it the number-two bass fishing lake in the world.

Scenic, sunny, and unassuming, Lake County is an undiscovered gem. Overshadowed by the chic attractions of nearby Napa and Sonoma, modest Lake County offers sunshine and spectacular natural beauty with virtually no traffic, parking problems, or long lines. It is also a hot spot for geysers, natural hot springs, and healing waters. In addition to the lake, wineries, and hot springs, each town in the area has a distinctive small-town feel, with unpretentious local eateries and an abundance of festivals and celebrations.

Located on the west side of the lake, about 20 miles east of Hopland on Highway 175, **Lakeport** is the oldest town in the county. As one of the larger towns in the area, Lakeport has many amenities, but it also has plenty of charm, the famous Courthouse Museum, and lodgings. Highway 29 follows the lake north of town, joining with Highway 20 at Upper Lake.

Upper Lake is at the intersection of Highways 20 and 29. The historic Old Town dates to 1854; it has country charm and multiple produce stands. The small Clear Lake lakefront villages of **Nice, Lucerne,** and **Clearlake Oaks** are south of Upper Lake along Highway 20.

The town of **Clearlake** is located on the southeast arm of the lake, south of Clearlake Oaks on Highway 53. The largest town in Lake County, Clearlake supports local services and tourist infrastructure. Lakeshore Drive, the main drag, follows the lake and is lined with hotels, restaurants, parks, and boat launches.

The town of **Lower Lake** is four miles south of Clearlake at the junction of Highways 53 and 29. It is most noted for its Schoolhouse Museum and Theater, and it is the location of Lake County's first permanent settler, C. Noble Copsey. Working-class **Kelseyville** is west of Clear Lake, 15 miles west of Lower Lake and seven miles south of Lakeport.

Middletown is one of the larger settlements of Lake County, located south of the lake, where Harbin Hot Springs lures visitors for relaxing and dining. Middletown is about 15 miles south of Lower Lake on Highway 29. Nearby **Hidden Valley Lake** is nine miles north of Middletown on Highway 29.

SIGHTS
◖ Clear Lake

The centerpiece of Lake County is Clear Lake, a natural freshwater lake estimated to be nearly 500,000 years old. With 68 square miles of surface area, it is the largest natural freshwater lake in California. Clear Lake is filled with bass and catfish, making it popular with anglers as well as swimmers and boaters who flock to its shores to cool off in summer. Clear Lake is shallow, which means sunlight easily reaches the bottom of the lake, and it's relatively easy for plants to grow in the water. The lake is often said to be

© HEATHER C. LISTON

sailing on Clear Lake

"nutrient-rich" (a euphemism for "stinky"), so be forewarned: When the weather gets hot, the smell can intensify.

Clear Lake State Park

Clear Lake State Park (5300 Soda Bay Rd., Kelseyville, 707/279-4293, www.parks.ca.gov, day use $8, boat launch $5) is on the shore of Clear Lake, about 3.5 miles northeast of Kelseyville. In addition to superior fishing, the park provides opportunities for swimming, boating, picnicking, and bird-watching. There is a visitors center and a boat launch, four camping areas, and several hiking trails, including the **Dorn Nature Trail** (2 miles, moderate) and the **Indian Nature Trail** (0.5 mile, moderate).

Courthouse Museum

The Courthouse Museum (255 N. Main St., Lakeport, 707/263-4555, www.co.lake.ca.us, 10 A.M.–4 P.M. Wed.–Sat., noon–4 P.M. Sun.,

$1–2 donation) celebrates the California Supreme Court case that gave Ethan Anderson the right to vote, making him the first Native American in the United States to have that right. The courtroom is also where the famous English actress and noted beauty Lillie Langtry was granted her divorce in 1897, after becoming part of the community as the owner of Langtry Estate and Vineyards. Other exhibits include a collection of baskets made by the local Pomo people, the Joe Waite Gun Room, the Victorian Parlor, the Rock and Mineral Room, and some interesting history and lore about Clear Lake. The museum is a California Registered Historic Landmark. Nearby are a Veterans Service Office and memorials to local Vietnam veterans and fallen firefighters and sheriffs.

Anderson Marsh State Historic Park

Anderson Marsh (8225 Hwy. 53, Lower Lake, 707/279-2267, www.parks.ca.gov, 9 A.M.–5 P.M.

Wed.–Sun., day use $4) was named for John Still Anderson, whose family had a cattle ranch here from 1885 until the 1960s. Today it is a nature preserve that protects the tule marsh, which in turn provides a habitat for many fish, birds, and mammals. Highlights of the park include ancient Pomo petroglyphs, a reconstructed Pomo village, and the Cache Creek, Ridge, and Anderson Flats hiking trails.

Schoolhouse Museum

The Schoolhouse Museum (16435 Main St., Lower Lake, 707/995-3565, www.co.lake.ca.us, 11 A.M.–4 P.M. Wed.–Sat., $1–2 donation) is a historic building as well as a history museum. Housed in an 1877 schoolhouse, the building was restored in 1992 and filled with period artifacts. A recreated schoolroom is complete with 19th-century desks and wall decor, while other rooms display farm implements and mining tools from the period as well as period garments and toys. An on-site **theater** stages community productions; scheduling is sporadic, so call ahead for details.

Taylor Observatory-Norton Planetarium

One of the most striking things about a rural area like Lake County is the breathtaking night sky filled with stars. For a little help interpreting the skies, plan a visit to the Taylor Observatory–Norton Planetarium (5725 Oak Hills Lane, Kelseyville, 707/262-4121, www.lake-coe.org). The observatory hosts public events (8–11 P.M. 3rd Sat. of the month, $3) that include a lecture, a show in the planetarium, and an opportunity to view the sky through a telescope (bring a flashlight and warm clothes).

Harbin Hot Springs

Harbin Hot Springs (18424 Harbin Springs Rd., Middletown, 707/987-2477 or 800/622-2477, www.harbin.org) is a clothing-optional resort and spiritual retreat. Harbin's 5,000-acres of wooded property include rolling hills, hiking trails, and a series of spring-fed pools. The largest pool is warm and about five feet deep. Behind it are two smaller pools—one very cold and the other very hot—best suited to quick dips. There is also a large lap pool, a small kid-friendly heart-shaped pool, a sauna, a steam room, and multiple sundecks. Free movies are shown every evening in a comfy, intimate theater with floor pillows and a few old couches. Massages and other bodywork treatments are also available, including Watsu (aquatic massage). Yoga classes, chanting sessions, sweat lodges, and other activities are frequently on offer.

Membership ($10 per month or $30 per year) is required. A six-hour pass (Mon.–Thurs. $20, Fri.–Sun. and holidays $25) includes use of all the pools and facilities. The 24-hour pass (Sun.–Thurs. $25, Fri.–Sat. $35) is a better deal as it allows guests to camp overnight. Accommodations ($75–260) in a private guest room or cabin, or in a dome up on the mountain, can be reserved by phone. The on-site restaurant, **Stonefront,** serves organic meals that are healthy and very fresh; some of the food is grown in the gardens outside.

Wineries

Lake County may never compete with Napa and Sonoma as a wine-tasting destination, but many growers and producers have long found this less expensive region compatible with their needs. These days wine consumers are gradually discovering the special pleasures of pursuing their passion here. Some wineries to visit include **Mt. Konocti Winery** (2550 Big Valley Rd., Kelseyville, 707/279-4213, www.mtkonoctiwines.com, noon–5 P.M. Thurs.–Sun. May–Oct., noon–5 P.M. Fri.–Sun. Nov.–Apr., tasting $5), **Langtry Estate & Vineyards** (21000 Butts Canyon Rd., Middletown, 707/987-9127, www.langtryestate.com, daily 11 A.M.–5 P.M., 5 flights $5), **Shannon Ridge**

Winery (12599 E. Hwy. 20, Clearlake Oaks, 707/998-9656, www.shannonridge.com, daily 10:30 A.M.–5 P.M. year-round, tasting $5), and **Gregory Graham Wines** (13633 Point Lakeview Rd., Lower Lake, 707/995-3500, www.ggwines.com, 11 A.M.–5 P.M. Fri.–Sun. summer, 11 A.M.–5 P.M. Sat.–Sun. winter, tasting free), all of which are relatively large and welcome visitors.

Lake County Wine Tours (707/355-2762, www.lakecountywineries.org) offers information about the 25 wineries and vineyards as well as tours and tastings in the region. **Eleven Roses Ranch** (5456 New Long Valley Rd., Clearlake Oaks, 707/998-4471, www.elevenrosesranch.com) also offers a variety of tours—from a historic look at the wine business from the seat of a horse-drawn carriage to a comfortable, air-conditioned bus ride that takes you to all the best tasting spots.

ENTERTAINMENT AND EVENTS

Lake County loves festivals. One of the biggest is the annual **Lake County Wine Adventure** (707/355-2762, www.lakecountywineries.org, late July, $35 pp in advance, $40 day of event) with more than 30 local wineries over two days of tasting, music, and food. Designated drivers are strongly encouraged and can participate in many activities free of charge. The annual **Lake County Wine Auction** (Ceago Vinegarden, 5115 E. Hwy. 20, Nice, 866/279-9463, www.winealliance.org, Sept., $75–150) benefits a number of local nonprofit organizations. And no true wine connoisseur would miss the **People's Choice Wine Awards** (707/355-2762, www.lakecowineawards.org, $30–35), which takes place in the fall.

Wild West Day (707/275-2000 or 800/525-3743, www.lakecounty.com, first Sat. in June) takes in Upper Lake's Historic Main Street district, with a pancake breakfast at the Odd Fellows Hall, contests for the best period costumes, and a Wild West–style shootout. The

Old Time Bluegrass Festival (Anderson Marsh State Historic Park, 8225 Hwy. 53, Lower Lake, 707/995-2658, www.andersonmarsh.org, Sept.) features a broad slate of musicians, both local and from elsewhere, to raise money to benefit the nonprofit Anderson Marsh Interpretive Association (AMIA). Also, check out the **Kelseyville Pear Festival** (707/279-9022, www.pearfestival.com, Sept.); the **Festival of Tulips** (4900 Bartlett Springs Rd., Nice, 707/274-9373, www.tuliphillwinery.com, Mar.), sponsored by the Tulip Hill Winery; **Wild West Day** (Upper Lake, www.northshorebusinessassociation.com, June); **Middletown Days,** held on Father's Day weekend in June in Middletown since 1961; the **Cattails & Tules Wine & Food Pairing Festival** (Gregory Graham Winery and Vigilance Winery and Vineyards, Lower Lake, www.lakecountywineries.org, mid-June); and the **Heron Festival and Wildflower Brunch** (Clear Lake State Park, 5300 Soda Bay Rd., Kelseyville, 707/279-2267 or 707/263-8030, www.parks.ca.gov or www.heronfestival.org) in late spring.

SPORTS AND RECREATION
Boating and Waterskiing

Clear Lake is a major destination for boaters and water-skiers, and there are a number of free public boat launches:

- **Clear Lake Avenue Extension** (Lakeport, 707/263-5615)
- **Library Park** (Lakeport, 707/263-5615)
- **Clear Lake Avenue** (next to Skylark Motel, Lakeport, 707/263-5615)
- **Rodman Slough Park** (small boats only, Hwy. 20, Nice–Lucerne cutoff, 707/262-1618)
- **Crystal Lake Way Extension** (North Lakeport, 707/263-5615)
- **Keeling Park** (1000 Lakeshore Blvd., Nice, 707/262-1618)
- **Lucerne Harbor Park** (6225 E. Hwy. 20, Lucerne, 707/262-1618)

- **Clearlake Oaks Boat Launch** (12684 Island Dr., Clearlake Oaks)
- **Redbud Park** (14655 Lakeshore Dr., Clearlake, 707/994-8201)
- **Clear Lake State Park** (5300 Soda Bay Rd., Kelseyville, 707/279-42935)

County-owned **Holiday Harbor Marina** (3605 Lakeshore Blvd., Nice, 707/263-2580, $8 per day, $20 per week) will store your boat for a reasonable price.

If you prefer to have someone else pilot the boat, take a pontoon-boat tour of the lake with **Indian Beach Resort** (9945 E. Hwy. 20, Clearlake Oaks, 707/998-3760, www.indianbeachresort.com, daily year-round, 1st hour $195, additional $90 per hour for up to 10 people). **Eyes of the Wild** (707/262-2401 or 707/349-0026, www.eyesofthewild.us, 2.5-hour tour $40 pp, minimum 4 people) offers customized pontoon-boat tours and specializes in wildlife viewing from the water.

You can rent kayaks year-round at **Kayak Adventures** (6316 E. Hwy. 20, Lucerne, 707/274-2170, $15 per hour, half day $45, full day $75); in the spring and summer (Mar.–Aug.), join a guided group at no extra charge. **Kayaks 2 Go** (707/349-9618, www.kayaks2go.net, by appointment only, $60–75 per day) also rents kayaks and canoes. **Disney's Watersports** (401 S. Main St., Lakeport, 707/263-0969, www.disneyswatersports.com, 9 A.M.–6 P.M. daily June–Aug., hours vary Apr.–May and Sept.–Oct.) rents all sorts of watercraft, including Jet Skis and WaveRunners ($75 per hour, $335 per day), kayaks and pedal boats ($25 per hour, $75 per day), and patio boats (3 hours $195, $345 per day).

Fishing

There's no sport pursued with more enthusiasm in Lake County than fishing. Clear Lake is often called the "bass capital of the West." Bass aren't the only fish in the lake, though—it's also well stocked with catfish, crappie, trout, sunfish, bluegill, and carp. If you're thinking of trying a little fishing but want some help, call a fishing guide. They'll provide the boat, tackle, and expertise; you can just relax and reel them in.

If it's bass you're after, contact **Bassin' with Bob** (Bob Myskey, Nice, 707/274-0373, www.fishclearlake.com, five-hour trip $250 for 1 person, $300 for 2, $350 for 3), who fishes Clear Lake year-round.

Bob Thein of **Bob Thein's Fishing Guide Service** (Clearlake, 707/994-4886 or 707/350-1493, www.bobtheinguide.com, Mar.–Oct., $40 per hour, 5-hour minimum) will take you out to chase bass on Clear Lake in the summer.

Catfish specialist Tommy Wheeler of **Gut Buckets Catfish'n Guide Service** (530/671-1415 or 530/300-3336, www.gutbucketsclearlakecatfishn.com, 4 hours $120 pp, 7 hours $220 pp) will take you out day or night and provides instruction, bait, and tackle.

For more about fishing tournaments in the area, check out **Holder Ford Team Bass Tournament** (707/263-5603, www.lakcochamber.com, Mar.), **Blue Lakes Trout Derby** (707/275-2718, www.thenarrowsresort.com, Apr.), **Catfish Derby** (707/998-3795, www.clearlakeoaks.org, May), and **Professional Club Tournaments** (www.dfg.ca.gov/fish).

Hiking

The natural beauty of Lake County makes it a fine place for hiking. Walk the **Red Hills Terroir Trail** (1.25 miles) at the Vigilance and Gregory Graham Wineries (13888 Point Lakeview Rd., Lower Lake). The trail is on their private land, so respect any posted rules. It provides a good vantage point to watch for migrating bald eagles, especially in January, and you'll see the Anderson Marsh wetlands, Clear Lake, hills formed from ancient lava flows, grazing sheep, and maybe even egrets and pelicans as you traverse the well-marked trail. If the wineries' tasting rooms are open, you can have a sip at the end of your journey.

NORTH COAST

The **Dorn Nature Trail** in Clear Lake State Park (5300 Soda Bay Rd., 707/279-2267, www. parks.ca.gov) is an easy 1.5-mile loop that's pleasant for walkers of all ages and fitness levels.

Across from Clear Lake is **Mount Konocti,** a 4,300-foot mountain that is actually a volcano—more evidence of the geothermal activity in this area. The mountain is between the towns of Lakeport and Clearlake; with five peaks and numerous caves, this interesting little mountain looks different from every angle. Lake County recently bought 1,520 acres of the top of this mountain and plans a major hiking network. Check with the Lucerne Visitors Center (707/274-5652 or 800/525-3743, www. lakecounty.com) for updates.

Hikers should be forewarned that deer-hunting season is around mid-August–mid-October. Check online (www.dfg.ca.gov) to confirm before hitting the trails.

Golf
Hidden Valley Lake Golf Course (19210 Hartman Rd., Middletown, 707/987-3035, www.golfhvl.com, daily 6:30 A.M.–dusk summer, daily 7:30 A.M.–6:30 P.M. winter, $30–55) is the only 18-hole golf course in the county, and its beautiful views of Mount St. Helena, the Geysers, and the surrounding mountains and vineyards may make it the only one you need.

ACCOMMODATIONS
Lakeport
One of the most popular places to stay is the lovely ◖ **Lakeport English Inn** (675 N. Main St., 707/263-4317, www.lakeportenglishinn. com, $150–200). You can choose among the Robin Hood Room, the Prince of Wales, the Langtry Room, or even the Roll in the Hay. Or rent the whole two-room Schilling Cottage, which comes with its own gardens, porch, and fireplace. In addition to a full English breakfast, guests are served tea and scones at 4 P.M. If the room rates sound a little high, rest assured that

they're worth it—this is the ultimate special-occasion getaway. The English Inn does weddings, and they have a special Mother's Day Garden Tea and a Victorian Christmas Fair in November.

Upper Lake
The historic **Tallman Hotel** (9550 Main St., 707/275-2245, www.tallmanhotel.com, $159– 275), built in 1896 and thoroughly renovated in 2006, offers elegant features, including high ceilings and period-style fixtures. Select a garden room, a verandah room, or a suite in the Farmhouse or the Caretaker's Bungalow. The Tallman is also eco-friendly, with an electric-car charging station, solar panels, geoexchange heating and cooling systems, organic cleaning products, and composting. There's a lovely swimming pool; pets can sometimes be accommodated (call ahead to confirm). The hotel is next door to the excellent **Blue Wing Saloon** (9520 Main St., 707/275-2233, www.bluewingsaloon.com).

Clearlake Oaks and Vicinity
For a whimsical overnight, try the **Gingerbread Cottages** (4057 E. Hwy. 20, Nice, 707/274- 0200, www.gingerbread cottages.com, $125– 195). Right on the lake, the cottages are painted yummy colors such as mint green and tangerine; some have giant gingerbread people on their sides. Most cottages have kitchens, decks, lake views, and gas barbecues, and each has its own special charm. Breakfast pastries are delivered each morning, and there's a swimming pool on the premises.

The **Lake Point Lodge** (13470 E. Hwy. 20, Clearlake Oaks, 707/998-4350 or 800/900- 4350, www.lakepointlodge.net, $89–150) is one of the more attractive places to stay along the lake. It's across the highway on its own large well-groomed campus, close enough to offer outstanding views of the lake in all its splendor but removed enough that you won't be bothered by roaring motorboats. Amenities include free continental breakfast and a juice bar, free

© HEATHER C. LISTON

Twin Pine Casino

wireless Internet access, blow-dryers, microwaves, fridges, a pool and spa, and even smoking and nonsmoking guest rooms.

Clearlake

The **Best Western El Grande Inn** (15135 Lakeshore Dr., 707/994-2000 or 800/538-1234, www.bestwestern.com, $159) is bigger and grander than anything else in the area. The Spanish-style hotel has been in this location for 26 years; it's well maintained, with clean, polished interiors and manicured trees lining the large parking lot. There are 68 guest rooms, a lounge with a pool table and a bar, and an atrium with a fountain. It fills up occasionally with tournament participants and business travelers at conferences, so plan ahead to be sure of getting a room.

The Clearlake **Travelodge** (4775 Old Hwy. 53, 707/994-1499, www.travelodge.com, $80–90) is near the center of town and has a pool, wireless Internet access, and breakfast included. A locally run budget option, the **Lamplighter Motel** (14165 Lakeshore Dr., 707/995-9700, www.lamplighterclearlake.com, $60–65), has parking right on the lake as well as a small outdoor pool.

Lower Lake

One of the loveliest places to stay is 🌙 **Spirit Lake** (11865 Candy Lane, 707/995-0909, www.spiritlakebnb.com, $95–145) is a bed-and-breakfast run by locally renowned massage teacher and practitioner Elaine Marie. All guest rooms have queen beds and private baths. Your stay includes free use of a canoe, a paddle boat, and a rowboat on the pristine lake. Package deals are available and may include a massage in addition to lodging and breakfast. This is a marvelous spot for romance or a peaceful solo retreat; pets are not permitted.

Middletown

Hotel rooms in the **Twin Pine Casino** (2223 Hwy. 29, 707/987-0297 or 800/564-4872,

NORTH COAST

www.twinpine.com, $100–280) are large, smoke-free, and have all the amenities—refrigerators, microwaves, blow-dryers, Internet access, and flat-screen TVs. There aren't a lot of places to stay in Middletown apart from the casino and **Harbin Hot Springs** (18424 Harbin Springs Rd., 707/987-2477 or 800/622-2477, www.harbin.org, $75–260). Both have their appeal, but neither is for everyone. If you're looking for a simple motel, your best bet may be the **Eagle & Rose Inn** (21299 Calistoga St., 707/987-7330, www.eagleandroseinn.com, $70–125). Its 22 renovated guest rooms are basic but serviceable; some have microwaves and fridges.

CAMPING

Clear Lake State Park (5300 Soda Bay Rd., Kelseyville, 800/444-7275, www.reserveamerica.com, $30–45) has 138 sites in four campgrounds. The Kelsey Creek Campground is right on the lake; Lower and Upper Bayview Campgrounds are near Dorn Cove; and Cole Creek Campground is along Cole Creek. Amenities include restrooms, showers, fire rings, and boat launches. Reservations are accepted April 1–September 30.

You can also camp at **Harbin Hot Springs** (18424 Harbin Springs Rd., Middletown, 707/987-2477 or 800/622-2477, 24-hour pass $25–35) on a raised camping deck, along Harbin Creek, or on a sleeping deck (summer only). Campers have full use of the pools and facilities; membership fees apply. Harbin does not rent tents or equipment, and fires and camp stoves are not permitted.

The Narrows Lodge Resort (5690 Blue Lakes Rd., Upper Lake, 707/275-2718, www.thenarrowsresort.com), on the shore of Upper Blue Lake, has campsites for tents ($28) and RVs ($30–35).

FOOD

Lake County has its own small chain of full-service grocery-and-more stores called **Hardester's;** the largest is in Middletown (21088 Calistoga Rd., Middletown, 707/987-2325, 7 A.M.–9 P.M. Sun.–Thurs., 7 A.M.–10 P.M. Fri.–Sat.), and there is another in Hidden Valley (18983A Hartmann Rd., Hidden Valley Lake, 707/987-2200).

Lakeport

Angelina's Bakery (365 N. Main St., 707/263-0391, 7 A.M.–5 P.M. Mon.–Fri., 8 A.M.–2 P.M. Sat.) has the best home-baked muffins in the county (try the blackberry–cream cheese). Angelina's also serves Dreyer's hard-pack ice cream and quiche; It also offers catering and specialty cakes to order. The shop includes unusual preserves, made by the Penna Olive Company of Orland, such as olive spread, meyer lemon, and spicy bean.

Upper Lake

Blue Wing Saloon & Café (9520 Main St., 707/275-2233, www.bluewingsaloon.com, daily 11 A.M.–9 P.M., $11–24), at the intersection of Highways 20 and 29, serves down-home cuisine on the site of the town's first saloon, built in the 1880s and torn down during Prohibition. The current incarnation resembles the historic one but with modern touches like solar panels, geoexchange heating and cooling systems, and an ultramodern kitchen. The outstanding menu features fresh in-season ingredients served with beef tenderloin medallions, chicken cordon bleu, and risotto with white truffle oil. Vegetarians will be happy too, as the veggie selection is excellent and varied. This restaurant is quite popular, so reservations are definitely recommended, especially for dinner.

Clearlake Oaks and Vicinity

Happy Garden Restaurant & Bar (13440 E. Hwy. 20, Clearlake Oaks, 707/998-0398, 11 A.M.–9:30 P.M. Sun.–Thurs., 11 A.M.–10 P.M. Fri.–Sat., $8–15) is one of the few places to eat in the Clearlake Oaks area, and their Chinese and Thai cuisine is quite good; both the food and the service get consistently positive reviews.

It's conveniently located next door to the Lake Point Lodge. The coolest place for coffee is **Harley Hippie's Coffee Shop & Internet Café** (6260 E. Hwy. 20, Lucerne, 707/274-0400), featuring coffee drinks, smoothies, ice cream, homemade soup, vegetarian sandwiches, and information about biker events.

Clearlake
One of the most popular restaurants in Clearlake is the **Main Street Bar & Grill** (14084 Lakeshore Dr., 707/994-6450, 6 A.M.–9 P.M. Thurs.–Tues., 6 A.M.–3 P.M. Wed., $8–20), a casual family place. Burgers, fish-and-chips, and chicken-fried steak are customer favorites, but those in the know are enthusiastic about the steak and prawns with fried mushrooms. Breakfast is served all day, and there's a large selection of local wines and a variety of beers.

Howard's Grotto Steakhouse (14732 Lakeshore Dr., 707/994-0441, 11 A.M.–9 P.M. Mon.–Thurs., 11 A.M.–10 P.M. Fri., 9 A.M.–10 P.M. Sat., 9 A.M.–9 P.M. Sun., $13–49) is a popular local place with standard American fare. Dinners—mostly steak and seafood—come with soup and salad bar, and the portions are generous. The top-ticket item is the lobster and filet mignon combo. There's also a full bar and a good dessert menu. Breakfast is available on weekends only.

The best Mexican food is at the **Cactus Grill** (3900 Baylis Ave., 707/994-0905, 11 A.M.–9 P.M. Mon.–Sat., $9–14) with dependable burritos, tacos, and specialty combination platters. It serves beer and wine, but the agave margaritas and *horchata* are something special. On Saturday, the *menudo* is popular.

Lower Lake
You can get a good cup of coffee at the **Lower Lake Coffee Co.** (16195 Main St., 707/995-2558, 6:30 A.M.–4:30 P.M. Mon.–Fri., 8 A.M.–2 P.M. Sat.). The deli (10 A.M.–4 P.M. Sat.–Sun.) serves salads and decent sandwiches.

Kelseyville
Studebakers Coffeeshop and Delicatessen (3990 Main St., 707/279-8871, www.studebakersdeli.com, 6 A.M.–4 P.M. Mon.–Fri., 7 A.M.–4 P.M. Sat., 7 A.M.–2 P.M. Sun.) is the place to go for a good sandwich and free Internet access in Kelseyville. They also have homemade baked goods and an extensive selection of sodas.

Middletown and Hidden Valley Lake
The cheerful orange-and-yellow **La Parrilla Mexican Grill** (21389 Stewart St., Middletown, 707/987-4663, noon–9 P.M. Wed.–Mon., $8–12) is a family-run business offering reasonably priced burritos and Del Sur de México ("from the South of Mexico") platters. All dishes can be prepared vegetarian at no extra charge. La Parrilla has ample seating indoors, but on a nice day the picnic tables on the patio are even more attractive.

For fine dining in the area, your best bet is **Boar's Breath Restaurant and Bar** (21148 Calistoga St., Middletown, 707/987-9491, www.boarsbreathrestaurant.com, 5–9 P.M. Tues.–Sat., $20–30), with a menu featuring pork chops, steaks, salmon, and pasta, all expertly prepared. Specials might include linguine with prawns or a grilled New York strip steak dinner. An imaginative salad selection brings out the staff's creativity. The elegant decor includes an interior brick wall, hardwood floor, a long wooden bar, and sturdy tables. In the back, under the same ownership, is the more casual **Steam City Backdoor Pizza** (21148 Calistoga St., Middletown, 707/987-9491, 5–9 P.M. Tues.–Sat., $20).

The **Little Cowpoke Café** (21118 Calistoga Rd., Middletown, 707/987-0661, daily 6 A.M.–2 P.M., $7–20) is an old-school Western diner that has been around forever. Expect grass-fed Black Angus cheeseburgers and breakfast omelets served at red vinyl booths and counter stools, friendly staff, a convenient location, and breakfast served all day.

Mount St. Helena's Brewing (21167

HEATHER C. LISTON

Boar's Breath Restaurant and Bar

Calistoga Rd., Middletown, 707/987-2106, 11 A.M.–8:30 P.M. Sun.–Thurs., 11 A.M.–9:30 P.M. Fri.–Sat., $6–20) is a restaurant, brewery, and pizza joint with decent food and a lively sports-bar atmosphere.

Grinders Steep (21187 Calistoga St., Middletown, 707/987-8810, www.grinderssteep.com, 5:30 A.M.–6 P.M. Mon.–Fri., 6:30 A.M.–6 P.M. Sat.–Sun.) offers organic sustainable coffee, a variety of loose leaf-teas, ice cream treats, pastries, breakfast burritos, and Internet access. **Mug Shots Espresso** (21159 Calistoga Rd., Middletown, 707/987-8991, daily 6 A.M.–6 P.M.) has a wonderful selection of drinks—coffee, tea, frappés, milk shakes, Italian sodas, and *macchiato*.

For surprisingly good Thai food, try **Ting's Thai Kitchen** (Hardester's Plaza, 18983D Hartmann Rd., Hidden Valley Lake, 707/987-1063, noon–9 P.M. Tues.–Sun., $10–15). Owners Charlie McFarling and his wife, Ting, who is Thai, provide customer service as excellent as the food. Ting's does a brisk take-out business, but the restaurant is quiet and peaceful enough that you can sit and enjoy the ambience.

The best treats are at ◖ **Big Chill Frozen Yogurt** (18990 Coyote Valley Rd., Suite 16, Hidden Valley Lake, 707/987-3377, noon–10 P.M. Mon.–Sat., 2–7 P.M. Sun.), a cheerful lavender-and-mint-colored palace where you can make your own sundae. **Mountain High Coffee & Books** (18983 Hartmann Rd., Suite 1, Hidden Valley Lake, 707/987-8086, www.mthicoffee.com, 5:30 A.M.–6 P.M. Mon.–Fri., 6:30 A.M.–5 P.M. Sat.–Sun.) offers a cool welcoming atmosphere, coffee and other beverages, juices, smoothies, and bagels. They also sell used books on consignment.

INFORMATION AND SERVICES
Visitors Centers
Lake County maintains a **Visitors Information Center** (6110 E. Hwy. 20, Lucerne, 707/274-5652 or 800/525-3743, www.lakecounty.com, 9 A.M.–5 P.M. Mon.–Sat., noon–4 P.M. Sun.), staffed with knowledgeable Lake County enthusiasts.

Banks and Post Office
Lakeport has a **Bank of America** (500 N. Main St., Lakeport, 707/263-6149). **West America Bank** has locations in Clearlake (15342 Lakeshore Dr., 707/995-4140, 9 A.M.–4 P.M. Mon.–Thurs., 9 A.M.–6 P.M. Fri., Sat. 9 A.M.–1 P.M.), Upper Lake (9470 Main St., 707/275-8170, 9 A.M.–4 P.M. Mon.–Thurs., 9 A.M.–6 P.M. Fri.), Lakeport (150 S. Main St., 707/262-5714, 9 A.M.–4 P.M. Mon.–Thurs., 9 A.M.–6 P.M. Fri., Sat. 9 A.M.–1 P.M.), Kelseyville (4025 Main St., 707/279-6850, 9 A.M.–4 P.M. Mon.–Thurs., 9 A.M.–6 P.M. Fri.), and Middletown (21058 Calistoga Rd., 9 A.M.–4 P.M. Mon.–Thurs., 9 A.M.–6 P.M. Fri.). Middletown has a **post office** (21177 Calistoga St., 707/987-3201, www.usps.com, 8:30 A.M.–5 P.M. Mon.–Fri.).

Media and Communications
The main newspaper for the area is the *Lake*

County Record-Bee (www.lakeconews.com), published Tuesday–Saturday. **Watershed Books** (305 N. Main St., Lakeport, 707/263-5787, www.watershedbookco.com, 10 A.M.–5:30 P.M. Mon.–Fri., 11 A.M.–5:30 P.M. Sat.) is an independent bookstore offering new and used books; it also hosts various community events.

Medical Services

There are two hospitals in Lake County: **St. Helena Hospital** (15630 18th Ave., Clearlake, 707/994-6486, www.sthelenahospitals.org) and **Sutter Lakeside Hospital** (5176 Hill Rd. East, Lakeport, 707/262-5000, www. sutterlakeside.org). St. Helena Hospital also operates family health centers in Middletown and Kelseyville.

GETTING THERE AND AROUND

Clear Lake is east of U.S. 101, about 40 miles east of Ukiah via Highway 20 and 20 miles east of Hopland via Highway 175. Highways 29 and 20 circumnavigate the lake.

Arriving by air, fly into **Sacramento International Airport** (SMF, 6900 Airport Blvd., Sacramento, 916/929-5411, www.sacramento.aero). It takes an hour and 40 minutes to reach Clearlake from Sacramento.

The Redwood Coast

Of all the natural wonders California has to offer, the one that seems to inspire the purest and most unmitigated awe is the giant redwood. *Sequoia sempervirens,* also called coast redwood, grows along the California coast from around Big Sur in the south and into southern Oregon in the north. Coast redwoods hold the records for the tallest trees ever recorded, and they also include some fine examples of the world's oldest and all-around most massive living things. The two best places to experience extensive wild groves of these gargantuan treasures are Humboldt Redwoods State Park, in Humboldt County, and Redwood National and State Parks, near the north end of California around Eureka and Crescent City.

Most of the major park areas along the Redwood coast can be accessed via U.S. 101 and U.S. 199. To get to the redwood parks from the south, drive up U.S. 101 or the much slower but prettier Highway 1. The two roads merge at Leggett, north of Fort Bragg, and continue north as U.S. 101.

LEGGETT

As Highway 1 heads inland toward Leggett, the ocean views are replaced with redwoods. This part of the road is curvy, winding, and sun-dappled. It's a beautiful drive, so take it slow.

A local commercial attraction might thrill the kids: the **Chandelier Drive-Thru Tree** (67402 Drive-Thru Tree Rd., Leggett, 707/925-6464, www.drivethrutree.com, daily 8:30 A.M.–8 P.M. June–Aug., daily 8:30 A.M.–5 P.M. Sept.–May, $5) at the junction of Highway 1 and U.S. 101. The tree opening is about six feet wide and a little over six feet high. And, of course, there's a gift shop.

If you're coming through Leggett early in the day, bring some provisions with you. Otherwise, stop at **Angelo's Pizza Parlor** (67658 Drive-Thru Tree Rd., Leggett, 707/025-6200, 4–8:30 P.M. Mon.–Fri., 2–9 P.M. Sat.–Sun., $15), which gets pretty good reviews from most visitors.

Leggett is at the junction of Highway 1 and U.S. 101. The town is not accessible by public transportation, but it's easy to reach by car.

GARBERVILLE
Richardson Grove State Park

Even if your main destination is Humboldt Redwoods State Park or another redwood park, save time for a stop at Richardson Grove

NORTH COAST

SAVE THE REDWOODS

The stereotype of tree-hugging California conservationists is often of long-haired college students carrying protest signs, blocking bulldozers, and tying themselves to trees. Thus you might think that it was a bunch of hippies and starving artists who saved the huge swaths of redwoods in the North Coast region. Nothing could be farther from the truth. The California redwoods were saved by some very rich people.

Powerful rich white men poured their power, political connections, and, in some cases, millions of their own dollars into a group called the **Save the Redwoods League** (www.savetheredwoods.org). The three founders were a paleontologist and University of California professor named John C. Merriam and his fellow conservationists Madison Grant and Henry Fairfield Osborn, both of whom were scientists and eugenicists. After surveying the destruction of the forests surrounding the then-new U.S. 101 in 1917, the three decided that something had to be done, and the organization was born.

For 90 years the Save the Redwoods League has aggressively pursued the conservation of redwood forests in California. Using high-level political connections, the group has successfully lobbied the U.S. government to create Redwood National Park and to expand the territory protected by Sequoia National Park. They're also major players at the state level, creating and expanding state parks all over the landscape.

How did they get hold of all these groves? They bought them. The resources of league members, plus significant donations from others, have given the group the ability to buy thousands of acres of redwood forest and then donate them to various parks. They're still doing it to this day, and in the 21st century the league has made several major purchases to expand Sequoia National Park, Redwood National Park, and several state parks.

Got some spare change in your car? You can donate to Save the Redwoods and help the group preserve and expand California's fabulous redwoods.

(1600 U.S. 101, 707/247-3318, www.parks.ca.gov, $8), the first of the old-growth redwood forests you come across driving north on U.S. 101. The park has special features all its own, like a tree you can walk through and the ninth-tallest coast redwood. The Eel River flows through the park, so there's good fishing as well as camping, swimming, and hiking. The **visitors center** (May–Sept.) in the 1930s Richardson Grove Lodge has cool exhibits and a nature store. Richardson Grove State Park is seven miles south of Garberville.

Accommodations

The place to stay is the **C Benbow Inn** (445 Lake Benbow Dr., 707/923-2124 or 800/355-3301, www.benbowinn.com, $99–605). A swank resort backing onto Lake Benbow, this inn has it all: a gourmet restaurant, an 18-hole golf course, and a woodsy atmosphere that blends perfectly with the ancient redwood forest surrounding it. Guest rooms glow with dark polished woods and jewel-toned carpets. Wide king and comfy queen beds beckon guests tired after a long day of hiking in the redwoods or golfing beside the inn.

Several small motels offer reasonable guest rooms, and many have outdoor pools where weary guests can cool off during the heat of summer. The best of these is the **Best Western Humboldt House Inn** (701 Redwood Dr., 707/923-2771 or 800/780-7234, www.bestwestern.com, $140–200). Guest rooms are clean and comfortable, the pool is sparkling and cool, and the location is convenient to restaurants and shops in Garberville. Most guest rooms have two queen beds, great for families and pairs of couples traveling together on a budget.

Camping

Richardson Grove State Park (1600 U.S. 101, 800/444-7275, www.parks.ca.gov, camping $35) has 169 campsites in three campground areas surrounded by redwoods and the Elk River.

You can park your RV year-round at the 112 sites of the posh **Benbow Hotel and Resort**'s RV park (7000 Benbow Dr., 707/923-2777 or 866/236-2697, www.benbowinn.com, $34–54). Premium sites come with complimentary tea and scones at the nearby Benbow Inn.

Food

The restaurant at the [C] **Benbow Inn** (445 Lake Benbow Dr., 707/923-2124 or 800/355-3301, www.benbowinn.com, daily breakfast and dinner 6–9 P.M., $31–50) matches the lodgings for superiority in the area. It serves upscale California cuisine, with a vegan menu available on request, and features an extensive wine list with many regional wineries represented. The white-tablecloth dining room is exquisite, and the expansive outdoor patio overlooking the water is the perfect place to sit as the temperature cools on a summer evening.

Garberville has several modest eateries that appeal to weary travelers and families with kids. One of these is the **Woodrose Café** (911 Redwood Dr., 707/923-3191, www.woodrosecafe.com, 8 A.M.–2 P.M. Mon.–Fri., 8 A.M.–1 P.M. Sat.–Sun., $9–14). You can get a traditional American-style breakfast and lunch at this small independent eatery, and a lot of the food is organic, local, and healthy, but it doesn't come cheap.

Sicilito's (445 Conger St., 707/923-2814, www.asis.com/sicilitos, daily 4:30–10 P.M. fall–spring, 4:30–10 P.M. Mon.–Fri., 11:30 A.M.–100 P.M. Sat.–Sun. summer, $16–21) has some decent examples of Italian and Mexican food. The pizzas and taco salads are tasty, and the beer and wine selection helps make diners happy with their choices. The small dining room's walls are crowded with patriotic memorabilia, and the establishment sometimes fills with biker types making their way north on U.S. 101.

Need a pick-me-up? You won't find too many Starbucks around here, so enjoy a taste of local Humboldt-roasted coffee instead. The **Signature Coffee** (3455 Redwood Dr., Redway, 707/923-2661, www.signaturecoffee-company.com, 7 A.M.–5 P.M. Mon.–Fri.) takes pride in its organic product and sustainable practices, and they sell bagged coffee too, so you can stock up for use at the campsite.

Information and Services

The **Garberville Redway Area Chamber of Commerce** (782 Redwood Dr., 800/923-2613, www.garberville.org, 9 A.M.–4 P.M. Mon.–Fri. Labor Day–Memorial Day, 9 A.M.–4 P.M. Mon.–Fri., 10 A.M.–4 P.M. Sat.–Sun. Memorial Day–Labor Day) is happy to help visitors get acquainted with the area. There is a convenient **post office** (3400 Redwood Dr., Redway, 707/923-3784, www.usps.com, 8:45 A.M.–4:45 P.M. Mon.–Fri.) in nearby Redway. The nearest hospital with an emergency room is **Redwood Memorial Hospital** (3300 Renner Dr., Fortuna, 707/725-3361, www.stjosepheureka.org).

Getting There and Around

Garberville is located 65 miles south of Eureka and 200 miles north of San Francisco on U.S. 101. The best way to get to Humboldt Redwoods State Park from either direction is via U.S. 101. You can also approach the center of the park from Mattole Road from the Lost Coast (Shelter Cove to Mattole). Road signs point to the Avenue of the Giants. Bicycles are not permitted on U.S. 101, but you can ride the Avenue of the Giants and Mattole Road.

The little towns of the Humboldt redwoods region can be short on necessary services such as gas stations. There is a **76 Gas Station** (790 Redwood Dr.) well off the highway.

The **Redwood County Transit** (707/464-6400, www.redwoodtransit.org) bus system offers limited service to Garberville from the north.

THE LOST COAST

From Shelter Cove to Mattole is the "Lost Coast," the remote rugged coastline accessible by few roads and no highways. Even GPS navigators lose connectivity with the trees out here, so bring an old-fashioned map if you plan to explore this unspoiled wilderness. The reason people make the arduous trek out to the Lost Coast is to hike the miles of wilderness trails.

Mattole Road

One of the few drivable routes from which to view the Lost Coast is Mattole Road, a narrow, mostly paved two-lane road that affords views of remote ranchland, unspoiled forests, and a few short miles of barely accessible cliffs and beaches. In sunny weather, the vistas along Mattole Road are spectacular. This road also serves as access to the even smaller tracks out to the trails and campgrounds of the Sinkyone Wilderness.

Big Black Sands Beach

Big Black Sands Beach (King Range National Conservation Area, www.blm.gov) is one of the most beautiful and accessible features of the Lost Coast. Just north of the town of Shelter Cove, the long walk across the dark sands of Big Black Sands Beach to either Horse Creek or Gitchell Creek is relatively easy. This beach also serves as the south end of the Lost Coast Trail.

Cape Mendocino Lighthouse

At Mal Coombs Park in Shelter Cove (www.sheltercoveca.info), the 43-foot tower of the Cape Mendocino Lighthouse (www.lighthousefriends. com) is quiet and dark. It began life on Cape Mendocino—a 400-foot cliff that marks the westernmost point of California—in 1868. In 1951 the tower was abandoned in favor of a light on a pole, and in 1998 the tower was moved to Shelter Cove, becoming a museum in 2000. When docents are available, you can take a tour of the lighthouse (daily 10:30 A.M.–3:30 P.M. Memorial Day–Labor Day). The original first-order Fresnel lens is now on display in nearby Ferndale.

Hiking and Backpacking

Mattole Beach (707/825-2300, www.

publiclands.org) is a broad sandy beach that's perfect for an easy contemplative stroll of any length. The **Chemise Mountain Trail** (1.5 miles) gives hikers beautiful views of beaches and mountains from the top of Chemise Mountain. For a schedule of guided day hikes, contact the **Sanctuary Forest** (707/986-1087, sanctuaryforest.org).

Serious Lost Coasters bring their backpacks and spend days on the trail, enjoying the serenity of a place where few others come to disturb them. The ultimate Lost Coast experience is the 26-mile **Lost Coast Trail,** which takes about three days. The trail is within the King Range National Conservation Area, and there are trailheads at Usal Campground, Big Black Sands Beach, and Mattole Beach. Bringing drinking water is a must, as is a current tide table, since the beach areas of the trail dwindle and disappear in some spots at high tide. Campsites, many with restroom facilities and small usage fees, are clustered along the trail, making it easy for backpackers to rest when they need to. You need a backcountry permit, but they are free as long as you're not an organized group or a commercial enterprise, and they double as fire permits. You can get a permit at a self-service box at one of the trailheads, at the King Range office in Whitethorn, or at the field office in Arcata (707/986-5400, www. ca.blm.gov/arcata/kingrange). Bear canisters are mandatory, but if you don't have one you can rent one ($5) with a major credit card at the Petrolia General Store (40 Sherman Rd., Petrolia, 707/629-3455).

For another great hike, take the **King Crest Trail,** a mountain hike from the southern Saddle Mountain Trailhead to stunning King Peak and on to the North Slide Peak Trailhead. A good solid 10-mile one-day round-trip can be done from either trailhead. An arduous but gorgeous loop trail, the eight-mile Hidden Valley–Chinquapin–Lost Coast Loop Trail can be done in one day, or in two days with a stop at water-accessible Nick's Camp. **Buck Creek**

Trail includes an infamous grade, descending more than 3,000 vertical feet on an old logging road to the beach. The many other trails include **Rattlesnake Ridge, Kinsey Ridge, Spanish Ridge,** and **Lightning.**

Fishing and Whale-Watching

The Lost Coast is a natural fishing haven. The harbor at Shelter Cove offers charter services for ocean fishing. Kevin Riley of **Outcast Sportfishing** (Shelter Cove, 707/986-9842, www.outcastsportfish.com, Apr.–Sept., $225 pp per day) can help plan a charter fishing trip chasing whatever is in season. The cost includes gear, tackle, and filleting and packaging your fish at the end of the day, but bring your own lunch. Another reputable charter service is **Shelter Cove Sport Fishing** (707/923-1668, www.codking.com, fishing trips $150–225 pp, whale-watching trips $85), offering excursions to hunt halibut, albacore, and salmon or just to watch whales.

If shellfish is your favorite, come to the Shelter Cove area in the springtime to enjoy the Northern California abalone season. Ask locally for this year's best diving spots, and be sure to obtain a license: The state Department of Fish and Game (888/773-8450, www.dfg.ca.gov) can explain the rules about taking abalone, which is strictly regulated.

Surfing

Big Flat is a legendary surf spot about eight miles north of Shelter Cove. While the hike in is challenging, hard-core surfers will find it worth the effort. Other surf breaks along the Lost Coast are **Deadman's, No Pass,** and **Gale Point.**

Accommodations

Shelter Cove offers several nice motels for those who aren't up for roughing it in the wilderness overnight. At the **Shelter Cove Beachcomber Inn** (412 Machi Rd., 707/986-7551 or 800/718-4789, www.sojourner2000.com, $65–105),

each guest room has its own character along with views of the coast or the woods. The inn is an easy stroll to the airstrip and downtown.

The Tides Inn of Shelter Cove (59 Surf Point, 707/986-7900 or 888/998-4337, www.sheltercovetidesinn.com, $155–220) has standard guest rooms and luxurious suites with fireplaces and full kitchens. Most guest rooms face the sea, only steps from the inn. The Tides Inn is centrally located within walking distance of the airstrip, local shops, and restaurants.

The **Inn of the Lost Coast** (205 Wave Dr., 707/986-7521 or 888/570-9676, www.innofthelostcoast.com, $135–225) has an array of large and airy guest rooms and suites with stellar views to suit even luxurious tastes. Ask about discounts for AOPA pilots and AARP members, as well as the usual AAA discount. Package deals with Salmon King Charters are available.

The **Cliff House at Shelter Cove** (141 Wave Dr., 707/986-7344, www.cliffhousesheltercove.com, $160–180) is perched atop the bluffs overlooking the black-sand beaches. Only two suites are available; each has a full kitchen, living room, bedroom, gas fireplace, and satellite TV. These suites are a perfect spot for a romantic vacation or family getaway.

Camping

For many, staying on the Lost Coast means camping in the wilderness near the trails. If you're planning to camp in the backcountry, you need a permit. Permits are free and can be obtained from self-service boxes at the trailheads, or by visiting the local office of the Bureau of Land Management (BLM, 768 Shelter Cove Rd., Whitethorn, 707/986-5400, www.ca.blm.gov). Bear canisters are mandatory, but if you don't have one, you can rent one ($5) with a major credit card at the Petrolia General Store (40 Sherman Rd., Petrolia, 707/629-3455).

If you prefer a developed campground with amenities like restrooms, grills, fire rings, picnic tables, bear boxes, and potable water, there are a number of sites in the King Range National Conservation Area (no permit required). Campgrounds are open year-round, and reservations are not available; the odds of getting a site are pretty good, given the fairly small number of people who come here, even in high season. Some of the larger BLM camping areas (707/986-5400, www.ca.blm. gov) in the King Range are **Wailaki** (Chemise Mountain Rd., 13 sites, $8), **Nadelos** (Chemise Mountain Rd., tents only, 8 sites, $8), **Tolkan** (King Peak Rd., 5 RV sites, 4 tent sites, $8), **Horse Mountain** (King Peak Rd., 9 sites, no water, $5), and **Mattole Campground** (end of Lighthouse Rd., 14 sites, $8). Trailers and RVs (up to 24 feet) are allowed at most sites except Nadelos, although it's wise to check road conditions beforehand.

In Sinkyone Wilderness State Park, you can stay at the **Needle Rock Barn Campground** (Whitethorn, 707/986-7711, www.parks. ca.gov, no reservations, $35). There's also a trail camp ($5) for walk-in visitors; all sites are first come, first served. The campground is open year-round but is only intermittently staffed; self-register in the park at the Usal Campground (south side) or at Needle Rock Visitors Center (north side).

For more developed camping, the nearby **Shelter Cove RV Campground** (492 Machi Rd., Whitethorn, 707/986-7474, RVs $43, tents $33) is attractive. They've even got a deli and store (daily 8 A.M.–6 P.M. summer, daily 10 A.M.–5 P.M. winter, grill daily 8 A.M.–5 P.M. summer, daily 10 A.M.–4 P.M. winter) on-site so you don't have to bring all your own food.

Food

Most Lost Coast dining options are in or around Shelter Cove. For a delicious seafood meal, visit the glass-fronted A-frame **Chart Room** (210 Wave Dr., 707/986-9696, www.chartroom.cc, 5–8:30 P.M. Sun.–Wed., 5–9 P.M. Sat., $20–25). In addition to seafood, hearty meat and pasta dishes are available along with vegetarian fare, sandwiches, and soups. Be sure to check out the nautical and aeronautical gift shop.

At the **Cove Restaurant** (10 Seal Court, 707/986-1197, www.sheltercoveoceanfrontinn. com, 5–9 P.M. Thurs.–Sun., $13–30), a solid hearty American menu, heavy on the seafood, is perfect after a hard day of hiking, fishing, and beachcombing.

Enjoy a slice of pizza or a whole pie at **Costa Cucina** (205 Wave Dr., Whitethorn, 707/986-7672, 4:30–9 P.M. Tues.–Sat.). For a hot cup of coffee or tea, try **Cape Mendocino Tea** (1176 Lower Pacific Dr., 707/986-1138, www.capemendocinotea.com, 11 A.M.–4 P.M. Sat.–Mon., $7–21).

Practicalities

The **Sinkyone Wilderness State Park Visitors Center** (Needle Rock Campground, Usal Rd., www.parks.ca.gov, day use areas sunrise–sunset, day use $6) is the largest information center in the area. For regional information, call the Sinkyone Wilderness State Park information line (707/986-7711) or Richardson Grove State Park (707/247-3318). Mattole Campground and several other large campgrounds have information posted at the parking areas. Emergency services are coordinated through the Shelter Cove Fire Department (9126 Shelter Cove Rd., Whitethorn, 707/986-7507, www. sheltercove-ca.gov).

You can drive to the coast via Highway 1 or U.S. 101. Contact the State Parks department for maps and information about the trailheads in the Sinkyone and King's Range wilderness areas.

If you're up for a one-way journey through the Lost Coast Wilderness, look into a shuttle from one of the trailheads back to your car. **Lost Coast Trail Transport Service** (707/986-9909, www.lostcoasttrail.com) offers rides from the Shelter Cove Black Sands Beach to Usal Beach, Mattole Beach, and many other points along the trail.

HUMBOLDT REDWOODS STATE PARK

Surprisingly, the largest stand of unlogged redwood trees isn't on the coast, and it isn't in the Sierras; it's here in Humboldt, bisected by U.S. 101. Come to this park to hike beneath 300-foot-plus old-growth trees that began their lives centuries before Europeans knew California existed. Start your visit at the **Humboldt Redwoods State Park Visitors Center** (707/946-2263, www.parks.ca.gov or www.humboldtredwoods.org, daily 9 A.M.–5 P.M. Apr.–Oct., daily 10 A.M.–4 P.M. Nov.–Mar.), located along the Avenue of the Giants (Hwy. 254), between the towns of Weott and Myers Flat. It's a nice visitors center, with plenty of information for anyone new to the region or looking for hiking or camping information. You can also enjoy the theater, interpretive museum, and gift shop. There is no entrance fee for Humboldt Redwoods State

Founder's Grove in Humboldt Redwoods State Park provides an up-close introduction to coast redwoods.

© SABRINA YOUNG

Park and no fee to use the visitors center; the only day-use fee in the park is for the Williams Grove Day Use Area ($8 per vehicle).

◀ Avenue of the Giants

The most famous stretch of redwood trees is the Avenue of the Giants (www.avenueofthegiants.net), paralleling U.S. 101 and the Eel River for about 33 miles between Garberville and Fortuna; look for signs on U.S. 101. Visitors come from all over the world to drive this stretch of road and gaze in wonder at the sky-high old-growth redwoods along the way. Campgrounds and hiking trails sprout among the trees off the road. Park your car at various points along the way and get out to walk among the giants.

The Avenue's highest traffic volume is in July–August, when you can expect bumper-to-bumper stop-and-go traffic along the entire road. That's not necessarily a bad thing, as slowly is the best way to see the sights. But if crowds aren't your thing, you might try visiting in spring or fall, or even braving the rains of winter to gain a more secluded redwood experience.

Hiking and Biking

Stop at the Humboldt Redwoods State Park Visitors Center (707/946-2263, www.parks.ca.gov or www.humboldtredwoods.org, daily 9 A.M.–5 P.M. Apr.–Oct., daily 10 A.M.–4 P.M. Nov.–Mar.) to pick up a trail map showing the number of hikes accessible on or near this road. Many are very short, so you can make a nice day of combined driving and walking without having to commit to one big trek.

Many visitors start with the **Founder's Grove Nature Loop Trail** (0.6 mile, easy), at mile marker 20.5 on the Avenue of the Giants. This sedate, flat nature trail gives walkers a taste of the big old-growth trees in the park. Sadly, the onetime tallest tree in the world, the Dyerville Giant, fell in 1991 at the age of about 1,600. But it's still doing its part in this astounding ecosystem, decomposing before your

NORTH COAST

eyes on the forest floor and feeding new life in the forest.

Right at the visitors center, you can enjoy the **Gould Grove Nature Trail** (0.6 mile, easy)—a wheelchair-accessible interpretive nature walk with helpful signs describing the denizens of the forest.

If you're looking for a longer walk in the woods, try the lovely **River Trail** (Mattole Rd., 1.1 miles west of Ave. of the Giants, 7 miles round-trip, moderate). It follows the South Fork Eel River, allowing access to yet another ecosystem. Check with the visitors center to be sure that the summer bridges have been installed before trying to hike this trail.

Hard-core hikers who like to go at it all day can get their exercise at Humboldt Redwoods State Park. Start at the **Grasshopper Multiuse Trailhead** (Mattole Rd., 5.1 miles west of Ave. of the Giants) to access the newer **Johnson Camp Trail** (10.5 miles round-trip, difficult) that takes you to the abandoned cabins of railroad tie makers. Or pick another fork from the same trailhead to climb more than 3,000 feet to **Grasshopper Peak** (13.5 miles, difficult). From the peak, you can see 100 miles in any direction, overlooking the whole of the park and beyond.

You can bring your street bike to the park and ride the Avenue of the Giants or Mattole Road. A number of the trails around Humboldt Redwoods State Park are designated multiuse, which means that mountain bikers can make the rigorous climbs and then rip their way back down.

Swimming and Kayaking

The Eel River's forks meander through the Humboldt redwoods, creating lots of great opportunities for cooling off on hot summer days. Check with the park's visitors center for this year's best swimming holes, but you can reliably find good spots at **Eagle Point,** near Hidden Valley Campground; **Gould Bar;** and **Garden Club of America Grove.** In addition to the usual precautions for river swimming,

during August–September a poisonous (if ingested) blue-green algae can bloom late in the summer, making swimming in certain parts of the river hazardous.

Events

Humboldt Redwoods State Park is the site of a couple of the best marathons and half-marathons around. It offers flat courses, cool weather, and world-class scenery. If you're looking for an unintimidating place to try your first marathon, or if you need a fast time for a personal record or to qualify for Boston, this is an ideal choice. These events are also less crowded than the famous marathons, and you can camp right in the park where they begin. October has the **Humboldt Redwoods Marathon** (www.redwoodsmarathon.org, $55–65) with a related half-marathon ($50–60) and a 5K ($25). The **Avenue of the Giants Marathon** (www.theave.org, marathon $60, half-marathon $50, 10K $30) is held each May.

Camping

There are few lodging options close to the park. Fortunately, the camping at Humboldt Redwoods State Park (707/946-2263, www.reserveamerica.com, $35) is good, with three developed car-accessible campgrounds; there are also primitive backcountry campsites ($5). Each developed campground has its own entrance station, and reservations are strongly recommended, as the park is quite popular with weekend campers.

Burlington Campground (707/946-1811, year-round) is adjacent to the visitors center and is a convenient starting point for the marathons and other races that traverse the park in May and October. It's dark and comfortable, engulfed in trees, and has ample restroom facilities and hot showers. **Albee Creek** (Mattole Rd., 5 miles west of Ave. of the Giants, 707/946-2472, mid-May–mid-Oct.) offers some redwood-shaded sites and others in open meadows, which can be nice in the summer if you want to get a little sun. ◖**Hidden Springs Campground** (Ave. of the Giants, 5 miles south of the visitors center, 707/943-3177, early May–Labor Day) is large and popular. Minimalist campers will enjoy the seclusion of hike-in trail camps at **Johnson** and **Grasshopper Peak.**

Equestrians can also make use of the multiuse trails, and the **Cuneo Creek Horse Camp** (old homestead on Mattole Rd., 8 miles west of Ave. of the Giants, May–mid-Oct., 1 vehicle and 2 horses $35) provides a place for riders who want to spend more than just a day exploring the thousands of acres of forest and meadowland.

FERNDALE

Ferndale was built in the 19th century by Scandinavian immigrants who came to California to farm. Dairy pastures and farmland still surround the town today, and many cows munch grass near Ferndale. In town, little has changed since the immigrants constructed their fanciful gingerbread Victorian homes and shops.

The main sight in Ferndale is the town itself, since the whole thing is a designated historical landmark. Ferndale is all Victorian, all the time—just ask about the building you're in and you'll be told all about its specific architectural style, its construction date, and its original occupants. Even the public restrooms are housed in a small Victorianesque structure, surrounded by Main Street's shops, galleries, inns, and restaurants—all set into scrupulously maintained and restored late-19th-century buildings. Architecture buffs can spend hours just strolling around downtown.

Sights

The **Ferndale History Museum** (515 Shaw St., 707/786-4466, www.ferndale-museum. org, 11 A.M.–4 P.M. Tues.–Sat., 1–4 P.M. Sun. June–Sept., 11 A.M.–4 P.M. Wed.–Sat., 1–4 P.M. Sun. Oct.–Dec. and Feb.–May, $1) is a block off Main Street and tells the story of

the town. Life-size dioramas depict period life in a Victorian home, and an array of antique artifacts brings history to life. Downstairs, the implements of rural coast history vividly display the reality that farmers and craftspeople faced in the preindustrial era.

To cruise farther back into the town's history, consider wandering out into the **Ferndale Cemetery** on Bluff Street. Well-tended tombstones and mausoleums wend up the hillside behind the town. Genealogists will love reading the scrupulously maintained epitaphs that tell the human history of the region.

Entertainment and Events

Ferndale is a quiet town where the sidewalks roll up early. But for visitors who like to be out and about after 6 P.M., there are a few options. The **Ferndale Repertory Theater** (447 Main St., 707/786-5483 or 800/838-3006, www.ferndale-rep.org, $13–18) puts on a number of shows each year. Most are wholesome and suitable for the whole family, and many are put on by local kids and teens, but be sure to check what's on when you're in town. Late into the night, you can fill the slots at the **Bear River Casino** (11 Bear Paws Way, Loleta, 707/733-9644 or 800/761-2327, www.bearrivercasino.com, 9 A.M.–5 A.M. Mon.–Thurs., 24 hours Fri.–Sat.).

Ferndale has hosted the **Humboldt County Fair** (1250 5th St., www.humboldtcountyfair. org, adults $8, seniors and students under $8) each August since 1896. For 10 days people from all around the county come to celebrate at the old-fashioned fair, complete with livestock exhibits and horse racing, competitions, a carnival, musical entertainment each night, and a variety of shows for kids and adults on the fairground stages. If you're in the area, come join the fun.

The **Kinetic Sculpture Museum** (580 Main St., 707/733-3841, usually daily 10 A.M.–5 P.M.) salutes wacky modernity in all its colorful, weird glory. As the end of the annual Kinetic Grand Championship sculpture race (www.

kineticgrandchampionship.com), Ferndale has the honor of housing a number of these sculptures. The museum is a repository of more than 40 years' worth of artifacts from the great race; docents do not interpret the art, so visitors are free to make what they will of the duckies, froggies, airplanes, and bicycles.

Shopping

A tour of Ferndale's Main Street shops makes for an idyllic morning stroll. The Victorian storefronts house antiques stores, jewelry shops, clothing boutiques, and art galleries. Ferndale is also a surprisingly good place to buy a hat.

The **Golden Gait Mercantile** (421 Main St., 707/786-4891, 10 A.M.–5 P.M. Mon.–Sat.) has it all: antiques, candies, gourmet foodstuffs, clothing, hats, souvenirs, and more. Antiques and collectibles tend to be small and reasonably priced. By comparison, **Silva's Fine Jewelry** (400 Ocean Ave., 707/786-4425, www.silvasjewelry.com, daily 8:30 A.M.–9 P.M.), on the bottom floor of the Victorian Inn, is not a place for the faint of wallet. But the jewels, both contemporary and antique, are classically gorgeous. Another jewel is the **Blacksmith Shop** (455 Main St., 707/786-4216, www.ferndaleblacksmith.com, daily 10 A.M.–5:30 P.M., sometimes later) which displays a striking collection of useful art made by top blacksmiths and glassblowers from around the country. The array of jewelry, furniture, kitchen implements, fireplace tools, and metal things defies description. A gentler warmth comes from the **Golden Bee Candleworks** (451 Main St., 707/786-4508, 10 A.M.–5 P.M. Wed.–Sat., 11 A.M.–4 P.M. Sun.), purveyor of fine products made with honey and beeswax. The candles, soaps, and much more make the whole store smell delicious.

Accommodations

In Ferndale, lodgings tend to be, of course, Victorian-style inns, mostly bed-and-breakfasts.

Guests of the **Shaw House Inn** (703 Main St., 707/786-9958 or 800/557-7429, www.shawhouse.com, $125–275) must walk a block or two to get to the heart of downtown Ferndale, but the reward for staying outside the town center is a spacious garden worth a stroll. In the heat of the afternoon, huge shade trees and perfectly positioned garden benches make a lovely spot to sit and read a book, hold a quiet conversation, or just enjoy the serene beauty of garden and town. A lush morning breakfast fortifies shoppers and hikers alike.

The **Victorian Inn** (400 Ocean Ave., 707/786-4949 or 888/589-1808, www.victorianvillageinn.com, $105–480) is an imposing structure at the corner of Ocean Avenue and Main Street that also houses Silva's Jewelry. The inn comprises 13 guest rooms, all decorated with antique furnishings, luxurious linens, and pretty knickknacks. Package deals are available, including a rare chance to spend a night in the famous Carson House in Eureka, which is not open to the public.

Hotel Ivanhoe (315 Main St., 707/786-9000, www.ivanhoe-hotel.com, $95–145) is kitty-corner across from the Victorian Inn. In a town full of history, the Ivanhoe is the oldest extant hostelry. Plaques on the building's exterior describe its rich legacy. Fully refurbished in the 1990s, the four guest rooms are done in rich colors that revive the Western Victorian atmosphere of the original hotel.

If bric-a-brac and scented soaps make your skin itch, an inexpensive not-an-inn lodging option in Ferndale is the **Redwood Suites** (332 Ocean Ave., 707/786-5000 or 888/589-1863, www.redwoodsuites.com, $95–145). Only a block off Main Street, the property has guest rooms that are simple but comfortable. Family suites with full kitchens are available, and the room rates are reasonable.

Food

The restaurant at the **Hotel Ivanhoe** (315 Main

St., 707/786-9000, www.ivanhoe-hotel.com, 5–9 P.M. Wed.–Sun., bar from 4 P.M. Wed.–Sun., $12–23) is a favorite for diners from as far away as Eureka. It's all about the hearty home-made Italian dishes and friendly personal service. A more casual Italian dining experience can be had down the street at the **Ferndale Pizza Co.** (607 Main St., 707/786-4345, 11:30 A.M.–9:30 P.M. Tues.–Thurs., 11:30 A.M.–10 P.M. Fri.–Sat., noon–9:30 P.M. Sun., $16–21).

If your accommodations don't include break-fast, stop in at the local favorite **Poppa Joe's** (409 Main St., 707/786-4180, 6 A.M.–2 P.M. Mon.–Fri., 6 A.M.–noon Sat.–Sun., $5.50–9). The interior is dim and narrow, but the break-fast and lunch offerings are delicious.

Don't forget to stop at the heavenly candy store **Sweetness and Light** (554 Main St., 707/786-4403 or 800/547-8180, www.sweetnessandlight.com, 10 A.M.–5 P.M. Mon.–Sat., 11 A.M.–4 P.M. Sun.).

Information and Services

The **Ferndale Enterprise** (707/786-4611, www.ferndaleenterprise.us, $1) is published once a week on Thursday. The paper also puts out a free souvenir edition once a year just for visitors. Many inns and shops carry the souvenir edition all year long.

If you need medical care, the **Humboldt Medical Group** (528 Washington St., 707/786-4028, www.humboldtmedical-group.com) can assist you. Ferndale has a **post office** (536 Main St., 707/786-4642, www.usps.com, 8:30 A.M.–5 P.M. Mon.–Thurs., 9:30 A.M.–5 P.M. Fri., 10 A.M.–noon Sat.).

Getting There and Around

Ferndale, like much of the Lost Coast, is not directly accessible from the U.S. 101; from U.S. 101 at Fernbridge, follow Highway 211 to Ferndale. Mattole Road leads out of town south toward the Sinkyone Wilderness area, while Centerville Road heads out to the beach. Walking provides the best views and feel of the town.

EUREKA

The town of Eureka began as a seaward access point to the remote gold mines of the Trinity area. Almost immediately, settlers realized the value of the redwood trees surrounding them and started building a logging industry as well. By the late 19th century, people were getting rich, and some built lovely Victorian homes and downtown commercial buildings. Today, lumber is still a major industry in Eureka, but tourism is another, with people coming to enjoy the water-front wharf, the charming downtown shopping area, and the Victorian lumber-baron history that pervades the town. Active outdoors enthusiasts can fish, whale-watch, and hike, while history buffs can explore museums, Victorian mansions, and even a working historic mill.

◖ Blue Ox Historic Park

Even in a town that thrives on the history of lumber, the Blue Ox Millworks and Historic Park (1 X St., 707/444-3437 or 800/248-4259, www.blueoxmill.com, tours 9 A.M.–5 P.M. Mon.–Fri., 9 A.M.–4 P.M. Sat. summer, 9 A.M.–5 P.M. Mon.–Fri. winter, adults $7.50, over age 64 $6.50, ages 6–12 $3.50) is special. Blue Ox has a working lumber mill, an upscale wood and cabinetry shop, a ceramics studio, a blacksmith forge, an old-fashioned print shop, a shipbuilding yard, school, a rose garden, and a historic park. It also has the world's largest collection of human-powered woodworking tools made by the historic Barnes Equipment Company. The Blue Ox owners, Eric and Viviana Hollenbeck, didn't intend to start an immense historical enterprise; they just couldn't afford new power tools for their shop, so they rescued and rehabilitated 19th-century human-powered jig-saws, routers, and other woodworking tools. Today, the rambling buildings are filled with purchased, donated, and rehabbed tools of all kinds, which craftspeople use to create ornate custom items for homes and historic buildings

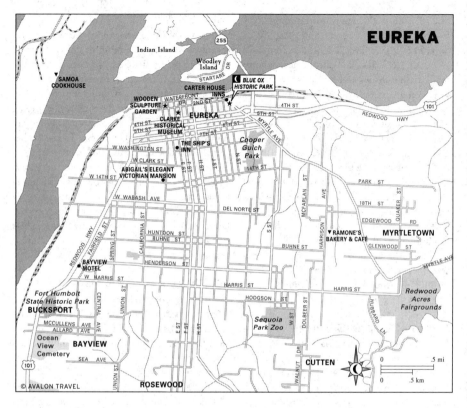

EUREKA

Indian Island

Woodley Island

STARTARE DR

SAMOA COOKHOUSE

BLUE OX HISTORIC PARK

CARTER HOUSE INNS

WOODEN SCULPTURE GARDEN

WATERFRONT DR 2ND ST

4TH ST

REDWOOD HWY

101

EUREKA

CLARKE HISTORICAL MUSEUM

5TH ST

6TH ST

7TH ST

MYRTLE AVE

THE SHIP'S INN

W WASHINGTON ST

Cooper Gulch Park

W CLARK ST

ABIGAIL'S ELEGANT VICTORIAN MANSION

14TH ST

PARK ST

W 14TH ST

W WABASH AVE

DEL NORTE ST

18TH ST

McFARLAN AVE

QUAKER ST

EDGEWOOD RD

HUNTOON ST

BUHNE ST

HARRISON ST

RAMONE'S BAKERY & CAFE

MYRTLETOWN

CALIFORNIA ST

SPRING ST

FAIRFIELD ST

HENDERSON ST

BUHNE ST

GLENWOOD ST

BAYVIEW MOTEL

MYRTLE AVE

W HARRIS ST

HARRIS ST

HARRIS ST

Redwood Acres Fairgrounds

Fort Humbolt State Historic Park

BUCKSPORT

UNION ST

CENTRAL AVE

HODGSON ST

DOLBEER ST

MCCULLENS AVE

ALLARD AVE

E ST

H ST

Sequoia Park Zoo

HUBBARD LN

Ocean View Cemetery

BAYVIEW

SEA AVE

WALNUT DR

CUTTEN

0 .5 mi

101

UNION ST

ROSEWOOD

0 .5 km

© AVALON TRAVEL

across the country. The school teaches high school students about things like digging their own clay, making pottery, and hand-setting type to print their own yearbooks. Newer workshops feature a glassblowing kiln and a darkroom where students can learn "historic" (that is, nondigital) photography methods, making their own photosensitive paper and developing black-and-white and sepia prints "just the way they did at Gettysburg." Visitors to the Blue Ox learn about the real lives and times of craftspeople of the late 1800s and early 1900s as they tour the facilities and examine the equipment. If you ask, you might even be allowed to touch and even work a piece of wood of your own. Also, be sure to stop in at the gift shop—a converted lumberjack barracks—to check out the ceramics and woodwork the students have for sale.

Clarke Historical Museum

The privately owned Clarke Historical Museum (240 E St., 707/443-1947, www.clarkemuseum. org, 11 A.M.–4 P.M. Wed.–Sat., $1, under age 5 free) is dedicated to preserving the history of Eureka and the surrounding area. Visitors get a view of changing exhibitions that illuminate the Native American history of the area as well as the gold rush and logging eras. The Nealis Hall annex displays one of the best collections of Northern California Native American artifacts in the state.

Fort Humboldt State Historic Park

Established in 1853 to protect white

settlers—particularly gold miners—from the local Native Americans, the original Fort Humboldt lasted only 17 years as a military installation. Today, Fort Humboldt State Historic Park (3431 Fort Ave., 707/445-6567, www.parks.ca.gov, daily 8 A.M.–5 P.M.) gives visitors a glimpse into the lives of 19th-century soldiers and loggers. The original fort hospital now serves as a museum. A sedate but fairly long walking tour takes you through re-creations of historic fort buildings, then out to the logging display, where you'll find several "steam donkeys," a piece of equipment that revolutionized the logging industry, along with examples of the type and size of redwood trees loggers were cutting and removing from 19th-century forests. Finally, you can spend a few minutes enjoying the tranquil historic garden, where master gardeners maintain the type of garden fort residents kept here 150 years ago.

Sequoia Park Zoo

The Sequoia Park Zoo (3414 W St., 707/442-6552, www.sequoiaparkzoo.net, daily 10 A.M.–5 P.M. summer, 10 A.M.–5 P.M. Tues.–Sun. winter, adults $5.50, ages 3–12 $3.50) might seem small, but its mission is a big one: It seeks not only to entertain visitors but also to preserve local species and educate the public about their needs. The "Secrets of the Forest" exhibit recreates the ecology of the Northern California forest while allowing visitors to see the multifarious species that live there. Be sure to say hi to Bill the Chimpanzee.

Wooden Sculpture Garden

Conveniently located downtown in the shopping district, the Wooden Sculpture Garden of Romano Gabriel (315 2nd St.) is behind a glass wall for all to see. Romano Gabriel was a furniture maker, carpenter, and gardener who immigrated from Mura, Italy, to Eureka in 1913, creating the bright colorful artworks over many years and placing them in his front yard. The

Eureka Heritage Society now preserves and maintains this sculpture garden for all to enjoy.

Humboldt Botanical Gardens

Humboldt Botanical Gardens (College of the Redwoods, 7351 Tompkins Hill Rd., 707/442-5139, www.hbgf.org, 10 A.M.–2 P.M. Sat., adults $5, under age 13 free) are the product of years of work by staff and volunteers to create gardens that celebrate the ecosystems of Humboldt County.

Entertainment and Events

The biggest and most popular restaurant and bar in Eureka is definitely the **Lost Coast Brewery & Café** (617 4th St., 707/445-4480, www.lostcoast.com, 11 A.M.–10 P.M. Sun.–Thurs., 11 A.M.–11 P.M. Fri.–Sat.). The tall cream-and-green building is perched off by itself on the main drag, easy to spot as you you're passing through town. The brewery draws crowds, especially on weekends. One thing that makes it special is that the brewery makes all the beers you can get on tap, all of which are award winners in various microbrew competitions and at the California State Fair. Come for tasty brewpub-style food, and try one or more of the delicious beers.

For a good solid dive-bar experience on the North Coast, complete with occasional live music, spend an evening at **The Shanty** (213 3rd St., 707/444-2053, daily noon–2 A.M.). You'll find all the proper dive-bar accoutrements: loud young drinkers, older locals, vintage arcade games, funky decor that includes light-up penguins at Christmastime, and plenty of cheap booze. On the rare warm evenings in summer, you can lounge outside on the patio for a smoke. Be sure to stop in for a before-dinner drink during the extended happy hour (4–7 P.M. Mon.–Fri., noon–4 P.M. Sat.–Sun.), when the prices are rock-bottom and some of the beers and liquors are top-shelf.

Eureka's **North Coast Repertory Theater** (300 5th St., 707/442-6278, www.ncrt.net,

$15–20, cash only) performs a mix of musicals, comedies, and the occasional Shakespeare or heavy-duty drama. Many performances benefit local charities.

Music lovers flock to Eureka each year for a number of big music festivals. **Blues by the Bay** (707/445-3378, www.bluesbythebay.org, all-weekend pass $70–90, individual events $20–50) is one of the largest. Held at Halvorsen Park on Humboldt Bay, the two-day festival in early September features many of the finest blues musicians alive playing in a spectacular setting. Accompanying the wailing blues are art, food, and microbrew booths. Another big event is the **Redwood Coast Jazz Festival** (707/445-3378, www.redwoodjazz.org, all-event pass $25–80, individual events $10–50). For four days in March, music lovers can enjoy every style of jazz imaginable, including Dixieland, zydeco, and big band. The festival also features dance contests and silent-movie screenings.

Shopping

The Eureka antiques scene is the largest California antiques market north of the Bay Area. In Old Town and downtown, seekers find treasures from lumber baron–era and Victorian delights, from tiny porcelain figurines to huge pieces of furniture. **Annex 39** (610 F St., 707/443-1323, noon–5:30 P.M. Mon.–Fri.) specializes in vintage linens and laundry products and also has a great selection of art deco and mid-century modern pieces. **Heritage Antique & Coins** (521 4th St., 707/444-2908, 10 A.M.–5 P.M. Tues.–Sat.) is a coin shop that also carries jewelry and Native American artifacts. Generalists will love rooting through the huge **Antiques and Goodies** (1128 3rd St., 707/442-0445, www.antiquesandgoodies.com, 10 A.M.–5 P.M. Wed.–Sat. and by appointment) and **Old Town Antiques** (318 F St., 707/442-3235, 10:30 A.M.–5:30 P.M. Mon.–Sat.).

For an afternoon of shopping in Eureka, head down toward the water to 2nd Street. Most of the buildings here are historic, and you might find an unassuming brass plaque describing the famous brothel that once inhabited what is now a toy store. Literature lovers have a nice selection of independent bookstores: **Eureka Books** (426 2nd St., 707/444-9593, www.eurekabooksellers.com, daily 10 A.M.–6 P.M.) has a big airy room in which to browse a selection of new and used books. **Booklegger** (402 2nd St., at E St., 707/445-1344, 10 A.M.–5:30 P.M. Mon.–Sat., 11 A.M.–4 P.M. Sun.), just down the street, is a small but well-organized new-and-used bookshop that specializes in antique books.

Galleries and gift shops abound, highlighting various aspects of California culture. The **Shorelines Gallery** (434 2nd St., 707/443-7272, www.shorelinesgalleryeureka.com, hours vary) specializes in fun sea-themed art and jewelry. Prices start out quite reasonable—with handmade jewelry from $10—and run up to five figures for the whimsical glass octopus coffee table. Native American art, including blankets, pottery, clothing, and jewelry, is sold at **Amerind Bay** (326 2nd St., 707/442-3042, 10:30 A.M.–6 P.M. Mon.–Sat., 4–11 P.M. Sun.). **Many Hands Gallery** (438 2nd St., 707/445-4700 or 877/445-0455, www.manyhandsgallery.net, 9:30 A.M.–9 P.M. Mon.–Sat., 10 A.M.–6 P.M. Sun.) represents approximately 100 local artisans and also displays work from national and international artists cooperatives, fair-trade organizations, and commercial importers. The offerings are very eclectic, as the gallery tries to include merchandise representative of many cultural, spiritual, and religious traditions from around the globe.

Sports and Recreation
FISHING

Eureka is a serious fishing destination. Oodles of both ocean and river fishing opportunities abound all over the region, and several fishing tournaments are held each year. As everywhere in California, you must have a valid state fishing license to fish in either the ocean or the rivers surrounding Eureka. Be sure to check with your charter service or guide to be sure they provide a day license with your trip. If they don't, you will have to get your own.

For deep-sea fishing, **Celtic Charter Service** (Woodley Island Marina, Dock D, 707/442-7115, www.shellbacksportfishing.com, fishing mid-May–Sept., crabbing Nov.) offers excursions leaving daily at 6:30 A.M. and returning at 2–3 P.M. Prices vary, as different fishing methods allow for different numbers of people on the boat. Salmon and rockfish trips are $130 pp, halibut fishing is $160 pp, albacore is $200 pp, and crabbing costs $60 pp. The company rents out tackle and sells day licenses as well. **Full Throttle Sportfishing** (Woodley Island Marina, 707/498-7473, www.fullthrottlesportfishing.com, $150–250) supplies all needed tackle and can take you out to fish for salmon, rockfish, tuna, or halibut. Trips last all day, and most leave at 6:30 A.M. If you're launching your own boat, public launches are the **Samoa Boat Ramp** (New Navy Base Rd., daily 5 A.M.–midnight) and the **Fields Landing Boat Ramp** (Railroad Ave.), both managed by Humboldt County Public Works (1106 2nd St., 707/445-7651, 8 A.M.–noon and 1–5 P.M. Mon.–Fri.).

Eureka also has good spots for pier fishing. In town, try the K Street Pier, the pier at the east end of Commercial Street, or the pier at the end of Del Norte Street. Farther north, the north jetty (Hwy. 255, across Samoa Bridge) also has a public pier open for fishing.

BIRD-WATCHING

The national, state, and county parks lacing the Eureka area create ideal bird-watching conditions. The **Humboldt Bay National Wildlife Complex** (1020 Ranch Rd., Loleta, 707/733-5406, www.fws.gov/humboldtbay) encompasses several wildlife-refuge sites where visitors are welcome. At the Salmon Creek Unit, you'll find the **Richard J. Guadagno Headquarters and Visitors Center** (daily 8 A.M.–5 P.M.), which is an excellent starting place for a number of wildlife walks. To get to the visitors center from U.S. 101, take the exit for Hookton heading north and turn left onto Eel River Drive. Take the first right onto Ranch Road, and you'll find the visitors center parking lot.

HIKING AND BIKING

Not only is there a vast system of trails in the state and national parks, the city of Eureka maintains a number of multiuse biking and hiking trails as well. Most familiar is the Old Town Boardwalk, part of the **Waterfront Trail** that comprises disconnected sections along Humboldt Bay. **Sequoia Park Trail** begins at the Sequoia Park Zoo and wends through redwood forests, past a duck pond, and through a meadow. This trail is paved and friendly for strollers and wheelchairs. The unpaved **Elk River Trail** (end of Hilfiker Lane) stretches for one mile through wild meadows along the coast. **Cooper Gulch Trail** is a more sedate stroll than a strenuous hike, circling the Cooper Gulch park playing fields.

KAYAKING AND RAFTING

The water is cold, but getting out on it in a kayak can be exhilarating. If you're new to the sport or just want a guided trip of the area, guided paddles, lessons, rentals, and kayak fishing trips are available through **Humboats Kayak Adventures** (Woodley Island Marina, 707/443-5157, www.humboats.com, canoe and kayak rentals $25–75, 2-hour full-moon kayak tour $50). Guides lead a huge variety of tours, from serene paddles in the harbor suitable for children to 30-mile-plus trips designed for experienced kayakers.

River rafters and kayakers have great opportunities for rapids fun on the Klamath and Trinity Rivers. **Bigfoot Rafting Company** (Willow Creek, 530/629-2263 or

© HEATHER C. LISTON

the driftwood-covered coast near Eureka

800/722-2223, www.bigfootrafting.com, $35–85) leads half-day, full-day, and multiday trips on both rivers as well as on the Cal-Salmon and the Smith Rivers. Experts can take inflatable kayaks down the Class IV rapids, and newcomers can find a gentle paddle with just enough white water to make things interesting.

Accommodations

With such a wealth of Victorian houses, Eureka is a natural location for classic bed-and-breakfast accommodations. Chain motels are also available in abundance, many of them quite cheap. But for a real taste of the town, try one of the charming inns.

Halcyon Inn Bed & Breakfast (1420 C St., 707/444-1310 or 888/882-1310, www.halcyoninn.com, $105–155) welcomes guests to a small Victorian house and a friendly, intimate Eureka experience. The brown-shingled exterior and well-kept verdant lawns give way to a gracious home. Since there are only three guest rooms, you can expect a quiet and uncrowded experience. Each guest room has its own four-poster bed and collection of antique furniture, floral bedspreads, and a private bath. In the morning, come to the cozy dining room to enjoy a sumptuous and health-conscious breakfast. Then wander out into the small but pretty gardens with flowers blooming in summer and tables and chairs set up to encourage reading, card games, or just lounging with an extra cup of coffee or glass of wine.

The Ship's Inn (821 D St., 707/443-7583 or 877/443-7583, www.shipsinn.net, $130–175) is a newish B&B in an oldish recently restored Victorian home on the east side of town. Few guest rooms and a friendly innkeeper make a stay at this inn delightfully like staying in a friend's grand home. Breakfast is particularly good, and the small garden is the perfect place to sit out in the afternoon reading a good book. Each of the four guest rooms has its own decoration and theme; the Captain's Quarters take the inn's name to heart with a blue-and-gold nautical design, while the other guest rooms tend more toward classic Victorian floral. Unlike many B&Bs, you'll find TVs in every room, along with fireplaces, plush robes, and private baths.

If B&Bs just aren't your style, get a room at the **Bayview Motel** (2844 Fairfield St., 707/442-1673 or 866/725-6813, www.bayviewmotel.com, $109–175). This hilltop motel has lovely views of Humboldt Bay from many of the guest rooms and from the grounds. Guest rooms are spacious and decorated in slightly more elegant colors and fabrics than at the average chain motel. You'll find wonderful whirlpool suites, free Wi-Fi, cable TV, wet bars, and coffeemakers. If you're traveling with the family, you can rent a double suite—two rooms with an adjoining door and separate baths. Although not right in downtown Eureka, it's an easy drive from the Bayview for dinner, shopping, and strolling by the harbor.

For the most Victorian experience you can have, book a room at **Abigail's Elegant Victorian Mansion** (1406 C St., 707/444-3144, www.eureka-california.com, $135–250). Originally built by one of the founders of the town, the inn has retained many of the large home's original fixtures. The owners took pains to learn the history of the house and the town and have added appropriate decor to create a truly Victorian mansion, right down to the vintage books in the elegant library. Each of the three guest rooms comes with its own story and an astonishing collection of antiques. All guest rooms have private baths, although it might be just across the hall.

The ◖ **Carter House Inns** (301 L St., 800/404-1390, www.carterhouse.com, $159–595) comprises two inns and two smaller cottages, the large mansions seen on either side of the street in downtown Eureka. The unusual smaller butter-yellow mansion is not a true Victorian dwelling; it's a reproduction built in the 1980s. The guest rooms in each building

are elegantly appointed, the dark wooden furniture evocative of the Victorian era, while the minimal floral gewgaws caters to modern sensibilities. Standard guest rooms are small and stylish with particularly attractive baths. Larger suites are decorated with antiques, and some have gorgeous soaking tubs set in windowed alcoves. Between the two buildings, the large inn offers nearly 30 guest rooms. Enjoy a truly magnificent dinner at the attached Restaurant 301, book an in-room massage, or even go for a wine-tasting package that delves into the Carter House's remarkable cellars.

Food

The ◖ **Samoa Cookhouse** (511 Vance Rd., Samoa, 707/442-1659, www.samoacookhouse.net, daily 7 A.M.–9 P.M. summer, daily 7 A.M.–8 P.M. winter, adults $16) is a historic Eureka institution. Red-checked tablecloths cover long rough tables to recreate the atmosphere of a logging-camp dining hall. The all-you-can-eat meals are served family-style from huge serving platters. Diners sit on benches and pass the hearty fare down in turn. Think big hunks of roast beef, mountains of mashed potatoes, and piles of cooked vegetables. This is the place to bring your biggest appetite. After dinner, browse the small Historic Logging Museum and gift shop.

Restaurant 301 (301 L St., 800/404-1390, www.carterhouse.com, daily 6–9 P.M., $18–29) at the Carter House Inns seems like a top-shelf San Francisco or Los Angeles eatery lost on the distant North Coast. The chef creates an ever-changing menu of delectable delicacies, with tasting menus that give diners the best chance to experience this great restaurant. You'll find everything from exotic duck dishes to simple local seafood preparations to items from the restaurant's own on-site kitchen garden on the succession of plates served at a relaxed pace. For a special treat, try the wine flights suggested with the menus.

Another high-end Eureka restaurant that

impresses even the most discriminating Bay Area–trained palates is **Avalon** (239 G St., 707/445-0500, www.avaloneureka.com, lunch 11:30 A.M.–2 P.M. Wed.–Fri., dinner 5–9 P.M. Tues.–Sat., $20–28), a restaurant that speaks to the hearts of eco-conscious carnivores with sustainably sourced steaks, mixed grills, and game meats prominent on the menu.

Some of the best Mexican food in Eureka can be had at **Chapala Café** (201 2nd St., 707/443-9514, daily 11 A.M.–9 P.M., $8.50–10.50). The large menu offers many Mexican classics, all available in both meat and vegetarian versions. The atmosphere at Chapala is friendly and festive, and you can't miss the gorgeous and colorful mural or the live entertainment on weekend evenings. Whether you order a classic taco-enchilada combination or one of the house-made slow-cooked chilies, be sure to get a margarita to go with it. Kids and teetotalers may prefer the imported Mexican Jarritos sodas. Chapala prides itself on its fast and excellent service, actually promising a free meal should your food not arrive in a timely fashion. The fish tacos are highly recommended.

Café Marina (601 Startare Dr., Woodley Island, 707/443-2233, www.samoacookhouse. net, daily breakfast, lunch, and dinner) provides a California coastal dining experience. Located on Woodley Island overlooking the harbor, the place has outdoor seating, which is beautiful on rare sunny days. From here, you can watch the sea lions lazing near the docks as the fishing boats come and go. The seafood is good, and the menu also includes burgers and sandwiches, plus a few additional entrées at dinner. Portions are large, and preparations are basic but tasty. The service is decent and the prices are reasonable, but the main reason to come is the location.

Ramone's Bakery & Café (2223 Harrison Ave., 707/442-1336, www.ramonesbakery. com, 7 A.M.–7 P.M. Mon.–Thurs., 7 A.M.–9 P.M. Fri.–Sat., 8 A.M.–6 P.M. Sun.) is a genuine local North Coast chain. All locations (including 209 E St. and 430 N. St., one in Arcata, and one in McKinleyville) sell fresh from-scratch baked goods and candies. Come in the morning to enjoy a fresh cup of coffee roasted in-house and a danish or a scone, indulge in an afternoon pastry, or even get a whole tart, cake, or loaf of fresh-baked bread to take out for an afternoon picnic.

Information and Services
The **Humboldt County Convention and Visitors Bureau** does not operate a public visitors center, but if you need something, drop by the business office (1034 2nd St., 707/443-5097, www.redwoods.info, 8:30 A.M.–5 P.M. Mon.–Fri.) and they'll do their best to help you. The website is an ideal place to do research on vacation plans anywhere in the Redwood Coast region, and you can call the travel hotline (800/346-3482) for information.

The **Eureka Chamber of Commerce** (2112 Broadway, 707/442-3738, www.eurekachamber.com, 8:30 A.M.–5 P.M. Mon.–Fri. fall–spring, 8:30 A.M.–5 P.M. Mon.–Fri., 10 A.M.–3 P.M. Sat.–Sun. summer) runs a helpful facility, with plenty of literature about things to do in town and beyond.

The local daily paper is the *Times-Standard* (www.times-standard.com, Mon.–Fri. $0.50, Sun. $1.50). It covers both national and local news and includes information about events in the North Coast region. You can pick up a copy at many businesses around the region. Check the entertainment section for the latest hot spots and live events during your stay.

As the big urban area on the North Coast, Eureka and Arcata have the major services travelers may need. You'll find branches of major banks, complete with ATMs, which are also available at supermarkets, pharmacies, and other businesses.

Naturally, you'll find **post offices** (337 W. Clark St., 707/442-1768, 8:30 A.M.–5 P.M.

Mon.–Fri., noon–3 P.M. Sat.; 514 H St., 707/442-0856, 9 A.M.–5 P.M. Mon.–Fri.).

Eureka has a full-service hospital, **St. Joseph Hospital** (2700 Dolbeer St., 707/445-8121, www.stjosepheureka.org), with an emergency room and an urgent care center for less serious issues.

Getting There and Around

Eureka is on U.S. 101, easily accessed by car from north or south. From Crescent City, Eureka is less than an hour's drive south on U.S. 101.

In Eureka, driving is the only option if you're not staying downtown, especially if you want to head out to Woodley Island. You can easily visit the 2nd Street shops and restaurants on foot. Parking downtown is metered or free on the streets, and not too difficult to find except on holiday or event weekends.

Bus service in and around Eureka is operated by the **Humboldt Transit Authority** (HTA, www.hta.org, adults $1.40, children and seniors $1.10). The HTA's **Eureka Transit System** (ETS) runs within town limits, and the Redwood Transit System (RTS, www.redwoodtransit.org, adults $2.75, children and seniors $2.50) can take around the area, from Eureka north to Crescent City, south to Ferndale, and east to Willow Creek.

Eureka has a small commercial airport, **Arcata-Eureka Airport** (ACV, 3561 Boeing Ave., McKinleyville, 707/839-5401, http://co.humboldt.ca.us/aviation), that serves the North Coast region. You can fly in and out on Horizon Air (a division of Alaska) or United Airlines. Expect flights to be expensive but convenient.

ARCATA

Arcata is just eight miles north of Eureka on U.S. 101 and is populated with students from Humboldt State University.

Arcata Marsh and Wildlife Sanctuary

Hundreds of animal species live in the Arcata area, and more migrate through in spring and fall. The Arcata Marsh and Wildlife Sanctuary (569 S. G St., 707/826-2359, www.cityofarcata.org) is an especially good birding spot. Visitors can join a free guided walk or enjoy exhibits at the **Interpretive Center** (1–5 P.M. Mon., 9 A.M.–5 P.M. Tues.–Sun.) and the **Headwaters Forest Reserve** (707/825-2300, www.blm.gov/ca, 7:45 A.M.–4:30 P.M. Mon.–Fri.).

Kinetic Grand Championship

An unusual event is the Kinetic Grand Championship sculpture race (707/733-3841, www.kineticgrandchampionship.com), a three-day, 42-mile race from Arcata to Main Street in Ferndale held each year on Memorial Day Weekend in May. Even if creating your own colorful and ridiculous human-powered locomotive sculpture isn't your thing, it's worth taking a spot along the racecourse to see what the artists have come up with this year. Be prepared for dinosaurs, donkeys, dung beetles, and other sublimely silly things. The sculptures cross pavement, sand, water, and mud over the course of the three-day race. Nowadays other towns have their own kinetic sculpture races (and yes, there's one at the Burning Man festival in Nevada), but the North Coast claims the original event, and this remains the grand championship of them all. For a great view, try to get a spot to watch Dead Man's Drop or the Water Entry.

PATRICK'S POINT STATE PARK

Patrick's Point State Park (4150 Patrick's Point Dr., Trinidad, 707/677-3570, www.parks.ca.gov, day use $8) is a rambling coastal park 25 miles north of Eureka replete with campgrounds, trails, beaches, landmarks, and history. It's not the biggest of the many parks along the North Coast, but it is one of the best. The climate remains cool year-round, making it perfect for hiking and exploring, if not for ocean swimming. There's a native plant garden, a visitors center, and three campgrounds ($35), plus a recreated Yurok Village. Because

Patrick's Point is small in comparison to the other parks, it's easy to get around. Request a map at the gate and follow the signs along the tiny and often nameless park roads.

Sights

Prominent among the local landmarks is the place the park was named after: **Patrick's Point,** which offers panoramic Pacific views and can be reached by a brief hike from a convenient parking lot. Another popular spot is **Wedding Rock,** adjacent to Patrick's Point in a picturesque cove. People really do hike the narrow trail out to the rock to get married, and you might even see a bride and groom stumbling along holding hands on their way back from a ceremony.

The most fascinating area in the park is **Sumeg Village,** a re-creation of a native Yurok village based on an actual archaeological find east of here. Visitors can crawl through the perfectly round hobbit-like hole-doors into semi-subterranean homes, meeting places, and storage buildings. Or check out the native plant garden, a collection of local plants the Yurok people used for food, basketry, and medicine. Today, the local Yurok people use Sumeg Village as a gathering place for education and celebrations, and they request that visitors tread lightly and do not disturb this tranquil area.

Those who want to dip a toe in the ocean rather than just gaze at it from afar will be glad to know that Patrick's Point has a number of accessible beaches. The steep trail leading down to **Agate Beach** deters few visitors. This wide stretch of coarse sand bordered by cliffs shot through with shining quartz veins is perfect for lounging, playing, and beachcombing. The semiprecious stones for which it is named really do appear here. The best time to find good agates is in the winter, after a storm.

Hiking

Only six miles of trails thread their way through Patrick's Point. Choose from the **Rim Trail,** which will take you along the cliffs for a view of the sea, and if you're lucky a view of migrating whales. Tree-lovers might prefer the **Octopus Tree Trail,** which provides a great view of an old-growth Sitka spruce grove.

Camping

The three campgrounds at Patrick's Point (information 707/677-3570, reservations 800/444-7275, www.reserveamerica.com, $35) have a total of 124 sites. It can be difficult to determine the difference between **Agate Beach, Abalone,** and **Penn Creek,** so be sure to get good directions from the park rangers when you arrive. Most campsites are pleasantly shaded by the groves of trees; all include a picnic table, a propane stove, and a food storage cupboard, and you'll find running water, restrooms, and showers nearby.

Information and Services

You can get a map and information at the **Patrick's Point State Park Visitors Center** (707/677-1945, usually daily 9 A.M.–4:30 P.M.), immediately to the right when you get to the entry gate. Information about nature walks and campfire programs is posted on the bulletin board.

Getting There and Around

Patrick's Point State Park is located on the coast 25 miles north of Eureka and 15 miles south of Orick on U.S. 101.

◖ REDWOOD NATIONAL AND STATE PARKS

The lands of Redwood National and State Parks (www.nps.gov/redw, day use and camping free) meander along the coast and include three state parks—Prairie Creek Redwoods, Del Norte Coast Redwoods, and Jedediah Smith. This complex of parkland encompasses most of California's northern redwood forests. The main landmass of Redwood National Park

© HEATHER C. LISTON

Redwood National Park

gigantic wooden sculptures of Paul Bunyan and his blue ox, Babe, from U.S. 101. The Trees of Mystery (15500 U.S. 101 N., 707/482-2251 or 800/638-3389, www.treesofmystery.net, daily 8:30 A.M.–6:30 P.M. June–Aug., daily 9:30 A.M.–4:30 P.M. Sept.–May, adults $14, ages 4–11 $7) doesn't disappoint as a great place to take a break from the road to let the family out for some good cheesy fun. Visitors can enjoy the original Mystery Hike, the SkyTrail gondola ride through the old-growth redwoods, and the palatial gift shop. Perhaps best of all, at the left end of the gift shop is a little-known gem: the Native American museum. A large collection of artifacts from ethnic groups across the country and indigenous to the redwood forests grace several crowded galleries. The restrooms here are large and well-maintained, which makes Trees of Mystery a nice stop en route.

Hiking

One of the easiest, most popular ways to get close to the trees is to walk the **Lady Bird Johnson Trail** (Bald Hills Rd., 1.4 miles, easy). This nearly level loop provides an intimate view of the redwood and fir forests that define this region. It's not far from the **Thomas H. Kuchel Visitors Center** (U.S. 101, west of Orick, 707/465-7765, daily 9 A.M.–6 P.M. summer, daily 9 A.M.–4 P.M. winter), and the staff there can direct you to the trailhead and provide a simple map. Another easy-access trail is **Trillium Falls** (Davison Rd. at Elk Meadow, 2.8 miles, easy). You may not see elk or trillium flowers, but the redwood trees along this cool, dark trail are striking, and the small waterfall is a nice treasure in the woods. This little hike is lovely any time of year but best in spring, when the water volume over the falls is at its peak.

The **Lost Man Creek Trail** (east of Elk Meadow, 1 mile off U.S. 101, 0.5 mile, easy–difficult) has it all. The first 0.5 mile is perfect for wheelchair users and families with small

is just south of Prairie Creek State Park along U.S. 101, stretching east from the coast and the highway. To get to the park from the south, drive along Bald Hills Road.

Thomas H. Kuchel Visitors Center

If you're new to the Redwood National and State Parks, the Thomas H. Kuchel ("KEE-kul") Visitors Center (U.S. 101, west of Orick, 707/465-7765, daily 9 A.M.–6 P.M. summer, daily 9 A.M.–4 P.M. winter) is a large facility with a ranger station, clean restrooms, and a path to the shore. You can get maps, advice, permits for backcountry camping, and books. In the summer, rangers run patio talks and coast walks that provide a great introduction to the area for children and adults. You can also have a picnic at one of the tables outside the visitors center, or you can walk a short distance to Redwood Creek.

Trees of Mystery

Generations of kids have enjoyed spotting the

children. But as the trail rolls along, the grades get steeper and more challenging. You can customize the length of this out-and-back trail by turning around at any time. If you reach the Lost Man Creek picnic grounds, your total round-trip distance is 22 miles with more than 3,000 feet of elevation gain and several stream crossings.

Another fabulous long hike is the **Redwood Creek Trail** (Bald Hills Rd. spur off U.S. 101, difficult), which follows Redwood Creek for eight miles to the **Tall Trees Grove.** If you have someone willing to act as a shuttle driver, you can pick up the **Tall Trees Trail** and walk another six miles (a total of 14 miles) to the **Dolason Prairie Trail,** which takes you back out to Bald Hills Road.

Accommodations and Camping

If you want to sleep indoors but still stay close to the national park, your best bet is the **Palm Café & Motel** (121130 U.S. 101, Orick, 707/488-3381, $60–90). It's a far cry from fancy, but it's a great location, and the food in the attached café (daily 6 A.M.–8 P.M. summer, $10–12) is good, and service is friendly at both. The **Green Valley Motel** (120784 U.S. 101, Orick, 707/488-2341, $44) is nearby in Orick.

There are no designated campgrounds in Redwood National Park, but free backcountry camping is allowed; permits may be necessary in certain areas. The **Elam Camp** and the **44 Camp** are both hike-in primitive campgrounds along the Dolason Prairie Trail.

Contact the **Crescent City Information Center** (1111 2nd St., Crescent City, 707/465-7335, daily 9 A.M.–6 P.M. summer, daily 9 A.M.–5 P.M. spring and fall, daily 9 A.M.–4 P.M. winter) if you're planning a backcountry camping trip. The center can help you determine whether you need a permit and issue one if you do.

Getting There and Around

The Redwood National and State Parks line U.S. 101 from Prairie Creek Redwoods in the south all the way up to Jedediah Smith near Crescent City at the northern end.

PRAIRIE CREEK REDWOODS STATE PARK

At the junction of the south end of the Newton B. Drury Scenic Drive and U.S. 101, Prairie Creek Redwoods State Park (Newton B. Drury Dr., 25 miles south of Crescent City, 707/465-7347, campground 707/488-2171, www.parks.ca.gov, day use $8) offers 14,000 acres of lush and shady hiking trails through redwoods as well as several large campgrounds ($35).

One of the cool things that makes a drive to Prairie Creek worth the effort is the herd of **Roosevelt elk.** These big guys with their huge racks hang out at—where else?—the Elk Prairie, a stretch of open grassland along the highway. To find the viewing platform, watch for the road signs. The best times to see the elk out grazing in the field are early morning and around sunset. The park asks that you stay in the viewing area and let the elk enjoy their meals in peace.

Prairie Creek Visitors Center

Just beyond the entrance off U.S. 101, the Prairie Creek Visitors Center (Newton B. Drury Dr., 707/488-2171, usually daily 9 A.M.–5 P.M.) includes a small interpretive museum describing the history of the California redwood forests. A tiny bookshop adjoins the museum, well stocked with books describing the history, nature, and culture of the area. Many ranger-led programs originate at the visitors center, and permits are available for backcountry camping in the park.

Newton B. Drury Scenic Drive

A gorgeous scenic road through the redwoods, Newton B. Drury Scenic Drive, off U.S. 101 about five miles south of Klamath, features old-growth trees lining the roads, a close-up view of the redwood forest ecosystem, and a grove or trailhead every hundred yards or so. A great place to turn off is at the **Big Tree Wayside.** The eponymous tree is only a short walk from the parking area, and several trails radiate from the little grove.

Hiking

Perhaps the single most famous hiking trail along the redwood coast is **Fern Canyon** (Davison Rd., Prairie Creek Redwoods State Park), near Gold Bluffs Beach. This hike runs through a narrow canyon carved by Home Creek. Ferns, mosses, and other water-loving plants grow thick up the sides of the canyon, creating a beautiful vertical carpet of greenery. It's so unusual, in fact, that Steven Spielberg used this canyon in both *Jurassic Park 2* and *Return of the Jedi.* The second most famous thing about this little area, after its sheer explosion of greenness, is the presence of the very large and relatively rare Roosevelt elk; look for them especially around Gold Bluffs Beach.

To get to the trailhead, take U.S. 101 three miles north of the town of Orick and then, at the Prairie Creek visitors center, turn west onto Davidson Road (no trailers allowed) and travel two more miles. This rough dirt road takes you through the campground and ends at the trailhead 1.5 miles later.

Take an easy one-mile loop here to experience Fern Canyon. You can extend this hike into a longer (6.5 miles, moderate) loop by starting at the same place; when the trail intersects with James Irvine Trail, bear right and follow that spur. Bear right again onto **Clintonia Trail** and walk through a redwood grove to Miners Ridge Trail. Bear right onto Miners Ridge, an old logging road, and follow it down to the ocean. Walk 1.5 miles along Gold Bluffs Beach to complete the loop.

Miners Ridge and **James Irvine Loop** (12 miles, moderate) covers some of the same ground but starts from the visitors center instead of the Fern Canyon trailhead, avoiding the rough dirt terrain of Davison Road. Start out on **James Irvine Trail** and bear right when you can, following the trail all the way until it joins Fern Canyon Trail. Turn left when you get to the coast and walk along Gold Bluffs Beach for 1.5 miles. Then make a left onto the Clintonia Trail and head back toward the visitors center.

If you're starting at the visitors center but don't want to do the entire 12-mile loop, you can cut this hike roughly in half. When you get to the Clintonia Trail on your way out to the coast, make a left instead of continuing on the James Irvine Trail. This will take you over to Miners Ridge, where you make another left to loop back to the starting point, for a total of about six miles. This is a pleasant hike with plenty of great trees; the drawback is that you don't get to see Fern Canyon.

If you're hiking the **California Coastal Trail** (www.californiacoastaltrail.info), you can do a leg here at Prairie Creek. The Coastal Trail runs along the northern coast of this park. Another way to get to the campground is via the **Ossagon Creek Trail** (north end of Newton B. Drury Dr., 2 miles round-trip, moderate). It's not long, but the steep grade makes it a tough haul in spots, and the stunning trees along the way make it worth the effort.

Camping

The **Elk Prairie Campground** (127011 Newton B. Drury Dr., Orick, campground 707/488-2171, reservations 800/444-7275, www.reserveamerica.com, vehicles $35, hikers and cyclists $5) has 75 sites for tents or RVs and a full range of comfortable camping amenities. You can get a shower and purchase wood for your fire ring. Several campsites are wheelchair-accessible, so be sure to ask for one if you need it when you reserve your site. A big campfire area is north of the campground, an easy walk for campers interested in the evening programs put on by rangers and volunteers.

For a sand camping experience, head out to **Gold Bluffs Beach Campground** (Davidson

Rd., 3 miles north of Orick, www.nps.gov/ redw, no reservations, $35). There are about 25 sites for tents or RVs. Amenities include flush toilets, water, solar showers, and wide ocean views. The surf can be quite dangerous here, so be extremely careful if you go in the water.

Backcountry camping is allowed in Prairie Creek, but only in two designated camping areas, **Ossagon Creek** and **Miners Ridge** (3 sites each, $5). Permits are available at the campground kiosk or the Prairie Creek Visitors Center (Newton B. Drury Dr., 707/488-2171, usually daily 9 A.M.–5 P.M.).

Getting There

Prairie Creek Redwoods is located 50 miles north of Eureka and 25 miles south of Crescent City on U.S. 101. Newton B. Drury Drive traverses the park and can be accessed from U.S. 101 north or south.

DEL NORTE COAST REDWOODS STATE PARK

South of Crescent City, Del Norte Coast Redwoods State Park (Mill Creek Campground Rd., off U.S. 101, 707/465-2146, www.parks. ca.gov, $8) encompasses a variety of ecosystems, including eight miles of wild coastline, second-growth redwood forest, and virgin old-growth forests. One of the largest in this system of parks, Del Norte is a great place to get lost in the backcountry with just your knapsack and your fishing rod, exploring the meandering branches of Mill Creek.

Del Norte State Park has no visitors center, but you can get information from the **Crescent City Information Center** (1111 2nd St., Crescent City, 707/465-7335, daily 9 A.M.–6 P.M. summer, daily 9 A.M.–5 P.M. spring and fall, daily 9 A.M.–4 P.M. winter). Minimal restroom facilities are available at the Del Norte campgrounds, and the park has an RV dump station but no RV hookups.

Hiking

Guided tours, nature trails, and wheelchair-accessible trails and campgrounds are all available at Del Norte. You'll want to dress in layers to hike as it can get down into the 40s even in summer. There are several rewarding yet gentle and short excursions that start and end in the Mill Creek Campground.

The **Trestle Loop Trail** (1 mile, easy) begins across from the campfire center in the campground. Notice the trestles and other artifacts along the way; the loop follows the route of a defunct railroad from the logging era. It's OK to eat the berries along this path; just keep in mind that bears and other animals like them as much as you do, so the more abundant the food, the more likely you'll have company. If you want more after this brief walk, take the nearby **Nature Loop Trail** (1 mile, easy), which begins near the campground entrance gate. This trail features interpretive signage to help you learn about the varieties of impressive trees you'll be passing.

These coastal parks are a cherished destination for serious hikers as well as sightseers, so it is possible to get a great workout along with the scenery. The northern section of the great **California Coastal Trail** (CCT, www.californiacoastaltrail.info) runs right through Del Norte Coast Redwoods State Park. The trail has been under development since 1972 and is ultimately envisioned as a 1,200-mile pathway along beaches and forests all the way from the Oregon border to the Mexican border. Not all of it will be completed for some time to come, but the parts available for use in Del Norte offer a great illustration of what the project is meant to be. The Coastal Trail is reasonably well marked; look for signs with the CCT logo.

The "last chance" section of the California Coastal Trail (Enderts Beach–Damnation Creek, 14 miles, strenuous) makes a challenging day hike. To reach the trailhead, turn west from U.S. 101 onto Enderts Beach Road in Del Norte, three miles south of Crescent City. Drive 2.3 miles to the end of the road, where the trail begins.

The trail follows the historic route of U.S. 101 south to Enderts Beach. You'll walk through fields of wildflowers and groves of trees twisted by the wind and saltwater. Eventually, the trail climbs about 900 feet to an overlook with a great view of Enderts Beach. At just over two miles, the trail enters Del Norte Coast Redwoods State Park, where it meanders through Anson Grove's redwood, fir, and Sitka spruce trees. At 4.5 miles, cross Damnation Creek on a footbridge, and at 6.1 miles, cross the Damnation Creek Trail. (For a longer hike, take the four-mile round-trip side excursion down to the beach and back.) After seven miles, a flight of steps leads up to milepost 15.6 on U.S. 101. At this point, you can turn around and return the way you came, making for a gloriously varied day hike of about 14 miles round-trip.

Camping

The **Mill Creek Campground** (U.S. 101, 7 miles south of Crescent City, 800/444-7275, www.reserveamerica.com, May 1–Sept. 7, vehicles $35, hikers and cyclists $5) is in an attractive setting along Mill Creek. There are 145 sites for RVs and tents, and facilities include restrooms and fire pits. Feel free to bring your camper to the Mill Creek campground; it has spots for RVs and a dump station on-site. Call in advance to reserve a spot and to be sure that your camper does not exceed the park's length limit. There are no designated backcountry campsites in Del Norte, and backcountry camping is not allowed.

Getting There

Del Norte Coast Redwoods is located seven miles south of Crescent City on U.S. 101. The park entrance is on Hamilton Road, east of U.S. 101.

JEDEDIAH SMITH REDWOODS STATE PARK

The best redwood grove in the old growth of Jedediah Smith Redwoods State Park (U.S.

199, 9 miles east of Crescent City, 707/458-3018, www.parks.ca.gov, $8 per vehicle) is the **Stout Memorial Grove**. This bunch of coastal redwood trees is, as advertised, stout—although the grove was named for a person, not for the size of the trees. These old giants make humans feel small as they wander in the grove. These are some of the biggest and oldest trees on the North Coast and were somehow spared the loggers' saws. Another great thing about this grove is the lack of visitors, since its far-north latitude makes it harder to reach than some of the other big redwood groves in California.

Visitors Centers

There are two visitors centers in Jedediah Smith, about five minutes apart. Both offer similar information and include materials about all of the nearby parks. One is the **Jedediah Smith Visitors Center** (U.S. 101, Hiouchi, 707/458-3496, hours vary mid-May–mid-Sept.), and the other is the **Hiouchi Information Center** (U.S. 199, Hiouchi, 707/458-3294, daily 9 A.M.–6 P.M. summer, hours vary fall–spring).

Hiking

The trails running through the trees make for wonderful cool and shady summer hiking. Many trails run along the river and the creeks, offering a variety of ecosystems and plenty of lush scenery to enjoy. Wherever you hike, stay on the established trails. Wandering into the forest, you can trample the delicate and shallow redwood root systems, unintentionally damaging the trees you're here to visit.

The **Simpson Reed Trail** (U.S. 199, 6 miles east of Crescent City, 1 mile, easy) takes you from U.S. 199 down to the banks of the Smith River.

To get a good view of the Smith River, hike the **Hiouchi Trail** (2 miles, moderate). From the Hiouchi Information Center and campgrounds on U.S. 199, cross the Summer Footbridge and then follow the river north. The Hiouchi Trail

NORTH COAST

© HEATHER C. LISTON

Jedediah Smith Redwoods State Park

then meets the Hatton Loop Trail and leads away from the river and into the forest.

If you're looking for a longer and more aggressive trek, try the **Mill Creek Trail** (7.5 miles round-trip, difficult). A good place to start is at the Summer Footbridge. The trail then follows the creek down to the unpaved Howland Hill Road.

If it's redwoods you're looking for, take the **Boy Scout Tree Trail** (5.2 miles, moderate). To get to the trailhead, you have to drive a rugged unpaved road for a couple of miles, but there are plenty of impressive trees to enjoy. The trail is usually quiet, with few hikers, and the gargantuan forest will make you feel truly tiny. About three miles into the trail, you'll come to a fork. If you've got time, take both forks: first the left, which takes you to the small, mossy, and very green Fern Falls, and then the right, which takes you to the eponymous Boy Scout Tree, one of the impressively huge redwoods.

Boating and Swimming

You'll find two boat launches in the park: one at Society Hole and one adjacent to the Summer Footbridge that's only open in winter. Down by the River Beach Trail, you'll find **River Beach** (immediately west of the Hiouchi Information Center), a popular spot for swimming in the river. Swimming is allowed throughout the park, but be very careful—rivers and creeks move unpredictably, and you might not notice deep holes until you're on them. Enjoy the cool water, but keep a close eye on children and other loved ones to ensure a safe time.

Fishing

With the Smith River and numerous feeder creeks running through Jed Smith, it's not surprising that fishing is one of the most popular activities. Chilly winter fishing draws a surprising number of anglers to vie for king salmon up to 30 pounds and steelhead up to 20 pounds. Seasons for both species run October–February. In the summer you can cast into the river to catch cutthroat trout.

Camping

The Ⓒ Jedediah Smith Campground (U.S. 199, Hiouchi, 800/444-7275, www.reserveamerica.com) is beautifully situated on the banks of Smith River, with most sites near the River Beach Trail (immediately west of the Hiouchi Information Center). There are 106 RV and tent sites (vehicles $35, hike-in or cycle-in primitive sites $5). Facilities include plenty of restrooms, fire pits, and coin-operated showers. Reservations are advised, especially for summer and holiday weekends. The campground is open year-round, but reservations are accepted only Memorial Day–Labor Day. Jedediah Smith has no designated backcountry campsites, and camping outside the developed campgrounds is not allowed. If you're backpacking, check at one of the visitors centers for help in finding the nearest place to camp overnight.

Getting There

Jedediah Smith Redwoods State Park (U.S. 199, 9 miles east of Crescent City, 707/458-3018, www.parks.ca.gov, $8 per vehicle) is north of Crescent City along the Smith River, next door to the immense Smith River National Recreation Area (U.S. 199 west of Hiouchi).

Crescent City

The northernmost city on the coast of California perches on the bay whose shape gave the town its name. Cool and windswept, Crescent City is a perfect place to put on a parka, stuff your hands deep in your pockets, and take a long contemplative walk along a wide beautiful beach. Serious deep-sea fishing aficionados will feel at home, and hikers will love the uncrowded redwood forests.

In 1964 much of Crescent City was destroyed in a tsunami caused by an Alaskan earthquake. The damage was estimated at $7–15 million, 10 local people died, and many were injured, making this the most severe tsunami in modern history on the West Coast of the United States. More than 40 years have passed, but the ripples of the event still shudder through the small community. Look to the tops of utility poles to see old tsunami warning sirens, now rusted with disuse but not yet removed.

SIGHTS
Point St. George

The wild, lonely, beautiful Point St. George (end of Washington Blvd.) epitomizes the glory of the North Coast of California. Walk out onto the cliffs to take in the deep blue sea, wild salt- and flower-scented air, and craggy cliffs and beaches. On a clear day, you can see all the way to Oregon. Short steep trails lead across wild beach prairie land down to broad, flat, nearly deserted beaches. In spring–summer wildflowers bloom on the cliffs, and swallows nest in the cluster of buildings on the point. On rare and special clear days, you can almost make out the St. George Reef Lighthouse alone on its perch far out in the Pacific. The St. George Reef Lighthouse Preservation Society offers occasional helicopter trips out to the site (707/464-8299, www.stgeorgereeflighthouse.us, $225 pp, cash or check only). Call ahead to reserve a spot and check the schedule and cost.

Battery Point Lighthouse Park

West of the downtown Crescent City, past the visitors center, is Battery Point Lighthouse Park (end of A St., 707/464-3089, daily 10 A.M.–4 P.M., tides permitting, Apr.–Sept., 10 A.M.–4 P.M. Sat.–Sun., tides permitting, Oct.–Mar.). Plan carefully and pick up a recent tide schedule, since the lighthouse is not always accessible. The "tides permitting" caveat

© ANDERM/123RF.COM

Battery Point Lighthouse Park

means access may be possible for as little as a couple of hours on any given day. At high tide, the causeway that connects the city to the lighthouse is underwater. But if you catch the tide when it's lower, you'll get an unadvertised treat as you walk out to the lighthouse: tide pools. The Battery Point tide pools are rife with life, including sea stars, sea anemones, worm colonies, and barnacle clusters. Small fish trapped by the receding tides hunt for food in the pools until the waters rise again. Up in the lighthouse, built in 1856, a tiny bookstore features local- and lighthouse-themed books and souvenirs. There's a free self-guided tour of the lighthouse, which is now both a museum and a working private light station.

Ocean World

Are the kids bored with all the gorgeous scenery? A great family respite is Ocean World (304 U.S. 101 S., 707/464-4900, www.oceanworldonline.com, daily 9 A.M.–9 P.M. summer, daily 10 A.M.–6 P.M. winter, adults $10, children $6). Tours of the small sea park depart about every 15 minutes and last about 40 minutes. Featured attractions are the shark petting tank, the 500,000-gallon aquarium, and the sea lion show. After the tour, take a stroll through the immense souvenir shop, which sells gifts of all sizes, shapes, and descriptions, many with nautical themes.

Del Norte County Historical Society Museum

The Del Norte County Historical Society Museum (577 H St., 707/464-3922, www.delnortehistory.org/museum, 10 A.M.–4 P.M. Mon.–Sat. Apr.–Sept., 10 A.M.–3 P.M. Mon.–Oct.–Mar., free) provides an educational respite from the chilly sea breezes. The Historical Society maintains this small museum that features the local history of both the Native Americans who were once the only inhabitants Del Norte County and the encroaching white settlers. Featured exhibits include the wreck of the *Brother Jonathan* at Point St. George, the story of the 1964 tsunami, and artifacts of the local Yurok and Tolowa people.

ENTERTAINMENT AND EVENTS

If you're looking for varied and rocking night-life, Crescent City is not your town, but a few options exist for insomniacs. Most of the action after 9 P.M. is at **Elk Valley Casino** (2500 Howland Hill Rd., 707/464-1020 or 888/574-2744, www.elkvalleycasino.com, daily 24 hours) at the eastern edge of town. Elk Valley is a bit more upscale than other local Native American casinos, with genuine aluminum-siding walls, poker and blackjack tables, a VIP card room, and a small nonsmoking slots area. The on-site restaurant is the **Full House Bar & Grill** (7 A.M.–10 P.M. Sun.–Thurs., 7 A.M.–11 P.M. Fri.–Sat., $7–29); a late-night food menu (daily 7 A.M.–2 A.M.) is available from the bar.

The **Tsunami Lanes Bowling Center** (760 L St., 707/464-4323, www.tsunamilanes.com, daily noon–10 P.M. Sept. 1–May 23, hours vary Mon. and Wed.–Sat. May 24–Aug., adults $3 per game, seniors and children $2) is a straight-up bowling alley, serving beer and greasy fries to all comers late into the evening.

A less physical evening is available at performances of the **Lighthouse Repertory Theater** (707/465-3740, www.dnlrt.org). The **Del Norte Association for Cultural Awareness** (707/464-1336, www.dnaca.net) hosts several live musical acts and other performances each year and provides a community arts calendar. Check this year's schedule for upcoming shows, which take place at the Crescent Elk Auditorium (994 G St.). If all else fails, you can take in a first-run movie at the **Crescent City Cinemas** (375 M St., 707/570-8438).

For almost 50 years, the Yurok people have held a festival to honor a creature most precious to them: the mighty salmon. The **Klamath Salmon Festival** (www.yuroktribe.org) takes place in August each year and includes a parade, live music, games, and, of course, salmon dinners served all day.

SPORTS AND RECREATION
Beaches

The sands of Crescent City are a beachcomber's paradise. Wide, flat, sandy expanses invite strolling, running, and just sitting to contemplate the broad crashing Pacific. **South Beach,** as advertised, is located at the south end of town. Long, wide, and flat, it's perfect for a romantic stroll, as long as you're bundled up. The adventurous and chill-resistant can try surfing and boogie boarding. Farther south, **Crescent Beach** and **Enderts Beach** (Enderts Rd.) offer picnic spots, tide pools, and acres of sand to walk and play on. The sand is dark, soft, and perfect for families. The trails down to the beach are steep and rocky, so take care. Hikers enjoy the trails that lead away from the beach into the national forest.

It might look tempting on rare sunny days, but swimming from the beaches of Crescent City is not for the faint of heart. The water is icy cold, the shores are rocky, and as elsewhere in Northern California, undertow and rip currents can be dangerous. No lifeguards patrol these beaches, so you are on your own.

Bird-Watching

Birders flock to Crescent City because the diverse climates and habitats nourish a huge variety of avian residents. The parks and preserves have become destinations for enthusiasts looking for "lifers" hard to find anyplace else. Right in town, check out **Battery Point Lighthouse Park** and **Point St. George.** For a rare view of an Aleutian goose or a peregrine falcon, journey to **Tolowa Dunes State Park** (1375 Elk Valley Rd., 707/465-2145, www.parks.ca.gov, daily sunrise–sunset, free), specifically the shores of Lake Earl and Kellog Beach. South of town, **Enderts Beach** is home to another large bird habitat.

Fishing and Whale-Watching

Anglers on the North Coast can choose

between excellent deep-sea fishing and exciting river trips. The Pacific yields ling cod, snapper, and salmon, while the rivers are famous for chinook (king) salmon, steelhead, and cutthroat trout. Mammal-loving travelers can choose whale-watching over fishing. The *Tally Ho II* (1685 Del Mar Rd., at the harbor, 707/464-1236) is available for a variety of deep-sea fishing trips (May–Oct., half-day trip $100 pp), whale-watching (Feb.–Mar., 3-hour trip $50), or a combination of the two.

River fishers have a wealth of guides to choose from. **Ken Cunningham Guide Service** (50 Hunter Creek, Klamath, 707/391-7144, www.salmonslayer.net, $175 pp) will take you on a full-day fishing trip; the price includes bait, tackle, and the boat. **North Coast Fishing Adventures** (1657 Childrens Ave., McKinleyville, 707/498-4087 or 707/839-8127, www.norcalriverfishing.com, $200 pp, minimum $400 per day) covers the Klamath and Smith Rivers as well as smaller waterways.

Hiking

The redwood forests that nearly meet the wide sandy beaches make the Crescent City area a fabulous place to hike. The hikes at **Point St. George** aren't strenuous and provide stunning views of the coastline and surrounding landscape. **Tolowa Dunes State Park** (1375 Elk Valley Rd., 707/465-2145, www.parks.ca.gov, daily sunrise–sunset, free), north of Point St. George, offers miles of trails winding through forests, across beaches, and meandering along the shores of Lake Earl.

Horseback Riding

The rugged land surrounding Crescent City looks even prettier from the back of a horse. Casual riders enjoy a guided riding adventure through redwoods or along the ocean with **Crescent Trail Rides** (2002 Moorehead Rd., 707/951-5407, www.crescenttrailrides.com, 1.5 hours $60, 4 hours $160). Under the same management, **Fort Dick Stable** (2002 Moorehead Rd., 707/951-5407, www.fortdickstable.com) offers boarding and riding lessons.

A great place to ride is **Tolowa Dunes State Park** (1375 Elk Valley Rd., 707/465-2145, www.parks.ca.gov, daily sunrise–sunset, free), which maintains 20 miles of trails accessible to horses. Serious equestrians with their own mounts can ride in to a campsite with corrals at the north end of the park off Lower Lake Road.

Surfing

For surfers and bodysurfers willing to don heavy wetsuits and brave the cold North Coast waters, some great waves can be found at **South Beach.** Longboard legend Greg Noll hosted the Annual Noll Longboard Classic contest here for many years, and his son's **Noll Surf & Skate** (275 L St., 707/465-4400, www.noll.net, 10 A.M.–5 P.M. Mon.–Sat., noon–4 P.M. Sun.) is still going strong on the nearby wharf. The beach at **Point St. George** isn't always reliable, but in the right conditions it's got a rideable break.

ACCOMMODATIONS

Accommodations in Crescent City are affordable even during midsummer high season and can be surprisingly comfortable.

The aptly named **Curly Redwood Lodge** (701 U.S. 101 S., 707/464-2137, www.curlyredwoodlodge.com, $68–93) is constructed of a single rare curly redwood tree. You'll get to see the lovely color and grain of the tree in your large, simply decorated guest room. A 1950s feel pervades this friendly unpretentious motel, conveniently located right on U.S. 101 near some of the area's best restaurants.

Few frills decorate the family-owned **Pacific Inn** (220 M. St., 707/464-9553 or 800/977-9553, $63–73), but the guest rooms are clean, inexpensive, and comfortable. Its central downtown location makes for easy access to restaurants, museums, and points of interest.

The **Lighthouse Inn** (681 U.S. 101 S.,

707/464-3993 or 877/464-9035, www.light-house101.com, $89–145) has an elegant but whimsical lobby filled with dolphins and dollhouses to welcome guests, and the enthusiastic staff can help with restaurant recommendations and sights. Stylish appointments and bold colors grace each guest room. Corner suites with oversize whirlpool tubs make a perfect romantic retreat for couples at a reasonable nightly rate, while standard double rooms are downright cheap, given their comfort.

The **Anchor Beach Inn** (880 U.S. 101 S., 800/837-4116, www.anchorbeachinn.com, $59–118), at the south end of town, offers great access to South Beach, the harbor, and several good seafood restaurants. The ocean views overlook a wide swath of asphalt RV park, but the guest rooms have attractive decor and are clean and well maintained; continental breakfast and Internet access are included.

For a more personal, intimate experience, try the **Castle Island Getaway** (1830 Murphy Ave., 707/465-5102, www.castleislandgetaway.com, $100–150), offering lodgings to only one party of up to four people at a time, the innkeepers take special care of guests. You'll get to choose your breakfast from a menu of options, and it will be served at your convenience. Light, bright, private guest rooms and a short walk to Pebble Beach make for a delightful romantic getaway.

FOOD

Not surprisingly, standard fare in Crescent City tends to be seafood, but family restaurants and even one or two ethnic eateries offer some appealing variety as well.

The **Apple Peddler** (308 U.S. 101 S., 707/464-5630, daily 24 hours, $8–18) is a 24-hour family restaurant with an extensive classic American menu and great local dessert specials such as summertime blackberry cobbler. Next door to Ocean World, it's the perfect place to take a weary family for a hearty lunch or a mid-afternoon slice of pie. The service can be spotty,

and the place can get crowded on summer weekends, but it's still the favored diner in the area.

Northwood's Restaurant (675 U.S. 101 S., 707/465-5656, daily 6 A.M.–9 P.M., $8–20) prides itself on serving the freshest fish available, and in Crescent City that can mean the fillet you're eating for dinner was caught that very morning by a local fishing boat. The varied menu also includes imported exotic fish plus a number of land-based entrées to appeal to every palate.

Fishermans Restaurant (700 U.S. 101 S., 707/465-3474, daily 6 A.M.–9 P.M., $11–26) is a great place to walk in wearing jeans and sandy sneakers to get a bite of great fresh fish. Breakfasts feature biscuits and gravy, pancakes, and thick juicy bacon, all delicious—and big enough—to sustain you through a long day of hauling nets.

The **Harbor View Grotto** (150 Starfish Way, 707/464-3815, 11 A.M.–9 P.M. Sun.–Thurs., 11 A.M.–9:30 P.M. Fri.–Sat., $7–29) is popular with locals. The fish is always fresh and the portions large, but the preparation is not top quality, and food tends to be overcooked. Most dinners come with lavish sides, including soup, salad, vegetables, and bread. Even meals on the "light menu" include all the trimmings; only the size of the fish is somewhat reduced.

For better seafood still at a reasonable price, the best bet is **The Chart Room** (130 Anchor Way, 707/464-5993, www.chartroomcrescentcity.com, 11 A.M.–4 P.M. Mon., 6:30 A.M.–8 P.M. Tues.–Sat., 6:30 A.M.–7 P.M. Sun., $8–23). It's very casual, the food is excellent, and it's right on the ocean, so you can watch sea lions cavort on the pier while you eat. If anyone in your party is not a seafood lover, the lasagna is excellent.

One of the best places to enjoy an impressive variety of fresh and healthy food is at **The Good Harvest Cafe** (575 U.S. 101 S., 707/465-6028, 7:30 A.M.–9 P.M. Mon.–Sat., 8 A.M.–9 P.M. Sun., $10–35). Even though the atmosphere could be called casual, this comfortable airy restaurant feels a little upscale. With fruit salad,

© HEATHER C. LISTON

The Chart Room serves delicious seafood.

yogurt, and fresh oatmeal, this is the best place around for a light healthy breakfast. For dinner, the steak-and-lobster dinner is at the high end of the menu, but there are also burgers, pasta, vegetarian entrées, and big salads to satisfy nearly any palate.

The **Java Hut** (437 U.S. 101 N., 707/465-4439, daily 5 A.M.–10 P.M., $5) is a drive-through and walk-up coffee stand that serves a wide array of coffee drinks, including some alcoholic treats (yes, at the drive-through). Beware of long lines of locals during the morning hours. Downtown, check out **Coffee Corner** (530 L St., 707/464-9255, daily 5 A.M.–3 P.M.); excellent pastries and sandwiches make this local shop stand out.

The small family-owned award-winning **Rumiano Cheese Co.** (511 9th St., orders 707/465-1535 or 866/328-2433, www.rumianocheese.com, call for hours) has been part of Crescent City since 1921. Come to the tasting room for the cheese and stay for, well, more cheese. The dry jack cheese is a particular favorite, though lots of varieties are available.

Like many California towns, Crescent City runs a **farmers market** (Del Norte County Fairgrounds, 451 U.S. 101 N., 707/464-7441, 9 A.M.–1 P.M. Sat. June–Oct.). While the harvest season is more restricted here than points south, veggie lovers can still choose from an array of fresh local produce all summer long.

INFORMATION AND SERVICES

The **Crescent City and Del Norte County Chamber of Commerce Visitors Center** (1001 Front St., 707/464-3174 or 800/343-8300, www.exploredelnorte.com, daily 9 A.M.–5 P.M. May–Oct., 9 A.M.–5 P.M. Mon.–Fri. Nov.–Apr.) is a good place to visit when you arrive. You'll find knowledgeable staffers who can advise you on "secret" local sights as well as the bigger attractions advertised in the myriad brochures lining the walls.

Also in town is the **Crescent City**

NORTH COAST

Information Center (1111 2nd St., 707/465-7335, daily 9 A.M.–6 P.M. summer, daily 9 A.M.–5 P.M. spring and fall, daily 9 A.M.–4 P.M. winter), run by Redwood National and State Parks. This friendly place has maps, souvenirs, and rangers who can chat about hiking, camping, and exploring the parks.

The Daily Triplicate (707/464-2141, www.triplicate.com, $0.75), the local newspaper of Crescent City, is published Tuesday, Thursday, and Saturday. You can pick up a Del Norte County Map and a copy of *101 Things to Do in Del Norte/Southern Oregon* (www.101things.com) at the visitors center and many local businesses.

GETTING THERE AND AROUND

The main routes in and out of town are U.S. 101 and U.S. 199. Both are well maintained but are twisty in spots, so take care, especially at night. From San Francisco, the drive to Crescent City is about 350 miles (6.5 hours). It is 85 miles (under 2 hours) from Eureka north to Crescent City on U.S. 101. Traffic isn't a big issue in Crescent City, and parking is free and easy to find throughout town.

Jack McNamara Field (CEC, 5 miles northwest of town, 707/464-7288, www.flycec.com) is also called Del Norte County Airport and is the only airport in Crescent City. United Express has daily nonstop flights to San Francisco and Sacramento.

Redwood Coast Transit (RCT, 707/464-6400, www.redwoodcoasttransit.org, adults $0.75, seniors and disabled $0.50, punch passes $10) handles bus travel in and around Crescent City. Make sure to have exact change handy. Four in-town routes and a coastal bus from Smith River to Arcata provide ample public-transit options for travelers without cars. Pick up a schedule at the visitors center (1001 Front St.) or local stores for current fares and times.

SHASTA AND LASSEN

The mountains in the far northern reaches of California are some of the most unspoiled areas in the state, protected by a wealth of national and state parks and forestlands. The most prominent features of this region are two iconic mountains: Shasta and Lassen. The stunning snow-capped peak of Mount Shasta may look familiar—it often graces calendars, postcards, and photography books. Shasta is a dormant volcano, which means it's not extinct—it will erupt again—but unlike an active volcano, it probably won't do so soon. Mount Shasta, and the town and lake that share its name, are easy to get to. The mountain itself, though, is daunting to climb and should be attempted only by experienced climbers.

South of Mount Shasta is the major resort area of Shasta Lake, which attracts boaters and water enthusiasts from far and wide.

Mount Lassen, about 150 miles southeast of Shasta, is classified as an active volcano, and the national park that surrounds it includes many volcanic features—boiling mud pots, steam vents, and sulfur springs. Both mountains make great vacation destinations, beautiful to behold and surrounded by recreation opportunities. Not quite as many visitors flock to Lassen as they do to Shasta, yet scaling Mount Lassen's peak is only a moderate day hike, accessible to almost anyone who is fit and game to try it.

As you drive up into this remote area, you'll

© HEATHER C. LISTON

HIGHLIGHTS

© AVALON TRAVEL

LOOK FOR (TO FIND RECOMMENDED SIGHTS, ACTIVITIES, DINING, AND LODGING.

(Lake Shasta Caverns: A lovely cruise across Shasta Lake is just a prelude to the exploration of these wondrous caverns, filled with natural limestone, marble, and crystal-studded stalactites and stalagmites (page 382).

(Shasta Dam: A marvel of human engineering, the massive dam that created Lake Shasta is even more interesting if you catch the outstanding informational tour (page 383).

(Lassen Peak: Lassen is an active volcano whose last major eruption, in 1914-1915, changed the landscape of the area and altered the shape of the craggy peak itself. The 10,462-foot mountain now offers a rewarding hike to the top, or a dramatic view from below (page 393).

(Loomis Museum and Manzanita Lake: This small but lovely museum offers a history of Lassen's volcanic eruptions through a series of startling and revealing photographs (page 394).

(Bumpass Hell: A two-mile hike leads through this hotbed of geothermal activity, from boiling mud pots and steaming springs to fumaroles and bubbling, hissing puddles and ponds (page 395).

(Mount Shasta: This dazzling glacier-topped mountain peak is truly one of the greatest visions the country has to offer (page 407).

(Castle Crags State Park: A longtime favorite of rock climbers, this park also offers great hiking, camping, and scenic views that everyone can enjoy (page 422).

(McArthur-Burney Falls: Touted as the "the most beautiful waterfall in California," this 129-foot cascade is accessible year-round via a short, easy path (page 423).

(Lava Beds National Monument: With more than 700 natural caves, famous Native American battle sites, ancient rock art, and 14 thriving species of bats, this strange and amazing place has something to thrill almost anyone (page 426).

discover a number of quirky places worth a visit of their own. Go underground at Lava Beds National Monument, scale the cliffs at Castle Crags, feel the spray of waterfalls at McArthur-Burney Falls, and discover the sad and shameful history of a World War II Japanese "segregation center" at Tulelake.

PLANNING YOUR TIME

Either Shasta or Lassen make a fabulous weekend getaway—particularly if you've got a three-day weekend. Mount Shasta offers fairly easy and reliable year-round access along I-5 with both winter and summer outdoor recreation. The weather on and near Shasta can get

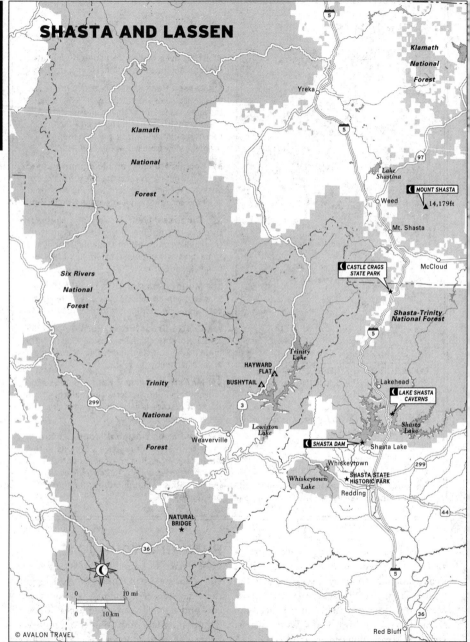

SHASTA AND LASSEN

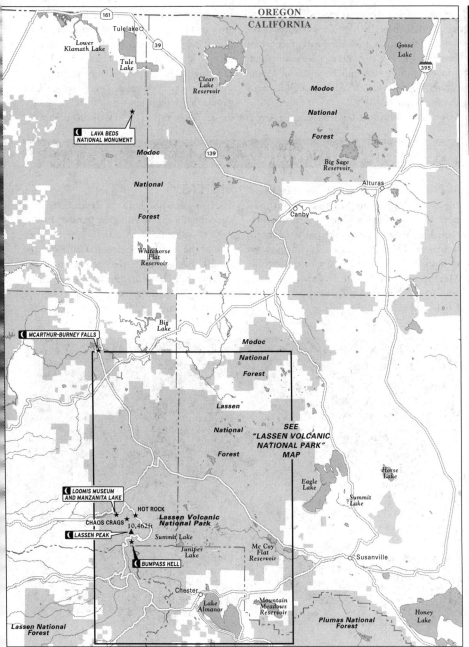

OREGON
CALIFORNIA

161
Tulelake
39

Lower
Klamath Lake
Tule
Lake

Clear
Lake
Reservoir

Goose
Lake

395

Modoc

National

LAVA BEDS
NATIONAL MONUMENT

Modoc

Forest

139

Big Sage
Reservoir

National
Alturas

Canby

Forest

Whitehorse
Flat
Reservoir

Big
Lake

McARTHUR-BURNEY FALLS

Modoc

National

Forest

Lassen

National

SEE
"LASSEN VOLCANIC
NATIONAL PARK"
MAP

Forest

Horse
Lake

LOOMIS MUSEUM
AND MANZANITA LAKE

Eagle
Lake

Summit
Lake

HOT ROCK
CHAOS CRAGS

Lassen Volcanic
National Park

10,462ft
LASSEN PEAK

Summit Lake

Juniper
Lake

Mc Coy
Flat
Reservoir

Susanville

BUMPASS HELL

Chester

Lake
Almanor

Mountain
Meadows
Reservoir

Honey
Lake

Lassen National
Forest

Plumas National
Forest

extreme; expect winter storms half the year and occasionally brutally high temperatures in the summer months. Check the weather reports so you can pack the right clothes for your trip. If you're planning to climb even part of Mount Shasta, be aware that it's high enough to create its own weather.

The best time to visit Mount Lassen is mid–late summer. Lassen is in the remote eastern part of the state, where the weather gets extreme; it can still be snowy on Lassen as late as June, so keep that in mind when you make your camping plans. During winter the main road through the park closes, making a visit to the region far less interesting—unless you've brought snowshoes or skis to explore the backcountry.

Redding and Vicinity

The biggest city in the region, Redding has all the amenities you might need on your journey. The town has a lot of turnover, so establishments that were here last time might have moved or been replaced. If you just want to get off I-5 for some quick food, skip the Market Street exit; the largest concentration of food and shops is west of the Lake Boulevard exit.

SIGHTS

The best-known sight in the Redding region is undoubtedly the magnificent **Sundial Bridge** (800/887-8532, daily 6 A.M.–midnight, free). Part of the Turtle Bay Exploration Park, the Sundial Bridge crosses the Sacramento River. This beautiful bit of architecture was designed by Santiago Calatrava and opened in 2004. For pedestrians only, the bridge features a single

Redding's Sundial Bridge

large pylon structure that anchors suspension cables that fan out over the bridge. Most people get to the bridge from Turtle Bay and walk north across its 200 tons of green glass, strips of granite, and ceramic tiles from Spain.

Turtle Bay Exploration Park (840 Sundial Bridge Dr., 530/243-8850 or 800/887-8532, www.turtlebay.org, daily 9 A.M.–5 P.M. summer, 9 A.M.–4 P.M. Wed.–Sat., 10 A.M.–4 P.M. Sun. winter, adults $14, ages 4–12 $10) is also worth a visit, although along with the rest of Redding, it gets blisteringly hot in summer. To escape the heat, spend some quality time in the Turtle Bay Museum, with its air-conditioning, art and nature displays, Native American exhibits, and traveling exhibits and shows. Much of the museum is designed to please young visitors, enabling kids to learn by listening, touching, and occasionally even smelling. Admission to the museum is included with park admission.

Outside the museum, the Exploration Park includes the spacious **McConnell Arboretum and Gardens** (daily 9 A.M.–5 P.M.), a 20-acre botanical garden that's perfect for spring and fall strolling, although it gets a bit hot in high summer. Beautiful plantings and areas include a children's garden, a medicinal garden, and two charming water features. Lots of butterflies are attracted to the flower plantings, so you'll get to see swallowtails, monarchs, and many other species. The arboretum is a 200-acre expanse of trees, and you can enjoy their shade as you explore the sustainable forest. Children enjoy the play areas and equipment in **Paul Bunyan's Forest Camp,** and one of the most interesting historical sites is the **Monolith**—a remnant of one of the concrete-processing plants that helped build Shasta Dam in the 1930s and 1940s.

ENTERTAINMENT AND EVENTS

Redding hosts a number of monthly and annual events. The annual **Redding Rodeo** (715 Auditorium Dr., 530/241-8559, www.

reddingrodeo.com, $13–63) is the star, with a weeks' worth of events each May. The rodeo runs Thursday–Saturday and includes the traditional riding, roping, and racing events. For a different kind of day out in Redding, come for the **Beer and Wine Festival** (530/243-7773, www.vivadowntownredding.org, mid-Sept., $35–40).

Monroe's Nightclub & Grill (Casino Club, 1885 Hilltop Dr., 530/221-5015, www.reddingpoker.com, noon–11 P.M. Sun.–Thurs., noon–midnight Fri.–Sat., $6–10) is one of the more popular nightspots in Redding, offering loud music, karaoke, and regular poker tournaments in addition to chicken, burgers, pasta, and plenty of alcohol.

ACCOMMODATIONS
Under $100

The **Motel 6 Redding South** (2385 Bechelli Lane, 530/221-0562, www.motel6.com, $55–66) is known to regular travelers as one of the best examples of a Motel 6 anywhere—it's definitely better than the other two in the Redding area. What you will get is a clean room with a clean bath and a comfortable bed for the night, and an outdoor pool that is clean and totally swimmable.

One tier up in the hierarchy of chain motels, the **Redding Travelodge** (540 N. Market St., 530/243-5291, reservations 800/243-1106, www.reddingtravelodge.com, $85–105) offers a few more amenities for a little more money. Guest rooms have queen or king beds, flowery comforters, dark carpets, white walls, and plenty of space; some guest rooms include fridges and partial kitchens, and all have free Internet access. Take a dip in the heated outdoor pool or soak in the indoor whirlpool tub (year-round). A hot breakfast at the nearby restaurant **Lumberjacks** (501 E. Cypress Ave., 530/223-2820, www.lumberjacksrestaurant.com, daily 6–11 A.M.) is included.

$100-150

If you're looking for something more than a

standard-issue motel, stay at the **Tiffany House B&B** (1510 Barbara Rd., 530/244-3225, www.tiffanyhousebb.com, $125–170). High on a hill in a quiet residential neighborhood, the Tiffany House shows off the best of Redding's views, accommodations, and people. All the guest rooms offer charm and comfort as well as views of Redding and all the way to Mount Lassen on a clear day. The spacious Cottage Room has a huge spa tub, a separate bath, a private porch, and comfortable amenities. The inn's common spaces include shady gardens and an outdoor pool, a music room, a parlor, and plenty of cozy nooks to sit and read a book. A two-course gourmet breakfast is included.

Another lovely little inn is the **Bridge House Bed and Breakfast** (1455 Riverside Dr., 530/247-7177, www.reddingbridgehouse.com, $119–179). The distinctive yellow house with a steeply pitched roof is along the Sacramento River just a block or two from historic downtown Redding. You can walk to some of the nicest restaurants and quirkiest shops in the neighborhood. Inside, you'll find a tranquil haven in one of four guest rooms. Each guest room is named after a bridge and is decorated with prints of its namesake, complementary colors, and attractive furniture. All guest rooms have TVs, spa bathrobes, and lots of amenities—the two largest guest rooms boast upscale "massage tubs" in the baths. The Bridge House acts primarily as a romantic retreat for couples, so babies and small children are not allowed.

FOOD

If you're planning to camp on Lassen or Shasta, or houseboat on the lake, the cheapest options for groceries are in Redding. For a generous array of groceries, head for one of two **Safeways** (2275 Pine St., 530/247-3030; 1070 E. Cypress Ave., 530/226-5871), both open 24-hours daily, which can be a lifesaver on road trips and camping expeditions. For local produce, visit the **Redding Certified Farmers Market** (Redding City Hall, 777 Cypress Ave., 530/226-7100, http://shastagrowersassociation.com, 7:30 A.M.–noon Sat. Apr.–Dec.).

Bakeries and Cafés

It's always a treat to find something original. **For the Love of Pie** (351 Northpoint Dr., 530/226-7437, www.4theloveofpie.com, 8:30 A.M.–8 P.M. Mon.–Sat., $15–16) is a local business opened in 2010 by the mother-daughter team Adrienne and Kirsten Sherman. "Treat" barely begins to describe it, though; a snack here may be one of your vacation highlights. If you have a personal favorite must-have pie, chances are they've got it. If you don't, try the key lime. And if one dessert isn't enough, try the coffee cake, cheesecake, or blackout chocolate cake. The owners serve organic fair-trade Equator Coffee, and you can also get homemade tamales, enchiladas, and pot pies to eat in or take out. A smaller pie ($5–6), which serves 1–2 people, is also available. They also carry gluten-free and wheat-free pies made locally by **Sorelle Bakery** (530/276-3965), and you can pull up to the drive-through window to pick up a pie to take with you. There's a second location (2931 Churn Creek, 530/246-7437, 8:30 A.M.–8 P.M. Mon.–Sat.), also in Redding.

From the Hearth Artisan Bakery (1292 College View Dr., 530/245-0555 or 530/245-0466, www.fromthehearthbakery.com, 7 A.M.–9 P.M. Mon.–Fri., 7 A.M.–6 P.M. Sat.–Sun., $3.75–10) offers homemade sourdough bread, chocolate croissants, and other carefully baked goods as well as smoothies and sandwiches.

HomeCraft Breads is another Redding favorite; its bakery and sandwich shop, **Kelsey's on the River** (2633 Park Marina Dr., 530/246-1301, www.homecraftbreads.com, 8 A.M.–6 P.M. Mon.–Fri., 10 A.M.–4 P.M. Sat., $6–9) can be difficult to find. From I-5 north, take the Redding Convention Center exit to Highway 299 west. Make a left on Auditorium Drive and another left onto Park Marina Drive.

Proceed to the cute little round building near the end of the road.

Casual Dining

Bartel's Giant Burger (75 Lake Blvd. E., 530/243-7313, 10 A.M.–9 P.M. Mon.–Sat., 11 A.M.–9 P.M. Sun., $4.75–9) has plenty of raving fans, and a sprinkling of disappointed customers who think the burgers aren't as fresh or as big as they recall. If you're extra hungry, ask for double or triple—rumor has it they'll even make you a stack with six patties on one bun. Enjoy it with lots of onions and the highly recommended "special sauce."

For a decent diner, take I-5's Cypress Avenue exit east and proceed to Hilltop Drive, where you'll find the local iteration of the **Black Bear Diner** (2605 Hilltop Dr., 530/221-7600, www.blackbeardiner.com, 6 A.M.–11 P.M. Mon.–Fri., 6 A.M.–midnight Fri.–Sat.). This Northern California chain began in the mountains and offers classic American dishes made fresh with better ingredients than at similar chains. The menu includes American breakfast classics, salads, sandwiches, chicken, fries, and potatoes; the list goes on. Breakfast is served all day, as are the thick, real-ice-cream milkshakes (try the huckleberry). Service is friendly, although it can get crowded on weekends.

Fine Dining

Fancy restaurants are hard to come by in Redding, but there's one that gets some buzz. The **Old School Restaurant** (1135 Pine St., Suite 119, 530/244-4600, www.oldschoolrestaurant.com, 11 A.M.–9 P.M. Mon.–Fri., 4–10 P.M. Sat., $12–20) was opened in 2011 by the owners of the defunct Rivers Restaurant, formerly one of Redding's fine-dining destinations. The Old School includes comfort foods like macaroni and cheese with crushed Ritz crackers along with more uptown offerings like macadamia tilapia and cornish game hen. After a day outdoors, sometimes you just need a big ol' steak. **Jack's Grill** (1743 California St., 530/241-9705, www.jacksgrillredding.com, 5–11 P.M. Mon.–Sat., $16–33) can hook you up. This locally owned favorite has been serving steaks for more than 70 years. Don't expect the high-end cuts and preparations of big-city steakhouses; instead, look for tasty and less expensive steaks, ground steak, and skewers. All meals come with soup or salad and a baked potato or fries. Jack's has a full bar that serves beer, wine, and cocktails.

In the mood for a hearty Italian meal? **Gironda's Restaurant** (1100 Center St., 530/244-7663, www.girondas.com, lunch 11:30 A.M.–2 P.M. Mon.–Fri., dinner 4:30–9 P.M. Sun.–Thurs.,. 4:30–10 P.M. Fri.–Sat., $13–25) serves ravioli and other pasta as well as big Italian-style entrées for lunch and dinner. Dine in the casually elegant dining room, or order takeout to enjoy elsewhere—even at your campsite.

INFORMATION AND SERVICES

For visitors camping at Shasta Lake or Mount Lassen, Redding is the last serious outpost of civilization before trekking to the more remote reaches of the state. The **Redding Convention & Visitors Bureau** (Turtle Bay Exploration Park, 840 Sundial Bridge Dr., 530/243-8850 or 800/887-8532, www.visitredding.com, daily 9 A.M.–5 P.M. summer, 9 A.M.–4 P.M. Wed.–Sat., 10 A.M.–4 P.M. Sun. winter) is a good first stop.

The local daily newspaper is the *Record Searchlight* (530/243-2424, www.redding.com). The paper covers national and local news and devotes lots of space to local outdoor recreation.

The best place to find ATMs and bank branches is Redding. A **Bank of America** (1300 Hilltop Dr., 530/226-6172, www.bankofamerica.com, 9 A.M.–5 P.M. Mon.–Thurs., 9 A.M.–6 P.M. Fri., 1–6 P.M. Sat.) and a **Wells Fargo** (830 E. Cypress Ave., 800/869-3557, 9 A.M.–6 P.M. Mon.–Sat.) are near I-5 for easy access.

Redding has a **post office** (2323 Churn Creek

Rd., 530/223-7523, www.usps.com, 8:30 A.M.–5:30 P.M. Mon.–Fri., 9 A.M.–3 P.M. Sat.).

Redding has the only major medical services available in the entire Shasta-Lassen region. **Mercy Medical Center Redding** (2175 Rosaline Ave., 530/225-6000, www.redding.mercy.org) has a 24-hour emergency room with a full trauma center for major medical problems.

GETTING THERE AND AROUND

Redding is on I-5 about 160 miles (3 hours) north of Sacramento and acts as the gateway to the Shasta and Lassen region. Redding is easy to navigate by car and parking is plentiful and free.

The **Redding Municipal Airport** (RDD, 6751 Woodrum Circle, 530/224-4320, http://ci.redding.ca.us) offers flights on United Express, which runs multiple daily nonstop trips to and from San Francisco. Flying in and out of the small airport isn't cheap, but there are short ticketing and security lines.

Most visitors to the region will need a car to explore further. Outside of the nearby airports, the best opportunities to rent a car are in Redding at **Hertz** (773 N. Market St., 530/241-2257; 6450 Lockheed Dr., 530/221-4620, www.hertz.com, $250–425 per week) and **Budget** (2945 Churn Creek Rd., 530/225-8652; 6751 Woodrum Circle, 530/722-9122, www.budget.com, $225–1,100 per week). **Avis** (6751 Woodrum Circle, 530/221-2855, www.avis.com, $195–500 per week) has an office at the airport. **Enterprise** (217 Cypress Ave., 530/223-0700, www.enterprise.com, $165–366 per week) has a full range of cars in stock; with advance notice, they can often accommodate special requests for trucks, vans, and large SUVs.

SHASTA STATE HISTORIC PARK

Believe it or not, the Shasta region was once more populous than it is now; the area was once crowded with 19th-century gold miners and the people providing goods and services to them. Today, Shasta State Historic Park (Hwy. 299,

5 miles west of I-5, 530/243-8194, www.parks.ca.gov, daily 6 A.M.–6 P.M.) honors that regional history. Two on-site museums, the **Litsch Store Museum** (10 A.M.–5 P.M. Fri. and Sun., free) and the **Courthouse Museum** (530/243-8194, 10 A.M.–5 P.M. Fri. and Sun., adults $3, ages 6–17 $2) allow history buffs to dig deeper into the life and times of early Shasta residents. See everything from an extensive collection of California landscape paintings to the area's original gallows. Outdoors, you'll get the chance to wander through the remains of historic cottages and read the human history of Shasta through the grave markers in the cemeteries. The park also features brick ruins of a former town.

WHISKEYTOWN

Whiskeytown National Recreation Area comprises 39,000 acres of wilderness for hiking, biking, and water sports just 10 miles west of Redding.

Whiskeytown Visitors Center

Exhibits at the visitors center (Hwy. 299 and John F. Kennedy Memorial Dr., 530/246-1225, www.nps.gov/whis, daily 10 A.M.–5 P.M. Memorial Day–Labor Day; daily 10 A.M.–4 P.M. Labor Day–Memorial Day, $5) illuminate the area's history as a gold-mining destination. It's also a good place to get maps, advice, and information about camping, hiking, and tours in the park.

Whiskeytown Lake

Whiskeytown Lake is the centerpiece of this delightfully uncrowded outdoor playground in Northern California. The lake, formed by the Whiskeytown Dam on Clear Creek, has 30 miles of shoreline. Its capacity is 241,100 acre-feet, plenty of room for fish, and the lake is stocked with rainbow and brown trout; largemouth, smallmouth, and spotted bass; and kokanee salmon. Bald eagles nest and breed nearby. Personal watercraft are prohibited on the lake, but nearly every other kind of water

SACRAMENTO NATIONAL WILDLIFE REFUGE COMPLEX

Whether you're a world-class bird-watcher or just like to catch a glimpse of a jackrabbit in the wild, you should know about the network of wildlife refuges managed by the U.S. Fish and Wildlife Service. The Sacramento National Wildlife Refuge Complex (530/934-2801 or 800/344-9453, www.fws.gov/sacramentovalleyrefuges) is the name for five National Wildlife Refuges (NWRs) and three Wildlife Management Areas (WMAs) spread out over the Sacramento Valley. Altogether, the Sacramento NWR Complex comprises about 35,000 acres of land and has been home to more than 300 species of birds since it was established in 1937.

Driving north on I-5 toward the Shasta area, you pass by several of these refuges, possibly without even noticing. They tend to keep a fairly low profile; the less human activity, buildings, and commerce, the more likely that birds and other animals will remain in these places and continue to use them during their migrations. Although the refuges are designed to preserve, protect, and showcase wildlife, none of these habitats are actually "natural" at this point. The Sacramento Valley used to be covered in wetlands, marshes, and ponds—all migration-friendly stopovers. Over the years, however, most of the land has been drained for agriculture or urban development; the former wetlands are being redeveloped and actively managed to ensure they remain stable.

The five individual refuges are: **Delevan NWR,** nine miles north of Williams on I-5 and four miles east along Maxwell Road; **Colusa NWR,** one mile west of Colusa on Highway 20; **Sutter NWR,** six miles south of Yuba City; **Sacramento NWR** (752 County Rd. 99W, Willows, $3 per vehicle), 20 miles north of Williams; and **Sacramento River NWR,** along the Sacramento River for 77 miles from Red Bluff to Princeton. Each refuge offers short hiking trails, viewing platforms, and self-guided auto tours. All but the Sacramento Refuge are free to visitors and are usually unstaffed; simple exhibits and helpful bulletin boards and brochures are available to make the most of your visit. Amenities include basic restrooms and picnic tables. The Sacramento Refuge also serves as the headquarters for the complex and is the only refuge that has a **visitors center** (752 County Rd. 99W, Willows, 530/934-2801, daily 9 A.M.-4 P.M. Nov.-Feb., 9 A.M.-4 P.M. Mon.-Fri. Mar.-Oct.).

Even if wildlife viewing is not the main purpose of your trip, a slight detour to drive through one or more of these treasure troves of fauna can be very rewarding. Plan to show up any time from two hours before sunrise until 1.5 hours after sunset. If you'd like to join a tour at one of the refuges, or learn more about the birds that frequent them, check out the offerings of the **Altacal Audubon Society** (www.altacal.org), based in Chico. The society runs birding talks, hikes, and other programs, some of which take place in the wildlife refuges.

activity is encouraged—feel free to kayak, canoe, swim, sail, water-ski, fish, or scuba dive.

One of the coolest features on the lake are the free 2.5-hour ranger-led **kayak tours** (reservations 530/242-3462, 9:30 A.M. and 6 P.M. Mon.–Fri., 9:30 A.M., 12:30 P.M., and 6 P.M. Sat.–Sun. summer). Note that "summer" is defined by the weather and other conditions, but it's usually at least mid-June–Labor Day. Call ahead to check availability and reserve space. The parks service provides kayaks, paddles, and life jackets.

There are two marinas on Whiskeytown Lake, both run by the National Park Service concessionaire, Forever Resorts. **Oak Bottom Marina** (12485 Hwy. 299 W., Whiskeytown, 530/359-2671, www.whiskeytownmarinas.com, year-round) is the larger of the two. Rentals include kayaks and canoes (4 hours $20–40, 8 hours $30–60); a 16-foot fishing boat suitable for five people (4 hours $100, 8 hours $175); and tubes, wakeboards, ski boats, water skis, and other conveyances. There is also a small campground store (530/359-2269, daily 8 A.M.–8 P.M. mid-Apr.–mid-Oct., daily 8 A.M.–4 P.M. mid-Oct.–mid-Apr.). **Brandy Creek Marina** (530/359-2671, www.whiskeytownmarinas.com, 1 month $195, mid-Apr.–mid-Oct. season $875, annually $1,595) is located on the south side of the lake. Boat-slip rental is the only service provided; no watercraft rentals are available.

Steve Huber (530/623-1918, www.stevehuberguideservice.com, $200 pp) uses a drift boat or powerboat to take anglers out on Whiskeytown Lake. He'll supply the gear and assist with fly-fishing, bait casting, or trolling.

Hiking

Park rangers lead a number of hikes in Whiskeytown National Recreation Area. A helpful list of hikes for a variety of fitness levels is available online (www.nps.gov/whis). An unusual hike is the ranger-led **Walk in Time** history tour (visitors center, Hwy. 299 and John F. Kennedy Memorial Dr., 530/246-1225, 3 P.M. Wed. and Sat.–Sun.). You can even pan for gold.

The **Mount Shasta Mine Loop Trail** (3.1 miles, moderate) is a short loop, but it climbs about 1,200 vertical feet, so it's not an easy hike. It's interesting because in addition to the great exercise, the trail passes the Whiskeytown Cemetery and the Mount Shasta Mine. The mine shaft is fenced for safety, but there's a sign to explain what it's all about. You'll also pass Orofino Creek (you might want to take a quick dip if it's a hot day) and get good views of Whiskeytown Lake. To get to the trailhead, take Kennedy Drive to Paige Bar Road. Follow Paige Bar Road about one mile. On the left-hand side, you'll see the parking area, and the trail begins from here, near the bath.

The hike to **Whiskeytown Falls** (3.4 miles, moderate) is one of four great waterfall hikes in the park (and if you do them all, you can pick up a free "I Walked the Falls" bandanna at the visitors center). Oddly enough, this beautiful 220-foot waterfall was "lost" for about 40 years. It was recently rediscovered, and park officials developed and reopened the access trail, called the James K. Carr Trail; it has become one of the most popular in the area. It's steep in places and not an easy hike. Group hikes are sometimes offered, beginning with a carpool to the trailhead from the visitors center; call 530/242-3451 to check the schedule.

Biking

Nearly all of the trails in the Whiskeytown National Recreation Area are open for mountain biking; pick up free trail maps at the visitors center (Hwy. 299 and John F. Kennedy Memorial Dr., 530/246-1225, www.nps.gov/whis, daily 10 A.M.–5 P.M. Memorial Day–Labor Day; daily 10 A.M.–4 P.M. Labor Day–Memorial Day). One of the most scenic rides is **The Chimney** (8.3 miles, moderate–challenging), which is difficult and steep in places but worth it. The hilly trail leads over bridges, along Brandy Creek, and up to some great views. Though technically an out-and-back ride, the trail includes two loops along the way, so you don't have to retrace your path. The Chimney is very popular with intermediate and skilled riders.

The **Oak Bottom Water Ditch Trail** (5.5 miles, easy) is ideal for beginners. It's both flat and attractive and runs along Whiskeytown Lake with lots of good spots to pull over and take a break—or even swim—if you get tired of riding. Parking is available at the trailhead, about five miles west of the Whiskeytown visitors center, near the Oak Bottom Campground.

If you like group activities, check out the **Redding Mountain Biking Club** (530/209-4707, Redding, www.reddingmountainbiking.com). They lead rides most Saturdays year-round, and visitors of all levels are welcome. There's no charge to join in, but you can become a member for $20. The group rides all over the area, including the Whiskeytown trails.

Accommodations and Camping

For an indoor overnight, there is a pleasant option nearby—the **French Gulch Hotel and Bed & Breakfast** (14138 Main St., French Gulch, 530/359-2112, wwww.frenchgulch-hotelbandb.com, $70–160). There's also a $250 option, but that's for a three-room suite on a Saturday night, with Sunday brunch included. To get from Whiskeytown to French Gulch, which is technically a town, although the population in the 2010 census was just 346, travel west on Highway 299 about 5.2 miles, then turn right onto Trinity Mountain Road and go another 3.1 miles on the partially unpaved road.

The **Oak Bottom Campground** (530/359-2269 or 800/365-2267, www.whiskeytown-marinas.com) is located within Whiskeytown National Recreation Area but managed by a for-profit concessionaire called Forever Resorts. This is the only campground on the shores of Whiskeytown Lake, and it offers 100 tent sites and 17 RV sites. The sites right on the lake—where you can actually tether a boat at your campsite—are $18; the other tent sites are $16, and RV sites are $14 in summer. October–April all sites are $10, and no reservations are needed. A beach for swimming and shower facilities are available. Cold showers are free, but hot ones cost a little.

Getting There

Whiskeytown is 10 miles (15 minutes) straight west of I-5 in Redding on Highway 299.

WEAVERVILLE

Located about 50 miles west of Redding, Weaverville is the county seat of Trinity County and is listed on the National Register of Historic Places. Weaverville is on the south side of the Trinity Alps Wilderness Area in the Klamath Mountains. A charming little town in its own right, it is also a good starting point for hikes and other adventures in the Trinity Alps.

Sights

Weaverville Joss House State Historic Park (southwest corner of Hwy. 299 and Oregon St., 530/623-5284, www.parks.ca.gov, 10 A.M.–5 P.M. Thurs. and Sat.–Sun., adults $4, ages 6–17 $2) has been part of California's state park system since 1956, but the temple it preserves and celebrates has been around much longer. The Temple of the Forest beneath the Clouds, also known as Joss House, is California's oldest Chinese temple in continual use. A Taoist house of worship, it is now a museum as well. The current building was erected in 1874 as a replacement for a previous incarnation that was lost in a fire. Through displays of Chinese art, mining tools, and weapons used in the 1854 Tong War, this museum tells some of the Chinese immigrant history in California. Admission includes a tour of the temple (hourly 10 A.M.–4 P.M.).

Accommodations

The rustic **Red Hill Motel-Cabins** (50 Red Hill Rd., 530/623-4331, www.redhillresorts.com, motel $37, cabins $48–95) have the woodsy feel of a forest vacation, yet they're right in the town of Weaverville, walking distance to local restaurants and museums—all at reasonable rates. What more could you ask for? At the west end of town, look behind the county library on Red Hill Road.

Southwest of Weaverville near the small town of Hayfork is an unusual lodging. The **Forest Glen Guard Station** (Hwy. 36, Forest Glen, 877/444-6777, www.recreation.gov, mid-Apr.–Dec., $35–75) was built in 1916 and is the oldest Forest Service building in the Shasta-Trinity National Forest. The two-story building has an indoor kitchen and bath, a large porch, and sleeps up to eight. It's near the South Fork of the Trinity River, so both the swimming and hiking nearby are excellent.

Food

Red House Coffee (86 S. Miner St., 530/623-1635, www.vivalaredhouse.com,

6:30 A.M.–5:30 P.M. Mon.–Fri., 7:30 A.M.–
5:30 P.M. Sat., $5–12) is a cute, friendly diner
in a historic 1930s building, serving breakfast,
lunch, and the gamut of coffee beverages, including a few house specialties.

The **Nugget Restaurant** (622 Main St.,
530/623-6749, daily 6 A.M.–9 P.M., $5–12) does
a fine job with basic hearty American breakfasts; it's also noted for its excellent pies.

At the slightly more upscale end of the small-
town dining spectrum, you'll find **La Grange
Café** (520 Main St., 530/623-5325, 11:30 A.M.–
9:30 P.M. Mon.–Fri., 11:30 A.M.–10 P.M. Sat.–
Sun., $12–28), with a varied American menu,
an Old West feel, and even a hook to hang your
miner's hat.

Stock up on picnic supplies at **Tops Super
Food** (1665 S. Main St., 530/623-2494, daily
6 A.M.–10 P.M.).

Information and Services

The U.S. Forest Service maintains **Weaverville
Ranger Station** (360 Main St., 530/623-2121,
www.fs.usda.gov, 8 A.M.–4:30 P.M. Mon.–Fri.).
One good reason to stop in: The Forest Service
offers free recreation maps and boating safety
maps for Shasta Lake and Trinity Lake if you
come to the office in person. And if you get here
after hours, don't despair: They have a self-service
center in front of the office where you can get a
campfire permit or a Trinity Alps Wilderness
permit even when the office is closed.

Getting There

Weaverville is due west of Shasta Lake. The
nearest airport is in Redding, and the drive
from Redding to Weaverville, west on Highway
299, takes about an hour. If you're driving from
San Francisco's airport or elsewhere in the Bay
Area, take I-80 east to I-505 north to I-5 north.
At Redding get onto Highway 44 west, and
then follow signs for Highway 299 west to
Weaverville. From Sacramento, the trip is just
over 200 miles (3.5 hours).

TRINITY ALPS

The Trinity Alps Wilderness (530/226-2500,
www.fs.usda.gov) is one of the five federally
designated wilderness areas within the Shasta-
Trinity National Forest. At 517,000 acres, it's
the second-largest wilderness area in California.
The Alps themselves are part of the Klamath
Mountain Range, and their highest point is
Thompson Peak (8,994–9,002 feet, depending on who you ask). This area seems somewhat resistant to climate change, and the Alps
encompass various small glaciers and permanent snowfields, including a 15-acre glacier on
the north side of Thompson Peak. The forest
is noted for its wide variety of conifers: subal-
pine fir, ponderosa pine, foxtail pine, and incense cedar are just a few of the trees you'll find.
Wildflower enthusiasts will find the rare Trinity
penstemon (*Penstemon tracyi*)—almost worth a
trip on its own. Naturally enough, given the
relatively minimal human usage of this area,
birds, fish, and wildlife abound as well. You're
likely to encounter black bears as well as deer,
California newts, and maybe even the Trinity
Alps giant salamander, an elusive alligator-size
creature that may or may not exist but holds a
place in the annals of cryptozoology—our own
Loch Ness Monster of the woods.

Natural Bridge

The striking Natural Bridge of Trinity-Shasta
National Forest has both geological and historic
significance. This natural limestone arch spans a
200-foot ravine near Hayfork. Names and dates
engraved in the limestone attest to the fact that
early pioneers used this as a picnic site. This is also
the site of the infamous Bridge Gulch Massacre of
1852, in which a conflict between a band of Wintu
people and some prominent Weaverville settlers
ended with the deaths of most of the Wintu people
living in the area. Striking to behold, this limestone phenomenon is worth a side trip—but be
respectful. Descendants of the Wintu still consider
this a place of cultural significance. Water, wind,

© HEATHER C. LISTON

Trinity Alps

and other forces alter the bridge's natural formation, but the more gently we treat it, the longer it will be around for others to marvel at.

Natural Bridge is about 32 miles southwest of Weaverville. From Weaverville, follow Highway 3 south for 26 miles. Turn left onto Wildwood Road, and in another five miles the road transitions onto Bridge Gulch Road. Natural Bridge is 1.2 miles south on Bridge Gulch Road.

Lewiston Lake

Lewiston Lake is an artificial reservoir created by a dam on the Trinity River. Located less than two miles north of the town of Lewiston (www.lewistonca.com), east of Weaverville, Lewiston Lake has a surface area of 750 acres. It's a popular spot for water sports and is particularly celebrated as a fly-fishing destination.

Trinity Lake

In an area rife with clear blue mountain lakes, Trinity Lake still manages to stand out. Formed by Trinity Dam, the lake is one of California's largest reservoirs, with 145 miles of shoreline and a capacity of about 2.5 million acre-feet. Trinity Lake was formerly called Clair Engle Lake, in honor of U.S. senator Clair Engle of California, who died in office in 1964. That name never really caught on, and it's easiest to refer to it as Trinity Lake.

Most people value this large lake as an aquatic playground, and it's particularly popular with water-skiers and houseboaters. If you're interested in renting or docking a houseboat, there are three marinas on the lake: **Trinity Alps Marina** (530/286-2282, www.trinity-alpsmarina.com, daily 9 A.M.–5 P.M. May–mid-Oct., $414–517 per day) in the south offers 50-foot houseboat rentals in midsummer; **Cedar Stock Marina** (530/286-2225 or 800/255-5561, www.trinitylakeresort.com, daily 8 A.M.–6 P.M. Apr.–Oct., $542 per day) in the west also has 50-foot houseboat rentals; and **Trinity Center Marina** (530/286-2225 or 800/255-5561, www.trinitylakeresort.com, daily 8 A.M.–6 P.M. May–Oct.), near the north end, offers private moorings (full season $700) but no boat rentals.

For technical data about reservoirs, storage capacity, precipitation, and climate, check http://cdec.water.ca.gov/reservoir.html. Trinity Lake is located along Highway 3 at the eastern edge of the Trinity Alps, north of the also-large Lewiston Lake and west of Shasta Lake.

Hiking

Hiking opportunities in the Trinity Alps abound. However, this is not the place to go for short easy hikes; it is largely a backpacking destination, and if your interest in hiking is more about communing with nature, you can go for days in the wilderness without seeing anyone else. That said, there are a couple hikes that start near Weaverville that can get you into the Trinity Alps.

One of the most popular hikes in the Trinity Alps is the **Granite Peak Trail** (9 miles round-trip). This trek to the summit of Granite Peak gains more than 4,000 feet of elevation in a fairly short distance—if you're into views, this is the way to get them. From the summit, you can survey vast areas of the Trinity Alps plus Trinity Lake, Mount Shasta, and Mount Lassen. To reach the trailhead from Weaverville, drive north on Highway 3 and look for the signed Stoney Ridge Trailhead. Shortly after the sign, turn left onto Granite Peak Road (Forest Rd. 35N28Y) and continue approximately three miles until you reach a spacious turnaround area; park here to start the hike.

For a particularly rewarding backcountry hike, head for the **Rush Creek Lakes Trail** (8 miles, moderate–strenuous). The trail passes Lower, Middle, and Upper Rush Creek Lakes along its route. Each of the three lakes provides enough fish (especially brook trout) for a good supper if you're a patient angler and don't mind cleaning and cooking a bunch of little ones instead of

one big one. Much of the terrain along this hike is rocky, uphill, or both, but it's well worth the trouble if you like cool mountain lakes and a serious break from civilization. This trail is great for an overnight backpacking trip but is good as a challenging day hike as well. To reach the trailhead from Weaverville, follow Highway 3 north for about eight miles. Turn right onto unmarked Kenney Camp Road, a dirt road about one mile north of Rush Creek Camp Road.

The **Stuart Fork Trail** leads to beautiful Emerald and Sapphire Lakes; this is a good trail into the heart of the Trinity Alps. The whole trail is approximately 30 miles out and back (2–4 days) with 3,000–4,000 feet of elevation gain. However, you can opt for just a short day hike and turn around when you've had enough of the mountains, valleys, and forest. The trailhead is north of Weaverville; take Highway 3 north for 13 miles until it becomes Trinity Lake Boulevard, and then turn left onto Trinity Alps Road.

Fishing

Trinity and Lewiston Lakes are good places to catch rainbow trout, brown trout, and smallmouth bass. The McCloud, Upper Sacramento, and Trinity Rivers are also rife with trout. Fishing licenses are required and are available for a day or for life; prices and requirements vary. For more information, contact the California Department of Fish and Game (601 Locust St., Lewiston, 530/225-2300, www.dfg.ca.gov, 8 A.M.–4:30 P.M. Mon.–Fri.).

John Gray, who calls himself **The Maine Guide** (530/739-0242, www.snowcrest.net/themaineguide, $360 per day for 2 people including lunch), takes visitors on fishing trips to Lewiston Lake and Trinity Lakes. Gray will also help design a personal fishing adventure, which might include hiking to nearby alpine lakes instead of going out on his boat.

Scott Stratton at **Trinity River Adventures** (361 Ponderosa Pines Rd., Lewiston, 530/623-4179, www.trinityriveradventures.com, $400 per day for 1–2 people including lunch) takes anglers out on his 16-foot Lowe jet boat on Lewiston Lake or the Trinity River. Trips include a gourmet lunch as well as fly-fishing instruction.

Friendly and helpful Bruce McGregor of **North Coast Outfitters** (530/694-9444, www. northcoastoutfitter.com, $250 per day for 1 person, $400 per day for 2) will take you out in a drift boat on the Trinity River and supply top-quality gear for your trip.

Versatile **Steve Huber** (530/623-1918, www.ste-vehuberguideservice.com, $200 pp) takes anglers out on the Trinity River in a drift boat or power-boat, as well as on the Rogue, Oregon, Klamath, and Sacramento Rivers. Huber supplies the gear and assists with fly-fishing, bait casting, or trolling—you name it. Plan to bring your own lunch.

Camping

A good campground near Trinity Lake, with easy access to the boat dock, is the U.S. Forest Service's **Bushytail Campground** (near Hwy. 3, 16 miles north of Weaverville, 877/444-6777, www.recreation.gov, May 15–Sept., tents $16, RVs $24–55). Of Bushytail's 12 large wooded sites, nine have electrical hookups. Amenities include flush toilets, drinking water, and showers.

There is a two-night minimum on weekends and a three-night minimum on holidays.

Also located near Trinity Lake is the larger **Hayward Flat** campground (near Hwy. 3, 15 miles north of Weaverville, 877/444-6777, www.recreation.gov, mid-May–mid-Sept., $17). Amenities include flush toilets and drinking water, and there is an amphitheater and ranger programs. It is popular due to its proximity to Trinity Lake, which makes it a great spot for swimming, fishing, and family vacations.

Information and Services

In Lewiston, stock up on supplies at the **Lewiston Mini Mart** (4789 Trinity Dam Blvd., Lewiston, 530/778-3268, 6:30 A.M.–9 P.M. Mon.–Sat., 7 A.M.–9 P.M. Sun.).

Getting There

The Trinity River Scenic Byway (Hwy. 299) stretches from Redding west through Whiskeytown, Weaverville, and all the way to Arcata on the coast. In Weaverville, Highway 3 runs north–south through the Trinity Alps region, past Trinity and Lewiston Lakes, and as far north as Yreka, where it connects with I-5.

Shasta Lake

Shasta Lake doesn't look like most lakes. Rather than a bowl shape, the lake is fed by three major rivers—the Sacramento, the Pit, and the McCloud—plus Squaw Creek, and each of these has an arm of the lake named after it. To create this sprawling artificial lake, not one but five towns were drowned. The remains are still down there, most sunk so deep that even scuba divers cannot explore them. Altogether, the lake has 29,500 acres of surface area, and it's 517 feet deep when it's full. It also has 369 miles of shoreline, which means lots of great places for camping in a tent or an

RV as well as hiking and wildlife-viewing. The unusual layout of this lake makes it all the more interesting for houseboats, waterskiing, fishing, swimming, canoeing, and wakeboarding.

The lake's four main arms and its many inlets all have their own characters, shapes, and surprises. Surrounding many fingers of the lake and some of the bigger pools are marinas, campgrounds, resorts, cabins, and restaurants for lakeside vacations. Marinas dot the shores of the lake's fingers, offering boat rentals, gas, snacks, water, ice, and more. For those few who don't want to spend all day every day on the water, hiking trails and 4WD roads thread through the forested wilderness areas surrounding the lake.

There are several very small towns close to Shasta Lake and Shasta Dam. At the south side of the lake is the tiny City of Shasta Lake. You won't find much besides a couple of motels and a pizza parlor. At the north side of the lake is Lakehead, right on I-5 midway between Redding to the south and the City of Mount Shasta to the north.

SIGHTS
◖ Lake Shasta Caverns

Summer lake visitors can find themselves longing for cool air—hard to come by at Shasta in August. The best natural air-conditioning in the region is inside the Lake Shasta Caverns (20359 Shasta Caverns Rd., Lakehead, 530/238-2752 or 800/795-2283, www.lakeshastacaverns.com, daily 9 A.M.–4 P.M. Memorial Day–Labor Day, daily 9 A.M.–3 P.M. Apr.–May and Sept., tours daily 10 A.M., noon,

Lake Shasta Caverns

© MARIUSZ JURGIELEWICZ/123RF.COM

and 2 P.M. Oct.–Mar., adults $22, ages 3–15 $13). Tours begin across the lake from the caverns at the Caverns Park and gift shop. In summer, tours leave every 30 minutes 9 A.M.–4 P.M. When your tour is called, you walk down to the boat launch and board a broad flat-bottomed ferry with plenty of bench seats and a canopy. On the quick ride across a narrow section of the lake, the pilot regales you with tales of the caverns. At the dock, where boaters can meet their tour groups, if they prefer, you board a bus and take a staggeringly steep drive 800 feet up to the cavern entrance. The road has some fabulous views out over the lake and all the way to Mount Shasta.

Your cavern tour guide meets you at the entrance and leads you into an artificial tunnel. You'll head up a bunch of stairs and into a series of natural limestone and marble caverns. The guide describes the amazing formations that spring from the walls, the ceiling, and the floor. The cathedral size of most of the cavern areas and the railed walkways help to remind visitors not to touch the delicate stalactites, drapes, pancakes, and ribbons of "cave bacon" that decorate each space. You're welcome to bring a camera to record the marvels here, but memories may provide better lighting.

Both kids and adults enjoy the tour of the Lake Shasta Caverns, but you'll want to keep an eye on younger children throughout the trip for their safety. No matter how hot it is outside, bring a jacket or sweater for your tour; the caverns remain cold year-round. While the tour isn't extremely strenuous, you need to be able to walk and to climb 100 stairs at a time. To get to Shasta Caverns, take the exit for O'Brien Road on I-5 north of Redding.

Shasta Caverns also offers a **Lake Shasta Dinner Cruise** (530/238-2752 or 800/795-2283, www.lakeshastadinnercruises.com, 6–8 P.M. Fri.–Sat. Memorial Day–Labor Day, adults $60, under age 12 $35). The cruises depart from the Lake Shasta Caverns' Gift Store, the same location as the regular cavern boat trips, 17 miles north of Redding, near I-5 exit 695. Dinner cruises may also be available at a slightly earlier time for a few weeks after Labor Day; call for reservations.

◖ Shasta Dam

Completed in 1945 and operated by the U.S. Bureau of Reclamation, Shasta Dam is a massive concrete dam that is second in size only to Hoover Dam. At 60 stories high and weighing 30 billion pounds, it is an impressive sight, and the water it stores is one of the reasons California has such fertile farmland.

Even if you're not fascinated by engineering statistics and superlatives, the one-hour dam tour (daily 9 A.M., 10:15 A.M., 11:30 A.M., 1 P.M., 2:15 P.M., and 3:30 P.M. Memorial Day–Labor Day, daily 9 A.M., 11 A.M., 1 P.M., and 3 P.M. Labor Day–Memorial Day, free) is a great experience, and it offers one of the best ways to get a broad view of Shasta Lake. Tours are limited to 40 people; it's recommended to arrive 30 minutes before start time. The tours begin at the **visitors center** (530/275-4463, daily 8 A.M.–5 P.M.); it's a bit of a walk from the parking lot. To explore the area yourself, you can walk across Shasta Dam daily 6 A.M.– 10 P.M. to take in the views of the lake and Mount Shasta. This is a beautiful walk, especially at sunset, and one of many wonderful vantage points to see and photograph the mountain.

Shasta Dam is officially located at 16349 Shasta Dam Boulevard. To get here, take I-5 exit 685 onto Shasta Dam Boulevard. Drive west six miles on Highway 151 to the Shasta Dam visitors center.

SPORTS AND RECREATION
Houseboating and Marinas

Most of the marinas along the shores of Shasta Lake provide all the rentals and services you'll need. If you've got a vacation rental or a campsite on or near the lake, you'll probably want to

© HEATHER C. LISTON

Shasta Dam is second in size only to Hoover Dam.

HOUSEBOATING ON SHASTA LAKE

Shasta Lake PR agencies have named the lake "the houseboating capital of the world." That bold statement may or may not be true, but Shasta Lake certainly is California's most popular houseboating destination. Most of the houseboats rented on Shasta range in size from "silly" to "absurd"—it's quite difficult to find a houseboat that sleeps fewer than 10 people, and most sleep 14-18, and a few true leviathans can hold more than 20 partiers. The beds aren't big, and private bedrooms are few, so for true comfort it's best to pile in no more than half to two-thirds the recommended number of overnight guests.

You can rent a houseboat at almost any marina on the lake. No special boating knowledge is required to rent a houseboat, though you may be required to provide a valid driver's license. Most marina websites post photos and price lists; for example, **Houseboats.com** (877/468-7326, www.houseboats.com), which works with the Jones Valley Resort on Lake Shasta, includes blogs, photos, and information about the lake while you shop online. Whichever marina you rent from, expect to pay anywhere from $850 per weekend for a small minimal craft to $8,500 per weekend for a huge luxury boat. Weekly rates, which include one weekend, are often a bargain at double or less the cost of a single weekend.

Expect to find a fair amount of luxury; many Shasta houseboats come with upper-deck hot tubs, waterslides, barbecues, satellite TV, and high-end entertainment systems. Your houseboat will also come with some necessities—most have fully equipped kitchens, basic cleaning supplies, and basic sanitary supplies (meaning toilet paper). But you'll need to bring a bunch of your own stuff too, such as pillows, towels, sheets, paper towels, folding chairs, ski-quality life jackets, and first-aid kits—as well as food and booze, of course. Talk to your rental company about the full list of supplies they recommend to bring.

Piloting a mammoth houseboat on the waters of Shasta Lake is a bit like driving a big RV up I-5. Take it slow, carefully follow all the instructions you're given at the marina, and you'll do fine. Most Shasta houseboaters pull their craft into small inlets and moor them for the night. Your marina staff can advise you on how to maneuver your houseboat safely toward shore in the evening and back out again the next morning.

Many Shasta houseboats have the equipment to tow smaller watercraft along behind them. If you choose, you can rent a ski boat, personal watercraft, or fishing boat and bring it along with you as you explore Shasta Lake.

---

pick one of the marinas near your lodgings for convenience; Shasta Lake really is that big and definitely that spread out. But not all marinas offer public gas docks or public launch facilities, and one or two of them are maintained for the owners of private slips.

SHASTA MARINA RESORT

One of the nearest marinas to the Shasta Caverns gift shop and loading dock is the Shasta Marina Resort (18390 O'Brien Inlet Rd., Lakehead, 800/959-3359, www.shastalake.net, Mar.–Oct.). Easily accessed from I-5 toward the south end of the lake, this marina offers midsize houseboats and SeaSwirl BowRider ski boats

with wakeboard towers. A 56-foot houseboat, which sleeps 14 people and has a hot tub, satellite TV, gas fireplace, and swim slide, rents for $3,060 for three nights; there's a three-night minimum in summer. Marina facilities include a gas dock, a convenience store with ice and swimsuits, and a boat launch (free with moorage or houseboat rental). This middle-of-the road rental spot definitely offers friendly service, so be sure to ask about good houseboating spots if you're new to Shasta Lake.

PACKERS BAY MARINA

The Packers Bay Marina (16814 Packers Bay Rd., Lakehead, 530/275-5570 or 800/331-3137, www.packersbay.com, 9 A.M.–5 P.M. Mon.–Sat., weekly houseboat rentals $1,395–7,135) is located in Packers Bay, a couple of miles west of I-5 near the big bridge. Getting to the marina from Redding is tricky; you must get off northbound I-5 at the exit for Shasta Caverns and O'Brien Road, then get back on I-5 southbound to reach the Packers Bay Road exit. A small independent operator, this marina offers some of the rare honest-to-goodness modest houseboats on Shasta Lake. These can sleep 10 people but are really comfortable for groups of 4–6 and are less expensive than the bigger models. Packers Bay Marina offers only houseboats and fewer services than the larger places. But houseboat renters can expect more personal service and nicer boats than at the big marinas. No pets are allowed on any boats.

BRIDGE BAY RESORT MARINA

You can see the Bridge Bay Resort Marina (10300 Bridge Bay Rd., Redding, 530/275-3021 or 800/752-9669, www.sevencrown.com,

patio boat $72 for 2 hours, $840 per week; ski boat with tower $130 for 2 hours, $1,280 per week) from the big bridge on I-5. This huge marina, the largest on the lake, is part of a full-scale resort that sees some real crowds in the summer. Bridge Bay Marina has a large rental fleet, which includes small–medium houseboats, closed-bow speedboats, patio boats, and ski boats with or without a tower, most of which can be rented by the day or by the week, as well as for two-hour or four-hour periods. Fishing boat rentals, for example, start at $31 for two hours. If you bring your own boat, it's $15 per day to launch it here, but you get one free launch with any guest room or other rental. You can also moor your boat temporarily. Three docks are available for service of various kinds: the Gas Dock, where you can also get ice, propane, and pump-outs of your holding tank; the Load-out Dock, for houseboat customers of Bridge Bay only; and the Courtesy Dock, which is open to the public and located next to

Bridge Bay Resort Marina

the launch ramp. If you pull up and park your boat at the Courtesy Dock, it's just a short walk to the store (daily 7 A.M.–6 P.M. summer, daily 8 A.M.–4 P.M. fall–spring) where you can get groceries, bathing suits, bait and tackle, and souvenirs. You can also walk to the marina's restaurant, the **Tail O' the Whale** (10300 Bridge Bay Rd., Redding, 800/752-9669, www.sevencrown.com, $13–20). There's good fishing all year; around Bridge Bay, anglers hook catfish, trout, sturgeon, and bass. In winter Bridge Bay hosts bass-fishing tournaments.

JONES VALLEY MARINA

One of the few year-round marinas on Shasta Lake, the Jones Valley Marina (22300 Jones Valley Marina Dr., Redding, 530/275-7950 or 877/468-7326, www.houseboats.com, houseboats $3,361–6,115 weekly; 30-foot 10-passenger patio boat $220 per day) is situated on the secluded Pit River Arm, away from the higher-traffic areas near the bridge, but it is still easily accessible from Redding and I-5. The McCloud Arm and the Squaw Creek Arm adjoin this marina, which is one of the few that sells gas in this part of the lake. Jones Valley Marina is part of a larger resort and includes a floating recreation area in addition to wheelchair-accessible docks and houseboats. Should you find yourself needing a three-deck houseboat that sleeps 22 people with eight flat-screen TVs, you can rent it—it's called *The Titan*—at Jones Valley. They've also got more modest houseboats, plus the usual array of patio party boats and smaller craft, including a top-tier wakeboard-ready speedboat.

SUGARLOAF RESORT

If you have your own boat and need a place to dock it for the summer, contact Sugarloaf Resort (19761 Lakeshore Dr., Lakehead, 877/468-7326, www.houseboats.com, May–Oct., full season $995) on the Sacramento River Arm. Formerly a full-service marina,

Sugarloaf now operates only as a moorage for small private boats. Their modern wheelchair-accessible concrete docks are an appealing starting point for boating adventures, and the docks are a little distance from the busier boating areas on the lake, making it a relatively quiet place to get used to the water before you have to contend with serious traffic.

Fishing and Patio Boating

If you just want to go out and putter on the lake for a day or host a sunset cocktail party, and all those beds and kitchens in the houseboats seem like overkill, what you want is a patio boat. These flat-bottomed pontoon-style boats rent by the hour and by the day and are much cheaper than houseboats. Most come with plenty of seating and canopies for shade. Larger patio boats might have barbecues and storage chests as well. You're free to bring your own coolers, fishing gear, stereo, and friends.

Bridge Bay Resort (10300 Bridge Bay Rd., Redding, 530/275-3021 or 800/752-9669, www.sevencrown.com) rents patio boats ($190 per day) and fishing boats ($89 per day). At **Jones Valley Marina** (22300 Jones Valley Marina Dr., Redding, 503/275-7950 or 877/468-7326, www.houseboats.com), you can rent a 30-foot patio boat ($220–275 per day). There are two options with capacity for 10 people; one boat is slightly larger and has a shower on board. Jones Valley also rents 14-foot aluminum fishing boats ($50 per day). For planned fishing trips, contact John Gray, **The Maine Guide** (530/739-0242, www.snowcrest.net/themaineguide, $360 per day for 2 people including lunch). In addition to fishing trips on Shasta Lake, Gray also plans trips to Lewiston and Trinity Lakes.

Waterskiing and Wakeboarding

Shasta Lake is an ideal place to water-ski and wakeboard; even on crowded weekends, chances are good that you'll find a place to water-ski. Most marinas rent recreation equipment for waterskiing and wakeboarding. **Bridge Bay Resort** (10300 Bridge Bay Rd., Redding, 530/275-3021 or 800/752-9669, www.sevencrown.com) rents wakeboards ($37 for up to 4 hours, $45 per day, $205 per week), ski boats ($290 per day, with tower $310 per day), and water skis ($30 per day). **Jones Valley Marina** (22300 Jones Valley Marina Dr., Redding, 503/275-7950 or 877/468-7326, www.houseboats.com) rents wakeboards, water skis, tubes, and other water play equipment ($50 per day each). Ski boat rentals include a 21-foot Malibu Wakesetter ($515 per day), a 20-foot Malibu Sportster ($475 per day), and a 19-foot Sea Ray ($395 per day). **Shasta Marina Resort** (10300 Bridge Bay Rd., Redding, 530/275-3021 or 800/752-9669, www.sevencrown.com) rents wakeboards ($20 per day) and water skis ($15 per day). Ski boat rentals (3 nights $900) include one pair of water skis as long as you rent a houseboat for the same period of time. They also rent personal watercraft ($350 per night, $1,500 per week), but you must also rent a houseboat for the same period.

You can put your own boat in at any number of public launches and rent a slip from one of the marinas. If you don't, you'll find that most of the marinas around the lake rent both speedboats and personal watercraft; a wide selection is available. Personal watercraft are mostly WaveRunners and the occasional Sea-Doo (get a Sea-Doo if you can; they're better machines). Prices run about $70–120 per hour, with good half-day, full-day, and full-week rates available at most marinas. Be aware that no matter what marina you work with, these are high-performance rental boats, and problems sometimes crop up.

If you'd like a guided boating adventure on a 22-foot professional series Sanger wakeboard boat, check with the **Fun Factory** (Weed, 530/925-1465 or 530/926-5387, www.funfactoryrentals.com, $140 per hour, reservations required). The same friendly people who bring you snowmobile rentals and tours in winter will take you out on their boats in summer. They operate on five lakes: Shasta, Shastina, Siskiyou, McCloud Reservoir, and Iron Gate Reservoir, so you can take your pick. Training in water and boat safety is included.

ENTERTAINMENT AND EVENTS

The main entertainment in the Shasta Lake area centers on the lake itself. The cool thing to do is to rent a patio boat or houseboat and throw your own party on the water. The major festival at Shasta Lake each year is the annual **Shasta Damboree** (530/949-2759, www.shastadamboree.org). Each May, a three-day weekend is devoted to family-friendly events that bring out the community and draw visitors to the region. The events are typical of a good small-town celebration, with spaghetti feeds, pancake breakfasts, an arts-and-crafts area, and a parade and evening party with fireworks and live music.

Some of the best drinking, pool playing, and occasional live music happens up on the northern Sacramento River Arm, just off the I-5 at **The Basshole** (20725 Lakeshore Dr., Lakehead, 530/238-2170, www.bassholebarandgrill.com, breakfast 8 A.M.–noon Sat.–Sun. and holiday Mon., $6.50–10, grill 11 A.M.–10 P.M. Wed.–Mon., 11 A.M.–5 P.M. Tues., $5.50–9, dinner 5–10 P.M. Wed.–Mon., $13–21). This bar, restaurant, and pool hall are all in one large hall, with the bait shop hiding in a tiny room just off the dining area. The food is nothing special, although for dinner they put out an array of slightly fancier entrées. But locals don't come here to eat; they come for the beer.

Another option for a little nightlife is the **Wonderland Tavern** (15041 Wonderland Blvd., Redding, 530/275-5669, noon or 2 P.M.–about 10 P.M. Mon.–Sat., $4) just off I-5, where they serve drinks and inexpensive appetizers. Wonderland has karaoke on Friday night and often stays open until 11:30ish if it's going strong—but there is no guarantee about the business hours. The owner makes the decision every night depending on the crowd.

You could try the **Idle Hour Bar & Grill** (14961 Bear Mountain Rd., Redding, 530/275-0230, daily 11 A.M.–8 P.M., $5–14), south of the Silverthorn Resort, close to the intersection of Bear Mountain Road and Silverthorn Road. There is beer, wine, burgers, and a rotating menu of dinner specials—Friday is prime-rib night.

ACCOMMODATIONS

Lakehead's cutest motel is the bright-yellow **Lakehead Lodge** (21417 Main St., Lakehead, 530/238-9688, www.lakeheadlodge.com, Memorial Day–Labor Day $70–95, Labor Day–Memorial Day $50–75), which offers small but adequate guest rooms with free wireless Internet access. The distinctive hand-painted smiley-face tables help make this is a cheerful oasis in a quiet woodsy area, and the motel has the advantage of being very close to the lake. It's also a good alternative if your goal is to go to Mount Shasta but you can't find lodging available there. The City of Mount Shasta can get crowded on holiday weekends, and this place is quite close.

If your main purpose is to visit Shasta Dam, a good place to stay is the **Shasta Dam Motel** (1529 Cascade Blvd., Shasta Lake, 530/275-1065, www.shastadammotel.com, $49–67). Just four miles from the dam, this is a simple little motel without many amenities, but it does have an outdoor pool. Free Internet access is also on the menu, although management does not guarantee that it's always working.

Because it's out in the woods one mile south of the lakeshore, the **Fawndale Lodge & RV Park** (15215 Fawndale Rd., 530/275-8000, www.fawndale.com, $73–123) offers comfortable lodge rooms and cabins at bargain prices. You can't see the lake from the lodge, but the surrounding forest has its own charm, and the garden and pool offer plenty of beauty nearby. All guest rooms include a fridge, a microwave, and a private bath. Suites have full kitchens, bed space for six, and air-conditioning. The decor is rustic wood walls and furniture and simple amenities, and small TVs offer minimal entertainment and subtle encouragement to get outside to play. Tent campers and RV travelers are welcome at Fawndale ($27–30); full-hookup RV spots are available, although you may need a reservation to guarantee a spot.

Toward the north end of the lake, the **Shasta Lake Motel** (20714 Lakeshore Dr., Lakehead, 530/238-2545, www.shastalakemotel.com, $75–135) is a favorite for regular visitors. For low rates you'll get some big lodge amenities, including air-conditioning, cable TV, microwaves, mini fridges, and coffeemakers. Each guest room glows softly with dark honey-colored wood-paneled walls and furniture, and the decor is rustic prints and artifacts. One special amenity will thrill tall travelers: All the twin and double beds are "extra-long," making them a treat for people over six feet tall. Outdoors, you can enjoy the motel pool or take a quick walk down to the shores of the lake. The motel is only a few minutes off I-5, close enough for convenience but not so near that you'll be listening to the trucks all night.

The ◖ **Bridge Bay Resort** (10300 Bridge Bay Rd., Redding, 800/752-9669, www.sevencrown.com, $115–190) has one of the best locations of any resort here, right where the big I-5 bridge crosses the lake. It's close to the center of the lake's arms, making its full-service marina a perfect spot from which to launch a boat. Bridge Bay also includes a restaurant and a store with groceries, souvenirs, and bait and tackle. The lodgings aren't terribly stylish; guest rooms are decorated in budget-motel chic with colorful bedspreads, particle-board furniture, and generic prints on the walls. But this is a cheerful family-friendly place—many of the guest rooms sleep 4–6, and some guest rooms have full kitchens—and its beautifully situated as a home base for all sorts of lake vacations.

Well east of I-5, out on the tip of a small peninsula in the Pit River Arm, the **Silverthorn Resort** (16250 Silverthorn Rd., Redding, 530/275-1571, www.silverthornresort.com, $935–1,690 per week) definitely has the advantage of a location right on the water. The views from the common areas and guest cabins are phenomenal, and the resort has its own full-service marina with houseboats for rent. Just don't expect to blow in and get a cabin for a single night in high season. At Silverthorn, cabins rent only by the week in summer and require a three-day minimum the rest of the year. Each cabin sleeps 4–6 people, except for the large family cabin that can handle eight. Inside, you'll find the ubiquitous wood-paneled interior walls and simple but attractive lodge-style decor. All cabins include a full kitchen, thus making the by-the-week rental requirement a bit more attractive, with a full-size fridge. Bedrooms are small but cute, and the atmosphere is woodsy and restful. Be sure to book your boat rentals with the marina at the same time you book your cabin to ensure that you get what you want when you want it. A small grocery store and a "Pizza and Pub" room offer easy dining and shopping on-site.

CAMPING

If you have a 4WD vehicle, you can really experience the full beauty of Shasta Lake's McCloud Arm. For a nominal fee, the U.S. Forest Service rents ☾**Hirz Mountain Lookout Tower** (information 530/275-8113, reservations 877/444-6777, www.recreation.gov, late Apr.–mid-Oct., up to 4 people $50). Located in the Shasta-Trinity National Forest, this 20-foot tower is on top of a 3,540-foot peak, so the views are phenomenal. In addition to the vast overview of the McCloud Arm, you can see both Mount Lassen and Mount Shasta. Getting here is a little tricky; you drive five miles down a dirt road (Forest Rd. 35N04) in a high-clearance 4WD vehicle, then walk the

breakfast in the Hirz Mountain Lookout Tower

last 0.25 miles, then climb a couple of flights of metal steps to tower.

For more traditional camping in the vicinity of Shasta Lake, one of the best places around is the **Hirz Bay Campground** (Gilman Rd., 20 miles northeast of Redding, information 530/275-1589, www.fs.usda.gov, reservations 877/444-6777, www.recreation.gov, mid-May–Labor Day, $18). This 48-site U.S. Forest Service family campground was renovated in 2009 and has nice amenities such as flush toilets, picnic tables, and paved parking. It also offers easy access to the lake via the Hirz Bay boat ramp.

FOOD

The **Tail O' the Whale** (10300 Bridge Bay Rd., Redding, 800/752-9669, www.sevencrown.com, daily breakfast, lunch, and dinner, $7–20) at the Bridge Bay Resort, west of I-5, has a casual dining room that's perfect for lakeside vacationers. The lengthy menu has plenty of American favorites, with something to please almost everybody. Breakfast ($7–14) is ordinary but hearty, with a bit of a Southern accent: Biscuits and gravy are served along with the usual eggs and pancakes. Lunch ($8–11) is the usual burgers, BLTs, and chicken salads with the addition of a Pacific Northwest salmon entrée and some fish-and-chips; and dinner ($13–20) has the full range of surf-and-turf, from calamari and salmon to prime rib and pork loin. Seating is on the porch or inside with views of Lake Shasta through the large windows. Upstairs above the restaurant is the **Pelican's Perch Cocktail Lounge** (4:30 P.M.–close Wed.–Sat., noon–4 P.M. Sun.), with its own share of views.

On the east side of the lake, the Silverthorn Resort has the only pizza along the lake at the **Silverthorn Pizza and Pub** (16250 Silverthorn Rd., Redding, 530/275-1571 or 800/332-3044, www.silverthornresort.com, 11 A.M.–9 P.M. Thurs. and Sun.–Mon., 11 A.M.–2 A.M. Fri.–Sat. late May–early Sept., $12–25). This ultra-casual eatery offers ice-cold beer and piping-hot pizzas.

A huge deck overlooking the lake lures people out for cocktails, and then bar games like pool and live music bring them back inside as night falls.

In the little town of Shasta Lake, you'll find the usual fast food joints as well as one local place with a little character, the **Old Mill Eatery** (4132 Shasta Dam Blvd., Shasta Lake, 530/275-0515, 7 A.M.–3 P.M. Wed.–Mon., $8–11), noted for its large portions of basic fare such as hamburgers, omelets, and pancakes, its low prices, and its friendly hometown atmosphere.

The **Lakeshore Village Market** (20750 Lakeshore Dr., Lakehead, 530/238-8615, daily 7 A.M.–9 P.M. year-round) has plenty of food plus basic camping, fishing, and outdoor recreation supplies for visitors staying at the north end of the lake.

INFORMATION AND SERVICES

Stop in at the **Shasta Lake Visitors Center** (Holiday Rd., Mountain Gate, 530/275-1589, www.fs.usda.gov, 8 A.M.–4:30 P.M. Wed.–Sun. Memorial Day–Labor Day), a U.S. Forest Service facility set up specifically to provide information for visitors. During the off-season (Labor Day–Memorial Day), when the visitors center is closed, go across the street to the **Shasta Lake Ranger Station** (530/275-1587, www.fs.usda.gov, 8 A.M.–4:30 P.M. Mon.–Fri. year-round) for campfire permits and permits to enter the Trinity Alps Wilderness. Note that these are not just backcountry camping permits; in a few wilderness areas, including Trinity Alps, you need a permit just to enter. For the Shasta Wilderness, go to the **Mount Shasta Ranger Station** (204 W. Alma St., Mount Shasta, 530/926-4511, 8 A.M.–4:30 P.M. Mon.–Fri. Labor Day–Memorial Day, 8 A.M.–4:30 P.M. Mon.–Sat. Memorial Day–Labor Day).

Shasta Lake has its own tiny local paper—the **Shasta Lake Bulletin** (530/275-1716, www.shastalake.ws, Wed., $0.50), which comes out once a week. The company also puts out a monthly magazine called *After Five* (free) that lists local entertainment and event options, and an annual *Visitor's Guide* (free) that comes out once a year around Memorial Day and has good information for travelers.

There is a **post office** (20856 Antlers Rd., Lakehead, 530/238-2681, www.usps.com, 8:30 A.M.–12:30 P.M. and 1–4 P.M. Mon.–Fri.), but the nearest major medical facilities are in Redding.

GETTING THERE AND AROUND

Most people come to Shasta Lake by car via I-5, which runs over the lake in two different places. Bridge Bay is one of the more popular spots on the lake due to its proximity and easy access to I-5. The Sacramento Arm to the north is also easily accessible from I-5.

Many people bring their own boats to Shasta Lake rather than paying the high fees to rent

from the marinas. Check local maps to find the public launch nearest to your accommodations, and expect to pay a small launching fee. Before you launch, your boat may be inspected both for proper state licensing and for pernicious mussels. A special license is not required to pilot a boat in California. All drivers of boats over 15 horsepower (that includes personal watercraft) must be age 16 or older. Children ages 12–15 can drive if directly supervised by an adult. All children under age 13 must wear a life jacket at all times when on board a boat. For more information about boating rules, visit www.dbw.ca.gov.

The nearest full-service airport is **Redding Municipal Airport** (RDD, 6751 Woodrum Circle, Redding, 530/224-4320), where you can rent a car to drive out to the lake.

Lassen Volcanic National Park

Lassen Volcanic National Park (www.nps.gov/lavo, information 530/595-6100, 8 A.M.–4:30 P.M. Mon.–Fri., visitors center 530/595-4480, daily 8 A.M.–6 P.M. summer, 8 A.M.–5 P.M. winter, $10) resulted from the merger of two National Monuments—Cinder Cone and Lassen Peak—in 1916. As such, it is one of the oldest national parks in the United States; it is also one of the remotest and most primitive. A paved road runs through the middle of the park, making it easy in summer for visitors to enjoy many of the major attractions—including the park's active volcanic features. The rugged weather and isolated location mean that a visit to Lassen Volcanic National Park is a trip to a largely unspoiled wilderness rather than an overdeveloped amusement park with rocks. A good half of the park has only minimal dirt-road access and offers its rugged beauty only to those travelers willing to hike for miles into the backcountry. Even the trails and campgrounds accessible by the paved main road maintain a kind of charm that's hard to find in the more popular California parks.

Mount Lassen itself is an active volcano with a long recorded history of eruptions, the last of which took place in 1914–1917. The mountain is a beautiful sight, and it's only accessible to most people during the short summer months when the temperatures rise and the snow melts.

SIGHTS

Lassen Volcanic National Park has ample hiking trails, lovely little ponds scattered throughout, and many campsites that let visitors settle in and really enjoy the amazing panoramas of Mount Lassen. A wonderful loop drive through the park takes you from the stark slopes and jagged brand-new rocks of the most recent eruption around the back to an enormous ancient crater, the remains of a long-gone volcano as big as or bigger than Mount Shasta. Beyond the bounds of the national park, national forest lands allow for additional exploration.

Although it is officially open year-round, snow chokes the area from as early as October until as late as June, closing the main road

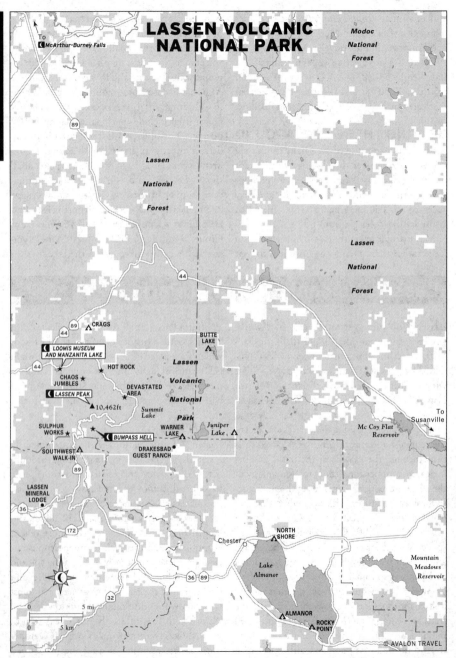

LASSEN VOLCANIC NATIONAL PARK

To McArthur-Burney Falls

Modoc
National
Forest

Lassen

National

Forest

89

44

Lassen

National

Forest

89 CRAGS

44
LOOMIS MUSEUM
AND MANZANITA LAKE

BUTTE
LAKE

44 HOT ROCK

CHAOS
JUMBLES

DEVASTATED
AREA

Lassen

Volcanic

LASSEN PEAK

10,462ft

National

SULPHUR
WORKS

Summit
Lake

Park

WARNER
LAKE

Juniper
Lake

BUMPASS HELL

SOUTHWEST
WALK-IN

DRAKESBAD
GUEST RANCH

To
Susanville

Mc Coy Flat
Reservoir

89

LASSEN
MINERAL
LODGE

36

172

Chester

NORTH
SHORE

Lake
Almanor

Mountain
Meadows
Reservoir

36 89

32

ALMANOR

ROCKY
POINT

0   5 mi

0   5 km

© AVALON TRAVEL

through the park and making even the lower-altitude campground snowy and cold. The only time to visit Lassen is the height of summer; most visitors pick August and early September. Call 530/595-4480 for updates on road conditions before planning a trip.

Kohm Yah-mah-nee Visitors Center

Lassen's first permanent year-round visitors center (530/595-4480, www.nps.gov/lavo, daily 9 A.M.–6 P.M. summer, daily 9 A.M.–5 P.M. winter) opened in 2008, which was 92 years after the park was created. The name Kohm Yah-mah-nee is from the language of the local Maidu people and means "snow mountain," which was their name for Lassen Peak.

Awarded the highest level of Leadership in Energy and Environmental Design (LEED) certification, this modern, comfortable, state-of-the-art facility was worth the wait. It's got an auditorium showing new films about the park, interactive exhibits illuminating local geology and ecology, an unusually well-stocked snack bar

and grill, a souvenir-and-sundries shop, an attractive amphitheater, a first-aid center, and large modern restrooms. Outside, strategically placed benches make great spots to enjoy lunch or a snack while you take a load off and enjoy gorgeous views of the mountains. One of the best features for a group with mixed ages and abilities is the very short interpretive trails just outside, with paved walkways and informative signage.

Located near the southwest entrance to the park on Highway 89, the visitors center is open every day except Thanksgiving and Christmas, and it's accessible even when other roads in the park are closed due to snow (which is common). It's convenient to the Sulphur Works and to the trailheads for Brokeoff Mountain and Ridge Lakes.

◖ Lassen Peak

It's not as tall as it used to be, but Lassen Peak still reaches 10,462 feet into the sky. Even if you're not up to climbing it, it's worth stopping at the parking lot at the trailhead to crane your neck and enjoy the view. The craggy broken

© HEATHER C. LISTON
Lassen Peak

mountain peak is what's left after the most recent eruption, hence the lack of vegetation. The starting elevation for the summit trail is 8,000 feet, which means the Lassen Peak trailhead tends to be cool even in the heat of summer. You may need to break out a windbreaker or light sweater if you plan to explore at length. The **Lassen Peak Trail** (5 miles, difficult) leads to the highest point on Mount Lassen.

◖ Loomis Museum and Manzanita Lake

As you enter the northwestern edge of the park on Highway 89, almost immediately you'll find Loomis Museum (530/595-6140, daily 9 A.M.–5 P.M. Memorial Day–Oct., free) and Manzanita Lake. Inside the museum is a wonderful opportunity to learn about the known history of Mount Lassen, focusing heavily on the 1914–1915 eruptions photographed by Mr. B. F. Loomis. Prints of those rare and stunning photos have been enlarged and captioned to create these exhibits; the museum was named for the photographer, who later became a major player in the push to make Mount Lassen a national park. This interpretive museum offers a rare chance to see, through photos, the devastation and following stages of regrowth of the ecosystem on the volcanic slopes.

Chaos Jumbles

This broken and decimated area may seem like another spot that was splashed with rocks and lava during the 1915 eruption of Mount Lassen, but rather than a volcanic eruption, this interesting formation was actually caused by a massive avalanche about 300 years ago. The results look similar to the regions affected by volcanoes, with devastation of the living ecosystem, displacement of massive rocks, and the general disorder of the landscape. The avalanche that occurred here was so big and came down so fast that it actually trapped a pocket of air underneath it, adding to the destruction. Now

visitors can enjoy a wealth of new life, including a broader-than-average variety of coniferous trees. The newness of the living landscape has allowed a greater variety of competing types of plants to get a foothold.

Hot Rock

No, it's not hot anymore, but this huge boulder was untouchable back when the Loomises explored the eruption zone soon after the 1915 blast. Frankly, the site isn't all that amazing now, except when you think that that big rock remained warm to the touch for months. The Hot Rock turnout also offers more great views of the Devastated Area.

Devastated Area

It seems like an odd name for a point of interest, but in fact the Devastated Area is one of the most fascinating geological and ecological sites in California. When Mount Lassen blew its top in 1915 after nearly a year of sporadic eruptions, a tremendous part of the mountain and all the life on its slopes was destroyed. Boiling mud and exploding gases tore off the side of Lassen's peak and killed all the vegetation in the area. A hail of lava rained down, creating brand-new rocks, in sizes from gravel to boulders, across the north side of the mountain.

Today, visitors can easily see how a volcano's surface ecosystem recovers after an eruption. First, park at the Devastated Area lot and take the interpretive walk through a small part of the recently disrupted mountainside. You'll see everything from some of the world's youngest rocks to grasses and shrubs through tall pine trees. Be sure to check out the photos in the Loomis Museum that depict the area during and immediately after the eruption for a great comparison to the spot as it looks now.

The Devastated Area offers ample parking, and the interpretive walk is flat and wheelchair accessible. Don't pick up any of the red and black volcanic rocks; they are part of the redeveloping ecosystem and necessary to the area's recovery.

Summit Lake

Lassen National Park is dotted with tiny lakes, although many might better be called ponds or puddles. One of the most popular and most easily accessible of these is Summit Lake, along the main road. The bright and shining small lake attracts many campers to its two forest-shaded campgrounds. There's an easy walk around the lake that lets you see its waters and the plants that proliferate nearby. You can also find one of the small trails down to the edge of the water to eke out a spot on the miniscule beach with all the other visitors who come to escape the heat. You can swim and fish in Summit Lake, and even take rafts and canoes out to paddle around. No power boats are permitted on any lake in Lassen Volcanic National Park.

◖ Bumpass Hell

This place belongs on the list of "Top 10 Best Place Names in California." The best and most varied area of volcanic geothermal activity on Lassen is at a location called Bumpass Hell (6 miles from the southwest entrance). The region

was named for Kendall Vanhook Bumpass, who, during his explorations, stepped through a thin crust over a boiling mud pot and severely burned his leg, ultimately losing the limb. In fact, the tale of the unfortunate Bumpass illustrates a good point for travelers visiting the mud pots and fumaroles: Stay on the paths! The dangers at Bumpass Hell are real, and if you step off the boardwalks or let your children run wild, you are risking serious injury.

Still, a hike down to Bumpass Hell on the Bumpass Nature Trail is fun. As long as you're careful, it's worth the risk. You'll need to walk about two miles from the parking lot and trailhead out to the interesting stuff—boiling mud pots, fumaroles, steaming springs, and pools of steaming boiling water cluster here. Prepare for the strong smell of sulfur, more evidence that this volcano is anything but extinct. Boardwalks are strategically placed through the area, creating safe walking paths for visitors.

The spacious parking lot at Bumpass offers stunning views to the east and south, giving

© LINDSAY DOUGLAS/123RF.COM

Bumpass Hell

you a hint at the scope of the ancient volcano that once stood here. Right at the parking lot you can see a famous "glacial erratic," a boulder carried along by a glacier; this one is about 10 feet high, demonstrating, once again, the colossal forces of nature that have been at work in this park over the millennia. There are also primitive toilet facilities in the parking lot.

Sulphur Works

For visitors who can't quite manage the trek out to Bumpass Hell, the Sulphur Works offers a peek at the geothermal features of Lassen from the main road. A boardwalk runs along the road, and a parking area is nearby, making it easy for visitors to get out of the car and examine the loud boiling mud pots and small steaming stream. The mud pots both look and sound like a washing machine, sending up steam and occasional bursts of boiling water. Keep hold of your children.

Starting from the Sulphur Works is a two-mile round-trip trail to Ridge Lakes. It's a fairly steep climb, but the payoff at the top is a view of two alpine lakes between Brokeoff Mountain and Mount Diller. Along the way, you'll walk through beautiful green meadows dotted with bright yellow wildflowers and then into a forest before reaching the lakes.

RECREATION
Hiking

Most of the easy interpretive walks and short day hikes run out to the sights of Mount Lassen Volcanic National Park. For hikers who want to get out and away from the more heavily visited areas but still make it back to the car before dark, several moderate–difficult hiking trails offer adventure, challenge, and maybe even a touch of solitude.

Be aware that the lower elevations of Mount Lassen's trails are still more than 7,000 feet above sea level. If you're planning to do serious hiking, it's good to come a day early, if you can, to acclimate to the elevation.

LASSEN PEAK TRAIL

The must-do hike for any serious hiker is Lassen Peak Trail (5 miles, difficult). A large

Lassen Peak Trail, overlooking Lake Helen

© BRAD CHRISTIE

parking lot with chemical-toilet facilities is at the trailhead, and you're likely to see a lot of other cars here. This path not only takes you to the highest point on Mount Lassen, it's also a starkly beautiful unusual trail that offers long views of the rest of the park and beyond.

The climb to the top is dramatic, challenging, and worth it. It's not actually a long hike—only five miles round-trip—but the trail gains more than 2,000 vertical feet in only 2.5 miles on the way up. The trail is well graded and has many switchbacks, which help manage the steepness. And some good news: Exhibits along the way explain some of the fascinating views of volcanic remains, lakes, wildlife, and rock formations.

The recent (by geologic standards) eruption and prevailing weather conditions leave this peak without much plant life, which means nothing blocks your views downward and outward, and the rocky terrain is visually interesting. Only the last 0.25 mile or so actually involves any scrambling over large rocks; most of the trail is just a steady upward walk. When you get to the top, *oh la la!* Be sure to turn all the way around to get 360-degree views back down to the newest volcanic landscape, across to the remains of the giant caldera of a huge extinct volcano, and then out west toward the Cascade Range, where you'll see Mount Shasta shining in the distance.

KINGS CREEK FALLS TRAIL

The Kings Creek Falls Trail (Hwy. 89, road marker 32, 3 miles round-trip, moderate) starts out easy. The initial walk begins downhill to the falls. Be sure to stop to admire the small cascade and pool and maybe sit down and have a snack as you prepare for the 700-foot climb back up to the trailhead. This is a good hike for fit day-hikers who've already been on the mountain for a few hours.

SUMMIT LAKE TO ECHO AND TWIN LAKES

It's the length of the trail that runs from Summit Lake to Echo and Twin Lakes (east side of Summit Lake, 8 miles round-trip, moderate–difficult) that makes it challenging. But you can choose how many little lakes you really want to see if you run short of breath. The elevation gain over the course of this long trail is only 500 feet in total—a gentle slope in these mountainous reaches. A pleasant and sedate four-mile walk is out to Echo Lake. It's another two miles to get to Upper Twin Lake and back, and two more miles to reach Lower Twin Lake. You might want to wear a swimsuit under your hiking clothes on hot summer days to cool off in one of the lakes before trekking back to base.

BROKEOFF MOUNTAIN

For a good solid all-day hike with some invigorating uphill stretches, climb Brokeoff Mountain (Hwy. 89, road marker 2, 7.5 miles round-trip, difficult). Brokeoff makes a good second- or third-day Lassen hike, after you've seen the sights and climbed Mount Lassen. It's near the Kohm Yah-mah-nee Visitors Center and the southern entrance to the park along Highway 89, so it can serve as a last big adventure before you head back to the Bay Area or points south. Brokeoff involves a 2,600-foot ascent from a mile-high starting point, so the thin air and rigorous climb can be quite difficult for hikers who are unused to altitude or are out of shape. On the other hand, if you're ready for it, this is one of the prettiest and most serene hikes in the more visited section of the park. Enjoy the pretty mountain streams and stellar views out over the mountains and valleys of Northern California.

Backpacking

Some of the most beautiful and interesting remote hiking in California can be found in Lassen's expanse of backcountry. Check with the ranger station when you enter the park to obtain any necessary backcountry permits and get the season's scoop on trail conditions. While you might not be the only backpacker out here,

SHASTA AND LASSEN

© BRAD CHRISTIE

Brokeoff Mountain, from Lassen Peak

you'll definitely leave the crowds on the main road behind and find yourself with more trees, birds, and other mountain critters than people. You might even get lucky enough to have a pristine lake or mountain stream to yourself.

No major park in California would be complete without a hunk of the **Pacific Crest Trail** (www.pcta.org) running through it. This high-altitude stretch (17 miles, difficult) of the continent-spanning trail offers lots of challenge and solitude and a fairly short window in which you can traverse this part of California. If you're doing the California leg of the Pacific Crest Trail, try to hit Lassen June–September, and be prepared for extreme weather conditions from blistering heat to snowstorms.

For a radical change of scenery, take the **Cinder Cone Trail** from Butte Lake (west end of Butte Lake Campground, 4–5 miles, moderate). Be sure to wear your sturdiest ankle-covering hiking boots on this adventure, since the ground on the Cinder Cone is...well...cinders.

Watch your footing so you don't slide down; even cold cinders can cut you up. The trail rises 800 vertical feet over two miles; to lengthen the hike, walk down the south side of the cone. Geology and photography buffs particularly like this hike, which is accessible by dirt road and shows off some of the more interesting and less-seen volcanic history of Mount Lassen.

If you can't get enough of Lassen's geothermal features, enter the park from Warner Valley Road and take a hike to **Boiling Springs Lake** (Warner Campground parking lot, 3 miles, easy–moderate). You'll get to see bubbling mud pots and check out the boiling springs from a safe distance. The walk out and back is reasonably short and nonstrenuous. Just be very careful once you reach the geothermal area; unlike Bumpass Hell, this region has no nice safe boardwalks encircling the mud pots and fumaroles. These features, along with the hot springs, can be extremely dangerous. This might not be a hike for young spirited children, but it's heaven for serious nature lovers who want to see what volcanic geothermal features look like in their wild state. Needless to say, trying to swim in sulfurous, acidic, 125°F Boiling Springs Lake is a very bad idea.

Looking for a more serious, multiday backcountry trek? Check the park website for maps and feel free to call the park to get advice on route planning and necessary equipment before you come. Once you're in the park, the visitors centers can issue a free wilderness permit for backcountry hiking and camping and provide last-minute pointers and current trail information.

Boating and Fishing

If you've got a canoe, a kayak, or a rowboat, bring it to Lassen in the summer. Many of the small–midsize lakes on the mountain allow unpowered boating and fishing. While most of the lakes on the west side of the park near the road are too small to boat, in the east part of the park, Juniper, Snag, and Butte Lakes have plenty of space to row or paddle out and enjoy the serenity of the water. No boat rentals are available inside Lassen Volcanic National Park.

Several varieties of trout inhabit the larger Lassen lakes. All you need is a pole, some bait, and a valid California fishing license. Manzanita Lake offers catch-and-release fishing only, but at all the other fishable lakes you're welcome to take a state limit of rainbows and browns. Fishing at several of the campgrounds makes it easy to enjoy the freshest dinner possible.

Fishing licenses are available online (www.dfg.ca.gov) and at the Redding office of the California Department of Fish and Game (601 Locust St., Redding, 530/225-2300, 8 A.M.–4:30 P.M. Mon.–Fri.).

ACCOMMODATIONS

Accommodations near Lassen Volcanic National Park are few and far between. Plan to camp in the park, or stay near Redding or Chester and take day trips into the park. The nearest lodgings are about nine miles south in Mineral.

Lassen Mineral Lodge (Hwy. 36, Mineral, 530/595-4422, www.minerallodge.com, year-round, $80–110) is on Highway 36 near the southwest entrance to the park. The lodge offers small motel-style guest rooms with private baths and few frills; pets are not allowed. The lack of TVs and telephones encourages visitors to get out and enjoy the park and its surrounding landscape. Hiking and fishing are favorite pastimes of lodge guests. The on-site **Mineral Lodge Restaurant** (daily 8 A.M.–8 P.M. summer, 8 A.M.–8 P.M. Sat.–Sun. winter, $15) has a bar and is open to nonguests.

Located near the southern entrance station is the **((Drakesbad Guest Ranch** (end of Warner Valley Rd., Chester, 866/999-0914, www.drakesbad.com, June–2nd Mon. in Oct., $176–201). This all-inclusive ranch includes three meals per day in the room rates, although the national park entrance fee is not included. The ranch maintains its own stable, making horseback riding on the trails of Lassen Volcanic National Park an easy proposition. Guided trail rides are $30 per hour. You're also within easy reach of any number of hiking trails, many of which are not accessible from the park's main paved roads. Bring your tackle along on a walk or a ride to take advantage of the fishing available in the local lakes and streams. Some anglers enjoy the guided fly-fishing program offered by the ranch, which teaches fly-fishing and practices catch-and-release sustainable fishing ($225 per day for 1–2 people). The ranch even has a wonderful pool that's fed by the water from a local hot spring, making it healthful for soaking as well as for swimming laps.

CAMPING

Lassen has eight campgrounds, four of which are accessible via the paved park road. The remaining four campgrounds offer primitive facilities or are accessible via a short hike.

Backcountry camping is permitted at Lassen; several hike-in campgrounds offer some minimal facilities and a way to lessen your impact on the landscape. You need a wilderness permit to camp in the backcountry, but the permit is free, and there are no quotas. To apply for a backcountry permit, download an application from www.nps.gov/lavo and mail or fax it prior to your trip. Permits are also available in the park from the Loomis Museum (530/595-6140, daily 9 A.M.–5 P.M. Memorial Day–Oct.) and Kohm Yah-mah-nee Visitors Center (530/595-4480, www.nps.gov/lavo, daily 9 A.M.–6 P.M. summer, daily 9 A.M.–5 P.M. winter); self-registration is possible at the Loomis, Butte Lake, Warner Valley Ranch, and Juniper Lake Ranger Stations.

MANZANITA LAKE

Closest to the park entrance along Highway 89 is the pleasant and serene Manzanita Lake Campground (179 sites, 877/444-6777, www.recreation.gov, May–Sept., $18). By far the largest campground in Lassen, Manzanita Lake has a full slate of amenities, including flush toilets, potable running water, fire rings or pits, picnic tables in all campsites, and an RV dump station, and it's the only place in the park where showers are available, in the nearby camp store (quarters required). Trailers and campers up to 35 feet are allowed. Advance reservations are recommended at this popular campground.

CRAGS

Five miles south of Manzanita Lake, the more primitive Crags Campground (45 sites, first-come, first-served, June–Sept., $12) offers a more out-in-the-woods style of camping. Crags has potable running water and pit toilets but no showers. Each site has a picnic table, a metal food locker, and a fire pit.

SUMMIT LAKE NORTH AND SOUTH

Farther south along Highway 89 at Summit Lake, **◖ Summit Lake North** (46 sites, 877/444-6777, www.recreation.gov, late June–Sept., $18) and **◖ Summit Lake South** (48 sites, 877/444-6777, www.recreation.gov, late June–Oct., $16) campgrounds are some of the most popular spots in the park, so reservations are recommended. Visitors can swim in Summit Lake, easily accessing its banks from trails and campsites. These two developed campgrounds have flush toilets, fire pits, and tables, but to be safe bring enough potable water for the length of your trip for drinking and washing. At 6,650 feet elevation, the Summit Lake campgrounds are among the highest in the park. Be sure to take it easy setting up camp on your first day so that you can get used to the thin air.

BUTTE LAKE

Out in the backcountry, well away from the main road, the Butte Lake Campground (42 sites, 877/444-6777, www.recreation.gov, June–Oct., $16) shows off the beauty of Lassen to its best advantage. Despite its remote location at the northeast corner of the park, you'll find this to be a fairly well-developed campground, with pit toilets and running water. Check with the National Park Service to be sure the water at this campground is drinkable. Each site has a fire pit and a table. Trailers and RVs up to 35 feet that can negotiate the road can camp at Butte Lake. To reach the campground, take Highway 44 to the dirt road, then drive six miles to the campground. Reservations are recommended.

JUNIPER LAKE

The Juniper Lake Campground (18 sites, June–Oct., $10) takes campers farther off the beaten path. Since the campground is located on the east side of the park, at the end of a rough dirt road near Chester, you'll do much better if you're a tent camper rather than with an RV or trailer.

This small campground beside beautiful Juniper Lake has pit toilets, fire pits, and tables, but the water isn't drinkable. Either bring purifying agents or your own drinking water in containers. Because it is at almost 7,000 feet elevation, definitely take it easy during your first day.

If you're bringing your horses with you, you can reserve space at the Juniper Lake Corral ($10 plus $4 per animal).

WARNER VALLEY

Warner Valley (18 sites, June–Oct., $14) is along the south edge of the park. Another small gem of a semi-developed campground, Warner Valley has pit toilets and drinking water as well as tables and fire pits at each site. Trailers are not allowed: Although the dirt road is only one mile long, it's too rough for large campers and RVs to navigate.

SOUTHWEST WALK-IN

The only campground open year-round is the Southwest Walk-in Campground (18 sites, tents only, first-come, first-served, $14). Plumbing is turned off in this campground when the snows come, so don't expect flush toilets and drinking water unless it's summer. However, you won't be far from the Kohm Yah-mah-nee Visitors Center, so you can use the facilities and get water there. The restrooms are located outside the main building, so they're accessible all night. "Walk-in," by the way, doesn't mean this is for backpackers only. The parking lot for this campground is quite close to the campsites; you just can't park right beside your tent.

FOOD

Mount Lassen offers precious little in the way of dining options. If you're camping, shop in Redding and bring in lots of food. Don't expect to get to a restaurant during your stay unless you're willing to drive a long way. The best food available in the park is at **Kohm Yah-mah-nee Visitors Center** (Hwy. 89, 530/595-4480,

www.nps.gov/lavo, daily 9 A.M.–6 P.M. summer, daily 9 A.M.–5 P.M. winter), where the snack bar sells burgers, slices of pizza, hot coffee, and ice cream.

In the summer, a small **camp store** (daily 8 A.M.–5 P.M.) opens near Manzanita Lake; it sometimes stays open until 8 P.M. in the busiest part of the season.

INFORMATION AND SERVICES

The **Kohm Yah-mah-nee Visitors Center** (Hwy. 89, 530/595-4480, www.nps.gov/lavo, daily 9 A.M.–6 P.M. summer, daily 9 A.M.–5 P.M. winter) is located at the south entrance station of the park, and there's a ranger station at the Highway 44/89 entrance. At either station you can get wilderness permits for backcountry camping, any other necessary permits, and advice about where you can and cannot hike, ride, swim, fish, and camp in Lassen.

Park rangers can provide first aid and help you get phone access to emergency services in Redding. If you're planning on serious hiking or camping, bring a well-stocked first-aid kit for minor injuries and illnesses.

GETTING THERE AND AROUND
By Air

The nearest major airport to Lassen is the **Reno-Tahoe International Airport** (RNO, 2001 E. Plumb Lane, Reno, NV, 775/328-6400, www.renoairport.com). You can also fly into **San Francisco International Airport** (SFO, Hwy. 101, San Francisco, 650/821-8211 or 800/435-9736, www.flysfo.com), or **Sacramento International Airport** (SMF, 6900 Airport Blvd., Sacramento, 916/929-5411, www.sacramento.aero), either of which involves a somewhat longer but still fairly easy drive to Lassen.

By Car

Lassen Volcanic National Park is about four hours' drive from Bay Area and three hours from Sacramento, most of it spent traveling north on I-5. At the town of **Red Bluff**, exit I-5 onto Highway 36 and head east for about 43 miles before making a left onto Highway 89, which leads into the park.

On Mount Lassen, winter usually begins in November and continues through May. Highway 89 through the park closes from about October until May, June, or July depending on the weather and snowfall in any given year. Highway 89 serves as the main road through the park, and the visitors center, campgrounds, trailheads, and lakes cluster along it. You can get a good feel for Lassen by taking a day trip along Highway 89.

South of Lassen, roads run from the tiny town of **Chester** to the park. Warner Valley Road is paved, but other roads from the town to the park are good old-fashioned dirt. On the northeast side of the park, Highway 44 leads from the remote town of **Susanville**; dirt roads lead from Highway 44 into the park.

However you get to Lassen, be sure to bring a good map and possibly a GPS device as well. Note that there are no gas stations in the park. Gas up in Red Bluff, Chester, or Susanville before driving up to Mount Lassen.

RED BLUFF

Red Bluff is just one hour west of the entrance to Lassen Volcanic National Park, and it's also a good stopping place on the way to Shasta. The town has a quaint and lively Main Street, good for shopping, and multiple parks and recreation opportunities for fishing, hiking, and camping.

Sights

William B. Ide Adobe State Historic Park

(21659 Adobe Rd., near I-5 exit 650, 530/529-8599, www.ca.parks.gov, day use and parking $6) was established in 1951 and is one of the area's proudest attractions. The park celebrates William Brown Ide (1796–1852), who came to California in 1845 and took part in the Bear Flag Revolt. There is a historic house and barn to tour, and the **visitors center** (daily 8 A.M.–5 P.M.) provides information about this fascinating part of California history.

The **Sacramento River Discovery Center** (1000 Sale Lane, Red Bluff, 530/527-1196, www.srdc.tehama.k12.ca.us, 11 A.M.–4 P.M. Tues.–Sat.) is the go-to spot for information about the river and wildlife in the area. In addition to a garden and greenhouse, the Discovery Center also offers guided bird tours (8 A.M. 1st Sat. of the month, rain or shine), and there's a special evening program (7 P.M. 3rd Thurs. of the month).

Entertainment and Events

The **Red Bluff Round-Up** (530/527-8700 or 800/545-3500, www.redbluffroundup.com, Apr.) is one of this town's biggest attractions. For several days each April, Red Bluff throws a rodeo, chili cook-off, and more events that turn the town into a bustling Western party. If you think that's interesting, check out the **Red Bluff Round-Up Museum** (670 Antelope Blvd., 530/528-1477, 1–4 P.M. Thurs.–Sat., free) to see photographs and memorabilia related to the event since it began in 1921.

Red Bluff is justifiably proud of its renovated **State Theatre for the Arts** (333 Oak St., 530/529-2787, www.statetheatreredbluff.com). In 1908 an opera house opened on this spot; in 1928 the building was renovated and turned into a popular theater. After the theater burned down in 1944, the State Theatre was rebuilt and reopened soon afterward. The beautiful art deco movie and live-entertainment palace underwent its most recent rebirth in October 2011.

If you can, time your visit to celebrate **Adobe Day** (3rd Sat. in Aug.) at William B. Ide Adobe State Historic Park. The Ide Adobe Players perform period music and offer instruction in pioneer crafts and other activities. Or come for the **Ide's Ferry Champion Horseshoe Pitchers**

Contest (2nd Sat. in Oct.). Park officials will lend you an appropriate 1850s costume, and you'll get a shot at winning a gold-filled pocket watch. You can also take part in the **Pioneer Christmas Party** (3rd Sat. in Dec.).

Sports and Recreation

About one mile south of Red Bluff is the **Red Bluff Recreation Area** (530/527-2813, www.fs.usda.gov), within Mendocino National Forest. The volunteer organization Red Bluff Trails United develops and maintains the trails here so that hikers can enjoy the wildlife and views while getting some exercise. Soon after entering the recreation area, you'll come to the trailhead for the **Shasta View Trail** (2 miles, easy), a mostly flat loop that delivers the views it promises. You can even see the Yolla Bolly Mountains from some places, worth it just so you can say it. The trail is a great leg-stretcher for people passing through town, or a morning jog for those staying in the **Sycamore Grove Campground** (877/444-6777, www.recreation.gov). In 0.5 miles is a parking lot with pit toilets, picnic tables, and a boat launch ($6). The visitors center doubles as the **Sacramento River Discovery Center** (1000 Sale Lane, 530/527-1196, www.srdc.tehama.k12.ca.us, 11 A.M.–4 P.M. Tues.–Sat.).

Bird-watching is a big attraction in the Red Bluff Recreation Area, and the park is home to great blue herons, great egrets, great horned owls, wood ducks, Anna's hummingbirds, and many other species. It also features bobcats, western pond turtles, Pacific tree frogs, opossums, woodchucks, and more. Various short nature trails, some of which are paved, make for easy forays into the best wildlife-viewing spots.

Accommodations and Camping

Red Bluff offers the standard hotel chains such as **Super 8** (30 Gilmore Rd., 530/529-2028 or 877/260-5783, www.super8.com, $51) and **Comfort Inn** (90 Sale Lane, 877/287-4809, www.comfortinn.com, $90). For something more specific to the area, try the **Sportsman Lodge** (768 Antelope Blvd., 530/527-2888 or 866/573-4235, www.redbluffsportsmanlodge.com, $75). It's nothing fancy, but it has an outdoor pool, free wireless Internet access, and friendly local owners.

If you've got your own bed on wheels, the place to park it is the upscale **Durango RV Resort** (100 Lake Ave., 530/527-5300 or 866/770-7001, www.durangorvresorts.com, $43, more for fountain sites or riverfront sites), which offers a lap pool, a sauna, free wireless Internet access, paddle tennis, boccie ball courts, two laundries, a lodge and concession center, and facilities to wash your dog *and* your vehicle. The resort is on the Sacramento River and is surrounded by woods. Due to underground watering, this is not a place for tents.

Within the Red Bluff Recreation Area, **Sycamore Grove Campground** (Sale Lane, 2 miles southeast of Red Bluff, 530/934-3316, www.fs.usda.gov, reservations 877/444-6777, www.recreation.gov, $16, with electricity $25, year-round) offers 30 sites for tents and trailers with up to eight people allowed per site; it also has a large group site that accommodates 16 people. Coin-operated showers are available in the modern restrooms.

Food

The Riverside Bar and Grill (500 Riverside Way, 530/528-0370, 11 A.M.–9 P.M. Mon.–Thurs., 11 A.M.–10 P.M. Fri.–Sat., 4–8 P.M. Sun., $20) has the best view in town, overlooking the Sacramento River. Sit inside or out on the patio while you enjoy the full bar, steaks, burgers, tacos, and salads. This is also the place to go for a DJ dance party on Friday night.

The Green Barn (5 Chestnut Ave., 530/527-3161, 11 A.M.–9 P.M. Mon.–Thurs., 11 A.M.–10 P.M. Fri.–Sat., 4–9 P.M. Sun., $18–25), with its aged steaks and divine homemade sticky buns, has been satisfying locals since 1959. It is

© HEATHER C. LISTON

The Green Barn in Red Bluff

located at the corner of Chestnut and Antelope Avenues, and you can see Mount Shasta as you arrive. Inside is a warm, mellow, and comfortable atmosphere.

La Nueva Taqueria (360 S. Main St., 530/527-1380, daily 7 A.M.–3 P.M., $8) is fairly new in town and already popular. **Casa Ramos** (2001 Main St., 530/527-2684, www.casaramos.net, 11 A.M.–9:30 P.M. Sun.–Thurs., 11 A.M.–10:30 P.M. Fri.–Sat., happy hour 3–6 P.M. Mon.–Fri., $8–15) is part of a small family-owned chain; this branch is a favorite of the employees of the Red Bluff–Tehama County Chamber of Commerce.

Information and Services
The **Red Bluff-Tehama County Chamber of Commerce** (100 Main St., 530/527-6220, www.redbluffchamber.com, 8:30 A.M.–5 P.M. Mon.–Thurs., 8:30 A.M.–4:30 P.M. Fri.) welcomes visitors to stop in, pick up literature about local attractions, and chat with the staff.

Getting There and Around
Red Bluff is 130 miles north of Sacramento, right on I-5. It is about 30 miles south of Redding and 50 miles west of the southern entrance to Lassen Volcanic National Park.

CHESTER
The tiny town of Chester is 25 miles east of the southwest entrance to Lassen Volcanic National Park on Highway 89/36. From Red Bluff, the 70-mile drive takes about one hour. The primary interest is Chester's proximity to the southwest entrance station of the national park and activities on nearby Lake Almanor.

Drakesbad Guest Ranch (Chester Warner Valley Rd., 866/999-0914, www.drakesbad.com, June–2nd Mon. in Oct., $176–201) offers the closest lodging to Lassen Volcanic National Park. The all-inclusive rates include meals, and there are stables, hiking trails, and fishing opportunities nearby. Drakesbad is 17 miles north of Chester on Chester Warner Valley Road.

North Shore Campground (Hwy. 36/89, 530/258-3376, www.northshorecampground.com, Apr.–Oct., tents $35, RVs $38–50) is two miles east of Chester with 34 sites for tents and RVs. Facilities include picnic tables, fire rings, drinking water, restrooms with flush toilets and showers, and a small store.

Rocky Point Campground (916/386-5164, www.pge.com, May–Sept., $25) is at the southwest end of Lake Almanor, with 130 sites for tents and RVs. Facilities include picnic tables, fire rings, drinking water, and vault toilets.

Almanor North and South Campgrounds (877/444-6777, www.recreation.gov, May–Oct., $18–36) are operated by the Almanor Ranger District (530/258-2141, www.fs.fed.us). Situated directly on the lake, the 104 campsites offer great views of Lassen as well as biking, hiking, and fishing. Facilities include picnic tables, fire rings, drinking water, vault toilets, and a boat ramp. To reach the campgrounds, turn right on Highway 89 two miles west of Chester and drive six miles to County Road 310; turn left for the campground.

SUSANVILLE

The small town of Susanville (www.cityof-susanville.org) is the seat of Lassen County, and you're likely to pass through it if you're approaching Lassen Volcanic National Park from the east. The town is located on the Susan River, and although it's unfortunately known as the home of two large prisons, Susanville has a certain Old West charm. It made a recent list compiled by *Outdoor Life* magazine as one of the best "outdoor towns" to live in.

Susanville is home to the **Lassen Historical Museum** (115 N. Weatherlow St., 530/257-3292, 10 A.M.–4 P.M. Mon.–Fri., 11 A.M.–2 P.M. Sat. summer, 10 A.M.–2 P.M. Tues.–Thurs., 11 A.M.–2 P.M. Sat. winter, and by appointment, free). The museum promises "Susanville ephemera," which may sound a little dubious to those with no connection to the town, but the cabin next door to the museum, called Roop's Fort, has an interesting history. Built in 1854 and lovingly cared for to the present day by the local historical society, it was once a trading post on the Emigrant Trail to the West. There's a lot to learn here about the history of the lumber and ranching businesses as well. If you ever find yourself in Susanville, don't miss it.

At the far end of Bizz Johnson Trail is the **Westwood Museum** (311 Ash St., Westwood, 530/256-2233, hours vary, free). The Westwood Museum depends on volunteer staff, so they cannot commit to specific days or times when they'll be open; call ahead to check before visiting. If you're lucky, you can learn about the Red River Lumber Company, once the largest pine lumber mill in the world. It was the reason the railroad was built through here.

Susanville is the main trailhead for the famous 25.4-mile **Bizz Johnson National Recreation Trail** (530/257-0456, www.bizz-johnsontrail.com), a favorite with hikers and cyclists that winds along the Susan River following the Fernley and Lassen Branch Line of the former Southern Pacific Railroad route. The trail begins at the **Susanville Depot Trailhead Visitors Center and Museum** (601 Richmond Rd., 530/257-3252, 9 A.M.–5 P.M. Tues.–Sat. May–Oct., 9 A.M.–5 P.M. Wed.–Sat. Nov.–Apr., free), and winds its way toward the small community of Westwood. At the depot visitors center you'll find trail maps, exhibits about the trail and the area, and a bookstore.

Susanville's wide outdoor spaces and beautiful scenery make it a natural for golfers. **Diamond Mountain Golf Course** (470–895 Circle Dr., 530/257-2520, www.golfsusanville.com, daily sunrise–sunset Mar.–Nov., $20–27, cart rental $10–15) offers 18 holes with mountain views. The on-site **Shag Bag Bar & Grill** (530/251-3670, daily 8 A.M.–6 P.M. summer, daily 10 A.M.–4 P.M. spring and fall, $10–15) provides inexpensive breakfast, lunch, and snacks.

Accommodations and Food

The River Inn (1710 Main St., 530/257-6051, $59–62) was built in the 1970s; it's a simple motel without many frills, but if you're tired of chains, you'll appreciate the chance to stay in a locally owned business with an unusually helpful and pleasant staff. The location is good too—right on Main Street beside several restaurants. The beds don't sag, the guest rooms are clean, and you can get the senior citizen rate and AAA discount whether you qualify or not. If you like bargains, this place is hard to beat.

The **Sports Bar & Grill** (900 Skyline Rd., 877/319-8514, $13–24) inside the Diamond Mountain Casino (www.diamondmountaincasino.com) has special theme buffets (Asian, Pow-Wow, Down Home) as well as a regular menu of steaks and other American comfort food. They're open for breakfast through late-night dining. There are discount drinks at happy hour (daily 5–7 P.M.).

The **Lassen Steakhouse** (1700 Main St., 530/257-7220, daily 5–10 P.M., $14–30) is popular, with favorites like the flat-iron and the porterhouse; this lively place can please nearly any carnivore. Although they don't have any vegetarian entrées, the same owner—self-professed workaholic Esther Faustino—also runs **El Tepeyac Grille** (1700 Main St., 530/257-7220, daily 6 A.M.–10 P.M., $6–23), a coffee shop and Mexican restaurant next door.

Getting There and Around

Susanville is on Highway 36, just a few miles east of where Highways 36 and 44 split and begin making a loop around Lassen. The fastest way to get to the national park from here is to stay on Highway 36, called Main Street as it passes through Susanville, and travel 60 miles to Highway 89. Make a right and the park entrance is just over five miles. To get to Susanville from the Bay Area, take I-80 east to I-505 north to Highway 36 east. The trip is about 290 miles (5 hours). Susanville is about 90 miles east of Red Bluff and 90 miles north of Reno, Nevada.

Mount Shasta and Vicinity

When I first caught sight of Mount Shasta, over the braided folds of the Sacramento Valley, I was fifty miles away and afoot, alone and weary. Yet all my blood turned to wine, and I have not been weary since.

John Muir, 1874

One of the most iconic natural formations in the United States, Mount Shasta is stunning from every angle at any time of day. Like Utah's Delicate Arch or the Grand Canyon, Shasta is immediately recognizable from calendars, book covers, and photographs on the walls of hotels and restaurants—but you need to see it with your own eyes. Once you experience it in person, you'll never forget it, and you'll find yourself longing to see it again and again.

The gorgeous sunny village known as Mount Shasta City is a shining jewel of Northern California. A visit is a must for hikers, boaters, skiers, anglers, and others who revel in the outdoors. The main street of Mount Shasta City is Mount Shasta Boulevard, and nearly every business in town includes "Shasta" in its name. A plaque outside the Mount Shasta Police Department (303 N. Mt. Shasta Blvd.) proclaims "Mount Shasta—Where Heaven and Earth Meet," while an inscription in the town center, near a coin-operated telescope aimed at the mountain, is a quote from Joaquin Miller that reads "Lonely as God and white as a winter moon."

© HEATHER C. LISTON

Mount Shasta

◖ MOUNT SHASTA

Mount Shasta is a tremendous dormant volcano that last erupted in 1786. Although it may someday erupt again, for now it's a delightful playground and a magnetic attraction. At 14,162 feet, Mount Shasta is the 49th highest peak in the country, the fifth highest in California, and the second tallest volcano in the Cascade Range. It has a 17-mile perimeter and stands pretty much alone, with no close neighbors of anywhere near similar stature. In winter, snow covers much of the mountain; in summer a series of glaciers make the mountain appear white and glistening.

Mount Shasta is covered with snow, at least in places, year-round. This makes it an appealing, if not always accessible, destination for skiers of all kinds. Some people like to go to the back side of the mountain (the "bowl"), climb as high as they can with skis strapped to their backpacks, and then ski down. Families with children can bring plastic sleds, hike a little less far up the mountain, and then let everyone sled down. The **Bunny Flat Trailhead** (6,900 feet) is recommended for this kind of activity.

SPORTS AND RECREATION
Hiking
Some of the best hiking in California can be found on and around Mount Shasta. This beautiful region abounds with waterfalls, pine forests, rivers, streams, and fascinating geology. Informal camping and backpacking (wilderness permits required) can create a wonderful multiday hiking trip. Day hikes offer everything from easy strolls great for kids to strenuous miles that can take you up to minor mountain peaks for tremendous views of the whole southern Cascade mountain region.

If you want to hike on Mount Shasta but don't have the time or the training to go all the way to the top, try a nice day hike to **Gray Butte** (3.4 miles, moderate), an intermediate peak on the south slope of the mountain. The

© HEATHER C. LISTON

the hike up Mount Shasta

trail runs east across Panther Meadow, which is quite beautiful and full of heather and other wildflowers, and into the nearby forest. At the first fork in the trail (just past 0.5 miles), choose the fork to the right. In 1.5 miles, you'll come to a saddle—a good place for views, but there are more to come. From the saddle, bear right again to reach the peak of Gray Butte in less than 0.25 miles. Not only can you see the peak of Mount Shasta, but on a clear day you can see all the way to Castle Crags, Mount Eddy, and even Lassen Peak. Return the same way. To reach the trailhead, take I-5 to the Central Mount Shasta exit. Turn east onto Lake Street, which becomes Everitt Memorial Highway. In 13.5 miles, you'll reach Panther Meadows Campground, which has extensive trail signage and plenty of information about the ecology and wildlife of the area.

For an unlikely extension of a story told way down on the Central Coast, take a walk along the **Ah-Di-Na Historic Trail** (0.25 miles, easy).

Follow the signs from Squaw Valley Creek Road at the reservoir to this odd little resort area along the McCloud River. The William Randolph Hearst family built a retreat here, and you'll see photos of their property on the interpretive signs marking the short flat trail. It's a bit of a drive out to Ah-Di-Na on slow dirt roads. It is possible to get there in a regular passenger car, but not an RV or towing a trailer; expect the drive to take some time.

While the name of the **Sims Flat Historic Trail** (Sims Rd., south of the river, 1 mile, easy) refers to the name of a former logging town, the trail itself is flat too. Sims Flat was once a bustling town with the railroad running through it to carry products from the busy sawmill to the big cities that needed lumber. Nearly a century later, a few historic signs tell the story of this diverse former town. Another great thing about this walk is the up-close views of Mount Shasta, which looms over Sims Flat.

On the other end of the hiking spectrum is

the **Sisson-Callahan National Recreation Trail** (North Shore Rd., 18 miles round-trip, difficult). Just past Deer Creek Bridge, take the left fork and park off the road. Starting near Lake Siskiyou, this trail gains almost one mile in elevation, peaking at over 8,000 feet at Deadfall Summit, and then dropping 1,000 feet to Deadfall Lakes. Be sure to dress in layers, since you might start out in the intense summer heat of the lower elevations and end up making snowballs on the summit. Because it is long, steep, and challenging, many hikers prefer to do this trail over more than one day. A number of campsites are along the North Fork of the Sacramento River and beyond, welcoming weary travelers with a spot to pitch a tent and enjoy a night's rest. In fact, the Sisson-Callahan links up with the Pacific Crest Trail (www.pcta.org) near Deadfall Lakes, so backpackers can keep going if they choose to.

If you like hikes that are big on views and not so much about climbing, the place for you is the **Lake Siskiyou Trail.** This mostly flat seven-mile loop circumnavigates the spectacular lake and offers changing perspectives on the nearby mountains, bridges, and shorelines. You can start from any one of several well-marked parking areas and enjoy four rest stops with pit toilets and helpful signage along the way. This gently undulating, easy-to-follow trail is also a great place for a run. To get to one of the main trailheads, start from the town of Mount Shasta and head west on W. A. Barr Road until you see signs for Lake Siskiyou Trail.

For a lovely long hike that takes you up to views of the whole of the Far North mountain region and into Oregon, trek up **Mount Eddy** (Forest Rd. 17, Mount Shasta Ranger Station 530/926-4511, 10 miles round-trip, difficult). This steep trail takes you up to the 9,000-foot peak, where you can turn around and check out the various highlights of the Cascade range: Mount Shasta, Mount Lassen, the Trinity Alps, and even Mount McLoughlin in Oregon. Bring plenty of water as there's none at the Deadfall Lake trailhead, where the hike starts. Along the way, Deadfall Lake and Deadfall Creek both offer what appears to be very clear, clean water, but, as always, it's best to treat it before you drink it. The early part of the trail is mostly mild climbing, and there's some shade to keep you cool as you do it. The last 0.8 miles is the hard part: It's a serious of steep exposed switchbacks, guaranteed to give you a workout no matter how fit you are. The reward is worth it, though: You'll soon be on a truly exceptional mountaintop with views you'll remember for a long time. If you're not up for such a long day hike, consider an overnight camping trip; the lake makes a great informal primitive campground.

For serious hikers, **Black Butte** is a great half-day adventure. This odd cinder-cone peak stands at 6,325 feet and looks like a giant cone of black pepper. (The U.S. Forest Service says it's actually made of hornblende andesite.) From some angles, the butte looks almost as impressive as its neighbor, the famous Mount Shasta, but the climb is not nearly as daunting; no ice axes or other special equipment is needed. Still, the hike up Black Butte is rocky, steep, and mostly unshaded. And although it's only 2.56 miles to the top, you gain 1,845 feet in elevation in that short distance. Take sunscreen, plenty of water, binoculars, and a camera. And if you're on a schedule, leave a little more time than you think you'll need, since finding the trailhead can be a little confusing. To get here from Mount Shasta Boulevard in the center of Mount Shasta City, turn east onto Lake Street, which soon becomes Everitt Memorial Highway. Drive a total of just under three miles and look for a small sign that says "Black Butte Trail." Make a left onto the gravel road (Forest Rd. 41N18). From here, the road winds through the forest (go slowly, if you value your car's undercarriage and windshield) on narrow, uneven, rocky roads. If someone has given you detailed instructions about turning left and right and bearing north and so on, feel

Alpine Lodge, the Sierra Club's warming hut

free to try to follow them, but it's easy to make a mistake if you're overthinking the twists and turns. The best advice is to stick to the main narrow gravel road all the way to the trailhead. Don't be distracted by forks off to the sides, and you will eventually get there.

Note that the 2.5-mile trail to popular **Mossbrae Falls** has been closed. The city of Dunsmuir is working with Union Pacific on a project to reroute the trail to a safer place, develop new parking, and make it all wheelchair accessible. For updates, contact the **Dunsmuir Chamber of Commerce and Visitors Center** (5915 Dunsmuir Ave., Dunsmuir, 530/235-2177, www.dunsmuir.com, 10 A.M.–3 P.M. Mon.–Sat.).

Climbing

Climbers come from all over the world come to tackle Shasta's majestic 14,162-foot peak. Be sure to pack your sturdiest hiking boots and your strongest leg muscles; fewer than one-third of the 15,000 intrepid mountaineers who try to conquer Mount Shasta each year actually make it to the top. Shasta's steep and rocky slopes, its long-lasting snowfields, and the icy glaciers that persist year-round all contribute to making this one of the most difficult climbs in the country. On top of all that, the thin air at this altitude makes breathing a challenge. If you're serious about doing the climb, you can get plenty of help from the locals.

Bagging this peak is not for everyone, but for healthy, well-trained, and well-equipped climbers, this can be the adventure of a lifetime; you'll see Mount Shasta up close in ways that most casual visitors could never imagine. The main climbing season is June–August, but do not expect sunny weather and easy footing. Casual visitors should exercise care accessing even the trailheads that lead to Shasta's peak. Some of the dirt roads around the base of the mountain require a 4WD vehicle, and weather conditions can have severe effects on the roads. Contact the **Mount Shasta Climbing Advisory**

(530/926-9613, www.shastaavalanche.org) before your trip for current weather and climbing conditions.

More than a dozen routes lead to the top. You can pick a quick, hard-core climb that takes you from the base camp up to the top in a single day, or choose a longer and more leisurely trail and spend two days making the trek, camping overnight in the wilderness. The most popular route begins near the Mount Shasta **Alpine Lodge** at Horse Camp and runs along Avalanche Gulch. The Alpine Lodge is lovely 1923 building made of local volcanic rock and wood from the Shasta forest. It is owned by the Sierra Club Foundation (www.sierraclub.org) and is sometimes called the Sierra Club hut, but it's much more solid than the word "hut" implies. Located at an altitude of 7,900 feet on the mountain's southwest side, this is a great destination for a modest day hike on the mountain or a good base camp for a mountaineer heading toward the summit.

Mountaineering and glacier classes are available, and several guides and outfitters can provide equipment and even lead you up the mountain. Private mountain guide Robin Kohn (530/926-3250, www.climbingmt-shasta.org) maintains a comprehensive website with up-to-date information and helpful advice. Contact her for help hiring a guide or arranging trip plans. **Shasta Mountain Guides** (Mount Shasta, 530/926-3117, www.shastaguides.com, $500–700 pp) has been taking climbers to the top for decades. Join one of their scheduled group trips along various routes up the mountain, or call to arrange a custom expedition. Snowboard and backcountry skis tours ($150 pp, minimum 2 people) are also available. **Sierra Wilderness Seminars** (210 Lake St., 888/797-6867, www.swsmtns.com, Apr.–Oct., $485–645 pp) leads groups of up to eight people up Mount Shasta. If you want to learn as well as climb, check out the Ice & Snow Expedition Course (June–Oct., 5 days

$895). The rigorous training on the use of ice axes and crampons, and what to do if someone falls into a crevasse, may come in handy during the climb to Shasta's summit along a "glaciated north-side route." If you're new to this, start with one of the company's one-day courses, such as the Ice Ax Clinic (Jan.–Aug., $125), which teaches basic snow-climbing techniques. Or make a weekend of it by combining this with the Basic Mountaineering Clinic (2 days $220). All clinics and climbs take place on Mount Shasta. **Alpine Skills International** (530/582-9170, www.alpineskills.com, $455–595 pp) provides training and guides for climbers of various skill levels. The founder, Bela Vadasz, recently won a lifetime achievement award from the American Mountain Guides Association and was instrumental in establishing certification programs for mountain guides in the United States. His company still takes training as seriously as adventure. One of their challenging courses on Mount Shasta is the four-day Glacial Ice Seminar (June–Aug., $725), which takes place on the Hotlum or Whitney Glaciers near the top of the mountain.

Fishing

Almost all the major rivers and feeder streams running through the Mount Shasta region are open for fishing. You can tie your fly on and cast into the McCloud, Sacramento, and Trinity Rivers, among many others. These rivers carry salmon, steelhead, and trout. If you want a guide to help you navigate these waters, contact one of the many services that can take you out to the perfect fishing holes. For fly-fishing or scenic rafting tours, call **Jack Trout International Fly Fishing Guide Service** (530/926-4540, www.jacktrout.com, year-round, $375 for 2 people). Jack will take you out on the McCloud, Klamath, Upper and Lower Sacramento, Pit, or Trinity Rivers, or to Hat Creek. Jack supplies all the gear and brings a gourmet lunch complete with wine and homemade strawberry shortcake for you to enjoy by the side of the river. It you're an expert fly-fisher who wants to improve your technique, he can help you. If you've never done it before but think you might like to try, give him a call—he loves beginners and says they always catch something. See his blog, complete with great photos, at www.mtshasta.com to help you visualize your fishing trip. You have to bring a California fishing license, available online at www.dfg.ca.gov.

Outdoor Adventures Sport Fishing (530/221-6151 or 800/670-4448, www.sacriverguide.com, year-round by appointment only, $150–200 pp per day) takes anglers on fly-fishing drift trips on the Sacramento and Trinity Rivers, where they specialize in salmon, trout, and steelhead; they'll also guide you on a jet-boat trip on Shasta Lake, where you can catch salmon and trout.

Rafting and Kayaking

In the Cascades, the best white-water rafting is definitely on the Trinity River. A good guide service to take you out onto this river is **Trinity River Rafting** (530/623-3033 or 800/307-4837, www.trinityriverrafting.com, guided trips $65–180 per day, kayak rental $40 per day). In addition to its flagship runs on the Trinity, this major rafting company runs on the Klamath, Salmon, and Upper Fork Sacramento Rivers as well as Canyon Creek. Depending on where you're staying and what level of rafting you can handle, you can choose the river to paddle. Half-day to three-day trips are available, and you can choose from a placid Class I–II float suitable for the whole family to a Class IV–V run for fit, experienced rafters only. Trinity Rafting also rents rafts and 1–2-person inflatable kayaks for paddlers who want to go off on their own.

Another major player in the northern mountains rafting scene is the **Bigfoot Rafting Company** (530/629-2263 or 800/722-2223, www.bigfootrafting.com, $65–149). With day trips on the Trinity and Salmon Rivers, and multiday rafting campouts on the Trinity and

Klamath Rivers, Bigfoot presents a depth of knowledge of the rivers it runs. Your guide will know a great deal about the history and natural surroundings of your chosen river, and as a bonus can cook you up fabulous meals on the full-day and multiday trips. Bigfoot also rents equipment.

Skiing and Snowboarding

The snowpack on Mount Shasta each winter creates a haven for downhill skiers, cross-country skiers, snowboarders, and snowshoers. The place to go for all this is the **Mount Shasta Ski Park** (Ski Park Hwy., off Hwy. 89 between McCloud and Mount Shasta, 530/926-8600, www.skipark.com, 9 A.M.–9 P.M. Thurs.–Sat., 9 A.M.–4 P.M. Sun.–Wed. mid-Dec.–mid-Apr., adults $20–50, ages 8–12 and seniors $12–31, under age 8 $7–10). This small but exciting downhill park has 425 skiable acres, three chairlifts, and a towrope. Nearly half the runs are open for night skiing, and the Marmot lift in the beginner area makes a perfect spot for beginners of all ages to gain their snow legs (at a fraction of the cost of the resorts at Lake Tahoe). Half-day discount lift tickets and night-skiing-only lift tickets make skiing here even more attractive for snow-loving bargain hunters.

Cross-country skiers can also get their fix at the **Mount Shasta Nordic Center** (Ski Park Hwy., 1 mile before downhill park, 530/926-2142, www.mtshastanordic.org, 9 A.M.–4 P.M. Wed.–Sun., donation adults $10, youth and seniors $5). Since 2006 this lovely ski center has been a not-for-profit organization dedicated to the promulgation of physical and mental health through cross-country skiing. It's open for the winter season, as determined by when the snow comes, usually in late December, and closes in mid-April. The center has 16 miles of groomed trails for cross-country skiing, and there's ample backcountry where you're welcome to explore off-trail. Snowshoers are allowed on the groomed trails as long as they stay to the side. Call the hotline (530/926-2142) for conditions and grooming updates. If you plan to come often, you can buy an annual membership, priced from $40 (individual out-of-towner) to $450 (family, with an extra donation). Memberships and other donations are tax-deductible. The organization sponsors clinics, demos, races, and other events. Ski and snowshoe rentals and lessons are available.

Horseback Riding

The wilderness around Mount Shasta beckons to anyone with a penchant for trail rides. One good outfit that serves the area is the **Rockin Maddy Ranch** (11921 Cram Gulch Rd., Yreka, 530/340-2100, www.rockinmaddyranch.com, year-round, by reservation only, 1.5 hours $48 pp, full day $175 pp). Choose rides that include the popular 90-minute Shasta View ride featuring grand vistas of the mountain all the way up to a full-day excursion into the Marble Mountains that includes tracks along rivers, past waterfalls, and with time to stop and fish while. Rockin Maddy allows smaller children to ride double on the same horse. You can even book a pony party for your children, a horse-drawn carriage ride for a wedding or special event, or a hayride led by a team of powerful Percherons.

ENTERTAINMENT AND EVENTS
Nightlife

The Gold Room (903 S. Mt. Shasta Blvd., 530/926-4125, daily 11 A.M.–2 A.M., cash only) is Mount Shasta's most authentic old-time locals bar, with two pool tables in the back, a couple of old-fashioned pinball and video games, and comfy vinyl-covered high chairs at the bar so you can settle in and get some hard-core drinking done. The jukebox often plays loud country music during the daytime hours for what the bartender describes as her "professional drinkers," but the atmosphere changes in the evening, as the crowd gets younger and more varied and includes visitors to the area. Note that the address is the same as the one for the **Lai Lai**

Chinese American Restaurant, located next door. The two businesses are not affiliated, except that there's a window between them, which allows bar patrons to order Chinese food and have it served to them right where they sit.

The Goat Tavern (107 Chestnut St., 530/926-0209, www.thegoatmountshasta.com, 11:30 A.M.–9 P.M. Tues.–Sat.) offers 12 beers on tap at any given time, and it rotates through 60–70 different microbrews on a regular basis.

Festivals and Events

Summer is the big season here, and the **Fourth of July** weekend is a big deal in Mount Shasta. The all-city celebration attracts visitors from near and far with its festive parade, street fair, and new-car raffle. One of the centerpieces of the day is a five-mile running or walking event (www.mtshastarunners.com, $18): As the T-shirts say, it's "The largest small town race in America." Whether it is or not might be hard to prove, but the race is definitely one of the best demonstrations of the festive congenial spirit most small towns are striving for. It goes without saying that the course is beautiful. There are special divisions for larger men (Clydesdale) and women (Athena), and everyone hangs around afterward to watch the emcee announce the dozens of awards for children and adults of all ages. Hotel prices go up and parking spaces get a little scarce around this weekend, but if you plan ahead you can enjoy one of the country's best small-town parties.

SHOPPING

As the name promises, **The Fifth Season** (300 N. Mt. Shasta Blvd., 530/926-3606, www.thefifthseason.com, 9 A.M.–6 P.M. Mon.–Fri., 8 A.M.–6 P.M. Sat., 10 A.M.–5 P.M. Sun.) is a year-round source for outdoor equipment, including mountain bikes, skis, snowboards, and any other recreation gear. The main focus, though, is mountain climbing equipment and the advice you need if you want to scale Mount

Shasta. You can start at the website before you come in, and then go to the storefront in town to rent or purchase everything from boots to ice axes and crampons. Before you start up the mountain, call 530/926-5555 for a recording that describes the current conditions approaching Mount Shasta's summit.

If it's ski and snowboard equipment, adjustment, rental, or repair you need, another good choice is **The Sportsman's Den** (402 N. Mt. Shasta Blvd., 530/926-2295, www.mt-shastasports.com, 9 A.M.–6 P.M. Mon.–Fri., 9 A.M.–5 P.M. Sat., 10 A.M.–4 P.M. Sun.), a shop that specializes in fine-tuning high-end snowboards and fitting skis to perfection. In the summer, the Sportsman's Den offers fishing tackle and some sporting equipment.

Village Books (320 N. Mt. Shasta Blvd., 530/926-1678, www.villagebooks-mt-shasta.com, 10 A.M.–7 P.M. Mon.–Thurs., 10 A.M.–8 P.M. Fri.–Sat., 11 A.M.–5 P.M. Sun.) is a very pleasant well-lit independent bookstore in the middle of town, with candy, coffee, home-baked muffins and cookies, and a few small tables. There is no Internet access, but you can bring your laptop and write your memoirs while you enjoy the coffee. The store features the best of new fiction, nonfiction, and poetry; an ample children's section complete with candy and toys; and a selected assortment of magazines focusing on health, outdoor life, and travel. The store specializes in metaphysics and New Age texts and has only a small section of classic literature. You can also find postcards, photos of the mountain, coffee mugs, and a few other souvenirs.

Village Books made a decision not to compete in travel books, deferring to the specialized **Language Quest** (309 N. Mt. Shasta Blvd., 530/918-9540, www.languagequest.com, 9 A.M.–5:30 P.M. Mon.–Fri., 9 A.M.–4:30 P.M. Sat.) nearby, which promises "everything for language and travel." They offer maps, software, audio, and videos in addition to travel books.

The **Mount Shasta Book Nook** (331 N. Mt. Shasta Blvd., 530/926-6660, 11 A.M.–6:30 P.M. Mon.–Sat., 11 A.M.–6 P.M. Sun.), for "previously loved books" fills the used-bookstore niche. Handily located across the street from Village Books, it also sells vinyl records and buys books, CDs, and video games at designated times; call ahead to ask before you bring over a load. Even the regular business hours aren't guaranteed: Despite listing business hours, the sign on their door says, "Open when we're here. Closed when we aren't."

Sereni-Tea (319 N. Mt. Shasta Blvd., 530/926-1688, www.sereni-tea.net, 10 A.M.–6 P.M. Mon.–Fri., 10 A.M.–5 P.M. Sat. Apr.–Nov., 10 A.M.–5 P.M. Mon.–Sat. Nov.–Mar.) is the place to buy all sorts of tea and tea accessories. Enjoy a hot beverage in the pleasant little shop, buy some to take home, or order online.

On Morgan Way, just a couple of blocks west of Mount Shasta Boulevard, **Mount Shasta Shopping Center** (134 Morgan Way) is a decent strip mall with a multiplex cinema, some chain eateries, and the large **Mount Shasta Do-it-Best Hardware** (128 Morgan Way, 530/926-2635, 8 A.M.–6 P.M. Mon.–Fri., 9 A.M.–5 P.M. Sat.–Sun.), full of all sorts of practical things you may need for your vacation, from flashlights to lawn chairs. You'll find the shopping center tucked in behind the Black Bear Diner and right across the street from the Best Western.

ACCOMMODATIONS
Under $100

One of the first lodgings you'll come across as you arrive from the south is the **Finlandia Hotel and Lodge** (1621 S. Mt. Shasta Blvd., 530/926-5596, www.finlandiamotelandlodge.com, $70–135), offering comfortable guest rooms from a single with a queen bed at the low end to a suite with king bed and a kitchen at the top. The hotel is pet-friendly, and you can book online.

One of the friendliest of the cheap motels on

the south end of town is the **Evergreen Lodge** (1312 S. Mt. Shasta Blvd., 530/926-2143, $49–99). The hosts, Bill and Bharti, are warm and welcoming, and the place is more than adequate as long as you're not looking for luxury. There are a table and chairs even in the smaller guest rooms, and easy-to-access free Internet service, make it a good place to stay if you need to do any kind of work. There are large TVs in the guest rooms and a small pool outside. The no-pets and no-smoking policies help keep the place clean and pleasant.

One of the most pleasant inexpensive lodging options at Shasta is the ◖ **Mount Shasta Ranch Bed & Breakfast** (1008 W. A. Barr Rd., 530/926-3870 or 877/926-3870, www.stayin-shasta.com, $60–130), offering homey luxury just slightly out of town. The budget-friendly guest rooms in the Carriage House offer small spaces, queen beds, and shared baths. The separate Cottage ($180) is the largest option, with two bedrooms that can comfortably sleep up to six. The four guest rooms in the Ranch House are spacious and furnished with a clutter of country-Victorian antiques and tchotchkes, and each has its own big private bath. All guest rooms include a full country breakfast served around 9 A.M. to get you up, moving, and fueled for a long day out in the Shasta wilderness.

Another bargain spot on the outskirts of the village is the **A-1 Choice Inn** (1340 S. Mt. Shasta Blvd., 530/926-4811, $59–149). Everything seems to have been ordered from the cheap basic motel kit, including the standard pink-and-green polyester bedspreads and the cheesy framed photo prints on the walls, but these aren't the smallest of budget rooms—there's room to walk around the beds. With a coffeemaker, fridge, and microwave in each guest room, a small pool and a hot tub beside the highway, and views of the top of Mount Shasta, it has everything you need, as long as you don't need anything fancy.

As you progress toward the town center, you'll eventually come to the **Travel Inn** (504 S. Mt. Shasta Blvd., 530/926-4617, $49–99), one of the budget motels closest to the restaurants and shopping. The Travel Inn can meet your basic needs for as low as $49 in winter, $69 in summer.

The cute **Dream Inn** (326 Chestnut St., 530/926-1536, www.dreaminnmtshastacity.com, $80–160) offers bed-and-breakfast accommodations at the base of the magnificent mountain. The four small inexpensive upstairs guest rooms have shared hallway baths. Downstairs, a bigger white antique bedroom has its own private bath and a view of Mount Eddy out the lace-curtained window. Next door, two large suites share space in a Spanish adobe–style home; each has its own living space, bath, and truly homelike cluttered decor. Guest rooms at the Dream Inn include a scrumptious full breakfast each morning.

The **Alpine Lodge** (908 S. Mt. Shasta Blvd. 530/926-3145, www.alpinelodgeca.com, $59–129) is on the not-so-fancy end of the spectrum, but it does offer Internet access, in-room coffeemakers, and a small outdoor pool and hot tub. The higher-end option ($129) is a two-bedroom unit with three beds and a kitchenette.

If you drive north through the center of town to the other side (which will take less than five minutes, unless there's a festival going on in the middle), you'll find the **Cold Creek Inn** (724 N. Mt. Shasta Blvd., 530/926-9851 or 800/292-9421, www.coldcreekinn.com, $59–140), a small motel with 19 simple but comfortable guest rooms and suites, some of which have mountain views. Amenities include free wireless Internet access, continental breakfast with organic coffee, and a little sundeck for those who want to get out of the room for a while. The Cold Creek Inn prides itself on using environmentally friendly cleaning products. All guest rooms are nonsmoking, and pets are welcome. Cold Creek offers discounts for travelers who stay more than four nights.

$100-150

If you're looking for something just a little more upscale than the string of budget motels, the **Mount Shasta Inn & Suites** (710 S. Mt. Shasta Blvd., 530/918-9292, www.mtshastainn.com, $69–199) may be for you. This place was built in 2000, making it one of the newer facilities in the area. The sparkling clean appearance is in part because all guest rooms are nonsmoking and pet-free. The beyond-the-basics amenities include an outdoor hot tub, a complimentary light breakfast, and guest rooms with free wireless Internet access, blow-dryers, fridges, and microwaves. Prices range from $69 for one person in winter to $199 for three people in a two-room suite in June–August.

To get a real sense of life in this region, book one of the guest rooms at the ◖ **Shasta MountInn Retreat & Spa** (203 Birch St., 530/926-1810, www.shastamountinn.com, $125–175). The big white farmhouse exterior fits perfectly into its semi-alpine setting, while the guest rooms ooze country charm and modern comforts. Each of the four guest rooms has its own private bath and high-end memory-foam mattress, which tempt guests to loll in bed all morning rather than heading downstairs for a healthy continental breakfast and a cup of organic coffee. The "spa" part comes with on-site massage services and a barrel-shaped redwood sauna. And if you're serious about taking a spiritual retreat into the local woods and waterways, your hosts can guide you to the sacred spots that dot this area, or you can strike out on your own to find your own sites.

The **Woodsman Hotel & Lodge** (1121 S. Mt. Shasta Blvd., 530/926-3411, www.mtshasta-hotels.net, $109–369) is a large complex with a variety of options for travelers, offering small guest rooms with one bed ($149 summer, as low as $109 fall–spring), suites with kitchenettes, and a cabin ($369) that sleeps eight, with two leather couches and a full kitchen. The Woodsman has warm and helpful staff; a large,

comfortable hunting lodge-style lounge complete with a fireplace and stuffed animal heads; and a bit more personality than the standard-issue motels nearby. On the other hand, the low-end guest room is even smaller than many of those at the cheaper motels, without enough space for a table or chair, and the price can be three times as much. Continental breakfast is included in the room rates, which you walk across the street to find at the Woodsman's sister hotel, the Strawberry Valley Inn.

The **Strawberry Valley Inn** (1145 S. Mt. Shasta Blvd., 530/926-2052, www.mtshasta-hotels.net, $129–189), under the same ownership as the Woodsman across the street, is an attractive property with a large green lawn and well-kept garden beside the Native Grounds Nursery and Mount Shasta Florist. The inn has an English feel to it, encouraging you to sit among the flowers and have tea before retiring to your charming, smallish, but lovely guest room. Continental breakfast is included in the room rates, as is complimentary beer or wine in the evening. The breakfast room can get crowded, and the overworked staff may fall behind in restocking, so try to get here early, and consider taking your breakfast out to the lawn.

$150-250

In a location and a class by itself is the **Tree House** (111 Morgan Way, 530/926-3101 or 800/780-7234, www.bestwestern.com, $150–180), a Best Western Plus hotel. It is slightly off the main drag near the Mount Shasta Shopping Center. Best Western hotels are individually owned and operated, but most of them tend to be at the upper-middle end of the chain hotel spectrum, and the ones designated "Plus" are a little nicer than average. The Mount Shasta version is a large, full-service hotel with an indoor pool, a hot tub, and a fitness center; full hot breakfast included; microwaves, fridges, and blow-dryers in the guest rooms; wireless Internet access; and a computer station in the lobby for travelers who didn't bring their own. The on-site **Tree House Restaurant** (daily 6:30–10:30 A.M. and 4:30–9 P.M., $15–25) serves breakfast and dinner, while **Tree House Lounge** (11 A.M.–10 P.M. Fri.–Sun., 3–10 P.M. Mon.–Thurs., $6–11) serves nachos, burgers, cocktails, wine, and beer.

Off the beaten Shasta Boulevard path are a few more elegant and more pricey places to stay, often with spacious grounds and lots of beautiful scenery. One of the nicest of these is **Mount Shasta Resort** (1000 Siskiyou Lake Blvd., information 530/926-3030, reservations 800/958-3368, www.mtshastaresort.com, summer $199–259, winter $159–219). If you're looking for a spa treatment or a golf course (530/926-3052, 18 holes $45–75) in addition to a beautiful suite to sleep in, this is the place for you. The **Evergreen Day Spa** (530/925-0422, www.mtshastaresort.com, by appointment daily 9 A.M.–6 P.M., 1-hour massage $90) on the premises offers massages, facials, and hair and nail care. Every guest room is special at the Mount Shasta Resort. If you want a lakeside deck, a fireplace, a jetted tub, two TVs, or a kitchenette or full kitchen, just ask, and the resort can probably accommodate you. All guest rooms come with free wireless Internet access, ironing boards and irons, blow-dryers, and all the other amenities expected from upscale lodgings.

CAMPING
Mount Shasta
The Shasta-Trinity National Forest (Shasta Ranger District, 530/926-4511, www.fs.usda.gov, 8 A.M.–4:30 P.M. Mon.–Fri.) manages three campgrounds on Mount Shasta. All are popular and fill quickly on summer weekends. Reservations are not accepted; weekdays are when it's easiest to find space.

McBride Springs (10 sites, first-come, first-served, May–Oct., $10) is conveniently located on the mountain at 5,000 feet just four miles

from Mount Shasta City. Facilities include drinking water, vault toilets, and picnic tables.

◖ **Panther Meadows** (Everitt Memorial Hwy., 1.7 miles past Bunny Flat, 10 sites, first-come, first-served, mid-July–Sept., free) is 14 miles northeast of Mount Shasta City at an elevation of 7,500 feet on the slopes of Mount Shasta. Due to the high elevation, it can be cold at night and snowed-in well into summer. Although this is a walk-in campground, it is only 100–500 feet from the parking lot to the campsites. Facilities include picnic tables, fire rings, and vault toilets; bring your own water. Because this is the most popular campground on Mount Shasta, there is a maximum stay of three nights.

The third campground is **Red Fir Flat** (530/926-4511, $12), a group site (8–75 people) available by reservation. Facilities include picnic tables, fire rings, and vault toilets; there is no drinking water.

Dispersed camping is allowed throughout the Shasta-Trinity National Forest. A wilderness permit is required on Mount Shasta itself. Otherwise, anywhere you want to sleep is fair game, although you do need a campfire permit, available for free at any ranger station. For permits and information, contact the **Mount Shasta Ranger Station** (204 W. Alma St., 530/926-4511, www.fs.usda.gov, 8 A.M.–4:30 P.M. Mon.–Fri.).

Vicinity of Mount Shasta
If the campgrounds on Mount Shasta are full, there are several options on the west side of I-5. The McCloud area also has developed camping.

Lake Siskiyou Camp & Resort (4239 W. A. Barr Rd., 530/926-2618 or 888/926-2618, Apr.–Oct.) is located on the shore of glacier-fed Lake Siskiyou, just three miles west of Mount Shasta City. There are hundreds of tent sites ($20) and RV sites ($26–29) with partial and full hookups as well as cabins ($108–153). Plentiful amenities include a beach, boat and equipment rentals, a Splash Zone for kids ($7 per hour, $18 per day), a Snack Shack (daily 10 A.M.–6 P.M. Memorial Day–Labor Day), and the on-site Lake Sis Grille & Brew (530/926-1865, 8 A.M.–9 P.M. Sun.–Thurs., 8 A.M.–10 P.M. Fri.–Sat. Memorial Day–Labor Day).

Castle Lake Campground (Castle Lake Rd., 6 sites, first-come, first-served, May–Oct., free) is about nine miles southwest of Mount Shasta City on beautiful Castle Lake. Facilities include picnic tables, fire rings, and vault toilets; there is no drinking water.

Gumboot Lake (Forest Rd. 26, 6 sites, first-come, first-served, June–Oct., free) is an undeveloped campground located on Gumboot Lake about 12 miles west of Mount Shasta City. Facilities include fire rings and a vault toilet but no picnic tables or drinking water. A campfire permit is required.

Sims Flat (I-5 exit 718, 19 sites, May–Nov. 15, $15) is 20 miles south of Mount Shasta City, but has the advantage of being on the Sacramento River; fishing is one of its main attractions. The campground has sites for tents or medium-size RVs; facilities include flush toilets, fire rings, and drinking water.

In addition to Lake Siskiyou Camp & Resort, **Chateau Shasta Mobile Home & RV Park** (704 S. Old Stage Rd., 530/926-3279, year-round, $25) offers a great location to park your vehicle and enjoy the area. Some of the spots are a bit crowded and exposed, but they all have great views.

FOOD

To stock up on groceries for camping and picnics, stop by the **Berryvale Grocery** (305 S. Mt. Shasta Blvd., 530/926-1576, www.berryvale.com, 8:30 A.M.–7:30 P.M. Mon.–Sat., 10 A.M.–6 P.M. Sun.). You can pick up high quality international foods, enjoy a cup of coffee at the café, and then feast like a king back at your campsite. From their attractive storefront in the center of town, **Mountain Song Natural Foods** (314 N. Mt. Shasta Blvd., 530/926-3391,

www.mountainsong.biz, 10 A.M.–6:30 P.M. Mon.–Sat., noon–6 P.M. Sun.) offers health-food groceries plus a large selection of trail mix varieties, an impressive gallery of organic spices and herbs, homemade bread from the Oven Bakery, and local beans from Northbound Coffee Roasters, along with the best dried mango ever. For those who can hang around longer than the weekend, the regular Monday **farmers market** (411 N. Mt. Shasta Blvd., 530/436-2532, www.mtshastafarmersmarket.com, 3:30–6 P.M. Mon. early June–mid-Oct.) is a treat. In years with abundant crops, the market is sometimes held on Thursday as well.

Bakeries and Cafés

The best coffee shop in Mount Shasta is ◖ **Snowcrest Internet Café** (333 N. Mt. Shasta Blvd., 530/926-4019, 7 A.M.–5 P.M. Mon.–Fri., 8 A.M.–4 P.M. Sat., extended hours July 4). Conveniently located in the middle of town, Snowcrest has a commendably friendly and accommodating staff who will set you up with two hours of free wireless Internet access on request. The scones, flavors of which vary daily, can feed a family of four. And Snowcrest's egg-and-cheese sandwich is surprisingly tasty on a homemade cranberry bagel.

Seven Suns Coffee and Café (1011 S. Mt. Shasta Blvd., 530/926-9701 or 530/926-9700, www.mtshastacoffee.com, daily 6 A.M.–4 P.M., $8–12) is very pleasant, if it's really coffee you want and not just an excuse to check your email. Breakfast and lunch are available in the form of local baked goods, burritos, wraps, and salads. You can also have all sorts of coffee and espresso drinks, and buy coffee beans by the pound (roasted in Chico by Has Beans Coffee). There's a spacious porch on the south side with umbrella-shaded tables, but the prime spot is the front sidewalk, with two small tables. Across the street, Seven Suns also maintains a small coffee outpost with drive-through and walk-up windows.

For those who like inspiration with their stimulation, **The Coffee Connection** (408 N. Mt. Shasta Blvd., 530/926-2622, www.thecoffeeconnection.org, 10 A.M.–4 P.M. Wed.–Fri., 11 A.M.–4 P.M. and 7–10 P.M. Sat.) is the place. Calling itself a Christian coffeehouse, it's operated by a not-for-profit organization, and all the workers are volunteers. They serve sandwiches, ice cream, and Christian music. Visit the website information on upcoming entertainment.

Some travelers may be glad to know that the enchanting City of Mount Shasta is free of the corporate chains like Starbucks and Peet's. But if you do crave the brew you're used to, you can get a cup of Peet's coffee at **Mount Shasta Pastry** (610 S. Mt. Shasta Blvd., 530/926-9944, www.mtshastapastry.com, 6 A.M.–2:30 P.M. Mon.–Sat., 7 A.M.–1 P.M. Sun., $6–12). Although the place looks like a small bakery, it actually has a full menu of selections for both breakfast (eggs, oatmeal, and croissant sandwiches) and lunch (focaccia sandwiches, salads, and pizza by the slice).

The best baked goods in town come from the **Oven Bakery** (214 N. Mt. Shasta Blvd., 530/926-0960, www.theoven-bakery.com, 7:30 A.M.–noon Mon., Wed., and Fri., 7:30 A.M.–5 P.M. Tues. and Thurs., 2–5 P.M. Sun., $2–6), which not only supplies the local coffee shops and grocery stores but also has its own storefront where you can come in, sit down, and enjoy a hot scone and a cup of coffee while you smell the baking in the background.

American

As you drive through California, you'll see lots of signs for Black Bear Diners. Since its founding in 1995, it has grown into a chain of nearly 50 franchises concentrated in the Western states. The Mount Shasta **Black Bear Diner** (401 W. Lake St., 530/926-4669, www.blackbeardiner.com, 5:30 A.M.–10 P.M. Sun.–Thurs., 5:30 A.M.–10:30 P.M. Fri.–Sat., $12–30), was the original Black Bear, and sure enough, it has

the feel of a local joint. The food is the usual diner fare, served up fast to guests in oversize red vinyl booths. The staff is helpful and willing to make good recommendations, and best of all, it's open late; like many small towns, businesses in Mount Shasta tend to close a little early.

The Goat Tavern (107 Chestnut St., at Mt. Shasta Blvd., 530/926-0209, www.thegoatmountshasta.com, 11:30 A.M.–9 P.M. Tues.–Sat., $9–15) offers microbrews, finger foods, burgers, sandwiches, and vegetarian specialties. You're sure to pass by it while walking around town, and the laughter from the outdoor deck will let you know just how much fun everyone is having. Popular especially with the young and active crowd, it's recommended as part of an after-fishing or after-hiking recovery.

At the south end of town is the **Wayside Grill** (2217 S. Mt. Shasta Blvd., 530/918-9234, www.waysidegrill.com, 4–9 P.M. Mon.–Thurs., 11 A.M.–10 P.M. Fri.–Sun., $11–30) a big casual place that's so popular there's sometimes a wait in spite of its size. Reservations at busy times of year are a good idea. It has lots of brick-oven pizza plus burgers, sandwiches, pasta, steak, tacos, 12 beers on tap, and wine. All menu items are also available to take out, there's an outdoor patio with mountain views, and there's live music on weekends.

At the north edge of the town center is the retro **Burger Express Frosty & Grill** (415 N. Mt. Shasta Blvd., 530/926-3950, http://burgerexpressmtshasta.com, 11 A.M.–7 P.M. Mon.–Fri., 11 A.M.–6 P.M. Sat., noon–4 P.M. Sun., $7–15). With great 1950s-style red stools and tables, a cheerful red-and-white counter, and a checkerboard floor, the place feels up-to-the-minute and delightfully old-fashioned at the same time. It serves basic burgers and hotdogs, shakes, sundaes, and soft-serve ice cream in cones. Eat in or take your food out to the small patio and enjoy the sun and the community. Either way, the eating and the nostalgia are good.

The **Tree House Restaurant** (111 Morgan

Way, 530/926-3101, daily 6:30–10:30 A.M. and 4:30–9 P.M., $15–25), inside the Best Western hotel, is one of the better places in town to have dinner, with a generous selection of seafood, steak, and pasta entrées.

Asian
Andaman Healthy Thai Cuisine (313 N. Mt. Shasta Blvd., 530/926-5288, 11 A.M.–2 P.M. and 5–8:30 P.M. Mon.–Fri., 5–8:30 P.M. Sat.–Sun., $10–30) promises "a marriage of centuries-old Eastern and Western influences harmoniously combined." And sure enough, they deliver tasty Thai food better than you might expect so far from a big city.

If you're in the mood for Chinese, most people agree that **Chen & Lee's** (1328 S. Mt. Shasta Blvd., 530/926-9815, 11 A.M.–3 P.M. and 5–9 P.M. Tues.–Sun., $8–13) is the best choice, with light nongreasy food, if a little heavy on the garlic, and a clean cheerful atmosphere. It's good for takeout, lunch, and dinner.

Lai Lai Chinese American Restaurant (903 S. Mt. Shasta Blvd., 530/926-1728, lunch 11:30 A.M.–3 P.M. Mon.–Fri., dinner daily 4–9 P.M., $6–11) has a bargain lunch buffet ($7) on weekdays and good prices for large quantities of food at dinner. The food is nothing spectacular, but the place is convenient to the town center and an easy place to pick up some quick takeout.

Italian
For carbo-loading in preparation for climbing Mount Shasta, get a table at **Mike & Tony's Restaurant and Bar** (501 S. Mt. Shasta Blvd., 530/926-4792, www.mikeandtonysms.com, 5–9 P.M. Thurs. and Sun.–Mon., 5–10 P.M. Fri.–Sat., brunch 9 A.M.–2 P.M. Sun., $13–24), which has been serving delicious dinners since 1945. The food is good solid Italian-American: pasta with excellent homemade sauces, veal and chicken armigiana, all the other basics you'd expect, and plenty of them. Even the à

la carte meat entrées include vegetables, pasta, and bread and butter. The family-style version includes minestrone, salad, and an antipasto plate. The restaurant is in two rooms, one with a long lively bar and comfortable booths and tables with views to the outside, the other a simple windowless room with light wood paneling and plain tables. If you're making a reservation (recommended), specify that you want to be seated in the room with the bar and the windows.

Mexican
Casa Ramos (1136 S. Mt. Shasta Blvd., 530/926-0250, www.casaramos.net, 11 A.M.–9:30 P.M. Sun.–Thurs., 11 A.M.–10:30 P.M. Fri.–Sat., happy hour 3–6 P.M. Mon.–Fri., $8–15) is a small chain of 11 authentic Mexican family restaurants in Northern California. The local incarnation is particularly cheerful and welcoming. "It's Taco Time!" says the sign out front, and when you see the place, you'll probably agree. Prices are reasonable, portions are ample, and the whole family is welcome. There are specials for kids and lots of choices, including steak, chicken, and cheeseburgers, to satisfy anyone who isn't in the mood for Mexican.

Dos Geckos Burrito Bar (401 N. Mt. Shasta Blvd., 530/926-4843, 11 A.M.–2 P.M. Mon.–Tues. and Thurs.–Sat., $10) offers beer and wine in addition to casual, affordable Mexican meals. Some of the selling points: big burritos, lots of choices, fast service, and ample patio seating with mountain views.

Fine Dining
At the white-tablecloth end of the dining spectrum in Mount Shasta is **Lily's** (1013 S. Mt. Shasta Blvd., 530/962-3372, www.lilysrestaurant.com, daily 8 A.M.–2:30 P.M. and 4–9:30 P.M., $18–25), a lovely spacious place with a white picket fence outside and a varied menu. Lily's serves breakfast, lunch, and dinner seven days a week and does catering as well. Breakfast is the full selection of omelets,

pancakes, and other American favorites, plus huevos rancheros, biscuits and gravy, and healthier choices like tofu and fruit. Lunch is burgers, salads, and a few slightly more unusual choices like the eggplant hoagie and the walnut dal burger. Dinner has char-grilled filet mignon au poivre flambéed with brandy, finished in a green peppercorn sauce and wrapped in bacon; or try the tofu vegetable curry. This place is a great for a mixed group of vegetarians and carnivores ready to splurge on something special.

INFORMATION AND SERVICES
Visitor Information
At the **Mount Shasta Visitors Bureau** (300 Pine St., 530/926-4865 or 800/926-4865, http://visitmtshasta.com) you'll find information about hotels, restaurants, and local recreation; the staff is also helpful with driving directions to nearby sites.

For wilderness permits and trail advice, head for one of the local ranger stations. The **Mount Shasta Ranger Station** (204 W. Alma St., 530/926-4511, www.fs.usda.gov, 8 A.M.–4:30 P.M. Mon.–Fri. fall–spring, 8 A.M.–4:30 P.M. Mon.–Sat. summer) can supply wilderness and summit passes, plus park maps and information about current mountain conditions. A summit pass ($20) is required when hiking above 10,000 on Mount Shasta, and it allows you to climb to the summit; you can buy one at the ranger station during business hours. You also have the option of self-registering at the trailhead and leaving payment in an envelope as long as you have a check or cash. In person at the ranger station you can use a credit card as well. California state campfire permits are free, but you must get them in person, so plan to come to the ranger station during business hours. The Shasta Wilderness requires you to have a permit just to enter, even if you're not spending the night. Those permits are also available here for free, and you can get them inside or from a self-service station out front.

Banks and Post Office
The local **Mount Shasta Post Office** (301 S. Mt. Shasta Blvd., 530/926-1343, www.usps.com, 8:30 A.M.–5 P.M. Mon.–Fri.) is easy to find. Several banks have branches in Mount Shasta, and you'll have ample access to ATMs. **Bank of America** (100 Chestnut St., 530/926-8950, www.bankofamerica.com, 10 A.M.–4 P.M. Mon.–Thurs., 10 A.M.–5 P.M. Fri.) is near the center of town. A branch of **Chase** (168 Morgan Way, 530/926-8910, www.chase.com, 9 A.M.–6 P.M. Mon.–Fri., 9 A.M.–4 P.M. Sat.) is near the Mount Shasta Shopping Center.

Media and Communications
The Mount Shasta region has its own newspaper, the **Mount Shasta Herald** (530/926-5214, www.mtshastanews.com, $0.75), published weekly on Wednesday and available at racks and stores all over town. In the center of Mount Shasta, a good place to get Internet access is at the **Snowcrest Internet Café** (333 N. Mt. Shasta Blvd., 530/926-4019, 7 A.M.–5 P.M. Mon.–Fri., 8 A.M.–4 P.M. Sat.).

Medical Services
The town of Mount Shasta has a full-service hospital, **Mercy Medical Center Mount Shasta** (914 Pine St., 530/926-6111, www.mercymtshasta.org), with a 24-hour emergency room.

GETTING THERE AND AROUND
Mount Shasta is on I-5; from Sacramento it's 220 miles (3.5 hours). Parking in the town is usually easy, except during local events that draw numerous visitors. The nearest commercial airport is 60 miles (1 hour) away: **Redding Municipal Airport** (RDD, 6751 Woodrum Circle, 530/224-4320, http://ci.redding.ca.us) is served by United Express.

VICILITY OF MOUNT SHASTA
[Castle Crags State Park

Castle Crags State Park (20022 Castle Creek Rd., Castella, 530/235-2684, www.parks. ca.gov, day use $8 per vehicle) is one of the greats in California's extensive network of state parks. With 4,350 acres of land, 28 miles of hiking trails, and some very dramatic granite peaks and cliffs, it is a wonderful destination or a convenient place to camp while you enjoy Mount Shasta to the north or Shasta Lake to the south. You can fish and swim in the Sacramento River, rock-climb the spectacular 6,000-foot crags, take a variety of hikes, or just enjoy stunning views of Shasta and other nearby mountains and ranges.

If you don't have much time, you can still have a nice little walk and a great Castle Crags experience. After you enter at the gate, drive through the park following the signs for "Vista Point." A paved walk of no more than 0.25 mile from the Vista Point parking lot leads to

a spectacular overlook with views all around. Bring your binoculars and your camera.

If you can stay longer, drive to the Vista Point parking lot and use it as access to the Crags Trailhead. The **Crags Trail to Castle Dome** (5.5 miles round-trip) is strenuous and worth every step. If you're a strong hiker with a brisk pace, it will take about two hours on the way up and 1–1.5 hours on the way down. Feel free to go slower, though—it's a steep climb with memorable views all along the way. Pull out your camera for an excuse to take lots of breaks. About two miles up the trail is a sign for Indian Springs, a 0.25-mile jaunt off the main trail.

Castle Crags has more than 40 established **rock climbing** routes plus plenty of wide, open formations for explorers who prefer to make their own paths. You'll get to tackle domes, spires, and walls of granite that reach 6,000 feet into the sky. The crags first thrust upward and then broke off and were scrubbed by glaciers into the fascinating climbable formations

Castle Crags State Park

© HEATHER C. LISTON

visible today. Some of the known favorite climbs at Castle Crags are the Cosmic Wall on Mount Hubris, Castle Dome, and Six Toe Crack.

The park also has a **campground** (reservations accepted at www.reserveamerica.com May–Sept., first-come, first-served the rest of the year, $30) with 76 sites as well as six environmental sites ($15).

Castle Crags is easy to find. Take I-5 north toward the city of Mount Shasta and follow signs for the park. From the Bay Area, it's a 170-mile trip on I-5 north to exit 724 at Castella. Turn left onto Castle Creek Road, and the park is less than 0.5 mile. If you're coming from the north, note that the park is just six miles south of Dunsmuir and about 13 miles (15 minutes) south of the City of Mount Shasta.

McCloud

A wonderful regional waterfall to visit is **McCloud Falls** (McCloud Ranger Station, 530/964-2184, www.shastacascade.com) on the McCloud River. At Lower McCloud Falls you'll see roiling white water pouring over a 30-foot rock wall into an aerated river pool below. Middle McCloud Falls resembles a tiny Niagara, a level fall of water that's wider than it is tall. Upper McCloud Falls cascades powerfully but briefly down into a chilly pool that can double as a swimming hole if you're feeling brave. The loop trail that takes you past all three is about 3.5 miles long. To get here, take the McCloud exit from I-5 onto Highway 89 east. After about five miles, look for a sign on the left directing you to Fowler's Camp and Lower McCloud Falls. After another mile is the Lower Falls picnic area, where you can park.

Little Mount Hoffman Lookout Tower (Hwy. 89, east of McCloud, McCloud District Office 530/964-2184, reservations 877/444-6777, www.recreation.gov, July–mid-Oct., $75) is in the northeast corner of the Shasta-Trinity National Forest near Medicine Lake.

This 1920s-era lookout tower was used regularly until 1978 and is sometimes still employed in fire emergencies. Meanwhile, you can rent it for a romantic vacation, writer's retreat, or hiking base camp. The views are outstanding—from the tower's height of more than 7,300 feet, you can see Mount Shasta, Mount Lassen, Mount McLoughlin, and more.

The McCloud area has several campgrounds with access to the McCloud River as well as nearby Mount Shasta. Popular **Fowlers Camp** (39 sites, first come, first served, Apr.–Nov., $15) is at 3,400 feet elevation on the Upper McCloud River. Facilities include picnic tables, fire rings, vault toilets, and drinking water. Fowlers Camp is five miles east of McCloud on Highway 89.

At 3,700 feet elevation, **Cattle Camp** (24 sites, first come, first served, Apr.–Nov., $15) is the second campground on the Upper McCloud River. Facilities include picnic tables, fire rings, vault toilets, and drinking water. Cattle Camp is 10 miles east of McCloud on Highway 89.

Ah-Di-Na (17 sites, first-come, first-served, Apr.–Nov., $10) is a remote campground located at 2,300 feet elevation on the Lower McCloud River. Facilities include picnic tables, flush toilets, and drinking water. The campground is located 10 miles south of McCloud; access is via a rough dirt road.

◖ McArthur-Burney Falls Memorial State Park

Often billed as the most beautiful waterfall in California, even by regular visitors to Yosemite, **Burney Falls** in McArthur-Burney Falls Memorial State Park (24898 Hwy. 89, Burney, 530/335-2777, www.parks.ca.gov, $8) has been thrilling viewers for generations. No less a naturalist than Theodore Roosevelt declared these falls one of the wonders of the world. The park is the second oldest in the California State Park system and is about halfway between Mount Lassen and Mount Shasta.

Unlike many California waterfalls, Burney

Burney Falls

© JEFFREY BANKE/123RF.COM

Falls flows strong and true year-round and is just as beautiful in September as in April. More good news: You don't have to hike to reach the falls; they're right by the parking lot. Still, it's more than worth your time to get out of your car and take a walk around the wide sheets of water that almost look like a miniature Niagara; it's only a quick walk to the pool at the base of the falls. For the best views, take the one-mile hike around the 129-foot waterfall.

The McArthur-Burney Falls **campground** (Hwy. 89, 530/335-2777, reservations May–Sept. 800/444-7275, www.recreation.gov, year-round, $35) has 128 campsites and 7 primitive hike-in sites. There are also 24 cabins ($72) with heaters and platform beds. Facilities include restrooms with flush toilets, showers, picnic tables, and fire rings.

McArthur-Burney Falls Memorial State Park is on Highway 89 near Burney; from Redding, take Highway 299 east to Burney, then head north on Highway 89 for six miles.

Weed

◀ **Stewart Mineral Springs** (4617 Stewart Springs Rd., Weed, 530/938-2222, www.stewartmineralsprings.com, $70–160) is a rustic resort nestled in the woods about 20 minutes north of the town of Mount Shasta. Secluded and peaceful yet close to local attractions, Stewart Mineral Springs offers a variety of sleeping options. Four private cabins ($90–110) each have a queen bed, full bath, woodstove, and kitchenette. Campers can choose among tent sites ($35), RV sites with electrical hookups ($55), or one of the five tepees ($45, optional cot rental $5). Other options include guest rooms in a small motel ($70), apartments of various sizes with kitchenettes ($80–160), and a whole A-frame house that sleeps up to 15 ($460 plus $20 pp beyond 10). For a truly restful getaway, there are no phones, TVs, or wireless Internet on the premises, and cellphone coverage is spotty. Overnight guests can enjoy the clothing-optional sundeck and the

4

"last dry-wood sauna in Northern California." Massages and indoor mineral baths are available for an additional fee, and members of the local Karuk Tribe lead traditional Sweat Lodge Purification Ceremonies (1 P.M. Sat., donation $25) on the premises. The **Glorified Roots Juice Bar** (noon–4 P.M. Sat.–Sun. May–Sept., $4–12) offers smoothies and vegetarian wraps on the patio between the creek and the bathhouse. For more formal dining, the **Creekside Café** offers lunch and dinner indoors or out (530/938-2221, 5–9 P.M. Thurs.–Sat. Memorial Day–Sept.). The fare is carefully prepared vegetarian, vegan, pasta, and seafood with beer and wine. Visitors to Stewart Mineral Springs are advised to bring their own coffee, breakfast, and lunch.

Tulelake

From 1942 to 1946 Tule Lake was the name of one of the 10 internment camps where Japanese Americans were held during World War II. In commemoration of the events that went on here and in the other camps, in December 2008 a total of nine sites were made into one national monument, collectively called the **World War II Valor in the Pacific National Monument Tule Lake Unit** (530/260-0537, www.nps.gov/tule). This is the site of the largest and most controversial of the internment locations, where a "segregation center" stayed open even after the war, incarcerating Japanese Americans who had given unsatisfactory answers to the infamous loyalty questionnaire.

The temporary **visitors center** (800 Main St., 8:30 A.M.–5 P.M. Fri.–Sun.) is in the Tulelake–Butte Valley Fairgrounds Museum (daily 8:30 A.M.–5 P.M.). You can get a tour (530/260-0537, Fri.–Sat. or by appointment) of the very interesting **Tule Lake Segregation Center Jail** and **Camp Tulelake.**

There are five guest rooms in the simple homey **Winema Lodge** (5215 Hill Rd., 530/667-5158, www.winemalodge.com, $65–75), which sleep up to five people each and have access to a bath down the hall. Ten motel rooms with private baths are available, and there are RV sites with full hookups ($25). Family-style meals ($15–25) are also available.

Captain Jack's Stronghold (45650 Hwy. 139, 530/664-5566, 9 A.M.–8 P.M. Tues.–Thurs. and Sun., 9 A.M.–8:30 or 9 P.M. Fri.–Sat., $8–21) is a popular spot in Tulelake. The menu includes brisket and chicken-fried steak, but there's also a salad bar and some vegetarian options. If you like Americana, stop in at **Jolly Kone Burgers** (223 Main St., 530/667-2622, 7 A.M.–7 P.M. Mon.–Fri., 9 A.M.–6 P.M. Sat.,

TULE LAKE

Near the very tip of California, north of Lava Beds National Monument, is large and lovely Tule Lake, visible from a long distance across the high desert landscape. While the lake you see today is still beautiful, blue, and deep, it is much smaller than it used to be. One of the early projects of the U.S. Bureau of Reclamation was to "reclaim" the land beneath Tule Lake and Lower Klamath Lake and make it available for homesteading. What was once underwater, and later homestead land, is now mostly farmland.

You can still see some striking evidence of the lake's original size from Petroglyph Point, a section of Lava Beds National Monument located east of the lake and separate from the main lava beds area. Along Petroglyph Point Trail, you may wonder how the ancient markings on the rock walls high above got up there. Tule Lake was much bigger 5,000–6,000 years ago, and what is now hot dry land was all underwater. The Modoc artists simply steered their boats to the edge of the lake and worked on the lakeshore rock face—now far out of reach.

11 A.M.–5 P.M. Sun., $6.25–10) for hamburgers, ice cream, and homemade pies and cakes.

◖ Lava Beds National Monument

One of the best places to see the results of volcanic activity is at Lava Beds National Monument (Hill Rd., 530/667-8113, www. nps.gov/labe, sunrise–sunset daily, visitors center daily 8 A.M.–6 P.M. Memorial Day–Labor Day, daily 8:30 A.M.–5 P.M. Labor Day–Memorial Day, day use $10). This fascinating 47,000-acre park is delightfully undervisited no doubt owing to its remote location. With ancient Native American petroglyphs, an unrivalled series of deep and twisting "tube" caves, primordial piles of lava, and an abundance of desert wildlife, it is a mother lode of history, nature, and awe-inspiring sights.

Over the course of about 500,000 years, Medicine Lake Volcano has created an amazing landscape. Among the hiking trails, Modoc battle sites, and scrubby high-desert wilderness are more than 700 caves created by underground lava flows. Some of the caves have been developed for fairly easy access—outfitted with ladders, walkways, and lights—while others remain in their original condition. All are home to whole ecosystems that thrive in the damp darkness.

In summer about 200,000 bats live in the park; two of the 14 species represented here live in trees, and the other 12 live in caves. Park officials monitor where and when bats are likely to be concentrated, and they'll steer you away from those places, mainly for the safety of the bats.

HIKING AND CAVING

The **visitors center** (530/667-8113, daily 8 A.M.–6 P.M. Memorial Day–Labor Day, daily 8:30 A.M.–5 P.M. Labor Day–Memorial Day) recommends bringing up to three flashlights per person to explore the caves, as well as caving or bicycle helmets (it's easy to hit your head on the low ceilings of the caves). The visitors

© HEATHER C. LISTON

Lava Beds National Monument

WHITE-NOSE SYNDROME

Lava Beds National Monument has one of the largest bat habitats in the United States—a thriving population of approximately 200,000 bats in 14 different species. Park officials are extremely concerned about white-nose syndrome, a lethal fungus that infects the skin of bats. Since 2006 this devastating disease has been wiping out bat colonies all over the East Coast and in Canada. White-nose syndrome thrives in places with low temperatures and high humidity, such as the caves and mines where bats tend to hibernate. The U.S. Fish and Wildlife Service states that "scientists believe white-nose syndrome is responsible for the most dramatic decline of North American wildlife in 100 years, with potentially dire environmental consequences."

To help preserve these small mammals, park officials question all visitors about any recent cave visits before being allowed to enter the park. If you have entered or explored any caves in the eastern United States or in Canada, leave any boots, equipment, and clothing used during those visits at home and make sure you have thoroughly washed your belongings, including your body, your vehicle or camping gear, and anything else. To date, it remains unclear exactly how contamination is transported, but the park is adamant about preventing its entrance here. For more information, contact the U.S. Fish and Wildlife Service (www.fws.gov).

themselves. Three more caves are accessible via a short hiker-only trail beside the visitors center. The park recommends **Mushpot Cave** (770 feet) as an introductory cave; it's well-lit and easy to get into.

In addition to the numerous caves are 12 hiking trails. One of the best-known trails is **Captain Jack's Stronghold** (1.5 miles, moderate); the interpretive signage will help you understand the contentious history of this area. Start at the visitors center and take the park's main road seven miles north.

The wide, easy **Schonchin Butte Trail** (1.4 miles round-trip, moderate) leads to a working fire tower, along with the trail built by the Civilian Conservation Corps between 1939 and 1941. If there is a ranger present when you get to the top, you may be able to go up to the fire tower's lookout deck. To get to the Schonchin Butte Trail from the visitors center, turn left onto the main park road and drive 3.2 miles to the trail sign on the right. From here, it's a 0.5-mile drive on a gravel road to the parking area.

CAMPING

Lava Beds National Monument (Hill Rd., 530/667-8113, www.nps.gov/labe) features one campground, **Indian Well** (43 sites, first-come, first-served, $10), close to the visitors center. The campground has ample potable water, modern restrooms with flush toilets (no showers), and an amphitheater; don't expect much shade at the campsites, however. One of the best features for history buffs are the picnic tables, built by hand out of local lava stone by the Civilian Conservation Corps in the 1930s.

GETTING THERE

Lava Beds National Monument is in the remote northeastern corner of the state about 70 miles from Mount Shasta City. To get here from I-5, take U.S. 97 north at Weed. Drive 50 miles north, and at the state line just north of Dorris, turn east onto Highway 161. Continue 16 miles

center will lend you a large flashlight and sells a simple helmet ($6.50). For the more challenging caves, gloves, knee pads, a cave map, and a compass are also recommended.

However, you don't necessarily need a lot of equipment to visit the caves here. The short, paved **Cave Loop Trail** (2.25 miles) outside the visitors center leads past 16 different caves—their cool rocky entrances are fascinating in

east on Highway 161 to Hill Road, then turn right (south) and drive nine miles to the park entrance. Plan at least two hours for the drive from Weed, and note that U.S. 97 gets snow at high elevations.

Yreka

The town of Yreka is on I-5 near the Oregon border about 40 miles north of Mount Shasta. With a population of more than 7,000, it offers some standard chain motels and a few B&Bs. **Best Western Miner's Inn** (122 E. Miner St., 530/842-4355, www.bestwesterncalifornia. com, $99) offers a dependable night's sleep.

Yreka claims the northernmost **Black Bear Diner** (1747S. Main St., 530/842-9324, www. blackbeardiner.com, daily 6 A.M.–10 P.M., $8–15) in the chain. At this better-than-average diner, you can get a hearty breakfast, lunch, or dinner even when everything else is closed. For slightly more local color, try **Poor George's** (108 Oberlin Rd., 530/842-4664, 6 A.M.–7:45 P.M. Mon.–Fri., 7 A.M.–1:45 P.M. Sat.–Sun., $12–19) for breakfast. It has real country atmosphere, homemade food, and large portions. For a hearty Italian meal, eat at **Strings Italian Café** (322 W. Miner St., 530/842-7704, www.stringsyreka.com, 11 A.M.–9 P.M. Sun.–Thurs., 11 A.M.–9:30 P.M. Fri.–Sat. summer, daily 11 A.M.–9 P.M. winter, $10–23).

LAKE TAHOE

The San Francisco Bay Area is a top vacation destination for people from all over the world. So where do people who live there take their vacations? Answer: Tahoe. Sparkling blue Lake Tahoe and its surrounding mountains, lakes, ski resorts, hiking trails, hot springs, charming mountain towns, casinos, and varied wilderness areas says "vacation" to just about anyone.

Lake Tahoe is 22 miles long, 12 miles wide, and 1,645 feet deep at its deepest point, with a surface elevation of 6,225 feet. It's the 10th-deepest lake in the world and the second-deepest in the United States, after Crater Lake in Oregon. Sixty-three streams flow into the lake, and the Truckee River flows out, carrying Lake Tahoe's waters to Pyramid Lake. Even though

Lake Tahoe's water temperature ranges 41–68°F, the lake is a great place for all sorts of water activities.

The Tahoe area has an international reputation as a skiing paradise, with some of the finest ski resorts in the nation—second only to the Rockies for vertical drop, quality of snow, and the number of resorts. There are many opportunities for skiers, snowboarders, cross-country skiers, snowshoers, and just to play in the snow with the kids.

Even if you're not a skier, don't rule out Tahoe as a great vacation spot. It is slightly less crowded in the summer months than during ski season, and the weather is gorgeous every day. Between the pristine lake and the unspoiled wilderness areas, it is a delight for

© HEATHER C. LISTON

HIGHLIGHTS

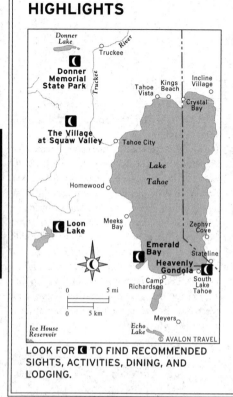

◖ **Heavenly Gondola:** Winter or summer, a ride up the gondola at Heavenly ski resort rewards with views from 9,163 feet (page 432).

◖ **Emerald Bay:** The most beautiful section of the "Most Beautiful Drive in America," Emerald Bay sparkles year-round. Whether you hike the trails of the state park of the same name, or just stop to gaze down at it from a highway overlook, the bay is Tahoe at its best (page 434).

◖ **Loon Lake:** Whether you like to swim, sail, kayak, hike, or just watch the sun set, peaceful Loon Lake is a great getaway sanctuary nestled in the Eldorado National Forest (page 457).

◖ **The Village at Squaw Valley:** This adorable mountainside village is the perfect place to while away a winter day amid boutiques, galleries, and restaurants (page 463).

◖ **Donner Memorial State Park:** Donner offers a lake that's perfect for recreation, along with interpretive trails and monuments illuminating one of the most compelling stories about the settlement of the West (page 473).

LOOK FOR ◖ TO FIND RECOMMENDED SIGHTS, ACTIVITIES, DINING, AND LODGING.

wakeboarders, water-skiers, campers, hikers, and families to swim, sun, play in the sand, rent kayaks, or just be in a beautiful place.

Californians often refer to Lake Tahoe simply as Tahoe, but the locals get more specific—it's all about the North Shore, with ski resorts, and the South Shore, with its sprawling town and glittering casinos just across the state line in Nevada.

It's possible to drive all the way around the lake, stopping at both the South and North Shores and enjoying the eastern and western perspectives as well as the attractions and natural beauty of both California and Nevada. Whether you're looking for radical recreation or

traditional relaxation of the more restful kind, you can find it at Tahoe year-round.

PLANNING YOUR TIME

Lake Tahoe has numerous recreation options and is usually accessible year-round. Weekend jaunts are popular, but many people take even longer trips to Tahoe; 1–2-week vacations are common because there's so much to see and do.

The number-one reason people come to Tahoe is for the snow. The North Shore boasts the most downhill ski resorts, many of them clustered near the small historic town of Truckee.

Summers are usually sunny and clear, but thanks to the 5,000–7,000-foot elevation

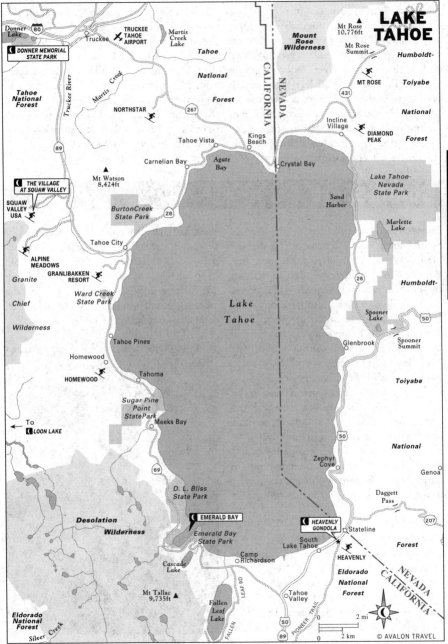

LAKE TAHOE

© AVALON TRAVEL

around the lake, the temperature never gets too high. In the summer months the average highs stay around 80°F with nights getting down to the 40s. The South Shore offers great lakeshore parks with numerous opportunities to enjoy the water in the summer. The lake is not exactly warm, but in the summer it's usually warmer than the Pacific Ocean, and people do enjoy swimming in it for a few months of the year.

One thing to remember about mountain regions—summer doesn't last as long as it does elsewhere. In Tahoe, summer usually means June–August, and sometimes less. When the Donner Party was famously delayed here by severe weather in 1846, it was only October. In midsummer, when all is wildflowers and bikinis, the ubiquitous winter road signs may look odd: "Beware of Ice," "Slippery," "Chains Required." It's not unheard of to run into a snowstorm on Memorial Day, so unless you're going for Fourth of July weekend, put your chains in the car. It doesn't hurt to be prepared.

South Shore

Part resort area and part working-class city, the South Shore is what you make of it. If you seek out good restaurants, you'll have a good time. But if fast food joints, low-budget superstores, run-down motels, and congested traffic get you down, then you may want to just stock up on groceries and move on toward the North Shore.

Approaching Tahoe from the Bay Area or Sacramento to the west, the South Shore will likely be your point of entry on U.S. 50 to the town of South Lake Tahoe. If you're looking for basic services such as supermarkets, banks, and drugstores before heading elsewhere, this is the place to stop. On the South Shore you'll find lively restaurants and bars, upscale lodging options, and lovely lake views and beaches. Just west of the California-Nevada border is the ski resort of Heavenly Village, jam-packed throughout the summer as well as winter.

SIGHTS
◖ Heavenly Gondola
The ride up the Heavenly Gondola (Heavenly Mountain Resort, 3860 Saddle Rd., South Lake Tahoe, 775/586-7000, www.skiheavenly.com, daily 10 A.M.–5 P.M. mid-June–Labor Day, 10 A.M.–4 P.M. Fri.–Sun. Labor Day–early Oct., adults $34, seniors and ages 13–18 $28, ages 5–12 $21) is a must in any season. The gondola travels 2.4 miles up the mountain to an elevation of 9,163 feet, stopping at an observation deck along the way. From here, you can view the whole of Lake Tahoe, the surrounding Desolation Wilderness, and more. Season passes (adults $52, children, youth, and seniors $42) allow multiple rides June–October.

Heavenly Gondola

© HEATHER C. LISTON

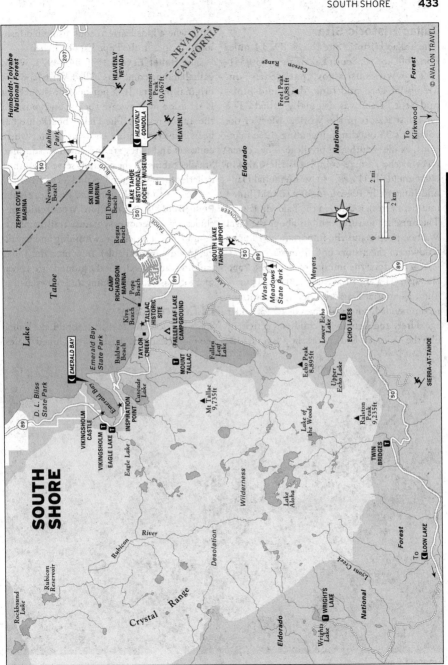

© AVALON TRAVEL

NEVADA
CALIFORNIA

SOUTH SHORE

Humboldt-Toiyabe National Forest

Carson Range

Freel Peak 10,881ft

Eldorado

National

To Kirkwood

HEAVENLY NEVADA

Monument Peak 10,067ft

HEAVENLY GONDOLA

HEAVENLY

Kahle Park

ZEPHYR COVE MARINA

Nevada Beach

SKI RUN MARINA

El Dorado Beach

Regan Beach

LAKE TAHOE HISTORICAL SOCIETY MUSEUM

South Lake Tahoe Airport

Washoe Meadows State Park

Meyers

To Kirkwood

Lake

Tahoe

CAMP RICHARDSON MARINA

Pope Beach

Kiva Beach

TALLAC HISTORIC SITE

Baldwin Beach

TAYLOR CREEK

FALLEN LEAF LAKE CAMPGROUND

MOUNT TALLAC

Fallen Leaf Lake

Lower Echo Lake

ECHO LAKES

Echo Peak 8,895ft

Upper Echo Lake

SIERRA-AT-TAHOE

Emerald Bay State Park

EMERALD BAY

D.L. Bliss State Park

VIKINGSHOLM CASTLE

VIKINGSHOLM

EAGLE LAKE

INSPIRATION POINT

Emerald Bay

Eagle Lake

Cascade Lake

Mt Tallac 9,735ft

Lake of the Woods

Ralston Peak 9,235ft

TWIN BRIDGES

To LOON LAKE

Rubicon

River

Rockbound Lake

Rubicon Reservoir

Crystal

Range

Desolation

Wilderness

Lake Aloha

Lyons Creek

Forest

Eldorado

National

Forest

WRIGHTS LAKE

Wrights Lake

2 mi

2 km

Tallac Historic Site

The Tallac Historic Site (Hwy. 89, 3.1 miles north of U.S. 50, South Lake Tahoe, 530/541-5227, www.fs.usda.gov, park Sat.–Sun. Memorial Day–mid-June, daily mid-June–mid-Sept., free) was originally called "The Grandest Resort in the World." Most of the complex's 33 buildings, including three mansions, exude wealth and privilege. The centerpiece of the 74-acre complex is the **Baldwin Museum** (daily 11 A.M.–4 P.M. Memorial Day–mid-June, daily 10 A.M.–4:30 P.M. mid-June–mid-Sept., free), located in the Baldwin Estate. The museum features exhibits about the local Washoe people and the importance of Lucky Baldwin to the history of California.

You can tour the interior of the 1894 **Pope Mansion** (11 A.M., 1 P.M., and 2:30 P.M. Thurs.–Tues. Memorial Day–mid-Sept., reservations recommended, adults $8, ages 6–12 $3, under age 6 free) and sign up for children's activities, like the "Kitchen Kids" workshop (ages 6–12, $10), where kids learn to cook using old-fashioned recipes in the Pope Estate kitchen.

The **Heller Estate** (530/541-4975, www.valhallatahoe.com) was called Valhalla by its original owners. It is not open for tours but is set aside to showcase the art and music of the Tahoe region. The Heller boathouse has been converted into a 164-seat theater where concerts and plays are presented in summer. Smaller cabins on the grounds serve as summer galleries for photographers and local artists.

Next to all that history and grandeur is the **Pope-Baldwin Recreation Area,** which includes a number of easy nature trails, a picnic ground, and a beach for swimming and kayaking (rentals are available). In winter, the Tallac buildings are closed, but the grounds are a great spot for cross-country skiing and snowshoeing.

◖ Emerald Bay

Some have called the road around Lake Tahoe the most beautiful drive in the United States.

Emerald Bay

© HEATHER C. LISTON

Whether that's true or not, the horseshoe-shaped inlet of Emerald Bay is its epicenter. Driving north from South Lake Tahoe, Highway 89 passes through Emerald Bay State Park. Even if you don't have plans to visit the park, try to pull over at one of the several scenic overlooks, such as **Inspiration Point** (Hwy. 89, 8 miles north of South Lake Tahoe). Emerald Bay offers views you won't want to miss.

Emerald Bay State Park

Emerald Bay State Park (Hwy. 89, 10 miles north of South Lake Tahoe, 530/541-3030 or 530/525-3345, www.parks.ca.gov, year-round, $10) was designated an "underwater" state park in 1994. It now encompasses the historic Vikingsholm mansion; Fannette Island (June–Feb.), the only island in Lake Tahoe; the Eagle Point Campground; and a boat-in campground on the north side of the bay. In addition, there are miles of hiking trails, including the **Rubicon Trail,** from Emerald Bay State Park to nearby D. L. Bliss State Park. Some visitors still enjoy the underwater aspect—scuba divers can see the remains of boats, cars, and some artifacts that date back to the turn of the 20th century.

Vikingsholm Castle

Wealthy benefactor Lora Josephine Knight had summered on the North Shore for 16 years when she decided to build her dream home on Emerald Bay. The result was the elegant Scandinavian-style mansion Vikingsholm (Emerald Bay State Park, Hwy. 89, 530/525-9530, www.vikingsholm.org or www.parks.ca.gov, tours daily 10:30 A.M.–4:30 P.M. Memorial Day–late Sept., grounds free, tours adults $8, ages 6–12 $5, cash or check only). This architectural gem is an intriguing reminder of a world gone by. Built by a Swedish architect in 1929, the castle-like structure is composed of granite boulders and includes towers, hand-cut timbers, and sod roofs green with growing grass. The interior

LAKE TAHOE

© HEATHER C. LISTON

Vikingsholm Castle

is furnished with authentic Scandinavian period reproductions.

Visitors are welcome to enjoy the beach, the grounds, and the exterior of Vikingsholm at no charge; the mansion is only accessible on the tours. Access is via a steep one-mile trail from the Harvey West parking lot at the Emerald Bay Overlook (Hwy. 89, day use $8). You can also reach Vikingsholm via the Rubicon Trail (1.7 miles one-way) from Eagle Point Campground in Emerald Bay State Park (day use $10).

D. L. Bliss State Park

D. L. Bliss State Park (Hwy. 89, 2 miles north of Emerald Bay, 530/525-3345 or 530/525-7277, www.parks.ca.gov, spring–fall, day use $8) has some of the best views in Tahoe. The park is directly north of Emerald Bay State Park, and the two are sometimes considered one unit. Hiking is a popular activity; trails include the **Rubicon-Lighthouse Trail** to Rubicon Point's lighthouse, built in 1919 and restored and stabilized in 2001; it was once the highest-elevation lighthouse on a navigable body of water in the world. Swimming is great at the Lester and Calawee Cove Beaches, and trout and salmon fishing are also popular from D. L. Bliss's shores. There are also three campgrounds within the park.

SPORTS AND RECREATION
Ski Resorts

Skiing can be an expensive hobby, and the cost of lift tickets may be a key factor in your vacation planning. The prices listed are subject to change, and the cost of lift tickets sometimes changes substantially and more often than other expenses. Check with the resort directly to confirm prices and availability before planning a trip.

HEAVENLY

On the less-skied South Shore, the queen bee of the few resorts is undoubtedly Heavenly (Wildwood Rd. and Saddle Rd., South Lake Tahoe, 775/586-7000, www.skiheavenly.com, 9 A.M.–4 P.M. Mon.–Fri., 8:30 A.M.–4 P.M. Sat.–Sun. and holidays Dec.–Apr., depending on snow; adults $61, children $35–46, seniors $46). At 10,067 feet, Heavenly offers the highest elevation of any mountain at Tahoe, along with the longest tubing hill on the West Coast, and one ski run that's five miles long.

Heavenly sprawls more than most resorts. Skiers can choose from four lodge and village access points up to the ski area: Heavenly Village down by the lake, California Lodge in the South Shore downtown area, and Boulder Lodge and Stagecoach Lodge inland. Ninety-seven runs snake down the mountainside, taking advantage of the more than 3,500 vertical feet. Beware: Even the lowland ski area near the California Lodge has mostly black-diamond runs. Approach the Killebrew and Mott Canyons carefully—gates at the head of these runs underscore the fact that only expert skiers should take them on. About 20 percent of Heavenly's runs are for beginners, and most of the beginner area is served by the gondola and the Powderbowl Express Six Chair. Freestylers have four terrain parks—High Roller, Groove, Ante Up, and Player's. In the works is a new adventure zone just for newbies and youngsters, called Black Bear Hollow, and a ski school lodge for children.

Heavenly is an intensely popular resort, so prepare to find parking a challenge at whichever lodge you choose. Crowding and lines at the lifts, especially at the bottom of the mountain, can get bad on weekends and holidays. On the other hand, once you're out of your car and on the mountain, you'll have access to nearly every service and amenity you need. Even better, take the **BlueGo Shuttle** (530/541-7149, www.bluego.org, free), which picks up at all the major lodging areas around town and drops skiers off at any of Heavenly's four lodges.

GETTING DISCOUNT LIFT TICKETS

The prices for skiing the famous mountains at Tahoe have earned their own infamy. New skiers quickly learn that spending a day on the slopes of Squaw, Alpine, or Heavenly can cost almost as much as spending the night in the nearby hotels. So what's a budget-conscious boarder to do?

Go coupon hunting: Check the racks of leaflets in Tahoe hotels or go to the visitors centers. Advertisements for the various ski resorts often include discount coupons for lift tickets or free rides on the resort ski shuttles. In supermarkets and pharmacies, look at the soda cans and popular snack products—some of these include a lift ticket coupon with proof of purchase. This type of coupon gets popular every winter in Sacramento and the Bay Area. Mine the Internet by searching for "discount coupon" with the name of the resort to find any online discounts or tips to obtain paper coupons.

Sign up for daily deals online: Groupon (www.groupon.com), for example, has been doing business with Tahoe vacation resorts. If you register online to receive its daily deals, you might get spam in your inbox, but you might also hit the jackpot if they offer half-price or better deals on lift tickets. Other companies in the online coupon business include Living Social (www.livingsocial.com), Amazon (www.local.amazon.com), Yelp (www.yelp.com), and HomeRun (http://homerun.com).

Look for membership or special-group discounts: Many discounts are available for students, active military personnel, seniors age 65 or older, and members of the American Automobile Association (AAA, www.aaa.com) or AARP (www.aarp.org). Bring valid membership or identification cards with you, and ask about these discounts when making reservations or purchasing tickets.

Ski in the afternoon: If you're a casual skier who only needs a couple of hours on the slopes to feel satisfied, check with your favorite resort for its afternoon rates. Most resorts offer lower-priced lift tickets after 2 or 3 P.M.

Ski a lot in one place: Find your favorite resort and stick to it, taking advantage of the discounts built into two-day and three-day (or more) lift passes.

LAKE TAHOE

KIRKWOOD

The South Shore's mid-tier resort is Kirkwood (1501 Kirkwood Meadows Dr., off Hwy. 88, Kirkwood, 209/258-6000, www.kirkwood.com, daily 9 A.M.–4 P.M. Dec.–Apr., depending on snow, adults $62–79, seniors $40–51, ages 13–18 $51–61, ages 6–12 $20–51). Kirkwood offers dozens of downhill runs, plus everything from pipes to a cross-country space. Lift-ticket prices change seasonally, and the pricing scheme is complex, with special rates for military personnel and college students, multiday packages, and more.

Both the easiest runs and the ski school **Tahoe Learning Center** (209/258-7754) are located near the Timber Creek Day Lodge. The Kirkwood Mountain Lodge lifts lead to more intermediate and advanced runs; the back of the mountain is devoted to double-black-diamond runs. Kirkwood features terrain parks for skiers and boarders, including a boarder-skier cross course, half-pipes, beginner terrain, and areas with sound systems and music to complete the atmosphere. For a more sedate adventure, check out the snowshoe and cross-country park; you can rent equipment for both at the **Cross Country and Snowshoe Center** (209/258-7248, daily 10 A.M.–4 P.M. winter) and the **High Alpine Adventure Center** (8:30 A.M.–12:30 P.M. Mon.–Thurs., 8:30 A.M.–6 P.M. Fri.–Sun. winter).

You'll find plenty of sustenance in and around Kirkwood. The resort includes three restaurants: The **Off the Wall Bar & Grill** (209/258-7365) is in the Lodge at Kirkwood; **Bub's Pub** (209/258-7225) is in the Kirkwood Village; and the **Kirkwood Inn** (209/258-7304) is at the entrance to Kirkwood, next to the Nordic Center. The **Red Cliffs Day Lodge** at the Nordic Center also has a cafeteria. If you prefer to stay where you ski, look into Kirkwood's array of lodges and vacation rentals.

SIERRA-AT-TAHOE

For a smaller and less crowded South Shore ski experience, check out Sierra-at-Tahoe (1111 Sierra-at-Tahoe Rd., Twin Bridges, 530/659-7453, www.sierraattahoe.com, 9 A.M.–4 P.M. Mon.–Fri., 8 A.M.–4 P.M. Sat.–Sun., late Nov.–Apr., depending on snow, rates vary), with plenty of long sweeping advanced runs as well as many good intermediate tracks. The "Easy Street" area is 100 acres of beginner-only terrain; slightly advanced beginners can enjoy the Sugar 'n Spice Trail, which runs all the way from the top. The Grandview Express quad chairs take skiers to the very top; the Nob Hill double chair lands midway up the mountain and also provides access to the backside, while the Rock Garden and Easy Rider Express lifts handle those who want to stay lower on the mountain. It's all black-diamond runs on the east side of the big quads, and mostly blues with a few black diamonds for spice in the west, coming off the West Bowl Express quad or the Puma triple chair. A few more beginning and intermediate runs go down the back of the mountain.

Sierra-at-Tahoe offers **Huckleberry Cat Tours** (daily 10 A.M.–2 P.M., $79), taking expert skiers and boarders directly into the backcountry and providing them with instruction, avalanche gear, and lunch. **Burton Riglet Park** is a new mini snowboard park where children age three and up can learn and practice on a board.

Sierra-at-Tahoe prides itself on being "the most affordable mountain in Lake Tahoe," so check website for rates and discounts.

There are six different eateries (530/659-7453) at the Base Lodge, from **Java Junction** to **Mama's Kitchen,** with its hearty breakfasts and hot soups, to the **Tiki Bar & Grill,** where you can sit outside on sunny days. The Grandview Lodge features the **360 Smokehouse BBQ.** One of the most popular eateries is the **Baja Grill,** located at the West Bowl.

Cross-Country Skiing and Snowshoeing

In some places, cross-country skiers feel like the poor cousins of downhillers, noodling around the edges of the "main" resorts and trails. Not so in Tahoe: The perfect combination of deep snow and ample wildlands make for a variety of cross-country options. You can find groomed and maintained trails at numerous cross-country centers, easy trails for a glide through the woods, or opportunities for some serious backcountry adventures.

A **Sno-Park** parking pass (recording 916/324-1222, information 916/324-4442, www.ohv.parks.ca.gov, $5 per day, all-season $25) is required for many forest ski trailheads November 1–May 30. You can pick up the pass at the Placerville Ranger Station (4260 Eight Mile Rd., Camino, 530/644-2324, 8 A.M.–4:30 P.M. Mon.–Fri.), the Kyburz Mini-Mart (13686 U.S. 50, Kyburz, 530/293-3232), and the Roadrunner Gas Station (2933 U.S. 50, South Lake Tahoe, 530/577-6946). The website lists additional vendors, and you can buy Sno-Park passes online (www.ohv.parks.ca.gov).

Those planning overnight ski-camping trips must first get a **wilderness permit** from the Placerville Ranger District's El Dorado Information Center (4260 Eight Mile Rd., Camino, 530/644-2324, 8 A.M.–4:30 P.M. Mon.–Fri.). While snow conditions are generally best in the morning, moonlight skiing is allowed in some areas.

Sections of the beautiful **Tahoe Rim Trail** (775/298-0012, www.tahoerimtrail.org) can be ideal for snowshoeing, depending on conditions, which are never predictable. The west (California) side of the lake gets a lot more snow than the east. The first snowfall usually hits the trail sometime in November, and some places will still have a little snow as late as July. The Rim Trail office suggests calling close to your planned trip dates for an updated report on conditions and specific advice on where to go. In the heart of winter (Jan.–Mar.), the Tahoe Rim Trail Association (775/298-0012, www.tahoerimtrail.org) offers guided snowshoe hikes on Saturday.

A number of cross-country trails that really do cross some country are maintained by the U.S. Forest Service. Some of these trails offer short single-day excursions, while others lead miles back into the ominously named Desolation Wilderness and may appeal to hard-core ski-campers who want a multiday adventure. Beginner explorers can have the safest backcountry fun at **Taylor Creek** (Hwy. 89, just north of Camp Richardson, 530/543-2600, www.fs.usda.gov or www.parks.ca.gov), an uncongested but reasonably populous area with many flat marked trails to help newcomers get a feel for the forest. Lots of trails for skiers of all levels run along the South and West Shores of Lake Tahoe. If you're planning to camp in Desolation Wilderness, the most popular trailhead takes you past **Echo Lakes** (U.S. 50 at Echo Lake Rd.) and then into the backcountry along the Pacific Crest Trail.

Snowmobiling

Operating from the town of Meyers on the South Shore, **Lake Tahoe Adventures** (3071 U.S. 50, Meyers, 530/577-2940 or 800/865-4679, www.laketahoeadventures.com, daily 8 A.M.–5 P.M. year-round, $50–200) specializes in snowmobile tours of all kinds—for groups, individuals, and even children (drivers must be at least eight years old). Snowmobile tours are usually available November–April; the company also offers Jeep and ATV tours. A shuttle will take riders from the tour center up to the base camp in Hope Valley, where a fleet of Arctic Cat snowmobiles awaits to explore the

high-elevation backcountry Sierra terrain. First-time drivers and families with children can pick one of the more sedate trail tours or practice on the snowmobile track at the company's home base in Meyers. Expert snowmobile enthusiasts prefer the "ultimate" off-trail tours that go deep into the backcountry and offer rougher riding. Reservations are required for all tours; drop-ins are welcome at the snowmobile track.

Sledding and Snow Play

Just a couple of miles from Heavenly Valley in a cute residential area is the **Tube & Saucer Hill at Hansen's Resort** (1360 Ski Run Blvd., South Lake Tahoe, 530/544-3361, www.hansensresort.com, daily 9 A.M.–5 P.M. mid-Dec.–Mar., $10 per hour, cash only). An annual favorite, Hansen's offers more features than many impromptu snow-play spots. Don't bother stacking a bunch of equipment in the car, since the hourly cost includes the use of a Hansen's saucer or tube. With constructed runs, you'll definitely get some thrills as you slip down the hill through the scattered pine trees. The resort also has a snack bar and a redwood hot tub available to customers.

In the South Shore area past Meyers, **Adventure Mountain Lake Tahoe** (21200 U.S. 50, Echo Summit, 530/577-4352, www.adventuremountaintahoe.com, 10 A.M.–4:30 P.M. Mon.–Fri., 9 A.M.–5 P.M. Sat.–Sun. and holidays late Nov.–Apr., $15 per vehicle) has the best groomed sledding area in Tahoe. With 40 acres of sled runs and play areas, plus restrooms and a concession stand that sells hot coffee and new sleds, Adventure Mountain also has access to the Pacific Crest Trail as well as a few other cross-country skiing and snowshoeing trails for those who want a quieter but more labor-intensive day in the snow. Feel free to bring your own sled and tubes.

Sleigh Rides

Catch a ride with **Wilderness Sleigh Rides at**

the **Camp Richardson Corral** (Hwy. 89, between Camp Richardson Resort and Fallen Leaf Rd., 530/541-3113, www.camprichardsoncorral.com, call for hours, Dec.–Feb., depending on snow, adults $30, under age 4 free). Rides are about 45 minutes long, and it's best to call ahead for reservations.

Ice Skating

Each year at the South Shore, **Heavenly Gardens** (1021 Heavenly Village Way, South Lake Tahoe, 530/542-4230, www.theshopsatheavenly.com/skating, daily 10 A.M.–8 P.M. mid-Nov.–early Apr., adults $39, children $15) turns part of its landscape into a winter wonderland. The outdoor rink appeals especially to kids, newbies, and those more serious about having fun than being great skaters. As Tahoe attractions go, this is an entertainment bargain, since your pass includes skate rental and in-and-out access all day long. They turn off the phones in the summer, but that doesn't mean things won't be ready to go as soon as the season arrives.

For serious skaters and hockey players who want to indulge while vacationing in Tahoe, the **South Lake Tahoe Ice Arena** (1176 Rufus Allen Blvd., South Lake Tahoe, 530/542-6262, www.tahoese.com, 9:30 A.M.–4 P.M. Mon.–Thurs., hours vary Fri.–Sun., adults $7.50, ages 5–18 $6.50, skate rental $3) can hook you up. This year-round center offers drop-in hockey, public skating, a skate school (drop-in lessons $12 per hour), and even an Adult Coffee Club skating hour.

Boating, Waterskiing, and Wakeboarding

Once the summer sunshine has warmed the air—if not the waters of the lake—thoughts turn to other kinds of skiing and boarding. The vast clear waters of Lake Tahoe are irresistible to water-skiers, wakeboarders, Jet Skiers, and powerboaters. There are miles of open water

power boats next to the *Tahoe Queen* at the Ski Run Marina

© HEATHER C. LISTON

to cross, a number of docks and marinas, and a lovely coastline to explore. Dive deeper than 18 inches into the lake and you'll find that the water is ice-cold—in the 40s—even in the height of summer. But that's no matter if you're sunning yourself on the bow of a speedboat or flying along on a wakeboard.

Be aware that the community and the governments around Tahoe take water quality very seriously—not only that of Lake Tahoe but also of Falling Leaf, Echo, and the other small lakes nearby. If you plan to bring your own powered watercraft, it's wise to familiarize yourself with the rules and restrictions governing all waterways in the Tahoe Basin at http://boattahoe.com/trparegs.htm.

Full-service **Tahoe Keys Marina** (2435 Venice Dr. E., South Lake Tahoe, 530/541-2155, www.tahoekeysmarina.net) is one of the largest marinas, selling gas, providing launch access, and renting slips as well as offering boat rentals and charter fishing trips. You can also dock your boat ($2.50 per foot per day plus $3 per day water quality and dredging fee, $12.50 per foot per week plus $21 in fees).

Tahoe Keys Boat & Charter Rentals (2435 Venice Dr. E., South Lake Tahoe, 530/544-8888, www.tahoesports.com) operates out of the Tahoe Keys Marina and offers boat rentals of various kinds: a 49-passenger 52-foot yacht, pontoon boats, powerboats, kayaks, and Yamaha Jet Skis. Powerboats rent for $120–205 per hour; if you want one for the whole day, the company will charge for six hours and let you keep it for eight.

The **Ski Run Boat Company** (Ski Run Marina, 900 Ski Run Blvd., South Lake Tahoe, 530/544-0200, www.tahoesports.com) is a sister company to the Tahoe Keys Boat & Charter Rental, operating out of a different location with even more variety. In addition to Jet Skis, pontoon boats, and 18–24-foot Reinell powerboats, you can rent canoes, ocean kayaks, stand-up paddleboards, a Catalina sailboat,

and even a double hydrobike ($25 per hour) or a water tricycle ($22 per hour). At this location you can also get a parasail ride ($50–75 pp).

The marina at **Camp Richardson** (1900 Jameson Beach Rd., South Lake Tahoe, 530/542-6570, 8 A.M.–8 P.M. daily June 25–mid-Sept., 9 A.M.–5 P.M. daily mid-Sept.–mid-Oct.) rents kayaks ($20–30 per hour), pontoon boats ($160 per hour, $960 per day), paddleboards ($30 per hour), Sea-Doos ($125 per hour), and more. You can also take the 1.5-hour Rum Runner Emerald Bay Cruise (530/542-6570, daily 1 P.M. and 3:30 P.M. June 25–mid-Oct., adults $32, children $19).

For a guided kayak tour of Emerald Bay, contact **Kayak Tahoe** (Timber Cove Marina, 3411 Lake Tahoe Blvd., South Lake Tahoe, 530/544-2011, www.kayaktahoe.com, daily 9 A.M.–1 P.M., by reservation only, $65 pp, minimum 6 people). You'll paddle the entire perimeter of the bay with a knowledgeable guide, stopping at Vikingsholm and Fannette Island. The company has four locations, including Nevada Beach, Pope Beach, and Baldwin Beach (530/523-3322, daily 9 A.M.–4 P.M.). Beginners are welcome, but the minimum age is eight.

Fishing

Several companies offer charter trips on Lake Tahoe for anglers looking to score mackinaw, rainbow, and brown trout or kokanee salmon. Operating out of the Ski Run Marina (900 Ski Run Blvd., South Lake Tahoe, www.skirunmarina.com) and the Zephyr Cove Marina (760 U.S. 50, Zephyr Cove, NV, 775/586-9338, www.zephyrcove.com), **Tahoe Sport Fishing** (530/541-5448 or 800/696-7797, www.tahoesportfishing.com, $85–135) offers half-day and full-day fishing trips tailored to suit all styles of lake fishing. The fishing boats have heated cabins and modest restroom facilities, and trips include all the trimmings: bait and tackle, cleaning and bagging services, cold beer and soda on board, and a choice of morning or afternoon half-day trips.

With the proliferation of rivers and streams surrounding Lake Tahoe, it's easy to find a good place to cast if you prefer fly-fishing to lake fishing. **Tahoe Fly Fishing Outfitters** (2705 Lake Tahoe Blvd., South Lake Tahoe, 530/541-8208, www.tahoeflyfishing.com, $175–375) can take you on an expert-guided fly-fishing or spin-fishing trip on one of the smaller lakes, Walker River, Carson River, Truckee and Little Truckee Rivers, or the Pleasant Valley Fly Fishing Preserve.

Hiking
TALLAC HISTORIC SITE
Along the South Shore, hikes range from easy walks along the shore at the Tallac Historic Site to hard-core treks up the **Mount Tallac Trail** (Hwy. 89 at Baldwin Beach, South Lake Tahoe, 10 miles round-trip, difficult). This long hike starts out easy, taking casual strollers past the Floating Island and Cathedral Lakes, and then gets steeper and harsher as it ascends up the front face of the mountain. To access the trail, turn off Highway 89 away from the beach toward a dirt road to the trailhead parking lot. For a more moderate but equally beautiful hike, choose the **Echo Lakes Trail** (Johnson Pass Rd. at Lower Echo Lake, 5–12 miles, moderate–strenuous, wilderness permit may be required). You can pick your distance on this route, depending on how many small alpine lakes you want to see. Start with a short walk to Upper Echo Lake, where you have the option to catch a water taxi rather than continuing on the trail along the lake. If you keep going, you'll see Tamarack Lake, Lucille and Margery Lakes, Lake in the Woods, and maybe even Aloha Lake.

EMERALD BAY STATE PARK
Emerald Bay State Park is a treasure trove of easy–moderate hiking trails. Near campsite 28 in Eagle Point Campground is the beginning

Emerald Bay, as seen from the Rubicon Trail

© HEATHER C. LISTON

of the **Overlook Trail,** a short (0.5 mile) walking trail to a camera-ready spot. Near campsite 34 and the campfire center amphitheater you can park in a lot and take one of two trails. The first is another short walk to an overlook; the second is the **Rubicon Trail** (1.7 miles), which takes you to Vikingsholm. This is the longer route, as opposed to the steep 0.5-mile trail to Vikingsholm that you can pick up from the Harvey West Parking Lot. The well-marked trail features undulating terrain, shade, and gorgeous views. The first mile is a gentle downhill slope, overlooking the lake on the right. The water at the edge is so shallow and clear that you can see the lake bottom from your perch on the trail. If it's been a wet year, some sections may be muddy, so wear boots. From the bridge, take a brief (0.2 mile) detour to your left to visit Lower Eagle Falls; or turn right to reach the visitors center in less than one mile. At the visitors center, you can buy tickets for a Vikingsholm tour or just walk another 0.2 mile to explore the Vikingsholm grounds on your own. Bring food, water, money for the tour, and a bathing suit to take a dip in the very cold water near the sandy beach beside Vikingsholm.

Altogether, the Rubicon Trail runs 4.5 miles along the shoreline of Emerald Bay; hikers who complete it will see osprey nests and an old wooden lighthouse in addition to the many other highlights.

D. L. BLISS STATE PARK

Hiking trails within D. L. Bliss State Park include the **Rubicon-Lighthouse Trail** to Rubicon Point's lighthouse, which was built in 1919 and restored and stabilized in 2001. You can take a short portion of this trail, from Calawee Cove Beach to the lookout at Rubicon Point, or walk a little farther to see the lighthouse. For a longer adventure, follow the Rubicon Trail all the way down around the bay, past Vikingsholm, and on to its end point at Upper Eagle Point Campground in Emerald

Bay State Park. The complete trail has a total distance of about 4.5 miles one-way, but the terrain is mostly easy.

There's a short (0.5 mile) self-guided **nature trail** to Balancing Rock on the west side of D. L. Bliss that nearly anyone can enjoy. Nineteen numbered signs along the way illuminate the history and geology of the area.

TAHOE RIM TRAIL

If you're in good shape and like a challenge, you will definitely want to experience the 165-mile Tahoe Rim Trail (775/298-0012, www.tahoerimtrail.org). This beautiful and varied trail, built between 1984 and 2001, encircles the entire lake through six counties in California and Nevada, one state park, three national forests, and three wilderness areas; 49 miles of it overlap the Pacific Crest Trail. You can hike the trail in segments, or if you're up for a little planning, do it in a multiday loop. Casual day-hikers can pick one portion of the trail and tackle it, either doing an out-and-back or using a shuttle service to get back at the end of the day.

The Tahoe Rim Trail is managed and maintained by the nonprofit Tahoe Rim Trail Association (TRTA, 948 Incline Way, Incline Village, NV, info@tahoerimtrail.org). The TRTA organizes a number of events, including trail maintenance work parties, workshops on backcountry skills, and informative Trail Talks. They're the people to contact if you want to volunteer, become an official member of the 165-Mile Club, or get information about the trail. Note that horseback riding is permitted on the Tahoe Rim Trail, and mountain biking is permitted on certain sections. For details, check the website (www.tahoerimtrail.org), which includes regular updates and specifics.

In summer, the TRTA runs several 14-day through-hikes (775/298-0231, $1,250), during which participants cover all 165 miles and bag elevation gains and losses totaling 27,500 feet. The cost includes food, trip leaders,

LAKE TAHOE

transportation to and from the trail, and delivery of meals and supplies to key locations along the way by a group of "Trail Angels"—which greatly reduces the weight of your backpack on a trek of this length. These trips fill up fast, so call early to get on the list.

If you're not up for hiking the whole trail in one bite, you might love the TRTA's Segment Hiking Program (membership fee $350), where you can join the expert guides as they hike the whole trail on Friday or Saturday over the course of eight weeks through the summer. This program also fills quickly; register through the website or contact the trail-use director (775/298-0231, jaimes@tahoerimtrail.org).

Biking

A great place to get out and cycle in summer is **Kirkwood** (1501 Kirkwood Meadows Dr., off Hwy. 88, Kirkwood, www.kirkwood.com, 209/258-7360 or 209/258-7210, July 4–Labor Day). When there's no snow, the slopes of this ski resort become great mountain biking tracks. Two lifts run on weekends in the summer (10 A.M.–4 P.M. Sat., 10 A.M.–3 P.M. Sun., adults $32), and a third lift operates occasionally on holidays. At the General Store (daily 9 A.M.–5 P.M. summer) at Kirkwood, you can rent high-end mountain bikes (adults $45–79, children $19–25). When the lifts aren't running, there's no charge to ride the trails. Kirkwood also offers several mountain-bike clinics through the season to help hone your skills.

Much of the **Tahoe Rim Trail** on the California side is not open to bicycles as the trail is in the Desolation Wilderness and along the Pacific Crest Trail. The one segment that's accessible is the five miles from Big Meadow to Echo Summit and Echo Lake. To reach the trailhead from South Lake Tahoe, drive south on U.S. 50 to Highway 89; continue south on Highway 89 for about five miles until the Tahoe Rim Trail crosses the road at Big Meadow, where you can park. The trail starts

out heading south but soon turns northwest up to Echo Summit and then Echo Lake. When you near the lake, you'll see a sign warning that the trail is about to join the Pacific Crest Trail, and cyclists must turn around. This round-trip is a scenic and invigorating 10-mile ride.

Horseback Riding

For travelers who prefer to explore the forests and trails on horseback, a few stables offer guided rides. On the west side of the South Shore, find the **Camp Richardson Corral** (Emerald Bay Rd. between Fallen Leaf Rd. and Valhalla Rd., 530/541-3113 or 877/541-3113, www.camprichardsoncorral.com, $40–78). Choose a one- or two-hour trail ride to explore the meadows and the forest, or a ride with a meal included. Camp Richardson offers an early-morning ride that culminates in a hearty hot cowboy-style breakfast and a two-hour evening ride with a steak barbecue. Riders must be at least six years old and weigh 225 pounds or less. Camp Richardson also offers horse boarding by the day, week, and month.

To get out and see the Sierra Foothills and mountains from the back of a horse, **Kirkwood** (1501 Kirkwood Meadows Dr., off Hwy. 88, Kirkwood, www.kirkwood.com, mid-June–Labor Day) has what you need. Kirkwood Corrals (775/790-5929) will take you out for a 0.5–1.5-hour ride ($35–85). If you're more advanced and want a gorgeous guided trail ride out into the Mokelumne Wilderness, join Kirkwood Sierra Outfitters (209/258-7433, www.kirkwoodsierraoutfitters.com) for a ride of half a day or more.

Golf

For golfers looking to play a few holes on the cheap, **Tahoe Paradise Golf Course** (3021 U.S. 50, South Lake Tahoe, 530/577-2121, www.tahoeparadisegc.com, daily 8 A.M.–7 P.M. May–Oct., daily 6 A.M.–8 P.M. midsummer, $25–55) offers a pleasant course as well as pleasantly low greens fees. Conveniently located on U.S. 50 on the South Shore, this course has pretty mountain views and plenty of lovely pine trees along with 18 holes of moderate golf that provides a good game for beginners and intermediates. There's also a pro shop, a practice area, and a modest snack bar with hot dogs and beer.

The **Lake Tahoe Golf Course** (2500 Emerald Bay Rd., South Lake Tahoe, 530/577-0788, www.laketahoegc.com, daily sunrise–sunset spring–fall, 18 holes and cart $84) offers a full-service restaurant and bar, cart service on the course, a grass driving range, pros and a pro shop, and—the main selling point—gorgeous views, but the greens fees are higher. If you want to save a little money, go later for the "twilight" (from 2 P.M., $69) and "super twilight" (from 4 P.M., $39) prices for 18 holes and a cart. The course closes for the winter around November 1.

Spas

The welcoming and soothing **BioSpirit Day Spa** (1116 Ski Run Blvd., South Lake Tahoe, 530/541-5511, www.massagetahoe.com, 10 A.M.–2 P.M. Mon., 9 A.M.–6 P.M. Tues.–Sat.) is a stand-out in the area. With a full menu of massages, facials, waxing, and wrapping, and more, you're sure to find something to make you feel good. BioSpirit is the only place in the area that does eyelash tinting and extensions, and use of their eucalyptus steam room is included with any service. There are special facials just for men and teens; you can also get a discount on services if you schedule a Pamper Party for a small group of friends or if you book in advance. In addition to their regular hours, BioSpirit is usually open on Sunday holiday weekends. Fans of the defunct Shannon's Day Spa will be pleased to find that BioSpirit is of similar quality and welcomes former Shannon's clients.

If you want your nails done, head for **Tahoe Nail Spa** (2176 Lake Tahoe Blvd., Suite 7, South Lake Tahoe, 530/541-1230, $42). Be aware that it's tough to ferret out in the strip-mall complex

it's located in, but don't give up. The aestheticians at this small salon will give you great attention as they work on your feet and hands, clipping, buffing, and polishing to perfection.

ENTERTAINMENT AND EVENTS
Nightlife

The casinos over the Nevada border in Stateline are nearby, but the South Shore has its own entertainment. The **Brewery at Lake Tahoe** (3542 Lake Tahoe Blvd., South Lake Tahoe, 530/544-2739, www.brewerylaketahoe.com, daily 11 A.M.–close, $10–21) is a casual, comfortable bar with a menu of local microbrews, including the signature Bad Ass Ale and the popular Washoe Wheat Ale, as well as a selection of seasonal brews. The food includes pizza, pasta, salads, salmon, steaks, and barbecued ribs. The Brewery is across the street from the lake; the outdoor picnic tables are a great place to watch the scenery.

A happening place is **Whiskey Dick's Saloon** (2660 Lake Tahoe Blvd., South Lake Tahoe, 530/544-3425, daily 11 P.M.–2 A.M.), with a full bar that has about 70 varieties of beer and live bands several times a week. Cover charges range from free to $15, depending on the band. **Fat City** (2660 Lake Tahoe Blvd., South Lake Tahoe, 530/542-2780, www.fatcityfood.com, daily 11 A.M.–9 or 10 P.M., $8–22), shares the building, and you can order pizza, sandwiches, and wings to be delivered in the bar.

Festivals and Events

Each August, the Lake Tahoe Airport (TVL, 1901 Airport Rd., South Lake Tahoe) is the site of the annual **Lake in the Sky Air Show** (530/541-0480, www.lakeintheskyairshow.com), with aerobatic performers, a search-and-rescue aircraft demonstration, some vintage war birds and World War II fighter planes, a CALSTAR helicopter flight simulator, a 5K run, and a pancake breakfast. There's free bus transportation (8 A.M.–4 P.M.) from the transit station at the South Y shopping center. If you walk or take the bus, admission is $5 (free if you're under 12); if you drive to the airport for the show, the cost is $15 per vehicle.

If you enjoy costumes and want to dive into the living history of the early-20th-century wealth and privilege that surrounded Lake Tahoe, hit the **Great Gatsby Festival** (530/541-0332, www.tahoeheritage.org, 2nd weekend in Aug.) at the Tallac Historic Site. In the heat of summer each year, actors and volunteers dress in period attire and stroll the grounds of the estates as 1920s vacationers. The most popular event of this two-day festival is the Gatsby Tea ($35) on Sunday afternoon, a sumptuous high tea spiced up by entertainment that culminates in a vintage fashion show.

SHOPPING

You won't find a lot of high-fashion boutiques or glittering malls, but South Lake Tahoe is a good place to stock up on batteries and basic foodstuffs before heading out. Many of the region's small quaint towns don't have much in the way of practical services.

If you're in need of basic necessities, head to the **Factory Outlet Stores at the Y** (2014–2062 Lake Tahoe Blvd., at Hwy. 89 and U.S. 50, South Lake Tahoe). For athletic equipment and apparel, check out the **Great Outdoor Clothing Company** (2050 Lake Tahoe Blvd., South Lake Tahoe, 530/541-0664, www.greatoutdoorclothing.com, daily 10 A.M.–6 P.M.). For après-ski apparel for women, **Blue Willow** (2020 Lake Tahoe Blvd., South Lake Tahoe, 530/543-3436, daily 10 A.M.–6 P.M.) offers sexy lingerie.

You can rent or buy a wide array of winter equipment at **Powder House Ski & Snowboard** (main store 4045 Lake Tahoe Blvd., next to Heavenly Gondola, 530/542-6222; Marriot Hotel, 1001 Park Ave., Suite 20, Heavenly Village, 530/541-6422; www.tahoepowderhouse.com, 7 A.M.–10 P.M. daily), with seven locations in South Lake Tahoe.

At the upscale **Shops at Heavenly Village** (1001 Heavenly Village Way, www.theshopsatheavenly.com) you'll find a **Patagonia** (Unit 16, 530/542-3385, www.patagonia.com, 10 A.M.–7 P.M. Mon.–Thurs., 10 A.M.–8 P.M. Fri.–Sat.) and a **Great Outdoor Clothing Company** (Unit 22, 530/543-0682, www.greatoutdoorclothing.com, 10 A.M.–6 P.M. Mon.–Thurs., 10 A.M.–7 P.M. Fri.–Sat.). You'll pay a premium for equipment here, but the atmosphere is fun, and there are food and gift shops and other attractions all around, making shopping a sport in itself.

At Heavenly Mountain Village, there's a good-size **North Face** (4118 Lake Tahoe Blvd., 530/544-9062, www.skiheavenly.com, daily 8 A.M.–8 P.M.), where you can rent recreational gear as well as buy it. Whether you're planning to hit the slopes or just hang around looking cool, you may want to check out the selection of goggles and sunglasses available at **Heavenly Eyes** (4080 Lake Tahoe Blvd., 775/586-6116, www.skiheavenly.com, 9 A.M.–7 P.M. Mon.–Fri., 9 A.M.–8 P.M. Sat.–Sun. summer, 8 A.M.–7 P.M. Mon.–Fri., 8 A.M.–8 P.M. Sat.–Sun. winter).

ACCOMMODATIONS
Under $100

South Lake Tahoe has quite a few basic motels that offer a guest room for the night without breaking the bank. One of the nicer ones is the **Matterhorn Motel** (2187 Lake Tahoe Blvd., South Lake Tahoe, 530/541-0367, $49). The guest rooms are clean and adequate, with free Internet access, and there's a small outdoor pool. It's family-owned, and the proprietors are warm and helpful beyond expectations.

For inexpensive guest rooms year-round, check in to the **Ambassador Motor Lodge** (4130 Manzanita Ave., South Lake Tahoe, 530/544-6461, www.laketahoeambassadorlodge.com, $72–100, under age 16 free with adult). With its private beach access and associated water-recreation options, rates are a little higher in the summer months and bargain-basement in the winter. Guest rooms have a basic motel feel, but a few soft touches make them prettier than the average bargain chain. Amenities are reminiscent of most chain motels—coffee and coffeemaker, TV, private bath—and offer little in the way of extras. The good news for summer visitors is that the Ambassador is right on the lake; winter guests may be happy to know it's only a short walk to the Heavenly Gondola.

The **Apex Inn** (1171 Emerald Bay Rd., South Lake Tahoe, information 530/541-2940, reservations 800/755-8246, www.apexinntahoe. com, $49–60) offers the winning combination of a good location and rates almost on par with camping. There's a small outdoor hot tub, free Internet access, and breakfast is included.

Another reasonable option is the **High Country Lodge** (1227 Emerald Bay Rd., 530/541-0508, $65). The yellow standard-issue motel could use some paint, but the gardens and lawn are well-kept, and the new owners have plans for hot tubs and picnic tables, with the goal of becoming a choice family destination. The place is pet-friendly and conveniently located.

The **Pine Cone Acre Motel** (735 Emerald Bay Rd., South Lake Tahoe, 530/541-0375, www.pineconeacremotel.com, rooms $55–100, cabin $170–200) has a great location on Highway 89 (Emerald Bay Rd.), just north of where Highway 89 crosses U.S. 50—which means the motel is very close to the center of South Lake Tahoe, but it's also out of the traffic in the attractive rustic vicinity of Emerald Bay. Guest rooms have microwaves and fridges, and there is a pool and picnic tables on the grounds. Prices vary seasonally, but they're always reasonable.

$100-150

The small rustic **Lazy S Lodge** (609 Emerald Bay Rd., South Lake Tahoe, 530/541-0230 or 800/862-8881, www.lazyslodge.com, $94–140)

is in a great location away from the center of town and has some of the most reasonable room rates in the region. The 20 guest rooms all have microwaves, wet bars, TVs, telephones, and private baths. Choose from a studio room with a nice bed, bath, and bar or a two-room cabin with sleeping room for several people, a kitchenette, and a nice fireplace. Facilities include a year-round hot tub, a summer-only swimming pool, barbecue grills and outdoor picnic tables, and easy access to hiking and biking trails, swimming, and the Heavenly ski resort.

$150-250

Perhaps the most famous place to stay in the area is **⚫ Camp Richardson** (1900 Jameson Beach Rd., South Lake Tahoe, 530/541-1801 or 800/544-1801, www.camprichardson.com, year-round, $105–275). This full-spectrum resort is located a few miles north of South Lake Tahoe along the West Shore. Guest rooms and suites vary considerably in price, but all feature rustic furnishings smoothed out by the luxurious fabrics and appointments. Guest rooms in the refurbished 1920 hotel are comfortable and quaint, with private baths and upscale amenities. Individual cabins, which can only be rented weekly in summer, offer full kitchens and linens but no TVs or phones. Staying in the RV Village costs ($40–45). Accommodations include use of the beach, the lounge, a group recreation area, and the marina. On-site facilities include the excellent **Beacon Bar and Grill,** the **Mountain Sports Center,** a coffee and candy shop, a general store, and the southern edge of the Tallac Historic Site. Cross-country ski and snowshoes rentals are available in winter, and paddleboats in summer. The large comfortable lounge has Internet access and work tables, or you can rent a small DVD player and watch some movies. Oh, and there are bears: Somehow all this development has not interfered with the ambience of the surrounding nature.

The **Timber Cove Best Western** (3411 Lake Tahoe Blvd., 530/541-6722, www.timbercovetahoe.com or www.bestwestern.com, $110–300) has the advantage of being right on the lake. There are more than 200 guest rooms and a complicated pricing structure that varies with the week. One thing stays constant: You pay an extra $30 for a guest room with a partial view of the lake and a $60-per-night surcharge for a full lake view.

Over $250

Dedicated B&Bers will enjoy the hospitality of the ☾ **Black Bear Inn** (1202 Ski Run Blvd., South Lake Tahoe, 530/544-4451 or 877/232-7466, www.tahoeblackbear.com, $215–450). Located on the road to Heavenly, the exterior accents of this lovely large building feature lodgepole pine and river rock that blend right in with the surrounding nature. A giant fireplace dominates the great room, and smaller but equally cozy river-rock fireplaces are in each of the upstairs lodge guest rooms. Rooms feature king beds, plush private baths, free Internet access, and an energy-building full breakfast. Appointments throughout are luxurious, with cushy comforters and rustic-elegant furnishings. Be sure to take a few moments to stroll along the tree-lined paths and serene green lawns surrounding the inn. The Black Bear Inn has a fine restaurant, the **Restaurant at Black Bear Inn** (530/327-9339, 6–8 P.M. Wed.–Mon., $25–45), complete with a sommelier and specializing in local and organic cuisine.

Hard-core skiers should book guest rooms at the **Deerfield Lodge at Heavenly** (1200 Ski Run Blvd., 530/544-3337 or 888/757-3337, www.tahoedeerfieldlodge.com, $200–329). This resort drips luxury, from the whirlpool tubs in every slate-and-granite bath to the stone fireplaces in the spacious living areas of most guest rooms. Contemporary furniture and striking black-and-white linens complement the comfy beds, and TVs, DVD players, and

wireless Internet access help make you comfortable in every way. The lodge gives guests a tray on arrival that features breakfast breads from a local bakery, fruit, energy bars, apple cider, coffee, and tea. The popular après-ski happy hour takes place in the common area, providing drinks, snacks, and time for guests to socialize in the afternoon.

Cabin and Condo Rentals

South Lake Tahoe's Marriott Resort (1001 Heavenly Village Way) has about 60 condos available for rent through **Condos at Tahoe** (775/586-1587 or 888/666-0773, www.condosattahoe.com). All units here have full kitchens and provide easy access to the Heavenly Gondola. Studios run about $200, and three-bedroom units—which are huge and sleep up to 14 people—are around $700.

Spruce Grove Cabins (3599–3605 Spruce Ave., South Lake Tahoe, 530/544-0549 or 800/777-0914, www.sprucegrovetahoe.com, $159–205) offers a gay-friendly and dog-friendly Tahoe vacation experience. Since there are only seven cabins on the property, you're guaranteed peace and privacy throughout your stay. The 1–2-bedroom cabins all have full kitchens, dining rooms, and living rooms with pull-out sofas to accommodate extra guests. Each cabin has its own wilderness-based decoration theme, including Snowshoe, Steamboat, and Washoe Native American. As one of the closest resorts to the Heavenly ski resort (Ski Run Blvd.), Spruce Grove gets its heaviest traffic in the winter.

For homey cabin living on the West Shore, you can't beat **The Tahoma Lodge** (7018 W. Lake Blvd., Tahoma, 866/819-2226, www.tahomalodge.com, $170–240), a series of 11 distinctive cabins, including studios and 1–2-bedroom units. Each cabin has a modern kitchen, and there are picnic tables, barbecues, and a heated swimming pool outside to help you enjoy your stay in summer. The pool is open mid-June–September, and if you visit in winter for the ski season, you'll appreciate the fireplace in each unit and the year-round outdoor hot tub.

For a condo on the South Shore, head on over to **The Lodge at Lake Tahoe** (3840 Pioneer Trail, South Lake Tahoe, 530/541-6226 or 800/874-9900, www.lodgeatlaketahoe.com, $120–230). The guest rooms have the elegant look of proper vacation condos, with colorful furnishings and tasteful prints on the walls. The smallest studios have only kitchenettes, but the larger condos offer fully equipped kitchens with utensils provided as well as a nice table and chairs. Complex amenities include a summertime pool and spa, a swing set, a horseshoe pit, and outdoor barbecues near the pool area. Heavenly skiers will have easy access to the resort, and gamblers can get to the Stateline casinos in Nevada in a few minutes.

CAMPING

Camping at Lake Tahoe in the summer is so easy and gorgeous that you almost wonder why anyone would sleep indoors. June–August, the weather is usually perfect and the prices are reasonable, with campsites just minutes from mountain-bike trails or beaches.

The two great state parks of the South Shore both have gorgeous campgrounds. **Emerald Bay State Park** (Hwy. 89, north of South Lake Tahoe, 22 miles south of Tahoe City, 800/444-7275, www.reserveamerica.com, $35–45) has the 100-site Eagle Point Campground and a Boat-in Campground (July–Sept.) on the north side of the bay. Campsites include fire rings, and restrooms and showers are available in the park. ◖ **D. L. Bliss State Park** (Hwy. 89, 800/444-7275, www.parks.ca.gov, May–Sept., $35–45) has some of the best campsites around. There are 165 sites; beachfront campsites have a premium price of $45, and they're worth it, whether you just like to stand outside and gaze at the views or jump right into the water. All campsites have picnic tables, bear-proof food lockers, and grills. Hot showers,

© HEATHER C. LISTON

D. L. Bliss State Park is a great camping location.

LAKE TAHOE

flush toilets, and potable water are available in the park. **Camp Richardson Resort** (530/541-1801 or 800/544-1801, www.camprichardson.com, $35–45) offers sites for tents, campers, and RVs. Amenities include a beach, a group recreation area, and a marina. On-site facilities include the Beacon Bar and Grill and the Mountain Sports Center.

The U.S. Forest Service runs 206 sites at **Fallen Leaf Lake Campground** (Fallen Leaf Lake Rd., off Hwy. 89, 3 miles north of U.S. 50, 530/543-2600 or 877/444-6777, www.recreation.gov, mid-May–mid-Oct., $32–34). RVs up to 40 feet are welcome, although there are no hookups or dump stations. Each campsite has a barbecue grill, a picnic table, and a fire ring. And not only are there modern baths with flush toilets, some restrooms even have free showers. The campground is just 0.25 mile north of Fallen Leaf Lake, where you can swim at your own risk.

The **Tahoe Valley RV Resort** (1175 Melba Dr., South Lake Tahoe, 530/541-2222 or 877/570-2267, www.rvonthego.com, May–Sept. $35–65, weekly $205–325, Oct.–Apr. $30, weekly $175, monthly $670–1,325) has 413 sites that can accommodate everything from small tents to big-rig RVs with water, electric, and cable TV hookups. Tall pine trees give each site some shade and privacy. Amenities include tennis courts, a swimming pool, an ice cream parlor serving Tahoe Creamery products, activities for children and families, a dog run, and free wireless Internet access.

FOOD
Breakfast and Cafés

For a classic American breakfast, it's tough to do better than the **❰ Original Red Hut Café** (2723 Lake Tahoe Blvd., South Lake Tahoe, 530/541-9024, www.redhutcafe.com, daily 6 A.M.–2 P.M., $6–12). This down-home waffle spot serves classic crispy thin waffles (if you're looking for huge fat Belgian waffles, this isn't the place),

plus biscuits and gravy, omelets, and plenty more. Locals recommend the waffle sandwich, which is a complete breakfast in a single dish. Expect to wait for a table or a seat at the counter on weekend mornings, as this spot is very popular with visitors and locals. If you can't get in, try the **New Red Hut Café** (3660 Lake Tahoe Blvd., 530/544-1595, daily 6 A.M.–9 P.M.).

Rude Brothers Bagel & Coffee Haus (3117 Harrison Ave., Suite B, 530/541-8195) looks and feels just right for an indie coffee shop and sandwich bar. It has a big open room for hanging out, outstanding breakfast burritos, and plenty of lunch goodies. All the usual espresso drinks are available at the counter. Rude Brothers is in the same little shopping center as the also-excellent **Sprouts Café** (3123 Harrison Ave., South Lake Tahoe, 530/541-6969, daily 8 A.M.–9 P.M., $8–15).

One of the most pleasant spots for a light breakfast is **Camp Richardson's Coffee & Confectionery** (1900 James Beach Rd., South Lake Tahoe, 530/542-6555, daily 6:30 A.M.–close summer, 6:30 A.M.–close Sat.–Sun. and holidays fall–spring). This small friendly spot, right across Highway 89 from the main lodge at Camp Richardson, has been around since 2009, and it fills a need for good coffee, good pastries, and a no-hassle Internet connection outside of town.

If you're a loyalist who wants your **Starbucks** (4000 Lake Tahoe Blvd., 530/543-3391, www.starbucks.com, 5:30 A.M.–11 P.M. Sun.–Fri., 5:30 A.M.–midnight Sat.), vacation or not, you'll be reassured to know you can find it at Heavenly Village. There are two other Starbucks locations (1064 Emerald Bay Rd., 530/544-4490; Safeway, 1020 Johnson Dr., 530/542-7740).

Asian

The **Dragon Buffet** (2397 Lake Tahoe Blvd., South Lake Tahoe, 530/541-3888, 7–10:30 A.M., 11 A.M.–4 P.M., and 5–9 P.M. Mon.–Sat., 11 A.M.–9 P.M. Sun., $7–13) is located in a former Denny's, and it looks it. The all-you-can-eat steam tables full of Mongolian barbecue, sweet-and-sour everything, chicken, and pork go on forever. There's also sushi and soft-serve ice cream.

California

For a great combination of delicious healthy food and budget dining, check out **Sprouts Café** (3123 Harrison Ave., South Lake Tahoe, 530/541-6969, daily 8 A.M.–9 P.M., $8–15). This cute, casual walk-up eatery offers ultra-healthy dishes made with fresh, mostly organic ingredients. Despite the wheatgrass growing on the shelves and the giant juicer on the rear counter, Sprouts has plenty of items that appeal to less health-conscious diners. Breakfast is served all day, and the lunch and dinner menus run to several pages. Choose among salads, burritos, rice bowls, and tasty vegetarian and vegan desserts.

An unassuming local joint with great food and veggie options is **Freshies Restaurant & Bar** (3330 Lake Tahoe Blvd., Suite 3, South Lake Tahoe, 530/542-3630, www.freshiestahoe.com, daily 11:30 A.M.–9 P.M., $10–27). This small yet popular Hawaiian-themed restaurant has been voted the "Best Place for Dinner" and "Best Place for Lunch" by the *Tahoe Daily Tribune*. The main dining room is accessed through a mall, but the best way to experience Freshies is to go to the side entrance and add your name to the list for a rooftop table, where you can see the lake.

Boasting a *Wine Spectator* Award of Excellence and a creative California cuisine menu that includes wild boar chops, Asian chicken mandarin orange stir-fry, and summer *ragu* bolognese, **Nepheles** (1169 Ski Run Blvd., South Lake Tahoe, 530/544-8130, www.nepheles.com, daily by reservation, $25–35) is the perfect place for a romantic dinner or a celebration of any kind.

One of the great restaurants in town is the **Tahoe Grille** (2543 Lake Tahoe Blvd., South

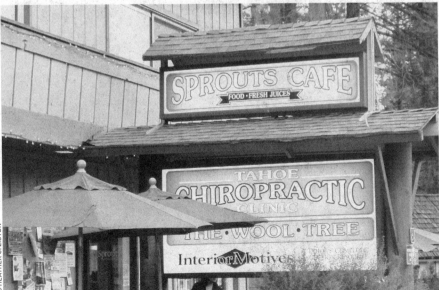

© HEATHER C. LISTON

Sprouts Café offers healthy food.

Lake Tahoe, 530/544-0400, www.tahoegrille. com, 5–9 P.M. Sun.–Thurs., 5–10 P.M. Fri.–Sat., $10–32). The menu is heavy on steak, but there's plenty of variety. Diners applaud the Tahoe Grille's food, wine, service, and ambience; there's nothing not to like.

Italian

If the crowds at Heavenly have you longing for a more intimate evening, book one of the seven tables at **Café Fiore** (1169 Ski Run Blvd., Suite 5, South Lake Tahoe, 530/541-2908, www. cafefiore.com, daily 5:30 P.M.–close, $18–35). This tiny bistro serves upscale Italian fare with a fabulous wine list. The exterior charms with its alpine-chalet look, while the interior is the definition of a romantic restaurant. Located on Ski Run Boulevard, Café Fiore is convenient to both the Heavenly ski resort and the lakeshore resorts of South Lake Tahoe.

For delicious, dependable Italian food at family-friendly prices, **Passaretti's** (1181 Emerald Bay Rd., South Lake Tahoe, 530/541-3433, www.passarettis.com, 11 A.M.–9 P.M. Sun.–Thurs., 11 A.M.–9:30 P.M. Fri.–Sat., $13–20) is a good bet. Extensive choices include hand-tossed pasta in a fresh homemade sauce, a children's menu, and daily lunch specials ($8). The back dining room seats 40, but if you're bringing a bus or a party, they'd appreciate a call first.

If you're hungry and approaching South Lake Tahoe from the west, you can get a decent pizza next door to the visitors center in Meyers at **Bob Dog Pizza** (3141 U.S. 50, Suite C2, Meyers, 530/577-2364, www.bobdogpizza. com, daily 10 A.M.–9 P.M., $7–20).

Seafood

Serious sushi aficionados might be concerned about eating raw ocean fish so far from the Pacific, but **Off the Hook** (2660 Lake Tahoe

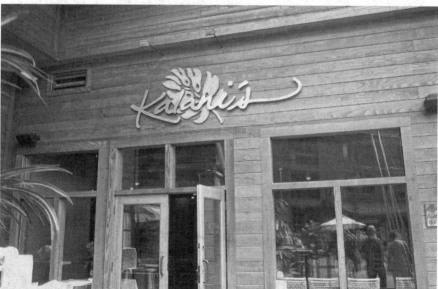

© HEATHER C. LISTON

Kalani's serves Pacific Rim fusion cuisine.

Blvd., Suite E., 530/544-5599, www.offthe-hooksushi.com, daily 5–10 P.M. fall–spring, daily 11:30 A.M.–2:30 P.M. and 5–10 P.M. summer, $13–23) offers good rolls and fresh *nigiri* for reasonable prices. Don't expect too much of some of the traditional Japanese dishes and you'll have an enjoyable dining experience.

For an all-around fine dining experience and some of the best fish ever, try **Kalani's** (1001 Heavenly Village Way, Suite 26, South Lake Tahoe, 530/544-6100, www.kalanis.com, daily 11:30 A.M.–close, $27–39). Serving Pacific Rim fusion cuisine, Kalani's offers subtly spiced salmon, mahimahi, sushi, barbecued ribs, and house specialties like the *kalua* smoked pork quesadilla and Portuguese bean soup. The sushi bar is open all day, as is Kalani's Puka Lounge, which serves wine, sake, and cocktails. Off the Hook is located in the Shops at Heavenly Village complex.

Good fish, good views, and entertainment too: That would be **Fresh Ketch** (2435 Venice Dr., South Lake Tahoe, 530/541-5683, www.thefreshketch.com, daily 5:30 P.M.–close, $13–37), located in the Tahoe Keys. Prices are reasonable, from fish tacos ($13) to halibut stuffed with a mash of shrimp, lobster, scallops, brie, dill, mascarpone, and chives ($37). The salads, sandwiches, and other light fare are good too, so you don't have to save this place for a fancy-dinner night. The Seafood Bar and Lounge is open for lunch (11:30 A.M.–close Mon.–Sat., 11 A.M.–close Sun.). Check the website for details on live music evenings (Tues. and Thurs.–Sat.).

One of the area's best restaurants, the **C Beacon Bar & Grill** (1900 Jameson Beach Rd., South Lake Tahoe, 530/541-0630, www.camprichardson.com, daily lunch, brunch, and dinner, $25–40) is located inside Camp Richardson, a just a few miles north of South Lake Tahoe on Highway 89. If you're driving Highway 89 from the north, look for the entrance on the left, seven miles south of Emerald Bay State Park. In addition to excellent food (filet mignon, fresh seafood, and a great spinach salad), the Beacon offers a beachfront patio and live music (Wed.–Sun. summer, Fri.–Sat. winter).

INFORMATION AND SERVICES

The best reason to stop in Meyers, seven miles south of South Lake Tahoe, is the **Meyers Interagency Visitors Center** (3071 Lake Tahoe Blvd, Meyers, 530/573-1804, www.tahoesouth.com, daily 9 A.M.–4 P.M.). This is a great first stop to answer any questions about the region.

The Lake Tahoe Visitors Authority (LTVA) maintains the spacious, welcoming, and well-staffed **LTVA Visitors Center** (3066 Lake Tahoe Blvd., South Lake Tahoe, 530/544-5050, www.tahoesouth.com, daily 9 A.M.–5 P.M.), across from the *Tahoe Daily Tribune* office.

Right next to the visitors center is the **Lake Tahoe Historical Society Museum** (3058 Lake Tahoe Blvd., South Lake Tahoe, 530/541-5458, www.laketahoemuseum.org, 11 A.M.–3 P.M. Wed.–Mon. Memorial Day–Labor Day, 11 A.M.–3 P.M. Sat. Labor Day–Memorial Day, donation).

The Lake Tahoe region has its own daily newspaper, the *Tahoe Daily Tribune* (530/541-3880, www.tahoedailytribune.com). Pick up a copy at any newsstand, or ask for it at your hotel.

South Lake Tahoe has two post offices (950 Emerald Bay Rd., 530/541-4365, 9 A.M.–5 P.M. Mon.–Fri.; 1046 Al Tahoe Blvd., 530/544-5867, 8:30 A.M.–5 P.M. Mon.–Fri., noon–2 P.M. Sat.).

For medical attention off-slope, go to **Barton Memorial Hospital** (2170 South Ave., South Lake Tahoe, 530/541-3420, www.barton-health.org) or the **Tahoe Urgent Care Center** (2130 Lake Tahoe Blvd., South Lake Tahoe, 530/541-3277, daily 8 A.M.–6 P.M.). A local drugstore is **Rite Aid** (1020 Al Tahoe Blvd., South Lake Tahoe, 530/541-2530).

GETTING THERE AND AROUND
Air

South Lake Tahoe has its own airport (1901 Airport Rd., www.laketahoeairport.com), but it has no commercial flights. So if you don't have a private plane, the nearest commercial airport is the **Reno-Tahoe International Airport** (RNO, 2001 E. Plumb Lane, Reno, NV, 775/328-6400, www.renoairport.com) or the **Sacramento International Airport** (SMF, 6900 Airport Blvd., Sacramento, 916/929-5411, www.sacramento.aero).

Bus and Train

Amtrak's *Capital Corridor* (877/974-3322, www.amtrak.com, $34 one-way) will take you to South Lake Tahoe from Sacramento by bus in about two hours and 20 minutes. From San Francisco, you must take a bus to Emeryville, then a train to Sacramento, and then a bus to South Lake Tahoe ($50 one-way). The bus will drop you off at one of two locations in South Lake Tahoe: the Y (1000 Lake Tahoe Blvd.), or the Stateline Transit Center (4114 Lake Tahoe Blvd.).

Car

U.S. 50 provides the quickest access to South Lake Tahoe. From the San Francisco Bay Area, the drive takes about five hours in good weather without traffic; from Sacramento it's only about two hours. However, don't expect good weather or light traffic if you plan to drive to Tahoe on a Friday in winter. Everybody else will be on the road with you, significantly slowing down the routes. Be sure to check traffic reports before you hit the road.

In winter, carry tire chains that fit your vehicle (unless you have a 4WD vehicle and you know how to navigate in snow). Chains are often required near and around Tahoe in winter, and there are many spots on I-80 and U.S. 50 where you can pull off the road to attach your chains. You can also buy chains on the road, but the closer you get to Tahoe, the more expensive they are.

In winter, highways can close during major storms, and smaller roads surrounding the lake can shut down for weeks at a time. Traffic reports both on the radio and online offer information about road closures and alternate routes. If you're planning a winter trip, be aware of the weather and plan for some uncertainty.

CAR RENTALS

Avis-Budget (4130 Lake Tahoe Blvd., South Lake Tahoe, 530/544-5289, www.avis.com, 8 A.M.–5 P.M. Mon.–Fri., 8 A.M.–3 P.M. Sat.–Sun.) is next door to the Stateline Transit Center bus station. You can also try **Enterprise** (2281 Lake Tahoe Blvd., 530/544-8844, www.enterprise.com, 8 A.M.–5 P.M. Mon.–Fri., 9 A.M.–1 P.M. Sat.), which has a full range of cars and small–midsize SUVs.

Public Transportation

In the South Lake Tahoe area, local public transportation is provided by **BlueGO** (530/541-7149, www.bluego.org, adults $2), which runs buses, trolleys, and ski shuttles. The cheerful-looking trolley (daily July–Labor Day, Sat.–Sun. June and Sept.) can help you get around the South Shore without driving. Routes and schedules vary, so consult the website for details.

Ski Resort Shuttles

Parking at the ski resorts, especially on weekends, can be a serious hassle. A much better option is a ski-resort shuttle. Most of the major ski resorts maintain shuttles that bring skiers and their equipment up to the mountains in the morning and back down to their hotels in the late afternoon. Look for seasonal brochures in major hotels and resorts or check online for the shuttles for Heavenly (www.skiheavenly.com) and Kirkwood (www.kirkwood.com), among others.

Tours and Cruises

If exploring on your own isn't enough, take one of any number of cruises and tours offered all around Lake Tahoe. To get out on the water in a big boat, book a cruise with

Lake Tahoe Cruises (800/238-2463, www. laketahoecruises.com or www.zephyrcove. com). Two honest-to-goodness paddle-wheel riverboats cruise Lake Tahoe on a near-daily basis—even in winter. The first boat, *Tahoe Queen,* sails from Ski Run Marina (900 Ski Run Blvd., South Lake Tahoe, 530/543-6191) and offers a 2.5-hour sightseeing cruise (adults $39, children $15) around Emerald Bay, complete with a "captain" character narrating stories about the lake's history and folklore. This is a beautiful way to see the lake, with photo opportunities that never end. If you really want to luxuriate, try the *Tahoe Queen's* sunset cruise (daily 7 P.M., adults $75, children $41), which lasts three hours. It includes a gourmet dinner onboard followed by dancing to live music.

The other boat is the **MS Dixie II**, a rear paddle wheeler that was imported from the Mississippi River. It sails from the Zephyr Cove Marina (750 U.S. 50, Zephyr Cove, NV, 775/589-4901, www.zephyrcove.com) and offers a two-hour morning or afternoon cruise (adults $39, ages 3–11 $15). If you're lucky, Mark Twain may even be your narrator. On Sunday, the *MS Dixie II* offers a special bargain: Take the brunch cruise (10:30 A.M.–12:30 P.M. Sun., adults $39, ages 3–11 $15) and enjoy an onboard buffet for the same price as the regular cruise. The Captain's Dinner Dance (adults $65, children $35) includes an on-board narrator, a live band, and a four-course meal. Like most things in Tahoe, weather can affect the cruise schedules, so be sure to check in advance.

A company that can take you to see the lovely Emerald Bay is **Bleu Wave** (866/413-0985, www.tahoebleuwave.com, adults $49–59, children $26–30), which operates from the Round Hill Pine Beach & Marina (325 U.S. 50, Zephyr Cove, NV, 775/588-3055, www.

LAKE TAHOE

© HEATHER C. LISTON

MS Dixie II

LAKE TAHOE

NATIONAL FORESTS AND WILDERNESS AREAS

What is a national forest? The U.S. Forest Service, a division of the U.S. Department of Agriculture, manages 155 national forests and 20 national grasslands in 44 states plus Puerto Rico and the Virgin Islands. Altogether, they account for 193 million acres, or about 9 percent of the total land of the United States. Usage rules vary by forest but are often less stringent than the rules for national parks and national monuments. For example, it is often OK to bring your pet, to hunt, and to gather firewood. It's also common for national forests, which tend to be large and sprawling, to contain within their borders national and state parks, recreation areas, and even towns that include private homes and businesses.

Lake Tahoe is surrounded by a network of national forests that abut one another. Directly to the north, south, and east of the lake is the **Humboldt-Toiyabe National Forest,** the largest national forest in the continental United States. Located mostly in Nevada, this 6.3-million acre preserve spills over into eastern California near Lake Tahoe, extending as far north as Loyalton and Sierraville, and down the eastern border of California through the Sierra to Mono Lake. To the west of Lake Tahoe is the **Eldorado National Forest,** which encompasses much of the Desolation Wilderness; to the northwest is the **Tahoe National Forest.** A little farther north, beyond the Tahoe and Toiyabe forests, is the **Plumas National Forest.** This large wilderness area eventually connects with the Lassen National Forest to the north.

For more information on the U.S. Forest Service and its activities, visit www.fs.fed.us. To explore specific activities, make reservations, or apply for permits, visit www.recreation.gov.

rhpbeach.com). You'll see many popular sights on the lake during this two-hour lunch cruise with an all-you-can-eat buffet, drinks included. For winter cruises, enjoy the on-board fireplace and spacious heated cabin.

ELDORADO NATIONAL FOREST

West of Tahoe, below the Tahoe National Forest, is a vast area called the Eldorado National Forest. This varied, mixed-use forest of about 600,000 acres is located in the Central Sierra Nevada, with elevations ranging 1,000–10,000 feet. The American and Rubicon Rivers run through the forest and there are many beautiful lakes, abundant hiking and cycling trails, and even one of the nation's most popular off-highway vehicle trails. The nearest town is Placerville, where the forest supervisor's office, the U.S. Forest Service (100 Forni Rd., 530/622-5061 or 530/655-6048 for general forest information, www.fs.usda.gov/eldorado), is located.

Desolation Wilderness

The eerily named Desolation Wilderness is second only to Death Valley for evoking images of darkness and intrigue in a vacation spot. This 63,960-acre subset of the Eldorado National Forest and the Lake Tahoe Basin Management Unit is every bit as beautiful, and as worthy of exploration, as the rest of Tahoe's surroundings. The Desolation is 99 square miles, with 108 miles of streams, 125 alpine lakes, and 123 miles of trails, including segments of the Tahoe Rim Trail and the Pacific Crest Trail.

Before venturing into the Desolation Wilderness, it's best to stop at the **Taylor Creek Visitors Center** (Hwy. 89, three miles north of South Lake Tahoe, 530/543-2674, www.fs.usda.gov, hours vary, Memorial Day–Oct.). Operated by the U.S. Forest Service, this modern visitors center has nature programs, interpretive hikes, and a nice big gift shop. Smokey the Bear sometimes appears live, and a number of programs are designed just for kids. This is also the place to get wilderness and campfire permits and up-to-date information on conditions in the Desolation. Permits are required year-round for day hikers as well as for backpackers. Memorial Day–Labor Day, there's a quota on how many permits are issued. Half the permits available on any given day are reserved for walk-in customers on a first-come, first-served basis at the permit office (8 A.M.–5:30 P.M. daily Memorial Day–Labor Day). You can also reserve a permit (877/444-6777, www.recreation.gov, $6) before you arrive.

Backcountry camping in the Desolation Wilderness requires a permit ($5 pp per night, ages 12 and under free) for the first two nights, and free thereafter up to 14 nights. It costs $5 to park your vehicle at Eagle Falls or Pyramid Creek while you're in the Desolation. For backcountry information, call 530/543-2736 summer or 530/543-2694 winter; for reservations call 877/444-6777. You are not required to have a bear canister for your food in the Desolation Wilderness. If you want to use one, you can borrow one free of charge at the visitors center. (Canisters are often the easiest way to protect your provisions from animals, but in the Desolation you're still allowed to hang your food up in trees. Just bring adequate ropes to secure your food at least 12 feet off the ground, 10 feet out from the trunk, and 5 feet below the level of any branch.) Some things you need to bring include a water filter and a GPS unit.

Loon Lake

One of the most popular and beautiful places to visit in the Eldorado National Forest is the 76,000-acre Loon Lake, a reservoir created in 1963 with the damming of Gerle Creek. The lake gives every appearance of being a fully natural part of the landscape, and it's a delightful place to camp, swim, sail, or kayak.

© GEORGE JEN

beautiful Loon Lake

LAKE TAHOE

To get here, take U.S. 50 to the Eldorado National Forest, west of Tahoe. About 23 miles east of Placerville, turn north on Forest Road 3 (Ice House Rd.). Travel about 30 miles along this winding but wide and well-paved road to Loon Lake.

Sports and Recreation
HIKING
Hikers can access many trails within the Desolation Wilderness and in the broader Eldorado National Forest, which has more than 350 miles of trails. One stimulating hike follows the **Loon Lake Trail** (14 miles, moderate) in the Pacific Ranger District of Eldorado all the way to Rockbound Lake in the Desolation. From the trailhead in Loon Lake Campground, walk alongside Loon Lake for a while, enjoying views of the sailboats out on the peaceful blue water. The trail then weaves in and out of the woods past small lakes tucked among the trees, and then back out to wide granite slabs from which you can look down on the larger valleys and bodies of water below. You'll pass Buck Island Lake and arrive at Rockbound Lake in about seven miles. A large flat overlook at Rockbound Lake is a great place for lunch before you turn around and head back. Although this hike is long, it does not have any major climbs, hence the moderate rating. You'll gain and lose a total of 800–1,000 feet of elevation each way along rolling terrain. Since this is an out-and-back hike, you can cut it short by turning around at any point along the way.

One of the most popular hikes in the Desolation is **Twin Lakes Trail** (7 miles round-trip, 1,200 feet elevation gain, moderate). The trailhead at Wright's Lake is marked with a sign and has its own parking lot. After heading up this trail for three miles, you'll reach Twin Lakes, a nice place to stop and have lunch. An even better idea is to continue another 0.5 mile to Island Lake instead. This scenic pool, beautiful in any season, is at 8,200 feet, so it often has a little snow in spring and fall. When hiking in the Desolation, you must have a wilderness pass; there is a self-registration box at the Twin Lakes trailhead.

A shorter and easier, but still scenic, trail on the border between the Tahoe and Eldorado National Forests is the **Hell Hole Trail** (4.3 miles, easy–moderate). The trail runs along the reservoir and then the Rubicon River, ending at Upper Hell Hole Campground. The total elevation gain is only 200 feet, making this a fairly easy hike in spite of the rocky terrain. To reach the trailhead at Hell Hole Dam, take Wentworth Springs Road 15 miles east of Georgetown and turn north onto Eleven Pines Road. From here, it's another 45 miles to Hell Hole Dam.

BIKING
The Eldorado National Forest is an excellent place to bring your road or mountain bike—as long as you stay out of the Desolation and Mokelumne Wilderness Areas, which do not allow bicycles. One great trail is the **Union Valley Bike Trail** (11.6 miles, easy), which runs between Jones Fork Campground and Tells Creek. This paved two-lane bikeway runs past great forest scenery without demanding extraordinary effort. To get here, take U.S. 50 east of Placerville for 23 miles, and make a left onto Ice House Road (Forest Rd. 3). Travel another 14 miles and park at Jones Fork Campground.

Another good ride is the **Ice House Bike Trail** (4 miles, easy–moderate), which connects Ice House Campground to Strawberry Campground. This trail is shorter than the Union Valley Bike Trail, but it's a little rougher and is unpaved, with some steep sections. To get to the trailhead, take U.S. 50 east of Placerville for 23 miles, and turn north onto Ice House Road (Forest Rd. 3). Drive 11 miles, and then turn east onto Wrights Lake Tie Road

(Forest Rd. 32). Go another two miles east to Ice House Reservoir.

Accommodations

The privately owned **Ice House Resort** (9199 Ice House Rd./Forest Rd. 3, Pollock Pines, 23 miles east of Placerville, 15 miles north of U.S. 50, 530/293-3221, late Apr.–Oct., $88–98) can set you up in one of five simple motel rooms. Guest rooms do not have TVs or phones; the resort generates its own electricity so its use is pretty controlled. You can also park your RV at the resort ($45) or set up a tent in the Silver Creek campground ($20). The "resort" complex includes a small grocery store (9 A.M.–8 P.M. Mon.–Fri., 7 A.M.–9 P.M. Sat.–Sun.), a restaurant (7 A.M.–9 P.M. Thurs.–Mon. Apr.–Oct.), a bar (3–9 P.M. Mon. and Thurs.–Fri., 10 A.M.–close Sat.–Sun.), and a gas station. There's no Internet service at the resort, although AT&T and Verizon provide pretty good cell signals.

Camping

More than 60 campgrounds dot the Eldorado National Forest. One of the most attractive is the ◖ **Loon Lake Campground** (Ice House Rd./Forest Rd. 3, 23 miles east of Placerville, 15 miles north of U.S. 50, 877/444-6777, www.recreation.gov, mid-June–Sept., $22). The campground is very close to the beautiful lake itself, where you can swim, sail, kayak, and cool off. It's also near some hiking trails that lead to other lakes, mountains, granite cliffs, and all manner of natural wonders. Loon Lake has 53 campsites, vault toilets, tables, fire rings, and drinking water, but it does not have showers.

The only showers near Loon Lake and Ice House Road are in the **Fashoda Campground** (Ice House Rd./Forest Rd. 3, 23 miles east of Placerville, 16 miles north of U.S. 50, 877/444-6777, www.recreation.gov, Memorial Day–Labor Day, $22). Fashoda, together with its sister campground, **Sunset** ($22), is the largest in the area. The

campgrounds have a total of 161 sites as well as water, picnic tables, and vault toilets. One thing they don't have is bear lockers, so if you plan to stay, make sure to bring a bear canister. Fashoda is a walk-in campground; leave your car in the nearby parking lot and carry your gear to your site. The Sunset Campground does have drive-in access and a parking spot beside each site.

If you prefer a little more solitude to the comforts of a picnic table, a bear locker, and a nearby restroom, you can camp in the **Eldorado National Forest** (530/644-6048, www.fs.usda.gov/eldorado) outside of the designated campgrounds. Pick up a free California campfire permit from any ranger station, Bureau of Land Management office, or CAL FIRE office. Campfire permits are valid for a full calendar year. You will not need a wilderness permit unless you're planning to venture into one of the two designated wilderness areas within the forest (Desolation or Mokelumne).

Food

The nearest town with many food options is Placerville, but you can also pick up essentials in the smaller but closer town of Pollock Pines. For a casual meal in the forest, go to the **Ice House Resort** (9199 Ice House Rd./Forest Rd. 3, Pollock Pines, 23 miles east of Placerville, 15 miles north of U.S. 50, 530/293-3221). The privately owned ramshackle complex of amenities here includes a restaurant (7 A.M.–9 P.M. Thurs.–Mon. Apr.–Oct., $10–25) and a bar (3–9 P.M. Mon. and Thurs.–Fri., 10 A.M.–close Sat.–Sun.) that serves some finger food. The place is particularly popular with off-highway vehicle (OHV) riders and hunters, so it can get a little rowdy, but the food is hot and decent. A small grocery store (9 A.M.–8 P.M. Mon.–Fri., 7 A.M.–9 P.M. Sat.–Sun.) can also help supplement your food supplies—just don't expect a wide selection or much food that isn't in boxes and cans.

Getting There and Around

The closest commercial airport to the Desolation Wilderness is the **Reno-Tahoe International Airport** (RNO, 2001 E. Plumb Lane, Reno, NV, 775/328-6400, www.renoairport.com); somewhat farther is the **Sacramento International Airport** (SMF, 6900 Airport Blvd., Sacramento, 916/929-5411, www.sacramento.aero).

To reach the Eldorado National Forest, including the Desolation Wilderness, from Sacramento or San Francisco, travel east on U.S. 50. About 23 miles past Placerville, right after the small town of Pollock Pines, turn left (north) onto Forest Road 3 (Ice House Rd.). Ice House Road is surprisingly well maintained for a forest road; you'll find it wide, smooth, and well-marked with signage for trails, campgrounds, and turnoffs, making it easy to get around in this large forest. Coming from Tahoe, travel west on U.S. 50 and make a right turn onto Ice House Road. Traffic to and from the Tahoe area can be very heavy both in summer and winter, especially around the holidays.

North and West Shores

The North and West Shores are often considered the most desirable areas of Lake Tahoe, filled with ski resorts, beachfront property, and tall pines. One of the larger towns on the West Shore is Tahoe City, a lively happening place with good restaurants, bars, and entertainment and a sparkling waterfront. The smaller communities of Lake Forest, Sunnyside, Tahoe Pines, Homewood, and Tahoma are close by and easy to access.

SIGHTS
Ed Z'berg Sugar Pine Point State Park

The Tahoe area has more than its share of outstanding state parks, and Ed Z'berg Sugar Pine Point State Park (Hwy. 89, Tahoma, 530/525-7982, www.parks.ca.gov, year-round, day use $8) is one of the greats. Located on the West Shore, north of Emerald Bay and a few miles south of the town of Homewood, the park features tours of the historic Ehrman Mansion, ski trails from the 1960 Winter Olympics, and great camping, among other attractions.

The park is split into two sections. Sugar Pine Point includes the General Creek Campground, the Ehrman Mansion, and the visitors center and gift shop. The smaller Edwin L. Z'berg Natural Preserve features the Sugar Pine Point Lighthouse. You can camp in both sections for just the day-use fee. Note that if you can't find "Sugar Pine Point" on the state park website, try a search for "Ed Z'berg."

Ehrman Mansion

A fine example of a former home of the wealthy turned tourist attraction, the Ehrman Mansion (Hwy. 89, 1 mile south of Tahoma, 530/525-7232, www.parks.ca.gov) is located within the day-use area of Sugar Pine Point State Park. This beautifully preserved 12,000-square foot house was built in 1903 and is now owned by the State of California. You can take a tour (on the hour daily 10 A.M.–3 P.M. Memorial Day–Labor Day; noon, 1 P.M., and 2 P.M. Mon.–Fri., on the hour Sat.–Sun. Sept., adults $8, ages 6–17 $5, under age 6 free).

Tahoe Maritime Museum

The Tahoe Maritime Museum (5205 W. Lake Blvd., Homewood, 530/525-9253, www.tahoemaritimemuseum.org, 10 A.M.–5 P.M. Thurs.–Tues. Memorial Day–Sept., 10 A.M.–5 P.M. Fri.–Sun. Oct.–Memorial Day, adults $5, under age 13 free) seeks to illuminate the significant marine history of Lake Tahoe. Located

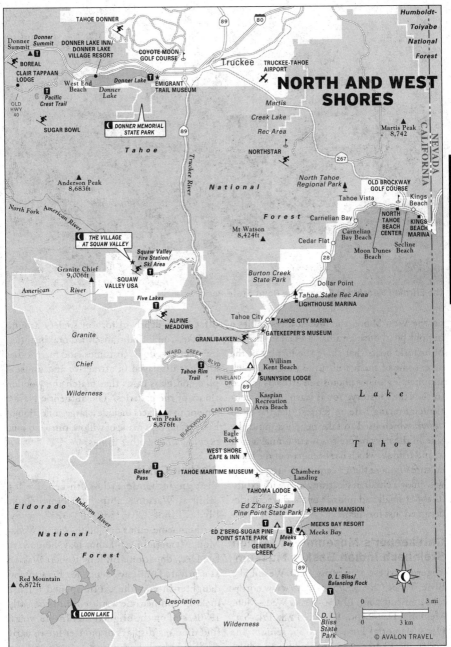

NORTH AND WEST SHORES

LAKE TAHOE

Humboldt-Toiyabe National Forest

Tahoe Donner

Donner Summit

Donner Summit

DONNER LAKE INN/ DONNER LAKE VILLAGE RESORT

BOREAL

CLAIR TAPPAAN LODGE

West End Beach

Pacific Crest Trail

OLD HWY 40

SUGAR BOWL

COYOTE MOON GOLF COURSE

Truckee

TRUCKEE-TAHOE AIRPORT

Donner Lake

Donner Lake

EMIGRANT TRAIL MUSEUM

DONNER MEMORIAL STATE PARK

Martis

Creek Lake

Rec Area

NORTHSTAR

Martis Peak 8,742

NEVADA CALIFORNIA

Tahoe

Anderson Peak 8,683ft

North Fork American River

Truckee River

National

Mt Watson 8,424ft

North Tahoe Regional Park

OLD BROCKWAY GOLF COURSE

Tahoe Vista

Forest

Carnelian Bay

Cedar Flat

Kings Beach

NORTH TAHOE BEACH CENTER

KINGS BEACH MARINA

Carnelian Bay Beach

Moon Dunes Beach

Secline Beach

THE VILLAGE AT SQUAW VALLEY

Granite Chief 9,006ft

Squaw Valley Fire Station/ Ski Area

SQUAW VALLEY USA

American River

Five Lakes

ALPINE MEADOWS

Granite

Chief

Wilderness

Tahoe Rim Trail

WARD CREEK BLVD

PINELAND DR

GRANLIBAKKEN

Tahoe City

TAHOE CITY MARINA

GATEKEEPER'S MUSEUM

Burton Creek State Park

Dollar Point

Tahoe State Rec Area

LIGHTHOUSE MARINA

28

Lake

William Kent Beach

SUNNYSIDE LODGE

89

Kaspian Recreation Area Beach

Tahoe

Twin Peaks 8,876ft

BLACKWOOD CANYON RD

Eagle Rock

WEST SHORE CAFE & INN

Barker Pass

TAHOE MARITIME MUSEUM

Chambers Landing

TAHOMA LODGE

Ed Z'berg-Sugar Pine Point State Park

EHRMAN MANSION

Eldorado

Rubicon River

National

ED Z'BERG-SUGAR PINE POINT STATE PARK

GENERAL CREEK

Meeks Bay

MEEKS BAY RESORT

Meeks Bay

Forest

Red Mountain 6,872ft

89

D. L. Bliss/ Balancing Rock

LOON LAKE

Desolation

Wilderness

D. L. Bliss State Park

0   3 mi

0   3 km

© AVALON TRAVEL

the Ehrman Mansion in Sugar Pine Point State Park

© HEATHER C. LISTON

on the West Shore, the museum resembles a big old boathouse and has a great collection of historic boats that share the history of the lake; some of them still run on the lake each summer. It also has photos and artifacts related to the lake's history. You'll learn about "gentlemen's racing"; steam ferries, like the 1896 *Tahoe,* which used to take people around the lake in the days before roads circumnavigated it; and fishing, which has been part of the lake's culture for more than a century. Young visitors will enjoy a children's learning area with exhibits about small and midsize boats and activities designed just for them.

Gatekeeper's Museum and Marion Steinbach Indian Basket Museum

Together, these museums (130 West Lake Blvd., Tahoe City, 530/583-1762, www.north-tahoemuseums.org, 10 A.M.–5 P.M. Wed.–Mon. Memorial Day–Sept., 11 A.M.–5 P.M. Fri.–Sat. Oct.–Memorial Day, adults $5, seniors $4, under age 13 free accompanied by an adult)

offer an in-depth history of society around the lake. You'll find transcribed oral histories, photographs, dolls, costumes, and many other artifacts displayed in attractive and unusual pine-and-glass cases that match the wooden floors of the galleries. The authentic Native American artifacts include a large collection of baskets and caps made of willow, tule, and pine needles, among other things.

Watson Cabin

Visit an authentic early-20th-century log cabin at Watson Cabin (560 North Lake Blvd., Tahoe City, 530/583-8717, www.northtahoemuseums.org, noon–4 P.M. Wed.–Mon. Memorial Day–Labor Day, hours vary late Dec., donation). Built by Robert Watson as a private family residence for his son and daughter-in-law, the cabin opened for use in 1909 and became a museum in the early 1970s, still on the original site. Inside, you'll find diorama displays of pioneer life in early modern Lake Tahoe.

◖ The Village at Squaw Valley

You might think of the Village at Squaw Valley (1750 Village East Rd., Olympic Valley, 530/584-1000, www.thevillageatsquaw.com) as a ski area, but it's actually a small upscale town designed to mimic a European Alpine village. There's no need to hit the slopes to enjoy what the village has to offer. Spend hours rambling around the colorfully painted clusters of buildings or strolling the cute exclusive boutiques and galleries. Souvenir seekers can go straight to **Squaw One Logo Company** (530/452-6250, www.squaw.com, daily 10 A.M.–6 P.M.). Those craving more outdoor gear and clothing can stop in at **North Face** (530/452-4365, www.northface.com, daily 10 A.M.–6 P.M.) or **Marmot** (530/584-6253, www.marmot.com, daily 10 A.M.–6 P.M.). For something local, visit the aromatic **Lather & Fizz Bath Boutique** (530/584-6001, www.latherandfizz.com, daily 10 A.M.–6 P.M.) for soaps, lotions, and face products made in nearby Truckee as well as luxurious signature pajamas, among other great gifts.

More than half a dozen restaurants, snack bars, and coffee shops offer sushi, pizza, high-end wine, and more. Entertainment options include skiing and ice skating in the winter, hiking in summer, and the **Cable Car** (hours vary, daily winter and summer, Sat.–Sun. spring and fall, adults $29, youth and seniors $22, under age 13 $10) up to **High Camp** (1960 Squaw Valley Rd., Olympic Valley, 530/584-1000, www.squaw.com) at 8,200 feet elevation. At High Camp, you can play tennis or paintball, roller-skate, soak in a hot tub, browse the **Olympic Museum** (www.squaw.com/olympic-museum, free with cable car ride), or just stand outside and enjoy the tremendous views. In summer there's often live music at the base of the mountain; various other special events offer year-round fun for adults and kids.

SPORTS AND RECREATION
Ski Resorts
SQUAW VALLEY

Squaw Valley (1960 Squaw Valley Rd., Olympic Valley, 530/583-6985, www.squaw.com, adults $55–73, youth $55, under age 12 $10) was the headquarters for alpine sports during the 1960 Winter Olympics. Today it is perhaps the most popular ski resort in California, with practically every amenity and plenty of activities, from geocaching to ziplining; but skiing and snowboarding remain the most important pursuits. Squaw Valley has a great ski school with plenty of fun for new skiers and boarders of all ages along with a wide selection of intermediate slopes. Some slopes are long, such as those served by the Squaw Creek, Red Dog, and Exhibition-Searchlight lifts—perfect for skiers who want to spend more time on the snow than on the lifts. But the jewels of Squaw are the many black-diamond and double-black-diamond slopes and the three terrain parks. Whether you prefer trees, moguls, narrow ridges, or wide-open vertical bowls, you'll find your favorite at Squaw. The slopes off KT-22 are legendary with skiers around the world. If you want to try freestyle for the first time, head for Belmont Park. Hard-core freestylers go for the Ford Freestyle Park and the 22-foot Superpipe.

Squaw Valley offers night skiing free with a daytime or half-day lift ticket; they'll also sell a nighttime-only ticket. During the day, especially weekends and holidays, expect long lines at the lifts, crowds in the nice big locker rooms, and still more crowds at the numerous restaurants and cafés.

ALPINE MEADOWS

Just one ridge over from Squaw Valley is the other grand ski resort at Tahoe, Alpine Meadows (2600 Alpine Meadows Rd., Tahoe City, 530/583-4232 or 800/441-4423, www.skialpine.com, mid-Nov.–mid-May, check website for prices). This sprawling resort encompasses both sides of its two Sierra peaks, Scott and Ward. With a full range of trails, an all-day every-day ski school, and brand-new state-of-the-art rental equipment, Alpine is ideal for all levels of skiers. Beginners will particularly enjoy their new "rocker" skis, which make steering easier than ever, and the scenic network of green trails. An intermediate skier can have a great time at Alpine, especially coming off the Summit Six or the Roundhouse Chairlifts. On the south side, from Scott Peak off the Lakeview Chair, all ski runs are blue. Alpine devotes considerable space to what it refers to as "Adventure Ski Zones." These are large clusters of black-diamond and double-black-diamond bowls and runs intended for expert skiers only. Fourteen lifts serve the mountains, including three high-speed chairs. If you're an expert, take just about any chair up the mountain, and you'll find exhilarating ways down. The Scott Chair leads to a bunch of single black-diamond runs on the front of the mountain, as does the Summit Express six-passenger chair at the back of Ward Peak. You can get to Art's Knob from the Sherwood Express. Alpine has three terrain parks: Tiegel, with small snow features for beginners and young adventurers; Kangaroo Ridge, for medium-level skiers and snowboarders; and Shreadows Terrain Park, where experts will find new challenges.

GRANLIBAKKEN

Many large, famous, and modern ski resorts around Tahoe overshadow each other in their own ways. But in the history of Tahoe, none is more venerable than Granlibakken (725 Granlibakken Rd., Tahoe City, 530/583-4242 or 800/543-3221, www.granlibakken.com, lift tickets $16–24, lodging $143–400). Actually called the Granlibakken Conference Center and Lodge, this lovely, historic resort dates to the turn of the 20th century, when the original

the totem at Granlibakken

© HEATHER C. LISTON

Tahoe Tavern was built on this site. In 1928 the Tavern stayed open through winter for the first time for vacationers who wanted to play in the snow, and the facilities grew quickly afterward. Soon there was an ice rink and a toboggan run, and then a ski jump used for demonstrations by traveling Norwegian ski jumpers entertaining the local community. The Tahoe Tavern was the site of the 1932 and 1936 U.S. Olympic trials, and over the years it has hosted various national championships, Junior Olympics, and other competitions. After World War II the famous Norwegian ski jumper Kjell "Rusty" Rustad moved here, renamed the place Granlibakken after a ski area from his youth, and developed a mountain for skiers. Later, Rusty helped the developers of Squaw Valley get started and lived to see other resorts become grander than his own.

Today, Granlibakken is unable to compete as a major downhill ski destination, but it still has much to offer. With a large outdoor pool and hot tub, the on-site **Lighthouse Spa** (530/583-8111, www.lighthousespa.com), a ropes course, bicycles, hiking and cross-country ski trails, and one of the best groomed sledding hills anywhere (saucer-sled provided, $10 per day), this is an ideal spot for family vacations, retreats, and corporate events. Most of the 84 condos on the site are managed by the company and are available for rent year-round. Granlibakken still offers some downhill skiing, but those who crave the excitement of bigger mountains should sleep here and take advantage of the package deals with other resorts, which include discount lift tickets and shuttle transportation to one of seven other ski areas.

Granlibakken's **Cedar House Pub** (530/583-4242 or 800/543-3221, 5–9 P.M. Fri.–Sat. and holidays mid-Dec.–Apr. 1, $10–18) serves German comfort food, while the **Ski Hut Snack Bar** (10 A.M.–3 P.M. Fri.–Sun. and holidays winter) offers Mexican food and hot dogs. A lavish buffet breakfast is included for overnight guests.

Cross-Country Skiing and Snowshoeing

One of the best cross-country ski trails for beginners is the **General Creek Trail,** also known as the 1960 Winter Olympiad X-C Ski Trail. A lot of the Olympic facilities in the area were neglected or forgotten for many years, but some of the ski trails were rediscovered and restored in connection with the 50th anniversary celebration in 2010. The first-ever Olympic biathlon competition was held on this trail, a 20K course designed by the former U.S. Olympian Wendall "Chummy" Broomhall and Allison "Al" Merrill, who was the head coach of the U.S. Ski Team 1963–1968. The trailhead is located inside Sugar Pine Point State Park (Hwy. 89, Tahoma, 530/525-7982, www.parks.ca.gov, day use $8) just a few miles south of the town of Tahoma. On entering the park, drive through the campground to campsite 148. Signs and a trail map are posted and explain a little about the trail's Olympic history. The trail is largely

LAKE TAHOE

© HEATHER C. LISTON

the bridge across General Creek

flat, so it's not too challenging for skiers at most levels—it's also amazingly beautiful. It's an out-and-back trip, so you can glide silently through the woods for as long as you like then turn around before you get too tired. Snowshoers are welcome but must stay out of the ski tracks.

Snowshoeing enthusiasts will be happy to hear that rangers in Sugar Pine Point State Park (Hwy. 89, Tahoma, 530/525-7982, www.parks.ca.gov, day use $8) lead **full-moon snowshoe tours** (West Shore Sports, reservations 530/525-9920, $15, under age 12 free, includes snowshoe rental) on specific dates in winter; call for details.

Snowmobiling

If you're up on the North Shore, check out **Lake Tahoe Snowmobile Tours** (Hwy. 267, south of Northstar Resort, 530/546-4280, www.laketahoesnowmobiling.com, $130–370). With a fleet of Ski-Doo snowmobiles and more than 20 years of guided touring experience, this outfit offers everything from easy 90-minute tours with gorgeous lake views through private 3–4-hour adventures for expert riders who want to tackle ungroomed backcountry terrain. You'll see sweeping North Shore views and drive through miles of unspoiled forest. Reservations are strongly recommended. Drivers must be age 16 or older and have a valid driver's license; children under age five may not ride.

Sledding and Snow Play

Granlibakken (725 Granlibakken Rd., Tahoe City, 877/552-6301 or 800/543-3221, www.granlibakken.com, daily 9 A.M.–4 P.M., $10 per day, resort guests $5) is a great place for the whole family to spend a day sledding down the machine-groomed mountain on saucers (included). You may also want to join the Granlibakken staff and longtime Tahoe residents when they build their community of snow people each year.

If you love huskies, make a journey with

Wilderness Adventures Dog Sled Tours (530/550-8133, www.tahoedogsledtours.com, daily 10 A.M.–5 P.M., over 60 pounds $95–110, under 60 pounds $45–55). Tours begin at the Resort at Squaw Creek (400 Squaw Creek Rd., Olympic Valley). Most tours last one hour, but if you're not afraid of the cold and are around on a weekday, sign up for a two-hour tour or Wilderness Expedition that runs 15–20 miles through the backcountry snow. Ask about moonlight tours.

Fishing

Mickey's Big Mack Charters (530/546-4444 or 800/877-1462, www.mickeysbigmack.com, 5-hour trip $85 pp) operates out of the Sierra Boat Company on Highway 28 in Carnelian Bay. The 43-foot fishing boat goes out twice daily, in the early-morning and for a late-afternoon cruise that includes spectacular sunset views. The cabin and restroom on board add to the comforts of the trip as you fish for mackinaw, rainbow, and brown trout.

Hiking

Sugar Pine Point State Park (Hwy. 89, Tahoma, 530/525-7982, www.parks.ca.gov, $8 day use) offers trails suitable for all levels of hikers. One simple and pleasant hike is the **Edward F. Dolder Nature Trail** (1.5 miles, easy). To reach the trailhead, enter the northeast section of the park—the Edwin L. Z'Berg Natural Preserve—and begin hiking the paved Rod Beaudry trail. The Dolder Trail circles the Z'berg Preserve, with views of the subalpine meadow and wildlife habitats. Along the way you'll pass through trees, a sandy beach, and the world's highest-elevation operating navigational lighthouse, the Sugar Pine Point Lighthouse.

A good hike in the southwestern section of Sugar Pine Point State Park is along the 1960 Olympic Ski Trails out to **Lily Pond** (3–6 miles, easy–moderate). Start in General Creek Campground, near site 148, and take the

General Creek Trail, also known as the 1960 Winter Olympiad X-C Ski Trail. This sunny wooded path is wide enough that it almost feels like an unpaved forest road. After about 1.5 miles, you'll come to a wooden bridge curving off to the left across General Creek. If you're ready to turn around, take the bridge to complete the loop back to the trailhead for a total of three miles.

If you're up for a few more miles, bear right; at this point, the path becomes more trail-like, narrow and winding through the woods. In 0.5 mile you'll come to a trail marker directing you to Lily Pond on the right. The next 0.75 mile are a bit of climbing, but then you're at Lily Pond, a small lake that actually has lily pads. You can walk around the pond or just turn around and head back, rejoining the General Creek Trail for a total of 5–6 miles.

If you like easy terrain and great views, the **Lakeside Trail,** a kind of paved boardwalk, is a great place for a stroll or a hike. Building this trail is an ongoing project of the Tahoe City Public Utility District (530/583-3440, www. tcpud.org), but miles of it have already been completed. Access the trail from Heritage Plaza in the center of Tahoe City.

The 165-mile **Tahoe Rim Trail** (775/298-0012, www.tahoerimtrail.org) runs along the shore of the entire lake, including the north and west sides. There are two good trailheads where you can gain access and do a segment of the trail. The northern trailhead is at Brockway Summit. To get to the Brockway trailhead, start in Kings Beach at the junction of Highways 28 and 267. Travel north on Highway 267 for four miles. Look for a "Tahoe Rim Trail" sign on the right, and then park on the nearby dirt road or on the roadside pullout. There are no restrooms, water, or other services at this trailhead.

The southern trailhead is Barker Pass. To get to the Barker Pass trailhead from Tahoe City, travel about 4.25 miles south on Highway 89. Make a right (west) onto Blackwood Canyon Road. When the road splits, take the left fork.

Drive seven miles to the crest of the hill and then another 0.2 mile on a dirt road. There will be a pullout to the right where you can park. Pit toilets are available at this trailhead, but there is no water. Also note that the famous **Pacific Crest Trail** (916/285-1846, www.pcta. org) joins the Tahoe Rim Trail here at Barker Pass and runs concurrent with it for the next 50 miles into the Desolation Wilderness.

Spas

One of the most popular day spas on the North Shore is the **Lighthouse Spa** (850 N. Lake Blvd., Suite 20A, Tahoe City, 530/583-8100, www. lighthousespa.com, daily 9 A.M.–8 P.M., massage $60–175). Look for it behind the Safeway, even if it seems like an unlikely spot for a spa. Once inside, choose a Swedish, deep-tissue, or hot-stone massage; expectant moms can get a special prenatal massage. Lighthouse also offers facials, body wraps, luxurious foot treatments, and aesthetic services that include manicures, pedicures, and waxing. Late appointments (until 8 P.M.) are available for those in desperate need of après-ski TLC. To make its pampering more convenient, Lighthouse Spa has a second location at the Granlibakken Resort (725 Granlibakken Rd., Tahoe City, 530/583-8111, www.granlibakken.com). If you're anywhere in the North Shore or Truckee areas, they'll also come to you for an extra fee ($100–200).

FESTIVALS AND EVENTS

A great way to see the lake is by participating in the annual 72-mile **Tour de Tahoe-Bike Big Blue** (800/565-2704, www.bikethewest.com, $100) ride each September. Cyclists start and finish at Lake Tahoe's Horizon Casino Resort (50 U.S. 50, Stateline, NV, 775/588-6211 or 800/648-3322, www.horizoncasino.com) at 6:30 A.M. and ride all the way around the lake, enjoying the sights in both Nevada and California and the company of other enthusiasts. If you're really into baskets, you'll love the annual **Weavers Market** (Marion Steinbach Indian Basket Museum, 130 West Lake Blvd., Tahoe City, 530/583-1762, www.northtahoemuseums.org), which takes place on a Saturday in September. For the event the museum hosts members of California and Nevada indigenous groups (Washoe, Miwok, Yurok, and Northern Paiute) who make baskets for exhibit and for sale, while demonstrating the craft of basketmaking. The event also has basket appraisers on hand who will appraise up to three pieces of your Native American art for $10. The public enjoys a reduced ($2) entry fee to the museum that day, so it's a great event to bring the whole family to.

ACCOMMODATIONS
Under $100
Mother Nature's Inn (551 N. Lake Blvd., Tahoe City, 530/581-4278 or 800/558-4278, www.mothernaturesinn.com, $55–115) strives to bring the Tahoe camping experience inside while still providing the creature comforts that travelers expect. Guest rooms are themed based on a distinct wild creature, and you can expect plenty of decorative tchotchkes in keeping with your room's animal totem. You'll also find lodge-style furnishings and linens in cozy if somewhat cluttered arrangements. All guest rooms have private baths, fridges, and coffeemakers. Pets are welcome for a small additional fee. The inn is only a few steps from the shores of the lake and the conveniences of downtown Tahoe City.

$100-150
If you'd rather stay in town, Tahoe City's **Pepper Tree Inn** (645 N. Lake Blvd., Tahoe City, 530/583-3711, www.peppertreetahoe.com, summer $113–198, winter $91–171) is a reasonable choice. With whirlpool tubs, blow-dryers, and coffee grinders in each room, plus an outdoor swimming pool and free wireless Internet access, Pepper Tree has everything you'd expect in an above-average hotel. It also has the advantage of a great location across the

street from the lake, the Lakeside Trail, and some of the best restaurants in Tahoe City. This is a great base for local adventures.

$150-250
Devotees of Alpine Meadows vie for guest rooms at the exclusive and beautiful 🄲 **Stanford Alpine Chalet** (1980 Chalet Rd., Tahoe City, 530/583-1550, www.stanfordalpinechalet.com, $135–265), situated at the base of Alpine's mountain. With only 14 guest rooms, each is special enough to make you feel like a rock star during your stay. Guest rooms are decorated in a simple yet elegant style with real wood, private baths, and striking mountain views. Meals are served family-style at big communal tables. In summer the chalet offers a heated swimming pool, sports courts, and horseshoe pits; winter guests enjoy a private ski shuttle and the warmth of a giant great-room fireplace. An outdoor hot tub lures guests with its bubbling year-round warmth. If you happen to be a Stanford grad, you can get a discount with your alumni membership number.

Over $250
For that special vacation when you're willing to spend a little more to make everything perfect, try the **West Shore Inn** (5160 W. Lake Blvd., Homewood, 530/525-5200, www.skihomewood.com, $199–549). Each of the four suites and two guest rooms has distinctive luxury, with balconies, lake views, leather sofas, fireplaces, and flat-screen TVs. A freshly baked continental breakfast is included, as is door-to-door shuttle service to nearby attractions and use of the inn's fleet of bicycles, kayaks, and paddleboards.

Condo Rentals
For the ultimate convenience in ski vacations, get a condo at **The Village at Squaw Valley** (1750 Village East Rd., Olympic Valley, 866/818-6963, www.thevillageatsquaw.com, 1-bedroom condo $269-450, 3-bedroom $550–1,200) and never leave the vicinity of

the lifts. Elegant, modern condos range from compact studios perfect for singles or couples to three-bedroom homes that sleep up to eight. The Village condos have full kitchens with all appliances and utensils—some even have granite countertops—as well as a living room with a TV and maybe a fireplace, and a dining table. The skiers' favorite condo has heated tile floors in the kitchen and bath. Also included in the price is use of the Village's eight outdoor hot tubs, four saunas, three fitness rooms, and heated underground parking garage.

CAMPING

Sugar Pine Point State Park's 🌲**General Creek Campground** (Hwy. 89, Tahoma, 800/444-7275, www.reserveamerica.com, mid-May–mid-Sept., $35) is a great place to stay on a family vacation or an inexpensive overnight trip while exploring West Shore attractions. Every campsite in this wooded wildlife-filled park has a picnic table, a charcoal grill, and ample space for a tent or camper. Some sites are ADA-compliant. As a bonus, it has relatively new and clean showers, and you can get a strong hot five-minute shower for $0.50 (bring quarters). The campground can get crowded in midsummer, so make reservations in advance.

Not far from Sugar Pine Point State Park, the Washoe Tribe runs the **Meeks Bay Resort** (7901 Hwy. 89, Tahoma, 530/525-5588 or 877/326-3357, www.meeksbayresort.com, May–Oct., tent sites $25, RV sites $45). There are 11 tent sites and 22 RV sites, all with a two-night minimum; pets are not allowed. The resort features a sandy beach on the shores of Lake Tahoe and a marina (530/525-5588) where you can rent single kayaks and pedal boats ($20 per hour) and double kayaks, canoes, and paddleboards ($30 per hour). You can also launch your own boat ($15 one-way, $25 round-trip) or rent a slip ($60 per night, weekly $360, full season $2,600).

For great tree-lined campsites with easy beach access, the **William Kent Beach and Campground** (Hwy. 89, 2 miles south of Tahoe City, 877/444-6777, www.recreation.gov, mid-May–mid-Oct., $27–29) is a good choice. The 86 sites are suitable for tents or campers. There are no showers or electrical hookups, but there are restrooms with flush toilets and bear lockers for your food. The facility is operated by the state's Lake Tahoe Basin Management Unit.

If you don't mind giving up a woodsy camping experience, the **Tahoe State Recreation Area** (Hwy. 28, east of Tahoe City, 800/444-7275, www.reserveamerica.com, Memorial Day–Labor Day, $35) is a good choice. There are 26 sites, coin-operated showers, and you can walk to the lake or to the shops of Tahoe City. A utilitarian place to sleep is the **Lake Forest Campground** (Lake Forest Rd., 1.5 miles east of Tahoe City on Hwy. 28, 530/583-3796, www.tahoecitypud.com, mid-May–early Oct., $20), run by the Tahoe City Public Utilities District. The 20 sites are first-come, first-served; RVs up to 21 feet are welcome, although there are no hookups. Facilities include drinking water, flush toilets but no showers, and picnic tables, and the campground is next to the public **Lake Forest Boat Ramp** (530/583-3796, www.tahoecitypud.com, 5 A.M.–8 P.M. Mon.–Thurs., 5 A.M.–10 P.M. Fri.–Sun. mid-May–Sept., 6 A.M.–4 P.M. daily Oct.–mid-May, launch $10), also run by the Public Utilities District.

FOOD

More than half a dozen restaurants, snack bars, and coffee shops at **The Village at Squaw Valley** (1750 Village East Rd., Olympic Valley, 530/584-1000, www.thevillageatsquaw.com) offer sushi, pizza, high-end wine, and more. There's a **Starbucks** (530/584-6120), the restaurant **Mamsake Sushi** (1850 Village South Rd., Suite 52, 530/584-0110, www.mamasake.com, 11:30 A.M.–9:30 P.M. Mon.–Thurs., 11:30 A.M.–10 P.M. Fri.–Sun., $9–26), and **Fireside Pizza Co.** (1985 Squaw Valley Rd.,

LAKE TAHOE

LAKE TAHOE

Suite 25, 530/584-6150, www.firesidepizza.com, $13–26), plus several other eateries.

Bakeries and Cafés

To fuel up for a day out on the lake or in the mountains, head over to the **Fire Sign Café** (1785 W. Lake Blvd., Tahoe City, 530/583-0871, daily 7 A.M.–3 P.M., $8–15). This breakfast-and-lunch spot is a favorite with locals, serving up an enormous menu of hearty fare. Choose whole-grain waffles with fruit, a kielbasa omelet, crepes, or blueberry coffee cake. Expect a wait for a table on weekend mornings.

If you want to relax with some fine caffeine and really soak in the vacation vibe, you'll revel in **Syd's Bagelry & Espresso** (550 N. Lake Blvd., Tahoe City, 530/583-2666, daily 6 A.M.–5 P.M.). Syd's offers free wireless Internet access, and one of its best features is the location next door to Heritage Plaza, so you can take your latte outdoors while you watch the sunrise over the water.

A good choice for casual, inexpensive dining and drinking in Tahoe City is **Fat Cat Café** (599 N. Lake Blvd., Tahoe City, 530/583-3355, www.

fatcattahoe.com, food 11:30 A.M.–9 P.M. Sun.–Thurs., 11:30 A.M.–10 P.M. Fri.–Sat. summer, daily noon–9 P.M. winter, bar daily until 2 A.M. year-round, $10–13), especially if you like entertainment with your food. Thursday is karaoke night, while Friday–Saturday have live music starting around 10 P.M. The food includes decent sandwiches, salads, and burgers, and the. There's also free wireless Internet access.

Casual Dining

The Blue Agave (425 N. Lake Blvd., Sunnyside–Tahoe City, 530/583-8113, www.tahoeblueagave.com, daily 11 A.M.–11 P.M., $8.50–15) is the place to go for Mexican food on the West Shore. It's located in the Tahoe Inn, built circa 1934, which has a long history involving gold miners, bootleggers, and film stars. The ample and delicious food is absolutely current and draws loyal patrons from all over.

Fine Dining

The combination of ethnic cuisines may seem odd, but the taste tells the tale at **Wolfdale's**

Fat Cat Café

© HEATHER C. LISTON

(640 N. Lake Blvd., Tahoe City, 530/583-5700, www.wolfdales.com, daily 5:30–10 P.M. July–Aug., 5:30–10 P.M. Wed.–Mon. Sept.–June, $14–58). Wolfdale serves "cuisine unique" dishes that fuse Asian and Western to create tastes you can't find elsewhere. They've been doing it since 1978, so it seems to be working. The small seasonal menu is heavy on seafood, but there's also tasty beef and game meats in season. For light dining, try homemade soups, salads, and interesting small plates. Be sure to save room for the delicious desserts, most made in a light California style.

An ideal spot for a delicious dinner and some lake-watching is **(** **Christy Hill Lakeside Bistro** (115 Grove St., Tahoe City, 530/583-8551, www.christyhill.com, dinner daily 5:30–9:30 P.M. year-round, lunch Tues.–Sun. May–Oct., bar daily 3–8 or 9 P.M. year-round, $20–32) and its outdoor Sand Bar on the back deck. Entrées range from fresh cannelloni with homemade lemon ricotta to Moroccan spiced lamb loin.

For a light meal and a fabulous sunset, end your day at the Mountain Grill at the **Sunnyside Resort** (1850 West Lake Blvd., Sunnyside, 2 miles south of Tahoe City, 530/583-7200 or 800/822-2754, www.sunnysidetahoe.com, daily 11 A.M.–10 P.M., $8–16). The patio has an expansive view of the lake and the mountains beyond; it also has plenty of room. The menu is brief—mostly appetizers, salads, and burgers—and the food is good, though not great. For a relaxing drink and a chance to mellow out by the water, this place is hard to beat.

Whether great views or great food is your goal, you'll be very happy at the **(** **West Shore Café & Inn** (5160 West Lake Blvd., Homewood, 530/525-5200, www.skihomewood.com, daily 11:30 A.M.–9:30 P.M., $13–33). The indoor atmosphere is classy, with white tablecloths and well-dressed patrons, but on the back patio it's sublime. Sit at the outdoor bar and watch the sun go down over the lake, or grab a table out on the pier, where strings of lights illuminate the railings and sailboats bob around. The West Shore Burger ($14) is the dish you'll be talking about when you get home, and the

outdoor seating at the West Shore Café & Inn

service is both professional and friendly. If you don't have time for dinner, stop for one of the signature cocktails, such as the West Shore Margarita or the Mango Zombie.

The **River Grill** (River Rd. at Hwy. 89 and Hwy. 28, 530/581-2644, www.rivergrilltahoe.com, daily 5:30 P.M.–close, $19–32) is located where the Truckee River meets Tahoe City. Eat outside on the rustic heated wooden porch, enjoying the river view while listening to live music, or sit indoors in the casually elegant dining room, complete with a fireplace. Happy hour (daily 5–6:30 P.M.) features discounted drinks and food in the bar and at the outdoor fire pit.

INFORMATION AND SERVICES

The Lake Tahoe Visitors Bureau maintains the **North Lake Tahoe Visitors Information Center and Chamber of Commerce** (380 N. Lake Blvd., Tahoe City, 530/581-6900, www.gotahoenorth.com, daily 9 A.M.–5 P.M.). Tahoe City has a Bank of America and ATMs as well as a **post office** (7005 N. Lake Blvd., Tahoe Vista, 530/546-5600, 8:45 A.M.–1:30 P.M. and 2:30–4:45 P.M. Mon.–Fri.). If you need medical attention, the **Tahoe Forest Hospital** (10121 Pine Ave., Truckee, 530/587-6011, www.tfhd.com) or its affiliate, **Incline Village Community Hospital** (880 Alder Ave., Incline Village, NV, 775/833-4100 or 800/419-2627, www.tfhd.com), are the nearest options for full-service emergency rooms. Kings Beach has a **Rite Aid** (8245 N. Lake Blvd., 530/546-2523).

GETTING THERE AND AROUND

Air

The nearest airports are **Reno-Tahoe International Airport** (RNO, 2001 E. Plumb Lane, Reno, NV, 775/328-6400, www.reno-airport.com) and **Sacramento International Airport** (SMF, 6900 Airport Blvd., Sacramento, 916/929-5411, www.sacramento.aero). Both are served by several major airlines.

Car

I-80 leads near the North Shore from Sacramento or the San Francisco Bay Area. From I-80, take Highway 89 south for 14 miles to Tahoe City. U.S. 50 runs along the West Shore from the south. From U.S. 50 in South Lake Tahoe, take Highway 89 north for 25 miles along the West Shore, passing Meeks Bay, Tahoma, and Tahoe Pines on the way to Tahoe City on the North Shore.

Bus

Tahoe Area Regional Transit (TART, 530/550-1212 or 800/736-6365, www.laketahoetransit.com) is the North Shore's public bus system. Buses (adults $1.75 one-way, 24-hour pass $3.75) run from Tahoma on the West Shore to Incline Village, Nevada, with many stops along the way. There are discounted fares for seniors, youth, and travelers with disabilities.

Ski Resort Shuttles

Many ski resorts maintain shuttles to bring skiers up to the mountains in the morning and back to their hotels in the late afternoon. Contact **Squaw Valley** (530/452-7181, www.squaw.com) and **Alpine Meadows** (530/525-2922, www.skialpine.com) for shuttle schedules.

In a few places there's even a free **Night Rider** (866/216-5222, northlaketahoeexpress.com, daily 7 P.M.–midnight, free) bus service, provided by North Lake Tahoe Express. The winter service goes to Squaw Valley, Tahoe City, Northstar, and the Biltmore in Crystal Bay, Nevada. In summer, the West Shore Night Rider offers service from the Tahoe City Y to Granlibakken, Sunnyside, Homewood, and Tahoma. Management of the Night Rider Service changes occasionally, so check www.laketahoetransit.com for updates.

Truckee-Donner

Gateway to the Tahoe ski world, Truckee is a historic Old West town that really has no off-season. Storefronts line the main street, Donner Pass Road, offering ski rentals, a bite to eat, and places to stay. Parking is hard to find and expensive, and both the prices and the lines at restaurants can resemble those in San Francisco. But this bustling small mountain town has its charms.

SIGHTS
Old Jail Museum

The Old Jail Museum (10142 Jibboom St., Truckee, 530/582-0893, www.truckeehistory.org, 11 A.M.–4 P.M. Sat.–Sun. June–Sept., donation $2–4) is such a cute little building that it's hard to believe it was an Old West jail in use until recently. Built in 1875, it housed prisoners continually until 1964. "Baby Face" Nelson and "Machine Gun" Kelly are among the notorious outlaws believed to have spent time here. Today, it has historical exhibits, cool information, and docents from the local Truckee-Donner Historical Society. In addition to the sometimes erratic weekend schedule, the museum is often open on Thursday evenings in summer during the citywide "Truckee Thursdays" events.

Donner Camp Picnic Ground Historical Site

You hear the word "Donner" around Tahoe a lot. If you want to learn more about what really happened to the infamous Donner party and where and how, visit the Donner Camp Picnic Ground Historical Site (Hwy. 89, 2.5 miles north of Truckee, www.fs.usda.gov/tahoe, free). The site is in the Tahoe National Forest, and it's a good place to stop for a picnic, a hike, or a mountain-bike ride. This is also where 25 members of the Donner party, who had left Springfield, Illinois, in April 1846 on their way to new lives in California, stopped to repair their wagons in the fall after being slowed down by an ill-fated shortcut through Hastings Cutoff. It was only October when they got here, but a blizzard hit hard. Some of the party ended up staying the whole winter, and some, as you may know, never left.

Your stop here need not be as difficult as theirs was. The interpretive **loop trail** that begins and ends here is short and pretty flat, with signs along the way that illuminate the Donner Party's history.

If you want to know more details about the Donner party story, read Ruth Whitman's book, *Tamsen Donner: A Woman's Journey.* In spite of the gruesome events that took place here, it's a beautiful spot among the trees, mountains, streams, and sunshine.

Donner Summit

Just west of Truckee, Donner Summit (I-80, 530/587-3558, www.exploredonnersummit.com or www.donnersummithistoricalsociety.org) is one of the legendary natural landmarks of the North Tahoe region. Come to see the Native American petroglyphs, to climb the varied rock faces, to ski the summit's snowy paths, or to watch the trains below, descendants of the first transcontinental railroad that went through here.

◖ Donner Memorial State Park

Donner Memorial State Park (12593 Donner Pass Rd., off I-80, 530/582-7892, www.parks.ca.gov, daily year-round, $8) is a great place to experience the lush beauty that the Donner party was heading to California to find. Near the entrance to the park is the **Pioneer Monument,** a massive structure celebrating the courage and spirit of the Donners and others who made their way west in harder times.

The **Emigrant Trail Museum** (daily

LAKE TAHOE

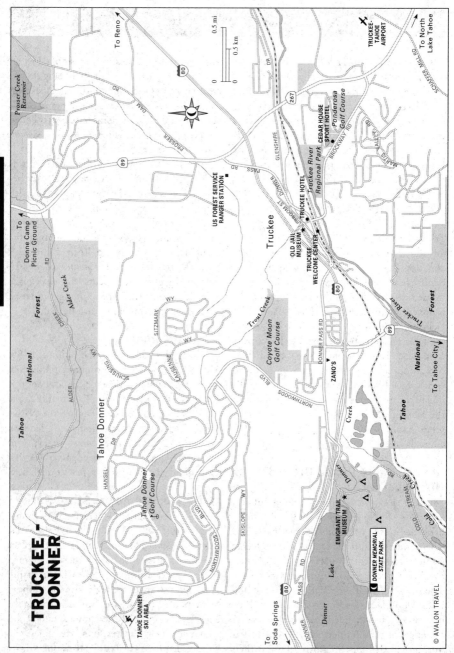

the Pioneer Monument, by sculptor John MacQuarrie

© HEATHER C. LISTON

SPORTS AND RECREATION
Ski Resorts
NORTHSTAR CALIFORNIA

Northstar California Resort (100 Northstar Dr., Truckee, 800/466-6784, www.northstarattahoe.com, lifts daily 8:30 A.M.–4 P.M. in season, adults $95–101, youth $86–88, children $56–58) is often a bit less crowded than the big resorts. Beginners can head up the mountain on the fast Vista Express quad chair and still find slopes heading gently all the way back to the village. Slow Zones provides good spots for young children fresh out of ski school and wobbly adults who haven't spent their whole lives on the slopes. Intermediate runs crisscross the front of the mountain, starting at the very peak off Comstock and running all the way down the mountain. The Backside, reachable via the Comstock Express quad chair and served by the Backside Express, is reserved for black-diamond skiers, although adventurous intermediates can test their ski legs here. Freestylers will find the most terrain right off the Vista Express quad, although a couple of other small areas dot the mountain elsewhere.

SUGAR BOWL

A great mid-tier ski area is Sugar Bowl (629 Sugar Bowl Rd., Norden, 530/426-9000, www.sugarbowl.com, lifts daily 9 A.M.–4 P.M. Nov.–May, adults $52, seniors $20–45, ages 13–22 $45, ages 6–12 $20, under age 5 free). With lots of skiable snow spread across a wide area and plenty of vertical drop, Sugar Bowl can satisfy skiers and boarders of all abilities. A mix of blue and black-diamond runs toward the top of the peaks offers intense variety, with a scattering of double-black-diamond runs out toward the edges and down the ridges. At the base, green and blue runs make it easy for younger and less experienced athletes to have a good time in the mountains. A gondola ferries visitors from the remote parking lot up to the village. The resort's Summit Chairlift brings visitors to

10 A.M.–5 P.M. year-round) and bookstore in the visitors center offer uplifting information about the human and natural history of the area. The 0.5-mile **Nature Trail** at the visitors center is an easy self-guided trek through a forest of Jeffrey and lodgepole pines past the site of the cabin built by the Murphy family during the Donner party's layover here in the winter of 1846–1847. A moving plaque at the cabin site lists those who perished and those who survived. The trail continues over a creek and through the campground (154 sites, reservations 800/444-7275, www.reserveamerica.com, Memorial Day–mid-Sept., $35).

Donner Lake is a paradise for children and adults alike, offering swimming, boating, fishing, and hiking. Walking or jogging the Lakeside Interpretive Trail along the shore is a great way to enjoy a little exercise, close-up views of the lake, and educational signage.

the top of Judah Peak for easy access to back-country trails. Sugar Bowl's General Admission Program offers a free two-hour group lesson and free rentals with the purchase of a lift ticket (Mon.–Fri. during non-holiday periods). The resort offers two base lodges: a day-lodge at Judah and the Lodge at Sugar Bowl, located in the village. The on-site **Lodge at Sugar Bowl** (750 Mule Ears Dr., Truckee, 530/426-6742, www.sugarbowl.com, $179–559) allows you to ski right up to your guest room door.

BOREAL MOUNTAIN RESORT

Boreal Mountain Resort (19659 Boreal Ridge Rd., Soda Springs, 530/426-3666, www.rideboreal.com, daily 9 A.M.–9 P.M. in season, adults $49–56, ages 13–18 $40–42, ages 5–12 $16) may not feel as fabulous as Squaw or Alpine, but many Californians find their snow legs here. The Accelerator Chair serves Boreal's Superpipe, its Core terrain park, and a night-skiing area, while the 49er Chair serves the intermediate and advanced terrain. Even on weekends, the lines at Boreal seem pleasingly short compared to the bigger resorts. In 2012 a new 33,000-square-foot complex, the **Woodward Tahoe Action Sports Training Facility** (530/426-3666, www.woodwardtahoe.com), opened to offer weeklong summer camps for skiers, snowboarders, bicycle motocross riders, cheerleaders, skateboarders, and gymnasts. In addition, there are trampolines, foam pits, an indoor skate park, and a digital-media learning center for complete training heaven. Boreal is very family-friendly, with ski and snowboard lessons for beginners and a lodge where parents can relax with a cup of coffee or a drink at the Upper Deck bar and watch their children ski; the cafeteria (daily 9 A.M.–9 P.M.) offers limited service after 4 P.M.

SODA SPRINGS

Soda Springs (10244 Soda Springs Rd., Soda Springs, 530/426-3901, www.skisodasprings. com, 9 A.M.–4 P.M. Thurs.–Mon., adults $36, under age 18 $25) is a great small family resort. Its claim to fame is tubing, included with every lift ticket, or you can buy a $25 tubing-only package. The Planet Kids area for young athletes (under age 9, $25) offers a safe place for the little ones to practice tubing, skiing, and snowboarding. Rentals and instruction are included in the price, and there are even two tubing carousels to add to the thrills. There's no on-site lodging at Soda Springs, but there is an adequate cafeteria.

TAHOE DONNER SKI AREA

Tahoe Donner Ski Area (11603 Snowpeak Way, Truckee, 530/587-9444, www.tahoedonner.com, hours vary Dec.–May, adults $25–35, children $10–15) prides itself on being "a great place to begin." With only five lifts, three of them conveyor belts, 14 runs, and 120 skiable acres, Donner will seem miniscule to skiers used to the big resorts. It's a great spot to bring your family, however, to get a feel for snowboarding or skiing, take lessons, and enjoy the snow in the beautiful Tahoe forest. To be truly family-friendly, Tahoe Donner offers lessons for children as young as age three, interchangeable lift tickets for parents, and even kid-friendly items on the snack-bar menu.

Cross-Country Skiing and Snowshoeing

The granddaddy of Tahoe cross-country ski areas, the **Royal Gorge Cross Country Ski Resort** (Summit Station, Soda Springs, 530/426-3871 or 800/500-3871, www.royalgorge.com, daily 9 A.M.–4 P.M. in season, adults $34, ages 13–17 $20, ages 6–12 $8, under age 6 free) has a truly tremendous chunk of the Sierra—9,000 acres—within its boundaries. Striving to provide a luxurious ski experience comparable to what downhillers expect, the Royal Gorge offers lodging, food, drink, a ski school, equipment rentals, equipment care facilities and services, and much more. With the most miles of groomed trails anywhere in the Tahoe area, Royal Gorge offers two stride tracks and a skate track on every trail to allow easy passing. They even have a surface lift for skiers who want to practice downhill technique or try telemarking.

The Royal Gorge Summit Station is the central lodge. However, you'll also find two overnight lodges, Ice Lakes Lodge (www.icelakeslodge.com) and Rainbow Lodge (www.rainbowlodge.com), and eight warming huts dotting the cross-country wonderland. Each lodge has a restaurant, and there's also a ski-in snack bar, the Summit Station Café. Pick up a map before you head out for the day; patches of the mountains are off-limits due to avalanche danger, and it's best to know where they are before you get deep into your cross-country ski adventure.

Tahoe Donner Cross Country (15275 Alder Creek Rd., Truckee, 530/587-9484, www.tdxc.com or www.tahoedonner.com, hours vary, adults $15–25, ages 60–69 $13–19, under age 13 free) offers some of the better cross-country ski action in the area. Tahoe Donner has almost 5,000 acres crisscrossed with trails ranging from easy greens all the way up through double-black-diamond trails; there are also two trails set aside just for snowshoers. A cross-country ski school introduces newcomers to the sport and helps more experienced skiers expand their skills. There is a separate day lodge just for cross-country skiers and a snack bar, the **Cookhouse** (11 A.M.–3 P.M. Sat.–Sun. and holidays in season, $5), halfway up the mountain in Euer Valley.

Snowmobiling

Several snowmobile outfits operate west of Truckee along the main roads—you'll see the tracks as you drive in and out of town. **Cold Stream Adventures** (11760 Donner Pass Rd., Truckee, 530/582-9090, www.coldstreamadventures.com, daily, hours vary, 2-hour tour $130–155) also offers tours into the mountains,

promising climbs up to 2,000 feet higher than the starting point. These guided tours run through private forest, so you'll see forested landscapes available no other way. Make reservations and grab your sunglasses.

Hiking

The **Donner Camp Picnic Ground Historical Site** (Hwy. 89, 2.5 miles north of Truckee, www.fs.usda.gov/tahoe, free) has two hikes, each excellent in its own way. A short educational interpretive loop trail begins in the picnic-area parking lot. The trail is very well maintained, with raised wooden planks above the grasslands in the sections that occasionally get wet. Six trailside signs explain the history. If you're a fast reader, you can do the whole trail in about 15 minutes.

Follow the coast of Donner Lake for an easy and scenic hike within **Donner Memorial State Park** (12593 Donner Pass Rd., 530/582-7892, www.parks.ca.gov, daily sunrise–sunset year-round); about 1.75 miles, or one-third, of the lake's coastline is within the park's boundaries. Start at the Lagoon parking area near the park entrance and follow the lakeshore to China Cove. Turn around and come back the same way for a 3.5-mile hike. Note that you can't hike all the way around the lake; some of the shore is located on private land outside the park. For a more physically strenuous hike, try the excellent Commemorative Emigrant Trail (15 miles round-trip), also accessible from the parking lot at the Donner Picnic Ground. This mostly flat trail leads to Prosser Creek and the Stampede Reservoir and is popular with mountain bikers and equestrians as well as pedestrians.

For serious hikers, an outstanding day trip is the hike from Sugar Bowl to Squaw Valley along the **Pacific Crest Trail** (18 miles one-way, challenging). To begin, take Donner Pass Road to the Sugar Bowl Ski Academy (19195 Donner Pass Rd., Norden, 530/426-1844) and park in the free lot on the right side of the highway. Find the Pacific Crest Trail (PCT) trailhead and start walking south. The trail's middle name is "Crest," so expect some magnificent high places with great views, varied terrain, and often chilly conditions. Snow as late as July is not uncommon. In midwinter, this trail section is best done as a cross-country ski adventure. This is a good hike to do as a car shuttle: Have someone in your party leave a car at Squaw Valley in the morning to ferry you, or arrange for a ride.

Golf
Coyote Moon (10685 Northwoods Blvd., Truckee, 530/587-0886, www.coyotemoongolf.com, $95–149) is not inexpensive, but according to expert golfers, it's more than worth it. Coyote Moon offers fairways dotted with granite boulders and lined by dense natural forest. No, the builders didn't make it that way; the designer created a layout that takes advantage of the natural features of this locale. While Coyote Moon tends to beckon advanced golfers, even beginners can play an enjoyable round here.

ENTERTAINMENT AND EVENTS
Nightlife
Truckee's **Pastime Club** (10096 Donner Pass Rd., 530/582-9219, daily 3 P.M.–2 A.M.) is open year-round with drinks every night and live music on Tuesday, Friday–Saturday, and occasionally Sunday. There's usually no cover on weekdays; weekend cover charges depend on the band but tend to run $3–10. The **Bar of America** (10040 Donner Pass Rd., Truckee, 530/587-2626, www.barofamerica. net, 11 A.M.–2 A.M. Mon.–Fri., 10 A.M.–2 P.M. Sat.–Sun., $9–17), in the Pacific Crest restaurant, offers an upscale atmosphere along with local beers, cocktails, food, and music. Bands tend to play here Friday–Sunday, and cover charges range from free to about $10.

Festivals and Events
Lake Tahoe hosts a number of festivals every year in both summer and winter, though undoubtedly summer has more. One of the biggest is the **Lake Tahoe Music Festival** (530/583-3101, www.tahoemusic.org). Performers such as Michael Bolton, Blues Traveler, and Big Bad Voodoo Daddy perform alongside symphony orchestras over a three-week stretch in late July–early August. In past years, the festival concerts were spread around at various venues, but now they're all held in one large and lovely location: the Village at Northstar in the Northstar-at-Tahoe Resort (5001 Northstar Dr., Truckee, 530/562-2267).

Truckee is the place to be on Thursday in the summer. Much of the historic downtown area is closed to traffic 5–8 P.M. for **Truckee Thursdays** (www.truckeethursdays.com or www.historictruckee.com, June–Aug.). Business as usual is replaced by a farmers market, a street fair, a bouncy house for the children, live bands, wine tasting, and more. The Old Jail Museum is often open to visitors during these festivals, and lots of local establishments participate with late hours, sidewalk sales, or whatever seems like fun at the time. For up-to-date details, check the websites.

SHOPPING
Donner Pass Road is the center of Truckee's historic district, and lots of little shops line both sides of the street. For summertime sports, the **Cycle Paths Bike Shop** (www.cyclepaths.com) has locations in Truckee (10200 Donner Pass Rd., 530/582-1890, daily 9 A.M.–6 P.M.) and Tahoe City (1785 West Lake Blvd., 530/581-1171, usually 9 A.M.–6 P.M. Sat.–Sun.) that can hook you up with bike rentals, sales, equipment, and repairs.

For women's clothing, gifts, and handmade jewelry, the woman-run family business **Mo Jo & Zoe** (10115 Donner Pass Rd., Suite B, Truckee, 530/587-3495, http://shop.m.ojozoe. com, daily 10 A.M.–6 P.M.) is a pleasant and friendly spot with reasonably priced goods. For your shopping convenience, they stay open till 8 P.M. on the first Friday of every month, and in the summer during the Truckee Thursdays festival, they're open until 8:30 P.M.

If your clothing tastes run to the more dramatic, you will enjoy the **Unique Boutique-Viviane's Vintage & Vogue** (10925 W. River St., Truckee, 530/582-8484, 11:30 A.M.–6 P.M. Tues.–Sat.). Viviane has been in business for nearly two decades, dressing partygoers, Burning Man attendees, and anyone else who's in or around Truckee looking for a little flair.

ACCOMMODATIONS
Under $100
In the town of Norden, just a few miles west of Truckee, is an unusual lodging option. Since 1934, the Sierra Club has run a large rustic mountain adventure headquarters, the **Clair Tappaan Lodge** (19940 Donner Pass Rd., 530/426-3632 or 800/679-6775, www.ctl.sierraclub.org). The lodge is a great starting point for cross-country skiing or hiking day trips, and odds are you'll meet other like-minded people looking to share a hike or a rafting trip. Accommodations are pretty basic: Most travelers sleep in the men's or women's dormitories, although there are a few small rooms for couples and larger rooms for families. Bring your own bedding, and expect to share a bath. You get overnight lodging plus three healthy home-cooked meals daily for a mere $50 (for Sierra Club for members; nonmembers $55, ages 4–13 $25, under age 4 free). Rates in winter and on weekends and holidays are usually $5 more. The shared facilities include a toasty library with a wood-burning stove, a hot tub, a recreation room, a dining room, and extensive grounds.

$100-150
The **Truckee Hotel** (10007 Bridge St., at Donner Pass Rd., Truckee, 530/587-4444 or 800/659-6921, www.truckeehotel.com,

© HEATHER C. LISTON

the historic Truckee Hotel

$69–189) offers fabulous period ambience for reasonable rates. The hotel has welcomed guests to the North Shore since 1873. Guest rooms show their age with high ceilings, claw-foot tubs, and little Victorian touches. Part of the historic charm includes third- and fourth-floor rooms without an elevator, so prepare for a climb. Most of the 37 guest rooms have shared baths in the hall that are clean and comfortable, with either a shower or a bathtub and a privacy lock. The few guest rooms with private baths are pricier. Breakfast is included, and the hotel also houses Moody's, the best restaurant in town, only steps from historic downtown Truckee.

Low-priced accommodations around Truckee are not easy to come by, especially in ski season. A decent basic hotel with affordable rates is the **Inn at Truckee** (11506 Deerfield Dr., Truckee, 530/587-8888, www.innattruckee.com, $145–175). It's pet-friendly ($15 per night) and offers a spa and sauna, included continental breakfast, and free wireless Internet access. The guest rooms are nothing special, but the convenience to major ski areas and other attractions makes it a good buy.

$150-250

If you prefer a longer stay, call the **Donner Lake Village Resort** (15695 Donner Pass Rd., Suite 101, Truckee, 855/979-0402, www.donnerlakevillage.com, $160–320), on the shores of Donner Lake. Choose from regular motel rooms without kitchens or studio, one-bedroom, and two-bedroom condos with full kitchen facilities. Guest rooms include all the amenities of a nicer motel, including tea and coffee, private baths, phones, and TVs with DVD players. Donner Lake Village has its own marina with rental ski boats, fishing boats, and slips if you've brought your own watercraft; a bait and tackle shop is across the street. The nearby North Shore ski resorts beckon in wintertime, an easy drive from your condo.

The **Donner Lake Inn** (10070 Gregory Place,

Truckee, 530/587-5574, www.donnerlakeinn. com, $159–179) is an intimate five-room and one-cabin B&B offering rustic charm beside Donner Lake. Each guest room has its own simple homey decorating scheme, private bath with a shower, private entrance, queen bed, large-screen TV with a DVD player, and free wireless Internet access. Each morning, the friendly and hospitable owners serve up a delicious full breakfast in the dining room.

The **C Cedar House Sport Hotel** (10918 Brockway Rd., Truckee, 866/582-5655, www. cedarhousesporthotel.com, $170–270) sports an exposed wood exterior and is landscaped with trees, fallen stumps, and a rusty steel girder. Inside, guest rooms are all about luxury, with light-wood platform beds, designer leather chairs and sofas, and shining stainless-steel fixtures in the private baths. Choose comfortable guest rooms with queen or king beds or fancy suites with flat-screen TVs and every possible amenity. The expert staff at Cedar House can help create your Tahoe dream expedition; call in advance and they'll happily put together guided hikes, bike rides, and rafting or kayaking trips.

CAMPING

Donner Memorial State Park (12593 Donner Pass Rd., off I-80 west of downtown Truckee, 800/444-7275, www.reserveamerica.com, Memorial Day–mid-Sept., $35) offers a spacious tree-filled campground with easy access to the lake, the Emigrant Trail Museum, and the trails in the park. There are 154 sites spread across three campgrounds: Ridge Campground (May–Oct.), Creek Campground (June–Sept.), and Splitrock (June–Sept.). Sites include fire rings and picnic tables, and there are restrooms with showers.

The Forest Service (877/444-6777, www. fs.usda.gov or www.recreation.gov) maintains three campgrounds along Highway 89 between Truckee and Tahoe City: **Granite Flat** (74 sites, Hwy. 89, 1.5 miles south of Truckee, mid-May–mid-Oct., $19) and **Goose Meadow**

LAKE TAHOE

© HEATHER C. LISTON

Jax at the Tracks, Truckee's famous diner

(25 sites, Hwy. 89, 4 miles south of Truckee, mid-May–Sept., $17) offer potable water and vault toilets; **Silver Creek** (19 sites, Hwy. 89, 6 miles south of Truckee, mid-May–Sept., $17) offers potable water and both flush and vault toilets. All three campgrounds get noise from the highway as well as the gentler sounds of the nearby Truckee River.

FOOD
Bakeries and Cafés

For a cool crisp salad or a relaxing espresso, you can't beat the simply named **CoffeeBar** (10120 Jibboom St., Truckee, 530/587-2000, www.coffeebartruckee.com, daily 6 A.M.–8 P.M., $5–9). Although it's located just one block from the main drag, Donner Pass Road, CoffeeBar feels calm and peaceful even when the nearby resorts emphatically do not. Expect lots of space, free wireless Internet access, and good food—homemade baked goods, crepes, paninis, salads, and breakfast calzones.

California

Jax at the Tracks (10144 W. River St., Truckee, 530/550-7450, www.jaxtruckee.com, daily 7 A.M.–10 P.M., $10–19) looks authentic inside and out. Housed in an actual 1940s diner, it has been thoroughly fixed up to be clean, fresh, and original. Jax has a creative California-style chef who puts his own stamp on comfort food, with homemade English muffins, Kobe beef meatloaf with root-beer raisin glaze, and a mean hollandaise.

Italian

Zano's Pizza (11401 Donner Pass Rd., Truckee, 530/587-7411, www.zanos.net, 4–9:30 P.M. Sun.–Wed., 11:30 A.M.–2 P.M. and 4–9:30 P.M. Thurs., 11:30 A.M.–2 P.M. and 4–10 P.M. Fri.–Sat., $12–30) serves huge pizzas and tremendous salads in a big casual dining room with sports playing on TV. The full menu includes pastas and Italian entrées; at lunch, the hot crisp *panini* tastes great. But it's the thin-crust pizzas that rule here; pick one of Zano's interesting combinations, or build your own from the list of fresh ingredients.

Fine Dining

The best restaurant in Truckee is ◖ **Moody's Bistro and Lounge** (10007 Bridge St., Truckee, 530/587-8688, www.moodysbistro.com, 11:30 A.M.–9 P.M. Sun.–Thurs., 11:30 A.M.–9:30 P.M. Fri., 11:30 A.M.–9:30 P.M. Sat., $22–34). This casual yet elegant eatery adjoins the historic Truckee Hotel, just off the main commercial drag. A wooden bar and a series of booths give the main lounge an old-time feel, while the white-tablecloth dining room in the back feels more classically elegant. The chef promises ingredients that are "fresh, local, seasonal, and simple" and then jazzes them up with creative preparations. You might find antelope or local fish on the menu with do-it-yourself s'mores for dessert (the hands-down favorite), with a burner and skewers brought to your table. Definitely make reservations for weekend evenings.

Pacific Crest Grill at Bar of America (10040 Donner Pass Rd., Truckee, 530/587-2626, www.pacificcrestgrill.com or www.barofamerica.net, 11:30 A.M.–3 P.M. and 5:30 P.M.–close Mon.–Fri., 11 A.M.–close Sat., 10:30 A.M.–close Sun., $17–32) is a fine restaurant serving fresh organic ingredients and daily specials as well as local beers and creative cocktails with professional service. Reservations are recommended.

Dessert

Bud's Ice Cream & Fountain (10108 Donner Pass Rd., Truckee, 530/214-0599, www.truckeeicecream.com, 11 A.M.–6 P.M. Mon.–Fri., 10 A.M.–8 P.M. Sat.–Sun.) delivers what its name promises—a counter, lots of ice cream, 1950s-era decor, and plenty of coffee drinks. At **Sweets** (10118 Donner Pass Rd., Truckee, 530/587-6556, 888/248-8840,

Moody's Bistro and Lounge

© HEATHER C. LISTON

www.sweetshandmadecandies.com, daily 10 A.M.–6 P.M.), you can watch the experts make fudge or come inside for a free sample. Sweets also offers hand-dipped chocolates and sundaes and cones made with Häagen-Dazs ice cream.

INFORMATION AND SERVICES

Truckee has a good comprehensive **California Welcome Center** (10065 Donner Pass Rd., 530/587-2757, www.visitcwc.com, 8:45 A.M.–6 P.M. Mon., 9 A.M.–6 P.M. Tues.–Sun.) featuring free Internet access on your computer or theirs, public baths, huge brochure racks, and friendly personal advice. The center is attached to the town's Amtrak station, perfect if you're coming from Reno or San Francisco.

Truckee has a number of banks and two **post offices** (10050 Bridge St., 530/587-7158, 8:30 A.M.–5 P.M. Mon.–Fri., 11 A.M.–2 P.M. Sat.; 11415 Deerfield Dr., 530/587-4835, 9 A.M.–4:30 P.M. Mon.–Fri.).

If you need medical attention, the **Tahoe Forest Hospital** (10121 Pine Ave., Truckee, 530/587-6011, www.tfhd.com) has a full-service emergency room, among other services. Truckee also has a **Rite Aid** (11230 Donner Pass Rd., Truckee, 530/587-5296, www.riteaid.com).

GETTING THERE AND AROUND
Air

The closest commercial airport is **Reno-Tahoe International Airport** (RNO, 2001 E. Plumb Lane, Reno, NV, 775/328-6400, www.reno-airport.com), about 32 miles east of Truckee via I-80. **Sacramento International Airport** (SMF, 6900 Airport Blvd., Sacramento, 916/929-5411, www.sacramento.aero) is about 105 miles west of Truckee, also via I-80. Both airports are served by several major airlines.

Train

Amtrak's Bay Area–Chicago *California Zephyr* (800/872-7245, www.amtrak.com, reservations required) departs Emeryville in the Bay Area daily at 9:10 A.M. and Sacramento at 11:09 A.M., arriving in Truckee at 2:38 P.M. It leaves Truckee daily at 9:37 A.M. to arrive in Sacramento at 2:13 P.M. and Emeryville at 4:10 P.M.—at least when all goes according to plan. This is a long-distance train covering a lot of ground, so delays are common. Fares from Truckee to Sacramento are $37 one-way, and to Emeryville $48 one-way.

Amtrak's *Capitol Corridor* (877/974-3322, www.capitolcorridor.org or www.amtrak.com) originates in San Jose, stopping at Oakland, Emeryville, Berkeley, Davis, and Sacramento before connecting via bus from Auburn to Truckee and Reno, Nevada, at the eastern end of the route. Reservations are not available; the one-way fare from Emeryville to Truckee is $41–45.

Car

Truckee is located on I-80. From San Francisco to Truckee is 185 miles, 3.25 hours' drive in good weather. From Sacramento, the trip is about 105 miles and (1.75 hours). If you're driving to Truckee from Reno, follow I-80 west for 32 miles (35 minutes).

Public Transit and Ski Shuttles

Truckee Transit (530/587-7451, www.townoftruckee.com or www.laketahoetransit.com, adults $2 one-way, day pass $4, seniors $0.50, under age 12 $1) handles routes between the Truckee Tahoe Airport, downtown Truckee, and the Donner Memorial State Park and Donner Lake.

The free **Night Rider** (866/216-5222, www.laketahoetransit.com, daily 7 P.M.–midnight) bus service runs in winter to Squaw Valley, Tahoe City, North Star, and the Biltmore in Crystal Bay, Nevada. In summer, the West Shore Night Rider offers service from the Tahoe City Y to Granlibakken, Sunnyside, Homewood, and Tahoma. Your ski resort may also run a shuttle service of its own, making it possible to enjoy a low-stress Truckee-area ski vacation without a car.

TAHOE NATIONAL FOREST

The Tahoe National Forest is sandwiched between the Plumas National Forest to the north and the Eldorado National Forest to the south. Along the eastern border is the Toiyabe National Forest, making what is essentially one vast wilderness area. The Tahoe National Forest contains 800,000 acres of public land interspersed with 400,000 acres of privately owned land in what the U.S. Forest Service describes as a "checkerboard ownership pattern." For example, Donner Memorial State Park is state-owned but surrounded by the forest, while the Donner Camp Picnic Ground is part of the forest. The town of Truckee is surrounded by forest, as are some of the privately owned ski resorts nearby.

Sierra Hot Springs

Sierra Hot Springs (521 Campbell Hot Springs Rd., Sierraville, 530/994-3773, www.sierrahotsprings.org, 3 hours $15, until midnight $20, ages 5–15 $7.50) is a rustic, minimally developed campus that truly makes you feel you're getting away from it all. Natural hot springs feed a large outdoor swimming pool and the small Temple Dome Hot (it's very hot). The pool area includes a sauna and is clothing-optional. Drugs, alcohol, and pets are not allowed, although several cats and a dog live here. Officially, Sierra Hot Springs is a nonprofit church—the New Age Church of Being—and at least one member of your party must join the church in order to visit. Nothing is required except a membership fee ($5 monthly, $20 yearly, lifetime $300).

Accommodations

If you want to spend the night in or around Sierra Hot Springs or the town of Sierraville, you have two basic choices, all of them owned by the hot springs organization. The **Main Lodge** (521 Campbell Hot Springs Rd., Sierraville, 530/994-3773, www.sierrahotsprings.org, private rooms $88 Sun.–Thurs., $110 Fri.–Sat. and holidays, dormitory $39 Sun.–Thurs., $50

Fri.–Sat. and holidays) on the resort premises was built in the 1870s. It has five private rooms with shared baths and one five-bed dormitory. The Main Lodge offers a lounge, a communal kitchen, a very small store (potato chips and toothbrushes), and best of all a gracious front porch and spacious lawn for sunbathing. Communal cats wander the premises.

You can also stay in the historic **Globe Hotel** (530/994-3773, www.sierrahotsprings.org, $88 Sun.–Thurs., $110 Fri.–Sat. and holidays) off the premises in the nearby town of Sierraville. The Globe offers a charming Old World parlor complete with a fireplace and a piano, a communal kitchen, and a large back deck. By the way, calling Sierraville a "town" is a bit of an exaggeration. If you choose to sunbathe on the porch, your privacy is unlikely to be interrupted much by people or passing cars. One of the hotel's selling points for allergy-prone visitors is the lack of cats and other animals.

Camping

The campgrounds at **Sierra Hot Springs** (521 Campbell Hot Springs Rd., Sierraville, 530/994-3773, www.sierrahotsprings.org, $27.50) are a rambling continuum of undeveloped meadows, woods, and ranchland with no designated campsites. Just find a place where you feel comfortable and pitch your tent. You can also bring an RV, but there are no hookups, and the mostly dirt roads can be bumpy and rutted. The camping fee includes full use of the pools and facilities; no reservations are needed.

The nearest U.S. Forest Service campground is **Lower Little Truckee Campground** (Hwy. 89, 11 miles north of Truckee, 877/444-6777, www.recreation.gov or www.fs.usda.gov, May–Oct., $17, Memorial Day, Independence Day, and Labor Day weekends $19). Quiet and remote, this campground does have potable water. Just a few miles farther north along Highway 89, is **Upper Little Truckee Campground** (Hwy. 89, 13.5 miles north of Truckee, 11.5

© HEATHER C. LISTON

the charming Globe Hotel

miles south of Sierraville, 877/444-6777, www.
recreation.gov or www.fs.usda.gov, May–Oct.,
$17, Memorial Day, Independence Day, and
Labor Day weekends $19) which offers the
same features plus a little more distance between you and urban life. Both campgrounds
have picnic tables and pit toilets.

Cold Creek Campground (Hwy. 89, 19 miles
north of Truckee, 4.5 miles south of Sierraville,
877/444-6777, www.recreation.gov or www.
fs.usda.gov, May–Oct., $12–14, holiday week-
ends $14–16) is a shady, attractive place with
minimal facilities but plenty of pine trees, nature trails, and streams. Pit toilets are available
in the campground, but there's no water, so
make sure to bring your own. Cold Creek is
located 20 miles north of Truckee and 4.5 miles
from Sierraville on Highway 89.

One of the particularly appealing U.S.
Forest Service campgrounds is **Chapman
Creek** (877/444-6777, www.recreation.gov,
$21). To get here, take Highway 89 north of

Truckee to Highway 49 west to Sierra City,
a small town in the Tahoe National Forest.
Eight miles before Sierra City is a quiet grove
of lodgepole pines with signs promising bears
and rattlesnakes and lots of water for fishing
and swimming. Chapman Creek runs through
the campground, and the North Yuba River is
across the street. Salmon Lake, Gold Lake, and
other picturesque mountain watering holes are
within easy driving or mountain-biking distance. In summer the place is usually sunny
without being too hot, thanks in part to the elevation—about 6,000 feet. With 27 sites in the
campground, there's likely to be space available,
although it's always best to make a reservation.

For an unusual overnight option, consider the **Calpine Lookout** (3 miles northwest of Calpine, near Hwy. 89, 877/444-6777,
www.recreation.gov or www.fs.usda.gov,
$45). This structure was built by the Civilian
Conservation Corps in 1934 and was used as
a forest-fire lookout until 1975. Now retired,

it's available for rent to overnight travelers. The observation cab sleeping area is on the top floor and is furnished with two single beds, a table, and chairs. A pit toilet and a picnic table are nearby. The tower is available year-round, but it can be difficult to reach in snowy weather. The last 1.5 miles to get to it are down an un-paved forest road, but if you've got the right vehicle—or are willing to walk, ski, or snowshoe the last bit—then winter can be a wonderful time to visit. Bring your own food, water, fire-wood, and first-aid kit, as the tower is not close to any services. For more information, contact the Sierraville Ranger Station (530/994-3401).

Food

When visiting Tahoe National Forest, it's best to stock up on food before you get too far from a supermarket. If you stay at Sierra Hot Springs or at the Globe Hotel in Sierraville, you'll be able to prepare food you bring in their kitchens.

The **Philosophy Café** (521 Campbell Hot Springs Rd., Sierraville, 530/994-3773, www.sierrahotsprings.org, 6:30–8:30 P.M. Fri., 8:30–10 A.M. and 6:30–8:30 P.M. Sat.–Sun., $10–15), located in the Main Lodge at the Sierra Hot Springs Resort, is a great place for both vegetarians and carnivores to eat fresh and fairly healthy food. Typical dinner options include the spinach–goat feta delight or the bacon lover's pizza, and prices are low. One drawback: It's open only on weekends.

In the town of Sierraville, across the street from the Globe Hotel, is the **Chuck Wagon Café** (101 Main St., Sierraville, 530/994-1000, daily 7 A.M.–2 P.M. summer, hours vary winter, $7–12). This old-time rural diner caters largely to local cattle ranchers. The food is filling if predictable, and service is sparse, but if you're hungry, you'll be glad you found this place.

About 13 miles northeast of Sierraville is Loyalton, where **Vicki's Blue Moon Bakery and Café** (700 Main St., Loyalton, 530/993-4634, 5 A.M.–2 P.M. Tues.–Fri., 7 A.M.–2 P.M.

Sat., $10) makes a mean breakfast in addition to homemade soups and baked goods.

Getting There and Around

Remoteness is part of the charm of the Tahoe National Forest—you'll need a car to get here. It's possible to take Amtrak to Truckee and rent a car there. Once you're in the countryside, bicycles, horses, and cross-country skis are great modes of transportation for moderate distances.

Most visitors travel on I-80 to Truckee; it is 185 miles from San Francisco, 105 miles from Sacramento, and 32 miles from Reno, Nevada. From Truckee, the main roads form a loop that roughly surrounds much of the Tahoe National Forest area. Highway 89 heads northwest from Truckee toward Sierraville (24 miles); to continue west, merge onto Highway 49 and follow the Yuba River through Sierra City (23 miles from Sierraville) and Downieville (12 more miles) before curving south. At Nevada City, 43 miles from Downieville, Highway 49 becomes Highway 20 and leads east to Norden, which is 42 miles from Nevada City, and Truckee, 15 miles east of Norden.

PLUMAS NATIONAL FOREST

The Plumas National Forest (530/283-2050, www.fs.usda.gov/plumas) is one of 18 national forests in California. Established in 1905 by President Theodore Roosevelt, it comprises almost 1.2 million acres in the Sierra Nevada south of the Cascade Mountain Range and north of Lake Tahoe and Truckee. The forest features hundreds of alpine lakes and streams, many of which are teeming with fish; challenging trails and memorable vistas created by the mountainous terrain; and sunny summer days with lots of elbow room. You may go to Plumas to pursue activities from boating to snowshoeing to mountain biking to horseback riding, or you may choose this as a great destination to just pitch a tent, breathe the mountain air, and listen to the quiet.

© HEATHER C. LISTON

Plumas National Forest

Plumas-Eureka State Park

Plumas-Eureka State Park (310 Johnsonville Rd., Blairsden, 530/836-2380, www.parks. ca.gov, free), five miles west of Blairsden on County Road A-14, is noteworthy for its historical and cultural significance in addition to its flat-out gorgeous natural setting. The 4,500-acre park is located near Eureka Peak, which used to be known as Gold Mountain; the area was originally developed because of gold mining in the late 1800s.

In the middle of the park is a **museum** (daily 9 A.M.–4:30 P.M. Memorial Day–Labor Day, 9 A.M.–4:30 P.M. Fri.–Sun. Labor Day–late Sept., donation), in a former bunkhouse for gold miners. Outside is the actual mining area, where you can visit two historic stamp mills, where ore was crushed to free gold, and watch demonstrations at a period blacksmith shop.

Plumas-Eureka State Park is well worth going out of your way for. From I-80 near Truckee, take Highway 89 north about 45 miles to Graeagle-Johnsville Road (County Rd. A-14). Turn left and follow the signs for about seven miles to Plumas-Eureka State Park.

Sports and Recreation

Hiking is one of the best reasons to go to Plumas County, and one of the best trails is located within Plumas-Eureka State Park. The **Eureka Peak Loop Trail** (6 miles round-trip) is believed to be the site where two 19th-century miners discovered the gold that was to make the place a sensation. From the park's visitors center and museum, follow County Road A-14 for one mile through Johnsville to the Ski Area. At the Ski Area parking lot, you'll see a fire road heading to Eureka Lake. Friday–Sunday, start from the parking lot and walk up the dirt road, where you'll find the trailhead for the Eureka Peak Loop Trail. Monday–Thursday, you're allowed to drive up the fire road to the lake and begin walking from there for a shorter hike (3 miles round-trip). If you hike the whole six miles, you'll gain 1,800 feet of elevation in a fairly short time, so the steepness makes this hike fairly strenuous. It's worth it, though—from the top of Eureka Peak is a broad view of the forests and mountains of the region, extending as far as Mount Lassen.

With its expansive grasslands and relatively small human population, Plumas County is a thriving region for cattle and horse ranches. Many local operators offer guided trail rides, lessons, pack trips, and stables to accommodate the horses. One operator with a good reputation is **Gold Lake Stables** (7000 Gold Lake Rd., Lakes Basin Recreation Area, 530/836-0940, www.reidhorse.com), near the town of Bassets Station along Highway 89. Gold Lake offers guided trail rides ranging from one hour ($33 pp) to an multiple-night backcountry trips ($255–350 pp per night).

Gold Lake Stables operates another facility that's a little more kid-oriented. **Graeagle Stables** (Hwy. 89, Graeagle, 530/836-0430, wwww.reidhorse.com, reservations required), a few miles north, offers private lessons ($45 per hour) and pony rides ($14 per hour) in addition to guided trail rides for adults.

Accommodations

If you want a comfortable place to rest after your daytime adventures, you'll find **Chalet View Lodge** (72056 Hwy. 70, Graeagle, 530/832-5528 or 800/510-8439, www.chaletviewlodge.com, $99–215), a lovely place to stay in the Plumas area. With 49 guest rooms, suites, and cabins, wireless Internet access, a day spa, an outdoor pool, a nine-hole golf course, and a mountain-bike track, this place has everything you need for a great vacation—even if you never leave the premises.

Camping

As many as 50 different campgrounds are scattered throughout the Plumas National Forest (www.fs.usda.gov), some for groups, some just for 4WD vehicles, and one specifically for equestrians. These campgrounds do not tend to fill up, even in the busy midsummer season, so chances are you'll find a place to sleep if you're willing to wing it.

One of the most scenic and peaceful Plumas National Forest campgrounds is ◖ **Gold Lake Campground** (9 miles southwest of Graeagle, June–Sept. $10, Oct.–May free) within the Lakes Basin Recreation Area. This is a great launching point for waterskiing, kayaking, canoeing, fishing, and even ice fishing in winter if you bring your snowmobile. There are 37 campsites with fire rings; parking and a boat dock are available at no charge. There is no drinking water available, so bring your own, and the restroom facilities are pit toilets and portables. To get here from Graeagle, take Highway 89 southeast for two miles, and then head south on Gold Lake Highway for 10 miles.

You can camp in one of the 67 sites at **Plumas-Eureka State Park** (310 Johnsonville Rd., Blairsden, 800/444-7275, www.reserveamerica.com, $35), five miles west of Blairsden on County Road A-14. Sites here are available by reservation Memorial Day–Labor Day; the rest of the year they're on a first-come, first-served basis. The campground features baths with flush toilets and hot showers. A number of streams and lakes are within a short drive or hike from the campground, and Jamison Creek meanders right through it, making fishing, especially for trout, as easy as rolling out of bed.

One of the more unusual places to stay in the Plumas National Forest is the **Black Mountain Lookout** (Beckwourth Ranger District, 530/836-2575, reservations 877/444-6777, www.recreation.gov, up to 8 people $60). The lookout offers views of Honey Lake and Last Chance Creek to the south. It is located near Milford, 10 miles from U.S. 395.

Food

Restaurants and supermarkets are not

abundant; bring some food of your own to make sure you don't get stuck out in the woods hungry and frustrated. The **Grizzly Grill** (250 Bonta St., Blairsden, 530/836-1300, www.grizzlygrill.com, daily 5–9 P.M. summer, hours vary fall and spring, closed Jan.–Mar., $17–25) is a comfortable woodsy eatery that feels like a cross between a hunting lodge and an upscale family diner. From homemade meatloaf to the fresh catch of the day and generous portions of pasta, you'll probably find something you'll like. There are also early-bird specials (5–6 P.M.) and a special children's menu for smaller appetites.

If you're looking for lunch, you can find it at **Mountain Cuisine** (250 Bonta St., Blairsden, 530/836-4646, www.mountaincuisine.com, 11:30 A.M.–5 P.M. Tues.–Sun., $4–7), next door to the Grizzly Grill and under the same ownership. Mountain Cuisine is also open until 8 P.M. for catering and takeout.

For good locally roasted coffee, espresso, muffins, and wraps, try the **Coffee Tree Express** (196 E. Sierra Ave., Portola, 530/832-4563, 6 A.M.–2:30 P.M. Mon.–Fri., 7 A.M.–2:30 P.M. Sat.).

Getting There and Around

Highways 89 and 70 are the main routes into the Plumas National Forest. The nearest airport is the **Reno-Tahoe International Airport** (RNO, 2001 E. Plumb Lane, Reno, NV, 775/328-6400, www.renoairport.com).

LAKE TAHOE

Nevada Shore

Lake Tahoe straddles California and Nevada, and so do visitors to the area. Heading east on U.S. 50 from the South Shore, the town of South Lake Tahoe becomes Stateline, Nevada, with barely a sign announcing the transition. On the North Shore, shortly west of the intersection of Highways 28 and 267, Crystal Bay marks the California-Nevada border crossing. The drive along the Nevada side of Lake Tahoe is beautiful, woodsy, and quiet, with fewer towns and stopping points along the way. You'll often find yourself deep in the pines with fewer lake views, although they certainly exist.

If you're driving the perimeter of the lake, many locals recommend driving the route clockwise, northbound on the west side and southbound on the east. The obvious advantage is that your car stays on the lake side, making it easier to admire the views and to pull over at beaches and scenic overlooks. But either direction provides a lovely excursion.

THUNDERBIRD LODGE

If you're seeking Native Americana, you're in for a surprise. On the Nevada side of the lake is the Thunderbird Lodge (5000 Hwy. 28, Incline Village, NV, 775/832-8750 or 800/468-2463, www.thunderbirdlodge.org, tours Tues.–Sat. June–mid-Oct., adult $39, children $19), built in 1936 by a Tahoe resident called the Captain who intended to create a luxury hotel and casino on his vast lakeside acreage. It was one of the last great upscale residential mansions constructed beside the lake and includes several outbuildings.

You won't be able to drive directly to Thunderbird Lodge. Instead, park at the Crystal Bay Visitors Center (969 Tahoe Blvd., Incline Village, NV, 800/468-2463, 8 A.M.–5 P.M. Mon.–Fri., 10 A.M.–4 P.M. Sat.–Sun.) to meet the tour guide and bus. You'll be driven out to the lodge for a 1.25-hour walking tour of the grounds and several of the buildings. The 600-foot underground tunnel from the mansion to the boathouse and card house is one of the tour highlights, especially for kids. Another highlight is the unbelievable 1930s-era mahogany yacht *Thunderbird,* which still floats in the boathouse.

LAKE TAHOE

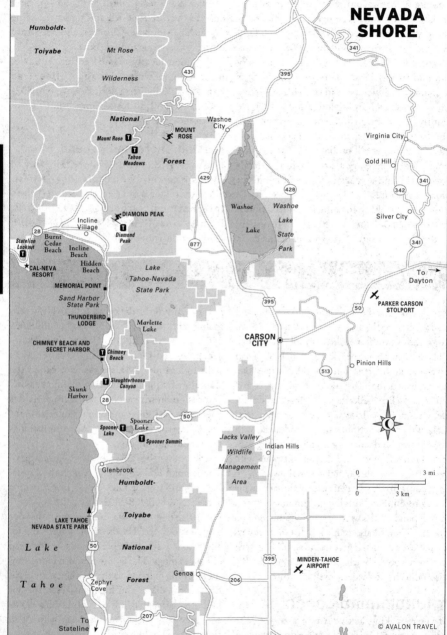

NEVADA SHORE

Humboldt-

Toiyabe

Mt Rose

Wilderness

National

Mount Rose

Mount Rose

Tahoe Meadows

Forest

DIAMOND PEAK

Incline Village

Diamond Peak

Stateline Lookout

Burnt Cedar Beach

Incline Beach

Hidden Beach

CAL-NEVA RESORT

MEMORIAL POINT

Sand Harbor State Park

THUNDERBIRD LODGE

CHIMNEY BEACH AND SECRET HARBOR

Chimney Beach

Slaughterhouse Canyon

Skunk Harbor

Spooner Lake

Spooner Lake

Spooner Summit

Glenbrook

Lake Tahoe-Nevada State Park

Marlette Lake

Humboldt-

Toiyabe

National

LAKE TAHOE NEVADA STATE PARK

Lake

Tahoe

Forest

Zephyr Cove

To Stateline

Washoe City

Virginia City

Gold Hill

Silver City

Washoe Lake

Washoe Lake State Park

To Dayton

PARKER CARSON STOLPORT

CARSON CITY

Pinion Hills

Jacks Valley Wildlife Management Area

Indian Hills

Genoa

MINDEN-TAHOE AIRPORT

28

431

341

395

429

428

877

395

50

513

341

342

341

50

28

50

50

207

206

395

0   3 mi

0   3 km

© AVALON TRAVEL

If you're staying on the west side of the lake, book a **boat tour** (Tahoe Keys Marina, South Lake Tahoe, 775/588-1881 or 888/867-6394, www.tahoeboatcruises.com, 10 A.M. Tues.–Sat. summer, reservations required, adults $135, ages 6–11 $55) on a historic wooden powerboat across the lake and along the eastern shore. The boat docks at the Thunderbird Lodge, and the walking tour continues from there. A continental breakfast is served on board the ship, and a buffet lunch at Thunderbird is included with the five-hour tour. Children under age six are not permitted. Both tours operate in summer only, with exact dates set by the Lodge.

SPORTS AND RECREATION
Ski Resorts
MT. ROSE
Mt. Rose (22222 Mt. Rose Hwy., Reno, NV, 775/849-0704 or 800/754-7673, www.mtrose.com, lift daily 9 A.M.–4 P.M. in season, adults $55–69, seniors $55, ages 13–17 $55, ages 6–12 $19) offers the most choice in terms of both variety and beginner routes. Many different ski school packages and private-lesson options are available for children ages three and older as well as seniors who want to cut it up on a snowboard. Sign the kids up for ranger-guided exploration programs as well as ski or board camps where they will have a great time, learn lots, and make ski buddies their own age.

Novices should beware of the center of Mt. Rose, an area called Chutes with a morass of double-black-diamond runs and names like Detonator and Yellow Jacket. If you're looking for green runs, park at the Main Lodge and take the Ponderosa or the Galena Chairs up to beginner territory. For lots of great long intermediate tracks, start at Slide Lodge (the second access point for the Mt. Rose resort) and take the Blazing Zephyrs Six-Chair almost to the top of the mountain. You can enjoy a hot cocoa and a meal or use restrooms at either lodge.

DIAMOND PEAK
Smaller Diamond Peak (1210 Ski Way, Incline Village, NV, 775/832-1177 or 877/468-4397, www.diamondpeak.com, lift daily 9 A.M.–4 P.M. in season, adults $38–49, seniors $14–39, ages 15–17 $30–39, ages 7–14 $14–18, under age 7 free) is easy to access from Incline Village and has two—count 'em, two—green runs at the bottom of the hill. It's probably not the best place to bring young children or beginners on as there isn't as much variety. However, if you're an intermediate skier or boarder, take the Crystal Express quad up to the top of the peak. Stop for a moment and enjoy the amazing vistas before taking a wonderfully long run down the blue Crystal Ridge, or cut into one of the black-diamond chutes that branch off through the forest. You'll start your day down at the Base Lodge, where you can also eat, drink, and make merry. In the middle of the day, the Snowflake Lodge on the ridge is the perfect setting for looking out onto the lake as you sip a drink or just sit with your feet up.

Cross-Country Skiing and Snowshoeing
For cross-country skiing, check out **Spooner Lake Cross Country** (Spooner Lake entrance, Lake Tahoe–Nevada State Park, Hwy. 28, 0.5 mile north of U.S. 50, 775/749-5349, www.spoonerlake.com, lift daily 9 A.M.–5 P.M. in season, adults $12–22, youth $12, under age 13 and over age 69 free), a cross-country and snowshoe resort. You can stride and glide by two small lakes in this region, Spooner and Marlette. Less experienced and more sedate skiers tend to stick to the well-groomed easy and moderate trails near Spooner Lake, Spooner Meadow, and the Lodge. The buns-of-steel crowd can head up North Canyon to Saints Rests beside Marlette Lake, or go all out and circle the aptly named Big Loop—a 21-mile advanced monster that will definitely give you a full day's workout. Big Loop may or may not be groomed; when it's left all-natural, it's even more challenging. All cross-country ski trails at Spooner are snowshoe-accessible (be courteous by staying on the

LAKE TAHOE

outside edges), and the resort maintains narrow-marked snowshoe-only trails throughout the area. Rentals and lessons are available. If you want to stay right at Spooner Lake, inquire about rental cabins, available year-round.

Snowmobiling

It's hard to miss the presence of the **Zephyr Cove Snowmobile Center** (Zephyr Cove Resort, 760 U.S. 50, 775/589-4906, www.zephyrcove.com, $119–169) in Zephyr Cove. The free shuttle runs along the highway for all reserved riders to use at their convenience. A Lakeview or Sierra Summit tour on a new Ski-Doo snowmobile includes breathtaking views, easy riding on groomed trails, and plenty of stops to take pictures. Advanced riders can work with the guides to create a challenging personal tour.

Sledding and Sleigh Rides

Take an old-school sleigh ride at several locations around Tahoe. Just across the street from the Harrah's and MontBleu casinos in Stateline is **Borges Family Sleigh Rides** (55 U.S. 50, Stateline, NV, 775/588-2953, www.sleighride.com, 30-minute ride adults $20, under age 12 $10). The Borges have been giving sleigh rides on the South Shore for more than 30 years. They've got sleighs seating 2–20 passengers and lovely blond Belgian draft horses; hour-long tours and dinner rides are also available. Each ride runs through the woods to a spectacular lake view. Cuddle under blankets as you listen to stories and songs—but bring a thermos of cocoa. In summer, check out the carriage and hayrides.

Waterskiing and Wakeboarding

Zephyr Cove Marina (750 U.S. 50, Zephyr Cove, NV, 775/589-4901, www.zephyrcove.com, ski boats $149–189, WaveRunners $109–129) offers a full complement of services and watercraft rentals. For skiers and wakeboarders, Zephyr Cove has a small fleet of 22–24-foot Sea Ray open-bow ski boats, plus skis, boards,

and toys. Personal watercraft riders can rent one of the marina's three-person WaveRunners. Truly adventurous visitors can also sign up for a parasailing session with professional drivers.

Beaches

Sand Harbor Beach (Hwy. 28, 3 miles south of Incline Village, NV, 775/831-0494, www.parks.nv.gov, daily 8 A.M.–7 P.M. May 1–Memorial Day; daily 8 A.M.–9 P.M. Memorial Day–Labor Day; daily 8 A.M.–7 P.M. Labor Day–Sept. 30; daily 8 A.M.–5 P.M. Oct. 1–Apr. 30; $12 per vehicle Apr. 15–Oct. 15, $7 per vehicle Oct. 16–Apr. 14, walk-in $1 pp) is part of the Lake Tahoe–Nevada State Park, but people often refer to it as Sand Harbor State Park. The 55-acre sandy beach is one of the most popular places to swim at Lake Tahoe. Big boulders make great destinations to swim out to, dive off, and perch on top of to rest and take in the views. There's a large picnic area, and the on-site restaurant–snack bar **Char-Pit Sand Harbor** (530/546-3171, www.charpit.com, daily 10:30 A.M.–7 P.M. June–Labor Day, $4–23) specializes in burgers and ice cream—the ample barbecue ribs are popular with hungry families. If it's boating you're interested in, the people to see are **Sand Harbor Rentals** (530/581-4336, www.sandharborrentals.com, single kayak or paddleboard $25 per hour, $65 per day, double kayak $40 per hour, $95 per day, wakeboard or tube $35 per day, Jet Skis $110 per hour, $600 per day), the only officially sanctioned boat concessionaire in the park. Sand Harbor Rentals is right on the beach next to the boat ramp; you can walk up and try your luck at getting a rental, but reservations are recommended. The company also offers a morning East Shore tour ($90 pp), a sunset kayak tour ($65 pp), and a stand-up paddleboard tour ($30 pp), for which reservations are also required.

Fishing

At Zephyr Cove you can book a fishing trip

with **O'Malley's Fishing Charters** (775/588-4102, www.worldwidefishing.com, Apr.–Oct., $115 pp). You need your own fishing license, but O'Malley's supplies the bait, tackle, and equipment. A cozy 22-foot boat and lots of personal attention from your guide make for an intimate angling experience.

At **Spooner Lake** (Lake Tahoe–Nevada State Park, U.S. 50 and Hwy. 28, 775/831-0494, www.parks.nv.gov, daily 8 A.M.–9 P.M. Memorial Day–Labor Day, hours vary Labor Day–Memorial Day, Apr. 15–Oct. 15 $12, Nevada residents $10, Oct. 16–Apr. 14 $7, Nevada residents $5) you can fish year-round and experience ice fishing in winter. You can keep up to five trout; a Nevada state fishing license is required.

Nearby **Marlette Lake** (Lake Tahoe–Nevada State Park, summer $10, Nevada residents $8) is full of brook, rainbow, and cutthroat trout. Marlette fishing is catch-and-release only, and the season runs July 15–September 30. For more information, visit the Nevada Department of Wildlife (www.ndow.org).

Golf

The championship George Fazio course at **Edgewood Tahoe** (180 Lake Pkwy., Stateline, NV, 775/588-3566, www.edgewoodtahoe.com, daily May.–Oct., $120–240) has been called better than the Pebble Beach Golf Links. Not everyone agrees with that bold assessment, but the consensus is that Edgewood is one of the top courses in the West if not the nation. Walking the course, you'll enjoy views of the lake and mountains so wonderful that you may forget all about that pesky putting for a moment or two. Several holes are right on the shores of Lake Tahoe—the biggest water hazard around. The rather hefty greens fees include a golf cart; you can also rent clubs and hire a caddie. After your game, enjoy lunch and a stiff drink at the **Brooks' Golf Bar & Deck** (daily 7 A.M.–9 P.M.).

Hiking

For a serious lake-to-lake hike, try the **Marlette Lake Trail** (10 miles, moderate). The Spooner Lake trailhead is located in Lake Tahoe–Nevada State Park (775/831-0494, www.parks.nv.gov, $10, Nevada residents $8) at the junction of U.S. 50 and Highway 28. The hike slopes uphill for five miles to the Marlette Dam, but you're on a fire road much of the way, so the trail is easy to follow and the terrain never gets too rough.

For a shorter hike with less climbing and even more shoreline, try the **Spooner Lake Trail** (2 miles) from the Spooner Lake trailhead in Lake Tahoe–Nevada State Park. The level trail features interpretive signage and gets you some close-up views of birds and other wildlife, including—if you're lucky—eagles and ospreys. In winter, the Spooner Lake area of Lake Tahoe–Nevada State Park is run by a private concessionaire, Spooner Lake Cross-country (775/749-5349, www.spoonerlake.com, daily 9 A.M.–5 P.M. winter, adults $12–22, youth $12, under age 13 and over age 69 free).

There's additional pleasant hiking in the **Sand Harbor** (Apr. 15–Oct. 15 $12, Nevada residents $10, Oct. 16–Apr. 14 $7, Nevada residents $5) area of Lake Tahoe–Nevada State Park. The **Sandy Point Trail** starts near the visitors center and takes you down a paved-and-boardwalk path for 0.3 mile, with interpretive signs along the way.

Farther north, the scenic hiking continues. For a quick easy walk near Crystal Bay, Nevada, head up to the **State Lookout** (iron-pipe gate on Forest Rd. 1601, 1 mile, easy). At the lookout, you'll find summer volunteers who can give you information about the region, including the short self-guided nature trail that surrounds the lookout.

Horseback Riding

Equestrians can sign up for a ride with **Zephyr Cove Resort Stables** (U.S. 50, Zephyr

Cove, 775/588-5664, www.zephyrcovestable.com, daily 9 A.M.–5 P.M. summer, daily 10 A.M.–4 P.M. spring and fall, 1 hour $40, 2 hours $70). Enjoy a lovely scenic trail ride complete with panoramic views of the lake. Zephyr Cove also offers "food rides" (2–2.5 hours, $40–70) at breakfast (8 A.M.), lunch (11 A.M.), and dinner (5 P.M.). If you have dietary restrictions, call ahead to make arrangements in advance. As at many stables, restrictions include a weight limit (225 pounds) and a minimum age (age 7) for riders.

Mountain Biking

You can rent a mountain bike from **Flume Trail Mountain Bikes** (daily 8:30 A.M.–6 P.M., 775/749-5349, www.theflumetrail.com, $45–65 per day), inside the Spooner Lake State Park day-use area in the Toiyabe National Forest in Zephyr Cove. The company, owned by Patti McMullan and Mountain Bike Hall of Fame member Max Jones, provides shuttle services to certain trailheads and offers knowledgeable advice about mountain biking in the area. Reservations are recommended and can be made by phone or online.

The spectacular **Tahoe Rim Trail** (www.tahoerimtrail.org) provides mountain bikers access to about half of the 165 miles of rugged and varied terrain. You can't bike where the trail enters the Desolation or Mount Rose Wilderness Areas, or where it joins the Pacific Crest Trail. These areas are usually well signed. If you'd like to bike the particularly beautiful section from the Tahoe Meadows trailhead to Spooner Lake, a private shuttle service (775/749-5349, www.theflumetrail.com, mid-June–Nov., $20) is available. The shuttle, with a trailer for your bike, leaves from the parking lot at Spooner Lake State Park and delivers you to the Tahoe Meadows Rim Trail trailhead on the Mount Rose Highway. Signs at the trailhead indicate that this section of the trail—between Tahoe Meadows and beyond Spooner

Lake to Spooner Summit—is bikable only on even-numbered days of the month.

CASINOS

If you think casinos are smoke-filled holes sheltering lonely souls pouring their savings into slot machines, think again: On the South Shore, just over the Nevada state line, various casinos attract a young crowd looking for a lively hip night out. Note that the casinos sometimes call the town Lake Tahoe, Nevada, although it's legally Stateline.

MontBleu

The gaming floor of the MontBleu Resort Casino and Spa (55 U.S. 50, Stateline, NV, 775/588-3515 or 888/829-7630, www.montbleuresort.com) is great fun on weekend evenings, with go-go dancers and youthful gamblers enjoying free drinks as they hammer the slots. As with other casinos here, you'll find full-fledged table games of the Vegas variety: craps, roulette, blackjack, and Texas hold 'em, among others. The Zone contains the sports book and the poker room, while slots and video poker machines are everywhere. MontBleu's casino is better lit and less smoky than many others, making it easy to stay and play late into the night. If you get tired of gambling, wander around to the full-service salon and spa, pool, lingerie shop, art gallery, ski-rental shop, nightclub, or several restaurants.

Harrah's

Gambling fans should definitely bring their frequent-player cards to the casino floor at Harrah's Lake Tahoe (15 U.S. 50, Stateline, NV, 775/588-2411 or 800/427-7247, www.harrahslaketahoe.com), which has all the Vegas gaming favorites—classic craps, rapid roulette, and of course Keno pads and monitors scattered all over the place. The atmosphere is a bit more classic casino, with dim lights in the evening and a warren of slot machines that make it easy to get lost.

Harrah's is a classic casino.

Now that Harrah's has absorbed its neighbor, Harvey's, it has a solid lock on its block. When you've had enough gaming, check out the live entertainment or the popular nightclub.

Harvey's

For those who can't get enough, Harrah's affiliated casino Harvey's Lake Tahoe (18 U.S. 50, Stateline, 775/588-2411 or 800/427-8397, www.harveystahoe.com) is nearby. At Harvey's, you can play all the usual games of chance or enjoy state-of-the-art video screens while betting on football, NASCAR, and horse races in The Book, the nonsmoking racing and sports site. Harvey's also boasts a fitness center, a pool, and, of course, entertainment, from improv comedy to headliner musical acts (Wed.–Sun. year-round) and concerts in the outdoor arena in summer.

Lakeside

Smaller and less flashy, Lakeside Inn and Casino (168 U.S. 50, Stateline, NV, 775/588-7777 or 800/624-7980, www.lakesideinn. com) is a local favorite. Lakeside looks more like a mountain lodge than a high-rise gaming emporium, and it has won the most votes for Best Casino, Loosest Slots, and Friendliest Casino Employees. The casino offers all the usual games and machines, and it is particularly welcoming for beginners, who may want to attend the "University of Lakeside" (6 P.M. Wed.), a free seminar in the Poker Room where Lakeside employees teach the basics of blackjack, craps, and more. In a way, they pay you to come, with a free cocktail, souvenirs, and $5 worth of free play at the slots.

Cal-Neva

The Cal-Neva Resort, Spa, and Casino (2 Stateline Rd., Crystal Bay, NV, 775/832-4000 or 800/225-6382, www.calnevaresort.com, $119–169) claims to be the only property in the world located in two states. The casino part,

© HEATHER C. LISTON

Harvey's casino

naturally, is on the Nevada side of the line, as are most of the hotel's 199 guest rooms, but the cabins and chalets (late May–Sept.) are on the lakefront in California. The casino has 35 slot machines and one automated blackjack table, making it much smaller than the giant casinos of the South Shore, but if you want to enjoy a little gambling as part of a quiet getaway on the lake, this may be the best choice. Apparently a few other people—including Frank Sinatra, Marilyn Monroe, and their friends—once thought so. A favorite activity here is the Secret Tunnel Tour ($10 pp) that takes you into an underground hideaway where celebrities are said to have protected their privacy while visiting. Room rates vary widely, from as low as $39 on winter weeknights to as high as $269 for a suite in midsummer, but they're usually quite reasonable—even the large chalets, which come with fridges, fireplaces, and living rooms, are only $99–119. Four cabins (even those purported to be favored by Frank and Marilyn) are only $109–159. The

on-site **Lakeview Dining Room** (775/298-3090, daily 7 A.M.–4 P.M. and 5–9 P.M., $9–30) features standard American fare like burgers, chicken, steak, and fish, all complete with expansive views of the nearby lake.

ENTERTAINMENT AND EVENTS
Nightlife

Since the youthful snowboarding crowd packs Tahoe in winter and the wakeboarders fill the summer, it's no surprise that some noticeable nightlife crops up around the lake. The favorite clubs tend to be inside the Stateline casino resorts. Often the hip dancing crew spills out of the clubs and onto the casino floor throughout the evening.

A favorite nightclub for many locals is **Vex at Harrah's** (15 U.S. 50, Stateline, NV, 775/586-6705, www.harrahslaketahoe.com, 10:30 P.M.–4 A.M. Fri.–Sat., cover Fri. women $5, men $10, Sat. women $10, men $20). This late-night watering hole features dancing Vex

Girls on Friday–Saturday nights at midnight and aerial acts on Saturday. An in-house DJ provides a lively mix for dancing. Enjoy a cocktail at the bar, or for additional cost, enjoy table service by the lovely cocktail staff in a plush VIP booth. Friday is bachelor and bachelorette party night; if you schedule your party in advance, the whole group gets in free.

When it comes to late-night entertainment, **The Opal Ultralounge at MontBleu** (55 U.S. 50, Stateline, NV, 775/586-2000 or 888/829-7630, www.montbleuresort.com, 10 P.M.–4 A.M. Wed.–Sat., cover $10–20) is one of the most happening places around. Entertainment includes expert mash-up DJs, resident body painters (midnight Thurs.–Sat.), and go-go dancers (11:30 P.M. Thurs.–Sat.). If you'd like to be painted, you can have it done in private at no charge, although gratuities are accepted. There's no cover on Wednesday nights, all drinks are $1 on Thursday, women drink for free until 2 A.M. on Friday, and women pay no cover before midnight on Saturday.

Comedy

For an evening of laughter, get tickets to **The Improv at Harveys** (18 U.S. 50, Stateline, NV, 800/786-8208, www.harrahslaketahoe.com, 9 P.M. Wed.–Fri. and Sun., 8 P.M. and 10 P.M. Sat., $25–30). Each evening an old-school Budd Friedman comic showcase goes up; Howie Nave is the host and emcee. This is the place where many of today's major comedy stars honed their acts—come see who'll be famous next.

Festivals and Events

California theater-lovers have been known to drive for hours to see a show at the **Lake Tahoe Shakespeare Festival** (800/747-4697, www.laketahoeshakespeare.com, July–Aug., $15–85). A new stage facility was built in 1995 at the classic Sand Harbor State Park beach location (Hwy. 28, 3 miles south of Incline Village). Shuttle service (948 Incline Way, Incline Village, NV, 775/298-0163) to the park is offered. Expensive sections of the theater have reserved seating and chairs, but in the cheap seats you can bring your own chair or lie on a blanket in the sand. Gates open at 5 P.M. and performances begin at 7:30 P.M. Come early to enjoy food and drinks from Shakespeare's Kitchen.

ACCOMMODATIONS
Casinos

Tahoe's casino resorts are some of the spiffiest places to stay on the Nevada side, offering upscale attractive hotel rooms often at lower than expected rates. You'll also find the occasional noncasino lakeshore resort that focuses more on recreation than the slots.

The most popular casino resort on the Nevada side is **Harrah's** (15 U.S. 50, Stateline, NV, 775/588-2411 or 800/427-7247, www.harrahslaketahoe.com, $179–219), with upscale accommodations, all the nightlife and entertainment you need, and easy access to Heavenly and other South Shore ski resorts in winter and the lakeshore in summer. The high-rise hotel has more than 500 upscale guest rooms; even the lower-end guest rooms have ample space, a California king or two double beds, two baths, Wi-Fi, cable TV, premium movies (for a fee), and minibars. Premium Rooms are above the tree line and provide excellent views of the lake and the mountains. The decor is upscale and contemporary, with white linens and comforters, bright colorful accents, and sleek furnishings and wall art. Room rates vary widely depending on the season, local events, and the weekday or weekend you plan to visit.

Harvey's Casino (18 U.S. 50, Stateline, NV, 775/588-2411 or 800/427-8397, www.harveystahoe.com, $139–199), now under the same ownership as Harrah's, has guest rooms that tend to be a little less plush and a little less expensive than those at Harrah's. At Harvey's, midweek off-season rates can run as low as $79.

MontBleu Casino (55 U.S. 50, Stateline,

© HEATHER C. LISTON

MontBleu Casino

NV, 775/588-3515 or 800/648-3353, www.montbleuresort.com, $100–250 summer) definitely shines when it comes to attractive hotel rooms with top amenities. With 437 guest rooms, MontBleu is prepared to offer a range of affordable choices. Tower rooms include a comfortable bed, loud decor and fabrics, blackout curtains, room service, private baths, and all the conveniences. For luxury, try a spa room, which includes a pink-marble bath, walk-in shower, and two-person hot tub in the bedroom. On winter weekdays, rates for a spa room can run as low as $49. MontBleu used to be a Caesar's, and although they renovated beautifully, the walls remain paper-thin—bring earplugs. Wireless Internet access is also available ($12 for 24 hours).

Condo Rentals

Club Tahoe (914 Northwood Blvd., Incline Village, NV, 775/831-5750 or 800/527-5154, www.clubtahoe.com, $145–250) is a great place to rent a condo on the Nevada side of the lake. Each three-story unit includes two bedrooms and a loft with twin beds, perfect for families or a group traveling together. The decor isn't the most contemporary—expect 1970s–1980s-era sofas, bargain-basement wood furniture, and paneling on the walls—but the full-size kitchens are stocked with appliances and utensils, and a second bath makes sharing the condo easy. Amenities include an outdoor pool and spa, a tennis court, a racquetball court, an arcade, and a full bar with pool table for adults looking to unwind in the evening.

Resorts

If you prefer a Nevada ski resort to a casino, try the **Parkside Inn at Incline** (1003 Tahoe Blvd., Incline Village, NV, 775/831-1052 or 800/824-6391, www.innatincline.com, $129–159), with 38 guest rooms in a modest mid-century-style motel. The guest rooms are reminiscent of a low-end motel, with slightly shabby furniture, but they are clean, and the private baths are adequate. Amenities include an indoor pool and a hot tub available year-round, flat-screen TVs, and free wireless Internet access in all guest rooms.

Perhaps the best noncasino place to stay is **Zephyr Cove Resort** (760 U.S. 50, Zephyr Cove, NV, 888/896-3830, www.zephyrcove. com, $139–319). This resort has it all: lakefront property, lodge guest rooms and individual cabins, a full-service marina, a winter snowmobile shuttle and park, and restaurants. Guests of Zephyr Cove can choose a guest room inside the big lodge or a cabin down by the lake. The four lodge rooms all have private baths, attractive modern appointments, TVs, microwaves, small fridges, and coffeemakers. For a special treat, ask for the room with the spa tub. The 28 cabins run from cozy studios for couples to multistory chalets that sleep up to 10 people ($609). Although they look rustic and woodsy from the outside, inside you'll find modern furniture, phones, TVs, wireless Internet access, and all the amenities you'd expect from a nice lakeside resort, including daily maid service. Zephyr Cove offers pet-friendly lodgings; when making reservations, let them know which furry friends you'll bring.

CAMPING

Within the Spooner Lake area of Lake Tahoe–Nevada State Park, **Spooner Lake Inc.** (775/749-5349, www.spoonerlake.com or www.flumetrail.com, Sun.–Thurs. May–Oct. $95–188, Sun.–Thurs. Nov.–Apr. $160–319) offers two log cabins for foot travelers: Spooner Cabin and Wild Cat Cabin. Accessible only by snowshoe, cross-country skiing, or hiking, these backwoods cabins are pretty basic. Each sleeps four people with a queen bed upstairs and a futon downstairs, a wood stove for heat, a kitchen stove for cooking, and two gallons of water per day. Note that Friday–Saturday nights are a package deal; you must pay for both nights if you want to come on the

weekend. In winter, the package also includes a cross-country ski trail pass, rental of skis or snowshoes, and a cross-country ski lesson.

Nevada Beach Campground (Elks Point Rd., 3 miles north of Stateline, NV, 0.25 mile northwest of U.S. 50, summer 775/588-5562, www.fs.usda.gov; reservations 877/444-6777, www.recreation.gov, mid-May–mid-Oct., $28–34) is a U.S. Forest Service campground offering 54 lakefront sites on the Nevada side of Lake Tahoe. RVs up to 45 feet are welcome, although no hookups are available. Drinking water, flush toilets, and convenience to both Lake Tahoe and the nightlife of Stateline are all attractions here.

FOOD
Stateline

The popular **Red Hut Café Nevada** (229 Kingsbury Grade, Stateline, NV, 775/588-7488, daily 6 A.M.–2 P.M., $10) opened an outpost in Stateline. **Starbucks** is served inside the Horizon Casino Resort (50 U.S. 50, Stateline, NV, 775/588-6211 or 800/648-3322, www.horizoncasino.com) and inside Harrah's (15 U.S. 50, Stateline, NV, 775/588-2411 or 800/427-7247, www.harrahslaketahoe.com).

The **Ciera Steakhouse at the MontBleu** (55 U.S. 50, Stateline, NV, 775/588-3515 or 800/648-3353, www.montbleuresort.com, 5:30–10 P.M. Wed.–Sun., $26–49) provides precisely the experience diners expect from a casino steak house. On the menu are plenty of steak and nonsteak options, with preparations designed to appeal to visitors from around the country. The coolest part of the Ciera dining experience is the coffee, complete with a fabulous tray of fixings, including delicious flavored whipped creams. Finally, you'll be presented with a complimentary dish of chocolate-covered strawberries resting atop a frothing container of dry ice.

With decor as cute as its name, **Thai One On** (292 Kingsbury Grade, Suite 33, Stateline, NV,

775/586-8424, www.thaioneontahoe.com, 7 A.M.–2:30 P.M. Mon., 7 A.M.–9 P.M. Tues.–Sun., $12–17) serves delicious food at reasonable prices. The menu is eclectic: french toast, tacos, egg rolls, and curry in addition to traditional Thai favorites such as pad thai. Most of the food is prepared on the premises with fresh ingredients, and the results are tantalizing.

The best French food in the area is at **Mirabelle's** (290 Kingsbury Grade, Stateline, NV, 775/586-1007, www.mirabelletahoe. com, 5:30 P.M.–close Tues.–Sun., $20–33). Mirabelle's offers a three-course Epicurean Menu ($35) or an á la carte dinner menu with entrées such as venison, lobster, and ostrich.

One of the best dining experiences is at **◖ Edgewood Tahoe Restaurant** (100 Lake Pkwy., Stateline, NV, 775/588-2787, www. edgewoodtahoe.com, 5:30 P.M.–close daily summer, 5:30 P.M.–close Wed.–Sun. winter, $27–40). Located on the world-famous Edgewood golf course, the restaurant features elk chops, macadamia-crusted sea bass, and rack of spring lamb. The prices are reasonable considering the quality of the food. For dessert, try the handmade chocolate truffle plate or the nightly crème brûlée.

Incline Village

Jack Rabbit Moon (893 Tahoe Blvd., Suite 600, Incline Village, NV, 775/833-3900, dinner 5:30–9 or 10 P.M. Wed.–Sun. year-round, lunch 9 A.M.–1 P.M. Sat.–Sun. June–Aug., $15–30) is a small but popular fine-dining establishment noted for its extensive wine list, fresh contemporary menu, and seafood specialties such as lobster tamales and wild salmon. Brunch is served in summer only, when they can open the doors and offer patio seating.

If your tastes run to the creative and pleasantly surprising, you'll enjoy **Fredrick's Fusion Bistro** (907 Tahoe Blvd., Incline Village, NV, 775/832-3007, www.fredricksbistro.com, 5–9 P.M. Tues.–Wed., 5–10 P.M. Thurs.–Sat.,

$13–32), where lobster dogs share a table with surf-and-turf sushi rolls. The fusion is mostly French and Asian, but there's a definite California feeling to the seasonal menus, which make good use of the fresh and the local.

A good place to splurge on a meal with an exceptional lake view is the **Lone Eagle Grille** (111 Country Club Dr., Incline Village, NV, 775/886-6899, www.loneeaglegrille.com, 11:30 A.M.–3 P.M. and 5:30–9 P.M. Mon.–Thurs., 11:30 A.M.–3 P.M. and 5:30–9:30 P.M. Fri.–Sat., 10:30 A.M.–3 P.M. and 5:30–9 P.M. Sun. winter, 11:30 A.M.–3 P.M. and 5:30–10 P.M. Mon.–Thurs., 11:30 A.M.–3 P.M. and 5:30–10:30 P.M. Fri.–Sat., 10:30 A.M.–3 P.M. and 5:30–10 P.M. Sun. summer, $35–47). Entrées on the main menu include steak, lamb, and veal, but there's a special menu just for vegetarians with up to four choices for every course; fresh creative soups, salads, and vegetables are prominent on both.

INFORMATION AND SERVICES

The **Lake Tahoe Visitors Authority Visitors Center** (169 U.S. 50, Stateline, NV, 775/588-5900, www.tahoesouth.com) is across from the Lakeside Inn and Casino. It's a big spacious place with maps, brochures, and clean restrooms. The **Incline Village Crystal Bay Visitors Bureau** (969 Tahoe Blvd., Incline Village, NV, 775/832-1606 or 800/468-2463, www.gotahoenorth. com, 8 A.M.–5 P.M. Mon.–Fri., 10 A.M.–4 P.M. Sat.–Sun.) is another source of information.

The Lake Tahoe region has its own daily newspaper, the *Tahoe Daily Tribune* (www. tahoedailytribune.com). Pick up a copy at any newsstand, or ask for it at your hotel.

To get cash, hit the ATMs in Stateline; the towns on the Nevada side of the lake are small and far apart. The casinos have plenty of cash machines too. Stateline has a **post office** (223 Kingsbury Grade, Stateline, NV, 775/588-1943, 9 A.M.–5 P.M. Mon.–Fri.).

Incline Village Community Hospital (880

Alder Ave., Incline Village, NV, 775/833-4100 or 800/419-2627, www.tfhd.com) is the place to go for help on the Nevada side. The hospital has a 24-hour emergency room.

GETTING THERE AND AROUND
Air
The closest commercial airport to Lake Tahoe is in Reno, the **Reno-Tahoe International Airport** (RNO, 2001 E. Plumb Lane, Reno, NV, 775/328-6400, www.renoairport.com). It is particularly convenient for travelers heading to the Nevada side of the lake. To get to Incline Village from the airport, take U.S. 395 south for eight miles to Highway 431 south for another 24 miles. The airport is open year-round, but be sure to check on your flights in advance in the winter since storms delay and sometimes cancel flights.

Car
I-80 and U.S. 50 are the main roads to the Nevada side of Lake Tahoe from points west. To reach the North Shore on the Nevada side, take I-80 to Truckee, then follow Highway 267 south to Kings Beach (still in California). Take Highway 28 east, which quickly enters Nevada, toward Incline Village. Highway 28 continues south along the lake, meeting U.S. 50 at the Spooner Lake area; continue south on U.S. 50 to reach Stateline, Nevada, in about 12 miles.

From South Lake Tahoe, follow U.S. 50 east for about three miles into Stateline, Nevada. U.S. 50 runs to Carson City, Nevada in another 12 miles. To continue circumnavigating the lake, bear left onto Highway 28 toward Incline Village and Highway 431 in about 12 miles.

From Reno, you can reach the North Shore on the Nevada side in 45–60 minutes, depending on the weather. Always check road conditions before attempting any route in winter, as storms may cause chain requirements or even road closures.

Cruises
Bleu Wave (866/413-0985, www.tahoebleuwave.com, adults $49–59, children $25–30) operates from the Round Hill Pine Beach & Marina (325 U.S. 50, Zephyr Cove, NV, 775/588-3055, www.rhpbeach.com) in Stateline. Their Emerald Bay cruise lasts two hours with an all-you-can-eat lunch buffet, drinks included.

LAKE TAHOE

SACRAMENTO AND GOLD COUNTRY

The capital of California, Sacramento is a cosmopolitan city with a friendly vibe and a low-key, fun entertainment scene. The city grew along the Sacramento River during the Gold Rush era and provided a vital transit link between the mining country and the port of San Francisco. Today, politics is the new gold, and it permeates Sacramento with its constant presence.

Most California mining history is outside the city in the small boomtowns that sprang up in the 19th century near major mines. With the closing of the mines, these towns declined for decades but were eventually rediscovered by tourists and travelers. A wealth of mining museums in the Gold Country region informs visitors about the backbreaking work of gold mining, while ghost stories entertain locals and visitors alike. For travelers who want less history and more action, this is also prime whitewater rafting and kayaking country.

While Sacramento pumps as California's political heart, down south in the Central Valley is its agricultural artery and the staple of the state's economy. The huge flat valley is where the majority of California's crops grow, as it offers a prime climate for a huge array of foods, especially citrus.

History buffs will enjoy visiting the Capitol Building and the historic sights around Old Sacramento before taking a road trip through the various Gold Rush towns and mining

HIGHLIGHTS

LOOK FOR ◖ TO FIND RECOMMENDED SIGHTS, ACTIVITIES, DINING, AND LODGING.

◖ **Capitol Building:** This iconic building is the epicenter for the city's political history, past and present. Be sure to check out the museum's im-

pressive collection of art and antiques (page 505).

◖ **Old Sacramento:** Take a tour of Old Sacramento for a sense of how the state capital grew during its 150 year existence (page 507).

◖ **Empire Mine State Historic Park:** The best example of Gold Country mining is this living history museum and park (page 526).

◖ **Marshall Gold Discovery State Historic Park:** This is the place that started it all—the spot where gold was discovered in 1848. The rest is literally history (page 539).

◖ **Apple Hill:** This 20-mile swath of grower heaven includes dozens of orchards, vineyards, and pit stops for dining and relaxing along the way (page 540).

◖ **Rafting:** The Gold Country has several mighty rivers with churning Class III-V rapids. Both rookie rafters and experienced paddlers will find rafting opportunities, especially on the American River near Placerville (page 543).

◖ **Daffodil Hill:** This private ranch is carpeted in golden color every March, when visitors can explore the more than 300 species of daffodils on display (page 559).

◖ **Columbia State Historic Park:** A former Gold Rush town, Columbia is now an indoor-outdoor museum experience with exhibits, shops, and even a saloon—all preserved in homage to the area's mining history (page 569).

SACRAMENTO

museums along Highway 49. Outdoors enthusiasts can start with a multiple-day river rafting trip, and then work their way north, hiking, kayaking, and spelunking. Epicureans and wine aficionados will find new delights along the farm trails of El Dorado County, through the Shenandoah Valley and Fair Play, and down to Fresno and the citrus belt. Whatever your pleasure, this diverse region of California has something for you.

PLANNING YOUR TIME

Sacramento makes a nice day trip or weekend getaway from the Bay Area, or a fun 1–2-day start to a longer Gold Country and Sierra adventure. Winters are mild here, while summers get blisteringly hot.

The Gold Country is physically too large to experience in one day, or even in a weekend. Highway 49 runs more than 100 miles through the precious metal–bearing Sierra

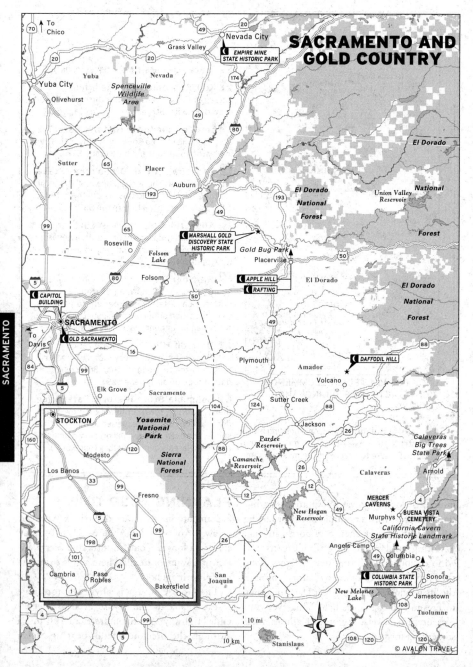

SACRAMENTO

SACRAMENTO AND GOLD COUNTRY

© AVALON TRAVEL

Foothills, and it's impossible to resist side trips to smaller towns and specific caverns, mines, and museums along the way. If you've got one day, pick a specific Gold Country town as your destination, and one or two of the major parks and attractions nearby. In a weekend, you can get an overview of either the northern or southern Gold Country, driving from town to town and making short stops along the way. Visiting season in Gold Country runs late spring–late fall, when the weather is best. Winter brings snow to many of the Sierra foothill towns, which draws skiers and other winter-sports enthusiasts.

Sacramento and Vicinity

Many people outside the state don't realize that Sacramento is California's state capital. Despite the fact that this river town is hundreds of miles from Hollywood, many actors have made their homes here—the office of governor has been occupied by the likes of actors Ronald Reagan and Arnold Schwarzenegger. This surprisingly lovely town has lots to offer visitors, from white-water rafting along the Sacramento River to one of the best music festivals in the state.

SIGHTS
Capitol Building

The California State Capitol Building (10th St. and L St., 916/324-0333, http://capitolmuseum. ca.gov, daily 9 A.M.–5 P.M., free) displays a grandeur befitting the great state of California. On the ground floor, the museum's magnificent art collection includes California art and artifacts, oil portraits of the state's governors, two murals, and a collection of antiques. You can take a free tour that highlights the neoclassical architecture of the building, or learn about some important legal decisions made for the state.

Once you've finished absorbing the history of California from inside the museum, go outside and take a stroll around the grounds. At the rear of the building is an unusual treat—the **Arbor Tour.** An amazing array of trees from around the world are planted in the sweeping space, creating a garden that's perfect for exploring, if you love botany, or just for finding a nice place to sit and relax in the shade. The Arbor Tour is self-guided during the winter months; docents offer guided tours spring–fall.

Governor's Mansion State Historic Park

Schoolchildren from all over the state journey to Sacramento to tour the Governor's Mansion (1526 H St., 916/323-3047, www.parks.ca.gov, 10 A.M.–5 P.M. Wed.–Sun., adults $5, children $3). The mansion served as the residence of California's governors 1903–1967; Governor

Capitol Building

© CHRISTOPHER ARNS

SACRAMENTO

SACRAMENTO

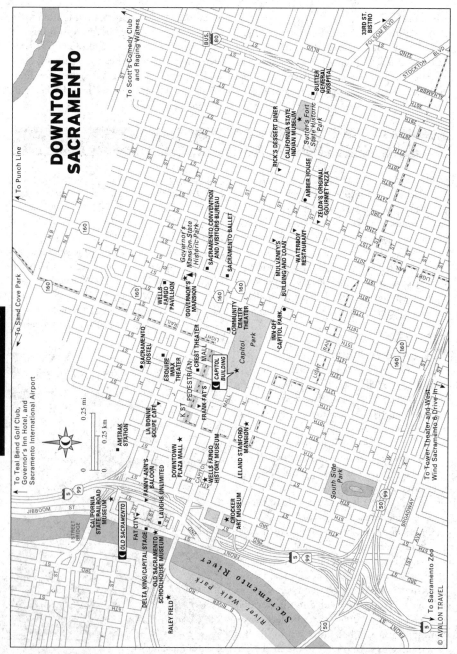

DOWNTOWN SACRAMENTO

To Punch Line

To Scott's Comedy Club and Raging Waters

33RD ST. BISTRO

SUTTER GENERAL HOSPITAL

RICK'S DESSERT DINER

CALIFORNIA STATE INDIAN MUSEUM

Sutter's Fort State Historic Park

AMBER HOUSE

ZELDA'S ORIGINAL GOURMET PIZZA

SACRAMENTO CONVENTION AND VISITORS BUREAU

SACRAMENTO BALLET

WATERBOY RESTAURANT

MULVANEY'S BUILDING AND LOAN

Governor's Mansion State Historic Park

WELLS FARGO PAVILLION

GOVERNOR'S MANSION

Capitol Park

COMMUNITY CENTER THEATER

INN OFF CAPITOL PARK

SACRAMENTO HOSTEL

CREST THEATER

ESQUIRE IMAX THEATER

Capitol Building

CAPITOL BUILDING

FRANK FAT'S

LA BONNE SOUPE CAFE

To Teal Bend Golf Club, Governor's Inn Hotel, and Sacramento International Airport

AMTRAK STATION

DOWNTOWN PLAZA MALL

WELLS FARGO HISTORY MUSEUM

LELAND STANFORD MANSION

To Tower Theater and West Wind Sacramento 6 Drive-In

South Side Park

FANNY ANN'S SALOON

LAUGHS UNLIMITED

CALIFORNIA STATE RAILROAD MUSEUM

OLD SACRAMENTO

FAT CITY

DELTA KING/CAPITAL STAGE

OLD SACRAMENTO SCHOOLHOUSE MUSEUM

CROCKER ART MUSEUM

RALEY FIELD

To Sacramento Zoo

Sacramento River

River Walk Park

0   0.25 mi

0   0.25 km

To Sand Cove Park

JIBBOOM ST.

I STREET BRIDGE

To Sacramento Zoo

© AVALON TRAVEL

© CHRISTOPHER ARNS

the historic Governor's Mansion

Ronald Reagan and his wife, Nancy, were the last couple to live in the mansion, and they stayed only three months. Since then, the mansion has become an educational tool and a visitor attraction. To enter the Governor's Mansion, you must buy tickets and sign up for a guided tour, held frequently throughout the day. Guests get to see the ornate European interior decor, evidence of different tastes and different generations, and the grandeur that has traditionally surrounded the governors of the state.

Old Sacramento

Sacramento became an important town as the Gold Rush progressed and supplies were sent up the Sacramento River from San Francisco. The most important part of the early town were the piers along the river, and that's still where Old Sacramento (visitors center, 1002 2nd St., 916/442-7644, daily 10 A.M.–5 P.M.) is today. The charming cobblestone streets and clattery wooden sidewalks pass old-time

shops, restaurants, and attractions. You can take a carriage ride through the streets or walk the wharf and wander the decks of the *Delta King.* Check out the tiny **Wells Fargo History Museum** (1000 2nd St., 916/440-4263) and **Old Sacramento Schoolhouse Museum** (Front St. and L St., 916/483-8818, www.oldsacschoolhouse.org), or lighten your wallet in the shops and boutiques. To really get into the spirit of the location, look for the Old Sacramento Living History (916/445-3101, www.oslhp.net) activities that take place every month. Join a Living History Walk (Sat.–Sun. June–Oct.), where a costumed guide will tell you the story of this area from the point of view of a 19th-century resident. You can also roam beneath the city's cobbled streets with **Old Sacramento Underground Tours** (916/808-7059, www.historicoldsac.org, hours vary Mar.–Nov., adults $15, children $10). Back in the 1860s, Sacramento was repeatedly inundated by catastrophic floods, so officials raised the city one story to escape the ravaging waters of the Sacramento River. Underground tours reveal the hidden corridors and passageways that were buried when the city was elevated. The tour schedule frequently changes; check the website for current times.

California State Railroad Museum

If you've ever felt a lick of romance for the rails, stop at the California State Railroad Museum (111 I St., 916/445-6645, www.csrmf.org, daily 10 A.M.–5 P.M., adults $9, children $4). Inside the mammoth museum buildings are artifacts and models that illustrate the building of the railroads to the West, especially the all-important Transcontinental Railroad. The main floor plays host to the museum's fabulous collection of rolling stock—locomotives, freight and passenger cars, and cabooses. It's strange to see mammoth locomotives standing still inside these walls; machines that made so much industry possible seem to belong outdoors. The

SACRAMENTO

museum occasionally lends its stock for photography and films.

You can look in on the stylish appointments of the private rail cars of the wealthy and stand next to the immense wheels of mighty steam locomotives. Climb aboard the open cars and locomotives for a look inside the railroad that made the growth and expansion of California possible. Along the edges of the room are memorabilia from the heyday of the railroads, including timetables and fine china. A gift shop offers souvenirs for visitors of all ages, including Thomas the Tank Engine toys for young kids, replica china for collectors, and thick tomes of railroad history for history buffs.

Cross the plaza to board the steam-powered **Excursion Train** (916/445-6645, 11 A.M.–5 P.M. Sat.–Sun. Apr.–Sept., adults $10, children $5) for a 40-minute ride along the riverfront.

Sutter Fort State Historic Park

Sutter Fort State Historic Park (2701 L St., 916/445-4422, www.parks.ca.gov, 10 A.M.–5 P.M. Tues.–Sun., adults $5, youth $3), situated in the middle of downtown Sacramento, was originally the center of John Sutter's "New Helvetia" settlement. A tour of the park begins with the mazelike museum at the entrance. Inside the fort structure, the story of John Sutter is told in photos, artifacts, and placards. After perusing the interpretive area, wander outside into the sunlight and enjoy the living history all around. Wander the inner walls of the fort to see how the early settlers lived—from dragging their luggage from the East to their bedrooms at the settlement. Denizens of the park, dressed in 19th-century costumes, engage in the activities that filled the days of California's settlers. With their help, you can try your hand at making rope, baking bread, and doing all sorts of pioneer activities. Afterward, stop at the gift shop, which evokes a small 1800s store, filled with historic costume patterns, books, and period toys.

Sutter Fort was an important colony during the Gold Rush.

© CHRISTOPHER ARNS

Leland Stanford Mansion

Railroad baron and Stanford University founder Leland Stanford and his family spent a number of years living in the capital city at what is now the Leland Stanford Mansion State Historic Park (800 N St., 916/324-0575, www.stanfordmansion.org, 10 A.M.–5 P.M. Wed.–Sun., adults $5, children $3). Some years after Leland Stanford's death, his wife, Jane Stanford, donated the family mansion to the Catholic Church for use as a children's home. It was eventually purchased by the state, and the current museum was constructed in the 1990s. Tours begin in the visitors center, next to the museum store outside the mansion. From here you'll journey inside the lavish main building, where you can admire the lovingly restored furnishings, carpets, walls, and antiques. Visitors get a hint of what it might have been like to live as one of the wealthiest people in the country in some of the most exciting years of California's history.

Mansion tours are wheelchair accessible, and assistive listening devices and other aids are available on request. You must be part of a tour to explore the mansion; the visitors center, store, and parts of the gardens can be visited for free.

Crocker Art Museum

Ten centuries of fine art are collected at the Crocker Art Museum (216 O St., 916/808-7000, www.crockerartmuseum.org, 10 A.M.–5 P.M. Tues.–Wed. and Fri.–Sun., 10 A.M.–9 P.M. Thurs., adults $10, seniors and students $8, children $5), and traveling exhibitions visit on an ongoing basis. The original gallery was donated to the city of Sacramento by the Crocker family—one of the "Big Four" railroad and industry barons who made a fortune building California's early infrastructure. That fortune paid for the international art collection that Margaret Crocker donated to the public. Today, wander the galleries filled with paintings from Europe and Asia, ceramics

SACRAMENTO

© CHRISTOPHER ARNS

Crocker Art Museum

from around the world, photographs, drawings, and specifically California art. The galleries—housed inside Victorian mansions—are works of art themselves. The museum recently expanded, allowing the Crocker to house even more exhibitions and paintings.

Sacramento Zoo

Take a trip to visit the animals at the Sacramento Zoo (Sutterville Rd. and Land Park Dr., 916/808-5888, www.saczoo.org, daily 9 A.M.–4 P.M. Feb.–Oct., daily 10 A.M.–4 P.M. Nov.–Jan., adults $11.25, children $7.25). A fabulous array of animals awaits, including big cats and other mammals, funky frogs and amphibians, big ol' snakes, a small-fish aquarium, and many more. Take cover from the summer heat under the shade of the century-old oak trees as the critters enjoy their own custom-grown garden habitats. Monthly zoo activities include educational talks, guided walks, special festivals, and other events.

ENTERTAINMENT AND EVENTS
Bars and Clubs

Before the city's Midtown district began its current renaissance, Sacramento's hottest lounge was **Harlow's** (2708 J St., 916/441-4693, www.harlows.com, shows age 21 and over, tickets $10–30). Sacramento's nightlife has grown since then, but Harlow's is better than ever. The sleek, urbane interior has a big-city feel and a moneyed vibe; make sure to spiff up before rubbing elbows with the swanky crowd. The live acts range from local favorites like Tainted Love and Irish rockers Young Dubliners to hot new DJs at the city's Electronic Music Festival (usually May). Harlow's often has a line to get in, especially if there's a show, so plan to arrive early if you don't want to wait.

Mix (1525 L St., 916/442-8899, www.mix-downtown.net) is a great place to rub elbows with Sacramento's power elite. Lobbyists and lawmakers come after office hours to let loose or haggle over state business; it's also a great

spot to meet friends for a night on the town. Polished wooden ceilings and wall panels give the decor a minimalist European feel with California flair. A rooftop patio with fire pits and comfy chairs invites relaxing with a glass of wine or a beer—perfect after a long day of strolling Sacramento's sidewalks. Mix is popular on weekends; there will definitely be a line if you arrive later in the evening.

De Vere's Irish Pub (1521 L St., 916/231-9947, http://deverespub.com) exudes Irish history and for good reason—most of the vintage photographs and mementos adorning the walls belong to the owners. If that's not authentic enough, all of the furniture and fixtures were designed and imported from Ireland, including the towering wooden bar that spans two rooms. The 20-ounce pints of Guinness are popular, but you can also order from a sizable cocktail list. There's also a full menu of Irish and British cuisine. One word of caution: De Vere's is one of the busier stops for Sacramento's singles scene, so be prepared for a meat market on weekends.

There's no secret password, but the **Shady Lady Saloon** (1409 R St., 916/231-9121, http://shadyladybar.com) still feels like a speakeasy with a Gold Rush vibe. The Shady Lady is in the heart of Midtown's up-and-coming R Street Historic Corridor, Sacramento's old industrial district. Bartenders don vintage vests and wear garters on their sleeves, all while serving up libations like the White Linen or the Horse Neck. There's a stylish decadence to the bar decor, and you can catch a variety of live acts nightly. The bar also serves dinner and weekend brunch. The Southern-inspired menu is delicious, but plan to order early; service can lag once the cocktail crowd arrives.

Live Music

For a night of impeccable classical music, buy tickets for a concert by the **Sacramento Philharmonic Orchestra** (916/732-9045, http://sacphil.org, $18–100). The

Philharmonic performs all over the area, most often in the Community Center Theater (1301 L St.) and Three Stages at Folsom Lake College (10 College Parkway, Folsom, 916/608-6888).

Each May, music lovers from around the state flock to the capital for the **Sacramento Music Festival** (www.sacjazz.com). Every Memorial Day Weekend, more than 100 acts—including classic, zydeco, big band, western, skiffle, and funk—descend on Sacramento to perform in venues ranging from the lush Convention Center stage to the wooden planks of the Old Sacramento sidewalks. Festival organizers also book blues, bluegrass, rock, and R&B bands, giving the event an inclusive feel. Be sure to get tickets in advance; this is one of the best events that Sacramento has to offer.

Comedy

Sacramento has three major comedy clubs. The **Punch Line** (2100 Arden Way, 916/925-5500, www.punchlinesac.com, shows Wed.–Sun., tickets $15–35), a sister club to the San Francisco Punch Line, brings in top national talent. You might see the likes of Dana Carvey and Wayne Brady live and in person. Shows run nightly Wednesday–Sunday, with hot local and up-and-coming national acts such as Gabriel Iglesias and Amy Schumer. All tickets are general admission, so you'll be able to find a seat at a table when the doors open.

In the middle of Old Sacramento, **Laughs Unlimited** (1207 Front St., 916/446-8128, www.laughsunlimited.com, shows Wed.–Sun., tickets $3–24) brings hilarity to the waterfront with comics such as Todd Paul and Chris Titus doing multiple-night engagements every week and occasional shows by comedy legends such as local resident Jack Gallagher, Shawn Wayans, and Alonzo Bodden. You'll have a great time at this classic comedy venue. There's a two-drink minimum, and a reasonable appetizer and dessert menu can satisfy appetites grown large from laughter.

If you're a sucker for improv comedy, head to the **Sacramento Comedy Spot** (1050 20th St., 916/444-3137, http://saccomedyspot.com, shows Wed.–Sun., tickets $10). Attend an improv class to sharpen your comedic skills, or watch the mostly local and occasionally national acts run through their skits. The Comedy Spot is open to all ages, although shows can sometimes get a little salty.

Cinema

Sacramento is a great place to go to the movies. For a larger-than-life cinematic experience, get tickets for the **Esquire IMAX Theater** (1211 K St., 916/443-4629, www.imax.com/sacramento, $8–17.50). The Esquire shows IMAX documentary films in traditional 2-D and mind-blowing 3-D.

If you're looking for a classic night out at the movies, drive in to the **West Wind Sacramento 6 Drive-In** (9616 Oates Dr., 916/363-6572, www.westwinddriveins.com, $5–7). This six-screen drive-in plays first- and second-run Hollywood films. You won't get a speaker for your car; instead you'll tune in to a radio channel. Bring your own pillows and blankets for a truly luxurious movie experience. The old-school circular building at the center of the facility sells inexpensive movie concessions and includes a fun, cheap arcade.

For your indie film pleasure, hit **The Crest** (1013 K St., 916/442-7378, www.thecrest.com, $9.50). The interior of the theater is a show in itself—it was restored in the 1990s to the glitzy heights of its 1940s art deco glory. In addition to films, the Crest occasionally puts on a live stand-up comedy show with a major star such as Carrot Top or Sam Kinison.

The Tower (2508 Land Park Dr., 916/442-0985, www.thetowertheatre.com, $9.50–11) is a quirky three-screen art house that shows popular, foreign, and independent films. It's not quite as grand as the Crest, but at the Tower you can enjoy an old-fashioned elegant cinematic atmosphere and a first-run Hollywood flick all at the same time.

Theater

Live theater is an important part of the nightlife of Sacramento. The **Capital Stage** (2215 J St., 916/995-5464, http://capstage.org, $18–32) strives and succeeds at taking regional theater to the next level. This professional company has a small space to perform works by up-and-coming playwrights and classic, less-often-produced plays by heavy hitters like Sam Shepard. All the plays Capital Stage puts on are geared for the over-18 set, so they may include adult language and sexual situations.

On board the *Delta King,* **Suspects Murder Mystery Dinner Theater** (1000 Front St., 916/443-3600, www.suspectstheater.com, $40–43) combines dinner and a fun show. As dinner begins, gunshots ring out, and you'll spend the rest of your meal laughing as you participate in an Agatha Christie–style murder mystery. You might find yourself a suspect, or possibly a victim. However the story plays out, you'll enjoy the comedy, the mystery, and the tasty food and drink at this fun, kitschy night.

For musical theater, get tickets for the latest show at **California Musical Theater** (CMT, 916/557-1999, www.calmt.com, $19–86). CMT uses the Wells Fargo Pavilion (1419 H St.), the Cosmopolitan Cabaret (1000 K St.), and the Community Center Theater (1301 L St.) for its productions. The Broadway Series features iconic Broadway musicals—*Phantom of the Opera* and *Mamma Mia.* The Music Circus series shows off the classic musicals such as *Aida, Annie,* and *The Best Little Whorehouse in Texas.* Purchase single-show tickets online at the website or over the phone.

Dance

Classical dance lovers can enjoy a night out at the **Sacramento Ballet** (1631 K St., 916/552-5800, www.sacballet.org, performances Thurs.–Sun., adults $18–65, children $9–32). For 50 years, this company has brought high-level dance spectacles to the capital; the Sacramento Ballet went fully professional in 1986. For the last 20 years it has produced an array of famous ballets, including classics such as *Sleeping Beauty* and *The Nutcracker* as well as any number of new and interpreted works, including the world premiere of *A Woman's Journey: The Tamsen Donner Story* and *A Streetcar Named Desire.* Purchase individual tickets directly from the box office, by phone, or the website. Most performances are held at the Sacramento Community Center theater—a large space with multiple tiers of seats.

Festivals and Events

The California State Fair takes place annually at the mammoth **California Exposition & State Fair Center** (Cal Expo, 1600 Exposition Blvd., 916/263-3000, www.calexpo.com). The property is used for large-scale retail shows as well as shows and festivals that require plenty of exhibition space. The Quilt, Craft, and Sewing Festival is held here, along with RV shows, landscape shows, gun shows, and boat shows. Year-round, horseracing fans can come to the Cal Expo Sports & Wagering Center at the Miller Lite Grandstand to place bets on their favorite ponies. Races play on the hundreds of flat-screen TVs set up all around the center.

The highlight of each year at Cal Expo is the **California State Fair** (www.bigfun.org). The fair lasts for two weeks, usually at the end of August. During that period, nearly one million people pass through the gates of Cal Expo. They might come for the musical concerts performed by national acts, the horse races at the Miller Lite Grandstand, the carnival, the exhibitions, or the contests. A major wine competition is held at the fair each year, and the biggest and most impressive wineries from around the state take it very seriously. Be sure to wear sunblock during the day and drink plenty of water any time you're here—it gets frighteningly hot in Sacramento in August.

SHOPPING
Antiques

If you prefer the old to the new, come to the **57th Street Antiques Mall** (855 57th St., 916/451-3110, www.57thstreetantiquerow.com, 10 A.M.–5 P.M. Tues.–Sun.). With more than 50 dealers selling their wares, you're likely to find whatever antique or collectible you're looking for. The Mall specializes in smaller items such as linens, jewelry, glass and china, and vintage clothing—perfect for nonlocal shoppers who'd like to pack their treasures into a suitcase. Inside the Mall, you'll find several unique antiques shops with their own specialties. Discovery Antiques has furniture, Asian and French imported antiques, and a fine collection of estate jewelry. Sekula's features 20th-century vintage collectibles with a distinctive West Coast–California bent.

Art Galleries

Between H Street and Capitol Avenue are a number of storefronts displaying works of local and worldwide artists in a variety of media. The best way to explore these is through **2nd Saturdays** (5–9 P.M. Sat. 2nd Sat. of the month, free), an art walk when galleries stay open late and residents crowd the streets filled with vendors, live music, and food.

If you're looking for gifts to bring home to family and friends, check **Zanzibar Imports & Jewelry** (1731 L St., 916/443-2057, www.zanzibartribalart.com, 11 A.M.–6 P.M. Mon.–Fri., 10–6 P.M. Sat., 10 A.M.–3 P.M. Sun.) for international art.

Clothing

The revitalized Midtown (www.midtowngrid.com) offers an array of boutiques, galleries, and shops that please shoppers. Fashionistas have a range of choices, from the sleek **Cuffs** (2523 J St., 916/443-2881, daily 11 A.M.–7 P.M.) to the truth-in-advertising **Cotton Club** (2331 J St., 916/442-2990, 10 A.M.–6 P.M. Mon.–Sat., 11 A.M.–4 P.M. Sun.), which specializes in clothing made from its named material. Thrift and vintage hunters head for **French Cuff Consignment** (2527 J St., 916/442-3724, www.frenchcuffbtq.com, daily 10 A.M.–6 P.M.).

Department Stores

For a standard urban-style shopping mall in Sacramento, go to the **Arden Fair** (1689 Arden Way, 916/920-1167, www.ardenfair.com, 10 A.M.–9 P.M. Mon.–Sat., 10 A.M.–7 P.M. Sun.). It's perfectly located near the junction of I-80 and U.S. 50. In this typical American mall, anchored by Sears, J. C. Penney, Macy's, and Nordstrom, you'll find all your favorite midrange chain clothing stores, shoe stores, specialty shops, and a food court filled with junk food from around the world.

SPORTS AND RECREATION
Amusement Parks

Kids and adults alike can escape the summer's heat at **Raging Waters** (1600 Exposition Blvd., 916/924-3747, www.rwsac.com, $22–31). With rides like Shark Attack, Hurricane, and Cliffhanger, thrill-seekers can get a full day of excitement. For a more sedate day at the water park, ride a slow tube down the Calypso Cooler River, play in Hook's Lagoon, or catch a wave at Breakers Beach.

Golf

You'll find more than a dozen golf courses in Sacramento and surrounding communities. For information about public courses in the city, check the Capital City Golf website (www.capitalcitygolf.com).

In town, perhaps the most beloved public course is the **Bing Maloney Golf Course** (6801 Freeport Blvd., 916/808-2283, www.bingmaloney.com, $11–46), with two courses: the historic 18-hole course that's been on the property since 1952, and the newer par-29 nine-hole executive course, a genuine bargain on weekdays and perfect for beginners. Make reservations for a tee time up to eight days in advance online or over by phone for either course. The par-72 18-hole course has been described as "what you see is what you get"—a straightforward course that will challenge your game with sloping greens and huge heritage oak trees, but not frustrate you with gimmicks or unwelcome surprises.

A newer course in town, the **Teal Bend Golf Club** (7200 Garden Hwy., 916/604-8563, www.tealbendgolf.com, $20–65) has been around since 1997. Conveniently located near the airport and the river, you can slip in a quick round of golf no matter how little time you have. As you walk and play, look out for the teal duck—the course's namesake—as well as deer, geese, and hawks, all of which make their home on the course. You might want to watch your step in the rough too. This course, a local favorite, is famous for its many water features. Make tee time reservations by phone or online up to eight days in advance, or consider enrolling in one of the club's many annual tournaments. After the game, relax at the Bar and Grille, enjoying a casual meal of a burger or a salad and a nice cold beer.

Just outside town, still more golf courses invite politicians, pros, visitors, and amateurs alike. The **Empire Ranch Golf Club** (1620 E. Natoma St., Folsom, 916/790-1595, www.empireranchgolfclub.com, $25–65) is the suburb of Folsom's first golf course, designed by Brad Bell (also the designer of the Teal Bend). The 18-hole course offers challenging play, especially on a windy day, and spectacular views out toward the Sierras. If you're just looking to hone your skills, Empire Ranch offers a full range of practice facilities—putting greens, chipping ranges, and a driving range.

Hiking

A trip to Sacramento wouldn't be complete without a hike along the **American River Parkway** (www.msa2.saccounty.net, 23 miles, easy–moderate). The parkway is actually a series of paved trails that run through wetlands, oak woodlands, and several regional parks along the American River. The trails start at **Discovery Park,** a grassy 302-acre park at the confluence of the Sacramento and American Rivers, and end 23 miles away in the city of Folsom. Along the way, you'll pass cyclists pedaling along river levees, families pushing strollers by the water, and plenty of dog owners taking their pets for a walk. If you're hiking on the trail near Folsom, stop by the **Nimbus Fish Hatchery** (2001 Nimbus Rd., Gold River, 916/358-2820, www.dfg.ca.gov), where the hatchery raises fingerling steelhead trout and salmon in dozens of tanks. The parkway has more than just hiking and biking trails; anglers will find plenty of fishing opportunities along the river, and boating enthusiasts can launch from various points.

One of the more popular Sacramento-area parks actually runs through the separate town of West Sacramento. **River Walk Park** (651 2nd St., www.cityofwestsacramento.org, 0.5 mile, easy) features a paved pathway along the river. Walk the path and read the interpretive plaques to learn about the flora and fauna that inhabit this part of the Sacramento River ecosystem. Bring a cooler and have a picnic at one of the various picnic areas, or bring your rod and tackle onto the fishing dock. A major boat dock lets private boaters moor at the park. River Walk Park also encourages swimming in the river, a refreshing break from the summer heat.

Swimming and Fishing

The heat of Sacramento's summers can make anyone want to jump in a lake—or the river, as the case may be. For a fun and refreshing day out on the banks of the Sacramento River, head for **Sand Cove Park** (2005 Garden Hwy., 916/264-5200). Walk from the parking lot down the trail to the sandy river beach, a

THE SACRAMENTO RIVER

At more than 375 miles long, the Sacramento River is California's largest. Its headwaters begin near Mount Shasta in the north and flow all the way to San Francisco Bay, where it enters the Pacific Ocean, watering the crops of the fertile Central Valley along the way. Immensely popular with boaters, anglers, swimmers, and vacationers of all sorts, the river attracts an estimated eight million visitors per year.

Originally called the Jesús María by Spanish explorers, in 1808 it was renamed by the explorer Gabriel Moraga as *El Rio de los Sacramentos*. The Sacramento River played an important role in the Gold Rush of the 1850s, and it was changed forever as trails, settlements, and cities developed along its shores as a result of the enormous influx of gold miners.

One of many good places to access and enjoy the Sacramento River is the **Colusa-Sacramento River State Recreation Area** (Hwy. 20, Colusa, 9 miles east of I-5, 530/458-4927, www.parks.ca.gov, daily year-round, day use $6, boat launch $5), which offers riverside camping ($25) and picnicking and specializes in boating. Campsites are close together and a bit exposed; don't expect much privacy, shade, or scenery. What you do get is a picnic table, a grill, room for a tent or trailer, access to well-maintained public restrooms, and proximity to the river. Wildlife lovers may be interested to know that this part of the river is a good place to spot great blue herons, mallards, Canada geese, mergansers, muskrats, and river otters, among other permanent residents and migratory visitors. The park is particularly busy in winter for fishing, when salmon and stripers are the main catch.

perfect spot to swim or fish. The park also has a grassy lawn area, shade trees, hiking trails, and a boat dock at the north end, although there's no launch here. Bring a picnic and while away the day alternately swimming in the water, sunning yourself, and fishing for dinner. The river shelters bass, sturgeon, and salmon; you'll need a California fishing license. Amenities at this municipal park are minimal—expect portable toilet facilities and no food vendors.

Spectator Sports

Sacramento is the home of professional sports teams at all levels. It's easy to take in a game while you're visiting. Basketball is a local favorite, and the NBA's **Sacramento Kings** (www.nba.com/kings, $10–190) play at **Power Balance Pavilion** (1 Sports Pkwy.). A fast-paced basketball game can be a great way to unwind after a long day of historical sights and museums. You can get tickets for cheap if you're willing to sit in the nosebleeds. Tickets are available online or at the arena box office. The arena has ample parking ($10).

The hot dry weather of Sacramento's summers just begs for a baseball game. The AAA minor-league **Sacramento River Cats** (www.rivercats.com) play **Raley Field** (400 Ball Park Dr., 916/376-4700, fee for parking), appropriately right by the Sacramento River. At a River Cats game, you'll see serious baseball played by up-and-coming young men, many of whom have a serious eye on the majors. You can take a shuttle ($3) to the field, buy a classic hot dog and a soda or a beer, sit back, and relax while the players do all the work. Ample paid parking is a short-to-medium walk from the stadium entrances.

ACCOMMODATIONS

Sacramento tends to be a working town, with folks coming in for meetings and conventions and staying at big-box chain motels and hotels. Your best bet for a cheap-and-easy guest room is the various Holiday Inns, Quality Inns, and Sheratons.

Under $100

For budget accommodations in Sacramento, you can't beat the **Sacramento Hostel** (925

H St., 916/443-1691, www.norcalhostels.org/ sac, $29–92), in a grand old Victorian home downtown. You'll love the parlor, drawing room, and recreation room—all with high ceilings and historic-style moldings. A full shared kitchen welcomes cooks with all the equipment needed to create tasty and inexpensive meals. On warm evenings, take your dinner out to the wraparound porch to enjoy the weather as the sun goes down. Lodgings include both coed and single-sex dorms, plus a few private guest rooms for a higher rate. Note that only one private guest room includes a private bath—all the other hall baths are shared. The attractive wooden bunks do not include linens, so you'll need to bring your own sheets or a sleeping bag. However, the hostel does have free wireless Internet access, laundry, on-site parking, and 24-hour guest access.

The **Governors Inn** (210 Richards Blvd., 916/448-7224, www.governorsinnhotel.com, $90–145), with classic motel styling, is near the Capitol Building. Walk from the Governors to the Capitol, or take a five-minute drive to Old Sacramento or Midtown, a perfect base for your stay. Whether you book a standard guest room or a two-room suite, you'll enjoy the understated elegance of this motel. Kids enjoy the outdoor pool in the hot summer months, and adults take advantage of the fitness center, free Wi-Fi, continental breakfast, and more. Check the website or ask at the desk for a plethora of recommendations for shopping, restaurants, golf courses, and sights around town.

$100-150

At the **Inn off Capitol Park** (1530 N St., 916/447-8100, www.innoffcapitolpark.com, $115–145), you'll find attractive luxury at moderate prices. The inn is within easy walking distance of the Capitol and the Sacramento Convention Center. The linens, wall art, and paint all match tastefully, and the furniture and lighting feel more like home than a motel.

With an eye toward business and pleasure travelers, amenities include free Wi-Fi and voicemail plus a continental breakfast and dinner recommendations. If you're planning a stay in Sacramento during major events, book at the inn early—with only 38 guest rooms, this friendly boutique hotel can fill up fast during conventions. The Inn off Capitol Park is 100 percent nonsmoking.

If you want to stay on a piece of history, book a stateroom on the **Delta King** (1000 Front St., 916/444-5464, www.deltaking.com, $140–260). An integral part of the Old Town neighborhood, the *Delta King* is at once a hotel, restaurant, theater, and gathering space. To stay on the *Delta King* means stepping back into the Prohibition era, when the *King* plied the Sacramento River between Sacramento and San Francisco. Drinks, jazz, and dancing were the order of the evening then. Today you can stay in the very same staterooms, albeit refurbished to modern, elegant standards. Be aware that the less expensive staterooms can be quite small, as is common onboard ships. All rooms have their own private bathrooms, and for a slightly higher fee you can stay in a much larger and more luxurious stateroom or suite.

$150-250

For a touch of luxury near the Capitol, stay at the **Inn and Spa at Parkside** (2116 6th St., 916/658-1818, www.innatparkside.com, $170–240). Each of the dozen guest rooms features unique decorations with vibrant colors and sumptuous fabrics. Pick from guest rooms named Kiss, Passion, Refresh, and Extravagant. You'll feel as though you're in a cross between a small bed-and-breakfast and an elegant luxury hotel. Many guest rooms have spa tubs and showers, flat-screen TVs, balconies, fireplaces, and other great amenities. This inn is set up for romantic evenings for couples, so consider choosing a different lodging if you're traveling with children. To add extra pampering to your Sacramento stay, book a treatment at Spa Bloom—the attached luxury spa that offers beautifying facials and relaxing massages. Some guest rooms at the inn are set up for in-room massage; check when you book.

Over $250

For luxury digs, the best B&B in Sacramento has long been the (**Amber House** (1315 22nd St., 916/444-8085, www.amberhouse.com, $170–280), located on a quiet residential street in Midtown within walking distance of shopping, restaurants, and nightlife. Consisting of two separate houses, the Amber House prides itself on a level of service you'd find at international upscale hotel chains. The owner and innkeepers will see to your every need from the moment you enter the front door. Every guest room at the inn has either a jetted tub or a deep-soaking bathtub, a very comfortable bed, a subtly tucked-away TV, and top-end amenities. The stellar comfort and service extends to the food as well.

FOOD
Bakeries and Cafés

Consider skipping dessert elsewhere in order to hit (**Rick's Dessert Diner** (2322 K St., 916/444-0969, http://ricksdessertdiner.com, 10 A.M.–11 P.M. Mon., 10 A.M.–midnight Tues.–Thurs., 10 A.M.–1 A.M. Fri.–Sat., noon–11 P.M. Sun., $6), a unique eatery serving all desserts, all the time in a 1950s diner–style restaurant. Open late, Rick's finds favor with local teenagers as well as plenty of older patrons, and there's often a line out the door on weekends after 10 P.M. The pies are nothing special, but the impossibly high layer cakes have wonderful flavors and textures in a wide variety of styles. An ice cream freezer makes pie and cake à la mode possible, as well as hot fudge sundaes and banana splits. You can take it out or eat in the diner at one of the rather small booths clad in sparkling red vinyl upholstery.

American

An outgrowth of the original Frank Fat's is Old Sacramento's (**Fat City Bar and Cafe** (1001 Front St., 916/446-6768, www.fatsrestaurants.com, 11:30 A.M.–2:30 P.M. and 4–9 P.M. Mon.–Fri., 11:30 A.M.–2:30 P.M. and 5–9 P.M. Sat.–Sun., $12–20). You'll imagine you've walked into an Old West saloon from the gold-mining heyday. Award-winning stained glass graces the windows, the lamps, and almost anything else it could be affixed to. Dark furniture and linens complete the atmosphere in the high-ceilinged dining room, across the street from the *Delta King*. But it's the menu that makes Fat City stand out. A diverse selection of dishes appeals to any palate. You can get a plate of chow mein, an order of tacos, or an enormous gooey cheeseburger (the Bourbon Barbecue Burger is the best of these). At dinner, the entrées are American comfort food, including meatloaf, pot pie, and racks of ribs. Lighter eaters can get an entrée salad. On weekends, enjoy a mixed brunch menu that includes the best of the lunch menu, plus a number of Fat City breakfast specialties.

Another good Old Sac burger joint is in **Fanny Ann's Saloon** (1023 2nd St., 916/441-0505, http://fannyannsaloon.com, 11:30 A.M.–midnight Sun.–Wed., 11 A.M.–2 A.M. Thurs.–Sat., $8–20). Enjoy classic American grub in an Old West setting.

Asian

Frank Fat's (806 L St., 916/442-7092, www.fatsrestaurants.com, 11 A.M.–10 P.M. Mon.–Fri., 5–10 P.M. Sat.–Sun., $9–27) lives up to its reputation as a legendary Sacramento institution, the oldest restaurant in Sacramento, opened by Frank Fat in 1939. From the beginning, Fat's has served authentic upscale Chinese food. Also from the beginning, the cream of capital-city society came to eat at Fat's. On the menu are steaks to satisfy even the heartiest appetites, Chinese delicacies with and without meat or poultry, and more. Carnivores can sate their appetites at Fat's, and vegetarians can get a fabulous meal.

Enjoy a tranquil Japanese meal at **Zen Sushi** (900 15th St., 916/446-9628, www.zen-sushi.com, 11:30 A.M.–10 P.M. Sun.–Thurs., 11:30 A.M.–10:30 P.M. Fri.–Sat., $5–15). This small casual well-lit sushi joint beckons with its wide array of house specialty rolls, fresh sashimi and nigiri, and plentiful vegetarian and cooked dishes. Sacramento's proximity to the Bay Area guarantees the availability of the best fresh sushi-grade fish. Lunch and dinner combinations offer good value, plus lots of options for those who don't eat raw fish. The House Special Rolls are good, and with your meal you can quaff one of a variety of Japanese and American beers, a Japanese soda, or a glass of sweet fruity plum wine. Before you pick a time to eat, remember that Zen's downtown location is popular with the local business lunch crowd; the dinner hour has a smaller crowd.

Cajun

Hot & Spicy Café New Orleans (117 J St., 916/443-5051, 11 A.M.–9 P.M. Sun.–Thurs., 11 A.M.–10 P.M. Fri.–Sat., $10–17) brings a taste of Louisiana to Sacramento. With exposed brick and ductwork and bright colorful tablecloths, the atmosphere is friendly and fun. As for the food, when they say "hot and spicy," they mean it. The Cajun foods—jambalaya, gumbo, and many other New Orleans favorites—are riddled with hot peppers and other spices. To put out the fire, go downstairs for an after-dinner drink at the attached SpeakEasy bar.

California

The menus at ◖ **33rd Street Bistro** (3301 Folsom Blvd., 916/455-2233, http://33rdstreetbistro.com, 8 A.M.–10 P.M. Sun.–Thurs., 8 A.M.–11 P.M. Fri.–Sat., $7–29) are inspired by the foods of the Pacific Northwest, the training ground of executive

chef Fred Haines, and favorite dishes from around the country. The *panini* selection speaks to the northwestern connection, while the salads offer original and delectable healthy fare. The casual dining room features exposed brick, an open kitchen and pizza oven, and a fun party atmosphere. Feel free to wear your favorite jeans and T-shirt when you eat at this Sacramento locals' favorite, which is open lateish for dinner on weekends to accommodate people out for a night on the town.

Mulvaney's Building & Loan (1215 19th St., 916/441-6022, www.mulvaneysbl.com, 11:30 A.M.–2:30 P.M. and 5–10 P.M. Tues.–Fri., 5–10 P.M. Sat., $15–34) is a product of Midtown's renaissance, an upscale eatery showcasing the best of California cuisine. The menu changes often to take advantage of local seasonal produce. Go for a standard appetizer and main dish, or order small plates to share to satisfy a smaller appetite. The wine list offers a reasonable number of tastings and interesting vintages. Pick a seat in the lively and loud dining room or a quieter table on the garden-like back patio.

French

For a tasty and inexpensive French lunch near the Capitol Building, head for **La Bonne Soupe Café** (920 8th St., 916/492-9506, 11 A.M.–3 P.M. Mon.–Sat., $15–30). This is the kind of narrow-focus local favorite that visitors love to find. Be warned that if you come at noon, you'll likely spend some time standing in line with local businesspeople who come from miles around to have lunch here. La Bonne Soupe serves hot soups—from classics such as french onion to tasty treats made with in-season produce—while sandwiches are made with fresh ingredients. If you usually eat a smaller lunch, consider splitting an order of soup and a sandwich with a traveling companion—portions are pretty hefty.

For a fancier French restaurant experience, dine at the **Waterboy Restaurant**

(2000 Capitol Ave., 916/498-9891, www. waterboyrestaurant.com, lunch 11:30 A.M.–2:30 P.M. Mon.–Fri., dinner 5–9 P.M. Sun.–Mon., 5–9:30 P.M. Tues.–Thurs., 5–10:30 P.M. Fri.–Sat., $10–27). The light, bright dining room feels like the south coast of France, and the cuisine takes much from the culinary traditions of Provence as well as Tuscany and just a hint of California. If you've got a serious appetite, go for the full three courses: appetizer, first, and main. But if you've got a lighter appetite, the first-course options can be adequate entrées that leave room for dessert.

Italian

Zelda's Original Gourmet Pizza (1415 21st St., 916/447-1400, www.zeldasgourmetpizza.com, 11:30 A.M.–10 P.M. Mon.–Thurs., 11:30 A.M.–11 P.M. Fri., 5–11 P.M. Sat., 5–9 P.M. Sun., $10–22) serves deep-dish Chicago-style pies that locals just can't resist. You won't find much to help your cholesterol level or waistline at Zelda's, but if you've been on the road a while feasting on an endless stream of leafy green California cuisine, a Zelda's pizza might just be the perfect answer to your craving.

INFORMATION AND SERVICES
Visitor Information
Need help from local experts for your time in Sacramento? Visit the **Sacramento Convention and Visitors Bureau** (1608 I St., 916/808-7777, www.discovergold.org, 8 A.M.–5 P.M. Mon.–Fri.). Call or check the website in advance for deals on hotels, advance reservations for attractions, and information about what's going on in and around the city.

Media and Communications
The major metropolitan daily paper for Sacramento is the *Sacramento Bee* (www.sacbee.com). For arts and culture features, live music info, and events coverage, pick up a copy of the *Sacramento News and Review* (www.

newsreview.com/sacramento), the city's alternative weekly paper.

Major banks are well represented in Sacramento. You'll find ample ATMs and branches downtown near the capital and in Midtown and Old Sacramento. As a major metropolitan area, Sacramento has plenty of **post office** branches, including downtown (801 I St., Room 149).

Medical Services
Sutter General Hospital (2801 L St., 916/454-2222, http://suttermedicalcenter.org) is right downtown and has an emergency room. Another local emergency center is run by **UC Davis** (4150 V St., 916/734-2525).

GETTING THERE AND AROUND
Air
Major carriers fly into **Sacramento International Airport** (SMF, 6900 Airport Blvd., 916/929-5411, www.sacairports.org), a great starting point for trips into the Gold Country.

Train
If you're coming into Sacramento from the San Francisco Bay Area, one of the best ways is on the *Capitol Corridor* train run by **Amtrak** (www.amtrak.com, 800/872-7245). Serving the centrally located Amtrak station (401 I St.), this train runs from Sacramento to Oakland and on to San Jose and back several times each day. The Oakland–Sacramento trip takes two hours, and San Jose–Sacramento is just over three hours. You can also get to Sacramento on the *California Zephyr,* which crosses the country from Chicago to Emeryville, in the Bay Area, once daily in each direction, or the *Coast Starlight,* which runs from Seattle to Los Angeles, also once daily in each direction. The *San Joaquin* route runs several times daily up the middle of California's Central Valley, from Sacramento to Bakersfield.

Bus
Sacramento has a busy and reasonably extensive

SACRAMENTO

public transit system that includes both buses and a light-rail train system, **Sacramento Regional Transit** (SACRT, www.sacrt.com, single ride $2.50, day pass $6). Including the downtown trolley and the light rail lines, SACRT has nearly 100 routes; check the website for schedules and maps.

Car

I-80 runs through Sacramento roughly east–west, and the I-80 Business adjunct goes into downtown on a slightly different route. I-5 splits the city on its north–south route. U.S. 50 runs east to Lake Tahoe, and Highway 99 runs south to Los Angeles.

Parking in town can get difficult during major events, but otherwise spots aren't hard to come by. Near the Capitol Building, bring change to feed the meters; some meters also take credit cards. In Old Sacramento, spots right in the middle of the action can be at a premium during high season—you may have to walk a few blocks to get to Front Street, although there are pay lots at the north and south ends of Old Sacramento. The theaters and arenas tend to have ample parking lots, although you'll pay at many of those. Most hotels offer parking free with your room.

Tours

Enjoy sightseeing as you dine aboard the **Sacramento RiverTrain** (800/866-1690, www.sacramentorivertrain.com, $23–84). Outside the window or on the open-air observation deck, look down at the river and the stunning Fremont Trestle. Choose from a variety of rides, including a standard weekday lunch trip, an upscale weekend dinner party, or even a reenactment of the Great Train Robbery, complete with costumed robbers and a Western-style barbecue lunch. Most rides last 2–4 hours; check the website for departure times, ride lengths, and special-event rides that happen several times each year.

If you're looking for a laugh with your sidewalk tour, try one of the three **Hysterical Walks & Rides** (916/441-2527, www.hystericalwalks.com). These walking tours are evening affairs; the standard Hysterical tour leaves at 6 P.M. on Friday–Saturday and lasts for one hour. Standup comedian-guides give you the story of Old Sacramento in the funniest way possible. At 7:30–8:30 P.M. Friday–Saturday, a costumed guide starts the Hysterical Walk of the Dead tour. This hour-long walk through the back alleys of Old Sacramento alternately provides giggles and shivers as your guide relates all the best ghost stories from this historic area.

If you prefer a sleek smooth ride to using your own feet, sign up for the daily Segway tour that takes you through Old Town, to the Capitol Building and gardens, and past other historic Sacramento sights. Your standup comedian will share the history of the city as you glide along the sidewalk on your personal transport vehicle. This tour lasts two hours, and all riders must be at least age 16. Segway tours depart daily at 9 A.M., 1 P.M., and 4 P.M.

DAVIS

Davis is a bustling town with a lively nightlife and restaurant scene. It's also home to the region's agricultural brainpower—the University of California, Davis, home of the "Aggies." The town is among rice fields and orchards in the fertile valley between Sacramento and California's coastal mountains. Most of the region's organic and community-supported farms are just northwest of Davis, and much of this bounty can be found twice a week at the town's renowned farmers market.

Known for its progressive vibe and left-leaning politics, Davis also consistently earns national recognition as a top-notch cycling town with some of the country's most prolific and well-maintained bike paths. Downtown, you'll find plenty of arty boutiques and antiques stores scattered throughout the town's shady streets, a perfect place for avoiding the hot valley sun.

University of California, Davis

One of the country's most esteemed educational institutions is the University of California, Davis (Old Davis Rd., 530/752-1011, www.ucdavis.edu). Students at UC Davis are known as Aggies, a nod to the school's storied agricultural background. First opened in 1905 as a farm school, the expansive campus, California's largest at 7,156 acres, has an on-site dairy and a working farm. Today, UC Davis is renowned for its biological and political science programs, along with one of the nation's biggest engineering schools. Sports are also an important part of Aggie life, and the UC Davis athletic program has rivalries with other NCAA Division I schools like Stanford, UC Berkeley, and nearby Sacramento State. If you visit Davis, make sure to visit the beautiful campus for a stroll or to catch an Aggies game.

How many universities teach students how to brew their own beer? At the **Robert Mondavi Institute for Wine and Food Science** (392 Old Davis Rd., 530/754-6349, http://robertmondaviinstitute.ucdavis.edu, tours $3–25), the on-campus brewery is just one of the world-class research facilities dedicated to food and beverage-making at UC Davis. Completed in 2008 and named for the famed Napa winemaker who donated $25 million to build it, the sprawling agricultural complex also boasts a green-certified winery and an organic vegetable garden on-site. Many of the cutting-edge techniques developed here have been applied to California's top wineries. Foodies will love the institute's olive oil center, which offers courses in how to produce artisanal olive oils. Stop by for a student-led tour or pay a little more for a faculty member to guide you around the institute.

If you love bugs, check out the **Bohart Museum of Entomology** (1124 Academic Surge, 530/752-0493, http://bohart.ucdavis.edu, 9 a.m.–noon and 1–5 p.m. Mon.–Thurs., free, parking $7). With more than seven million insects, the museum has one of the largest collections in North America, and 50,000 new specimens are added every year. Kids will especially love checking out the museum's trove of wasps, bees, and California's native insects. If you're coming with a group, call ahead and book a special guided tour.

Entertainment and Events

Some of the world's greatest performers have dazzled audiences at the beautiful **Mondavi Center for the Performing Arts** (1 Shields Ave., 866/754-2787, www.mondaviarts.org, $10–89), including musicians like Joshua Bell and Anoushka Shankar as well as mainstream acts like Florence and the Machine and Wilco. For classical music fans, the center regularly hosts quartets and traveling symphonies, along with occasional concerts performed by the UC Davis Symphony Orchestra. You can also catch dramatic performances, documentaries, indie films, and headliners from the center's guest-speaker series—including big names that have included Apple cofounder Steve Wozniak and *This American Life* host Ira Glass. The center's architecture alone is worth the trip: Built of glass and sandstone bricks, the building is a stunning spectacle when lit at night.

Accommodations

Located between the university and downtown Davis, the **Aggie Inn** (245 1st St., 530/756-0352, www.aggieinn.com, $110–165) has a range of cozy, stylish accommodations options that include two-bedroom cottages. Every bed has a pillow-top mattress, so you'll sleep like a baby; if that's not relaxing enough, book a guest room with a jetted tub and soak away your aches and pains from a day of traveling. All guest rooms come with microwaves, mini fridges, coffeemakers, air-conditioning, and include Wi-Fi; some guest rooms include kitchenettes. The Aggie is a perfect place to stay if you dig the boutique-inn experience instead of crashing at a big-name motel.

COURTESY OF PRAYITNO

Mondavi Center for the Performing Arts

The most convenient option for visiting UC Davis is the **Hyatt Place UC Davis** (173 Old Davis Rd. Extension, 530/756-9500, http://ucdavis.place.hyatt.com, $140–180). Located on the university's campus, the Hyatt is also a five-minute walk from the city's downtown district. Upscale, modern, and one of the more luxurious accommodations in Davis, the Hyatt's large guest rooms include flat-screen TVs, mini fridges, coffeemakers, blow-dryers, and included Wi-Fi. In the morning, grab breakfast at the included continental buffet in the lobby; if you're still hungry, order a full meal or pick up some muffins at the hotel's café. On the downside, a train runs behind the hotel, so light sleepers might want to inquire about guest rooms farther away from the tracks.

The renovated **Hallmark Inn** (110 F St., 530/758-8623, www.hallmarkinn.com, $125–155) is a homey laid-back option near downtown Davis. The simple tasteful guest rooms feature plush beds, leather furniture, and decor that can feel refreshing after staying at corporate hotel chains. You'll find all the basic hotel room amenities here: included Wi-Fi, microwaves, mini fridges, coffeemakers, blow-dryers, plus a few extras like flat-screen TVs, marble baths, and a breakfast buffet. There's also an outdoor pool and complimentary bicycles for cruising around Davis.

The **Best Western Plus Palm Court Hotel** (234 D St., 530/753-7100, www.bestwestern-california.com, $140–180) is located on a leafy street corner in downtown Davis. Close to just about everything, this smaller hotel is a quiet, comfortable spot for business travelers or students visiting the university. The guest rooms have a classic elegant vibe with dark wood furniture and comfy beds. Couples or small families might do best booking a suite; the cozier guest rooms can feel a little cramped. Standard amenities include coffeemakers, blow-dryers, cable TV, and mini fridges. Underground parking is also provided. Sadly, this hotel doesn't allow pets; with only 27 guest rooms, it also fills up fast, so call ahead to reserve.

Food

The delicious fare at **Delta of Venus** (122 B St., 530/753-8639, www.deltaofvenus.org, 7:30 A.M.–10 P.M. Mon.–Wed., 7:30 A.M.–midnight Thurs.–Fri., 7:30 A.M.–6 P.M. Sat.–Sun., $4–11) is just part of this funky café's charm. Stopping here feels like visiting a colorful neighbor's house; artwork adorns the walls, and students lounge on the tree-covered patio. Meals are served all day; dinner focuses on Caribbean fare and shouldn't be missed (try the tofu with ginger and citrus chili sauce, or the coconut chicken with Jamaican curry). Omelets and breakfast burritos are what's for breakfast, while lunch includes mostly salads and sandwiches, such as the vegetarian-friendly Blue Lagoon (served with blue cheese, tomatoes, and marinated artichoke hearts). The café often hosts live bands.

With a name like **Burgers and Brew** (403 3rd St., 530/750-3600, http://burgersbrew.com, 11 A.M.–midnight Sun.–Wed., 11 A.M.–3 A.M. Thurs.–Sat., $8), you wouldn't expect many surprises. However, this is no ordinary brewpub: The burgers are made with all-natural meat and topped with plenty of mouthwatering fixings. Wash it down with one of the roughly 20 craft beers on tap, or select something from the long list of bottled brews. For dessert, spoil your taste buds with a slice of Nutella cheesecake. There is a menu for kids if you're bringing children, but it's pretty basic, with burgers, hot dogs, and a grilled-cheese sandwich.

There's more than just crepes at **Crepeville** (330 3rd St., 530/750-2400, www.crepeville. com, daily 7 A.M.–11 P.M., $6–10, cash only). Run by the same folks who own Burgers and Brew, the restaurant serves delightful omelets, egg scrambles, and sandwiches. Still, you can't visit Crepeville without trying a homemade breakfast or dessert crepe; the Hawaiian is especially good

for breakfast, though the banana chocolate crepe will have your eyes rolling in ecstasy.

Information and Services

The **Yolo County Visitors Bureau** (604 2nd St., 530/297-1900, www.yolocvb.net, 8:30 A.M.–4:30 P.M. Mon.–Fri.) provides information on the Davis, Woodland, and Winters area. Pop into the office or visit the website for a full list of events and attractions in Davis. They can also provide directions on navigating the array of local bike paths.

Grab a copy of the daily *Davis Enterprise* (www.davisenterprise.com) for a local perspective on the town; for a more collegiate take, UC Davis students publish *The California Aggie* (www.theaggie.org) four days a week. To stay updated on Davis nightlife, check out *The Davis Dirt* (www.davisdirt.blogspot.com), a local blog on the Davis arts and entertainment scene.

You can find plenty of ATMs and bank branches in Davis; the **Golden One Credit Union** (503 2nd St., www.golden1.com) is conveniently located near the Amtrak station and UC Davis. There is also a **post office** (424 3rd St., 9:30 A.M.–4:30 P.M. Mon.–Fri., 9:30–11 A.M. Sat.).

If you need medical attention in Davis, the major hospital is **Sutter Davis Hospital** (2000 Sutter Place, 530/756-6440, www.sutterdavis. org). You can find a wide array of services, including emergency and urgent care, pediatric care, and a birthing center.

Getting There and Around

Davis is 14 miles west of Sacramento on I-80; the Richards Boulevard exit provides easy access to downtown.

The closest airport is **Sacramento International Airport** (SMF, 6900 Airport Blvd., Sacramento, 916/929-5411, www.sacairports.org). The **Davis Airporter** (530/756-6715, www.davisairporter.com) provides door-to-door shuttle service to the airport.

The *Capitol Corridor* train run by **Amtrak**

(840 2nd St., 530/758-4220 or 800/872-7245, www.amtrak.com) stops several times daily in downtown Davis on the way to Oakland, San Jose, and Sacramento. **Unitrans** (1 Shields Ave., Davis, 530/752-2877, http://unitrans.ucdavis.edu, $1) provides student-run public transit around Davis and the university campus.

Davis Pedicab (530/771-7405, 7 P.M.–3 A.M. Thurs.–Sat., 2–10 P.M. Sun.) is a fun and reliable human-powered option for getting around Davis. Hours change during warmer months, and service can also extend to Wednesday; if you have a special request, Davis Pedicab can usually make arrangements ahead of time.

CHICO

The Sacramento Valley community of Chico is a thriving college town with outstanding urban parks, lush agricultural surroundings, and a living connection to its history. California State University, Chico, tends to dominate local culture.

Bidwell Mansion State Historic Park

Chico prides itself on having one of the largest and most diverse urban parks in the country. The original land for Bidwell Mansion State Historic Park (525 Esplanade, 530/896-7800, www.bidwellpark.org or www.friendsofbidwellpark.com) was donated by John and Annie Bidwell, the town's first and most prominent citizens. Their **Bidwell Mansion** (530/895-6144, www.parks.ca.gov, tours hourly noon–5 P.M. Mon.–Wed., 11 A.M.–5 P.M. Sat.–Sun., adults $8, ages 3–17 $3), a preserved 26-room Victorian house, is available for tours. Completed in 1868, this beautiful home features prime examples of the 19th-century furnishings and decor.

The park boasts 3,618 acres in two sections. The undeveloped Upper Park, in the Sierra Nevada foothills, includes Big Chico Creek and Horseshoe Lake and is great for hiking or horseback riding. It is also the location of the 18-hole par 72–73 **Bidwell Park Golf Course**

(3199 Golf Course Rd., 530/891-8417, www.bidwellpark.americangolf.com, daily sunrise–sunset, Mon.–Fri. $13–39, Sat.–Sun. $17–47). Amenities at the Lower Park include the **Sycamore Pool** (daily 11 A.M.–7 P.M. Memorial Day–Labor Day, free), **Caper Acres** (9 A.M.–sunset Tues.–Sun., free), a special play area for children under age 12, the **Chico Creek Nature Center** (1968 E. 8th St., 530/891-4671, 11 A.M.–4 P.M. Wed.–Sun., adults $1, children $0.50), the **Living Animal Museum** (11 A.M.–4 P.M. Wed.–Sun., free), and the **Howard Tucker Exhibit Hall** (11 A.M.–4 P.M. Fri.–Sun., free).

Sierra Nevada Brewing Company

The Sierra Nevada Brewing Company (1075 E. 20th St., 530/893-3520, www.sierranevada.com, tours noon–4 P.M. Sun.–Thurs., noon–5 P.M. Fri.–Sat., free) was founded in 1979. Sierra Nevada was at the forefront of the microbrew movement, and its original creation, Sierra Nevada Pale Ale, is still a star. The company continues to develop innovative new beers that win awards and fans. Sign up for the free tour.

Entertainment and Events

Chico's liveliest bar is **Madison Bear Garden** (316 W. 2nd St., 530/891-1639, www.madisonbeargarden.com, daily 11 A.M.–10 P.M., $5–11), mainly a student hangout, but all are welcome to enjoy its creative burgers and large variety of beers, shots, and iced teas.

The Butte Environmental Council of Chico hosts an **Endangered Species Faire** (530/891-6424, www.endangeredspeciesfaire.org) on a Saturday in May at Bidwell Park's Cedar Grove. See fascinating animals up close with explanations by their expert handlers, along with music performances, puppet shows, and presentations about endangered species.

The Sacramento River Preservation Trust of Chico hosts the **Snow Goose Festival** (Chico Masonic Family Center, 1110 W. East Ave.,

530/345-1865 or 530/342-7143, www.snow-goosefestival.org, Jan.), which includes art shows, a duck-calling class and competition, and seminars on everything from building a wooden duck box to drawing waterfowl and shorebirds. The highlight is the migration of thousands of snow geese on their way to warmer climes.

One of the biggest events for cyclists, the **Chico Wildflower Century** (530/343-8356 or 800/482-2453, www.chicovelo.org, $65) takes place in April or May. The route starts at the Silver Dollar Fairgrounds (2337 Fair St.) at 6 A.M. and ends 12 hours later with a celebratory dinner.

Accommodations

Elegant lodgings are at the **Hotel Diamond** (220 W. 4th St., 866/993-3100, www.hotel-diamondchico.com, Sun.–Thurs. $139–319, Fri.–Sat. $179–389). Built in 1904 and renovated in 2005, the Hotel Diamond is located in the downtown Chico just four blocks from the university. Free parking, Internet access, and an "expanded continental" breakfast are included. All guest rooms come with complimentary slippers and the use of a robe.

The **Oxford Suites Chico** (2035 Business Lane, 530/899-9090 or 800/870-7848, $120) offers all-suites lodging perfect for families visiting the university. Guest rooms feature queen or king beds, fridges, coffeemakers, and TVs. Amenities include wireless Internet access, parking, and an outdoor pool; breakfast is included in the rates.

In addition to chain motels, there are several B&Bs in the area. The **Goodman House Bed & Breakfast** (1362 Esplanade, 530/566-0256, $105–150) is a two-story craftsman home that dates to 1906. There are five guest rooms, each with queen beds, private baths, and decorated with tasteful antiques; some guest rooms have fireplaces. The **Grateful Bed** (1462 Arcadian Ave., 530/342-2464, $135–175) is a bed-and-breakfast housed in a 1905 Victorian with four guest rooms, each with a private bath. Enjoy a gourmet breakfast in the morning; in the afternoon, rock away on the inn's back porch.

Food

For gut-busting breakfasts, you can't go wrong at **Café Coda** (265 Humboldt Ave., 530/566-9476, daily 7 A.M.–2 P.M., $10). Choose between sweet specialties like banana Nutella french toast or "Masterpieces": scrambles with everything from basil pesto to red beans and Spanish rice. Live music (daily 8 P.M.) and free Wi-Fi access keeps it busy.

The Sierra Nevada Brewing Company's **C Taproom & Restaurant** (1075 E. 20th St., 530/345-2739, www.sierranevada.com, 11 A.M.–9 P.M. Sun.–Thurs., 11 A.M.–10 P.M. Fri.–Sat., $10–31) is an airy and attractive modern restaurant on the premises of the brewery. Dine on fresh seasonal food, including vegetarian choices; waiters can suggest ideal beer-and-food pairings to enhance your meal.

5th Street Steakhouse (345 W. 5th St., 530/891-6328, 4:30–9 P.M. Sun.–Thurs., 4:30–10 P.M. Fri.–Sat., $30–40) is the go-to place for steak in Chico, with unusual offerings like the mole-crusted rib eye. For casual food and tasty drinks, **The Banshee** (132 W. 2nd St., Chico, 530/895-9670, 11 A.M.–2 A.M. Mon.–Sat., 10 A.M.–2 A.M. Sun., $12–20) earns rave reviews, especially for the mac and cheese with bacon.

Getting There and Around

Chico is 90 miles north of Sacramento on Highway 99. It can be accessed from I-5: From Orland, exit I-5 onto Highway 32 east for about 20 miles to Chico. The *Coast Starlight* train, run by **Amtrak** (www.amtrak.com, 800/872-7245), runs from Seattle to Los Angeles once daily in each direction with a stop at the Chico platform (450 Orange St., no services).

Northern Gold Country

California's Gold Country is a great sprawling network of small towns and roads crisscrossing the Sierra Nevada foothills where much of California's modern history begins. It was the gold in these hills that drew migrants from the East Coast and around the world to come to work the fields, build the railroads, and drag the wild lands of California into the modern era.

When visiting, it's easiest to traverse the Gold Country from north to south. The northern Gold Country extends from Nevada City down into the Shenandoah Valley. I-80 can get you from Sacramento or the Bay Area to the northern Gold Country town of Auburn. Here you can pick up Highway 49 north to Grass Valley and Nevada City. On Highway 49 south of Auburn, head east to Placerville, Coloma, and Fair Play, and south down into the Shenandoah Valley where small highways and roads lead to other tiny dots on the map.

NEVADA CITY AND GRASS VALLEY
◖ Empire Mine State Historic Park

Arguably the best mining museum in the Gold Country is the Empire Mine State Historic Park (10791 E. Empire St., Grass Valley, 530/273-8522, www.empiremine.org, daily 10 A.M.–5 P.M., adults $7, children $3, tour included). Walking into the yard, you can see and feel the life of the 19th–20th-century miners who extracted tons of gold from the earth below your feet. Kids can run and shout in the yard, enjoying the open spaces and strange tools and machines. Keep a close eye on children; the museum contains many dangers both obvious and hidden. Adults can enjoy the history of the place and imagine a hard-rock life in the mine, or a privileged existence up in the owner's cottage.

The mine yard has a vast collection of tools

Empire Mine State Historic Park

© CHRISTOPHER ARNS

SACRAMENTO

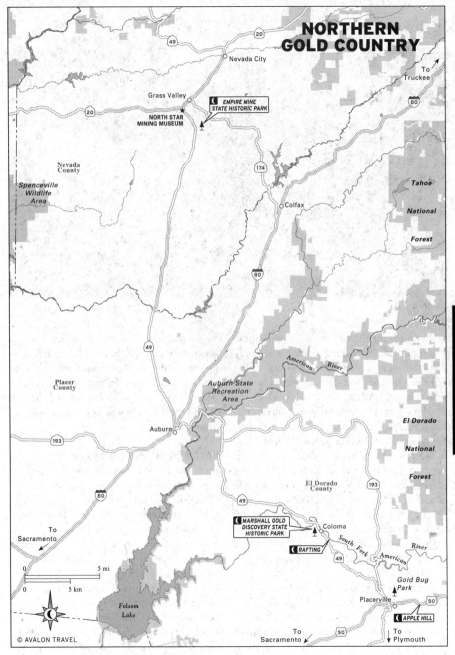

NORTHERN
GOLD COUNTRY

To
Truckee

Nevada City

Grass Valley

EMPIRE MINE
STATE HISTORIC PARK

NORTH STAR
MINING MUSEUM

Nevada
County

Spenceville
Wildlife
Area

Colfax

Tahoe

National

Forest

American   River

Placer
County

Auburn State
Recreation
Area

El Dorado

Auburn

National

Forest

El Dorado
County

MARSHALL GOLD
DISCOVERY STATE
HISTORIC PARK

Coloma

RAFTING

South Fork   American   River

Gold Bug
Park

Placerville

APPLE HILL

To
Sacramento

To
Sacramento

To
Plymouth

Folsom
Lake

0   5 mi

0   5 km

© AVALON TRAVEL

SACRAMENTO

© SABRINA YOUNG

Nevada City

and equipment used in the hard-rock mine shafts; the shop that kept the mine machinery functioning still works. If you come on the right day (usually Sat.–Sun.), you might find a blacksmith working away inside. Duck inside for a glimpse of the main mineshaft. You can go a few feet down into the shaft, then look deep down and imagine what it was like to perch in a metal car and shoot down thousands of feet into the darkness. The showpiece of the museum collection is the scale model of the Empire Mine and the various nearby interconnected tunnels. Turn on the lights surrounding the mammoth glass case to highlight and hear the stories of the different parts of the overwhelmingly vast and complex underground maze.

For something completely different, leave the mine yard and take the path up the slight rise to the "cottage"—the mine owner's home. In stark contrast to the dust, rust, and timber of the yard, you'll see acres of sweeping green lawn dotted with flowering shrubs and bisected by gently curving pathways. The garden leads up to the mammoth brick mansion. Check the park schedule inside the museum for regular tours of the inside of the cottage and the surrounding gardens as well as occasional living history events.

North Star Mining Museum

Much smaller and more intimate than Empire Mine, the North Star Mining Museum (10933 Allison Ranch Rd., Grass Valley, 530/273-4255, http://nevadacountyhistory.org, 10 A.M.–4 P.M. Tues.–Sun. May–Oct., donation) is a low-key alternative. History fans will love this fascinating tribute to the industrial machinery that once powered the North Star Mine, one of California's most successful mines during the Gold Rush. Miners used some of the most advanced technology of the era to construct sprawling hydraulic operations or burrow deep into the hillsides to find the quartz

© CHRISTOPHER ARNS

North Star Mining Museum

deposits; gigantic water cannons blasted canyon walls with thousands of gallons per minute. The museum has plenty of mining relics from those operations, such as the largest Pelton wheel in the world, a crude form of hydraulic power that once helped power the mine. The museum even has a working stamp mill, a towering machine once used to crush hundreds of tons of gold ore per day with an awe-inspiring engine of gears and pistons.

The museum is closed in winter, so plan your visit accordingly. Some of the machines are outside, so you can still walk around the grounds if the museum isn't open. Walking on the dirt and gravel paths is easy, but part of the museum is on a slope; families with strollers or individuals who have difficulty walking might have trouble. If you have kids, ask the helpful park guides to demonstrate how some of the machinery works. There's also a shady picnic area next to a rushing creek, so pack a lunch and enjoy the leafy setting.

Entertainment and Events

Nightlife in the northern Gold Country involves the classic saloons dotted along the main streets of each little town. In Grass Valley, the saloon on the ground floor of the historic Holbrook Hotel offers some of the best drinks and company in town. The **Golden Gate Saloon** (212 W. Main St., Grass Valley, 530/273-1353, http://holbrookehotel.com/saloon) boasts of being the oldest continually operating saloon west of the Mississippi River. Yup, the Golden Gate braved possible federal raids and kept serving liquor through Prohibition. Today, the old-time saloon features a light lunch and dinner menu, a full bar with beer on tap, high-end wines, and plenty of cocktails. It's also got lots of locals, many of whom stop in to enjoy the live music Wednesday–Saturday.

Most regional theater in the Gold Country is performed at the **Nevada Theatre** (401 Broad St., Nevada City, 530/265-6161, www.

nevadatheatre.com, films $8, plays $25) in Nevada City. Professional companies such as the Community Asian Theatre of the Sierra (www.catsweb.org) and LeGacy Productions (www.legacypresents.com) produce big-name works in the historic 1865 theater, with an occasional show in Grass Valley as well. The regular season can include Broadway musical hits such as *Urinetown,* classics such as *On Golden Pond,* and unusual newer works such as *Doubt: A Parable* by John Patrick Shanley. In summer, the Nevada Theatre Film Series as well as current and independent films grace the screen. Check the website for current shows.

Every small town seems to have a local fair, but the **Nevada County Fair** (11228 McCourtney Rd., Grass Valley, 530/273-6217, www.nevadacountyfair.com, early Aug., adults $9, children $6) stands out for its atmosphere. For one week every August, while the rest of Northern California steams under the summer sun, this rustic and charming little fair takes place under a shady canopy of towering evergreens. Attractions include the usual assortment of carnival games for kids, plus crafts, musical acts, art exhibitions, a rodeo, and appearances by the Budweiser draft horses. If you're hungry, stop by the food court and grab a homemade corn dog at a booth run by the local chapter of Job's Daughters. Don't miss the livestock exhibits from the Nevada County farms and the local high school FFA clubs, many of whom earn top prizes at the California State Fair later in the year. While the fair is a great place for families and kids, pets are not allowed. If you visit the fair in the evening, make sure to pack a light jacket—even in August the foothills can be slightly chilly. Children under age five get in free; on Thursday all children under age 13 get in free.

Shopping

Both Nevada City and Grass Valley are chock-full of tiny boutiques, art galleries, and quirky gift stores. In Nevada City, most shopping is on Broad and Commercial Streets; in Grass Valley, head for Main and Mill Streets. Parking in either town can be a challenge and is mostly on the street, so be patient and check side streets for empty spaces.

If you've always dreamed of surrounding yourself in leather and fur, **Nevada City Fur Traders** (319 Broad St., Nevada City, 530/265-8000, www.furtraders.com, daily 10 A.M.–6 P.M.) will satisfy that craving. From the fringed to the furry, Fur Traders definitely has something to catch your eye. Apparently, one store wasn't enough; there are three Fur Traders on Broad Street within a block of each other, and each store has slightly different merchandise.

At **Utopian Stone** (301 Broad St., Nevada City, 530/265-6209, www.utopianstone.com, daily 10 A.M.–5:30 P.M.), the jewelers divide their work into two categories: one-of-a-kind pieces and everything else. Five master goldsmiths produce some of the most luminous fine jewelry you'll ever see—and if you don't see it, they'll build anything on commission. Some of the gold comes from nuggets found in the nearby Yuba River and quartz from Nevada County mines. Besides the gold work, Utopian Stone's superb gemstone carvings are also quite unique.

For a unique gift for any occasion, stop by **Yuba Blue** (116 Mill St., Grass Valley, 530/273-9620, www.yubablueonline.com, daily 10 A.M.–6 P.M.). Part boutique and part knickknack novelty, this store is a little pricy, but it has everything from exquisite jewelry and clothing to housewares and decorations. Some of the items do seem a little random, like the stack of gourmet jellies next to the gag books section, but that's part of the fun.

Booktown Books (107 Bank St., Grass Valley, 530/272-4655, 10 A.M.–6 P.M. Mon.–Sat., 11 A.M.–5 P.M. Sun.) is truly the mother lode for rare and used tomes. More co-op than store, 12 independent booksellers share the same open space. Every genre is represented,

© CHRISTOPHER ARNS

Booktown Books in Grass Valley

from science fiction to romance and comic book art. If you're pressed for time, grab a store directory at the front counter to find each bookseller; there's nothing separating them from each other, and the different sections blend together.

Sports and Recreation

In addition to its fabulous historic park and museum, the **Empire Mine State Historic Park** (10791 E. Empire St., Grass Valley, 530/273-8522, www.empiremine.org) doubles as an outdoor hiking park. With 800 acres of former mining lands, this park offers both natural beauty and views of abandoned mines that are being overgrown as nature re-establishes dominance. The Hardrock Trails can run 1–3 miles, depending on how far you want to hike. Loop from the visitors center around to see the remains of the Pennsylvania, WYOD, and Orleans Mines before heading out to the Osborn Loop or back to the parking lot.

The Hardrock Trails and their offshoots are reasonably flat and easy to hike, but be aware that you can hit rocky stretches, and there are no restroom facilities on the trails. Along the trail you'll see the remains of the major hardrock mines that once produced gold. From the Hardrock Trails Area, you can head farther afield on the Osborn Hill Loop Trail to check out several more abandoned mines and their detritus. This loop runs about one mile and is a bit steeper and more challenging than the Hardrock Trails.

Looking to cool off after traipsing through the foothills? Head to the **South Yuba River State Park** (17660 Pleasant Valley Rd., Penn Valley, 530/273-3884, park daily sunrise–sunset, visitors center 11 A.M.–3 P.M. Thurs.–Sun., free). This 20-mile stretch of the Yuba River winds all the way from Malakoff Diggins State Historic Park to the picturesque covered bridge at Bridgeport. There are plenty of Gold Rush ruins on the river, including an old mining camp and several sections of the Virginia Turnpike, a 14-mile-long toll road. A short nature walk leads through oak woodlands and wildflowers that include California poppies and purple lupine; during spring, the visitors center offers guided wildflower walks on weekends. Come on the last Sunday in April and October, when the park offers wagon rides and exhibits on pioneer life and the indigenous Maidu people that lived in the canyon before gold was discovered. In summer, explore a small gravel beach just a short hike east of the covered bridge and the nearby rocks, where more adventurous visitors can jump into the river. Parking is provided in a fenced lot ($5); street parking on Pleasant Valley Road is not allowed.

One of the most beautiful hikes in South Yuba River State Park is the **Independence Trail** (Hwy. 49, 5.5 miles north of Nevada City, 10 miles round-trip, easy), which was used as an old mining flume during the Gold Rush era; it has since been converted into a flat stroll along the river canyon. The best time to visit is in spring, when live oaks cover the path in a lime-green canopy and wildflowers bloom. It's also the best time to spot California newts crawling on their orange bellies through puddles beside the trail. The trail is actually two separate hikes that both start from Highway 49; each is roughly five miles round-trip. The eastern section ends near a bucolic picnic area with a creek and plenty of shade. Parking is permitted in turnouts along the highway, so keep an eye on traffic.

Hike through the eerie but colorful canyon at **Malakoff Diggins State Historic Park** (Tyler Foote Rd., 26 miles north of Nevada City, 530/265-2740, www.parks.ca.gov, daily sunrise–sunset, day use $8 per vehicle), once the site of California's largest hydraulic mine. During the Gold Rush, miners blasted the hillsides with water to find gold buried deep in the ground, leaving behind strange land formations streaked with red and orange mineral deposits.

The best way to explore the park is by hiking the **Diggins Loop Trail** (3 miles round-trip). This is also the easiest route if you have kids; there are several other more challenging hikes if you really want to explore further. The park includes the ghost town of **North Bloomfield,** which has several historic structures, including a one-room schoolhouse, an old cemetery, St. Columncille's Church, and a small museum.

Malakoff Diggins is about 26 miles north of Nevada City, but it can take almost an hour to drive. To reach the park from Nevada City, take Highway 49 north for 11 miles toward the small town of Downieville. Turn right onto Tyler-Foote Road and follow the road into the park.

Accommodations

For elegance in the land of gold, you can't beat the **Emma Nevada House** (528 E. Broad St., Nevada City, 530/265-4415, www.emmanevadahouse.com, $170–250). History permeates this large Victorian house, which once belonged to the family of a noted opera singer named Emma Nevada. You'll see real antiques in the front rooms, and charming collectibles in the six uniquely styled guest rooms, all with comfortable beds, attractive appointments, and plush baths, some with claw-foot tubs. Breakfast is served each morning—come out early to get a seat in the sunroom, definitely the best breakfast seat in the house. You'll get a multicourse gourmet treat to fortify yourself for a day out exploring El Dorado and Amador Counties.

Located just a short stroll from downtown Nevada City is the **Outside Inn** (575 E. Broad St., Nevada City, 530/265-2233, www.outsideinn.com, $80–200). Converted from a 1930s motor-court motel, each guest room has a different outdoor theme, including the Single Track Room and the romantic Creekside Hideaway cabin—officially Nevada City's smallest house. A natural creek gently runs through the laid-back patio area, which includes a pool and a brick fire pit. The Outside

Inn is pet-friendly; for kids, ask about the quirky scavenger hunt for lawn trolls hiding on the neatly tended hotel grounds.

If themed guest rooms aren't your style, check out the **Sierra Mountain Inn** (816 W. Main St., Grass Valley, 530/273-8133, www.sierramountaininn.com, $80–180). Just minutes from downtown Grass Valley, these charming motel-style accommodations offer a romantic and relaxing option to get away from it all. The guest rooms combine rustic decor with luxurious touches like marble baths and vaulted ceilings for a quirky farmhouse feel. Most guest rooms offer kitchenettes with mini fridges, sinks, and microwaves. If you plan to stay only one night, call and reserve over the phone instead of booking online—the inn usually requires a two-night minimum. Note that if you bring a dog, it's at least $25 extra, depending on the guest room.

Food

Any trip to Grass Valley would be incomplete without visiting ◖ **Cousin Jack Pasties** (100 S. Auburn St., Grass Valley, 530/272-9230, www.historichwy49.com, 11 A.M.–5 P.M. Mon.–Sat., 11 A.M.–4:15 P.M. Sun., takeout 10:30 A.M.–6 P.M. Mon.–Sat., 11 A.M.–5 P.M. Sun., $6). Opened in 1989, this adorable café serves up delicious pasties, a hearty meat pie filled with piping-hot ingredients. Try the turkey pasty, or look for unusual specials; the Greek pasties are amazingly good. Cousin Jack's is also a savory way to experience Grass Valley history— the pasty was introduced by Cornish mine workers who immigrated to the area during the Gold Rush. You can also order traditional British fare like fish-and-chips and English tea.

Unpretentious and unassuming, the ◖ **Flour Garden Café and Bakery** (999 Sutton Way, Grass Valley, 530/272-2043, 5 A.M.–7 P.M. Mon.–Sat., 6 A.M.–6 P.M. Sun.) serves homemade pastries, soups, sandwiches, and cakes to a mostly local crowd who prefer something

good to something trendy. Part of what makes this Gold Country mini chain great is that they use natural organic ingredients. If you're looking for an early-morning continental breakfast, purchase an unbelievably flaky and delicious pastry—made with real butter and homemade fruit fillings—plus an espresso drink or a plain old cup of Fair Trade coffee. For lunch, pick up any number of to-go prepared items, have a sandwich made, grab a baguette to make your own sandwich, or order a bowl of the fresh homemade soup of the day. A monthly menu describes the hearty hot soups, which are a meal in themselves. The Flour Garden is loved by locals, and there's often a line at mealtime. Best of all, the Flour Garden has three locations; check out the downtown Grass Valley location (109 Neal St., Grass Valley) and the Auburn store (340C Elm Ave., Auburn).

For delicious and inventive Italian food, go to **Cirino's** (309 Broad St., Nevada City, 530/265-2246, www.cirinosbarandgrill.com, 5–9 P.M. Mon.–Thurs., 11:30 A.M.–10 P.M. Fri.–Sat., 11:30 A.M.–9 P.M. Sun., $20). This cute, locally favored restaurant offers plenty of tables, a full bar, a relaxed atmosphere, and a large, innovative, reasonably priced menu. Start with a cocktail from the bar, which doubles as the local watering hole. Enjoy a salad or an appetizer from the antipasti menu, then move on to the main event. The portions, especially the pasta, are enormous. Despite this, you'll have a hard time resisting the array of delectable pasta dishes, plus the yummy entrées made with seafood, poultry, and meat, including veal. The service is friendly and helpful, and the overall feel of the place will encourage you to sit back and enjoy your meal without rushing.

Looking for a good taco or burrito? Enjoy a meal at **Las Katarinas Mexican Restaurant** (311 Broad St., Nevada City, 530/478-0275, 11 A.M.–9 P.M. Wed.–Mon., $10–15). Located right in the middle of the main drag, Las Katarinas serves enchiladas, tacos, and tostadas, plus *chile colorado* and *chile verde* all made with fresh whole ingredients. Vegetarians can order lard-free dishes. Beware: The salsa's got some kick to it. The full bar serves Mexican beers, California wines, and strong margaritas.

The last thing you might expect in Nevada City is high-quality sushi. Before opening **Sushi in the Raw** (315 Spring St., Nevada City, 530/478-9503, 5:30–9 P.M. Tues.–Sat. spring–fall, 5–9 P.M. Tues.–Sat. winter, $6–15) in 2002, owner Ru Suzuki already had a dedicated following as one of Gold Country's premier sushi chefs, and he's topped himself with this cozy authentic location. Start with the scallop shooters and then order Ru's white-truffled sashimi; your taste buds will swear they're in Tokyo. Call several days ahead for a reservation; the restaurant is small and very popular with locals.

Lefty's Grill (221 Broad St., Nevada City, 530/265-5838, www.leftysgrill.com, daily 11:30 A.M.–9 P.M., $15) has some of the best upscale bar food you'll ever sink your teeth into. The restaurant is located in a handsome brick building, a historic landmark that was once a bank during the Gold Rush. Inside, cheerful lighting and spotless white tablecloths give the restaurant a hip urban feel, and the food definitely measures up. For starters, order a side of sweet-potato fries slathered in apricot chipotle sauce. Leave room for the Napa pizza (named Best in the West at the 2009 International Pizza Expo).

The relaxed vibe at **Diego's Restaurant** (217 Colfax Ave., Grass Valley, 530/477-1460, daily 11 A.M.–9 P.M., $14) will make you feel right at home. This eatery leans heavily to the local crowd and with an eclectic funky interior that makes a nice break from tourist-oriented joints. The cuisine is Chilean with a Californian flair and shouldn't be missed. Try the *panqueque especial,* a tasty mishmash of pineapple, chorizo, cheese sauce, and rice rolled in a crepe and slathered with tomatillo sauce. The menu has a few vegetarian options besides salads, like the stuffed portobello with tofu and quinoa, but most entrées are meat-heavy.

Information and Services

The **Nevada City Chamber of Commerce** (132 Main St., Nevada City, 530/265-2692, www.nevadacitychamber.com, 9 A.M.–5 P.M. Mon.–Fri., 11 A.M.–4 P.M. Sat., 11 A.M.–3 P.M. Sun.) doubles as the visitors center.

For a local take on Nevada City and Grass Valley, read *The Union* (www.theunion.com), the Nevada County daily newspaper. A great online visitors guide to the Nevada County area is **Nevada County Gold** (www.ncgold.com). Most of the Gold Country is covered in the pages of *Sierra Heritage* magazine (www.sierraheritage.com).

You'll find ATMs and a few bank branches in Nevada City and Grass Valley. There are also **post offices** (200 Coyote St., Nevada City; 185 E. Main St., Grass Valley).

The major hospital with an emergency room is **Sierra Nevada Memorial Hospital** (155 Glasson Way, Grass Valley, 530/274-6000, www.snmh.org).

Getting There and Around

Grass Valley and Nevada City are on Highway 49, north of I-80 and Auburn. To reach the area by car, take I-80 to Auburn and follow Highway 49 (Golden Chain Hwy.) northwest. Grass Valley is 25 miles from Auburn, and Nevada City is four miles farther north. Note that weekend traffic on I-80 between San Francisco and Tahoe can be quite congested, and the area can receive heavy snowfall in winter. Check on the weather, road conditions, and traffic reports with **Caltrans** (http://dot.ca.gov) before heading out.

The local **Nevada County Airport** (13083 John Bauer Ave., Grass Valley, 530/273-3347, www.nevadacountyairport.com) has no scheduled commercial flights. The closest airports served by the airlines are **Sacramento International Airport** (SMF, 6900 Airport Blvd., Sacramento, 916/929-5411, www.sacairports.org), 60 miles south, and **Reno-Tahoe International Airport** (RNO, 2001 E. Plumb

Lane, Reno, NV, 775/328-6400, www.renoairport.com), about 90 miles east.

Car rentals are available with **Hertz** (139 Joerschke Dr., Grass Valley, 530/272-7730) and **Enterprise** (1611 Nevada City Hwy., Grass Valley, 530/274-7400).

Gold Country Stage (http://new.mynevadacounty.com/transit, adults $1.50, day pass $4.50, under age 6 free) runs buses and minibuses through Nevada City, Grass Valley, Auburn, and points north of the Gold Country.

AUBURN
Placer County Museum

Located on the first floor of the historic Placer County courthouse, the Placer County Museum (101 Maple St., 530/889-6500, www.placer.ca.gov, daily 10 A.M.–4 P.M., free) offers a glimpse into the town's rustic past. While small, the museum is a worthwhile stop before heading farther into the Gold Country

to visit other historical sites. The exhibits span different themes and time periods in Placer County history, such as the women's jail, a recreated sheriff's office, and the stagecoach that ran from Auburn up into the mountains. There's also a video about the history of I-80, the transcontinental highway through Auburn, plus different art pieces depicting the indigenous Maidu and Miwok people that lived in the Auburn area before the pioneers arrived. Outside the museum, views from the courthouse are photo-worthy, and it's just a short walk to the restaurants and bars in Auburn's Old Town. The museum is closed on holidays, so call ahead for hours.

Gold Country Museum

Auburn was one of California's first mining settlements, built after gold was discovered in 1848. Learn more about the area's history at the Gold Country Museum (1273

© CHRISTOPHER ARNS

Auburn's Old Town, with the historic Placer County courthouse in the background

SACRAMENTO

High St., 530/889-6500, www.placer.ca.gov, 11 A.M.–4 P.M. Tues.–Sun., free). Many standard Gold Country exhibits are on display, including a reconstructed mine, a stamp mill, and a mining-camp saloon. Kids can pan for gold in the museum's indoor stream ($3). You might be underwhelmed by the displays after visiting some of the region's larger historic sites, but the attentive docents are knowledgeable about Auburn's place in Gold Rush lore. Note that finding the museum's location can be challenging; it's tucked near the back of the Gold Country Fairgrounds in a one-story building.

Entertainment and Events

Brilliantly restored, the **Auburn Placer Performing Arts Center** (985 Lincoln Way, 530/885-0156, www.livefromauburn.com, tickets $5–25) brings a dash of Hollywood glamour to the foothills. The center offers concerts, community theater productions, classic flicks like *Dirty Harry,* and more contemporary films like *The Shawshank Redemption.* The center is located in the historic State Theatre, which first opened in 1930; the renovated marquee conjures memories of glitzy movie premieres from a bygone era. On stage, the center hosts a bevy of musical and dramatic events, from country-music crooners to Shakespeare. There are even family-friendly improv performances that will keep you cracking up all evening. The performance hall currently seats 130, so order tickets online to avoid missing a show.

Sports and Recreation

Tucked inside stunning American River canyon, **Auburn State Recreation Area** (www.parks.ca.gov, daily 7 A.M.–sunset, day use $10) should be a priority for outdoors enthusiasts. More than 100 miles of trails wind through leafy oak woodlands amid California poppies in spring and past seasonal waterfalls like Codfish Falls. The area is used by hikers, joggers, mountain bikers, dirt bikers, and horseback riders. Parking is easiest at the confluence of the American River's North and Middle Forks, and it's also where most of the trails begin. This area is arguably one of the best local places for water sports: rafting, kayaking, and boating are all available along various stretches of the river. Pack a swimsuit in summer and enjoy the cooling waters of the river confluence, which has plenty of swimming holes and jumping rocks. Keep your eyes peeled for wildlife; white-tailed deer, bald eagles, river otters, black bears, and even the occasional mountain lion roam the park.

History buffs will enjoy exploring the Gold Rush sights, such as the ancient railroad bridge spanning the lower Middle Fork. Farther upriver at **Upper Lake Clementine** (Apr. 15–Oct. 15), look for a jagged rock formation named Robber's Roost—local outlaws once used it for a hideout. The **Lower Clementine Trail** (10.5 miles, moderate) is an exhilarating way for mountain bikers to check out the canyon's scenery. Part of the trail plunges down an old stagecoach road, providing unrivaled views of the canyon. A word of caution: Beaches south of the Highway 49 bridge, about 0.5 mile downstream from the river confluence, are unofficially clothing optional. Parking in the area is limited, so arrive early in the summer to find a spot close to the confluence.

Lance Armstrong wannabes will love the **Auburn Century** (early June, www.wildestride.com, $40–95), a one-day cycling event through many of the region's historic mining towns. This is no easy pedal; riders choose one of four grueling courses, the shortest of which is 40 miles and climbs 3,000 feet. There are no bike lanes, and cyclists ride all day on hair-raising backcountry roads, so it's best to have some experience before tackling the Auburn Century. Still, it's a chance to bike through picturesque scenery and historic Gold Rush towns, including ghost towns like Gold Run and Iowa Hill. Participants receive a souvenir cycling jersey

© CHRISTOPHER ARNS

The American River flows through the Auburn State Recreation Area.

SACRAMENTO

RAFTING

From Auburn, it's a 15–20-minute drive to either the Middle Fork or the North Fork of the mighty American River; the South Fork is about 30 minutes away. Most guided trips in the area are run by companies based near Placerville or in Calaveras County, and they usually meet just east of Auburn for river excursions. If guided tours aren't your thing, it's possible to rent rafts and kayaks from outfitters in Auburn sans guides, although it's best to steer clear of more dangerous Class IV–V rapids, especially on the North Fork, on your own. The season usually runs April–October, and outfitters can advise about the best spots to put in on the river.

If you'd rather hit the rapids without a guide, **Canyon Raft Rental** (133 Borland Ave., 530/823-0931, www.canyonraftrentals.com,

and bragging rights for braving one of the toughest bike rides in the West.

rafts $42–250, kayaks $35–70) offers inflatable kayak and raft rentals. It's certainly much cheaper to go guideless, but this option is best for rafters with some experience. Canyon Raft has a shuttle service providing transport to the Middle Fork and back to Auburn, but make sure to reserve it beforehand; occasionally, you can arrange shuttle pickup on the North Fork. If you're not using the shuttle, it's easy to pack a raft into your trunk and inflate it at the river; air pumps are included with all rentals.

You can also rent equipment from **Sierra Outdoor Center** (440 Lincoln Way, 530/885-1844, www.sierraoutdoorcenter.com, rafts $80–235, kayaks $19–69). Rentals include paddles, helmets, an air pump, and life jackets. If you're not sure where to ride the river, just ask the friendly staff; everyone in the shop has paddling experience. If you need extra instruction before heading out on the water, Sierra Outdoor Center also offers lessons in basic kayaking and rafting.

Accommodations

The **Best Western Golden Key** (13450 Lincoln Way, 530/885-8611, www.bestwesterngoldenkey.com, $65–115) has tidy and comfortable accommodations in a location perfect for exploring nearby Gold Country attractions. There's a hot tub and a heated outdoor pool that's enclosed during winter. Wi-Fi is included, and a hearty continental breakfast with hubcap-size waffles is another perk. The hotel is also pet-friendly but charges an additional $15 per night.

The slightly more upscale **Auburn Holiday Inn** (120 Grass Valley Hwy., 530/887-8787, www.auburnhi.com, $100–165) has an outdoor pool and large, well-equipped guest rooms with flat-screen TVs and king beds. Inside, the hotel is comfortable without being lavish. The convenient location is less than one mile from Auburn's historic town center, and you'll have a decent view of the town's historic courthouse. Amenities include free Wi-Fi, on-site laundry pickup, room service, and a fitness center. Pets are welcome for a one-time $20 surcharge.

Food

Across the street from the historic Placer County courthouse, **C Latitudes** (130 Maple St., 530/885-9535, http://latitudesrestaurant.com, 11:30 A.M.–3 P.M. and 5–9 P.M. Wed.–Thurs., 11:30 A.M.–3 P.M. and 5–10 P.M. Fri.–Sat., 10 A.M.–3 P.M. Sun., $10–27) is the Indiana Jones of restaurants. Each month, chef Pete Enochs prepares delicious healthy cuisine with a different culinary theme from around the world—hence the restaurant's name. There's also a fairly extensive wine list with local varietals that also change monthly to reflect the restaurant's current regional focus. The charming Victorian building was constructed in 1880 around a 200-year-old oak tree, and it oozes history; both the dining room and the downstairs bar are supposedly haunted. During warm evenings, sit outside on the second-story patio and watch sunset. The restaurant is a local favorite, so plan to arrive early or call ahead to make reservations for dinner.

Located inside a former Gold Rush saloon in Old Town Auburn, **C Carpe Vino** (1568 Lincoln Way, 530/823-0320, www.carpevino-auburn.com, 5–10 P.M. Wed.–Sat., $10–29) feels like a place John Wayne might have enjoyed had he been a wine drinker. The building dates to 1855, and the current owner took pains to restore the rustic vaulted ceiling and aged brick walls, giving Carpe Vino a polished Old West vibe. On the menu, you'll find only sustainably grown ingredients from local farms and vendors; the red-wine braised beef, Muscovy duck breast, and roasted Angus strip loin are all standout dishes. Don't forget the superb wine list; the restaurant's owner and wine guru Gary Moffat spends hours camping in his Airstream trailer to find new varietals from all over Northern California. If the restaurant is full, pull up a chair at the gleaming mahogany bar, a replica of the original from the old saloon. Carpe Vino opens at noon Tuesday through Saturday for wine-tasting only.

For delicious fast food with an Asian twist, head to **Ikeda's California Country Market** (13500 Lincoln Way, 530/885-4243, www.ikedas.com, 11 A.M.–7 P.M. Mon.–Thurs., 10 A.M.–8 P.M. Fri.–Sun., $8–10). This roadside burger joint and fruit stand has become a de facto rest stop for travelers headed to Lake Tahoe. The food is a culinary mash-up of traditional diner fare and Japanese cuisine; menu options include everything from pot pies to teriyaki bacon burgers. The turkey burger—showered with a tasty mix of secret spices—is delicious. Lunch and dinner hours can bring quite a crowd, so expect a short wait for your food.

Information and Services

Auburn has all the amenities of a small city, complete with gas stations, ATMs, big-box stores, and a **post office** (371 Nevada St., 9 A.M.–5:30 P.M. Mon.–Fri., 10 A.M.–3 P.M. Sat.). Auburn's daily newspaper is the **Auburn**

Journal (http://auburnjournal.com), which covers foothill and Placer County government news. *Sierra Heritage* (www.sierraheritage.com), a travel magazine dedicated to the Sierra Nevadas and the foothill region, sometimes profiles Auburn and surrounding areas. A great website for local visitor information is the **Placer County Visitors Bureau** (www.visitplacer.com).

For medical assistance, **Sutter Auburn Faith Hospital** (11815 Education St., 530/888-4500, www.sutterauburnfaith.org) offers an emergency room and a full range of hospital services.

Getting There and Around

Auburn is located on I-80 and provides access to Highway 49 north and south. As such, it experiences heavy weekend traffic as well as snow in winter. Check weather, road conditions, and traffic reports online with **Caltrans** (http://dot.ca.gov) before traveling in winter.

The closest major airport is **Sacramento International Airport** (SMF, 6900 Airport Blvd., Sacramento, 916/929-5411, www.sacairports.org), 30 miles south. The local **Auburn Municipal Airport** (13626 New Airport Rd., 530/386-4211), has no scheduled commercial flights.

The *Capitol Corridor* train run by **Amtrak** (www.amtrak.com, 800/872-7245) departs several times a day on its way to Sacramento, Oakland, and San Jose at Auburn Station (277 Nevada St.), but there are no ticket services. The **Gold Country Stage** (http://new.mynevadacounty.com/transit, adults $1, day pass $3, under age 6 free) runs buses and minibuses through Nevada City, Grass Valley, Auburn, and to points north of the Gold Country.

PLACERVILLE AND VICINITY
◖ Marshall Gold Discovery State Historic Park

One day in 1848, a carpenter named James W. Marshall took a fateful stroll by the sawmill he was building for John Sutter on the American River and found gold specks shining

© CHRISTOPHER ARNS

a replica of Sutter's Mill in Coloma, where gold was first discovered in California

in the water. Marshall's discovery sparked the California Gold Rush and one of the greatest migrations in history. See where it all began at Marshall Gold Discovery State Historic Park (310 Back St., Coloma, 530/622-3470, www. parks.ca.gov, daily 8 A.M.–7 P.M. summer, call for hours fall–spring, $8 per vehicle). Start inside the **visitors center** (10 A.M.–4 P.M. Tues.–Sun. Apr.–Nov., 10 A.M.–3 P.M. Tues.–Sun. Dec.–Mar.) for a quick lesson on the park's storied past, complete with artifacts from the indigenous Nisenan and Miwok people that lived in the area before the Gold Rush. Outside the visitors center, history buffs will love the park's interactive exhibits—catch a live pioneer cooking demonstration, or help load a real wagon with mining supplies like a true forty-niner.

Feel like recreating Marshall's discovery for yourself? Take a gold-panning lesson at the park's Eureka Experience Center, and then try your luck by the river. Kids will especially love getting elbow-deep in the mud for a chance to strike it rich. The park also provides nature walks and hikes through the scenic American River canyon; the **Gold Discovery Loop Trail** (3.6 miles) takes you to the very spot where Marshall made his discovery. Surrounded by beautiful wildflowers in spring, a full-size replica of **Sutter's Mill** stands near several immaculately restored historic buildings, like the tiny one-bedroom Mormon cabin, the Chinese-operated Wah Hop and Man Lee stores, the old blacksmith shop, and the Price-Thomas home.

Gold Bug Park

If you're traveling with your kids and want them to experience a gold-mining museum, visit Placerville's Gold Bug Park (Bedford Ave., 530/642-5207, www.goldbugpark.org, daily 10 A.M.–4 P.M. Apr.–Oct., adults $5, children $2, audio tour $5). This smaller mine, originally called the Hattie, dates from the 1850s. Today, the museum offers lessons in history, including tours of the mine, an interpretive

museum, and a gift shop. For a small fee, you can pan for gold in a manufactured sluice. Many of the tour features and exhibits are designed for children, combining education and entertainment as kids don their hard hats, check out the mine shaft, and learn the function of a stamp mill.

◖ Apple Hill

Aptly named Apple Hill (Apple Hill Scenic Dr., north of U.S. 50, between Placerville and Pollack Pines, 530/644-7692, www.applehill.com) produces many of the apples grown in California. Dozens of orchards cluster in the apple-friendly climate of this part of the Sierra Foothills. More recently, some of the orchards and vacant land have been converted to vineyards to help feed the insatiable appetite for wine. For a scenic tour, download a map from the website or visit in person by taking exits 48 or 54 from U.S. 50 onto Apple Hill Scenic Drive. Charming country roads and cute farm buildings fronted by orchards fill the landscape. At some orchards you can pick your own apples in season. At others you'll find a large shop stuffed with homemade pies frozen and ready to be baked, as well as preserves, cookbooks, and every type of apple product you can imagine. Come in the middle of summer to enjoy the raspberry, blackberry, and blueberry crops, and in summer–fall for the dozens of apples varieties grown in the region. Check the website for information about events and festivals that draw crowds out to Apple Hill, including country fair–style activities, arts and crafts shows, food and drink tastings, and more.

Wineries
APPLE HILL
The Apple Hill region grows more than just Fujis and Granny Smiths. The region, just northeast of Placerville, is also home to a number of vineyards that feed the local wineries.

Among the largest of the Apple Hill

wineries is **Boeger Winery** (1709 Carson Rd., 800/655-2634, www.boegerwinery.com, daily 10 A.M.–5 P.M., tasting free). Visit the elegant tasting room for a regular or reserve tasting of Boeger's best current-release wines. Better yet, bring a picnic to enjoy in the redwood grove. Owner and vineyard manager Greg Boeger bought his vines to follow a family tradition; more than a century ago, his grandfather had a winery in the Napa Valley to serve the new residents of California during the Gold Rush. Today, Boeger's specialties tend to be big hearty reds, although you can taste the occasional delicate white wine here too.

At the opposite end of the spectrum, tiny **Fenton Herriott Vineyards** (120 Jacquier Court, 530/642-2021, www.fentonherriott. com, daily 11 A.M.–5 P.M.) makes only a few hundred cases of wine each year. When visiting the little tasting room off the main drag, you'll get to try a small variety of tasty and reasonably priced red wines that you won't find in retail shops. The tasting staff knows a lot about the wines they're pouring and can tell you the story of each one.

Toward the east end of Apple Hill is **Primus Vineyards** (2875 Larsen Dr., 530/647-9463, www.primuswinery.com, daily 11 A.M.–5 P.M.). A cute red barn houses a surprisingly elegant tasting room, complete with a wooden tasting bar and shelving to hold bottles for sale. The elegance extends to the wines, all small-lot reds. Primus releases only about five wines each year. While sipping, be sure to check out the unusual and extensive collection of antique wine tools.

Wofford Acres Vineyards (1900 Hidden Valley Lane, Camino, 530/626-6858, www. wavwines.com, 11 A.M.–5 P.M. Thurs.–Sun.), another red specialist, exemplifies the new era of small family wineries in California. Open since 2003, Wofford Acres is owned and operated by the Wofford family, and you're likely to run into one or more Woffords when you visit the small tasting room. Look for low-priced but high-flavored red table wines, red varietals, and possibly even a yummy dessert port to finish off your tasting experience.

FAIR PLAY
Fitzpatrick Winery & Lodge (7740 Fairplay Rd., 530/620-6838, www.fitzpatrickwinery. com, 11 A.M.–5 P.M. Wed.–Mon.) was Fair Play's first winery, opened in 1980. Fitzpatrick focuses on "earth-friendly" wines, using organically grown grapes and producing wines in small lots to preserve the essence of the *terroir* where the grapes were grown. Going further, the wine is bottled in recycled glass with untreated cork, and then stored in a warehouse running almost entirely on solar energy on land maintained with tractors running 90 percent vegetable oil. The lengthy wine list features some California classics in the way of zinfandels, chardonnays, and merlots. To get into this winery properly, try some of the less common vintages, which can range from Irish-style white and red blended wines to a surprisingly complete array of ports in both red and white. The estate also operates a bed-and-breakfast inn. Stay for the Ploughman's Lunch (noon–4 P.M. or until the food runs out Sat.–Sun.), hearty hot fare that will set you up for an afternoon of tasting elsewhere in Fair Play and the northern Gold Country.

Charles B. Mitchell Vineyards (8221 Stoney Creek Rd., 530/620-3467, http://charlesb-mitchell.com, 11 A.M.–5 P.M. Sat.–Thurs., 11 A.M.–9 P.M. Fri. spring–fall, 11 A.M.–5 P.M. Tues.–Thurs. and Sat.–Sun., 11 A.M.–9 P.M. Fri. winter) is one of the more recognizable names in the Fair Play American Viticultural Area. In the tasting room, you'll get a chance to try a wide variety of wines, including sparkling, white, Amador County–grown reds, and lush dessert ports. You can take a tour of the winery as well, but for a special treat, book ahead to bottle your own wine.

A winery with a great name, **Toogood Estate**

SACRAMENTO

Wine Caves (7280 Fairplay Rd., 530/620-1910, www.toogoodwinery.com, daily 11 A.M.–5:30 P.M.) beckons visitors with its unique winery and distinctive wines. To get to the tasting room, enter the famed Toogood Caves. All wines here are aged in 5,000 square feet of underground space, which maintains a perfect cool temperature year-round. Bring a coat if you're sensitive to cold. You'll find almost all reds with a number of intriguing blends, some fun varietals like barbera and cabernet franc, plus a couple of unusual dessert wines, such as malbec port (really). Bottle prices range from a moderate $20 up to $80 for the rarest ports.

Cantiga Wineworks & Deli (5980 Meyers Lane, Somerset, 530/621-1696, www.cantigawine.com, 11 A.M.–5 P.M. Fri.–Sun.) brings innovation and history to the world of small-batch wine-making. If you're lucky, you'll find one of the owners and winemakers in the tasting room and can learn of the true passion that goes into Cantiga's wines. Many of the whites and several of the reds here are not malolactically fermented—highly unusual for California wines. Some grapes are grown on the Cantiga estate, but most are lovingly chosen from vineyards around California, especially at Lodi, where Cantiga maintains a second tasting room, and Monterey County.

Entertainment and Events

If you're looking for something in the old-school biker-bar department, try **PJ's Roadhouse** (5641 Mother Lode Dr., Placerville, 530/626-0336, daily 11 A.M.–2 A.M.). Off the main drag, PJ's features cheap beer and shots, a small dance floor, and the occasional DJ or live band designed to drag drinkers off their barstools. Expect lots of Harleys out front, precious little light inside, and perhaps a whiff of marijuana emanating from the back porch.

If you crave some serious exercise, plan to visit in late fall for the **Apple Hill Harvest Run** (Camino, www.applehillrun.org). This annual event includes an 8.5-mile loop run, a 3.5-mile loop, and 0.25-mile and 0.5-mile kids fun runs. Depending on your fitness level, pick one of the races and get running. The race starts early in the morning and finishes equally early, allowing racers to spend their afternoons perusing the orchards and wineries of Apple Hill. This race, which includes some major hills on the longer loop to challenge runners, benefits local schools.

During the Gold Rush, mining camps attracted all kinds of roguish performers seeking to entertain bored and homesick prospectors with colorful melodramas. The **Olde Coloma Theatre** (380 Monument Rd., Coloma, 530/626-5282, www.oldecolomatheatre.org, $10) is a throwback to those days. Built in a ramshackle cabin just down the street from where gold was first discovered, the theater offers whimsical productions like *It Just Ghost to Show* and *There's Snow Time Like the Present*. The shows are family-friendly, and many productions are staged with kids in mind. Best of all, catcalls are encouraged—audience members can boo and yell at the actors, just like melodrama attendees did in the Gold Rush era.

A stuffed buffalo looks down from the wall as you walk into **Buford's** (835 Lotus Rd., Coloma, 530/626-8096, www.sierranevadahouse.com, 5–10 P.M. Wed.–Sun. fall–spring, 5–8 P.M. Wed.–Sun. winter), the bar at Sierra Nevada House. Remodeled to resemble an Old West saloon, you won't find dirty prospectors or gunslingers in this drinking establishment; the gleaming wooden interior and immaculate bar give Buford's an upscale vibe. Still, it's a lively place to spend an evening after a day on the river, especially if you're staying in the adjoining hotel. The bar offers an extensive list of local wines and beer along with reasonably priced cocktails. Coloma's nightlife isn't exactly hopping, so Buford's is probably your best bet for evening fun in this tiny town.

Shopping

Good retail opportunities abound on Main

Street in Old Hangtown (central Placerville). The main shopping blocks run from Center Street to Cedar Ravine Road and are easily walkable. Placerville is a great place to look for antiques and vintage collectibles. There are several antiques shops clustered on Main Street—start at **Empire Antiques** (432 Main St., Placerville, 530/642-1025, daily 10:30 A.M.–5 P.M.) or **Placerville Antiques and Collectibles** (448 Main St., 530/626-3425, daily 10 A.M.–6 P.M.).

Like most Gold Country towns, Placerville has a smattering of art galleries that appeal to a variety of shoppers. The **Bennett Gallery** (6200 Pleasant Valley Rd., El Dorado, 530/621-1164, www.bennettgallery.net, 10 A.M.–3 P.M. Mon.–Fri.) displays art in a variety of media, from modern painting to handblown glass pieces. Only local artists show and sell their work at the **Gold Country Artist's Gallery** (379 Main St., Placerville, 530/642-2944, www.goldcountryartistsgallery.com, daily 11 A.M.–5 P.M.). These foothill artists create everything from painting and sculpture to pottery and gourd art.

Just like the apparel shops, the bookstores of Placerville are unique to the town; make sure to stop by **The Bookery** (326 Main St., 530/626-6454, 10 A.M.–5:30 P.M. Mon.–Thurs., 10 A.M.–7 P.M. Fri.–Sat., 10 A.M.–4 P.M. Sun.) if you need a new read.

You won't find any big chain clothing stores in the Gold Country. Instead, shop in cute one-of-a-kind boutiques like **Lighthouse** (451 Main St., Suite 1, 530/626-5515, 9 A.M.–6 P.M. Sat.–Thurs., 9 A.M.–9 P.M. Fri.), **Treehouse** (327 Main St., 530/295-0102, 10 A.M.–5:30 P.M. Mon.–Sat., 11 A.M.–4 P.M. Sun.), or **Winterhill** (321 Main St., 530/626-6369, www.winterhillfarms.com, 10 A.M.–6 P.M. Mon.–Sat., 11 A.M.–5 P.M. Sun.).

If you're looking for a sweets shop in Placerville, head to **CandyStrike: Old Tyme Candy & More** (398 Main St., 530/295-1007, www.candystrike.com, 11 A.M.–6 P.M. Mon.–Tues. and Thurs., 11 A.M.–8 P.M. Fri., 10 A.M.–8 P.M. Sat., 11 A.M.–5 P.M. Sun.) for goodies like black licorice, saltwater taffy, and fudge. For something heartier, get some great cheese and artisanal bread from **Dedrick's Main Street Cheese** (312 Main St., 530/344-8282, www.dedrickscheese.com, 10 A.M.–6 P.M. Mon.–Sat., 11 A.M.–5 P.M. Sun.).

Sports and Recreation
◖ RAFTING

For guided river trips, Placerville is the white-water capital of the Gold Country. From here, outfitters can take you to all three forks of the American River, including the rugged Class IV–V rapids of the North Fork and the more moderate Class III–IV white water of the Middle Fork. Rafting trips are designed for all experience levels, and you can even book overnight excursions; if you're a rookie rafter, try a more leisurely half-day trip down the lower section of the South Fork. The season usually runs April–October, except for trips on the North Fork, which usually run April–May or June, depending on weather and water levels. Check online for specific dates.

All-Outdoors Whitewater Rafting (925/932-8993, www.aorafting.com, $110-495) offers half-day, full-day, and multiday trips on the North, Middle, and South Forks of the American River. If you have time, take a 2–3-day jaunt and camp deep in the stunningly beautiful river canyons. Guides prepare all your meals, and it's an excellent way to experience a different side of the Gold Country. You can also book full-day trips on any of the three forks if a multiday expedition isn't feasible. If you have small kids or just want to calmly drift down the river, consider the full-day Tom Sawyer Float Trips along the rapids-free section of the South Fork.

Beyond Limits Adventures (530/622-0553,

www.rivertrip.com, $100–300) offers mostly half-day and one-day excursions to the North, Middle, and South Forks; you can also take two-day trips on the South Fork with complementary wine and beer served at dinner. Two-day trips also include a stop at a riverside resort where you can fish, play basketball, and try your hand at panning gold.

American Whitewater Expeditions (800/825-3205, www.americanwhitewater.com, $85–395) offers half-day, full-day, and multiday trips to all three forks of the American River. All expeditions come with delicious meals, friendly guides, and jaw-dropping Sierra Nevada scenery.

O.A.R.S. (800/346-6277, www.oars.com, $110–360) offers trips to all three forks of the American River. They are one of the most experienced rafting companies in the West, and the guides are extremely knowledgeable. O.A.R.S. offers full-day trips with a picnic on the Middle and North Forks; you can also take half-day, full-day, and two-day trips on the South Fork with meals included. Or enjoy a two-day wine-and-raft tour that includes side trips to several El Dorado County wineries.

Whitewater Connection (530/622-6446, www.whitewaterconnection.com, $95–340) offers the standard full-day trips to the North, Middle, and South Forks, along with multiday expeditions. You can also book half-day trips on the South Fork if time is an issue. Whitewater Connection also offers two-day trips combining one day on the North Fork with another day on either the Middle or South Fork.

Accommodations
PLACERVILLE
You could picture Ernest Hemingway or Rudyard Kipling staying at **Eden Vale Inn** (1780 Springvale Rd., 530/621-0901, http://edenvaleinn.com, $150–310). More safari resort than bed-and-breakfast, this renovated hay barn somehow combines a rustic foothill vibe with Napa-style luxury. Inside are

seven guest rooms, each named after native California trees, with gas fireplaces and lavish amenities. Five of the guest rooms have private hot tubs and enclosed patios; soak away a long day in the Gold Country before slipping into unbelievably comfortable beds. If that's not decadent enough, book a relaxing massage or a facial at the on-site spa. In the morning, don't miss a homemade breakfast buffet made from locally grown ingredients and herbs from the inn's garden. The Eden Vale Inn is only a 10-minute drive from Coloma.

The **Historic Cary House Hotel** (300 Main St., 530/622-4271, www.caryhouse. com, $100–160) is an imposing brick building in the heart of downtown Placerville. It was constructed in 1857, and plenty of famous guests have slept here, including Elvis Presley and Mark Twain. The guest rooms are small but still bristle with character; the decor invokes the Gold Rush with period antiques and old tintype photographs on the walls. From the elaborately decorated lobby, complete with wooden paneling and plush furniture, a 1920s-style elevator lifts visitors to the upstairs guest rooms. Amenities include included Wi-Fi, Continental breakfast, fridges, and cable TV. With more than 150 years of history, it's unsurprising that guests frequently report ghost sightings and other strange activity—the second floor is supposedly the most haunted. The Historic Cary House is just steps from world-class restaurants and tiny boutiques; you won't find accommodations closer to the heart of Placerville. Note that live bands play most weekends, so noise may be a factor.

Step back into the Gilded Age at the **Albert Shafsky House** (2942 Coloma St., 530/642-2776, www.shafsky.com, $140–185), a cozy Victorian bed-and-breakfast built in 1902. Each guest room boasts luxurious handmade furniture and antiques from the late 19th century. You'll drool over the mouthwatering

CHRISTOPHER ARNS ©

Albert Shafsky House

breakfasts, fixed entirely with local gourmet ingredients. Guests are treated to a complementary bottle of El Dorado wine and an artisanal cheese plate. Keep your eyes peeled before hitting the sheets; the house was originally built for a wealthy Placerville businessman whose friendly ghost supposedly still haunts the guest rooms. The Shafsky House has only three delightful decadent guest rooms, so call well ahead to reserve.

The **Mother Lode Motel** (1940 Broadway, 530/622-0895, www.placervillemotherlodemotel.com, $50–80) has clean and reasonably priced accommodations halfway between Placerville and Apple Hill. Don't be discouraged by the motel's cheap-looking sign; inside, the guest rooms are comfortable and tastefully decorated. You'll find modern amenities like included Wi-Fi, microwaves, mini fridges, and private hot tubs. There's also a decent-size pool and lounge area that offers relief during the sweltering foothill summers.

COLOMA

The **Coloma Country Inn** (345 High St., 530/622-6919, www.colomacountryinn.com, $125–235) has the white picket fence and wide veranda of a bucolic country ranch. Surrounded by willows and immaculate lawns on the bank of a small lake, the property is tucked back from the road, giving the place a secretive private feel. Built in 1852, the Inn has six guest rooms, each charmingly decorated in a 19th-century farmhouse theme. For a true farmhouse experience, book one of the two studios inside the property's original carriage house. Breakfast is a treat; if you're lucky, homemade blackberry pie will be waiting for you in the morning. The Coloma Country Inn is a short walk from the Marshall Gold Discovery State Park and several of the town's historic buildings, including a crumbling cemetery that's almost 200 years old.

The **Sierra Nevada House** (835 Lotus Rd., 530/626-8096, www.sierranevadahouse.com, $90–105) is just a stone's throw from the South Fork of the American River and offers charming and romantic accommodations. The six Western-themed guest rooms each have a different Gold Rush theme. Overall, this roadside inn is actually more of a couples' retreat—families with children might do better to stay elsewhere. The hotel is right on Highway 49 and can be somewhat noisy; if you stay in the Bordello Room, beware: Your quarters are right above the bar. The location is convenient to the area's historic and recreational attractions, and the room rates are quite reasonable for the area.

For more casual accommodations, camp at the **American River Resort** (6019 New River Rd., 530/622-6700, http://americanriverresort.com, cabins $150–280, campsites $25–35, RV hookup sites $45). More than just a drab RV park, the resort is located on the South Fork of the American River and gives visitors the chance to feel closer to nature. Restrooms and showers are available near all 85 campsites,

SACRAMENTO

along with a swimming pool—although there's always the river for taking a dip. The riverside cabins have been remodeled, and kitchens are fully stocked with appliances and utensils, although bed linens are not provided.

FAIR PLAY

For an up-to-date bed-and-breakfast experience plus great access to a fabulous wine region, book a room at **Lucinda's Country Inn** (6701 Perry Creek Rd., 530/409-4169, www. lucindascountryinn.com, $175–225). Each of the five guest rooms welcomes visitors with the style of a luxury hotel. You'll find classy understated decor, a fireplace, a fridge, a microwave, a coffeemaker, plush robes to relax in, and a two-person spa tub in some guest rooms. Outside the inn is the Fair Play wine region, and not too far away is the Shenandoah Valley.

The **Fitzpatrick Winery and Lodge** (7740 Fairplay Rd., Somerset, 530/620-3248, www. fitzpatrickwinery.com, $90–165) takes its Irish roots seriously—right down to the green eggs and ham served at breakfast. Inside, two of the five guest rooms feature Celtic-themed decor with patterned cushions and Fitzpatrick family photos. Most of the guest rooms include a clawfoot tub and a woodstove, providing a comfortable homespun vibe with log-cabin decor that still feels lavish. The log-cabin theme continues inside the Great Room, which has a vaulted log ceiling and plush sofa set before a fireplace. Breakfast is homemade with ingredients from the local farmers market and the Fitzpatrick's own garden. On steamy summer days, take a dip in the Olympic-length lap pool; at night, you can ease into the lodge's hot tub for a relaxing soak.

Food
PLACERVILLE

The Shoestring (1320 Broadway, 530/622-7125, 11 A.M.–8 P.M. Mon.–Sat., 11 A.M.–7 P.M. Sun., $10) is a roadside hole-in-the-wall serving savory fare—burgers, hot dogs, and culinary guilt-inducers like chili cheese fries. There's also a small children's menu, but most of the food (cheeseburgers, corn dogs, chicken nuggets) is already kid-friendly. Diners will be conveniently located near the northern tip of downtown Placerville, making it easy to swing by on the way to Apple Hill. The Shoestring doesn't have restrooms, so factor that into your plans before dropping in.

The Heyday Café (325 Main St., 530/626-9700, www.heydaycafe.com, 11 A.M.–9 P.M. Tues.–Thurs., 11 A.M.–10 P.M. Fri.–Sat., 11 A.M.–8 P.M. Sun., $17–26) has quickly gained a reputation as one of the best eateries in Placerville. From the street, it's easy to miss Heyday's modest entrance; inside, the stripped-brick interior and rough-hewn wooden ceiling gives the café a rugged yet hip vibe. The California bistro–style food is fused with Asian, Italian, and Mediterranean influences. Try the bacon-artichoke-pesto pizza or the lemon salsa skewers; pair with a crisp riesling from Apple Hill to sample the extensive wine list.

For upscale Mexican food in the heart of Gold Country, grab a table at **Cascada** (384 Main St., 530/344-7757, www.cascadaonmain-street.com, 11 A.M.–8:30 A.M. Sun.–Thurs., 11 A.M.–9:30 P.M. Fri.–Sat., $10–23). Located in downtown Placerville, Cascada is Mexican with a California-bistro twist. You'll find familiar Mexican favorites like burritos, tacos and enchiladas; if you're feeling adventurous, try the pork medallions with raspberry chipotle sauce. Since the restaurant is elegant-casual, you might want to freshen up before arriving, and reservations are probably a good idea.

COLOMA

The **Café Mahjaic** (1006 Lotus Rd., 530/622-9587, www.cafemahjaic.com, 5–8 P.M. Wed.–Sat., $19–25), housed inside a historic brick building constructed in 1855, offers fine dining near the banks of the American River. Menu items are served with natural and

APPLE HILL EATERIES

There's plenty of good healthy food to be had in the Apple Hill region. But what if you need more than a nice fresh apple to keep hunger away? Stop at one of the orchard-based restaurants along the meandering trails. A number of these offer a variety of foods such as sandwiches to hot handmade apple pies. The area maps available at almost every orchard point out which establishments offer a restaurant.

Perhaps the best place for lunch in Apple Hill is the kitschy **Bavarian Hills Orchard** (3100 N. Canyon Rd., Camino, 530/642-2714, www. bavarianhills.com, 11 A.M.-5 P.M. Sat.-Sun. June-Aug., daily 11 A.M.-5 P.M. Sept.-Dec.). Oompah music blares from speakers outside the white-gingerbread-trimmed brown barn buildings that house the store and the restaurant. Walk into the unprepossessing cafeteria-style restaurant, with its linoleum floor, walk-up counter with refrigerator cases, and tile-lettered menu on the wall. Order a sausage on a roll with some traditional German side dishes, and strap in for one of the best surprises you'll encounter on your trip to Gold Country. Your food will be brought on paper plates to whatever table you can find, inside or out. The sausages are phenomenal, and the side dishes—warm German potato salad, sauerkraut, and braised red cabbage—are homemade from scratch daily. The owner brought the recipes to Apple Hill from her Bavarian home, and her dedication to creating great authentic German food shows. Finally, your dessert can be any sort of apple pastry, though there's no reason to avoid the home-made strudel from the orchard's own apples.

A "lunch" includes a sausage on a roll, a side dish, and a dessert. Portions are eminently reasonable. If you've got a hearty appetite, order an extra side dish or two—they're tasty enough to make it worth it. Or you can get an extra portion of strudel for dessert.

If you're just looking for a fresh slice of pie, some of the best you'll find is sold at the **Apple Pantry Farm** (2310 Hidden Valley Lane, Camino, 530/318-2834, www.applepantryfarm.com, 9 A.M.-5 P.M. Fri.-Sun.). First you'll see the attractive small store, selling apples and an array of frozen uncooked pies ready to be baked in your home oven. Just up and to the right of the main store, a small trailer exudes aromas that draw visitors as if by magic. You can buy just a slice or a whole apple, apple-blackberry, or other seasonal fruit pie the likes of which your grandmother wished she could bake. Ask the proprietress if she buys her crusts premade, and she'll look at you as though you'd asked her if she enjoys torturing puppies. Every crumb of every Apple Pantry pie gets made from scratch and slices are sold hot out of the industrial ovens in the trailer. While some say that the apple-blackberry with the crumble crust is the best, everyone has their own take on which pie rules the Pantry. The frozen ready-bake pies in the shop below are made by the same team; if you've got the means to transport them, pick up as many as you can.

organic ingredients, and the restaurant's cuisine competes with anything in Napa or the Bay Area. The New American fare includes subtle Mediterranean touches—the Hillbilly salad is a delicious twist on a traditional Greek favorite, and the grilled flatbread with *tzatziki* sauce and hummus is wonderful. The white tablecloths and a decidedly cosmopolitan interior will make you want to spiff up before dinner. The last reservation is at 8 P.M.; make sure to reserve a table, as this restaurant is very popular. Note that Café Mahjaic is closed the first week of July and the first two weeks of January.

You can't go wrong at the **Sierra Nevada House** (835 Lotus Rd., 530/626-8096, www. sierranevadahouse.com, 5–10 P.M. Wed.–Sun., $8–23). The mostly American steak house food is surprisingly good for this tiny Gold Rush town. Try the pear chutney pork chops sprinkled with chunks of blue cheese and pair it with a bottle of local zinfandel from El Dorado County. The haute fig chicken is also a treat, made with a tasty house fig and thyme jam.

Vegetarians might feel left out, as the menu isn't overflowing with meatless options, but the gourmet salads are meals in themselves.

The **Argonaut** (331 Hwy. 49, 530/626-7345, 10 A.M.–4 P.M. Tues.–Sun., $8) is a tiny shack just steps from where James Marshall discovered gold in 1848. The food is reasonably priced; you can order homemade sandwiches, soups, chili, and pie made nearby in Apple Hill. On sunny days, grab a picnic table behind the Argonaut, or just sit at one of the small tables on the café's side patio with views of the South Fork of the American River. The Argonaut is conveniently located across Highway 49 from the visitors center at the Marshall Gold Discovery State Park.

FAIR PLAY

From the outside, the **Gold Vine Grill** (6028 Grizzly Flat Rd., 530/626-4042, www.gold-vinegrill.com, 11 A.M.–3 P.M. and 5–9 P.M. Wed.–Sun., $8–23) looks like a run-of-the-mill roadside café. Inside, the gleaming wooden tables and exquisite artwork give this restaurant a stylish feel. The mostly California cuisine—blackened salmon with Cajun cream sauce, pork chops with jalapeño and honey, and macadamia-crusted mahimahi—is mouthwateringly good. And if you're staying at any of Fair Play's bed-and-breakfasts, there's no need to drive into Placerville for dinner.

For a quick espresso or a sandwich, stop by **Crossroads Coffee and Cafe** (6032 Grizzly Flat Rd., 530/344-0591, www.gr8espresso. biz, 6 A.M.–3 P.M. Mon.–Fri., 7 A.M.–3 P.M. Sat.–Sun., $9), serving breakfast and lunch along with excellent espresso drinks. There are about 20 different sandwiches to choose from on the menu; almost all of the sandwiches include meat, so vegetarians will have to stick to salads. For live entertainment in the Fair Play area, come by the café the second Saturday of the month; Crossroads stays open in the evening for open-mic night, and a variety of local musicians usually play.

Information and Services

Placerville is the largest town in El Dorado County, and it's your best bet for major services. You can find gas stations, banks, ATMs, supermarkets, and a **post office** (3045 Sacramento St., 8:30 A.M.–5 P.M. Mon.–Fri., 10 A.M.–1 P.M. Sat.).

For local news, the **Mountain Democrat** (www.mtdemocrat.com), one of the oldest daily newspapers in California, covers Placerville and El Dorado County. Many of the smaller towns also have their own weekly newspapers, often free. For arts and entertainment events, pick up the free **Sierra Lodestar** (www.sierralodestar. com), which advertises upcoming concerts and cultural events.

For medical assistance, **Marshall Hospital** (1100 Marshall Way, 530/622-1441, www.mar-shallmedical.org) offers an emergency room and a full range of hospital services in Placerville.

If you're low on fuel and deep in the countryside, **Riverside Mini Mart** (7215 Hwy. 49, Lotus, 530/642-9715) provides gas for travelers in Coloma, while **Gray's Mart** (6713 Mount Aukum Rd., Melsons Corners, 530/620-5510) is the place to stop near Fair Play.

Getting There and Around

Placerville is located 45 miles east of Sacramento at the intersection of U.S. 50 and Highway 49. Stoplights on U.S. 50 can cause traffic to back up on weekends; winter snows can close the roads in the winter. To reach Apple Hill, take U.S. 50 two exits east of Placerville. Coloma is almost nine miles north of Placerville on Highway 49; the Marshall Gold Discovery State Historic Park is the easiest landmark. It snows in Coloma November–April, and sometimes even into May, so check road conditions before driving with Caltrans (http://dot.ca.gov).

Fair Play is up in the Sierra Foothills well off Highway 49. It's a good idea to have a full tank of gas before you take the winding country roads into this mountainous area. To reach Fair Play from Placerville, take Highway 49 south to Pleasant Valley Road. Follow Pleasant Valley Road east for about 10 miles to Pleasant Valley, and then head south on County Road 16 (Plymouth–Shenandoah Rd.). County Road 16 winds almost 30 miles up to Omo Ranch Road; turn east and then left onto Fair Play Road.

Shenandoah Valley

The best-known wine region in the Gold Country is the Shenandoah Valley. Dozens of wineries are near the towns of Plymouth, Amador City, Sutter Creek, Jackson, and even tiny Volcano, and most use locally grown grapes that show the best of what the Sierra Foothills can produce.

PLYMOUTH
Amador Flower Farm
Nearly 1,000 different kinds of daylilies grow at the Amador Flower Farm (22001 Shenandoah School Rd., 209/245-6660, www.amadorflowerfarm.com, daily 9 A.M.–4 P.M.). Take a serene

© CHRISTOPHER ARNS

Amador Flower Farm

and colorful walk through the eight acres of farmland and four acres of demonstration gardens, flowers, and perennials. If you brought a picnic, enjoy it in the gardens shaded by heritage oak trees. In the gift shop, get a single lily for your sweetheart, or pick up a bundle of bulbs to take home.

Shenandoah Valley Museum
If you're a history buff with a few extra minutes on your hands, you can find a wealth of 15-minute museums in northern Gold Country. In these tiny galleries, learn about little-explored aspects of California pioneer life. The Shenandoah Valley Museum (14430 Shenandoah Rd., 209/245-4455, www.sobonwine.com, free) describes the wine-making process that began in Gold Country almost as soon as the first miners arrived. It's part of the Sobon Estate—a winery that has been in continuous operation in the Shenandoah Valley since 1856.

Wineries
Arguably the best of the small–medium Shenandoah wineries is **Story Winery** (10525 Bell Rd., 800/713-6390, www.zin.com, tasting daily 11 A.M.–5 P.M. summer, noon–4 P.M. Mon.–Fri., 11 A.M.–5 P.M. Sat.–Sun. winter, free), where you can begin to taste the true history of Amador County wines. Some of the Story vineyards have been around for nearly 100 years and still produce grapes (albeit in tiny quantities) for wines made today. The specialty of the house at Story is zinfandel—check out the amazing selection of old-vine

SACRAMENTO

SACRAMENTO

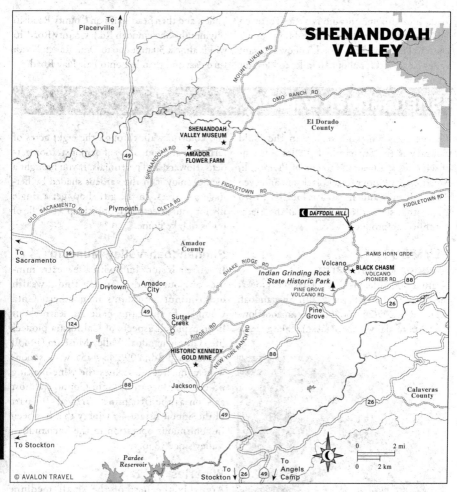

single-vineyard zins. Tasting takes place in a charming, casual environment where you'll feel at home even if you're new to high-end wine. Walk outside to admire the estate vineyards ranging down the hills.

With only the barest of nods to California favorite varietals, **Bray Vineyards** (10590 Shenandoah Rd., 209/245-6023, www.bray-vineyards.com, 10 A.M.–5 P.M. Wed.–Mon.) goes its own way, pouring wines made from grapes even savvy wine lovers won't find

familiar. Taste a wine made from verdelho, tempranillo, alicante bouschet, or an intriguing blend of Portuguese grapes largely unknown in the United States. To really get a feel for what Bray does, go outside the tasting room and into the vineyards; Bray grows its own grapes, plus olives for estate olive oil, and has a number of native oak trees.

One of the biggest names in the Shenandoah Valley, **Montevina** (20680 Shenandoah School Rd., 209/245-6942, www.montevina.com, daily 10 A.M.–4:30 P.M.) lives up to its reputation and prides itself on its zinfandels, boasting that it makes "the best in the world." That's a bold claim in Amador County, which is the zinfandel heartland, but Montevina doesn't box itself in—you can taste white wines, light red wines, medium red wines, blends, and more at this fun tasting room. Check out something from each of the three labels: the standard Montevina, reserve Terra d'Oro, and the fun, inexpensive Wild Bunch blends.

For a small winery experience, hit the cute barn at **Deaver Vineyards** (12455 Steiner Rd., 290/245-4099, www.deavervineyard.com, daily 10:30 A.M.–5 P.M.). Deaver produces a couple of white and rosé wines and some flavored sparklers, but reds are unquestionably the mainstay. At the tasting bar you can sip a range of intense layered zins and syrahs, or get bold with a carignan or a barbera. Even if you're not a wine fan, you can't help but be charmed by the farm-style atmosphere, complete with decrepit outbuildings and sweeping green fields (under the vines, of course).

Wilderotter Vineyard (19890 Shenandoah School Rd., 209/245-6016, www.wilderottervineyard.com, 10 A.M.–5 P.M. Wed.–Mon.) brings great grapes from a loving grower out of the vineyard and into the tasting room. Wilderotter started as a vineyard that sold all its grapes to various winemakers and only transformed into a winery in its own right in 2002. The production is limited both in quantity and in scope. Zinfandel, grenache, viognier, and barbera are what's planted in the vineyards, so that's what's available in the bottles.

Accommodations

The 🅒 **Amador Harvest Inn** (12455 Steiner Rd., 800/217-2304, www.amadorharvestinn.com, $150–170) brings a bit of uptown Napa to the Shenandoah Valley while retaining the down-home feel of Amador County. The exterior of the inn feels perfectly unpretentious—a simple farmhouse set on a green lawn surrounded by trees and water. Inside you'll find four guest rooms named after wine grapes, each decorated in a charming country style. The dining room continues the farmhouse charm, with kitchen-style tables and chairs and a home-cooked breakfast each morning. The Amador Harvest Inn makes a perfect base from which to explore the whole of the Shenandoah Valley wine country.

The romantic **Plymouth House Inn** (9525 Main St., 209/245-3298, www.plymouthhouseinn.com, $90–180) blends Amador wine culture with a dash of Gold Rush past. There's an old mineshaft underneath the building where gold was discovered in the late 1800s; you can still see the old mine in the basement while visiting the inn's antiques shop. The seven Victorian-style guest rooms feature quaint wood stoves, handmade antique furniture, and quilted linens as well as ceiling fans and TVs. There's also a full breakfast in the morning, a complementary wine hour, and plenty of country charm in the plush but understated common room. And unlike some older bed-and-breakfasts in the Gold Country, each guest room has air-conditioning. Note that you'll probably want to leave the kids at home since the ambiance, while perfect for couples, is less so for families.

For a more Californian experience, book a cabin at **Rancho Cicada Retreat** (10001 Bell Rd, 209/245-4841, www.ranchocicadaretreat.com, $85–159) in the backwoods of the foothills. The retreat offers both tent cabins and wood-sided cabins, most of which share common single-sex restrooms. The main attraction of the Rancho, the Cosumnes River, runs along the tent cabins. Visitors can swim, inner-tube, and fish in the river, and your hosts will happily show you good spots to bag a trout and peaceful holes to enjoy a relaxing dip. Or you can visit the riverside hot tubs, perhaps after an old-fashioned sweat in the Mi-Wok sweat

© CHRISTOPHER ARNS

The Plymouth House Inn is steps away from downtown Plymouth.

lodge. Rancho Cicada offers primitive lodgings—bring your own sleeping bags or bedding, pillows, towels, and food to cook, plus ice chests for drinks.

For casual accommodations at the right price, consider the **49er Village** (18265 Hwy. 49, 800/339-6981, www.49ervillage.com, cabins $110–230). Primarily an asphalt-covered RV park, the 49er Village also rents studio and one-bedroom vacation cabins at reasonable rates. Cabins include private baths, private decks, full kitchens with utensils, and full access to the park's pools and amenities. One-bedroom cabins sleep 5–6 people.

Food

Stepping into **Restaurant Taste** (9402 Main St., 209/245-3463, http://restauranttaste. com, 4:30 P.M.–close Mon. and Thurs.–Fri., 11:30 A.M.–2 P.M. and 5 P.M.–close Sat.–Sun., $8–42) can be quite a shock. Set in a modest building off Plymouth's dusty main drag, this surprising bistro has an upscale vibe that feels like eating out in downtown San Francisco. Chef Mark Berkner's menu is stocked with gourmet food made from seasonal healthy ingredients; the entrées are meat-heavy upscale fare done to perfection. The wine list is a balanced selection of Amador wines and California varietals with some international labels thrown in. If you're vegan or have gluten sensitivities, make sure to call ahead, and the restaurant will create a special menu.

The **Amador Vintage Market** (9393 Main St., 209/245-3663, www.amadorvintagemarket.com, 10 A.M.–6 P.M. Wed.–Sun., $10) whips up gourmet sandwiches and take-out cuisine in this downtown Plymouth eatery. For lunch, try the Miner's Reuben with pastrami and pepperjack cheese on grilled focaccia. Locals recommend the half-pound balsamic pork tenderloin along with the potato of the day.

If you're craving burgers, pop into **Marlene and Glen's Diner** (18726 Hwy. 49, 209/245-5778, daily 7 A.M.–2:30 P.M., $4–14). This quirky roadside stop is like a scene from *Happy Days*—polished chrome and red leather seats at the counter, homey curios on the wall, and heaping portions of good ol' American diner food. For breakfast, there are nine different choices of eggs benedict, including the steak benedict with Cajun hollandaise sauce. The menu has plenty of greasy but tasty lunch choices; the Kelly Blue Cheese Burger is a standout. The service can slow down considerably on weekends, so either come early or be ready to wait.

Information and Services

Plymouth is a small town without many of the services found in larger cities, so the best place for news and events is online (http://plymouthcalifornia.com). If you're planning to visit local wineries, a good place to start is the **Amador Vintner's Association** (9310 Pacific St., 209/245-6992, daily 10 A.M.–4 P.M.) to pick up brochures and directions; the **Amador 360 Wine Collective** (18590 Hwy. 49, 209/267-4355, www.amador360.com, daily 11 A.M.–5 P.M.) offers tasting and advice about smaller boutique wineries that can be hard to find.

There aren't many bank branches in Plymouth, but you can find an ATM at the **El Dorado Savings Bank** (18726 Hwy. 49, 209/245-3000, www.eldoradosavingsbank.com, 9 A.M.–5 P.M. Mon.–Thurs., 9 A.M.–6 P.M. Fri.). To fill up your tank before heading into the wine country, there's a Shell **gas station** (17699 Village Dr.) just south of town on Highway 49. You can also find a **post office** (9477 Main St., 9–11 A.M. and 11:30 A.M.–4:30 P.M. Mon.–Fri.).

Getting There and Around

Plymouth is just off Highway 49, north of Jackson and Sutter Creek. If you're driving from the north, follow Highway 49 south from Placerville for about 20 miles. From Sacramento, take Highway 16 southeast to Highway 49 and then head northeast. These highways are all two-lane roads and can become packed on weekends, so adjust your travel time accordingly.

Amador Transit (209/267-9395, http://amadortransit.com, $2) runs buses between Plymouth and Sutter Creek, where you can catch connections to Jackson and other towns in the region.

SUTTER CREEK
Monteverde Store Museum

Miners, their wives, and everybody else who came to live in the bustling boomtowns of Gold Country needed supplies: food, cloth, tools, and medicines. In 19th-century California, many of those supplies were sold at the general store. The Monteverde Store Museum (11A Randolph St., 209/267-1344, www.suttercreek.org, by appointment) sold staples to Sutter Creek residents for 75 years. After its last shopkeepers, Mary and Rose Monteverde, died, the city took over the building. The sisters had stipulated that it was to become a museum, and so it is—a look into the hub of town life in the 19th century.

Entertainment and Shopping

You'll find a mix of live theater and live musical performance at the **Sutter Creek Theatre** (44 Main St., 916/425-0077, www.suttercreektheater.com, $17–25). Music acts include folk, flamenco, and country-western; performers can really connect with the audience in this intimate venue. Plays are performed several times a year, generally family-friendly classics such as *A Christmas Carol* and *The Velveteen Rabbit*. Occasionally you might get a chance to see a new work by a local playwright.

At **Chaos Glassworks** (121 A Hanford St., 209/267-9317, www.chaosglassworks.com, noon–7 P.M. Wed.–Fri., 10 A.M.–7 P.M. Sat., 10 A.M.–6 P.M. Sun.), you can purchase handmade works of glass art and watch the glassblower create new pieces before your very eyes.

SACRAMENTO

To shop Sutter Creek, simply take a stroll down historic Main Street. You'll find cluttered antiques shops filled with treasures great and small. For something fun to spruce up the house, walk into **Water Street Antiques** (74 Main St., 209/267-0585, www.waterstreetantiques.com, 10 A.M.–4 P.M. Mon. and Wed.–Fri., 10 A.M.–5 P.M. Sat., 11 A.M.–5 P.M. Sun.). Peruse imported furniture, housewares, and hundreds of decorative items.

Accommodations

With the ethos of a classic B&B and the fun touches of a hostel, you'll find the perfect lodging mix at **Hanford House** (61 Hanford St., 209/267-0747, www.hanfordhouse.com, $110–290). Hanford House is a brick manor house with nine guest rooms, each decorated in a floral country style with unique furnishings and textiles. Beds are large and comfy, and baths squeak with cleanliness and feel a little bit like home. Enjoy the hearty breakfast in the morning and pass your morning reading the walls and ceiling of the inn. Guests have signed and commented on the plain white walls over the years; they're almost full now, so if you feel a

need to add your own John Hancock, you'll have to hunt for a bare spot.

The **Imperial Hotel** (14202 Hwy. 49, Amador City, 209/267-9172, www.imperial-amador.com, $105–190) shows off the brick facade and narrow-column architecture of a classic Old West hotel. You'll get a true mining town hotel experience in one of six guest rooms on the second floor of the building, or in one of three new guest rooms in the "cottage" out back. These guest rooms have been updated to include private baths and are done in a simple antique style that makes use of the redbrick interior walls. Each guest room is a haven of peace and quiet, without a TV or even a phone to bother you. Music and literature are the entertainment at the Imperial. You can take all your meals downstairs, including the full hot breakfast that's included in the room rate. Dinner is a special time, featuring gourmet California cuisine made with local organic produce, natural meats, and sustainable seafood.

Food

Pizza Plus (20 Eureka St., 209/267-1900, daily 11 A.M.–9 P.M., $12–22) serves the best pies

historic Sutter Creek

© CHRISTOPHER ARNS

Pizza Plus in downtown Sutter Creek

in Amador in some of the best ambiance. The pizza is great, but the cheese-covered breadsticks are just as famous. Vegetarians will be pleasantly surprised by the small mountain of tomatoes, olives, yellow onions, mushrooms, artichoke hearts, and green bell peppers on the veggie pizza. There are no big-screen TVs on the walls, making Pizza Plus the perfect place for families more interested in eating together than watching a game.

Andrae's Bakery (14141 Hwy. 49, Amador City, 209/267-1352, www.andraesbakery.com, 8 A.M.–4 P.M. Thurs.–Sun., $8) feels like eating at a your grandmother's house. Locals order the gourmet sandwiches—the turkey is a standout, made with locally raised meat, cheese, and veggies on house-baked focaccia bread. For dessert, you absolutely, positively must have one of the pastries; any of the cookies are dangerously good, but the seasonal scones (strawberry and peach in summer, cranberry in winter) themselves are worth the trip. You can order to go at Andrae's, but a better alternative is to sit outside on the back patio. There's a fair number of

old-fashioned sodas in the drink case to wash down your meal; after lunch, browse the artisanal salts and sauces on the café shelves.

Do you love a traditional afternoon tea? Indulge your whims at the **Tea Eras Tea Room & Gifts** (34 Main St., 209/267-0333, www.teaerastearoom.com, daily 11 A.M.–3 P.M.), a white wood-frame house in old downtown Sutter Creek that exudes a Victorian atmosphere. Order a full tea service with scones, finger sandwiches, salad, savories, and desserts, plus tea, of course—a charming alternative to a plain ol' lunch. Several alternative tea services cater to all appetites, while the à la carte menu offers salads and sandwiches.

Information and Services

The **Sutter Creek Visitors Center** (71A Main St., 209/267-1344, http://suttercreek.org, 11 A.M.–2:30 P.M. Mon.–Wed., 10 A.M.–5 P.M. Thurs.–Sun.) has a helpful website with loads of travel advice and tips on local sights, along with an events list for upcoming cultural happenings. The visitors center is staffed by volunteers, so the daily hours may fluctuate; call ahead to make sure someone is there.

In Amador, the local newspaper, the *Ledger-Dispatch* (www.ledger-dispatch.com), provides information about entertainment happenings. For entertainment and cultural events in Amador, Calaveras, and Tuolumne Counties, pick up a free copy of the *Sierra Lodestar* (www.sierralodestar.com).

There are ATMs and several bank branches in Sutter Creek, as well as a **post office** (3 Gopher Flat Rd., 9 A.M.–4:30 P.M. Mon.–Fri.).

Getting There and Around

Sutter Creek is 10 miles south of Plymouth and roughly 5 miles north of Jackson on Highway 49. From Placerville, head south on Highway 49 for about 30 miles to reach Sutter Creek. From the Central Valley, take Highway 88 northeast from Stockton and drive 42 miles to Highway 49; turn north for 2.5 miles to Sutter Creek.

The local **Westover Field-Amador County Airport** (12380 Airport Rd., Jackson, 209/223-2376, www.co.amador.ca.us) is between Jackson and Sutter Creek, but it has no scheduled commercial flights. The closest airport served by the airlines is **Sacramento International Airport** (SMF, 6900 Airport Blvd., Sacramento, 916/929-5411, www.sacairports.org), 55 miles west.

If you're interested in the exploring the mines, drive along the **Sutter Creek Gold Mine Trail** (209/267-1344, www.suttercreek.org). Highways 49 and 88 are the main thoroughfares through the Amador County gold-mining district—a commercial map of the area makes a good companion to the hand-drawn map in the official brochure.

Amador Transit (115 Valley View Way, 209/267-9395, http://amadortransit.com, $2) runs several bus routes all over Amador County and to Sacramento from its station.

JACKSON
Historic Kennedy Gold Mine

The Historic Kennedy Gold Mine (Hwy. 49 and Hwy. 88, 209/223-9542, www.kennedy-goldmine.com, guided tours 10 A.M.–3 P.M. Sat.–Sun. Mar.–Oct.) is a great place to learn about life in a California gold mine. The Kennedy Mine was one of the deepest hard-rock gold mines in the state, extending more than a mile into the earth. Tour the stately Mine House, marvel at the size of the head frame, and learn how a stamp mill worked to free the gold from the rocks. For the best experience, take a guided tour and learn the true stories of the mine.

Indian Grinding Rock State Historic Park

Indian Grinding Rock State Historic Park (14881 Pine Grove–Volcano Rd., 209/296-7488, www.parks.ca.gov, daily sunrise–sunset, day use $8 per vehicle) focuses on the history of the state before the European influx. This park, 12 miles east of Jackson, celebrates the life and culture of the Miwok people, specifically the Northern Sierra Miwok who inhabited the foothills for centuries. One of the central aspects of Miwok life was grinding acorns, their principal food. Women came to the grinding rock to grind and then soak their acorns for the day's meals. The park's focal point is a huge grinding rock, one used by all the women of the group who lived in the adjacent meadow and forest. The dozens of divots in the rock, plus the fading petroglyphs drawn over generations, attest to the lengthy use of this chunk of marble. The grinding rock's marble is frail, so don't walk on it.

Follow the pathways past the grinding rock to the reconstructed roundhouse, a sacred space in current use by local Miwoks, implying that visitors should be respectful. Walk farther toward the **Miwok village,** where you can enter the dwellings to see how these native

Californians once lived. If you're up for a longer hike, the **North Trail** winds around most of the park. For a deeper look into Miwok history, spend some time in the visitors center and museum.

Sports and Recreation

Golf addicts can find plenty to keep themselves busy at the highly rated public **Castle Oaks Golf Club** (1000 Castle Oaks Dr., Ione, 209/274-0167, www.castleoaksgolf.com, $20–52). This 18-hole par-71 championship course offers five different levels of tee, making it fun for golfers of any skill level. Lots of water features keep the game interesting, and the relatively flat terrain makes for a lovely walk. Located in Ione, west of Jackson and Plymouth, Castle Oaks makes a perfect diversion from the endless museums, mines, and wineries of the area. If you're just looking for practice, Castle Oaks has a driving range, chipping green, and putting green. The club recommends that you book your tee time at least one week in advance.

At **Lake Camanche** (2000 Camanche Rd., Ione, 209/763-5121, www.camancherecreation. com), you can zip around the lake on a personal watercraft, try your skills at waterskiing or wakeboarding, or enjoy a relaxing afternoon or evening of fishing. You can fish at Camanche all year. Beautiful scenery and plentiful fishing combine at **Pardee Lake Recreation Area** (4900 Stony Creek Rd., Ione, 209/772-1472, www.pardeelakerecreation.com).

Accommodations

El Campo Casa (12548 Kennedy Flat Rd., Jackson, 209/223-0100, http://elcampo-casa.com, $50–60) is a throwback motel with Old World character. If you're burned out on Victorian-style inns or restored Gold Rush flophouses, pull into this white stucco *ranchería* for a change. The 15 simple guest rooms evoke a mid-century motel feel, and have ceiling fans, air-conditioning, and TVs; there's also an outdoor pool and a shady patio area. It's quite reasonable for the rates and makes a perfect base for excursions in the Shenandoah Valley. On the downside, the guest rooms are somewhat Spartan, and the baths are a little too cozy. Note that all guest rooms are nonsmoking.

For a place with modern conveniences, stay at the **Best Western Amador Inn** (200 S. Hwy. 49, 209/223-0211, www.bestwestern. com, $70–110), actually a homey place to crash after touring the area's wineries. If visiting during the scorching summer months, take a dip in the outdoor pool and enjoy the patio area. Guest room amenities include coffeemakers, air-conditioning, fridges, and cable TV; some guest rooms also have gas fireplaces. The continental breakfast is included, and you can even make decent-size waffles. Make sure to ask specifically for a nonsmoking room.

The **Holiday Inn Express** (101 Clinton Rd., 209/257-1500, $115–200) is a modern and comfortable hotel just off Highway 49. Guest rooms are well stocked with anything you'll need, including microwaves, fridges, cable TV, and blow-dryers. It also has a business center and a fitness room. In the morning, start your day with a trip to the hotel's breakfast buffet, included in the rates.

Food

The **Mother Lode Market and Deli** (36 Main St., 209/223-0652, 8 A.M.–3 P.M. Mon.–Sat., $5) is a local institution that serves down-home meals and some local history. This quaint rustic café is in downtown Jackson and makes a perfect stop for coffee or a bite to eat. The menu is filled with standard Americana café fare sandwiches, deli items, salads, and soups—it's nothing fancy, but everything is prepared from scratch. Order a sandwich with freshly baked bread and a heaping pile of homemade potato salad; the tri-tip beef and the Italian sausage sandwiches are excellent choices.

Thomi's Café (627 S. Hwy. 49, 209/257-0800, www.thomiscafe.net, 8 A.M.–9 P.M. Mon.–Sat., 8 A.M.–8 P.M. Sun., $10–17) is the kind of old-fashioned family restaurant you probably ate at as a kid. Meals are served pretty much any time of the day, but make sure to come hungry—to say the portions are hearty is an understatement. The menu is typical American surf-and-turf, although Thomi also has an astonishingly good stir-fry menu. Locals like the breakfasts here, especially the California benedict with eggs, tomato, bacon, and avocado. One thing you won't find is vegetarian options, other than some salads and a few meatless pasta dishes.

For good take-out food in Jackson, it's hard to beat the **Vinciguerra Ravioli Company** (225 Sutter St., 209/223-7654, 11 A.M.–6 P.M. Wed.–Sat., $8). There's no sit-down service, just a window where you pick up buckets of ravioli to cook later—but this hole-in-the-wall is a gem. The ravioli comes frozen, so you need either a stove or a microwave to cook it. Any of options are excellent, although the pumpkin ravioli with sage butter sauce is ahead of the pack.

Information and Services
The **Amador Chamber of Commerce** (115 Main St., 209/223-0350, http://amadorcountychamber.com, 8 A.M.–4 P.M. Mon.–Fri., 10 A.M.–2 P.M. Sat.–Sun.) is also the visitors bureau in Jackson, and it's the best place to learn about what's happening in town.

Jackson is the nerve center for Amador County politics, and the *Ledger-Dispatch* (www.ledger-dispatch.com) covers local government news. Cultural events can be found weekly in the pages of the *Sierra Lodestar* (www.sierralodestar.com).

Jackson is one of the region's largest towns and has plenty of services available, including ATMs, banks, gas stations, and supermarkets. There's also a **post office** (424 Sutter St., 9 A.M.–4 P.M. Mon.–Fri., 10 A.M.–2 P.M. Sat.).

For medical emergencies and health needs, visit **Sutter Amador Hospital** (200 Mission Blvd., 209/223-7500, www.sutteramador.org).

Getting There and Around
Jackson is near the intersection of Highways 49 and 88 and is fairly easy to reach by car. From the north or south, take Highway 49; from the Bay Area or the Central Valley, Highway 88 is the best bet. Note that both highways are two-lane roads that become congested during summer and on weekends. Jackson can also receive snowfall, which can complicate travel plans; check weather and traffic reports with Caltrans (http://dot.ca.gov) before traveling.

The local **Westover Field–Amador County Airport** (12380 Airport Rd., 209/223-2376, www.co.amador.ca.us) is between Jackson and Sutter Creek, but it has no scheduled commercial flights. The closest airport served by the airlines is **Sacramento International Airport** (SMF, 6900 Airport Blvd., Sacramento, 916/929-5411, www.sacairports.org), 60 miles west.

Public transit options are limited in the area, but **Amador Transit** (209/267-9395, http://amadortransit.com, $2) runs several bus routes between Sutter Creek and Jackson Monday–Friday.

VOLCANO
Black Chasm
For an underground experience in nature, take an easy one-hour tour of the Black Chasm Caverns (Volcano–Pioneer Rd., 866/762-2837, www.caverntours.com, daily 9 A.M.–5 P.M. June–Aug., daily 10 A.M.–4 P.M. Sept.–May, adults $15, children $7.50). This tour isn't accessible to strollers or wheelchairs, but young children can enjoy the reasonably sedate stroll into the immense chasm filled with amazing calcite formations. In the Landmark Room, you'll get a chance to check out the rare helictite formations (a crystalline cave formation) that made Black Chasm famous. Enjoy the visitors center on the way out or as you wait for

your tour. Many visitors enjoy the video that describes how the creators of *The Matrix* used the look and feeling of Black Chasm in their films. You can even see some of the immense stalagmite props made for the movie.

◖ Daffodil Hill

Spring is the time to visit the famed Daffodil Hill (18310 Rams Horn Grade, 209/296-7048, http://suttercreek.org, daily late Mar.–mid-Apr., free). Perfect for travelers who love the greenery aboveground as much as the minerals beneath it, Daffodil Hill explodes each March into a profusion of sunny yellow that lasts for about a month. Daffodil Hill is actually the private working ranch of the McLaughlin family, which has been planting daffodil bulbs on their property since they first acquired the land in 1887. Today, you'll see more than 300,000 flowers blooming, and more are planted each year. In addition to the more than 300 different species of daffodils, other bulb flowers and plants help create carpets of color across the meadows and hills. Even among the many fabulous landscapes and gardens of California, Daffodil Hill is special; out here, you can't help but feel the joy and promise of spring.

Daffodil Hill opens to the public only during daffodil season. Exact opening and closing dates vary each year; call ahead to get the latest information.

Entertainment and Events

Only in the Gold Country would a town as tiny as Volcano need to maintain its own theater company, complete with both indoor and outdoor performance spaces. At the **Volcano Theatre Company** (Main St., 209/296-2525, www.volcanotheatre.org, shows 8 P.M. Fri.–Sat., 2 P.M. Sun.), the wall of the outdoor amphitheater spans nearly half of Volcano's main street; the indoor space uses a storefront on the other side of the street. Highly regarded throughout the region, the amateur Volcano

Theatre Company takes on some serious plays, such as William Nicholson's *Shadowlands* and John Steinbeck's *Of Mice and Men,* plus unusual comedies like John Cecil Holm's *Gramercy Ghost* and Barbara Pease Weber's *Delval Divas.* You'll see the summer plays in the amphitheater; bring your own chairs, thermoses of a warm beverage, and blankets and coats to bundle up as the night cools off. In the spring and fall, shows are performed at the 50-seat Cobblestone Theatre—the smallest fixed-seat theater in California. You have to purchase tickets early if you want to get in.

Accommodations and Food

For a budget hotel adventure deep in the northern Gold Country, get off the highway and head for the **Union Inn and Pub** (21375 Consolation St., 209/296-7711, www.volcanounion.com, $110–140). This is the only hotel in tiny Volcano, and there are only four guest rooms, but each one is exquisitely decorated with a different luxurious theme. Modern amenities include flat-screen TVs, radios with iPod docks, and DVD players in each guest room; for a truly romantic stay, ask for a guest room with a sunken porcelain tub. In the morning, the Union serves up a gourmet breakfast (the owner is the chef at Restaurant Taste in Plymouth) with fresh fruit, homemade pastries, and something special that's whipped up just for the day. The Union is best for couples looking for a romantic getaway; children and pets are not allowed. If you're staying at the Union, you don't have to go too far for food and entertainment. The Volcano Theatre Company performs in the amphitheater across the street, and some of the best food in Amador County is served in the hotel's restaurant (5–8 P.M. Mon., 3–9 P.M. Fri., noon–9 P.M. Sat., noon–8 P.M. Sun., $18).

Information and Services

In Volcano you won't find much in the way of services; the closest bank branches and gas stations are located four miles southwest in Pine

Grove, or eight miles east in Pioneer, both on Highway 88. You will find a **post office** (16120 Main St., 8:30 A.M.–4 P.M. Mon.–Fri.).

Getting There and Around

Volcano is on the eastern edge of Gold Country where the elevation starts to climb among towering pine trees that blanket the hillsides. By car, take Highway 88 northeast from Jackson for about nine miles; turn left on Pine Grove–Volcano Road. Volcano will appear in about three miles. Due to the higher elevation, Volcano often has heavy snowfall in winter, and chains may be required. Check weather and traffic reports with Caltrans (http://dot.ca.gov) before planning your trip.

Southern Gold Country

The southern Gold Country runs from the town of Jackson down almost to Yosemite Valley. Every few miles along Highway 49 and on the roads through Sonora and Jamestown are historic plaques commemorating everything from the local hanging tree to the prostitutes who made life more, um, bearable for the rough men working the mines. You'll also find museums, caverns, mines, parks, wineries, great restaurants, and quirky hotels.

Southern Gold Country runs south from Jackson and includes the towns of Murphys, Angels Camp, Sonora, Columbia, Jamestown, and Arnold. Highway 49 can take you north–south through the region. Highway 4 runs northeast–southwest, intersecting Highway 49 at Angels Camp and running east to Murphys. Highway 4 also runs south from Vallecito to Columbia and then south to Sonora. You can also drive Highway 49 all the way to Jamestown, then pick up Highway 108 east to Sonora.

ANGELS CAMP
California Caverns

California Caverns (9565 Cave City Rd., Mountain Ranch, 866/762-2837, www.caverntours.com, daily 10 A.M.–5 P.M. Apr.–Oct.,

Highway 49 winds through Angels Camp.

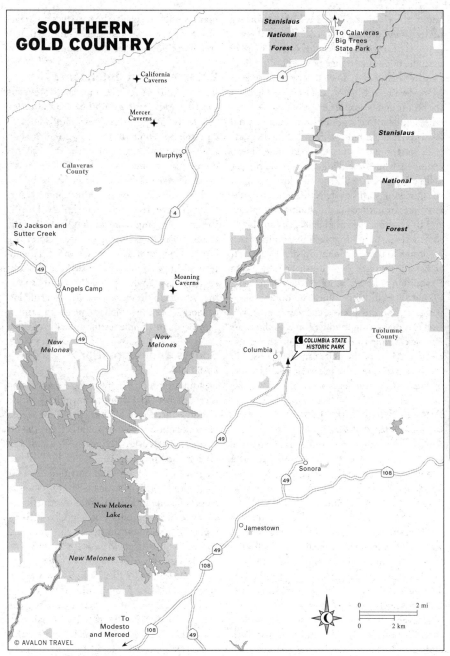

SOUTHERN GOLD COUNTRY

Stanislaus
National
Forest

To Calaveras
Big Trees
State Park

(4)

+ California
Caverns

Stanislaus

+ Mercer
Caverns

National

Murphys

Calaveras
County

Forest

(4)

To Jackson and
Sutter Creek

(49)

+ Moaning
Caverns

Angels Camp

New Melones

(49)

*New
Melones*

Tuolumne
County

COLUMBIA STATE
HISTORIC PARK

Columbia

*New
Melones*

(49)

Sonora

(49)

(108)

*New Melones
Lake*

Jamestown

New Melones

(49)

(108)

To
Modesto
and Merced

(108)

(49)

© AVALON TRAVEL

0   2 mi
0   2 km

SACRAMENTO

adults $15, children $7.50) has been welcoming underground explorers for more than 150 years. An Army captain discovered the caves in 1850 when he noticed a strange breeze blowing from a rocky outcropping; since then, visitors such as Mark Twain and John Muir have wondered at the bizarre and beautiful formations in these caverns. The basic tour is geared toward families and lasts just over an hour; a knowledgeable guide leads you through a wonderland of subterranean chambers while describing the cavern's history and geology. Kids will especially love gazing at the numerous forms of stalactites, especially the vine-like formations in the **Jungle Room** cavern. If you're not claustrophobic, you can also do some serious spelunking, spending hours with a guide as you plunge into murky depths and raft across underground pools on the **Middle Earth Expedition** (4 hours, $130). Make sure to bring hiking shoes or boots, since the underground paths can be quite slippery, and wear clothes you won't mind getting muddy; some of the tours involve crawling through damp wormholes and crevices. Many of the tours can't be accessed in certain seasons, so call the cavern visitors center or check the website for more information.

Angels Camp Museum and Carriage House

Among the many museums that litter the Gold Country, the Angels Camp Museum and Carriage House (753 S. Main St., 209/736-2963, www.angelscamp.gov, 10 A.M.–4 P.M. Thurs.–Mon. Mar.–Nov., 10 A.M.–4 P.M. Sat.–Sun. Nov.–Feb.) still offers a unique experience. Inside the main museum building, you'll get to see meticulously preserved artifacts of the mining era. Outside you'll find old, and in some cases decrepit, mining equipment. The huge waterwheel sits in its original position in Angels Camp. A treat for transportation lovers, the Carriage House shelters more than 30 horse-powered vehicles of the 19th and early 20th centuries. Better restored than

many similar displays, the carriages and wagons here show off the elegance and function of true horse-powered transportation.

Entertainment and Events

Each May in Angels Camp, the **Calaveras County Fair and Jumping Frog Jubilee** (209/736-2561, www.frogtown.org, adults $7, children $5) comes to town. During the fair, frogs jump on command in the contest that honors the famous Mark Twain story. You'll also find all sorts of other classic fair activities, such as livestock shows, baking contests, auctions, historic readings, and exhibits. During the frog-jumping contest, you'll see literally thousands of frogs leaping toward victory. The top 50 from all heats compete in a final contest; all hope to beat the world record, a feat that carries a $5,000 prize. Practically speaking, visitors to the fair and jubilee will find lots of food at the concessionary, places to camp if they need, and ample restroom facilities.

Sports and Recreation
RAFTING

Heading south on Highway 49, Angels Camp is yet another Gold Country town that's within a short shuttle ride of churning white water. Here the options change slightly from the excursions offered farther north. You can still take guided tours on the South Fork of the American River with local outfitters, but the North Fork of the Stanislaus River is closer to Angels Camp and offers more intermediate–advanced trips through roaring Class III–IV rapids. The season is shorter on the Stanislaus and runs mid-April–May, weather and river conditions permitting; be sure to call ahead.

All-Outdoors (925/932-8993, www.aor-afting.com, $110–340 pp) runs full-day trips to the North Fork of the Stanislaus. You can plunge through Class IV rapids with hair-raising names like Beginner's Luck, Rattlesnake, and Maycheck's Mayhem; the last rapid is a

MOANING CAVERN

Along with the tremendous network of artificial mine shafts, the southern Sierra Foothills are honeycombed with natural tunnels and caverns. Children and adults love the cavern tours. If you choose to visit one of these caverns, be aware that you'll need to climb hundreds of stairs and squeeze through tight spots, and that the total walk may be more than 0.5 miles. Check with the tour operators when you buy your tickets to be sure you're up for the trek. Also, the temperature inside the cavern hovers steadily at about 55°F, so bring a coat and hat to keep yourself warm.

The popular Moaning Cavern (5350 Moaning Cavern Rd., Vallecito, 866/762-2837, www.caverntours.com, 10 A.M.-6 P.M. Mon.-Fri., 9 A.M.-6 P.M. Sat.-Sun. Apr.-Sept., 10 A.M.-4 P.M. Mon.-Fri., 9 A.M.-4 P.M. Sat.-Sun. Sept.-Apr., adults $15, children $8) is still fun to visit, despite the damage done to make it into a tourist attraction. Unlike the other caverns you can traverse in California, Moaning Cavern has only one major chamber, and it's a big one. Even folks with claustrophobia can get comfortable in the palatial chamber filled with great formations. You can take the basic 45-minute walking tour, rappel 165 feet down into the cavern if you are in good shape, or sign up for a three-hour adventure tour, if you're in good shape and not claustrophobic, that takes you through narrow passages to see things you'd miss completely from the regular tour.

But however you visit the Moaning Cavern, you'll never hear it moan. When it was first discovered and made into a visitor attraction, a big draw was the strange "moaning" sounds of air flowing through the cavern. It became so popular that the operators decided to widen the narrow mouth of the chamber to allow more people to enter at once. But when the rock was chiseled away and the mouth made wide and group-friendly, the famous moan disappeared. The shape of the rock had created the eerie sounds, which have never recurred. So come to Moaning Cavern for what you can see rather than what you can no longer hear.

partial Class V drop. You can also take full-day and two-day trips on the calmer South Fork of the American River if the Stanislaus is beyond your experience level.

O.A.R.S. (209/736-4677, www.oars.com, $110–360) also offers trips to the mighty North Fork of the Stanislaus River. The guides are knowledgeable and friendly, and lunch is provided. If you'd rather raft the South Fork of the American River, O.A.R.S. offers half-day, full-day, and two-day excursions.

Accommodations

If you're traveling with family or a group of friends, consider staying at the **Greenhorn Creek Resort** (711 McCauley Ranch Rd., 209/736-9372, www.greenhorncreekvacation-cottages.com, $300–375). You can rent a condo or, better yet, a 2–3-bedroom "cottage" that's really your own full-fledged vacation home. Cottages have full kitchens, dining areas, and living rooms decorated in light, bright homey styles. Each bedroom has its own separate bath; most bedrooms have king beds, though some have two twins. These cottages are perfect if you're planning a longer stay in the region and really want to settle in and get comfortable. The Greenhorn Creek Resort property offers a variety of amenities, including an on-site restaurant, an 18-hole golf course, and tennis courts. The pool facilities sparkle on hot summer days, with a shallow family pool, a large main pool, and a nice hot whirlpool tub.

It's impossible not to feel spoiled at the **Cooper House Inn** (1184 Church St., 888/330-3764, www.cooperhouseinn.com, $140–300), a renovated Victorian-era country home. Staying here is like taking a couples' getaway back to the Gilded Age with a few modern upgrades. The three guest rooms feature locally made linens, biodegradable

SACRAMENTO

bath kits, pillow-top mattresses, and private showers, plus 21st-century conveniences like free wireless Internet access and flat-panel TVs. Downstairs, take a complementary bottle of wine outside onto the patio and relax in the padded lounge chairs. Breakfast is made with organic ingredients and might include homemade frittatas, apple-chicken sausage, and foothill-grown produce. The Chardonnay suite is the only guest room with a king bed; otherwise, the only downside to the fabulously luxurious Cooper House is the lack of en suite baths, which means you have to walk down the hall to find one.

Food

For a truly homemade deli sandwich, go to the **Pickle Barrel** (1225 S. Main St., 209/736-4704, www.pickle-barrel.com, daily 11 A.M.–3 P.M.). The sandwich meats are barbecued out on the back porch of the deli, and the carrot cake is made from the owner's grandmother's recipe. If you're eating on-site, get a hot *panini* sandwich. If you're looking to carry out food for a picnic, choose from cold sandwiches, prepared salads, and other tasty treats.

Sidewinder's Café (1252 S. Main St., 209/736-0444, 11 A.M.–8 P.M. Tues.–Sat., $10) serves all-natural food that's a mash-up of Californian, Mexican, and Basque cuisines. Belly up to the counter to customize your order; there's an eye-popping amount of mostly organic and local ingredients to choose from. Top choices include the chili-lime chicken wrap with beer-battered fries and chipotle dip. If those fries make you thirsty, browse the stacked beer list for one of the many microbrews on tap. The relaxed decor means Sidewinders has a laid-back vibe, so you can feel comfortable grabbing a table in flip-flops and a T-shirt. If there's a downside, it's the long line that forms at night; try to call ahead if you're on the road, or prepare for a wait.

Crusco's (1240 S. Main St., 209/736-1440, www.cruscos.com, 11:30 A.M.–3 P.M. and 5–9 P.M. Thurs.–Mon., $17–26) serves hearty homemade Italian food fixed with local ingredients. This isn't your average spaghetti and meatballs kind of place—Crusco's does Italian with a Californian flair, serving dishes like wild salmon with orange madeira cream sauce and New York steak topped with crab and butter sauce. Save room for the chocolate truffle torte for dessert. The best part about this restaurant is the Old World hospitality and attentive service from the owner, who is usually on hand to greet you.

Information and Services

Begin your trip at the **Calaveras County Visitors Bureau** (1192 S. Main St., 800/225-3764, www.gocalaveras.com). The **BBVA Compass** bank (479 S. Main St., 209/736-4561) has a 24-hour ATM.

For urgent medical needs and health issues, go to **Angels Camp Prompt Care** (23 N. Main St., 209/736-9130, daily 8 A.M.–6 P.M.). Note that while Angels Camp Prompt Care can treat medical conditions such as broken bones or infections, it is not equipped to handle major emergencies.

Getting There and Around

Angels Camp is in the heart of Gold Country, on Highway 49 about 28 miles south of Jackson. From Stockton, take Highway 4 east for 50 miles and turn south on Highway 49; Angels Camp is another two miles. Sacramento is 75 miles away, and Placerville is 60 miles north.

If you have your own plane, or have access to one, you can fly into the **Calaveras County Airport** (3600 Carol Kennedy Dr., San Andreas, 209/736-2501). There's isn't much in the way of public transportation in Angels Camp, but **Calaveras Transit** (209/754-4450, www.calaverastransit.com, $2) runs four bus routes to the surrounding area Monday–Friday, including trips to Arnold and Murphys.

MURPHYS AND VICINITY
Mercer Cavern

One of the fascinating caverns that pock the

© SABRINA YOUNG

Murphys is home to wineries and caverns.

Sierra Foothills, Mercer Cavern (1665 Sheep Ranch Rd., 209/728-2101, www.mercercaverns. com, daily 10 A.M.–4:30 P.M. Jan.–Memorial Day, daily 9 A.M.–5 P.M. Memorial Day–Labor Day, adults $14, children $8) winds into the mountains just outside of Murphys. Mercer Caverns has been in continuous operation as an attraction for more than 125 years. Visitors descend 172 steps into the narrow cavern, crowding the numerous walkways that run 162 feet down from the surface entrance. The 45-minute standard tour is a fun family activity, provided that everyone is reasonably fit and mobile. Kids love "seeing" objects like fruit, vegetables, and people's faces in the myriad limestone formations that populate the various rooms of the cavern.

Buena Vista Cemetery

Overlooking a small hill outside downtown Murphys, the Buena Vista Cemetery (Cemetery Lane, 209/728-2387, http://murphyscemetery.com) has been in continuous use since the 1850s. The cemetery is adjacent to an old schoolhouse museum; visitors can drive through many parts of the graveyard, or spend hours wandering the historic plots. Despite its size and regular maintenance, Buena Vista has plenty of ghostly atmosphere. A parade of slightly crooked marble and granite markers meander across the acres, and a few elderly oak trees provide light shade. You can piece together the Gold Rush history of Murphys by reading the town's collection of tombstones; you'll find the graves of war veterans, Masons, miners, immigrants, wives, mothers, and children. Locals whose time in Murphys has ended are still buried here, and the modern markers stand out in stark contrast to the softened lines of the older stones.

Calaveras Big Trees State Park

Take some time away from mining history to visit Calaveras Big Trees State Park (Hwy. 4, 3 miles east of Arnold, 209/795-2334, www.bigtrees.org, daily sunrise–sunset, $8). Highlights of the park include the North and South

Groves of rare giant sequoia trees; be sure to take a walk in both groves to check out the landmark trees and stumps. Beyond the sequoias, you can hike and bike in 6,000 acres of pine forest crisscrossed with trails and scattered with campgrounds (reservations 800/444-7275) and pretty groves set up for picnicking. Feel free to take a dip in the cool refreshing Stanislaus River running through the trees, or cast a line out to try to catch a rainbow trout. In the winter, break out the snowshoes and cross-country skis—the trails are marked for winter sports as well as summer.

Start your day at the visitors center, where you can talk to rangers about the best hikes for you, and pick up trail maps for several of the major hiking areas in the park. In winter, many of the roads through the park are closed, but drive in as far as you can and snowshoe or ski from there. The visitors center operating hours fluctuate depending on the season, so call ahead (209/795-3840) for the current schedule.

Wineries

There are a number of tasting rooms in downtown Murphys, and out in the countryside a few vineyards boast major estates. The largest estate belongs to **Ironstone Vineyards** (1894 Six Mile Rd., 209/728-1251, www.ironstonevineyards.com, daily 10 A.M.–5 P.M.). This huge complex of vineyards, winery buildings, a museum, an amphitheater, and gardens can draw hundreds of visitors in a single day. Inside the vast tasting room are three bars and a pleasant surprise. The complimentary regular tasting includes any number of wines, most priced at $10 per bottle. The reserve tasting bar shows off the higher-end vintages, but it's the lovely and shockingly reasonable low-end wines that make visitors buy their favorites by the case. In summer, the winery hosts a summer concert series; buy tickets early, as the concerts tend to be local favorites.

The tiny elegant **Black Sheep** (221 Main St.,

209/728-2157, www.blacksheepwinery.com, daily 11 A.M.–5 P.M.) tasting room offers higher-end red wines at a bar that could fit maybe six people—if they're friendly. Black Sheep's specialty is zinfandel made from Calaveras County and Amador County grapes, but they also make cabernet sauvignon, cabernet franc, and more unusual varietals like cinsaut.

With a focus on Spanish and Rhône varietals and an unlikely rubber-chicken mascot, check out **Twisted Oak Winery** (4280 Red Hill Rd., at Hwy. 4, Vallecito, 209/736-9080, www.twistedoak.com, 11:30 A.M.–5:30 P.M. Sun.–Fri., 10:30 A.M.–5:30 P.M. Sat.). While Twisted Oak takes pride in being truly twisted, their wines are straight-up award winners.

Entertainment and Events

Drama is the new gold at **Murphys Creek Theatre Company** (580 S. Algiers St., 209/728-8422, http://murphyscreektheatre.org, $12–18), a surprisingly professional acting group deep in the foothills. The small company does wonderful productions of everything from Shakespeare's *Tempest* to contemporary shows like *Almost Maine*. For years the company performed outside during the summer until building a permanent home at the Black Bart Theatre in Murphys; the group now performs year-round. During warmer months, catch a play from the company's Under the Stars series at the Albeno Munari Vineyard and Winery.

Shopping

There's a bustling shopping district in the heart of this old mining town, with antiques shops, small boutiques, and a few surprises. Most shops are between the parallel Church and Main Streets, with a few stores farther out along Highway 4. On weekends, parking can be a frustrating challenge, so arrive earlier in the day if you can.

Tea an'Tiques (419 Main St., 209/728-8240, 11 A.M.–5 P.M. Sun.–Fri., 10:30 A.M.–6 P.M.

Sat.) serves tea while you browse their wonderful selection of old knickknacks and curios. Stepping through the bright yellow door is like stepping into an English country cottage—only with a self-serve tea bar stocked with 100 different varieties of fine tea.

At the **Sierra Nevada Adventure Company General Store** (448 Main St., 209/728-9133, www.snacattack.com, daily 10 A.M.–6 P.M.), you'll find gear for any kind of trek, climb, or walkabout imaginable. It's the perfect place to pick up hiking shoes, a new backpack, or cool-weather fleece before heading into the foothills.

If you need a summer reading book or travel journal, stop by **Sustenance Books** (416 Main St., 209/728-2200, 11 A.M.–5 P.M. Mon. and Wed., 11 A.M.–6 P.M. Thurs.–Sun.). Whether new or used, you can find tomes from every genre on the shelves here. Sustenance specializes in children's books; they also have a wide selection of books on nature and volumes on sustainability.

At **Marisolio Tasting Bar** (488 Main St., 209/728-8853, www.marisolio.com, noon–5 P.M. Tues., 10 A.M.–5 P.M. Wed.–Mon.), you can belly up to a different kind of bar—one that serves tastings of artisanal olive oils and vinegars. The oils and vinegars are mostly from California, but the shop also has imported products made with fair-trade and sustainable ingredients from all over the world. Try either the white or the black truffle extra virgin olive oil, and if you taste the vinegars, don't miss the delicious black cherry.

Your nose will have no trouble finding **The Spice Tin** (457 N. Algiers St., 209/728-8225, www.thespicetin.com, daily 11 A.M.–5 P.M.). Spices aren't the only goods; sauces, salts, dips, and rubs also line the tangy shelves.

Sports and Recreation

In summer, the **Bear Valley** (2280 Hwy. 207, Bear Valley, 209/753-2301, www.bearvalley.com, daily 9 A.M.–4 P.M., adults $62, youth $49, children $19) ski resort turns its runs into tracks and its slopes into trails. Everyone from the most sedate walkers and road bikers to the most dedicated backpackers and off-road vehicle riders will find fun at Bear Valley. Check the website for maps and information about the acres of road-biking areas, mountain-biking tracks, and hiking trails.

When winter snows come to the southern Gold Country, the skiers and boarders come out to play. Only a few miles past Arnold, the mountain lures snow lovers with a big mountain filled with great runs and tracks. You can take lessons on the wide gentle beginner slopes near the lodge. If you prefer to take your chances, head up the hill to the array of intermediate and advanced trails that make up 75 percent of the skiable terrain at Bear Valley. Ten different lifts make lines short on weekdays. If you're looking for something edgier, take your snowboard out to the "Cub" terrain parks.

Accommodations and Camping

Murphys Inn Motel (76 Main St., 888/796-1800, www.centralsierralodging.com, $85–210), centrally located in downtown Murphys, makes a perfect base of operations for Gold Country. Most of the 37 guest rooms have two queen beds, furnished and decorated in traditional motel style. Outside your room, you can take a cooling dunk in the pool or enjoy a hard workout in the small fitness room.

From the outside, the blocky square structure of **Dunbar House 1880** (271 Jones St., 209/728-2897, www.dunbarhouse.com, $200–275) evokes a Dickensian air in the unlikely locale that is Murphys. Inside you'll find a plethora of modern comfort and Victorian elegance that calls to mind Dickens's richer characters. Each of the guest rooms boasts flowers, stripes, wallpaper, fabrics, and furniture reminiscent of the decorative excesses of the Victorian era. In the bath you might find an antique claw-foot tub and vintage shower, or the most modern of two-person whirlpool tubs. All guest rooms have English towel warmers—the very height of luxury on chilly winter mornings. For breakfast, you'll feast on homemade baked goods, a delicious hot entrée, coffee, tea, and specially blended hot chocolate. You can dine in the dining room, the garden, or if you're in one of the suites, in the privacy of your own room.

Calaveras Big Trees State Park (Hwy. 4, 3 miles east of Arnold, 800/444-7275, www.parks.ca.gov or www.reserveamerica.com, reservations Memorial Day–Labor Day, reservation fee $7, sites $35) has two seasonal campgrounds for tents and RVs. The North Grove Campground (Mar.–Nov.) lies closest to the park entrance on Highway 4 and has 73 sites. Forested Oak Hollow Campground (May–Sept.) is four miles inside the park and two miles from the Stanislaus River. The 55 sites are set on a hill and are a bit quieter. All campsites include a fire ring, a picnic table, and parking; flush toilets, coin-operated showers, and drinking water are available in the campgrounds. Reservations are accepted up to seven months in advance and are strongly recommended in summer; off-season, campsites are first-come, first-served.

Food

Grounds (402 Main St., Suite A, 209/728-8663, www.groundsrestaurant.com, 7 A.M.–10:30 P.M. Mon.–Fri., 7 A.M.–11:15 P.M. Sat., 8 A.M.–11:15 P.M. Sun., $14–29) was one of the first gourmet restaurants to open when Murphys began its renaissance in the 1990s, and it's still one of the best places to eat in town. The food is modern California cuisine; standard dishes include the grilled eggplant sandwich for lunch or the seared swordfish steak over linguini. If you can't stop by for dinner, come for breakfast and make your own omelet from ingredients like sweet Italian sausage, black olives, gouda, and cheddar. This

restaurant is one of the busiest in Murphys, so reservations are recommended.

At **Firewood** (420 Main St., 209/728-3248, www.firewoodeats.com, daily 11 A.M.–9 P.M., $6–14), you're playing with fire—from wood-fired pizzas to the ax handles that grace the front doors, the restaurant, in a former fire station, has a fiery theme. You can't go wrong with the chicken pesto with basil and parmesan pizza; or try the gorgonzola burger or the fish tacos. There's also a children's menu with chicken strips and sweet-potato fries.

Come to **Mineral Restaurant** (419 Main St., 209/728-9743, www.mineralrestaurant.com, 5–8:30 P.M. Thurs., noon–8 P.M. Fri.–Sat., 10 A.M.–3 P.M. Sun., $10–16) for mind-blowing vegetarian fare. Chef Steve Rinauros knows how to turn food into art. The menu constantly changes; all dishes are made from seasonal ingredients, and the menu you saw last month might be completely different a few weeks later. The brew list at Mineral includes a good selection of award-winning beers.

Information and Services

Murphys doesn't have much in the way of visitor services or a local newspaper, so the best place for information is online (www.visitmurphys.com). For financial needs, try **El Dorado Savings** (245 Tom Bell Rd., 209/728-2003, www.eldoradosavingsbank.com) for an ATM and banking services.

There are several gas stations in Murphys along Highway 4, which is the main thoroughfare in town. If you need groceries, head to **Sierra Hills Market** (117 E. Hwy. 4, 209/728-3402, 7 A.M.–8:30 P.M. Sun.–Thurs., 7 A.M.–9 P.M. Fri.–Sat.). There is also a **post office** (140 Big Trees Rd., 8:30 A.M.–4:30 P.M. Mon.–Fri.).

Getting There and Around

By car, you can reach Murphys by taking Highway 4 northeast from Angels Camp for 10 miles. It is a fair drive from any major city;

you'll have to drive 84 miles from Sacramento and 62 miles from Modesto to reach Murphys. If you need public transportation, **Calaveras Transit** (209/754-4450, www.calaverastransit.com, $2) runs round-trip bus routes between Murphys and Angels Camp Monday–Friday.

SONORA AND COLUMBIA
Columbia State Historic Park

A stroll down Main Street in Columbia State Historic Park (11255 Jackson St., Columbia, 209/588-9128, www.parks.ca.gov, daily year-round, most businesses daily 10 A.M.–5 P.M., free) is a stroll into California's boomtown past. Start with the **Columbia Museum** (Main St. and State St., daily 10 A.M.–4 P.M.) to discover the history of this fascinating place, one of the early California mining towns. Gold was discovered here in the spring of 1850, and the town sprang up as miners flowed in, growing to become one of California's largest cities for a short time. It inevitably declined as the gold ran out, and in 1945 the state took it over and created the State Historic Park. In the museum, you'll see artifacts of the mining period, from miners' equipment and clothing to the household objects used by women who lived in the bustling city. After the museum, walk the streets, poking your head into the exhibits and shops selling an array of period and modern items. Examine the contents of the Dry Goods Store, imagine the multiculturalism of another age in the Chinese Store Exhibit, or grab a bite to eat in the City Hotel Saloon.

This large indoor-outdoor museum experience is an easy flat walk, with plenty of wheelchair-accessible areas. The horses, carriages, and staff in pioneer costumes delight children. It can get hot in the summer and cold in winter, and you'll be on your feet a lot, so dress accordingly and wear sensible shoes. Docent-led tours happen at 11 A.M. Saturday–Sunday. Check the park schedule for the dates of living history events.

Tuolumne County Museum

If you can hit only one local museum in your journey through southern Gold Country,

SACRAMENTO

© CHRISTOPHER ARNS

Columbia State Historic Park

make it the Tuolumne County Museum (158 W. Bradford St., Sonora, 209/532-1317, www.tchistory.org, 10 A.M.–4 P.M. Sun.–Fri., 10 A.M.–3:30 P.M. Sat., free). The county leaders took entertaining advantage of the museum's location in the old Sonora jailhouse; a number of exhibits are inside cells, and one cell has been recreated as an exhibit of what incarceration might have been like in 19th-century Tuolumne County (hint: unpleasant). Appropriate homage is paid to Tom Horn, a prisoner who died in a jailhouse fire—one that he set himself in an ill-conceived escape attempt.

Throughout the rest of the museum, you'll find plenty of artifacts from the mines, shops, and homes of the county. Interpretive areas describe the process of hard-rock mining, the arduous journey the would-be gold miners took to get from the East to California, and the history of the county.

Entertainment and Events

It's only fitting that the land where thousands gambled their futures on finding a fortune in gold should play host to a casino or two. If you're already in Sonora, take a detour to the **Black Oak Casino** (19400 Tuolumne Rd. N., Sonora, 877/747-8777, www.blackoak-casino.com) in Tuolumne County. This full-service family-friendly casino features games for kids and adults alike. While the under-21 crowd bowl at the Black Oak Lanes or spend their quarters in the Underground Arcade, the grown-ups can play over 1,000 slots and video poker machines, plus a small array of table games. When you're ready for a break, you can eat and drink at any one of Black Oak's seven restaurants and bars, take in some live weekend entertainment at the Willow Creek Lounge, or even spin a few more slots in the smoke-free Jumping Coyote Bar on the second floor.

In Columbia, the **What Cheer Saloon** (22768 Main St., Columbia, 209/532-1479, www.briggshospitalityllc.com, 3–9 P.M.

Mon.–Fri., noon–10 P.M. Sat.–Sun.) is the only full-service watering hole in town; the place still has the original cherrywood bar shipped from Boston in 1857. If you need a drink, ask for a Columbia Gold—it's the bar's most popular libation, but don't bother asking the bartender for the recipe; the ingredients are top secret. Since the saloon serves hard liquor (there's an eye-popping selection of cognacs and single-malt Scotch), along with beer and wine, it's mostly for adults.

In Sonora, you'll also find a vibrant theater community that produces some of the best entertainment in the foothills. At the **Stage 3 Theatre** (208 S. Green St., Sonora, 209/536-1778, www.stage3.org, 7 P.M. Thurs.–Sat., 2 P.M. Sun., $12–20), the regular season can include plays by Broadway heavyweights like Arthur Miller, David Mamet, and Neil Simon. Even though Stage 3 is miles from drama hot spots like San Francisco or Los Angeles, theater fans will love the surprisingly professional company. Stage 3 is a small venue, which means you'll probably enjoy the intimate atmosphere; at the same time, note that tickets may sell out quickly for more popular plays.

Broadway might be miles away, but the nonprofit **Sierra Repertory Theatre** (13891 Mono Way, East Sonora, 209/532-3120, www.sierrarep.org, 2 P.M. Wed. and Sun., 7 P.M. Thurs.–Fri., 2 P.M. and 8 P.M. Sat., $20–32) also stages big-name hits in town. For a small company, the performances are immensely enjoyable. You can watch plays at two different venues—there's the East Sonora Theatre, a converted tin warehouse, and the Historic Fallon House up the road in Columbia. Seasonal shows have included *Oklahoma!, Hairspray,* and *Fiddler on the Roof.* If you like new twists on classic plays, the company has been known to get creative; they once staged *Romeo and Juliet* with a New Orleans theme.

Shopping

Looking for some Wild West mementos straight

from the Gold Country? You won't find anywhere better than the gift shops in Columbia's old buildings. Hard-core travelers might pick up a tourist-trap vibe, but families traveling with children will get a kick out of the old-timey shops staffed by their costumed clerks. If Columbia is too kitschy for you, head for Sonora's more refined downtown to browse the abundant boutiques and antiques shops along Highway 49. Be careful while driving through the city's narrow streets or finding parking downtown; on crowded weekends, the two-lane main drag often feels like all of California is visiting.

Need some fixings for the homestead? At the **Fancy Dry Goods and Clothing Store** (22733 Main St., Columbia, 209/532-1066, www.columbiacalifornia.com, 10 A.M.–5 P.M. Wed.–Mon. summer, 10 A.M.–5 P.M. Wed.–Sun. winter), you can browse the "supplies" on hand like a true forty-niner. Everything here would have been in style 150 years ago, including the bonnets, calico dresses, and men's hats on the store's shelves. You can also check out the mock weapons and mining tools. Still, this isn't a museum; you can buy gifts for men, women, and kids, including sewing kits for quilting or knitting your very own Wild West wardrobe.

The next best thing to stepping back in time is visiting **Kamice's Photographic Establishment** (22729 Main St., Columbia, 209/532-4861, www.photosincolumbia.com, 10 A.M.–5 P.M. Thurs.–Tues., by appointment Wed.). Bring the family and snap a sepia-toned portrait like true pioneers. Kids will love posing in fake miner's outfits or posing with a six-shooter; you can even bring along the family dog.

You can't leave town without visiting **Nelson's Columbia Candy Kitchen** (22726 Main St., Columbia, 209/532-7886, www.columbiacandykitchen.com, 9 A.M.–5 P.M. Mon.–Fri., 9 A.M.–6 P.M. Sat.–Sun.). The store has been serving candy for more than 100 years, and they've just about perfected the recipes. Everything here is diet-busting, finger-licking

good; make sure to try the homemade marshmallow bars or a piece of whipping cream fudge. Luckily, Nelson's also has a few sugar-free candies if your sweet tooth can't indulge in the other goodies.

You'll quickly find that **Legends** (131 S. Washington St., Sonora, 209/532-8120, 11 A.M.–5 P.M. Wed.–Mon.) is a different kind of bookstore. Instead of just books and a coffee bar, this fun little shop also has an old-fashioned soda fountain. Grab some ice cream or a hot dog while browsing the rare books and antiques, or settle into the comfy bar stools for a sandwich.

If you've toured the Gold Country from top to bottom, you've probably breezed through quite a few antiques stores, but **Antique Den** (163 S. Washington St., Sonora, 209/533-1012, www.antiqueden.net, 10 A.M.–5 P.M. Mon.–Thurs., 10 A.M.–6 P.M. Fri.–Sat., 11 A.M.–4 P.M. Sun.) is one of the best. It's actually a collective of several antiques dealers, many specializing in vintage American and European furniture. For collectors, this place will yield all sorts of finds, like a German gun cabinet or a Victorian kerosene chandelier. Besides furniture, the collective has the standard lineup of antique glassware, porcelain, jewelry, and clocks.

Sports and Recreation

For a peaceful fishing trip in the Gold Country, go to **Pinecrest Lake** (Hwy. 108, 30 miles east of Sonora, www.fs.fed.us). The Stanislaus National Forest permits boating, and a launch is available for your convenience. There's also a pier; bring your pole and bait, and fish in peace from dry land. The U.S. Forest Service stocks the lake with rainbow trout. As long as you have a California fishing license, you're good to go.

Fishing and boating are also allowed on a number of other lakes. **New Melones Lake** (6850 Studhorse Flat Rd., Sonora, 209/536-9094, www.usbr.gov) has beautiful hiking and biking trails along its edges. Dive in for a swim, go out on your boat, or cast a line to catch your dinner.

Many native Californians cut their first turns in the snow at **Dodge Ridge** (1 Dodge Ridge Rd., Pinecrest, 209/965-3474, www.dodgeridge.com, daily 9 A.M.–4 P.M. in season, adults $64, youth $52, children $20). Only a few miles from Sonora, Dodge Ridge is a reasonable drive from the Bay Area, and an easy drive from Gold Country towns. A major bowl served by three different chairlifts has all beginner and advanced-beginner runs. The peewee area is reserved for kids learning to ski, while Ego Alley offers a chance for adventurous new skiers to try a slightly steeper slope. The rest of the mountain beckons to intermediate and advanced skiers and boarders. Intermediates love this resort, since you can get all the way down the mountain on blue slopes from almost every lift in the park. For experts, a few double-black-diamond runs nestle at the top of Chair 3. Freestylers have fun on the five terrain parks scattered throughout the park.

Adjacent to Dodge Ridge, the **Gooseberry** area calls to hard-core cross-country skiers. Trails range from "more difficult" to "most difficult" at this park. The tiny parking lot fits only about eight cars, but there is a restroom for weary skiers needing a break.

Accommodations

For history in your hotel room, you can't beat the **Gunn House Hotel** (286 S. Washington St., Sonora, 209/532-3421, http://gunnhousehotel.com, $75–120). The original home of Dr. Lewis Gunn—a gold prospector and newspaper owner—the building has been a home, a hospital, and a hotel in its more than 150 years. A dozen guest rooms are done up in elegant jewel tones and rich fabrics, each with a king or queen bed with a teddy bear to welcome you. The Gunn House offers cable TV in every room, plus full heating and air-conditioning. Each morning, partake in the included sumptuous Innkeeper's Breakfast.

Barretta Gardens Inn (700 S. Barretta St., Sonora, 209/532-6039, www.barrettagardens.com, $110–390) is a restored farmhouse with some of the most lavish digs in the Gold Country. The eight guest rooms feature serious luxury—Persian carpets, mahogany bed frames, and polished antique furnishings. Enjoy a glass of wine outside into the sprawling one-acre garden or play croquet on the lawns.

The **Bradford Place Inn** (56 W. Bradford St., Sonora, 800/209-2315, www.bradfordplaceinn.com, $140–265) feels like an authentic Gold Rush home. First built in 1889 for a Wells Fargo agent, the house has been a bed-and-breakfast since the 1980s. Four guest rooms are decorated with Victorian-style floral wallpaper, plush furniture, and vintage wooden headboards. Each guest room has private heating and air-conditioning, a flat-screen TV, Wi-Fi, and a phone. Breakfast is included. With only four guest rooms, call well in advance to book your stay.

There are two authentic Wild West hotels in town, and they've been restored in similar fashion. The **Columbia City Hotel** (22768 Main St., Columbia, 209/532-1479, www.briggshospitalityllc.com, $120–150) is located near the north end of the state park. The **Fallon Hotel** (11175 Washington St., Columbia, 209/532-1470, www.briggshospitalityllc.com, $80–150) is near the park's southern boundary on the county road. The cozy guest rooms in each hotel have been faithfully restored with Victorian-style wallpaper, handmade furniture, Gold Rush–era photos, and double beds. There's a strict no-pets policy at both hotels, so leave your furry friends at home.

Food

One of the top picks in the region, the 🄲 **Diamondback Grill** (93 S. Washington St., Sonora, 209/532-6661, www.thediamondbackgrill.com, 11 A.M.–9 P.M. Mon.–Thurs., 11 A.M.–9:30 P.M. Fri.–Sat., 11 A.M.–8 P.M. Sun., $10) serves good grill food at extremely reasonable prices. Everyone loves the burgers and the sweet-potato fries, and the garlic fries are a treat. Fresh salads feed lighter appetites, and you can enjoy a glass of wine with your meal. Expect a wait, especially on weekends.

The place for tea is **Babcia's Tea Room** (31 S. Washington St., Sonora, 209/532-1306, daily breakfast and lunch). The best time to come is in the afternoon, when you can order a full high tea, with finger sandwiches, scones, sweets, and, a pot of hot tea.

With costumed bartenders, old-time piano music, and a fully restored bar from the 1800s, the **Jack Douglass Saloon** (22718 Main St., 209/533-4176, daily 10 A.M.–6 P.M., $5–10) feels like a place where duels might happen. These days, the only conflict comes from deciding between the homemade sarsaparilla or the wild cherry soda. For lunch, choose from sandwiches, hot dogs, salads, or the gigantic nachos, a saloon specialty.

The **Columbia City Hotel Restaurant** (22768 Main St., Columbia, 209/532-1479, 5–8 P.M. Fri.–Sun. winter, 10 A.M.–2 P.M. and 5–9 P.M. Tues.–Sun. summer, $20–36) is the place for gourmet meals in Columbia's historic district. You'll find dishes like lobster whiskey in bourbon sauce and pan-roasted duck sautéed in red-wine sauce. If you're staying in the hotel, don't miss dinner or brunch in the elegantly decorated dining room.

Information and Services

Sonora is one of the largest towns in the southern Gold Country and has plenty of services. For the central municipal visitors center, head for the **Tuolumne County Visitors Bureau** (542 W. Stockton St., Sonora, 209/533-4420, www.tcvb.com, 10 A.M.–5 P.M. Mon.–Sat., 10 A.M.–4 P.M. Sun.).

For local news during the week, the **Union Democrat** (www.uniondemocrat.com) publishes headlines Monday–Friday about Tuolumne County. There's also a local website (http://tuolumne.virtualsierra.com) packed with plenty of recreation and travel advice.

In Sonora, there is a main **post office** (781 N. Washington St. 800/275-8777, 8:30 A.M.–5 P.M. Mon.–Fri. 10 A.M.–2 P.M., Sat.), with easy to access for downtown visitors.

Sonora Regional Medical Center (1000 Greenley Rd., Sonora, 209/532-5000, www.sonorahospital.org) has an emergency room.

Getting There and Around

Sonora is at the tip of the southern Gold Country. By car, it's about 15 miles south of Angels Camp on Highway 49; south of Sonora, it's 55 miles to Mariposa. From the Central Valley, take Highway 108 from Modesto for 48 miles and then head north on Highway 49 for another 2 miles to reach Sonora. If you need to rent a car, **Enterprise** (14860 Mono Way, Sonora, 209/533-0500) or **Hertz** (13413 Mono Way, Sonora, 209/588-1575) have rentals available.

There are several public transit options in Sonora. Don't miss a ride on the **Historic 49**

© CHRISTOPHER ARNS

Jack Douglass Saloon is inside Columbia State Historic Park.

SACRAMENTO

Trolley (209/532-0404, www.tuolumnecountytransit.com, daily summer, Sat.–Sun. fall–spring, adults $1.50, day pass $4, under age 13 free), an old-fashioned (but air-conditioned) way to see local sights in Sonora, Columbia, and Jamestown. For bus rides during the week, **Tuolumne County Transit** (209/532-0404, www.tuolumnecountytransit.com, adults $1.50, day pass $4) runs four bus routes in Sonora and the immediate vicinity.

JAMESTOWN
Railtown 1897 State Historic Park
Much of Railtown 1897 (Hwy. 108, 209/984-3953, www.railtown1897.org, daily 9:30 A.M.–4:30 P.M. Apr.–Oct., daily 10 A.M.–3 P.M. Nov.–Mar., free, museum and guided tour adults $5, children $3) is scattered on tracks outdoors, but the best plan is to start inside; the old depot waiting room includes artifacts and a video describing the filmography of the Railtown trains. You'll see signs from *Petticoat Junction* (a 1960s black-and-white Wild West TV sitcom) and locomotives used in films and TV shows. Prize locomotives sit in the century-old roundhouse. Train fans, history lovers, film buffs, and children all love this unusual indoor-outdoor museum. Behind the roundhouse you can check out the functioning turntable, then wander out to the rolling stock (some of it in fairly decrepit condition) and poke around a little.

Want to ride in the classic cars behind the great old steam locomotives you've seen? You can take a six-mile, 40-minute ride out into the woodsy Sierra Foothills. Trains depart on the hour (11 A.M.–3 P.M. Sat.–Sun. Apr.–Oct., adults $13, youth $6). In winter, check for holiday-themed rides in November–December. Note that Railtown may be affected by the state's ongoing budget crisis; call ahead for the park's current status.

Accommodations
For a reasonable nightly rate in an upscale Victorian inn, try the **Royal Carriage Inn** (18239 Main St., 209/984-5271, www.abvijamestown.com, $80) and stay in a uniquely decorated guest room furnished with antiques and collectibles. All guest rooms have private baths, and several have adjoining doors for families or couples traveling together. Enjoy the hospitality in the parlor by the fireplace or out on one of the two balconies overlooking the town.

The at-times infamous 🌙 **National Hotel** (18183 Main St., 800/894-3446, www.national-hotel.com, $140) has operated almost continuously since 1859—either as a hotel, a brothel, a small casino, or as a Prohibition–era bar. Each of the nine guest rooms features antique furniture and comfy linens and comforters on the one queen bed. All guest rooms have their own baths with a shower and access to the soaking room, which the hotel describes as its "1800s Jacuzzi." An upscale gourmet restaurant is downstairs, while the Gold Rush Saloon serves up signature cocktails and wines.

The **Victorian Gold B&B** (10382 Willow St., 888/551-1851, www.victoriangoldbb.com, $110–185) is a stunningly renovated Gilded Age mansion built in the 1890s. The eight guest rooms are charmingly decorated with modern amenities and include a private bath with either a shower or a claw-foot tub; some guest rooms have both. The inn is fully air-conditioned, and there's included Wi-Fi in every room. Don't miss the homemade breakfast with fresh fruit and made-to-order omelets.

Food
Get a hearty American breakfast or lunch at the **Mother Lode Coffee Shop** (18169 Main St., 209/984-3386, 7 A.M.–2:15 P.M. Mon.–Sat., 8 A.M.–2:15 P.M. Sun., $8), next door to the old Jamestown Hotel. This local favorite offers traditional coffee shop fare: egg and pancake breakfasts, sandwiches, and burgers. The medium-size dining room can get crowded on weekend mornings.

One of the best Mexican spots in the area is **Morelia** (18148 Main St., 209/984-1432, daily 11 A.M.–9 P.M., $12) for enchiladas, Mexican grilled meat dishes, good beans and guacamole, and plenty of other tasty classic fare.

In a town thick with Gold Rush atmosphere, Jamestown's 🚻 **Willow Steakhouse and Saloon** (Willow St. and Main St., 209/984-3998, 11 A.M.–2:30 P.M. and 5–8:30 P.M. Mon.–Fri., $20–35) fits right in. The steaks are good rather than great, but the baked potatoes and the bucket of fixings make up for it. For an after-dinner cocktail, head into the Saloon and have a drink with the locals. You might have to wait for a table on weekend evenings.

Information and Services

Jamestown doesn't have a visitors center, but you can find plenty of information online (www.jamestown-ca.com) for loads of travel advice and maps of the town. Jamestown doesn't have many services, but you can still get gas and quick cash in town. To fill up your car, stop by **Chip's Chevron Mini Mart and Car Wash** (18151 Hwy. 108, 209/984-5245) on the main drag. There's also a 24-hour ATM at **Umqua Bank** (18281 Main St., 209/984-3971). If you need to mail something, there's a **post office** (18303 Main St., 8:30–4:30 P.M. Mon.–Fri.).

Getting There and Around

By car, Jamestown is less than four miles south of Sonora on Highway 49. If you're driving from Modesto, take Highway 108 northeast for 43 miles and then head north on Highway 49 for three more miles to reach Jamestown. **Enterprise** (209/533-0500) or **Hertz** (209/588-1575) has rental cars available.

There are two bus routes in Jamestown and Sonora. For a more whimsical ride that families will especially love, hop on the **Historic 49 Trolley** (209/532-0404, www.tuolumnecountytransit.com, daily summer, Sat.–Sun. fall–spring, adults $1.50, day pass $4, under age 13 free). **Tuolumne County Transit** (209/532-0404, www.tuolumnecountytransit.com, adults $1.50, day pass $4) runs Monday–Friday.

Central Valley

The Central Valley, bisected by I-5 and Highway 99 from Sacramento to Bakersfield, is an agrarian heat bowl sunk between the Coast Range to the west and the Sierra Nevadas to the east. This is the major north–south route for travelers and truckers to Yosemite, Sequoia, and Kings Canyon National Parks, and eventually to Los Angeles. If you need a place to stay for the night, Stockton, Fresno, and Bakersfield provide basic lodgings and places to eat; Yosemite-bound travelers may find Merced and Modesto convenient gateways.

STOCKTON

Stockton serves as a commuter town for the Bay Area. While not an inspired visitor haven, it is at the confluence of several highways, making it a convenient place to fill up on gas or food, or find a cheap motel for the night. The **Stockton Asparagus Festival** (www.asparagusfest.com, adults $12, youth $7) takes place in late spring in downtown Stockton. Enjoy tasty asparagus dishes, live entertainment, and local vintages and brews.

Accommodations

Motel 6 (817 Navy Dr., 209/946-0923, www.motel6.com, $40–55) has basic guest rooms with double or queen beds and an outdoor pool. The pet-friendly **Best Western Plus Heritage Inn** (111 E. March Lane, 209/474-3301, www.bestwesterncalifornia.com, $70–130) is somewhat nicer and has a pool, a fitness center, and an outdoor spa. Guest room amenities include comfortable beds, a coffeemaker, and high-speed Internet access. The on-site Venetian Restaurant makes it easy to grab a drink or a meal.

La Quinta (2710 W. March Lane, 209/952-7800, www.lq.com, $62–75) offers sizeable guest rooms with a king bed or two doubles, a coffeemaker, and free high-speed Internet access. There's a pool, included continental breakfast, and pets are welcome.

At the **Residence Inn Stockton** (3240 March Lane, 209/472-9800, www.marriott.com, $140–180), you'll get a suite that includes a full kitchen, included Wi-Fi access, an outdoor pool and spa, and included continental breakfast daily.

Food

Cocoro Japanese Bistro & Sushi (2105 Pacific Ave., 209/941-6053, www.cocorobistro.com, 11:30 A.M.–2 P.M. and 5:30–9 P.M. Mon.–Sat., $10–30) serves fresh and original sushi. In addition to fabulous rolls and a variety of sashimi and sushi, Cocoro offers teriyaki, *udon, donburi,* and tempura. There's also a second location that does takeout (3499 Brookside Rd., Suite B, 209/451-0398, daily 11:30 A.M.–8 P.M., $10–30).

One of the best cheeseburgers in Stockton can be had **Chuck's Burgers** (6034 Pacific Ave., 209/473-9977, 5 A.M.–5:30 P.M. Mon.–Fri., 5 A.M.–5 P.M. Sat., $10). This comfy downtown joint has vinyl booths, a classic counter, and eclectic decor. In addition to gourmet burgers, they also serve breakfast.

Practicalities

Stockton is bordered by I-5 and Highway 99; Highway 4 runs east from Antioch in the East Bay; and I-205 connects west to Tracy and Livermore via I-580. Stockton is served by **Amtrak**'s (800/872-7245, www.amtrak.com) *San Joaquin* train, which runs many times daily to Sacramento from Cabral Station (949

E. Channel St.) and to Oakland, Fresno, and Bakersfield from San Joaquin Street Station (735 S. San Joaquin St.).

The **Stockton Record** (www.recordnet.com) provides daily local and national news. For emergency medical care, go to **Dameron Hospital** (525 W. Acacia St., 209/944-5550, www.dameronhospital.org).

MODESTO

Modesto is located along Highway 99 in the San Joaquin Valley. In addition to dairies and vineyards, Modesto also functions as a stopping place on the way to Yosemite, less than two hours east. The **Gallo Center for the Arts** (1000 I St., Modesto, 209/338-2100, www.galloarts.org) is a large and impressive facility that brings a rich variety of performing arts to the area.

Accommodations

A large and modern **Doubletree Hotel** (1150 9th St., 209/526-6000, www.doubletree.com, $124–149) towers over the downtown area. Since it is primarily a business hotel, the weekend rate ($99) is often lower than weekdays. Amenities include a gym, a pool, and valet parking; Internet access is available at extra cost. The hotel is within easy walking distance of the Gallo Center for the Arts as well as the restaurants, shops, and visitors center downtown.

Food

The best restaurant in Modesto is **C Galletto Ristorante** (1101 J St., 209/523-4500, www.galletto.biz, 11:30 A.M.–9:30 P.M. Mon.–Thurs., 11:30 A.M.–10:30 P.M. Fri., 4:30–10:30 P.M. Sat., 11 A.M.–9 P.M. Sun., $12–30). The owners, Tom and Karyn Gallo of the Gallo winery family, take pride in running a "farm-to-fork" restaurant that buys from local purveyors, thereby ensuring fresh meals and supporting local businesses. The ivy-covered 1930s art deco building is just right for the offbeat elegance of the place.

© HEATHER C. LISTON

Gallo Center for the Arts

Carino's Italian Restaurant (3401 Dale Rd., 209/578-9432, www.carinos.com, 11 A.M.–9 P.M. Sun.–Thurs., 11 A.M.–10 P.M. Fri.–Sat., $14–18) offers Italian food on a budget. The food is dependable and generously portioned, and the atmosphere is warm and friendly.

The British-style pub **Firkin & Fox** (1111 I St., 209/575-2369, www.firkinfoxmodesto. com, noon–1 A.M. Sun.–Thurs., noon–2 A.M. Fri.–Sat., $10–20) is across the street from the Gallo Center for the Arts, serving bangers, beans, and mash before or after the show. An extensive menu includes everything from steaks and chops to quesadillas and Italian subs.

Practicalities

Modesto is at the junction of Highways 99 and 132, 30 miles south of Stockton. The **Modesto Convention & Visitors Bureau** (1150 9th St., Suite C, 209/526-5588 or 888/640-8467, www.visitmodesto.com, 8 A.M.–5 P.M. Mon.–Fri.) is downtown.

MERCED

The beautiful Merced River flows through small and lively Merced, for which the city was named. Although it has a branch of the University of California and a strong agricultural sector, it is best known as the "Gateway to Yosemite." The **Merced County Courthouse Museum** (21st St. and N St., 209/723-2401, www.mercedmuseum.org, 10 A.M.–4 P.M. Wed.–Sun., free) was dedicated in 1875 and is listed on the National Register of Historic Places. Inside are exhibits about the early history of Merced County and the Central Valley. Right across from the Courthouse Museum is the **Merced County Veterans Memorial,** with separate monuments dedicated to local soldiers from a long list of wars.

Accommodations

Many of Merced's chain hotels and motels are situated right on Highways 140 and 99, on the way to Yosemite. For something a little special,

SACRAMENTO

SACRAMENTO

© HEATHER C. LISTON

the Merced County Courthouse Museum

try the **Hooper House Bear Creek Inn** (575 W. North Bear Creek Dr., 209/723-3991, www. hooperhouse.com, $139–169), a colonial-style bed-and-breakfast with three suites in a preserved mansion. There is also one private cottage on the grounds nearby. All guest rooms have private baths and down comforters as well as full breakfast in the dining room.

Food

Merced has all the standard fast food and chain restaurants. One stand-out is **Toni's Courtyard Café** (516 W. 18th St., 209/384-2580, www. toniscourtyardcafe.com, 7 A.M.–3 P.M. Mon.– Fri., 7:30 A.M.–2 P.M. Sat., $7–10). Toni's serves omelets, sandwiches, and salads, but the bakery items really make this place special.

Fernando's Bistro (510 W. Main St., 209/381-0290, www.fernandosbistro.com, 11 A.M.–9 P.M. Tues.–Sat., $16–27), located in Bob Hart Square, serves California cuisine at patio tables beside the pleasant Susie Rossi Memorial Fountain. Entrées include salmon,

sirloin, and lamb complemented by selections from the martini bar menu.

Practicalities

Merced is 40 miles south of Modesto at the junction of Highways 99 and 140. The Arch Rock entrance to Yosemite Park is about 70 miles east on Highway 140. Merced is a transportation hub served by Amtrak, Greyhound, Yosemite Area Rapid Transit (YARTS), and the local Merced Transit system. The **Merced Transportation Center** (710 W. 16th St.) is home to both the **Greyhound** bus station (station 209/722-2121, reservations 800/231-2222, www.greyhound. com, 8 A.M.–5:30 P.M. Mon.–Fri.) and the **YARTS** depot (877/989-2787, www.yarts.com). You can catch the YARTS bus to Yosemite from the **Amtrak** station (324 W. 24th St., at K St., www.amtrak.com, 7:15 A.M.–9:45 P.M. daily), served several times daily by the *San Joaquin* train from Bakersfield, Oakland, and Sacramento.

Merced has a large and welcoming **California Welcome Center** (710 W. 16th

St., 209/724-8104 or 800/446-5353, www. visitmerced.travel or www.visitcwc.com, 8:30 A.M.–5 P.M. Mon.–Thurs., 8 A.M.–4 P.M. Sat., 10 A.M.–3 P.M. Sun.), with brochures, maps, and even a copy of the *Yosemite Guide.*

FRESNO

Fresno sprawls along Highway 99; it's the largest city between Sacramento and Bakersfield. Despite recent growth, the culture of Fresno still revolves around the fields that surround it. The Orange Belt starts here, and many other warmweather crops enjoy the hot summer sunshine.

Accommodations

Conveniently located near the airport, the **EconoLodge Fresno** (445 N. Parkway Dr., 559/485-5019, www.econolodge.com, $50–55) has modestly decorated guest rooms with TVs and DVD players, air-conditioning, phones, Internet access, and a basic but welcoming outdoor pool.

The **Rodeway Inn Fresno** (6730 N. Blackstone Ave., 559/431-3557, www.rodeway-inn.com, $60–90) has reasonably clean low-end motel rooms and basic amenities. The free Wi-Fi is a bonus, and pets are welcome.

The **Picadilly Shaw Inn** (2305 W. Shaw Ave., 559/348-5220, www.piccadillyinn.com, $90) is a slightly more upscale motel offering guest rooms with a king or two queen beds, decorated in fairly standard chain-motel chic. Amenities include free Wi-Fi, small fridges, and coffeemakers.

Food

A true local legend, **Grandmarie's Chicken Pie Shop** (861 E. Olive Ave., 559/237-5042, 7 A.M.–8 P.M. Mon.–Fri., 7 A.M.–3 P.M. Sat.–Sun., $10) is referred to as "Fresno's Chicken Pie Shop." From the avocado green booths to the giant plastic chickens, this vintage spot looks like it hasn't changed since the 1960s. The delectable pot pies are made fresh daily. For dessert, grab a slice of homemade fruit pie.

For a burger and fries, head to **Dog House Grill** (2789 E. Shaw Ave., 559/294-9920, 11 A.M.–10 P.M. Sun.–Thurs., 11 A.M.–11 P.M. Fri.–Sat., $10–30) for classic American food in a casual atmosphere. The Dog House has big TVs showing popular sporting events.

Try the tasty Armenian cuisine at **Nina's Bakery** (2022 W. Shaw Ave., 559/449-9999, 8 A.M.–6 P.M. Mon.–Sat., 10 A.M.–5 P.M. Sun., $10–20), an unlikely gem tucked in Fresno. If you like your *lahmajoun* spicy, you won't be disappointed.

Practicalities

Fresno is at the junction of Highway 99, Highway 180, and Highway 41. **Amtrak**'s *San Joaquin* route stops several times daily at Fresno Station (2650 Tulare St., www.amtrak.com) on the way to Sacramento, Oakland, or Bakersfield. Major airlines serve the **Fresno Yosemite International Airport** (FAT, 5175 E. Clinton Way, 800/244-2359, www.flyfresno.com), the major Central Valley air hub.

The local daily newspaper is the *Fresno Bee* (www.fresnobee.com). For medical services, go to **St. Agnes Medical Center** (1303 E. Herndon Ave., 559/450-3000, www.samc.com) at the north end of town, or try the **Community Regional Medical Center** (2823 Fresno St., 559/459-6000, www.community-medical.org), in central Fresno.

BAKERSFIELD

Bakersfield is the last major town on Highway 99 before you hit the infamous Grapevine and head down into the Los Angeles area. It's a good place to stop for gas and a meal. For local entertainment, check out the **Buck Owens Crystal Palace** (2800 Buck Owens Blvd., 661/328-7560, www.buckowens.com, 5 P.M.–close Tues.–Sat., 9:30 A.M.–2 P.M. Sun., $10–30), where you can visit a museum, take in a live show, and grab a meal. In the museum are Buck's favorite guitars, fabulous performance outfits, a collection of album covers, and endless photos and memorabilia chronicling his lengthy music career. Live music plays almost every night.

Accommodations

The **Motel 6 Bakersfield Airport** (5241 Olive Tree Court, 661/392-9700, www.motel6.com, $35–45) is a good option for an overnight stay. Another reasonable choice is the **Rodeway Inn & Suites** (3400 Chester Lane, 661/328-1100, www.rodewayinn.com, $55–90). For a few dollars more, you can get a few more amenities at the **Sleep Inn & Suites** (6257 Knudsen Dr., 661/399-2100, www.sleepinn.com, $60–80). In Bakersfield, luxury appears at the **SpringHill Suites** (3801 Marriott Dr., 661/377-4000, www.marriott.com, $100–140).

Food

Treat yourself to an upscale meal at the **Valentine Restaurant** (3310 Truxtun Ave., Suite 160, 661/864-0397, lunch 11:30 A.M.–2 P.M. Tues.–Fri., dinner 5–8 P.M. Mon., 5–9 P.M. Tues.–Sat., $10–30), with treats like sake-braised short ribs and a great range of California wines.

For delectable home-style Mexican, you can't beat **Don Pepito's Restaurant** (1201 Chester Ave., 661/326-1250, 11 A.M.–3 P.M. Mon., 11 A.M.–8 P.M. Tues.–Sun., $10), which serves both Mexican and Salvadoran dishes. For a quick burger, stop at **John's Burger** (2637 River Blvd., 661/873-8036, daily 7 A.M.–11 P.M., $3–8), often voted the Best Burger in Bakersfield.

Buck Owens Crystal Palace (2800 Buck Owens Blvd., 661/328-7560, www.buckowens. com, 5 P.M.–close Tues.–Sat., 9:30 A.M.–2 P.M. Sun., $10–30) serves up great American grill food that matches perfectly with the music. Try the barbecue pizza or a burger, and be sure to save room for dessert.

Practicalities

Highway 99 runs north through Bakersfield, and is one of the major corridors through the Central Valley. From I-5, get to Bakersfield on the Stockdale Highway, which becomes Highway 58 in the middle of town and heads east.

Bakersfield is a stop on the **Amtrak** (601 Truxton Ave., 800/872-7245, www.amtrak. com) *San Joaquin* line, and is the southern terminus for the route. From Bakersfield, the train runs several times daily north to Stockton, Oakland, and Sacramento. **Meadows Field** (BFL, 3701 Wings Way, 661/391-1800, www. meadowsfield.com) is the local commercial airport with flights on United and US Airways.

The *Bakersfield Californian* (www.bakers-field.com) is an independent family-owned daily. For medical attention, try **Bakersfield Memorial Hospital** (420 34th St., 661/327-4647, www. bakersfieldmemorial.org), which has a full emergency room. On the other side of town is **Mercy Southwest Hospital** (400 Old River Rd., 661/663-6000, www.mercybakersfield.org).

YOSEMITE AND THE EASTERN SIERRA

Of all the wondrous sights, natural and otherwise, that Northern California has to offer, few are more iconic than Yosemite National Park. This 1,200-square-mile playground has been immortalized in the photographs of Ansel Adams and in the words of the naturalist John Muir, who called it "the grandest of all the special temples of Nature I was ever permitted to enter." It was Muir who introduced Yosemite to President Theodore Roosevelt, an event that eventually resulted in its national park designation in 1890.

No one seems to visit Yosemite without being profoundly affected by it. If this is your first visit, prepared to be overwhelmed. If you're a regular visitor, then you already know you're going to see something new this time that will knock your polar-fleece socks off. Whether you scale a legendary granite precipice, wake at dawn to watch bear cubs frolic in a glistening meadow, hike under a crashing waterfall, or sit by the fire in one of the park's rustic lodges and watch the snow fall in the moonlight, you'll be different by the time you leave; enjoy the transformation.

East of the great park, Mono Lake greets visitors with an eerie stillness. This treeless, alkaline, and salt-filled lake is home to odd calcite (tufa) formations—mute testament to the extraordinary mineral content of the water. The rough High Sierra climate, with its deep winter snows and summer heat, attracts

© HEATHER C. LISTON

HIGHLIGHTS

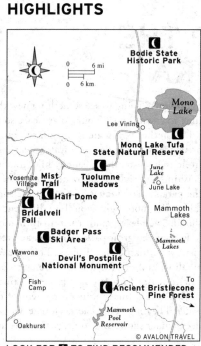

© AVALON TRAVEL

LOOK FOR ◖ TO FIND RECOMMENDED SIGHTS, ACTIVITIES, DINING, AND LODGING.

◖ **Half Dome:** Even in a park filled with iconic monuments, Half Dome towers over all others. Whether you come to scale its peak or just to see the real-life model for all those wonderful photographs, Half Dome lives up to the hype (page 586).

◖ **Bridalveil Fall:** One of the most monumental—and the most accessible—of Yosemite's marvelous collection of waterfalls (page 586).

◖ **Mist Trail:** The best way to experience Yosemite Valley's grandeur is on one of its many scenic trails. A hike along the Mist Trail to the top of Vernal Fall, or even Nevada Fall, brings the waterfalls and valley views alive (page 590).

◖ **Badger Pass Ski Area:** California's first-ever downhill ski area is as popular as ever, with affordable downhill and cross-country skiing, sledding hills for the kids, and full-moon snowshoe walks (page 600).

◖ **Tuolumne Meadows:** Explore the wonders of the park's high elevations at this rare alpine meadow. Numerous hiking trails thread through Yosemite's backcountry while the adjoining campground gives weary hikers a place to rest their heads (page 609).

◖ **Mono Lake Tufa State Natural Reserve:** Freestanding calcite towers, knobs, and spires dot the alien landscape of Mono Lake. Several interpretive trails provide history and access to what is undoubtedly one of the most unusual lakes you will ever see (page 636).

◖ **Bodie State Historic Park:** A state of "arrested decay" has preserved this 1877 gold-mining ghost town. Tours of the abandoned mine provide background on the settlement's sordid history (page 640).

◖ **Devils Postpile National Monument:** One visit to these strange natural rock formations and you'll understand how they got their name. A mix of volcanic heat and pressure created these near-perfect, straight-sided hexagonal posts that have to be seen to be believed (page 646).

◖ **Ancient Bristlecone Pine Forest:** The oldest trees on earth are on view in this quiet, fascinating section of the Inyo National Forest. Take a self-guided nature trail past Methuselah, a 4,750-year-old tree (page 657).

YOSEMITE

© HEATHER C. LISTON

Bodie State Historic Park

few year-round residents, although the mining town of Bodie—now California's biggest ghost town—once sheltered 10,000 gold-hungry adventurers.

South of Mono Lake, the picturesque town of Mammoth Lakes supports the Mammoth Mountain ski area. Winter tourism plays a big part in the local economy, but there's much more to do around Mammoth than just skiing and snowboarding. Hiking, mountain biking, fishing, backpacking, and sightseeing are great in this part of the Eastern Sierra, and you can find bargains on lodging in the summertime "off-season."

PLANNING YOUR TIME

Yosemite National Park (209/372-0200, www. nps.gove/yose, $20 per vehicle, $10 pp pedestrians, bicycles, motorcycles, noncommercial buses) is open daily year-round. There are five park entrances, two of which close in winter, and entrance fees are valid for seven days. The park website provides the best source of comprehensive, well-organized, and seasonal information along with the downloadable *Yosemite Guide.*

Try to plan at least two or three days just in Yosemite Valley, with an excursion to Glacier Point. With a week, add the Tuolumne (summer only), Hetch Hetchy, and Wawona sections of the park. To explore the Eastern Sierra, visit in summer and plan a full weekend to explore Mono Lake and Bodie State Historic Park. Mammoth Lakes makes a great ski getaway in winter, but you'll need a three-day weekend here at the very least.

Summer is traditionally high season, and during the height of summer, traffic jams and parking problems plague the park, making it hard to get around. Consider parking at the

YOSEMITE

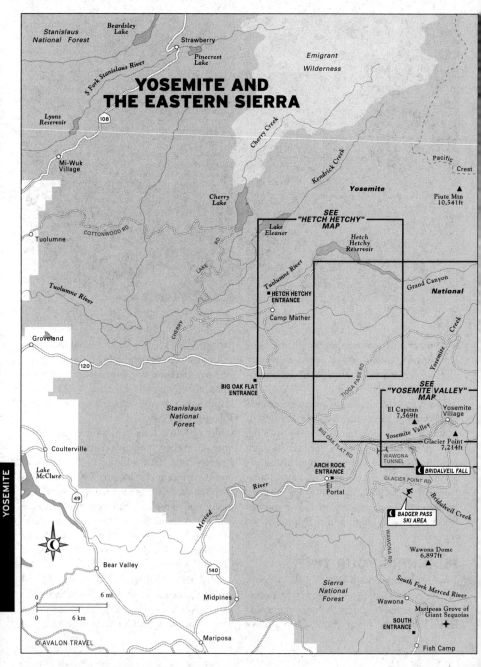

YOSEMITE

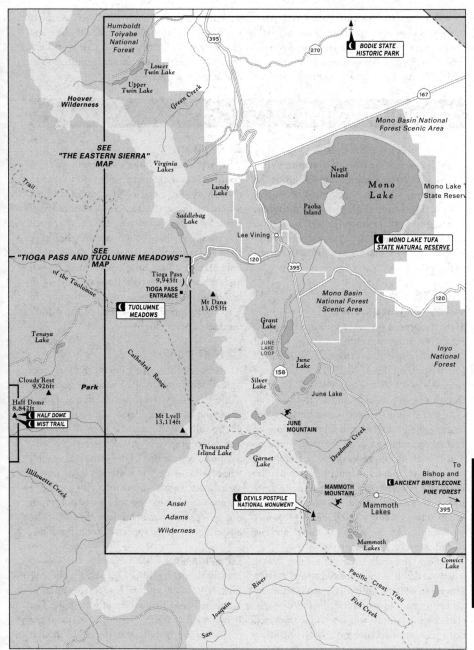

Humboldt
Toiyabe
National
Forest

395

270

BODIE STATE
HISTORIC PARK

167

Hoover
Wilderness

Lower
Twin Lake

Upper
Twin Lake

Green Creek

Mono Basin National
Forest Scenic Area

SEE
"THE EASTERN SIERRA"
MAP

Trail

Virginia
Lakes

Lundy
Lake

Negit
Island

Mono
Lake

Mono Lake
State Reserv

Saddlebag
Lake

Paoha
Island

Lee Vining

MONO LAKE TUFA
STATE NATURAL RESERVE

of the Tuolumne

SEE
"TIOGA PASS AND TUOLUMNE MEADOWS"
MAP

120

395

Tioga Pass
9,945ft
TIOGA PASS
ENTRANCE

TUOLUMNE
MEADOWS

Mt Dana
13,053ft

Mono Basin
National Forest
Scenic Area

120

Tenaya
Lake

Grant
Lake

Inyo
National
Forest

Cathedral Range

JUNE
LAKE
LOOP

June
Lake

Clouds Rest
9,926ft

Park

158

Silver
Lake

Half Dome
8,842ft

HALF DOME
MIST TRAIL

June Lake

Mt Lyell
13,114ft

JUNE
MOUNTAIN

Illilouette Creek

Thousand
Island Lake

Garnet
Lake

Deadman Creek

To
Bishop and
ANCIENT BRISTLECONE
PINE FOREST

Ansel
Adams
Wilderness

DEVILS POSTPILE
NATIONAL MONUMENT

MAMMOTH
MOUNTAIN

Mammoth
Lakes

395

Mammoth
Lakes

San

Joaquin

River

Pacific Crest Trail

Fish Creek

Convict
Lake

YOSEMITE

visitors center in Yosemite Valley and using the free shuttles to travel around the park. Tuolumne and Tioga Pass are less congested than the valley, making it a good summer option (it's closed in winter). Spring is best for waterfalls and wildflowers, and there are fewer crowds, as in fall. In Winter, roads close and crowds are minimal, but the park is still enchanting. The Badger Pass ski area offers a fun and affordable getaway.

Yosemite Valley

The first place most people go when they reach the park is the floor of Yosemite Valley (Hwy. 140, Arch Rock Entrance). From the valley floor, you can check out the visitors center, the theater, galleries, the museum, hotels, and outdoor historic exhibits. It's the most visited place in Yosemite, and many hikes, ranging from easy to difficult, begin in the valley.

SIGHTS
Valley Visitors Center
After the scenic turnouts through the park, your first stop in Yosemite Valley should be the visitors center (Yosemite Village, off Northside Dr., 209/372-0299, www.nps.gov/yose, 9 A.M.–7:30 P.M. daily late May–mid-Oct., 9 A.M.–5 P.M. daily mid-Oct.–late May). Here you'll find an interpretive museum describing the geological and human history of Yosemite in addition to all the usual information, books, maps, and assistance from park rangers. The complex of buildings includes the **Yosemite Museum** (9 A.M.–5 P.M. daily, free) and store, the **Yosemite Theater LIVE,** the **Ansel Adams Gallery** (209/372-4413, www.anseladams.com, 9 A.M.–6 P.M. daily), and the all-important public restrooms.

A short, flat walk from the visitors center takes you down to the recreated **Miwok Native American Village.** The village includes many different types of structures, including some made by the later Miwoks, who incorporated European architecture into their building techniques.

El Capitan
The first natural stone monument you encounter as you enter the valley is El Capitan (Northside Rd., west of El Capitan Bridge), a massive hunk of Cretaceous granite that's named for this formation. This craggy rock face rises more than 3,000 feet above the Valley floor and is accessible two ways: You can take a long hike westward from Upper Yosemite Fall and up the back side of El Capitan, or you can bring your climbing gear and scale the face. El Cap boasts a reputation as one of the world's seminal big-face climbs.

◖ Half Dome
At the foot of the valley, one of the most recognizable features in all of Yosemite rises high above the valley floor. Ansel Adams's famed photographs of Half Dome, visible from most of the valley floor, made it known to hikers and photography lovers all over the world. Scientists believe that Half Dome was never a whole dome—the way it appears to us now is actually its original formation. This piece of a narrow granite ridge was polished to its smooth dome-like shape tens of millions of years ago by glaciers, giving it the appearance of half a dome.

◖ Bridalveil Fall
Bridalveil Fall (Southside Dr., past the Hwy. 41 turnoff) is many visitors' first introduction to Yosemite's famed collection of waterfalls. The **Bridalveil Fall Trail** (0.5 mile, 20 minutes) is a pleasantly sedate walk up to the fall. Although the 620-foot waterfall runs year-round, its fine

Half Dome

Bridalveil Fall

mist sprays most powerfully in the spring—expect to get wet!

The trailhead has its own parking area, which is west of the main lodge and visitors center complex, so it's one of the first major sights people come to upon entering the park. It's a great first stop as you travel up the valley.

Yosemite Falls

Spring and early summer are the best times to view the many waterfalls that cascade down the granite walls of Yosemite. Most of the major waterfalls require at least a short hike to the best viewing points. Yosemite Falls, however, is visible from the valley floor near Yosemite Lodge. Actually three separate waterfalls—Upper Fall, Lower Fall, and middle cascades—this dramatic formation together creates one of the highest waterfalls in the world. The flows are seasonal; if you visit Yosemite Valley during the fall or the winter, you'll see just a trickle of water on the rocks or nothing at all. The best time to

see water gushing is the spring, when the snow-melt swells the river above and creates the beautiful cascade that makes these falls so famous.

Mirror Lake

Past the end of Southside Drive in Yosemite Valley lies still, perfect Mirror Lake. This small lake offers a stunningly clear reflection of the already spectacular views of Tenaya Canyon and the ubiquitous Half Dome. A short, level **hiking and biking path** circumnavigates the lake (2 miles round-trip, 1 hour). But come early in the season—this lake is gradually drying out, losing its water and becoming a meadow in the late summer and fall. Take the shuttle from anywhere in Yosemite Valley to stop 17 to get to the start of the paved pathway to the lake.

RECREATION
Hiking

Yosemite Valley is the perfect place for a day hike, no matter how energetic you feel. Valley

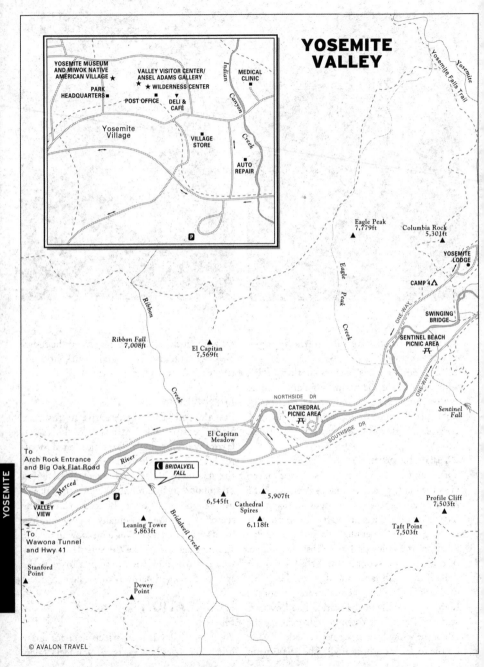

YOSEMITE

YOSEMITE VALLEY

YOSEMITE MUSEUM AND MIWOK NATIVE AMERICAN VILLAGE ★

PARK HEADQUARTERS ■

VALLEY VISITOR CENTER/ ANSEL ADAMS GALLERY ★
★ **WILDERNESS CENTER**

MEDICAL CLINIC ■

POST OFFICE ■

■ **DELI & CAFÉ**

Yosemite Village

■ **VILLAGE STORE**

■ **AUTO REPAIR**

Indian Canyon Creek

Yosemite Falls Trail

Eagle Peak 7,779ft ▲

Columbia Rock 5,301ft ▲

● **YOSEMITE LODGE**

CAMP 4 △

SWINGING BRIDGE

Eagle Peak Creek

SENTINEL BEACH PICNIC AREA ⊼

ONE-WAY

ONE-WAY

Ribbon Fall 7,008ft

Ribbon Creek

El Capitan 7,569ft ▲

NORTHSIDE DR

CATHEDRAL PICNIC AREA ⊼

SOUTHSIDE DR

Sentinel Fall

El Capitan Meadow

To Arch Rock Entrance and Big Oak Flat Road ←

Merced River

P

☾ **BRIDALVEIL FALL**

Bridalveil Creek

VALLEY VIEW

P

6,545ft ▲

Cathedral Spires 6,118ft ▲

5,907ft ▲

Profile Cliff 7,503ft ▲

To Wawona Tunnel and Hwy 41

Leaning Tower 5,863ft ▲

Taft Point 7,503ft ▲

Stanford Point

Dewey Point

© AVALON TRAVEL

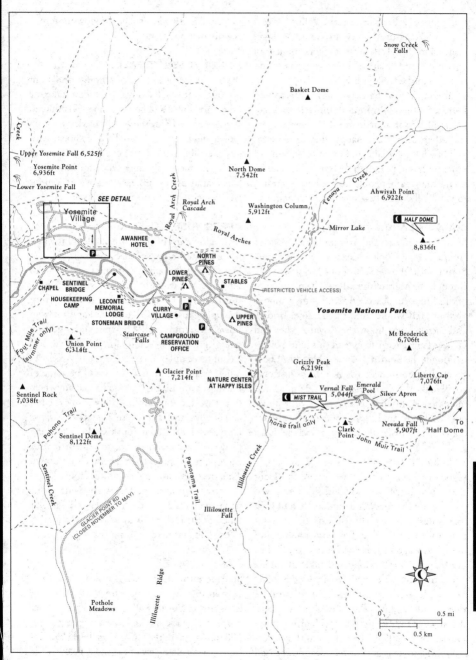

Snow Creek Falls

Basket Dome ▲

Creek

Upper Yosemite Fall 6,525ft

Yosemite Point 6,936ft

Lower Yosemite Fall

North Dome 7,542ft ▲

Royal Arch Creek

Royal Arch Cascade

Washington Column 5,912ft ▲

Tenuya Creek

Ahwiyah Point 6,922ft ▲

SEE DETAIL

Yosemite Village

Royal Arches

Mirror Lake

☾ **HALF DOME**

8,836ft

AWANHEE HOTEL ●

P

NORTH PINES ⛺

CHAPEL

SENTINEL BRIDGE

LOWER PINES ⛺

STABLES

(RESTRICTED VEHICLE ACCESS)

Yosemite National Park

HOUSEKEEPING CAMP

LECONTE MEMORIAL LODGE

STONEMAN BRIDGE

CURRY VILLAGE ●

P

UPPER PINES ⛺

Four Mile Trail (summer only)

Union Point 6,314ft

Staircase Falls

CAMPGROUND RESERVATION OFFICE

P

Mt Broderick 6,706ft ▲

Glacier Point 7,214ft ▲

NATURE CENTER AT HAPPY ISLES

Grizzly Peak 6,219ft ▲

Liberty Cap 7,076ft ▲

Sentinel Rock 7,038ft ▲

Vernal Fall 5,044ft ▲

Emerald Pool

Silver Apron

☾ **MIST TRAIL**

To Half Dome

Pohono Trail

Sentinel Dome 8,122ft ▲

horse trail only

Clark Point

Nevada Fall 5,907ft ▲

John Muir Trail

Sentinel Creek

Panorama Trail

Illilouette Creek

GLACIER POINT RD (CLOSED NOVEMBER TO MAY)

Illilouette Fall

Illilouette Ridge

Pothole Meadows

0   0.5 mi

0   0.5 km

YOSEMITE

hiking maps are available at the Valley Visitors Center (Yosemite Valley at Valley Village, Northside Dr.). Talk to the rangers about trail conditions and be sure to bring you map—and water—on the trail with you.

In addition to the easy hikes to **Bridalveil Fall** (0.5 mile, 20 minutes) and **Mirror Lake** (2 miles, 1 hour, shuttle stop 17), there are several other valley hikes that provide a good sampler of what's available in Yosemite—plenty of other trails wind through this gorgeous area. Be aware that many people love the valley trails, so you likely won't be alone in the wilderness.

COOK'S MEADOW

Soak in quintessential Yosemite Valley views from the easy Cook's Meadow Loop (1 mile, 30 minutes, shuttle stop 5 or 9), a short walk through the heart of the valley. The main point of this hike is to observe Ansel Adams's famous view of Half Dome from the Sentinel Bridge, and then to gaze up at the Royal Arches and Glacier Point. You can extend this hike a bit by making it the **Sentinel-Cook's Meadow Loop**. By circling both meadows instead of just one, you'll make the whole trip about 2.25 miles and increase the number of angles for your photo ops. Trail signs, and the plethora of other hikers doing these trails, make it easy to find the turns.

VALLEY FLOOR

If you've got several hours, take the Valley Floor Loop (Northside Dr. and Southside Dr., paved path beside the road). The moderate **half loop** (6.5 miles, 3 hours, shuttle stop 6) traverses the El Capitan Bridge, following the path of many old wagon roads and historic trails. The **full loop** is 13 miles long and takes about six hours to hike. It's a great moderate day hike, and you'll see the most beautiful parts of the valley while escaping the crowds on the roads. If you want to hike the Valley Floor Loop, it's a good idea to talk to the rangers at the visitors center; the route is not entirely clear on the trail

map, and getting lost in the meadows or forests is a distinct possibility.

LOWER YOSEMITE FALL

If you're staying at Yosemite Lodge and want an easy, gentle walk with a great view, take the Lower Yosemite Fall Loop (1.1 miles, 30 minutes, shuttle stop 6). Enjoy the wondrous views of both Upper and Lower Yosemite Falls, complete with lots of cooling spray. If you can, hike this trail in the spring or early summer, when the flow of the falls is at its peak. This easy trail works well for families with children who love the water.

UPPER YOSEMITE FALL

Naturally, some of the more challenging hikes in Yosemite Valley are also the most rewarding. One of these is the strenuous trek up to Upper Yosemite Fall (7.2 miles, 6–8 hours, shuttle stop 7). You can start this hike from the Upper Yosemite Fall trailhead or walk from Lower Yosemite Fall. The trail starts getting steep right away—you'll climb 2,700 vertical feet in three miles to reach the top of America's tallest waterfall. Your reward will be some of the most astonishing views to be had anywhere in the world. You can look down over the fall and out over the valley, with its grassy meadows far below. Plan all day for this hike, and bring plenty of water and snacks to replenish your energy for the potentially tricky climb down. This trail is well marked and much used, and the steep parts are made passable with stone steps, switchbacks, and occasional railings. But much of the trail tends to be wet and slippery, so hold on and take it slow.

◖ MIST TRAIL

Starting at the Happy Isles Nature Center (shuttle stop 16), the moderate-strenuous Mist Trail leads first to **Vernal Fall** (3 miles, 3 hours) over much steep, slick granite—including more than 600 stairs—up to the top of Vernal Fall. Your reward is the stellar view of the valley below while

© HEATHER C. LISTON

the Mist Trail to Vernal Fall

relaxing on the flat granite boulders that abut the Merced River. If you packed a lunch, stop and eat here before returning back the same way. Hardier souls should continue another steep and strenuous 1.5–2 miles of switchbacks to the top of **Nevada Fall** (5.4 miles, 5–6 hours) and return via the John Muir Trail. Plan six hours for this hike, with a 2,000-foot elevation gain, and consider taking a lightweight rain jacket since this aptly named trail gives hikers a shower in the spring and early summer months.

Note that the Mist Trail is closed in winter due to ice and snow and can be dangerous in the spring months when the river is at its peak; hikers have been lost in the waters here. Exercise caution in extreme conditions, and obey all trail signage.

HALF DOME
The most famous climb in Yosemite Valley takes you to the top of monumental Half Dome (14–16 miles, 10–12 hours, May–Oct. only, shuttle stop 16). But before you start, a word of warning: This hike can be dangerous. With a round-trip distance of 14 miles by

the Mist Trail or 16 miles by the John Muir Trail, and with a very strenuous 4,800-foot elevation gain, this arduous, all-day hike is not for small children, the elderly, or anyone remotely out of shape. The trek is significantly riskier in rain, snow, high wind, or other adverse conditions, and rangers will not be able to rescue you should you become stranded at the top. Attempt this hike only in the summer (Memorial Day–Columbus Day) when the cables are up (you must hold onto cables to help pull yourself up the last 400 feet of steep granite to the top of the dome). Most importantly, obey all signage on the trail. If the park posts that the trail is closed or unsafe, heed the conditions and turn back. Continuing when conditions deem otherwise risks your life and others, including those who will try to rescue you.

Before you commit to Half Dome, make sure you're ready, mentally and physically, for a long and sometimes treacherous challenge. Check weather conditions and sunrise and sunset times before you hike, and establish a turn-around point so that you aren't hiking back in darkness. Take a well-organized pack with

YOSEMITE

water (1 gallon pp), food, a topo map and compass, a headlamp or flashlight (with batteries), and other safety essentials. Wear hiking shoes that have been broken in and bring a hat.

From the Happy Isles shuttle stop, follow the Mist Trail to Nevada Fall (or, alternately, take the John Muir Trail instead), and then follow the signs for Half Dome. Once you stagger to the top, you'll find a restful expanse of stone on which to sit and rest and enjoy the scenery.

Yosemite requires all hikers to have a **permit** (877/444-6777, www.recreation.gov, $1.50 pp) to climb Half Dome. There are 400 permits issued per day; 300 permits are allotted for day hikers, and the rest are for backpackers. You can reserve up to four permits during each phone call or online visit. Reservations must be made in advance; permits are not available first-come, first-served, so don't show up at the trailhead expecting to get lucky. However, there are a few almost-last-minute options: Check the website at 7 A.M. Pacific Time the day before you want to climb. If the next day's allotment of permits isn't all taken, a batch of permits will be released. If someone cancels their permit at the last minute, the park will continue issuing permits to replace those canceled until midnight the night before.

Backpacking

If you're a serious hiker and you have time for just one big hike in Yosemite, you can't go wrong with the **Snow Creek Trail** (13 miles round-trip, 5–7 hours, shuttle stop 17) from Mirror Lake to the granite domes above Tenaya Canyon. From the shuttle stop, walk 350 yards on a paved sidewalk to Tenaya Bridge. Here the trail splits; keep left and cross the bridge to take the northern trail. In another 0.5–0.75 miles you'll see Mirror Lake. Look straight down into this aptly named pool and you'll notice that the view of Half Dome and the other natural wonders nearby is stunningly clear. Eventually, you'll leave Mirror Lake behind and continue walking northeast, following a wide trail for

about a mile through a cool, swampy forest. The terrain is mostly easy, but soon the trail joins the Tenaya Lake and Tuolumne Meadows Trail and begins a long series of switchbacks, climbing up through rocks, streams, redwoods, ponderosa pines, and manzanitas. In the spring, gradual snowmelt seeps across the trail, making for a few shallow water crossings and an abundance of wildflowers.

The trail is a little steep but never impassable. The switchbacks keep the grade reasonably consistent, discreet rock stairs help you over the rough spots, and water bars and contouring guide water off the trail, helping to contain erosion as well as keeping your feet dry and your footing secure. As you climb, take in the hillside teeming with forest life, and vast sweeping views of the mountains and rock faces to the east and south.

Just when you've had enough of climbing (about 2.5 miles of switchbacks and nearly 3,000 feet of elevation gain), you'll notice that the trail flattens out and enters a forest. Look for a clearing to your right after about 0.25 miles and head in that direction through fallen trees and low brush. In just a couple of minutes you'll find yourself on top of a massive granite slab, the end of the hike. This enormous rock provides a perfect lunch spot with 360-degree views of Mount Watkins to the east with Clouds Rest beyond it, Snow Creek Falls across the valley, and the rarely seen north side of Half Dome. When you're ready, return by the same route.

Biking

Biking is a great way to get out of the car, off the crowded roads, and explore Yosemite at a quicker-than-walking (and sometimes even quicker than driving) pace. Twelve miles of paved trails are mostly flat. You can bring your own bike, or rent one in Yosemite Village from the in-park concessionaire, Delaware North Companies (209/372-4386, www.yosemitepark.com, 9 A.M.–6 P.M. daily, $10 per hour, $28 per day). Check at Yosemite Lodge

(801/559-5000, shuttle stop 8) for more information about rentals and to get a bike trail map.

Horseback Riding

Two different rides begin at the **Yosemite Valley Stables** (end of Southside Dr., 209/372-8348, www.yosemitepark.com/Activities_ MuleHorsebackRides.aspx, 7 A.M.–5 P.M. daily May–Oct., $64–85). The sedate two-hour trek to Mirror Lake works well for children and beginning riders. Along the way, your guide will explain the geologic forces that are slowly drying out the lake. A half-day ride takes you out to Clark Point, from where you can admire Vernal Fall, Nevada Fall, and the valley floor. This ride takes about four hours but isn't terribly difficult.

Ice-Skating

Curry Village (end of Southside Dr., 209/372-8319, www.yosemitepark.com, 3:30–6 P.M. and 7–9:30 P.M. Mon.–Fri., 8:30–11 A.M., noon–2:30 P.M., 3:30–6 P.M., and 7–9:30 P.M. Sat.–Sun. mid-Nov.–Mar., adults $8, children $6, rentals $3) has an ice-skating rink in winter.

Rock Climbing

The rock climbing at Yosemite is some of the best in the world. **El Capitan,** the face of **Half Dome,** and **Sentinel Dome** in the high country are challenges that draw climbers from all over. If you plan to climb one of these monuments, check with the Yosemite park rangers and the Mountaineering School well in advance for necessary information and permits.

Note that many of the spectacular ascents are not beginners' climbs. If you try to scale El Capitan as your first-ever climb, you'll fail (if you're lucky). The right place to start climbing in Yosemite is the **Yosemite Mountaineering School** (209/372-8344, www.yosemitepark. com/activities_mountaineeringschool.aspx). Here you'll find "Go Climb a Rock" classes for beginners, perfect for older kids or adult

© GEORGE JEN

rock climbing on Yosemite's granite walls

team-building groups. You'll also find guided climbs out of Yosemite Valley and Tuolumne Meadows, and if you're looking for a one-on-one guided climb experience, you can get it through the school. Also available are guided hikes and backpacking trips as well as cross-country skiing lessons and treks in winter.

ENTERTAINMENT AND EVENTS

LeConte Memorial Lodge (Southside Dr., 10 A.M.–4 P.M. Wed.–Sun., shuttle stop 12) hosts evening programs (8 P.M. Fri.–Sun. summer, free) and has a library, a children's play area, and seasonal exhibits. Check the *Yosemite Guide* for a list of programs.

Ranger Programs are popular with the kids. Park rangers give talks, lead guided walks, and host evening programs throughout the valley; check the *Yosemite Guide* for a list of programs.

Theater and Music

The **Yosemite Valley Auditorium and**

YOSEMITE AT NIGHT

Yosemite National Park does not roll up its meadows and trails at sunset. In fact, some aspects of the park come alive only at nightfall. Many of the animals that live in the park are crepuscular by nature—they're most active in the twilight hours of dawn and dusk. Take a quiet stroll in the park early in the morning or just as darkness is falling and you're likely to see more wildlife than you'll run into during the day.

If you prefer a guided tour, come in the spring or early fall to join the **Night Prowl** (209/372-4386, www.yosemitepark.com/Activities_EveningPrograms_NightProwl.aspx, 90 minutes, $5). This guided tour takes you along easy trails near Yosemite Lodge at the Falls and explains the nightlife of the valley floor's inhabitants. Night Prowl takes place once or twice a week, starting at various times and places, and is good for both children and adults. Purchase your tickets at any activity desk in Yosemite, or call 209/372-4386, and you'll get all the information on where and when to meet.

If astronomy is your interest, join experienced guides for the **Starry Skies** (209/372-4386, summer-fall, $5) program. Equally well suited for beginners and more experienced stargazers, this 90-minute program takes you out to the meadows to look at the stars and the moon free of light pollution. You'll learn about constellations, comets, and meteors and enjoy the myths and legends about the night sky. Starry Skies happens several times each week in Yosemite Valley and once a week in Wawona.

For families tired after a long day of running around the park, more sedentary evening programs are available. The **Campfire Program** (209/372-4386, summer-fall, 90 minutes, $5 pp or $20 per family) does it old-school—groups gather around a nice big campfire (bring blankets and bug repellent) for stories, singing, and marshmallow toasting. You might need to take a short walk to get to the fire near Camp Curry. If you're out at one of the more primitive lodges or campsites, check with the local rangers or office for campfire programs at the site, since many spring up in the summer and early fall months. **Fireside Storytelling** (fall-spring, free) focuses on, well, telling stories around the big fire inside the Ahwahnee Great Lounge. Take refuge from the bugs and the cold and listen to great tales in a comfortable indoor environment during the off-season. Check the *Yosemite Guide* for more information about these and other programs.

Yosemite Theater (Northside Dr.) share a building behind the visitors center in the heart of Yosemite Village. Check the copy of *Yosemite Guide* you received at the gate for a list of what shows are playing during your visit. The John Muir Performances (209/372-0731, 7 P.M. Wed.–Thurs. May–mid-Nov., adults $8, children $4), starring Yosemite's resident actor Lee Stetson, have been running for 25 years. Stetson's repertoire includes *Conversation with a Tramp: An Evening with John Muir* about Muir's battle to preserve Hetch Hetchy, *The Spirit of John Muir, John Muir Among the Animals,* and a two-person show, *The Tramp and the Roughrider,* about Muir's relationship with Theodore Roosevelt. Any or all of these may be offered during a given season in the park.

Other programs in the theater and auditorium include presentations by Shelton Johnson (who appeared in the Ken Burns documentary *The National Parks: America's Best Idea*) about the Buffalo Soldiers, films about climbing, and—on Monday evenings—Tom Bopp singing historic songs of Yosemite. For more details on upcoming programs, visit www.yosemiteconservancy.org; for background on Lee Stetson and John Muir in particular, visit www.johnmuirlive.com.

Photography and Art Classes

The unbelievable scenery of Yosemite inspires visitors young and old to create images to take home with them. Knowing this, Yosemite offers art and photography classes to help people find their inner Ansel Adams. In summer, free art classes are offered by the **Yosemite Art and Education Center** (Yosemite Village, 209/372-1442, www.yosemiteconservancy. org, 10 A.M.–2 P.M. Tues.–Sat. Apr.–Oct., $5 per day donation), a program of the Yosemite Conservancy. Check the *Yosemite Guide* or the website for a list of classes during your visit. You must bring your own art supplies, a chair or cushion to sit on, and walking shoes (you'll take a brief walk out to a good location to see the scenery). If you don't have supplies, you can buy them at the Village Store (9 A.M.–4:30 P.M.) just before class. Also check the *Yosemite Guide* for guided tours of the **Ansel Adams Gallery** (Yosemite Village, 209/372-4413, www.anseladams.com, 9 A.M.–5 P.M. daily) and walks throughout the park led by staff from the gallery.

ACCOMMODATIONS

All lodgings, including campsites, fill up quickly—up to months in advance. In Yosemite Valley, **Delaware North Companies** (801/559-5000, www.yosemitepark.com) handles reservations for the lodgings at Curry Village, Housekeeping Camp, Yosemite Lodge at the Falls, and the Ahwahnee Hotel.

Curry Village

Curry Village (801/559-5000, www.yosemitepark.com) offers some of the oldest lodgings in the park. Often called Camp Curry, this sprawling array of wood-sided and canvas-tent cabins was originally created in 1899 to provide affordable lodgings so that people of modest means could visit and enjoy the wonders of Yosemite. At Curry Village, you can rent a tent cabin or a wood cabin, with or without heat and with or without a private bath, depending on your budget and needs. You can also reserve a motel room if you prefer. Curry Village has showers ($5) and several eateries (most open in summer), so you won't lack for food choices. The Curry Village breakfast buffet (7–10 A.M.)

is included in some special "hiker's packages"; it can also be added to any accommodations option for $12. You won't find any TVs or telephones in the Curry Village lodgings, which is part of the appeal for many people.

The 56 **Yosemite Cabins** (year-round, $171 d) are hard to come by, and they're usually booked far in advance. These wood structures include one or two double beds (some have a double and a single) that sleep up to five. Cabins have private baths, electricity, decks or patios, and maid service. There are 14 cabins without private baths; these share a central bathhouse instead.

In addition, there are 319 **Canvas Tent Cabins** ($70–120), the most affordable option. These are small, wood-frame, canvas-covered structures that sleep 2–4 in a combination of single and double cot beds. A small dresser, sheets, blankets, and pillows are provided, but there is no electricity or heat. Bear-proof lockers are available outside each tent cabin. Shared showers and restrooms are found within Curry Village. A few **Heated Tent Cabins** (801/559-4884, late Sept.–mid-May, $120) are available on a limited basis.

The 18 guest rooms in the **Stoneman Motel** ($192 d) sleep 2–6 and have heat, private baths, and daily maid service. There's an extra charge of $10–12 for each person beyond the first two.

Dining options include the **Pavilion Buffet** (209/372-8303, 7–10 A.M. and 5:30–8 P.M. daily Mar.–Nov., $10–12); **Coffee Corner** (6 A.M.–10 P.M. daily summer, 7–11 A.M. Sat.–Sun. winter); the **Curry Village Bar** (noon–10 P.M. daily summer); **Pizza Deck** (noon–10 P.M. daily summer, 5–9 P.M. Fri., noon–9 P.M. Sat. winter); and the **Taqueria** (11 A.M.–5 P.M. daily summer).

Housekeeping Camp

Want to camp, but don't want to schlep all the gear into the park? Book a tent cabin at Housekeeping Camp (801/559-5000, www.yosemitepark.com, mid-Apr.–mid-Oct., $100).

YOSEMITE

Located on the banks of the Merced River, Housekeeping Camp has its own sandy river beach for playing and sunbathing. Cabins have cement walls, white canvas roofs, and a white canvas curtain that separates the bedroom from the covered patio that doubles as a dining room. Every cabin has a double bed plus two bunks (with room for two additional cots), a bear-proof food container, and an outdoor fire ring. You can bring your own linens, or rent a "bed pack" (no towels, $3). No maid service is provided, but you won't miss it as you sit outside watching the sunset over Yosemite Valley.

Yosemite Lodge at the Falls

◖ **Yosemite Lodge at the Falls** (801/559-5000, www.yosemitepark.com, $192–219), situated near Yosemite Village on the Valley floor, has a location perfect for touring all over the park. The motel-style rooms are light and pretty, with polished wood furniture, bright-colored bed linens, and Native American design details. Lodge rooms with king beds offer romantic escapes for couples, complete with balconies overlooking the valley, while the standard rooms can accommodate singles, couples, or families. Enjoy the heated pool in the summer and free shuttle transportation up to the Badger Pass ski area in winter. The amphitheater at the middle of the lodge runs nature programs and movies all year. The lodge is central to the Yosemite shuttle system and has a post office, an ATM, the on-site **Mountain Room Restaurant** (209/372-1499, 5:30–9:30 P.M. Sun.–Fri. May–Oct., 5–8:30 P.M. Sun.–Thurs., 5–9 P.M. Fri. Oct.–May), the **Mountain Room Lounge** (4:30–11 P.M. Mon.–Fri., noon–11 P.M. Sat.–Sun.), and a food court (6:30–11 A.M., 11:30 A.M.–2 P.M., 5–9:30 P.M. daily summer).

Ahwahnee Hotel

If you're looking for luxury among the trees and rocks, check in to the ◖ **Ahwahnee Hotel** (801/559-5000, www.yosemitepark. com, $493–1,102). Built as a luxury hotel in the early 20th century, the Ahwahnee lives up

Ahwahnee Hotel

© FRANK KOVALCHEK

THE BEARS OF YOSEMITE

© FRANK KOVALCHEK

Although grizzlies have not been seen in California since 1922, the smaller but still impressive black bears (*Ursus americanus californiensis*) are plentiful, especially in Yosemite. Black bears do not seek out humans and they're usually not looking for trouble. They are, however, looking for food, and this often leads them into campgrounds and other places frequented by humans.

To protect both people and bears, National and State Park rangers are very strict about enforcing rules to minimize contact between the species. Yosemite is particularly vigilant about its bear rules. The park provides metal bear-proof storage lockers and all visitors must store any food, ice chests, or anything that looks or smells like food in these lockers. Remember that garbage, toothpaste, shampoo, deodorant, beer, and soda all smell like food even if they don't seem like it to you—don't ever put any of these items in a tent. Even if you're only in a park for the day, you must use these lockers or at least put all your food in the trunk of your vehicle, out of sight. If it looks like food to a bear, it can lead to trouble and visitors have been known to get expensive tickets for having even an empty grocery sack within view inside a locked car. Note that bears do not hibernate in Yosemite during the winter; the visitors center and lodge display disturbing videos of bears tearing apart car doors and rooftops in winter to get at food inside.

If you see a bear at least 50 yards away, be quiet and keep your distance. If the bear approaches you or your campsite, actively discourage it by banging on pots and pans, yelling, and waving your arms. If you're carrying food or a backpack or other parcel, drop it and move slowly away. The bear will probably switch its attention to the pack and leave you alone. For backpacking, Yosemite requires the use of approved bear-resistant canisters; these can be bought at any outdoor supply store, and sometimes you can borrow or rent one at a trailhead or visitors center. Note that bear spray and pepper spray are not permitted in the park.

YOSEMITE

to its reputation with a gorgeous stone facade, striking stone fireplaces, and soaring ceilings in the common rooms. The guest rooms, in both the hotel and the cottages, drip with sumptuous appointments. The theme is Native American, and you'll find intricate, multicolored geometric and zoomorphic designs on linens, furniture, and pillows. The Ahwahnee includes 24 cottages and 99 hotel rooms in the main building. All bedrooms come with either one king bed or two doubles; guest rooms in the main hotel may be combined with a parlor to make a suite. The cottages come with small stone patios as well as TVs, telephones, small refrigerators, and private baths. Whether you're seeking a romantic getaway or a family vacation, you're likely to find a room that feels just right.

A bonus is the on-site **Ahwahnee Dining Room** (Ahwahnee Hotel, 209/372-1489, www.yosemitepark.com, 7–10:30 A.M., 11:30 A.M.–3 P.M., and 5:30–9 P.M. Mon.–Sat., 7 A.M.–3 P.M. and 5:30–9 P.M. Sun., $27–46).

CAMPING

There are four campgrounds in Yosemite Valley, and they are deservedly popular. Upper Pines, Lower Pines, and North Pines require **reservations** (877/444-6777, www.recreation.gov), sometimes up to five months in advance; leashed pets are permitted at these three campgrounds. Campground reservations in Yosemite Valley are very competitive. At 7 A.M. eastern time on the 15th of each month, a new batch of campsites become available for a period up to five months in advance. A few minutes after 7 A.M., choice sites and dates—maybe even all of them—will be gone. If you need a reservation for a specific day, get up early and call or check online diligently starting at 7 A.M. eastern time.

If you're in the valley and don't have a campsite reservation, call the **campground status line** (209/372-0266) for a recording of what's open, what's closed, what's full, and what's available that day. Or try one of the first-come, first-served campgrounds (but get there early).

Lower Pines

The Lower Pines campground (60 sites, Mar.–late Oct., $20) is across from Curry Village. Sites accommodate tents and RVs up to 40 feet and include fire rings, picnic tables, a bear-proof food locker, water, flush toilets—and very little privacy. Supplies and showers ($5) are available in Curry Village. Reservations are required and are available up to five months in advance.

Upper Pines

Upper Pines campground (238 sites, year-round, $20) is the largest campground in the valley. It lies immediately southwest of Lower Pines and is encircled by the park road. Sites accommodate tents and RVs up to 35 feet and include fire rings, picnic tables, a bear-proof food locker, water, and flush toilets. Supplies and showers ($5) are available in Curry Village. Reservations are required March 15–November and are available up to five months in advance. Sites are available first-come, first-served December–March 15.

North Pines

Set along the Merced River and Tenaya Creek, North Pines (81 sites, Apr.–Sept., $20) offers slightly more privacy than its Upper and Lower Pines siblings. Sites accommodate tents and RVs up to 40 feet and include fire rings, picnic tables, a bear-proof food locker, water, and flush toilets. Supplies and showers ($5) are available in Curry Village, and the Yosemite Valley Stables are right nearby. Reservations are required and are available up to five months in advance.

Camp 4

Camp 4 (35 campsites, first-come, first-served, $5) stays open year-round. Yes, you can camp in the snow! Bring a tent—no RVs or trailers are allowed. You'll find showers nearby at Curry Village, and food and groceries at Yosemite Lodge. Sites include fire pits, picnic tables, and a shared bear-proof food locker. Restrooms with water and flush toilets are nearby. Pets are not permitted.

Reservations are not accepted. Spring–fall, hopeful campers must register with a park ranger. Plan to wait in line at the campground kiosk well before the ranger arrives at 8:30 A.M. Sites are available first-come, first-served and hold six people each, so you may end up camping with new friends.

FOOD
Casual Dining

For casual food options, head to Yosemite Village for **Degnan's Loft** (209/372-8381, noon–9 P.M. daily June–Aug., 5–9 P.M. Mon.–Fri. and noon–9 P.M. Sat.–Sun. Apr.–May and Sept.–Oct., $8–20) for hot pizza, soups, and appetizers. **Degnan's Deli** (209/372-8454, 7 A.M.–5 P.M. daily year-round, $6.50–7.50) offers an array of sandwiches, salads, and other take-out munchies, and **Degnan's Cafe** (Apr.–Sept.) has coffee and baked goods. The **Village Grill** (11 A.M.–5 P.M. daily spring–fall, $5–15) offers standard burgers and grilled food.

Curry Village is where to go for relatively cheap fast food. Hiking clothes are expected! The Curry Village **Pavilion Buffet** (209/372-8303, 7–10 A.M. and 5:30–8 P.M. daily Mar.–Nov., $10–12) hosts an all-you-can-eat buffet for breakfast and dinner. There is also **Coffee Corner** (6 A.M.–10 P.M. daily summer, 7–11 A.M. Sat.–Sun. daily winter), the **Curry Village Bar** (noon–10 P.M. daily summer), a **Pizza Deck** (noon–10 P.M. daily summer, 5–9 P.M. Fri., noon–9 P.M. Sat. winter), the **Taqueria** (11 A.M.–5 P.M. daily summer), and the **Happy Isles Snack Stand** (11 A.M.–7 P.M. daily summer) at shuttle stop 16.

The **Yosemite Lodge Food Court** (Yosemite Lodge, 6:30–11 A.M., 11:30 A.M.–2 P.M., and 5–9:30 P.M. daily summer, $5–15) offers basic meals in a cafeteria-style setting. A casual bar menu is available at the **Mountain Room Lounge** (4:30–11 P.M. Mon.–Fri., noon–11 P.M. Sat.–Sun., $5–21), immediately across from the Mountain Room Restaurant.

Fine Dining

The **◀ Ahwahnee Dining Room** (Ahwahnee Hotel, 209/372-1489, www.yosemitepark. com, 7–10:30 A.M., 11:30 A.M.–3 P.M., and 5:30–9 P.M. Mon.–Sat., 7 A.M.–3 P.M. and 5:30–9 P.M. Sun., $27–46) enjoys a reputation for fine cuisine that stretches back to 1927. The grand dining room features expansive ceilings, wrought-iron chandeliers, and a stellar valley view. The restaurant serves three meals daily, with dinner the highlight. The California cuisine of an Ahwahnee dinner mirrors that of top-tier San Francisco restaurants (with a price tag to match). Reservations are recommended for all meals, though it's possible to walk in for breakfast and lunch. For dinner, "resort casual" attire is requested, which means something like semiformal. Specifically, all the dress code really says is no shorts on anyone, and men should wear collared shirts with their long pants, but some people dress up quite a bit more than that, and it's fun to join in and make an elegant evening of it.

At the other side of the valley, you can enjoy a spectacular view of Yosemite Falls at the **Mountain Room Restaurant** (209/372-1499, 5:30–9:30 P.M. daily May–Oct., 5–8:30 P.M. Sun.–Thurs., 5–9 P.M. Fri.–Sat. Oct.–May, $16–32), part of Yosemite Lodge at the Falls. The glass atrium lets guests at every table take in the view. The menu runs to American food, and drinks are available from the full bar.

GETTING THERE AND AROUND
Car

From the San Francisco Bay Area, Yosemite Valley is about 195 miles, and the drive takes about 4.5 hours. The most efficient way to get to the valley from the Bay Area is to take I-580 east to I-205 to I-5 to Highway 120, and enter through Groveland and the **Big Oak Flat Entrance** on the west side of the park. After you enter the park, it's another 25 miles to the valley, which takes about 45 minutes.

If you plan to drive to most places in Yosemite Valley, be aware that in summer—especially on weekends—traffic and parking can be slow and stressful. If possible, it's a good idea to leave your car parked somewhere during those busy times and use the free shuttle buses to get around.

Bus

The **Yosemite Area Regional Transportation System** (YARTS, 877/989-2787, www.yarts. com) runs daily buses from Mariposa ($8–12 round-trip, $4–6 one-way) and Merced ($18–25 round-trip, $9–13 one-way) to Yosemite Valley.

If you enter the park on one of these buses, you won't have to pay the entrance fee ($20). You can buy tickets on the bus, as well as from several businesses in the area. No reservations are necessary, and children under 12 ride free. You can also take your bicycle on the bus, making a complete no-car vacation a real possibility. Buses run more frequently in summer. Check the YARTS website for current schedules.

Shuttle Services

The free Yosemite Shuttle is particularly active in Yosemite Valley. The **Yosemite Valley** shuttle (7 A.M.–10 P.M. daily year-round) runs every 10–20 minutes, stopping at Yosemite Lodge, the Valley Visitors Center, Curry Village, all campgrounds, and the Happy Isles trailhead. Check the map in the *Yosemite Guide* for a list of numbered shuttle stops.

Glacier Point

The best view of Yosemite Valley may not be from the valley floor. To get a different look at the familiar formations and falls, drive up Glacier Point Road to Glacier Point (16 miles from Chinquapin junction). The trail from the end of the road to the actual point is an easy one—paved and wheelchair accessible—but the vista down into Yosemite Valley is anything but common. The first part of Glacier Point Road stays open all year, except when storms make it temporarily impassable, to allow access to the Badger Pass ski area, but chains may be required.

In summer, park rangers host evening programs at Glacier Point. Check the *Yosemite Guide* for specific listings.

BADGER PASS

Five miles east of Wawona Road on the way toward Glacier Point is Badger Pass, a beautiful section of Yosemite and probably the only one

that's actually busier in winter than in summer. This is the site of the Badger Pass Ski Area, which was California's first-ever downhill ski hill; it is one of only three areas with ski lifts in any national park. In winter, Badger Pass is bustling with downhill skiers, cross-country skiers, ice skaters, sledders, and people drinking hot chocolate. In summer, it's a good starting place for hikes to Glacier Point and nearby.

RECREATION
Badger Pass Ski Area

Downhill skiing at Badger Pass (Glacier Point Rd., 5 miles from Chinquapin turnoff and 15 miles from Wawona, www.yosemitepark.com, 9 A.M.–4 P.M. daily mid-Dec.–mid-Mar. or early Apr.) is a favorite wintertime activity at Yosemite. Badger Pass was the first downhill ski area created in California, and today, it's the perfect resort for families and groups who want a relaxed day or three of moderate skiing. With plenty of beginner runs and classes, Yosemite has helped thousands of children and adults learn to ski and snowboard as friends and family look on from the sundecks at the lodge. There are enough intermediate runs to make it interesting for mid-level skiers as well. Double black-diamond skiers may find Badger Pass too tame for their tastes since there are just a few advanced runs. But everyone agrees that the prices are more reasonable than at Tahoe's big resorts, and the focus is on friendliness and learning rather than showing off and extreme skiing. Downhill ski lessons are available (1 lesson $44–83). Lift tickets run $23–42 for a full day and $18–34 for a half-day. Season passes are also available ($169–434). Ski rentals are available (adults $32.50–42, ages 13–17 $30–37, ages 7–12 $18–22, under age 7 free with a paying adult, over age 64 $30–37, free nonholiday weekdays).

And here's a snowshoe adventure to remember: If you're lucky enough to be in Yosemite during a full moon, or the four days leading up to one, do your best to reserve a spot on one of the **Full Moon Snowshoe Walks** (Badger Pass Day Lodge, reservations 209/372-1240, weather 209/372-1000, Jan.–Mar., $18.50 includes snowshoe rental, $5 if you bring your own, reservations required). These two-hour treks into the snowy forest, not recommended for children under 10, include an expert guide who can help you with your snowshoes and also discuss survival techniques, winter wildlife, folklore about full moons, and more.

Cross-Country Ski School

Glacier Point Road is the only place in Yosemite with groomed tracks for cross-country skiing, but the park has more than 800 miles of trails, and nearly all of them are skiable when the snow gets deep enough. In fact, many places in Yosemite are accessible in winter only on cross-country skis or snowshoes. The Cross-Country Ski School (www.yosemitepark.com/badger-pass_crosscountryskiing.aspx) has classes, rentals (adults $19–23, youths $15–17, under age 13 $7–11), and guided cross-country ski tours.

© HEATHER C. LISTON

Badger Pass in winter

Skiers of any level can have a good day out in the snow on the groomed trails from Badger Pass to Glacier Point. This 21-mile run is wide and well maintained; much of it is flat, so beginners can enjoy it slowly while experts fly past at top speed on skating skis or carry backpacks for overnight hut-to-hut ski trips. Many tributary trails branch off into the backcountry from this main trail; they're much less crowded and can be very beautiful. Just make sure you have a trail map if you decide to explore them, and don't go alone. Conditions can change rapidly in the woods, and things can get hazardous when frozen streams start melting, tree branches block a trail, or darkness falls faster than expected.

Cross-country skiing lessons ($35–49, with rental $46–60) are available, and tours and packages ($120–350 pp) include an overnight trip to **Glacier Point Hut.** The school also offers guided hikes and winter camping trips. In winter, guides from the Nordic Center lead group snowshoe walks to **Dewey Point** (9 A.M.–3 P.M. Wed. and Sun., $50, with snowshoe rental $60).

Hiking

If you love the thrill of heights, head up Glacier Point Road and take a hike up to or along one of the spectacular and slightly scary granite cliffs. Hikes in this area run from quite easy to rigorous, but note that many of the cliff-side trails aren't appropriate for rambunctious children.

PANORAMA TRAIL

The very difficult Panorama Trail (17 miles) runs all the way from Glacier Point to Yosemite Valley with 3,000–4,000 feet of elevation change each way, and can be impassable in winter when snows are heavy. But if you like a challenge, and the views that go with it, you may want to give it a try. The Panorama Trailhead is located at Glacier Point; the road is usually open late May–October. Two miles into the hike, you'll see Illilouette Fall, cross Illiloutte

Creek, and begin walking along Panorama Cliff. In about 0.5 mile, there will be an unmarked turn-off that leads out to Panorama Point. (There is a sheer drop-off at the Point and there are no guardrails, so this detour is not for everyone!) Those who brave it will be rewarded with views of Half Dome, the Mist Trail, Upper and Lower Yosemite Falls, and a sweeping vista of the Valley. Return to the main trail and continue until mile six, where you turn left to join the Mist Trail. Follow the Mist Trail down to the Happy Isles trailhead in Yosemite Valley.

If this sounds like a bit much, you can park a car at one end of the trail and then take the **Glacier Point Tours Bus** (209/372-4386, www.yosemitepark.com, 8:30, 10 A.M., and 1:30 P.M. daily, spring–fall, $25 one-way) to the other end and hike back.

SENTINEL DOME

The two-mile round-trip hike up Sentinel Dome starts at the trailhead just southwest of the end of Glacier Point Road. It is a surprisingly easy walk; the only steep part is climbing the dome at the end of the trail. You can do this hike in 2–3 hours, and you'll find views at the top to make the effort and the high elevation (over 8,000 feet at the top) more than worthwhile. On a clear day, you can see from Yosemite Valley to the High Sierras and all the way to Mount Diablo in the Bay Area to the west. Be sure to bring a camera! Be aware that there are no guardrails or walls to protect you from the long drops along the side of the trail and at the top of the dome.

TAFT POINT AND THE FISSURES

Another not-too-long walk to a magnificent vista point is the hike to Taft Point and the Fissures. To get here, park 1–2 miles southwest of Glacier Point on Glacier Point Road. This two-mile round-trip hike takes you along unusual rock formations called the Fissures, through the always lovely woods, and out to Taft Point. This precarious precipice does not have any walls, only a rickety set of guardrails to keep visitors from plummeting off the point down 2,000 feet to the nearest patch of flat ground. Thrill seekers enjoy challenging themselves to get right up to the edge of the cliff to peer down. Happily for more sedate hikers, the elevation gain from the trailhead to the point is only about 200 feet.

FOUR MILE TRAIL

If you're looking for a mid-level or challenging hike, plus the most spectacular view of all of Yosemite Falls in the park, take the misnamed Four Mile Trail (9.6 miles round-trip) that connects Glacier Point to Southside Drive in Yosemite Valley. It's actually 4.8 miles each way, but who's counting? In summer, the easiest way to take this hike is to start from Glacier Point and hike down to the valley. You can then catch a ride back up to your car on the **Glacier Point Tour Bus** (209/372-4386, www.yosemitepark.com, 8:30 A.M., 10 A.M., and 1:30 P.M. daily spring–fall, adults $25 one-way), but be sure to buy tickets in advance. The steep climb up the trail from the valley can be much harder on the legs and the lungs, but it affords an ascending series of views of Yosemite Falls and Yosemite Valley that grow more spectacular with each switchback.

OSTRANDER LAKE

For a longer high-elevation hike, take the 12.5-mile walk to Ostrander Lake and back. The trailhead is approximately two miles past Bridalveil Creek Road on Glacier Point Road. You can also cross-country ski to the lake in the winter and stay overnight at the local ski hut. This trek can take all day if you're going at a relaxed pace—especially if you're visiting during June–July and stopping to admire the wildflowers in bloom all along the trail. The lake itself is a lovely patch of shining clear water surrounded by granite boulders and picturesque pine trees. Consider starting up the trail in the morning and packing a picnic lunch to enjoy beside the serene water. And remember to bring bug repellent since the still waters of the lake and nearby streams are mosquito breeding grounds during hiking season.

ACCOMMODATIONS AND FOOD

If you're planning an extended stay at Yosemite with friends or family, it might be convenient and economical to rent a condo or house through the **Yosemite West Condominiums** (Yosemite West Community, 7519 Henness Circle, 800/669-9300, www.yosemitelodging.com, $135–155), off Glacier Park Road. Modular buildings can be divided into a number of separate units—or not, if you want to rent a large space for a big group. The studio and loft condos sleep 2–6 and have full kitchens and access to all complex amenities. Luxury suites are actually one-bedroom apartments with full kitchens, pool tables, hot tubs, four-poster beds, and all sorts of other amenities. Two- and three-bedroom apartments sleep 6–8. And a duplex house ($1,180) can actually fit up to 22 guests, so you could fit an entire family reunion or college ski party into one huge house.

The **Glacier Point Snack Stand** (9 A.M.–4 P.M. daily Memorial Day–Oct., $5–10) sells snacks and hot chocolate.

CAMPING

Bridalveil Creek (110 sites, first-come, first served, mid-July–early Sept., $14) is halfway up Glacier Point Road, eight miles from Chinquapin junction and 45 minutes south of the valley. Its season is fairly short due to the snow that blankets this area, but its location along Bridalveil Creek makes it an appealing spot. Sites permit tents and RVs up to 35 feet and include fire pits, picnic tables, a shared bear-proof food locker, and a bathroom with water and flush toilets nearby. In addition, there are three equestrian campsites (877/444-6777, $25, reservations required) and two group sites (www.recreation.gov, $40, reservations required).

GETTING THERE
Car
Glacier Point is in the southwestern quadrant of the park, about an hour's drive from Yosemite Valley. From the Valley Visitors Center, drive 14 miles south to Chinquapin junction, and then make a left turn onto Glacier Point Road. Drive another 16 miles to the end of the road, and park in the lot on the left.

If you're driving from San Francisco directly to Glacier Point, allow at least five hours; it's 213 miles. The most efficient route is to enter through Big Oak Flat, and once you're inside the park, turn right (south) onto Wawona Road (Hwy. 41). In 9.2 miles, you'll come to Glacier Point Road. Turn left and take it 16 miles to the point itself.

If you enter through the South Entrance (Hwy. 41), drive 20 miles to Chinquapin junction, make a right turn onto Glacier Point Road, and take it all the way to the end, about 16 miles.

Glacier Point Road is closed approximately November–May. You can get as far as Badger Pass Ski Area (5 miles) on the road whenever the ski area is open, which is usually December–March; chains may be required.

Bus
The Yosemite Shuttle system does not serve Glacier Point, but during the season when conditions allow, the park's official concessionaire, Delaware North Companies, operates four-hour trips from Yosemite Valley to Glacier Point and back: **Glacier Point Tour Bus** (209/372-4386, www.yosemitepark.com, 8:30 A.M., 10 A.M., and 1:30 P.M. daily spring–fall, adults $41 round-trip, $25 one-way). Tickets can be purchased by telephone (209/372-4386) or in person at the tour desks in Yosemite Lodge, Curry Village, or the Yosemite Village Grocery Store.

Wawona

The small town of Wawona is only four miles from the South Entrance of Yosemite. The historic Wawona Hotel was built in 1917 and also houses a popular restaurant and a store.

SIGHTS
Wawona Visitors Center at Hill's Studio
The Wawona Visitors Center at Hill's Studio (209/375-9531, 8:30 A.M.–5 P.M. daily mid-May–mid-Oct., 9:30 A.M.–4 P.M. Fri.–Sun. mid-Oct.–late Nov.) is right next to the Wawona Hotel, in the former studio and gallery of Thomas Hill, a famous landscape painter from the 1800s. The visitors center is perfect for information gathering; you can also get free wilderness permits (self-register outside

in the off-season) and rent bear-proof canisters ($5 for 2 weeks).

Pioneer Yosemite History Center
Wawona is home to the Pioneer Yosemite History Center (near Wawona Store parking lot, daily year-round). The first thing you'll see as you enter this outdoor display area is a big open barn housing an array of vehicles used over a century ago in Yosemite, including big cushiony carriages for wealthy tourists and oil wagons once used in an ill-conceived attempt to control mosquitoes on the ponds. Farther along, walk under the Vermont-style covered bridge to the main museum area. This rambling, uncrowded stretch of land contains many of the original structures built in the

park. Most were moved here from various remote locations. Informative placards describe the history of Yosemite National Park through its structures, from the military shacks used by the soldiers who were the first park rangers through homes lived in by early settlers in the area presided over by stoic pioneer women.

In summer, visitors can take a 10-minute tour by **horse-drawn carriage** (adults $4, ages 3–12 $3). If you want more help understanding it all, you can also buy a self-guided tour brochure ($0.50) nearby. Check your *Yosemite Guide* for listings of living history programs and live demonstrations held here during the summer.

Mariposa Grove of Giant Sequoias

One of three groves of rare giant sequoia trees in Yosemite, the Mariposa Grove (Wawona Rd./ Hwy. 41, dogs and bicycles not permitted) offers a view of these majestic trees. During high season, a one-hour open-air tram ride meanders through the grove, complete with an audio tour describing the botany and history of this area. You can also walk throughout the grove, taking your time to admire the ecology of the giant sequoia forest. The **Wawona to Mariposa Grove Trail** entails a moderate walk of about six miles from the Wawona Hotel; there are also shorter loop walks that allow you to see some of the most impressive trees in a mile or less. The **Mariposa Grove Museum** (Upper Mariposa Grove, 10 A.M.–4 P.M. daily May–Sept.) is another good place for visitors interested in Sequoias. The museum building is a replica of the cabin of Galen Clark, a former Guardian of Yosemite National Park who is credited as the first nonnative to see Mariposa Grove.

It's best to take the free **Mariposa Grove & Wawona shuttle** (9 A.M.–6 P.M. daily spring–fall, free) to the grove from Wawona or Yosemite Valley in high season to cut down on auto traffic and minimize use of the limited grove parking areas. Note that you cannot

drive all the way to the museum. Either take a short walk to it from the grove's parking lot or take the tram.

RECREATION
Hiking

It's not quite as popular (or crowded) as Yosemite Valley, but the hikes near Wawona in southern Yosemite can be just as scenic and lovely. In addition to the numerous trails that weave throughout the **Mariposa Grove of Giant Sequoias,** there are easy walks along the **Swinging Bridge Loop** (4.8 miles, 2 hours), from the trailhead at the Wawona Store, and up to the more strenuous **Alder Creek Trail** (12 miles, 6–8 hours) from the trailhead on Chilnualna Falls Road.

WAWONA MEADOW LOOP

From the trailhead at the Pioneer Yosemite History Center, start with the easy Wawona Meadow Loop (3.5 miles, 2 hours), a flat and shockingly uncrowded sweep around the lovely Wawona meadow and a somewhat incongruous nine-hole golf course. This wide trail was once fully paved and is still bikeable, but the pavement has eroded over the years, and you'll find much dirt and tree detritus. It is best in late spring because the wildflowers bloom in profusion. For a longer trip, you can extend this walk to five miles, with about 500 feet of elevation gain, by taking the detour at the south end of the meadow.

CHILNUALNA FALLS

If you're up for a hard-core hike and a waterfall experience few who visit Yosemite ever see, take the difficult 8.5-mile trail to Chilnualna Falls, with a 2,300-foot elevation gain. The trailhead is near the Pioneer Yosemite History Center. Plan for 4–6 hours and bring water, snacks, and a trail map. You'll see a few fellow hikers and many tantalizing views of the cascades. Sadly, there's no viewing area, so you'll need to peek through the trees to get the best looks and photos of the falls. The trail runs all the way up to the top of the falls, but be careful to avoid the stream during spring and summer high flow—it's dangerous, what with the waterfall and everything!

Horseback Riding

You'll find more horses than mules at **Wawona Stable** (Pioneer Yosemite History Center, Wawona Rd., 209/375-6502, www.yosemitepark.com/Activities_MuleHorsebackRides_WawonaStable.aspx, 8 A.M.–5 P.M. daily May–Oct., $64–128), and more travelers too— reservations for the rides out of Wawona are strongly recommended. From Wawona you can take a sedate two-hour ride around the historic wagon trail running into the area. Or try the five-hour trip out to Chilnualna Falls. Both of these rides are fine for less experienced riders, and the wagon-trail ride welcomes children with its easy, flat terrain.

Snowshoeing and Cross-Country Skiing

Mariposa Grove maintains winter trails for snowshoeing and cross-country skiing in winter. A popular trail is the **Loop Road** (8 miles round-trip) from the South Entrance to the Mariposa Grove of Sequoias. Pick up a copy of the *Mariposa Grove Winter Trails* guide ($0.50) at the visitors center, or download a copy from the park's website (www.nps.gov/yose).

ENTERTAINMENT AND EVENTS

Listen to the delightful piano music and singing of the legendary Tom Bopp in the **Piano Lounge at the Wawona Hotel** (209/375-1425, Tues.–Sat. Apr.–Dec.) five nights a week throughout Wawona's season. Older visitors especially love his old-style performance and familiar songs, but everyone enjoys the music and entertainment he provides. **Ranger Programs** include "Coffee with a Ranger" (8–8:45 A.M. summer) at the Wawona Campground Amphitheater,

and a nightly campfire. Check the *Yosemite Guide* for specific listings.

ACCOMMODATIONS AND FOOD

The charming **Wawona Hotel** (801/559-5000, www.yosemitepark.com, Mar.–Nov. and Dec. 14–Jan. 1, $225, $148–168 shared bath) opened in 1879 and has been a Yosemite institution ever since. The black-and-white exterior of the hotel complex may remind visitors of a 19th-century Mississippi riverboat. The interior matches the outside well, complete with Victorian wallpaper, antique furniture, and a noticeable lack of in-room TVs and telephones. The Wawona feels more like a huge European pension than an American motel, including guest rooms with shared baths for the more economically minded traveler.

The ◖ **Wawona Dining Room** (Wawona Hotel, 209/375-1425, 7–10 A.M., 11:30 A.M.– 1:30 P.M., and 5:30–9 P.M. daily Apr.–Dec., $19–30) serves upscale California cuisine for reasonable prices to all comers. No reservations are accepted—all seating is first come, first served. The large, white-painted dining room is family-friendly, and the menu offers options for vegetarians as well as devout carnivores; breakfast is always a lavish buffet. You'll probably have to wait for a table on high-season weekends, but the large common area offers seating, drinks, and live piano music (Tues.–Sat.). Note that dining hours for each meal may be slightly shorter in the off-season (late Oct.–Dec.); if you plan to eat at the beginning or the end of a shift, call ahead to make sure they're open.

The **Wawona Golf Shop & Snack Stand** (9 A.M.–5 P.M. daily in season) and the **Wawona Store & Pioneer Gift Shop** (8 A.M.–8 P.M. daily in season) fills the gap when the Wawona Dining Room is closed.

CAMPING

Camp at the lovely and forested **Wawona Campground** (93 sites, 877/444-6777, www.

© CHEE-ONN LEONG/123RF.COM

the Wawona Hotel

recreation.gov, reservations required Apr.–Sept., $20; first-come, first-served Oct.–mid-Apr., $14), one mile north of Wawona. RVs are welcome, although there are no hookups on-site. If you want to camp with your horse, Wawona offers two equestrian sites. The small grocery store in town can provide a few basics, but most services (including showers) can't be found closer than Yosemite Valley.

GETTING THERE

Enter the park at the **South Entrance** (year-round) and continue four miles up Highway 41 (Wawona Rd.) to Wawona. From Wawona, it's another 1.5 hours to Yosemite Valley. Wawona is well served by the Yosemite Shuttle bus system. The **Mariposa Grove & Wawona shuttle** (9 A.M.–6 P.M. daily spring–fall, free) takes passengers among the Wawona Store, the South Entrance, and the Mariposa Grove of Giant Sequoias, where it drops them off at the Mariposa Grove Gift Shop. The **Wawona to Yosemite Valley** shuttle (daily Memorial Day–Labor Day, free) leaves the Wawona Hotel at 8:30 A.M. and the Wawona Store at 8:35 A.M., delivering passengers to Yosemite Valley. It returns to Wawona in the afternoon, leaving Yosemite Lodge at 3:30 P.M.

Tioga Pass and Tuolumne Meadows

Tioga Road (Hwy. 120), Yosemite's own "road less traveled," crosses Yosemite from west to east, leading from the more visited west edge of the park out toward Mono Lake in the eastern Sierra. Along the road, you'll find a number of developed campgrounds, plus a few natural wonders that many visitors to Yosemite never see.

SIGHTS

In the spring, walk out to view the wildflowers at **White Wolf,** about 15 miles east of the Tioga Road junction (turn north on a dirt road to get to the parking lot). Another 12 miles east along Tioga Road, bring out your camera to take in the vista at **Olmstead Point.** Stroll along the sandy beach at **Tenaya Lake,** two miles east

YOSEMITE

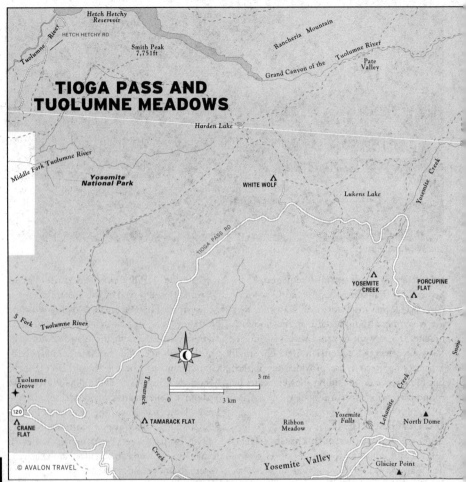

TIOGA PASS AND TUOLUMNE MEADOWS

© AVALON TRAVEL

of Olmstead, while staring up toward **Clouds Rest.** Nearby Tuolumne Meadows is bracketed by **Pothole Dome** on its west end and **Lembert Dome** to the east.

Tuolumne Meadows Visitors Center

The Tuolumne Meadows Visitors Center (209/372-0263, 8 A.M.–7 P.M. daily in summer, 9 A.M.–6 P.M. daily in fall) is in a rustic building not far from the campground and the Tuolumne Meadows Store. Frequent ranger

talks are held in the parking lot throughout the summer; details on upcoming programs are available in the *Yosemite Guide.* Wilderness permits are available year-round, and a separate structure across the parking lot houses large handicapped-accessible restrooms.

Soon after entering the park through the west entrance, you'll come to the **Big Oak Flat Information Station** (209/379-1899, 8 A.M.–5 P.M. daily mid-May–mid-Oct.) on the right. You can get a free wilderness permit

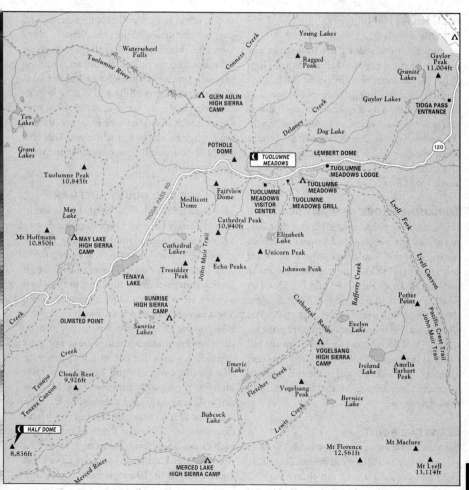

here in the summer when it's open; in winter you can self-register for a permit right outside.

◖ Tuolumne Meadows

Tuolumne Meadows lies along Tioga Road (summer only), about 40 miles from the Crane Flat junction. After miles of soaring rugged mountains, it's almost surprising to come upon these serene grassy High Sierra alpine meadows. In tones of brilliant green, and dotted with wildflowers in spring, the waving grasses support a variety of wildlife. Stop the car and get out for a quiet, contemplative view of the meadows. Or if you prefer a long trek, Tuolumne Meadows serves as a good base camp for high-country backpacking. The short, easy trail to **Soda Springs** and **Parsons Lodge** (1.5 miles, 1 hour), from the trailhead at Lembert Dome, leads past a carbonated spring to the historic Parsons Lodge (10 A.M.–4 P.M. daily in season) before leading to the Tuolumne Meadows Visitors Center.

RECREATION
Hiking

For smaller crowds along the trails, take one or more of the many scenic hikes along Tioga Road. Just be aware that they don't call it "high country" for nothing; the elevation starts at 8,500 feet and goes higher on many trails. If you're not in great shape, or if you have breathing problems, take the elevation into account when deciding which trails to explore.

Trailheads are listed in west-to-east order along Tioga Road.

TUOLUMNE GROVE OF GIANT SEQUOIAS

If you're aching to see some giant trees but were put off by the parking problems at Mariposa Grove, try the Tuolumne Grove of Giant Sequoias. Parking and the trailhead are at the junction of Tioga Road and Old Big Oak Flat Road. This 2.5-mile round-trip hike takes you down about 400 vertical feet into the grove, which contains more than 20 mature giant sequoias. (You do have to climb back up the hill to get to your car.) While you'll likely see other visitors, the smaller crowds make this grove an attractive alternative to Mariposa, especially in the high season.

OLMSTEAD POINT

For nonathletes who just want a short walk to an amazing view, Olmstead Point (Tioga Rd., 1–2 miles west of Tenaya Lake, shuttle stop 12) may be the perfect destination. The trail is only 0.5 mile round-trip from the parking lot to the point, and it exists to show off Clouds Rest in all its grandeur. Half Dome peeks out behind Clouds Rest, and right at the trail parking lot, a number of large glacial erratic boulders draw almost as many visitors as the point itself.

TENAYA LAKE

A great place to start your high-country exploration, the loop trail to Tenaya Lake (Tioga Rd., 12 miles west of the east entrance, shuttle stop 9) offers an easy walk, sunny beaches, and possibly the most picturesque views in all of Yosemite. The trail around the lake is about 2.5 miles, and the only difficult part is fording the outlet stream at the west end of the lake, since the water gets chilly and can be high in the spring and early summer. If the rest of your group is sick of hiking and scenery, you can leave them on the beach while you take this easy 1–2-hour stroll. Just remember the mosquito repellent.

MAY LAKE AND MOUNT HOFFMAN

May Lake (May Lake Trailhead, 1 mile southwest of Tenaya Lake on Tioga Rd., shuttle stop 11) sits peacefully at the base of the sloping granite of Mount Hoffman. While the hike to May Lake is only two miles round-trip, the elevation gain from the trailhead up to the lake is a steady, steep 500 feet. One of Yosemite's High Sierra camps is located here, which makes this hike popular with the sort of visitors who enjoy the lesser-known high-country areas. For more energetic hikers, a difficult trail leads from the lake another two miles and 2,000 vertical feet higher to the top of Mount Hoffman. Much of this walk is along granite slabs and rocky trails, and some of it is cross-country, but you'll have clear views of Cathedral Peak, Mount Clark, Half Dome, and Clouds Rest along the way. As you pass May Lake, you'll see May Lake High Sierra Camp at the lake's southeast corner. The final part of the climb to Mount Hoffman's summit, at 10,850 feet, is very rocky, but there is a narrow trail through the boulders. On top is a nice flat plateau where you can relax and stay awhile, enjoying outstanding vistas of the entire park. Mount Hoffman is right in the center, so all of Yosemite is laid out around you.

ELIZABETH LAKE

The trail to Elizabeth Lake, from the trailhead at Tuolumne Campground and John Muir Trail (shuttle stop 5), begins at Tuolumne Meadows and climbs almost 1,000 vertical feet up to the lake, with most of the climb during the first mile of the 4.8-mile, 4–5-hour round-trip. Evergreens ring the lake, and the steep granite Unicorn Peak rises high above it. This stunning little lake makes a perfect photo op that your friends won't necessarily recognize as Yosemite.

GAYLOR LAKES

Hikers willing to tackle somewhat longer, steeper treks will find an amazing array of small scenic lakes within reach of Tioga Road. Gaylor Lakes Trail, from the trailhead on Tioga Road at the Yosemite Park border (seasonal shuttle), starts high, at almost 10,000 feet, and climbs a steep 600 vertical feet up the pass to the Gaylor Lakes valley. Once you're in the valley, you can wander around the five lovely lakes, stopping to admire the views out to the mountains surrounding Tuolumne Meadows or visiting the abandoned 1870s mine site above Upper Gaylor Lake. The total hike is about three miles (2 hours) if you don't wander around the valley. The crowd-averse will enjoy this trek, which is one of Yosemite's less-populated scenic hikes.

NORTH DOME

For an unusual look at a classic Yosemite landmark, take the strenuous North Dome Trail from the trailhead at Porcupine Creek, through the woods, and out to the dome, which is right across the valley from Half Dome. You'll hike almost nine miles round-trip, with a few hills thrown in, but getting to stare right at the face of Half Dome and Clouds Rest just beyond at what feels like eye-level makes the effort worth it.

CATHEDRAL LAKES

If you can't get enough of Yosemite's granite-framed alpine lakes, take the moderate to strenuous long walk out to one or both of the Cathedral Lakes (7 miles round-trip, 4–6 hours) from the trailhead at Tuolumne Meadows Visitors Center. From Tuolumne Meadows, you'll climb about 800 vertical feet

over 3.5 miles, depending on which lake you choose. These picture-perfect lakes show off the dramatic alpine peaks, surrounding lodgepole pines, and crystalline waters of Yosemite to their best advantage. Be sure to bring your camera, water, and food for a lovely picnic.

GLEN AULIN TRAIL

The strenuous Glen Aulin Trail, from the trailhead at Tuolumne Stable to Tuolumne Fall and White Cascade, is part of the John Muir Trail, and several of its forks branch off to pretty little lakes and other nice spots in the area. From Tuolumne Meadows to Tuolumne Fall and back is 11 miles round-trip (6–8 hours), with some steep and rocky areas. But if you've got the lungs for it, you'll be rewarded by fabulous views of the Tuolumne River alternately pooling and cascading right beside the trail. This hike may get a bit crowded in the high season. In the summer, many trekkers trade their dusty hiking clothes for swimsuits and cool off in the pools at the base of both White Cascade and Tuolumne Fall. A great way to do this hike is to enter the High Sierra Camp lottery, and if you win, arrange to stay the night at the Glen Aulin camp. If you do this, you can take your hike a few miles farther, downstream to California Fall, Le Conte Fall, and finally Waterwheel Fall.

Horseback Riding

The **Tuolumne Meadows Stable** (209/372-8427, www.yosemitepark.com, 8 A.M.–5 P.M. daily May–Oct., $64–85) is accessible on a short dirt road on the north side of Tioga Road past the Tuolumne Visitors Center. You can get the perfect overview of the Yosemite high country by taking the introductory-level two-hour ride. For a longer ride deeper into the landscape, do the four-hour trip that passes Twin Bridges and Tuolumne Falls. An all-day ride with a variable route beckons the adventurous traveler, but you need to be in good shape and be an experienced rider for this one. To customize a longer pack trip, call 209/372-8348.

Snowshoeing and Cross-Country Skiing

Crane Flat has a variety of ungroomed winter trails for snowshoeing and cross-country skiing. Pick up a copy of the *Crane Flat Winter Trails* guide ($0.50) at the visitors center or download a copy from the park's website (www.nps.gov/yose).

ACCOMMODATIONS AND FOOD

Tuolumne Meadows Lodge (801/559-5000, www.yosemitepark.com, early June–mid-Sept., $104) offers rustic lodgings and good food in a gorgeous subalpine meadow setting. Expect no electricity, no private baths, and no other plush amenities. What you will find are small, charming wood-frame tent cabins that sleep up to four, with wood stoves for heat and candles for light. Central facilities here include restrooms, hot showers, and a dining room. The location is perfect for starting or finishing a backcountry trip through the high-elevation areas of the park.

The **Tuolumne Meadows Lodge Restaurant** (5:45–8 P.M. daily early June–mid-Sept., $7–27) serves dinner nightly in a rustic central building near the tent cabins. The quality of the food is better than you'd expect in what feels like a summer-camp mess hall, and it's priced accordingly. Order the Sierra flatiron steak, wild salmon linguine, or the chef's special nightly creations; everything comes with generous sides of salad, potatoes, and vegetables. Seafood is selected in accordance with the Monterey Bay Aquarium's recommendations for health and sustainability, and the vegetables are locally grown and organic. If you don't want a big meal, or don't want to spend too much money, the good news is that anyone, not just children or early birds, can order from the "Lighter Eaters" menu, with its low-priced small-portions of hot dogs, hamburgers, and macaroni and cheese.

Right next to Tuolumne Campground, **Tuolumne Meadows Grill** (8 A.M.–5 P.M. daily June–Sept., $10) offers sustenance for hungry campers. Breakfasts include filling egg and biscuit sandwiches and pancakes, while lunch

Tuolumne Meadows Lodge

© HEATHER C. LISTON

YOSEMITE

offers burgers and chili. Eat outside on the accompanying picnic benches with views of Tuolumne Meadows across the road.

Another rustic high-country lodging option, the **White Wolf Lodge** (801/559-5000, www.yosemite-park.com, mid-June–Sept., $95–115) sits back in the trees off Tioga Road. Here you can rent either the standard wood-platform, wood stove–heated tent cabin with use of central restroom and shower facilities, or a solid-wall cabin with a private bath, limited electricity, and daily maid service. All cabins and tent cabins at White Wolf include linens and towels. Breakfast and dinner ($20, reservations required) are served family-style in the White Wolf dining room; they'll also make you a box lunch to take along on your day hikes. Amenities are few, but breathtaking scenery is everywhere. Take a day hike to Harden Lake or a horseback ride through the backcountry. White Wolf works well for visitors who prefer smaller crowds, since the lodge has only 24 tents and four cabins.

CAMPING

Yosemite visitors who favor the high country tend to prefer to camp rather than to stay in a lodge. Accordingly, most of Yosemite's campgrounds are north of the valley, away from the largest crowds (excluding the High Sierra Camps, which are also up north).

If you're entering the park from the west side on Highway 120, the first campground you'll come to is **Hodgdon Meadow** (102 sites, 877/444-6777, www.recreation.gov, reservations required mid-Apr.–mid-Oct., $20; first-come, first-served late Oct.–early Apr., $14). This can be an excellent choice for people who drive up Friday night after work; you can set up camp right after entering the park and won't have to drive for miles in the dark. At 4,900 feet, Hodgdon Meadow can accommodate tents or RVs, although there are no hookups for electricity, water, or sewage. Sites include fire rings and picnic tables, and there are bear-proof food lockers, water, and flush toilets. Supplies are

available at Crane Flat, and the closest showers are in Yosemite Valley. Pets are permitted.

At the intersection of Big Oak Flat Road and Tioga Road is **Crane Flat** (166 sites, reservations required, 877/444-6777, www.recreation.gov, mid-July–Sept., $20). Crane Flat is 17 miles from Yosemite Valley at 6,200 feet elevation. Although it does allow RVs up to 35 feet as well as tents, there are no electric, water, or sewer hookups. Sites include fire pits and picnic tables, and there are bear-proof food lockers, water, and flush toilets. Pets are permitted. There is a small grocery store down the road at Crane Flat gas station; the closest showers are in Yosemite Valley.

Heading east along Tioga Road, **Tamarack Flat** (52 sites, Tioga Rd., first-come, first-served, July–early Oct., $10) keeps you reasonably close to Yosemite Valley, but still in a fairly primitive environment. Tamarack Flat is at 6,300 feet elevation and is a tent-only campground. Although there are picnic tables and bear-proof food lockers, there are no restroom facilities except pit toilets, and you must bring your own water or be prepared to treat the water you find.

Serene **White Wolf** (74 sites, first-come, first-served, late July–early Sept., $14) is at 8,000 feet elevation on Tioga Road; the turnoff is on the left down a narrow side-road. Sites accommodate tents and RVs up to 27 feet and include fire pits and picnic tables, and there are bear-proof food lockers, water, and flush toilets; pets are permitted. Crane Flat is the closest place for supplies.

Ditch the traffic and the crowded central visitor areas and head for **Yosemite Creek** (75 sites, first-come, first-served, late July–mid-Sept., Sat.–Sun. only mid-Sept.–mid-Oct., $10). Yosemite Creek flows right through this tent-only campground, a perfect spot for cooling off on a hot day. Yosemite Creek offers few amenities—fire pits, picnic tables, and bear-proof food lockers but no groceries, showers, or water, and only vault toilets. In the same vicinity is **Porcupine Flat** (52 sites, first-come, first-served, June 1—Oct. 15, $10) at 8,100 feet with some limited RV sites, but no water.

◖**Tuolumne Meadows** (304 sites, Tioga Rd. at Tuolumne Meadows, 877/444-6777, www. recreation.gov, July–late Sept., reservations strongly advised, tents and RVs $20, equestrian sites $25) has one of the largest campgrounds in the park, with more than 300 sites, including four horse sites. Half of the sites are available by reservation; the remaining half are first-come, first-served. Tuolumne can be crowded for the whole of its season, and the campground does tend to fill up every night, so don't just show up and assume you will find a spot. Tuolumne is accessible for RVs up to 35 feet, although it does not have electric, water, or sewage hookups. Sites include fire rings and picnic tables, and there are bear-proof food lockers, water, and flush toilets. Leashed pets are permitted. Food is available at nearby Tuolumne Meadows Lodge and the Tuolumne Grill, but the closest showers are in Yosemite Valley. Tuolumne Meadows is at about 8,600 feet elevation, which means nights can get quite chilly even in midsummer; you're might wake up to frost on your tent by the end of the season in late September.

The ◖**High Sierra Camps** (801/559-5000, www.yosemitepark.com/accommodations_highsierra_howtoapply.aspx, June or July–Sept., lodging, dinner, and breakfast adults $151, ages 7–12 $91, sack lunches adults $15.25, children $7.75) at Yosemite offer far more than your average backcountry campground. Want to get into the wilderness, but don't want to carry a heavy pack with all your stuff? The High Sierra Camps provide tent cabins with amenities, breakfast and dinner in camp, and a sack lunch to take along during the day. Choose from among the Merced Lake, Vogelsang, Glen Aulin, May Lake, and Sunrise Camp—or hike from one to another if you're lucky enough to get a spot. Why do you need luck? Because you can't just walk up to a High Sierra Camp and expect to find a bed. Starting September 1, a lottery takes place for spots at High Sierra Camps through the following summer. You must submit an application to join the lottery; even if you get a spot, there's no guarantee you'll get your preferred dates. Check the website during the high season (June–Sept.) to see if any dates are available. The High Sierra camps have a limited number of spaces available for hikers looking for dinner and breakfast (801/559-4909, adults $46, ages 7–12 $23), but not for overnight campers.

The bottom line? If you want to take advantage of the Yosemite backcountry, it's best to plan for a summer when you can be flexible with your dates, and start making your arrangements a year in advance.

GETTING THERE AND AROUND
By Car

Tuolumne Meadows is located along Tioga Road (Hwy. 120), which runs all the way across the park to the eastern boundary. At Tioga Pass, the east entrance, Highway 120 becomes Tioga Pass Road. Although you'll sometimes hear it referred to as Tioga Pass Road, technically that name does not apply within Yosemite.

From the west, Highway 120 becomes Big Oak Flat Road at the Big Oak Flat park entrance. In nine miles, at Crane Flat junction, the left fork becomes Tioga Road. The Tuolumne Meadows Visitors Center is 38 miles from the west entrance. To get to Tioga Road from Yosemite Valley, take Northside Road to Big Oak Flat Road. At the Tioga Road junction, turn east.

Tioga Road is always closed in winter, and remember that "winter" can come at almost any time at this elevation. To check weather conditions and road closures, call 209/372-0200.

Shuttle and Bus

In summer, the free **Tuolumne Meadows** shuttle (7 A.M.–7 P.M. daily June–mid-Sept., weather permitting) runs along Tioga Road between Olmstead Point and the Tuolumne

Meadows Lodge. Trips begin at 7 A.M. at Tuolumne Meadows Lodge and run every half hour, stopping at the Dog Lake Parking area, the Tuolumne Meadows Wilderness Center, Lembert Dome, Tuolumne Meadows Campground and Store, Tuolumne Meadows Visitors Center, Cathedral Lakes Trailhead, Pothole Dome, the east end of Tenaya Lake, Sunrise Lakes Trailhead at the west end of Tenaya Lake, May Lake Trailhead, and Olmsted Point. Going the other direction, the first bus leaves Olmstead Point at 7:30 A.M. daily. Limited service is available to the Mono Pass Trailhead and Tioga Road–Gaylor Lakes Trailhead, on the east end of this route.

July–September, Delaware North Companies offers a **guided bus tour** (209/372-4386, www.yosemitepark.com, adults $5–23, children half price) between Yosemite Valley and Tuolumne Meadows. The coach makes multiple stops, starting from Curry Village (8 A.M.) and ending at Tuolumne Meadows Lodge (arriving at 10:35 A.M.). It departs Tuolumne Meadows again at 2:05 P.M. for the return trip. Fares are prorated if you only want to travel part of the way.

Hetch Hetchy

One of the most politically controversial areas in California, Hetch Hetchy (Hetch Hetchy Rd. past the Hetch Hetchy park entrance), about 30 minutes north of Highway 120, was once a valley similar to Yosemite Valley. It is now Hetch Hetchy Reservoir, with 1,972 acres of surface area, a maximum depth of 312 feet, and a capacity of 117 billion gallons. Hetch Hetchy supplies famously clean, clear water (plus some hydroelectric power) to the city of San Francisco and other parts of the Bay Area. But many environmental activists—beginning with the patron saint of Yosemite himself, John Muir, who opposed the project before it had even begun—see the reservoir's existence as an affront, and lobby to have O'Shaughnessy Dam torn down and

© HEATHER C. LISTON

Hetch Hetchy

YOSEMITE

the valley returned to its former state of natural beauty. For those of us who didn't have the privilege of seeing this spot before the dam was built, it's almost difficult to imagine how it could be even more beautiful than it is today. The water is deep and blue, the trees around its perimeter cast stunning reflections into its calm surface, the gushing waterfalls along the sides are some of the most gorgeous in the whole park, and the hikes surrounding Hetch Hetchy are outstanding.

O'SHAUGHNESSY DAM

Named for Michael M. O'Shaughnessy, the original chief engineer of the Hetch Hetchy Project, O'Shaughnessy Dam is a massive curved gravity dam that turns part of the Tuolumne River into Hetch Hetchy Reservoir. It originally opened in 1923 at 344 feet high; a later phase of construction, completed in 1938, raised it to its current size of 426 feet high and 900 feet long.

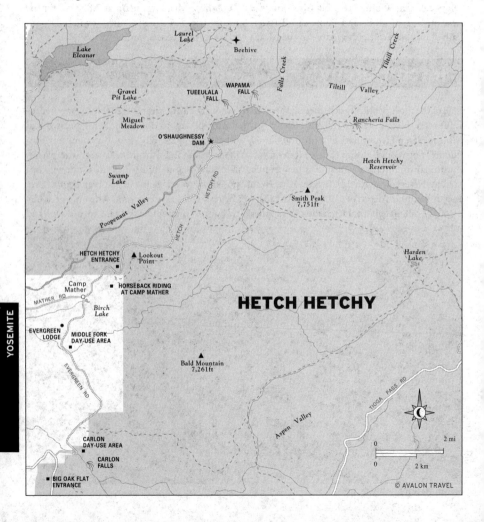

© GEORGE JEN

O'Shaughnessy Dam

RECREATION
Hiking

At less than 4,000 feet in elevation, Hetch Hetchy is one of the lowest parts of Yosemite; it gets less snow and has a longer hiking season than many other areas of the park. It's also warmer here in summer, so you may want to plan a spring or fall visit. The relative warmth, combined with the abundance of water, may be one reason rattlers and other snakes seem particularly common in this area. Do not let that deter you—snakes really, really do not want to mess with people, and they'll get off the trail in time to avoid an encounter as long as they sense you coming.

In addition to the hikes listed are the moderate-to-difficult trails to **Lookout Point** (2 miles, 1 hour) and the more strenuous **Smith Peak** (13.5 miles, 6–8 hours) and **Poopenaut Valley** (3 miles, 2 hours), all starting from the Hetch Hetchy Entrance Station.

WAPAMA FALL

If you like waterfalls, you'll love the easy-to-moderate hike to Wapama Fall (5 miles round-trip, 2 hours). Begin by crossing O'Shaughnessy Dam and then follow the Wapama Falls Trail (also known as Rancheria Falls Camp Trail) through the tunnel and along the shore of the reservoir. Along the way, you'll also see close-up views of the spectacular **Tueeulala Fall.** Tueeulala is set back in the hillside a little, so you can get some great photos of it. Wapama Falls comes splashing down right onto the trail, so you'll experience it in a whole different way—and you'll probably want to keep your camera safely packed away. For a longer hike, bring a large poncho or rain gear to protect yourself and your pack before stepping onto the wooden bridge that crosses under these falls. On a hot day, the shower could be a very welcome treat.

A word of warning: The amount of water flowing over Tueeulala and Wapama Falls varies greatly with the season and recent

YOSEMITE

JOHN MUIR

The best known among our nation's conservationists is John Muir, a Scottish immigrant raised and educated in Wisconsin. It was while roaming the fields and woods there that he first developed his love of nature. After three years at the University of Wisconsin, Muir traveled the northern United States and Canada and then later from Indianapolis to the Gulf of Mexico, a trip which he recounted in *A Thousand-Mile Walk to the Gulf*. After contracting malaria in Florida, Muir abandoned plans to travel to South America and sailed to California instead, arriving in San Francisco in 1868. He immediately made for Yosemite and was never the same.

"I have run wild," he later wrote of Yosemite's ruggedness. "As long as I live, I'll hear waterfalls and birds and winds sing. I'll interpret the rocks, learn the language of flood, storm, and the avalanche. I'll acquaint myself with the glaciers and wild gardens, and get as near the heart of the world as I can." Muir focused his energy toward Yosemite Valley for the following decade. He became noted for tales of his adventures traveling throughout the valley and for encouraging others to visit. He was the first to theorize that the valley was carved by glacier; in 1871, he found an active glacier in the Sierra Nevada, adding credence to this theory. Muir remained in the valley and continued to explore what it had to offer, to sketch and write, and to shape what historian Kevin Starr called a "distinctly Californian relationship to the outdoors." He would go on to write 300 articles and 10 books on his travels around the world and into the Sierra Nevada.

Muir married in 1880 and settled in Martinez, spending his time as a fruit rancher alongside his father-in-law—but that did not take hold of his attention quite like the Sierra Nevada. Muir and *Century Magazine* editor Robert Underwood Johnson were in northern Yosemite in 1889 when the two planned a campaign to transform Yosemite Valley into a national park. The campaign was successful and Congress established Yosemite National Park in 1890.

Muir knew that an organization would be needed to protect Yosemite. As it so happened, a group of University of California professors, artists, and attorneys others were interested in promoting recreation by making the Sierra Nevada and Yosemite Valley more accessible. Muir joined these and others interested in forming an alpine club, which ultimately became the Sierra Club. Incorporated on May 28, 1892, the Sierra Club was formed "to explore, enjoy, and render accessible the mountain regions of the Pacific Coast; to publish authentic information concerning them." It also meant to "enlist the support and cooperation of the people and government in preserving the forests and other natural features of the Sierra Nevada." Muir was the Sierra Club's president until his death in 1914.

Muir's writing expressed his spiritual connection with the outdoors and drew the attention of a wide range of people, including at least one president. Muir's 1901 book *Our National Parks* attracted the interest of Theodore Roosevelt. The president visited with Muir in Yosemite two years later and it was there that the two laid the base for Roosevelt's conservation programs.

There were many battles waged by Muir and the Sierra Club to protect the Sierra Nevada, but perhaps none so striking as the one to prevent the damming of Hetch Hetchy within Yosemite National Park. Hetch Hetchy Valley contained one of the most unique and diverse ecosystems in the world—Muir called it "one of nature's rarest and most precious mountain temples." However, in 1913 San Francisco won congressional approval to build O'Shaughnessy Dam in order to provide water for burgeoning San Francisco. The dam would hold back the pristine Tuolumne River and submerge the valley's meadows and ancient forests under 300 feet of water. Muir was heartbroken and died the following year in Los Angeles while on a visit to his daughter.

The fight to protect Hetch Hetchy Valley may have failed, but Muir's efforts spurred an international conservation movement that continues to this day. There remains an active effort to restore the Hetch Hetchy Valley (www.hetchhetchy.org). Today Muir's name and legacy graces numerous schools, colleges, libraries, boulevards, wilderness areas, and national monuments. A vast collection of Muir's writings and sketches are held at the John Muir Center in the Holt-Atherton Special Collections section of the University of the Pacific Library in Stockton. Muir's home in Martinez is now the **John Muir National Historic Site** (www.nps.gov/jomu/index.htm).

© HEATHER C. LISTON

Tueeulala and Wapama Falls

precipitation in the park. In spring, water can be especially abundant and powerful. Although thousands of hikers have passed through here safely over the years, and many families with young children enjoy playing in the falls, there are times when they can be quite dangerous. In June 2011 two experienced male backpackers were killed when they tried to cross under the falls during an unusually high runoff. If you go, follow any posted restrictions and use good judgment to stay safe.

RANCHERIA FALLS
A longer day hike, also a recommended backpacking trip, is the 13.4-mile round-trip (6–8 hours) Rancheria Falls Camp Trail, which begins at O'Shaughnessy Dam and continues past Wapama Falls along the shore of Hetch Hetchy Reservoir. This trail can be done comfortably in one day by fit hikers. The terrain is rolling, with some up and some down each way, and the total elevation gain is less than 700 feet.

Along the way, you'll pass Tueeulala Fall and become one with Wapama Falls (remember to bring your rain gear). You'll continue along the same path, but with far fewer people around as you complete the journey to Rancheria Falls. Beautiful views of Hetch Hetchy Reservoir continue most of the way. You'll walk through pine forests, on stone stairs, across creeks, and past sunny overlooks. Large flat granite slabs beside Rancheria Falls make a great place for lunch before you turn around to return the same way.

CARLON FALLS
For a short, easy hike that still includes a nice waterfall at the end, try the hike to Carlon Falls (4 miles, easy). The actually trail begins outside the Yosemite park boundaries, in the Stanislaus National Forest, but enters the park soon after. The trail follows the South Fork of the Tuolumne River and blooms with wildflowers in the spring. The payoff at the end, after one brief uphill climb, is the lovely Carlon

YOSEMITE

Falls. This year-round waterfall is much smaller than dazzling superstars like Bridalveil Fall, but it's no less attractive in its own way and much more approachable. You may even want to play in the river nearby or have a picnic on the rocks. To get to the trailhead from the Big Oak Flat Entrance, drive north on Highway 120 for one mile. Bear right onto Evergreen Road, toward Mather and Hetch Hetchy, and continue another mile. Just past the Carlon Day Use Area is a pullout on the right with room for a few cars.

Backpacking

A great backpacking destination from Hetch Hetchy is Rancheria Falls. This 6.5-mile (one-way) trek along the **Rancheria Falls Camp Trail** begins at O'Shaughnessy Dam and continues past Wapama Falls along the shore of Hetch Hetchy Reservoir. The terrain is rolling, meaning there's some up and some down each way, but no major mountains to climb on the way to your destination. The total elevation gain is less than 700 feet. When you get to Rancheria Falls, you'll find a beautiful woodsy area with plenty of space for multiple visitors to set up tents and enjoy some peace. The sense of privacy and seclusion here is enhanced by the sound of the nearby falls, which muffles the noise of human activity. Rancheria Falls isn't the kind of waterfall that crashes down from high atop a mountain; it's a wide expanse with water flowing gradually over massive rocks. You can wade in and fill your water bottle as long as you treat the water before drinking it. This area makes a good base camp for challenging day hikes.

ACCOMMODATIONS

The **Evergreen Lodge** (33160 Evergreen Rd., Groveland, 209/379-2606, www.evergreen.com, $170–370) has 88 cabins in a variety of styles and sizes available for rent. The location on Evergreen Road is only one mile from the Hetch Hetchy Entrance to the park and seven miles from the Big Oak Flat Entrance. Although

most visitors to Evergreen Lodge are here for the easy access to Yosemite, it is almost a destination in itself with a summer camp atmosphere and organized activities like campfire sing-alongs, bingo, and s'mores-making. The largest accommodation onsite is the 2,500-square foot John Muir House ($575–1,050 per night, sleeps 10), which has three bedrooms and a loft, plus a private deck with a hot tub.

CAMPING

There are no developed campgrounds in the Hetch Hetchy region of the park. The **Hetch Hetchy Backpackers' Campground** is next to the overnight parking lot at the end of Hetch Hetchy Road. To backpack overnight in the Hetch Hetchy area, you need a bear canister for your food and a wilderness permit (reservation $5 plus $5 pp) from the Hetch Hetchy Entrance Station (209/372-0200, 7 A.M.–9 P.M. daily May 1–Labor Day).

GETTING THERE

Hetch Hetchy is in the northwest corner of Yosemite National Park. The Hetch Hetchy Entrance is about 10 miles north of the Big Oak Flat Entrance on Highway 120. From Highway 120, take the Hetch Hetchy turnoff onto Evergreen Road, then follow Evergreen Road north for 7.2 miles. At the town of Mather, turn onto Hetch Hetchy Road and proceed another 16 miles through the gate and to the parking lot near O'Shaughnessy Dam.

If you're already in the park, you have to leave through the Big Oak Flat Entrance and onto Highway 120 before reentering at the Hetch Hetchy Entrance. It takes about 1.25–1.5 hours to get to Hetch Hetchy from Yosemite Valley, a distance of about 40 miles.

Hetch Hetchy Reservoir is about 185 miles from San Francisco, and the drive takes about four hours. The road to Hetch Hetchy is open year-round, except in extreme weather conditions, but the park gate is only open 8 A.M.–7 P.M.

Practicalities

RESERVATIONS

If you plan to spend the night in the park, advance reservations for overnight accommodations are essential. All lodgings, including campsites, fill up quickly—up to months in advance. For reservations and details on lodging in the park, you must contact Yosemite's concessionaire, **Delaware North Companies** (DNC, 801/559-5000, www.yosemitepark. com). DNC books reservations for Yosemite as well as many other national parks, but they are not located near Yosemite and cannot answer park-specific questions. The website list lodging rates, but always confirm prices and other details with a reservation agent.

Yosemite has 13 campgrounds, seven of which are available by reservation. Campground reservations are required March 15–November and are absolutely necessary April–September. Yosemite National Park campgrounds are managed by **Recreation.gov** (877/444-6777, www.recreation. gov, 7 A.M.–9 P.M. daily Mar.–Oct., 7 A.M.–7 P.M. daily Nov.–Feb.). Campsite availability is released in one-month blocks, and you can book up to five months in advance. Only two site reservations at a time are permitted per booking.

When reservations become available in the campgrounds, booking can become competitive. You'll want to be online, or to start calling, first thing in the morning the day sites become available. Note that the reservation system works on Eastern time. If you're on Pacific time, and new sites become available at 10 A.M., you need to get on the phone at 7 A.M.

INFORMATION AND SERVICES
Banks and Post Offices

A number of ATMs are available throughout Yosemite. **Citizens Bank** (www.citizensbank. com) maintains cash machines inside the park at the Village Store, Degnan's Deli, the lobby of Yosemite Lodge at the Falls, the Curry Village Gift and Grocery Store, the Wawona Pioneer Gift & Grocery, the Crane Flat Store, the Ahwahnee Lodge, the Tuolumne Meadows store (seasonal), and the Badger Pass Ski Area (seasonal). In addition, there is a **Yosemite Credit Union** ATM in Yosemite Village at the Yosemite Art & Education Center.

Several **post offices** provide mailing services. Look for a post office in Yosemite Village (8:30 A.M.–5 P.M. Mon.–Fri., 10 A.M.–noon Sat.), inside Yosemite Lodge (12:30–2:45 P.M. Mon.–Fri.), in El Portal (8:30 A.M.–12:30 P.M. and 1:30–5 P.M. Mon.–Fri.), and in Wawona (9 A.M.–5 P.M. Mon.–Fri., 9 A.M.–noon Sat.).

Gas and Automotive Services

There is no gas available anywhere in Yosemite Valley. The nearest gas stations in the park are at **El Portal, Wawona,** and **Crane Flat,** and at **Tuolumne Meadows** (June–Oct.). All gas stations are open 24 hours and are pay-at-the-pump with debit or credit cards. There's gas in Mariposa at **Pioneer Texaco** (5177 Hwy. 140, Mariposa, 209/966-2136), which also has a minimart.

If your car breaks down, you can take it to the **Yosemite Village Garage** (9002 Village Dr., off Northside Dr., Yosemite Village, 209/372-8320, 8 A.M.–5 P.M. daily, towing 24 hours daily). Because it's the only game in town, expect to pay a high premium for towing and repairs.

Laundry, Groceries, and Showers

There are laundry facilities available at the **Housekeeping Camp** (8 A.M.–10 P.M. daily Apr.–Oct.) inside the Curry Village complex. Several expensive, crowded, and limited-stock grocery stores are located in the park: the **Curry Village** Gift and Grocery (8 A.M.–9 P.M. daily), the **Yosemite Lodge** Gift and Grocery

(8 A.M.–8 P.M. daily), the **Crane Flat Store** (9 A.M.–5 P.M. daily), and the **Wawona Store and Pioneer Gift Shop** (8 A.M.–6 P.M. daily). In summer, you can also get groceries in the **Housekeeping Camp** grocery (8 A.M.–6 P.M. daily Apr.–Oct.) and the **Tuolumne Meadows** store (9 A.M.–6 P.M. daily spring–late Sept.).

Showers are available at **Curry Village** (24 hours daily year-round, $5) and **Housekeeping Camp** (8 A.M.–10 P.M. daily Apr.–Oct., $5).

Media and Communications

The official *Yosemite Guide* is published several times a year by the park. This paper provides general information about the park and its services. More important, it has a detailed schedule of all classes, events, programs, and so on for the upcoming weeks. You'll receive a copy when you enter the park at one of the entrance stations; you can also download it (www.nps.gov/yose) ahead of time.

Internet access is available in a few spots in Yosemite Valley. The only place you can connect your own laptop is inside Yosemite Lodge. Guests of the lodge can use the wireless service at no extra charge; nonguests are charged $5.95. In Curry Village, wireless Internet access is available in the lounge for Curry Village guests only. Guests of the Ahwahnee Hotel have access to wireless Internet service. Internet kiosks are available in Degnan's Deli (209/372-8454, 7 A.M.–5 P.M. daily year-round, $0.25 per minute, summer only), and free Internet access is available at the Yosemite Valley Branch Library (Girls Club Bldg., 9000 Cedar Ct., 209/372-4552, www.mariposalibrary.org/yosemite, 2–5 P.M. Mon., 8:30 A.M.–12:30 P.M. Tues., 2–6 P.M. Wed., 4–7 P.M. Thurs.) in Yosemite Valley.

Medical Services

The park maintains its own clinic, the **Yosemite Medical Clinic** (209/372-4637) in Yosemite Village at the floor of the valley. It's got a 24-hour emergency room, other services available 9 A.M.–7 P.M., and a domestic violence crisis center. **Dental services** (209/372-4200) are also available adjacent to the medical center.

Wilderness Permits

There is a wilderness center near each of the visitors centers (at Big Oak Flat, both are in the same building). The Tuolumne wilderness center closes at the end of September, and the others close at the end of October; they all reopen in April or May. In summer, you can get a free wilderness permit in any of the wilderness offices. The permit allows access to backcountry trails anywhere in the park. When the wilderness centers are closed, you can get permits in the visitors centers. And when the visitors centers are closed, you can self-register for permits right outside each visitors center. To self-register during the off-season, you need to go to the office in the district where you plan to hike. When wilderness offices and visitors centers are open, they rent bear-proof canisters ($5 for up to 2 weeks, $95 security deposit required), which are required in the backcountry. Separate campfire permits are not necessary in Yosemite, but no fires are allowed above the tree line.

GETTING THERE

Yosemite's regions are accessible via five park entrances: Big Oak Flat, Arch Rock, South, Tioga Pass, and Hetch Hetchy. The **Arch Rock** Entrance (Hwy. 140) and the **Big Oak Flat** Entrance (Hwy. 120 west) are usually open year-round. The **Tioga Pass** (Hwy. 120 east) Entrance is just a few miles from Tuolumne Meadows and is the eastern access to Yosemite from U.S. 395. Tioga Road closes in November or December each year and reopens in the spring, usually in May or June. The **Hetch Hetchy** Entrance is to the northwest of the park and also closes in winter. The **South** Entrance is open year-round.

In winter it is always possible that roads can close unexpectedly and chains may be required on any road at any time. Check the park website (www.nps.gov/yose) or call 209/372-0200 for current road conditions.

Car
BIG OAK FLAT ENTRANCE
The most popular route into the park, particularly for those coming from the Bay Area, is through the Big Oak Flat Entrance. **Highway 120** leads through Modesto, Manteca, and Groveland. Inside the park, Highway 120 becomes Big Oak Flat Road; if you follow it to the right (southeast), it will lead you into the famed **Yosemite Valley.** The trip from the entrance to the valley is only about 25 miles, but allow at least 45 minutes. Speed limits in the park are set low to protect animals and people, and they are strictly enforced.

The drive to Big Oak Flat is about 170 miles from San Francisco and takes at least four hours; however, traffic, especially in summer and on weekends, has the potential to make it much longer. Try to time your drive for weekdays or early mornings to avoid the biggest crowds. For the most efficient route to Yosemite from San Francisco, take I-580 east to I-205 east. In Manteca, take I-5 to Highway 120 and follow it south to Big Oak Flat Road.

If you're headed for **Tioga Road** or Tuolumne Meadows, the Big Oak Flat Entrance is a good way to get there. About nine miles into the park, take the left fork east off Big Oak Flat Road onto Tioga Road (closed in winter). **Tuolumne Meadows** is 38 miles from the Big Oak Flat Entrance, and it will take about 1.5 hours to reach (maybe a little less if traffic is light). If you continue on Tioga Road another eight miles past Tuolumne, you'll get all the way to Tioga Pass, the east entrance to the park.

ARCH ROCK ENTRANCE
The most direct route into **Yosemite Valley** is through the Arch Rock Entrance. This gateway, south of the Big Oak Flat Entrance, is reached via **Highway 140** from Merced and Mariposa. From San Francisco, take I-580 east to I-205 east. In Manteca, take Highway 99 south for 56 miles to Merced. In Merced, turn right onto Highway 140 east. Highway 140 will take you right to the Arch Rock Entrance. After you enter the park you're on El Portal Road, which follows the Merced River.

TIOGA PASS ENTRANCE
The Tioga Pass Entrance is on the east side of Yosemite, 12 miles west of **U.S. 395.** The entrance road is **Tioga Road** west of the entrance, and Tioga Pass Road to the east. The town of Lee Vining is near the east entrance. Tioga Pass is closed in winter (usually Oct.–May or early June), but closing dates can vary depending on the weather. To check on weather and road closings in Yosemite, call 209/372-0200.

SOUTH ENTRANCE
Yosemite's South Entrance is accessed from **Highway 41,** coming north from Fresno and Oakhurst. Inside the park, Highway 41 becomes Wawona Road. The road is open year-round, although chains may be required in winter. The smaller Mariposa Grove Road, which leads off to a giant sequoia grove to the east, is closed to vehicles in winter (but you can walk it). You can take Wawona Road farther north to Yosemite Valley (from the South Entrance to the Yosemite Valley Visitors Center is about 35 miles, or 1.25 hours); or you can make a right turn from Wawona Road onto Glacier Point Road and reach the Badger Pass Ski Area (about 17 miles from the South Entrance). At the end of that road is Glacier Point.

HETCH HETCHY ENTRANCE
The northernmost route on the west side of Yosemite is the Hetch Hetchy Entrance. This is the entrance for Hetch Hetchy Reservoir, and it accesses much of the vast backcountry in the less developed section of the park. To get here from **Highway 120,** make a left

(north) onto Evergreen Road before the Big Oak Flat Entrance. After about seven miles, Evergreen Road passes through the tiny town of Mather and becomes Hetch Hetchy Road, which leads right through the entrance and on to O'Shaughnessy Dam, Hetch Hetchy Reservoir, and the Hetch Hetchy Backpackers Camp. Note that this entrance, and Hetch Hetchy Road, are open year-round but only at limited times. The road tends to be open sunrise–sunset; in summer (May 1–Labor Day) that translates to 7 A.M.–9 P.M.

Train

It is possible to reach Yosemite via **Amtrak** (800/872-7245, www.amtrak.com, $37–68 one-way from San Francisco, $56 from Los Angeles). From San Francisco (7 hours), you must take a bus to the Amtrak station in the East Bay (5885 Horton St., Emeryville, 45 minutes) and connect to the San Joaquin line to Merced. From Los Angeles (8.5 hours), take the bus from Union Station downtown (800 N. Alameda St., Los Angeles, 3 hours) to Bakersfield and then the Amtrak San Joaquin line to Merced.

All trains terminate at the Merced Amtrak station (324 W. 24th St. at K St., Merced, www.amtrak.com, 7:15 A.M.–9:45 P.M. daily). From Merced, the YARTS bus takes passengers into Yosemite (2.5 hours), making stops at Curry Village, the Ahwahnee Lodge, the Yosemite Valley Visitors Center, and Yosemite Lodge (year-round); and Crane Flat, White Wolf Lodge, and Tuolumne Meadows (summer only).

Bus

Greyhound (Merced station 209/722-2121, reservations 800/231-2222, www.greyhound.com, Merced station 8 A.M.–5:30 P.M. Mon.–Fri., $39–50 from San Francisco, $40–50 from Los Angeles) can get you as close as Merced. From the **Merced Transportation Center** (710 W. 16th St., Merced), you must then catch the YARTS bus into Yosemite.

The **Yosemite Area Regional Transportation System** (YARTS, 877/989-2787, www.yarts.com) runs daily buses into Yosemite. The Highway 140 bus ($12–25) picks up passengers in Merced, Mariposa, Midpines, and El Portal on the way into Yosemite. The Highway 120 bus (daily July–Aug., Sat.–Sun. June and Sept., $3–20) runs in summer only, picking up passengers at Mammoth Lakes, June Lake, and Lee Vining on the way to Tuolumne and Yosemite Valley. Schedules vary and change often; check the YARTS website for the most up-to-date information before your trip.

GETTING AROUND

Once you've reached Yosemite, most of the popular sights, attractions, and trailheads are accessible by road, at least in the summer. However, summer traffic and parking in Yosemite can be every bit as frustrating as it is in a big city. Preserve your good mood and help save the air by leaving your car behind and relaxing on one of Yosemite's free, comfortable, and efficient shuttle buses.

In winter (Nov.–May), Tioga Road, Glacier Point Road, and Mariposa Grove Road are closed, and chains may be required on any park road at any time. Check the park website (www.nps.gov/yose) or call 209/372-0200 for current road conditions.

Shuttle Services

Yosemite runs an extensive network of free shuttle buses in various areas of the park. The system works extremely well and frees up visitors to enjoy the park and decrease the traffic.

- **Yosemite Valley** shuttle (7 A.M.–10 P.M. daily year-round, free) provides access to numbered shuttle stops in the valley, including Yosemite Lodge, the Valley Visitors Center, Curry Village, all campgrounds, and the Happy Isles trailhead. Shuttles run about every 10–20 minutes; check the map in the *Yosemite Guide* for stops.
- **El Capitan** shuttle (9 A.M.–6 P.M. daily

mid-June–early Sept., free) runs during the summer season and stops at the Valley Visitors Center, El Capitan, and the trailhead for Four Mile.

- **Wawona-Mariposa Grove** shuttle (spring–fall, free) transports travelers between Wawona and the Mariposa Grove, picking up passengers at the South Entrance, the Wawona Store, and the Mariposa Grove gift shop.
- **Wawona to Yosemite Valley** shuttle (Memorial Day–Labor Day, free) leaves the Wawona Hotel at 8:30 A.M. for Yosemite Valley. The shuttle picks up passengers at Yosemite Lodge at 3:30 P.M. for the return trip to Wawona.
- **Badger Pass** shuttle (Dec.–Mar., free) runs twice daily between Yosemite Valley and the Badger Pass ski area during the winter ski season.
- **Tuolumne Meadows** shuttle (7 A.M.–7 P.M. daily June–mid-Sept., free) runs along Tioga Road, making multiple stops between Olmstead Point and the Tuolumne Meadows Lodge.

In-Park Bus Tours

Separate from the Yosemite shuttle system, a few commercial operators provide bus services in the park for a fee. **Glacier Point Tours** (209/372-4386, www.yosemitepark.com, 8:30 A.M., 10 A.M., and 1:30 P.M. daily spring–fall, adults $25 one-way, $41 round-trip, discounts for children, seniors, and groups) runs daily trips from Yosemite Valley Lodge to Glacier Point (4 hours round-trip). A popular choice for the hardy is to take the bus one way and then hike back to the valley.

July–September, Glacier Point Tours offers a luxurious guided bus tour between Yosemite Valley and Tuolumne Meadows. The coach makes multiple stops from Curry Village (8 A.M.) all the way to Tuolumne Meadows Lodge (arriving at 10:35 A.M.). It departs Tuolumne Meadows again at 2:05 P.M. and heads back. You don't have to take the whole journey; you can travel any segment and get off when you like. Round-trip fares range $5–23

for adults, depending on the distance traveled, and children ages 5–12 are half price.

GATEWAYS TO YOSEMITE
Groveland

The little town of Groveland, 26 miles outside the north entrance to Yosemite National Park on **Highway 120**, is the perfect place to stop for a last fill-up of gas, food, coffee, and anything else you may need. If you're trying to avoid rush hour traffic or getting a jump on your weekend trip to Yosemite by driving up late the night before, it can be a great idea to sleep in Groveland and enter the park the next morning, rested and ready to go.

The most elegant option is Groveland is the historic ◖ **Groveland Hotel** (18767 Main St., 800/273-3314, www.groveland.com, $145–339), built in 1849 and located right in the center of town. The proprietor, Peggy A. Mosley, oversees a seamless blend of historical intrigue that includes gold miners, gambling, and ghosts along with the modern comfort of the hotel's 17 guest rooms, each furnished with down comforters, feather beds, and charming touches like flocked floral wallpaper, hand-sewn quilts, and china chamber pots—and large flat-screen HD TVs, discreetly mounted on the wall. Amenities include fresh coffee beans, in-room coffeemakers; chocolate chip cookies waiting on the beds; and an open-door policy for dogs and cats in all guest rooms. Free wireless Internet service throughout the facility also helps workaholics ease gradually toward their wilderness vacation.

The best feature of the **Yosemite Riverside Inn** (11399 Cherry Lake Rd., Groveland, 209/962-7408 or 800/626-7408, www.yosemiteriversideinn.com, $69–295) is its proximity to Yosemite—it's located just 11 miles west of the Big Oak Flat Entrance. Rooms range from simple ($69–149) to deluxe ($99–160), with kitchenettes and river or courtyard views. One- and two-bedroom suites ($225–295) and cabins with full kitchens ($99–160)

© HEATHER C. LISTON

Groveland Hotel

are also available. Yosemite Riverside Inn offers a woodsy setting and a free continental breakfast; wireless Internet is available for a fee ($5).

The modern **Yosemite Westgate Lodge** (7633 Hwy. 120, Groveland, 209/962-5281, www.yosemitewestgate.com, $145–300 in summer; $64–139 in winter) is a convenient overnight spot, just 13 miles from the Big Oak Flat Entrance. This independently owned lodge is part of the America's Best Value Inn network, and its 45 rooms are all non-smoking and pet-free. A heated pool and spa and free wireless Internet are some of the notable amenities.

Camp in Big Oak Flat along Highway 120 at the Thousand Trails Campground at **Yosemite Lakes** (31191 Harden Flat Rd., 800/533-1001, ranger station 209/962-0103, www.1000trails.com, RVs $49, tents $59). This sprawling wooded campground beside the Tuolumne River has more than 250 RV sites with full hookups, 130 tent sites, a few dozen cabins, tent cabins, yurts, and a 12-bed hostel. It's only

five miles from the park entrance, and it has a full slate of recreational amenities, laundry facilities, and Internet service.

The **Iron Door Saloon** (18761 Main St., 209/962-6244, www.iron-door-saloon.com, 11 A.M.–9 P.M. daily year-round, $11–20) claims to be the oldest bar in California. It served gold prospectors sometime in the 1850s, and through the early 20th century it was the saloon of choice for the engineers who built the O'Shaughnessy Dam at Hetch Hetchy. With live music every weekend, it's still arguably the center of nightlife for many miles around. The food is standard, but the drinks are strong. The bar stays open until 2 A.M., but may close earlier in the off-season.

Stop in at **Dori's Tea Cottage** (18744 Main St., 209/962-5300, www.doristeacottage.com, 11 A.M.–3 P.M. Mon. and Wed.–Thurs., 11 A.M.–7 P.M. Fri.–Sat., $9–16), a sweet little place with a "traditional English tea luncheon in a quaint and comfortable atmosphere." Wine,

YOSEMITE

champagne, and dessert are always available and there are vegetarian options. Reservations are recommended for lunch in the summer.

In the tiny community of Big Oak Flat, the **Big Oak Restaurant and Bar** (17820 Hwy. 120, 209/962-6015, 7:30 A.M.–2:30 P.M. daily, $8–10) is near the junction of Highways 120 and 108. Dark, cool, and quiet by day, the place feels more like a bar than a restaurant. The food is nothing special, but quantities are generous.

The **Cellar Door** (18767 Main St., 800/273-3314, www.groveland.com, 8–10 A.M. and 5:30–9:30 P.M. daily, Dec. hours shorter, $17–27, reservations suggested in summer) is the excellent restaurant at the Groveland Hotel. Outdoor tables are equipped with sun umbrellas and surrounded by lush gardens of roses and local flora. On cool evenings, propane heaters ensure that the patio stays comfortable, and indoor tables are also available in the hotel's oak-paneled dining room.

Mariposa

Mariposa lies about 32 miles from the **Arch Rock Entrance** and 44 miles from Yosemite Valley. You can't miss the **River Rock Inn and Deli Garden Café** (4993 7th St., 209/966-5793, www.riverrockncafe.com, $65–159) with its vivid orange-and-purple exterior in the heart of Mariposa. What was once a rundown 1940s motor lodge is now a quirky, whimsical motel with unusually decorated guest rooms. Two suites provide enough space for families, while the other five guest rooms sleep couples in comfort. The River Rock is a 45-minute drive from the west entrance to Yosemite.

If you prefer cozy seclusion to large lodge-style hotels, stay at the **Highland House** (3125 Wild Dove Lane, 209/966-3737, www.highlandhouseinn.com, $115–150), outside Mariposa and west of Yosemite. The house is set deep in the forest far from town, providing endless peace and quiet away from civilization. This tiny B&B has only three guest rooms,

each decorated in soft colors and warm, inviting styles. All guest rooms have down comforters, sparkling clean bathtubs and showers, free wireless Internet access, and TVs with DVD players.

Another lovely small B&B, **Poppy Hill Bed and Breakfast** (5218 Crystal Aire Dr., 209/742-6273 or 800/587-6779, www.poppyhill.com, $135–150) is 27 miles from the west entrance to the park. The four airy guest rooms are done in bright white linens, white walls, lacy curtains, and antique furniture. No TVs mar the sounds of birds from the expansive gardens surrounding the old farmhouse, but you can take a dip in the totally modern hot tub any time. A full gourmet breakfast served on your schedule gives the right start to a day spent exploring Yosemite or the Mariposa County area.

Several campgrounds surround the Arch Rock Entrance near Mariposa. The **Yosemite Bug Rustic Mountain Resort** (6979 Hwy. 140, 209/966-6666 or 866/826-7108, www.yosemitebug.com, dorm $22–25, tent cabin $45–75 for 2–4 people, private cabin $75–155 for 2–4 people) is part hostel, part rustic cabin lodge. This facility includes five hostel dormitories, a number of attractively appointed tent cabins with real beds (but bring your own sleeping bag), and a few cabins with private guest rooms, some with private baths. Solo travelers and families on tight budgets favor Yosemite Bug for its comfortable and cheap accommodations.

El Portal

El Portal is less than four miles from the **Arch Rock Entrance** and just 15 miles from Yosemite Valley, making it one of the closest places for a final overnight on the way to the park. With a population of fewer than 500 people, it's smaller than Mariposa, so don't expect too much in the way of services.

RVers aiming for the Arch Rock Entrance flock to the **Indian Flat RV Park** (9988 Hwy. 140, 209/379-2339, www.indianflatrvpark.com, tents $20–25, RVs $32–42, tent cabins

$30–59, cottages $65–109, pet fee $5). This park is a full-service low-end resort, with everything from RV sites (with water and electricity; some with sewer hookups) to tent cabins and full-fledged cottages. Showers are available ($3), and you can stop in for a shower even if you're not spending the night. The lodge next door has extended an invitation to all Indian Flat campers to make use of their outdoor pool. Because Indian Flat is relatively small (25 RV sites and 25 tent sites), reservations are strongly recommended for May–September. You can book up to a year in advance; this kind of planning is a good idea for summertime Yosemite visitors.

Oakhurst

Oakhurst lies less than 15 miles from the **South Entrance** of Yosemite National Park. The **Best Western Plus Yosemite Gateway Inn** (40530 Hwy. 41, Oakhurst, 559/683-2378 or 888/256-8042, www.yosemitegatewayinn.com, $126–137) offers both indoor and outdoor pools and spas, free wireless Internet, and better-than-your-average-chain rooms. If you're bringing a group, consider one of their two-room "family suites" which feature four queen beds ($200/night in summer). The on-site **Yosemite Gateway Restaurant** (6:30–11 A.M. and 5–9 P.M. Mon.–Sat., 6:30 A.M.–1 P.M. and 5–9 P.M. Sun., $8–20) serves breakfast and dinner daily with brunch on Sunday. Dinner features steaks and a full salad and soup bar.

The family-owned **Oakhurst Lodge** (40302 Hwy. 41, Oakhurst, 559/683-4417 or 800/655-6343, www.oklodge.com, $150–165) is within walking distance to the shops and restaurants of Oakhurst. Wireless Internet service and a continental breakfast are included and the unheated outdoor pool is open year-round.

Chateau du Sureau (48688 Victoria Ln., Oakhurst, 559/683-6800 or 559/683-6860, www.chateausureau.com, closed two weeks in Jan., $385–585) is a breathtakingly beautiful lodge with just 10 rooms, each spectacularly appointed. Request a canopy bed, a French balcony, a Jacuzzi tub, a garden view—whatever your fantasy of luxury is, you can probably find it here. This Forbes five-star and AAA five-diamond property was built in 1991 and has all the modern conveniences, but with the charm of a country house. Free wireless is available throughout the property, and all room rates include an elegant European-style breakfast.

The best restaurant in the Oakhurst area is **Erna's Elderberry House** (48688 Victoria Ln., Oakhurst, 559/683-6800, www.elderberryhouse.com, 5:30 P.M.–close Mon.–Sat., 11 A.M.–1 P.M. and 5:30 P.M.–close Sun., closed mid-Jan., $95) on the grounds of the Chateau du Sureau. This astonishingly chic establishment features the classical French cuisine and farm-to-table sensibility of its executive chef Gunnar Thompson, who has trained in fine restaurants around the world but forages locally. The five-course prix fixe dinner features a different menu nightly ($95), and the four-course Sunday brunch ($58) includes a glass of wine.

Fish Camp

Fish Camp is 40 miles from Yosemite Valley via the **South Entrance**, a little over an hour's drive. The **Narrow Gauge Inn** (48571 Hwy. 41, 559/683-7720 or 888/644-9050, www.narrowgaugeinn.com, $79–195) is a charming 26-room mountain inn offering one- and two-bed nonsmoking guest rooms done in wood paneling, light colors, white linens, and vintage-style quilts. Each guest room has its own outdoor table and chairs to encourage relaxing outside with a drink on gorgeous summer days and evenings. The restaurant and common rooms feature antique oil lamps, stonework, and crackling fireplaces. Step outside your door and you're in the magnificent High Sierra pine forest.

For inexpensive lodge-style accommodations east of Fish Camp, check in to the **White Chief Mountain Lodge** (7776 White Chief Mountain

Rd., 559/683-5444, www.whitechiefmountain-lodge.com, $120–160). The basic guest rooms feature light wood paneling, tribal-design textiles, and small TVs. Guest rooms in the main lodge have wireless Internet access, but the cottages do not.

The **Tenaya Lodge** (1122 Hwy. 41, 559/683-6555 or 888/514-2167, www.tenayalodge.com, $245–400) offers plush lodge-style accommodations at a reasonable price. Guest rooms in the lodge are styled with rich fabrics in bright oranges and other bold, eye-catching colors; the three dozen cottages have a Native American–themed decor. The modern wall art evokes the woods and vistas of Yosemite. The beds are comfortable, the baths attractive, and the views forest-filled. Tenaya Lodge focuses on guest care, offering five dining venues on-site, from pizza to deli to fine dining, with three meals daily; a full-service spa that specializes in facials; and daily (and nightly) nature walks complete with costumed guides.

The **Pines Resort** (54432 Rd. 432, Bass Lake, 559/642-3121 or 800/350-7463, www.basslake.com, June–Aug. $159–299) is perfectly located for your angling convenience right on the shores of Bass Lake. You can choose a suite (a split-level king room with dark floors, light walls, fireplaces, some with spa tubs) or rent a chalet (a two-story cabin in rustic mountain style that sleeps up to 6, with a full kitchen, a deck, and an outdoor mini barbecue). The Pines is a full-service resort, with a lake-view restaurant, **Ducey's on the Lake** (7–11 A.M. and 4–9 P.M. Mon.–Fri., 7 A.M.–noon and 4–9 P.M. Sat.–Sun., $18–37), a grocery store (8 A.M.–9 P.M. Mon.–Fri., 8 A.M.–10 P.M. Sat.–Sun. June–Aug., shorter hours Sept.–May), all-weather tennis courts, a swimming pool (in summer), hot tubs (year-round), massage services, a fitness room, s and meeting facilities.

A mile and a half south of the South Entrance, is the small, attractive **Summerdale Campground** (Hwy. 41, northeast of Fish Camp, 877/444-6777, www.recreation.gov, $20). This lovely spot has a two-night minimum on weekends and a three-night minimum on holiday weekends, only 29 campsites, and a strict limit on RV size (24 feet), making it a bit quieter and less city-like than the mega-campgrounds. You'll have a fire ring and a grill at your site, plenty of room under mature shade trees, and maybe even a water spigot (although boiling the water before drinking it is recommended).

The Eastern Sierra

LEE VINING AND VICINITY

Whether you've been camping out in the backcountry for weeks, or you've just driven across it, you'll be glad to come upon the lively town of Lee Vining on the eastern edge of the park. Although it's not large (pop. 222) and some of its services close down in the winter months, Lee Vining couldn't be a more welcoming place for travelers. Set right on the southwest edge of Mono Lake, convenient to the ghost town of Bodie and the recreational paradise of June Lake, and a good stopover for travelers heading south to Mammoth Lakes and Bishop, Lee Vining takes tourism seriously, offering a variety of restaurants and lodgings, and even *two* top-quality visitors centers.

Accommodations

Soon after exiting the Tioga Pass entrance on the east side of the park, you'll come to the rustic ◖ **Tioga Pass Resort** (85 Hwy. 120 W., Lee Vining, www.tiogapassresort.com, summer only, $105–210, cash or check only), which offers both charm and convenience. Whether your plan is to play in Yosemite itself, explore the treasures of the Eastern Sierra like Bodie

YOSEMITE

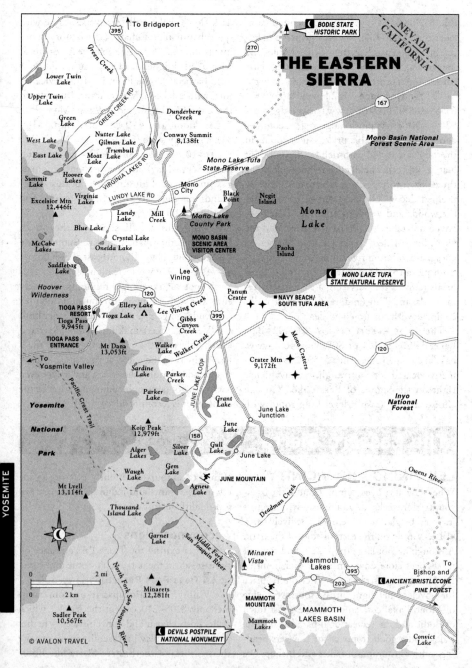

© STAN NESTER

Tioga Pass Resort

and Mono Lake, or do some of both, this is a great spot. Tioga Pass Resort offers 10 cabins and four guest rooms. The guest rooms do not have kitchens or showers but do have access to showers in a shared facility. One thing the resort does not have on a reliable basis is telephone and Internet access, which means they cannot accept credit cards.

To make a reservation, send an email to tiogapassresortllc@gmail.com with the requested dates. If you don't get an answer within a week, email again. When you receive a reservation confirmation, print it out and bring it with you. The resort has closed in recent winters, but they hope to get their infrastructure back up to snuff so they can be a year-round resort once again.

For clean, comfortable, affordable lodgings, try **Murphey's Motel** (51493 U.S. 395, 760/647-6316 or 800/334-6316, www.murpheysyosemite.com, $58–123). Open all year, this motel provides double-queen and king beds with cozy comforters, TVs, tables and

chairs, and everything you need for a pleasant stay in the Mono Lake area. Its central location in downtown Lee Vining makes dining, shopping, and trips to the visitors center and chamber of commerce convenient.

El Mono Motel (1 3rd St. at U.S. 395, 760/647-6310, www.elmonomotel.com, late May–Oct. 31, depending on weather, $67–92 shared bath, $85–95 private bath) offers comfy beds and clean guest rooms at very reasonable prices. Enjoy the location in downtown Lee Vining, and start each morning with a fresh cup of organic coffee from the on-site Latte Da Coffee Café (7 A.M.–8 P.M. daily summer).

At the junction of Highway 120 and U.S. 395, stay at the comfortable and affordable **Lake View Lodge** (51285 U.S. 395, 760/647-6543 or 800/990-6614, www.lakeviewlodgeyosemite.com, $122–255). This aptly named lodge offers cottages, which can be rented in summer only, and motel rooms, available year-round. Whether you choose a basic guest room for a night or two or a larger option with a kitchen

YOSEMITE

for more than three days, you'll enjoy the simple country-style decor, the outdoor porches, and the views of Mono Lake. All guest rooms have TVs with cable, and Internet access is available in the motel rooms but not the cottages.

Named for its main claim to fame—its proximity to the park, only 14 miles from Yosemite's east gate—the **Yosemite Gateway Motel** (51340 U.S. 395, 760/647-6467, www.yosemitegatewaymotel.com, $99–159) offers a charming rustic experience for travelers to the Eastern Sierra. The red and white exterior is echoed in the decoration of the guest rooms, which are supplemented with gleaming wood, new furnishings, and clean baths. TVs and Internet access provide entertainment on chilly evenings, and the wonderful outdoor recreation opportunities of the Eastern Sierra are just outside the door.

Camping

There are a number of campgrounds in the Inyo National Forest on the east side of Yosemite, near U.S. 395 and Tioga Pass. You can stay at **Ellery Campground** (Hwy. 120, Upper Lee Vining Canyon, ranger station 760/873-2400, www.fs.fed.us/r5/inyo, $19), which has 12 campsites at an elevation of 9,500 feet with drinking water, pit toilets, and garbage cans. It's not possible to reserve these sites, so get here at dawn if you want a site on a weekend. Another option is **Sawmill Walk-In** (Saddlebag Rd., on Forest Rd. 04, 1.6 miles north of Hwy. 120, ranger station 760/873-2400, www.fs.fed.us/r5/inyo, June–Oct., $14). This primitive hike-in campground, at an elevation of 9,800 feet, has 12 sites and no water, so walk in slowly. It's not possible to reserve these sites.

Food

Tioga Pass Resort's simple diner-restaurant, the **Tioga Pass Resort Café** (85 Hwy. 120 W., Lee Vining, www.tiogapassresort.com, 8 A.M.–8 P.M. Mon.–Fri., 7 A.M.–9 P.M.

Sat.–Sun. summer, $20), offers breakfast, lunch, and dinner, served with plenty of good cheer.

The best way to kick off any vacation in the Eastern Sierra is with a memorable meal (and a tank of gas) at the ◖ **Whoa Nellie Deli** (Hwy. 120 and U.S. 395, 760/647-1088, www.whoanelliedeli.com, 6:45 A.M.–9 P.M. daily end of Apr.–end of Oct., $12–14) at the Tioga Gas Mart. The Whoa Nellie and Tioga Gas Mart are right at the east entrance to Yosemite, so it's the perfect place to stop when leaving the park or heading in. You'll get a full hearty meal of fish tacos, buffalo meatloaf, or pizza; a pleasant place to eat it all; and an all-around friendly, festive atmosphere. Expect to wait in line for a while at the counter to order, as Whoa Nellie is justifiably popular. Seating is available both inside and out, so there are usually enough tables to go around. There's a fairly large grocery store and souvenir shop, and the large, clean restrooms are also a draw, especially for those who've been camping for a while. The place is closed in winter, though, since Tioga Pass tends to be closed.

Lee Vining has several charming independent coffee shops. The **Latte Da Coffee Café** (1 3rd St. at U.S. 395, 760/647-6310, 7 A.M.–8 P.M. daily summer) uses organic coffee and local fresh water to create delicious coffee drinks at the El Mono Motel. Over at the Lake View Lodge, enjoy a cup of joe at the **Garden House Coffee Shop** (51285 U.S. 395, 760/647-6543, www.lakeviewlodgeyosemite.com, 7–11 A.M. daily summer–fall). To get a great start to your day, you can pick up a smoothie or a fresh pastry in addition to your favorite espresso drinks.

A classic American diner, **Nicely's** (U.S. 395 and 4th St., Lee Vining, 760/647-6477, 7 A.M.–9 P.M. daily summer, 7 A.M.–9 P.M. Thurs.–Mon. winter, $10–20) offers friendly service and familiar food. Inside, you'll find a large dining room with half-circle booths upholstered in cheerful red vinyl. The

© HEATHER C. LISTON

Whoa Nellie Deli at the Tioga Gas Mart

cuisine includes eggs and pancakes in the morning; salads and sandwiches for lunch; and steak, trout, and salmon in the evening. Portions are more than generous. Nicely's is open earlier in the morning, later in the evening, and more in the winter than most places in the area. This is a good place to take the kids for comfort foods like burgers, fries, and macaroni and cheese.

If you're looking for a Wild West atmosphere and a good spicy sauce, have lunch or dinner at **Bodie Mike's Barbecue** (51357 U.S. 395 at 4th St., Lee Vining, 760/647-6432, 11:30 A.M.–10 P.M. daily June–Sept.). Use your fingers to dig into barbecued ribs, chicken, beef, brisket, and more. A rustic atmosphere with rough-looking wood, red-checked tablecloths, and local patrons in cowboy boots completes your dining experience. Just don't expect the fastest service in the world. At the back of the dining room is the entrance to a small, dark bar populated by local characters.

Information and Services

There's a fine visitors center in the middle of Lee Vining, the **Mono Lake Committee Information Center & Bookstore** (U.S. 395, 760/647-6595, 9 A.M.–5 P.M. daily) with a big selection of free maps and brochures and helpful staff. The **Mono Basin National Forest Scenic Area Visitor Center** (U.S. 395, 0.5 mile north of Lee Vining, 760/647-3044, www.monolake.org, May–Nov.) is nearby at Mono Lake.

You can use mail services at the **Lee Vining Post Office** (121 Lee Vining Ave., 760/647-6371, www.usps.com, 9 A.M.–2 P.M. and 3–5 P.M. Mon.–Fri.). Lee Vining has few ATMs, but you can find one or two places to get cash (which you'll need, because many places out here don't take plastic). Try the gas stations, the visitors center, and the local grocery-minimart.

YOSEMITE

© MARINA TROOST

Mono Lake Committee Information Center & Bookstore

Getting There

AIR

The nearest airport to Lee Vining is the **Mammoth Yosemite Airport** (MMH, 1200 Airport Rd., Mammoth Lakes, 760/934-3813, www.ci.mammoth-lakes.ca.us). Alaska Airlines serves this airport year-round; United and Horizon fly in December 15–April 30. For more options at a major hub, book a flight to **Reno-Tahoe International Airport** (RNO, 2001 E. Plumb Lane, Reno, NV, 775/328-6400, www.renoairport.com). From Reno, drive south on U.S. 395; Lee Vining in about 137 miles (3 hours).

From the **Sacramento International Airport** (SMF, 6900 Airport Blvd., Sacramento, 916/929-5411, www.sacramento.aero) you can get to Lee Vining in about four hours. From the **San Francisco International Airport** (SFO, U.S. 101, San Francisco, 650/821-8211 or 800/435-9736, www.flysfo.com) it takes approximately 5.5 hours.

CAR

Lee Vining is located just north of the junction of Highway 120 (also known as Tioga Pass Rd.) and U.S. 395. In summer the drive is quite beautiful, if not always fast. From the Bay Area, take I-580 east to I-205 east to Highway 120. Follow Highway 120 east as it becomes Tioga Road and across Yosemite National Park. When you reach U.S. 395, turn left, and you'll find yourself in Lee Vining. Expect the trip to take about 5.5 hours, but don't be surprised if it's longer. Traffic near and through Yosemite can be intense—especially on summer weekends—and many of the other travelers are enjoying the scenery, stopping to take photos along the way. When the snow comes, Tioga Road is closed.

From the Bay Area or Sacramento, you can take an alternate route to avoid Tioga Road, which is closed in winter. Take I-80 east for about 80 miles before turning onto U.S. 50 east for about 100 miles. Turn right onto Highway 89/88 and drive about 30 miles until you reach U.S. 395. Turn right (south) onto U.S. 395, and you'll arrive in Lee Vining in another 93 miles. The total distance is about 300 miles, a travel time of about six hours, depending on traffic and weather.

MONO LAKE

Mono Lake, eerie in its stillness, is the main attraction in the northern part of the Eastern Sierra, just east of Yosemite. This unusual and beautiful lake is 2.5 times as salty as the ocean and is 1,000 times more alkaline.

The reason for Mono Lake's odd appearance? It is fed by only about seven inches' worth of rain and snowfall each year; the rest of the water inflow is from various streams. No streams or tributaries flow out of Mono Lake, but it loses about 45 inches of water each year to evaporation. Meanwhile, any salt and minerals that have been carried into the lake stay in the lake as water evaporates. Over time, the lake has collected huge stores of calcium carbonate, which solidifies into strange-looking tufa towers.

The lake surrounds two large islands: **Negit Island,** a volcanic cinder cone and nesting area for California gulls, and **Paoha Island,** which was created when volcanic activity pushed sediment from the bottom of the lake up above the surface. Mono Basin, where the lake is located, is part of the Inyo National Forest. In 1984 the U.S. Congress designated Mono Basin a National Forest Scenic Area, which gives it additional protections.

If you're visiting the Eastern Sierra, you won't want to miss this natural wonder. It's large enough that you can see it from a distance—in fact, you can get a pretty good view just by driving by on U.S. 395, but stop to take a closer look if you can. One of the best viewpoints is on the grounds of the Mono Basin National Forest Scenic Area Visitors Center (U.S. 395, 0.5 mile north of Lee Vining, 760/647-3044, www.monolake.org, May–Nov.). Another good spot for looking through binoculars and taking photos is the lookout area on the east side

© HEATHER C. LISTON

Mono Lake

YOSEMITE

of U.S. 395 near the junction with Highway 120, right across from the Whoa Nellie Deli. Look for a grassy hill with a parking lot, a large American flag, and a "Mono Lake" sign with a big hunk of volcanic rock hanging from it. If you want to do more than just look, come in summer and enjoy an oddly buoyant swim in its heavily salted waters or a boat trip around the silent, uninhabited islands.

Mono Basin National Forest Scenic Area Visitors Center

The large building that houses the visitors center for Mono Lake is only a short drive from the highway. The Mono Basin National Forest Scenic Area Visitors Center (U.S. 395, 0.5 mile north of Lee Vining, 760/647-3044, www.monolake.org, 8 A.M.–5 P.M. daily May–Sept., 9 A.M.–4:30 P.M. Thurs.–Mon. Oct.–Nov.) is the perfect place to learn about Mono Lake, to take a walk around the lake, and to photograph the landscape. The interpretive museum inside details the natural and human history of the lake, from the way tufa towers form to the endless litigation involving the lake. Original films, interactive exhibits, a bookstore, and friendly staff are all available to help get you up to speed on this beautiful and unusual area. Walk out the back of the building to take one of several brief interpretive walks through the landscape or to sit on a bench and gaze down at the lake for a while. Talk to the staff to learn about the best hikes and spots to visit, swim, launch a boat, or even cross-country ski.

At the visitors center, you can also learn about various guided walks and hikes at Mono Lake, which can give you a more in-depth look at the wonders of the area.

◖ Mono Lake Tufa State Natural Reserve

The tufa formations—freestanding calcite towers, knobs, and spires—make Mono Lake one of the most unusual lakes you'll ever see. The

Mono Lake Tufa State Natural Reserve

© MARINA TROOST

YOSEMITE

Mono Lake Tufa State Natural Reserve (U.S. 395, just north of Lee Vining, 760/647-6331, www.parks.ca.gov, 24 hours daily, free) educates and amazes visitors. Free tours are offered at 10 A.M. daily in summer. Among other reasons to visit, the California State Parks service has declared it the "best place to watch gulls in the state." About 85 percent of the entire population of California gulls nests here in the spring.

A boardwalk trail provides access to the North Tufa area. Enjoy wandering through the different chunks of this preserve, which appear along the shore all the way around the lake. Be aware that much of the land adjacent to the State Reserve areas is restricted—help take care of this delicate terrain by not venturing out of the designated visiting areas. Also, to access some of the reserve at the east side of the lake, you'll need either a boat or a 4WD vehicle, since no paved roads circle Mono Lake.

South Tufa

The South Tufa area (off Hwy. 120, 11 miles east of Lee Vining, $3 pp, free with Federal Parks Pass) on the—where else?—south shore of Mono Lake is one of the best places to view the spectacular tufa towers and a good place for newcomers to start exploring. This area is managed by the U.S. Forest Service, which charges a fee even though most of the state-run areas around here do not. But the good news is that all summer long, naturalists lead a one-mile, one-hour **walking tour** (6 P.M. daily summer) around South Tufa, and it's free.

If you're hiking on your own, a good place to start is the one-mile **interpretive trail** (southeast of the visitors center, adjacent to Navy Beach) that winds through the South Tufa area and describes the natural history of the area and the formations.

Old Marina

Years ago, the stillness of Mono Lake was broken by quite a bit of boat traffic. Private boats and small tour operators still travel the lake in the summer, but no major commercial water traffic remains. The hub of this activity was the marina north of Lee Vining. Today, the Old Marina (1 mile north of Lee Vining, off U.S. 395, www.monolake.org/visit/oldmarina, $3 per car) is a good spot to take a short stroll down to the edge of the lake and to enjoy outstanding views of the lake's two large islands and several nearby tufa towers. There's a 1.5-mile trail from the Mono Basin Scenic Area Visitors Center to the Old Marina, and an even shorter boardwalk trail that's wheelchair-accessible.

Panum Crater

Even if you aren't a professional geologist, the volcanic Panum Crater (Hwy. 120, 3 miles east of U.S. 395) is worth visiting. This rhyolite crater, accessed from a parking area down a short dirt road off Highway 120, is less than 700 years old—a mere baby on geologic time scales. Take a hike around the rim of the crater, and if you're feeling up to it, climb the trail to the top of the plug dome. Be sure to slather on the sunscreen, since no trees shade these trails and it gets quite warm in the summer. Check the Mono Lake website (www.monolake.org) for occasional guided tours of Panum Crater.

Hiking

Mono Lake is not like Yosemite and its clusters of trailheads everywhere. But the hiking near Mono Lake is usually quieter, with fewer other travelers around, and the scenery is unlike anything you'll find anywhere else. Note that the trails around the Mono Basin National Forest Scenic Area Visitors Center and the South Tufa area are open year-round, even when the visitors centers are closed.

You can get a quick and informative introduction to the ecosystem around the lake by taking the 0.25-mile **Secrets of Survival Nature Trail** right outside the Mono Basin National Forest Scenic Area Visitors Center (U.S. 395, 0.5 mile north of Lee Vining, 760/647-3044, www.monolake.org). This trail offers interpretive signage and long views of the lake.

For an easy walk along the lake, go to the **Mono Lake County Park** (Cemetery Rd.), where the trailhead is 0.5 mile east of Cemetery Road, and take the boardwalk trail 0.25 mile down to the tufa formations. Wandering through the tufa will add distance to your walk, but the ground is flat and the scenery is diverting.

A lovely interpretive trail, the **Tioga Tarns Nature Walk** (Hwy. 120, east of Tioga Lake) is about 0.5 mile long and includes numerous signs describing the flora, fauna, and geology of the area.

A nature walk that offers both gentle exercise and increased knowledge is the **Lee Vining Creek Trail.** This easy-to-moderate 1.6-mile (one-way) walk stretches from the Mono Basin National Forest Scenic Area Visitors Center (U.S. 395, 0.5 mile north of Lee Vining, 760/647-3044, www.monolake.org) to the south end of Lee Vining, following Lee Vining Creek, which is currently under restoration to return it to its natural state after decades of diversion. If you start at the visitors center, you can pick up a free trail guide. The total round-trip walk is just over three miles and takes an hour or two, depending on how much time you spend admiring the revitalized ecosystem.

You can find any number of moderate hikes in the Mono Lake vicinity. The **Lundy Canyon Trail** (Lundy Lake Rd.), from the trailhead at the dirt lot, can be anywhere from 0.5 mile of fairly easy walking through Lundy Canyon to a strenuous seven-mile hike all the way out to Saddlebag Lake. Another trail leads out to **Parker Lake** or **Parker Bench** (Parker Lake Rd., off Hwy. 158). This hike is a minimum of four miles round-trip, and it can be 10 miles if you take the left fork of the trail out to Silver Lake and Parker Bench. Steep sections make this trek a bit demanding, but you'll love the scenic, shady trail that follows Parker Creek along the shorter right fork to Parker Lake. If one or two lakes just aren't enough, take the longish but only moderately tough **20-Lakes Basin Trail** (Saddlebag Lake Rd.) from the parking area across from the dam. This six-mile loop trail will take you out past many of the lakes for which the basin is named. If you're tired of all that water, take a moderate two-mile round-trip pilgrimage out to the remains of the mining town at **Bennettville** (Junction Campground Rd.). You can prowl around the abandoned mine, but be careful—old mine shafts and abandoned buildings can be extremely hazardous.

Boating and Swimming

Go ahead and bring your powerboat, canoe, kayak, or even a sailboat out to Mono Lake. You can launch from **Navy Beach** (0.5 mile east of South Tufa), although there's no direct access to the water from the parking lot, so you'll have to carry your canoe or kayak about 30 yards to get it into the water. If you're putting a heavier boat into the lake, check with the staff at the Mono Basin National Forest Scenic Area Visitors Center (U.S. 395, 0.5 mile north of Lee Vining, 760/647-3044, www.monolake.org, 8 A.M.–5 P.M. daily May–Sept., 9 A.M.–4:30 P.M. Thurs.–Mon. Oct.–Nov.) for directions to the launch ramp near Lee Vining Creek. Also note that, for the protection of nesting California gulls, you cannot beach any kind of boat on the islands April 1–August 1. Outside that protected timeframe, the islands of Mono Lake can be a great destination for boaters.

Swimming is allowed (and even encouraged) in Mono Lake in the summer. You can swim from your boat or from any of the unrestricted shore access points. You'll find yourself floating easily since the salt content of Mono Lake is several times higher than the ocean. But take care and watch kids closely: No lifeguards patrol the area, and you're swimming at your own risk.

Bird-Watching

The birds of the Eastern Sierra are so varied and abundant that three organizations—the

Eastern Sierra Audubon Society (www.es-audubon.org), the Mono Lake Committee (760/647-6595, www.monolake.org), and the Owens Valley Committee (760/876-1845, www.ovcweb.org)—got together to produce the wonderful *Eastern Sierra Birding Trail Map*. The map covers 200 miles of territory from Bridgeport Reservoir (near the junction of U.S. 395 and Hwy. 182) in the north to Cactus Flat and the Haiwee Reservoir in the south (near Olancha and the junction of U.S. 395 and Hwy. 190). Along the way, 38 stops identify good birding habitats, and callouts provide details on the natural habitat of each area and the species to look out for. For an online version of the map, visit www.easternsierrabirdingtrail.org. To get your own free hard copy, contact the Mono Lake Committee (707/647-6595, birding@monolake.org).

Entertainment and Events

It's called the **Ghosts of the Sagebrush Tour** (760/647-6461, www.monobasinhs.org, late Sept., $25 per day), but this annual education-and-entertainment weekend event, produced by the Mono Basin Historical Society, is much more than just a tour. Friday evening, there's a dinner at The Historic Mono Inn (U.S. 395, Lee Vining, 760/647-6581, www.mononinn.com) with a presentation by a living history interpreter. Saturday is a full day of activities that include walks, talks, special exhibits, and lunch from the Tioga Lodge at Mono Lake (54411 U.S. 395, Lee Vining, 760/647-6423, www.tiogalodgeatmonolake.com).

Accommodations and Food

Just across the freeway from Mono Lake, the **Tioga Lodge at Mono Lake** (54411 U.S. 395, Lee Vining, 760/647-6423, www.tiogalodgeatmonolake.com, late May–mid-Oct., $99–139) offers a view of the lake from every room. This old lodge offers the perfect location for sightseeing and outdoor adventures, plus heated rooms and comfortable beds. Guest rooms are simple and appealingly decorated, each with tile floors and a full private bath. Some rooms sleep two, and others have room for up to four. The two-bedroom suites are perfect for families. Don't expect to find TVs or other digital entertainment—in keeping with the area, you're encouraged to get outside to find your entertainment.

The **Hammond Station Restaurant** (54411 U.S. 395, Lee Vining, 760/647-6423, reservations 619/320-8868, www.tiogalodgeatmonolake.com, 7:30–10 A.M. and 5–9:30 P.M. daily late May–early Oct., $10–24), at the Tioga Lodge, offers an excellent variety of good food. Choose from the health-conscious vegetarian and spa menu, which includes a number of vegan, gluten-free, and dairy-free options; the California Casual menu; or the Drinks & Desserts menu. Expect a small dining room with attractive wrought-iron furniture plus an ample outdoor seating area perfect for warm summer evenings. The food is tasty, and the service makes you feel like a local even if you're from far out of town.

A great place to get a to-go breakfast or lunch is the **Mono Market** (51303 U.S. 395, 760/647-1010, 7 A.M.–10 P.M. daily summer, 7:30 A.M.–8 P.M. daily winter). Breakfast sandwiches and pastries are made fresh daily, as are the sandwiches, wraps, and messier napkin-requisite entrées you can carry out for lunch or dinner.

Information and Services

The **Mono Basin National Forest Scenic Area Visitors Center** (U.S. 395, 0.5 mile north of Lee Vining, 760/647-3044, www.monolake.org, 8 A.M.–5 P.M. daily May–Sept., 9 A.M.–4:30 P.M. Thurs.–Mon. Oct.–Nov.) is an excellent resource for information about the area. It includes an interpretive museum that describes the creation of Mono Lake and the strange tufa formations that define it. This visitors center also has a ranger station with knowledgeable staff who can help you with the best seasonal trail and lake advice.

Right in the center of Lee Vining is another fine visitors center that's about much more than just the lake. The **Mono Lake Committee Information Center & Bookstore** (U.S. 395, Lee Vining, 760/647-6595, 9 A.M.–5 P.M. daily) is a pleasant and welcoming place, with endless free maps and brochures, helpful staff, and souvenirs available for purchase.

The nearest medical facility to Mono Lake is to the south in Mammoth Lakes at **Mammoth Hospital** (85 Sierra Park Rd., Mammoth Lakes, 760/934-3311, emergency services 760/924-4076, www.mammothhospital.com), which has a 24-hour emergency room.

Getting There and Around

Mono Lake is very close to the junction of Tioga Pass Road and U.S. 395. Getting here from San Francisco, Los Angeles, or anyplace else in California with a major airport usually requires a long drive.

Tioga Road is closed November–May each year, sometimes longer if snows are heavy. Check the Yosemite National Park website (www.nps.gov/yose) or call 209/372-0200 for updates on road closings in and around Yosemite. U.S. 395 remains open all year, although storms can close it briefly until the plows do their work. But accessing U.S. 395 from the north or south involves long drives from most places. You might want to consider flying in Reno or even Las Vegas and approaching Mono Lake from the north or east. From the **Reno-Tahoe International Airport** (RNO, 2001 E. Plumb Lane, Reno, NV, 775/328-6400, www.renoairport.com), you can drive 140 miles south on U.S. 395 and get to Mono Lake in about three hours. From **McCarran International Airport** (LAS, 5757 Wayne Newton Blvd., Las Vegas, 702/261-5211, www.mccarran.com), the 350-mile trip takes about six hours, mostly on U.S. 95 north.

Very little public transit of any kind gets as far as Lee Vining and Mono Lake. To adequately explore this region, you need a vehicle of your own. On the bright side, parking in Lee Vining and around the lake tends to be both easy and free.

◖ BODIE STATE HISTORIC PARK

Bodie State Historic Park (end of Hwy. 270, 13 miles east of U.S. 395, 760/647-6445, www.parks.ca.gov, 9 A.M.–6 P.M. daily Memorial Day–Labor Day, 9 A.M.–5 P.M. daily Oct., 9 A.M.–3 P.M. daily winter, adults $7, ages 6–16 $5) is the largest ghost town in California and possibly the best-preserved in the whole country. Its preservation in a state of "arrested decay" means you get to see each house and public building just as it was when it was abandoned. What you see is not a bright shiny museum display; you get the real thing: dust and broken furniture and trash and all. It would take all day to explore the town on foot, and even then you might not see it all. If you take a tour, you can go into the abandoned mine and gain a deeper understanding of the history of the buildings and the town.

The town of Bodie sprang up around a gold mine in 1877. It was never a nice place to live at all. The weather, the work, the scenery, and, some say, the people all tended toward the bleak or the foul. By the 1940s mining had dried up, and the remote location and lack of other viable industry in the area led to Bodie's desertion.

A visit to Bodie takes you back in time to a harsh lifestyle in an extreme climate, miles from the middle of nowhere. As you stroll down the dusty streets, imagine the whole town blanketed in 20 feet of snow in winter and scorched by 100°F temperatures in summer with precious few trees around to provide shade or a hint of green in the unending brown landscape. In a town filled with rough men working the mines, you'd hear the funeral bells tolling at the church every single day—the only honor bestowed on the many murder victims Bodie saw during its

© HEATHER C. LISTON

Bodie State Historic Park

existence. Few families came to Bodie (though a few hardy souls did raise children in the hellish town), and most of Bodie's women earned their keep the old-fashioned way: The prostitution business boomed while mining did.

Today, most of the brothels, stores, and houses of Bodie aren't habitable or even tourable. Structures have been loosely propped up, but it's dangerous to go inside, so doors remain locked. You can peer in the windows at the remains of the lives lived in Bodie, however, and get a sense of hard-core California history.

To reach Bodie, take U.S. 395 to Highway 270 and turn east. Drive 10 miles to the end of the paved road, then continue another three miles on a rough dirt-and-gravel road to the ghost town.

HOOVER WILDERNESS

The Hoover Wilderness (Bridgeport Ranger District, 760/932-7070, www.fs.usda.gov) is a 48,600-acre section of Mono County within the Inyo and Humboldt-Toiyabe National Forests with plenty of room for hiking and camping, and with some sweet mountain lakes to help you enjoy it all. It's a narrow strip of land east of Yosemite and west of Mono Lake that runs into the Ansel Adams Wilderness and Tioga Pass to the south, near the Emigrant Wilderness and Sonora Pass to the north.

Travertine Hot Springs

A delightful treasure in the Eastern Sierra, Travertine Hot Springs (www.monocounty. org) is a naturally occurring series of spring-fed pools hidden in the hills. Only one of the pools has a concrete bottom, added by human hands. The rest are pretty much the way nature made them, with uneven rocky sides. They can be slippery with moss or smelly from sulfur, but if you like to relax outdoors in a peaceful setting, especially under a full moon, you'll find a visit a memorable experience. Temperatures in the small pools vary from warm to extremely hot, so explore the area until you find one that's

YOSEMITE

© MARINA TROOST

Travertine Hot Springs

just right for you. The population varies too: It's not uncommon to have the whole isolated backcountry spot to yourself, but around sunset on a summer weekend you might find the pools crowded with people. And not everyone who visits here wears a bathing suit.

The pools are accessible by car, although finding them can be tricky. To reach Travertine Hot Springs, drive north from Lee Vining on U.S. 395. In about 24 miles, just south of the town of Bridgeport, you'll see a ranger station on the right-hand side, and then a sign that says "Animal Shelter." Turn right at that sign onto Jack Sawyer Road. After a few hundred yards, make a left onto a dirt road and follow it for about a mile until you come to the springs.

Hiking

The strenuous hike from **Glines Canyon to Virginia Pass** (10 miles) starts at an elevation over 8,000 feet and climbs more than 2,500 vertical feet, making it a pretty serious workout among wildflowers, waterfalls, and mountain lakes. Start by walking alongside Green Creek for about 2.5 miles to Green Lake. On the north side of the lake, begin climbing Glines Canyon all the way to Virginia Pass (about 10,500 feet), which is between Yosemite National Park and Hoover Wilderness. From here, you can see Twin Peaks, Matterhorn Peak, and Camiaca Peak, the two small Par Value Lakes, and Soldier Lake, all spread out in various directions far below.

Another strenuous hike that's not quite as long is **Lundy Canyon Trail** (7 miles), although it still gains more than 2,000 feet of elevation. The trail begins by crossing Mill Creek and continues up above Lundy Lake. From here, continue climbing alongside Mill Creek until you reach Blue Lake, then Crystal Lake, and then Oneida Lake. Along the way, you'll see remains of the May Lundy Mine as well as a beaver pond, two waterfalls, and plenty of alpine lakes. This is an out-and-back hike, so turn around when you start to get tired. The trailhead is at the end of Lundy Lake Road; to get here, drive seven miles north of Tioga Pass on U.S. 395. Turn right on Lundy Lake Road and go 6.3 miles, passing the Lundy Lake Resort along the way.

Camping

There's plenty of room for camping throughout the Hoover Wilderness, but you do need a wilderness permit. Pick one up in either of the two National Forests (Humboldt-Toiyabe and Inyo) that share management of the Hoover. Closest to Lee Vining, and much of the rest of this area, is the **Bridgeport Ranger Station** (U.S. 395, Bridgeport, 760/932-7070, www.fs.usda.gov, 8 A.M.–4:30 P.M. Mon.–Fri.). If the Bridgeport Ranger Station is closed, you can self-register there. You can also order a permit by mail up to three weeks in advance of your trip. You can also contact the Inyo National Forest Permit Reservation line (760/873-2483, 8 A.M.–4:30 P.M. daily summer, 8 A.M.–4:30 P.M. Mon.–Fri. winter) or download an application (www.fs.usda.gov) and fax it in (760/873-2484).

Food

The **Bridgeport Inn** (205 Main St., Bridgeport, 760/932-7380, 8 A.M.–9 P.M. Thurs.–Tues. mid-Mar.–mid-Nov., $10–30) offers the most genteel dining experience around here, with steaks, fish, and salads in a historic-inn sort of atmosphere. For something more youthful and budget-friendly, the place to go is **Rhinos Bar & Grille** (226 Main St., Bridgeport, 760/932-7345, 11 A.M.–9 P.M. Sun.–Thurs., 11 A.M.–10 P.M. Fri.–Sat. Mar.–Dec., $10).

Information and Services

In this northern section of the Eastern Sierra, the best place for information is the **Bridgeport Ranger Station** (U.S. 395, Bridgeport, 760/932-7070, www.fs.usda.gov, 8 A.M.–4:30 P.M. Mon.–Fri.). There's also the small **Bridgeport Museum and Visitors Center** (123 Emigrant St., 760/932-7500, www.bridgeportcalifornia.com, 8 A.M.–6 P.M. daily May–Oct.) in downtown Bridgeport, run by the local Chamber of Commerce.

Getting There and Around

Green Lakes, Bodie, and the Hoover Wilderness are all on the east side of Yosemite National Park. If you're traveling from the Bay Area in summer, you have a choice of routes. You can cut through Yosemite on Tioga Road (closed in winter); or you can take the northern route along Sonora Pass, also known as Highway 108 (closed in winter). The route along Tioga Road takes about six hours. From San Francisco, take I-580 east to I-205 east to Highway 120 east. Enter the park through the Big Oak Flat Entrance and drive south to the junction with Tioga Road. Take Tioga Road east for almost 60 miles to U.S. 395. Drive north on U.S 395, and in 26 miles you'll come to the town of Bridgeport, the most significant town of any size near the Hoover Wilderness.

To travel via the Sonora Pass, when Highway 108 splits from Highway 120, east of Oakdale, stick with Highway 108 and head north. When you get to U.S. 395, turn right and drive south. After a total of about 228 miles (5 hours), you'll reach Bridgeport. To get from Bridgeport to Bodie, take U.S 395 south another seven miles, then make a left onto Highway 270, also known as Bodie Road (Bodie lies 12.8 miles down this partly unpaved road).

In winter, when Tioga Road and Highway 108 are closed, take I-80 east from the Bay Area for about 80 miles before turning onto U.S. 50 east for about 100 miles. Turn right onto Highway 89/88 and drive about 30 miles until you reach U.S. 395. Turn right (south) onto U.S. 395, and you'll arrive in Lee Vining in another 93 miles. The total distance is about 300 miles, a travel time of about six hours, depending on traffic and weather.

YOSEMITE

JUNE LAKE

The small community of June Lake lies east of Yosemite, just 15 minutes south of Mono Lake and Lee Vining. Although less famous than Mammoth Lakes, its neighbor to the south, June Lake is a popular ski destination, thanks primarily to June Mountain, which offers everything you need in a ski resort, yet manages to hold onto the feeling of an unspoiled outdoor wonderland. Although the town is named for just one of the alpine lakes nearby, there are actually four: Gull Lake, Silver Lake, and Grant Lake. Each has its own style of beauty. If you don't have time to stop by for a swim, you can still enjoy driving the scenic 15-mile June Lake Loop.

June Lake Loop

The 15-mile scenic June Lake Loop (Hwy. 158), accessible from U.S. 395 south of Lee Vining, takes you away from the high-traffic, heavily visited areas of the Eastern Sierra. Along the way, you get the full-fledged alpine experience. Once you get out of the car, the loop's namesake—June Lake—offers good recreation. You can take a hike, go fishing, or even plan to stay overnight at one of the campgrounds. Next you'll come to Gull Lake, and then to Silver Lake, two other popular boating and angling waterways. As you drive north on the loop, stop at least once to admire Reversed Peak, a 9,500-foot Sierra mountain. Finally, you'll come to Grant Lake. There are no resorts or major trailheads here, but you'll find a boat launch and some spectacular alpine trout fishing. Finally, take a break at the Mono Craters Monument before heading back out to U.S. 395 toward Lee Vining or Mammoth Mountain.

June Mountain

Like so many other parts of the Eastern Sierra, June Lake as a vacation destination is largely about skiing. Although the lake and the others nearby make lovely summer recreation spots, most people who come here are headed for the snow. One of the most popular places to hit the slopes in this area is the **June Mountain Ski Resort** (3819 Hwy. 158, 760/648-7733, www. junemountain.com, lifts 8:30 A.M.–4 P.M. daily, adults $72, seniors $36, ages 13–18 $54, ages 7–12 $20). About 20 miles north of Mammoth Lakes, June Mountain offers seven lifts (two quads, four doubles, and a carpet) and more than 2,500 feet of vertical drops on 500 skiable acres. The resort caters to beginners and intermediate skiers, and 80 percent of its trails are green or blue. Beginners can even take a lift up to the top of Rainbow Summit and enjoy a long run down the Silverado Trail. However, a number of black and double black-diamond slopes make a trip to June Mountain fun for more advanced skiers and boarders as well. Thrill-seeking experts and adventurous intermediates head up to the top of June Mountain Summit and then plummet down the bowl (hard-core double black diamond) or slide along the ridgeline (blue). Be sure to check your trail map before going up this way unless you're very sure of your abilities. For a cup of coffee or hot chocolate, stop at the June Meadows Chalet (top of Chair J1, breakfast and lunch from 8 A.M. daily) at the center of the ski area.

Accommodations and Food

June Lake has plenty of cabins and lodges available. One particularly nice one is the **Double Eagle Resort and Spa** (5587 Hwy. 158, June Lake, 760/648-7004, www.doubleeagle.com, year-round, $199–349). Its 15 two-bedroom cabins ($349) sleep up to six, and all come complete with decks and fully equipped kitchens. The 16 luxurious lodge rooms ($199–229) come with breakfast, free Internet access, and whirlpool tubs. The on-site Creekside Spa includes an indoor pool and a fitness center, and the resort's **Eagle's Landing Restaurant** (7 A.M.–9 P.M. daily, $20–30) helps make this an everything-you-need destination, whether you're seeking an active trip or a relaxing getaway.

A little more rustic but also very pleasant is **The Four Seasons** (24 Venice St., 760/648-7476, www.junelakesfourseasons.com, late Apr.–Oct., $129–195), which, ironically, is only open in summer. The five A-frame cabins each sleep up to six, with a master bedroom and a sleeping loft as well as a full kitchen, a living room, and a large deck. The resort is just two miles from the town of June Lake and a short drive to all the lakes.

Camping

The U.S. Forest Service maintains several campgrounds near June Lake in the Inyo National Forest. A particularly good one is **Silver Lake Campground** (Hwy. 158, 7 miles west of U.S. 395, reservations www.recreation.gov, mid-Apr.–mid-Nov., $18). Each of the 39 sites has a bear-proof food locker, a picnic table, and a fire ring; the campground has flush toilets, drinking water, and even a small store. The best part is that the campground is right on the shore of lovely Silver Lake, which is a good place to fish, watch for wildlife, or just sit and enjoy the view.

Information and Services

The small **June Lake Visitors Center** (U.S. 395 and Hwy. 158, 760/648-1917, summer only) is staffed by volunteers, so there's no guarantee of when it is open. Call first before planning a visit.

Getting There

June Lake is located east of Yosemite, west of U.S. 395, south of Lee Vining, and north of Mammoth Lakes. To get to June Lake, take U.S. 395 and turn west onto Highway 158 at the June Lake Loop. June Mountain Ski Resort is about four miles west of U.S. 395.

Mammoth Lakes

The town of Mammoth Lakes, located east of Yosemite and about 28 miles south of Tioga Pass, started out as a gold mining settlement and then became a logging site. The gorgeous mountain scenery, however, along with multiple alpine lakes, natural hot springs, and dependable snowfall, soon helped to establish Mammoth Lakes as a prime tourist destination. Today, outdoor sports—and skiing in particular—is the town's main reason for existing. Ski and snowboard season can last up to 11 months, so don't be surprised if you come for hiking in July and see lifts running and skiers gliding down the hills. Even when the snow stops, this idyllic town and its surrounding nature do not grind to a halt. In winter, the roads are subject to the whims of weather, although they rarely close. It's best to carry chains and to check weather reports before starting out.

SIGHTS
The Village at Mammoth Lakes

Like many large ski resort areas, the Village at Mammoth Lakes (www.thevillageatmammoth.com) is a hybrid of a real town, an overly planned shopping mall, and a clean, upscale amusement park. Its central purpose, of course, is to provide support services for people who come to enjoy Mammoth Mountain, most of whom are skiers. To that end, the Village offers lodging (including the Juniper Springs Resort), dining (the standard chains plus a few local places), and shopping—all organized around a central pedestrian plaza. In summer, the plaza is sprinkled with outdoor benches, tables with umbrellas, and recently planted greenery as it tries to impersonate an actual village square. Concerts and outdoor movies are presented here in the warmer months.

YOSEMITE

Gondola Rides

Mammoth Mountain, like all ski resorts, has plenty of gondolas, chairlifts, and other ways to get up to the mountain while relaxing and enjoying the view. Of the two main gondolas, one is open only in winter: **Village Gondola** takes you from the Village at Mammoth Lakes to Canyon Lodge. The other gondola, **Panorama Gondola,** sometimes called the Scenic Gondola Ride, operates in summer and winter. Panorama runs from the Main Lodge at Mammoth to McCoy Station and then, after a stop there, goes all the way to the top of the mountain. In winter, the gondola is extremely popular with skiers: Intermediate-level skiers get off at McCoy to access the trails there; the top of the mountain is for experts only. In summer (9 A.M.–4 P.M. daily June–Sept., adults $21, ages 13–18 $17, under age 13 free with an adult) it serves sightseers, mountain bikers, hikers, and anyone else who wants to get to the top of the 11,053-foot mountain. From the top, you can see as far as 400 miles on a clear day.

The ride all the way to the top takes about 20 minutes. Some people do it just for the thrill of the ride; others stop for a meal or a snack at the **Top of the Sierra Café** (9:30 A.M.–4 P.M. daily summer, 8:30 A.M.–3:30 P.M. daily winter, $8–20), open when the gondola is running.

One of the most popular reasons to ride up is to ride down—on your mountain bike. In summer, 70 miles of trails are open for biking and 25 miles of hiking trails are available. You can buy a day pass (over age 12 $43, under age 13 $22) to bike the trails, which includes all-day access to both the Panorama Gondola and the shuttle. Hikers only pay to ride the gondola, and then they're free to walk down. If you're not a skier, you can still ride the Panorama Gondola to the top and back in winter (ages 18–64 $24, over age 64 $20, ages 13–17 $19, ages 7–12 $8).

The Panorama Gondola is usually closed only in October for maintenance between the two big seasons.

Inyo Craters

California is full of volcanic action, and some of the most interesting results to behold are the three Inyo Craters (www.fs.usda.gov). These phreatic craters on and near Deer Mountain were created by explosions of steam. Scientists believe that all three craters came into being at about the same time, around A.D. 1350. Two of the three craters are about 200 feet deep and large enough that they actually have lakes inside them. The third crater is smaller, but all are worth seeing. If you can, make time for this geologic side trip.

To reach Inyo Craters, drive five miles north of Mammoth Lakes on Highway 203. Turn right (east) onto the Mammoth Scenic Route (Dry Creek Rd.) and continue about 3.2 miles until you see the sign for the Inyo Craters. Turn right at the sign and drive about 1.3 more miles on a dirt road (not plowed, or advised, in winter). Park in the lot and walk 0.3 mile to the crater site.

◖ Devils Postpile National Monument

Compared to the area's other national parks, Devils Postpile National Monument (Minaret Vista Rd., 760/934-2289, www.nps.gov/depo, mid-June–mid-Oct., park 24 hours daily, ranger station 9 A.M.–5 P.M. daily, adults $7, ages 3–15 $4) is small, but what you'll see is worth a visit. The park is named for the strange natural rock formation called the Devils Postpile. It's hard to fathom that the near-perfect, straight-sided hexagonal posts are a natural phenomenon created by volcanic heat and pressure; you have to see it to believe it. Less heavily traveled than many other parks, Devils Postpile has hikes to serene meadows and unspoiled streams, and you're likely to see the occasional deer or maybe even a bear meandering through the woods. Free

© STAN NESTER

Devils Postpile National Monument

guided ranger walks are held at 11 A.M. most days throughout the summer, starting from the ranger station.

Also part of the monument is the beautiful crystalline **Rainbow Falls.** The thick sheet of water cascades 101 feet down to a pool, throwing up stunning rainbows of mist. For the best rainbows at the waterfall, hike the three miles (round-trip) from Red Meadow near the middle of the day when the sun is high in the sky.

The $7 park entry fee includes the Reds Meadow–Devils Postpile Shuttle. Visitors are required to access the park via the shuttle, which runs hourly 7–11 A.M. daily from the Village at Mammoth Lakes and every 15–30 minutes 7 A.M.–7 P.M. daily mid-June–early September from the Mammoth Mountain Adventure Center and Main Lodge area. When the shuttle stops running for the season in September, visitors may drive their cars into the park, but the $7 fee still applies.

Old Mammoth Road

Like most of the Eastern Sierra region, Mammoth Lakes became of interest to miners in the 19th century after the gold rush began—miners got out this far in 1877. Along Old Mammoth Road (south off Hwy. 203/ Main St.) you'll find a number of old mining sites. At the height of the short-lived boom, about 20 different small mines operated in the area. Along this road, you can see the grave of a miner's wife, a stamp mill's flywheel, and then the meager remains of Mammoth City and the nearby Mammoth Mine. The highlight of this summertime half-day trip is the ruins of the Mammoth Consolidated Mine. You can still see some bits of the camp and its housing buildings, the assay office, the mill, and mining equipment. The mine shaft is also visible, but do not attempt to get around the security features to head down there. Old mine shafts are unbelievably dangerous and should not be entered for any reason.

YOSEMITE

SPORTS AND RECREATION
Skiing
MAMMOTH MOUNTAIN

The premier downhill ski and snowboard mountain is, aptly, Mammoth Mountain (1 Minaret Rd., information 760/934-2571, lodging and lift tickets 800/626-6684, snow report 888/766-9778, www.mammothmountain.com, lift 8:30 A.M.–4 P.M. daily, 2011–2012 rates adults $96, ages 7–12 $30). Whether you're completely new to downhill thrills or a seasoned expert looking for different terrain, you'll find something great on Mammoth Mountain. More than two dozen lifts, including three gondolas and nine express quads, take you up 3,100 vertical feet to the 3,500 acres of skiable and boardable terrain; there are also three pipes. If you're staying at Eagle Lodge, Canyon Lodge, Mammoth Mountain Inn, or the Village at Mammoth Lakes, enjoy the convenience of a lift or gondola right outside your door. All these, plus the Mill Café and McCoy Station halfway up the mountain, offer hot drinks, tasty snacks, and a welcome spot to rest during a long day of skiing.

The easiest runs on the mountain mostly cluster around the ski school and the lower area near the Mammoth Mountain Inn; they are recognizable by their cute nursery-school names. If you're an intermediate skier, runs swing down all over the mountain just for you. Build your confidence by taking the Panorama Gondola up to Panorama Lookout at the top of the mountain then skiing all the way down the east side of the mountain along the intermediate-to-harder ridge runs. Advanced skiers favor the bowls and chutes at the front of the mountain, and hard-core experts go west from Panorama Lookout to chase the dragon.

TAMARACK CROSS-COUNTRY SKI CENTER

Here's your chance to explore the snow-covered Mammoth Lakes Basin in winter. Tamarack (163 Twin Lakes Rd., 760/934-2442, www.tamaracklodge.com, 8:30 A.M.–5 P.M. daily mid-Nov.–Apr., adults $22–27, youths and seniors $17–21, children $12–15) offers 19 miles of groomed cross-country ski tracks, some with groomed skating lanes, for all abilities and levels. This lovely resort also has a restaurant, a lounge, and a bar where you can enjoy a nice cup of hot chocolate and good book if you get tired of skiing. And getting here from Mammoth Lakes is free: Just take the Orange shuttle line from Mammoth Village hourly on the half-hour 8:30 A.M.–5 P.M. daily in winter.

BLUE DIAMOND TRAILS

The Blue Diamond Trails (www.mammoth.us/winter/blue_diamond_trail.shtml) system starts just behind the Mammoth Lakes Welcome Center (Hwy. 203, 3 miles west of U.S. 395, 760/924-5500, www.visitmammoth.com, 8 A.M.–5 P.M. daily), at the entrance to Mammoth Lakes, and winds through 25 miles of Inyo National Forest, marked by signs bearing a blue diamond on the trees. Pick up a free trail map in the Welcome Center before you set out. Some trails are not groomed, so be prepared to deal with varying snow conditions and unbroken trails. There's plenty of relatively flat land here for beginners, however. The Shady Rest Trails (Hwy. 203, just before the Welcome Center) might sound like a cemetery, but in fact it's a group of beginner loops with plenty of shade trees to keep skiers cool through their exertions. The Knolls Trail (Mammoth Scenic Loop, 1.5 miles north of Hwy. 203) makes a good intermediate day out, passing through lovely stands of lodgepole and Jeffrey pines. Beginners beware of the deceptively named Scenic Loop Trail (Mammoth Scenic Loop, across from Knolls Trail); this reasonably short trail—about four miles long—includes steep descents and some difficult terrain.

Hiking

Hikers will find plenty of worthwhile terrain

around Mammoth Lakes for both short day hikes and longer backpacking adventures. The **Mammoth Mountain Bike Park** (1 Minaret Rd., 800/626-6684, www.mammothmountain.com/bike_ride, 8 A.M.–6 P.M. daily summer) includes a number of great hiking trails. For an all-downhill walk, take the Panorama Gondola (9 A.M.–4 P.M. daily June–Sept., adults $21, ages 13–18 $17, under age 13 free with an adult) up to the Panorama Overlook and hike back down to town. Just be sure to get a trail map at the **Mammoth Adventure Center** (1 Minaret Rd., 800/626-6684, www.mammothmountain.com/bike_ride, daily 8 A.M.–6 P.M. June–Sept.) so you can keep to the hiking areas and avoid being flattened by fast-moving mountain bikers.

Mammoth Lakes also acts as a jumping-off point for adventurers who want to take on the **John Muir Wilderness** (south of Mammoth Lakes to Mount Whitney, www.sierranevadawild.gov/wild/john-muir). John Muir pioneered the preservation of the Sierra Nevadas, and more than 500,000 acres in the area have been designated national wilderness areas in his honor. Day hikers are welcome, and there's plenty to see. Check with the Inyo and Sierra National Forests (www.fs.usda.gov) for trail maps of the area. The main attractions to the John Muir, as it's called locally, are the **John Muir Trail** (JMT, 215 miles Yosemite–Mount Whitney, www.johnmuirtrail.org) and the **Pacific Crest National Scenic Trail** (PCT, 2,650 miles Mexican border–Canadian border, www.pcta.org), both among the holiest of grails for backpacking enthusiasts from around the world.

If you're planning an overnight camping trip in the John Muir, Ansel Adams, Dinkey Lakes, or Kaiser Wilderness areas of the Sierra National Forest, you must first obtain a wilderness permit. You can apply for these up to one year in advance by downloading an application from www.fs.usda.gov/sierra or by calling 559/297-0706. If you reserve in advance, there

is a charge of $5 pp for the permit. On the other hand, if you're willing to be flexible, you can just show up at a ranger station no more than 24 hours before your trip begins and apply in person. There is no charge for these "walk-up" permits, although their availability is not guaranteed. The main office is the **High Sierra Ranger District Office** (29688 Auberry Rd., Prather, 559/855-5355, 8 A.M.–4:30 P.M. daily).

If you're planning an overnight in the Inyo National Forest, you can apply for your permit in person at the **Mammoth Lakes Welcome Center** (Hwy. 203, 3 miles west of U.S. 395, 760/924-5500, www.visitmammoth.com, daily 8 A.M.–5 P.M.), at the entrance to Mammoth Lakes, or apply online (www.fs.usda.gov/inyo).

Biking

Come summertime and melting snow, Mammoth Mountain transforms from a ski resort to a mountain bike mecca. The **Mammoth Mountain Bike Park** (1 Minaret Rd., 800/626-6684, www.mammothmountain.com/bike_ride, 8 A.M.–6 P.M. daily, $10 for trail access, $43 for trail, gondola, and shuttle access) spans much of the same terrain as the ski areas, with almost 90 miles of trails that suit all levels of biking ability. The park headquarters is at the **Mammoth Adventure Center** (Main Lodge, 1 Minaret Rd., 760/934-0706 or 800/626-6684, 8 A.M.–6 P.M. daily June–Sept.), at the Main Lodge at Mammoth Mountain. You can also buy bike park tickets at the Mountain Center at the Village (760/924-7057).

You can take your bike onto the Panorama Gondola and ride all the way to the top of Mammoth Mountain, then ride all the way down (3,000-plus vertical feet) on the single tracks. Be sure to pick the trails that best suit your fitness and experience level. Several other major lodges offer rider services, including the Village at Mammoth Lakes, Juniper Springs, the Panorama Lookout, and Outpost 14. If you value scenery as much as extreme adventure,

YOSEMITE

pack your camera and plan to rest at the various scenic overlooks throughout the trail system.

If you need to rent a bike or buy park tickets, go to the **Mammoth Adventure Center** (Main Lodge, 1 Minaret Rd., 760/934-0706) or to the **Mammoth Mart at the Village** (6201 Minaret Rd., inside the Village, 760/934-2571, ext. 2078). Both locations offer new high-end bikes for adults and kids. These shops can also help with parts and repairs for bikes you've brought up with you, and they sell accessories.

Horseback Riding

Perhaps the most traditional way to explore the Eastern Sierra is on the back of a horse or mule. Early pioneers to the area came on horseback, and you can follow their example from several locations near Mammoth Lakes. From the **McGee Creek Pack Station** (2990 McGee Creek Rd., Crowley Lake, June 1–Sept. 30 760/935-4324, Oct. 1–May 31 760/878-2207, www.mcgeecreekpackstation.com, $35 per hour, $125 9 A.M.–5 P.M.), 10 miles south of Mammoth Lakes on U.S. 395, you can ride into McGee Canyon, a little-visited wilderness area. Other day-trip destinations include Baldwin Canyon and Hilton Lakes. Standard rides range from one hour to a full day, but McGee's specialty is multiday and pack trips that let you really get out beyond the reach of paved roads to camp for a number of days by one of the many pristine lakes dotting the mountains. If you love the outdoors and really want a vacation as far away from it all as you can get, consider a few days' camping in Convict Basin or near Upper Fish Creek in the John Muir Wilderness. The McGee Creek guides will help you pack your gear and guide you through the incredible backcountry of the Eastern Sierra.

Snowshoeing

If you prefer walking to all that sliding around on planks, rent or bring your own snowshoes to Mammoth and enjoy a snowy hike through the mountains and meadows. Check the cross-country ski areas first—many have specifically designated snowshoe trails. Or head out to the backcountry and explore Mammoth Lakes Basin or the Sherwin Range. Groomed trails start right behind the Mammoth Lakes Welcome Center.

ATVs and Snowmobiles

ATVs, dirt bikes, and snowmobiles are a big no-no in most national parks and wilderness areas; not so at Mammoth Lakes. Here you'll find miles of trails set aside for motorized fun. Eighty miles of groomed trails and 75,000 acres of snow-covered meadows and mountainsides await snowmobilers each winter. Much of the same territory is open to ATV and dirt-bike traffic in the summer. Get a copy of the *Mammoth Lakes Winter Recreation Guide* for a complete trail and area map to find the best (and legal) places to play. The guide is available at local hotels and businesses and at the **Mammoth Lakes Welcome Center** (Hwy. 203, 3 miles west of U.S. 395, 760/924-5500, www.visitmammoth. com or www.fs.usda.gov/inyo, 8 A.M.–5 P.M. daily) at the entrance to Mammoth Lakes.

To rent snowmobile equipment, ATVs, and other sporty vehicles in Mammoth Lakes, visit the Mammoth location of **Bishop Motosports** (58 Commerce Dr., 760/872-4717, www. bishopmotosports.com, by appointment early morning–10 P.M. daily, $225–275 for 3 hours, $400–500 full day). Maps, helmets, and trailers for off-road vehicles are included with all rentals.

Golf

If you're in the Mammoth Lakes area in the summer, you can enjoy a round of golf at a beautiful course with stunning mountain views. The 18-hole, par 70 **Sierra Star Golf Course** (2001 Sierra Star Pkwy., 760/924-4653, www.mammothmountain.com, $99–129) is open to the public. Walk this wonderful course for the best views of the surrounding Sierra Nevadas, or concentrate all your efforts on the game. Amenities include a full-service pro shop, a PGA golf pro on-site, and a café with a full bar.

Spas

If you want to enjoy some pampering after a hard day of skiing, book a treatment at one of Mammoth Lakes's day spas. The **Bodyworks Mountain Spa** (3343 Main St., 760/924-3161, www.bodyworksmountainspa.com, $60–95 for a 1-hour Swedish massage), located upstairs at the Luxury Outlet Mall, offers massage therapy, spa treatments, and facials, plus a wide range of combination packages to maximize your time and money at the spa.

The **InTouch MicroSpa** (3325 Main St., 760/934-2836, www.intouchmicrospa.com, $85 for a 1-hour massage) offers a full menu of treatments with a focus on the four elements of earth, air, fire, and water. Exclusively using Aveda products, InTouch caters to spa-goers who care about what's put on their skin. A number of different styles of facials and aesthetic treatments are available.

Located inside the Best Western Hotel, the day spa **BellaDonna** (3228 Main St., 760/934-3344, www.belladonnamammoth.com, $85 for a 1-hour massage) offers a crackling fireplace, a serene setting, and all sorts of massages, facials, manicures, and pedicures. If you're looking for romance, check out the couples side-by-side fireside massage.

ENTERTAINMENT AND EVENTS
Bars and Clubs

For possibly the best evening in Mammoth, try the **Clocktower Cellar Pub** (Alpenhof Lodge, 6080 Minaret Rd., 760/934-2725, www.alpenhof-lodge.com, 4:30 P.M.–midnight daily winter, 5 P.M.–midnight daily summer, food service 4:30–10 P.M. daily, $3–12). This happening nightspot offers a full bar with more than 125 whiskeys, 26 brews on tap, and 50 different bottled beers. They also provide

glasses of fine wine cadged from Petra next door, and a casual atmosphere complete with sports on TV, vintage video games, and a pool table. Instead of an obnoxious pickup joint, the Clocktower acts as a refuge for locals looking for some after-work relaxation and a pint or two. Expect informal dress and friendly conversation up at the bar, along with the delicious and unusual variety of beers. The location is perfect—in the basement of the Alpenhof just across the street from the Village. Note that the Clocktower closes for a few weeks in what they call the "shoulder seasons." If you're visiting in October or May–June, call ahead to be sure they're open.

If you prefer a French-style wine bar experience to a noisy British-style pub, try the vintages at the **Side Door Bistro** (100 Canyon Blvd., Suite 229, 760/934-5200, www.sidedoormammoth.com, 7 A.M.–10:30 P.M. Sun.–Thurs., 7 A.M.–midnight Fri.–Sat. winter, 11 A.M.–9 P.M. daily summer, $8–11). Not only can you enjoy glasses of California's top wines in the evening, you can order up a delicious dinner or dessert crepe to go with your favorite varietal. Or you can show up in the morning in the winter and enjoy a breakfast crepe with your coffee. The crepes are excellent, and the wine list is often called the best in the Village. Note that the hours at many places in Mammoth Lakes, including the Side Door, can vary considerably with the seasons. The manager of the Side Door notes that they're open "till 9 P.M. or later" in summer and winter, and also that they often close a few days a week during spring and fall; but they're always open on weekends.

Didn't get enough sports during your day at Mammoth? Spend the evening at **Grumpy's** (361 Old Mammoth Rd., 760/934-8587, www.grumpysmammoth.com, 11 A.M.–1:30 A.M. Mon.–Thurs., 11 A.M.–1:30 A.M. Fri.–Sat., 10 A.M.–1:30 A.M. Sun., food service until 10 P.M., $10–24). This sports bar has the usual array of TVs showing major sporting events, along with pool tables and an arcade. Grumpy's has a full bar and serves up a lunch and dinner menu of Mexican and American specialties.

The **Lakanuki Tiki Bar** (6201 Minaret Rd., 760/934-7447, www.lakanuki.com, 3 P.M.–2 A.M. Mon. and Thurs., 10 A.M.–2 A.M. Fri.–Sun., food service until 10 P.M., $6–22) serves fresh fish, steaks, and stir-fries, but it's the nightlife in the tacky tiki bar that packs the place, especially on weekends, with the young male snowboarding crowd. Note that hours may vary, so call ahead to be sure they're open.

Live Music

For an exceptional evening of classical music in the mountains, check out a performance of **Chamber Music Unbound** (760/934-7015, www.felicitrio.com, late July–early Aug., adults $25, seniors $17, students $10, season passes $190). This nonprofit group mixes the familiar with out-of-the-way classical pieces and performs at several locations in Bishop and Mammoth Lakes. Most of the annual festival takes place at Cerro Coso Community College (101 College Pkwy.).

Festivals and Events

Whatever the season, Mammoth is about vacations and recreation, and locals plan plenty of special events each year to celebrate. In late September, the Village at Mammoth Lakes throws an **Oktoberfest** (760/924-1575, www.villageatmammoth.com). "Roktoberfest" is 6–9 P.M. on Friday night and features concerts, food, and drink, and there are events all day Saturday—keg-tossing, Bavarian food tasting, and children's activities.

We probably don't need to tell you when **The Village 4th of July Festivities** (760/924-1575, www.villageatmammoth.com) take place. This all-weekend party includes concerts and rubber ducky races; everyone is welcome. The town's official Independence Day event is the **Mammoth Lakes 4th of July Celebration**

(888/466-2666, www.mammothfestivals.com), which features a Lion's Club Pancake Breakfast, a parade, fireworks, and Pops in the Park.

If music is your thing, check out the **Sierra Summer Festival** (760/935-3837, www.sierrasummerfestival.org, $20–30, discounts for students) in August. The Eastern Sierra Symphony Orchestra, under musical director Bogidar Avramov, performs during this weeklong festival, along with special guests. For art enthusiasts, the **Labor Day Arts Festival** (760/937-2942, www.monoarts.org) has been going on for more than 40 years, showcasing both fine artists and craftspeople.

Not surprisingly, there are plenty of special sporting events around here too. Late August brings the **Mammoth Mud Run** (Village at Mammoth, 100 Canyon Blvd., 800/626-6684, www.mammothmountain.com, adults $49–60, ages 5–12 $15), a 6K race for adults and a 1K for kids, both full of obstacles and chances to get dirty.

A Saturday in August brings the **Mammoth Lakes Challenge Triathlon** (415/335-0179, www.sierra-nevada-races.com, $40), and the next day the same organization—that is, Bay Area schoolteacher and runner Gail Pavlich, whose passions include triathlons and Mammoth Lakes scenery—puts on the **Quake & Shake 10K & Half-Marathon** ($30). The Quake & Shake takes place in Inyo Crater, three miles north of Mammoth Lakes. It's a beautiful but not-too-hilly course through changing scenery. Pavlich's third event each year is called **George's Tri** ($40), which she believes may be the highest-elevation triathlon anywhere. It's run at 9,000 feet, with a 0.25-mile swim in Horseshoe Lake, three laps of the lake on a mountain bike, and a two-mile run on a loop trail up and down Mammoth Pass. Wetsuits and mountain bikes are strongly recommended in this rugged region, but if you're concerned about your abilities in one area, don't worry: Families and friends often do this event as a relay, so one person bikes, one swims, and one runs.

On the Sunday of Labor Day weekend,

the High Sierra Triathlon Club puts on the **Mammoth Rock Race 10K** (760/717-0176, www.highsierratri.org, $30–40), which it claims is California's highest-elevation 10K. The race starts and ends in Mammoth Creek Park and has an average elevation of about 8,000 feet. For cyclists, there's the **High Sierra Fall Century** (760/914-0396, www.fallcentury. org, $60) held on a Saturday in September. This gorgeous 100-mile course with its autumn scenery is almost entirely free of stop-and-signs; the entry fee includes a lavish lunch, five rest stops, and plenty of snacks.

And what's a festival roundup without beer? In early August, the annual **Mammoth Festival of Beers and Bluespalooza** (888/992-7397, www.mammothbluesbrewsfest.com, $35 individual events, $135 weekend pass) gives attendees the chance to sample the work of more than 60 craft breweries and listen to major performers like Robert Cray and Blues Traveler.

SHOPPING

While it's not a big shopping town, Mammoth Lakes has some upscale boutiques and galleries and a small outlet mall that allows weary adventurers to take a day off the slopes and engage in some retail therapy.

In downtown Mammoth Lakes, visit the **Mammoth Gallery** (501 Old Mammoth Rd., 760/934-6120 or 888/848-7733, www.mammothgallery.com, 10 A.M.–5 P.M. daily) to see the work of a number of local photographers and watercolor artists plus a large collection of vintage ski poster reproductions. Another photo gallery in Mammoth Lakes, formerly located in Bishop, is the **Vern Clevenger Gallery** (220 Sierra Manor Rd., Unit 4, 760/934-5100, www.vernclevenger.com, 1–5 P.M. Mon. and Wed.–Sat., and by appointment), which features only the nature photography of Mr. Clevenger himself. What you see in his work is all natural, with no digital enhancement to the images or colors. Inexpensive note cards and

posters are available for purchase in addition to the lovely framed fine-art prints. You can also take a workshop to learn how to create these gorgeous images yourself.

ACCOMMODATIONS
Under $100

Want to ski the slopes of Mammoth, but can't afford the hoity-toity condo resorts? Stay at the **Innsbruck Lodge** (Forest Trail between Hwy. 203 and Sierra Blvd., 760/934-3035, www.innsbrucklodge.com, $95–165). Economy rooms offer twin beds, a table and chairs, and access to the motel whirlpool tub and lobby with a stone fireplace at very reasonable nightly rates. Other rooms have queen or king beds, some can sleep 2–6, and some include kitchenettes. The quiet North Village location is on the ski area shuttle route for easy access to the local slopes. It's also an easy walk to most restaurants and other Village attractions.

The inexpensive **Boulder Lodge** (2282 Hwy. 158, 760/648-7533 or 800/458-6355, www.boulderlodgejunelake.com, Oct.–May $88–265, June–Sept. $98–365) provides an array of options, from simple motel rooms for short stays to multiple-bedroom apartments and even a five-bedroom lake house for longer trips and larger groups. The Boulder Lodge takes guests back a few decades with its decorating style— the browns, wood paneling, and faux leather furniture recall the 1950s. But the views of June Lake, the indoor pool and spa, and the wonderful outdoor recreation area surrounding the lodge are timeless.

$100-150

The **Sierra Lodge** (3540 Main St., 760/934-8881 or 800/356-5711, www.sierralodge.com, $119–129) offers reasonably priced all-non-smoking guest rooms located right on the ski shuttle line, and only 1.5 miles from the Juniper Ridge chair lift. This small motel's rates are rock-bottom in the off-season and on weekdays

YOSEMITE

in winter. Guest rooms have either a king or two double beds, a kitchenette with a microwave and dishes, and plenty of space for your snow and ski gear. The decor is simple motel styling in cool, relaxing blues. Breakfast, cable TV, and Internet access are included with your room.

One of the best things about the **Tamarack Lodge & Resort** (163 Twin Lakes Rd., Mammoth Lakes, 760/934-2442, www.tamaracklodge.com) is that you can cross-country ski right up to your door. There are 11 lodge rooms ($100–200) and 35 cabins ($200–799), ranging from studios to three-bedroom units that sleep up to nine. Lodge rooms sometimes go for as low as $79 per night on weeknights. Tamarack prides itself on its rustic atmosphere, so accommodations have fireplaces or wood stoves, but no televisions.

$150-250

From the outside, the ornate, carved-wood, fringed **Austria Hof** (924 Canyon Blvd., 760/934-2764 or 866/662-6668, www.austriahof.com, $150–170) might be a ski hotel tucked into a crevice of the Alps. But on the inside, you'll find the most stylish American appointments. Winter is high season for these peaceful, sea-green motel rooms—some with king beds and spa bathtubs—and rates can be considerably more on weekends and holidays. In summer, however, guest rooms can be rented for less than $100. Austria Hof's location adjacent to the Canyon Lodge and the free gondola to the Village make it a great base camp for winter skiing or summer mountain biking. In the evening, head down to the Austria Hof Restaurant ($25) for some hearty German fare.

Across the street from Mammoth Mountain's Main Lodge and right beside the Panorama Gondola, is the **Mammoth Mountain Inn** (1 Minaret Rd., Mammoth Lakes, 760/934-2581, 800/626-8684, www.mammothmountain.com). The main building at the Inn features standard hotel rooms ($159–249) in various sizes. The nearby East-West Building (also part of the Inn) features condos that range from studios ($299) to one-bedrooms ($329) to deluxe two-bedrooms with lofts that can sleep up to 11 people ($749/night in ski season). All rooms and condos have flat-screen TVs in addition to all the amenities you'd expect in an upscale ski lodge.

Over $250

It's not cheap, but the ◖ **Juniper Springs Resort** (4000 Meridian Blvd., reservations 760/924-1102 or 800/626-6684, www.mammothmountain.com/lodging/juniperspringsresort, $300–900 winter, $119–269 off-season) has absolutely every luxury amenity you could want to make your ski vacation complete. Condos come in studio, 1–3-bedroom, and townhouse sizes, sleeping up to eight. The interiors have stunning appointments, from snow-white down comforters to granite-topped kitchen counters and 60-inch flat-screen TVs. Baths include deep soaking tubs, perfect to relax aching muscles privately after a long day on the slopes. The resort also features heated pools year-round and three outdoor heated spas—there's nothing like jumping into a steaming hot tub on a snowy evening, and then jumping back out to find the cold perfect and refreshing. The on-site **Talons Restaurant** (760/934-0797 or 760/934-2571, ext. 3797, 7:30 A.M.–5 P.M. daily Nov.–Apr.) serves breakfast and lunch in winter only, and the **Daily Grind** (7 A.M.–1 P.M. daily summer, 7 A.M.–10 P.M. daily winter) provides coffee and snacks year-round. Juniper Springs is located next door to the Eagle Lodge, which serves as one of the Mammoth Mountain base lodges, complete with a six-seat express chairlift up to the main ski area.

The company that owns Juniper Springs also owns the luxury condo complex at **The Village Lodge** (1111 Forest Trail, 760/934-1982 or 800/626-6684, www.mammothmountain.com, $349–900 winter, $139–429 off-season), which is even a little closer to the ski mountain. Check them out if you can't get the condo of your dreams at Juniper.

For another fine condo rental, check out **Mountainback** (435 Lakeview Blvd., 800/468-6225, www.mountainbackrentals.com, $265–420 winter, two-night minimum, $35 booking fee). This complex has an array of all-two-bedroom units, some of which sleep up to six. Every individual building has its own outdoor spa, and the complex has a heated pool and a sauna. Every condo is decorated differently (you might even be able to buy and redecorate one if you have the cash). Check the website for photos to find what you like—big stones everywhere, wood paneling, gentle cream walls, or even red-and-green holiday-themed furniture.

FOOD

The very popular **Whiskey Creek** (24 Lake Mary Rd., 760/934-2555, 4 p.m.–close daily Nov.–Mar., 5 p.m.–close daily Apr.–Oct., $12–30) offers fine food and good drinks on two levels. Order a fine steak or a simple burger, and sample the wide selection of wines and beers. Whiskey Creek maintains its own small on-site brewery, so some of the beers they serve really are as local as it gets. The crowd feels warm and friendly, as do the hearty dishes served to hungry après-skiers. Be sure to make reservations on winter weekends as it can get crowded. If you've just come for a drink and a good time, enjoy a DJ in the bar (Wed. and Fri.–Sat. winter, Wed. summer). The music starts around 9 p.m. and usually keeps playing long past midnight. Whiskey Creek is only half a block from the Village, so you can walk over from most places.

Petra's Bistro and Wine Bar (6080 Minaret Rd., 760/934-3500, www.petrasbistro.com, 5:30 p.m.–close Tues.–Sun.) offers a seasonal menu that's designed to please the palate and a wine list that's worth a visit itself. The by-the-glass offerings change each night, and your server will happily cork your unfinished bottle to take home. Two dining rooms and a wine bar divide the seating nicely, and the atmosphere succeeds in feeling romantic without being cave-dark. Petra's stays open all year, so if you're visiting in the off-season, you'll get a pleasantly uncrowded treat. Reservations are a good idea during ski season.

The popular gourmet establishment **Skadi** (587 Old Mammoth Rd., Suite B, 760/934-3902, www.skadirestaurant.com, 5:30–9:30 p.m. Wed.–Sun., $24–32) describes its menu as "alpine cuisine." The restaurant, co-owned by a chef and a rancher, offers a creative menu of fresh local meat (venison, for example) and plants (macadamias) to their best advantage. Everything on the list looks tasty, but if you're not ready for a heavy entrée, consider ordering a couple of items from the ample selection of appetizers for a "small plates" experience. Oh, and don't skip dessert!

Even Californians who eat Mexican food on a regular basis tend to agree on that **Roberto's Mexican Café** (271 Old Mammoth Rd., 760/934-3667, www.robertoscafe.com, 11 a.m.–close daily, $7–15) is special. This casual spot serves classic California-Mexican food in great quantities but includes specialty items like lobster burritos and duck tacos to shake things up. Whatever you order, it's perfect for skiers and boarders famished after a long day on the slopes. For a quiet meal, stay downstairs in the main dining room. To join a lively younger crowd, head upstairs to the bar, which has tables and serves the full restaurant menu.

INFORMATION AND SERVICES
Visitor Information

The town of Mammoth Lakes has an awesome visitors center at the entrance to Mammoth Lakes, the **Mammoth Lakes Welcome Center** (Hwy. 203, 3 miles west of U.S. 395, 760/924-5500, www.visitmammoth.com or www.fs.usda.gov/inyo, hours vary). The facility is jointly run by the U.S. Forest Service, the

YOSEMITE

town of Mammoth Lakes tourism bureau, and the National Parks Service, so they can help you with everything from condo rentals and restaurant reservations before you arrive to the latest bar openings and best seasonal recreation options when you get here. They're also your best resource for camping information, weather travel advisories, updates on snowmobile trails, and even backcountry passes for your backpacking trip.

Banks and Post Offices

Plenty of ATMs crowd Mammoth Lakes at gas stations, minimarts, and bank branches. Check the Village, Main Street, and Minaret Road for banks and cash machines. Mammoth Lakes has a **post office** (3330 Main St./Hwy. 203, 760/934-2205, www.usps.com, 8 A.M.–4 P.M. Mon.–Fri.).

Media and Communications

Mammoth Lakes has its own weekly newspaper, the **Mammoth Times** (www.mammothtimes.com), which comes out on Thursday and serves the whole of the Eastern Sierra region. Check for local events and good nightspots, and visit the website for up-to-date weather and road conditions.

Despite its small size, the town of Mammoth Lakes has a cosmopolitan atmosphere that includes plenty of Internet access. Many of the condos and hotel rooms have some form of Internet access, and you can find a couple of **Starbucks** (481 Old Mammoth Rd., 760/934-4536, and 6201 Minaret Rd., 760/934-0698) with dependable wireless service.

Medical Services

Need medical service beyond that offered at the ski resorts? You can get it at **Mammoth Hospital** (85 Sierra Park Rd., 760/934-3311, www.mammothhospital.com), which has a 24-hour emergency room.

GETTING THERE AND AROUND
Air

The nearest airport to Mammoth Lakes is the **Mammoth Yosemite Airport** (MMH, 1200 Airport Rd., 760/934-3813, www.ci.mammoth-lakes.ca.us). Alaska Airlines serves this airport year-round; United Express and Horizon fly in December 15–April 30. In winter, nonstop flights run to Mammoth from Los Angeles, San Francisco, and San Jose. For a major transportation hub, fly to the **Reno-Tahoe International Airport** (RNO, 2001 E. Plumb Ln., Reno, NV, 775/328-6400, www.renoairport.com). From there, you can drive 166 miles south on U.S. 395 and get to Mammoth Lakes in about 3.5 hours.

Car

U.S. 395 is the main access road to the Mammoth Lakes area. To get to the town of Mammoth Lakes from U.S. 395, turn onto Highway 203, which will take you right into town. Expect a seven-hour drive from San Francisco if the traffic and weather cooperate. If you fly into Reno, the drive out to Mammoth takes about 3.5 hours.

In the winter, be aware that it snows at Mammoth Lakes more than it does in almost any other place in California. Carry chains! Even if the weather is predicted to be clear for your visit, having chains can prevent a world of hurt and the need to turn back in a sudden storm. The longer you plan to stay, the more you should stock your car with items such as ice scrapers, blankets, water, food, and a full tank of gas whenever possible. For the latest traffic information, including chain control areas and weather conditions, call Caltrans (800/427-7623).

Parking in Mammoth Lakes in the off-season is a breeze. In the winter, it can get a bit more complicated, as constant snow removal means that parking on the street is illegal throughout town. Most of the major resorts and hotels offer heated parking structures, and many of the restaurants, bars, and ski resorts have plenty of parking in their outdoor lots.

Shuttles and Buses

The **Eastern Sierra Transit Authority** (ESTA, 760/924-3184, www.estransit.org) runs a number of bus lines, including the CREST line, which takes passengers from Lone Pine through Bishop, Mammoth, Lee Vining, and other stops on the way to the Reno Greyhound station and the Reno-Tahoe International Airport. The trip from the Reno Airport to Mammoth Lakes takes 3.5 hours (adults $50, children and seniors $44). The ESTA also operates local bus routes around Mammoth Lakes, including the **June Mountain Express** ($11.50–13.25 round-trip), which takes skiers from Mammoth Lakes to the June Lake ski area.

The **Mammoth Transit System** (www.visitmammoth.com, Nov.–May, free) offers complimentary rides all over town in the winter, freeing visitors from their own cars most of the time. You can download a copy of the transit map from the website.

Devils Postpile National Monument (760/934-2289, www.nps.gov/depo, adults $7, children $4) runs a shuttle that's mandatory for all visitors during high season (vehicles with handicap placards excepted). The shuttle runs hourly 7–11 A.M. daily from the Village at Mammoth Lakes, and every 15–30 minutes 7 A.M.–7 P.M. daily mid-June–early September from the Mammoth Mountain Adventure Center at the Main Lodge area.

BISHOP

Bishop is located west of the Inyo and White Mountains, southeast of Yosemite, and northeast of Kings Canyon, and is a great jumping-off point for travelers to explore some of the natural wonders of this area. Bishop is the largest city in Inyo County. Its quaint western main street offers some low-key hotels and restaurants and ample places to rent equipment for a variety of active sports. Additional local color—and nightlife—are provided by the Paiute and Shoshone peoples who have a large reservation nearby and operate a casino in Bishop. With an elevation of just over 4,000 feet, Bishop doesn't get as cold, or anywhere near as snowy, as nearby Mammoth Lakes, which is twice its height. Still, the area is pretty remote so it's best to be prepared for emergencies. Carry chains, food, and water in your car, and don't pass up a chance to fill the gas tank on the way.

Laws Railroad Museum and Historic Site

If you've got a railroad buff in the family (and who doesn't?) make time to visit the Laws Railroad Museum and Historic Site (Silver Canyon Rd., off U.S. 6, 760/873-5950, www.lawsmuseum.org, 9:30 A.M.–4:30 P.M. daily summer–Labor Day, 10 A.M.–4 P.M. winter, donation), 4.5 miles north of Bishop. There's more here than just trains—in fact, there's a whole historic village with artifacts from the area's history well preserved and on display. But the center of the village is the railroad depot, which is pretty much how towns were organized back when residents depended on the railroads not only for transportation but also for commerce and communication with the outside world. Come and see the self-propelled Death Valley Car from 1927, a caboose from 1883, model railroad displays, and more.

◖ Ancient Bristlecone Pine Forest

Directly to the east of Bishop near the Nevada border is yet another amazing California wilderness area. Little visited but worth a trip on its own, Ancient Bristlecone Pine Forest is a section of the Inyo National Forest in the White Mountains where the world's oldest trees reside. The bristlecone pines can be even older than the coastal redwoods and sequoias. The most famous bristlecone pine, **Methuselah,** at the ripe age of about 4,750, is believed to be 1,000

YOSEMITE

© MIKE NORTON/123RF.COM
a bristlecone pine

years older than any other tree in the world. To protect the tree, the Forest Service has chosen not to mark it or produce maps directing people to it, but don't worry—almost all the trees around here are beautiful to behold.

There are two main groves of trees that you won't want to miss. The **Schulman Grove** is where you'll find the **Bristlecone Pine Forest Visitors Center** (Hwy. 168, 23 miles east of Big Pine, 760/873-2500, www.fs.usda.gov/inyo, 10 A.M.–5 P.M. daily Memorial Day–Sept. 30, $3 pp or $6 per car).

The second notable grove, 12 miles north of Schulman on a dirt road, is the **Patriarch Grove.** Here you'll see the Patriarch Tree, which is the world's largest bristlecone pine. A self-guided nature trail in the Patriarch Grove enables you to get out among the trees and learn more about them.

Three hiking trails begin right outside the Bristlecone Pine Forest Visitors Center. The **Discovery Trail** is an easy one-mile loop with

helpful signs along the way. The **Methuselah Trail** is a loop of about 4–5 miles, also easy. Yes, you will see the world's oldest tree if you take this walk—you just won't know exactly which tree it is. Its secret identity is protected, but you can have fun admiring *all* the noble specimens here and guessing which is most ancient. Finally, the **Mexican Mine Trail** is an out-and-back hike of about five miles in total that leads past some abandoned mine buildings made out of tough bristlecone pine wood, of course, in addition to still more living trees.

You can get to the Ancient Bristlecone Pine Forest by car from the town of Bishop in about an hour. Take U.S. 395 south to Big Pine and turn left (east) onto Highway 168. Take Highway 168 for 13 miles to White Mountain Road. Turn left (north) and drive 10 miles to the visitors center in Schulman Grove.

Horseback Riding

Operating out of Bishop, **Rainbow Pack Outfitters** (off Hwy. 168, west of Bishop, 760/873-8877, www.rainbowpackoutfit.com) offers a wide range of options for horse lovers. At the stables, small children can enjoy their "Li'l Cowpoke" ride ($20) on a pony or horse with an expert leading. Options for bigger kids and adults include the Rainbow Meadow Ride (1 hour, $35), the South Lake Vista Ride (2 hours, $50), the Long Lake Scenic Ride (4 hours, $75), the All-day Ride (9 A.M.–5 P.M., $105), and the All-day Fishing Ride (9 A.M.–5 P.M., $125), which is a mini–pack trip. If you're looking for a longer horseback vacation, check into Rainbow's options for full-service multiday riding trips, with hunting, fishing, photography, birding, and more. Rainbow provides service into the John Muir Wilderness, the Inyo National Forest, and Sequoia and Kings Canyon National Parks. Another part of Rainbow's business is displaying the historic side of packing. Free facility tours are available during the summer season when the pack station is open. Reservations are recommended for any of the rides. The best way to reach Rainbow is by telephone; since the pack station has no electricity, they don't get their email until they head into town for a break.

Snowmobiling

Given the heavy snows, great scenery, and wide-open spaces, snowmobiling in Bishop is a given. To rent equipment and get some help getting started, stop into **Bishop Motosports** (107 S. Main St., 760/872-4717, www.bishopmotosports.com, daily, $225–275 for 3 hours, $400–500 full day). Maps, helmets, and trailers (for off-road vehicles) are included with all rentals. The management at Bishop Motosports declines to list hours since they make themselves available to customers from early in the morning till late at night every day of the week. If you make an appointment, they'll be there. Another location in Mammoth offers similar services.

Entertainment and Events

Each September for more than 20 years, the Inyo Council for the Arts has put on the sort of music festival you'd expect to find in a much larger metropolitan center. The **Millpond Music Festival** (Millpond Park, Sawmill Rd., 5 miles northwest of Bishop, 760/873-8014, www.inyo.org, day pass $25–35 adults, K–12 students $15, weekend pass $75–90 adults, K–12 students $25) has performers as varied as Los Lobos, Ray Bonneville, and the Marc Atkinson Trio. In addition to amazing music in a beautiful mountain setting, you'll find work by local artists, arts and crafts activities for children, food and drink booths, and musician workshops.

If an hour or three at the slots or the blackjack tables sounds like a good way to unwind, go to the **Paiute Palace Casino** (2742 N. Sierra Hwy., 888/372-4883, www.paiutepalace.com,

24 hours daily), owned by the Bishop Paiute Tribe. You can play more than 300 slots plus table blackjack and poker. Look for Texas hold 'em tournaments every Wednesday and Sunday. The in-house restaurant, **TuKaNovie** (7 A.M.–midnight Sun.–Thurs., 7 A.M.–10 P.M. Fri.–Sat., $8–15), serves steak, pork chops, and liver and onions, with a prime rib special on Friday and Saturday nights starting at 5 P.M.

Camping

A nice place to stay near Bishop is **Keough's Hot Springs** (800 Keough Hot Springs Rd., 760/872-4670, www.keoughshotsprings.com, $20–115). The 100- by 30-foot swimming pool is heated by natural hot springs, so it's open year-round, as is the campground and other facilities. Lodging options include "dry" tent or RV sites ($20), campsites with water and electricity ($25), four tent cabins ($75), and a mobile home ($115). To get to Keough's, travel six miles south of Bishop on U.S. 395. When you see the big blue sign on your left, turn right. You'll be there in less than 10 minutes.

A number of campgrounds are available in the Inyo National Forest near Bishop. One of the most popular is **Bishop Park** (Hwy. 168, 12 miles west of Bishop, 760/872-7018, www.fs.usda.gov, 20 sites, first-come, first-served, Apr.–Oct., $21). It's right on the banks of Bishop Creek with flush toilets and space for RVs. Another nice option is **Intake Two** (Hwy. 168, 16 miles west of Bishop, 8 sites, first-come, first-served, Apr.–Oct., $21), located near Intake Two Lake. Swimming is not advised because the water is so cold, but you can catch trout here. **Sabrina Campground** (Hwy. 168, 18 miles west of Bishop, 18 sites, first-come, first-served, late May–Oct., $21) is at 9,300 feet elevation, making it low on oxygen but high on views. Lake Sabrina is nearby, and it's a good trout-fishing destination. Showers are not available at any of the National Forest campgrounds, but you can buy a shower at a

© STAN NESTER

Keough's Hot Springs

YOSEMITE

couple of places nearby: **Bishop Creek Lodge** (2100 S. Lake Rd., 760/873-4484, www. bishopcreekresort.com, Apr.–Oct., $6 for a 10-minute token, $1 for soap and towel) and **Parchers Resort** (5001 S. Lake Dr., 760/873-4177, www.parchersresort.net, Memorial Day–Oct., $6 for a 10-minute shower, $1 for soap and towel).

Food

Even if you don't usually like casinos, consider having a meal at **TuKaNovie** (2742 N. Sierra Hwy./U.S. 395, 888/372-4883, www.paiute-palace.com, 7 A.M.–midnight Sun.–Thurs., 7 A.M.–10 P.M. Fri.–Sat., $8–15), the restaurant at the Paiute Palace Casino. The food, service, and prices are all better than you might expect, and the restaurant is smoke-free. Expect basic American food, with a prime rib special on Friday and Saturday nights starting at 5 P.M. The absence of sales tax on Native American land makes the place even more affordable.

Another hopping place to eat in Bishop is **Whiskey Creek** (524 N. Main St., 760/873-7174, 11 A.M.–10 P.M. Mon.–Thurs., 11 A.M.–10:30 P.M. Fri., 7 A.M.–10:30 P.M. Sat., 7 A.M.–10 P.M. Sun. summer, 11 A.M.–9 P.M. Mon.–Thurs., 11 A.M.–10 P.M. Fri., 8 A.M.–10 P.M. Sat., 8 A.M.–9 P.M. Sun. winter, $11–30). This branch of the popular Whiskey Creek in Mammoth serves burgers, steaks, salads, and a full menu of beer and wine.

Information and Services

The **Bishop Chamber of Commerce and Visitors Bureau** (690 N. Main St., Bishop, 888/395-3952, www.bishopvisitor.com, 10 A.M.–5 P.M. Mon.–Fri., 10 A.M.–4 P.M. Sat.–Sun.) offers friendly advice on lodgings, local attractions, and more.

Getting There

The nearest airport to Bishop is the **Mammoth Yosemite Airport** (MMH, 1200 Airport

Rd., Mammoth Lakes, 760/934-3813, www. ci.mammoth-lakes.ca.us). Alaska Airlines serves this airport year-round, and United Express and Horizon fly in December 15–April 30.

Bishop is not located near a major city, so expect it to take a while to get here from almost anywhere else. Bishop is located at the junction of U.S. 395 and U.S. 6, west of Sequoia National Forest and east of the Inyo National Forest's Ancient Bristlecone Pine Forest. From the San Francisco Bay Area, in summer, cross through Yosemite on Highway 120 (Tioga Rd., closed in winter), or drive north and cross on Highway 108 via the Sonora Pass (closed in winter). Once you get to U.S. 395, follow it south to Bishop, about 64 miles from Tioga Pass or 107 miles from Sonora Pass. Plan on at least 6.5 hours to drive the 300–320 miles. Since both mountain passes are closed in winter (usually Nov.–May), the only way to get here during those months is to take I-80 to U.S. 50 all the way to Lake Tahoe, then cross over into Nevada on Highway 88/89 and connect with U.S. 395. From this point, the trip south to Bishop is 157 miles. Altogether, this winter route is about 370 miles and will take at least seven hours.

The route from Sacramento to Bishop is shorter than the winter route from San Francisco. Take U.S. 50 to Lake Tahoe, then turn onto Highway 88/89. Go south on U.S. 395 for the final 157 miles. The total trip is 285 miles and takes about 5.5 hours.

SEQUOIA AND KINGS CANYON

Kings Canyon and Sequoia National Parks offer rugged mountain scenery, some of the tallest and oldest trees on earth, numerous and varied hiking trails, thriving wildlife, and far smaller crowds than their surpassingly famous neighbor. Among other wonders, these two parks showcase the largest tree in the world, the deepest canyon in the country, and the highest peak in the continental United States.

The area actually encompasses two distinct parks, a forest, and a monument: Kings Canyon National Park to the north, Sequoia National Park to the south, Sequoia National Forest surrounding much of the parkland, and Giant Sequoia National Monument, a subset of the national forest to the south and west of the parks.

In Sequoia National Park, the trees are the main attraction. Groves of giant sequoias, including the largest known tree on earth—General Sherman—soar out of the fertile Sierra soil. These *Sequoiadendron giganteum* grow only in a narrow 60-mile band on the western slope of the Sierra Nevada range between 5,000 and 8,000 feet elevation. The species is distinct from the magnificent coast redwoods (*Sequoia sempervirens*) that grow along the Pacific Coast. The giant sequoias are truly massive, from stalwart trunk to hefty branches to towering top.

Kings Canyon National Park is characterized by rough granite slabs and dramatic canyons—in fact, Kings Canyon is deeper than the Grand Canyon. In both parks, expect marble caverns,

© HEATHER C. LISTON

HIGHLIGHTS

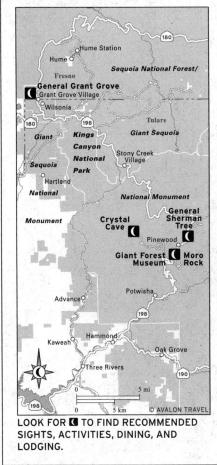

◖ General Grant Grove: A paved 0.5-mile walkway leads to the General Grant Tree, the world's second-largest tree and the country's only living war memorial; other trails within the grove include natural wonders such as the Fallen Monarch, a tree you can walk through (page 665).

◖ General Sherman Tree: The biggest tree on the face of the earth is here in Sequoia National Park—easy to walk to and thrilling to see (page 678).

◖ Giant Forest Museum: It's great to wander outside and see all the big trees, but if you want to learn more about what you're seeing, the Giant Forest Museum in Sequoia National Park is the place to be (page 678).

◖ Crystal Cave: Well-lit tunnels lead into the grand chambers of this dramatic cavern, filled with dramatic calcite formations and polished marble (page 679).

◖ Moro Rock: An invigorating climb up the stairs to the top of Moro Rock leads to some of the best views in the park (page 679).

LOOK FOR ◖ TO FIND RECOMMENDED SIGHTS, ACTIVITIES, DINING, AND LODGING.

rushing rivers, and an astounding variety of ecosystems from chaparral to alpine meadow.

Sequoia National Park was California's first national park, dating to 1890. The same year, the small General Grant National Park was born with the goal of preserving the giant sequoia known as the General Grant Tree. Kings Canyon National Park was established in 1940,

encompassing a large tract of land north of Sequoia. At that point, the small General Grant Park, though separated from the main body of Kings Canyon by forestland, was absorbed into it. Today, Sequoia and Kings Canyon are jointly administered by the National Park Service, and together they encompass more than 864,000 acres.

SEQUOIA & KINGS CANYON

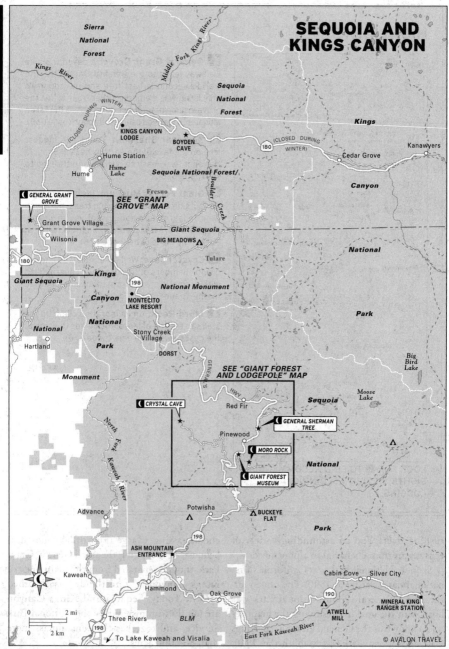

SEQUOIA AND KINGS CANYON

Sierra National Forest

Kings River

Middle Fork Kings River

Sequoia National Forest

Kings

(CLOSED DURING WINTER)

KINGS CANYON LODGE

BOYDEN CAVE

180

(CLOSED DURING WINTER)

Kanawyers

Hume Station

Hume Lake

Hume

Cedar Grove

Sequoia National Forest/

Canyon

Fresno

GENERAL GRANT GROVE

SEE "GRANT GROVE" MAP

Grant Grove Village

Giant Sequoia

Wilsonia

BIG MEADOWS

National

180

Tulare

Giant Sequoia

198

Kings

National Monument

Park

National

MONTECITO LAKE RESORT

Canyon

National

Hartland

Stony Creek Village

Big Bird Lake

Park

DORST

Monument

SEE "GIANT FOREST AND LODGEPOLE" MAP

Moose Lake

GENERAL'S HWY

Sequoia

North Fork Kaweah River

CRYSTAL CAVE

Red Fir

GENERAL SHERMAN TREE

Pinewood

MORO ROCK

National

GIANT FOREST MUSEUM

Advance

Potwisha

BUCKEYE FLAT

Park

ASH MOUNTAIN ENTRANCE

198

Kaweah

Cabin Cove   Silver City

Hammond

190

MINERAL KING RANGER STATION

Oak Grove

ATWELL MILL

0   2 mi

0   2 km

Three Rivers

BLM

East Fork Kaweah River

198   To Lake Kaweah and Visalia

© AVALON TRAVEL

PLANNING YOUR TIME

Together, Sequoia and Kings Canyon National Parks are so large and spread out that even a trip limited to driving past the major sights, photographing the most famous trees, and stopping in the visitors centers could easily occupy several days. To explore the parks in depth plan to stay 3–4 days and take some of the many long hikes. In the main campgrounds, it's common for vacationers to set up a tent for a 1–2-week vacation and use that as a base for exploring the parks.

Grant Grove

SIGHTS

The Grant Grove area of Kings Canyon National Park is located near the Big Stump Entrance, accessed via Highway 180. It is home to three campgrounds, lodging, a visitors center, and several hikes.

Grant Grove Village

Grant Grove Village (year-round) is one of the busiest visitor areas in Kings Canyon and one of the best places to come if you need services. There's a large visitors center, a restaurant, a gift shop (9 A.M.–6 P.M. Sun.–Thurs., 9 A.M.–7 P.M. Fri.–Sat.), a grocery market, public showers, a lodge, and cabins. Three of the park's nicest campgrounds are close by, as is the famous attraction that gives the place its name: the gargantuan General Grant Tree. Grant Grove cannot be called central, exactly; physically it's on the west side of the park area, separated from the much larger section of Kings Canyon by a gulf of national forest. Still, Grant Grove may well be central to your Kings Canyon experience. It's just 3.5 miles from the Big Stump park entrance on Highway 180, and it works well as a home base from which to venture out on explorations.

Kings Canyon Visitors Center

The large visitors center in Grant Grove, Kings Canyon Visitors Center (83918 Hwy. 180 E., 559/565-4307, daily 8 A.M.–6 P.M. Apr.–Oct., daily 9 A.M.–4:30 P.M. Nov.–Mar.) is three miles from the Highway 180 entrance and is run by the National Park Service (unlike other parts of Grant Grove Village, which are managed by a commercial concessionaire). This is the place to get maps, information about camping and hiking, ranger talks, and other park activities; check weather conditions and road closures for the whole park; explore the well-designed exhibits about park ecology and history; and chat with park rangers.

◖ General Grant Grove

The tree after which the whole grove is named is not only the second-largest tree by volume in the world, it's also the nation's only living war memorial, as declared by President Dwight Eisenhower who made it a national shrine in 1956. (That's after Calvin Coolidge ennobled it as the "Nation's Christmas Tree," in 1926.) This 1,700-year-old tree is about 268 feet tall, with a diameter of 40 feet and a volume of 46,608 cubic feet. Of all the giant sequoias that have been discovered and studied, this is the widest. Note that you'll still see some references to General Grant as the third-largest tree on earth, but its ranking improved in 2005, when the Washington tree lost some of its stature in a fire. Now Grant is second only to General Sherman, its compatriot at the other end of the Generals Highway. From the visitors center, head north on Kings Canyon Road then turn left (signed).

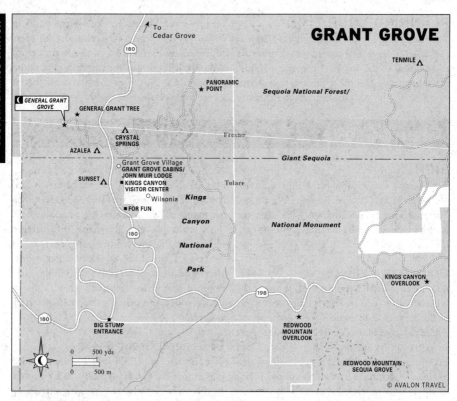

Panoramic Point

Just like it sounds, this is one of the best viewpoints in the parks. To get here, drive east through the Kings Canyon Visitor Center parking lot; turn left at the meadow and then turn right onto the steep and winding road marked Panoramic Point. (This route is closed in winter and is not appropriate for trailers.) In 2.3 miles you'll reach the parking lot and the 0.25-mile walk to the ridge. From your perch at more than 7,500 feet you'll see Hume Lake, Kings Canyon, and mountains and trees galore. The **Park Ridge Trail** also starts here and leads to a fire lookout.

Redwood Mountain Overlook

From Grant Grove, travel south on Generals Highway for six miles and look for the signed Redwood Mountain Overlook. Pull over to look out over one of the world's largest groves of giant sequoias. It's fun to see them from above for once. The trailhead for the **Redwood Mountain Grove** is two miles farther down a dirt road.

Kings Canyon Overlook

Kings Canyon Overlook is very close to Redwood Mountain Overlook and about six miles southeast of Grant Grove. Watch for signs (they're large and easy to spot) along Generals Highway and pull over into the ample roadside parking area. Descriptive signs help identify the peaks and groves surrounding you. Break out the binoculars if you've got a pair.

RECREATION
Hiking
General Grant Grove

General Grant Grove (0.1 mile northwest of the Kings Canyon Visitors Center) is home to dozens of monumental sequoias. The largest of these is the General Grant Tree, which truly lives up to its hype. The **General Grant Trail** (0.5 mile, easy) leads past many other stunning sights on the way to and from its namesake tree in just a short distance.

Along this trail is the **Fallen Monarch,** an immense tree lying on its side and hollowed out in the middle. You can actually walk lengthwise through the tree, and no matter how tall you are it's unlikely you'll have to duck. If ever you wanted to feel like a Keebler elf, this is your chance—it's amazing.

You'll also pass the **Gamlin Cabin,** built in 1872 and later used as the living quarters for the first ranger stationed here back when this was General Grant National Park. Farther along the trail lies **Centennial Stump,** so large that whole Sunday School classes have been held on top of it.

The General Grant Trail is a paved, short, and easy walk and is accessible for wheelchairs. It's not always easy to follow, though, since a few turns, side trails, and distractions can pull you off the main thoroughfare if you're not careful. Trail guides ($1.50) are available at the trailhead and can help keep you on track as well as give you more background about what you're seeing. The trailhead has a large parking lot, suitable for buses and crowds, with restrooms and informative signs. From the visitors center, head north on Kings Canyon road then turn left (signed).

NORTH GROVE LOOP

After visiting the General Grant Tree, take the North Grove Loop Trail (1.5 miles), which starts from the same parking lot. Most of the loop is along an old park road

© HEATHER C. LISTON

General Grant Grove

© HEATHER C. LISTON

Kings Canyon Overlook

through the grove. You might find yourself on the North Grove Loop even if you didn't intend to; it's not well differentiated from the General Grant Tree Trail and it covers much of the same area.

PARK RIDGE TRAIL

Enjoy the vistas from the Park Ridge Trail (Panoramic Point Rd. parking area, 2.5 miles east of Grant Grove Village, closed in winter, 4.7 miles, easy). If you pick a clear day, you can see all the way out to the Coast Range of mountains in the San Francisco Bay Area from this trail. While there's little elevation change on this walk, and much of it is on a wide, easy-to-follow fire road, the altitude can make this it a little challenging. To reach the trailhead, drive east through the Kings Canyon Visitor Center parking lot; turn left at the meadow and then turn right onto the steep and winding road marked Panoramic Point.

SEQUOIA LAKE OVERLOOK-DEAD GIANT LOOP

For a different view on the life and death of the giant sequoias and human intervention in this area, hike the Sequoia Lake Overlook–Dead Giant Loop (lower end of General Grant Tree parking area, 2.2 miles, easy). This trail takes you to the Dead Giant, a first-growth giant sequoia that was mostly likely killed by loggers who tried and failed to cut it for lumber. The trail continues to an overlook of Sequoia Lake, actually an old mill pond from the logging days.

SUNSET TRAIL

For a longer, more demanding day hike, check out the Sunset Trail (across the street from Kings Canyon Visitors Center, 6 miles, strenuous). From the visitors center, cross Kings Canyon Road entering the Sunset Campground (the trail leaves the campground at site 118) After 1.25 miles, follow the South Boundary Trail for 0.25 mile to Voila Falls.

Then, on the Sunset Trail, hike downhill to Ella Falls. Altogether, you'll climb about 1,400 vertical feet round-trip through magnificent mixed forests. To return to the trailhead, either return the way you came or follow the fire road north to the General Grant Grove trailhead.

BIG STUMP TRAIL

Immediately outside the Big Stump Entrance (three miles south of Grant Grove Village), take the Big Stump Trail (1 mile round-trip) through a grove that was heavily logged in the late 19th century, but is now reclaiming its true nature as a sequoia grove. One of the sights along here is the Mark Twain stump, the remains of a 26-foot wide tree that was cut in 1891.

REDWOOD MOUNTAIN SEQUOIA GROVE

Redwood Canyon is home to the largest grove of giant sequoias in the world. There are 16 miles of trails within the canyon, making it a good place to wander around and see the trees up close. At the trailhead, turn left to begin the **Hart Tree and Fallen Goliath Loop.** This easy 6.5-mile trek leads across Redwood Creek and past the former logging site of Barton's Post Camp. About halfway around the loop, you'll come to a short spur trail that takes you to the Hart Tree, the largest in the grove and the 25th largest known in the world. Fallen Goliath, a little farther along, is another impressive site, even lying down.

To get here, take Generals Highway seven miles south of Grant Grove Village. When you see the sign for Redwood Canyon, turn right onto the dirt road and travel another two miles along Quail Flat. At the end of this road, you'll find ample room for parking, since this area is rarely crowded.

BUENA VISTA PEAK

Buena Vista Peak is an ideal spot for gazing out at the Western Divide, Mineral King, and Farewell Gap and pondering the regrowth of a sequoia forest after a fire. (This area had a prescribed burn in 2004.) The hike to reach the peak is a fairly easy two miles. Park at the Buena Vista trailhead, which is near the Kings Canyon Overlook, three miles north of Montecito-Sequoia Lodge on Generals Highway and six miles south of Grant Grove.

BIG BALDY TRAIL

The Big Baldy Trail (4 miles, easy–moderate) is a popular out-and-back hike with only 600 feet of elevation gain; it's one of the most rewarding hikes in the park, considering the relatively small effort you have to expend for the major views. From the granite summit of Big Baldy, you'll be able to see far into Redwood Canyon. The trailhead and parking area are along the Generals Highway, eight miles south of Grant Grove.

Horseback Riding

If you love horses, the place to go is **Grant Grove Stables** (Hwy. 180, 0.25 mile north of Grant Grove Village, summer 559/335-9292, winter 559/799-7247, www.nps.gov/seki, $50 per hour). Expert equestrians lead 1–2-hour trail rides to the General Grant Tree or deep into the sequoia forests. If you're up for a multiday trip, ask about the affiliated pack station in Cedar Grove.

ACCOMMODATIONS

While reservations at Grant Grove lodgings are not as competitive as those in Yosemite, the popular rooms do to fill up 4–6 months in advance. This includes the Camp Cabins (which are economical) and the Bath Cabins (which are warm, private, and very nice). (Note that the concessionaire is considering closing the Bath Cabins in the winter.) Tent Cabins and the John Muir lodge usually need to be reserved about three months in advance.

Grant Grove Cabins

The Grant Grove Cabins (866/522-6966 or 866/565-6343, www.sequoia-kingscanyon.com) offer an array of lodging styles at a variety of prices. Many of these cabins have been around awhile—some since the early days of what was then the General Grant National Park. The economy option is the **Tent Cabins** (17 cabins, June–Sept., $62–77), which are short on amenities, with no electricity or heat and with shared central baths. They have a great location, however, right in Grant Grove Village, with easy access to the Grant Grove Restaurant and all the other services and attractions in the neighborhood, making these a fine option for travelers on a budget.

The so-called **Camp Cabins** (May–Nov., $77–91) are at the low end of the fully enclosed cabins. They have solid walls, unlike the Tent Cabins, plus electricity, a propane heater, and daily maid service, but they do not have private baths. Each Camp Cabin comes with 2–3 double beds. **Rustic Cabins** (May–Nov., $87) also come with 2–3 double beds and are a step up from Camp Cabins—they have carpets and insulation, which makes them considerably warmer during the chilly seasons. The **Bath Cabins** (8 duplex cabins, 1 single, year-round, $129–140) have all of the above plus private baths with a tub and shower.

If you're visiting in the spring or fall, remember that winter weather can come early; Grant Grove is at an altitude of 6,600 feet. Consider whether you're willing to chance an unheated or minimally heated cabin should a storm arrive.

John Muir Lodge

The attractive, simple, and sturdy John Muir Lodge (Grant Grove Village, 866/565-6343, www.jmlodge.com, 36 rooms, year-round, summer $172–186, winter as low as $69) is both a comfortable motel and a classic woodsy lodge. Big timber poles combine form and function in the large common room, which has a fireplace, wireless Internet access, tables, sofas, and board games. Guest rooms are simply decorated in an alpine theme, with comfortable beds, private baths, and good views

© HEATHER C. LISTON

John Muir Lodge

out into the forest. Soda machines, free ice, and clean baths are available inside the building, making this a comfortable place to hang out. You don't have to be a guest of the lodge to enjoy it; campers in the area are welcome to use the Internet access or relax by the fire. Since you're up at the edge of Grant Grove Village, you'll find plenty of nearby food and services, including the Grant Grove restaurant, a market, a gift shop, and the Kings Canyon Visitors Center. The lodge is convenient to hiking and to Generals Highway. Note that John Muir Lodge is two stories and there's no elevator; if anyone in your party has a problem with stairs, be sure to mention that when you book.

The check-in desk at John Muir Lodge (daily 7 A.M.–midnight Memorial Day–Labor Day, daily 7 A.M.–10 P.M. Labor Day–Memorial Day) is located inside the building that houses the gift shop and restaurant, near the entrance to Grant Grove Village. John Muir Lodge and cabins are managed by a park concessionaire,

Sequoia–Kings Canyon Park Services Company, and it's their helpful staff who run the check-in desk. They know a lot about the parks, but they're not the source for camping information; contact the park-run visitors center across the way.

CAMPING

The **Sunset** (157 sites, summer only, $18) and ◖**Azalea** (110 sites, year-round, summer $18, winter $10) campgrounds are both located 3.5 miles from the Kings Canyon park entrance and are close to the visitors center and Grant Grove Village. Only slightly farther, on the east side of Highway 180, is **Crystal Springs** (50 sites, summer only, $18). All campgrounds are supplied with picnic tables, fire rings, bear lockers, drinking water, and restrooms with flush toilets; they are all beautifully decorated in top-of-the-line national park scenery, with towering trees, artistically jumbled boulders, and winding paths. There are no showers in

Azalea Campground

the campgrounds, but showers are available at Grant Grove Village nearby.

Campgrounds are first-come, first served and fill up on weekends in July–August. To confirm campground opening and closing dates, call 559/565-3341 prior to your visit.

FOOD

Grant Grove Restaurant (Hwy. 180 at Generals Hwy., 559/335-5500, daily 7–10:30 A.M., 11 A.M.–3 P.M., and 5–9 P.M. summer, daily 8–10:30 A.M., 11 A.M.–2 P.M., and 5–8 P.M. winter, $10–25) serves three meals each day and is closed between. The basic dining room offers standard American fare (hamburgers, pasta, steak) with prime rib on Friday–Saturday at pretty high resort prices. The food is nothing special, but you can get a palatable meal and a glass of wine or beer.

You'll find a minimart at **Grant Grove Village** (86728 Hwy. 180, 8 A.M.–8 P.M. Sun.–Thurs., 8 A.M.–9 P.M. Fri.–Sat. summer, 9 A.M.–6 P.M. Sun.–Thurs., 9 A.M.–7 P.M. Fri.–Sat. fall–spring) selling a few staples, soda, beer, s'mores fixings, and some packaged food suitable for reheating over a campfire. You can also get some nonfood supplies like batteries, flashlights, and moleskin.

GETTING THERE

Grant Grove is located in Kings Canyon National Park, four miles east of the Big Stump Entrance on Highway 180.

Cedar Grove

Cedar Grove Village (May–Oct., weather permitting) is located within Kings Canyon National Park, 30 miles northeast of Grant Grove on Highway 180. In mid–late October, the eastern part of Highway 180 closes past the junction of Highway 180 with Generals Highway, near the Princess Campground in Sequoia National Forest. If you visit when the road is open, the drive out to Cedar Grove is a treat in itself. This section of Highway 180 is known as the **Kings Canyon Scenic Byway,** and it offers tremendous views of the vast canyons that give the park its name. The drive starts at 6,600 feet at Grant Grove, weaving down as far as 3,000 feet around Convict Flat before climbing back up to 5,000 feet before its terminus at Road's End. While curvy, the road is not treacherous; it is wide with shoulders most of the way, and most vehicles maintain a reasonable-to-slow speed. Ample roadside pull-outs are available on both sides of the highway, so you'll find it easy to stop for photos along the way.

SIGHTS
Cedar Grove Visitors Center

Located next to the Sentinel Campground near Cedar Grove Village, the Cedar Grove Visitors Center (559/565-3793, daily 9 A.M.–5 P.M. summer) has books, maps, first aid, and park rangers. Like the rest of the facilities in Cedar Grove, it is open only in summer.

Cedar Grove Village

The centerpiece of Cedar Grove Village (daily 8 A.M.–8 P.M. midsummer, daily 8 A.M.–7 P.M. spring and fall) is the **Cedar Grove Lodge** (559/565-0100, May–Sept.) and restaurant (daily 8 A.M.–8 P.M. midsummer, daily 8 A.M.–7 P.M. spring and fall). Other services in the village include a snack bar, a gift shop, a small grocery market, a laundry, showers, and an ATM.

Cedar Grove Pack Station

Cedar Grove Pack Station (1 mile east of Cedar Grove Village, summer 559/565-3464, www.nps.gov/seki, May–Oct., weather permitting) offers customized backcountry horseback riding trips for up to two weeks. They will provide the food and do the cooking, bring all the gear (except your sleeping bag), and will take care of the horses along the way. Backcountry pack trips are $250 pp per day, and the minimum trip is three days for four people. Short trips in the Cedar Grove area are also possible, provided horses are still available after the pack trips have left. Day trips include one hour along the Kings River ($50), a half-day ride to Mist Falls or the Kings Canyon Overlook ($100), and an all-day trip ($125).

Day trips are first-come, first-served; you can show up at the stable or call one day in advance. Reservations are required for multiday trips, which can go anywhere in the High Sierra, and you can help design the itinerary. For information in the off-season, contact Tim and Maggie Loverin (559/337-2314).

Canyon View

On Kings Canyon Road, approximately one mile east of Cedar Grove Village, pull off the road and really take in the shape of this stunning canyon. The U-shaped canyon was carved through these soaring peaks by glaciers; the Kings River now flows through its dramatic descent.

Knapp's Cabin

Small but picturesque Knapp's Cabin was built in the 1920s by George Knapp, a Santa Barbara businessman who stored the extensive gear he used on fishing expeditions here. To get there, take the Kings Canyon Scenic Byway and pull over two miles east of the Cedar Grove Village turnoff. The cabin is just a short walk from the road.

Zumwalt Meadow

The largest meadow in Kings Canyon, Zumwalt is one of the most beautiful areas to view native grasses, colorful wildflowers, and the birds and animals that live here. Zumwalt Meadow is also the best vantage point for

Grand Sentinel and North Dome, two of the canyon's most impressive granite formations.

Roads End

Roads End is one of those great place names that tells you exactly what it is. Yes, this really is the end of Highway 180 (E. Kings Canyon Rd.). Roads End is located deep in the middle of Kings Canyon, a few miles past Cedar Grove Village and about 35 miles from Grant Grove. Beyond Roads End, the park is trails, canyons, forests, and lakes.

What you will find at the end of the road is the **Roads End Permit Station** (daily 7 A.M.–3:30 P.M. late May–late Sept.). This small wooden building is the place to get your permit and to talk to the rangers about trail conditions, recommended routes, and food storage and bear management regulations before you begin your backcountry adventure. A wilderness permit ($15) is required for any overnight camping outside of the official campgrounds. During high season (May–Sept.), there's a quota for permits, and you must obtain your permit at the station nearest to the trailhead you plan to use. You can reserve a permit up to two weeks in advance by downloading the application form online (www.nps.gov/seki) and sending it in with payment; or you can stand in line at 1 P.M. the day before your hike for a first-come, first-served permit. When the quota season ends in late September, permits are free and you can self-register at the permit station.

Note: Park personnel must continually remind visitors that there is no way to cross the Sierra through Kings Canyon by car. To reach points east of the park, you need to take the long way around or hike.

RECREATION
Hiking
SHEEP CREEK CASCADE
Moderate hikes abound in this area. A good place to bring a picnic is Sheep Creek Cascade.

The hike to Sheep Creek (2 miles, 1.5 hours) ascends 600 vertical feet to a picturesque shaded glen that's perfect for taking a load off your feet and enjoying the serene surroundings.

DON CECIL-LOOKOUT PEAK

One of the more challenging day hikes in the Cedar Grove area is Don Cecil Trail to Lookout Peak (13 miles, strenuous). As you climb 4,000 feet to the top, you'll see long distances into the wild parts of Sequoia. The Don Cecil trailhead is well marked with a large sign along Highway 180 near Sheep Creek, 0.2 mile east of Cedar Grove Village.

HOTEL CREEK-LEWIS CREEK LOOP

The Hotel Creek–Lewis Creek Loop (8 miles, moderate) has only 1,200 feet of elevation gain and offers a variety of forest and mountain scenery in addition to two creeks. You'll still be able to discern effects of a major 1980 forest fire; the rejuvenated forest that's grown since is inspiring. Expect to pop in and out of the woods along the way and be prepared for sun, as significant portions of the trail are exposed. Enjoy long views of the canyon, and look for Monarch Divide in the distance. The hike starts from the Lewis Creek Trailhead on the north side of Kings Canyon Scenic Byway, just before you get to Cedar Grove.

ROARING RIVER FALLS

Even if you're not really a hiker, you'll want to get out of the car and stroll the negligible distance (less than 0.25 mile) from the parking area three miles east of Cedar Grove Village to the Roaring River Falls. The whole tiny trail is under a canopy of trees, making it cool even in the hottest parts of summer, and just looking at the falls feels refreshing after driving the Generals Highway.

ZUMWALT MEADOW TRAIL

The Zumwalt Meadow Trail (1.5 miles, easy) leads through the meadow for optimal viewing, and continues through a grove of heavenly smelling incense cedar and pine trees along the Kings River. The trailhead parking lot is one mile west of Roads End.

MIST FALLS

The Mist Falls Trail (park at the Roads End trailhead) is a popular jumping-off point for backpackers destined for the Kings Canyon backcountry. You can hike to Mist Falls (8 miles round-trip, moderate–strenuous), or keep going the way to Paradise Valley (14 miles, strenuous). Plan for dust and heat on the first couple of miles of the trail, and then steep switchbacks that take you up 1,500 vertical feet to the falls. If you're passing through on your way to the John Muir Trail, keep going past the falls all the way to Paradise Valley and then on to the trail crossing at Upper Woods Creek.

Backpacking

Without a doubt, the most famous backpacking trip in this region is to Mount Whitney. Whitney's not for everyone, though. For more moderate backpackers, the premier trip in these parks is the **Rae Lakes Loop** in Kings Canyon. This is a 46-mile loop trail with more than 5,000 feet of elevation gain. How difficult it is depends largely on how quickly you try to complete it. Ten days or more is ideal. The trail is shady and beautiful, with terrain that varies from flat and pleasant to rolling to some mettle-testing rock-scrambling and stream-crossing. If you don't have the time or the stamina to do it all, don't think you can't still enjoy Rae Lakes. Hiking in for a day or two and turning around to return the same way makes for a very good short trip.

Backcountry permits ($15) are required and are available at the permit station at Roads End. There's a quota for permits during high season (May–Sept.). You can reserve a permit up to two weeks in advance by downloading the application form online (www.nps.gov/seki) and sending it in with payment; or you can stand in line at 1 P.M. the day before your hike for a first-come, first-served permit. When the quota season ends in late September, permits are free and you can self-register at the permit station. Bear canisters are required, but you can rent one from the ranger station if you don't have your own.

ACCOMMODATIONS AND FOOD

Cedar Grove Lodge (559/565-0100, reservations 866/522-6966, May–Sept., $119–135) has 18 guest rooms in the main building, each with two queen beds, private baths, telephones, and air-conditioning. It also offers three patio rooms, each with one queen bed, a private bath, a phone, and a patio looking directly on the Kings River.

The restaurant at Cedar Grove (559/565-0100, daily 8 A.M.–8 P.M. midsummer, daily 8 A.M.–7 P.M. spring and fall, $10–20) is a no-frills place. Diners walk up to a window to place their orders and then take their food on a tray out to a group table in the casual dining room, or out onto the porch. The food isn't bad, though; in addition to simple hamburgers

MOUNT WHITNEY

One of the most famous climbing or backpacking trips in Northern California is Mount Whitney (www.nps.gov/seki). At 14,500 feet, Whitney is the highest peak in the continental United States, and this must-do trek draws intrepid hikers and climbers from around the world. Whitney also marks the southern end of the John Muir Trail and makes for a dramatic end or beginning for through-hikers doing the whole trail.

Mount Whitney is located at the far eastern edge of Sequoia National Park, just west of the town of Lone Pine. You can see the impressive peak from a few places in the backcountry of Sequoia and Kings Canyon, but you can't get there from within the parks. There is no road that crosses the parks all the way from west to east. If you're coming from the west, you have to circle around the parks and enter from the eastern side.

While Mount Whitney is a very challenging climb, it need not be a technical one. You can climb all the way to the top of Mount Whitney and back in one day if you're in good shape and prepared properly for the journey. Very fit hikers can walk the trail to the top, even without ropes and carabiners. The climbs up the steep East Face of the mountain or up the Needles are not beginners' journeys, but the East Face isn't out of reach for intermediate climbers. Most of the East Face is rated a Class 3, with the toughest bits rated 5.4. It's important to plan ahead, start early, bring all the right safety gear, and prepare for extreme weather.

Permits are required for anyone entering the Mount Whitney Zone—even day hikers. May–October, there's a quota for hikers; those who want to hike must enter the February lottery in order to have a good chance of getting a permit for the following summer. For more information about the lottery, and to download an application, visit www.fs.fed.us/r5/inyo or call the wilderness permit information and reservation line for Inyo National Forest (760/873-2483). November–April, hikers still need a permit, but there are no quotas in place. Pick up a permit in person at the **Mount Whitney Ranger Station** within the **Interagency Visitors Center** (U.S. 395 and Hwy. 136, 1 mile south of Lone Pine, 760/876-6200, www.fs.fed.us/r5/inyo, daily 8 A.M.-4:30 P.M. Nov. 1-Apr., daily 8 A.M.-5 P.M. Apr.-Oct.). During the off-season, you can self-register for a permit if the visitors center is closed.

Hikers should plan to stay nearby and get an early start in the morning—very early if you're planning to summit. The nearest campground is **Whitney Portal** (end of Whitney Portal Rd., 6 miles west of Lone Pine, 877/444-6777, www.recreation.gov, 43 sites, late May–late Oct., $17) in the Inyo National Forest; it's seven miles from the trailhead. If you're planning to climb the summit, you'll want to stay even closer to wake up in the wee hours and start your ascent. There are 13 walk-in sites located near the **Mount Whitney Trailhead** (first come, first-served, one-night limit, $10).

and other snack-bar items, they occasionally have fresh trout and other specials in season.

The lodge and restaurant at Cedar Grove are run by Sequoia–Kings Canyon Park Services Company (866/565-6343, www.sequoia-kingscanyon.com), the same company that runs the facilities at Grant Grove and Stony Creek.

CAMPING

Several attractive campgrounds are available within a short distance of Cedar Grove Village, making food, showers, and access to ranger programs a breeze. In order, the campgrounds are **Sheep Creek** (111 sites, May–Nov., $18), **Sentinel** (83 sites, Apr.–Sept., $18), **Canyon View** (12 group sites, no RVs or trailers, May–Oct., $35), and **Moraine** (120 sites, May–Sept.,

$18). Campgrounds are first-come, first-served and have drinking water, flush toilets, and food lockers; most are open in summer only, as this section of the park is inaccessible once the snows come. To confirm seasonal opening and closing dates, call 559/565-3341 prior to visiting.

GETTING THERE

Cedar Grove is 30 miles northeast of Grant Grove on Highway 180, less than 35 miles from the Big Stump Entrance to Kings Canyon. Only the first six miles of the road are open in winter, so this section of the park is unreachable October–April. Exact opening and closing dates depend on snowfall, and chains can be required at any time; call the park (559/565-3341) to confirm road conditions and seasonal status.

Giant Forest and Lodgepole

If you have limited time to spend in Sequoia, the first place to visit is the Lodgepole and Giant Forest area. Here you can see and learn about some of the most impressive living things on earth, all within a fairly small geographical area. The Giant Forest contains some of the best natural attractions, and the Lodgepole complex provides support services and human comforts to help you enjoy and appreciate it all.

The Giant Forest was named by the patron saint of California wilderness, John Muir. The childlike simplicity of his description reflects the way many people feel when they encounter this extraordinary grove of giant sequoias. The General Sherman Tree, believed to be the largest tree on earth, is the star here—but it is my no means the only impressive sight. The sheer abundance of awe-inspiring trees all in one place makes visiting an amazing experience. It's interesting to note that many of the trees are named for people and even the groups

of trees are personified—one grove is called "Congress" and another is "The Senate," as if they've gathered together for meetings. To understand more about the natural history of these trees, start your visit with a trip to the Giant Forest Museum. But whatever you do, make sure to save time for one of several short trails that make it easy to see an enormous amount in a short time.

SIGHTS
Wuksachi Village

Wuksachi Village (open year-round) is located near Generals Highway, about two miles north of Lodgepole. Of all the accommodations and restaurants in the parks, those at Wuksachi Village are the most upscale and elegant, and the drive here (1 hour from Grant Grove) may well be worth it for at least one really nice meal. Other services at Wuksachi include a luxurious lodge, a gift shop (daily 8 A.M.–8 P.M.), wireless Internet access, and an ATM.

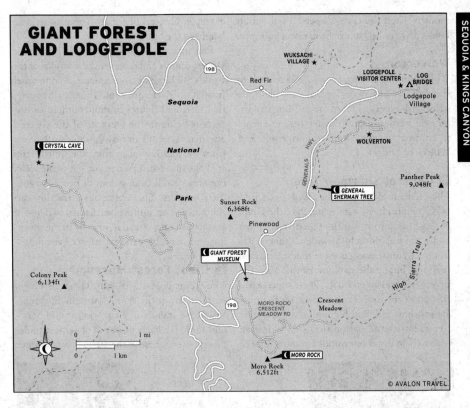

Lodgepole Village

Lodgepole Village (559/565-3301) contains the major visitor services for Sequoia National Park, including a large visitors center, a market, a deli, a gift shop, a coin laundry, an ATM, shuttle services, and a post office. The snack bar and deli (daily 8 A.M.–8 P.M. Memorial Day–Labor Day) are open in summer only. The market, gift shop, and laundry ($0.50–1) stay open mid-April–end of October (daily 8 A.M.–8 P.M. Memorial Day–Labor Day, daily 10 A.M.–4:30 P.M. spring and fall). Showers are also available (daily 9 A.M.–1 P.M. and 3–5:30 P.M. spring–late Sept., daily 9 A.M.–1 P.M. and 3–4 P.M. late Sept.–late Oct., $3 for 10 minutes).

Many of the facilities here are closed in winter, so check the website before you come.

Lodgepole Visitors Center

The Lodgepole Visitors Center (Lodgepole Rd., 559/565-4436, daily 7 A.M.–7 P.M. summer, daily 8 A.M.–4:30 P.M. spring and fall, 9 A.M.–4:30 P.M. Fri.–Mon. Nov.–Apr.) is one of the major information centers run by the National Park Service. Visitors can get books, maps, and souvenirs and join a ranger talk or walk. Wilderness permits (summer $15, off-season free) are available inside the visitors center when it's open; self-register outside when it's closed. Crystal Cave tour tickets are sold here (daily 8 A.M.–4 P.M. mid-May–late Oct.) during the months when the cave is open. It's about an hour's drive to Lodgepole from either entrance.

Wolverton

Wolverton is a picnic area two miles north of the General Sherman Tree. It's a wide-open space with plenty of room for sledding in winter and barbeque and dinner theater events in summer (tickets sold at Lodgepole and Wuksachi Lodge).

◖ General Sherman Tree

The General Sherman Tree (Wolverton Rd., off Generals Hwy., 4 miles north of the Giant Forest Museum) is not the tallest tree, at just under 275 feet, nor is it the widest, at about 103 feet in circumference, nor the oldest, at 2,200 years old, but by sheer volume of wood it is the largest tree known on earth. These superlatives are part of the fun. It can be difficult to imagine just how tall, and big, and old these trees are; scientists and park officials have devised ways to help us get our minds around it all. For example, General Sherman is about the same height as the Statue of Liberty.

Pick up some of the literature available at the visitors centers and discover the locations of the worlds' 30 largest giant sequoias, among other fun facts. There are some things, of course, that facts and figures cannot communicate—such as being in the presence of the General Sherman Tree. It's an easy 0.5-mile walk down from the parking lot or from the shuttle stop at Wolverton Road. When you get to the viewing area, you'll find masses of people paying their respects. This enormous attraction can get crowded on summer weekends, so if you're able to visit on a weekday, or early in the morning, you may enjoy the experience even more.

◖ Giant Forest Museum

The Giant Forest Museum (Generals Hwy., 16 miles from the Ash Mountain Entrance, 559/565-4480, daily 9 A.M.–5 P.M. mid-May–mid-Oct.) is a lively place full of giant sequoias that grow only here in the Sierra Nevada range.

© HEATHER C. LISTON

General Sherman Tree

Children and adults alike love the touchable exhibits that provide context to all the facts and figures about the trees. This museum goes into great detail about the importance of fire in the life of a giant sequoia (and other plants and trees that grow in the same areas). You'll also learn how the park used to look, and why many of the buildings have been removed to make way for more trees. This is a great stop for families, especially if the kids need a rest from hiking or from long intervals in the car. Numerous hikes branch out into the Giant Forest Sequoia Grove.

◖ Crystal Cave

Magical Crystal Cave (Generals Hwy., 3 miles south of the General Sherman Tree) is one of the most beautiful of the 200 or so caves that occur naturally in the park. Its immense underground rooms are filled with sparkling stalagmites and stalactites made of limestone that has metamorphosed into marble over time. The Sequoia Natural History Association (559/565-3759, www.sequoiahistory.org) offers 45-minute guided tours of the cave (daily mid-May–late Oct., adults $13, over age 61 $12, ages 5–12 $7). A more challenging two-hour tour takes you deeper into the caverns and gives you a much more detailed lesson on the cave's history and geology. Best of all, serious spelunkers can sign up for the Wild Cave Tour (559/565-4251, $135), a 4–6-hour crawl off the well-lit trails and into the depths of Crystal Cave. You must be at least 16 years old and in good physical condition to join this expedition. Caving gear is provided.

You can't buy a ticket for a tour at the entrance to Crystal Cave: You need to stop at either the Foothills or the Lodgepole Visitors Center (Lodgepole Rd., 559/565-4436, daily 7 A.M.–7 P.M. summer, daily 8 A.M.–4:30 P.M. spring and fall, 9 A.M.–4:30 P.M. Fri.–Mon. Nov.–Apr.) in advance to purchase tickets. Then

drive the long, winding, dirt road to the cave parking lot; note that the trip can take more than an hour from either visitors center. No trailers or RVs over 22 feet are allowed on the road to Crystal Cave. Be aware that even in the fall, tours fill up quickly, so if possible get your tickets early in the morning or even a day in advance.

◖ Moro Rock

Moro Rock stands starkly alone in the middle of the landscape, providing an amazing vantage point for much of the park. This granite dome was formed by exfoliation, a repetitive process in which outer layers drop off, the remaining rock is no longer as compressed, so it expands further, and further peeling occurs. The end result is the rock's smooth, rounded dome. If you can, try to be here for one of the ranger talks that occasionally happen on top; or visit at sunset to see it in full color.

For maximum impact, park in the lot at the base of the rock and climb the 400 steps to the top, a distance of about 0.25 mile. (The climb to Moro Rock is not for those with an extreme fear of heights, but most people should be able to manage it.) The stairs are solid, and there are handrails all along the way. You'll want to take it slow, in any case; the entire route is filled with photo ops as you look down on the canyons of the Great Western Divide and across the canyons to some of the most beautiful peaks of the Sierra Nevada—Triple Divide Peak, Mount Silliman, Alta Peak, and Castle Rocks.

To reach the parking area from Generals Highway, take Moro Rock/Crescent Meadow Road south. There are restrooms and interpretive signage in the large parking lot. A free shuttle is available in summer (9 A.M.–6 P.M.); the road is closed to vehicles weekends and holidays.

Crescent Meadow

A sort of oasis beside the Giant Forest, Crescent Meadow is a bright green and yellow plain, thick

Moro Rock

© HEATHER C. LISTON

with grasses and teeming with wildlife. You can walk around the whole meadow in about an hour, watching for all manner of birds, squirrels, chipmunks, marmots, and even black bears. To reach the parking area from Generals Highway, take Moro Rock/Crescent Meadow Road south, past Moro Rock to the road's terminus. A free shuttle is available in summer (9 A.M.–6 P.M.); the road is closed to vehicles weekends and holidays.

RECREATION
Hiking

Numerous trails characterize this region, offering options for hikers of all levels and abilities. Hard-core hikers willing to brave steep climbs at high altitudes can either take day hikes or obtain overnight backcountry passes for the region's major trails. The following are just a sample; pick up trail maps ($1.50–3.50) at the visitors centers for even more hikes.

LITTLE BALDY

How can you resist a hike to a granite formation called Little Baldy (nine miles north of the General Sherman Tree, 3.4 miles round-trip)? This moderate climb takes you up about 700 feet to the top of the granite dome. Look down from the peak, which tops out at over 8,000 feet, into the Giant Forest and snap a few photos.

TOKOPAH FALLS

To cool off, head for Tokopah Falls (trailhead near Marble Fork Bridge in Lodgepole Campground, 3.4 miles round-trip, easy). Early summer, when the flow is at its peak, is the best time to trek out the almost two miles along the Marble Fork of the Kaweah River to this fantastic 1,200-foot waterfall.

LAKES TRAILS

The Lakes Trails (trailhead at Wolverton Picnic Area, 8–12.5 miles, strenuous) vary in length, but you're definitely going to have to climb a ways up to the glacial lakes. From the trail, you can visit Heather Lake, Emerald Lake, and Pear Lake. The minimum distance round-trip for a day hike to **Heather Lake** is eight miles. To go all the way to **Pear Lake** and back is at least 12.5 miles. Note that there is a daily quote of

Crescent Meadow

25 people; request a first-come, first-served wilderness permit from Lodgepole Visitors Center before beginning this hike.

ALTA TRAIL

Peak-baggers choose the Alta Trail (trailhead at Wolverton Picnic Area, 14–15 miles, very strenuous) which ascends all the way up to the 11,204-foot summit of Alta Peak. Pick a clear day for this challenging hike and you'll get a view of Mount Whitney across the Great Western Divide. As you climb, you'll also see Pear Lake, Moose Lake, and the granite Tablelands below. If you make it all the way, you'll gain more than 4,300 feet in altitude—but do not feel shy about turning around if conditions feel treacherous. (There's some rock-scrambling near the top that is not for the faint of heart, and at this altitude it is likely you'll run into snow and ice year-round.) Exercise caution, especially if you encounter large ice fields; they can be slippery and dangerous to traverse. Tharp's Rock, at

10,400 feet, is an impressive destination in itself, and a good place to stop and turn around if you've had enough.

CONGRESS TRAIL

One of the best short trails in the whole area is the Congress Trail (trailhead at General Sherman Tree, 2 miles, easy), which begins from the parking lot for the General Sherman Tree off Wolverton Road. Pick up a pamphlet and map to get the best experience on this trail, which includes many of the park's most famous giant sequoias—Chief Sequoyah, General Lee, and President McKinley—as well as the House and Senate Groups. This round-trip trail is paved, making it wheelchair accessible and an easy walk even for people who usually aren't big hikers.

BIG TREES TRAIL

This level loop hike (trailhead at Giant Forest Museum, under 1 mile, easy) travels around Round Meadow near the Giant Forest Museum. Interpretive panels make this

Alta Trail

a fun walk for kids and the paved boardwalk is wheelchair accessible. Accessible parking is available at the Big Trees trailhead; otherwise, park at the Giant Forest Museum and follow the hike from the Trail Center trailhead.

HAZELWOOD NATURE TRAIL

For a charming interpretive walk, head down the Hazelwood Nature Trail (trailhead at Giant Forest Museum, 1 mile, easy). Signs along this flat stroll detail the history of humans' relationship with the giant sequoia trees—both beneficial and destructive. This walk works well for families with children. From the Giant Forest Museum, take the Alta Trail to the Hazelwood Loop.

In the same vicinity, you can putter along the 0.25-mile **Trail for All People.** This interpretive nature walk is best in spring, when the wildflowers bloom.

MORO ROCK

If you do only one hike, it should be the 300-foot ascent to the summit of Moro Rock at 6,725 feet. From the parking lot off Morro Rock/Crescent Meadow Road, climb the 400 steps to the top (0.25 mile, moderate) where you'll be greeted by the canyons of the Great Western Divide and the Sierra Nevada peaks. To extend this hike another three miles, start instead from the Giant Forest Museum and hike the Moro Rock Trail 1.5 miles south along a mostly wooded trail to the base of Moro Rock, enjoying a couple of spectacular overlooks along the way.

You can also begin this hike at the General Sherman Tree for a 10-mile loop with Moro Rock in the middle. Begin by taking the Congress Trail past The Cloister, then follow the Alta Trail south past the Bedrock Mortars. At the second junction, follow the Soldiers Trail south, walking along Circle Meadow and continuing all the way to the base of Moro Rock. After your climb, follow the Moro Rock Trail to turn east onto Sugar Pine Trail. You'll walk alongside Crescent Meadow, Log Meadow, past Tharp's Log (the oldest pioneer cabin still in the park) and the Chimney Tree. At

© GEORGE JEN

the junction of the Huckleberry Trail with the Crescent Meadow Loop, hike north to return to the Congress Trail and your starting point near the General Sherman Tree.

CRESCENT MEADOW-LOG MEADOW LOOP TRAIL

The Crescent Meadow–Log Meadow Loop Trail (1.6 miles, easy) starts at the Crescent Meadow parking lot and picnic area. This short loop lets you experience more wildflowers and forest; it also takes you past Tharp's Log, the park's oldest cabin. Start by following the High Sierra Trail a short distance to its intersection with the Crescent Meadow Loop (you'll see signs for Tharp's Log). Take the Tharp's Log Trail north to the namesake cabin along Log Meadow. Explore the "cabin," then turn west to visit the Chimney Tree at the northern edge of Crescent Meadow. Follow the Crescent Meadow Loop south to return to the parking area.

ACCOMMODATIONS

Built in 1999, the C **Wuksachi Lodge** (64740 Wuksachi Way, off Generals Hwy. west of Lodgepole, 559/565-4070 or 888/252-5757, www.visitsequoia.com, 866/786-3197, www. visitsequoia.com, $200–270) offers the most luxurious accommodations available inside the parks. With 102 guest rooms in various sizes, the Wuksachi Lodge offers ample luxury housing for tree-lovers who just can't give up their creature comforts. Guest rooms have a woodsy-motel decor, with colorful Native American print bedspreads and mission-style wooden furniture. Each guest room has a private bath, a TV, a phone, a coffeemaker, a fridge, ski racks, and daily maid service, and Internet access is available at no extra charge both in the guest rooms and in the common areas. The Wuksachi's superior guest rooms offer space and comfort, particularly for families who like digital entertainment on their vacations. An on-site restaurant (the best in the

parks), a Native American–themed gift shop, and close access to the Lodgepole visitors complex round out the attractions of this popular lodge. While it's a bit pricey in summer, the Wuksachi can be quite affordable in winter, with nonholiday rates as low as $93. Ask for the bed-and-breakfast special year-round, which adds an excellent buffet breakfast ($25) for two to your room rate.

CAMPING

Lodgepole Campground (205 sites, year-round, reservations summer only 877/444-6777, www. recreation.gov, summer $20, spring and fall $18, winter $10) is located along the Kaweah River, 21 miles from the Ash Mountain park entrance. The campground has flush toilets, picnic tables, and bear-proof containers, and it's less than 0.25 mile from Lodgepole Village, where you'll find showers, laundry, and groceries. Off-season, there are only 24 first-come, first-served walk-in tent sites available.

Dorst Creek Campground (210 sites, reservations 877/444-6777, www.recreation.gov, late June–Labor Day, $20) is located along Generals Highway, six miles north of Wuksachi Village. This is only one of two campgrounds (the other is Lodgepole) in the parks that accepts reservations, and they are definitely recommended; Dorst fills up fast in summer. The campground has flush toilets, drinking water, picnic tables, fire rings, bear-proof containers, and a dump station.

Adventurous campers should check out the **Bearpaw Meadow High Sierra Camp** (DNC, 888/252-5757, www.visitsequoia.com, July–mid-Sept., 2 people $350). This camp takes a leaf from Yosemite's book with its accommodations and amenities, featuring six tent cabins that sleep two people apiece with bedding, towels, and sleeping pads. (You can even fit a third person on the floor of your cabin.) A bathhouse offers flush toilets and hot showers, and each stay comes with a full dinner and breakfast, served family-style. You can even buy a box lunch to take with you on your next day's journey. To reach this backcountry camp from the Crescent Meadow parking area, hike the wide, well-marked High Sierra Trail for 11.5-miles to Bearpaw Meadow at 7,800 feet.

If you have overnight reservations at High Sierra Camp, you do not have to pay the $15 wilderness camping fee, but you do still need a wilderness permit from the Lodgepole Visitors Center.

FOOD

The closest thing to an upscale restaurant in Sequoia and Kings Canyon is the ◖ **Wuksachi Lodge Restaurant** (64740 Wuksachi Way, off Generals Hwy. two miles north of Lodgepole, 559/565-4070 or 888/252-5757, www.visitsequoia.com, daily 7–10 A.M., 11:30 A.M.–2:30 P.M., and 5–10 P.M. summer, daily 7:30–9:30 A.M., 11:30 A.M.–2:30 P.M., and 5:30–8:30 P.M. winter, $10–30). The elegant dining room features white tablecloths and sweeping forest views outside the picture windows. The Wuksachi Restaurant offers three meals daily and nonguests are welcome. Dinner is especially good, with creative menus and fine California-style ingredients, and includes vegan options. Make a reservation if you plan to dine at the Wuksachi on a summer weekend.

You'll find basic groceries and other necessary camping supplies at the **Lodgepole Market** (Generals Hwy., Lodgepole, 559/565-3301, daily 8 A.M.–8 P.M. Memorial Day–Labor Day, daily 10 A.M.–4:30 P.M. Apr.–Memorial Day and Labor Day–Oct.). There's also a gift shop in the **Wuksachi Lodge** (daily 8 A.M.–8 P.M.).

The snack bar and deli (559/565-3301, daily 8 A.M.–8 P.M. Memorial Day–Labor Day) at Lodgepole Village are open in summer only, serving pizza, pre-made sandwiches, and other light snacks.

GETTING THERE

Lodgepole is located on Generals Highway 22 miles north of the Ash Mountain (south) Entrance and 27 miles south of the Big Stump (northwest) Entrance. It takes about an hour to drive to Lodgepole from either entrance. Wuksachi Village is just two miles northwest of Lodgepole, and the General Sherman Tree parking lot is 2.5 miles south of Lodgepole off Wolverton Road.

Foothills

The Foothills area of Sequoia National Park is in the southern part of the park, with lower elevations and drier snow-free weather. It is accessed from the Ash Mountain Entrance on Highway 123, east of Three Rivers.

SIGHTS
Foothills Visitors Center

The Foothills Visitors Center (559/565-4212, daily 8 A.M.–6 P.M. Memorial Day–Labor Day, daily 8 A.M.–4:30 P.M. Labor Day–Memorial Day) is located one mile north of the Ash Mountain Entrance and also serves as the park headquarters. It includes a bookstore and exhibits about the nearby area, and ranger talks and walks begin here. You can also buy Crystal Cave tickets (daily 8 A.M.–4 P.M. mid-May–late Oct.) or get a wilderness permit (late May–late Sept., $15 for up to 15 people); check the office behind the visitors center in summer, or self-register for a permit outside the rest of the year for free.

Hospital Rock

Hospital Rock is the former home of the Western Mono people. Exhibits help identify the markings they left behind when they vacated the area in the 1870s. One of the major indicators of their way of life are the grinding holes on the rocks, where they ground flour out of acorns. The short **Hospital Rock River Trail** is nearby and there is a picnic area. Hospital Rock is on Generals Highway six miles northeast of the Foothills Visitors Center.

RECREATION
Hiking
MARBLE FORK TRAIL

For a vigorous adventure with a big payoff, take the Marble Fork Trail (7.4 miles, moderate–strenuous) to Marble Falls. This hike starts in the Potwisha Campground near site 14. (You aren't allowed to park in Potwisha unless you're camping here, but there's some room across the street for parking.) The trail is named after the Marble Fork of the Kaweah River, and you'll hear its pleasant sounds as you hike. Start out on a forest road, and you'll soon see a sign directing you to keep left; the way becomes more trail-like, winding upward through the woods. After 2.5 miles, you'll emerge from the trees for sweeping views of the canyons around you and the water below. In four miles or less you'll come to Marble Falls. The falls are beautiful, noisy, and dramatic, and you'll see why they got their name—the viewpoint actually looks like a very large slab of white marble. Sit and enjoy the falls for a while as you rest up from your climb, and then return the way you came.

PARADISE CREEK

A nice short nature walk in the Foothills area starts in Buckeye Flat Campground and leads alongside Paradise Creek (3 miles, easy). Start by crossing the footbridge near campsite 28 and then bear right to follow the trail beside the creek. The Middle Fork of the Kaweah River heads off to the left. In about 1.5 miles the trail will start to peter out. At that point, turn around and return the same way.

CAMPING

Potwisha (40 sites, year-round, $18) is on the Kaweah River, about four miles north of the Ash Mountain Entrance. Amenities at this first-come, first-served campground include flush toilets, drinking water, a dump station, and bear-proof containers.

Just a few miles farther north along Generals Highway, and on a little spur to the east, you'll find **Buckeye Flat** (28 sites, May–Sept., $18) in a lovely spot along the Kaweah River. This tent-only campground is first-come, first-served and has flush toilets; it does not accommodate RVs or trailers.

The **South Fork** is a tent-only campground (10 sites, year-round, May–Oct., $12, Nov.–Apr. free) 13 miles off Highway 198 on South Fork Drive near Three Rivers. The campground is first-come, first-served with pit toilets and bear-proof containers, but no drinking water.

GETTING THERE

The Foothills area is easily accessed from the south via Highway 198; it's the first part of the park you encounter after the Ash Mountain Entrance.

Mineral King

All of the national park and national forest lands here have extensive unspoiled natural beauty and are remote from civilization, but the Mineral King section (Mineral King Rd., 25 miles east of Hwy. 198) of Sequoia National park is really out there. This glacial valley was annexed into the park in 1978 and is now its southernmost section. The region includes just a few examples of human intervention: the Mineral King Ranger Station, the Silver City Mountain Resort, a few private cabins, and two campgrounds (Atwell and Cold Springs). Otherwise, you're fully communing with nature, so plan accordingly. The nearest food and gas are in the town of Three Rivers, and the 22-mile road to get there is so rough that it takes at least 1.5 hours to drive—and that's in good weather. It's a one-lane road open to two-way traffic, so expect to pull over and wait now and then.

Interestingly, the once booming town of Mineral King never had a successful mining industry nearby. Silver was discovered here in the 19th century, and mining began in 1873, but not many minerals moved out of the mountain. Instead, the road built in 1879 attracted loggers and the hydroelectric industry, and the town managed to flourish for a while. Today, visitors drive up the long winding road to enjoy the resurgence of nature at the expense of human construction. Mineral King Valley draws both geology and botany buffs with its glacier-carved array of rocks and minerals, some overgrown with a variety of native plants. The Atwell Mill that once cut first-growth sequoia timber has been reduced to a few relics—a steam engine, a wheel, miscellaneous junk—while all around, young giant sequoias reclaim their territory. High above the former town, Sawtooth Peak, at more than 12,000 feet, looms large and reminiscent of similar mountains in the Rockies. The peak is perfect for intrepid day hikers and backpackers.

Marmots frequent the Mineral King area, and these furry critters won't seem quite so cute after you discover they've chewed through your radiator hoses. Check with the ranger station about their current activity, and notify the rangers if your car has been disabled.

SIGHTS
Mineral King Ranger Station

The Mineral King Ranger Station (Mineral King Rd., 559/565-3768, daily 8 A.M.–4 P.M. May–Sept.) is located near the end of Mineral King Road, beyond the Silver City Resort and close to Cold Springs Campground. You can get information and wilderness permits here, and there is a self-service wilderness permit box ($15 summer, free winter) on the porch so you can get a permit even when the ranger station is closed.

RECREATION
Hiking

Many hikes begin in Mineral King Valley, and you can visit a number of charming alpine lakes if you're up for a hike of 7–12 miles. However, at 7,500 feet elevation hikes in the Mineral King area are demanding and strenuous. Bring lots of water and honestly gauge the fitness level of yourself and others before hitting the trail.

COLD SPRINGS NATURE TRAIL

A good place to start walking in Mineral King is the Cold Springs Nature Trail (1 mile). This easy interpretive walk describes and displays the natural wonders and the formation of the valley.

TIMBER GAP

The Timber Gap Trail (4 miles round-trip) follows an old mining road through a forest of red fir trees. You'll enjoy pretty views out to Alta Peak and the Middle Fork of the Kaweah River. Remember that you're at over 7,500 feet elevation, so you may feel you're getting a workout even on this short hike.

MONARCH LAKES

Upper and Lower Monarch Lakes (8.5 miles round-trip) sit nestled beneath majestic Sawtooth Peak. The trek is mostly flat and easy walking through forest and meadows with views of the Great Divide; consider bringing a picnic to enjoy beside the lakes.

For hikers in great shape and looking for tremendous views, keep hiking 1.3 miles past the lakes to the top of **Sawtooth Peak** (11,700 feet). This trail isn't for the faint of breath or shaky of leg—it climbs 1,200 vertical feet in just over a mile of loose difficult ground. But once you're at the top, you'll get a fine chance to rest as you soak in the majestic peaks all around.

Another option is to explore the trail to **Crystal Lake** (10 miles round-trip) where it splits from the Monarch Lakes hike at Chihuahua Bowl. The trail passes the relics of an old mine before climbing steeply to end at the lake.

EAGLE AND MOSQUITO LAKES

Plan to spend all day on the hike out to Eagle and Mosquito Lakes (7 miles round-trip), which lies in the backcountry beyond the Mineral Creek Ranger Station. The Eagle and Mosquito Lakes Trailhead is at the end of Mineral King Road. From the trailhead, climb two miles up Mineral King Valley to Eagle Basin. Where the trail splits, head left to Eagle Lake (3.4 miles from trailhead) or right to Mosquito Lake (3.6 miles from trailhead).

WHITE CHIEF TRAIL

The White Chief Trail (5.8 miles round-trip) begins at the Eagle and Mosquito Lakes Trailhead at the end of Mineral King Road. The trail leads to the abandoned mine site at White Chief Bowl. It's a fairly steep climb at times, but the rewards include scenic views of the Mineral King Valley and a look at some remnants from the area's mining history, including the Crabtree Cabin, which dates to the 1870s.

ACCOMMODATIONS AND FOOD

Silver City Mountain Resort (559/561-3223, www.silvercityresort.com, May–mid-Oct.) is the sort of place that isn't supposed to exist: a privately owned resort on national park land. That's because it was already there when the Mineral King area was annexed to the southern part of Sequoia National Park in the 1970s, and so it was grandfathered in. The resort has 13 different cabins. The most economical are the three small "historical cabins" built in the 1930s ($120–150). A step up in comfort are the three "family cabins" that sleep up to five people ($195). Finally, five luxurious modern "chalets" ($250–395) are outfitted with decks, fireplaces, showers, phones, and outstanding mountain views. Wi-Fi is included in the rates, and it sometimes works outdoors near the cabins and chalets.

The **Silver City Resort Restaurant** (8 A.M.–8 P.M. Thurs.–Mon., 8 A.M.–5 P.M. Tues.–Wed., $8–17.50) is the only place to get food, thus it's important to know that the only thing they serve on Tuesday–Wednesday is pie and beverages. The homemade pies are very good, but if you want a real meal, make sure you bring food of your own. There is actually no food left on the premises by the time Tuesday rolls around, and the kitchen staff is off making the long drive into town to restock. The food is good while it lasts, though, and they have a liquor license allowing them to serve beer and wine. There's a souvenir shop (8 A.M.–8 P.M. Thurs.–Mon., 8 A.M.–5 P.M.

Tues.–Wed.) in the restaurant building, but the only snacks available are usually energy bars and sodas.

CAMPING

There are two campgrounds in the Mineral King area: **Atwell Mill** (21 sites, May–Oct., $12) and **Cold Springs** (40 sites, May–Oct., $12). Both are first-come, first-served and have vault toilets. If you want showers or food, you can drive to Silver City, 0.5 mile east of Atwell Mill and 2.5 miles west of Cold Spring. Both campgrounds have drinking water available, however the water is turned off mid-October to April, so bring your own if you plan to visit then. The Mineral King Ranger Station is located beside the Cold Spring campground;

summer ranger programs (www.nps.gov/seki) serve campers from both areas.

GETTING THERE

To get to Mineral King, approach Sequoia National Park from the south on Highway 198, and instead of entering the park, make a right turn onto Mineral King Road, two miles before the Ash Mountain Entrance, and drive 25 miles east. It will take about 30 minutes to come to the end of this narrow winding road; trailers and RVs are not allowed. Along the way, you will enter the boundaries of Sequoia National Park through the small Lookout Point entrance (May–Oct., $20) and pay the entrance fee at a self-serve station. November 1–April, the gate is locked for the season.

Sequoia National Forest

As you explore Kings Canyon and Sequoia National Parks, you'll find yourself crossing in and out of park boundaries almost without noticing. Signs announce the entrance of Sequoia National Forest, then a national park, and then back again. While both the national forest and the parks are full of scenery, hiking trails, and interesting things to do, the rules in each are a little different. For example, inside national park boundaries, you can camp only in designated campgrounds; in Sequoia National Forest, you can camp almost anywhere as long as you have a wilderness permit. Services also vary. Companies doing business on national park land must either work for the National Park Service or be an official concessionaire hired by the National Park Service and subject to its restrictions. In Sequoia National Forest, the government can lease areas to private operators who are free to run their businesses their own way. The Hume Lake Christian Camp and the Kings Canyon Lodge are two such properties; they're located in the Sequoia

National Forest, but they are privately owned and operated. In addition, Sequoia–Kings Canyon Park Services Company operates the Montecito–Sequoia Lodge and Stony Creek Village in the Sequoia National Forest.

Free dispersed camping (camping outside developed campgrounds) is allowed throughout most of the Sequoia National Forest. The only areas where it is not allowed are the Hume Lake and Stony Creek recreation areas. Be careful to check where you're camping; forest lands run seamlessly into the national parks here, and dispersed camping in Sequoia and Kings Canyon National Parks is not allowed unless you have a backcountry permit. You do not need a backcountry permit to camp in the national forest, but you do need a campfire permit if you want to have a fire or use a stove. You can pick one up at the **Kings Canyon Visitors Center** (Grant Grove, 83918 Hwy. 180 E., Miramonte, 559/565-4307, daily 8 A.M.–6 P.M. Apr.–Oct., daily 9 A.M.–4:30 P.M. Nov.–Mar.) or the **Hume Lake Ranger District** (Hwy. 180, 19 miles west of the Big Stump Entrance, 559/338-2251, 8 A.M.–4:30 P.M. Mon.–Fri.).

HUME LAKE

The **Hume Lake Ranger District** office (35860 E. Kings Canyon Rd., Dunlap, 559/338-2251, 8 A.M.–4:30 P.M. Mon.–Fri.) for the Sequoia National Forest and Giant Sequoia National Monument is located 19 miles west of Kings Canyon National Park on Highway 180. At the district office, you can get forest information and free campfire permits. You may want to stop by even if they're closed; not only is there a self-serve station for permits, there are outdoor exhibits about the area, and information about the 13 giant sequoia (*Sequoiadendron giganteum*) groves that lie within the Hume Lake Ranger District. The 1882 Dolbeer Donkey displayed outside dates from Hume Lake's past as a logging site. Plenty of literature is available outside to take with you as well.

Hume Lake Christian Camp

Hume Lake is a lovely 87-acre body of water located along the Generals Highway about eight miles northeast of Grant Grove Village. The lake itself is part of the national forest, and anyone may use it. Most of the facilities on the lake are owned and operated by the private Hume Lake Christian Camp (559/305-7770, www.humelake.org), which has been here since 1946. The Christian Camp is a lively bustling place with a lodge, a dining room, a conference center, four swimming pools, a snack shop, a general store, a small laundry, and fleets of bicycles, kayaks, and golf carts. Most of the facilities are primarily for the use of the organization and its constituents. However, when the camp isn't full, it becomes available to visitors.

The **Lodge at Hume Lake Christian Camp** (800/965-4863, www.humelake.org, $105–125, including breakfast) rents guest rooms to

© HEATHER C. LISTON

Hume Lake

the public whenever space is available beyond the needs of their own programs. Guest rooms are spacious and modern, with phones, ceiling fans, coffeemakers, and other niceties. They're tastefully decorated in woodsy style, so you won't feel you're in a generic motel. Guests at the Lodge can use the camp's swimming pools at no extra charge.

The **Pine Tree Dining Room** at Hume Lake Christian Camp (daily 6:30–8:30 A.M., 11:30 A.M.–1:30 P.M., and 4:30–6:30 P.M. summer, daily 6:45–7:30 A.M., 11:45 A.M.–12:30 P.M., and 4:45–5:30 P.M. fall–spring, $5.50–9.50) is open to the public when space is available. Meals are served buffet-style in a large modern building with wonderful views of the lake and forest from its picture windows. If you're staying in the Grant Grove area, this can be a nice alternative to the village offerings; in good weather the drive takes less than 30 minutes. There's also a snack shop (daily 7 A.M.–11 P.M. summer, limited hours Sat.–Sun. fall–spring) on the premises, serving ice cream, pizza, and a few other things at a walk-up counter.

Groceries and other basic supplies, as well as fishing licenses, are available at the **Hume Lake General Store** (559/305-7770, www.humelake.org, 8 A.M.–5 P.M. Sun.–Fri., 8 A.M.–7:30 P.M. Sat. year-round). A **gas station** (64144 Hume Lake Rd., 559/336-2542, with credit card daily 24 hours year-round) and a post office (64144 Hume Lake Rd., 559/336-2542, 9:15 A.M.–2 P.M. Mon.–Fri. June–Aug.) are located in the middle of the Hume Lake development, and both are open to the public.

Camping

Campgrounds are managed by the Hume Lake Ranger District of the Sequoia National Forest/Giant Sequoia National Monument (559/338-2251, www.fs.fed.us/r5/sequoia). To check weather and to verify campground availability, call 559/565-3341. Campgrounds in the area include **Princess Campground** (Hwy. 180, 877/444-6777, www.recreation.

gov, June–Sept., $18), six miles north of Grant Grove Village, with 90 sites and vault toilets; **Hume Lake** (Generals Hwy., 877/444-6777, www.recreation.gov, May–Sept., $20), 10 miles northeast of Grant Grove, with 74 sites and flush toilets; **Tenmile** (Generals Hwy., May–Sept., $16), five miles northeast of Grant Grove, with 13 first-come, first-served sites. It allows RVs up to 22 feet long but has no drinking water and has vault toilets; **Landslide** (Generals Hwy., summer only, $16), 13 miles northeast of Grant Grove, with nine first-come, first-served sites and vault toilets; and **Convict Flat** (Hwy. 180, summer only, free) 19 miles northeast of Grant Grove, with five first-come, first-served sites.

KINGS CANYON LODGE

As you drive the scenic road from Grant Grove to Cedar Grove, you'll eventually come upon a large roadside sign that says "Caution Ice." It's not an unusual warning in these parts, but below, a sort of addendum to the sign continues: "Cream Ahead." Sure enough, you're just 0.25 mile from quirky Kings Canyon Lodge (67751 E. Kings Canyon Rd., 13 miles east of Grant Grove Village, 559/335-2405, Apr.–Nov., $99–199), which offers ice cream, beer, food, accommodations, and gas. If ever there was a mountain resort that time forgot, this is it. The main building is a ramshackle wooden cabin with a counter and about a dozen barstools inside. Upstairs are three guest rooms and two baths, while out on the grounds are seven cabins, each of which sleep 2–8 people. The main attraction is a pair of antique gas pumps, which date to 1928 and claim to be the country's oldest double gravity pumps. (The owners are a little touchy about people stopping by just to take pictures with the gas pumps, so enjoy a look but be respectful.) This family-owned and oddly charming complex has no Wi-Fi, no cell service, no laundry, and no guaranteed hours of operation.

Kings Canyon Lodge Restaurant (67751 E. Kings Canyon Rd., 13 miles east of Grant Grove Village, 559/335-2405, hours vary, usually daily 8:30 A.M.–7 P.M. Apr.–Nov., $6–9) is the only place to buy food between Grant Grove and Cedar Grove. It's far from fancy, but if you've ever fantasized about dining in an Old West saloon, you'll enjoy the experience. The food is mostly sandwiches, burgers, milk shakes, and ice cream, but the cold beer and soda will be especially welcome to summer travelers taking a break.

BOYDEN CAVE

Tucked back in the wilds of the Sequoia National Forest, between Grant Grove and Cedar Grove, Boyden Cave (74101 E. Kings Canyon Rd., 559/338-0959 or 888/965-8243, www.caverntours.com/boydenrt.htm, tours daily 10 A.M.–5 P.M. May–Sept., daily 11 A.M.–4 P.M. mid-Apr.–May and Sept.–mid-Nov., adults $13, under age 12 $8) gives visitors an up-close cave experience. Inside Boyden, "please try not to touch the formations" takes on a new meaning—you have to turn sideways to avoid the walls and duck to keep from hitting your head on stalactites that are many thousands of years old. The cavern network contains plenty of draperies, pancakes, stalactites, and other calcite structures; you can stare right at them, up into them, and in some cases walk all the way around them. For visitors who are very curious and physically fit, there's also a 2.5-hour "flashlight tour" ($35) that explores deeper into the nooks and crannies of the cave—expect to get dirty and to do some crawling. Note that some of the spaces are tight, making the tour difficult and uncomfortable for larger people.

Boyden Cave is operated on national forest land by Boyden Cavern Adventures and Tours, a private company. Due to its location along Highway 180 (Kings Canyon Scenic Byway/E. Kings Canyon Rd.), visitors must first enter Kings Canyon National Park and pay the park entry fee ($20) before driving to the cavern. However, the cavern is not in the park or operated by the government, so you must also pay a fee for the tour.

BIG MEADOWS

In the Big Meadows area, you'll find one of those funky one-of-a-kind lodging options that the U.S. Forest Service sometimes surprises you with. The 900-square-foot **Big Meadows Guard Station** (35860 Kings Canyon Rd., Dunlap, 877/444-6777, www.recreation.gov, June–Oct., $125) was built by the Civilian Conservation Corps between 1933 and 1935 as a residence for firefighting personnel. The one-story cabin has a refrigerator, a stove, a hot-water heater, pots, pans, and dishes, a table and chairs, and beds for six people (one queen, two bunks, and a double-size fold-out sofa); bring your own sleeping bags or blankets and all your own food. The station is located in one of the higher areas of the forest, at 7,600 feet elevation, so expect cool nights even in midsummer.

The U.S. Forest Service maintains the **Horse Camp** (Big Meadow Rd., June–Oct., first-come, first-served, free), 13 miles southeast of Grant Grove via Generals Highway, with five equestrian sites, no drinking water, and vault toilets; and the **Big Meadows Campground** (Big Meadow Rd., June–Oct., first-come, first-served, free), 13 miles southeast of Grant Grove via Generals Highway, with 25 sites, vault toilets, and no drinking water.

MONTECITO LAKE RESORT

Montecito Lake Resort (63410 Generals Hwy., 559/565-3388 or 800/227-9900, www.ms-lodge.com, year-round), also known as the Montecito-Sequoia Lodge, is a rustic full-service resort located on Generals Highway nine miles southeast of Grant Grove Village. The main lodge has 24 guest rooms, three smaller lodges that sleep up to five people each, and

© HEATHER C. LISTON

Montecito Lake Resort

eight heated cabins that sleep up to eight people each. The cabins do not have private baths, but bathhouses with free showers are nearby.

In summer, Montecito operates primarily as a family camp (800/227-9900, Sun.–Fri. mid-June–mid-Aug., six-day minimum). The weekly rates range from $1,495 for one person to $6,195 for a family of 3–8 people in one of the better suites. Lodging, meals, and all sorts of activities are included, from guided hikes to canoeing on the lake to swimming in the large outdoor pool. Supervised activities for children ages 2–17 are also included. In summer, the lodge is available to noncampers ($100–400) on Saturday only.

Outside the summer season, Montecito Lake Resort is a regular resort with nightly accommodations (mid-Aug.–mid-June, $99–296, meals included). The pool is closed, but the outdoor hot tub is open and can be ideal after a day of cross-country skiing, backcountry snowboarding, tubing on Montecito's 40 miles of groomed trails, or ice-skating on Montecito Lake. The resort rent skis, snowshoes, ice skates, and even "extreme snow bikes" ($15 per day), and lessons are available ($15). The staff also offers group activities for children, such as snow sculpture and igloo-building.

Free wireless Internet access is available in the lodge and there's a business center for guests that has a hard-wired computer and printer and satellite TV. A gift shop is located inside the **Mt. Top Ski Shop** (hours vary), but there are no groceries available. The nearest gas in summer is at Stony Creek, 3.5 miles south, or at Hume Lake the rest of the year.

The restaurant at **Montecito Lake Resort** (daily 7:30–9 A.M., noon–1:30 P.M., and 5:30–7 P.M. mid-June–mid-Aug., daily 8–9 A.M., noon–1 P.M., and 6–7 P.M. mid-Aug.–mid-June, $9–20) is open to nonguests year-round. Buffet-style meals are served at massive wooden tables that seat 10 people each, which encourages mingling among the campers. For those who plan to spend the day hiking or skiing, the staff will prepare trail lunches ($9–10) on request. The **Pine Box Bar** (daily noon–9:45 P.M. summer, daily noon–8:30 or 9 P.M. winter) is in the back room of the main lodge.

Montecito Lake Resort is run by Sequoia–Kings Canyon Park Services Company (866/565-6343). If you're staying at one of their other lodgings (Cedar Grove, Grant Grove, or Stony Creek), you can receive a 25 percent discount on meals here.

STONY CREEK

Stony Creek Village (May–Sept. or Oct.) is located in the Sequoia National Forest on Generals Highway, just north of the boundary of Sequoia National Park. Facilities here are operated by the Sequoia–Kings Canyon Park Services Company (866/565-6343) and include a lodge, a restaurant, a market and gift shop (daily 9 A.M.–6 P.M.), a coin laundry (daily 9 A.M.–6 P.M.), an ATM, and a gas station (with credit card daily 24 hours).

The **Stony Creek Lodge** (866/522-6966, www.sequoia-kingscanyon.com, $159–179) has 11 guest rooms, each with either one queen bed and a patio or a combination of queen and twin beds. Guest rooms include satellite TV, phones, private baths, maid service, and continental breakfast. The on-site **restaurant** (daily 11 A.M.–8 P.M., $10–25) specializes in pizza.

In addition, the U.S. Forest Service maintains two campgrounds near Stony Creek Village. **Stony Creek Campground** (Generals Hwy., 14 miles southeast of Grant Grove, 49 sites, 877/444-6777, www.recreation.gov, May–Oct., $20) has tent and RV sites with fire rings, flush toilets, water, and food storage. **Upper Stony Creek Campground** (Generals Hwy., 14 miles southeast of Grant Grove, 19 sites, first-come, first-served, $16) has fire rings, picnic tables, water, and pit toilets.

Practicalities

There are three entrances to Sequoia and Kings Canyon National Parks. The **entrance fee** is $20, good for up to seven days, and it is valid for both Sequoia and Kings Canyon National Parks. (No additional fees are necessary for access to Sequoia National Forest or Giant Sequoia National Monument.) Upon entering the park, you'll receive a glossy pamphlet with a basic map of the parks and an up-to-date park guide for Sequoia and Kings Canyon. These will provide you with all the in-park information you need to have a great time and keep up on any activities and events.

INFORMATION AND SERVICES
Banks and Post Offices

There are no banks inside the park, but you can find ATMs at the major visitors complexes at Grant Grove (inside the restaurant and in the grocery market), Lodgepole, Wuksachi, and Cedar Grove (summer only).

Although you can no longer mail a letter from the old log cabin post office, you can make use of the **Park Post Office at Lodgepole** (Lodgepole Visitors Center, 63228 General's Hwy., 559/565-3678, 8 A.M.–1 P.M. and 2–4 P.M. Mon.–Fri.). Another post office is beside the market in **Grant Grove Village** (86724 Hwy. 180, 559/335-2499, 9 A.M.–4 P.M. Mon.–Fri.), and there's another one within the **Hume Lake Christian Camp** (64144 Hume Lake Rd., 559/336-2542, 9:15 A.M.–2 P.M. Mon.–Fri. June–Aug.).

Fishing Licenses

Fishing is not a major sport in Kings Canyon and Sequoia, but the many lakes and streams in the park do allow fishing provided you have a valid California fishing license and follow state regulations. You can purchase tackle at the Lodgepole, Grant Grove, and Cedar Grove markets; licenses are available at the Hume Lake General Store. Get up-to-date information on fishing regulations in the parks at the various visitors centers, and ask for recommendations about good spots to try. In most of the parks, trout season is late April–mid-November. Check online with the Department of Fish and Game (www.dfg.ca.gov) for information on seasons and rules.

Gas and Automotive Services

Technically, there is no gas available within Sequoia or Kings Canyon National Parks. However, there are several gas-station locations outside and very close to the park boundaries.

The **Kings Canyon Lodge Gas Station** (67751 E. Kings Canyon Rd., 13 miles east of Grant Grove Village, 559/335-2405, Apr.–Nov.) can be found on Kings Canyon Road between Grant Grove and Cedar Grove, however it is in Sequoia National Forest rather than Kings Canyon National Park. Many visitors are dubious when they see the genuine antique gas pumps sitting outside the funky old lodge. The pumps actually work, although they're not self-service, so please ask the owners for assistance.

Two other gas stations are also located in Sequoia National Forest. One is at Hume Lake in the **Hume Lake Christian Camp** (64144 Hume Lake Rd., 559/305-7770, 24 hours with credit card, year-round), nine miles north of Grant Grove. The other gas station is at **Stony Creek Village** (Generals Hwy., 559/565-3909, 24 hours with credit card, summer only), between Wuksachi and Grant Grove.

West of the Big Stump Entrance, gas is available at the **Valero Station** (Hwy. 180, 866/565-6343, Squaw Valley, 20 miles west of Grant Grove); it's owned by the Sequoia–Kings Canyon Park Services Company. The station also has a grocery store, **Clingan's** (daily 7 A.M.–9 P.M. summer, daily 7 A.M.–8 P.M. winter), and it has free Wi-Fi access. There is also a **Chevron Station** (41907 Sierra Dr., Three Rivers), approximately six miles west of the Foothills Entrance off Highway 198.

Laundry and Showers

Laundry facilities are available at **Cedar Grove Village** (daily 8 A.M.–1 P.M. and 3–6 P.M., $1.75), **Stony Creek Resort** (daily 9 A.M.–6 P.M. summer, $1.75), and **Lodgepole Village** (daily 8 A.M.–8 P.M. in summer, shorter hours spring–fall, May–Oct., $0.50–1). There's also a very small coin laundry at Hume Lake in the Christian Camp facilities; nonguests are welcome to use it, but it's quite busy. At **Montecito Lake Resort** (63410 Generals Hwy., 559/565-3388 or 800/227-9900, www.mslodge.com, year-round), the housekeeping staff will launder items for a fee. If you drive out to Stony Creek Resort to do laundry, bring your own soap; only large boxes of laundry soap are available.

Cedar Grove Village (daily 7 A.M.–1 P.M. and 3–7 P.M. mid-Apr.–mid-Nov., $3.50) has seasonal showers. Showers are also available at **Grant Grove Village** (daily 11 A.M.–4 P.M. May–Oct., $1) in the Meadow Camp cabins area; ask for a map at the visitors center. **Stony Creek Village** has showers (daily 9 A.M.–6 P.M. May–Sept., $4) available seasonally. Campers can clean up at **Lodgepole Village** (daily 8 A.M.–1 P.M. and 3–5 P.M. May–Oct., $3). Bring quarters for all laundry services and showers.

Media and Communications

You're a long way from civilization when you visit Sequoia and Kings Canyon National Parks—don't expect cell-phone or 3G service. Instead, you'll rely on land lines at the visitors centers and the lodgings for the duration of your stay. **Pay telephones** are available outside most visitor centers, at Cold Springs

Campground and Silver City Mountain Resort in the Mineral King Area, at Stony Creek Village and the Dorst Campground on Generals Highway, and at Hume Lake and Kings Canyon Lodge (summer only).

Internet access is becoming reasonably common in heavily trafficked areas. Several park lodges (John Muir, Montecito-Sequoia, and Wuksachi) offer free unsecured wireless access; you can also connect in the Grant Grove Restaurant, in the lodging desk lobby area beside the restaurant, and at the Valero Station, 20 miles outside the park on Highway 180. Of course, it's also nice to forget about the laptop and unplug for a few days.

Medical Services

There are no medical services available in Sequoia and Kings Canyon beyond the first aid provided by rangers. In a medical emergency, dial 911. The nearest hospitals are in Fresno at **St. Agnes Medical Center** (1303 E. Herndon Ave., 559/450-3000, www.samc.com) or **Community Regional Medical Center** (2823 Fresno St., 559/459-6000, www.communitymedical.org).

GETTING THERE
Car

There are three entrances to Sequoia and Kings Canyon National Parks. Visitors can enter Sequoia National Park at the Ash Mountain Entrance on Highway 198. The Big Stump Entrance is north in Kings Canyon National Park on Highway 180. The main road running through the two parks is Generals Highway; it connects Highway 180 (Kings Canyon Hwy.) in the north to Highway 198 in the south. The little-used Lookout Point Entrance provides seasonal access to the Mineral King area of Sequoia National Park. There are no road entrances on the east side of the parks.

The closest major highway is Highway 99. From Highway 99, turn east onto Highway 180 at Fresno to reach the Big Stump Entrance of Kings Canyon National Park. From San Francisco, the drive to the Big Stump Entrance takes about 4.5 hours. If entering from the south, take Highway 99 to Visalia, and then turn east onto Highway 198 to reach the Ash Mountain Entrance of Sequoia National Park.

BIG STUMP ENTRANCE

The main portal on the west side of Kings Canyon National Park is the Big Stump Entrance, located on Highway 180. Big Stump is the most direct route to either park from the west or north.

At time of publication, a long-term road construction project was underway, and access can be a bit odd. Immediately upon entering the park boundary, all traffic is directed left off Highway 180 into a temporary entrance station. At the entrance station, pay the park entry fee ($20) and receive your park map and official *Guide*. When leaving the pay station, turn left to return to Highway 180 heading north into the park. If your goal is Kings Canyon National Park, continue straight; you'll be at Grant Grove Village in about 3.5 miles. To reach Sequoia National Park, turn right onto Generals Highway at the next junction and head south toward Lodgepole Visitors Center and Village.

ASH MOUNTAIN ENTRANCE

The Ash Mountain Entrance is located on Highway 198, which enters Sequoia National Park from the south. Once inside the park, Highway 198 becomes Generals Highway. As you continue north, you'll pass the Foothills Visitors Center, Giant Forest Museum, the General Sherman Tree, and after many curves and switchbacks, the Lodgepole Visitors Center and Village. This road can be slow going thanks to a combination of heavy traffic (especially in summer) as well as ongoing road construction.

In winter, the Ash Mountain Entrance is probably the better choice. This southern section of Generals Highway is plowed sooner and more thoroughly than the stretch from Grant Grove to Lodgepole. To check road conditions in advance, call 559/565-3341 or Caltrans Highway (800/427-7623).

LOOKOUT POINT ENTRANCE
Located on Mineral King Road, east of the Ash Mountain Entrance, the Lookout Point Entrance is only used by travelers headed for the Mineral King area of Sequoia National Park. It is much less trafficked than the other two entrances; the entrance fee ($20) can be paid at a self-serve kiosk. Mineral King Road is narrow, winding, and closed in winter (Nov. 1–May) and cannot be used by RVs or trailers.

Air
The nearest airport is the **Visalia Municipal Airport** (VIS, 9501 Airport Dr., Visalia, 559/713-4201, www.flyvisalia.com), with daily flights from Los Angeles and Las Vegas on Great Lakes Airlines. Driving distance from the airport to the park's Ash Mountain Entrance is about 36 miles.

The **Fresno-Yosemite International Airport** (FAT, 5175 E. Clinton Way, Fresno, 800/244-2359, www.fresno.gov) is served by a number of airlines; it is about 50 miles west of the Big Stump Entrance to Kings Canyon National Park. Larger airports include **Sacramento International Airport** (SMF, 6900 Airport Blvd., Sacramento, 916/929-5411, www.sacramento.aero) or **San Francisco International Airport** (SFO, Hwy. 101, San Francisco, 650/821-8211 or 800/435-9736, www.flysfo.com).

GETTING AROUND
Car
Generals Highway is the main road running north–south through the two parks; it connects Highway 180 (Kings Canyon National Park) in the north to Highway 198 (Sequoia National Park) in the south. It might be called it a "highway," but the Generals Highway is a steep, narrow, twisting mountain road that can be treacherous in bad weather or when driven too fast. Road construction may also create delays. The maximum allowed RV length on Generals Highway is 22 feet and trailers are not permitted. Neither RVs nor trailers are permitted on Mineral King Road or Moro Rock–Crescent Meadow Road.

Parking lots are available at most major attractions, but these can fill up quickly in summer; some parking is permitted along the roadside. In summer, various shuttles provide convenient access to some of the park's biggest sights.

Shuttles
Sequoia National Park provides free shuttle service (559/565-3341, www.nps.gov/seki, 9 A.M.–6 P.M.) within the park Memorial Day–September. The **Giant Forest Route** (30 min.) connects the Giant Forest Museum to the Lodgepole Visitors Center, stopping at the General Sherman Tree. The **Moro Rock-Crescent Meadow Route** (15 min.) connects the Giant Forest Museum to Moro Rock (outbound only) and Crescent Meadow. The **Lodgepole-Wuksachi-Dorst Route** (hourly) takes visitors from Lodgepole to the Dorst Creek Campground, stopping at Wuksachi Lodge.

The **Giant Forest-Visalia Route** is operated by Sequoia Shuttle (877/287-4453, www.sequoiashuttle.com, $15 round-trip, Memorial–Labor Day). Buses leave Visalia hourly (6–10 A.M., two hours on-way) for the Giant Forest Museum, returning in the afternoon (2:30–6:30 P.M.). And since you don't have to pay the $20 entry fee when you come in by bus, this is a real bargain. Call for reservations in advance.

Winter Access

Several of the park's roads close in winter. **Mineral King Road, Crystal Cave Road,** and **Panoramic Point** close from the beginning of November to the end of May each year. Generals Highway remains open, at least officially, however heavy snows make it difficult to predict how quickly even the major roads will be plowed. The top priorities for plowing are: Highway 198 from the Ash Mountain Entrance to Lodgepole; and Highway 180 from the Big Stump Entrance through Grant Grove Village and as far north as the Princess Campground junction. After that, the remainder of Generals Highway, through the middle of the parks, will be cleared if possible. If you have reservations in winter at Montecito Lake Resort (63410 Generals Hwy., 559/565-3388 or 800/227-9900, www.mslodge.com, year-round), don't worry. If the road conditions are difficult, call the resort when you get to Grant Grove and they will send an escort to help you get there safely. Check www.nps.gov/seki or call 559/565-3341 for current road conditions.

CENTRAL COAST

Here begins the California coast that movies and literature have made legendary. Soaring cliffs drop straight into the sea, making the white-sand beaches that occasionally appear beneath and beyond them all the more inviting. From north to south, the Pacific Ocean changes from slate gray to a gentler blue. Scents of salt and kelp waft up the beaches, and the endless crash of the breakers against the shore is a constant lullaby in the coastal towns.

The seacoast city of Santa Cruz, with its ultra-liberal culture, redwood-clad university, and general sense of funky fun, prides itself on keeping things weird. The beach and boardwalk are prime attractions for surfing and enjoying the sun.

Gorgeous Monterey Bay is famous for its sealife. Sea otters dive and play at the world-renowned aquarium while sea lions beach themselves for sunning pleasure on offshore rocks. The historic Cannery Row was immortalized by John Steinbeck in his novel of the same name, but the now-touristy wharf area bears only a superficial resemblance to its fishing past.

One of the most exclusive enclaves of the wealthy in California, nearby Carmel has charming ocean views, well-traveled beaches and parks, and unbelievably expensive real estate; Clint Eastwood was once mayor. The legendary Pebble Beach golf course and resort is just north of downtown.

CENTRAL COAST

HIGHLIGHTS

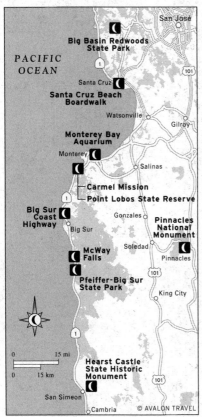

PACIFIC OCEAN

San José

Big Basin Redwoods State Park

Santa Cruz

Santa Cruz Beach Boardwalk

Watsonville

Gilroy

Monterey Bay Aquarium

Monterey

Salinas

Carmel Mission
Point Lobos State Reserve

Big Sur Coast Highway

Big Sur

Gonzales

Pinnacles National Monument

McWay Falls

Soledad

Pinnacles

Pfeiffer-Big Sur State Park

King City

0   15 mi
0   15 km

Hearst Castle State Historic Monument

San Simeon

Cambria

© AVALON TRAVEL

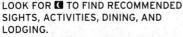

LOOK FOR ◖ TO FIND RECOMMENDED SIGHTS, ACTIVITIES, DINING, AND LODGING.

◖ **Santa Cruz Beach Boardwalk:** This seaside amusement park is the place to feel like a kid again. Watch the waves crash and hear the roller coaster rumble (page 701).

◖ **Big Basin Redwoods State Park:** Among the park's 80 miles of trails are some of the tallest redwoods in the world, along with gushing waterfalls, freshwater streams, steep mountain inclines, and backcountry camping (page 721).

◖ **Monterey Bay Aquarium:** The number-one attraction in Monterey brings the majestic world of the sea to a place where everyone can experience its raw beauty (page 722).

◖ **Pinnacles National Monument:** Replete with massive rock formations, caves, and water displays, Pinnacles offers hiking, rock climbing, picnicking, and camping (page 753).

◖ **Carmel Mission:** Father Junípero Serra's crown jewel is still a functioning church as well as a school and museum (page 755).

◖ **Point Lobos State Natural Reserve:** The reserve showcases the natural treasures of Monterey Bay, including an ancient cypress grove, China Cove, and a spellbinding coastline (page 757).

◖ **Big Sur Coast Highway:** Twisting Highway 1 is iconic, with jutting cliffs, crashing surf, and glorious views (page 766).

◖ **McWay Falls:** A river falls off a sheer cliff onto an ocean beach hundreds of feet below. A hiking trail winds high above the cove for dramatic views of the waterfall (page 770).

◖ **Pfeiffer Big Sur State Park:** The largest and most developed park in Big Sur offers Big Sur Lodge, a restaurant and café, a shop, an amphitheater, plenty of hiking-only trails, and lovely redwood-shaded campsites (page 773).

◖ **Hearst Castle State Historic Monument:** Newspaper mogul William Randolph Hearst built this dazzling mansion high above the sea (page 782).

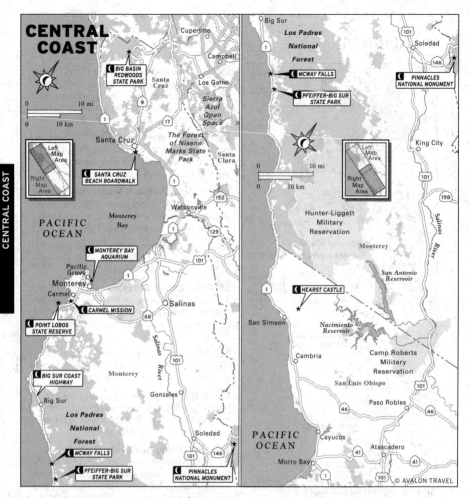

South of Carmel, Highway 1 begins its scenic tour down the Big Sur coast, perhaps the single most beautiful part of California. The rugged cliffs and protected forests have little development to mar their natural charms. Waterfalls and redwoods beckon hikers and campers while cliff-side resorts pamper guests.

Seaside Cambria makes a good base from which to visit much of the Central Coast, including San Simeon, home to the grand Hearst Castle, an homage to excess. The coast becomes less rugged here though no less beautiful.

PLANNING YOUR TIME

The Central Coast is a favorite for romantic weekend getaways. If you're coming to visit on a weekend, make hotel or campground reservations far in advance. The coast is popular, and places book up fast. Don't try to get everywhere in only two days—this is a big region, and driving from one spot to another can take hours. For a relaxed weekend with less travel, focus your trip in Santa Cruz, Monterey, or Big Sur. If you're up for more adventure, spend a day wine-tasting in Carmel or continue down the coast to San Simeon and Cambria.

Santa Cruz

Santa Cruz is the laid-back, fun-in-the-sun, hang-loose beach town where anyone can fit in, and there's no place like it. You'll find surfers on the waves year-round, hikers in the redwood forests, tattooed hipsters downtown, and families walking the dog along West Cliff Drive.

SIGHTS

Stretching half a mile out to sea, the **Santa Cruz Municipal Wharf** (831/420-5273 or 831/420-6025, www.santacruzwharf.com, fee for parking), was built in 1914 as a haven for ocean travelers. Today, you can walk its length and find caramel apples and fish markets, boat rentals and souvenir shops, and numerous restaurants. The Lifeguard Headquarters (831/420-6015) is located on the wharf, public restrooms are at the end of the wharf and at the entrance (on the right), and a public boat landing is on the boardwalk side of the wharf.

◖ Santa Cruz Beach Boardwalk

The Santa Cruz Beach Boardwalk (400 Beach St., 831/423-5590, www.beachboardwalk.com, daily 11 A.M.–close, parking $10) has an appeal that beckons young children, cool teens, and adults of all ages. The park contains 35 rides, including the Double Shot, a tower ride that launches thrill-seekers 125 feet into the air. The Hurricane creates 4.5 g's and banking angles of 80 degrees. Get caught up in the

CENTRAL COAST

© KRISTIN LEAL

Santa Cruz Beach Boardwalk

SANTA CRUZ AND VICINITY

© AVALON TRAVEL

swirling Tsunami—the ride runs both forward and reverse. The Haunted Castle takes the brave deep into the dungeons below the boardwalk. The ride has expanded its boundaries, taking horror to a new low by adding 10,000 square feet of basement space to the original site. Twelve rides in the park are dedicated to young children, including the Cave Train, a glow-in-the-dark experience. Avid gamers can choose between the lure of prizes from the traditional midway games and the large arcade. The traditional carousel from 1911 actually has a brass ring that you can try to grab.

Admission to the amusement park is free, but you must buy per-ride tickets or an unlimited-ride wristband.

Santa Cruz Surfing Museum

The Santa Cruz Surfing Museum (701 W. Cliff Dr., 831/420-6289, www.santacruzsurfingmuseum.org, noon–4 P.M. Thurs.–Mon. early Sept.–June, 10 A.M.–5 P.M. Wed.–Mon. July–early Sept., free) is located in the Mark Abbott Memorial Lighthouse. The museum is the first of its kind; it opened in the summer of 1986 to celebrate 100 years of surfing history with a focus on local heroes. Read stories of shark attacks and surf clubs, check out old-school surfboards, boards with shark bites, and plenty of nostalgia-inducing photos.

The lighthouse is located just above the boardwalk, nestled among exquisite Victorian homes and quaint beach bungalows. The size

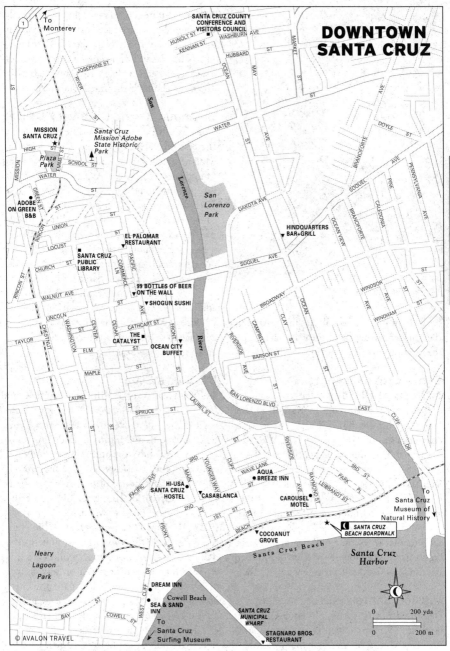

DOWNTOWN SANTA CRUZ

CENTRAL COAST

To Monterey

SANTA CRUZ COUNTY
CONFERENCE AND
VISITORS COUNCIL

HUNOLT ST
WASHBURN AVE
KENNAN ST
HUBBARD
OCEAN AVE
MAY
MARKET
AVE

DOYLE ST

BRANCHFORTE
SOQUEL
PINE ST
PENNSYLVANIA AVE
CALEDONIA ST

JOSEPHINE ST

RIVER ST

San Lorenzo

WATER ST

MISSION SANTA CRUZ ★

Santa Cruz Mission Adobe State Historic Park

HIGH
MISSION
EMMETT ST
SCHOOL ST
Plaza Park
WATER ST

San Lorenzo Park

DAKOTA AVE

BRANCHFORTE
OCEANVIEW
WINDSOR AVE
WINDHAM ST

ADOBE ON GREEN B&B

GREEN ST
RINCON ST
UNION ST
LOCUST

EL PALOMAR RESTAURANT

HINDQUARTERS BAR+GRILL

SANTA CRUZ PUBLIC LIBRARY

CHURCH ST

SOQUEL AVE

CHESTNUT ST
WASHINGTON
CENTER ST
CEDAR ST
ELM ST

WALNUT AVE

99 BOTTLES OF BEER ON THE WALL

PACIFIC AVE
COMMERCE LN

▼ SHOGUN SUSHI

BROADWAY
RIVERSIDE AVE
CAMPBELL ST
CLAY ST
OCEAN ST
BARSON ST

LINCOLN
TAYLOR

CATHCART ST
THE CATALYST
FRONT ST

OCEAN CITY BUFFET

River

MAPLE ST

LAUREL

SPRUCE ST

LAUREL ST

SAN LORENZO BLVD

EAST CLIFF DR

3RD ST
PARK ST

HI-USA SANTA CRUZ HOSTEL

WAVE LANE
AQUA BREEZE INN
RIVERSIDE
RAYMOND ST
LEIBRANDT ST

To Santa Cruz Museum of Natural History

PACIFIC AVE
MAIN ST
YOUNGER WAY
CLIFF ST
▼ CASABLANCA
2ND ST
1ST ST

CAROUSEL MOTEL

FRONT ST
BEACH ST

▼ COCOANUT GROVE

★ SANTA CRUZ BEACH BOARDWALK

Neary Lagoon Park

Santa Cruz Beach

Santa Cruz Harbor

DREAM INN
Cowell Beach
● SEA & SAND INN

CLIFF DR
WEST
BAY ST
COWELL ST

SANTA CRUZ MUNICIPAL WHARF

To Santa Cruz Surfing Museum

STAGNARO BROS. RESTAURANT

0   200 yds
0   200 m

© AVALON TRAVEL

Santa Cruz Surfing Museum

of the lighthouse is not all that impressive, but the brick construction against the backdrop of the ocean is postcard-worthy.

Santa Cruz Museum of Natural History

The Santa Cruz Museum of Natural History (1305 E. Cliff Dr., 831/420-6115, www.santacruzmuseums.org, 10 A.M.–5 P.M. Wed.–Fri. Memorial Day–Labor Day, 10 A.M.–5 P.M. Tues.–Sun. Labor Day–Memorial Day, adults $4, children and seniors $2) was the first public museum in the city, dating to 1904. Permanent and rotating exhibits include those on the Native American Ohlone people, geology of the Santa Cruz region, wildlife and habitats of the Santa Cruz region, marine life of Monterey Bay, and the Garden Learning Center.

Mission Santa Cruz

Dedicated in 1791, Mission Santa Cruz (126 High St., 831/426-5686, 10 A.M.–4 P.M. Tues.–Sat., 10 A.M.–2 P.M. Sun., donation) was one of the last California missions built; unfortunately, the original mission structures were destroyed in an earthquake. Today, an attractive white building with a classic red-tiled roof welcomes parishioners to the active Holy Cross church; built in 1889, the church is the fourth one on the site.

Seymour Marine Discovery Center

The large attractive gray building complex at the end of Delaware Avenue is the Seymour Marine Discovery Center at Long Marine Laboratory (Delaware Ave., 831/459-3800, http://seymourcenter.ucsc.edu, 10 A.M.–5 P.M. Tues.–Sat., noon–5 P.M. Sun., adults $6, children $3). Set on the edge of a cliff overlooking the ocean, the Seymour Marine Discovery Center is the public part of the lab; research is done primarily by students and faculty of the University of California, Santa Cruz. Kids particularly love the touch tanks, while curious adults enjoy the seasonal tank that contains the wildlife of Monterey Bay. Sign up an hour in advance to take a tour of the lab (1 P.M., 2 P.M., and 3 P.M. Tues.–Sun.).

UC Santa Cruz

The University of California, Santa Cruz (UCSC, Bay St., 831/459-0111, www.ucsc.edu) is set in the hills above downtown Santa Cruz. The classrooms and dorms sit under groves of coastal redwood trees and among tangles of ferns and vines. Visitors can tour the campus (831/459-4118, groups of 6 or more, reservations required), or simply enjoy wandering around the campus and woods.

The **UC Santa Cruz Arboretum** (1156 High St., 831/427-2998, www.arboretum.ucsc.edu, daily 9 A.M.–5 P.M., adults $5, children $2) is a research and teaching facility where visitors are welcome to explore the lush gardens. There are more than 300 plant varieties, including a large collection of rare and threatened species. Learn about plant diversity and conservation that you can apply in your own garden.

© KRISTIN LEAL

The current Mission Santa Cruz was built in 1889.

Call ahead to schedule a docent-led tour ($8 pp) for a behind-the-curtain experience; the additional cost is worth it as the guides are extremely knowledgeable.

Santa Cruz Mystery Spot

Since the early 1930s, visitors have been making their way to the Santa Cruz Mystery Spot (465 Mystery Spot Rd., 831/423-8897, www.mysteryspot.com, daily 9 A.M.–7 P.M. June–Aug., 10 A.M.–4 P.M. Mon.–Fri., 10 A.M.–5 P.M. Sat.–Sun. Sept.–May, $6, parking $5), where gravity seems to be off-kilter. Marvel as you walk up walls, balls roll uphill, brooms stand on end, and people seem to shrink. The cabin tends to be the highlight of the 45-minute tour. There are many theories about what makes the mystery spot so mysterious—including the idea of extraterrestrial intervention.

SPORTS AND RECREATION
Beaches

At the south end of Santa Cruz, near the harbor,

beachgoers flock to **Seabright Beach** (E. Cliff Dr. and Seabright Ave., 831/685-6500, www.santacruzstateparks.org, daily 6 A.M.–10 P.M., free) during summer. This miles-long stretch of sand, protected by the cliffs from heavy wind, is a favorite retreat for sunbathers and loungers. While there's little in the way of facilities, there's lots of soft sand, plenty of room to play football or volleyball, and, of course, easy access to the chilly Pacific Ocean. There's no surfing—Seabright has a shore break that delights skimboarders but makes wave-riding impossible.

With more than a mile of soft sand and a shipwreck at the end of the pier, **Seacliff State Beach** (west end of State Park Dr., 831/685-6442, www.parks.ca.gov, daily 8 A.M.–sunset, $10) is perfect for a stroll, sunbathing, catching some waves, casting a line from the pier or the shore for striped bass, and watching the sunset. There is a snack shack and a visitors center as well as RV camping right next to the beach.

MAIN BEACH

The most famous stretch of beach in the area is the Santa Cruz Main Beach (Beach St., 831/420-6015, www.santacruzparksandrec.com, free). Located on the back side of the Santa Cruz Beach Boardwalk, it graces countless postcards. Its reach is wide, from the wharf to the south end of the boardwalk. Volleyball courts are available year-round with plenty of action in the summer and on weekends, kids love to swim in the surf, the waves are just right for body boarding, and the beach beckons sun worshippers.

The section of beach that reaches north from the wharf is known as **Cowell Beach** (101 Beach St.). This section tends to be less crowded and is a good spot for first-time surfers. You can also see lifeguards doing their training on this beach, as their headquarters are located on the wharf. A small parking lot is located next to the Dream Inn. The free outdoor showers make it easy to hop in and out of the sea.

CENTRAL COAST

© LE DO/123RF.COM

Natural Bridges State Park

NATURAL BRIDGES STATE PARK

At the tip of the west side of Santa Cruz, Natural Bridges State Park (W. Cliff Dr., 831/423-4609, www.parks.ca.gov, daily 8 A.M.–sunset, $10) offers nearly every kind of beach recreation possible. The sand isn't wide, but it's deep and is crossed by a creek running into the sea. An inconsistent break makes surfing at Natural Bridges fun on occasion, while the near-constant winds bring out windsurfers nearly every weekend. Hardy sun-worshippers brave the breezes, bringing beach blankets, umbrellas, and sunscreen on rare sunny days (usually late spring and fall).

Back from the beach, a wooded picnic area has tables and grills. Even farther back, the visitors center can provide great stories about the various natural wonders of this surprisingly diverse state park. Rangers offer guided tours of the tide pools at the west side of the beach, accessed by a scrambling short 0.5-mile hike on the rocks. These odd little holes full of sealife aren't like most tide pools; many are nearly perfect round depressions in the sandstone cliffs worn away by harder stones in the tide. Don't touch the residents of these pools, as human hands can damage the delicate creatures.

Every year October–February, **monarch butterflies** travel to Natural Bridges State Beach, resting among the trees with their legs intertwined to resemble leaves. You can hike behind the scenes with a docent naturalist and discover the wonders of the Monarch Grove. There are hour-long guided tours (11 A.M. and 2 P.M. Sat. Oct.–Jan.) that depart from the visitors center, or take a self-guided tour on the boardwalk that leads directly into the grove.

Surfing

The cold waters of Santa Cruz demand full wetsuits year-round, and the shoreline is rough and rocky, unlike the flat sandy beaches of Southern California. But that doesn't deter the hordes of locals who ply the waves every chance they get.

Surfing culture pervades the town, symbolized by the cliff-top *To Honor Surfing* sculpture (W. Cliff Dr. and Pelton Ave.). **Cowell Beach** (350 W. Cliff Dr.) on the west side is all about surfing. The coastline geography and underwater features create a reliable small break that lures new surfers by the dozens. The waves are low and long, making for fun long-board rides and helpful for beginners just getting their balance. Because Cowell's break is an acknowledged newbie spot, the often sizable crowd tends to be polite to newcomers.

The most famous break in Santa Cruz can also be the most hostile to newcomers. **Steamers Lane** (W. Cliff Dr. between Cowell Beach and the lighthouse) has both a fiercely protective crew of locals and a dangerous break that actually kills someone every other year or so. But if you're into adrenaline and there's a swell coming in, you'll be hard-pressed to find a more exciting break.

For surf schools in Santa Cruz, check out **Santa Cruz Surf School** (131 Center St., 831/345-8875, www.santacruzsurfschool.com) or **Richard Schmidt School of Surfing** (849 Almar Ave., 831/423-0928, www.richardschmidt.com) for lessons. **O'Neill at the Boardwalk** (400 Beach St., 831/459-9230, www.oneil.com, 10 A.M.–5 P.M. Mon.–Fri., 10 A.M.–8 P.M. Sat.–Sun.), a prefab chain, specializes in surfboards, wetsuits, skateboards, accessories, and brand-name clothing. For 30 years, Pearson Arrow has been shaping custom high-quality surfboards at **Arrow Surf & Sport** (2322 Mission St., 831/423-8286, www.arrowsurfshop.com, 9 A.M.–7 P.M. Mon.–Sat., 9 A.M.–6 P.M. Sun.), where the emphasis is on surfboards, along with accessories and apparel. From the surf to the snow, **Pacific Wave Surf Shop** (1502 Pacific Ave., 831/458-9283, www.pacwave.com, 10 A.M.–8 P.M. Sun.–Thurs., 10 A.M.–9 P.M. Fri.–Sat.) carries a little of everything—surf, skate, and snowboard apparel plus accessories as well as a limited selection of surfboards and skateboards.

Windsurfing

Beginning windsurfers vie with long-boarders for space at **Cowell's** break (stairs at W. Cliff Dr. and Cowell Beach), next to the City Wharf. For a bigger breeze, head up West Cliff Drive to **Natural Bridges State Park** (W. Cliff Dr., www.parks.ca.gov), the easiest spot to set up. There are restroom facilities and ample parking. If you want to try windsurfing for the first time, contact **Club Ed** (831/464-0177, www.club-ed.com) to set up a lesson. They operate in the gentle breezes and small swells at Cowell's break and make it easy for first-timers to gain confidence.

Kayaking

Santa Cruz has secluded coves to discover, a wide harbor, open water near the wharf, and the possibility to fish. Bring your own gear and launch at numerous locations or pick up a rental boat. The local rental companies also offer self-guided and guided tours. Tours are especially helpful for beginners and first-timers in the area.

A great beginner spot is **Santa Cruz Main Beach** (Beach St., 831/420-6015, www.santacruzparksandrec.com, free) and **Cowell Beach** (101 Beach St.). Parking is close to the water, with easy drop-off points near Cowell's break and on the north side of the Boardwalk. The breakers tend to be smaller on Santa Cruz Main Beach and are easier to navigate through if you're looking for a relaxing paddle along the shore. If you are in the mood for a heart-pumping thrill ride, head to Cowell Beach and ride the waves. The showers in the parking lot are particularly appreciated after a day in the sea.

The easiest launch is at **Santa Cruz Harbor** (Santa Cruz Port District, 135 5th Ave., 831/475-6161, www.santacruzharbor.org). The launch ramps make unloading and putting in easy, and you can drive right to the water's edge. The harbor is fun to explore, as you can get a close look at the boats in port and the noisy sea lions. You can also easily head out past the breakwaters to the open sea for a more adventurous paddle.

You can pick up a rental or take a lesson at **Venture Quest Kayaking** (2 Municipal Wharf, 831/425-8445, www.kayaksantacruz. com, 10 A.M.–7 P.M. Mon.–Fri., 9 A.M.–7 P.M. Sat.–Sun., single sit-on-top kayak 3 hours $30). Access to the bay from the Santa Cruz Municipal Wharf is ideal; you don't have to break the surf, and wildlife encounters start right away with the large sea lions napping under the pier.

Kayak Connections (413 Lake Ave., Suite 3, 831/479-1121, www.kayakconnection.com, 10 A.M.–5 P.M. Mon.–Fri., 9 A.M.–5 P.M. Sat.–Sun., 4 hours single $35, double $50) is located on the harbor with rentals, repairs, and gear. They also have stand-up paddleboards, body boards, wetsuits, and other gear. Lessons are available for all skill levels on kayaks, surf kayaks, and stand-up paddleboards.

For lessons and multiple-day expeditions, try **Eskape Sea Kayaking** (740 30th Ave., Suite 117, 831/476-5385, www.eskapekayak.com). Since 1992 Eskape has paddled around Santa Cruz and knows the waters well. Eskape offers advanced and custom clinics, beginner classes, and American Canoe Association certification workshops, great for kayakers of any skill level. Classes are small, and kayaks are provided.

Fishing

Stagnaro Fishing Trips (32 Municipal Wharf, 831/427-2334, www.stagnaros.com) is a leader in charter fishing trips, with year-round excursions for commercial and recreational fishing. Seasonal catches include salmon, sand dabs, rock cod, and albacore. Rock cod trips are the most fun for children, as they are easy to hook, and everyone usually catches their limit. Stagnaro also runs whale-watching tours (daily year-round) to look for blue, humpback, and gray whales, a variety of dolphin species, and many other sea mammals and birds.

A variety of trips can be booked through **Monterey Bay Charters** (333 Lake Ave., 831/818-8808, www.montereybaycharters.

com). Depending on the season, salmon, halibut, tuna, lingcod, sea bass, and rock cod can be caught. Other options include marine-sanctuary sightseeing tours, on-the-water picnics, marine and wildlife ecotours, team building, and private "Day on the Bay" parties.

Captain Brad, owner and operator of **Ultimate Fish Charters** (departs Santa Cruz Harbor at 135 5th Ave., 831/566-9407, www.ultimatefishcharters.com), has been fishing the waters of Monterey Bay all his life and knows where the fish are biting. His trips go into Monterey Bay, Morro Bay, and Half Moon Bay. Spring trips fish near the shore for salmon, rock cod, and halibut; in summer, trips look for albacore tuna.

Sailing

Sailing on the bay can range from a restorative excursion to full-on racing. Either way, you can view the magnificent coastline and possibly encounter some wildlife. Set sail with **Chardonnay II Sailing Charters** (704 Soquel Ave., Suite A, 831/423-1213, www.chardonnay.com) and choose from 16 tour options for special events. Tours aboard the 70-foot *Chardonnay II* sailing yacht highlight the protected wildlife of Monterey Bay.

Lighthall Yacht Charters (934 Bay St., 831/429-1970, www.lighthallcharters.com) has two-hour tours for as little as $40. Shared tours and private charters operate on 34–47-foot sailing yachts. Lighthall has taken more than one million passengers out on the local seas. **O'Neill Yacht Charters** (2222 E. Cliff Dr., 831/457-1561, www.oneillyachtcharters.com, spring–summer, 1-hour sail $20 pp, 1.5-hour sail $30 pp) sails along the Santa Cruz shoreline while taking in the boardwalk, the wharf, Walton Lighthouse, local surfers, playful sea otters, and napping seals.

Learn to sail or take a private cruise with **Pacific Yachting Sailing** (790 Mariner Park Way, Suite 1, 831/423-7245 or 800/374-2626, www.pacificsail.com). Cruises (2 hours from

$230) accommodate up to six passengers and can be a leisurely sail, a whale-watching adventure, or a romantic sunset getaway.

Whale Watching

Stagnaro Fishing Trips, also known as **Santa Cruz Whale Watching** (32 Municipal Wharf and 3640 Capitola Rd., 831/427-2334 or 831/427-0230, www.stagnaros.com or www.santacruzwhale-watching.com, adults $45, children $31) runs 3–4 hour whale-watching trips in the bay, where you will most likely encounter several whales, dolphins, seals, sea otters, and a variety of marine birds. They also offer an inner-bay calm-water tour (1 hour, adults $20, children $13), a shorter ride along the shore that showcases some of Santa Cruz's sights from a different perspective. You can also see a plethora of marine animals, including seabirds, sea otters, harbor seals, sea lions, and possibly a dolphin or two.

ENTERTAINMENT AND EVENTS
Bars and Clubs

Down on Pacific Avenue, called "the Mall," walk upstairs to **Rosie McCann's** (1220 Pacific Ave., 831/426-9930, www.rosiemccanns.com) for a pint and a bite. This dark-paneled Irish-style saloon serves Guinness, black and tan, snakebites, and several tasty draft beers. Food includes sausages, mashed potatoes, and other hearty pub fare. A largely local crowd hangs out here, and you'll find the bar crowded and noisy, but the vibe is friendly and entertaining.

There is no better place in Santa Cruz for cold beer than **99 Bottles of Beer on the Wall** (110 Walnut Ave., 831/459-9999, daily 11 A.M.–midnight). Like the sign says, they serve 99 different varieties of beer and a few wine choices. The food isn't bad and pairs nicely with the brews. **Callahan's** (507 Water St., 831/427-3119, www.dhcallahans.com, daily 11 A.M.–2 A.M.) is a classic bar experience with 13 cold beers on tap, pool tables, and darts. Five high-definition TV screens play sports, including NFL Ticket and MLB Package offerings.

For drink specials and a dance floor grooving to DJ beats, look no farther than **Blue Lagoon** (923 Pacific Ave., 831/423-7117, www.thebluelagoon.com, daily 4 P.M.–2 A.M.). Thursday is stand-up comedy night with dancing to '80s music afterward. Friday music is a house and Top 40 mix.

Live Music

The Catalyst (1011 Pacific Ave., 831/423-1338, advance tickets 866/384-3060, www.catalyst-club.com, $12–35), downtown on the Mall, is *the* Santa Cruz live-rock venue for big-name acts. Catalyst also hosts DJ dance nights, teen nights, and other fun events (some shows are age 21 and over only). The main concert hall is a standing-room-only space, while the balconies offer seating. The vibe tends to be low-key; some of the more retro acts draw an older crowd, while the techno-DJ dance parties cater to university students.

The **Crow's Nest** (2218 E. Cliff Dr., 831/476-4560, www.crowsnest-santacruz.com) has a full bar and restaurant and functions as a venue for all kinds of live music (Wed.–Sat.). You might see a contemporary reggae-rock group one night and a Latin dance band the next. Most shows are free, but sometimes there's a cover. The Crow's Nest also has weekly stand-up performances (9 P.M. Sun.). **Moe's Alley** (1535 Commercial Way, 831/479-1854, www.moesalley.com, 4 P.M.–2 A.M. Tues.–Sun.) hosts blues, salsa, ska, and hip-hop. The dance floor is spacious, and the outdoor patio has heaters and a smoking area.

Theater

Santa Cruz is home to several community theater groups and an outdoor summer Shakespeare festival that draws theatergoers from around the Bay Area. The **Santa Cruz Actors' Theatre** (1001 Center St., 831/425-7529, www.sccat.org) is Santa Cruz's permanent local theater company, with a subscription season, theater arts workshops, playwriting contests for kids and adults, and improv shows.

CENTRAL COAST

UCSC puts on the annual summer **Shakespeare Santa Cruz** (831/459-2121, http://shakespearesantacruz.org, adults $15–30, under age 18 $14), a six-week festival in July–August. Both venues are on the UCSC campus: the indoor Theatre Arts Mainstage (1156 High St.) and the Festival Glen (Meyer Dr.), in a redwood forest. Each year the festival puts on at least two of Shakespeare's plays. At the outdoor Glen, audience members are encouraged to bring a picnic; this can make for a romantic date or a fun outing for the whole family.

Festivals and Events

For more than 25 years, the **Santa Cruz Kayak and Surf Festival** (Steamers Lane and Cowell Beach, just north of the Municipal Wharf, mid-Mar.) has been celebrated by locals and visitors. Watch stand-up paddleboard surfing, kayak surfing, and traditional surfing.

The West Coast's oldest and longest-running surfing competition is the **Santa Cruz Longboard Club Invitational** (Steamers Lane at Lighthouse Point, 831/324-2278, www. santa-cruz-longboard-union.com, late May). The event features amateur and professional surfers in 11 age groups.

Kick off the summer with the **Surf City Classic: Woodies on the Wharf** (Municipal Wharf, 831/420-5273, www.santacruzwharf.com, late June). The 20-year-old annual family-friendly event is all about classic cars and the surf spirit.

For car lovers, **Hot Rods at the Beach** (River parking lot, end of Beach St., 831/423-3720, www.hotrodsatthebeach.com, Oct.) brings over 500 classic cars and street hot rods in a display of shiny eye candy and roaring engines. There is food, local vendors, raffles, music, and scores of displays.

SHOPPING

Pacific Street, the town's main drag, is filled with an eclectic mix of shops that range from thrift stores to the Gap. The **Pacific Garden Mall** (Pacific Ave., 831/429-8433, www.downtownsantacruz.com) stretches along Pacific Avenue and its side streets. At the north end, shoppers peruse antiques, boutique clothing, and kitchenware. Near the middle of the Mall are independent places to eat, drink coffee, and have cocktails. The Mall has just a few chain stores; most stores are independent and local. A proudly independent local bookseller since 1966, **Bookshop Santa Cruz** (1520 Pacific Ave., 831/423-0900, www.bookshopsantacruz.com, 9 A.M.–10 P.M. Sun.–Thurs., 9 A.M.–11 P.M. Fri.–Sat.) sells new and used books in 20,000 square feet of space. There is an extensive magazine section, a special children's section, and an ongoing authors series.

On the Santa Cruz Beach Boardwalk is **O'Neill at the Boardwalk** (400 Beach St., 831/459-9230, www.oneill.com, 10 A.M.–5 P.M. Mon.–Fri., 10 A.M.–8 P.M. Sat.–Sun.), one of the chain's smaller stores, carrying a limited selection of surfboards, wetsuits, skateboards, and accessories.

ACCOMMODATIONS
Under $100

The **Santa Cruz Youth Hostel Carmelita Cottages** (321 Main St., 831/423-8304, www. hi-santacruz.org, dorm $25, private rooms $60) is clean, cheap, friendly, and close to the beach. Expect hostel-style amenities, a nice garden out back, free linens, laundry facilities, and a free Internet kiosk. You can store your surfboard or bike for free, parking is $1 per day, and a kitchen is open for guest use. Just across from the Boardwalk is the **Aqua Breeze Inn** (204 2nd St., 831/426-7878, www.santacruzaquabreezeinn.com, $50–69), with 50 clean and well-appointed guest rooms with mini fridges, microwaves, coffeemakers, sundecks, Internet access, and HBO on TV. There is an outdoor heated pool, and pets are welcome.

$100-150

The Spanish-style **Mission Inn** (2250 Mission

St., 831/425-5455 or 800/895-5455, www.mis-sion-inn.com, $135–150) is near Highways 1 and 9 for easy access to the Santa Cruz mountains; the beach is five minutes' drive. The inn has 53 nonsmoking guest rooms modestly equipped with coffeemakers, Wi-Fi, cable TV, and whirlpool tubs. Continental breakfast is included.

$150-250

Just steps away from the ticket booth of the Santa Cruz Beach Boardwalk is the **C Carousel Motel** (110 Riverside Ave., 831/425-7090 or 800/214-7400, www.santacruzmotels.com, $149–219), a basic motel with Internet access, continental breakfast, cable TV, and private balconies.

Sea & Sand Inn (201 W. Cliff Dr., 831/427-3400, www.santacruzmotels.com, $199–289) has an unbeatable location on the ocean side of West Cliff Drive at Bay Street in a residential neighborhood. Accommodations are basic, but guest rooms overlook the ocean. Amenities include private baths and Internet access. The **Inn at Pasatiempo** (555 Hwy. 17, 831/423-5000, www.innatpasatiempo.com, $170), next door to the Pasatiempo Golf Club, makes it easy to get in a round of golf. Guest rooms are decorated in country style with fireplaces and sitting areas. There is an outdoor pool and a decent restaurant on-site.

The four-room **Adobe on Green Street** (103 Green St., 831/469-9866, www.adobeongreen.com, $189–219) offers lovely bed-and-breakfast accommodations close to the heart of downtown Santa Cruz and within walking distance of the Pacific Garden Mall. Each guest room has a queen bed, a private bath (most with tubs), a small TV with a DVD player, and lots of other amenities. An expanded continental spread is set out in the dining room each morning (8–11 A.M.). In keeping with the Santa Cruz environmentalist ethos, the B&B runs on solar power.

High on a bluff with breathtaking views is the **Chaminade Resort and Spa** (1 Chaminade

© CHAMINADE RESORT & SPA

Chaminade Resort and Spa

Lane, 831/475-5600 or 800/283-6569, www.chaminade.com, $206–240), with a fitness center, tennis courts, a pool, a hot tub, and an all-inclusive spa. Guest rooms are open and elegant, with modern decor and outdoor patios.

Over $250

The **C Santa Cruz Dream Inn** (175 W. Cliff Dr., 831/426-4330 or 831/460-5007, www.dreaminnsantacruz.com, $399–419) is right on the beach, just steps from the wharf and the boardwalk. It has an outdoor pool and a hot tub, and guest rooms have private balconies and ocean views.

CAMPING

The Santa Cruz region has rich camping possibilities; in summer, make camping reservations far in advance. For any of the state parks, you can check availability and reserve sites through **Reserve America** (800/444-7275, www.reserveamerica.com).

CENTRAL COAST

Beachside RV and trailer camping can be found at **Seacliff State Beach** (west end of State Park Dr., 831/685-6442, www.parks.ca.gov, $55). Sites abut the beach, and many have water and electrical hookups. The sandy beaches are great for swimming and extend more than one mile north to the wooded bluffs of New Brighton State Beach. There is a snack shack along with a visitors center, and the park is known for its long fishing pier and a shipwreck at the end of the pier.

Surf in, surf out accommodations can be found at **Manresa State Beach** (400 San Andreas Rd., 831/761-1795, www.parks.ca.gov, May 16–Oct. 31, $35). There are 64 walk-in tent campsites, hot showers (bring quarters), flush toilets, great surf, and a wide sandy beach.

A little-known RV park is the **Santa Cruz Harbor RV Park** (Santa Cruz North Harbor, 7th Ave. and Brommer St., 831/475-3279, www.santacruzharbor.org, $40), with 12 full-hookup sites and an on-site dump station. Views of the north harbor are beautiful, and you are close to restaurants and kayak rentals. Reservations are advised as space is limited.

Just 0.5 mile from the beach, **Santa Cruz KOA Kampground** (1186 San Andres Rd., 831/722-0551 or 831/722-8051, www.santacruzkoa.com, $55–70) is a little like home, with a pool and a hot tub on-site, camping cabins, camping lodges, Airstream trailer rentals, the KOA fun train, an outdoor cinema, a climbing wall, miniature golf, banana bikes, a game room, an espresso bar, a pet play area, and planned recreation everyone can take part in.

FOOD
Bakeries and Cafés

For a casual sandwich or pastry, head for **Kelly's French Bakery** (402 Ingalls St., 831/423-9059, www.kellysfrenchbakery.com, 7 A.M.–7 P.M. Sat.–Thurs., 7 A.M.–8 P.M. Fri., $12). This popular bakery is in an old industrial warehouse space, and its dome shape, built

of corrugated metal, looks like anything but a restaurant. Full breakfasts and lunch sandwiches are served at both indoor and outdoor seating, and you can order to go.

Do as the locals do and stop in at **◖ Emily's Good Things to Eat** (1129 Mission St., 831/429-9866, www.emilysbakery.com, daily 7 A.M.–3 P.M., $8) for a cup of joe and mouthwatering savory or sweet pastries. The rear deck beckons for longer stays, especially on sunny days, and the inside seating is cozy.

For a traditional breakfast with a Mexican twist, **Walnut Avenue Café** (106 Walnut Ave., 831/457-2307, www.walnutavenuecafe.com, 7 A.M.–3 P.M. Mon.–Fri., 8 A.M.–4 P.M. Sat.–Sun., $10) does large three-egg omelets, eggs benedict with a shrimp and tomato spin, griddle classics, huevos Mexicanos, and *chilaquiles*. They also do a weekend brunch that is sure to satisfy.

For a cheap breakfast hot off the griddle, **Windmill Café** (21231 E. Cliff Dr., 831/464-4698, www.windmillcafesantacruz.com, 7 A.M.–3 P.M. Mon.–Sun., $5–8) does a little of everything, including scrambles, specialty bagels, vegetarian or carnivore breakfast burritos, and a daily waffle. The vegetables are fresh and organically grown in Windmill's own garden.

American

Carnivores, prepare for juicy bites at the **Hindquarters Bar and Grill** (303 Soquel Ave., 831/426-7770 or 831/426-7773, www.thehindquarter.com, 11:30 A.M.–2:30 P.M. and 5:30–9:30 P.M. Mon.–Sat., 10:30 A.M.–2:30 P.M. and 5:30–9:30 P.M. Sun., $20–37), serving numerous cuts of steak grilled any way you like it. Vegetarians can find menu options as well.

Asian

Local sushi lovers go to **Shogun Sushi** (1123 Pacific Ave., 831/469-4477, 5–9 P.M. Mon.–Wed., 5–10 P.M. Thurs.–Fri., 3–10 P.M. Sat., $12–25) on the Pacific Garden Mall. The *nigiri* comes in big fresh slabs, and there is an interesting collection of *maki* (rolls). Although service can be spotty, it is usually efficient. There's often a wait for a table in the evening, especially on weekends.

Ocean City Buffet (431 Front St., 831/426-8168, daily 10:30 A.M.–10 P.M., $11–30) is affordable Chinese with friendly service right downtown. There is a vast made-to-order sushi bar as well as a buffet of traditional Chinese favorites such as kung pao chicken, Singapore noodles, sweet-and-sour chicken, broccoli beef, grilled chicken legs, and pot stickers.

Seafood

The most famous place for seafood in Santa Cruz is ☾ **Stagnaro Bros. Restaurant** (Municipal Wharf, 831/423-2180, www.stagnarobros.com, daily 11 A.M.–close, $20), with over 20 different seafood dishes daily. They pride themselves on serving the freshest seafood possible. The upper deck of seating has a nautical feel, and the lower deck feels more traditional and intimate. The full menu is offered on both decks, and there are two bars.

The **Crow's Nest** (2218 E. Cliff Dr., 831/476-4560, www.crowsnest-santacruz.com, 11:30 A.M.–close Mon.–Sat., 11 A.M.–close Sun., $17–30) has a casual atmosphere upstairs with a full bar and cheap eats; downstairs is a little more formal, serving up steaks, local seafood, and specialty seafood salads.

A fantastic Mexican place with a menu of fresh seafood from local fisheries is ☾ **El Palomar Restaurant** (1336 Pacific Ave., 831/425-7575, www.elpalomarcilantros.com, daily 11 A.M.–10:30 P.M., $11–27). El Palomar has been a local favorite since the early 1980s, with homemade salsas, award-winning margaritas, and handmade corn tortillas.

Casablanca Restaurant (101 Main St. at Beach St., 831/426-9063, www.casablanca-santacruz.com, daily 5 P.M.–close, $10–27) has ocean views from every table, exquisite food, and a massive wine selection. The beachside

atmosphere is relaxed and graceful, and dishes include prime-cut steaks, tender chicken, pastas, and, of course, fine seafood. The chef is experienced and creative.

Soak in the views at **Johnny's Harborside** (493 Lake Ave., 831/479-3430, www.johnnysharborside.com, 11:30 A.M.–10 P.M. Mon.–Fri., 10 A.M.–9 P.M. Sat.–Sun., $15–30). Up to eight different choices of fresh fish are served daily, along with pastas, steaks, salads, and sandwiches.

INFORMATION AND SERVICES

While it can be fun to explore Santa Cruz on your own, those who want a bit more structure can visit the **Santa Cruz Visitors Center** (1211 Ocean Ave., 800/833-3494, www.santacruzca.org, 9 A.M.–4 P.M. Mon.–Fri., 11 A.M.–3 P.M. Sat.–Sun.) for maps, advice, and information.

Santa Cruz has its own daily newspaper, the *Santa Cruz Sentinel* (www.santacruzsentinel.com), with a dose of national wire-service news and current events, local news, and some good stuff for visitors. The *Sentinel* has a Food section, a Sunday Travel section, and plenty of up-to-date entertainment information.

Santa Cruz is, like, totally wired. You can access the Internet in a variety of cafés and hotels. Starbucks locations sell access, and the many indie cafés have sometimes-free Wi-Fi.

The **post office** (850 Front St., 831/426-0144, 9 A.M.–5 P.M. Mon.–Fri.) is near the Pacific Garden Mall. Santa Cruz has plenty of banks and ATMs, including ATMs on the arcade at the boardwalk. Bank branches are clustered downtown near the Mall. The west side is mostly residential, but you'll find a few ATMs in supermarkets and gas stations.

Despite its rep as a funky bohemian beach town, Santa Cruz's dense population dictates that it has at least one full-fledged hospital; get medical treatment and care at **Dominican Hospital** (1555 Soquel Ave., 831/426-7700, www.dominicanhospital.org).

CENTRAL COAST

GETTING THERE AND AROUND

To reach Santa Cruz from San Francisco (75 miles, 1.5 hours), take U.S. 101 south to I-280 south. I-280 meets Highway 17 south, which leads into the heart of Santa Cruz. Be forewarned that Highway 17 is a narrow road that may often close due to traffic accidents or inclement weather. Check traffic reports before heading out; the weekend beach traffic in the summer backs up fast in both directions.

For a more leisurely drive from San Francisco, opt for two-lane Highway 9, which travels through the forested Santa Cruz Mountains. The tight curves and endless switchbacks keep traffic at a reasonable speed; however, watch for bicyclists and motorcyclists on this highway. Coastal Highway 1 also leads directly into Santa Cruz from the north or south. In Santa Cruz, Highway 1 becomes Mission Street on the west side and acts as the main artery through Santa Cruz, Capitola, Soquel, Aptos, and points farther south.

Parking in Santa Cruz can be difficult. If you're driving into downtown, head straight for the parking structures one block from Pacific Avenue on either side. They're much easier to deal with than trying to find street parking. The same goes for the beach and boardwalk areas: At the boardwalk, just pay the fee to park in the big parking lot adjacent to the attractions. You'll save an hour of driving around trying to find street parking and possibly a break-in or theft in the sketchy neighborhoods that surround the boardwalk.

Transit buses are run by **Santa Cruz METRO** (831/425-8600 www.scmtd.com, adults $1.50, passes available). With 42 routes in Santa Cruz County, you can probably find a way to get nearly anywhere you'd want to go.

VICINITY OF SANTA CRUZ

Outside the city of Santa Cruz are a series of small beach towns; Aptos, Capitola, and Soquel are all south of Santa Cruz along the coast, and each has its own shopping district, restaurants, and lodgings.

Aptos

For more advanced surfers looking for smaller crowds in the water, **Manresa State Beach** (San Andreas Rd., www.parks.ca.gov), south of Santa Cruz, has a good beach break, and the waves can get big when there's a north swell. It is also known for its great negative tide. There are fire pits on the beach and open showers in the parking lot.

Just south of Santa Cruz is **The Forest of Nisene Marks** (Aptos Creek Rd. and Soquel Dr., 831/763-7063, www.parks.ca.gov, $10), 10,000 acres of semi-wilderness redwood and Douglas fir forest with 30 miles of hiking, jogging, and biking trails that climb as high as 2,600 feet. Picnic tables and barbecue pits are available, and there is primitive camping deep inside the park. Dogs are welcome on a leash. The hike-in campground is six miles from the parking lot; it's an easy day's hike in. Sites are first come, first served and must be arranged through the ranger station. Be prepared for changeable weather with limited resources; fires are not allowed, and there is no running water. Note that poison oak grows throughout the park, so beware of it encroaching on trails.

Off the beaten path but right on the beach, **Seascape Beach Resort-Monterey Bay** (1 Seascape Resort Dr., 831/688-6800 or 800/929-7727, www.seascaperesort.com, $229–774) is a luxury resort that feels like a beach house with dramatic views of the bay. Guest rooms are like private villas with all the necessities and services at your fingertips. Take advantage of in-room massages and specialty packages.

Cafe Sparrow (8042 Soquel Dr., 831/688-6238, www.cafesparrow.com, lunch 11:30 A.M.–2 P.M. Mon.–Sat., 9:30 A.M.–2 P.M. Sun., dinner daily 5:30 P.M.–close, $20) serves consistently tasty French country cuisine. The seafood is noteworthy, especially the Friday-night bouillabaisse, as are the steaks. Cafe Sparrow uses all fresh ingredients in its innovative preparations and sauces. The daily prix fixe menu is the best deal; for dessert, try the profiteroles.

Harking back to the 1950s origins of fast food, ◖ **Snow White Drive Inn** (223 State Park Dr., 831/688-4747, daily 6 A.M.–8:30 P.M. winter, daily 6 A.M.–9:30 P.M. summer, $8–12) should be a required stop on the way to Seacliff State Beach for dipped cones, corn dogs, chili fries, cheeseburgers, chicken sandwiches, fried calamari, onion rings, and chicken tenders. And, hello, they serve hot breakfasts too.

For an authentic Thai experience, try ◖ **Bangkok West** (2508 Cabrillo College Dr., 831/479-8297, lunch buffet 11 A.M.–2:30 P.M. Mon.–Fri., dinner daily 5–9:30 P.M., $10–20). The curries are mouthwatering and addicting, and the lunch buffet has a bit of everything, including great fresh spring rolls. The outdoor garden evokes Thailand; ask to sit in the little house (table 9) for a truly traditional encounter.

Capitola

For a bit of Capitola's past, visit the **Capitola Historical Museum** (410 Capitola Ave., 831/464-0322, www.capitolamuseum.org, Wed. and Fri.–Sun. noon–4 P.M., free), filled with an extensive collection of old photographs and significant artifacts from the seaside town. The museum also has a constant rotation of new exhibits that focus on the town's history and art.

A favorite sandy spot is **New Brighton State Beach** (1500 Park Ave., 831/464-6330, www.parks.ca.gov, daily 8 A.M.–sunset, $10). The park has hiking, swimming, and fishing possibilities year-round, and wildlife can be seen on the two miles of trails and the sandy beach; pelicans, playful harbor seals, sea otters, dolphins, and whales are all local to the area. A shaded campground ($35) has more than 100 sites for both tents and RVs along with ranger-led nature programs. Call in advance for reservations at this popular state park. New Brighton can get crowded on rare sunny summer days, but

it's nothing like the wall-to-wall people of popular Southern California beaches.

The Santa Cruz region boasts one seriously upscale eatery, the ◖ **Shadowbrook** (1750 Wharf Rd., 800/975-1511, www.shadowbrook-capitola.com, 5–8:45 P.M. Mon.–Fri., 4:30–9:30 P.M. Sat., 4:30–8:45 P.M. Sun., $25), perched on a cliff with an actual brook flowing through the dining room. It has perhaps the most impressive views and atmosphere of any restaurant in the region. The Shadowbrook is perfect for a romantic date, complete with roses, candlelight, and fine chocolate desserts.

Overlooking the water in Capitola is the **Paradise Beach Grill** (215 Esplanade, 831/476-4900, www.paradisebeachgrill.com, daily 11 A.M.–close, $18–32), with a mix of fine food, good service, and fun. Weekly specials are inspired fresh seasonal products, often in Californian-Hawaiian combinations. Catch a jazz and blues session with your meal every Tuesday 6–9 P.M.

Soquel

Pleasure Point (between 32nd Ave. and 41st Ave.) encompasses a number of different breaks, including The Hook (steps at 41st Ave.), a well-known paradise for experienced long-boarders. But don't mistake the Hook for a beginners break; locals feel protective of the waves and aren't always friendly toward inexperienced surfers. The break at 36th Avenue and East Cliff Drive (steps at 36th Ave.) is a better place on weekdays; on weekends the intense crowding makes catching your own wave a challenge. Up at 30th Avenue and East Cliff Drive (steps at 36th Ave.) are challenging sets and hot-dogging short-boarders.

Vine Hill Winery (2300 Jarvis Rd., 831/427-0436, www.vinehillwinery.com, noon–5 P.M. 3rd Sat. of the month, tasting $5 and $10) is in the hills above Soquel. The Vine Hill District, in the heart of the Santa Cruz Mountains, was originally established in 1867; the winery is dedicated to carrying on the tradition of creating outstanding artisanal wines while using sustainable vineyard and winery practices in crafting chardonnay, pinot noir, and syrah. From Vine Hill Winery, continue up the mountain to **Silver Mountain Vineyards** (Silver Mountain Dr., off Miller Cutoff, 408/353-2278, www.silvermtn.com, noon–5 P.M. Sat., tasting $5, waived with wine purchase), specializing in small lots of hand-crafted chardonnay, pinot noir, and Alloy, a Bordeaux-style blend.

At **Cafe Cruz** (2621 41st Ave., 831/476-3801, www.cafecruz.com, lunch 11:30 A.M.–2:30 P.M. Mon.–Sat., dinner daily 5:30 P.M.–close, $16–30), the menu features homey American favorites with a California twist: ribs, rotisserie chicken, bowls of pasta, and fresh crunchy salads. Cafe Cruz purchases fresh local produce, meat, and seafood.

Fine seaside dining is at the Dream Inn's **Aquarius** (173 W. Cliff Dr., 831/460-5012, www.aquariussantacruz.com, daily 7 A.M.–10:30 P.M., $20–30). Aquarius is a modern American bistro featuring sustainable seafood, local organic produce, and local vineyards. Large windows offer an expansive view of magical sunsets over the bay.

Wilder Ranch State Park

Just north of Santa Cruz is a place where the flavor of the Wild West lives on. Wilder Ranch State Park (1401 Old Coast Rd., 831/423-9703 or 831/426-0505, www.parks.ca.gov, daily year-round, $10) was once home to the Ohlone people. Later it became the home of the Wilder family, settlers who operated a dairy farm, and today, it is a huge state park with sections of the land leased to local farmers. Visitors can tour ranch structures (1 P.M. Thurs.–Sun.), including an adobe homestead, a bunkhouse, a garage, a chicken coop, a horse barn, and a cowboy cottage. The Farm Animal Program has sheep, goats, chickens, barn cats,

© KRISTIN LEAL

an old Victorian ranch house at Wilder Ranch State Park

and horses. Interacting with these animals is a great way for kids to get some exposure to farm animals. There are nature walks (Sat.), annual events, and holiday celebrations with live entertainment.

Wilder Ranch has hiking and horseback-riding trails that follow the rolling terrain. The 1.25-mile Old Cove Landing Trail is one of the more popular treks and leads to the Ohlone Bluff Trail. The trail runs above a gentle valley that leads to the coast.

Davenport Landing

Eleven miles north of Santa Cruz, the strong continuous wind of Davenport Landing (Hwy. 1, 831/454-7956, www.scparks.com, free) provides good opportunities to wind-surf. Kayakers, body boarders, and surfers are also seen here. The beach itself is pleasant and secluded with a few picnic tables and restrooms. Dogs are welcome, and there is plenty

© KRISTIN LEAL

the redwood forest of the Santa Cruz Mountains

of space for children to run around. Surf kayaking starts with an easy launch as the parking lot is very close to the beach. Although this is a well-known kayaking spot, there are plenty of waves for everyone. Views of the shore reveal hidden beaches among the cliffs. The cove is good place to drop a line to fish for rock cod, sometimes lingcod, and several other tasty fish.

SANTA CRUZ MOUNTAINS

Away from the beach, the Santa Cruz Mountains are home to majestic redwood forests. North of Santa Cruz, off Highway 1, is the small town of Bonny Doon, home to a winery worth the trip. Highway 17 north of Santa Cruz passes through Scotts Valley, while Highway 9 meanders through Felton, Ben Lomond, and Boulder Creek all the way up to Big Basin State Park. Within this region, you can take a train from the ocean to the forest,

hike and camp amid coastal redwoods, and fill up on a hearty German food.

There are a few ways to reach the Santa Cruz Mountains. Highway 9 from Santa Cruz runs north to Felton, Ben Lomond, and Boulder Creek. You can also take Highway 17 north of Santa Cruz and take the exit for Mount Herman Road, which leads to Graham Hill Road and then Highway 9. Big Basin Redwoods State Park is on Highway 236 west of Highway 9. You can also approach it from Highway 1 and Bonny Doon Road.

Throughout the Santa Cruz Mountains, transit buses are run by **Santa Cruz METRO** (831/425-8600 www.scmtd.com, adults $1.50 per ride, passes available).

Bonny Doon

Have a taste of the savory Santa Cruz Mountains at **Bonny Doon Vineyard's Cellar Door** (328 Ingalls St., 831/425-6737, www.bonnydoonvineyard.com, daily noon–5 P.M., tasting $5, waived with wine purchase). Known for its exceptional Rhône and Italian varietals, they craft a full line of reds, whites, rosés, and dessert wines.

Originally established in 1863 as the Jarvis Brothers Vineyard, **Santa Cruz Mountain Vineyard** (334-A Ingalls St., 831/426-6209, www.santacruzmountainvineyard.com, noon–5 P.M. Wed.–Sun. and by appointment) is located at one of the oldest continuously operated vineyards in California. In 1975, Ken Burnap started the winery, setting out to make the finest pinot noir possible. The first release under the Santa Cruz Mountain Vineyard label was the highly regarded 1975 vintage. Today, Ken continues to craft fantastic wines and has brought the tasting room to downtown Santa Cruz.

Redwood Croft Bed & Breakfast (275 Northwest Dr., 831/458-1939, www.redwoodcroft.com, $155–275) is a funky two-room B&B set back in a formerly beautiful redwood

CENTRAL COAST

forest that recently burned. The inn itself takes the woodsy theme indoors, using natural wood on the walls and furniture to create a serene retreat feeling. Both guest rooms have beautiful appointments, lovely stone baths, and views into the recovering woods.

It's all about fine organic cuisine and notable wines at Bonny Doon Vineyard's ☾ **Cellar Door** (328 Ingalls St., 831/425-6737, www.bonnydoonvineyard.com, lunch noon–3 P.M. Sat.–Sun., dinner 5:30 P.M.–close Wed.–Sun., $40–50). The menu changes daily according to what is fresh in the garden. The chef has a continual focus on local ingredients sourced from small growers in Santa Cruz and Monterey Counties. The prix fixe menu is beautifully paired with two-ounce pours of three wines through the meal.

Scotts Valley

As you climb into the Santa Cruz Mountains along Highway 17, stop in Scotts Valley to visit **Ivy's Porch** (5311 Scotts Valley Dr., 831/438-1228, www.ivysporch.com, 10 A.M.–5 P.M. Mon.–Sat., 11 A.M.–4 P.M. Sun.) to discover collectables, antiques, outdoor pieces, and garden goodies. A cottage-style collective, Ivy's is in a beautiful one-acre garden. Outside are magnificent arbors, birdbaths, gazebos, iron items, and fountains. Among the things inside are French antiques and early American furniture.

For a taste of Thailand in the Santa Cruz Mountains, **Kao Sook** (245 Mt. Hermon Rd., 831/439-9520, 11 A.M.–9 P.M. Mon.–Fri., noon–9 P.M. Sat.–Sun., $8–12) has addicting curries, noodle dishes, and salads.

Have a cup of coffee and a bite at the **Coffee Cat** (255 Mt. Hermon Rd., 6 A.M.–10 P.M. Mon.–Thurs., 6 A.M.–11 P.M. Fri.–Sat., $3–8). If you're camping, this comfortable lounge is a good space to catch up on Internet use. The coffee is roasted in-house and served any way you like it along with a full menu of homemade savory and sweet goodies.

Felton
ROARING CAMP RAILROADS

All aboard for an antique steam-train ride through the redwood forest or to the beach. Roaring Camp Railroads (5355 Graham Hill Rd., 831/335-4484, www.roaringcamp.com, daily year-round, check website for hours, adults $24–26, children $17–20, under age 3 free) is Wild West fun for the whole family deep in the Santa Cruz Mountains. Hop aboard an antique train, explore the Wild West Main Street, or rent a picnic area. The train winds through the redwoods up Bear Mountain on a one-hour route; other trips include a beach route, a seasonal haunted Halloween ride, and a holiday trip with Santa. This is a dog-friendly place—dogs are even allowed on the train.

There are playing fields on the Roaring Camp grounds that include a baseball field, a volleyball court, tetherball, and horseshoe pits. Lunch options include a birthday caboose, chuck wagon barbecue, and a food stand near the General Store.

BIGFOOT DISCOVERY MUSEUM

Located deep in the Santa Cruz Mountains among the towering redwoods, the Bigfoot Discovery Museum (5497 Hwy. 9, 831/335-4478, www.bigfootdiscoveryproject.com, 11 A.M.–6 P.M. Wed.–Mon. summer, 1–6 P.M. Wed.–Fri. fall, $3–5 donation) contains a full collection of local history tied to the creature, including actual evidence that the Sasquatch roams the Santa Cruz Mountains. There is a video presentation, and you can examine plaster casts of both the feet and the hands of the formidable beast.

HENRY COWELL REDWOODS STATE PARK

The northern redwood forest of Henry Cowell Redwoods State Park (101 N. Big Tree Rd., 831/335-4598 or 831/438-2396, www.parks.ca.gov, $10) offers a vast variety of outdoor activities. The 4,600-acre park has camping, biking, hiking, guided nature walks, swimming, picnicking, and horseback-riding trails. The large **Nature Center** has interactive and educational kid-friendly exhibits. There are sections dedicated to each of the four habitats of the park.

The main park has 15 miles of hiking and dirt-biking trails that weave among old-growth forests. The River Trail follows the San Lorenzo River, where there is swimming access. The northern part of the park, known as **Fall Creek,** has 20 miles of hiking trails deep into the wooded mountains, where giant trees abound. The Fall Creek Trail has a 3.2-mile loop with a 200-foot elevation gain; the longer option on this trail is a seven-mile round-trip route around Ben Lomond Mountain that gains 900 vertical feet. Dogs are allowed on the Pipeline Road, Graham Hill Trail, and Meadow Trail.

Several dirt roads allow bicycle riders to explore the park. Bikes are allowed on the Pipeline Road, Rincon Fire Road, Ridge Fire Road, and Powder Mill Fire Road. Helmets are required for riders under age 18. Horses and riders can travel many of the trails, except Redwood Grove Trail, Meadow Trail, Ox Trail, and Pipeline Rode south of the Rincon Fire Road. At the Powder Mill Trailhead is a parking lot where horses can be staged and trailers parked. The lot is in the southeast corner of the park on Graham Hill Road near the campgrounds.

WINERIES

Hallcrest Vineyards and the Organic Wine Works (379 Felton Empire Rd., 831/335-4441, www.hallcrestvineyards.com, daily noon–5 P.M., tasting $7) was established in 1941 where the soil and climate are ideal for producing premium California varietals. Chaffee Hall, a former attorney from San Francisco, established his own vineyard and released his first vintage in 1946. Soon after, Hallcrest Vineyards became known for its cabernet sauvignon and white riesling. After Hall's death, the vineyard was purchased in 1987 by its current owner, John Schumacher, and he stays true to handcrafting fine wines in small lots in the signature character of the Santa Cruz Mountain American Viticultural Area. Also known as the original producer of organic wines, Hallcrest bottles its organics under the Organic Wine Works label. They use certified organic grapes and use an organic wine-making process that naturally avoids the use of sulfites.

ACCOMMODATIONS AND FOOD

Escape into the majestic redwood forest at **Fern River Resort Motel** (5250 Hwy. 9, 831/335-4412, www.fernriver.com, $69–233), with snug private cottages equipped with fireplaces, small kitchens, and outdoor decks with barbecues. The river is close by, and a private beach has great swimming, especially in the heat of the summer.

Jaye's Timberlane Resort (8705 Hwy. 9, Ben Lomond, 831/336-5479, www.jayestimberlane.com, $85–175) has 10 cabins on seven attractive acres among towering redwoods. The property has a solar-heated pool, horseshoe pits, and tennis courts; it's great for a family stay, as kids are welcome.

Henry Cowell Redwoods State Park (101 N. Big Tree Rd., 831/335-4598 or 831/438-2396, www.parks.ca.gov, $35) has over 100 campsites deep in the redwood forest with freshwater streams nearby; there are also a number of group camps. The Junior Ranger and Campfire Programs are great for children, and the Little Ones Nature Club meets Friday–Sunday. The Nature Center in the park is also great for some hands-on discovery, and recreational opportunities abound.

For a hearty mountain breakfast that won't break the bank, **Rocky's Café** (6560 Hwy. 9, 831/335-4637, 7:30 A.M.–2:30 P.M. Mon.–Sun., $8–10) serves typical breakfast fare that includes oatmeal and banana pancakes, and the portions are large enough to hold you over until lunch and maybe even dinner.

Mama Mia's Ristorante Italiano (6231

Graham Hill Rd., 831/335-4414 www.mama-mias.com, daily 4–9 P.M., $18–32) has pizzas for the whole family and offers a full menu of pasta, Italian specialties, and steaks.

Don Quixote's International Music Hall (6275 Hwy. 9, 831/603-2294, www.donquiotesmusic.com, daily 11 A.M.–2 A.M., $10–26) is more about music than food, but they serve up Southern fried chicken, several seafood entrées, burritos, and other Mexican dishes. Families are welcome, with a kids menu to satisfy the little ones.

Ben Lomond

The small town of Ben Lomond is located 10 miles north of Santa Cruz along twisty Highway 9. Here, you can hunt for treasure throughout the 10,000-square-foot **Lacey Days Antiques** (9280 Hwy. 9, 831/336-2686, daily 11 A.M.–5 P.M.), which operates primarily as a furniture store and carries many larger pieces, such as kitchen tables, china cabinets, chairs, nightstands, chests, and bookcases. The furniture inside is mid-century to contemporary; some are antiques, but many are not.

Towne & Country Antiques (9280 Hwy. 9, Suite 22, 831/336-5993, daily 11 A.M.–5 P.M.) is a rustic country shop with treasures big and small and a constant influx of new items. The selection includes glassware, garden accents, jewelry, wall hangings, art, books, and kitchenware.

Overlooking the San Lorenzo River is the **Quality Inn & Suites Santa Cruz Mountains** (9733 Hwy. 9, 831/336-2292, www.qualityinn.com, $69–299), with 25 guest rooms, continental breakfast, an outdoor heated pool, free Wi-Fi, and fax services. The standard guest rooms are equipped with coffeemakers, irons and ironing boards, and blow-dryers. The suites are better for families.

One of the last American roadhouses, **Henflings Tavern** (9450 Hwy. 9, 831/336-9318, www.henflings.net, daily 11 A.M.–2 A.M., $15) serves traditional pub fare and has a full

bar. In the evening, expect live music or a little karaoke. The outdoor seating is nice, and the atmosphere is about as casual as it gets.

For a warm fire in a comfy chalet, head to the **Tyrolean Inn** (9600 Hwy. 9, 831/336-5188, www.tyroleaninn.com, 5–9 P.M. Tues.–Thurs., 4–10 P.M. Fri.–Sat., noon–9 P.M. Sun., $18) and enjoy authentic Bavarian cuisine. German menu favorites include sausage, *zigeuner schnitzel, rindsrouladen,* and *zwiebelrostbraten.* The service is always friendly, the German beers are large, and the food is comforting. On weekends, enjoy live Bavarian folk music.

Boulder Creek

A small community filled with charming antiques shops, Boulder Creek (Hwy. 9, www.boulder-creek.com) also has a local brewery, a few winemakers, state parks, and a majestic golf course surrounded by redwoods. It is just under an hour's drive from Santa Cruz but is much less visited. Boulder Creek began as a rough Western town of saloons, cathouses, gambling dens, and hotels, a hint of which remains today.

The largest antiques shop in the Santa Cruz Mountains is **Boulder Creek Antiques** (13164 Hwy. 9, 831/338-0600, www.bouldercreekantiques.blogspot.com, daily 11 A.M.–5:30 P.M.). The place seems to go on forever, a beautiful maze indoors and out. Several sections are targeted specifically at men, and there are jewelry cases, a garden section, laces, linens, furniture, antique radios, toy cars, and kitchenware.

Ahlgren Vineyard (20320 Hwy. 9, 831/338-6071, www.ahlgrenvineyard.com, noon–4 P.M. Sat., tasting free) started in the early 1970s when Valerie Ahlgren began to craft zinfandel in her suburban Silicon Valley garage. Today, along with her husband, Dexter, she produces limited runs of fine premium wines in their rustic mountain-cottage cellar, including sémillon, chardonnay, cabernet sauvignon, merlot, cabernet franc,

© SABRINA YOUNG

Lovely Berry Creek Falls is worth the hike.

zinfandel, nebbiolo, and syrah. They have earned a reputation for fine balance, fullness, and intensity of varietal flavor, firm structure, complex character, and extended life.

Since 1989 the **Boulder Creek Brewery & Café** (13040 Hwy. 9, 831/338-7882, www. bouldercreekbrewery.net, 11:30 A.M.–10 P.M. Mon.–Thurs., 11:30 A.M.–10:30 P.M. Fri.–Sat., $8–15) has served handcrafted beers and juicy burgers, all-American classics, soups, salads, espresso, and desserts. Boulder Creek Brewery has owned Santa Cruz Brewery since 2003 and uses its refurbished brew house and tanks at this location. It features a full bar and happy hour (4–6 P.M. Mon.–Fri., 9–10 P.M. Sat.).

For picnic supplies, head to locally owned **New Leaf Community Markets** (13159 Hwy. 9, daily 9 A.M.–9 P.M.). For nearly 20 years, owners Scott and Rex have been providing their customers with fresh local organic goods. The deli can provide lunch

goodies, the cracker isle is a must, and the beverage selection sprawls with specialty drinks and local brews.

◖ BIG BASIN REDWOODS STATE PARK

Established in 1902, Big Basin State Park (21600 Big Basin Way, 831/338-8860, www.parks. ca.gov, daily 8 A.M.–sunset, $10) is California's first state park. In addition to towering old-growth redwoods, oaks, madrones, and Douglas firs line the park's 80 miles of trails.

The most popular hike is to **Berry Creek Falls** (12 miles, 6 hours, strenuous), a series of three waterfalls in a primordial valley dense with old-growth redwoods. The **Skyline to the Sea Trail** to Waddell Beach (12.5 miles one-way, strenuous) is a rite of passage for many local outdoor enthusiasts. Shorter and more moderate hikes include the **Sequoia Trail** to Sempervirens Falls and the **Shadowbrook Trail** to the Sky Meadow backpacking camp.

There are 146 campsites ($35) spread among three **campgrounds**, including tent cabins ($75), walk-in campsites ($35), two group camps ($335), and two backpacking camps ($15). Facilities include restrooms with showers (bring quarters), drinking water, fire pits, picnic tables, and firewood for sale. Reservations can be made online (800/444-7275, www.reserveamerica.com), but backpacking sites must be reserved in advance (831/338-8861). Visitor services include a small grocery store, a gift shop, and a tiny museum. Docent-led hikes generally occur on Saturday mornings.

Big Basin is located is 25 miles northwest of Santa Cruz in the Santa Cruz Mountains. The closest town is Boulder Creek, nine miles south on Highway 9. To reach Big Basin from Santa Cruz, take Highway 9 north for about 14 miles to the town of Boulder Creek. Turn left onto Highway 236 and drive about nine miles to the park headquarters.

CENTRAL COAST

Monterey Bay

Home to the Monterey Bay Aquarium, plenty of ocean-side fairways, and world-class restaurants, the city of Monterey brings marine science, California history, and natural landscapes together with pampered luxury and gourmet cuisine. Destination restaurants are found alongside the favorite local doughnut shop. And just beyond where the land ends, world-renowned diving awaits under the surface of the bay, where rock cod dart around as you explore the underwater landscape.

SIGHTS

The location of Old Fisherman's Wharf (1 Old Fisherman's Wharf, 831/649-6544, www. montereywharf.com) dates back to 1770, when the harbor was discovered by Spaniard Gaspar de Portolà. The whaling industry took off in Monterey by the 1840s, and the wharf was a major hub of action. It was also home to a booming fishing industry through the mid-20th century. Today, you can walk the planks of the 1845 pier and enjoy its historic nautical charm.

◖ Monterey Bay Aquarium

The fantastic Monterey Bay Aquarium (866 Cannery Row, 831/648-4800, www.montereybayaquarium.org, 10 A.M.–6 P.M. Mon.–Fri., 10 A.M.–8 P.M. Sat.–Sun. summer, daily 10 A.M.–6 P.M. fall–spring, adults $35, seniors and students $32, children $22) explores the world below the waves, visiting the ocean depths through hands-on experiences, adventure programs, and conservation ethics. The two floors of exhibits can easily take an entire day to explore.

On the first floor, begin your visit at the two-story **Kelp Forest.** Leopard sharks and schools of sardines swim amid lengthy strands

of kelp while rockfish hide within the rocks. Greet the **giant octopus,** then explore the series of **Monterey Bay Habitats** before dipping your fingers in the **Touch Pools** to pet bat rays, feel a sea cumber, or pick up a knobby sea star.

Back in the center of the aquarium are the most popular personalities—the **sea otters.** The two-level exhibit provides views above and below the surface as the otters play, eat, and nap. Feeding times (daily 10:30 A.M., 1:30 P.M., and 3:30 P.M.) are action-packed and should not be missed; plan to get here early.

Upstairs are several must-see exhibits. Sardines swirl over the entrance to the **Jellies,** where lobed comb jellyfish move slowly and intricately together in beautifully lit tanks. The **Open Sea** is the largest tank in the aquarium. Scalloped hammerhead sharks circle, a

© KRISTIN LEAL

Monterey Bay Aquarium

CENTRAL COAST

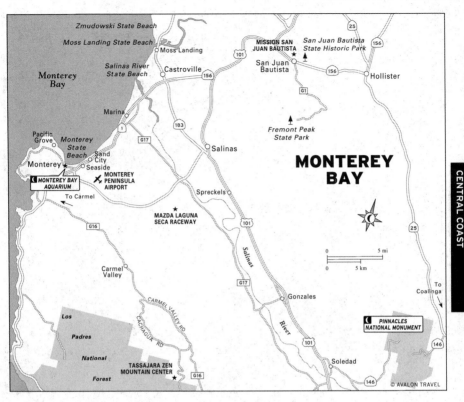

© AVALON TRAVEL

sea turtle combs the surface, and Pacific blue-fin tuna hustle in small schools while barracudas group together. Nearby are the **Puffins,** fluffy, short birds with bright yellow beaks and elegant feathers.

Also upstairs is the **Splash Zone,** where kids can roll up their sleeves and touch sea grapes, hold a starfish, and handle a rainbow star. This area is also home to the **Penguins** exhibit; their feeding times (daily 10:30 A.M. and 3 P.M.) are always fun to watch.

In addition to exhibits, the aquarium offers a variety of educational programs for children and adults, including tours and nighttime sleepovers. There is an on-site café and a restaurant, a gift store, and an auditorium for scheduled lectures.

Cannery Row

Famous for its rich fishing history and as the setting for one of John Steinbeck's classic novels, Cannery Row (831/649-6690, www.canneryrow.com) conveniently hugs the shores of the harbor. In the early 20th century it was an ideal setting to support the growing fishing industry on Monterey Bay, and it became home to 16 canning plants and 14 reduction plants that produced thousands of tons of sardines every year. The fishing industry collapsed in the mid-1950s, and today, Cannery Row serves visitors with waterfront accommodations, numerous restaurants, diving operators, jewelry shops, clothing stores, a wax museum, wine-tasting, and, of course, the Monterey Bay Aquarium. There is also a

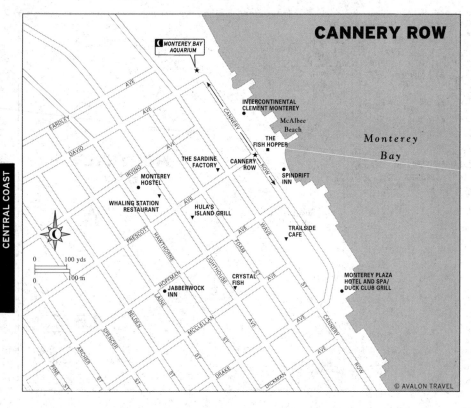

CANNERY ROW

beach with a tide pool and a chance to chase the waves.

Monterey State Historic Park

Enjoy a California history lesson on the Path of History at Monterey State Historic Park (831/649-7118, tour reservations 831/649-7172, www.parks.ca.gov, daily, free), a collection of 55 historic sites along a 2.5-mile trail. Many people find Colton Hall (570 Pacific St.) or Pacific House (Custom House Plaza) nice entry spots to the Path of History, as there are parking garages at both. The walk is self-guided, but guided tours can be purchased by calling the park office in advance. Enter the path at any point by simply looking for the round yellow tiles set in the sidewalks, and

begin your journey back in time. Free maps can be found at most of the historic sites along the way, or print one from the website.

Custom House Plaza (Custom House Plaza, 831/646-3866, www.mtycounty.com, daily) provides just a sample of the 55 historic sites along Monterey's Path of History. Located between downtown and Old Fisherman's Wharf, the plaza serves as the focal point for large public events throughout the year.

The **Custom House** (Custom House Plaza, 831/649-7118, www.parks.ca.gov, 10 A.M.–4 P.M. Sat.–Sun., free) was first used by the Mexican government, and it wasn't until 1846 that Commodore John Drake Sloat raised the American flag and claimed it for the United

Monterey's Cannery Row

States. The museum is styled as it would have been in the 1940s, and you can examine a variety of goods and tools that were used at the port. Through the windows upstairs you can watch as boats enter and leave the harbor.

Constructed in 1847, the **Pacific House Museum** (Custom House Plaza, 831/649-7181, www.parks.ca.gov, 10 A.M.–4 P.M. Sat.–Sun., free) was used as a hotel, an Army storage facility, a courthouse, offices, and a tavern. Today, it showcases exhibits that tell the story of Monterey Bay from the time when Native

SEAFOOD WATCH AND SUSTAINABILITY

Today, the health of our oceans is at risk. Around the world 75 percent of fisheries are overfished or fished to capacity, causing many species to become endangered. What you choose to eat has a direct impact on the world around you, and Monterey Bay Aquarium has developed a program to help you personally take action.

Your daily food choices affect the fishing industry, and sustainability is the key to ensuring the health of the oceans. The primary mission of the Monterey Bay Aquarium Seafood Watch program is promoting sustainable fishing to allow ecosystems to survive and remain diverse

and productive for the future. Seafood Watch is an inclusive vision that considers species, habitat, management, government reports, journal articles, and sustainability criteria to classify the consumption of species based on the impact their harvest has on marine ecosystems.

The Seafood Watch program has a pocket guide to assist you in making sustainable seafood choices, with seafood items ranked for their sustainability as "Best Choices," "Good Alternatives," and "Avoid." Carrying it with you can help you reduce the impact of your food choices on the environment.

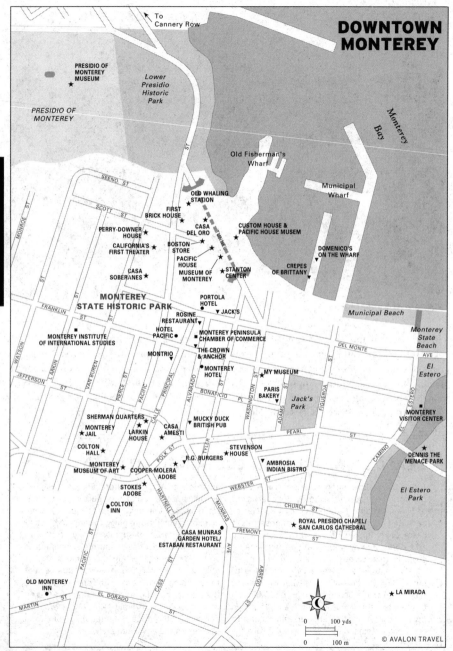

DOWNTOWN MONTEREY

To Cannery Row

PRESIDIO OF MONTEREY MUSEUM

Lower Presidio Historic Park

PRESIDIO OF MONTEREY

Monterey Bay

Old Fisherman's Wharf

Municipal Wharf

SEENO ST

OLD WHALING STATION

SCOTT ST

FIRST BRICK HOUSE

PERRY-DOWNER HOUSE

CASA DEL ORO

CUSTOM HOUSE & PACIFIC HOUSE MUSEM

CALIFORNIA'S FIRST THEATER

BOSTON STORE

PACIFIC HOUSE

DOMENICO'S ON THE WHARF

CASA SOBERANES

MUSEUM OF MONTEREY

STANTON CENTER

CREPES OF BRITTANY

MONTEREY STATE HISTORIC PARK

PORTOLA HOTEL

FRANKLIN ST

ROSINE RESTAURANT

JACK'S

Municipal Beach

MONROE ST

HOTEL PACIFIC

Monterey State Beach

MONTEREY INSTITUTE OF INTERNATIONAL STUDIES

MONTEREY PENINSULA CHAMBER OF COMMERCE

DEL MONTE AVE

El Estero

WATSON ST

MONTRIO

THE CROWN & ANCHOR

LARKIN ST

JEFFERSON ST

VAN BUREN ST

MONTEREY HOTEL

MY MUSEUM

MONTEREY VISITOR CENTER

PIERCE ST

PACIFIC ST

PRINCIPAL ST

CALLE

ALVARADO ST

BONAFICIO PL

WASHINGTON ST

ADAMS ST

PARIS BAKERY

Jack's Park

FIGUEROA ST

ESTERO

SHERMAN QUARTERS

MONTEREY JAIL

LARKIN HOUSE

CASA AMESTI

MUCKY DUCK BRITISH PUB

PEARL ST

CAMINO

DENNIS THE MENACE PARK

COLTON HALL

POLK ST

TYLER ST

R.G. BURGERS

STEVENSON HOUSE

MONTEREY MUSEUM OF ART

COOPER-MOLERA ADOBE

AMBROSIA INDIAN BISTRO

El Estero Park

STOKES ADOBE

WEBSTER ST

MUNRAS AVE

COLTON INN

HARTNELL ST

CHURCH ST

PACIFIC ST

CASA MUNRAS GARDEN HOTEL/ ESTABAN RESTAURANT

FREMONT ST

ROYAL PRESIDIO CHAPEL/ SAN CARLOS CATHEDRAL

CASS ST

ABREGO ST

OLD MONTEREY INN

MARTIN ST

EL DORADO ST

LA MIRADA

0   100 yds
0   100 m

© AVALON TRAVEL

Americans were the only residents through the present day. Explore Monterey's rich history on the two floors, and don't forget to head out back to the garden.

Home of the Boston Store and Picket Fence Garden Shop, **Casa del Oro** (210 Olivier St., off Pacific St., 831/649-3364, www.parks.ca.gov, 11 A.M.–3 P.M. Thurs.–Sun.) was constructed by Thomas O. Larkin in 1845 and served as a general store in 1850. Monterey's first safe was installed here in Joseph Boston & Co., and as the story goes, miners returning from the gold fields would store their assets in the safe, earning the two-story adobe the nickname "Casa del Oro" (Gold House). The store and garden shop, offering fresh herbs, seeds for planting, silverware, coffee mills, teas, and soaps, are operated by the Historic League of Monterey.

Visiting the **First Brick House** (20 Custom House Plaza, 831/649-7118, www.parks.ca.gov) has to be a walk-by visit, as it is closed until further notice due to ongoing state budget problems. In 1874 Gallant Duncan Dickenson arrived in California and introduced his fired clay bricks, which were much stronger and more durable that mud adobe. He never finished construction of his brick home, as the gold in the Sierras was calling him; he abandoned the structure, and the unused bricks were auctioned off for $1,000 in 1851.

Originally built as a home for David Wright and his family in 1847, it wasn't until 1855 that the Monterey Whaling Company used the **Old Whaling Station** (391 Decatur St., 831/375-5356, www.parks.ca.gov, daily 9 A.M.–5 P.M., free) as an employee residence and headquarters. Today, the building is a museum known for its whalebone walkway.

Due to structural damage, **California's First Theater** (Pacific St. and Scott St., www.parks.ca.gov) is closed to the public most of the year. Once a year, in early December, the theater's tavern opens its doors for the Christmas in the Adobes event. It was originally built as a tavern

and lodging house for sailors in 1847 by Jack Swan; in 1850, U.S. Army officers began producing plays as a moneymaking venture. The first night pulled in $500.

Casa Soberanes (Pacific St. and Del Monte Ave., 831/649-7118, www.parks.ca.gov, daily 9 A.M.–5 P.M., free) is an adobe with a blue gate leading to the garden. It was home to many families starting in the 1840s, with the Soberanes family being the longest residents, from 1860 to 1922. The garden is layered with pieces of Monterey: Whalebones, wine bottles, and abalone shells line the garden path. You can also tour the interior, which is filled with modern Mexican folk art, Chinese trade pieces, and early New England furnishings.

The first two-story building in California was the **Larkin House** (464 Calle Principal, 831/646-3991, www.parks.ca.gov, daily 9 A.M.–5 P.M., free), built by the merchant Thomas Oliver Larkin in 1835 as his home and storefront; later it was the headquarters for the U.S. military governor of California. It has a beautiful garden and two floors to tour inside. Many of the pieces inside originate with Alice Larkin Toulmin after she acquired the adobe from her grandfather in 1922 and furnished it with early-19th-century antiques from around the world.

A favorite subject for photographers is **Sherman Quarters** (Calle Principal, next to Larkin House, 831/649-7118, www.parks.ca.gov, daily 9 A.M.–4 P.M., free). The building is closed but can be viewed from the gardens of Larkin House. In 1847 it served as the living quarters of Lieutenant William T. Sherman, later General Sherman of Civil War fame, who was in charge of the troops constructing the Presidio of Monterey.

Visit the site where the first California Constitution was drafted, **Colton Hall** (351 Pacific St., 831/646-5640, www.monterey.org, daily 10 A.M.–4 P.M., closed holidays, free). The large building also served as a courthouse and public school for many years before becoming

CENTRAL COAST

© KRISTIN LEAL

Colton Hall

a museum. Located behind the building is the Old Monterey Jail, which dates to 1854.

The focus of many social events in the early days of Monterey was the **Stokes Adobe** (500 Hartnell St., 831/373-1110, www.mtycounty. com), one of the most pretentious homes in Monterey. In its heyday, the most important events were the cascarone balls, festive events where eggshells were smashed between dances. During the 1840s the adobe was the home of Monterey mayor and physician James Stokes. Today, visitors enjoy walking the around the property to admire the roses and possibly catch a glimpse of a ghost.

The **Cooper-Molera Adobe** (525 Polk St., at Alvarado St. and Munras St., 831/649-7118 or 831/649-7111, www.parks.ca.gov, daily 9 A.M.–4 P.M., free) is another garden and museum with two acres to explore, including the museum, barns, gardens, and a gift shop. It was the 19th-century home of the Cooper family, headed by Captain John Rogers Cooper, who was in the business of trading items like hides, otter pelts, tallow, and general merchandise.

Once a rooming house and later the French Hotel, **Stevenson House** (530 Houston St., 831/649-7118, www.parks.ca.gov, daily 9 A.M.–5 P.M., free) was where famed author Robert Louis Stevenson stayed in the 1870s while courting his future wife, Fanny Osbourne. Today, it is restored to what it would have looked like in Stevenson's era, with many rooms devoted to the author. The two-story adobe is worth a visit for the lovely gardens as well.

Known today as the San Carlos Cathedral, the original **Royal Presidio Chapel** (500 Church St., 831/373-2628, www.sancarloscathedral.net) was California's first cathedral. Founded by Father Junípero Serra in 1770, it was the birthplace of the Carmel Mission. A year later the mission was moved to Carmel, leaving the church behind as a royal chapel for the soldiers; the structure seen today was completed in 1774. Beautifully built in the

Spanish colonial style with ornamental arches and fine sandstone molding throughout, the cathedral was associated with the new Spanish Presidio. It is currently one of the oldest functioning churches in California. The **Heritage Center Museum** (10 A.M.–noon and 1:15–3:15 P.M. 2nd and 4th Mon., 10 A.M.–noon Wed., 10 A.M.–3 P.M. Fri., 10 A.M.–2 P.M. Sat., 1–3 P.M. Sun., donation) offers docent-led tours that explore a relic of the Vizcaíno-Serra Oak, old photos and drawings of the chapel, pieces of the whalebone sidewalk that led to the church, and other pieces recovered in an archaeological dig. The museum is on the east side of the chapel in the Parish Offices Building.

Museum of Monterey

The Museum of Monterey (5 Custom House Plaza, 831/372-2608, www.museumofmonterey.org, 10 A.M.–5 P.M. Tues.–Sun., $5) was renovated in 2011. Its various permanent collections include costumes and textiles, decorative arts, model ships, Monterey history archive, historical objects, and photography. It showcases new exhibitions as well.

Monterey Museum of Art

The Monterey Museum of Art (559 Pacific St., 831/372-5477, www.montereyart.org, 11 A.M.–5 P.M. Wed.–Sat., 1–4 P.M. Sun., closed holidays, $10) is a treasure trove in the downtown area, with eight galleries in a three-story structure that features rotating exhibits. You can admire photography, contemporary and early American art, and California paintings.

My Museum

The place for the whole family to come and play is at My Museum (425 Washington St., 831/649-6444, www.mymuseum.org, 10 A.M.–5 P.M. Mon.–Tues. and Thurs.–Sat., noon–5 P.M. Sun., $7). Interactive educational exhibits include My Day at the Beach for the little ones and My Go-Fore Golf for bigger

kids. There are always 75 bins filled with art and craft supplies, both recyclable and nonrecyclable, to create masterpieces. The staff are also experts at hosting special events, and it is a popular birthday-party spot.

Presidio of Monterey

From the time Europeans first saw Monterey Bay in 1602, the military has played a vital role that continues today. The Presidio of Monterey (between Hwy. 68/Holman Hwy. and Lighthouse Ave., 831/242-5555, www.monterey.army.mil) is a U.S. Army base known for its Defense Language Institute Foreign Language Center. The original Presidio building was located near Lake Estero in today's downtown area. In 1792, a small fort equipped with 11 cannons, El Castillo, was built to protect the original Presidio.

Within the Presidio today are two public attractions for visitors. The 26-acre **Lower Presidio Historic Park** has markers with information about the military presence in Monterey through the Spanish, Mexican, and American periods. Views of the bay abound throughout the park. All that remains of the Rumsen Native American village here is their burial grounds and a large ceremonial rain rock that was used to grind acorns. The 31-foot-tall granite Sloat Monument marks the location of Fort Mervine, which stood here during the Civil War era.

Located in Lower Presidio Historic Park is the **Presidio of Monterey Museum** (Bldg. 113, Corporal Ewing Rd., off Artillery St., 831/646-3456, www.monterey.org, 10 A.M.–1 P.M. Mon., 10 A.M.–4 P.M. Thurs.–Sat., 1–4 P.M. Sun., free), with information on Monterey's military history in a series of exhibits that includes the Rumsen people through the present-day military presence. Parking at the museum and park is free, but make sure to bring a picture ID, as you are entering a military base.

Art Galleries

Housed in an old green-shingled home,

the **Monterey Peninsula Art Foundation** (425 Cannery Row, 831/655-1267, daily 11 A.M.–5 P.M.) is a cooperative of about 30 local artists. Their pieces are in watercolors, acrylics, ceramics, jewelry, and sculpture. It's one of the few Monterey galleries that exhibits exclusively local art, and there is also a classy selection of greeting cards featuring works by the artists.

Venture Gallery (260 Alvarado St., 831/372-6279, www.venturegallery.com, daily 10 A.M.–6 P.M.) is owned and operated by local artists who specialize in capturing scenes of the Monterey Peninsula. The gallery is ever-changing as the artists manipulate a variety of media, including ceramics, sculptures, paintings, jewelry, and pottery.

Fine-art photography by Russell Levin can be found at the **Levin Gallery** (408 Calle Principal, 831/649-1166, www.russlevin.com, 11 A.M.–4 P.M. Mon.–Fri.). A California native and local photographer, Levin brings his love of art to Monterey. His passion lies in capturing people, action images, simple nudes, and environmental nudes.

If you have an interest in 19th-century photographs, **Willem Photographic** (426 Calle Principal, 831/648-1050, www.willemphotographic.com, Sat.–Sun. and by appointment) is the place to visit. The gallery contains an eclectic mix of 19th–20th-century photographs; artists include Ansel Adams, Norman Parkinson, Alvin Booth, and Ruth Orkin.

The place for Swarovski Crystal in Monterey is at **Crystal Fox Gallery** (381 Cannery Row, 831/655-3905, www.crystal-fox.com, 10 A.M.–6 P.M. Mon.–Sat., 10 A.M.–5 P.M. Sun.). Enjoy the Richard Satava jellyfish, art glass sculptures, and bronzed sculptures, many with marine inspirations.

SPORTS AND RECREATION
Beaches

Stretching from the southern reaches of Seaside to the Monterey Municipal Wharf, the Monterey Bay shoreline has numerous access points. **Monterey State Beach** (west of Seaside exit from Hwy. 1, 831/649-2836, www.parks.ca.gov) is the spot for surfing, boarding,

There is plenty to discover within Monterey's tide pools.

© KRISTIN LEAL

surf kayaking, kite flying, running, and shore fishing. The beach arcs west to the Monterey Municipal Wharf. It is the perfect place to head for a sunset walk and a beach bonfire, and a lifeguard is on duty during the summer months.

The Coast Guard Pier, between downtown and Cannery Row, has a small cove called **San Carlos Beach,** perfect for the little ones to get their toes wet or wrestle in the large grassy area. There is a secluded cove behind **Monterey Plaza** where you can avoid the crowds. **McAbee Beach** is along Cannery Row, with stairs next to the Fishhopper Restaurant (700 Cannery Row) that lead to the pale beach and a cluster of tide pools. If you like to snorkel, McAbee Beach has kelp mazes, rocky mounds, tiny pink starfish, quick rock cod, and the occasional harbor seal to swim around.

Fishing and Whale Watching

Randy's Whale Watching and Fishing Trips (66 Fisherman's Wharf, 831/372-7440, www.randysfishingtrips.com) offers tours year-round. The fishing voyages last about seven hours and have seasoned captains at the helm. Trip prices vary and can include rod and reel rentals along with a daily fishing license. Three-hour whale-watching tours ($30) head out daily year-round and are packed with adventure. The unique canyon and upwelling deep below the bay is rich with plant growth, making Monterey Bay an ideal spot for migratory and year-round species. Look forward to seeing gray (Dec.–Apr.), blue, and humpback (May–Nov.) whales along with porpoises and the killer whales that are known to hunt in Monterey waters.

Chris's Fishing and Whale Watching Trips (48 Fisherman's Wharf 1, 831/375-5951, www.chrisfishing.com or www.chriswhalewatching.com) has been fishing Monterey Bay since the 1940s, and the skippers know the local waters well, hitting the water at sunrise to return by early afternoon on the hunt for rock cod, albacore, salmon, crab, and Humboldt squid. The

whale-watching adventure ($32) starts at the mouth of the harbor, where the sea lions like to play on the rocks.

Keeping a lookout for whales year-round is the **Monterey Bay Whale Watch Center** (84 Fisherman's Wharf, 831/375-4658, www.montereybaywhalewatch.com, $38–47). Hitting the seas for 4–5 hours, there are many chances to get up close to these massive creatures. In addition to whales, the tour also focuses on the vast variety of marine animals within the bay. A naturalist is on board to educate you on the sea otters, harbor seals, minke whales, fin whales, pacific white-sided dolphins, Risso's dolphins, northern right whale dolphins, bottlenose dolphins, Dall's porpoises, harbor porpoises, and a vast variety of seabirds all known to make an appearance in the bay.

The largest whale-watching vessel on the wharf is the **Princess Monterey Whale Watching** (96 Fisherman's Wharf 1, 831/372-2203, www.montereywhalewatching.com, $40), and it is strictly dedicated to following the massive mammals. The boat's captains are experts at searching out the spouting whales, and the various companies keep in contact with each other to report where the elusive beasts have been sighted during the day, making the chances of sighting whales high.

Kayaking

Fisherman's Wharf offers both beginner and intermediate paddles. The launch begins with an easy paddle through the harbor, where bronzed sea lions balance on buoys and harbor seals blend into the rocks. The harbor at the Wharf is filled with curious seals that tend to follow kayakers.

Dolphins are also known to show off near **Cannery Row.** Crossing through the canopy of kelp where sea otters rest slows the kayak, and paddles can become entangled. During the spring, mother sea otters can also be seen holding baby pups on their bellies. Gaining a

kayaking the backside of Cannery Row, a popular paddle spot

© KRISTIN LEAL

different perspective on a much visited place, the ride through Cannery Row is tranquil.

Launch ramps are not the only way to access the ocean by kayak. **Del Monte Beach** off Casa Verde is a challenge, and many local paddlers compete for the waves alongside the surfers. **Monterey State Beach** is another great spot to paddle in the foamy surf; the waves are not huge but offer a mixed challenge.

A good place to start is with **Adventures by the Sea** (299 Cannery Row, 831/372-1807, www.adventuresbythesea.com, daily 9 A.M.–sunset, tours $50 pp, rentals $30 per day). All-day kayak rentals allow you to choose your own route in and around the magnificent Monterey Bay. If you're not confident enough to go off on your own, the tour of Cannery Row (2.5 hours, $50 pp) is filled with wildlife sightings. The sit-on-top tandem kayaks make it a great experience for school-age children. Reservations are recommended for all tours, including the Cannery Row tour (daily 10 A.M. and 2 P.M. summer).

Monterey Bay Kayaks (693 Del Monte Ave., 831/373-5357, www.montereybaykayaks.com, tours $50–60 pp) specializes in tours of both central Monterey and Elkhorn Slough to the north. You can choose between open-deck and closed-deck tour groups, beginning tours perfect for kids, romantic sunset or full-moon paddles, or even long paddles designed for more experienced sea kayakers.

AB Seas Kayaks of Monterey (32 Cannery Row, Suite 5, 831/647-0147, www.montereykayak.com, tours $60 pp, rentals $30 per day) also has plenty of sit-on-top single or double sea kayaks for rent, or take a tour of Monterey Bay with an experienced guide.

Sailing

Sailing is a stunning way to take in the beauty of Monterey. Year-round adventures can be had with **Monterey Bay Sailing** (78 Fisherman's Wharf 1, 831/372-7245, www.montereysailing.com, adults $39, children $25). With a fleet of seven sailboats, options range from daily cruises to weeklong trips. Monterey Bay Sailing is a member of the American Sailing Association Academy (ASA); all captains are certified instructors and teach a variety of sailing classes for any level.

Scuba Diving

Monterey Bay and Carmel offer a unique opportunity to experience an underwater habitat within a marine sanctuary, and several companies offer the chance to dive from shore or from a boat. All dive boats depart from the Monterey Harbor and Marina between Old Fisherman's Wharf 1 and 2, on K Dock. The water temperature in the bay tends to range from the high 40s to the mid-50s.

Eric's Pinnacle is best accessed by boat, off the shore of 17-Mile Drive. It is an 80–105-foot dive with lots of rock slivers shooting up. Most sealife is seen on the rocks, as many other animals bury themselves in the sand. Farther south, **Aumentos Reef** displays everything Monterey Bay has to offer. The pinnacles are a lush carpet, and strawberry anemones cover the rocks. **Break Water** is a great beginner spot, with nice walls that drop off quickly. **Tankers Reef** off Del Monte Beach is another location in the bay that offers a bounty of discovery.

Aquarius Dive Shop (2040 Del Monte Ave., 831/375-1933, www.aquariusdivers.com) offers everything you'll need to go diving in Monterey Bay: air and nitrox fills, equipment rentals, certification courses, and help booking trips on local dive boats. Aquarius works with four boats to create great trips for divers of all interests and ability levels. Another local favorite is **Bamboo Reef Enterprises** (614 Lighthouse Ave., 831/372-1685, www.bambooreef.com), a full dive shop with lessons and certification courses. They do clean repairs at a fair price and have all the latest dive equipment for purchase.

Get suited up at **Monterey Bay Dive Company** (225 Cannery Row, 831/656-0454,

www.mbdcscuba.com) and take a shore dive at the neighboring Coast Guard Wharf. It is a full-service dive shop and dive-chartering service; hitch a ride on their dive boat for a two-tank tour ($75). You can take dive classes year-round, get certified, rent equipment, and fill your own tanks. A popular dive boat is the **Monterey Bay Express** (831/915-0752, www.montereyexpress.com, $90). The morning and afternoon charters include two dives, and the Saturday-night trip has one. Depending on the surface conditions, trips head to the pinnacles off the shores of Pacific Grove or down to Point Lobos State Natural Reserve.

If you're looking for a dive in Point Lobos State Natural Reserve, sign up with the **Beachhopper II** (408/463-0585, www.beachhopper2.com, daily 6:30 A.M.–7:30 P.M., $90). It runs south to Point Lobos for a two-tank dive in the reserve and its natural glory.

Surfing

Whether you're just learning to harness the power of the ocean or are a longtime ripper, the Monterey Bay coastline offers gleaming shores with year-round endless waves. A great spot to avoid the weekend crowds is at **Marina State Beach** (Reservation Rd., off Hwy. 1, 831/649-2836, www.parks.ca.gov, free). Steady winds help to create moderate–hard surf that tends to be filled with strong riptides among heavy undertows. Be prepared with a full wetsuit, a hoodie, and booties on windy days.

Three separate beaches shared by Seaside and Monterey are known as **Monterey State Beach** (Seaside/Hwy. 218 exit from Hwy. 1, 831/649-2836, www.parks.ca.gov, free). This strip of shoreline is known for its fantastic beginner waves with long flat rollers. The Monterey Junior Lifeguards find the conditions ideal and use these beaches for their yearly summer programs. On the Seaside-Monterey boundary, this is the only beach that has an occupied lifeguard tower throughout summer;

the state beaches from Marina to Monterey are patrolled by lifeguards in a truck during summer. Locals love to surf the waters along the section known as Del Monte Beach off of Casa Verde Way. The waves are consistently changeling and get mellower farther west toward the wharf.

Get fully geared up for beach fun on Lighthouse Avenue. The local choice surf and skate shop on the peninsula is **Sunshine Freestyle Sports** (443 Lighthouse Ave., 831/375-5015, www.sunshinefreestyle.com, 10 A.M.–6 P.M. Mon.–Sat., 11 A.M.–5 P.M. Sun.). Officially the sponsor and creator of the Annual Surf About in Carmel, the shop has been owned by local surfers since the early 1980s.

A little more on the hip and trendy side is **On the Beach Surf Shop** (693 Lighthouse Ave., 831/646-9283, www.onthebeachsurfshop.com, 10 A.M.–7 P.M. Mon.–Sat., 10 A.M.–6 P.M. Sun.). It has a bit of everything, including surfboard and ski rentals, to prepare you for the surf or the snow. There is also a full line of clothing and accessories for the rider lifestyle.

Hiking

Within the city of Monterey, a ridge-top reserve awaits the outdoors addict. Hidden among thick pine forest, **Jacks Peak County Park** (25001 Jacks Peak Dr., off Hwy. 68, 831/372-8551, www.co.monterey.ca.us, $5) is a perfect escape for an afternoon ramble. Stunning wide views overlook Monterey Bay through the shaded woods.

At **Fort Ord Dunes State Park** (Lightfighter exit from Hwy. 1, 831/649-2836, www.parks.ca.gov, daily 8 A.M.–sunset, free), the newest addition to the California State Park system, hike a short trail to the beach or explore the interpretive panels along the new boardwalk. Fort Ord is located off Highway 1 north of Monterey Bay.

Biking

The **Monterey Bay Coastal Bike Trail** (www.mtycounty.com) is a fantastic way to take in the sights of the bay. As the trail runs through

You can find several bike trails both on and off the road.

Monterey, it follows the shore of the bay through the sandy dunes, crosses Old Fisherman's Wharf, and leads into Pacific Grove. Ocean views are pretty much constant. The northern leg of the trail presents plenty of challenging hills, and anyone can enjoy the flat stretch from the Naval Postgraduate School to Asilomar State Beach. The full trail runs 29 miles from Castroville to Pebble Beach.

A full-service bike shop that specializes in everything from BMX and triathlon to family fun is **Joselyn's Bicycles** (398 E. Franklin St., 831/649-8520, www.joselynsbicycles.com, 9:30 A.M.–6 P.M. Mon.–Fri., 9:30 A.M.–5 P.M. Sat., 11 A.M.–5 P.M. Sun., $20 per hour, half day $60, full day $100).

In operation for 29 years is **Aquarian Bicycles** (486 Washington St., 831/375-2144, www.aquarianbicycles.com, noon–5 P.M. Sun.–Mon., 10 A.M.–5:30 P.M. Tues.–Sat., $8 per hour, 4 hours $24, 24 hours $36). This is a full-service shop with knowledgeable technicians. **Bay Bikes** (585 Cannery Row, 831/655-2453, www.baybikes.com) offers a full line of rental bikes, including surreys, tandem bikes, Trail-a-Bikes, street bikes, mountain bikes, and accessories.

Dennis the Menace Park

Everyone has a chance to be a kid where the world of Dennis the Menace comes to life. Nestled in the center of Monterey, the **El Estero** complex (Pearl St. and Camino El Estero, www.montery.org) is a multiuse recreation area that includes Dennis the Menace Park, perfect for tiny tikes. Teenage skaters tear up the skate park, and there is a ball park, fishing piers, an exercise course, and paddleboat rentals. Grab a bite at the El Estero Snack Bar, next to the steam engine.

ENTERTAINMENT AND EVENTS
Nightlife

A hip young hangout with a full bar, a menu of local seafood and produce, and live entertainment is **The Mucky Duck** (479 Alvarado St., 831/655-3031, www.muckyduckmonterey.com, daily 11 A.M.–2 A.M.).

A favorite of locals and visitors alike is **Britannia Arms Pub and Restaurant** (444 Alvarado St., 831/656-9543, www.britanniaarmsofmonterey.com, daily 11 A.M.–2 A.M.), just the stop for a dark brew and a bite to eat. Local bands and DJs play every Friday–Saturday night, or check out the game on one of the many TV screens.

A British-style pub known for aged bourbons and vintage ports is **Crown & Anchor** (150 W. Franklin St., 831/656-9543, www.crownandanchor.net, daily 11 A.M.–2 A.M.). The patio is the perfect place to mingle throughout the day and into the night. The full menu is served until midnight, and appetizers are available until closing time, making it a great late-night stop.

The **Hippodrome** (321 Alvarado St., 831/262-2704, www.hippclub.com, 9 P.M.–2 A.M.

Thurs.–Mon.) is the place to get your groove on, with four dance floors, go-go cages, and 13 bar stations. An outside deck is the perfect cooling-off space. Live bands frequent the stages, and DJs rock the night away year-round.

Sly McFly's (700 Cannery Row, 831/649-8050, www.slymcflys.net, daily 11:30 A.M.–2 A.M., no cover) is one of the best venues for live music on Cannery Row, bringing in a wide variety of artists, some very well known, to play rock, blues, and soul seven nights a week. The stage is small, and the ambience is a little tired, but the music and the crowds spill out into the streets.

For a late-night brew, the **Cannery Row Brewing Company** (95 Prescott Ave., 831/643-2722, www.canneryrowbrewingcompany.com, 11 A.M.–11 P.M. Mon.–Thurs., 11 A.M.–midnight Fri.–Sun.) is a choice spot, with nearly 75 beers on tap and 25 in bottles. The industrial decor and concrete floors give it a bit of a rough feel; it can also be quite loud inside.

Live music on the weekends is on at **Captain Bullwackers Restaurant & Patio Pub** (653 Cannery Row, 831/373-1353, www.bullwackers.com, daily 11 A.M.–10:30 P.M. or later). Local bands play everything from reggae to rock and the blues. Inside is a full bar and restaurant.

Live bands rock the house Thursday–Saturday night at **Jose's Underground Lounge** (638 Wave St., 831/655-4419, daily 11 A.M.–10 P.M. or later). The inside or outdoor seating is intimate to listen to rock, punk, and indie jams, and there is a full bar mixing drinks along with beer on tap and by the bottle.

Theater

For live performances, check out the **Bruce Ariss Wharf Theatre** (Old Fisherman's Wharf 1, 831/649-2332, www.mctaweb.org, adults $25, under age 13 $10), which has been putting on lighthearted shows and musicals for 35 years, with occasional dramas and Broadway revues. Community-based shows

CENTRAL COAST

run Thursday–Friday evening with a Sunday matinee.

Festivals and Events

Come to the Monterey Bay Aquarium in late May for a food and wine adventure with **Cooking for Solutions** (831/644-7561, www.montereybayaquarium.org). World-renowned top chefs host live demonstrations in support of the aquarium's Seafood Watch program, and you get a chance to wander the aquarium's exhibits as you sample some fine sustainable dishes.

The annual **Monterey Wine Festival** (800/422-0251, www.montereywine.com) in early June has a number of tasting events, including a major event at the fairgrounds and a swank soiree at the Monterey Bay Aquarium. The festival offers the perfect introduction to Monterey and Carmel wineries, many of which have not yet made big news in wine circles.

In late June, blues lovers kick off summer with the **Monterey Bay Blues Festival** (Monterey County Fairgrounds, 831/394-2652, www.montereyblues.com), a three-day event with a sizzling lineup of artists from around the world. The large venue has multiple stages for varied entertainment and plenty of space to walk around.

At the end of July is one of the largest reggae festivals in California, **Monterey Bay Reggaefest** (831/394-6534, www.mbayreggaefest.net), held at the Monterey County Fairgrounds. More than 25 bands, including star performers, dancers, and dancehall acts, take to the stages. The event is a family-friendly celebration, with an entire area set aside for kids to play, including a bouncy house and a giant slide.

One of the biggest music festivals in California is the **Monterey Jazz Festival** (2000 Fairground Rd., 831/373-3366, www.montereyjazzfestival.org), which is also the longest-running jazz festival in the world. Concerts are held over a long weekend each September at the Monterey County Fairgrounds. Nine stages host acts day and night, making it easy to settle in for multiple acts or wander the grounds to sample performances at each venue.

SHOPPING

Like sardines in a can, **Cannery Row** (www.canneryrow.com) and Lighthouse Avenue are crammed with shopping possibilities. Shops include **Mackerel Jacks Trading Company** (799 Cannery Row, 831/655-2399, daily 9 A.M.–7:30 P.M.), carrying everything from treasure maps to books on local folklore; the **Cannery Row Antique Mall** (471 Wave St., 831/655-0264, 10 A.M.–5:30 P.M. Mon.–Fri., 10 A.M.–6 P.M. Sat., 10 A.M.–5 P.M. Sun.), with 150 vendors in a massive two-story warehouse; and **Monterey Bay Boatworks Company** (400 Cannery Row, 831/643-9482, daily 10 A.M.–7 P.M.) with resort wear.

Book Buyers (600 Lighthouse Ave., 831/375-4208, www.bookbuyers.com) is one of the last independent used bookstores in the area, with more than 30,000 titles in hardbacks and paperbacks.

Officially known as Alvarado Mall, **The Portola Plaza Mall** (Portola Plaza and Alvarado St.) has many specialty shops in the open air on either side of the promenade. There are several independent clothing stores, jewelry shops, art galleries, wine and gift shops, restaurants, brewpubs, a spa, and more. Many of the shops are independent.

ACCOMMODATIONS
Under $100

The **Monterey Hostel** (778 Hawthorne St., 831/649-0375, http://montereyhostel.com, $23–64) offers inexpensive accommodations within walking distance of the aquarium, Cannery Row, and the Monterey Bay Coastal Bike Trail. Rates include a pancake breakfast every morning, linens are included with your bed, and there are casual common spaces with couches, musical instruments, and monthly potluck dinners with guest speakers. There's no laundry on-site, and the dorms can be crowded, so if you like a little space, opt for a private room.

In downtown Monterey is a European-style property updated with a turn-of-the-20th-century ambiance. The **Monterey Hotel** (406 Alvarado St., 831/375-3184, www.monterey-hotel.com, $89–309) was built in 1904 and is furnished with pieces from that era; the guest rooms and suites have also been lavishly restored.

Offering guests amenities a cut above a standard beach-town motel is the **Colton Inn** (707 Pacific St., 831/649-6500, www.coltoninn.com, $99–279), located in the middle of downtown Monterey. The queen and king guest rooms boast attractive fabrics, designer baths, and pretty appointments. While you'll find restaurants and historic adobe buildings adjacent to the Colton, expect to drive or take public transit to Cannery Row and the aquarium.

$100-150

A historic hotel in the center of downtown is the **⊂ Casa Munras Hotel and Spa** (700 Munras Ave., 831/375-2411, www.hotelcasa-munras.com, $129–449), a beautifully restored building and one of the sights on the Path of History. There is an outdoor heated pool, a fitness center, and bikes available to borrow. Look forward to relaxing after a long day of exploration at the spa and restaurant.

$150-250

Be sure to call in advance to get a room at the popular **Jabberwock Inn** (598 Laine St., 831/372-4777, www.jabberwockinn.com, $169–299), a favorite with frequent visitors to Monterey. This *Alice in Wonderland*–themed B&B is both whimsical and elegant; expect to find a copy of an *Alice* novel in your tastefully appointed guest room. Be sure to take the owners up on their daily wine-and-cheese reception in the afternoon—they have extensive information about the area and will be happy to recommend restaurants and activities for all

tastes. Although it is located up a steep hill, the Jabberwock is within walking distance of Cannery Row and its adjacent attractions.

Guest rooms at the European-style **Spindrift Inn** (652 Cannery Row, 831/646-8900, www.insofmonterey.com, $199–459) are cozy and have wood-burning fireplaces and king canopy beds. Enjoy the nightly wine-and-cheese reception that features local wines before you head out for the evening.

Minutes from Monterey's primary attractions is the **Hotel Pacific** (300 Pacific St., 831/373-5700, www.hotelpacific.com, $159–429). All the guest rooms are luxurious suites with fireplaces in an authentic Spanish-style adobe. With its lovely gardens, it may exceed your expectations, and it is one of the few pet-friendly hotels on the peninsula.

Although the **⊂ Portola Hotel** (2 Portola Plaza, 831/649-4511, www.portolahotel.com, $189–550) is a big hotel, it feels smaller. About 40 percent of its 379 guest rooms offer prime views of the bay. There is also an on-site fitness room, a large round outdoor pool, and a hot tub. The hotel is conveniently located between downtown and Cannery Row. The guest rooms and baths are large and comfortable, with in-room coffeemakers and fridges on request. Many packages include local restaurants and attractions, but parking and Wi-Fi cost extra.

Over $250

You'll pay handsomely to stay right on Cannery Row overlooking the bay, but it's worth it at the **Monterey Plaza Hotel & Spa** (400 Cannery Row, 831/646-1700, www.montereyplazaho-tel.com, $250–3,500). The atmosphere is traditionally elegant and comfortable, and views of the ocean are the centerpiece. Guest rooms are spacious, and many have ocean views and balconies. There is a relaxing spa and four restaurants on-site.

The **InterContinental Clement Monterey** (750 Cannery Row, 831/375-4500, www.

ichotelsgroup.com, $250–1,300) is a comfortable minimalist hideaway. The modernist Asian-inspired interior belies the pragmatic Cannery Row exterior. There are 110 guest rooms on the bay side and another 98 on the inland side, connected by a covered walking bridge. The furnishings are clean and sleek—every guest room has its own orchid. The hotel has a full-service spa, a Kids Club with supervised day care, and a covered garage.

Visitors looking for elegant accommodations will love the ◖**Old Monterey Inn** (500 Martin St., 831/375-8284, www.oldmontereyinn.com, $250–449). The lovely old building stands in mature gardens that bloom all spring and summer, showing their sedate green side in fall and winter. Inside, the garden motif is echoed in the upscale bed linens and window treatments that complement the pretty furnishings and cozy fireplaces. Spa bathtubs pamper guests. Additional amenities include a full breakfast (often served in the garden) and a menu of spa treatments that can be enjoyed downstairs in the serene treatment room.

CAMPING

Within the City of Monterey are a few out-of-the-way campgrounds that welcome tents, RVs, and trailers. **Monterey Veteran's Memorial Park** (Veterans Dr. and Skyline Dr., 831/646-3865, www.monterey.org, first-come, first-served, $27) is located one mile up the hill from Cannery Row and Fisherman's Wharf in a quiet spot with wide views of the bay. Within the 50-acre park are hiking trails, a playground, a basketball court, picnic areas, barbecue pits, lawn areas, restrooms, and a dump station.

A little-known spot to park the RV with full hookups is the **Monterey County Fairgrounds RV Camping** (2004 Fairgrounds Rd., 831/372-5863, www.montereycountyfair.com, $40), a lovely spot if you're coming for an event at the fairgrounds or just want to get away from the crowds.

FOOD
Cannery Row and Old Fisherman's Wharf

For coffee, espresso, and beignets, head to the delightful **Trailside Café** (550 Wave St., 831/649-8600, www.trailsidecafe.com, daily 8 A.M.–4 P.M., $15–20). This Cannery Row restaurant offers breakfast, lunch, and dinner on a heated patio overlooking the bay. **Jacks** (2 Portola Plaza, 831/649-2698, www.portolahotel.com, daily 6–10:30 A.M., 11:30 A.M.–2 P.M., and 5–9 P.M., $30) is located in the Portola Plaza Hotel and serves up a fresh California coastal fare with sustainable ingredients. Dine fireside on the outdoor patio or enjoy the nautically themed interior.

Indulge in authentic Breton-style French crepes on Old Fisherman's Wharf at **Crepes of Brittany** (6B Old Fisherman's Wharf 1, 831/601-4847, www.vivelacrepemonterey.com, daily 8:30 A.M.–about 4 P.M., $10). Whether it's sweet or savory, they are made to satisfy. A tropical Hawaiian fusion restaurant in the heart of Monterey, **Hula's Island Grill** (622 Lighthouse Ave., 831/655-4852, www.hulastiki.com, 11:30 A.M.–4 P.M. Tues.–Sat., from 4:30 P.M. Sun.–Mon., $30) is known for featuring island fish, prime steaks, juicy burgers, and creative salads. There is a full bar featuring fruity cocktails that come with a heavy punch.

A must-stop is ◖**The Sardine Factory** (701 Wave St., 831/373-3775, www.sardinefactory.com, daily 5 P.M.–midnight, $40–50). There are several dining rooms: The Captain's Room pays tribute to brave sailors, the Conservancy is a glass room surrounded by greenery, and the Wine Cellar is the more exclusive private dining room downstairs. The abalone bisque is a must, and the fish entrées—such as Alaskan salmon topped with artichoke hearts and hollandaise sauce—are tremendous. The Sardine Factory has also received many awards for its impressive wine list.

From rolls to *nigiri* and sashimi, the sushi at

Crystal Fish (514 Lighthouse Ave., 831/649-3474, lunch 11:30 A.M.–2 P.M. Mon.–Fri., dinner daily 5–9 P.M., $25) is fresh and artfully prepared and served. There is a selection of vegetarian rolls as well as noodles and tempura. The *bento* boxes provide a nice sampling of everything.

For some fine steaks and seafood, make reservations at the **Whaling Station Restaurant** (763 Wave St., 831/373-3778, www.whalingstationmonterey.com, dinner daily 5–9:30 P.M., $35–45). The Whaling Station is famous for its beautiful thick cuts of meat. John Pisto, an international chef, brings his talents to Monterey with a casually sophisticated dining experience.

With a fresh Italian spin on seafood with prime steaks, **Domenico's on the Wharf** (50 Fisherman's Wharf, 831/372-3655, www.domenicosmonterey.com, daily 10:30 A.M.–10 P.M., $30) is all about the panoramic view of the harbor. It features locally caught seafood and fresh local produce from the owner's farm.

Downtown Monterey

Housed in an old firehouse, **C Montrio** (414 Calle Principal, 831/648-8880, www.montrio.com, daily 4:30 P.M.–close, $15–20) has high ceilings, graceful curved walls, and custom lighting. The menu emphasizes local sustainable and organic food in dishes like artichoke ravioli, seared scallops, rosemary-roasted portobello mushrooms, and the legendary crab cakes. It gets very busy and so can be noisy; reservations are recommended.

Locals love the family atmosphere of **Rosines Restaurant** (434 Alvarado St., 831/375-1400, www.rosinesmonterey.com, daily 8 A.M.–9 P.M., $10–15), the place for large plates and a menu that has a bit of everything. Don't leave without sharing a piece of the mile-high cake.

R.G. Burgers (570 Munras Ave., 831/372-4930, www.rgburgers.com, daily 11 A.M.–8 P.M., $15) is a good old American burger joint. Order a frosty shake and a double cheeseburger, or try

one of the more creative combinations from the all-embracing menu. The setting is comfortable, and the dress is casual.

Around the corner is the **East Village Coffee Lounge** (498 Washington St., 831/373-5601, daily 7 A.M.–9 P.M., $7), which has a comfortable lounge vibe as well as outdoor seating. There are plenty of coffee and tea drinks; pastry options include a tasty and moist chocolate scone and organic peach coffeecake. Parfaits, ham-and-cheese croissants, and tomato and basil *paninis* are also available. Free Wi-Fi means lots of laptops.

About as British as it gets in downtown Monterey is the **Crown and Anchor** (150 W. Franklin St., 831/649-6496, www.crownandanchor.net, daily 11 A.M.–2 A.M., $12), located below street level. Twenty British and international beers are on tap to complement lamb shanks, cottage pie, corned beef and cabbage, and, of course, fish-and-chips.

Visit **Paris Bakery** (271 Bonifacio Place, 831/646-1620, daily 6 A.M.–6 P.M., $8) for real French pastries, just the place to jump-start your morning with an espresso and a stuffed croissant. They also serve a fast lunch that you can take to go, or eat in the bustling café.

Tantalize your taste buds at the lunch buffet at **Ambrosia Indian Bistro** (565 Abrego St., 831/641-0610, www.ambrosiaib.com, daily 11:30 A.M.–close, $10, Sun. lunch buffet $12), one of the best deals in town. Regular dishes include flavorful butter chicken and tandoori chicken; vegetarians will find many options.

Three blocks of Alvarado Street close to traffic for the **Old Monterey Market Place** (Alvarado St., 831/655-8070, www.oldmonterey.org, 4–8 P.M. Tues. summer, 4–7 P.M. Tues. winter). The street fills with an organic rainbow of vendors and shoppers with over 150 stands lining the street. Produce vendors from all over California have sold their certified organic goods here, rain or shine, since 1991.

CENTRAL COAST

INFORMATION AND SERVICES

In Monterey, the **El Estero Visitors Center** (401 Camino El Estero, 877/666-8373, www.montereyinfo.org, 9 A.M.–6 P.M. Mon.–Sat., 9 A.M.–5 P.M. Sun. summer, 9 A.M.–5 P.M. Mon.–Sat., 10 A.M.–4 P.M. Sun. winter) is the local outlet of the Monterey Country Convention and Visitors Bureau. They put out a comprehensive annual guide to Monterey County; you can download the guide from the website or call the office to have one mailed.

The local newspaper is the *Monterey County Herald* (www.montereyherald.com), a daily that has a weekly Go section featuring all the current local happenings. The *Monterey County Weekly* (www.montereycountyweekly.com) is the alternative paper for area happenings, with a Club Grind section and a daily events calendar. **Post offices** are located at 565 Hartnell Street and at 686 Lighthouse Avenue.

The **Community Hospital of the Monterey Peninsula** (23625 Hwy. 68/Holman Hwy., 831/624-5311) provides emergency services to the area. Open daily 24 hours is the **Monterey Police Department** (3151 Madison St., 831/646-3914). In case of emergency, dial 911.

GETTING THERE AND AROUND

Air

The small and convenient **Monterey Peninsula Airport** (MRY, 200 Fred Kane Dr., 831/648-7000, www.montereyairport.com) has service by United, Allegiant, American Eagle, and America West along with car-rental companies. Taxi service is available through Central Coast Taxi (831/626-3333), or hire a limo through Arrow Luxury Transportation (831/646-3175).

San Jose International Airport (SJC, 2077 Airport Blvd., San Jose, 408/277-4859, www.sjc.org) is about 90 minutes inland along U.S. 101 in Silicon Valley. Major U.S. airlines serve this airport, and there are flights to Mexico as well. Hop on the Monterey-Salinas Air Bus (831/373-7777, http://montereyairbus.com,

$30–40) from San Jose Airport to Monterey, or rent a car from one of the many providers.

Train

For a more leisurely ride, **Amtrak**'s Seattle–Los Angeles *Coast Starlight* train travels through Salinas (Station Place and Railroad Ave., Salinas, daily 8 A.M.–10 P.M.) daily in both directions. For Amtrak travelers, there is free bus service (30 minutes) to downtown Monterey.

Bus

Monterey-Salinas Transit (MST, 831/899-2555, www.mst.org) runs buses in both Monterey and Santa Cruz Counties. Express route 55 (2.25 hours, one-way $5, round-trip $10) runs Monterey–San Jose. If you're coming to Monterey from Salinas, take route 20 (50 minutes, $1–2).

Downtown at the end of Alvarado Street is the **Monterey Transit Plaza,** where you can pick up a full bus schedule; view bus routes, fares, and timetables on the Monterey-Salinas Transit website (www.mst.org). Exact change is required on buses, and fares range $1.50–2. Once you're in Monterey, take advantage of the free **WAVE Trolley** (daily 9 A.M.–7:30 P.M. Memorial Day–Labor Day), which loops between downtown Monterey and the aquarium.

Car

Most visitors drive to Monterey via the scenic Highway 1. From the Bay Area (1.5 hours), take U.S. 101 south to Highway 156 west. Turn south at Highway 1 toward the Monterey Peninsula. From San Francisco (2.5 hours), another option is to take U.S. 101 south to San Jose, then Highway 85 south, and then Highway 17 south toward Santa Cruz. Eventually you merge on to Highway 1 heading south to Monterey.

PACIFIC GROVE

Pacific Grove, also known as "Butterfly Town USA," is one of the hidden gems of the Monterey Peninsula. This small town has

CENTRAL COAST

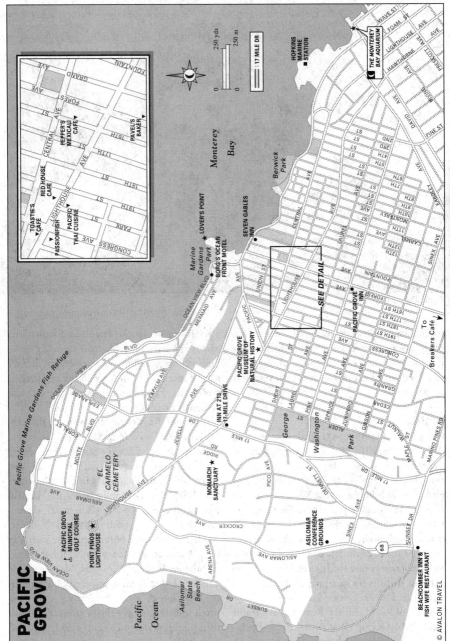

PACIFIC GROVE

Monterey Bay

Pacific Ocean

Pacific Grove Marine Gardens Fish Refuge

THE MONTEREY BAY AQUARIUM

HOPKINS MARINE STATION

WAVE ST
FOAM ST
LIGHTHOUSE AVE
HAWTHORNE
PRESCOTT AVE

Berwick Park

Marine Gardens Park

LOVER'S POINT

SEVEN GABLES INN

BORG'S OCEAN FRONT MOTEL

SEE DETAIL

PACIFIC GROVE INN

PACIFIC GROVE MUSEUM OF NATURAL HISTORY

EL CARMELO CEMETERY

INN AT 213 17-MILE DRIVE

MONARCH SANCTUARY

George Washington Park

ASILOMAR CONFERENCE GROUNDS

Asilomar State Beach

PACIFIC GROVE MUNICIPAL GOLF COURSE

POINT PINOS LIGHTHOUSE

BEACHCOMBER INN & FISH WIFE RESTAURANT

To Breakers Café

OCEAN VIEW BLVD
ASILOMAR AVE
CORAL ST
MONTE AVE
OCEAN VIEW BLVD
SEA PALM AVE
ESPLANADE
JEWELL AVE
LIGHTHOUSE AVE
17 MILE DR
RIDGE RD
PICO AVE
CROCKER AVE
ARENA AVE
ASILOMAR AVE
SINEX AVE
DEWMETT ST
17 MILE DR
SUNSET DR
MARINO PINES RD
MAPLE ST
WALNUT ST
GIBSON AVE
CEDAR
GRANITE
CONGRESS
19TH ST
18TH ST
17TH ST
16TH ST
15TH ST
FOUNTAIN AVE
FOREST AVE
LIGHTHOUSE
UNION ST
PINE
SPRUCE
JUNIPERO
ALDER
LAUREL
SHORT ST
PACIFIC
MERMAID AVE
CENTRAL AVE
LAUREL AVE
CARMEL AVE
12TH ST
13TH ST
11TH ST
10TH ST
9TH ST
8TH ST
7TH ST
6TH ST
5TH ST
4TH ST
3RD ST
2ND ST
PINE ST
DAVID AVE
FORGE AVE
RAMSEY AVE
SINEX AVE
MONTEREY AVE

68

N

0   250 yds
0   250 m

: 17 MILE DR

Inset (detail map):

GRAND AVE
FOUNTAIN AVE
FOREST AVE
CENTRAL AVE
CONGRESS AVE
PARK ST
LIGHTHOUSE
17TH ST
16TH ST
15TH ST
14TH ST
13TH ST
12TH ST
11TH ST

PEPPER'S MEXICALI CAFE
PAVEL'S BAKERY
RED HOUSE CAFE
TOASTIE'S CAFE
PASSIONFISH
PACIFIC THAI CUISINE

© AVALON TRAVEL

© KRISTIN LEAL

Point Piños Lighthouse

special attractions, including a monarch butterfly sanctuary, golf fairways on the ocean, a historical lighthouse, museums, and shopping, to fill a day and tempt you to extend your stay for a weekend.

Sights

Point Piños Lighthouse (Lighthouse Ave. and Asilomar Ave., 831/648-3176, www.ci.pg.ca.us/lighthouse, 1–4 P.M. Thurs.–Mon., $5 donation) has operated since 1855 and is the oldest extant lighthouse on the West Coast. The U.S. Coast Guard is in charge of the light, and volunteers operate the day-use facilities. Inside is a restored model of the living conditions of Emily Fish, one of the few women who worked as lighthouse keeper in that era. The original bathtub still sits on its sturdy metal feet, and the tea set Fish once owned is stored inside.

Located near Cannery Row, **Lovers Point Park** (630 Ocean View Blvd., daily dawn–dusk) offers views of Monterey to the right, Pacific Grove to the left, and Santa Cruz across the bay. There's access to sandy coves and stunning granite rock formations, and it's a great spot for a picnic. A walking and cycling path leads to the Monterey Bay Aquarium and Asilomar State Beach.

The **Pacific Grove Museum of Natural History** (165 Forest Ave., 831/648-5716, www.pgmuseum.org, 10 A.M.–5 P.M. Tues.–Sun., $3–5 donation) displays native wildlife and local plants in the botanical gardens. With more than 100 native plants and a "spirit nest" (a giant bird's nest created by a Big Sur artist), there is enough to entertain both adults and children.

Majestic monarch butterflies make their way to the **Monarch Sanctuary** (end of Ridge Rd. off Lighthouse Ave.) early November–late February. The fog-shrouded eucalyptus and pine forest is the best place to watch these magnificent creatures, and the trees seem to come alive with their fluttering wings. Docents offer free guided tours (831/648-5716, www.pgmuseum.org, daily

Pacific Grove is known as "Butterfly Town U.S.A."

noon–3 P.M. peak season, noon–3 P.M. Sat.–Sun. off-season) during the migration season, providing a behind-the-scenes look at the butterflies and answering questions.

Entertainment and Events

The Pacific Grove **Wildflower Show** (165 Forest Ave., 831/648-5716, www.pgmuseum.org, Apr. 15–17) is the largest in the Central Coast region. Growers bring more than 600 species for public display both inside and outside the museum.

The **Butterfly Criterium** (Lighthouse Ave., www.ghosttreeracing.com, May) is a 1970s Prestige Classic bicycle race, perfect for a weekend getaway before the summer rush. Spend your time watching the races during some of the best weather of the year.

The holiday season is a big deal in Pacific Grove, and there are several celebrations and extravagant decorations. Through the holiday season, residents along several streets transform their front yards into winter wonderlands for

Candy Cane Lane (bounded by Beaumont Dr. and Morse Dr.). The **Parade of Lights** (downtown, 831/373-3304, www.pacificgrove. org, Dec. 1) is an annual event with marching bands, holiday floats, dance teams, equestrian groups, and, of course, Santa Claus. Kids will enjoy the carolers, wagon rides, and a chance to meet Santa. Stores remain open, with plenty of gifts for sale.

Shopping

You'll find a trove of antiques at **Trotters Antiques** (590 Lighthouse Ave., 831/373-3505, 11 A.M.–5 P.M. Mon.–Sat.). Owner Lee Trotter has been in the business for 46 years, and her reputation for delivering unique finds is impeccable. **Pacific Grove Antiques** (472 Lighthouse Ave., 831/658-0488, daily 10 A.M.–5 P.M.) carries unique vintage furnishing and accessories on two floors, with a separate outdoor garden shop known as the **Trellis Garden Market** (472 Lighthouse Ave., 831/375-1115). Overflowing with antiques, **Blessings Boutique** (620 Lighthouse Ave., 831/641-0813, daily 10 A.M.–5 P.M.) specializes in local art, seaside souvenirs, and vintage furnishings.

Sunstudios (208 Forest Ave., 831/373-7989, daily 9 A.M.–5 P.M.) features a collection of artwork, crafts, and jewelry handcrafted by local artisans. **The Works** (667 Lighthouse Ave., 831/372-2242, www.theworkspg.com, 7 A.M.–6 P.M. Mon.–Sat.) is one of the last local bookstores, a hip place to pick up some hot beverages, purchase local art, and catch some live entertainment.

Sports and Recreation

The place for the fearless to catch the big waves is at **Lovers Point** (630 Ocean View Blvd.). The surf breaks near the rugged coastline, and some navigation skills are definitely required. This spot offers an intense rush, and the waves, rated moderate–hard, are among the most massive on the peninsula. In winter the waves are huge and epic. A nice location where the surf is almost always up is at **Asilomar State Beach** (south end of Sunset Dr. near Asilomar Blvd., 831/646-6440, www.parks.ca.gov, free) in Pacific Grove. The breakers are continuous, and the ride is moderate. The wide beach has a nice cove to walk along, and you can hang out all day. Parking is limited to the street, so check the tide table and arrive early.

Tee time in Pacific Grove is dreamy and an affordable alternative to Pebble Beach. **Pacific Grove Municipal Golf Links** (77 Asilomar Blvd., 831/648-5775, www.pggolflinks.com, day $40–48, twilight $20–25) is an 18-hole par-70 course with a Scottish links experience. Views on the back nine are incredible as the salty shoreline and Point Piños Lighthouse come into sight, and the greens seem to extend nearly into the surf.

Get geared up for great paddling on Pacific Grove's shores at **Adventures by the Sea** (Lovers Point Park, 831/372-1807, www.

adventuresbythesea.com, daily 9 A.M.–sunset, $30 pp), offering single and double kayaks to explore the coves of Asilomar, the back of the aquarium, Cannery Row, and Monterey Harbor. Along the rocky shoreline you'll see spotted harbor seals, sea otters, and may even catch sight of migrating whales.

The **Monterey Bay Coastal Bike Trail** runs to Pebble Beach and 17-Mile Drive, with countless coves, beach access, and tide-pools along the way. The trail is mostly flat with a few small hills that are barely noticeable. Bikes can be rented at Lovers Point Park through **Adventures by the Sea** (Lovers Point Park, 831/372-1807, www. adventuresbythesea.com, daily 9 A.M.–sunset, $7 per hour, half day $20, full day $25).

Accommodations

Just across the street from the ocean is the █ **Borg's Ocean Front Motel** (635 Ocean View Blvd., 831/375-2406, www.borgsoceanfrontmotel.com, $65–165). The views from the guest rooms are breathtaking, Lovers Point Park is nearby, and the Monterey Bay Coastal Bike Trail is steps from your guest room. The rates, the view, and the location are hard to beat.

Pacific Grove Inn (581 Pine Ave., 831/375-2825, www.pacificgroveinn.com, $119–379) is a romantic bed-and-breakfast blending Old World charm with modern-day luxury. There are 16 guest rooms and suites, many with ocean views. Wine and cheese is served daily, as are cookies and milk before bedtime.

Designed by architect Julia Morgan of Hearst Castle fame, █ **Asilomar Conference Grounds** (800 Asilomar Ave., 888/635-5310, www.visitasilomar.com, $175–750) was originally commissioned as a YWCA by Phoebe Apperson, William Randolph Hearst's mother. The original 65 guest rooms, built between 1913 and 1928, are small and face an outdoor courtyard. Built separately from the original structure, 259 larger, more modern guest rooms are Spartan, with no telephones or TVs.

There is an outdoor pool and Wi-Fi in the common areas along with a business center. A park ranger offers campfire talks in the early evenings. It's a short walk across the dunes to the beach in Pacific Grove.

The woodwork is spectacular at the **Inn at 213 Seventeen Mile Drive** (213 17-Mile Dr., 800/526-5666, www.innat17.com, $200–280 d), a classic craftsman home built in 1925. There are four upstairs guest rooms in the house, with an additional 10 in the separate coach house. Breakfast is served at 9 A.M., and evening wine and hors d'oeuvres are served at 5 P.M., all prepared by a Cordon Bleu–trained chef. The guest rooms are large, each with its own theme. Parking is off-street, and other amenities include Wi-Fi and a small hot tub in the garden.

The **Seven Gables Inn** (555 Ocean View Blvd., 831/372-4341, www.thesevengablesinn.com, $199–559) is a massive bed-and-breakfast on the shores of Monterey Bay. Every guest room has scenic ocean views, and a walk along the shore is only steps away.

Food

There are plenty of good eats in Pacific Grove. **The Red House Café** (662 Lighthouse Ave., 831/643-1060, 11 A.M.–2:30 P.M. and 5 P.M.–close Tues.–Fri., 8–11 A.M. and 5 P.M.–close Sat.–Sun., $20) offers New American cuisine with a European flavor and a strong emphasis on fresh, seasonal ingredients. Order a locally brewed Sparkies Root Beer; it packs a bite.

The moment you walk into **Pacific Thai Cuisine** (633 Lighthouse Ave., 831/646-8424, www.pacificthaicuisine.com, 11 A.M.–3 P.M. and 5 P.M.–close Mon.–Thurs., 11:30 A.M.–close Fri.–Sun., $20–30), the aroma will make your mouth water. This is the top stop for Thai iced tea and red curry, and the chicken satay and scrumptious salads are great starters.

There is nothing fancy about **Toasties Café** (702 Lighthouse Ave., 831/373-7543, 6:30 A.M.–3 P.M. Mon.–Sat., 7 A.M.–2 P.M.

Sun., $12), but the food is very good, and the line out the door speaks for itself.

Before an early morning surf at Asilomar State Beach, stop for a bite at **Breakers Café** (1126 Forest Ave., 831/375-8484, daily 7:30 A.M.–2 P.M., $8–12), a local favorite. Traditional breakfast and lunch café favorites are served in sizable portions.

Visit **Pavel's Bakery** (219 Forest Ave., 831/643-2636, daily 6:30 A.M.–2:30 P.M., $5) for a steaming cup of coffee as well as savory and sweet treats. Get here early, as the display case gets picked over by noon.

Grab a table early to dine with the locals at **Peppers MexiCali Café** (170 Forest Ave., 831/373-6892, 11:30 A.M.–9 P.M. Mon.–Thurs., 11:30 A.M.–10 P.M. Fri.–Sat., 4–9 P.M. Sun., $15). The decor is Southwestern, and the food is Latin American with an emphasis on seafood. Everything is made in-house with a spicy pepper kick.

There's no need to pull out your *Seafood Watch* card at **◖Passionfish** (701 Lighthouse Ave., 831/655-3311, www.passionfish.net, daily 5 P.M.–close, $30) as they pride themselves on serving only sustainable seafood. The menu changes regularly as Chef Ted Walter and his wife, Cindy, choose the finest ingredients according to local harvests.

The flavor of the **◖ Fish Wife** (1996½ Sunset Dr., 831/375-7107, www.fishwife.com, daily 11 A.M.–9 P.M., $12–25) is all California seafood with a twist of the Caribbean. The chef uses local produce from the Salinas Valley to present colorful daily specials, seafood, and pasta dishes. The atmosphere is casual, and there is a full bar.

Information and Services

A quick stop at the **Pacific Grove Chamber of Commerce** (Forest Ave. and Central Ave., 831/373-3304, www.pacificgrove.org, 9:30 A.M.–5 P.M. Mon.–Fri.) and the **Tourist Information Center** (100 Central Ave.,

831/373-3304, www.pacificgrove.org, daily 10 A.M.–5 P.M.) will get you a rundown on all the attractions of Pacific Grove. The **U.S. Post Office** (680 Lighthouse Ave., 831/373-2271) is centrally located.

For medical needs, the **Community Hospital of the Monterey Peninsula** (CHOMP, 23625 Hwy. 68/Holman Hwy., 831/624-5311) provides emergency services in the area. The main office of the **Pacific Grove Police Department** (580 Pine Ave., 831/648-3143) is open daily 24 hours.

Getting There and Around

There are two ways to enter Pacific Grove. Take Highway 1 to Highway 68 heading northwest to Sunset Boulevard; or get off at Highway 1's "Monterey Aquarium" exit and follow the signs to Cannery Row and the Monterey Bay Aquarium, where you will eventually run into Ocean View Boulevard in Pacific Grove. Alternately, once you reach Lighthouse Avenue, stay on it; it runs through both Monterey and Pacific Grove.

PEBBLE BEACH

While Pebble Beach's reputation is all about its championship golf course, there's more to this small unincorporated town than golf greens and sand traps. Some of the main attractions include picturesque 17-Mile Drive, the famed Lone Cypress, the multitude of multimillion-dollar homes, an extensive equestrian center, and, of course, the renowned golf courses.

The 17-Mile Drive

The 17-Mile Drive (starts at Sunset Dr./Hwy. 68, Pacific Grove, www.pebblebeach.com, daily sunrise–sunset, no motorcycles, cars $10) offers some of the most beautiful views on the Central Coast. Long ago, the locally all-powerful Pebble Beach Corporation realized what a precious commodity this road was and began charging a toll. The good news is that when you pay your fee at the gatehouse, you'll get a map of the drive

the Lone Cypress on 17-Mile Drive

© KRISTIN LEAL

that describes the parks and sights that you pass. These include the much-photographed Lone Cypress, the beaches of Spanish Bay, and Pebble Beach's golf course, resort, and housing complex. There are plenty of turn-outs where you can stop to take photos of the stunning ocean and the iconic cypress trees. You can picnic at many of the formal beaches, most of which have basic restroom facilities and ample parking lots. The only food and gas are at the Inn at Spanish Bay and the Lodge at Pebble Beach.

The best time to view this scenic seascape is at dusk, when the pinks of the fading sun accent the blues of the ocean. If you're in a hurry, you can get from one end of 17-Mile Drive to the other in 20 minutes—but that would defeat the main purpose the drive, which is to enjoy the beauty of the area. If you take your time and bring a picnic, it will take about two hours. The best picnic spots are between Point Joe and Seal Rock.

Golf Courses

Golf has been a major pastime here since the late 19th century, and today avid golfers come from around the world to tee off beside the ocean. Pebble Beach is home to five golf courses, with the Pebble Beach Company running four of them.

The 18-hole, par-72 **Pebble Beach Golf Links** (The Lodge at Pebble Beach, 1700 17-Mile Dr., 831/622-8723, $495, cart rental included for guests) is the priciest fairway in the county and what many consider to be the best course in the country. You can feel the energy of golf's greats, who have played here since 1919. Events include the annual AT&T Pebble Beach National Pro-Am and five U.S. Open Championships, with a return engagement scheduled for 2019.

One of the Pebble Beach Resort courses, the 18-hole par-72 **Spyglass Hill** (1700 17-Mile Dr., 800/654-9300, www.pebblebeach.com, $360, cart rental included for guests) gets its

CENTRAL COAST

© KRISTIN LEAL

Pebble Beach Golf Links

name from the Robert Louis Stevenson novel *Treasure Island*. But don't be fooled—the holes on this beautiful course may be named for children's characters, but that doesn't mean they're easy. Spyglass Hill boasts some of the most challenging play in the course-laden Carmel region. Expect a few bogeys, and tee off from the Championship level at your ego's own risk.

Designed in the image of true Scottish play from over 500 years ago is the 18-hole par-72 **Links at Spanish Bay** (The Inn at Spanish Bay, 2700 17-Mile Dr., 800/654-9300, www.pebblebeach.com, $260, cart rental included for guests). A bagpiper closes each evening with whimsical music, and the greens will impress. You'll have to hit your ball in a steady breeze; the Scottish term *links* actually means a sandy wasteland near the sea with bristly grasses and ever-prevailing winds.

The best deal and the easiest course in Pebble Beach is the nine-hole par-27 **Peter Hay Golf Course** (The Lodge at Pebble Beach, 1700 17-Mile Dr., 831/622-8723, www.pebblebeach.com, adults $30, ages 13–17 $10, under age 13 free with an adult). This is the place to take the kids for a lesson. It is the only public course on the peninsula, and it could not be in a better location; it is a good spot to work on your short game.

Another favorite with the golf crowd is the famed 18-hole par-72 **Poppy Hills Golf Course** (3200 Lopez Rd., 831/622-8239, www.poppyhillsgolf.com, day $200, twilight $65). Although it's not managed by the same company, Poppy Hills shares amenities with Pebble Beach golf courses, so you can expect the same level of care and devotion to the maintenance of the course and your experience as a player. If you're looking to improve your game, check out the two-day program that gets you onto both Poppy and Spyglass Hill for a chance to pick up some new skills and enjoy the incidentally gorgeous views.

Entertainment and Events

Held in mid-April, the **Pebble Beach Food &** **Wine** (26364 Carmel Rancho Lane, 800/907-3663, www.pebblebeachfoodandwine.com) has become the predominant culinary event between Los Angeles and San Francisco. Master chefs and high-end winemakers from across the nation converge on Pebble Beach for a three-day celebration of eating and drinking with cooking demonstrations, wine symposia, and vertical tastings of rare vintages, all against the gorgeous backdrop of Pebble Beach.

During the first two weeks of August, the **Concours d'Elegance** (1700 17-Mile Dr., www.pebblebeachconcours.net) celebrates the automobile. Hundreds of cars congregate on the 18th green at Pebble Beach, while others line the streets of Carmel. This is one of the largest events in the area, second only to the Monterey Jazz Festival, with nearly 10,000 people swamping the hamlet of Carmel. Plan well in advance, as getting reservations anywhere during this time is nearly impossible.

There are three major annual golf events at Pebble Beach that bring in the pros, celebrities, and up-and-coming juniors. The **AT&T Pebble Beach National Pro Am** (1700 17-Mile Dr., www.pebblebeach.com) in early February brings professional team talent to the greens. The second event is the **First Tee Open at Pebble Beach** (Peter Hay Golf Course, 1700 17-Mile Dr., www.pebblebeach.com) in early July, which brings past champions to the peninsula to golf alongside up-and-coming juniors. The **Callaway Pebble Beach Invitational** (1700 17-Mile Dr., www.pebblebeach.com) in mid-November is a unique tournament that brings together professionals from PGA, LPGA, Championships, and National Tours for fierce competition.

Accommodations

Pebble Beach has three elegant resorts with legendary service. At **The Inn at Spanish Bay** (1700 17-Mile Dr., 831/647-7500, Pebble Beach, www.pebblebeach.com, $595–3,450), take in views of the golf course with the ocean as the backdrop in the secluded bay. The decor is contemporary, and the accommodations are lavish. All guest rooms feature fireplaces, modern baths, included wireless Internet access, and flat-panel TVs. The magnificent and spacious suites come in five styles, with the Presidential suite the most luxurious.

The place to stay for ultimate decadence is 《The Lodge at Pebble Beach (1700 17-Mile Dr., 831/647-7500, www.pebblebeach.com, $675–3,275). The lodge has been legendary since opening in 1919; guest rooms and suites feature private patios or balconies, fireplaces, flat-panel TVs, plush towels, and fine linens.

Just beyond the lodge entrance is **Casa Palmero Pebble Beach** (1700 17-Mile Dr., 831/622-6650, www.pebblebeach.com, $845–2,750), an estate with the flair of Mediterranean architecture. There are 24 suites, a heated outdoor pool, a billiards room, and a library. Views overlook the Pebble Beach golf courses. Each guest room has a fireplace, an oversize soaking tub, and heavenly mattresses.

Food

Pebble Beach has a handful of dining options at The Inn at Spanish Bay and The Pebble Beach Lodge. The Lodge at Pebble Beach (1700 17-Mile Dr.) has four restaurants. The **Stillwater Grill** (831/625-8524, www.pebblebeach.com, daily breakfast, lunch, and dinner, $30) serves sizzling sustainable seafood and organic produce. At **The Tap Room** (831/625-8535, www.pebblebeach.com, $40–60) you will find a classic American-style tavern open for dinner and late-night dining. Fill up on tasty spirits and fine cuts of meat after a day of golf. The **Gallery Café** (831/625-8577, www.pebblebeach.com, daily breakfast and lunch, $12) is a cheaper place for home-style meals in a casual atmosphere; expect burgers, deli sandwiches, and the best milk shake in town. **The Terrance Lounge** (831/625-8524, www.pebblebeach.

com, daily) is the place to congregate for cocktails and close conversation. Come in to enjoy the full bar and cushy oversize chairs while you watch the sunset over Carmel Bay.

The Inn at Spanish Bay (2700 17-Mile Dr.) is home to five restaurants and bars. **Peppoli at Pebble Beach** (831/647-7433, www.pebblebeach.com, daily 6–10 P.M., $50) serves bold northern Italian seafood and meat dishes and features traditional pastas. 《Roy's at Pebble Beach** (831/647-7423, www.pebblebeach.com, daily breakfast, lunch, and dinner, $40–60) brings Hawaiian fusion to the table as you take in the beauty of the ocean view. Big flavor in a casual atmosphere is at **STICKS** (831/647-7470, www.pebblebeach.com, daily breakfast, lunch, and dinner, $30) for sports, food, and fun. **Taps** (831/647-7500, www.pebblebeach.com), a sports bar, has a full bar and serves dinner and late-night favorites like hot wings, burgers, fried chicken, and delectable desserts. **The Lobby Lounge** (831/647-7500, www.pebblebeach.com, daily lunch, dinner, and evening) has a full cocktail bar and food menu where you can enjoy a drink and an appetizer.

Getting There and Around

There are five entry gates to Pebble Beach. Stick to the main gates: the Pacific Grove Gate (Sunset Dr./Hwy. 68 and 17-Mile Dr.) and the Carmel Gate (N. San Antonio Ave. and 2nd Ave., Carmel). The best way to navigate Pebble Beach is by car, but you can also hitch a ride with one of the many tour companies that travel 17-Mile Drive. If you are feeling bold, you can hop on a bicycle and navigate this narrow road as well.

SALINAS

Made famous by John Steinbeck's *East of Eden,* Salinas has the rich soil and climate to make it "the salad bowl of the world," with a rainbow of fruits and vegetables growing on the farmland. Temperatures are generally hotter than on the peninsula, and life is a bit more rugged.

CENTRAL COAST

© KRISTIN LEAL

the National Steinbeck Center

National Steinbeck Center

In the heart of Old Town Salinas is the National Steinbeck Center (1 Main St., 831/775-4721, www.steinbeck.org, daily 10 A.M.–5 P.M., adults $11, seniors and students $9, ages 13–17 $8, ages 6–12 $6, under age 6 free), where you can explore Steinbeck's life and famous works. The interactive museum brings his writing to life and gives visitors a full sensory experience walking in the author's footsteps. The $15-million complex comprises two permanent exhibits, the John Steinbeck's Exhibition Hall and the Rabobank Agricultural Museum.

The six themed galleries of the **John Steinbeck's Exhibition Hall** showcase the life and times of Steinbeck through artifacts, film clips, photography, and interactive exhibits. Take a journey into the life of Salinas's native son and discover his inspiration for works that include *The Grapes of Wrath, Tortilla Flat, East of Eden,* and *Cannery Row.*

As you wander **The Rabobank Agricultural Museum,** you will learn why the Salinas Valley is considered the salad bowl of the world. The land is fertile and the weather ideal for growing everything from lettuce to strawberries. See how California's produce is brought from seed to table, and learn about the culture and history of Salinas's farming industry through the exhibit's many artifacts.

Serious Steinbeck scholars can also check out the **Steinbeck House** (132 Central Ave., Salinas, 831/424-2735, www.steinbeckhouse.com, call for hours, tours $10).

Mazda Laguna Seca Raceway

If you're feeling the need for speed, you can get lots of it at the Mazda Laguna Seca Raceway (1021 Monterey–Salinas Hwy., 831/242-8201, www.laguna-seca.com), one of the country's premier road-racing venues. Monterey has had a love affair with fast sexy cars and the obsession to race them since the Pebble Beach Road Races of the 1950s. Today, the races have expanded to several events year-round, including the Red Bull U.S. Grand Prix, Ferrari Racing Days, superbikes, and stock-car races, to name a few. The major racing season runs May–October most years. In addition to the big events, Laguna Seca hosts numerous auto clubs and smaller sports-car and stock-car races. Be sure to check the website for parking directions specific to the event you plan to attend—this is a big facility. You can camp here, and there are plenty of food concessions during big races.

Entertainment and Events

The world's premier Grand Prix motorcycle racing championship in the MotoGP class is the annual **Red Bull U.S. Grand Prix** (www.mazdaraceway.com), held at Laguna Seca Raceway in late July. Top manufacturers that participate include Honda, Suzuki, Ducati, Yamaha, Kawasaki, and Aprilia.

Steinbeck fans can mark the calendar for early August for the **Steinbeck Festival** (831/775-4721, www.steinbeck.org), an annual event that has been inspiring young and old for over 30 years. The four-day event has films, guest speakers, panels, performing arts, and bus and walking tours of Steinbeck's home turf.

Information and Services

The best place for information is the **Salinas Valley Chamber of Commerce** (119 E. Alisal St., 831/424-7611, www.salinaschamber.com, 9 A.M.–5 P.M. Mon.–Fri.). The **Old Town Salinas Association** (831/758-0725, www.oldtownsalinas.com) is here as well and can provide information on downtown events, shopping, and activities.

Getting There and Around

Salinas is on U.S. 101. From Monterey, take Highway 68 east. **Amtrak**'s Seattle–Los Angeles *Coast Starlight* train travels through Salinas (Station Place and Railroad Ave., daily 8 A.M.–10 P.M.) daily in both directions. For Amtrak travelers, there is free bus service (30 minutes) to downtown Monterey.

If you arrive on **Greyhound** (19 W. Gablin St., 831/242-4418 or 800/231-2222, www.greyhound.com), you can catch local buses to all the sights. **Monterey-Salinas Transit** (1 Ryan Ranch Rd., Monterey, 831/899-2555 or 831/242-7965, www.mst.org) has bus routes throughout the peninsula; check online for fares and schedules.

Salinas Municipal Airport (SNS, 30 Mortesen St., 831/758-7214, www.ci.salinas.ca.us) has no commercial flights but welcomes small aircraft. Major airlines have scheduled flights to the **Monterey Peninsula Airport** (MRY, 200 Fred Kane Dr., Monterey, 831/648-7000, www.montereyairport.com) and the larger **San Jose International Airport** (SJC, 2077 Airport Blvd., San Jose, 408/277-4859, www.sjc.org), just over an hour's drive north.

SAN JUAN BAUTISTA
Mission San Juan Bautista

The San Juan Bautista area was originally inhabited by the Mutsun people until the Spanish arrived and began building the mission in 1797. The location of Mission San Juan Bautista (406 2nd St., 831/623-4528, www.oldmissionsjb.org, daily 9:30 A.M.–4:30 P.M., donation) was chosen because of the fertile local soil and the distance of a day's walk to nearby missions. The Spanish forced the Mutsun people to build the mission; at one time there were 1,200 Native Americans working and living on the compound. There is a mass grave beside the mission with more than 4,300 Native Americans interred.

San Juan Bautista State Historic Park

Just across from Mission San Juan Bautista is the Plaza Hotel and San Juan Bautista State Historic Park (2nd St. between Washington St. and Mariposa St., 831/623-4526, www.

© KRISTIN LEAL

San Juan Bautista State Historic Park

parks.ca.gov, 10 A.M.–4:30 P.M. Tues.–Sun., adults $3, under age 17 free). The park is a tour through the San Juan Bautista old town, once the largest city in central California. The **Plaza Hotel** is an adobe structure that once served as barracks for soldiers and later as a hotel during the 19th century. **Plaza Hall-Zanetta House** displays furnishings from the 1800s along with many children's toys from the era. Horses were housed in the **Plaza Stables and Blacksmith Shop.** Today, the exhibit includes stagecoaches, a fire wagon, carriages, and wagons. The **Castro-Breen Adobe** was owned by General José Castro in the early 1840s, then sold to the Breen family, who survived the 1846 Donner Party incident.

Guided walking tours of San Juan Bautista Historic Park can be reserved in advance; the cost is $70 for groups of 1–10 plus $4 pp to tour the mission, and $7 pp for groups of 11–25 plus $3 pp to tour the mission.

Fremont Peak State Park

About 11 miles south of San Juan Bautista,

159-acre Fremont Peak State Park (park info 831/623-4255, observatory 831/623-2465, www.parks.ca.gov, daily 8 A.M.–sunset) is easily accessible from Highway 156. The **Fremont Peak Trail** (1 mile round-trip, easy) has mild elevation gains and leads up the peak for a 360-degree view. On a clear day, it's possible to see Monterey Bay, the Salinas Valley, the San Benito Valley, the Santa Cruz Mountains, the Diablo Range, the Gabilan Range, the Santa Lucia Mountains, and the Sierra Nevada Mountain Range from atop the 3,169-foot peak.

The park is known for awe-inspiring stargazing at the **Fremont Peak Observatory** (moonless Sat. Apr.–Oct.). The peak is high above the surrounding towns and away from urban lights, so the night sky glitters.

Accommodations and Food

For camping with great views, try **Fremont Peak State Park** (park info 831/623-4255, www.parks.ca.gov, reservations 888/444-7275, www.reserveamerica.com, $25), with 25

GILROY GARLIC

During the 19th century, thriving Gilroy farms produced apples, apricots, cherries, peaches, pears, plums, and all kinds of nut crops. At the turn of the 20th century, row-crop farming techniques were introduced by Italians and other southern Europeans who grew, canned, or dehydrated crops of tomatoes, peppers, onions, and garlic. With the arrival of Japanese farmers during World War I, garlic began to boom as a crop, and the bulbs were grown for the commercial market in massive quantities. Not until the late 1970s was the garlic harvest officially celebrated as a community event, attracting over 130,000 visitors annually.

The **Gilroy Garlic Festival** (Christmas Hill Park, 7100 Miller Ave., Gilroy, 408/842-1625, www.gilroygarlicfestival.com, adults $17, seniors $8, ages 6-12 $8, under age 6 free) is held for three days on the last full weekend in July and features flaming cook-offs, family fun, live entertainment, and more. Vendors sell their wares and lure you in with the aroma of garlic; you may go home with some tasty Gilroy garlic souvenirs. Watch for Miss Gilroy Garlic, rock out to live concerts all day long, and visit over 100 fine-art and crafts merchants.

The heart of the event is at Gourmet Alley, where chefs gather to showcase their garlic culinary techniques in an all-out competition that features pepper steak, stuffed mushrooms, calamari, garlic bread, fries, pasta con pesto, scampi, chicken stir-fry, combo plates, Italian sausage, and even some garlic-free grub.

---

campsites nestled among pine and oak trees. Trailer, RV, and tent sites are available, and water hookups and washrooms are nearby. There are 20 primitive campsites available on a first-come, first-served basis.

Locals love **Jardines de San Juan** (115 3rd St., 831/623-4466, www.jardinesrestaurant.com, 11:30 A.M.–9 P.M. Sun.–Thurs., 11:30 A.M.–10 P.M. Fri.–Sat., $7–12). There are tables outside in the exceptional garden; on weekends a local musician performs. **La Casa Rosa** (107 3rd St., 831/623-4563, www.lacasarosarestaurant.com, 11:30 A.M.–3 P.M. Thurs.–Sun., $15) provides Basque comfort cooking. Open since 1935, La Casa Rosa keeps things simple with a small menu and just four entrées: Old California Casserole, New California Casserole, Chicken Soufflé, and Seafood Soufflé.

Getting There

To reach San Juan Bautista from Monterey, take Highway 1 north to Highway 156 east, then U.S. 101 north to Highway 156 east to San Juan Bautista. To get to Hollister, continue on Highway 156 east of San Juan Bautista. From Salinas, take U.S. 101 north to Highway 156 east.

◖ PINNACLES NATIONAL MONUMENT

The 26,000 acres of rugged territory at Pinnacles National Monument (5000 Hwy. 46, Paicines, 831/389-4485, www.nps.gov, day use $5) has hiking and plenty of steep rock walls to climb. The rocky terrain of the park resembles another planet. Huge rocks shoot into the sky, boulders protrude from massive cracks, and there is much evidence of volcanic activity. Narrow trails traverse the sides of the monument. Be sure to bring plenty of water, as it is generally warm and dry year-round; expect blazing heat in the summer.

There are two sets of caves in the reddish rocks. The **Bear Gulch Cave** is located along the **Moses Spring-Rim Trail Loop** on the east side of the monument. This uphill hike gains 500 feet in elevation as it climbs through the dark cave system and leads to a reservoir. Open seasonally (mid-July–mid-May), only some sections of the cave system can be explored; this

© KRISTIN LEAL

Pinnacles National Monument

is to protect the resident rare Townsend's big-eared bats. The bats leave their caves completely for short periods in October and March, when the entire cave system is open, so be sure to check the status of the caves before you depart.

At the west entrance to the monument, the easy–moderate **Old Pinnacles Trail to Balconies Cave** is a 2.4-mile loop with an elevation gain of 100 feet; hiking it counterclockwise is less strenuous. The trail has sections of talus caves to get through, so bring a flashlight.

Camping

The Pinnacles Campground (831/389-4538, reservations 877/444-6777, www.reserveamerica.com, tents $23, RVs $36) is located on the east side of the monument with 134 sites, including groups sites. Oak trees shade some sites, while others are exposed to the hot summer sun.

Campsites include picnic tables and fire rings, and there are electrical hookups for the RV sites. Amenities include restrooms with flush toilets, drinking water, showers, a small on-site store, and a swimming pool that's open seasonally.

Getting There

There are two entrances to Pinnacles, but no road connects the two, and it can be a two-hour detour to drive around to the other entrance. For the **east entrance,** take U.S. 101 north from Salinas to Highway 25 through the town of Hollister. Drive 30 miles to Highway 146 and turn right. The campground entrance will be on the left; the Bear Gulch entrance is 3.5 miles farther.

For the **west entrance,** take U.S. 101 south from Salinas to Highway 146 east. Continue on Highway 146 east for 14 miles to the west entrance. Note that there are no services at this entrance.

Carmel

Carmel is divided into two distinct sections: Carmel-by-the-Sea, with quaint homes and small shops alongside sprawling estates and designer boutiques; and Carmel Valley, conjuring images of the Wild West with dusty hills and windswept seaside forests.

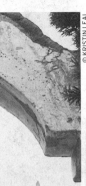

© KRISTIN LEAL

CENTRAL COAST

CARMEL-BY-THE-SEA

Carmel-by-the-Sea quickly charms with whimsical cottages, a historic mission, big-city entertainment, shopping, and outdoor fun. The main drag is Ocean Avenue, lined with art galleries, couture shops, and fine dining. But the charm of the town extends beyond Ocean Avenue. Make time to walk or drive through some of the winding streets of Carmel to see fairy-tale bungalows and gingerbread-style houses next to secret gardens and tiny castles.

House numbers are not used on the twisting streets of Carmel-by-the-Sea; rather, homes are named for locations from fairy tales. Today, the village still represents the original intention of its bohemian creators as a haven for artists, and the dwellings themselves are artworks. Many of the cottages are the original structures from Carmel's early days, and newer dwellings are built to mirror the whimsical forerunners. Along any street in the one-square-mile village, walking or driving reveals interesting houses.

◖ Carmel Mission

Mission San Carlos Borroméo de Carmelo (3080 Rio Rd., 831/624-3600, www.carmel-mission.org, 9:30 A.M.–5 P.M. Mon.–Sat., 10:30 A.M.–5 P.M. Sun., adults $6.50, seniors $4, ages 7–17 $2, under age 7 free) was Father Junípero Serra's favorite California mission. He lived, worked, and eventually died here; today visitors can see a replica of his room.

The Carmel Mission has a small memorial museum inside off the second courtyard, but

Carmel Mission

exhibits run through many of the buildings, illustrating the lives of the 18th- and 19th-century friars. The highlight is the church, with its gilded altar, shrine to the Virgin Mary, the grave of Junípero Serra, and an ancillary chapel dedicated to his memory. Round out your visit by walking in the gardens and reading the grave markers in the small cemetery. A working Catholic parish remains part of the complex, so be respectful on the self-guided tour.

Robinson Jeffers's Tor House

In 1919, Robinson Jeffers, the "dark prince of poetry," built a rugged-looking castle constructed from boulders unearthed on the shore of Carmel Bay. Tor House (26304 Ocean View Ave., 831/624-1813, www.torhouse.org) and its Hawk Tower is a fitting monument to his work and poetry, which often dealt with dark and

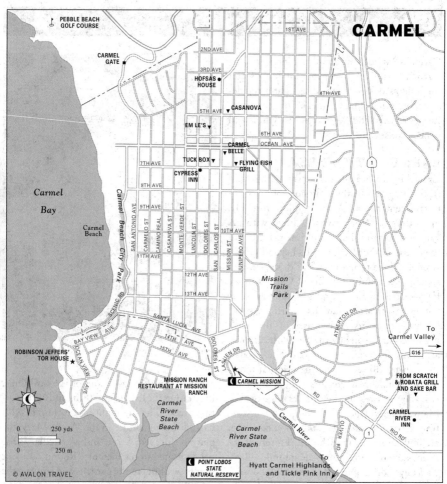

controversial topics in heavy blank verse. There is a fragrant, layered English cottage garden, and docents lead tours (hourly 10 A.M.–3 P.M. Fri.–Sat., adults $10, students $5).

Art Galleries

Carmel boasts more art galleries per capita than any other town in the United States. Of the many galleries in Carmel, the one with the greatest breadth of local talent is the **Carmel Art Association** (Delores St. between 5th Ave. and 6th Ave., 831/624-2176, www.carmelart. org, daily 10 A.M.–5 P.M.), a co-op of over 120 talented artists, all of whom live within 30 miles of town. The majority of pieces are oils and pastels, but there are other media, including wood and sculpture. Artists bring in new works on the first Wednesday of each month, ensuring constant rotation.

Gallery Diamante (Dolores St. between 5th Ave. and 6th Ave., 831/624-0852, www. gallerydiamante.com, call for hours) is

© KRISTIN LEAL

Tor House

representative, with a large collection of landscape paintings by different artists, interesting sculptures, and the most popular modern styles in painting and sculpture. Boban Bursac is the sole owner of the tiny **EX-tempore Gallery** (Dolores St. between 5th Ave. and 6th Ave., 831/626-1298, www.ex-temporegallery.com, call for hours). Bursac's amazing large-format paintings evoke emotional reactions from even the most casual passerby.

Trotter Galleries (San Carlos St. between Ocean Ave. and 7th Ave., 831/625-3246, www. trottergalleries.com, 11 A.M.–5 P.M. Tues.–Sat., by appointment Sun.–Mon.) specializes in early California and Americana with many featured Carmel artists since 1980. **Mountain Song Galleries** (Ocean Ave., just south of Mission St., 831/620-0600, www.mountainsonggalleries.com, 11 A.M.–7 P.M. Mon. and Wed.–Thurs., 11 A.M.–8 P.M. Fri.–Sat., noon–7 P.M. Sun.) displays an array of handblown glass, surfboards, sculpture, paintings, and guitar art from all over

the state. **Winfield Gallery** (Dolores St. between 7th Ave. and Ocean Ave., 831/624-3369, www. winfieldgallery.com, 11 A.M.–5 P.M. Mon.–Sat., noon–5 P.M. Sun.) is hands down the finest art gallery on the peninsula. Artist Chris Winfield and his wife offer a sophisticated collection of contemporary artists, including Andrea Johnson, Jack Zajac, and Bruce Beasley.

Perfect for the seaside town of Carmel is a branch of the **Wyland Galleries** (Ocean Ave., north of Mission St., 831/626-6223, www. wylandgallerycarmel.com, call for hours). Wyland is an accomplished photographer, writer, painter, and sculptor, and his shops are always worth a visit.

◖ Point Lobos State Natural Reserve

Five miles south of Carmel is Point Lobos State Reserve (Hwy. 1 at Riley Ranch Rd., 831/624-4909, www.pointlobos.org, daily 8 A.M.–sunset year-round, day use $10), a stunning piece of land abutting the ocean. The rugged, ragged cliffs and rocks, beautiful and malformed, are dotted with pine and cypress trees and scented by the pines and the fresh ocean breeze. Within the sheltered coves and twisting forests, history runs deep. Europeans arrived in the area at Point Lobos in 1796 and used this location as a whaling station, a shipping port, a cannery, a pasture for livestock, and residential lots. The whaler's cabin at the bottom of **Whalers Cove** was built by Chinese fishermen in the 1850s and is now a cultural history museum; adjacent to it is the whaling station museum.

Hiking trails within the park stretch for miles along the weathered coastline and wind among ancient cypress trees. **Cypress Grove Trail** (under 1 mile) is home to one of only two naturally occurring stands of Monterey cypress trees that exist. **Pine Ridge Trail** (0.5 mile) runs through open woods filled with coast live oaks and Monterey pines. A favorite path starts at South Shore Trail, hugs the beach for one mile,

CENTRAL COAST

CENTRAL COAST

© KRISTIN LEAL

Point Lobos State Natural Reserve

and runs into Bird Island Trail, which runs about one mile more to China Cove and Gibson Beach.

Cycling is allowed on all the paved roadways, and parking areas are available to lock up your bicycle if you want to continue on the dirt paths on foot. Motorized vehicles are limited to 15 mph in the park.

Point Lobos State Natural Reserve offers diving access to Whalers Cove and Blue Fish Cove, with many access points by boat or from shore. Inside the park is a boat ramp to launch kayaks or boats up to 18 feet long. The reserve is filled with large pinnacles emerging from the sandy ocean floor. A winding maze of giant kelp can be seen along the middle reef. The shoots can grab rocks as deep as 130 feet. Wolf eels, rockfish, and lingcod hide among the rocks and plantlife. Giant sunflower stars hunt for crabs, abalones, sea urchins, sea cucumbers, and other stars.

Beaches

At the west end of Ocean Avenue is the sparkling white sand of **Carmel Beach** (Ocean Ave., 831/624-4909, daily 6 A.M.–10 P.M.). This lovely south-facing stretch allows off-leash dog visitors, and bonfires are allowed south of 10th Avenue until 10 P.M. Surfing, wading, and sunbathing are especially popular in the fall. Parking is generally easy along Scenic Drive. This is the only beach in Carmel that is safe enough to surf and body-board, and the waves are appropriate for beginners and intermediates. **Carmel Surf Lessons** (831/915-4065, $100 pp includes equipment) has professional lessons for all skill levels and ages. Owner Noah Greenberg has been catching waves for over 20 years and is the surf instructor at California State University Monterey Bay.

A mile-long beach and lagoon, **Carmel River Beach** (end of Carmelo St., 831/649-2836, www.parks.ca.gov, free) is perfect for building sandcastles, and when the river is high, it cuts right through the beach to empty vigorously into the sea. Part of Carmel River State Beach is the dangerous **Monastery Beach** (just north of

Point Lobos State Natural Reserve). A popular site for shore divers, the waters can be unforgiving to recreational swimmers or waders; the undertow is swift, and the ocean floor drops quickly near shore.

Entertainment and Events

The General Store, also known as **Forge in the Forest** (Junipero St. and 5th Ave., 831/624-2233, www.forgeintheforest.com, 11:30 A.M.–9 P.M. Sun.–Thurs., 11:30 A.M.–10 P.M. Fri.–Sat.), has a rustic pioneer bar in the heart of Carmel-by-the-Sea. Enjoy a frothy brew or a classy cocktail next to the actually flaming forge or outside in the patio.

The bar is comfortable and the fire is cozy at **The Fuse Lounge** (Carmel Mission Inn, 3665 Rio Rd., 831/624-1841, www.carmelmissioninn.com, daily 5–10 P.M.). There is never a cover charge, and the weekend music will get you out on the dance floor in no time.

The **Pacific Repertory Theater** (PacRep, 831/622-0100, www.pacrep.org) is the only professional theater company on the Monterey Peninsula, performing most often in the Golden Bough Playhouse (Monte Verde St. and 8th Ave.). The company puts on classic and new dramas, comedies, and musicals. Each fall, PacRep puts on the **Carmel Shakespeare Festival,** a short showing of Shakespearean works.

The **Sunset Center** (San Carlos St. and 9th Ave., 831/620-2040, www.sunsetcenter.org) brings numerous big-city performances to its stage year-round. Annual events include the Carmel Bach Festival, Carmel Music Society concerts, Chamber Music Monterey Bay concerts, and performances of the Monterey Symphony.

In a town famed for art galleries, one of the biggest events of the year is the **Carmel Art Festival** (Mission St., www.carmelartfestival.org) in May, a four-day event celebrating visual arts in a variety of media with shows by internationally acclaimed artists at galleries, parks, and other venues around town. The festival also sponsors here-and-now contests, including the prestigious plein air (outdoor painting) competition. Visitors get a rare opportunity to witness the artists working outdoors. Perhaps best of all, the Carmel Art Festival is a great place to bring the family, as there are a wealth of children's activities.

One of the most prestigious festivals in Northern California is the **Carmel Bach Festival** (Sunset Center, www.bachfestival.org). For three weeks in July–August, Carmel-by-the-Sea and surrounding towns host dozens of classical concerts. The works of J. S. Bach are featured, but you can also hear Mozart, Vivaldi, Handel, and other heavyweights. Concerts and recitals are held daily.

Get a **Taste of Carmel** (Carmel Mission, 3080 Rio Rd., 831/624-2522, www.tasteofcarmel.com) in early October, when more than 30 restaurants come together to tempt your palate with local produce paired with wines from 20 local vineyards.

Shopping

There are three distinct shopping areas in Carmel. The main shopping street in downtown Carmel-by-the-Sea is Ocean Avenue and along its side streets all the way to the ocean. There are antiques shops, unique gifts, typical souvenirs, and clothing along with the jewel in the crown, **Carmel Plaza** (Ocean Ave. and Mission St., 831/624-0138, www.carmelplaza.com, 10 A.M.–6 P.M. Mon.–Sat., 11 A.M.–5 P.M. Sun.), a mall with 40 high-end chain stores on three levels.

The **Barnyard Shopping Village** (831/624-8886, www.thebarnyard.com, daily 10 A.M.–6 P.M.) is a whimsically well-designed two-story complex with bike shops, women's clothing, sparkly treasures, and full salons.

Crossroads Shopping Village (Hwy. 1 and Rio Rd., 831/625-4106, www.crossroadsshoppingvillage.com, 10 A.M.–6 P.M. Mon.–Sat., noon–5 P.M. Sun.) is the place for practicality and specialized stores. The mall contains over

50 stores, making it easy to lose track of time while wandering and browsing.

Accommodations

Hofsas House (San Carlos St. and 3rd Ave., 831/624-2745, www.hofsashouse.com, $120–260) is in a quiet residential neighborhood within easy walking distance of downtown Carmel-by-the-Sea. Guest rooms are surprisingly spacious, with nice furniture and linens that show just a touch of wear, along with adequate baths. If you can, get an ocean-view room with a patio or balcony.

Owned by Carmel's movie-star former mayor, Clint Eastwood, ◖ **Mission Ranch** (26270 Dolores St., 831/624-6436, www.missionranchcarmle.com, $120–310) is a high-end place to stay with wide views of the grassy ranch leading to the ocean. Postcard-worthy sheep graze, and the fog burns off slowly, exposing gaps of blue sky. There are tennis courts on-site, and guest rooms are country elegant with room to spread out.

At the **Carmel River Inn** (2600 Oliver Rd., 831/624-1575, www.carmelriverinn.com, $80–369) the spacious and comfortable guest rooms are equipped with kitchenettes, fireplaces, and in-room jetted tubs, and there is a pool on-site.

Staying at the all-inclusive resort **Hyatt Carmel Highlands** (120 Highland Dr., 831/620-1234, www.highlandsinn.hyatt.com, $225–695) feels like staying near edge of the world. Guest rooms have dramatic views of the rugged coastline and Point Lobos in the distance. The pool is delightful, and the hot tub feels great after a long day of hiking or horseback riding.

The cliff-top **Tickle Pink Inn** (155 Highland Dr., 831/624-1244, www.ticklepinkinn.com, $231–559) offers tasteful luxury. Each guest room has a view of the ocean, an array of high-end furniture and linens, and top-end amenities. For a special treat, book a spa-bath suite.

Doris Day is one of the owners of the ◖ **Cypress Inn** (Lincoln St. at 7th Ave.,

831/624-3871, www.cypress-inn.com, $225–575), one of the oldest and classiest places to stay in Carmel. Day's Hollywood memorabilia is on display throughout the property, and given her love of animals, it's no surprise that the inn is pet-friendly (for $30). The midsize guest rooms are well appointed, with fresh flowers, fruit, and cream sherry to welcome you. Many guest rooms have jetted tubs, and all have Wi-Fi. You can hear the ocean, four blocks away, from the charming outdoor patio.

Food

Em Le's (Dolores St. between 5th Ave. and 6th Ave., 831/625-6780, www.em-les.com, 7 A.M.–3 P.M. Mon.–Tues., 7 A.M.–3 P.M. and 4:30–8 P.M. Wed.–Sun., $20) is one of the oldest restaurants in Carmel, dating to 1955, with a menu focused on comfort foods like meatloaf, Caesar salad, pasta dishes, triple-decker clubs, and patty melts. The food is simple but fresh, the decor country comfortable, and the service attentive.

For the best Japanese food on the peninsula, go to ◖ **Robata Grill and Sake Bar** (3658 The Barnyard, 831/624-2643, lunch 11:30 A.M.–2 P.M. Mon.–Sat., dinner 5–8:30 P.M. Sun.–Thurs., 5–9:30 P.M. Fri.–Sat., $20–30). The sushi is fantastically creative, but there is also a full selection of hot items, including the barbecue ball with steamed vegetables and special sauce.

Breakfasts at **From Scratch** (3626 The Barnyard, 831/625-2448, daily 7:30 A.M.–2:30 P.M., $10–15) are made from scratch. Specialties include corned beef and hash, cheese blintzes, crab eggs benedict, granola, and oatmeal. There's a country feel to the small dining room, tucked downstairs from street level, but the best seats are out front under the vine-covered arbor.

The **Tuck Box** (Dolores St. between Ocean Ave. and 7th Ave., 831/624-0440, www.tuckbox.com, daily 7:30 A.M.–2:30 P.M., $12) reflects the storybook atmosphere of

Carmel-by-the-Sea. Celebrated as a historical landmark and serving hot meals for the last 70 years, generations of visitors have made it a stop.

The king of Jordan has dined at **C Casanova** (5th Ave. between San Carlos St. and Mission St., 831/625-0501, www.casanovarestaurant.com, daily 11:30 A.M.–3 P.M. and 5–10 P.M., $25), a Carmel institution. It's deceptively small from the outside but unfolds into several dining areas that include a fine-dining section, a large arbor-covered outdoor patio, several small intimate spaces, and the Van Gogh room, where you can eat at a table that once belonged to artist Vincent van Gogh. An excellent wine list complements the country French and Italian menu.

The **Flying Fish Grill** (Mission St. between Ocean Ave. and 7th Ave., 831/625-1962, 5–9 P.M. Sun.–Thurs., 5–9:30 P.M. Fri.–Sat., $30–40) serves Japanese-style seafood with a California twist in the Carmel Plaza open-air shopping mall. The service and the presentation of the plates make a visit worth the time and expense.

You can easily fill your picnic basket at **Bruno's Market and Delicatessen** (Junipero St. and 6th Ave., 831/624-3821, www.brunosmarket.com, daily 7 A.M.–8 P.M.). This full-service deli makes great sandwiches, barbecue ribs, and roasted chicken and has a massive selection of items like fine cheese, wine, produce, and sweets.

Carmel Belle (Doud Arcade, San Carlos St., 831/624-1600, www.carmelbelle.com, daily 8 A.M.–5 P.M., $5–18) has a large to-go menu of country-fresh and organic items.

Information and Services

The **Carmel Visitors Center** (San Carlos St. between 5th Ave. and 6th Ave., 831/624-2522, www.carmelcalifornia.org, daily 10 A.M.–5 P.M.) is right in downtown Carmel-by-the-Sea. For more information about the town and current events, pick up a copy of the local weekly newspaper, the *Carmel Pine*

Cone (www.pineconearchive.com). The nearest major medical center is in Monterey; for minor issues, head for the **Community Hospital of Monterey** (23625 Holman Hwy., Monterey, 831/622-2746, www.chomp.org).

Getting There

The **Monterey Peninsula Airport** (MRY, 200 Fred Kane Dr., Monterey, 831/648-7000, www.montereyairport.com) has nonstop scheduled flights from Los Angeles, San Diego, and San Francisco, but airfares are much higher than at **San Jose International Airport** (SJC, 2077 Airport Blvd., San Jose, 408/277-4859, www.sjc.org), which is a 90-minute drive north.

Amtrak's (800/872-7245, www.amtrak.com) Seattle–Los Angeles *Coast Starlight* train travels through Salinas (Station Place and Railroad Ave., Salinas, daily 8 A.M.–10 P.M.) daily in both directions. To reach Carmel, take the free shuttle bus to the Aquarium Bus Stop in Monterey, which is a curbside-only stop. From there, switch to the Monterey-Salinas Transit (MST, 888/678-2871, www.mst.org) bus to Carmel.

The most direct driving route from San Francisco to Carmel takes 2.5 hours (about 117 miles). Get on U.S. 101 south, exit onto Highway 156 west, and then get onto Highway 1 south. The coastal routes into Carmel are via Highway 1, which runs north–south. From Highway 1, take Ocean Avenue to downtown Carmel.

Getting Around

Monterey-Salinas Transit (MST, 888/678-2871, www.mst.org) has bus service that can transport you from Monterey to Carmel. They also operate a shuttle service through Carmel, a green-and-wood-colored bus that runs every 30 minutes.

The **Carmel Valley Grapevine Express** (888/678-2871, www.mst.org, daily 11 A.M.–6 P.M. year-round) shuttle bus stops at Cannery Row, downtown Monterey, and the Barnyard Shopping Center in Carmel and takes you to the Carmel Valley wineries for just

$6 round-trip. Buses run every hour. This is a great way to avoid the hassle of driving and finding parking.

Carmel Taxi (26080 Carmel Ranch Blvd., 831/624-3885) can take you anywhere on the peninsula.

CARMEL VALLEY

The laid-back side of Carmel is a 20-minute drive inland from the coast. The scenery shifts to wide ranches, rows of grapevines arcing over the hills, and the cool Carmel River. The hills, evergreen oak trees, and mild climate give way to vineyards and more outdoor recreation opportunities.

Sights

Earthbound Farms (7250 Carmel Valley Rd., 831/625-6219, www.ebfarm.com, 8 A.M.–6 P.M. Mon.–Sat., 10 A.M.–5 P.M. Sun.) offers visitors access to its facility in the Carmel Valley. Drive up to the farm stand and browse a variety of organic fruits, veggies, and flowers. Outside, you can walk into the fields to inspect the chamomile labyrinth and the kids garden (yes, kids can look and touch). Select and harvest your own fresh herbs from the cut-your-own garden, or leave the cooking to the experts and purchase delicious prepared organic dishes at the farm stand.

Carmel Valley Village (Carmel Valley Rd. and Esquiline Rd.) is an unincorporated little town with wine tasting, shopping, outdoor action, and good eats. Most of the valley's tasting rooms are here. Famed antiques shop Jan De Luz is in the center, and you can find an

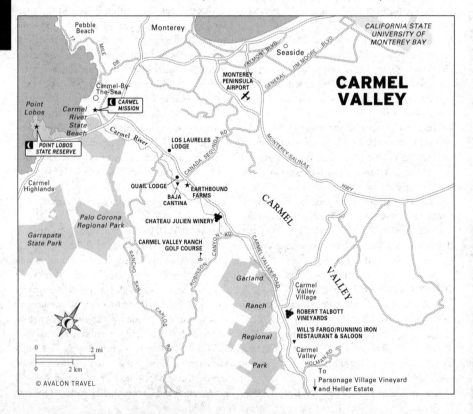

© AVALON TRAVEL

enjoying the view in Carmel Valley

assortment of Western-inspired restaurants as well as the old-fashioned Running Iron Saloon.

Wineries

There are a limited number of vineyards in the Carmel Valley, but it is a charming place for a wine-tasting day trip. Traffic is lighter and crowds are smaller than in larger wine districts, and many of the wineries are still family-owned.

Bernardus Winery (5 W. Carmel Valley Rd., 800/223-2533, www.bernardus.com/winery, daily 11 A.M.–5 P.M., tasting $5–10) also has a luxurious lodge and a gourmet restaurant. The short list of wines made from the grapes grown on the estate includes Marinus Vineyard, a Bordeaux-style blended red. Chardonnay, pinot noir, and sauvignon blanc varietals come from cooler coastal vineyards. If you're lucky, you might get to sip some small-batch vintages of single-vineyard wines that are available only in the tasting room.

The biggest name in the Carmel Valley is

Château Julien (8940 Carmel Valley Rd., 831/624-2600, www.chateaujulien.com, 8 A.M.–5 P.M. Mon.–Fri., 11 A.M.–5 P.M. Sat.–Sun.). The European-style estate building with a round turret is visible from the road. The light, airy tasting room is crowded with barrels, wine cases, souvenirs, and tasting glasses. You can taste a wide selection of chardonnays, cabernets, syrahs, merlots, and more. Call ahead to reserve a spot on the twice-daily free vineyard and winery tours.

Tiny **Parsonage Village Vineyard** (19 E. Carmel Valley Rd., 831/659-7322, www.parsonagewine.com, daily 11 A.M.–5 P.M., tasting $8) often doesn't make it onto Carmel Valley wine maps, which is a shame because arguably some of the best syrah in California comes from this unpretentious winery's nine-acre vineyard. The tasting room is along a tiny strip of shops in a glowingly lit space with a copper-topped bar. At the bar, taste wonderful syrahs, hearty cabernet sauvignons, and surprisingly deep and

CENTRAL COAST

complex blends; the Snosrap (that's "Parsons" spelled backwards) table wine is inexpensive for the region and very tasty.

Heller Estate Organic Vineyards (69 W. Carmel Valley Rd., 831/659-6220, www.heller-estate.com, daily 11 A.M.–5 P.M.) has been making wines for over 40 years, and the vineyard has been certified organic since 1996, producing exceptionally age-worthy wines. Among the hills overlooking the Cachagua area, Heller's mountain vineyard grows cabernet franc, cabernet sauvignon, chardonnay, chenin blanc, merlot, malbec, petit verdot, and pinot noir.

At **Robert Talbott Vineyards** (53 W. Carmel Valley Rd., 831/659-3500, www.talbott-vineyards.com, daily 11 A.M.–5 P.M., tasting $7.50), sample some of the featured chardonnay and pinot noir made from grapes grown on Talbott's 565-acre Sleepy Hollow Vineyard, in the Santa Lucia Mountains, and the 14-acre Diamond T Vineyard in Carmel Valley.

Handcrafted gold-medal wines are found at **Joyce Vineyards** (6 Pilot Rd., 831/659-2885, www.joycevineyards.com, 11 A.M.–5 P.M. Fri.–Sun.), with a tasting room and outdoor garden and featuring merlot, pinot noirs, cabernets, syrahs, chardonnays, and Pudding Wine.

An easy way to explore the wine tasting in the valley is the **Carmel Valley Grapevine Express** (888/678-2871, www.mst.org, daily 11 A.M.–6 P.M. year-round, $6 round-trip), a shuttle bus that can be boarded throughout Carmel and at the Monterey Transit Plaza (every hour at a quarter past the hour). Tours Monterey (831/624-1700, www.toursmonterey.com) has a relaxing **Wine Trolley** ($99) that includes a box lunch and a five-hour tour. Advanced reservations are required; tours start at 11 A.M. sharp at Portola Plaza in Monterey.

Entertainment and Events

A Carmel tradition is the **Art and Wine Celebration** (831/659-4000, www.carmel-valleychamber.com) in early June, with an open-house event in Carmel Valley Village that features live music. Stop in to the fine-art galleries, country antiques shops, cafés, and restaurants.

The fall season is all about the harvest; in Carmel Valley it kicks off with the **Harvest to Table Festival** (831/622-7770, www.harvest-carmel.com) in late September. More than 50 chefs show off their culinary skills with delectable bites to sample, and more than 100 wineries gather to pour their creations.

Shopping

The valley has fine antiquing prospects that are worth traveling inland for. The country charm of **Tancredi and Morgan** (Valley Hills Shopping Center, 7174 Carmel Valley Rd., 831/625-4477, www.tancredimorgan.com, 10 A.M.–5 P.M. Mon.–Sat., 11 A.M.–4 P.M. Sun.) includes continuously replenished antiques from Europe, unique paper art, and jewelry. Classic French style is at **Jan de Luz** (4 E. Carmel Valley Rd., 831/659-7966, www.jandaluz.com, 9 A.M.–5 P.M. Mon.–Sat.). Alongside linens and interior products are one-of-a-kind French antiques, wall fountains, fireplace hearths, and furniture.

Sports and Recreation

Garland Ranch Regional Park (Carmel Valley Rd., 8 miles east of Hwy. 1, 831/372-3196, www.mprpd.org, daily sunrise–sunset, day use free) has 4,462 acres of mountain biking and hiking trails, fishing, and picnic sites. Horse trails are accessible to hikers, and dogs are welcome throughout the park. The Kahn Ranch (831/372-3196, ext. 108) recently added 1,100 acres and many more trails to discover; access is via a private easement on Hitchcock Canyon Road.

One of the county's lesser-known hiking spots is **Arroyo Seco** (Arroyo Seco Rd., just outside Greenfield, 831/674-5726, camping reservations 877/444-6777, www.rocky-mountainrec.com, day use $7, camping $20, primitive sites $15). Arroyo Seco is in the Los

Padres National Forest in the Santa Lucia Mountains, and besides camping and hiking, it provides opportunities for swimming, seasonal fishing, and jumping off cliffs into the river. For white-water aficionados, the rapids on the Arroyo Seco River are rated Class III. You can do a full run of 14.5 miles if you put in at the Willowcreek Bridge and stop at the Arroyo Seco picnic area; a three-mile stretch has Class IV–V rapids. Riverfacts.com (http://riverfacts.com) can provide information on current conditions.

Rancho Cañada Golf Course (4860 Carmel Valley Rd., 800/536-9459, www.ranchocanada. com, $40–70) has two 18-hole courses known as the East Course and the West Course. The East Course is longer, but both have wide and narrow fairways that cross the Carmel River. There's a pro shop, dining, and bunkered chipping greens.

A par-71 course tucked in the hills of Carmel Valley is the **Quail Lodge** (8205 Valley Greens Dr., 831/620-8866, www.quaillodge.com, $100–150). This is a traditional course, with three sets of tees at each hole and a seven-acre driving range. The 10 lakes on the property and the Carmel River provide some challenges. PGA-certified pros are available to help improve your game.

Carmel Valley Ranch Golf Course (1 Old Ranch Rd., 831/620-6406, www.carmelvalleyranch.com, $100–195) is a semiprivate par-70 course, featuring a layout restored to Pete Dye's original design with T1 bentgrass, enlarged greens, tee boxes, and a clubhouse.

Accommodations

Los Laureles Lodge (313 W. Carmel Valley Rd., 831/659-2233, www.loslaureles.com, $125–650) offers affordable full-service accommodations. Amenities include free Internet access, family suites, a pool, in-room jetted tubs, fireplaces, and kitchenettes; pets are welcome. The guest rooms are spacious and rustic, and there is a restaurant and saloon on-site. Several room-and-wine-tasting packages are available.

Set amid seven acres of grapevines, the **Bernardus Lodge** (415 W. Carmel Valley Rd., 888/648-9463, www.bernardus.com, $295–1,970) is one of the nicest properties in Carmel Valley, with first-rate service and furnishings. Some guest rooms overlook the pool; others face the boccie and croquet lawn. There are two restaurants on-site; go for the Chef's Table, a small booth right in the kitchen where the chef prepares your meal in front of you. The walls have been signed by well-known guests, including Julia Child.

If you love to golf, book a room at the **Carmel Valley Ranch** (1 Old Ranch Rd., 831/625-9500, www.carmelvalleyranch.com, $359). Tucked amid stands of oak trees in the Santa Lucia Mountains, it is a peaceful location with over 500 acres to explore as well as a pool, a golf course, the Land Rover Driving School, and a spa.

Food

Step back into the classy West at the **Will's Fargo** (16 W. Carmel Valley Rd., 831/659-2774, www.bernardus.com, daily 4:30 P.M.–close, $28), a steak house and saloon with meat choices that include fish, veal, pork, lamb, quail, and chicken. For veggie eaters, the lasagna and the goat-cheese ravioli are mouthwatering.

For a good old country breakfast or lunch, the **Wagon Wheel** (7156 Carmel Valley Rd., 831/624-8878, daily 6:30 A.M.–2 P.M., $10–15) is a must. The oatmeal pancakes and corned beef hash are excellent. Wake up early to get a seat or be ready to wait.

With boots, saddles, and other Western paraphernalia hanging from the ceiling, the **Running Iron Saloon** (24 E. Carmel Valley Rd., 831/659-4633, 11 A.M.–10 P.M. Mon.–Fri., 10 A.M.–10 P.M. Sat.–Sun., $20) is true to its name even if it's rather out of place in the upscale Carmel Valley. There is live music on Friday and karaoke on Tuesday.

Baja Cantina (7166 Carmel Valley Rd.,

831/625-2252, 11:30 A.M.–10 P.M. Mon.–Fri., 11 A.M.–9 P.M. Sat.–Sun., $20) has an upbeat environment with an outside deck that's perfect for sunny days and a fireplace near the bar that's perfect when the fog rolls in. Menu favorites include the rosemary chicken burrito, mango chicken enchiladas, and halibut fish tacos. The chips and salsa are excellent.

For a taste of wine country cuisine, reserve a table at **Marinus at Bernardus Lodge** (415 W. Carmel Valley Rd., 831/658-3550, www.bernardus.com, daily 6–10 P.M., $45–80). The exquisite California cuisine features the produce, fish, and meat of local producers.

Open for breakfast, lunch, and dinner, the **Carmel Valley Ranch Lodge Restaurant** (1 Old Ranch Rd., 831/625-9500, www.carmel-valleyranch.com, daily 7 A.M.–10 P.M., $13–30) serves local organic sustainable food that is very good. Executive chef Tim Woods imbues every bite with his sense of adventure.

Getting There

To reach Carmel Valley, take Highway 1 to Carmel Valley Road, a major intersection with a stoplight; signs point the way. The **Carmel Valley Grapevine Express** (888/678-2871, www.mst.org, daily 11 A.M.–6 P.M. year-round) shuttle bus stops at Cannery Row, downtown Monterey, and the Barnyard Shopping Center in Carmel and takes you to the Carmel Valley wineries for just $6 round-trip; buses run every hour.

Big Sur

Big Sur is both the name of the town and of the coastal region along Highway 1 south of Carmel and north of San Simeon. Soaring cliffs dropping to sporadic white-sand beaches exemplify the Big Sur coastline made legendary in film and literature. From north to south, the Pacific Ocean changes from slate gray to a gentler blue, and the endless crash of the breakers on the shore is a constant lullaby in Big Sur's coastal towns. The region is explored via Highway 1, also called the Pacific Coast Highway, a road that hugs sheer cliffs and passes several state parks, resorts, and restaurants like Nepenthe, seemingly perched on the edge of the world.

SIGHTS
◖ Big Sur Coast Highway

The Big Sur Coast Highway, a 90-mile stretch of Highway 1, runs atop jagged cliffs and along rocky beaches, through dense redwood forest, over historic scenic bridges, and past several parks. Construction on this stretch of road was completed in the 1930s to connect Cambria to Carmel. You can start out at either end and spend a whole day winding your way along this road. There are plenty of wide turnouts on picturesque cliffs, which makes it easy to stop to admire the glittering ocean and stunning wooded cliffs.

Old Coast Road

Easily found on the left side of Highway 1, about 13 miles south of Carmel and just before Bixby Bridge, the Old Coast Road cuts high into the Coast Range of Big Sur. There are steep grades with areas of chunky quartz, slick muddy sections, tight turns through the redwoods, and narrow ledges. It is a little more than 10 miles to the end of the road and Andrew Molera State Park. The road is passable in dry weather, but in wet weather there are many flood-prone sections in the forest and steep loose grades. Most vehicles can handle the drive when it's dry. The road has a handful of drainage pipes that are somewhat bumpy; like large speed bumps, low-clearance vehicles should traverse these with caution.

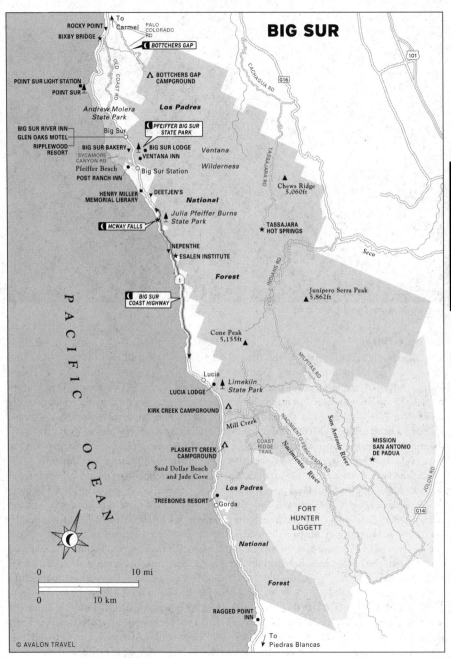

CENTRAL COAST

BIG SUR

To Carmel
ROCKY POINT
BIXBY BRIDGE
PALO COLORADO RD
BOTTCHERS GAP

OLD COAST RD
CACHAGUA RD
G16
101

BOTTCHERS GAP CAMPGROUND

POINT SUR LIGHT STATION
POINT SUR

Los Padres

Andrew Molera State Park

BIG SUR RIVER INN
GLEN OAKS MOTEL
RIPPLEWOOD RESORT
Big Sur
PFEIFFER BIG SUR STATE PARK

BIG SUR BAKERY
SYCAMORE CANYON RD
Pfeiffer Beach
POST RANCH INN
BIG SUR LODGE
VENTANA INN
Big Sur Station

Ventana
Wilderness

TASSAJARA RD

Chews Ridge 5,060ft

HENRY MILLER MEMORIAL LIBRARY
DEETJEN'S
National
Julia Pfeiffer Burns State Park
MCWAY FALLS

TASSAJARA HOT SPRINGS

Seco

NEPENTHE
ESALEN INSTITUTE

1
Forest

BIG SUR COAST HIGHWAY

INDIANS RD

Junipero Serra Peak 5,862ft

Cone Peak 5,155ft

MILPITAS RD

Lucia
LUCIA LODGE
Limekiln State Park

KIRK CREEK CAMPGROUND

Mill Creek

NACIMIENTO-FERGUSSON RD

San Antonio River

MISSION SAN ANTONIO DE PADUA

PLASKETT CREEK CAMPGROUND
COAST RIDGE TRAIL
Nacimiento River

P A C I F I C   O C E A N

Sand Dollar Beach and Jade Cove

Los Padres

TREEBONES RESORT
Gorda

FORT HUNTER LIGGETT

JOLON RD

National

G14

Forest

0   10 mi
0   10 km

RAGGED POINT INN

To
Piedras Blancas

© AVALON TRAVEL

© KRISTIN LEAL

Highway 1 along the Big Sur coast

Bixby Bridge

You'll probably recognize the Bixby Bridge when you come to it on Highway 1, about 18 miles south of Carmel. Among the world's highest, Bixby Bridge is over 260 feet high and more than 700 feet long. The cement open-spandrel arched bridge is one of the most photographed bridges in the nation, and it has been used in countless car commercials over the years. The bridge was built in the early 1930s as part of the massive New Deal government works project to complete Highway 1 and connect Northern California to the south along the coast. Today, you can pull out at either end of the bridge to take photos or just to view the attractive span and Bixby Creek flowing into the Pacific far below.

Point Sur Light Station

The Point Sur Light Station (Hwy. 1, 0.25 mile north of Point Sur Naval Facility, 831/625-4419, tours 10 A.M. and 2 P.M. Sat.–Sun. Nov.–Mar., 10 A.M. and 2 P.M. Wed. and Sat.–Sun. Apr.–June and Sept.–Oct., 10 A.M. and 2 P.M. Wed. and Sat.–Sun., 10 A.M. Thurs. July–Aug., adults $10, children $5) keeps watch over ships navigating the rocky waters of Big Sur. First lit in 1889, this now fully automated light station still provides navigational assistance; keepers stopped living and working in the tiny stone-built compound in 1974.

To tour the light station, check the tour times online. Parking is off the west side of Highway 1 by the locked farm gate. Tour guides meet here to take a limited number of visitors 0.5 miles up the paved road to the light station. Once at the station, you'll climb the stairs up to the light, explore the restored keepers homes and service buildings, and walk out to the cliff's edge. Be sure to dress in layers; it can be sunny and hot or foggy and cold in winter or summer, and sometimes both on the same tour. Tours last three hours and require more than one mile of walking, with a bit of incline and more than

© KRISTIN LEAL

Bixby Bridge

100 stairs. Take one of the moonlight tours (call for details) to learn about the haunted history of the light station buildings.

There is no access to the light station without a tour group. Tour schedules can vary from year to year and season to season; call ahead before showing up. For special assistance, call 831/667-0528 as far ahead as possible to make arrangements. No strollers, food, pets, or smoking are allowed on the property.

Big Sur Spirit Garden

A favorite among local art lovers, the Big Sur Spirit Garden (47504 Hwy. 1, Loma Vista, 831/238-1056, www.bigsurspiritgarden.com, daily 9 A.M.–6 P.M.) changes a little almost every day. The "garden" part includes a variety of plantlife, while the "spirit" part is modern and postmodern fair-trade art from nearby and as far away as India. The artwork tends toward brightly colored small sculptures done in exuberant naive style. The Spirit Garden

offers educational programs, community celebrations, and musical events.

Big Sur Station

Pull in at Big Sur Station (Hwy. 1, south of Pfeiffer Big Sur State Park, 831/667-2315, daily 8 A.M.–4:30 P.M.) for maps and brochures to all the major parks and trails of Big Sur; there is also a small bookshop. Several of the smaller parks and beaches (Limekiln, Garrapata, and Sand Dollar) have no visitor services, so Big Sur Station serves visitors traveling to one of those less-visited spots. You can also get a backcountry permit here for the Ventana Wilderness.

Henry Miller Memorial Library

Henry Miller lived and wrote in Big Sur for 18 years. He began to cultivate this region as an artists colony in 1944, and his utopian 1957 novel *Big Sur and the Oranges of Hieronymus Bosch* put his Big Sur dream on the map. Today, the Henry Miller Memorial Library (Hwy. 1,

© KRISTIN LEAL

Point Sur Light Station

0.25 mile north of Deetjens, 831/667-2574, www.henrymiller.org, 11 A.M.–6 P.M. Wed.–Mon.) celebrates the life and work of Miller and his peers in this quirky community center, museum, coffee shop, and gathering place. You can flip through the collection of literature, be entertained by local performances, attend short film festivals, and more. The library is easy to find on Highway 1—look for the hand-painted sign and funky fence decorations.

McWay Falls

A popular photo op is breathtaking McWay Falls at Julia Pfeiffer Burns State Park (831/667-2315, www.parks.ca.gov, daily sunrise–sunset, $10). A ribbonlike stream spews out of Anderson Canyon and falls some 200 feet to the pale beach below. The waterfall flows year-round, with heavier volume in winter and early spring. The hike is less than one mile and offers stunning views of the Big Sur coastline. The trail begins at Julia Pfeiffer Burns State Park, where the rolling hills drop dramatically to the sea and redwood forests protect the inland reaches. The trail ends at the ruins of the McWay Waterfall House, during the 1920s the home of Lathrop and Helen Hopper Brown. Today, a decaying foundation of the terrace is all that remains.

Esalen Institute

The Esalen Institute (55000 Hwy. 1, 831/667-3000, fax 831/667-2724, www.esalen.org, by reservation only) is a retreat from the world. People come from all over to this haven, sometimes called "the New Age Harvard," for lengthy courses and classes, but massages and use of the bathhouse are available to nonguests.

Esalen isn't a day spa. You must make an appointment for a massage (75 minutes, $150), which grants you access to the hot tubs for an hour before and an hour after your session. If you just want to sit in the bathhouse's hot tubs, you have to stay up late—very late. Access to

© KRISTIN LEAL

McWay Falls at Julia Pfeiffer Burns State Park

the Esalen tubs (831/667-3047, $20) is by reservation and is only possible 1–3 A.M.

The bathhouse, a motley collection of mineral-fed hot tubs with ocean views, is located down a rocky path on the edge of the cliffs overlooking the ocean. Once you've parked and been given directions, it's up to you to find your way down to the cliffs. You can choose the Silent Side to sink into the water and contemplate the Pacific, or the Quiet Side to get to know your fellow bathers. Esalen's bathhouse area is clothing-optional. You'll have to find your own towel, grab a shower, and then wander out to find a hot tub. Be sure to go all the way outside, past the individual claw-foot tubs, to the glorious shallow cement tubs right out on the edge of the cliff.

Limekiln State Park

There is plenty of outdoor action and good camping at 717-acre Limekiln State Park (Hwy. 1, 52 miles south of Carmel, 831/667-2403,

www.parks.ca.gov, $8). Besides the historical lime kilns, there are deep-woods hiking trails and beach kayaking, fishing, and swimming. Squirrels, deer, foxes, and raccoons are often seen, attracted by the two creeks in the park. Mountain lions, bobcats, and ring-tailed cats are much more elusive but are known to roam the area.

The day-use parking is limited to 12 spots, but you can park in the pullouts along Highway 1 just above the park. Day-use activities include picnicking, good shore fishing, and kayaking from the beach. Three hiking trails start just beyond the Redwood Campground. The **Limekiln Trail** (0.5 mile) is a hike to the cluster of historic lime kilns. The **Falls Trail** branches off the Limekiln Trail and leads to a 100-foot waterfall; be prepared to get your feet wet. The **Hare Creek Trail** is an easy hike through the majestic redwood forest alongside the rushing water.

In the thick redwoods and along a sheltered cove are campsites (summer by reservation, winter first-come, first-served, $35) that can accommodate tents and RVs up to 24 feet. The three sections of the campground are the Beach, Lower Creek, and Redwood Campgrounds.

Piedras Blancas

Six miles north of San Simeon is the **Piedras Blancas Lighthouse** (15950 Hwy. 1, 805/927-7361, www.piedrasblancas.org, tours 9:45 A.M. Tues., Thurs., and Sat., adults $10, children $5, under age 5 free), named after the white rock outcropping just off the point. It was completed in 1875, and the original tower was 110 feet tall. The beach around the lighthouse is a favorite resting spot for elephant seals. If you plan to take the tour, you may want to arrive early to ensure a spot, as space is limited. Tours meet at the old Piedras Blancas Motel, 1.5 miles north of the lighthouse.

The vista point with a parking lot just beyond the Piedras Lighthouse is a famous location to view elephant seals at the **Northern Elephant Seal Rookery** (Hwy. 1, www.elephantseal.org, 805/924-1628, daily sunrise–sunset, free). Home to roughly 15,000 giant northern elephant seals year-round, you can witness them molt, breed, give birth, and—their favorite pastime—rest. Much of the time the elephant seals are quite calm, but occasional sparring matches with deep guttural growling provide the best action. Be careful not to get too close to these creatures; remember that they are wild animals and can therefore be unpredictable and dangerous. A large parking area just off Highway 1 is alongside the beach, where you can view these impressive animals.

HIKING
Garrapata State Park

A narrow two-mile-long band of pretty light sand creates the beach at Garrapata State Park (Hwy. 1, gate 18 or 19, 831/624-4909, www.parks.ca.gov, free), north of the Point Sur Light Station. Stroll along the beach, scramble up the

cliffs for a better view of the ocean, or check out the seals, sea otters, and sea lions near Soberanes Point. In winter, use binoculars to look for the migrating gray whales that pass quite close to shore. Expect few to no facilities; at most you might find a pit toilet. Parking is in a wide spot on Highway 1. Within the park, dogs are allowed on Garrapata Beach.

Hiking in Garrapata State Park is inspirational. Coastal cliffs drop dramatically to sandy beaches, and mountains of the Santa Lucia Range rise above. There are several access gates, but the main parking area is along the strip of cypress trees. The **Soberanes Point Trail** (2 miles, strenuous), east of the highway, is one of the more challenging and fun hikes. The trail runs through open hillsides covered in cacti with willows lining the creek below. The trail eventually leads to the trickling sound of a creek and a valley of poppies, then into lush forest and up a peak with inspiring ocean vistas.

Part of the Sorberanes Canyon Trail, the **Rocky Ridge Trail** (4.5 miles) is a strenuous climb. The **North Fork Trail** (1 mile) and **Peak Trail** (1.5 miles) branch off to add more distance. The variety of microclimates along the Sorberanes Canyon Trail, part of the Rocky Ridge Trail, is amazing.

Whale Peak is a great place to search for migrating gray, blue, and humpback whales. Look for the spouts of water that shoot up one after another as they travel close to shore. Some trails lead down to the beach, but be cautious, as the tide comes in quickly and large waves often hit these beaches.

Andrew Molera State Park

The first park you encounter driving south from Carmel into the Big Sur region is Andrew Molera State Park (Hwy. 1, 22 miles south of Carmel, 831/667-2315, www.parks.ca.gov, day use $10). Once home to small camps of the Esselen people, this chunk of Big Sur eventually became the Molera ranch, used to grow crops and ranch animals as well as a hunting and fishing retreat for family and friends. In 1965 Frances Molera sold the land to the Nature Conservancy, and when she died three years later the ranch was sold to the California State Park system as per her will. Today, the **Molera Ranch House Museum** (831/620-0541, bshs@mbay.net, 11 A.M.–3 P.M. Sat.–Sun.) displays stories of the life and times of Big Sur's pioneers and artists as well as the wildlife and plants of the region. Take the road toward the horse tours to get to the ranch house.

The park has numerous hiking trails that run down to the beach and up into the forest along the river; biking and horseback riding are also allowed on many of the trails. Most of the park trails are west of the highway. The beach is down the multiuse **Trail Camp Beach Trail** (1 mile, easy). From here, climb back out on the **Headlands Trail** (0.25-mile loop) for a beautiful view from the headlands. If you want a better look at the Big Sur River, take the flat **Bobcat Trail** (5.5 miles round-trip, moderate), which leads right along the riverbank. Watch out for bicycles and the occasional horse and rider. For an even longer and more difficult trek up the mountains and down to the beach, take the **Ridge Bluff Loop** (8 miles). It starts at the parking lot on the Creamery Meadow Beach Trail, then makes a left onto the long and fairly steep Ridge Trail. Turn left again onto the Panorama Trail, which runs down to the coastal scrublands, and finally out to the Bluffs Trail, which takes you back to Creamery Meadow.

At the park entrance are restrooms, but there is no drinkable water. If you are camping here, bring plenty of your own water for washing as well as drinking. If you are hiking for the day, pack in bottled water and snacks.

You can also take a guided horseback ride with **Molera Horseback Tours** (831/625-5486, http://molerahorsebacktours.com, daily 9 A.M. spring–summer, $25–60). Call ahead to guarantee a spot on the 1–2.5-hour tours, or take a chance and just show up at the stables 15 minutes ahead of time. Each ride takes you from the modest corral area along multiuse trails through forests and meadows or along the Big Sur River and down to Molera Beach.

◖ Pfeiffer Big Sur State Park

The biggest and most developed park in Big Sur is Pfeiffer Big Sur State Park (47225 Hwy. 1, 831/667-2315, www.parks.ca.gov, day use $10). It has the Big Sur Lodge, a restaurant and café, a shop, an amphitheater, plenty of hiking-only trails, and lovely redwood-shaded campsites. This park is up in the coastal redwood forest, with a network of roads that can be driven or biked into the trees and along the Big Sur River.

Pfeiffer Big Sur has the tiny **Ernest Ewoldsen Memorial Nature Center,** which features examples of local wildlife. The **Homestead Cabin** was once the home of part of the Pfeiffer family—the first European immigrants to settle in Big Sur. Day-trippers and overnight visitors can take a stroll through the cabins of the Big Sur Lodge, built by the Civilian Conservation Corps during the Great Depression.

No bicycles or horses are allowed on trails in this park, which makes it quite peaceful for hikers. Take the **Nature Trail** (0.7-mile loop, easy) from Day Use Parking Lot 2. For a longer stroll, head out on the popular **Pfeiffer Falls Trail** (1.5 miles round-trip). You'll find stairs on the steep sections and footbridges across the creek, and then a lovely platform at the base of the 60-foot waterfall, where you can rest. For a longer and more difficult hike, start at the Homestead Cabin and head to the **Mount Manuel Trail** (10 miles round-trip, strenuous). From the Y intersection with the Oak Grove Trail, it's four miles to Mount Manuel, one of the most spectacular peaks in the area.

Julia Pfeiffer Burns State Park

One of the best-known and easiest hikes in the Big Sur region is in Julia Pfeiffer Burns State Park (Hwy. 1, 12 miles south of Pfeiffer Big Sur

CENTRAL COAST

State Park, 831/667-2315, www.parks.ca.gov, $10). The **Overlook Trail** (0.7 mile round-trip, easy) is along a level wheelchair-friendly boardwalk. Stroll under Highway 1, past the Pelton wheelhouse, and out to the observation deck for a stunning view of McWay Falls. The tiny Pelton wheel exhibit off the Overlook Trail has an interpretive exhibit, including the old Pelton wheel itself. If you're up for a longer hike, take the **Ewoldsen Trail** (4.5 miles round-trip, moderate–difficult). This trek takes you through McWay Canyon, and you'll see the creek and surrounding lush greenery on the walk. The trail then loops away from the water and climbs into the hills. Be sure to bring drinking water, as this hike can take several hours.

If you want to spend the day at Julia Pfeiffer Burns State Park, drive north from the park entrance to the Partington Cove pullout and park along the side of Highway 1. On the east side of the highway, start out along the **Tanbark Trail** (6.4 miles round-trip, difficult). You'll walk through redwood groves and up steep switchbacks to the top of the coastal ridge.

Ventana Wilderness

Savage terrain can be found in the remote Ventana Wilderness, part of the Los Padres National Forest (831/385-5434, www.fs.usda. gov). More than 200,000 acres are characterized by steep hillsides, sharp ridges, and deep V-shaped valleys with thermal springs, waterfalls, and deep pools. The climate is mild except in the winter months, when heavy storms drop massive amounts of water and make the area unpredictably rugged.

The visitors center at **Big Sur Station** (Hwy. 1, south of Pfeiffer Big Sur State Park, 831/667-2315, daily 8 A.M.–4:30 P.M.) can provide a map and information about the region. Hiking in the Ventana Wilderness is not to be undertaken casually, as the elevation gains range 600–5,750 feet. Entry points include the trailheads at Bottchers Gap, Big Sur Station, and Plaskett Creek Campground.

There are 273 miles of trails with access to 55 designated primitive camping sites. Palo Colorado Road runs eight miles from Highway

TASSAJARA HOT SPRINGS

Tassajara (information 415/865-1895, reservations 415/865-1899 or 888/743-9362, www.sfzc.org) was established in 1967 as a Zen center and retreat in the remote Ventana Wilderness. Though closed for practice periods in fall-winter, it is open to guests by reservation for day use (daily 9 A.M.-9 P.M. May-Sept., adults $30, children $12, cash or check only) to enjoy its rustic serenity, summer retreats, Zen practice, hiking, and use of the hot springs. Plan to bring your own towels and bathing suit; pack a lunch with you, or reserve lunch in advance (adults $12, children $8). Retreats require an additional fee and may focus on yoga, gardening, art expression, or meditation.

Overnight accommodations are available in cabins ($210-388) or dorms ($95-115); there is a two-night minimum Friday-Saturday. Most guest rooms have a toilet and sink, but all bathing facilities are in the clothing-optional bath-

house. All meals (breakfast, lunch, and dinner) are vegetarian and are included in the price of the cabin or dorm. Note that there is no electricity, no phones, and no Internet access or cell phone reception. A bathing suit is required for the hot springs. Pets are not permitted.

Tassajara is deep in the Ventana Wilderness, about 1.5 hours west of Carmel, and driving here can be an adventure in itself. The winding dirt Tassajara Road runs 14 miles into the Los Padres National Forest, with steep drop-offs and narrow brake-burning descents along the way. The hour-long drive is not suitable for all cars; visit the website for specific driving instructions. First-time visitors should opt for the Stage (daily 10:30 A.M., 8 passengers, $55 pp, reservations required), a shuttle that leaves from Jamesburg and starts the return trip from Tassajara at 3 P.M.

1 to **Bottchers Gap** (end of Polo Colorado Canyon Rd., 805/968-6640, day use $5), which has a small campground. Expect solitude in the thick redwood forest, chaparral meadows, rocky riverbanks, and deep canyons. One of the popular hikes off the Pico Blanco Trail is the **Little Sur Trail**, which picks up at the bottom of the Boy Scouts private property line. The **Skinner Ridge Trail** also has plenty of rugged camps and tricky terrain with primitive camping along the way.

In the backcountry of the Ventana Wilderness is popular **Sykes Hot Springs**, a hike on the Sykes Trail (20 miles round-trip) that requires at least an overnight stay at Sykes Campground. The best way to access the trail is at Big Sur Station No. 1 (47555 Hwy. 1, 831/667-2315, www.parks.ca.gov, parking $5 per night), where you can pick up a detailed map. The hike, through grand redwood groves and rolling chaparral, is breathtaking. The terrain is challenging in places, even for avid hikers, with steep inclines in both directions. At the end of the trail, the reward is nature's soothing riches—the Big Sur River and Sykes Hot Springs, natural hot-spring pools terraced above the Big Sur River. The largest is about 10 feet across and bubbles at an average temperature of 100°F; it can accommodate about six adults. Depending on the flow of the springs, you are likely to find other smaller pools marked by past visitors with cairns. This is a popular destination in peak months (Apr.–Sept.) but quieter midweek and in the off-season (Nov.–Mar.).

BEACHES

Across from the entrance to Big Sur Station, **Pfeiffer Beach** (Sycamore Canyon Rd., off Hwy. 1, 26 miles south of Carmel, 805/434-1996, www.campone.com, daily 9 A.M.–8 P.M., $5) is at the end of a winding road. The beach is easily accessed on a short sandy trail. Rocky islets rise beyond the foam of the surf with visible small caves and windows. The grainy white sand is marbled with red and black silt, creating unique textures and colors. Sunsets in the cove ignite the horizon with a surge of orange that blends into sheets of pink across the fading blue sky. Anglers are known to visit the beaches in the early morning, and surfers frequent the waves.

For an easy-access launch spot for your kayak along the Big Sur coast, try **Mill Creek** (53 miles south of Carmel, 805/434-1996, www.campone.com, daily sunrise–sunset). Parking is just a few steps from the water near the put-in spot, but be careful, as the path to the water is a bit rough with a cluster of rocks to walk over. Locals frequent this location to fish from the bluffs and rocks. There are no amenities besides pit toilets and the paved parking lot.

An impressive spot for surfing and lounging is **Sand Dollar Beach** (60 miles south of Carmel, www.campone.com, daily 30 minutes before sunrise–30 minutes after sunset, 805/434-1996). The breakers are far enough off shore to provide a pleasant ride. Sunbathers will find plenty of secluded spots on the longest beach in the region. At low tide, there is an interesting cave to explore, but keep an eye out for the incoming tide, as it floods the cave.

Several beaches in the southern part of the Big Sur region are known for jade, including **Jade Beach Reserve** (Hwy. 1, 9.7 miles south of Lucia, www.campone.com, daily sunrise–sunset), a U.S. Forest Service reserve marked by a road sign but not much else. Park in the dirt-and-gravel strip along the road, and walk past the fence into the park. A narrow path seems to lead to the edge of a cliff. From the top of the cliff, the short trail becomes rough. It's only 0.25 miles, but it's almost straight down a rocky, slippery cliff face. Don't climb down if you're not in reasonably good physical condition, and use your hands to steady yourself. At the bottom, you'll find huge boulders and smaller rocks, very little sand, and a small herd of people dressed in wetsuits and scuba gear

© KRISTIN LEAL

Pfeiffer Beach

hunting for jade. If you're a hard-core rock hound, you can join the locals scuba diving for jewelry-quality jade. As long as you find it in the water or below the high-tide line, it's legal to take whatever you find.

You can also find pieces of jade at **Willow Creek** (Hwy. 1, 62 miles south of Carmel, 831/385-5434, www.campone.com, daily 30 minutes before sunrise–30 minutes after sunset), tucked away under one of the many Highway 1 bridges where freshwater cuts through a dark pebbly beach and spills into the foam of the ocean. The combination of strong tides and a decaying hillside rich with natural deposits of jade makes it an ideal spot for digging. Willow Creek has parking practically on the sand, and dogs are allowed.

ENTERTAINMENT AND EVENTS

It probably won't be a surprise to learn that Big Sur is not a hotbed of cutting-edge clubs and bars. You can find some fun at the **Fernwood Resort** (Hwy. 1, 831/667-2422, noon–midnight Sun.–Thurs., noon–1 A.M. Fri.–Sat.). Most live music happens on the weekend, especially Saturday night, starting at 9 P.M. Even without the music, the tavern can get lively in the evening, with locals drinking at the full bar, eating, and holding parties in the meandering rooms.

ACCOMMODATIONS
$100-150

A lodge-style motel set in a redwood forest, the **Big Sur River Inn** (Hwy. 1, Pheneger Creek, 800/548-3610, www.bigsurriverinn.com, $125–170) first opened in the 1930s; the inn has been in continuous operation ever since. Today, it boasts 20 motel rooms, a restaurant, and a gift shop. Guest rooms are small but comfortable, with chain-motel comforters and curtains juxtaposed with rustic lodge-style wooden interior paneling. Budget-conscious guest rooms have one queen bed. Families and small groups can choose between standard guest rooms with two queen beds and two-room suites with multiple beds and attractive back decks that look out over the Big Sur River. All guests can enjoy the attractively landscaped outdoor pool with its surrounding lawn leading down to the river. The attached restaurant serves three meals a day. Be sure to make reservations in advance, especially for summer weekends.

For a rustic cabin experience, check into the **Ripplewood Resort** (47020 Hwy. 1, 831/667-2242 or 800/575-1735, www.ripplewoodresort.com, $95–185). The 17 cabins, most with kitchens, are simple redwood structures set along the Big Sur River deep in the redwoods and are suitable for young couples and small families. Advance reservations are strongly advised.

Riverside Campgrounds and Cabins (40720 Hwy. 1, 831/667-2414, www.riversidecampground.com, $100–200) has 11 cabins that can accommodate up to four people; some cabins allow dogs. Within the beautiful natural wood interiors are queen and double

beds. Many of the cabins have decks and outdoor fireplaces. The river is nearby, making an afternoon float in an inner tube a must.

Along Highway 1 in the village of Big Sur are a couple of small motels, including **Fernwood Resort** (Hwy. 1, 831/667-2422, www.fernwoodbigsur.com, $110–195). The resort includes 12 motel rooms, a small grocery store, and a restaurant and tavern. Farther down the small road is a campground with tent cabins as well as tent and RV sites. Motel rooms are modest spaces in a blocky one-level building beside the main store and restaurant buildings. Guest rooms have queen beds and attached private baths but no TVs. In winter, ask for a room with a gas stove. In the summer months, book in advance to be sure of getting a room, especially on weekends.

To stay at ◖ **Deetjens Big Sur Inn** (48865 Hwy. 1, 831/667-2377, www.deetjens.com, $90–260) is to enjoy a small part of Big Sur history and culture. The inn prides itself on

the cozy restaurant at Deetjens Big Sur Inn

its rustic historic construction, and your guest room will be unique, decorated with the art and collectibles chosen and arranged by Grandpa Deetjen many moons ago—expect thin weathered walls, funky construction, no locks on the doors, and an altogether Big Sur experience. Many guest rooms have shared baths; you can also request a guest room with a private bath. Deetjens prefers to offer a serene environment, and to that end does not permit children under 12 unless you rent both guest rooms in a two-room building. Deetjens has no TVs or phones in the guest rooms, and no cell-phone service, although two pay phones are available for emergencies.

$150-250

One of the most romantic and affordable digs is at **Glen Oaks Motel** (Hwy. 1, near Andrew Molera State Park, 831/667-2105, www.glenoaksbigsur.com, $155–300). You can stay at the lodge, a cozy cabin, or the Oak Tree Cottage. The guest rooms in the lodge are modern and spacious, while the cabins are fully functional, with full kitchens, outdoor decks, and plenty of space to spread out. There are cabins with river views and forest views.

The **Big Sur Lodge** (47225 Hwy. 1, 800/424-4787, www.bigsurlodge.com, $159–369), in Pfeiffer Big Sur State Park, was built in the 1930s as a New Deal government works project, and the cabins still evoke a classic woodsy feel. Set in a redwood forest, the cabins feature patchwork quilts, rustic furniture, understated decor, and simple but clean baths. Larger cabins are perfect for families or groups and may have fireplaces and kitchens. The lodge has a swimming pool and on-site restaurant, but the real attraction is access to the Pfeiffer Big Sur trails.

Where the Santa Lucia Mountains meet the sea you'll find the **Lucia Lodge** (62400 Hwy. 1, Lucia, 831/677-2391, www.lucialodge.com, $150–275). There are 10 updated shabby-chic

cabins and guest rooms. The guest rooms are tucked into the cliff side for stunning views; the cabins are more spacious and are farther from the cliffs.

For a high-end camping experience, book a yurt at **Treebones Resort** (71895 Hwy. 1, 877/424-4787, www.treebonesresort.com, $155–280). Yurts at Treebones tend to be spacious and charming, with polished wood floors, queen beds, seating areas, and outdoor decks for lounging. There are also five walk-in campsites ($65 for 2 people). In the central lodge are hot showers and usually clean restrooms. Treebones offers a casual dinner each night as well as basic linens. Children ages 12 and older are welcome in four of the yurts.

Ragged Point Inn (19019 Hwy. 1, 805/927-4502, http://raggedpointinn.net, $159–219) takes advantage of its location on one of Big Sur's famous cliffs to offer stellar views. Guest rooms feature private balconies or patios, and even the budget-friendly guest rooms still have plenty of space, a comfy king or two double beds, and ocean views. Enjoy a meal in the full-service restaurant, fill up at the on-site gas station, or peruse the works of local artists in the gift shop or jewelry gallery. A special treat is the hotel's hiking trail, which drops 400 feet past a waterfall to Ragged Point's beach.

Over $250

If money is no object, you cannot beat the lodgings at the ☾ **Ventana Inn** (48123 Hwy. 1, 800/628-6500, www.ventanainn.com, $600–1,350), where the panoramic ocean views begin in the parking lot. Guest rooms range from "modest" standard rooms with king beds, tasteful exposed cedar walls and ceilings, and attractive appointments to gorgeous spacious suites and full-size multibedroom houses. Home-baked pastries, fresh yogurt, in-season fruit, and organic coffee are delivered in the morning to be enjoyed outdoors on your private patio overlooking the ocean. There are two Japanese bathhouses (clothing-optional and gender segregated) and two swimming pools offer a cooler respite. Facilities include the on-site Cielo dining room and The Spa at Ventana (831/667-4222, www.ventanainn.com, daily 9 A.M.–7 P.M. fall–spring, daily 9 A.M.–8 P.M. summer).

Post Ranch Inn (47900 Hwy. 1, 800/527-2200, www.postranchinn.com, $550–2,285) is perched on the cliffs of Big Sur. The outdoors is highlighted throughout the handcrafted tree houses, guest rooms, and private houses with ocean and forest views. Guest rooms are far from modest but still have the rustic flair of Big Sur. The Sierra Mar restaurant is legendary, and the on-site spa offers massage, body, and facial work.

CAMPING
Andrew Molera State Park
Andrew Molera State Park (Hwy. 1, 22 miles south of Carmel, 831/667-2315, www.parks.ca.gov, $35) offers 24 walk-in tent-only campsites located 0.25–0.5 mile from the parking lot via a well-maintained level trail. Sites are first-come, first-served, in a pretty meadow near the Big Sur River, and have picnic tables and fire rings. No reservations are taken, so come early in summer to get one of the prime spots under a tree. Potable water is not available, and neither are showers. Toilets are a short walk from the camping area.

Fernwood Resort
The Fernwood Resort (Hwy. 1, 831/667-2422, www.fernwoodbigsur.com, campsites $45–75, tents $108, cabins $195) maintains a large campground area on both sides of the Big Sur River. Tent cabins are canvas spaces with room for four people in a double bed and two twins. Bring your own linens or sleeping bags, pillows, and towels. Hot showers and restrooms are a short walk away. Tent campsites are tucked in by the river or under shady redwood trees. RV sites include water and electric hookups. The resort has easy access to the river, where you can swim, inner tube, and hike. You'll also have access to the restaurant, store, and tavern.

Pfeiffer Big Sur State Park
The biggest and most developed campground in Big Sur is Pfeiffer Big Sur State Park (Hwy. 1, 800/444-7275, www.parks.ca.gov, reservations 800/444-7275, www.reserveamerica.com, $35, river view $50), with 212 individual sites, each of which can take two vehicles (RVs up to 32 feet or trailers up to 27 feet) and eight people. There is a dump station on-site and plenty of flush toilets and hot showers scattered throughout. During the summer, a grocery store and laundry facilities are open. In the evening, walk down to the Campfire Center for entertaining and educational programs. There are also hike-in and bike-in campgrounds. Pfeiffer Big Sur fills up fast in summer, especially on weekends. Advance reservations are strongly advised.

Ventana Wilderness and Los Padres National Forest
Los Padres National Forest offers good primitive camping at 55 primitive sites in the backcountry. Get a free wilderness and fire permit from the Los Padres National Forest District Office (805/385-5434, www.campone.com). Good trailheads with backcountry access are Bottchers Gap and Big Sur Station. Palo Colorado Road, off Highway 1, runs eight miles to **Bottchers Gap** (805/968-6640), where there are 12 campsites. Two major trails start here and lead in opposite directions into the wilderness. There are three primitive sites in the redwood forest at **Jackson Camp,** five miles in from Bottchers Gap; **Pico Blanco Camp** is seven miles in. Up the Skinner Ridge Trail are plenty of rugged campsites and difficult terrain to explore. **Apple Tree Camp** is a little over three miles in, and **Turner Creek Camp** is five miles in. Devils Peak has nice

campsites just one mile beyond **Cummings Camp.** For a good look at the Carmel watershed drainage, check out Pine Creek, 6.5 miles in, and Pat Springs, eight miles in. For the adventurous there is also the extreme 60-mile Big Sur loop; it has primitive camping all along the way.

Entering the Ventana Wilderness from the Big Sur Station (Hwy. 1, south of Pfeiffer Big Sur State Park, 831/667-2315, daily 8 A.M.–4:30 P.M.), you can hike in several directions into the heart of the backwoods. Stop in at the visitors center for a detailed map of the area before you head out. From this entrance, **Ventana Campground** can easily be reached in a day; **Barlow Flat Camp** is deep in the backcountry; and **Tassajara Camp,** near the Tassajara Hot Springs, is a well-known spot for a seriously relaxing soak at the Tassajara Zen Mountain Center.

Limekiln State Park

The small but pretty campground at Limekiln State Park (Hwy. 1, 2 miles south of Lucia, 831/667-2403, www.parks.ca.gov, $35) has 33 campsites with hot showers and flush toilets. On bluffs overlooking the ocean, **Kirk Creek Campground** (Hwy. 1, 55 miles south of Carmel, 805/434-1996, www.campone.com, reservations 877/444-6777, www.recreation.gov, $22) has 34 campsites with full panoramic views of the ocean. Reservations are a must to stay at this jewel of Big Sur. Tucked in the shade of Monterey pines and cypress trees, **Plaskett Creek Campground** (Hwy. 1, 60 miles south of Carmel, www.campone.com, reservations 877/444-6777, www. recreation.gov, $22) welcomes tents and RVs, with 44 sites, restrooms, fire rings, and grills.

RVs and trailers up to 24 feet are welcome, but hookups and dump stations aren't available. In the summer, make reservations early. In the winter, no reservations are taken, and many sites are closed.

FOOD
Casual Dining

The northernmost dining option on the Big Sur coast, **Rocky Point Restaurant** (36700 Hwy. 1, 831/624-2933, www.rocky-point.com, daily 9 A.M.–3 P.M. and 5 P.M.–close, $40) offers decent food and great views. Enjoy the smell of mesquite from the grill as you wait for your steak or fish. Meat eaters will find solid dishes for breakfast, lunch, and dinner, but vegetarian options are limited.

When the locals want to cool off in Big Sur, they grab a drink from the full bar at **Big Sur River Inn** (46840 Hwy. 1, Pheneger Creek, 831/667-2700 or 800/548-3610, www.bigsurriverinn.com, $15–37) and sit in the river.

The **Redwood Grill** (Hwy. 1, 831/667-2129, www.fernwoodbigsur.com, daily 11:30 A.M.–9 P.M., $25) at Fernwood Resort looks and feels like a grill in the woods ought to. Even in the middle of the afternoon, the aging wood-paneled interior is dimly lit and strewn with slightly saggy couches and casual tables and chairs. Walk up to the counter to order somewhat overpriced burgers and sandwiches, then on to the bar to grab a soda or a beer.

The **Big Sur Lodge Café and Restaurant** (47225 Hwy. 1, 800/242-4787, www.bigsurlodge.com, daily 7 A.M.–9 P.M., $25) has a dining room as well as a cute espresso and ice cream bar out front. The dining room dishes up a full menu of American classics for every meal, and you can grab a quick sandwich to go from the espresso bar.

The ◖ **Big Sur Bakery** (47540 Hwy. 1, 831/667-0520, www.bigsurbakery.com, lunch 11 A.M.–2:30 P.M. Tues.–Fri., 10:30 A.M.–2:30 P.M. Sat.–Sun., dinner 5:30 P.M.–close Tues.–Sun., $45) is an organic gourmet restaurant featuring local ingredients. Be sure to make reservations, or you're unlikely to get a table. In the morning, stop in at 8 A.M. for a freshly baked scone, homemade jelly doughnut, or a flaky croissant sandwich.

The best breakfast in the area is at ◖**Deetjens** (48865 Hwy. 1, 831/667-2377, www.deetjens.com, daily breakfast and dinner, $20–35). The funky dining room, with its mismatched tables, dark wooden chairs, and cluttered wall decor, belies the high quality of the cuisine served. Enjoy delectable dishes created from the freshest local ingredients for breakfast and then again at dinner.

At the Treebones Resort is the **Wild Coast Restaurant & Sushi Bar** (71895 Hwy. 1, 877/424-4787, www.treebonesresort.com, daily 6–8:30 P.M., $12–33). Globally inspired dishes created from ingredients grown in Wild Coast's own garden will tantalize your taste buds. You can get everything from fresh sushi to tender cuts of beef, roast chicken, and Japanese-inspired dishes.

For southbound drivers, the last dining stop atop the majestic jagged cliffs is at the **Ragged Point Resort Restaurant and Snack Bar** (19019 Hwy. 1, 805/927-4502, www.raggedpointinn.net, daily 8 A.M.–8 P.M., $15–60). The restaurant consists of a semitraditional California coastal cuisine; the local wine choices are delightful. You can also grab a quick bite at the snack bar (daily 8 A.M.–5 P.M., $5–20) serving espresso, sandwiches, and wine.

Fine Dining

When you dine at ◖**Nepenthe** (48510 Hwy. 1, 831/667-2345, www.nepenthebigsur.com, daily 11:30 A.M.–10 P.M., $35), be sure to ask for a table on the deck. The restaurant offers a short but tasty menu of meat, fish, and plenty of vegetarian dishes. On an outdoor patio, **Café Kevah** at Nepenthe (daily breakfast and lunch Mar.–Jan., $15–18) offers a similar sampling of breakfast items and sandwiches at slightly lower prices.

Enjoy a fine gourmet dinner at **The Restaurant at Ventana** (Hwy. 1, 831/667-4242, www.ventanainn.com, daily noon–3:30 P.M. and 6–9 P.M., $30–40). The spacious dining room has a warm wood fire, an open kitchen, and comfortable banquettes with throw pillows. The chef offers California cuisine made with organic produce and local meats as well as some seafood offerings. The best value is the prix fixe menu, with a choice of several courses; be sure to save room for dessert.

The **Sierra Mar** (47900 Hwy. 1, 831/667-2800, www.postranchinn.com, daily 8–10:30 A.M., noon–3 P.M., and 3–9 P.M., $110) restaurant at the Post Ranch Inn offers a decadent four-course prix fixe dinner menu in a stunning ocean-view setting. Casual lunch and snacks are served through the afternoon, but expect to dress up for a formal dinner at this very upscale restaurant.

Stop at the **Lucia Lodge Restaurant** (62400 Hwy. 1, Lucia, 831/688-4884 or 866/424-4787, www.lucialodge.com, daily 11 A.M.–4:30 P.M. and 5–9 P.M., $19–35) for a great view and a tasty meal. The menu is quite extensive, with dinner delights like bacon-wrapped filet mignon, award-winning fish-and-chips, and homemade chicken cordon bleu. For lunch, order a hearty salad, burger, or sandwich, or choose a few appetizers to go around.

INFORMATION AND SERVICES

There are two comprehensive visitors centers in Big Sur. The visitors center at **Pfeiffer Big Sur State Park** (47225 Hwy. 1, 831/667-2315, www.parks.ca.gov) is a good spot to get maps and information. Farther south at **Julia Pfeiffer Burns State Park** (Hwy. 1, 12 miles south of Pfeiffer Big Sur, 831/667-2315, www.parks.ca.gov), rangers at the visitors center can advise about activities in the region.

For trail maps, permits, and general information, head to the **Big Sur Station** (just south of Pfeiffer Big Sur State Park, 831/667-2315, daily 8 A.M.–4:30 P.M.). For current information about the trails throughout the Los Padres

National Forest, contact the **King City District Forest Service** (831/385-5434).

The **Big Sur Health Center** (46896 Hwy. 1, 831/667-2580, 10 A.M.–5 P.M. Mon.–Fri.) can take care of minor medical needs and provides an ambulance service and limited emergency care. The **Big Sur Volunteer Fire Brigade** (831/667-2113, www.bigsurfire.org) also has an ambulance and a 24-hour paramedic team.

There are no supermarkets anywhere in the Big Sur region. You can stock up on staples at the **Fernwood Resort** (Hwy. 1, 831/667-2422, www.fernwoodbigsur.com), which has a small market. You'll also find a seasonal market at Pfeiffer Big Sur State Park.

Be aware that your cell phone may not work in the Big Sur region. Emergency call boxes are placed at regular intervals along the highway.

GETTING THERE AND AROUND

Big Sur is 28 miles south of Monterey on Highway 1. To reach Big Sur from San Francisco (2 hours 45 minutes, 141 miles), take U.S. 101 south to Highway 85 south. Merge onto Highway 17 south, and then onto Highway 1 south. Note that in Big Sur, Highway 1 becomes a narrow twisting track that is breathtaking both for its beauty and its danger. Fog often comes in at sunset, limiting visibility considerably. If you must drive at night, take it slow.

You can get as far south as Nepenthe from Monterey, Carmel, or Salinas on **Monterey-Salinas Transit** (831/899-2555, www.mst.org, $1.50–3, exact change required) a few times a day. The bus route starts in downtown Monterey at the **Transit Plaza** (end of Alvarado St.) and runs through Carmel.

San Simeon and Cambria

The San Simeon area was made famous by William Randolph Hearst and his early-20th-century castle on the hill. Today, it remains much as it was back then, minus the celebrity guest list. The town of San Simeon is small and appropriate for an overnight or weekend stay, with a handful of camping, lodging, and dining options.

Cambria began as an artists colony. The windswept hills and sparkling ocean have always provided inspiration for painters, writers, sculptors, glassblowers, and other creative minds. The seaside town is a tight cluster of art galleries, antiques malls, shops, ocean-side accommodations, and restaurants.

SAN SIMEON

The tiny village of San Simeon was established primarily to support the construction efforts up the hill at Hearst Castle. The village dock provided a place for ships to unload tons of marble, piles of antiques, and scores of workers. The general store and post office acted as a central gathering place for the community. You can still walk up the weathered wooden steps to shop at **Sebastian's Store** (442 Slo San Simeon Rd., 805/927-3307, 11 A.M.–4 P.M. Wed.–Sun.), an old-fashioned shop with a variety of gifts. You can also grab a sandwich, a cup of coffee, or a burger and eat at one of the picnic tables.

◖ Hearst Castle State Historic Monument

Newspaper magnate William Randolph Hearst hired Julia Morgan, the first woman to graduate from the University of California, Berkeley, to design and build the regal Hearst Castle (Hearst Castle Rd., off Hwy. 1, 800/444-4445, www.hearstcastle.org, tours daily 9 A.M.–3:20 P.M., adults $25, children $12; evening tours adults $36, children $18), the grand Mediterranean-style mansion set on ranch-land his parents owned along the California coast. Morgan did a brilliant job with every detail, despite the ever-changing ideas of her employer. For decoration, Hearst relocated hundreds of medieval and Renaissance antiquities from Europe. He also created one of the largest private zoos in the nation on his thousands of Central Coast acres. Although most of the zoo is gone, you can still see the occasional zebra grazing peacefully along Highway 1. The sheer size and attention to detail is a marvel throughout the estate, from the rooftops to the gardens. The beauty and opulence of every room, filled with European art and antiques, amazes. The two swimming pools—the outdoor Greco-Roman style Neptune Pool and the indoor Roman Pool with blue Venetian glass and gold tiles—are a highlight, both surrounded by custom and antique statuary.

The Hearst Castle visitors center houses a gift shop, a restaurant, a café, the ticket booth, and a movie theater showing *Hearst Castle:*

Building the Dream, an overview of the construction. After buying your ticket, a shuttle bus takes you up the hill to begin the tour (no private cars are allowed on the roads up to the castle). There are four tours available, each focusing on different spaces and aspects of the castle. The **Grand Rooms Museum Tour** is recommended for first-time visitors; the **Evening Tour** is a seasonal tour with volunteers dressed in 1930s fashions who welcome guests as if to one of Hearst's legendary parties. Other tours include the **Upstairs Suites Museum Tour** and the **Cottages and Kitchen Tour.** All tours provide access to the two pools as well as the extensive gardens.

Visitors should reserve tour tickets a few days in advance, and far in advance for the Evening Tour and summer weekends. Restrooms and concessions are located in the visitors center; no food or drink are allowed on any tour. Expect to walk for 45–60 minutes and to climb up

CENTRAL COAST

© CALIFORNIA STATE PARKS

the Neptune Pool at Hearst Castle

Hearst Castle State Historic Monument

and down many stairs. For visitors with limited mobility, special wheelchair-accessible tours are available. Strollers are not permitted.

William Randolph Hearst Memorial State Beach

Directly across Highway 1 from Hearst Castle, William Randolph Hearst Memorial State Beach (750 Hearst Castle Rd., 805/927-2020, www.parks.ca.gov, daily dawn–dusk, $10) includes a small cove and the remaining structure of the old pier. The wide beach is appealing for sunbathers, as the winds are mild and the sand warm. The protected cove has mild waves for beginning surfers or body boarders, although the water temperature averages only 55–60°F. Kayaks and body boards are available for rent. A walk along the **San Simeon Bay Trail** (2 miles) to Simeon Point is a beautiful way to take in the bay; the trail begins just north of the fishing pier. There are 24 picnic sites with pedestal grills as well as

public restrooms and drinking water. Access to the beach is steps away at a 150-space parking lot.

Accommodations

The Morgan San Simeon (9135 Hearst Dr., 805/927-3878 or 800/451-9900, www.hotelmorgan.com, $79–199) has a contemporary design and a touch of elegance. Guest rooms are sizable, and the Morgan Suite has an extra room for lounging and entertaining. This is a full-service hotel, and guests are welcome to visit the on-site spa and dine at the El Chorlito Mexican Restaurant.

The beach-inspired **San Simeon Lodge** (9520 Castillo Dr., 805/927-4601, www.sansimeonbeachresort.net, $49–250) is located in the center of San Simeon, near Hearst Castle and only a block from William Randolph Hearst Memorial State Beach. Vibrant gardens surround the resort, and guest rooms are decorated in blond wood furniture and light blue, with room to move around. There is an outdoor pool and an on-site fitness center.

Stay alongside the ocean at the **Best Western Cavalier Resort** (9415 Hearst Dr., 805/927-4688, www.cavalierresort.com, $99–319). This oceanfront venue is known for its comfort and service, offering everything from family-size guest rooms to romantic escapes. Guest rooms have coffeemakers, minibars, DVD players, full baths, fridges, and blow-dryers; many have ocean views and some feature fireplaces and outdoor patios. The Cavalier Restaurant is on-site.

Food

For beachside dining indoors or out, the **San Simeon Beach Bar & Grill** (9520 Castillo Dr., 805/927-4604, www.sansimeonrestaurant.com, daily 7:30 A.M.–9:30 P.M., bar 7:30 A.M.–2 A.M. Fri.–Sat., $18–24) is casual and laid-back, with everything from early morning breakfast to late-night cocktails, salads, pastas, and pizzas. There is karaoke (9 P.M.–1 A.M. Fri.–Sat.) and happy hour (daily 4–6 P.M.).

With a great ocean view, **El Chorlito Mexican Restaurant** (9135 Hearst Dr., 805/927-3878 or 800/451-9900, www.elchorlito.com, $9–28) offers traditional dishes like burritos, tacos, *carnitas,* and enchiladas. House specialties include lamb shanks in a mild tomato sauce.

Reasonably priced American food is on offer at **The Cavalier Restaurant** (9415 Hearst Dr., 805/927-4688, www.cavalierresort.com, daily 7 A.M.–9 P.M. winter, daily 7 A.M.–10 P.M. summer, $5–19). Breakfast is strictly traditional with a few specialties like eggs benedict and eggs florentine served all day. Lunch and dinner entrées focus on comfort food such as chicken-fried steak.

Information and Services

For information about the area, visit the **San Simeon Chamber of Commerce** (250 San Simeon Ave., Suite 3A, 805/927-3500 or 805/927-0640, www.sansimeonchamber.org, daily 10 A.M.–4 P.M.). The closest emergency services are in Templeton at the **Twin Cities Hospital** (1100 Las Tablas Rd., Templeton, 805/434-3500, www.twincitieshospital.com), about 25 miles east of San Simeon.

Getting There and Around

San Simeon is located along Highway 1, 95 miles south of Monterey and 40 miles inland from Paso Robles via Highway 46.

CAMBRIA

Seaside Cambria is a tight cluster of art galleries, antiques malls, shops, ocean-side accommodations, and restaurants. Most of Cambria's amenities are downtown within walking distance, while coastal Moonstone Beach has some accommodations and food.

Sights

Local eccentric Arthur Harold Beal (aka "Captain Nitt Witt" or "Der Tinkerpaw") built **Nitt Witt Ridge** (881 Hillcrest Dr., 805/927-2690, tours by appointment, free) over five decades, scavenging trash to use as building supplies for this multistory home. It's weird, it's funky, and it's fun—an oddly iconic experience. Today, you can make an appointment with owners Michael and Stacey O'Malley to tour the property, but don't just drop in.

The **Cambria Cemetery** (6005 Bridge St., 805/927-5158, www.cambriacemetery.com) reflects the artistic bent of the town's residents in its tombstone decor. Graves are decorated with colorful personal objects such as panes of stained glass, wind chimes, and many other unique expressions of love, devotion, and art.

Art Galleries

Cambria is known as an artistic community, and each art gallery is unique, featuring both local and widely known artists. **The Vault Gallery** (2289 Main St., 805/927-0300, www.

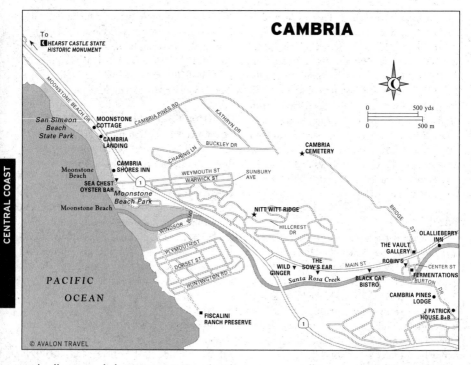

CAMBRIA

vaultgallery.com, daily 10:30 A.M.5:30 or 6 P.M.) showcases fine art produced by local artists. Come to the place where American imagination takes shape at **The Art of America Moonstones Gallery** (4070 Burton Dr., 805/927-3447 or 800/424-3827, www.moonstones.com, daily 10 A.M.–10 P.M.), with a bit of everything in a variety of media. Most afternoons you can visit the **Patricia Griffin Studio & Gallery** (880 Main St., 805/924-1050 or 805/927-1871, www.patriciagriffinstudio.com, daily from noon). Within the walls of a 100-year-old schoolhouse, Griffin creates contemporary pottery that reflects the beauty of nature in combinations of earthy tones. Call to make sure the studio doors are open.

Wineries

There are several tasting rooms in Cambria, including the west-village **Moonstone Cellars** (801 Main St., 805/927-9466, www.

moonstonecellars.com, daily 11 A.M.–5 P.M., tasting $5 for 6 flights), crafting an array of whites, reds, and dessert wines; varietals include albariño, viognier, chardonnay, syrah, tempranillo, cabernet sauvignon, merlot, zinfandel, and adularia.

Enjoy the Roaring '20s-themed tasting room of **Black Hands Cellars** (766 Main St., 805/927-9463, www.blackhandcellars. com, 11 A.M.–5 P.M. Thurs.–Mon. winter, 11 A.M.–5 P.M. daily summer) and enjoy red wines with clever names like Hit and Run, Alibi, and The Deal Maker.

In the east village, **Fermentations** (4056 Burton Dr., 805/927-7141, www.fermentations. com, 11 A.M.–7 P.M. Mon.–Thurs., 10 A.M.–10 P.M. Fri.–Sun. winter, daily 10 A.M.–10 P.M. summer, tasting $5, includes glass) carries everything from local gourmet food items to wine accessories.

For a relaxed wine-tasting experience with a

designated driver, take a ride on the **Wine Line** (805/610-8267, www.hoponthewineline.com, $60). This hop-on, hop-off shuttle service goes to San Simeon, Cambria, and Paso Robles. Service is door-to-door, with pickup times 10:30–11:30 A.M.; the end-of-day drop-off at your lodging is around 4–5 P.M. There are more than 60 wineries along the route; arrange for lunch ($15), or you can pack your own in a cooler.

Entertainment and Events

The Pewter Plough Playhouse (824 Main St., 805/927-3877, www.pewterploughplayhouse. org) stages productions of musicals, dramas, and comedies. You can usually catch a show at 7:30 P.M. Friday–Saturday, with matinees at 3 P.M. Sunday and the occasional Thursday performance. Get tickets early for Cambria's three-day **Art and Wine Festival** (www.see-cambria.com/artwine) in January. Be dazzled for two days and nights by local food, wine from 30 local wineries, live entertainment, an art show, a silent auction, and a raffle. There is a barbecue lunch on the last day.

Shopping

The bright yellow shop in the west village is **Caren's Corner** (755 Main St., 805/927-1161, 11 A.M.–5 P.M. Mon.–Tues. and Sat.–Sun., 11 A.M.–7 P.M. Wed.–Thurs.), with all kinds of trinkets such as seashells, wind chimes, garden flags, and postcards as well as an old-fashioned ice cream parlor.

A Matter of Taste in Cambria (4120 Burton Dr., 805/927-0286, www.amatteroftastecambria. com, daily 10 A.M.–5 P.M.) carries linens, bakeware, serving dishes, kitchen gadgets, and gourmet food. It also carries the works of local artist Barbara Katz Bierman, who specializes in creating colorful trays, tote bags, floor mats, and original paintings. If you are planning to be in Cambria for a while, check out the cooking classes.

GOWA Creative Arts (4009 West St., 805/927-1005, www.g-o-w-a.com, 11 A.M.–5 P.M. Mon.–Fri., 10 A.M.–5 P.M. Sat.–Sun.) are a series of colorful cottages that serve as art studios and an apparel store. Each piece of clothing is one of a kind, modern, fashionable, and wearable art fashioned and airbrushed by Christopher and Dinah Lee.

Sports and Recreation

Just south of Highway 1 is **Moonstone State Beach** (Moonstone Beach Dr., 805/927-2020, free), with a long shoreline ideal for a stroll. The boardwalk runs from Leffingwell Landing and Day Use area to just north of Weymouth Street. The beach stretches a bit farther than the boardwalk and includes the Santa Rosa Day-use Area to the south, where you can find additional parking.

Leffingwell Landing at Moonstone Beach offers tide pools to explore, a launch ramp, and a parking lot; you can do some shore fishing from the rocks. Dogs are welcome on the boardwalk and on the beach.

The 364-acre **Fiscalini Ranch Preserve** (4500 Windsor Blvd., www.ffrpcambria.org, daily sunrise–sunset, free) has 11 trails, some of which run along the bluffs above the ocean. You may see sea otters basking in the sun in Otter Cove, an abundance of seabirds such as egrets and herons, and elephant seals and migrating whales. The Friends of Fiscalini Ranch (www.cambriaranchwalks.com) host docent-led nature walks once a month (10 A.M.–noon Sat.).

Accommodations

The **Olallieberry Inn** (2476 Main St., 805/927-3222 or 888/927-3222, www.olallieberry.com, $135–225) is a charming 19th-century Greek Revival home and adjacent cottage. Each of the nine guest rooms features its own quaint Victorian-inspired decor with comfortable beds and attractive appointments. A full daily breakfast, complete with olallieberry jam, rounds out the experience. **Her Castle Homestay Bed and Breakfast Inn** (1978 Londonderry Lane,

Moonstone State Beach is perfect for a long walk.

805/924-1719, www.hercastle.cc, $120–160) has only two guest rooms and lots of personal attention from the owners. Ask about a half-day wine tour, dinner reservations, or even lunch and dinner provided by the inn. The Her Castle can be a perfect lodging for two couples traveling together.

Watch migrating whales from your ocean-view room at **Cambria Landing** (6530 Moonstone Beach Dr., 805/927-1619, www.cambrialanding.com, $100–275). Amenities include Wi-Fi access, continental breakfast, fireplaces, balconies or patios, and a bottle of wine at check-in. Some suites have spacious jetted tubs and roaring fireplaces. Standard guest rooms have partial ocean views. For a great selection from economical standard guest rooms up to sizable cabins, the **Cambria Pines Lodge** (2905 Burton Dr., 800/445-6868, www.cambriapineslodge.com, $69–389) has guest rooms with TVs, private baths, kitchenettes, and fireplaces in some rooms.

A charming log cabin structure houses the eight guest rooms of **J. Patrick House Bed and Breakfast** (2990 Burton Dr., 805/927-3812, www.jpatrickhouse.com, $165–215). Each guest room has modern-country decor, a private bath, and plenty of amenities. J. Patrick includes a big breakfast in the morning, hors d'oeuvres in the afternoon, and chocolate-chip cookies at bedtime. **Moonstone Cottages** (6580 Moonstone Beach Dr., 805/927-1366, http://moonstonecottages.com, $175–349) offers peace and luxury along with proximity to the sea. Expect your cottage to include a fireplace, a marble bath with a jetted tub, a flat-screen TV with a DVD player, Internet access, and breakfast delivered daily to your door. The views are stellar, and the guest rooms are cozy.

Just across the street from the beach is the **Cambria Shores Inn** (6276 Moonstone Beach Dr., 805/927-8644 or 800/433-9179, www.cambriashores.com, $180–310). Guest rooms are high-end, and breakfast is served in a basket at your door. Dogs are welcome.

Food

Enjoy a little taste of Italy at **Allocco's Italian Bakery** (1602 Main St., 805/927-1501, www.alloccos.com, daily 7 A.M.–5 P.M., $2–8). Along with imported items are freshly baked breads and pastries, Taralli Italian Gourmet Pretzels, Italian coffee ($1), Italian sodas, and freshly made sandwiches.

For a caffeine fix any time of day, head to **Cambria Coffee Roasting Company** (761 Main St., 805/927-0670, www.cambriacoffee.com, daily 7 A.M.–5:30 P.M., $2–6), serving carefully roasted coffee from around the world. Seating is limited upstairs and outside alongside the street, but it's a great grab-and-go stop; Wi-Fi is free.

One of the best food bargains in town is **C Wild Ginger** (2380 Main St., 805/927-1001, www.wildgingercambria.com, 11 A.M.–2:30 P.M. and 5–9 P.M. Fri.–Wed., $15–18), a tiny pan-Asian café with delicious fresh food at a few tables as well as take-out fare displayed in a glass case. Come early for the best selection. Part of a large local family business, **Linn's of Cambria** (2277 Main St., 805/927-0371, www.linnsfruitbin.com/restaurant, daily 8 A.M.–9 P.M., $10) serves tasty, unpretentious American favorites in a casual family-friendly atmosphere. The menu features meatloaf, rack of lamb, homemade soups, fresh salads, and all kinds of sandwiches. You can purchase a ready-to-bake homemade olallieberry pie, various jams, and homemade vinegar at this café or the original farm stand (6275 Santa Rosa Creek Rd.).

Locals love **C Robin's Restaurant** (4095 Burton Dr., 805/927-5007, www.robinsrestaurant.com, lunch and dinner daily 11 A.M.–9 P.M., brunch 11 A.M.–3 P.M. Sun., $11–26). Flowering vines, wooden birdhouses, and small lanterns decorate the walls. The food is homemade and combines creativity with local fresh ingredients. Dishes are beautifully presented; gluten-free and vegan options are available. **The Sow's Ear** (2248 Main St., 805/927-4865, www.thesowsear.com, daily 5–9 P.M., $15–38) serves upscale comfort food in a romantic atmosphere. Menu items such as lobster pot pie and chicken and dumplings provide a taste of old-fashioned Americana.

Sea Chest Oyster Bar (6216 Moonstone Beach Dr., 805/927-4514, daily 5:30–9 P.M., $25–40, cash only) serves fresh seafood with a good selection of raw oysters. Reservations are not accepted, so get here early or prepare to wait a while. The **Black Cat Bistro** (1602 Main St., 805/927-1600, www.blackcatbistro.com, 5 P.M.–close Thurs.–Mon., $25–45) has an interesting California-French menu offering both small and large portions, each with a suggested wine pairing. The menu features many unique dishes with a focus on seafood such as grilled ahi, Idaho rainbow trout, and sea scallops.

Information and Services

Cambria does not have a brick-and-mortar visitors center, but you can visit online (www.cambriavisitorsbureau.com or www.cambriacmaber.org). The nearest medical services are at **Twin Cities Hospital** (1100 Las Tablas Rd., Templeton, 805/434-3500), 24 miles inland near U.S. 101 just south of Highway 46. Mail service is at Cambria's **post office** (Main St. and Bridge St.).

Getting There and Around

Cambria is located on Highway 1, about 10 miles south of San Simeon and 30 miles inland from Paso Robles via Highway 46. A local transportation option is the **Cambria Village Trolley** (805/541-2228, www.cambriacsd.org, 9 A.M.–6 P.M. Thurs.–Mon. June–Sept. 4, 9 A.M.–6 P.M. Fri.–Mon. Sept. 5–May). There are 24 stops along the loop that starts and ends at San Simeon Pines Resort (7200 Moonstone Dr., Cambria).

BACKGROUND

The Land

GEOGRAPHY

Northern California's geographic profile is as diverse as its population. At nearly 159,000 square miles, California is the third-largest state in the United States, stretching 770 miles from the Oregon state line to its southern border with Mexico. Northern California includes the Sierra Nevada mountain range, numerous national parks and monuments, coastal and giant redwoods, volcanoes, the agricultural Central Valley, and the tallest mountain in the continental United States, Mount Whitney, at 14,505 feet. In addition, two major tectonic plates—the north-moving Pacific and south-moving North American Plate—give Northern California a reputation for shaking things up a bit.

Mountain Ranges

The Northern California coast is characterized by craggy cliffs, rocky beaches, and enormous coast redwoods (*Sequoia sempervirens*) that reach heights up to 380 feet. The coast is bounded by the aptly named Coast Range, ruggedly steep mountains formed 30 million years ago when part of the Pacific Plate jammed, folded, and compressed to form the Coast Range and

Transverse Range. In addition to the Coast Range, there are two other significant high-elevation regions in the state. In the north, the Cascade Mountains evolved through volcanic activity 10 million years ago when the Juan de Fuca Plate, earth's smallest tectonic plate caught between the North American and Pacific Plates, collided with the North American Plate and was forced under the larger plate. Magma from the melting plate raised a series of mountains, including California's two active volcanoes—Mount Lassen and Mount Shasta. Mount Lassen (10,462 feet) last blew its top in 1915; today, the surrounding park offers a glimpse into the earth's formation. Majestic Mount Shasta, along I-5 north of Redding, has not erupted in quite some time. At 14,179 feet, Mount Shasta's extreme height creates its own weather system.

To the east is the Sierra Nevada, stretching 400 miles north–south and forming the eastern spine of the state. Its peaks and valleys include Mount Whitney, Lake Tahoe, Yosemite, and the giant sequoias (*Sequoiadendron giganteum*) in Sequoia and Kings Canyon National Parks. The Sierra Nevada formed 60 million years ago when magma seeped up between the Pacific and North American Plates. It created a massive pool of granite that slowly cooled to form a batholith, a massive dome-shaped formation of intrusive igneous rock. For the past 12 million years the formation has been pushing upward.

Earthquakes and Faults

Earthquakes occur when the tectonic plates that compose the earth's crust shift along faults, the boundaries between the plates—and Northern California's seat on the Pacific Ring of Fire is well established. The North American Plate and Pacific Plate came together about 150 million years ago, causing compression and folding of the earth's crust that created the Sierra Nevada; it eventually eroded to fill with sediments what

BACKGROUND

PHOTO BY ARNOLD GENTHE: "SAN FRANCISCO: APRIL 18, 1906." FROM *AS I REMEMBER*

San Franciscans survey the damage to their city after the 1906 earthquake and resulting fire.

EARTHQUAKE TIPS

Visitors from outside California may have the impression that big earthquakes happen here all the time. Well, that's only partly correct. Earthquakes do happen all the time, but most shakers are measurable only by sophisticated equipment and remain unfelt by most residents. According to the California Emergency Management Agency, there are some things you can do to protect yourself during an earthquake:

- Drop! Cover! Hold on! California schoolchildren learn this early on through education programs. It means that if an earthquake begins, drop to the ground. Find cover under a sturdy desk or table, or stand in a corner or doorway. Hold on to something sturdy if the ground begins to pitch.

- If you're in a high-rise building, avoid elevators, windows, and outside areas.

- If you're outside, move to a clear area away from trees, buildings, overpasses, walls, and power lines—anything that could fall on you.

- If you're in a car, pull over to the side of the road. Make sure you're not parked underneath a structure that could collapse.

- If you're inside a crowded place, do not rush to the exit. Instead, squat down and protect your head and neck with your hands and arms.

It's important to stay as calm as possible after an earthquake; the ground may start shaking again. Aftershocks, usually smaller, often follow a sizable earthquake and originate near the same location. A mild earthquake might cause anxiety, but it should not affect your travel plans aside from slight delays in public transportation and other inconveniences. A major earthquake—magnitude 4.5 and larger—is a different story, but these earthquakes are pretty uncommon (it's more likely that you'll win the state lottery than experience a major earthquake).

For more information on what to do before, during, and after an earthquake, visit the California Emergency Management Agency (www.calema.ca.gov) and the U.S. Geological Survey (www.usgs.gov).

---

would become the Central Valley. About 30 million years ago a ridge of the Pacific Plate became jammed and caused the folding and compression that formed the Coast and Transverse Ranges. More importantly, the contact caused the Pacific Plate to change direction and move northward, forming the San Andreas Fault. This infamous strike-slip fault, where two tectonic plates move horizontally, the North American Plate moving mostly southward and the Pacific Plate moving mostly northward, runs along the North Coast, near San Francisco, and east of Los Angeles before branching off into Mexico and the Pacific Ocean.

The plates frequently catch as they move past each other, storing energy and causing tension to build. When the plates jolt past one another, they release this energy in the form of an earthquake. The San Andreas Fault is not the only fault in Northern California; earthquakes along numerous faults happen daily, 10,000–37,000 times each year. Most register less than magnitude 3 and go unnoticed by Californians used to the shake, rattle, and roll. However, there have been several significant earthquakes in Northern California history. The 1906 San Francisco earthquake had a magnitude of 7.7–8.3 and involved the "rupturing" of the northern 300 miles of the San Andreas Fault from San Juan Bautista to Cape Mendocino. The 1989 Loma Prieta earthquake, with an epicenter near Loma Prieta Peak in the Santa Cruz Mountains, was small by comparison at magnitude 6.9 and with only 25 miles of ruptured fault. California's stringent building codes, developed in the wake of deadly and destructive earthquakes, include an extensive seismic retrofit program that has brought older buildings,

Fog envelopes the Golden Gate Bridge.

overpasses, bridges, and other structures up to stringent standards.

CLIMATE

Vast in size and varied in geography, Northern California also has a vastly varied climate, from boiling heat in the Central Valley to subarctic temperatures at mountain summits.

Along the North Coast, the weather stays fairly constant: chilly, windy, and foggy. Summer days rarely reach 80°F, and winter rainstorms can pound the area. San Francisco shares its cool and foggy climate with temperatures in the 50s and 60s well into summer. South on the peninsula or across the Bay in Marin County and the East Bay, the temperature may rise 20–30 degrees and the fog often makes way for sun.

North of San Francisco, the Wine Country is graced with milder weather and warm summers, perfect for growing grapes. Inland, Sacramento and the Central Valley can be very hot. Daily temperatures in summer can peak well over 100°F and often worsen air quality, causing Spare the Air alerts. Winters in the Central Valley are cool and usually clear, however the nearby Sierra Nevada Foothills often receive snow in the winter, and roads can become impassable.

Expect harsh weather if you head to Yosemite, Lake Tahoe, Mount Shasta, Mount Lassen, or the Eastern Sierra in the winter. Snowfall in a 24-hour period can be measured in feet, forcing road closures and power outages that wreak havoc with travel plans. But activities such as skiing, snowboarding, sledding, snowshoeing, and snow camping abound. The short hot summers draw campers, hikers, and mountain bikers.

The Central Coast is a bit warmer than the San Francisco Bay Area, but still, expect cool temperatures and fog in summer. A chilly wind accompanies the rain in the winter, often closing mountain roads and highways, including Highway 1.

ENVIRONMENTAL ISSUES

Californians face several major environmental issues. The state battles drought and water for crops, farms, and human consumption is always in short supply. Conservations measures can include limiting development and urban sprawl, restricting water usage, and designating set periods for personal and recreational use, such as watering lawns.

Water pollution is also an issue. Most tap water is safe to drink, but swimming in California's plentiful bays, lakes, and rivers as well as the Pacific Ocean requires more caution. Pollution may cause *E. coli* outbreaks at beaches, affecting wildlife and beachgoers alike. Fishing is no longer permitted in San Francisco Bay due to high mercury levels in the Bay's fish.

Northern California's lakes have also been affected by infestations of invasive zebra mussels, which grow so quickly and profusely that they can clog water intakes and outcompete native mussels and clams. Many boat restrictions are in effect at coastal waterways and mountain lakes to control the spread of the infestation; check with the Department of Fish and Game (916/445-0411, www.dfg.ca.gov) for more information.

Many of state's grand oak trees have succumbed to sudden oak death, a disease that spreads through spores to eventually kill live oaks, black oaks, and tanoaks. To control its spread, travelers are advised to clean all camping equipment thoroughly and to buy and burn local firewood rather than importing it from elsewhere.

Flora and Fauna

FLORA
Redwoods

A visit to Northern California's famous redwoods should be on every traveler's list. The coast redwood (*Sequoia sempervirens*) grows along the North Coast as far south as Big Sur. Coast redwoods are characterized by their towering height, flaky red bark, and moist understory. Among the tallest trees on earth, they are also some of the oldest, with some individuals almost 2,000 years old. Coast redwoods occupy a narrow strip of coastal California, growing less than 50 miles inland to collect moisture from the ocean and fog. Their tannin-rich bark is crucial to their ability to survive wildfires and regenerate afterward. The best places to marvel at the giants are within the Redwood National and State Parks, Muir Woods, and Big Basin State Park.

The giant sequoia (*Sequoiadendron giganteum*) grows farther inland in a 260-mile belt at 3,000–8,900 feet elevation in the Sierra Nevada mountain range. Giant sequoias are the largest trees by volume on earth; they can grow to heights of 280 feet with a diameter up to 26 feet and can live for thousands of years. Giant sequoias share the ruddy bark of the coast sequoia as well as its fire-resistant qualities. The best places to see giant sequoias up close are at Sequoia and Kings Canyon National Parks, Calaveras Big Trees, and the Mariposa Grove at Yosemite National Park.

Oaks

Northern California is home to many native oaks. The most common are the valley oak, black oak, live oak, and coastal live oak. The deciduous valley oak (*Quercus lobata*) commonly grows on slopes, valleys, and wooded foothills in the Central Valley. The black oak, also deciduous, grows throughout the foothills of the Coast Range and Sierra Nevada; it is unfortunately one of the victims of sudden oak death. The live oak habitat is in the Central Valley, while the coastal live oak occupies the Coast Range. The acorns of all these oaks were an important food supply for California's

© SABRINA YOUNG

Sequoia sempervirens, or coast redwoods

Native American population and continue to be an important food source for wildlife.

Wildflowers

California's state flower is the California poppy (*Eschscholzia californica*). The pretty little perennial grows just about everywhere, even on the sides of the busiest highways. The flowers of most California poppies are bright orange, but they also appear occasionally in white, cream, and an even deeper red-orange.

FAUNA
Mountain Lions

Mountain lions (*Felis concolor*) are an example of powerful and potentially deadly beauty. Their solitary territorial hunting habits make them elusive, but human contact has increased as more homes are built in mountain lion habitat throughout California. Many parks in or near mountain lion territory post signs with warnings and advice: Do not run if you

come across a mountain lion; instead make noise and raise and wave your arms so that you look bigger. The California Fish and Game Department (www.dfg.ca.gov) offers a downloadable brochure on encounters and other tips.

Black Bears

Don't take the name black bear (*Ursus americanus*) too literally. The black bear can actually have brown and even cinnamon-colored fur, sometimes with a white patch on the chest. The black bear is pretty common throughout North America, including in the forests of Northern California south to Sonoma County, the Sierra Nevada, and the Transverse Range. While the black bear can appear cuddly from a distance, distance is exactly what should separate bears and humans—at least 25 feet or more. These are wild animals; do not attempt to feed or approach them, and never come between a mama bear and her cubs. Bears can run up to 30 mph, and they can definitely outrun you. Campers

a black bear in Sequoia National Park

© GEORGE JEN

should use bear-proof food lockers at campgrounds or a bear canister in the backcountry; never keep food or any scented products (toothpaste, energy bars, hair products) in a tent or in view inside a car. Bears can be crafty and destructive—some, especially in Yosemite National Park, have broken into cars and shredded the interiors looking for food. Bears are mostly nocturnal but can be seen out during the day, and they do not always hibernate in winter.

Tule Elk

Tule elk (*Cervus elaphus nannodes*, also known as wapiti, California elk, or dwarf elk) are the smallest elk in North America and once thrived in the Central Valley; tule elk were nearly hunted to extinction to feed Gold Rush settlers. There are now almost 3,000 tule elk in approximately 20 free-range and protected herds in several grassland habitats in the Central Valley and Point Reyes National Seashore. Usually pale gray, brown, or tan with thick chestnut brown necks, the male bull can grow antlers

that stretch five feet or more. In the fall, the bull gives a low bellow followed by a distinctive far-carrying whistle or bugle, while the female whistles in spring.

Whales

The massive, majestic gray whale (*Eschrichtius robustus*) was once endangered, but its numbers have rebound with international protection. The gray whale measures about 40 feet long and has mottled shades of gray with black fins; its habitat is inshore ocean waters, so there is a chance to get a glimpse at them from headlands up and down the coast. Gray whales generally migrate south along the coast November–January, and closer to shore February–June when they migrate northward. Mendocino County is a perfect place to watch the water for a glimpse of whales breaching.

Perhaps a more recognizable behemoth is the humpback whale (*Megaptera novaeangliae*). At 45–55 feet long, the humpback is the only large whale to breach regularly, then roll and crash back into the water, providing one of the best shows in nature; the whale also rolls from side to side on the surface, slapping its long flippers. Humpbacks generally stay a little farther from shore, so it may be necessary to take a whale-watching cruise to catch a glimpse of them, but their 20-foot spouts can help landlubbers spot them from shore. Look for humpbacks April–early December off the coast near Big Sur, particularly at Julia Pfeiffer Burns State Park.

The blue whale (*Balaenoptera musculus*) is the largest animal on earth. At 70–90 feet long, the blue whale even exceeds dinosaurs in size. With a blue-gray top and a yellowish bottom, the blue whale has a heart the size of a small car, two blowholes, but alas does not breach. They can be seen June–November off the Northern California coast, but especially at Monterey and north of Point Reyes.

California Sea Lions

Watching a beach full of California sea lions (*Zalophus californianus*) sunning themselves and noisily honking away can be a pleasure. Sea lions are migratory, so they come and go at will, especially in the fall when they head to the Channel Islands for breeding. If you have a serious hankering to see California sea lions, try Pier 39 near Fisherman's Wharf or on the coast at Seal Rocks, both in San Francisco.

Sea Otters

Much higher on the cuteness scale is the sea otter (*Enhydra lutris*), which can be spotted just off shore in shallow kelp beds. Once near extinction, the endearing playful sea otter has survived; now there are more than 2,000 in California waters. It can be a bit mesmerizing to witness a sea otter roll on its back in the water and use a rock to break open mollusks for lunch. Sea otter habitat runs mainly from Monterey Bay to Big Sur, but they have also been spotted in the waters near Mendocino.

Birds

California has a wide range of habitat with

Monterey Bay is famous for its large sea otter population.

accessible food and water that makes it perfect for hundreds of bird species to nest, raise their young, or just stop over and rest during long migrations. Nearly 600 species have been spotted in California, so it may be just the place for a bird-watcher's vacation.

Among the most regal of California's bird species are raptors. The red-tailed hawk (*Buteo jamaicensis*) is found throughout California and is frequently sighted perched in trees along the North Coast highway, in the Central Valley, and even in urban areas such as San Francisco. The red-tailed hawk features a light underbelly with a dark band and a distinctive red tail that gives the bird its name.

Although not as common as it once was, Swainson's hawk (*Buteo swainsoni*) has been an indicator species in California's environment. The Swainson's hawk population has declined due to loss of habitat and excessive pesticide use in agricultural lands in the Central Valley; its main diet consists of the locusts and grasshoppers that feed on these crops, passing the contaminants on to the birds. These hawks are smaller than the red-tailed hawk, with dark brown coloring and some white underparts either on the chest or under the tail.

Reptiles

Several varieties of rattlesnakes are indigenous to the state. The Pacific Northwest rattler makes its home in Northern California, while more than half a dozen different rattlesnake varieties live in Southern California, including the western diamondback and the Mojave rattlesnake.

If you spot California's most infamous native reptile, keep your distance. All rattlesnakes are venomous, although death by snakebite is extremely rare in California. Most parks with known rattlesnake populations post signs alerting hikers to their presence; hikers should stay on marked trails and avoid tromping off into meadows or brush. Pay attention when hiking, especially when negotiating rocks and

woodpiles, and never put a foot or a hand down in a spot you can't see first. Wear long pants and heavy hiking boots for protection from snakes as well as insects, other critters, and unfriendly plants you might encounter.

Butterflies

California's vast population of wildflowers attracts an array of gorgeous butterflies. The monarch butterfly (*Danaus plexippus*) is emblematic of the state. These large orange-and-black butterflies have a migratory pattern that's reminiscent of birds. Starting in August, they begin migrating south to cluster in groves of eucalyptus trees. As they crowd together and close up their wings to hibernate, their dull outer wing color camouflages them as clumps of dried leaves, thus protecting them from predators. In spring, the butterflies begin to wake up, fluttering lazily in the groves for a while before flying north to seek out milkweed on which to lay their eggs. Pacific Grove, Santa Cruz, and Cambria are great places to visit these California "butterfly trees."

© JEFFREY BANKE/123RF.COM

A monarch butterfly rests on a leaf during its migration through California

History

THE FIRST RESIDENTS

The diverse ecology of California allowed Native Americans to adapt to the land in various ways. Communities settled from the border of present-day Oregon south though the mountain ranges and valleys, along the coast, into the Sierra Nevada, and in the arid lands that stretch into Mexico. These groups include the Maidu, Miwok, Yurok, and Pomo. More than 100 Native American languages were spoken in California, and each language had several dialects, all of which were identified with geographic areas. There are about two dozen distinct Native American groups in the Del Norte–Humboldt–Mendocino area alone. Below is an overview of the groups most commonly encountered when traveling around the state.

Yurok

The Yurok people are the largest Native American population in California, and they continue to live along the Klamath River and the Humboldt County coast near Redwood National Park, north of Eureka and south of Crescent City. Spanish explorers arriving in 1775 were the Yurok's first contact with Europeans. Fur traders and trappers from the Hudson's Bay Company arrived in about 1827, but it wasn't until gold miners arrived in 1850 that the Yurok faced disease and destruction that diminished their population by 75 percent. Researchers put the 1770 population at 2,500–3,100, which dropped to 669–700 by 1910. Today, there are more than 5,000 Yurok living in California and about 6,000 in the United States overall.

Pomo

The name for the Pomo people and their language first meant "those who live at the red earth hole," possibly referring to the magnesite used for red beads or the reddish earth and clay mined in the area. It was also once the name of a village near the present-day community of Pomo in Potter Valley. The Pomo territory was large, bounded by the Pacific Ocean to the west and extending inland to Clear Lake in Lake County. Today, the territory includes present-day Santa Rosa and much of the Sonoma County wine country.

In 1800 there were 10,000–18,000 Pomo living in approximately 70 communities that spoke seven Pomo languages. But as the Pomo interacted and traded with the Russians at Fort Ross, added pressure came from the Spanish missionaries and American settlers pressing in from the south and east. European encroachment may have been the reason Pomo villages became more centralized and why many Pomo retreated to remote areas to band together in defense.

The Pomo suffered not only from lifestyle changes and loss of territory but from diseases for which they had no immunity. Missionaries, traders, and settlers brought with them measles, smallpox, and other diseases that devastated indigenous populations. In 1850 miners began settling in the Russian River Valley, and the Lake Sonoma Valley was homesteaded. As a result, the U.S. government forced the Pomo off their land and onto reservations. Historians believe there were 3,500–5,000 Pomo in 1851, but only 777–1,200 by 1910. There were nearly 5,000 Pomo by the early 1990s.

Miwok

Before contact with white settlers in 1769, the Miwok people lived in small bands in separate parts of California. The Plains and Sierra Miwok lived on the Sacramento–San Joaquin Delta, parts of the San Joaquin and Sacramento Valleys, and the foothills and western slopes of the Sierra Nevada. The Coast

BACKGROUND

Miwok—including the Bodega Bay Miwok and the Marin Miwok—lived in what is now Marin and southern Sonoma Counties. Lake Miwok people were found in the Clear Lake Basin of Lake County. The Bay Miwok were in present-day Contra Costa County. Miwok domesticated dogs and grew tobacco but otherwise depended on hunting, fishing, and gathering for food. Miwok in the Sierra exploited the California black oak for acorns, and it is believed that they cultivated the tree in parts of what is now Yosemite National Park.

Like so many indigenous people in California, the Miwok suffered after explorers, missionaries, miners, and settlers arrived. Historians estimate there were at least 11,000 Miwok in 1770, but in all four regions there were only about 671 Miwok in 1910 and 491 in 1930. Today, there are about 3,500 Miwok.

Ohlone

The Ohlone people once occupied what is now San Francisco, Berkeley, Oakland, Silicon Valley, Santa Cruz, Monterey, and the lower Salinas Valley. The Ohlone (a Miwok word meaning "western people") lived in permanent villages, only moving temporarily to gather seasonal foods such as acorns and berries. The Ohlone formed an association of about 50 different communities with an average of 200 members each. The villages interacted through trade, marriages, and ceremonies. Basket weaving, ceremonial dancing, piercings and tattoos, and general ornamentation indicated status within the community and were all part of Ohlone life. Like other Native Americans in the region, the Ohlone depended on hunting, fishing, gathering, and agrarian skills such as burning off old growth each year to get a better yield from seeds.

The Ohlone culture remained fairly stable until the first Spanish missionaries arrived to spread Christianity and to expand Spanish territorial claims. Spanish explorer Sebastián Vizcaíno reached present-day Monterey in December 1602, and the Rumsen group of Ohlone were the first they encountered. Father Junípero Serra's missionaries built seven missions on Ohlone land, and most of the Ohlone people were brought to the missions to live and work. For the next 60 years, the Ohlone suffered, as did most indigenous people at the missions. Along with the culture shock of subjugation came the diseases for which they had no immunity—measles, smallpox, syphilis, and others. It wasn't until 1834 that the California missions were abolished and the Mexican government redistributed the mission land holdings.

The Ohlone lost the vast majority of their population between 1780 and 1850 because of disease, social upheaval from European incursion, and low birth rates. Estimates are that there were 7,000–26,000 Ohlone when Spanish soldiers and missionaries arrived, and about 3,000 in 1800 and 864–1,000 by 1852. There are 1,500–2,000 Ohlone people today.

Yokut

The Yokut people have inhabited the Central Valley for at least 8,000 years; they may even have been the first people to settle here. The Yokuts live in the San Joaquin Valley from the Sacramento–San Joaquin River Delta south to Bakersfield and east to the Sierra Foothills. Sequoia and Kings Canyon National Parks are included in this area, as are the cities of Fresno and Modesto. Like other Native Americans, the Yokuts developed water transportation, harvesting abundant tule reeds to work them into canoes.

Spanish explorers entered the valley in 1772 and found 63 different Yokut groups scattered up and down the Central Valley. Many of the Yokuts were taken to the various missions, where they suffered from European subjugation and diseases. Later, as miners entered the region, the Yokut people were forced from their lands. There may have been as many as 4,500 Yokuts when the Spaniards arrived, but the last full-blooded member of the Southern Yokuts is said to have died in 1960. Yokut descendants today live on the Tule River Reservation near Porterville and at the Santa Rosa Rancheria near Lemoore.

Paiute

The Paiute people are grouped by their language—despite location, political connection, or even genetic similarity. For the Northern Paiutes and the Southern Paiutes, that language is the Numic branch of the Uto-Aztecan family of Native American languages. The Northern Paiutes live in the Great Basin; the Southern Paiutes lived in the Mojave Desert on the edge of present-day Death Valley National Park. Between the Northern Paiutes and the Southern Paiutes are the Mono Lake Northern Paiutes and the Owens Valley Paiutes.

The Northern Paiute lifestyle was well adapted to the harsh environment of the Great Basin. Each band occupied a territory usually centered around a lake or other water source that also provided fish and waterfowl. Food drives to capture rabbits and pronghorn were communal and often involved nearby bands. Piñon nuts were gathered and stored for winter, and grass seeds and roots were part of the diet. Because of their remoteness, the Northern Paiutes may have completely avoided the hardships of the mission period. Their first contact with European Americans may have occurred in 1820, but sustained contact did not happen until the 1840s; several violent confrontations over land and other conflicts occurred in this period. In the end, smallpox did more to decimate the Northern Paiutes than warfare. The Northern Paiutes established colonies that were joined by Shoshone and Washoe people and eventually received recognition by the federal government.

The Southern Paiutes were not as fortunate as the Northern Paiutes. The first contact with Europeans came in 1776, when the priests Silvestre Vélez de Escalante and Francisco Atanasio Domínguez met them while seeking an overland route to the California missions. The Southern Paiutes suffered slave raids by the Navajo and Ute before Europeans arrived, and the raids increased afterward. In 1851, Mormon settlers arrived and occupied local water sources, and the slave raids ended. Settlers and their agrarian practices such as cattle herding drove away game and limited the Southern Paiutes' ability to gather food, disrupting their traditional lifestyle.

EXPLORATION

Juan Rodríguez Cabrillo, a Portuguese explorer and adventurer, was commissioned in 1542 by the Viceroy of New Spain (Mexico) to sail into what is now San Diego Bay. He continued north as far as Point Reyes before heading to Santa Catalina Island in late November 1542 to winter and make repairs to his ship. On Christmas Eve, Cabrillo tripped, splintering his shin, and the injury developed gangrene.

members of a Paiute family, 1872

BACKGROUND

© SABRINA YOUNG

Signs of Spanish exploration are evident throughout Northern California.

He died on January 3, 1543, and is buried on Catalina. The rest of his party arrived in Barra de Navidad on April 14, 1543. Having found no wealth, advanced Native American civilization or agriculture, or northwest passage, Portuguese interest in exploring California lapsed for more than 200 years.

Francis Drake, an English explorer, claimed a chunk of the Northern California coast in 1579. It is thought that Drake landed somewhere along Point Reyes to make extensive repairs to his only surviving ship, *The Golden Hind*. Drakes Bay, just east of Point Reyes, is marked as the spot of his landing, but the actual location is disputed. Drake eventually left California and completed the second recorded circumnavigation of the world (Ferdinand Magellan's was the first).

THE MISSION PERIOD

In the mid-1700s, Spain pushed for colonization of Alta California, rushing to occupy

North America before the British beat them to it. The effort was overly ambitious and underfunded, but missionaries started to sweep into present-day California.

The priest Junípero Serra is credited with influencing the early development of California. A Franciscan monk, Serra took an active role in bringing Christianity and European diseases to Native American people from San Diego north to Sonoma County. The Franciscan order built a string of missions; each was intended to act as a self-sufficient parish that grew its own food, maintained its own buildings, and took care of its own people. However, mission structures were limited by a lack of suitable building materials and skilled labor. Later, the forced labor of Native Americans was used to cut and haul timbers and to make adobe bricks. By the time the missions were operating, they claimed about 15 percent of the land in California, or about one million acres per mission.

Spanish soldiers used subjugation to control

indigenous people, pulling them from their villages and lands to the missions. Presidios (royal forts) were built near some of the missions to establish land claims, intimidate indigenous people, and carry out the overall goal of finding wealth in the New World. The presidios housed the Spanish soldiers that accompanied the missionaries. The cities of San Francisco, Santa Barbra, San Jose, and later Santa Cruz grew from the establishment of these missions and the presidios.

In 1821, Mexico gained independence from Spain along with control of Alta California and the missions. The Franciscans resisted giving up the land and free labor, and Native Americans continued to be treated as slaves. From 1824 to 1834 the Mexican government handed out 51 land grants to colonists for land that had belonged to Native Americans and was held by nearby missions. From 1834 to 1836 the Mexican government revoked the power of the Franciscans to use Native American labor and to redistribute the vast mission land holdings.

In the 20th century, interest in the history of the missions was rekindled, and funds were invested to restore many of the churches and complexes. Today, many of the missions have been restored as Catholic parishes, with visitors centers and museum displays of various levels of quality and polish. Some have been restored as state parks.

THE BEAR FLAG REVOLT

Mexico gained independence in 1821, claiming the Spanish lands that would become California and the U.S. Southwest. Hostilities between U.S. and Mexican troops began in April 1846 when a number of U.S. Army troops in the future state of Texas were attacked and killed. The first major battle of the Mexican-American War was fought the following month, and Congress responded with a declaration of war.

Rumors of possible Mexican military action against newly arrived settlers in California led a group of 30 settlers to seize the small Sonoma garrison in 1846. The uprising became known as the Bear Flag Revolt after a hastily designed flag depicting a grizzly bear and a five-point star was raised over Sonoma as the revolutionaries declared independence from Mexico. John A. Sutter, who had received a land grant near present-day Sacramento, and his men joined and supplied the revolt.

Captain John C. Frémont, who was leading a U.S. Army Corps of Topographical Engineers Exploratory Force, returned to Northern California when he received word that war with Mexico was imminent and that a revolt had occurred. The Bear Flag Revolt was short-lived; Frémont took over the rebellion and replaced the Bear Flag with the U.S. flag. Without orders and without knowing about the declaration of war, Frémont went on to the San Francisco Presidio to spike, or disable, the canons there. More U.S. ships, marines, and sailors arrived and took control of California ports up and down the coast. Frémont's forces grew into the California Battalion, whose members were used mainly to garrison and keep order in the rapidly surrendering towns.

THE GOLD RUSH

James Marshall was a carpenter employed by John Sutter to build a sawmill in Coloma near Placerville. Marshall made a glittery discovery on January 24, 1848, in a nearby stream: gold. Soon news spread to Sacramento and San Francisco that chunks of gold were on the riverbeds for the taking, and the Gold Rush was on. Thousands of people streamed into Northern California seeking gold. After panning streams and water-blasting hillsides for gold, the famous hard-rock mines of California began construction. Although panning continued, by the 1860s most of the rough men had taken jobs working in the dangerous mines. The most productive region was a swath of land nearly 200 miles long, roughly from El Dorado south to Mariposa,

BACKGROUND

© SABRINA YOUNG

Sutter's Mill, the site where gold was discovered in California

known as the Mother Lode or Gold Country. Mining towns such as Sonora, Volcano, Placerville, Sutter's Creek, and Nevada City swelled to huge proportions, only to shrink back into obscurity as the mines eventually closed one by one. Today, Highway 49 winds from one historic Gold Rush town to the next, and gold mining has mostly given way to tourism.

As American and European men came to Northern California to seek their fortunes in gold, a few wives and children joined them, but the number of families in the average mining town was small. A few lone women joined in the rush to the gold fields in the oldest profession, serving the population of single male miners and laborers with female companionship.

Another major group of immigrants came to Northern California from China—not to mine but to labor and serve the white miners. Most were forced to pass through the wretched immigration facilities on Angel Island in the middle of San Francisco Bay before being allowed onto the mainland; others were summarily shipped back to China. San Francisco's Chinatown became a hub for the immigrants, a place where their language was spoken and their culture understood. Thousands headed east, becoming low-level laborers in the industry surrounding the mines or workers on the railroads continuously being built to connect Gold Country to the rest of the country.

The dramatic population boom caused by the Gold Rush ensured that California would be on the fast track to admission into the United States, bypassing the territorial phase. California became a state in 1850—it had gone from a Mexican province to the 31st U.S. state in little more than four years.

THE RAILROADS

California's population swelled to more than 250,000 within three years of the Gold Rush. To avoid the grueling cross-country trip, Eastern industrialists pushed for a railroad to open the West. While politicians argued, Theodore D. Judah got to work. Judah came to California from New York at the bidding of the promoters of the Sacramento Valley Railroad. The route linked the Embarcadero along the Sacramento River to Folsom, the jumping-off point to the gold fields. When the Sacramento Valley Railroad project ended in 1856, Judah became a passionate advocate for a transcontinental railroad. He lobbied in Washington DC and in 1861 convinced a group of merchants—men who would become known as the Big Four—to incorporate the Central Pacific Railroad in Sacramento.

The Big Four were Leland Stanford, Charles Crocker, Collis Huntington, and Mark Hopkins, and they were instrumental in developing the state railroad system from 1861 to 1900. Stanford operated a general store for miners before becoming an American tycoon, industrialist, politician, and the founder of Stanford University. Crocker founded a small independent iron forge, invested in the railroad venture, and eventually gained a controlling interest in Wells Fargo Bank before buying the rest of the bank for his son. Huntington was a Sacramento merchant who later went on to build other railroads. Hopkins was another Sacramento merchant who formed a partnership with Huntington before joining him in investing in the transcontinental railroad.

In mid-1862 President Abraham Lincoln signed the Pacific Railroad Act, giving the Central Pacific Railroad the go-ahead to build the railroad east from Sacramento and the Union Pacific Railroad to build west from Omaha. The government used land grants and government loans to fund the project. Workers for the two companies met May 10, 1869, at Promontory Summit, Utah, to complete the nation's first transcontinental railroad with a ceremonial golden spike.

THE GREAT DEPRESSION
The stock market crash of 1929 led to the Great Depression. Many property owners lost their farms and homes, and unemployment in California hit 28 percent in 1932; by 1935, about 20 percent of all Californians were on public relief.

The Great Depression transformed the nation. Beyond the economic agony was an optimism that moved people to migrate to California. Settling primarily in the Central Valley, these Midwest transplants preserved their ways and retained identities separate from other Californians. The Midwest migrant plight was captured in John Steinbeck's 1939 novel *The Grapes of Wrath*. Steinbeck, a Salinas native, gathered information by viewing firsthand the deplorable living and labor conditions under which Okie families existed. The novel was widely read and was turned into a movie in 1940. Government agencies banned the book from public schools, and libraries and large landowners campaigned to have it banned elsewhere. That effort lost steam, however, when Steinbeck won the 1940 Pulitzer Prize.

Even during the worst economic depression in U.S. history, Californians continued to build and move forward. The San Francisco–Oakland Bay Bridge was completed in 1936 and the Golden Gate Bridge in 1937, connecting the land around San Francisco Bay and putting people to work. The 1939 Golden Gate International Exposition on Treasure Island in San Francisco Bay helped show the Great Depression the door.

WORLD WAR II
During World War II, San Francisco become home to the liberty ships, a fleet of like-design ships built quickly to help supply the war effort. Some liberty ships, known as the Mothball Fleet, are now tied together farther up Carquinez Strait and can be seen while driving south on I-680 near one of the state's first capitals, Benicia.

Unfortunately, Northern California was also home to a deplorable chapter in the war— the internment camps for Japanese people and

Japanese Americans. In reaction to the attack on Pearl Harbor, President Franklin Roosevelt signed Executive Order 9066 in 1942, creating "military exclusion zones" for people of Japanese ancestry. Approximately 110,000 Japanese Americans were uprooted and sent to war relocation camps in desolate areas such as Manzanar, in the dry basin of the eastern Sierras, Tulelake, in the remote northeast corner of the state, and as far away as North Dakota and Oklahoma.

In San Francisco, the immigration station on Angel Island became a deportation center in addition to interring Japanese prisoners of war. Today, examples of their carved inscriptions on the prison walls remain as part of the museum in the old barracks building.

THE 1960S

Few places in the country felt the impact of the radical changes of the 1960s more than California. It's arguable that the peace and free-love movements began here, probably on the campus of the indomitable University of California, Berkeley. Certainly Berkeley helped to shape and foster the culture of hippies, peaceniks, and radical politics. The college campus was the home of the Black Panthers, anti–Vietnam War sit-ins, and numerous protests for many progressive causes.

If Berkeley was the de facto home of 1960s political movements, then San Francisco was the base of its social and cultural phenomena. Free concerts in Golden Gate Park and the growing fame of the hippie community taking over a neighborhood called Haight-Ashbury drew young people from across the country. Many found themselves living on Haight Street for months and experimenting with the mind-altering chemicals emblematic of the era. The music scene became the stuff of legend. The Grateful Dead—one of the most famous and

An activist protests on University of California's Sather Gate in 1969.

COURTESY OF SNAP MAN/FLICKR

longest-lasting of the 1960s rock bands—hailed from the Bay Area.

THE DOT-COM ERA

The spectacular growth of the electronics industry started in Silicon Valley, south of San Francisco. Many firms settled in the area of Palo Alto, Santa Clara, Sunnyvale, and San Jose, producing innovations such as personal computers, video games, and networking systems at an incredible pace. All these firms were based in the Santa Clara Valley, dubbed Silicon Valley after the material used to produce integrated circuits. Hewlett-Packard and Varian Associates were among the early companies that grew here. Even today, the tenant list is impressive: Facebook, YouTube, LinkedIn, Adobe Systems, Apple, Cisco Systems, Intel, Oracle Corporation, SanDisk, and Symantec.

The demand for skilled technical professionals was so great in the high-tech industry that firms had difficulty filling openings and began lobbying to have visa restrictions eased so they could recruit professionals from abroad. Later, however, the dot-com financial bubble that formed in the mid-1990s burst, and tech-industry stock values plummeted in April 2000; many tech companies went into bankruptcy or were sold for a fraction of their worth, and jobs evaporated overnight. Within a few years, it seemed that many of the coveted high-tech jobs were "off-shored" (sent to India for 10 percent of the U.S. labor cost) or "on-shored" by recruiting among newcomers from China and India.

Despite the dot-com bust, Silicon Valley continues to be the technological hub of the state. Among metropolitan areas, Silicon Valley has the highest concentration of tech workers, with nearly 286 out of every 1,000 private-sector jobs. And the money is good too—the San Jose–Sunnyvale–Santa Clara metropolitan area has the most millionaires and billionaires per capita in the United States.

Government and Economy

GOVERNMENT

Northern California is often viewed as a place where liberalism has run amok. It's true that Northern California is home to what many consider liberal views: political protests and free speech, legalized medical marijuana use, environmental activism, and gay and lesbian rights. These beliefs are not incorporated as a whole throughout the state, however. Major metropolitan areas, such as San Francisco, and areas along the coast have become havens for artists, musicians, and those seeking alternatives to mainstream America. Populations in the Central Valley and the Sierra Nevada Foothills often show more conservative leanings at the polls.

California is overwhelmingly Democratic, but when it comes to politics, not everything is predictable. In 2008 California voters approved Proposition 8, which outlawed same-sex marriage equality, by 52.2 percent to 47.8 percent; voters in some counties approved the ban by more than 75 percent. A ballot measure to legalize marijuana use was defeated that same year. Yet Californians also voted for Barack Obama as president the same year by a definitive majority, 61 percent to 37 percent.

ECONOMY

California boasts the eighth-largest economy in the world, although the ongoing global economic downturn may put a dent in that ranking in the years to come. Still, California's contribution to the United States outpaces even its immense size and population; it continues to be the country's number-one economy.

SAVING CALIFORNIA'S STATE PARKS

California's state finances are not ideal at present, and the budget for state parks continues to be under threat as a result. A few state parks closed in 2011, while others have had services or hours reduced or campgrounds shut. Much more significant state park closings loom in the future, and there is a fair amount of uncertainty about the future of many of California's parks.

Before planning your trip, check the status of state parks first to avoid disappointment. For updates on park closings and service changes, check online (www.parks.ca.gov), call the park directly, or contact the main office in Sacramento (800/777-0369, 8 A.M.-5 P.M. Mon.-Fri.).

To become involved in keeping California's parks open to the public, join the Save Our State Parks Campaign, run by the **California State Parks Foundation** (916/442-2119, www.savestateparks.org). Of course, nothing speaks louder about the value of our parks than visiting them. If you love the parks, use them: go camping, take a hike, learn about the state's cultural and natural history, or even volunteer. Using the parks is one of the best ways to signal your support and to help ensure that they'll thrive in the future.

Northern California's number-one economic sector is farming. The Central Valley's agricultural juggernaut supplies the world with crops that include grapefruit, grass-fed beef, rice, corn, and tomatoes. Sweet strawberries and spiky artichokes grow in abundance in the cooler Central Coast region. As the fog gets colder and drippier in Marin, ranchers take advantage of the naturally growing grasses for herds of cattle. Agriculture, including fruit, vegetables, nuts, dairy, and wine production, help make California the world's fifth-largest supplier of food and agriculture commodities.

Today, organic farms and ranches are proliferating across the state. In addition to the giant factory farms prevalent in the Central Valley, you'll also see an increasing number of small farms and ranches growing crops using organic, sustainable, and even biodynamic practices. Most of these farmers sell directly to consumers by way of farmers markets and farm stands—almost every town or county in the Northern California has a weekly farmer's market in the summer, and many last year-round.

And then there's the wine. It seems like every square inch of free agricultural land has a grapevine growing on it. The vineyards that were once seen primarily in Napa and Sonoma can now be found on the slopes of the Sierra Foothills, on the northern Mendocino coast, and in Carmel. It's actually the wine industry that's leading the charge beyond mere organic and into biodynamic growing practices—using sheep to graze and maintain vineyards weeds, providing natural fertilizer, harvesting grapes, and pruning vines.

ESSENTIALS

Getting There

BY AIR

Northern California is easy to fly to, particularly if you're heading for one of the major metropolitan areas. Reaching the more rural outlying regions is a bit trickier, and you'll probably find yourself driving—possibly for hours—from one of the major airports.

San Francisco's major airport is **San Francisco International Airport** (SFO, U.S. 101, San Mateo, 800/435-9736, www.flysfo.com), located approximately 13 miles south of the city. Plan to arrive at the airport up to three hours before your flight leaves. Airport lines, especially on weekends and holidays, are notoriously long, and planes can be grounded due to fog.

To avoid the SFO crowds, consider booking a flight into one of the Bay Area's less crowded airports. **Oakland International Airport** (OAK, 1 Airport Dr., Oakland, 510/563-3300, www.flyoakland.com) serves the East Bay with access to San Francisco via the Bay Bridge and commuter trains. **San Jose International Airport** (SJC, Airport Blvd., San Jose, 408/392-3600, www.sjc.org) is south of San Francisco in the heart of Silicon Valley. These airports are

© HARRIS SHIFFMAN/123RF.COM

quite a bit smaller than SFO, but service is brisk from many U.S. destinations.

Sacramento International Airport (SMF, Airport Blvd., Sacramento, 916/929-5411, www.sacramento.aero) is a good launching point for trips in the Central Valley, Gold Country, or the Sierra Nevada and Lake Tahoe areas.

If driving long distances is not for you, **Southwest Airlines** (www.southwest.com, 800/435-9792) offers many affordable connecting flights among these Northern California airports. To reach the small but user-friendly airports in Monterey, Eureka, Crescent City, and Redding from the Bay Area, check with United Airlines (www.united.com, 800/864-8331).

Airport Transportation

Several public and private transportation options can get you into San Francisco. **Bay Area Rapid Transit** (BART, www.bart.gov) connects directly with SFO's international terminal, providing a simple and relatively fast (under 1 hour) trip to downtown San Francisco. The BART station is an easy walk or a free shuttle ride from any point in the airport; a one-way ticket to any downtown station costs $8.10. **Caltrain** (www.caltrain.com) is a good option if you are staying farther south on the peninsula. To access Caltrain from the airport, you must first take BART to the Millbrae stop, where the two lines meet. This station is designed for folks jumping from one line to the other. Caltrain tickets range $2.75–12.75 depending on your destination.

Shuttle vans are another cost-effective option for door-to-door service, although these make several stops along the way. From the airport to downtown San Francisco, the average one-way fare is $17–25 pp. Shuttle vans congregate on the second level of SFO above the baggage claim area for domestic flights, and on the third level for international flights. Advance reservations guarantee a seat, but these aren't required and don't necessarily speed the process. Some companies to try include Bay Shuttle (415/564-3400, www.bayshuttle.com), Quake City Shuttle (415/255-4899, www.quakecityshuttle.com), and SuperShuttle (800/258-3826, www.supershuttle.com).

For **taxis,** the average fare to downtown San Francisco is around $40.

BY TRAIN

Several long-distance **Amtrak** (www.amtrak.com) trains rumble through Northern California daily. There are eight train routes that serve the region: The *California Zephyr* runs from Chicago and Denver to Emeryville; the *Capitol Corridor* serves Auburn, Sacramento, Emeryville, Oakland, and San Jose, and is a popular route with local commuters; the *Coast Starlight* travels down the West Coast from Seattle and Portland as far as Los Angeles; the *Pacific Surfliner* will get you to the Central Coast; and the *San Joaquin* serves the Central Valley. There is no train depot in San Francisco; the closest station is in Emeryville in the East Bay. Fortunately, comfortable coach buses ferry travelers to and from the Emeryville Amtrak station with many stops in downtown San Francisco.

BY CAR

The main transportation artery in Northern California is **I-5,** which runs north–south from Oregon through Sacramento and ending at the Mexican border.

Highway 1, also known as the Pacific Coast Highway, follows the North Coast from Leggett to San Luis Obispo on the Central Coast and points south. Running parallel and intertwining with Highway 1 for much of its length, **U.S. 101** stretches north–south from Crescent City on the North Coast through the Central Coast, meeting Highway 1 in San Luis Obispo. These alternate routes are longer but prettier than I-5.

The main east–west conduit is **I-80,**

BART (Bay Area Rapid Transit) provides efficient transportation around the San Francisco Bay Area.

which begins as part of the Bay Bridge in San Francisco and runs east through Sacramento to Tahoe and over the Sierra Nevada. I-80 can often close due to winter snows.

Highway speeds in Northern California are generally 55 mph, unless otherwise posted. Larger freeways, such as I-80 and I-5, may have posted speed limits of 65–70 mph.

California law requires that all drivers carry liability insurance for their vehicles.

Getting Around

BY AIR
Domestic flights can be an economical and faster option when traversing between major cities within the state. San Francisco International Airport (SFO, www.flysfo.com), Oakland International Airport (OAK, www.flyoakland.com), San Jose International Airport (SJC, www.sjc.org), and Sacramento International Airport (SMF, www.sacramento. aero) connect with several smaller regional airports in Northern California. These include the **Monterey Regional Airport** (MRY, www.montereyairport.com), the **Chico Airport** (CIC, www.chico.ca.us), the **Redding Municipal Airport** (RDD, www.ci.redding.ca.us), and the **Arcata-Eureka Airport** (ACV, http://co.humboldt.ca.us/aviation). Southwest Airlines (www.southwest.com) provides

WINTER DRIVING

It can snow in the Northern California mountains anytime between November and April; if you plan on crossing any high passes, make sure you have tire chains in your vehicle. In winter, the mountain passes on I-5 near Mount Shasta and on I-80 to Tahoe and over the Sierra Nevada can be very hazardous and may require chains, snow tires, or both. Close to Tahoe, many roadside chain installers set up in pullouts along the side of I-80 and will install tire chains for a hefty fee. Chains can also be rented at certain automotive stores and service stations.

Road closures elsewhere in the state can be common in winter. Highway 1 along the coast can shut down due to flooding or landslides. I-5 through the Central Valley can either close or be subject to hazardous driving conditions resulting from tule fog, which can reduce visibility to only a few feet. Some highways avoid these problems altogether by closing for part of the year. Highway 120, which runs over Tioga Pass and connects Yosemite Valley with the Eastern Sierra, is generally closed October-April.

The **California Department of Transportation** (Caltrans, 800/427-7623, http://dot.ca.gov) has a very user-friendly website to check current road conditions before your trip.

affordable flights among the larger airports, while United Airlines (www.united.com) has regular flights to regional airports. Geared toward commuters, flights are generally frequent but a bit pricy.

BY TRAIN

Amtrak (www.amtrak.com) runs several trains through the state. The *California Zephyr, Capitol Corridor, Coast Starlight,* and *San Joaquin* routes offer services to Auburn, Sacramento, Emeryville, Oakland, San Jose, the Central Coast, and the Central Valley. Trains are roomy, comfortable, and offer a dining car for affordable snacks and meals. While there is no train station in San Francisco, Amtrak provides bus service between downtown San Francisco and Emeryville in the East Bay, the main Amtrak hub for this part of the state. In the San Francisco Bay Area, **Bay Area Rapid Transit** (BART) is a high-speed train that runs from San Francisco south to the airport and across to the East Bay. **Caltrain** (www.caltrain.com) is largely a commuter train that runs from San Francisco down the peninsula as far as San Jose.

BY BUS

A very affordable way to get around Northern California is on **Greyhound** (800/231-2222, www.greyhound.com). The San Francisco Station (200 Folsom St., 415/495-1569) is a hub for Greyhound bus lines serving Northern California. Other major stations include Oakland (2103 San Pablo Ave., 510/823-4730), San Jose (70 S. Almaden Ave., 408/295-4151), and Sacramento (420 Richards Blvd., 916/444-6858). Greyhound routes generally follow the major highways, traveling up U.S. 101 through Santa Rosa to Arcata, along I-5 through Redding and Mount Shasta, near I-80 to Reno, and south through San Jose to Santa Cruz. Greyhound does not go to destinations like Wine Country, Gold Country, and the Monterey Peninsula.

Most counties and municipalities have bus service with routes to outlying areas.

BY CAR AND RV

California is great for road trips. Scenic coastal routes such as Highway 1 and U.S. 101 are often destinations in themselves, while inland I-5 is the most direct route north-south

©HEATHER C. LISTON

Tioga Pass, the eastern entrance to Yosemite National Park

through the state. However, traffic congestion, accidents, mudslides, fires, and snow can affect highways at any time. To explore Northern California safely, have a good map and check road conditions online with the **California Department of Transportation** (Caltrans, 800/427-7623, http://dot.ca.gov) before departure. The *Thomas Guide Road Atlas* (www.thomasguidebooks.com, $14) is a reliable and detailed map and road guide and a great insurance policy against getting lost.

Larger highways like I-5 and I-80 are relatively easy to navigate, but many smaller two-lane highways that connect Northern California's rural destinations offer scenic and leisurely alternatives. Note that mountain passes such as I-80 to Tahoe and I-5 in the Shasta and Lassen regions may require snow tires or chains at any time. In rural areas, gas stations may be few and far between.

The left lanes of most major Bay Area freeways become **carpool lanes** during the heaviest commute times (generally 7–10 A.M. and 3–7 P.M.). Posted signs list the hours of operation, the number of people you have to have in your car to use the lanes, and the often hefty fine for violating.

In addition, bridge tolls are charges to cross the **Bay Bridge** (westbound, $5), the **Richmond Bridge** (westbound, $5) and the **Golden Gate Bridge** (southbound, $6). Many savvy Bay Area commuters pay electronically via **FasTrak** (www.bayareafastrak.org), a transponder in their cars that deducts the toll from the user's account as they pass through the toll plaza.

Car and RV Rental

Most car-rental companies are located at each of the major Northern California airports. To reserve a car in advance, contact **Budget Rent A Car** (800/527-0700, www.budget.com), **Dollar Rent A Car** (800/800-4000, www.dollar.com), **Enterprise** (800/261-7331, www.enterprise.com), or **Hertz** (800/654-3131, www.hertz.com).

To rent a car, drivers in California must at least 21 years of age and have a valid driver's license. California law also requires that all vehicles carry liability insurance. You can purchase

ESSENTIALS

insurance with your rental car, but it generally costs an additional $10 per day, which can add up quickly. Most private auto insurance will also cover rental cars. Before buying rental insurance, check your car insurance policy to see if rental-car coverage is included.

The average cost of a rental car is $40 per day or $210 per week; however, rates vary greatly based on the time of year and distance traveled. Weekend and summer rentals cost significantly more. Generally, it is more expensive to rent from car rental agencies at an airport. To avoid excessive rates, first plan travel to areas where a car is not required, then rent a car from an agency branch in town to further explore more rural areas. Rental agencies occasionally allow vehicle drop-off at a different location from where it was picked it up for an additional fee.

If you rent an RV, you won't have to worry about camping or lodging options, and many facilities, particularly farther north, accommodate RVs. However, RVs are difficult to maneuver and park, limiting your access to metropolitan areas. They are also expensive, both in terms of gas and the rental rates. Rates during the summer average $1,300 per week and $570 for three days, the standard minimal rental. **Cruise America** (800/671-8042, www.cruiseamerica. com) has branches in San Jose, Sacramento, Santa Rosa, and San Mateo. **El Monte RV** (415/771-8770, www.elmonterv.com) operates out of Fisherman's Wharf in San Francisco.

Tips for Travelers

VISAS AND OFFICIALDOM
Passports and Visas

Visiting from another country, you must have a valid passport and a visa to enter the United States. If you hold a current passport from one of the following countries, you may qualify for the Visa Waiver Program: Andorra, Australia, Austria, Belgium, Brunei, Czech Republic, Denmark, Estonia, Finland, France, Germany, Greece, Iceland, Ireland, Italy, Japan, Latvia, Liechtenstein, Lithuania, Luxembourg, Malta, Monaco, the Netherlands, New Zealand, Norway, Portugal, San Marino, Singapore, Slovakia, Slovenia, South Korea, Spain, Sweden, Switzerland, and the United Kingdom. To qualify, you must apply online with the Electronic System for Travel Authorization and hold a return plane or cruise ticket to your country of origin dated less than 90 days from your date of entry. Holders of Canadian passports don't need visas or visa waivers.

In most other countries, the local U.S. embassy should be able to provide a tourist visa. The average fee for a visa is US$160. While a visa may be processed as quickly as 24 hours on request, plan at least a couple of weeks, as there can be unexpected delays, particularly during the busy summer season (June–Aug.).

Embassies

San Francisco has embassies and consulates from many countries around the globe. If you should lose your passport or find yourself in some other trouble while visiting California, contact your country's offices for assistance. To find an embassy, check online at www.state. gov/s/cpr/rls/dpl/32122.htm, which lists the websites for all foreign embassies in the United States. A representative will be able to direct you to the nearest embassy or consulate.

Customs

Before you enter the United States from another country by sea or by air, you'll be required to fill out a customs form. Check with the U.S. embassy in your country or the Customs and Border Protection website (www.cbp.gov) for an updated list of items you must declare.

If you require medication administered by injection, you must pack your syringes in a checked bag; syringes are not permitted in carry-ons coming into the United States.

Also, pack documentation describing your need for any narcotic medications you've brought with you. Failure to produce documentation for narcotics on request can result in severe penalties in the United States.

If you're driving into California along I-5 or another major highway, prepare to stop at Agricultural Inspection Stations a few miles inside the state line. You don't need to present a passport, a visa, or even a driver's license; instead, you must be prepared to present all your fruits and vegetables. California's largest economic sector is agriculture, and a number of the major crops grown here are sensitive to pests and diseases. In an effort to prevent known pests from entering the state and endangering crops, travelers are asked to identify all produce they're carrying in from other states or from Mexico. If you've got produce, especially homegrown or from a farm stand, it could be infected by a known problem pest or disease. Expect it to be confiscated on the spot.

You'll also be asked about fruits and veggies on your U.S. Customs form, which you'll be asked to fill out on the airplane or ship before you reach the United States.

CONDUCT AND CUSTOMS

The legal drinking age in California is 21. Expect to have your ID checked if you look under age 30, especially in bars and clubs, but also in restaurants and wineries. Most California bars and clubs close at 2 A.M.; you'll find the occasional after-hours nightspot in San Francisco.

Smoking has been banned in many places throughout California. Don't expect to find a smoking section in any restaurant or an ashtray in any bar. Smoking is illegal in all bars and clubs, but your new favorite watering hole might have an outdoor patio where smokers can huddle. Taking the ban one step further, many hotels, motels, and inns throughout Northern California are strictly nonsmoking, and you'll be subject to fees of hundreds of dollars if your room smells of smoke when you leave.

There's no smoking in any public building, and even some of the state parks don't allow cigarettes. There's often good reason for this; the fire danger in California is extreme in the summer, and one carelessly thrown butt can cause a genuine catastrophe.

ACCESS FOR TRAVELERS WITH DISABILITIES

Most Northern California attractions, hotels, and restaurants are accessible for travelers with disabilities. State law requires that public transportation must accommodate the special needs of travelers with disabilities and that public spaces and businesses have adequate restroom facilities and equal access. This includes national parks and historic structures, many of which have been refitted with ramps and wider doors. Many hiking trails are also accessible to wheelchairs, and most campgrounds designate specific campsites that meet the Americans with Disabilities Act standards. The state of California also provides a free telephone TDD-to-voice relay service; just dial 711.

If you are traveling with a disability, there are many resources to help you plan your trip. **Access Northern California** (http://accessnca.org) is a nonprofit organization that offers general travel tips, including recommendations on accommodations, parks and trails, transportation, and travel equipment. **Access-Able** (http://access-able.com) is another travel resource, as is **Gimp-on-the-Go** (www.gimponthego.com). The message board on the **American Foundation for the Blind** (www.afb.org) website is a good forum to discuss travel strategies for the visually impaired. For a comprehensive guide to wheelchair accessible beaches, rivers, and shorelines from Santa

ESSENTIALS

Cruz to Marin County, including the East Bay and Wine Country, contact the **California Coastal Conservancy** (510/286-1015, www.scc.ca.gov), which publishes a free and downloadable guide. San Francisco's **Wheelchair Getaways** (800/638-1912, www.wheelchairgetaways.com, $95–110 per day) rent wheelchair-accessible vans and offer pickup and drop-off service from San Francisco, Oakland, San Jose, and Sacramento airports ($100–300). Likewise, **Avis Access** (888/879-4273, www.avis.com) rents cars, scooters, and other products to make traveling with a disability easier; click on the "Services" link on the website.

TRAVELING WITH CHILDREN

Many spots in California are ideal destinations for families with children of all ages. Amusement parks, interactive museums, zoos, parks, beaches, and playgrounds all make for family-friendly fun. On the other hand, there are a few spots in the Golden State that beckon more to adults than to children. Frankly, there aren't many family activities in Wine Country. This adult playground is all about alcoholic beverages and high-end dining. Similarly, the North Coast's focus on original art and romantic B&Bs brings out couples looking for weekend getaways rather than families. In fact, before you book a room at a B&B that you expect to share with your kids, check to be sure that the inn can accommodate extra people in the guest rooms and whether they allow guests under age 16.

WOMEN TRAVELING ALONE

California is a pretty friendly place for women traveling alone. Most of the major outdoor attractions are incredibly safe, and even many of the urban areas boast pleasant neighborhoods that welcome lone female travelers. But you'll need to take some basic precautions and pay attention to your surroundings, just as you would in any unfamiliar place. Carry your car keys in your hand when walking out to your car. Don't

sit in your parked car in a lonely parking lot at night; just get in, turn on the engine, and drive away. When you're walking down a city street, be alert and keep an eye on your surroundings and on anyone who might be following you. In rural areas, don't go tromping into unlit wooded areas or out into grassy fields alone at night without a flashlight; many of California's critters are nocturnal. Of course, this caution applies to men as well; mountain lions and rattlesnakes don't tend to discriminate.

SENIOR TRAVELERS

California makes an ideal destination for older or retired folks looking to relax and have a great time. You'll find senior discounts nearly every place you go, including restaurants, golf courses, major attractions, and even some hotels, although the minimum age can range 50–65. Just ask, and be prepared to produce ID if you look young or are requesting a senior discount. You can often get additional discounts on rental cars, hotels, and tour packages as a member of **AARP** (888/687-2277, www.aarp.org). If you're not a member, its website can also offer helpful travel tips and advice. **Elderhostel** (800/454-5768, www.roadscholar.org) is another great resource for senior travelers. Dedicated to providing educational opportunities for older travelers, Elderhostel provides package trips to beautiful and interesting destinations. Called "Educational Adventures," these trips are generally 3–9 days long and emphasis history, natural history, art, music, or a combination thereof.

GAY AND LESBIAN TRAVELERS

California is known for its thriving gay and lesbian communities. In fact, the Golden State is a golden place for gay travel—especially in the bigger cities and even in some of the smaller towns around the state. As with much of the country, the farther you venture into rural and agricultural regions, the less likely you are to experience the liberal acceptance the state is known for. The **International Gay and Lesbian Travel Association** (www.iglta.org) has a directory of gay- and lesbian-friendly tour operators, accommodations, and destinations.

San Francisco has the biggest and arguably best **Gay Pride Festival** (www.sfpride.org) in the nation, usually held on Market Street on the last weekend in June. Year-round, the Castro District offers fun of all kinds, from theater to clubs to shopping, mostly targeted at gay men but with a few places sprinkled in for lesbians. If the Castro is your primary destination, you can even find a place to stay in the middle of the action.

Santa Cruz on the Central Coast is a quirky town specially known for its lesbian-friendly culture. A relaxed vibe informs everything from underground clubs to unofficial nude beaches to live-action role playing games in the middle of downtown. Even the lingerie and adult toy shops tend to be woman-owned and operated.

Many gay and lesbian San Francisco residents go to Guerneville for a weekend escape. This outdoorsy town on the Russian River has rustic lodges, vacation rentals, and cabins down by the river; rafting and kayaking companies offer summertime adventures, and nearby wineries offer relaxation. The short but colorful Main Street is home to queer-friendly bars and festivals.

The oh-so-fabulous California vibe has even made it to the interior of the state—Sacramento's newly revitalized Midtown neighborhood offers a more low-key but visible gay evening scene.

Health and Safety

MEDICAL SERVICES

For an emergency anywhere in California, dial 911. Inside hotels and resorts, check your emergency number as soon as you get to your guest room. In urban and suburban areas, full-service hospitals and medical centers abound, but in more remote regions, help can be more than an hour away.

If you're planning a backcountry expedition, follow all rules and guidelines for obtaining wilderness permits and for self-registration at trailheads. These are for your safety, letting the rangers know roughly where you plan to be and when to expect you back. National and state park visitors centers can advise in more detail on any health or wilderness alerts in the area. It is also advisable to let someone outside your party know your route and expected date of return.

Being out in the elements can present its own set of challenges. Despite Northern California's relatively mild climate, heat exhaustion and heat stoke can affect anyone during the hot summer months, particularly during a long strenuous hike in the sun. Common symptoms include nausea, lightheadedness, headache, or muscle cramps. Dehydration and loss of electrolytes are the common causes of heat exhaustion. If you or anyone in your group develops any of these symptoms, get out of the sun immediately, stop all physical activity, and drink plenty of water. Heat exhaustion can be severe, and if untreated can lead to heat stroke, in which the body's core temperature reaches 105°F. Fainting, seizures, confusion and rapid heartbeat and breathing can indicate the situation has moved beyond heat exhaustion. If you suspect this, call 911 immediately.

Similar precautions hold true for hypothermia, which is caused by prolonged exposure to cold water or weather. For many in California, this can happen on a hike or backpacking trip without sufficient rain gear, or by staying too long in the ocean or another cold body of water without a wetsuit. Symptoms include shivering, weak pulse, drowsiness, confusion, slurred speech, or stumbling. To treat hypothermia, immediately removing the wet clothing, cover the person with blankets, and feed him or her hot liquids. If symptoms don't improve, call 911.

You don't have to be outdoors to suffer from altitude sickness. A flu-like illness, it can affect anyone who has made a quick transition from low to high elevation. It occurs most commonly above 8,000 feet, but some individuals suffer at lower elevations. Headaches are the most common symptom, followed by nausea, dizziness, fatigue, and even the swelling of hands, feet, and face. Symptoms either go away once the individual has acclimated to the thinner air and lower oxygen levels or they don't, requiring either medical attention or a return to lower elevation. To prevent altitude sickness, avoid any strenuous exercise, including hiking, for the first 24 hours of your stay. Drinking alcohol also exacerbates altitude sickness because it can cause dehydration.

WILDERNESS SAFETY

Many places are still wild in California, making it important to use precautions with regard to wildlife. While California no longer has any grizzly bears, black bears thrive and are often seen in the mountains foraging for food in the spring, summer, and fall. Black bears certainly don't have the size or reputation of grizzlies, but there is good reason to exercise caution. Never get between a bear and her cub, and if a bear sees you, identify yourself as human by waving your hands above your head, speaking in calm voice, and backing away slowly. If a bear charges, do not run. One of the best precautions against an unwanted bear encounter is to keep a clean camp, store all food in airtight bear-proof containers, and strictly follow any guidelines given by the park or rangers.

Even more common than bears are mountain lions, which can be found in the Sierra Foothills, the Coast Range, and as well as grasslands and forests. Because of their solitary nature, it is unlikely you will see one, even on long trips in the backcountry. Still, there are a couple things to remember. If you come across a kill, probably a large partly eaten deer, leave immediately. And if you see a mountain lion and it sees you, identify yourself as human, making your body appear as big as possible, just as with a bear. And remember: Never run. As with any cat, large or small, running triggers its hunting instincts. If a mountain lion should attack, fight back; cats don't like to get hurt.

The other treacherous critter in the backcountry is the rattlesnake. They can be found in summer in generally hot and dry areas from the coast to the Sierra Nevada. When hiking in this type of terrain—many parks will indicate if rattlesnakes are a problem in the area—keep your eyes on the ground and an ear out for the telltale rattle. Snakes like to warn you to keep away. The only time this is not the case is with baby rattlesnakes that have not yet developed their rattles. Unfortunately, they have developed their fangs and venom, which is particularly potent. Should you get bitten, immediately try to suck out the venom with your

Stay alert when you're in mountain lion habitat.

mouth and then spit it out. Use a piece of cloth as a tourniquet on your upper arm or leg to reduce to blood flow to the bite. This will lessen the chance of the venom spreading. Next, get immediate medical help.

Mosquitoes can be found throughout the state, particularly in the Central Valley and the Sierra Nevada. At higher elevations they can be worse, prompting many hikers and backpackers to don head nets and apply potent repellents, usually DEET. The high season for mosquitoes in this area is late spring–early summer, at the end of snowmelt when there is lots of still freshwater to multiply in. In the Central Valley, there has been concern over West Nile virus, which can cause nausea, diarrhea, and fever for 3–6 days. In very rare cases, the illness becomes more serious, and medical attention becomes necessary.

Ticks live in many of the forests and grasslands throughout the state, except at higher elevations. Tick season generally runs late fall–early summer. If you are hiking through brushy areas, wear pants and long-sleeve shirts. Ticks like to crawl to warm moist places (armpits are a favorite) on their host. If a tick is engorged, it can be difficult to remove. There are two main types of ticks found in Northern California: dog ticks and deer ticks. Dog ticks are larger, brown, and have a gold spot on their backs, while deer ticks are small, tear-shaped, and black. Deer ticks are known to carry Lyme disease. While Lyme disease is relatively rare in California—there are more cases in the northernmost part of the state—it is very serious. If you get bitten by a deer tick and the bite leaves a red ring, seek medical attention. Lyme disease can be successfully treated with early rounds of antibiotics.

There is only one major variety of plant in California that can cause an adverse reaction in humans if you touch the leaves or stems: poison oak, a common shrub that inhabits forests throughout the state. Poison oak has a characteristic three-leaf configuration, with scalloped leaves that are shiny green in the spring and then turn yellow, orange, and red in late summer–fall. In fall the leaves drop, leaving a cluster of innocuous-looking branches. The oil in poison oak is present year-round in both the leaves and branches. Your best protection is to wear long sleeves and long pants when hiking, no matter how hot it is. A product called Tecnu is available at most California drugstores—slather it on before you go hiking to protect yourself from poison oak. If your skin comes into contact with poison oak, expect a nasty rash known for its itchiness and irritation. Poison oak is also extremely transferable, so avoid touching your eyes, face, or other parts of your body to prevent spreading the rash. Calamine lotion can help, and in extreme cases a doctor can administer cortisone to help decrease the inflammation.

CRIME AND SAFETY PRECAUTIONS

The outdoors is not the only place that harbors danger. In both rural and urban areas, theft can be a problem. When parking at a trailhead or in park or at a beach, don't leave any valuables in the car. If you must, place them out of sight either in a locked glove box or in the trunk. The same holds true for urban areas. Furthermore, avoid keeping your wallet, camera, and other expensive items, including lots of cash, easily accessible in backpacks; keep them within your sight at all times. Certain neighborhoods in San Francisco and Oakland are best avoided at night. However, many of them, like the Mission and Tenderloin districts in San Francisco or downtown Oakland, are also home to great restaurants, clubs, and music venues. If you find yourself in these areas after dark, consider taking a cab to avoid walking blocks and blocks to get to your car or to wait for public transportation. In case of a theft or any other emergency, call 911.

ESSENTIALS

Information and Services

MONEY

California businesses use the U.S. dollar ($). Most businesses also accept the major credit cards Visa, MasterCard, Discover, and American Express. ATM and debit cards work at many stores and restaurants, and ATMs are available throughout the region. In more remote areas, such as Gold Country and the North Coast, some business may only accept cash, so don't depend entirely on your plastic.

You can change currency at any international airport in the state. Currency exchange points also crop up in downtown San Francisco and at some of the major business hotels in urban areas.

California is not a particularly expensive place to travel, but keeping an eye on your budget is still important. San Francisco and the Wine Country are the priciest regions for visitors, especially with the amount of high-quality food and luxury accommodations. Advance reservations for hotels and marquee restaurants in these areas are recommended.

Banks

As with anywhere, traveling with a huge amount of cash is not recommended, which may make frequent trips to the bank necessary. Fortunately, most destinations have at least one major bank. Usually Bank of America or Wells Fargo can be found on the main drags through towns. Banking hours tend to be 8 A.M.–5 P.M. Monday–Friday, 9 A.M.–noon Saturday. Never count on a bank being open on Sunday or federal holidays. If you need cash when the banks are closed, there is generally a 24-hour ATM available. Furthermore, many cash-only businesses have an ATM on-site for those who don't have enough cash ready in their wallets. The unfortunate downside to this convenience is a fee of $2–4 per transaction. This also applies to ATMs at banks at which you don't have an account.

Tax

Sales tax in California varies by city and county, but the average rate is around 8.5 percent. All goods are taxable with the exception of food not eaten on the premises. For example, your bill at a restaurant will include tax, but your bill at a grocery store will not. The hotel tax is another unexpected added expense to traveling in California. Most cities have enacted a tax on hotel rooms largely to make up for budget shortfalls. As you would expect, these taxes are higher in areas more popular with visitors. In Wine County you can expect to add an additional 12–14 percent onto your hotel bill, while in San Francisco the tax tops 15 percent. Some areas like Eureka have a lower hotel tax of 10 percent.

Tipping

Tipping is expected and appreciated, and a 15 percent tip for restaurants is about the norm. When ordering in bars, tip the bartender or waitstaff $1 per drink. For taxis, plan to tip 15–20 percent of the fare, or simply round the cost up to the nearest dollar. Cafés and coffee shops often have tip jars out. There is no consensus on what is appropriate when purchasing a $3 beverage. Often $0.50 is enough, depending on the quality and service.

COMMUNICATIONS AND MEDIA

With the exception of rural and wilderness areas, Northern California is fairly well connected. Cell phone reception is good except in places far from any large town. Likewise, you can find Internet access just about anywhere. The bigger cities are well wired, but even in small towns you can log on either at a library or in a café with a computer in the back. Be prepared to pay a per-minute usage fee.

The main newspaper in Northern California

is the *San Francisco Chronicle*. You can usually find it on sale from Monterey to Crescent City and east to Lake Tahoe. Of course, there are other regional papers that may offer some international news in addition to the local color. As for radio, there are some news stations on the FM dial, and in most regions you can count on finding a National Public Radio (NPR) affiliate. While they will all offer some NPR news coverage, some will be more geared toward music and local concerns. KQED (88.5 FM) is the hometown San Francisco station that can also be heard in Sacramento (89.3 FM). Nearly all California radio stations report traffic conditions during commuting hours.

Because of California's size both geographically and in terms of population, you will have to contend with multiple area codes—the numbers that prefix the seven-digit phone number—throughout the state. In Northern California, 415 is San Francisco north to Novato; 650 is San Mateo County, including Palo Alto; 831 is Monterey County; 408 is San Jose; 510 is the East Bay; 925 is the far-east East Bay; 707 is Wine Country and the North Coast; 916 is Sacramento and part of Gold Country; and 530 is the Sacramento Valley north to Oregon and east to Lake Tahoe. The 800 or 866 area codes are toll-free numbers. Any time you are dialing out of the area, you must dial a 1 plus the area code followed by the seven-digit number.

To mail a letter, find a blue post office box, which are found on the main streets of any town. Postage rates vary by destination. You can purchase stamps at the local post office, where you can also mail packages. Stamps can also be bought at some ATMs and online at www.usps.com, which can also give you the location and hours of the nearest post office. Post offices are generally

open Monday–Friday, with limited hours on Saturday. They are always closed on Sunday and federal holidays.

MAPS AND TOURIST INFORMATION

When visiting California, you might be tempted to stop in at one of several **Golden State Welcome Centers** (www.visitcwc.com) scattered throughout the state. If you're in an area that doesn't have its own visitors center, the State Welcome Center might be a useful place to pick up maps and brochures. Otherwise, stick with local, regional, and national park visitors centers, which tend to be staffed by volunteers or rangers who feel a real passion for their locale.

If you are looking for maps, almost all gas stations and drugstores sell maps both of the place you're in and of the whole state. **California State Automobile Association** (CSAA, www.csaa.com) is the auto club for Northern California, and it offers free maps to auto club members.

Many local and regional visitors centers also offer maps, but you'll need to pay a few dollars for the bigger and better ones. But if all you need is a wine-tasting map in a known wine region, you can probably get one for free along with a few tasting coupons at the nearest regional visitors center. Basic national park maps come with your admission payment. State park maps can be free or cost a few dollars at the visitors centers.

The state's **California Travel and Tourism Commission** (916/444-4429, gocalif.ca.gov) also provides helpful and free tips, information, and downloadable maps and guides.

California is in the Pacific time zone (PST and PDT) and observes daylight saving time March–November.

RESOURCES

Suggested Reading

FICTION

Kerouac, Jack. *Big Sur.* New York: Penguin, 2011.

London, Jack. *The Valley of the Moon.* Los Angeles: Aegypan, 2007.

Muir, John, *The Mountains of California.* San Francisco: Sierra Club Books, 1988.

Muir, John. *My First Summer in the Sierra.* New York: Penguin Books, 1997.

Steinbeck, John. *The Grapes of Wrath.* New York: Penguin, 2006.

Stegner, Wallace. *Angle of Repose.* New York: Penguin, 2000.

Stevenson, Robert Louis. *The Complete Short Stories of Robert Louis Stevenson: With a Selection of the Best Short Novels.* New York: Modern Library, 2002.

FIELD GUIDES

Alden, Peter, and Fred Heath. *National Audubon Field Guide to California.* New York: Knopf, 1998.

Arno, Stephen F. *Discovering Sierra Trees.* Yosemite National Park: Yosemite Association and Sequoia Natural History Association, 1986.

Blackwell, Laird R. *Wildflowers of the Tahoe Sierra: From Forest Deep to Mountain Peak.* Redmond, WA: Lone Pine Publishing, 1997.

Hill, Mary. *Geology of the Sierra Nevada.* Berkeley, CA: University of California Press, 2006.

Horn, Elizabeth L. *Sierra Nevada Wildflowers.* Missoula, MT: Mountain Press Publishing Company, 1998.

Tekiela, Stan. *Birds of California Field Guide.* Cambridge, MN: Adventure Publications, 2003.

HISTORY

Belden, L. Burr, and DeDecker, Mary. *Death Valley to Yosemite: Frontier Mining Camps and Ghost Towns.* Bishop, CA: Spotted Dog Press, 2000.

Davis, Mike. *City of Quartz.* Brooklyn, NY: Verso, 2006.

Gutiérrez, Ramon A., and Richard J. Orsi, eds. *Contested Eden: California Before the Gold Rush.* Berkeley, CA: University of California Press, 1998.

Heizer, Robert F., and Albert B. Elsasser. *The Natural World of the California Indians.* Berkeley, CA: University of California Press, 1981.

Holiday, James. *The World Rushed In: The California Gold Rush Experience: An Eyewitness Account of a Nation Heading West.* Norman, OK: University of Oklahoma Press, 2002.

Reisner, Marc. *Cadillac Desert: The American West and Its Disappearing Water.* New York: Penguin, 1993.

Rice, Richard, William Bullough, and Richard Orsi. *The Elusive Eden: A New History of California*. Columbus, OH: McGraw Hill, 2001.

Sullivan, Charles. *A Companion to California Wine: An Encyclopedia of Wine and Winemaking from the Mission Period to the Present*. Berkeley, CA: University of California Press, 1998.

NATURAL HISTORY

Bakker, Elna, and Gordy Slack. *An Island Called California*. Berkeley, CA: University of California Press, 1985.

Barbour, Michael, Bruce Pavlik, Susan Lindstrom, and Frank Drysdale. *California's Changing Landscapes: Diversity and Conservation of California Vegetation*. Sacramento, CA: California Native Plant Society Press, 1991.

Gudde, Erwin G., and Bright, William O. *California Place Names: The Origin and Etymology of Current Geographical Names*. Berkeley, CA: University of California Press, 2010.

Guyton, Bill, *Glaciers of California: Modern Glaciers, Ice Age Glaciers, the Origin of Yosemite Valley, and a Glacier Tour in the Sierra Nevada*. Berkeley, CA: University of California Press, 2001.

McPhee, John. *Assembling California*. New York: Farrar, Straus and Giroux, 1994.

Schoenherr, Allan A. *A Natural History of California*. Berkeley, CA: University of California Press, 1995.

TRAVEL

Brown, Ann Marie. *Moon 101 Great Hikes of the San Francisco Bay Area*. Berkeley, CA: Avalon Travel, 2011.

Brown, Ann Marie. *Moon Tahoe*. Berkeley, CA: Avalon Travel, 2012.

California Coastal Commission, State of California. *The California Coastal Access Guide*. Berkeley, CA: University of California Press, 2003.

Leal, Kristin. *Moon Monterey & Carmel*. Berkeley, CA: Avalon Travel, 2012.

Soares, Marc J. *Best Coast Hikes of Northern California: A Guide to the Top Trails from Big Sur to the Oregon Border*. San Francisco: Sierra Club Books, 1998.

Stienstra, Tom, and Ann Marie Brown. *Moon California Hiking*. Berkeley, CA: Avalon Travel, 2012.

Stienstra, Tom. *Moon California Camping*. Berkeley, CA: Avalon Travel, 2011.

Internet Resources

CALIFORNIA

California Department of Transportation
www.dot.ca.gov
Contains state map and highway information.

Visit California
www.visitcalifornia.com
The official tourism site of the state of California.

REGIONAL SITES

Central Coast Regional Tourism
www.centralcoast-tourism.com
A guide to the Central Coast region, including Santa Cruz and Monterey.

NapaValley.com
www.napavalley.com
A Napa Valley tourism website from WineCountry.com.

Sacramento Convention and Visitors Bureau
www.sacramentocvb.org
The official website of the Sacramento Convention and Visitors Bureau.

Shasta and Lassen Regional Tourism
www.shastacascade.org
The California Travel and Tourism Information Network includes information and a downloadable visitors guide to Mount Shasta, Shasta Lake, Redding, and Lassen.

Visit California Gold Country
www.calgold.org
The website from the Gold Country Visitors Association, with information about Grass Valley, Nevada City, Placer Country, Sacramento, and Amador Country.

PARKS AND OUTDOORS

California Outdoor and Recreational Information
www.caoutdoors.com
This recreation-focused website includes links to maps, local newspapers, festivals, and events as well as a wide variety of recreational activities throughout the state.

California State Parks
www.parks.ca.gov
The official website lists hours, accessibility, activities, camping areas, fees, and more information for all parks in the state system.

Lassen Volcanic National Park
www.nps.gov/lavo
The official website for Lassen Volcanic National Park.

Recreation.gov
www.recreation.gov
Recreation.gov is the reservation website for numerous California campgrounds.

Redwood National Park
www.nps.gov/redw
The official website for all Redwood National and State Parks.

Sequoia and Kings Canyon National Parks
www.nps.gov/seki
The official website for Sequoia and Kings Canyon.

State of California
www.ca.gov/tourism/greatoutdoors.html
Outdoor resources for California state and government organizations. Check for information about fishing and hunting licenses, backcountry permits, boating regulations, and more.

Yosemite National Park
www.nps.gov/yose
The National Park Service website for Yosemite National Park.

Yosemite National Park Vacation and Lodging Information
www.yosemitepark.com
The concessionaire website for Yosemite National Park lodging, dining, and reservations.

Index

List of Maps

www.moon.com

DESTINATIONS | ACTIVITIES | BLOGS | MAPS | BOOKS

MOON.COM is ready to help plan your next trip! Filled with fresh trip ideas and strategies, author interviews, informative travel blogs, a detailed map library, and descriptions of all the Moon guidebooks, Moon.com is all you need to get out and explore the world—or even places in your own backyard. While at Moon.com, sign up for our monthly e-newsletter for updates on new releases, travel tips, and expert advice from our on-the-go Moon authors. As always, when you travel with Moon, expect an experience that is uncommon and truly unique.

KEEP UP WITH MOON ON FACEBOOK AND TWITTER
JOIN THE MOON PHOTO GROUP ON FLICKR

MAP SYMBOLS

▦ Expressway		◖ Highlight		✗ Airfield		⚲ Golf Course
Primary Road		○ City/Town		✈ Airport		℗ Parking Area
Secondary Road		◉ State Capital		▲ Mountain		◭ Archaeological Site
▪▪▪▪▪ Unpaved Road		⊛ National Capital		✚ Unique Natural Feature		⬤ Church
------ Trail		★ Point of Interest				
⋯⋯ Ferry		• Accommodation		﹅ Waterfall		⛽ Gas Station
▰▰ Railroad		▾ Restaurant/Bar		▲ Park		◠ Glacier
▦ Pedestrian Walkway		▪ Other Location		▮ Trailhead		〰 Mangrove
▥ Stairs		Λ Campground		⛷ Skiing Area		▨ Reef
						▤ Swamp

CONVERSION TABLES

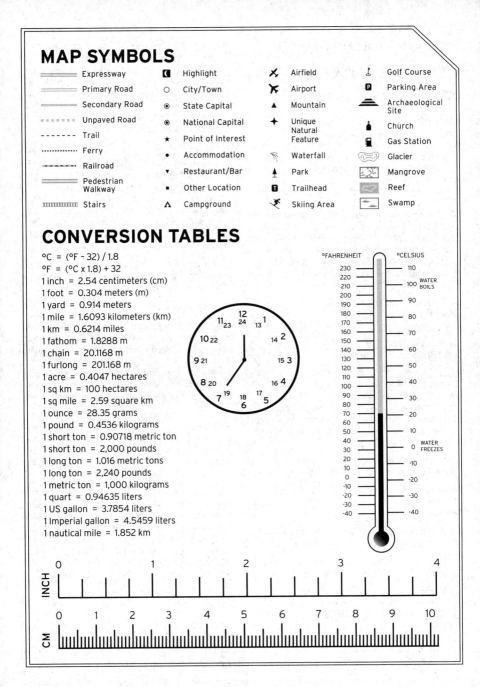

°C = (°F - 32) / 1.8
°F = (°C x 1.8) + 32
1 inch = 2.54 centimeters (cm)
1 foot = 0.304 meters (m)
1 yard = 0.914 meters
1 mile = 1.6093 kilometers (km)
1 km = 0.6214 miles
1 fathom = 1.8288 m
1 chain = 20.1168 m
1 furlong = 201.168 m
1 acre = 0.4047 hectares
1 sq km = 100 hectares
1 sq mile = 2.59 square km
1 ounce = 28.35 grams
1 pound = 0.4536 kilograms
1 short ton = 0.90718 metric ton
1 short ton = 2,000 pounds
1 long ton = 1.016 metric tons
1 long ton = 2,240 pounds
1 metric ton = 1,000 kilograms
1 quart = 0.94635 liters
1 US gallon = 3.7854 liters
1 Imperial gallon = 4.5459 liters
1 nautical mile = 1.852 km

MOON NORTHERN CALIFORNIA

Avalon Travel
a member of the Perseus Books Group
1700 Fourth Street
Berkeley, CA 94710, USA
www.moon.com

Editor: Sabrina Young
Series Manager: Kathryn Ettinger
Copy Editor: Christopher Church
Graphics and Production Coordinator: Elizabeth Jang
Cover Designer: Elizabeth Jang
Map Editor: Albert Angulo
Cartographers: Kaitlin Jaffe, Chris Henrick
Indexer: Greg Jewett
Contributing Writers: Christopher Arns (Sacramento and Gold Country), Liz Hamill (San Francisco), Elizabeth Linhart Money (San Francisco Bay Area, Wine Country, Essentials), Heather C. Liston (North Coast, Shasta and Lassen, Lake Tahoe, Yosemite and the Eastern Sierra, Sequoia and Kings Canyon), Keith Michaud (Background)

ISBN-13: 978-61238-149-7
ISSN: 1524-4148

Printing History
1st Edition – 2000
6th Edition – March 2013
5 4 3 2 1

Text © 2013 by Avalon Travel.
Maps © 2013 by Avalon Travel.
Text in the Central Coast chapter originally appeared in *Moon Monterey & Carmel*, fourth edition, © 2012 Kristin Leal and Avalon Travel. Used with permission. All rights reserved.

Front cover photo: Bristlecone Pine, White Mountains, Inyo National Forest, CA © Ed Callaert Photography/www.edcallaert.com

Title page photo: colorful Victorian homes in San Francisco © Frank Kovalchek

Interior color photos: p. 4 Golden Gate Bridge © Nickolay Stanev/Dreamstime.com; p. 5 Yosemite National Park © Mariusz Blac/123rf.com; p. 6 Redwoods National Park © Krzysztof Wiktor/123rf.com; p. 7 (inset) California poppy © Sabrina Young, (lower left) California poppy © Sabrina Young, (center) otter in Monterey Bay © Kristin Leal, (lower right) a relaxing way to view the Golden Gate Bridge © Rainer Junker/123rf.com; p. 8 © David Frederick; p. 9 (left) courtesy of Prayitno, (center) © Heather C. Liston, (right) © Sabrina Young; p. 10 © Sherri Camp/123rf.com; p. 11 © capturelight/123rf.com; p. 12 (left) © Eric Wolfinger/Courtesy Tartine Bakery and Postcardpr, (right) © Joerg Hackemann/123rf.com; p. 13 © Michael Klenetsky/123rf.com; p. 14 © Dwight Smith/123rf.com, p. 15 © Andrew Zarivny/123rf.com; p. 16 © Sabrina Young; p. 17 © Alexey Kamenskiy/123rf.com; p. 18 © Joerg Hackemann/123rf.com; p. 19 © Heather C. Liston; p. 20 © Stephen Goodwin/123rf.com; p. 21 © Heather C. Liston; p. 22 © Heather C. Liston; p. 23-24 © Sabrina Young

p. 261 artwork: "We are made of Stars" – Tara Heffernon; "Back to Brown - I & II" – James Jarret; "Forchetta Chandelier" – Allis Teegarden

Printed in Canada by Friesens

KEEPING CURRENT

If you have a favorite gem you'd like to see included in the next edition, or see anything that needs updating, clarification, or correction, please drop us a line. Send your comments via email to feedback@moon.com, or use the address above.